*seventh edition*

# Financial Markets *and* Institutions

# THE MCGRAW-HILL EDUCATION SERIES IN FINANCE, INSURANCE, AND REAL ESTATE

## FINANCIAL MANAGEMENT

Block, Hirt, and Danielsen
**Foundations of Financial Management**
*Sixteenth Edition*

Brealey, Myers, and Allen
**Principles of Corporate Finance**
*Twelfth Edition*

Brealey, Myers, and Allen
**Principles of Corporate Finance, Concise**
*Second Edition*

Brealey, Myers, and Marcus
**Fundamentals of Corporate Finance**
*Ninth Edition*

Brooks
**FinGame Online 5.0**

Bruner, Eades, and Schill
**Case Studies in Finance: Managing for Corporate Value Creation**
*Eighth Edition*

Cornett, Adair, and Nofsinger
**Finance: Applications and Theory**
*Fourth Edition*

Cornett, Adair, and Nofsinger
**M: Finance**
*Fourth Edition*

DeMello
**Cases in Finance**
*Third Edition*

Grinblatt (editor)
**Stephen A. Ross, Mentor: Influence through Generations**

Grinblatt and Titman
**Financial Markets and Corporate Strategy**
*Second Edition*

Higgins
**Analysis for Financial Management**
*Twelfth Edition*

Ross, Westerfield, Jaffe, and Jordan
**Corporate Finance**
*Eleventh Edition*

Ross, Westerfield, Jaffe, and Jordan
**Corporate Finance: Core Principles and Applications**
*Fifth Edition*

Ross, Westerfield, and Jordan
**Essentials of Corporate Finance**
*Ninth Edition*

Ross, Westerfield, and Jordan
**Fundamentals of Corporate Finance**
*Twelfth Edition*

Shefrin
**Behavioral Corporate Finance: Decisions that Create Value**
*Second Edition*

## INVESTMENTS

Bodie, Kane, and Marcus
**Essentials of Investments**
*Tenth Edition*

Bodie, Kane, and Marcus
**Investments**
*Eleventh Edition*

Hirt and Block
**Fundamentals of Investment Management**
*Tenth Edition*

Jordan, Miller, and Dolvin
**Fundamentals of Investments: Valuation and Management**
*Eighth Edition*

Stewart, Piros, and Heisler
**Running Money: Professional Portfolio Management**
*First Edition*

Sundaram and Das
**Derivatives: Principles and Practice**
*Second Edition*

## FINANCIAL INSTITUTIONS AND MARKETS

Rose and Hudgins
**Bank Management and Financial Services**
*Ninth Edition*

Rose and Marquis
**Financial Institutions and Markets**
*Eleventh Edition*

Saunders and Cornett
**Financial Institutions Management: A Risk Management Approach**
*Ninth Edition*

Saunders and Cornett
**Financial Markets and Institutions**
*Seventh Edition*

## INTERNATIONAL FINANCE

Eun and Resnick
**International Financial Management**
*Eighth Edition*

## REAL ESTATE

Brueggeman and Fisher
**Real Estate Finance and Investments**
*Sixteenth Edition*

Ling and Archer
**Real Estate Principles: A Value Approach**
*Fifth Edition*

## FINANCIAL PLANNING AND INSURANCE

Allen, Melone, Rosenbloom, and Mahoney
**Retirement Plans: 401(k)s, IRAs, and Other Deferred Compensation Approaches**
*Twelfth Edition*

Altfest
**Personal Financial Planning**
*Second Edition*

Harrington and Niehaus
**Risk Management and Insurance**
*Second Edition*

Kapoor, Dlabay, Hughes, and Hart
**Focus on Personal Finance: An active approach to help you achieve financial literacy**
*Sixth Edition*

Kapoor, Dlabay, Hughes, and Hart
**Personal Finance**
*Twelfth Edition*

Walker and Walker
**Personal Finance: Building Your Future**
*Second Edition*

*seventh edition*

# Financial Markets
# *and* Institutions

**Anthony Saunders**
*Stern School of Business*
*New York University*

**Marcia Millon Cornett**
*Bentley University*

Mc
Graw
Hill
Education

FINANCIAL MARKETS AND INSTITUTIONS

Published by McGraw-Hill Education, 2 Penn Plaza, New York, NY 10121. Copyright © 2019 by McGraw-Hill Education. All rights reserved. Printed in the United States of America. No part of this publication may be reproduced or distributed in any form or by any means, or stored in a database or retrieval system, without the prior written consent of McGraw-Hill Education, including, but not limited to, in any network or other electronic storage or transmission, or broadcast for distance learning.

Some ancillaries, including electronic and print components, may not be available to customers outside the United States.

This book is printed on acid-free paper.
1 2 3 4 5 6 7 8 9 LWI 21 20 19 18

ISBN 978-1-260-09195-3
MHID 1-260-09195-3

Cover Image: © *Shutterstock / Rudy Balasko*

mheducation.com/highered

To Ingo Walter: a mentor, coauthor, and friend.
—TONY SAUNDERS

To my parents, Tom and Sue.
—MARCIA MILLON CORNETT

### Anthony Saunders

Anthony Saunders is the John M. Schiff Professor of Finance and former chair of the Department of Finance at the Stern School of Business at New York University. Professor Saunders received his PhD from the London School of Economics and has taught both  undergraduate- and graduate-level courses at NYU since 1978. Throughout his academic career, his teaching and research have specialized in financial institutions and international banking. He has served as a visiting professor all over the world, including INSEAD, the Stockholm School of Economics, and the University of Melbourne.

Professor Saunders holds or has held positions on the Board of Academic Consultants of the Federal Reserve Board of Governors as well as the Council of Research Advisors for the Federal National Mortgage Association. In addition, Dr. Saunders has acted as a visiting scholar at the Comptroller of the Currency and at the International Monetary Fund. He is editor of the *Journal of Financial Markets, Instruments and Institutions,* as well as the associate editor of a number of other journals. His research has been published in all of the major finance and banking journals and in several books. He has just published a new edition of his textbook, with Dr. Marcia Millon Cornett, *Financial Institutions Management: A Risk Management Approach,* for McGraw-Hill/Irwin (ninth edition) as well as a third edition of his book on credit risk measurement for John Wiley & Sons. Professor Saunders was ranked the most prolific author out of more than 5,800 who have published in the seven leading finance academic journals from 1959 to 2008 ("Most Prolific Authors in the Financial Literature, 1959–2008," Jean Heck and Philip Cooley).

### Marcia Millon Cornett

Marcia Millon Cornett is the Robert A. and Julia E. Dorn Professor of Finance at Bentley University. She received her BS degree in economics from Knox College in Galesburg, Illinois, and her MBA and PhD degrees in finance from Indiana University in Bloomington, Indiana. Dr. Cornett has written and published several articles in the areas of bank performance, bank regulation, corporate finance, and investments. Articles authored by Dr. Cornett have appeared in such academic journals as the *Journal of Finance,* the *Journal of Money, Credit, and Banking,* the *Journal of Financial Economics, Financial Management,* and the *Journal of Banking and Finance.* She was recently ranked the 124th most published out of more than 17,600 authors and the number five female author in finance literature over the last 50 years. Along with Anthony Saunders, Dr. Cornett has recently completed work on the ninth edition of *Financial Institutions Management* (McGraw-Hill/Irwin).  With Troy A. Adair Jr. (Harvard University) and John Nofsinger (University of Alaska, Anchorage), she has also recently completed work on the fourth edition of *Finance: Applications and Theory* and the third edition of *M: Finance* (McGraw-Hill/Irwin). Professor Cornett serves as an associate editor for the *Journal of Banking and Finance,* the *Journal of Financial Services Research, Review of Financial Economics, Financial Review,* and *Multi-national Finance Journal.* Dr. Cornett has served as a member of the Board of Directors, the Executive Committee, and the Finance Committee of the SIU Credit Union. She has also taught at Southern Illinois University at Carbondale, the University of Colorado, Boston College, Southern Methodist University, and Boston University.

he last 30 years have been dramatic for the financial services industry. In the 1990s and 2000s, boundaries between the traditional industry sectors, such as commercial banking and investment banking, broke down and competition became increasingly global in nature. Many forces contributed to this breakdown in interindustry and intercountry barriers, including financial innovation, technology, taxation, and regulation. Then in 2008–2009, the financial services industry experienced the worst financial crisis since the Great Depression. Even into the mid-2010s, the U.S. and world economies have not recovered from this crisis. It is in this context that this book is written.

As the economic and competitive environments change, attention to profit and, more than ever, risk become increasingly important. This book offers a unique analysis of the risks faced by investors and savers interacting through both financial institutions and financial markets, as well as strategies that can be adopted for controlling and better managing these risks. Special emphasis is also put on new areas of operations in financial markets and institutions such as asset securitization, off-balance-sheet activities, and globalization of financial services.

While maintaining a risk measurement and management framework, *Financial Markets and Institutions* provides a broad application of this important perspective. This book recognizes that domestic and foreign financial markets are becoming increasingly integrated and that financial intermediaries are evolving toward a single financial services industry. The analytical rigor is mathematically accessible to all levels of students, undergraduate and graduate, and is balanced by a comprehensive discussion of the unique environment within which financial markets and institutions operate. Important practical tools such as how to issue and trade financial securities and how to analyze financial statements and loan applications will arm students with the skills necessary to understand and manage financial market and institution risks in this dynamic environment. While descriptive concepts so important to financial management (financial market securities, regulation, industry trends, industry characteristics, etc.) are included in the book, ample analytical techniques are also included as practical tools to help students understand the operation of modern financial markets and institutions.

## INTENDED AUDIENCE

*Financial Markets and Institutions* is aimed at the first course in financial markets and institutions at both the undergraduate and MBA levels. While topics covered in this book are found in more advanced textbooks on financial markets and institutions, the explanations and illustrations are aimed at those with little or no practical or academic experience beyond the introductory-level finance courses. In most chapters, the main relationships are presented by figures, graphs, and simple examples. The more complicated details and technical problems related to in-chapter discussion are provided in appendixes to the chapters (available through McGraw-Hill *Connect Finance* or your course instructor).

## ORGANIZATION

Since our focus is on return and risk and the sources of that return and risk in domestic and foreign financial markets and institutions, this book relates ways in which a modern financial manager, saver, and investor can expand return with a managed level of risk to achieve the best, or most favorable, return–risk outcome.

**Part 1** provides an introduction to the text and an overview of financial markets and institutions. Chapter 1 defines and introduces the various domestic and foreign financial markets and describes the special functions of FIs. This chapter also takes an analytical look at how financial markets and institutions benefit today's economy. In Chapter 2, we provide an in-depth look at interest rates. We first look at factors that determine interest rate levels, as well as their past, present, and expected future movements. We then review the concept of time value of money. Chapter 3 then applies these interest rates to security valuation. In Chapter 4, we describe the Federal Reserve System and how monetary policy implemented by the Federal Reserve affects interest rates and, ultimately, the overall economy.

**Part 2** of the text presents an overview of the various securities markets. We describe each securities market, its participants, the securities traded in each, the trading process, and how changes in interest rates, inflation, and foreign exchange rates impact a financial manager's decisions to hedge risk. These chapters cover the money markets (Chapter 5), bond markets (Chapter 6), mortgage markets (Chapter 7), stock markets (Chapter 8), foreign exchange markets (Chapter 9), and derivative securities markets (Chapter 10).

**Part 3** of the text summarizes the operations of commercial banks. Chapter 11 describes the key characteristics and recent trends in the commercial banking sector. Chapter 12 describes the financial statements of a typical commercial bank and the ratios used to analyze those statements. This chapter also analyzes actual financial statements for representative commercial banks. Chapter 13 provides a comprehensive look at the regulations under which these financial institutions operate and, particularly, the effect of recent changes in regulation.

**Part 4** of the text provides an overview describing the key characteristics and regulatory features of the other major sectors of the U.S. financial services industry. We discuss other lending institutions (savings institutions, credit unions, and finance companies) in Chapter 14, insurance companies in Chapter 15, securities firms and investment banks in Chapter 16, investment companies in Chapter 17, and pension funds in Chapter 18.

**Part 5** concludes the text by examining the risks facing a modern FI and FI managers and the various strategies for managing these risks. In Chapter 19, we preview the risk measurement and management chapters in this section with an overview of the risks facing a modern FI. We divide the chapters on risk measurement and management along two lines: measuring and managing risks on the balance sheet, and managing risks off the balance sheet. In Chapter 20, we begin the on-balance-sheet risk measurement and management section by looking at credit risk on individual loans and bonds and how these risks adversely impact an FI's profits and value. The chapter also discusses the lending process, including loans made to households and small, medium-size, and large corporations. Chapter 21 covers liquidity risk in financial institutions. This chapter includes a detailed analysis of the ways in which FIs can insulate themselves from liquidity risk and the key role deposit insurance and other guarantee schemes play in reducing liquidity risk.

In Chapter 22, we investigate the net interest margin as a source of profitability and risk, with a focus on the effects of interest rate risk and the mismatching of asset and liability maturities on FI risk exposure. At the core of FI risk insulation is the size and adequacy of the owner's capital stake, which is also a focus of this chapter.

The management of risk off the balance sheet is examined in Chapter 23. The chapter highlights various new markets and instruments that have emerged to allow FIs to better manage three important types of risk: interest rate risk, foreign exchange risk, and credit risk. These markets and instruments and their strategic use by FIs include forwards, futures, options, and swaps.

Finally, Chapter 24 explores ways of removing credit risk from the loan portfolio through asset sales and securitization.

## NEW FEATURES

- Tables and figures in all chapters have been revised to include the most recently available data.
- Revised "After the Crisis" boxes highlighting significant events related to the financial crisis have been added to chapters throughout the book.
- Updates on the major changes proposed for the regulation of financial institutions are included where appropriate throughout the book.
- Discussion of how financial markets and institutions continue to recover from the financial crisis has been added throughout the book. Virtually every chapter includes

new material detailing how the financial crisis affected risk management in financial institutions.

- Several chapters include a discussion of Brexit as its affects the risk and return for investors in financial markets and financial institutions.
- Several chapters include a discussion of the impact of initial interest rate increases by the Federal Reserve.
- Several chapters include a discussion of the impact of China's economic policies and economic slowdown on financial markets.
- Chapter 1 includes a new section on enterprise risk management. The chapter also provides an update on the implementation of the Wall Street Reform and Consumer Protection Act enacted as a result of the financial crisis.
- Chapter 4 provides an update on the Federal Reserve's actions intended to strengthen the U.S. economy, including the interest rate increases instituted by the Fed.
- Chapter 5 includes updates on the LIBOR scandal.
- Chapter 6 discusses China's and worldwide Treasury holdings and the potential impact of these holdings on the U.S. economy.
- Chapter 8 includes more on dark pools and Brexit's impact on worldwide stock markets.
- Excel spreadsheets containing bank financial statements and ratio calculations have been added to Chapter 12.
- Chapter 13 includes a discussion of how the Volcker Rule and Consumer Protection Regulation have affected the operations of financial institutions.
- Chapter 14 includes a discussion of new payday lending legislation
- Chapter 17 includes more on new regulations for money market mutual funds.
- Chapter 21 includes updates of the new international liquidity standards enacted as a result of the financial crisis.

## ACKNOWLEDGMENTS

We take this opportunity to thank all of those individuals who helped us prepare this and previous editions. We want to express our appreciation to those instructors whose insightful comments and suggestions were invaluable to us during this revision.

Keldon Bauer
*Tarleton State University*
Jen-Chi Cheng
*Wichita State University*
Kathy English
*Wilmington University*
Andrew Fodor
*Ohio University–Athens*
Robert Goldberg
*Adelphi University*
Walt Nelson
*Missouri State University*
Abdullah Noman
*Nicholls State University*

Ozde Oztekin
*Florida International University–Miami*
O. John Paskelian
*University of Houston Downtown*
Blaise Roncagli
*Cleveland State University*
Matthew Ross
*Western Michigan University–Kalamazoo*
Benjamin Thompson
*Lincoln Memorial University*
Ann Marie Whyte
*University of Central Florida–Orlando*
David Zalewski
*Providence College*

We would like to thank the staff at McGraw-Hill for their help and guidance, especially Chuck Synovec, executive brand manager; Noelle Bathurst, senior product developer; Heather Ervolino, content project manager; Tobi Philips, digital product developer; Trina Maurer, senior marketing manager; and Dave O'Donnell, marketing specialist. Additional thanks to Alex Marden for his editorial assistance.

**Anthony Saunders**

**Marcia Millon Cornett**

## Chapter Features

The following special features have been integrated throughout the text to encourage student interaction and to aid students in absorbing and retaining the material

### CHAPTER-OPENING OUTLINES

These outlines offer students a snapshot view of what they can expect to learn from each chapter's discussion.

> **OUTLINE**
>
> Major Duties and Responsibilities of the Federal Reserve System: Chapter Overview
>
> Structure of the Federal Reserve System
>
> > Organization of the Federal Reserve System
> >
> > Board of Governors of the Federal Reserve System

---

**Learning Goals**

**LG 4-1**  *Understand the major functions of the Federal Reserve System.*

**LG 4-2**  *Identify the structure of the Federal Reserve System.*

**LG 4-3**  *Identify the monetary policy tools used by the Federal Reserve.*

**LG 4-4**  *Appreciate how monetary policy changes affect key economic variables.*

**LG 4-5**  *Understand how central banks around the world adjusted their monetary policy during the recent financial crisis.*

---

**Federal Open Market Committee (FOMC)**

*The major monetary policy-making body of the Federal Reserve System.*

**open market operations**

*Purchases and sales of U.S. government and fed-*

The **Federal Open Mar** body of the Federal Rese members of the Federal Bank of New York, and basis). The chair of the required to meet at least scheduled meetings have

The main responsi employment, economic trade. The FOMC seeks operations. **Open marke** eral agency securities—i gets (although the opera Reserve Bank of New Y

### LEARNING GOALS

Learning goals (LGs) appear at the beginning of each chapter to provide a quick introduction to the key chapter material. These goals are also integrated with the end-of-chapter questions and problems, which allows instructors to easily emphasize the learning goal(s) as they choose.

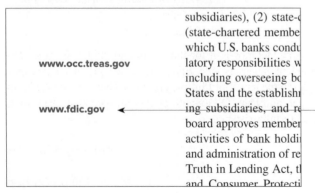

subsidiaries), (2) state-c (state-chartered membe which U.S. banks condu latory responsibilities w including overseeing bc States and the establishi ing subsidiaries, and re board approves member activities of bank holdi and administration of re Truth in Lending Act, t and Consumer Protecti

www.occ.treas.gov

www.fdic.gov

### BOLD KEY TERMS AND A MARGINAL GLOSSARY

The main terms and concepts are emphasized throughout the chapter by bold key terms called out in the text and defined in the margins

### PERTINENT WEB ADDRESSES

Website addresses are referenced in the margins throughout each chapter, providing additional resources to aid in the learning process.

# Pedagogical Features

## DO YOU UNDERSTAND:

1. What the main functions of Federal Reserve Banks are?
2. What the main responsibilities of the Federal Reserve Board are?
3. How the FOMC implements monetary policy?
4. What the main assets and

as the Fed took
and housing ma
rities (MBS) ba
MBS purchase
of agency MBS
through 2016. T
the financial ma

**Gold and Fore**
holds Treasury

### "DO YOU UNDERSTAND" BOXES

These boxes allow students to test themselves on the main concepts presented within each major chapter section. Solutions are provided in Connect.

### "IN THE NEWS" BOXES

These boxes demonstrate the application of chapter material to real current events.

### IN-CHAPTER EXAMPLES

These examples provide numerical demonstrations of the analytical material described in many chapters.

## IN THE NEWS

### The Financial Crisis: Toward an Expla

In the first half of 2007, as the extent of declining home prices became apparent, banks and other financial
l to reas-

off the company's balance
month, the board also ann
the creation of the Term S
Lending Facility (TSLF), sw

### EXAMPLE 4–1  Purchases of Securities by the Federal F

Suppose the FOMC instructs the FRBNY Trading Desk to purchase $5(
sury securities. Traders at the FRBNY call primary government securiti
commercial and investment banks (such as Goldman Sachs and Morg
provide a list of securities they have available for sale, including the de
seek to purchase th
ible price) until th
ernment bond dep

## AFTER THE CRISIS

### Goldman Reaches $5 Billion Settlement ov

In January 2016, Goldman Sachs agreed to pay more than $5 billion, the largest regulatory penalty in its history. In settling with the Justice Department and a collection of other state and

residential mortgages, and wh
banks deceived investors by
senting the quality of underlyi
The government's inquiry into
related to mortgage-backed s

### "AFTER THE CRISIS" BOXES

These boxes use articles pertaining to events caused or affected by the 2008–2009 financial crisis to elaborate on chapter material.

### INTERNATIONAL COVERAGE

An international icon appears in the margin to easily communicate where international material is being introduced.

## INTERNATIONAL MONETARY POLICIES AND STRATE

Central banks guide the monetary polic
European Central Bank (ECB) is the centr
of England is the central bank of the Unite
independent central banks whose decision
In contrast, the People's Bank of China, t
of Brazil are less independent in that the g
the operations of these central banks. Inde
the bank is free from pressure from poli

## EXCEL PROBLEMS

Excel problems are featured in selected chapters and are denoted by an icon. Spreadsheet templates are available in Connect.

### QUESTIONS

1. Describe the functions performed by Federal Reserve Banks. (*LG 4-1*)

2. Define the discount rate and the discount window. (*LG 4-2*)

3. Describe the structure of the Board of Governors of the Federal Reserve System. (*LG 4-2*)

4. What are the primary responsibilities of the Federal Reserve Board? (*LG 4-1*)

5. What are the primary responsibilities of the Federal Open Market Committee? (*LG 4-2*)

6. What are the major liabilities of the Federal Reserve System? Describe each. (*LG 4-2*)

7. Why did reserve deposits increase to the point that this account represented the largest liability account on the Federal Reserve's balance sheet in the late 2000s? (*LG 4-2*)

8. What are the major assets of the Federal Reserve System? Describe each. (*LG 4-2*)

9. Why did U.S. government agency securities go from nothing to being the largest asset account on the Federal Reserve's balance sheet in the late 2000s? (*LG 4-2*)

### PROBLEMS

1. Suppose the Federal Reserve instructs the Trading Desk to purchase $1 billion of securities. Show the result of this transaction on the balance sheets of the Federal Reserve System and commercial banks. (*LG 4-3*)

7. **eXcel** **Using a Spreadsheet to Calculate Mortgage Payments:** What is the monthly payment on a $150,000, 30-year mortgage if the mortgage rate is 5.75 percent? 6.25 percent? 7.5 percent? 9 percent? (*LG 7-4*)

| Present Value | Periods | Interest Rate | ⇒ | The Payment Will Be |
|---|---|---|---|---|
| $150,000 | 30 × 12 | 5.75%/12 | | $ 875.36 |
| 150,000 | 30 × 12 | 6.25%/12 | | 923.58 |
| 150,000 | 30 × 12 | 7.50%/12 | | 1,048.82 |
| 150,000 | 30 × 12 | 9.00%/12 | | 1,206.93 |

## END-OF-CHAPTER QUESTIONS AND PROBLEMS

The questions and problems in the end-of-chapter material appear in separate sections, allowing instructors to choose whether they prefer students to engage in quantitative or qualitative analysis of the material. Selected problems are assignable online in Connect.

## SEARCH THE SITE

Featured among the end-of-chapter material in most chapters, these Internet exercises weave the web, real data, and practical applications with concepts found in the book.

## SEARCH THE SITE

Go to the Federal Reserve Board website and find the latest information available on t the three-month T-bill rate using the following steps. Go to **www.federalreserve.gov**. click on "Selected Interest Rates." Click on the most recent date. The data will be in th

### Questions

1. What are the current levels for each of these interest rates?
2. Calculate the percentage change in each of these rates since June 2016.

**connect**®

McGraw-Hill Connect® is a highly reliable, easy-to-use homework and learning management solution that utilizes learning science and award-winning adaptive tools to improve student results.

## Homework and Adaptive Learning

- Connect's assignments help students contextualize what they've learned through application, so they can better understand the material and think critically.

- Connect will create a personalized study path customized to individual student needs through SmartBook®.

- SmartBook helps students study more efficiently by delivering an interactive reading experience through adaptive highlighting and review.

### Connect's Impact on Retention Rates, Pass Rates, and Average Exam Scores

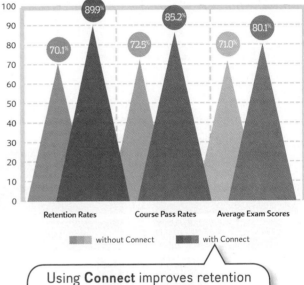

without Connect | with Connect

Over **7 billion questions** have been answered, making McGraw-Hill Education products more intelligent, reliable, and precise.

Using **Connect** improves retention rates by **19.8%**, passing rates by **12.7%,** and exam scores by **9.1%**.

73% of instructors who use **Connect** require it; instructor satisfaction **increases** by 28% when **Connect** is required.

## Quality Content and Learning Resources

- Connect content is authored by the world's best subject matter experts, and is available to your class through a simple and intuitive interface.

- The Connect eBook makes it easy for students to access their reading material on smartphones and tablets. They can study on the go and don't need internet access to use the eBook as a reference, with full functionality.

- Multimedia content such as videos, simulations, and games drive student engagement and critical thinking skills.

# Robust Analytics and Reporting

- Connect Insight® generates easy-to-read reports on individual students, the class as a whole, and on specific assignments.

- The Connect Insight dashboard delivers data on performance, study behavior, and effort. Instructors can quickly identify students who struggle and focus on material that the class has yet to master.

- Connect automatically grades assignments and quizzes, providing easy-to-read reports on individual and class performance.

©Hero Images/Getty Images

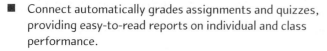

## Impact on Final Course Grade Distribution

| without Connect | | with Connect |
|---|---|---|
| 22.9% | **A** | 31.0% |
| 27.4% | **B** | 34.3% |
| 22.9% | **C** | 18.7% |
| 11.5% | **D** | 6.1% |
| 15.4% | **F** | 9.9% |

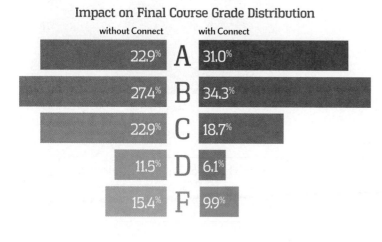

> More students earn **As** and **Bs** when they use **Connect**.

# Trusted Service and Support

- Connect integrates with your LMS to provide single sign-on and automatic syncing of grades. Integration with Blackboard®, D2L®, and Canvas also provides automatic syncing of the course calendar and assignment-level linking.

- Connect offers comprehensive service, support, and training throughout every phase of your implementation.

- If you're looking for some guidance on how to use Connect, or want to learn tips and tricks from super users, you can find tutorials as you work. Our Digital Faculty Consultants and Student Ambassadors offer insight into how to achieve the results you want with Connect.

**www.mheducation.com/connect**

# FOR THE INSTRUCTOR

Instructors will have access to teaching support such as electronic files of the ancillary materials, described below, available within Connect.

- **Instructor's Manual** Prepared by Tim Manuel, University of Montana, the Instructor's Manual includes detailed chapter contents and outline, additional examples for use in the classroom, and extensive teaching notes.
- **Test Bank** Prepared by Ohaness Paskelian, University of Houston–Downtown, the Test Bank includes nearly 1,000 additional problems to be used for test material.
- **Solutions Manual** Prepared by coauthor Marcia Millon Cornett, this manual provides worked-out solutions to the end-of-chapter questions. Author involvement ensures consistency between the approaches presented in the text and those in the manual.
- **PowerPoint** Developed by Courtney Baggett, Troy Univerity, the PowerPoint presentation includes full-color slides featuring lecture notes, figures, and tables. The slides can be easily downloaded and edited to better fit your lecture.

## Student Resources

The Students Resources page in Connect is the place for students to access additional resources. The Student Study Center offers quick access to the web appendixes, Excel files and templates, eBooks, and more.

## Student progress tracking

*Connect Finance* keeps instructors informed about how each student, section, and class is performing, allowing for more productive use of lecture and office hours. The progress-tracking function enables you to:

- View scored work immediately and track individual or group performance with assignment and grade reports.
- Access an instant view of student or class performance relative to learning objectives.
- Collect data and generate reports required by many accreditation organizations, such as AACSB and AICPA.

# MCGRAW-HILL CUSTOMER CARE CONTACT INFORMATION

At McGraw-Hill, we understand that getting the most from new technology can be challenging. That's why our services don't stop after you purchase our products. You can e-mail our Product Specialists 24 hours a day to get product-training online. Or you can search our knowledge bank of Frequently Asked Questions on our support website. For Customer Support, call 800-331-5094, e-mail hmsupport@ mcgraw-hill.com, or visit www.mhhe.com/support. One of our Technical Support Analysts will be able to assist you in a timely fashion.

# CONTENTS IN BRIEF

# CONTENTS

# Introduction

## Learning Goals

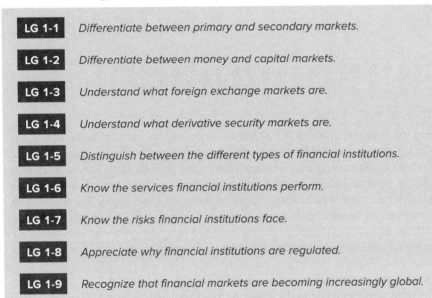

**LG 1-1**  *Differentiate between primary and secondary markets.*

**LG 1-2**  *Differentiate between money and capital markets.*

**LG 1-3**  *Understand what foreign exchange markets are.*

**LG 1-4**  *Understand what derivative security markets are.*

**LG 1-5**  *Distinguish between the different types of financial institutions.*

**LG 1-6**  *Know the services financial institutions perform.*

**LG 1-7**  *Know the risks financial institutions face.*

**LG 1-8**  *Appreciate why financial institutions are regulated.*

**LG 1-9**  *Recognize that financial markets are becoming increasingly global.*

## WHY STUDY FINANCIAL MARKETS AND INSTITUTIONS? CHAPTER OVERVIEW

In the 1990s, financial markets in the United States boomed. As seen in Figure 1–1, the Dow Jones Industrial Index—a widely quoted index of the values of 30 large corporations (see Chapter 8)—rose from a level of 2,800 in January 1990 to more than 11,000 by the end of the decade; this compares to a move from 100 at its inception in 1906 to 2,800 eighty-four years later. In the early 2000s, as a result of an economic downturn in the United States and elsewhere, this index fell back below 10,000. The index rose to over 14,000 in July 2007, but (because of an increasing mortgage market credit crunch, particularly the subprime mortgage market) fell back to below 13,000 within a month of hitting the all-time high. By 2008, problems in the subprime mortgage market escalated to a full-blown financial crisis and the worst recession in the United States since the Great Depression. The Dow Jones Industrial Average (DJIA) fell to 6,547 in March 2009 before recovering, along with the economy, to over 11,000 in April 2010. However, it took until March 5, 2013, for the DJIA to surpass its pre-crisis high of 14,164.53, closing at 14,253.77 for the day, and the DJIA rose to over 21,000 in mid-2017.

**Figure 1–1**   The Dow Jones Industrial Average, 1989–2016

During the financial crisis of 2008–2009, market swings seen in the United States quickly spread worldwide. Stock markets saw huge swings in value as investors tried to sort out who might survive and who would not (and markets from Russia to Europe were forced to suspend trading as stock prices plunged). As U.S. markets recovered in 2010–2013 and, as mentioned earlier, surpassed their pre-crisis highs, European stock markets struggled as Greece battled with a severe debt crisis that eventually spread to other European nations with fiscal problems, such as Portugal, Spain, and Italy. Even the growth in the robust Chinese economy slowed to 6.7 percent in 2016, the lowest level in seven years.

World markets were rocked again in June 2016 when the people of the United Kingdom voted to leave the European Union (EU) after 43 years (dubbed "Brexit"). The shock from the UK's surprise vote to leave the EU swept across global markets, triggering steep drops in stock markets and the British pound and a flight into safe assets such as U.S. bonds and gold. The pound fell more than 11 percent to its lowest point since 1985. The DJIA dropped 610.32 points, or 3.4 percent. The Stoxx Europe 600 index fell 7 percent, its steepest drop since 2008, while Japan's Nikkei Stock Average declined 7.9 percent. Bonds also sold off sharply, pushing UK government borrowing costs sharply higher, as traders and investors grappled with the market implications of Brexit. The UK had its credit rating outlook cut to "negative" by the ratings agency Moody's.

The UK's vote to leave the European Union shook the region, precipitating an immediate political crisis in Britain and shifting the path of a European project created to bind a continent torn by World War II. Prime Minister David Cameron, who had led the campaign to stay inside the 28-nation bloc, announced he would step down, setting off a leadership contest among Conservatives. Britain's decision, one of the most momentous by a Western country in the past 50 years, reverses the course of expansion for the EU. It had grown over decades to include most of Europe, absorbing former dictatorships in Greece, Spain, and Portugal, and the countries of the east, formerly under Soviet domination. The UK would be the first member nation to leave, a step some leaders warned beforehand would diminish the global influence of the UK and the EU and risk setting in motion the European bloc's eventual disintegration. The vote also raised questions about whether the UK itself would split. After a large majority of Scottish citizens voted to remain a part of the EU, Scotland's First Minister said the Scottish National Party would seek to hold a new referendum on the country's exit from the EU.

Originally the banking industry operated as a full-service industry, performing directly or indirectly all financial services (commercial banking, investment banking, stock investing, insurance provision, etc.). In the early 1930s, the economic and industrial collapse resulted in the separation of some of these activities. In the 1970s and 1980s new, relatively unregulated financial services industries sprang up (e.g., mutual funds, brokerage funds) that separated the financial service functions even further.

The last 30 years, however, have seen a reversal of these trends. In the 1990s and 2000s, regulatory barriers, technology, and financial innovation changes were such that a full set of financial services could again be offered by a single financial services firm under the umbrella of a financial services holding company. For example, J.P. Morgan Chase & Co. operates a commercial bank (J.P. Morgan Chase Bank), an investment bank (J. P. Morgan Securities, which also sells mutual funds), and an insurance company (J. P. Morgan Insurance Agency). Not only did the boundaries between traditional industry sectors change, but competition became global in nature as well. For example, J.P. Morgan Chase is the world's seventh-largest bank holding company, operating in 60 countries.

The financial crisis produced another reshaping of all financial institution (FI) sectors and the end of many major FIs (e.g., Bear Stearns and Lehman Brothers), with the two most prominent investment banks in the world, Goldman Sachs and Morgan Stanley, converting to bank holding company status. Indeed, as of 2010, all the major U.S. investment banks had either failed, been acquired by a commercial bank, or become bank holding companies. Further, legislation enacted as a result of the financial crisis represents an attempt to again separate FI activities. For example, the "Volcker Rule" provision of the Wall Street Reform and Consumer Protection Act prohibits bank holding companies from engaging in proprietary trading and limits their investments in hedge funds, private equity, and related vehicles. Despite these most recent changes, many FIs operate in more than one FI sector.

As economic and competitive environments change, attention to profit and, more than ever, risk becomes increasingly important. This book provides a detailed overview and analysis of the financial system in which financial managers and individual investors operate. Making investment and financing decisions requires managers and individuals to understand the flow of funds throughout the economy as well as the operation and structure of domestic and international financial markets. In particular, this book offers a unique analysis of the risks faced by investors and savers, as well as strategies that can be adopted for controlling and managing these risks. Newer areas of operations such as asset securitization, derivative securities, and internationalization of financial services also receive special emphasis. Further, as the United States and the world continue to recover from the collapse of the financial markets, this book highlights and discusses the impact of this crisis on the various financial markets and the financial institutions that operate in them.

This introductory chapter provides an overview of the structure and operations of various financial markets and financial institutions. Financial markets are differentiated by the characteristics (such as maturity) of the financial instruments or securities that are exchanged. Moreover, each financial market, in turn, depends in part or in whole on financial institutions. Indeed, FIs play a special role in the functioning of financial markets. In particular, FIs often provide the least costly and most efficient way to channel funds to and from financial markets. As part of this discussion, we briefly examine how changes in the way FIs deliver services played a major part in the events leading up to the severe financial crisis of the late 2000s. A more detailed discussion of the causes of, the major events during, and the regulatory and industry changes resulting from the financial crisis is provided in Appendix 1A to the chapter (available through Connect or your course instructor).

## OVERVIEW OF FINANCIAL MARKETS

**financial markets**

*The arenas through which funds flow.*

**Financial markets** are structures through which funds flow. Table 1–1 summarizes the financial markets discussed in this section. Financial markets can be distinguished along two major dimensions: (1) primary versus secondary markets and (2) money versus capital markets. The next sections discuss each of these dimensions.

**TABLE 1–1     Types of Financial Markets**

**Primary markets**—markets in which corporations raise funds through new issues of securities.
**Secondary markets**—markets that trade financial instruments once they are issued.
**Money markets**—markets that trade debt securities or instruments with maturities of less than
  one year.
**Capital markets**—markets that trade debt and equity instruments with maturities of more than
  one year.
**Foreign exchange markets**—markets in which cash flows from the sale of products or assets
  denominated in a foreign currency are transacted.
**Derivative markets**—markets in which derivative securities trade.

**LG 1-1**

### Primary Markets versus Secondary Markets

**primary markets**

*Markets in which corporations raise funds through new issues of securities.*

**Primary Markets.     Primary markets** are markets in which users of funds (e.g., corporations) raise funds through new issues of financial instruments, such as stocks and bonds. Table 1–2 lists data on primary market sales of securities from 2000 through 2016. Note the impact the financial crisis had on primary market sales by firms. New issues fell to $1,068.0 billion in 2008, during the worst of the crisis, from $2,389.1 billion in 2007, pre-crisis. As of 2015, primary market sales had still not recovered as only $1,843.2 billion new securities were issued for the year.

Fund users have new projects or expanded production needs, but do not have sufficient internally generated funds (such as retained earnings) to support these needs. Thus, the fund users issue securities in the external primary markets to raise additional funds. New issues of financial instruments are sold to the initial suppliers of funds (e.g., households) in exchange for funds (money) that the issuer or user of funds needs.[1] Most primary market transactions in the United States are arranged through financial institutions called investment banks—for example, Morgan Stanley or Bank of America Merrill Lynch—that serve as intermediaries between the issuing corporations (fund users) and investors (fund suppliers). For these public offerings, the investment bank provides the securities issuer (the funds user) with advice on the securities issue (such as the offer price and number of securities to issue) and attracts the initial public purchasers of the securities for the funds user. By issuing primary market securities with the help of an investment bank, the funds user saves the risk and cost of creating a market for its securities on its own (see the following discussion). Figure 1–2 illustrates a time line for the primary market exchange of funds for a new issue of corporate bonds or equity. We discuss this process in detail in Chapters 6 and 8.

**initial public offering (IPO)**

*The first public issue of a financial instrument by a firm.*

Primary market financial instruments include issues of equity by firms initially going public (e.g., allowing their equity—shares—to be publicly traded on stock markets for the first time). These first-time issues are usually referred to as **initial public offerings (IPOs).** For example, on June 16, 2015, Fitbit announced a $732 million IPO of its common stock.

**TABLE 1–2     Primary Market Sales of Securities** *(in billions of dollars)*

| Security Type | 2000 | 2005 | 2007 | 2008 | 2010 | 2012 | 2015 | 2016* |
|---|---|---|---|---|---|---|---|---|
| All issues | $1,256.7 | $2,439.0 | $2,389.1 | $1,068.0 | $1,024.7 | $1,401.0 | $1,843.2 | $318.9 |
| Bonds | 944.8 | 2,323.7 | 2,220.3 | 861.2 | 893.7 | 1,242.5 | 1,611.3 | 285.3 |
| Stocks | 311.9 | 115.3 | 168.8 | 206.8 | 131.0 | 129.5 | 174.0 | 33.2 |
| Private placements | 196.5 | 24.6 | 20.1 | 16.2 | 22.2 | 21.4 | 28.8 | n.a.† |
| IPOs | 97.0 | 36.7 | 46.3 | 26.4 | 37.0 | 40.9 | 29.1 | 0.4 |

*Through first quarter.
†n.a. = not applicable.

1. We discuss the users and suppliers of funds in more detail in Chapter 2.

**Figure 1–2** **Primary and Secondary Market Transfer of Funds Time Line**

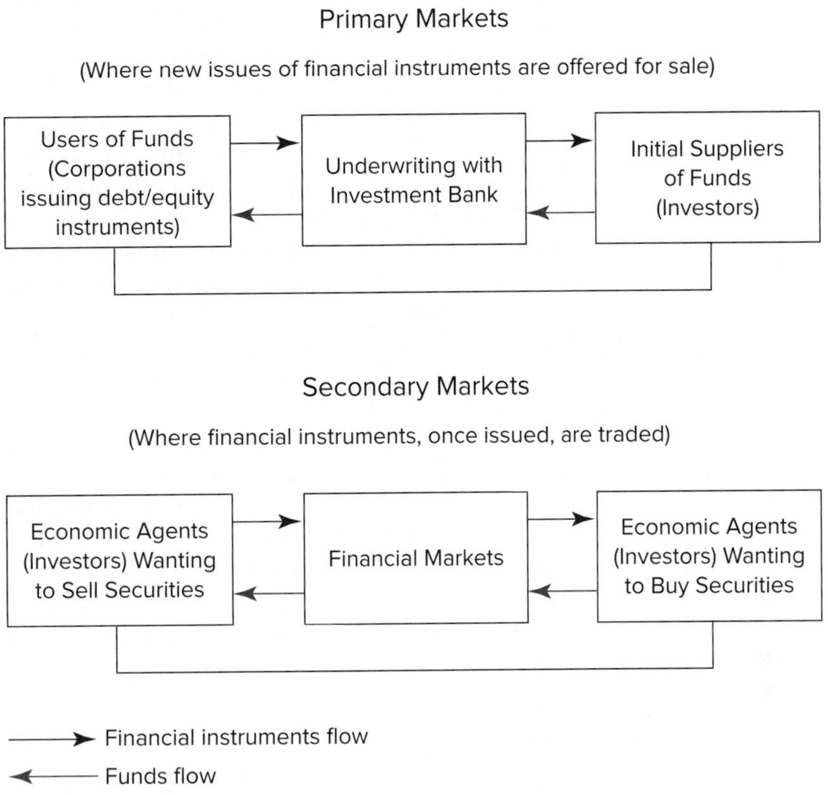

Primary Markets

(Where new issues of financial instruments are offered for sale)

Secondary Markets

(Where financial instruments, once issued, are traded)

⟶ Financial instruments flow

⟵ Funds flow

The company's stock was underwritten by several investment banks, including Morgan Stanley, Deutsche Bank, and Bank of America Merrill Lynch. Primary market securities also include the issue of additional equity or debt instruments of an already publicly traded firm. For example, on January 28, 2016, Molson Coors Brewing Company announced the sale of an additional 29.88 million shares of common stock underwritten by investment banks such as UBS, Bank of America Merrill Lynch, and Citigroup.

**secondary market**

*A market that trades financial instruments once they are issued.*

**Secondary Markets.**  Once financial instruments such as stocks are issued in primary markets, they are then traded—that is, rebought and resold—in **secondary markets.** For example, on April 12, 2016, 9.7 million shares of ExxonMobil were traded in the secondary stock market. Buyers of secondary market securities are economic agents (consumers, businesses, and governments) with excess funds. Sellers of secondary market financial instruments are economic agents in need of funds. Secondary markets provide a centralized marketplace where economic agents know they can transact quickly and efficiently.

These markets therefore save economic agents the search and other costs of seeking buyers or sellers on their own. Figure 1–2 illustrates a secondary market transfer of funds. When an economic agent buys a financial instrument in a secondary market, funds are exchanged, usually with the help of a securities broker such as Charles Schwab acting as an intermediary between the buyer and the seller of the instrument (see Chapter 8). The original issuer of the instrument (user of funds) is not involved in this transfer. The New York Stock Exchange (NYSE) and the National Association of Securities Dealers Automated Quotation (NASDAQ) system are two well-known examples of secondary markets for trading stocks. We discuss the details of each of these markets in Chapter 8.

**derivative security**

*A financial security whose payoffs are linked to other, previously issued securities or indices.*

In addition to stocks and bonds, secondary markets also exist for financial instruments backed by mortgages and other assets (see Chapter 7), foreign exchange (see Chapter 9), and futures and options (i.e., **derivative securities**—financial securities whose payoffs are linked to other, previously issued [or underlying] primary securities or indexes of primary securities) (see Chapter 10). As we will see in Chapter 10, derivative securities have existed for centuries, but the growth in derivative securities markets occurred mainly in the 1980s through 2000s. As major markets, therefore, derivative securities markets are among the newest of the financial security markets.

Secondary markets offer benefits to both investors (suppliers of funds) and issuing corporations (users of funds). For investors, secondary markets provide the opportunity to trade securities at their market values quickly as well as to purchase securities with varying risk-return characteristics (see Chapter 2). Corporate security issuers are not directly involved in the transfer of funds or instruments in the secondary market. However, the issuer does obtain information about the current market value of its financial instruments, and thus the value of the corporation as perceived by investors such as its stockholders, through tracking the prices at which its financial instruments are being traded on secondary markets. This price information allows issuers to evaluate how well they are using the funds generated from the financial instruments they have already issued and provides information on how well any subsequent offerings of debt or equity might do in terms of raising additional money (and at what cost).

**liquidity**

*The ease with which an asset can be converted into cash quickly and at fair market value.*

Secondary markets offer buyers and sellers **liquidity**—the ability to turn an asset into cash quickly at its fair market value—as well as information about the prices or the value of their investments. Increased liquidity makes it more desirable and easier for the issuing firm to sell a security initially in the primary market. Further, the existence of centralized markets for buying and selling financial instruments allows investors to trade these instruments at low transaction costs.

 LG 1-2 

### *Money Markets versus Capital Markets*

**money markets**

*Markets that trade debt securities or instruments with maturities of one year or less.*

**Money Markets.**   **Money markets** are markets that trade debt securities or instruments with maturities of one year or less (see Figure 1–3). In the money markets, economic agents with short-term excess supplies of funds can lend funds (i.e., buy money market instruments) to economic agents who have short-term needs or shortages of funds (i.e., they sell money market instruments). The short-term nature of these instruments means that fluctuations in their prices in the secondary markets in which they trade are usually quite small (see Chapters 3 and 22 on interest rate risk). In the United States, money markets do not operate in a specific location—rather, transactions occur via telephones, wire transfers, and computer trading. Thus, most U.S. money markets are said to be **over-the-counter (OTC) markets.**

**over-the-counter (OTC) markets**

*Markets that do not operate in a specific fixed location—rather, transactions occur via telephones, wire transfers, and computer trading.*

**Money Market Instruments.**   A variety of money market securities are issued by corporations and government units to obtain short-term funds. These securities include Treasury bills, federal funds, repurchase agreements, commercial paper, negotiable certificates of deposit, and banker's acceptances. Table 1–3 lists and defines the major money market securities. Figure 1–4 shows outstanding amounts of money market instruments in the United States in 1990, 2000, 2010, and 2016. Notice that in 2016 federal funds and repurchase agreements, followed by negotiable CDs, Treasury bills, and commercial paper, had the largest amounts outstanding. Money market instruments and the operation of the money markets are described and discussed in detail in Chapter 5.

**Figure 1–3**  **Money versus Capital Market Maturities**

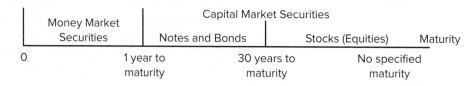

**TABLE 1–3**  Money and Capital Market Instruments

### MONEY MARKET INSTRUMENTS

**Treasury bills**—short-term obligations issued by the U.S. government.
**Federal funds**—short-term funds transferred between financial institutions usually for no more than one day.
**Repurchase agreements**—agreements involving the sale of securities by one party to another with a promise by the seller to repurchase the same securities from the buyer at a specified date and price.
**Commercial paper**—short-term unsecured promissory notes issued by a company to raise short-term cash.
**Negotiable certificates of deposit**—bank-issued time deposits that specify an interest rate and maturity date and are negotiable (i.e., can be sold by the holder to another party).
**Banker's acceptances**—time drafts payable to a seller of goods, with payment guaranteed by a bank.

### CAPITAL MARKET INSTRUMENTS

**Corporate stock**—the fundamental ownership claim in a public corporation.
**Mortgages**—loans to individuals or businesses to purchase a home, land, or other real property.
**Corporate bonds**—long-term bonds issued by corporations.
**Treasury bonds**—long-term bonds issued by the U.S. government.
**State and local government bonds**—long-term bonds issued by state and local governments.
**U.S. government agency bonds**—long-term bonds collateralized by a pool of assets and issued by agencies of the U.S. government.
**Bank and consumer loans**—loans to commercial banks and individuals.

**Figure 1–4**  Money Market Instruments Outstanding

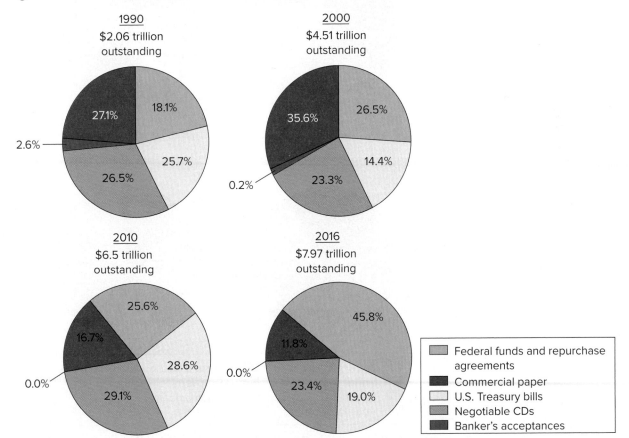

**Sources:** Federal Reserve Board, "Financial Accounts of the United States," *Statistical Releases,* Washington, DC, various issues. www.federalreserve.gov

**capital markets**

*Markets that trade debt (bonds) and equity (stocks) instruments with maturities of more than one year.*

**Capital Markets.**    **Capital markets** are markets that trade equity (stocks) and debt (bonds) instruments with maturities of more than one year (see Figure 1–3). The major suppliers of capital market securities (or users of funds) are corporations and governments. Households are the major suppliers of funds for these securities. Given their longer maturity, these instruments experience wider price fluctuations in the secondary markets in which they trade than do money market instruments. For example, all else constant, long-term maturity debt instruments experience wider price fluctuations for a given change in interest rates than short-term maturity debt instruments (see Chapter 3).

**Capital Market Instruments.**    Table 1–3 lists and defines the major capital market securities. Figure 1–5 shows their outstanding amounts by dollar market value. Notice that in 2000, 2010, and 2016, corporate stocks or equities represent the largest capital market instrument, followed by mortgages and corporate bonds. The relative size of the market value of capital market instruments outstanding depends on two factors: the number of

**Figure 1–5**   Capital Market Instruments Outstanding

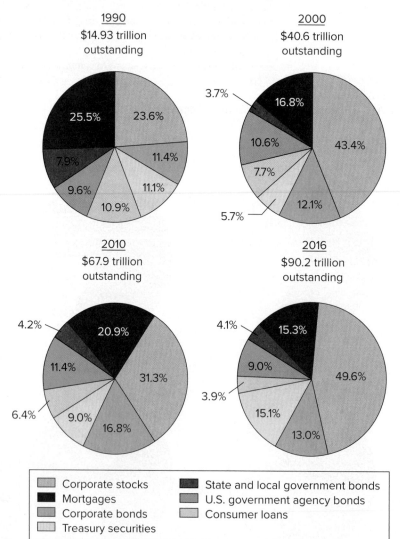

**Sources:** Federal Reserve Board, "Financial Accounts of the United States," *Statistical Releases*, Washington, DC, various issues. www.federalreserve.gov

securities issued and their market prices.[2] One reason for the sharp increase in the value of equities outstanding is the bull market in stock prices in the 1990s. Stock values fell in the early 2000s as the U.S. economy experienced a downturn—partly because of 9/11 and partly because interest rates began to rise—and stock prices fell. Stock prices in most sectors subsequently recovered and, by 2007, even surpassed their 1999 levels. Stock prices fell precipitously during the financial crisis of 2008–2009. As of mid-March 2009, the Dow Jones Industrial Average (DJIA) had fallen 53.8 percent in value in less than 1½ years, larger than the decline during the market crash of 1929 when it fell 49 percent. However, stock prices recovered, along with the economy, in the last half of 2009, rising 71.1 percent between March 2009 and April 2010. Capital market instruments and their operations are discussed in detail in Chapters 6, 7, and 8.

**LG 1-3**

### Foreign Exchange Markets

In addition to understanding the operations of domestic financial markets, a financial manager must also understand the operations of foreign exchange markets and foreign capital markets. Today's U.S.-based companies operate globally. It is therefore essential that financial managers understand how events and movements in financial markets in other countries affect the profitability and performance of their own companies. For example, in 2015 a strengthening dollar reduced profits for internationally active firms. IBM experienced a drop in its 2015 earnings per share of $1.10 due to foreign exchange trends. Coca-Cola, which gets the majority of its sales from outside the United States, saw 2015 revenues decrease by 5.1 percent as the U.S. dollar strengthened relative to foreign currencies.

Cash flows from the sale of securities (or other assets) denominated in a foreign currency expose U.S. corporations and investors to risk regarding the value at which foreign currency cash flows can be converted into U.S. dollars. For example, the actual amount of U.S. dollars received on a foreign investment depends on the exchange rate between the U.S. dollar and the foreign currency when the nondollar cash flow is converted into U.S. dollars. If a foreign currency depreciates (declines in value) relative to the U.S. dollar over the investment period (i.e., the period between the time a foreign investment is made and the time it is terminated), the dollar value of cash flows received will fall. If the foreign currency appreciates, or rises in value, relative to the U.S. dollar, the dollar value of cash flows received on the foreign investment will increase.

While foreign currency exchange rates are often flexible—they vary day to day with demand for and supply of a foreign currency for dollars—central governments sometimes intervene in foreign exchange markets directly or affect foreign exchange rates indirectly by altering interest rates. We discuss the motivation and effects of these interventions in Chapters 4 and 9. The sensitivity of the value of cash flows on foreign investments to changes in the foreign currency's price in terms of dollars is referred to as *foreign exchange risk* and is discussed in more detail in Chapter 9. Techniques for managing, or "hedging," foreign exchange risk, such as using derivative securities like foreign exchange (FX) futures, options, and swaps, are discussed in Chapter 23.

### DO YOU UNDERSTAND:

1.  The difference between primary and secondary markets?

2.  The major distinction between money markets and capital markets?

3.  What the major instruments traded in the capital markets are?

4.  What happens to the dollar value of a U.S. investor's holding of British pounds if the pound appreciates (rises) in value against the dollar?

5.  What derivative security markets are?

**LG 1-4**

**derivative security markets**

*The markets in which derivative securities trade.*

### Derivative Security Markets

**Derivative security markets** are markets in which derivative securities trade. A **derivative security** is a financial security (such as a futures contract, option contract, swap contract, or mortgage-backed security) whose payoff is linked to another, previously issued security such as a security traded in capital or foreign exchange markets. Derivative securities generally involve an agreement between two parties to exchange a standard quantity of an asset or cash flow at a predetermined price and at a specified date in the future. As the

2. For example, the market value of equity is the product of the price of the equity times the number of shares that are issued.

**derivative security**

*An agreement between two parties to exchange a standard quantity of an asset at a predetermined price at a specified date in the future.*

value of the underlying security to be exchanged changes, the value of the derivative security changes. While derivative securities have been in existence for centuries, the growth in derivative security markets occurred mainly in the 1990s and 2000s. Table 1–4 shows the dollar (or notional) value of derivatives held by commercial banks from 1992 through 2016. Note the tremendous growth in these securities between 1992 and 2013, and the large drop from 2013 to 2016. As we discuss in Chapter 10, part of the Wall Street Reform and Consumer Protection Act, passed in 2010 in response to the financial crisis, is the Volcker Rule which prohibits U.S. depository institutions (DIs) from engaging in proprietary trading (i.e., trading as a principal for the trading account of the bank). This includes any transaction to purchase or sell derivatives. Thus, only the investment banking arm of the business is allowed to conduct such trading. The Volcker Rule was implemented in April 2014 and banks had until July 21, 2015, to be in compliance. The result has been a reduction in derivative securities held off-balance-sheet by these financial institutions.

As major markets, derivative security markets are the newest of the financial security markets. Derivative securities, however, are also potentially the riskiest of the financial securities. Indeed, at the center of the recent financial crisis were losses associated with off-balance-sheet mortgage-backed (derivative) securities created and held by FIs. Losses from the falling value of subprime mortgages and the derivative securities backed by these mortgages reached $700 billion worldwide by early 2009 and resulted in the failure, acquisition, or bailout of some of the largest FIs and the near collapse of the world's financial and economic systems.

We discuss derivative security activity in Chapter 10. Derivative security traders can be either users of derivative contracts for hedging (see Chapters 10 and 23) and other purposes or dealers (such as banks) that act as counterparties in trades with customers for a fee.

### Financial Market Regulation

**www.sec.gov**

Financial instruments are subject to regulations imposed by regulatory agencies such as the Securities and Exchange Commission (SEC)—the main regulator of securities markets since the passage of the Securities Act of 1934—as well as the exchanges (if any) on which the instruments are traded. The main emphasis of SEC regulations (as stated in the Securities Act of 1933) is on full and fair disclosure of information on securities issues to actual and potential investors. Those firms planning to issue new stocks or bonds to be sold to the public at large (public issues) are required by the SEC to register their securities with the SEC and to fully describe the issue, and any risks associated with the issue, in a legal document called a prospectus.

The SEC also monitors trading on the major exchanges (along with the exchanges themselves) to ensure that stockholders and managers do not trade on the basis of inside information about their own firms (i.e., information prior to its public release). SEC regulations are not intended to protect investors against poor investment choices, but rather to ensure that investors have full and accurate information available about corporate issuers when making their investment decisions.

**TABLE 1–4**   **Derivative Contracts Held by Commercial Banks, by Contract Product**
*(in billions of dollars)*

|  | 1992 | 2000 | 2008 | 2013 | 2016 |
|---|---|---|---|---|---|
| Futures and forwards | $4,780 | $ 9,877 | $ 22,512 | $ 45,599 | $ 35,685 |
| Swaps | 2,417 | 21,949 | 131,706 | 138,361 | 107,393 |
| Options | 1,568 | 8,292 | 30,267 | 33,760 | 30,909 |
| Credit derivatives | — | 426 | 15,897 | 13,901 | 6,986 |
| Total | $8,765 | $40,544 | $ 200,382 | $231,621 | $180,973 |

**Note:** Em dashes represent values that are too small to register.
**Sources:** Office of the Comptroller of the Currency website, various dates. www.occ.treas.gov

## OVERVIEW OF FINANCIAL INSTITUTIONS

**financial institutions**

*Institutions that perform the essential function of channeling funds from those with surplus funds to those with shortages of funds.*

**direct transfer**

*A corporation sells its stock or debt directly to investors without going through a financial institution.*

**Financial institutions** (e.g., commercial and savings banks, credit unions, insurance companies, mutual funds) perform the essential function of channeling funds from those with surplus funds (suppliers of funds) to those with shortages of funds (users of funds). Chapters 11 through 18 discuss the various types of FIs in today's economy, including (1) the size, structure, and composition of each type; (2) their balance sheets and recent trends; (3) FI performance; and (4) the regulators who oversee each type. Table 1–5 lists and summarizes the FIs discussed in detail in later chapters.

To understand the important economic function financial institutions play in the operation of financial markets, imagine a simple world in which FIs do not exist. In such a world, suppliers of funds (e.g., households), generating excess savings by consuming less than they earn, would have a basic choice: they could either hold cash as an asset or directly invest that cash in the securities issued by users of funds (e.g., corporations or households). In general, users of funds issue financial claims (e.g., equity and debt securities or mortgages) to finance the gap between their investment expenditures and their internally generated savings such as retained earnings. As shown in Figure 1–6, in such a world we have a **direct transfer** of funds (money) from suppliers of funds to users of funds. In return, financial claims would flow directly from users of funds to suppliers of funds.

**TABLE 1–5**    Types of Financial Institutions

**Commercial banks**—depository institutions whose major assets are loans and whose major liabilities are deposits. Commercial banks' loans are broader in range, including consumer, commercial, and real estate loans, than are those of other depository institutions. Commercial banks' liabilities include more nondeposit sources of funds, such as subordinate notes and debentures, than do those of other depository institutions.

**Thrifts**—depository institutions in the form of savings associations, savings banks, and credit unions. Thrifts generally perform services similar to commercial banks, but they tend to concentrate their loans in one segment, such as real estate loans or consumer loans.

**Insurance companies**—financial institutions that protect individuals and corporations (policyholders) from adverse events. Life insurance companies provide protection in the event of untimely death, illness, and retirement. Property casualty insurance protects against personal injury and liability due to accidents, theft, fire, and so on.

**Securities firms and investment banks**—financial institutions that help firms issue securities and engage in related activities such as securities brokerage and securities trading.

**Finance companies**—financial intermediaries that make loans to both individuals and businesses. Unlike depository institutions, finance companies do not accept deposits but instead rely on short- and long-term debt for funding.

**Investment funds**—financial institutions that pool financial resources of individuals and companies and invest those resources in diversified portfolios of assets.

**Pension funds**—financial institutions that offer savings plans through which fund participants accumulate savings during their working years before withdrawing them during their retirement years. Funds originally invested in and accumulated in pension funds are exempt from current taxation.

**Figure 1–6**    **Flow of Funds in a World without FIs**

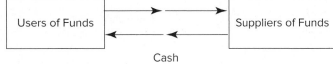

Financial Claims
(equity and debt instruments)

Users of Funds → Suppliers of Funds

Cash

In this economy without financial institutions, the level of funds flowing between suppliers of funds (who want to maximize the return on their funds subject to risk) and users of funds (who want to minimize their cost of borrowing subject to risk) is likely to be quite low. There are several reasons for this. First, once they have lent money in exchange for financial claims, suppliers of funds need to monitor continuously the use of their funds. They must be sure that the user of funds neither steals the funds outright nor wastes the funds on projects that have low or negative returns. Such monitoring is often extremely costly for any given fund supplier because it requires considerable time, expense, and effort to collect this information relative to the size of the average fund supplier's investment. Given this, fund suppliers would likely prefer to leave, or delegate, the monitoring of fund borrowers to others. The resulting lack of monitoring increases the risk of directly investing in financial claims.

Second, the relatively long-term nature of many financial claims (e.g., mortgages, corporate stock, and bonds) creates another disincentive for suppliers of funds to hold the direct financial claims issued by users of funds. Specifically, given the choice between holding cash and long-term securities, fund suppliers may well choose to hold cash for liquidity reasons, especially if they plan to use their savings to finance consumption expenditures in the near future and financial markets are not very developed, or deep, in terms of the number of active buyers and sellers in the market.

**price risk**

*The risk that an asset's sale price will be lower than its purchase price.*

Third, even though real-world financial markets provide some liquidity services, by allowing fund suppliers to trade financial securities among themselves, fund suppliers face a **price risk** upon the sale of securities. That is, the price at which investors can sell a security on secondary markets such as the New York Stock Exchange (NYSE) may well differ from the price they initially paid for the security either because investors change their valuation of the security between the time it was bought and when it was sold and/or because dealers, acting as intermediaries between buyers and sellers, charge transaction costs for completing a trade.

### Unique Economic Functions Performed by Financial Institutions

Because of (1) monitoring costs, (2) liquidity costs, and (3) price risk, the average investor in a world without FIs would likely view direct investment in financial claims and markets as an unattractive proposition and prefer to hold cash. As a result, financial market activity (and therefore savings and investment) would likely remain quite low.

**indirect transfer**

*A transfer of funds between suppliers and users of funds through a financial intermediary.*

However, the financial system has developed an alternative and indirect way for investors (or fund suppliers) to channel funds to users of funds.[3] This is the **indirect transfer** of funds to the ultimate user of funds via FIs. Due to the costs of monitoring, liquidity risk, and price risk, as well as for other reasons explained later, fund suppliers often prefer to

**Figure 1–7**     **Flow of Funds in a World with FIs**

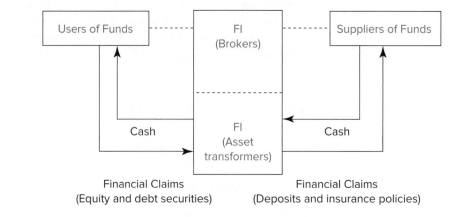

3. We describe and illustrate this flow of funds in Chapter 2.

hold the financial claims issued by FIs rather than those directly issued by the ultimate users of funds. Consider Figure 1–7, which is a closer representation than Figure 1–6 of the world in which we live and the way funds flow in the U.S. financial system. Notice how financial intermediaries or institutions are standing, or intermediating between, the suppliers and users of funds—that is, channeling funds from ultimate suppliers to ultimate users of funds.

How can a financial institution reduce the monitoring costs, liquidity risks, and price risks facing the suppliers of funds compared to when they directly invest in financial claims? We look at how FIs resolve these cost and risk issues next and summarize them in Table 1–6.

**LG 1-6**

**Monitoring Costs.**    As mentioned previously, a supplier of funds who directly invests in a fund user's financial claims faces a high cost of monitoring the fund user's actions in a timely and complete fashion. One solution to this problem is for a large number of small investors to group their funds together by holding the claims issued by a financial institution. The FI groups the fund suppliers' funds together and invests them in the direct financial claims issued by fund users. This aggregation of funds by fund suppliers in a financial institution resolves a number of problems. First, the "large" FI now has a much greater incentive to hire employees with superior skills and training in monitoring. This expertise can be used to collect information and monitor the ultimate fund user's actions because the FI has far more at stake than any small individual fund supplier. Second, the monitoring function performed by the FI alleviates the "free-rider" problem that exists when small fund suppliers leave it to each other to collect information and monitor a fund user. In an economic sense, fund suppliers have appointed the financial institution as a **delegated monitor** to act on their behalf. For example, full-service securities firms such as Morgan Stanley carry out investment research on new issues and make investment recommendations for their retail clients (or investors), while commercial banks collect deposits from fund suppliers and lend these funds to ultimate users such as corporations. An important part of these FIs' functions is their ability and incentive to monitor ultimate fund users.

**delegated monitor**

*An economic agent appointed to act on behalf of smaller investors in collecting information and/ or investing funds on their behalf.*

**TABLE 1–6**   **Services Performed by Financial Institutions**

**Services Benefiting Suppliers of Funds:**

**Monitoring costs**—aggregation of funds in an FI provides greater incentive to collect a firm's information and monitor actions. The relatively large size of the FI allows this collection of information to be accomplished at a lower average cost (economies of scale).

**Liquidity and price risk**—FIs provide financial claims to household savers with superior liquidity attributes and with lower price risk.

**Transaction cost services**—similar to economies of scale in information production costs, an FI's size can result in economies of scale in transaction costs.

**Maturity intermediation**—FIs can better bear the risk of mismatching the maturities of their assets and liabilities.

**Denomination intermediation**—FIs such as mutual funds allow small investors to overcome constraints to buying assets imposed by large minimum denomination size.

**Services Benefiting the Overall Economy:**

**Money supply transmission**—depository institutions are the conduit through which monetary policy actions impact the rest of the financial system and the economy in general.

**Credit allocation**—FIs are often viewed as the major, and sometimes only, source of financing for a particular sector of the economy, such as farming and residential real estate.

**Intergenerational wealth transfers**—FIs, especially life insurance companies and pension funds, provide savers with the ability to transfer wealth from one generation to the next.

**Payment services**—the efficiency with which depository institutions provide payment services directly benefits the economy.

**asset transformers**

*Financial claims issued by an FI that are more attractive to investors than are the claims directly issued by corporations.*

**Liquidity and Price Risk.**    In addition to improving the quality and quantity of information, FIs provide further claims to fund suppliers, thus acting as **asset transformers.** Financial institutions purchase the financial claims issued by users of funds—primary securities such as mortgages, bonds, and stocks—and finance these purchases by selling financial claims to household investors and other fund suppliers in the form of deposits, insurance policies, or other *secondary securities.* Thus, in contrast to a world without FIs, while funds are being transferred from suppliers of funds through FIs to users of funds, ownership of the financial claims is not directly transferred from users of funds to the suppliers of funds. For example, an individual investor in a mutual fund that purchases Apple stock is not a shareholder of Apple Inc. The mutual fund owns Apple shares and the individual investor owns shares of this mutual fund.

Often claims issued by financial institutions have liquidity attributes that are superior to those of primary securities. For example, banks and thrift institutions (e.g., savings associations) issue transaction account deposit contracts with a fixed principal value and often a guaranteed interest rate that can be withdrawn immediately, on demand, by investors. Money market mutual funds issue shares to household savers that allow them to enjoy almost fixed principal (depositlike) contracts while earning higher interest rates than on bank deposits, and that can be withdrawn immediately. Even life insurance companies allow policyholders to borrow against their policies held with the company at very short notice. Notice that in reducing the liquidity risk of investing funds for fund suppliers, the FI transfers this risk to its own balance sheet. That is, FIs such as depository institutions offer highly liquid, low price-risk securities to fund suppliers on the liability side of their balance sheets, while investing in relatively less liquid and higher price-risk securities—such as the debt and equity—issued by fund users on the asset side. Three questions arise here. First, how can FIs provide these liquidity services? Furthermore, how can FIs be confident enough to guarantee that they can provide liquidity services to fund suppliers when they themselves invest in risky assets? Finally, why should fund suppliers believe FIs' promises regarding the liquidity and safety of their investments?

**diversify**

*The ability of an economic agent to reduce risk by holding a number of different securities in a portfolio.*

The answers to these three questions lie in financial institutions' ability to **diversify** away some, but not all, of their investment risk. The concept of diversification is familiar to all students of finance. Basically, as long as the returns on different investments are not perfectly positively correlated, by spreading their investments across a number of assets, FIs can diversify away significant amounts of their portfolio risk. (We discuss the mechanics of diversification in the loan portfolio in Chapter 20.) Thus, FIs can exploit the law of large numbers in making their investment decisions, whereas because of their smaller wealth size, individual fund suppliers are constrained to holding relatively undiversified portfolios. As a result, diversification allows an FI to predict more accurately its expected return and risk on its investment portfolio so that it can credibly fulfill its promises to the suppliers of funds to provide highly liquid claims with little price risk. As long as an FI is large enough to gain from diversification and monitoring on the asset side of its balance sheet, its financial claims (its liabilities) are likely to be viewed as liquid and attractive to small savers—especially when compared to direct investments in the capital market.

### Additional Benefits FIs Provide to Suppliers of Funds

The indirect investing of funds through financial institutions is attractive to fund suppliers for other reasons as well. We discuss these below and summarize them in Table 1–6.

**economies of scale**

*The concept that cost reduction in trading and other transaction services results in increased efficiency when FIs perform these services.*

**Reduced Transaction Cost.**    Not only do financial institutions have a greater incentive to collect information, but also their average cost of collecting relevant information is lower than for the individual investor (i.e., information collection enjoys **economies of scale**). For example, the cost to a small investor of buying a $100 broker's report may seem inordinately high for a $10,000 investment. For an FI with $10 billion of assets under management, however, the cost seems trivial. Such economies of scale of information production and collection tend to enhance the advantages to investors of investing via FIs rather than directly investing themselves. Nevertheless, as a result of technological advances, the costs of direct access to financial markets by savers are ever falling and the relative benefits to the individual savers of investing through FIs are narrowing.

**Maturity Intermediation.**　An additional dimension of financial institutions' ability to reduce risk by diversification is their greater ability, compared to a small saver, to bear the risk of mismatching the maturities of their assets and liabilities. Thus, FIs offer maturity intermediation services to the rest of the economy. Specifically, by maturity mismatching, FIs can produce long-term contracts such as long-term, fixed-rate mortgage loans to households, while still raising funds with short-term liability contracts such as deposits. In addition, although such mismatches can subject an FI to interest rate risk (see Chapters 3 and 22), a large FI is better able than a small investor to manage this risk through its superior access to markets and instruments for hedging the risks of such loans (see Chapters 7, 10, 20, and 24).

**Denomination Intermediation.**　Some FIs, especially mutual funds, perform a unique service relating to denomination intermediation. Because many assets are sold in very large denominations, they are either out of reach of individual savers or would result in savers holding very undiversified asset portfolios. For example, the minimum size of a negotiable CD is $100,000, while commercial paper (short-term corporate debt) is often sold in minimum packages of $250,000 or more. Individual small savers may be unable to purchase such instruments directly. However, by pooling the funds of many small savers (such as by buying shares in a mutual fund with other small investors), small savers overcome constraints to buying assets imposed by large minimum denomination size. Such indirect access to these markets may allow small savers to generate higher returns (and lower risks) on their portfolios as well.

### Economic Functions FIs Provide to the Financial System as a Whole

In addition to the services financial institutions provide to suppliers and users of funds in the financial markets, FIs perform services that improve the operation of the financial system as a whole. We discuss these next and summarize them in Table 1–6.

**The Transmission of Monetary Policy.**　The highly liquid nature of bank and thrift deposits has resulted in their acceptance by the public as the most widely used medium of exchange in the economy. Indeed, at the core of the most commonly used definitions of the money supply (see Chapter 4) are bank and/or thrift deposit contracts. Because deposits are a significant component of the money supply, which in turn directly impacts the rate of economic growth, depository institutions—particularly commercial banks— play a key role in the *transmission of monetary policy* from the central bank (the Federal Reserve) to the rest of the economy (see Chapter 4 for a detailed discussion of how the Federal Reserve implements monetary policy through depository institutions).[4] Because depository institutions are instrumental in determining the size and growth of the money supply, they have been designated as the primary conduit through which monetary policy actions by the Federal Reserve impact the rest of the financial sector and the economy in general.

**Credit Allocation.**　FIs provide a unique service to the economy in that they are the major source of financing for particular sectors of the economy preidentified by society as being in special need of financing. For example, policymakers in the United States and a number of other countries such as the United Kingdom have identified *residential real estate* as

---

4. The Federal Reserve is the U.S. central bank charged with promoting economic growth in line with the economy's potential to expand.

**DO YOU UNDERSTAND:**

6.  *The three major reasons that suppliers of funds would not want to directly purchase securities?*

7.  *What the asset transformation function of FIs is?*

8.  *What delegated monitoring function FIs perform?*

9.  *What the link is between asset diversification and the liquidity of deposit contracts?*

10. *What maturity intermediation is?*

11. *Why the need for denomination intermediation arises?*

12. *The two major sectors that society has identified as deserving special attention in credit allocation?*

13. *Why monetary policy is transmitted through the banking system?*

14. *The payment services that FIs perform?*

needing special attention. This has enhanced the specialness of those FIs that most commonly service the needs of that sector. In the United States, savings associations and savings banks must emphasize mortgage lending. Sixty-five percent of their assets must be mortgage related for these thrifts to maintain their charter status (see Chapter 14). In a similar fashion, farming is an especially important area of the economy in terms of the overall social welfare of the population. Thus, the U.S. government has directly encouraged financial institutions to specialize in financing this area of activity through the creation of Federal Farm Credit Banks.[5]

**Intergenerational Wealth Transfers or Time Intermediation.**   The ability of savers to transfer wealth from their youth to old age as well as across generations is also of great importance to a country's social well-being. Because of this, special taxation relief and other subsidy mechanisms encourage investments by savers in life insurance, annuities, and pension funds. For example, pension funds offer savings plans through which fund participants accumulate tax-exempt savings during their working years before withdrawing them during their retirement years.

**Payment Services.**   Depository institutions such as banks and thrifts are also special in that the efficiency with which they provide payment services directly benefits the economy. Two important payment services are check-clearing and wire transfer services. For example, on any given day, over $4.5 trillion of payments are directed through Fedwire and CHIPS, the two largest wholesale payment wire network systems in the United States. Any breakdowns in these systems would likely produce gridlock to the payment system, with resulting harmful effects to the economy.

**LG 1-7**   *Risks Incurred by Financial Institutions*

As financial institutions perform the various services described previously, they face many types of risk. Specifically, all FIs hold some assets that are potentially subject to default or credit risk (such as loans, stocks, and bonds). As FIs expand their services to non-U.S. customers or even domestic customers with business outside the United States, they are exposed to both foreign exchange risk and country or sovereign risk as well. Further, FIs tend to mismatch the maturities of their balance sheet assets and liabilities to a greater or lesser extent and are thus exposed to interest rate risk. If FIs actively trade these assets and liabilities rather than hold them for longer-term investments, they are further exposed to market risk or asset price risk. Increasingly, FIs hold contingent assets and liabilities off the balance sheet, which presents an additional risk called off-balance-sheet risk. Moreover, all FIs are exposed to some degree of liability withdrawal or liquidity risk, depending on the type of claims they have sold to liability holders. All FIs are exposed to technology risk and operational risk because the production of financial services requires the use of real resources and back-office support systems (labor and technology combined to provide services). Finally, the risk that an FI may not have enough capital reserves to offset a sudden loss incurred as a result of one or more of the risks it faces creates insolvency risk for the FI. Chapters 19 through 24 provide an analysis of how FIs measure and manage these risks.

**LG 1-8**   *Regulation of Financial Institutions*

The preceding section showed that financial institutions provide various services to sectors of the economy. Failure to provide these services, or a breakdown in their efficient provision, can be costly to both the ultimate suppliers of funds and users of funds as well as to the economy overall. The financial crisis of the late 2000s is a prime example of how such a breakdown in the provision of financial services can cripple financial markets

---

5. The Farm Credit System was created by Congress in 1916 to provide American agriculture with a source of sound, dependable credit at low rates of interest.

worldwide and bring the world economy into a deep recession. For example, bank failures may destroy household savings and at the same time restrict a firm's access to credit. Insurance company failures may leave household members totally exposed in old age to the cost of catastrophic illnesses and to sudden drops in income upon retirement. In addition, individual FI failures may create doubts in savers' minds regarding the stability and solvency of FIs and the financial system in general and cause panics and even withdrawal runs on sound institutions. Indeed, this possibility provided the reasoning in 2008 for an increase in the deposit insurance cap to $250,000 per person per bank. At this time, the Federal Deposit Insurance Corporation (FDIC) was concerned about the possibility of contagious runs as a few major FIs (e.g., IndyMac and Washington Mutual) failed or nearly failed. The FDIC wanted to instill confidence in the banking system and made the change to avoid massive depositor runs from many of the troubled (and even safer) FIs, more FI failures, and an even larger collapse of the financial system.

FIs are regulated in an attempt to prevent these types of market failures and the costs they would impose on the economy and society at large. Although regulation may be socially beneficial, it also imposes private costs, or a regulatory burden, on individual FI owners and managers. Consequently, regulation is an attempt to enhance the social welfare benefits and mitigate the costs of the provision of FI services. Chapter 13 describes regulations (past and present) that have been imposed on U.S. financial institutions.

### Trends in the United States

In Table 1–7, we show the changing shares of total assets of financial institutions in the United States from 1948 to 2016. A number of important trends are clearly evident; most apparent is the decline in the total share of depository institutions—commercial banks and thrifts—since World War II. Specifically, while still the dominant sector of the financial institutions industry, the share of commercial banks declined from 54.5 percent in 1948 to 26.1 percent in 2016. Note the particularly large decrease in the share of commercial banks from 2010 (32.8 percent) to 2016 (26.1 percent). The effects of regulation imposed during the financial crisis (e.g., the Financial Institutions Reform and Recovery Act of 2010 and Basel 3 capital regulations discussed in Chapter 13) and historically low interest rates on bank deposits (discussed in Chapter 2) reflect this relatively large decline. Further, the share of thrifts (savings banks, savings associations, and credit unions) fell from 12.0 to 3.0 percent over the same period.[6] Similarly, insurance companies also witnessed a decline

**TABLE 1–7** Percentage Shares of Assets of Financial Institutions in the United States, 1948–2016

| | 1948 | 1960 | 1970 | 1980 | 1990 | 2000 | 2010 | 2016 |
|---|---|---|---|---|---|---|---|---|
| Commercial banks | 54.5% | 40.8% | 42.6% | 40.7% | 32.4% | 30.5% | 32.8% | 26.1% |
| Thrift institutions | 12.0 | 21.0 | 23.0 | 25.0 | 17.1 | 10.1 | 7.3 | 3.0 |
| Insurance companies | 26.0 | 24.2 | 19.0 | 16.2 | 18.0 | 15.6 | 14.8 | 10.9 |
| Investment companies | 0.3 | 0.7 | 0.7 | 2.0 | 9.2 | 15.8 | 18.0 | 24.5 |
| Pension funds | 3.8 | 7.7 | 8.0 | 9.5 | 10.5 | 8.8 | 7.6 | 24.5 |
| Finance companies and mortgage companies | 2.7 | 5.2 | 5.7 | 6.2 | 6.8 | 6.9 | 5.3 | 2.0 |
| Securities brokers and dealers | 0.7 | 0.4 | 0.7 | 0.3 | 5.7 | 12.1 | 13.4 | 8.0 |
| Real estate investment trusts | — | 0.0 | 0.3 | 0.1 | 0.3 | 0.2 | 0.8 | 1.0 |
| Total (percentage) | 100.0% | 100.0% | 100.0% | 100.0% | 100.0% | 100.0% | 100.0% | 100.0% |
| Total (trillions of dollars) | $0.324 | $0.810 | $1.375 | $4.066 | $11.557 | $29.105 | $51.385 | $73.124 |

**Sources:** Federal Reserve Board, "Financial Accounts of the United States," *Statistical Releases,* various issues. www.federalreserve.gov

6. Although commercial bank assets as a percentage of total assets in the financial sector may have declined in recent years, this does not necessarily mean that banking activity has decreased. Indeed, off-balance-sheet activities have replaced some of the more traditional on-balance-sheet activities of commercial banks (see Chapter 11). Further, as is discussed in Part Three of the text, banks are increasingly providing services (such as securities underwriting, insurance underwriting and sales, and mutual fund services) previously performed exclusively by other FIs.

in their share, from 26.0 to 10.9 percent. The most dramatic trend involves the increasing share of pension funds and investment companies and securities brokers and dealers. Investment companies (mutual funds and money market mutual funds) increased their share from 0.3 to 24.5 percent, while pension funds increased from 3.8 to 24.5 percent over the 1948 to 2016 period.

**The Rise of Financial Services Holding Companies.**    To the extent that the financial services market is efficient and the data seen in Table 1–7 reflect the forces of demand and supply, these data indicate a current trend: savers increasingly prefer investments that closely mimic diversified investments in the *direct* securities markets over the transformed financial claims offered by traditional FIs. This trend may also indicate that the regulatory burden on traditional FIs—such as banks and insurance companies—is higher than that on pension funds, mutual funds, and investment companies. Indeed, traditional FIs are unable to produce their services as cost-efficiently as they previously could.

Recognizing this changing trend, in 1999 the U.S. Congress passed the Financial Services Modernization (FSM) Act, which repealed the 1933 Glass-Steagall barriers between commercial banking, insurance, and investment banking. The bill, promoted as the biggest change in the regulation of financial institutions in 70 years, allowed for the creation of "financial services holding companies" that could engage in banking activities, insurance activities, and securities activities. After 70 years of partial or complete separation between insurance, investment banking, and commercial banking, the FSM opened the door for the creation of full-service financial institutions in the United States similar to those that existed before 1933 and that exist in many other countries. Thus, while Table 1–7 lists assets of financial institutions by functional area, the financial services holding company (which combines these activities in a single financial institution) has become the dominant form of financial institution in terms of total assets.

**The Shift Away from Risk Measurement and Management and the Financial Crisis.**
Certainly, the financial crisis of the late 2000s changed and reshaped today's financial markets and institutions. As FIs adjusted to regulatory changes brought about by the likes of the FSM Act, one result was a dramatic increase in the systemic risk of the financial system, caused in large part by a shift in the banking model from that of "originate and hold" to "originate and distribute." In the traditional model, banks take short-term deposits and other sources of funds and use them to fund longer term loans to businesses and consumers. Banks typically hold these loans to maturity and thus have an incentive to screen and monitor borrower activities even after a loan is made.

However, the traditional banking model exposes the institution to potential liquidity, interest rate, and credit risk. In attempts to avoid these risk exposures and generate improved return-risk tradeoffs, banks have shifted to an underwriting model in which they originate or warehouse loans and then quickly sell them. Figure 1–8 shows the growth in bank loan secondary market trading from 1991 through 2015. Note the huge growth in bank loan trading even during the financial crisis of 2008–2009. When loans trade, the secondary market produces information that can substitute for the information and monitoring of banks. Further, banks may have lower incentives to collect information and monitor borrowers if they sell loans rather than keep them as part of the bank's portfolio of assets. Indeed, most large banks are organized as financial services holding companies to facilitate these new activities.

More recently, activities of shadow banks, nonbank financial services firms (such as structured investment vehicles [SIVs] discussed in Chapter 24) that perform banking services, have facilitated the change from the originate-and-hold model of commercial banking to the originate-and-distribute banking model. In the shadow banking system, savers place their funds with money market mutual and similar funds, which invest these funds in the liabilities of shadow banks. Borrowers get loans and leases from shadow banks rather than from banks. Like the traditional banking system, the shadow banking system intermediates the flow of funds between net savers and net borrowers. However, instead of

**Figure 1–8** Bank Loan Secondary Market Trading 1991–2015

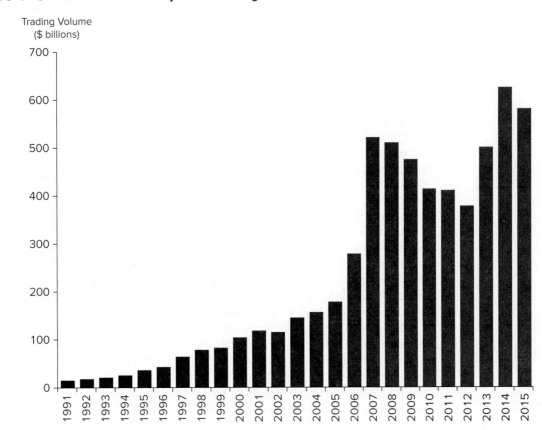

Source: Thomson Reuters LPC website, 2016. www.loanpricing.com

the bank serving as the intermediary, it is the nonbank financial services firm, or shadow bank, that intermediates. These innovations remove risk from the balance sheet of financial institutions and shift risk off the balance sheet and to other parts of the financial system. Since the FIs, acting as underwriters, are not exposed to the credit, liquidity, and interest rate risks of traditional banking, they have little incentive to screen and monitor the activities of borrowers to whom they originated loans. Thus, FIs' role as specialists in risk measurement and management has been reduced.

Adding to FIs' move away from risk measurement and management was the boom ("bubble") in the housing markets, which began building in 2001, particularly after the terrorist attacks of 9/11. The immediate response by regulators to the terrorist attacks was to create stability in the financial markets by providing liquidity to FIs. For example, the Federal Reserve lowered the short-term interest rate that banks and other financial institutions pay in the federal funds market. Perhaps not surprisingly, low interest rates and the increased liquidity provided by the central bank resulted in a rapid expansion in consumer, mortgage, and corporate debt financing. Demand for residential mortgages and credit card debt rose dramatically. As the demand for mortgage debt grew, especially among those who had previously been excluded from participating in the market because of their poor credit ratings, FIs began lowering their credit quality cut-off points. Moreover, to boost their earnings, in the market now popularly known as the "subprime market," banks and other mortgage-supplying institutions often offered relatively low "teaser" rates on adjustable rate mortgages (ARMs). These teaser rates provided exceptionally low initial interest rates. But after the expiration of the initial rate period two or three years later, if market rates rose, the loan rates increased substantially.

Under the traditional, originate-and-hold banking model, banks might have been reluctant to so aggressively pursue low-credit-quality borrowers for fear that the loans would default. However, under the originate-and-distribute model of banking, asset securitization and loan syndication allowed banks to retain little or no part of the loans, and hence little or no part of the default risk on loans that they originated. Thus, as long as the borrower did not default within the first months after a loan's issuance and the loans were sold or securitized without recourse back to the bank, the issuing bank could ignore longer-term credit risk concerns. The result was a deterioration in credit quality at the same time as there was a dramatic increase in consumer and corporate leverage.

Eventually, in 2006, housing prices started to fall. At the same time, the Federal Reserve started to raise interest rates as it began to fear inflation. Since many of the subprime mortgages that originated in the 2001–2005 period had adjustable rates, the cost of meeting mortgage commitments rose to unsustainable levels for many low-income households. The confluence of falling house prices, rising interest rates, and rising mortgage costs led to a wave of mortgage defaults in the subprime market and foreclosures that only reinforced the downward trend in housing prices. In 2007, the percentage of subprime mortgage-backed securities delinquent by 90 days or more was 10.09 percent, substantially higher than the 5.37 percent rate in May 2005. The financial crisis began. As previously mentioned, Appendix 1A (available through Connect or your course instructor) provides a detailed discussion of the causes of, the major events during, and the regulatory and industry changes resulting from the financial crisis.

The economy relies on financial institutions to act as specialists in risk measurement and management. The importance of this was demonstrated in the aftermath of the FIs' failure to perform this critical function during the global financial crisis. The result was a worldwide breakdown in credit markets, as well as an enhanced level of equity market volatility. When FIs failed to perform their critical risk measurement and management functions, the result was a crisis of confidence that disrupted financial markets.

**Enterprise Risk Management.** A major theme of this book is the measurement and management of FI risks. While FIs have traditionally examined risk measurement and management by functional area (e.g., credit risk or liquidity risk), more recently they have recognized the value of enterprise risk management. **Enterprise risk management (ERM)** recognizes the importance of prioritizing and managing the combined impact of the full spectrum of risks as an interrelated risk portfolio. The process also seeks to embed risk management as a component in all critical decisions throughout the FI.

**enterprise risk management (ERM)**

*Recognizes the importance of managing the combined impact of the full spectrum of risks as an interrelated risk portfolio.*

ERM came to the forefront for many FIs during and after the financial crisis, when their risk management practices came under intense scrutiny. Many FIs had invested heavily in advanced risk measurement and management systems only to have them fail to detect or control risk exposures that led up to the crisis. These failures resulted in significant examinations of what went wrong with risk management systems and practices. For example, since the financial crisis, global FI regulators, such as the Basel Committee on Banking Supervision, have moved to address risk culture, risk appetite setting, and risk governance more explicitly in regulatory standards. This was not the case prior to the crisis, when emphasis was predominantly placed on risk management processes and systems, believing that this ought to be sufficient. Prior to the financial crisis, FIs largely failed to take into account behavioral biases that play a critical role in senior management decisions which ultimately affect the risks that a company was willing to take or tolerate. Rather, the advancements in risk management had resulted in a highly analytical-focused discipline that largely ignored fundamental drivers of risk taking that are rooted in subtler behavioral characteristics. Using an ERM framework, decisions include how performance targets are set for staff, how incentive structures are designed, and the stature and resources that are provided to risk management functions within the FI. ERM stresses the importance of building a strong risk culture supported by governance arrangements that are explicitly aligned to a firm's risk appetite.

## GLOBALIZATION OF FINANCIAL MARKETS AND INSTITUTIONS

**LG 1-9**

Financial markets and institutions in the United States have their counterparts in many foreign countries. International debt and equity markets are those markets that trade debt and equity securities issued by domestic and foreign firms. While U.S. markets are the world's largest, international markets have seen rapid growth in recent years. Table 1–8 lists U.S. dollar equivalent values of money market and debt securities outstanding in countries throughout the world from 1996 through 2015. Notice that U.S. markets dominate the world debt markets. In 2015, for example, 14.9 percent of the world's debt securities were issued in the United States. The next two most active issuers (the United Kingdom and Germany) had fewer debt securities outstanding than the U.S. market. Table 1–9 reports U.S. dollar equivalent market capitalization on major worldwide stock exchanges. U.S. stock exchanges are again the largest equity markets, followed by Japan and the United Kingdom.

While U.S. financial markets have historically been much larger in value, size, and trading volume than any foreign market, financial markets became truly global in the 1990s as technological improvements resulted in more immediate and cheaper access to real-time data worldwide by domestic and international investors. Added to this was investors' demand for international securities and international portfolio diversification (such as through the growth of U.S. mutual funds that invest in offshore bonds and stocks). As a result, the volume and values of stocks and other securities traded in foreign markets soared.

The significant growth in foreign financial markets is the result of several other factors as well. First is the increase in the pool of savings in foreign countries (e.g., the European

**TABLE 1–8**  World Financial Markets, International Debt Outstanding, by Issuer *(in billions of dollars)*

| Country | Long-Term Debt | | | | Money Market Securities | | |
|---|---|---|---|---|---|---|---|
| | 1996 | 2000 | 2010 | 2015* | 2000 | 2010 | 2015* |
| Argentina | $ 29.0 | $ 68.1 | $ 53.8 | $ 50.9 | $ 0.4 | $ 0.1 | $ 0.1 |
| Australia | 77.4 | 94.1 | 571.5 | 599.1 | 17.9 | 31.1 | 22.8 |
| Austria | 62.5 | 82.2 | 335.6 | 240.4 | 9.3 | 12.4 | 13.9 |
| Belgium | 42.1 | 65.3 | 573.9 | 287.7 | 12.4 | 18.3 | 10.9 |
| Brazil | 23.1 | 48.9 | 172.6 | 304.5 | 3.5 | 2.8 | 7.5 |
| Canada | 177.8 | 202.8 | 649.8 | 746.8 | 5.8 | 18.3 | 14.2 |
| China | n.a. | 17.6 | 71.8 | 413.5 | 0.2 | 2.8 | 76.1 |
| France | 204.4 | 346.5 | 75.8 | 1,489.3 | 12.7 | 117.5 | 78.2 |
| Germany | 319.8 | 769.8 | 23.9 | 1,648.9 | 104.4 | 121.9 | 163.6 |
| Hong Kong | 15.9 | 28.4 | 85.1 | 126.4 | 2.5 | 1.2 | 5.5 |
| Ireland | 20.0 | 32.0 | 491.0 | 286.7 | 4.1 | 43.4 | 6.7 |
| Italy | 88.6 | 198.1 | 316.2 | 921.8 | 12.6 | 40.5 | 8.7 |
| Japan | 325.6 | 274.2 | 399.7 | 369.3 | 7.4 | 19.6 | 46.2 |
| Luxembourg | 8.4 | 16.4 | 88.5 | 124.4 | 5.4 | 4.2 | 10.2 |
| Mexico | 41.5 | 63.7 | 105.1 | 207.7 | 2.9 | 0.8 | 2.1 |
| Netherlands | 112.2 | 267.2 | 257.7 | 1,192.8 | 26.2 | 91.6 | 63.7 |
| Norway | 19.5 | 39.1 | 204.2 | 241.5 | 1.8 | 4.8 | 3.9 |
| South Korea | 38.9 | 48.7 | 138.1 | 175.6 | 0.8 | 5.0 | 10.7 |
| Spain | 44.2 | 137.0 | 720.4 | 933.6 | 11.3 | 60.0 | 20.4 |
| Sweden | 99.6 | 90.6 | 9.3 | 435.7 | 7.5 | 47.8 | 36.2 |
| Switzerland | 39.5 | 89.3 | 451.9 | 366.7 | 8.1 | 10.5 | 30.3 |
| United Kingdom | 258.7 | 519.2 | 3,020.5 | 2,555.5 | 48.1 | 98.2 | 58.6 |
| United States | 372.4 | 1,662.7 | 7,074.7 | 3,083.7 | 40.9 | 108.3 | 51.4 |
| Total debt | $2,982.5 | $5,907.7 | $26,750.8 | $20,666.7 | $370.1 | $913.5 | $884.4 |

*As of the end of the first quarter.
**Source:** Bank for International Settlements, "International Banking and Financial Market Developments," BIS Statistics Explorer. www.bis.org

**TABLE 1–9**   World Financial Markets, Market Capitalization *(in billions of dollars)*

| Country | 2003 | 2010 | 2013 | 2016 |
|---|---|---|---|---|
| Buenos Aires SE (Argentina) | $ 35.0 | $ 63.9 | $ 43.2 | $ 52.3 |
| Australian SE | 585.5 | 1,454.5 | 1,513.3 | 1,095.7 |
| TMX Group (Canada) | 910.2 | 2,170.4 | 2,032.2 | 1,551.2 |
| Deutsche Börse (Germany) | 1,079.0 | 1,429.7 | 1,566.4 | 1,563.4 |
| NYSE Euronext (Europe) | 2,076.4 | 2,930.1 | 3,016.2 | 3,190.9 |
| Hong Kong Exchanges | 714.6 | 2,711.3 | 2,883.1 | 2,808.0 |
| Irish SE | 85.1 | 60.4 | 128.7 | 114.6 |
| Japan Exchange Group—Tokyo | 2,953.1 | 3,827.8 | 4,223.3 | 4,522.8 |
| Luxembourg SE | 37.3 | 101.1 | 62.5 | 44.4 |
| Mexican Exchange | 122.5 | 454.3 | 556.2 | 386.6 |
| Oslo Børs (Norway) | 95.9 | 295.3 | 250.6 | 183.5 |
| Korea Exchange | 298.2 | 1,091.9 | 1,146.7 | 1,197.1 |
| BME Spanish Exchanges | 726.2 | 1,171.6 | 1,014.0 | 703.4 |
| SIX Swiss Exchange | 727.1 | 1,229.4 | 1,397.4 | 1,395.7 |
| London SE | 2,425.8 | 3,613.1 | 3,821.9 | 3,541.3 |
| NYSE Euronext (U.S.) | 11,328.0 | 13,394.1 | 15,571.6 | 16,813.4 |
| **WFE Total** | **$30,721.0** | **$54,891.1** | **$58,538.9** | **$61,434.5** |

**Source:** World Federation of Exchanges. www.world-exchanges.org

Union). Second, international investors have turned to U.S. and other markets to expand their investment opportunities and improve their investment portfolio risk and return characteristics. This is especially so as the retirement value of public pension plans has declined in many European countries and investors have turned to private pension plans to boost their long-term savings. Third, information on foreign investments and markets is now more accessible and thorough—for example, via the Internet. Fourth, some U.S. FIs—such as specialized mutual funds—offer their customers opportunities to invest in foreign securities and emerging markets at relatively low transaction costs. Fifth, while the euro has had a significant effect throughout Europe, it is also having a notable impact on the global financial system. Despite challenges resulting from the Greek (and to some extent, the European) debt crisis of the 2010s, the euro is still one of the world's most important currencies for international transactions. Sixth, economic growth in Pacific Basin countries, China, and other emerging countries has resulted in significant growth in their stock markets. Finally, deregulation in many foreign countries has allowed international investors greater access and allowed the deregulating countries to expand their investor bases (e.g., until 2012, individual foreign investors faced severe restrictions on their ability to buy Indian stocks). As a result of these factors, the overall volume of investment and trading activity in foreign securities is increasing, as is the integration of U.S. and foreign financial markets.

Table 1–10 shows the extent of the growth in foreign investment in U.S. financial markets. From 1992 through 2015, foreign investors' holdings of U.S. financial market debt securities outstanding increased from $989.3 billion to $10,470.7 billion, while foreign financial market debt securities held by U.S. investors increased from $315.8 billion to $3,077.4 billion. While U.S. financial markets dominate world markets, the growth of U.S. financial markets depends more and more on the growth and development of other economies. In turn, the success of other economies depends to a significant extent on their financial market development. Further, for the same reasons discussed earlier (i.e., monitoring costs, liquidity risk, and price risk), financial institutions are of central importance to the development and integration of markets globally. However, U.S. FIs must now compete not only with other domestic FIs for a share of these markets, but increasingly with foreign FIs. Table 1–11 lists the 10 largest banks in the world, measured by total assets, as of 2016. Only 2 of these are U.S. banks.

**TABLE 1–10    Financial Market Securities Holdings** *(in billions of dollars)*

|  | 1992 | 1996 | 2000 | 2010 | 2015* |
|---|---|---|---|---|---|
| **U.S. Financial Market Instruments Held by Foreign Investors** | | | | | |
| Open market paper | $  12.9 | $  57.9 | $  114.3 | $  191.0 | $  102.7 |
| U.S. government securities | 595.0 | 1,293.9 | 1,462.8 | 5,550.6 | 7,048.2 |
| U.S. corporate bonds | 251.5 | 453.2 | 1,073.6 | 2,523.3 | 3,116.3 |
| Loans to U.S. corporate businesses | 129.9 | 126.2 | 117.3 | 160.4 | 203.5 |
| Total | 989.3 | 1,931.2 | 2,768.0 | 8,425.3 | 10,470.7 |
| U.S. corporate equities held | 326.2 | 666.6 | 1,632.0 | 3,475.8 | 6,289.1 |
| Total financial assets held | $1,315.5 | $2,597.8 | $4,400.0 | $11,901.1 | $16,759.8 |
| **Foreign Financial Market Instruments Held by U.S. Investors** | | | | | |
| Commercial paper | $  78.4 | $  67.5 | $  120.9 | $  398.6 | $  444.8 |
| Bonds | 147.2 | 347.7 | 572.7 | 1,689.5 | 2,271.5 |
| Bank loans | 23.9 | 43.7 | 70.5 | 115.1 | 328.0 |
| Other loans & advances | 66.4 | 60.0 | 50.3 | 22.1 | 33.1 |
| Total | 315.8 | 518.8 | 814.4 | 2,225.3 | 3,077.4 |
| Foreign corporate equities held | 314.3 | 1,006.0 | 1,852.8 | 4,646.9 | 6,732.0 |
| Total financial assets held | $630.1 | $1,524.8 | $2,667.2 | $6,872.2 | $ 9,809.4 |

*As of the end of the first quarter.
**Sources:** Federal Reserve Board, "Financial Accounts of the United States," *Statistical Releases,* various issues. www.federalreserve.gov

**TABLE 1–11    The Largest (in Total Assets) Banks in the World** *(in trillions of dollars)*

| Bank | Country | Total Assets |
|---|---|---|
| 1.  Industrial Commerce Bank of China | China | $3.42 |
| 2.  China Construction Bank | China | 2.83 |
| 3.  Agricultural Bank of China | China | 2.74 |
| 4.  Bank of China | China | 2.59 |
| 5.  Mitsubishi UFJ Financial | Japan | 2.46 |
| 6.  HSBC Holdings | United Kingdom | 2.41 |
| 7.  J.P. Morgan Chase | United States | 2.35 |
| 8.  BNP Paribas | France | 2.17 |
| 9.  Bank of America | United States | 2.14 |
| 10.  Credit Agricole | France | 1.85 |

**Source:** Authors' research.

As a result of the increased globalization of financial markets and institutions, U.S. financial market movements now have a much greater impact on foreign markets than historically. For example, in mid-August 2007, overseas markets experienced dramatic selloffs as a result of increasing concern among investors that the credit market problems in the United States could trigger a slowdown in global economic growth. What started as a major decline in the U.S. bond markets led to fears of a wider credit crunch that could affect economies from South Korea to Mexico to China. The global selloff began late Wednesday August 15, 2007, in the United States as credit market worries hit Countrywide Financial Corp., one of the country's biggest mortgage lenders. The selloff continued on to hit worldwide markets in Asia, where the Japanese stock market fell 2 percent, the Hong Kong stock market fell 3.3 percent, and the South Korean stock market fell 6.9 percent. European stock markets followed, with UK stock markets falling 4.1 percent and German markets by 2.4 percent. The selling continued in the United States, with the Dow Jones

Industrial Average falling more than 300 points at the beginning of trading on Thursday, August 16.

Conversely, global events now have an impact on U.S. financial markets. For example, by the mid-2010s, after years of rapid growth, China was the world's second-biggest economy. However, by late 2015, as China matured into a more developed market, demand for raw materials eased significantly. This raised concerns that China's economy was slowing at a much faster pace than previously thought. For example, a private report released in January 2016 showed China's manufacturing sector contracted in December 2015 following two months of stabilization. As a result, the Shanghai Composite plummeted nearly 7 percent in one day. This negative news about China had global ramifications and the sharp selling spread overseas. The DJIA fell by as much as 467 points on January 4, 2016, closing below the 17,000 level for the first time since October 2015. Most recently, and as mentioned in the introduction, the June 2016 vote by the citizens of the UK to leave the European Union sent shockwaves around the world as the fate of the 43-year-old unified Europe was brought into question. Britain's vote to leave the European Union set in motion an unprecedented and unpredictable process that could unsettle markets for many years.

## SUMMARY

This introductory chapter reviewed the basic operations of domestic and foreign financial markets and institutions. It described the ways in which funds flow through an economic system from lenders to borrowers and outlined the markets and instruments that lenders and borrowers employ to complete this process. In addition, the chapter discussed the need for FI managers to understand the functioning of both the domestic as well as the international markets in which they participate.

The chapter also identified the various factors impacting the specialness of the services FIs provide and the manner in which they improve the efficiency with which funds flow from suppliers of funds to the ultimate users of funds. Currently, however, some forces—such as technology and especially the Internet—are so powerful that in the future FIs that have historically relied on making profits by performing traditional special functions such as brokerage will need to expand the array of financial services they sell as well as the way that such services are distributed or sold to their customers.

## QUESTIONS

1. Classify the following transactions as taking place in the primary or secondary markets: (*LG 1-1*)
   a. IBM issues $200 million of new common stock.
   b. The New Company issues $50 million of common stock in an IPO.
   c. IBM sells $5 million of GM preferred stock out of its marketable securities portfolio.
   d. The Magellan Fund buys $100 million of previously issued IBM bonds.
   e. Prudential Insurance Co. sells $10 million of GM common stock.

2. Classify the following financial instruments as money market securities or capital market securities: (*LG 1-2*)
   a. Banker's acceptances
   b. Commercial paper
   c. Common stock
   d. Corporate bonds
   e. Mortgages
   f. Negotiable certificates of deposit
   g. Repurchase agreements
   h. U.S. Treasury bills
   i. U.S. Treasury notes
   j. Federal funds

3. How does the location of money markets differ from that of capital markets? (*LG 1-2*)

4. Which of the money market instruments is the largest in terms of dollar amount outstanding in 2016? (*LG 1-2*)

5. What are the major instruments traded in capital markets? (*LG 1-2*)

6. Which of the capital market instruments is the largest in terms of dollar amount outstanding in 2016? (*LG 1-2*)

7. If a U.S. bank is holding Japanese yen in its portfolio, what type of exchange rate movement would the bank be most concerned about? (*LG 1-3*)

8. What are the different types of financial institutions? Include a description of the main services offered by each. (*LG 1-5*)

9. How would economic transactions between suppliers of funds (e.g., households) and users of funds (e.g., corporations) occur in a world without FIs? (*LG 1-6*)

10. Why would a world limited to the direct transfer of funds from suppliers of funds to users of funds likely result in quite low levels of fund flows? (*LG 1-6*)

11. How do FIs reduce monitoring costs associated with the flow of funds from fund suppliers to fund investors? (*LG 1-6*)

12. How do FIs alleviate the problem of liquidity and price risk faced by investors wishing to invest in securities of corporations? (*LG 1-6*)

13. How do financial institutions help individuals diversify their portfolio risks? Which financial institution is best able to achieve this goal? (*LG 1-6*)

14. What is meant by maturity intermediation? (*LG 1-6*)

15. What is meant by denomination intermediation? (*LG 1-6*)

16. What other services do FIs provide to the financial system? (*LG 1-6*)

17. What types of risks do FIs face? (*LG 1-7*)

18. Why are FIs regulated? (*LG 1-8*)

19. What events resulted in banks' shift from the traditional banking model of originate-and-hold to a model of originate-and-distribute? (*LG 1-6, LG 1-7, LG 1-8*)

20. How did the boom in the housing market in the early and mid-2000s exacerbate FIs' transition away from their role as specialists in risk measurement and management? (*LG 1-6, LG 1-7, LG 1-8*)

21. What countries have the most international debt securities outstanding? (*LG 1-9*)

22. What countries have the largest commercial banks? (*LG 1-9*)

---

## SEARCH THE SITE

Go to the New York Stock Exchange Facts & Figures: Interactive Viewer website at **www.nyxdata.com/nysedata/asp/factbook/viewer_interactive.asp** and find the latest figures for top NYSE volume days using the following steps: Click on "Market Activity." Click on "NYSE Group Volume Records—Top 10 Days." This brings up a file that contains the relevant data.

**Questions**

1. What is the largest number of daily shares traded on the NYSE? On what day did this occur?
2. Calculate the percentage change in daily trading volume since the 3.3 billion shares traded on April 18, 2016.

---

**APPENDIX 1A: The Financial Crisis: The Failure of Financial Institutions' Specialness**

This appendix is available through Connect or your course instructor.

# chapter

# Determinants of Interest Rates

## Learning Goals

| | |
|---|---|
| **LG 2-1** | *Know who the main suppliers of loanable funds are.* |
| **LG 2-2** | *Know who the main demanders of loanable funds are.* |
| **LG 2-3** | *Understand how equilibrium interest rates are determined.* |
| **LG 2-4** | *Examine factors that cause the supply and demand curves for loanable funds to shift.* |
| **LG 2-5** | *Examine how interest rates change over time.* |
| **LG 2-6** | *Know what specific factors determine interest rates.* |
| **LG 2-7** | *Examine the different theories explaining the term structure of interest rates.* |
| **LG 2-8** | *Understand how forward rates of interest can be derived from the term structure of interest rates.* |
| **LG 2-9** | *Understand how interest rates are used to determine present and future values.* |

## INTEREST RATE FUNDAMENTALS: CHAPTER OVERVIEW

**Nominal interest rates** are the interest rates actually observed in financial markets. These nominal interest rates (or just interest rates) directly affect the value (price) of most securities traded in the money and capital markets, both at home and abroad. Changes in interest rates influence the performance and decision making for individual investors, businesses, and governmental units alike. Figure 2–1 illustrates the movement in several key U.S. interest rates over the past 40 years: the federal funds rate used for interbank borrowing, the three-month T-bill rate, the AAA-rated corporate bond rate, and the home mortgage rate. Notice in Figure 2–1 the variability over time in interest rate levels. For example, the federal funds rate was as low as 3.29 percent in the early 1970s, yet hit highs of almost 20 percent in the early 1980s, was well below 10 percent throughout much of the 1990s,

**Figure 2–1**   Key U.S. Interest Rates, 1972–2016

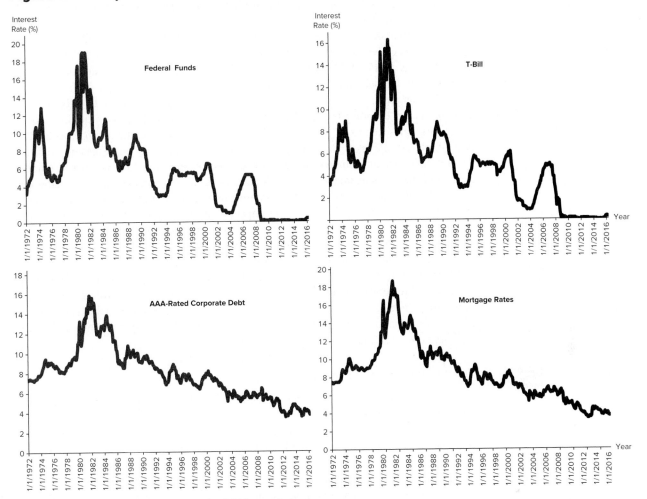

**Source:** Federal Reserve Board website, May 2016. www.federalreserve.gov

**nominal interest rates**

*The interest rates actually observed in financial markets.*

and fell back to and was even below 4 percent in the early and late 2000s. As we discuss in detail in Chapter 4, in 2008 through 2016, the Federal Reserve lowered interest rates to historic lows as it took steps to stimulate the U.S. economy (which was suffering from its worst recession since the Great Depression).

This chapter examines factors that drive the level of current and future interest rates, as well as the link between interest rates and the time value of money. Sections 1 through 5 (as listed in the Learning Goals for this chapter) generally deal with the levels of interest rates, while Sections 6 through 8 are more concerned with differences among various interest rates. Finally, Section 9 demonstrates how interest rates affect the value of financial securities by reviewing time value of money concepts.

## LOANABLE FUNDS THEORY

Interest rates play a major part in the determination of the value of financial instruments. For example, in June 2013 the Federal Reserve announced that it expected to be able to reduce its efforts to support the U.S. economy as it recovered from the financial crisis of 2008–2009 by the end of 2013. The financial markets reacted significantly: the Dow Jones Industrial Average (which had previously posted three consecutive days of gains in value) declined over 200 points, 1.35 percent in value, the interest rate (for bond instruments the interest rate is most often referred to as the yield to maturity[1] or just yield) on Treasury securities increased (i.e., the yield on two-year T-notes increased from 0.126 percent to 2.308 percent, the highest rate in over a year), gold prices dropped 3.4 percent, and the U.S. dollar strengthened against foreign currencies. When the Fed eventually raised interest rates in December 2015 (for the first time in 10 years), the DJIA jumped 224.18 points, or 1.3 percent, to 17,749.09, with only two of the 30 blue-chip companies on the index trading lower. Global equity markets rallied in volatile trading, while the dollar rose after the Fed's statement. However, this rate increase was highly anticipated. In a Reuters poll of more than 90 economists taken between December 4 and 9, the probability that the Fed would raise rates rose to 90 percent. Further, in its announcement, the Fed stressed that the pace of interest rate hikes would be gradual. Thus, benchmark 10-year Treasury notes that yielded 2.294 percent minutes ahead of the announcement, rose to 2.31 percent immediately after the announcement, before falling back to 2.2995 percent. Likewise, gold held steady after the announcement that the interest rate increase was a tentative beginning to a "gradual" tightening cycle. Given the impact a change in interest rates has on security values, financial institution and other firm managers spend much time and effort trying to identify factors that determine the level of interest rates at any moment in time, as well as what causes interest rate movements over time.

One model that is commonly used to explain interest rates and interest rate movements is the **loanable funds theory.** The loanable funds theory views the level of interest rates as resulting from factors that affect the supply of and demand for loanable funds. It categorizes financial market participants—consumers, businesses, governments, and foreign participants—as net suppliers or demanders of funds.

**loanable funds theory**

*A theory of interest rate determination that views equilibrium interest rates in financial markets as a result of the supply of and demand for loanable funds.*

**LG 2-1**

### Supply of Loanable Funds

The *supply of loanable funds* is a term commonly used to describe funds provided to the financial markets by net suppliers of funds. In general, the quantity of loanable funds supplied increases as interest rates rise. Figure 2–2 illustrates the supply curve for loanable funds. Other factors held constant, more funds are supplied as interest rates increase (the reward for supplying funds is higher). Table 2–1 presents data on the supply of loanable funds from the various groups of market participants from U.S. flow of funds data as of 2016.

The household sector (consumer sector) is one of the largest suppliers of loanable funds in the United States—$70.33 trillion in 2016. Households supply funds when they have excess income or want to reallocate their asset portfolio holdings. For example, during times of high economic growth, households may replace part of their cash holdings with earning assets (i.e., by supplying loanable funds in exchange for holding securities). As the total wealth of a consumer increases, the total supply of loanable funds from that

**Figure 2–2**  **Supply of and Demand for Loanable Funds**

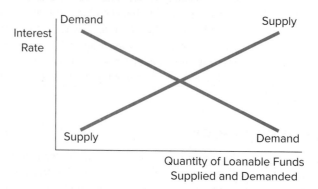

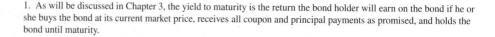

---

1.  As will be discussed in Chapter 3, the yield to maturity is the return the bond holder will earn on the bond if he or she buys the bond at its current market price, receives all coupon and principal payments as promised, and holds the bond until maturity.

**TABLE 2–1** Funds Supplied and Demanded by Various Groups *(in trillions of dollars)*

| | Funds Supplied | Funds Demanded | Net Funds Supplied (Funds Supplied— Funds Demanded) |
|---|---|---|---|
| Households | $70.33 | $14.51 | $55.82 |
| Business—nonfinancial | 23.20 | 55.85 | −32.65 |
| Business—financial | 85.91 | 96.90 | −10.99 |
| Government units | 5.22 | 23.19 | −17.97 |
| Foreign participants | 23.03 | 17.24 | 5.79 |

**Source:** Federal Reserve Board website, "Financial Accounts of the United States," May 2016. www.federalreserve.gov

consumer will also generally increase. Households determine their supply of loanable funds not only on the basis of the general level of interest rates and their total wealth, but also on the risk of securities investments. The greater the perceived risk of securities investments, the less households are willing to invest at each interest rate. Further, the supply of loanable funds from households also depends on their immediate spending needs. For example, near-term educational or medical expenditures will reduce the supply of funds from a given household.

Higher interest rates will also result in higher supplies of funds from the U.S. business sector ($23.20 trillion from nonfinancial business and $85.91 trillion from financial business in 2016), which often has excess cash, or working capital, that it can invest for short periods of time in financial assets. In addition to the interest rates on these investments, the expected risk on financial securities and their businesses' future investment needs will affect their overall supply of funds.

Loanable funds are also supplied by some governments ($5.22 trillion in 2016). For example, some governments (e.g., municipalities) temporarily generate more cash inflows (e.g., through local taxes) than they have budgeted to spend. These funds can be loaned out to financial market fund users until needed. During the recent financial crisis, the federal government significantly increased the funds it supplied to businesses and consumers as it attempted to rescue the U.S. economy from a deep economic recession (see Appendix 1A).

Finally, foreign investors increasingly view U.S. financial markets as alternatives to their domestic financial markets ($23.03 trillion of funds were supplied to the U.S. financial markets in 2016). When interest rates are higher on U.S. financial securities than they are on comparable securities in their home countries, foreign investors increase their supply of funds to U.S. markets. Indeed the high savings rates of foreign households (such as Japanese households) has resulted in foreign market participants being major suppliers of funds to U.S. financial markets in recent years. Similar to domestic suppliers of loanable funds, foreigners assess not only the interest rate offered on financial securities, but also their total wealth, the risk on the security, and their future expenditure needs. Additionally, foreign investors alter their investment decisions as financial conditions in their home countries change relative to the U.S. economy and the exchange rate of their country's currency changes vis-à-vis the U.S. dollar (see Chapter 9). For example, during the recent financial crisis, investors worldwide, searching for a safe haven for their funds, invested huge amounts of funds in U.S. Treasury securities. The amount of money invested in Treasury bills from this "flight to quality" was so large that the yield on the three-month Treasury bill went below zero for the first time ever. Investors were essentially paying the U.S. government to borrow money.

**LG 2-2**

### Demand for Loanable Funds

The *demand for loanable funds* is a term used to describe the total net demand for funds by fund users. In general, the quantity of loanable funds demanded is higher as interest rates fall. Figure 2–2 also illustrates the demand curve for loanable funds. Other factors held constant, more funds are demanded as interest rates decrease (the cost of borrowing funds is lower).

Households (although they are net suppliers of funds) also borrow funds in financial markets ($14.51 trillion in 2016). The demand for loanable funds by households reflects the demand for financing purchases of homes (with mortgage loans), durable goods (e.g., car loans, appliance loans), and nondurable goods (e.g., education loans, medical loans). Additional nonprice conditions and requirements (discussed below) also affect a household's demand for loanable funds at every level of interest rates.

Businesses demand funds to finance investments in long-term (fixed) assets (e.g., plant and equipment) and for short-term working capital needs (e.g., inventory and accounts receivable) usually by issuing debt and other financial instruments ($55.85 trillion for non-financial businesses and $96.90 trillion for financial businesses in 2016). When interest rates are high (i.e., the cost of loanable funds is high), businesses prefer to finance investments with internally generated funds (e.g., retained earnings) rather than through borrowed funds. Further, the greater the number of profitable projects available to businesses, or the better the overall economic conditions, the greater the demand for loanable funds.

www.ustreas.gov

Governments also borrow heavily in the markets for loanable funds ($23.19 trillion in 2016). For example, state and local governments often issue debt instruments to finance temporary imbalances between operating revenues (e.g., taxes) and budgeted expenditures (e.g., road improvements, school construction). Higher interest rates can cause state and local governments to postpone borrowings and thus capital expenditures. Similar to households and businesses, governments' demand for funds varies with general economic conditions. The federal government is also a large borrower partly to finance current budget deficits (expenditures greater than taxes) and partly to finance past deficits. The cumulative sum of past deficits is called the national debt, which in the United States in 2016 stood at a record $19.21 trillion. Thus, the national debt and especially the interest payments on the national debt have to be financed in large part by additional government borrowing. Chapter 4 provides details of how government borrowing and spending impacts interest rates as well as overall economic growth.

Finally, foreign participants (households, businesses, and governments) also borrow in U.S. financial markets ($17.24 trillion in 2016). Foreign borrowers look for the cheapest source of dollar funds globally. Most foreign borrowing in U.S. financial markets comes from the business sector. In addition to interest costs, foreign borrowers consider nonprice terms on loanable funds as well as economic conditions in their home country and the general attractiveness of the U.S. dollar relative to their domestic currency (e.g., the euro or the yen). In Chapter 9, we examine how economic growth in domestic versus foreign countries affects foreign exchange rates and foreign investors' demand and supply for funds.

**LG 2-3**

## Equilibrium Interest Rate

The aggregate supply of loanable funds is the sum of the quantity supplied by the separate fund supplying sectors (e.g., households, businesses, governments, foreign agents) discussed above. Similarly, the aggregate demand for loanable funds is the sum of the quantity demanded by the separate fund demanding sectors. As illustrated in Figure 2–3, the aggregate quantity of funds supplied is positively related to interest rates, while the aggregate quantity of funds demanded is inversely related to interest rates. As long as competitive forces are allowed to operate freely in a financial system, the interest rate that equates the aggregate quantity of loanable funds supplied with the aggregate quantity of loanable funds demanded for a financial security, $Q^*$, is the equilibrium interest rate for that security, $i^*$, point $E$ in Figure 2–3. For example, whenever the rate of interest is set higher than the equilibrium rate, such as $i^H$, the financial system has a surplus of loanable funds. As a result, some suppliers of funds will lower the interest rate at which they are willing to lend and the demanders of funds will absorb the loanable funds surplus. In contrast, when the rate of interest is lower than the equilibrium interest rate, such as $i^L$, there is a shortage of loanable funds in the financial system. Some borrowers will be unable to obtain the funds they need at current rates. As a result, interest rates will increase, causing more suppliers of loanable funds to enter the market and some demanders of funds to leave the market. These

**Figure 2–3** **Determination of Equilibrium Interest Rates**

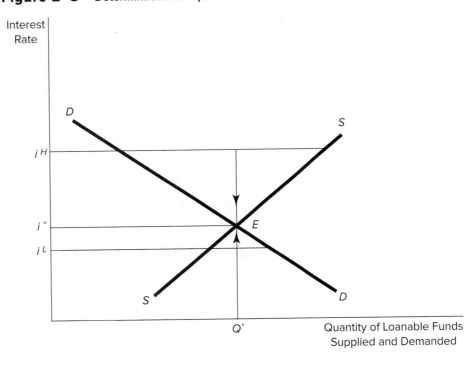

competitive forces will cause the quantity of funds supplied to increase and the quantity of funds demanded to decrease until a shortage of funds no longer exists.

### Factors That Cause the Supply and Demand Curves for Loanable Funds to Shift

While we have alluded to the fundamental factors that cause the supply and demand curves for loanable funds to shift, in this section we formally summarize these factors. We then examine how shifts in the supply and demand curves for loanable funds determine the equilibrium interest rate on a specific financial instrument. A shift in the supply or demand curve occurs when the quantity of a financial security supplied or demanded changes at every given interest rate in response to a change in another factor besides the interest rate. In either case, a change in the supply or demand curve for loanable funds causes interest rates to move. Table 2–2 recaps the factors that affect the supply and demand for loanable funds discussed in this section, their impact on the supply and demand for loanable funds for a specific security, and the impact on the market clearing (or equilibrium) interest rates holding all other factors constant.

**Supply of Funds.**   We have already described the positive relation between interest rates and the supply of loanable funds along the loanable funds supply curve. Factors that cause the supply curve of loanable funds to shift, at any given interest rate, include the wealth of fund suppliers, the risk of the financial security, near-term spending needs, monetary policy objectives, and economic conditions.

*Wealth.*   As the total wealth of financial market participants (households, businesses, etc.) increases, the absolute dollar value available for investment purposes increases. Accordingly, at every interest rate, the supply of loanable funds increases, or the supply curve shifts down and to the right. For example, as the U.S. economy grew in the early and mid-2010s, total wealth of U.S. investors increased as well. Consequently, the supply of funds available for investing (e.g., in stock and bond markets) increased at

**TABLE 2–2** Factors That Affect the Supply of and Demand for Loanable Funds for a Financial Security

| Panel A: The supply of funds | | |
|---|---|---|
| Factor | Impact on Supply of Funds | Impact on Equilibrium Interest Rate* |
| Interest rate | Movement along the supply curve | Direct |
| Total wealth | Shift supply curve | Inverse |
| Risk of financial security | Shift supply curve | Direct |
| Near-term spending needs | Shift supply curve | Direct |
| Monetary expansion | Shift supply curve | Inverse |
| Economic conditions | Shift supply curve | Inverse |
| Panel B: The demand for funds | | |
| Factor | Impact on Demand for Funds | Impact on Equilibrium Interest Rate |
| Interest rate | Movement along the demand curve | Direct |
| Utility derived from asset purchased with borrowed funds | Shift demand curve | Direct |
| Restrictiveness of nonprice conditions | Shift demand curve | Inverse |
| Economic conditions | Shift demand curve | Direct |

*A "direct" impact on equilibrium interest rates means that as the "factor" increases (decreases) the equilibrium interest rate increases (decreases). An "inverse" impact means that as the factor increases (decreases) the equilibrium interest rate decreases (increases).

every available interest rate. We show this shift (increase) in the supply curve in Panel a of Figure 2–4 as a move from $SS$ to $SS''$. The shift in the supply curve creates a disequilibrium between demand and supply. To eliminate the imbalance or disequilibrium in this financial market, the equilibrium interest rate falls, from $i*$ to $i*''$, which is associated with an increase in the quantity of funds loaned between fund suppliers and fund demanders from $Q*$ to $Q*''$.

Conversely, as the total wealth of financial market participants decreases, the absolute dollar value available for investment purposes decreases. Accordingly, at every interest rate, the supply of loanable funds decreases, or the supply curve shifts up and to the left. The decrease in the supply of funds due to a decrease in the total wealth of market participants results in an increase in the equilibrium interest rate and a decrease in the equilibrium quantity of funds loaned (traded).

*Risk.* As the risk of a financial security decreases (e.g., the probability that the issuer of the security will default on promised repayments of the funds borrowed), it becomes more attractive to suppliers of funds. At every interest rate, the supply of loanable funds increases, or the supply curve shifts down and to the right, from $SS$ to $SS''$ in Panel a of Figure 2–4. Holding all other factors constant, the increase in the supply of funds, due to a decrease in the risk of the financial security, results in a decrease in the equilibrium interest rate, from $i*$ to $i*''$, and an increase in the equilibrium quantity of funds traded, from $Q*$ to $Q*''$.

Conversely, as the risk of a financial security increases, it becomes less attractive to suppliers of funds. Accordingly, at every interest rate, the supply of loanable funds decreases, or the supply curve shifts up and to the left. Holding all other factors constant, the decrease in the supply of funds due to an increase in the financial security's risk results in an increase in the equilibrium interest rate and a decrease in the equilibrium quantity of funds loaned (or traded). For example, during the financial crisis, the

**Figure 2–4**    The Effect on Interest Rates from a Shift in the Supply Curve of or Demand Curve for Loanable Funds

(a) Increase in the supply of loanable funds

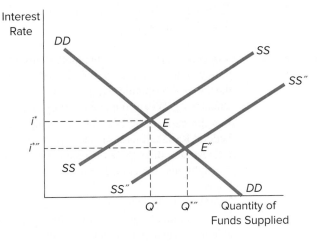

(b) Increase in the demand for loanable funds

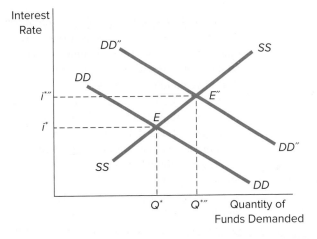

Baa corporate bond rates spiked and 10-year T-note rates dropped significantly as suppliers of funds moved away from riskier investments (Baa corporate bonds) to the safest possible investments (Treasury notes). In the loanable funds framework, this can be interpreted as a reduction in the supply of funds, due to investor uncertainty about credit quality of firms in the corporate bond market and as an increase in the supply of funds in the Treasury notes market, as investors fled to quality investments. Consequently, the equilibrium interest rate was higher in the corporate bond market and lower in the Treasury notes market.

*Near-Term Spending Needs.*    When financial market participants have few near-term spending needs, the absolute dollar value of funds available to invest increases. For example, when a family's son or daughter moves out of the family home to live on his or her own, current spending needs of the family decrease and the supply of available funds (for investing) increases. At every interest rate, the supply of loanable funds increases, or the supply curve shifts down and to the right. The financial market, holding all other factors constant, reacts to this increased supply of funds by decreasing the equilibrium interest rate and increasing the equilibrium quantity of funds traded.

Conversely, when financial market participants have increased near-term spending needs, the absolute dollar value of funds available to invest decreases. At every interest rate, the supply of loanable funds decreases, or the supply curve shifts up and to the left. The shift in the supply curve creates a disequilibrium in the financial market that results in an increase in the equilibrium interest rate and a decrease in the equilibrium quantity of funds loaned (or traded).

www.federalreserve.gov *Monetary Expansion.*    One method used by the Federal Reserve to implement monetary policy is to alter the availability of funds, the growth in the money supply, and thus the rate of economic expansion of the economy (we explain this process in detail in Chapter 4). When monetary policy objectives are to allow the economy to expand (as was the case in the late 2000s, during the financial crisis, and in the early 2010s), the Federal Reserve increases the supply of funds available in the financial markets. At every interest rate, the supply of loanable funds increases, the supply curve shifts down and to the right, and the equilibrium interest rate falls, while the equilibrium quantity of funds traded increases.

Conversely, when monetary policy objectives are to restrict the rate of economic expansion (and thus inflation), the Federal Reserve decreases the supply of funds available in the financial markets. At every interest rate, the supply of loanable funds decreases, the supply curve shifts up and to the left, and the equilibrium interest rate rises, while the equilibrium quantity of funds loaned or traded decreases.

*Economic Conditions.*    Finally, as the underlying economic conditions themselves (e.g., the inflation rate, unemployment rate, economic growth) improve in a country relative to other countries, the flow of funds to that country increases. This reflects the lower risk (country or sovereign risk) that the country, in the guise of its government, will default on its obligation to repay funds borrowed. For example, the severe economic crisis in Greece in the early 2010s resulted in a decrease in the supply of funds to that country. An increased inflow of foreign funds to U.S. financial markets increases the supply of loanable funds at every interest rate and the supply curve shifts down and to the right. Accordingly, the equilibrium interest rate falls and the equilibrium quantity of funds loaned or traded increases.

Conversely, when economic conditions in foreign countries improve, domestic and foreign investors take their funds out of domestic financial markets (e.g., the United States) and invest abroad. Thus, the supply of funds available in the financial markets decreases and the equilibrium interest rate rises, while the equilibrium quantity of funds traded decreases.

**Demand for Funds.**    We explained above that the quantity of loanable funds demanded is negatively related to interest rates. Factors that cause the demand curve for loanable funds to shift include the utility derived from assets purchased with borrowed funds, the restrictiveness of nonprice conditions on borrowing, and economic conditions.

*Utility Derived from Assets Purchased with Borrowed Funds.*    As the utility (i.e., satisfaction or pleasure) derived from an asset purchased with borrowed funds increases, the willingness of market participants (households, businesses, etc.) to borrow increases and the absolute dollar value borrowed increases. Accordingly, at every interest rate, the demand for loanable funds increases, or the demand curve shifts up and to the right. For example, suppose a change in jobs takes an individual from Arizona to Minnesota. The individual currently has a convertible automobile. Given the move to Minnesota, the individual's utility from the convertible decreases, while it would increase for a car with heated seats. Thus, with a potential increased utility from the purchase of a new car, the individual's demand for funds in the form of an auto loan increases. We show this shift (increase) in the demand curve in Panel b of Figure 2–4 as a move from *DD* to *DD"*. The shift in the demand curve creates a disequilibrium in this financial market. Holding all other factors constant, the increase in the demand for funds due to an increase in the utility from the purchased asset results in an increase in the equilibrium interest rate, from $i^*$ to $i^{*\prime\prime}$, and an increase in the equilibrium quantity of funds traded, from $Q^*$ to $Q^{*\prime\prime}$.

Conversely, as the utility derived from an asset purchased with borrowed funds decreases, the willingness of market participants (households, businesses, etc.) to borrow decreases and the absolute dollar amount borrowed decreases. Accordingly, at every interest rate, the demand for loanable funds decreases, or the demand curve shifts down and to the left. The shift in the demand curve again creates a disequilibrium in this financial market. As competitive forces adjust, and holding all other factors constant, the decrease in the demand for funds due to a decrease in the utility from the purchased asset results in a decrease in the equilibrium interest rate and a decrease in the equilibrium quantity of funds loaned or traded.

*Restrictiveness of Nonprice Conditions on Borrowed Funds.* As the nonprice restrictions put on borrowers as a condition of borrowing decrease, the willingness of market participants to borrow increases and the absolute dollar value borrowed increases. Such nonprice conditions may include fees, collateral, or requirements or restrictions on the use of funds (so-called restrictive covenants; see Chapter 6). The lack of such restrictions makes the loan more desirable to the user of funds. Accordingly, at every interest rate, the demand for loanable funds increases, or the demand curve shifts up and to the right, from $DD$ to $DD''$. As competitive forces adjust, and holding all other factors constant, the increase in the demand for funds due to a decrease in the restrictive conditions on the borrowed funds results in an increase in the equilibrium interest rate, from $i^*$ to $i^{*\prime\prime}$, and an increase in the equilibrium quantity of funds traded, from $Q^*$ to $Q^{*\prime\prime}$.

Conversely, as the nonprice restrictions put on borrowers as a condition of borrowing increase, market participants' willingness to borrow decreases, and the absolute dollar value borrowed decreases. Accordingly, the demand curve shifts down and to the left. The shift in the demand curve results in a decrease in the equilibrium interest rate and a decrease in the equilibrium quantity of funds traded.

*Economic Conditions.* When the domestic economy experiences a period of growth, such as that in the United States in the mid-2000s and early 2010s, market participants are willing to borrow more heavily. For example, state and local governments are more likely to repair and improve decaying infrastructure when the local economy is strong. Accordingly, the demand curve for funds shifts up and to the right. Holding all other factors constant, the increase in the demand for funds due to economic growth results in an increase in the equilibrium interest rate and an increase in the equilibrium quantity of funds traded.

Conversely, when domestic economic growth is stagnant, market participants reduce their demand for funds. Accordingly, the demand curve shifts down and to the left, resulting in a decrease in the equilibrium interest rate and a decrease in the equilibrium quantity of funds traded.

---

**DO YOU UNDERSTAND:**

1. Who the main suppliers of loanable funds are?

2. Who the major demanders of loanable funds are?

3. What happens to the equilibrium interest rate when the demand for loanable funds increases?

4. What happens to the equilibrium interest rate when the supply of loanable funds increases?

5. How supply and demand, together, determine interest rates?

---

## MOVEMENT OF INTEREST RATES OVER TIME

**LG 2-5**  As discussed in the previous section of this chapter, the loanable funds theory of interest rates is based on the supply of and demand for loanable funds as functions of interest rates. The equilibrium interest rate (point *E* in Figure 2–4) is only a temporary equilibrium. Changes in underlying factors that determine the demand for and supply of loanable funds can cause continuous shifts in the supply and/or demand curves for loanable funds. Market forces will react to the resulting disequilibrium with a change in the equilibrium interest rate and quantity of funds traded in that market. Refer again to Panel a of Figure 2–4, which shows the effects of an *increase in the supply curve* for loanable funds, from *SS* to *SS″* (and the resulting *decrease in the equilibrium interest rate,* from *i\** to *i\*″*), while Panel b of Figure 2–4 shows the effects of an *increase in the demand curve* for loanable funds, from *DD* to *DD″* (and the resulting *increase in the equilibrium interest rate,* from *i\** to *i\*″*).

## DETERMINANTS OF INTEREST RATES FOR INDIVIDUAL SECURITIES

**LG 2-6**

So far we have looked at the general determination of equilibrium (nominal) interest rates for financial securities in the context of the loanable demand and supply theory of the flow of funds. In this section, we examine the specific factors that affect differences in interest rates across the range of real-world financial markets (i.e., differences among interest rates on individual securities, given the underlying level of interest rates determined by the demand and supply of loanable funds). These factors include inflation, the "real" risk-free rate, default risk, liquidity risk, special provisions regarding the use of funds raised by a security's issuance, and the term to maturity of the security. We examine each of these factors in this section and summarize them in Table 2–3.

### Inflation

**inflation**

*The continual increase in the price level of a basket of goods and services.*

The first factor to affect interest rates is *actual or expected inflation* in the economy. **Inflation** of the general price index of goods and services (*IP*) is defined as the (percentage) increase in the price of a standardized basket of goods and services over a given period of time. The higher the level of actual or expected inflation, the higher will be the level of interest rates. The intuition behind the positive relationship between interest rates and inflation rates is that an investor who buys a financial asset must earn a higher interest rate when inflation increases to compensate for the increased cost of forgoing consumption of real goods and services today and buying these more highly priced goods and services in the future. In other words, the higher the rate of inflation, the more expensive the same basket of goods and services will be in the future. In the United States, inflation is measured using indexes such as the consumer price index (*CPI*) and the producer price index (*PPI*). For example, the annual inflation rate using the CPI index between years *t* and *t* + 1 would be equal to:

$$\text{Inflation } (IP) = \frac{CPI_{t+1} - CPI_t}{CPI_t} \times 100$$

**real risk-free rate**

*The risk-free rate that would exist on a default-free security if no inflation were expected.*

### Real Risk-Free Rates

A **real risk-free rate** is the interest rate that would exist on a risk-free security if no inflation were expected over the holding period (e.g., a year) of a security. The real risk-free

**TABLE 2–3**  **Factors Affecting Nominal Interest Rates**

**Inflation**—the continual increase in the price level of a basket of goods and services.
**Real risk-free rate**—nominal risk-free rate that would exist on a security if no inflation were expected.
**Default risk**—risk that a security issuer will default on the security by missing an interest or principal payment.
**Liquidity risk**—risk that a security cannot be sold at a predictable price with low transaction costs at short notice.
**Special provisions**—provisions (e.g., taxability, convertibility, and callability) that impact the security holder beneficially or adversely and as such are reflected in the interest rates on securities that contain such provisions.
**Term to maturity**—length of time a security has until maturity.

rate on an investment is the percentage change in the buying power of a dollar. As such, it measures society's relative time preference for consuming today rather than tomorrow. The higher society's preference to consume today (i.e., the higher its time value of money or rate of time preference), the higher the real risk-free rate (*RFR*) will be.

**Fisher Effect.**   The relationship among the real risk-free rate (*RFR*), the expected rate of inflation [*E(IP)*], described above, and the nominal interest rate (*i*) is often referred to as the Fisher effect, named for the economist Irving Fisher, who identified these relationships early last century. The Fisher effect theorizes that nominal risk-free rates observed in financial markets (e.g., the one-year Treasury bill rate) must compensate investors for (1) any reduced purchasing power on funds lent (or principal lent) due to inflationary price changes and (2) an additional premium above the expected rate of inflation for forgoing present consumption (which reflects the real risk-free rate discussed above), or

$$(1 + i) = [1 + E(IP)](1 + RFR)$$

Rearranging this relation, when an investor purchases a security that pays interest, the nominal risk-free rate exceeds the real risk-free rate because of inflation.

$$i = RFR + E(IP) + [RFR \times E(IP)]$$

where $RFR \times E(IP)$ is the inflation premium for the loss of purchasing power on the promised nominal risk-free rate payments due to inflation. For small values of *RFR* and *E(IP)* this term is negligible.

Thus, the Fisher effect formula is often written as:

$$i = RFR + E(IP) \tag{2-1}$$

The approximation formula, in Equation (2-1), assumes $RFR \times E(IP)$ is small. Thus, the nominal risk-free rate will be equal to the real risk-free rate only when market participants expect the inflation rate to be zero—$E(IP) = 0$. Similarly, nominal risk-free rates will be equal to the expected inflation rate only when real risk-free rates are zero. Note that we can rearrange the nominal risk-free rate equation to show the determinants of the real risk-free rate as follows:

$$RFR = i - E(IP) \tag{2-2}$$

---

**EXAMPLE 2–1**   **Calculations of Real Risk-Free Rates**

The one-year Treasury bill rate in 2007 averaged 4.53 percent and inflation (measured by the consumer price index) for the year was 4.10 percent. If investors had expected the same inflation rate as that actually realized (i.e., 4.10 percent), then according to the Fisher effect the real risk-free rate for 2007 was:

$$4.53\% - 4.10\% = 0.43\%$$

The one-year T-bill rate in 2015 was 0.32 percent, while the CPI change for the year was 0.70 percent. This implies a real risk-free rate of −0.38 percent, that is, the real risk-free rate was actually negative.

---

stats.bls.gov/cpi/home.htm

Panel a of Figure 2–5 shows the nominal risk-free rate (one-year T-bill rate) versus the change in the CPI from 1962 through 2016. Panel b shows the difference in the two rates (i.e., the real risk-free rate over the period). Because the expected inflation rate is difficult to estimate accurately, the real risk-free rate can be difficult to estimate accurately as well, since investors' expectations are not always realized. Figure 2–5 shows the realized inflation and real risk-free rates.

**default risk**

*The risk that a security issuer will default on that security by being late on or missing an interest or principal payment.*

### Default or Credit Risk

**Default risk** is the risk that a security issuer will fail to make its promised interest and principal payments to the buyer of a security. The higher the default risk, the higher the interest rate that will be demanded by the buyer of the security to compensate him or her for this default (or credit) risk exposure. Not all securities exhibit default risk. For example, U.S. Treasury securities are regarded as having no default risk since they

**Figure 2–5** Nominal Interest Rates versus Inflation

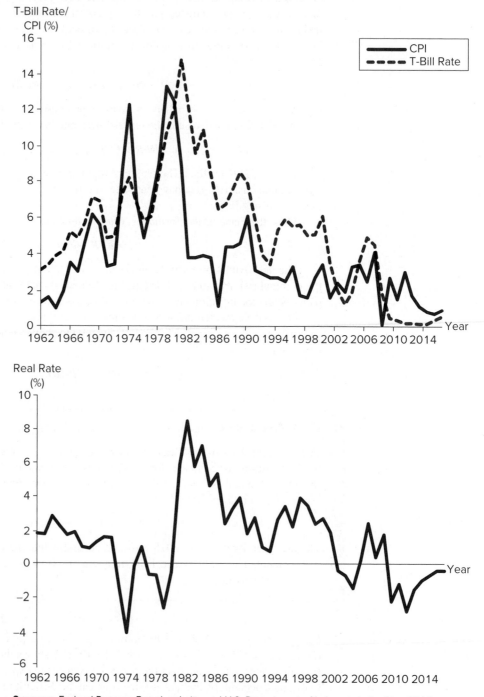

**Sources:** Federal Reserve Board website and U.S. Department of Labor website, May 2016. www.federalreserve.gov and stats.bls.gov/cpi/home.htm

are issued by the U.S. government, and the probability of the U.S. government defaulting on its debt payments is practically zero given its taxation powers and its ability to print currency. Some borrowers, however, such as corporations or individuals, have less predictable cash flows (and no taxation powers), and therefore investors charge them an interest rate risk premium reflecting their perceived probability of default and the potential recovery of the amount loaned. The difference between a quoted interest rate on a security (security *j*) and a Treasury security with similar maturity, liquidity, tax, and other features (such as callability or convertibility) is called a *default* or *credit risk premium* (*DRP_j*). That is:

$$DRP_j = i_{jt} - i_{Tt} \qquad\qquad (2\text{-}3)$$

where

$i_{jt}$ = interest rate on a security issued by a non-Treasury issuer (issuer *j*) of maturity *m* at time *t*

$i_{Tt}$ = interest rate on a security issued by the U.S. Treasury of maturity *m* at time *t*

www.moodys.com

www.standard
andpoors.com

The default risk on many corporate bonds is evaluated and categorized by various bond rating agencies such as Moody's and Standard & Poor's. (We discuss these ratings in more detail in Chapter 6.)

In May 2016, the 10-year Treasury interest rate, or yield, was 1.77 percent. On Aaa-rated and Baa-rated corporate debt, interest rates were 3.61 and 4.78 percent, respectively. Thus, the average default risk premiums on the Aaa-rated and Baa-rated corporate debt were:

$$DRP_{Aaa} = 3.61\% - 1.77\% = 1.84\%$$
$$DRP_{Baa} = 4.78\% - 1.77\% = 3.01\%$$

Figure 2–6 presents these risk premiums from 1977 through 2016. Notice from this figure and Figure 2–5 that default risk premiums tend to increase when the economy is contracting and decrease when the economy is expanding. For example, from 2008 to 2009 real risk-free rates (T-bills/CPI in Figure 2–5) decreased from 1.73 percent to −2.23 percent. Over the same period, default risk premiums on Aaa-rated bonds increased from 1.97 percent to 2.05 percent and on Baa-rated bonds from 3.78 percent to 4.03 percent. Conversely, from 2009 to 2010, the real risk-free rate increased from −2.23 percent to −1.18 percent. Over this period, default risk premiums on Aaa-rated bonds decreased from 2.05 percent to 1.67 percent and on Baa-rated bonds from 4.03 percent to 2.92 percent.

**Figure 2–6**  **Default Risk Premium on Corporate Bonds**

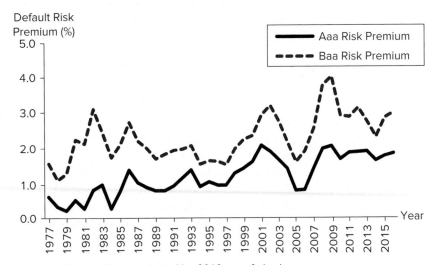

**Source:** Federal Reserve Board website, May 2016. www.federalreserve.gov

### Liquidity Risk

A highly liquid asset is one that can be sold at a predictable price with low transaction costs and thus can be converted into its full market value at short notice. If a security is illiquid, investors add a **liquidity risk** premium (LRP) to the interest rate on the security that reflects its relative liquidity. In the United States, liquid markets exist for most government securities and the stocks and some bonds issued by large corporations. Many bonds, however, do not trade on a regular basis or on organized exchanges such as the NYSE. As a result, if investors wish to sell these bonds quickly, they may get a lower price than they could have received if they had waited until maturity to sell the bonds. Consequently, investors demand a liquidity premium on top of all other premiums to compensate for the bond's lack of liquidity and the potential price discount from selling it early. Thus, the liquidity risk premium might also be thought of as an "illiquidity" premium.

A different type of liquidity risk premium may also exist (see below) if investors dislike long-term securities because their prices (present values) are more sensitive to interest rate changes than short-term securities (see Chapter 3). In this case, a higher liquidity risk premium may be added to a security with a longer maturity simply because of its greater exposure to price risk (loss of capital value) on the security as interest rates change.

### Special Provisions or Covenants

Numerous special provisions or covenants that may be written into the contract underlying a security also affect the interest rates on different securities (see Chapter 6). Some of these special provisions include the security's taxability, convertibility, and callability.

For example, for investors, interest payments on municipal securities are free of federal, state, and local taxes. Thus, the interest rate required by a municipal bond holder is smaller than that on a comparable taxable bond—for example, a Treasury bond, which is taxable at the federal level but not at the state or local (city) levels, or a corporate bond, whose interest payments are taxable at the state and local levels as well as federal levels.

A convertible (special) feature of a security offers the holder the opportunity to exchange one security for another type of the issuer's securities at a preset price. Because of the value of this conversion option, the convertible security holder requires a lower interest rate than a comparable nonconvertible security holder (all else equal). In general, special provisions that provide benefits to the security holder (e.g., tax-free status and convertibility) are associated with lower interest rates, and special provisions that provide benefits to the security issuer (e.g., callability, by which an issuer has the option to retire—call—a security prior to maturity at a preset price) are associated with higher interest rates.

### Term to Maturity

Interest rates are also related to the term to maturity of a security.[2] This relationship is often called the **term structure of interest rates** or the yield curve. The term structure of interest rates compares interest rates on securities, assuming that all characteristics (i.e., default risk, liquidity risk) *except maturity* are the same. The change in required interest rates as the maturity of a security changes is called the maturity premium (MP). The MP, or the difference between the required yield on long- and short-term securities of the same characteristics except maturity can be positive, negative, or zero. The term structure of interest rates for U.S. Treasury securities is the most frequently reported and analyzed yield curve. The shape of the yield curve on Treasury securities has taken many forms over

---

2. As we discuss in Chapter 3, only debt securities have an identifiable maturity date; equity securities do not.

**Figure 2–7** Common Shapes for Yield Curves on Treasury Securities

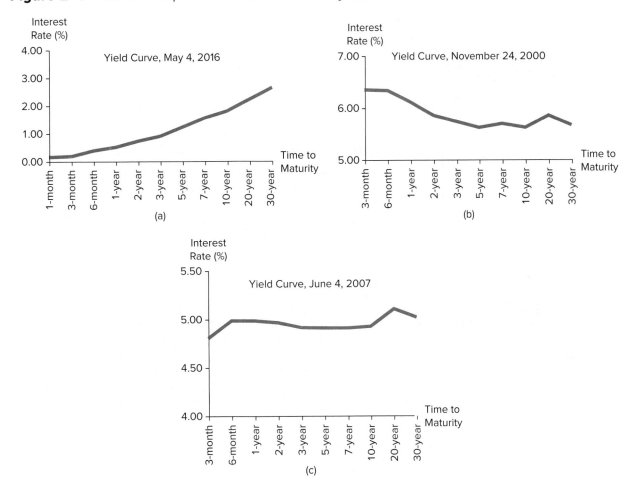

**Source:** U.S. Treasury, Daily Treasury Yield Curves, various dates. www.ustreas.gov

the years, but the three most common shapes are shown in Figure 2–7. In Panel a, the yield curve on May 4, 2016, yields rise steadily with maturity when the yield curve is upward sloping. This is the most common yield curve, so that on average the MP is positive. Panel b shows an inverted or downward-sloping yield curve, reported on November 24, 2000, for which yields decline as maturity increases. Inverted yield curves do not generally last very long. Finally, Panel c shows a flat yield curve, reported on June 4, 2007, in which the yield is virtually unaffected by the term to maturity.

Note that these yield curves may reflect factors other than investors' preferences for the maturity of a security, since in reality there may be liquidity differences among the securities traded at different points along the yield curve. For example, yields on newly issued 30-year Treasury bonds may be less than yields on (seasoned issues) 10-year Treasury bonds if investors prefer new ("on the run") securities to previously issued ("off the run") securities. Specifically, since (historically) the Treasury issues new 10-year notes and 30-year bonds only at the long end of the maturity spectrum, an existing 10-year Treasury bond would have to have been issued 20 years previously (i.e., it was originally a 30-year bond when it was issued 20 years previously). The increased demand for the newly issued "liquid" 30-year Treasury bonds relative to the less liquid 10-year Treasury bonds can be large enough to push the equilibrium interest rate on the 30-year Treasury bonds below that on the 10-year Treasury bonds and even below short-term rates. In the next section, we review three major theories that are often used to explain the shape of the yield curve.

Putting the factors that impact interest rates in different markets together, we can use the following general equation to determine the factors that functionally impact the fair interest rate ($i_j^*$) on an individual ($j$th) financial security:

$$i_j^* = f(IP, RFR, DRP_j, LRP_j, SCP_j, MP_j) \qquad (2\text{-}4)$$

where

## DO YOU UNDERSTAND:

**6.** *What the difference is between inflation and real risk-free rates?*

**7.** *What should happen to a security's equilibrium interest rate as the security's liquidity risk increases?*

**8.** *What term structure of interest rates means?*

$$
\begin{aligned}
IP &= \text{Inflation premium} \\
RFR &= \text{Real risk-free rate} \\
DRP_j &= \text{Default risk premium on the } j\text{th security} \\
LRP_j &= \text{Liquidity risk premium on the } j\text{th security} \\
SCP_j &= \text{Special feature premium on the } j\text{th security} \\
MP_j &= \text{Maturity premium on the } j\text{th security}
\end{aligned}
$$

The first two factors, *IP* and *RFR,* are common to all financial securities, while the other factors can be unique to each security.

## TERM STRUCTURE OF INTEREST RATES

**LG 2-7**

As discussed previously in the context of the maturity premium, the relationship between a security's interest rate and its remaining term to maturity (the term structure of interest rates) can take a number of different shapes. Explanations for the shape of the yield curve fall predominantly into three theories: the unbiased expectations theory, the liquidity premium theory, and the market segmentation theory. Table 2–4 summarizes the theories. We discuss them in detail below. Review again Panel a in Figure 2–7, which presents the Treasury yield curve as of May 4, 2016. As can be seen, the yield curve on this date reflected the normal upward-sloping relationship between yield and maturity.

### Unbiased Expectations Theory

According to the unbiased expectations theory of the term structure of interest rates, at a given point in time the yield curve reflects the market's current expectations of future short-term rates. As illustrated in Figure 2–8, the intuition behind the unbiased expectations theory is that if investors have a four-year investment horizon, they could either buy a current, four-year bond and earn the current or spot yield on a four-year bond ($_1R_4$, if held to maturity) each year, or invest in four successive one-year bonds—of which they know only the current one-year spot rate ($_1R_1$), but form expectations of the unknown future one-year

**TABLE 2–4  Explanations for the Shape of the Term Structure of Interest Rates**

**Unbiased expectations theory**—at any given point in time, the yield curve reflects the market's current expectations of future short-term rates. According to the unbiased expectations theory, the return for holding a four-year bond to maturity should equal the expected return for investing in four successive one-year bonds (as long as the market is in equilibrium).

**Liquidity premium theory**—long-term rates are equal to geometric averages of current and expected short-term rates, plus liquidity risk premiums that increase with the security's maturity. Longer maturities on securities mean greater market and liquidity risk. So, investors will hold long-term maturities only when they are offered at a premium to compensate for future uncertainty in the security's value. The liquidity premium increases as maturity increases.

**Market segmentation theory**—assumes that investors do not consider securities with different maturities as perfect substitutes. Rather, individual investors and FIs have preferred investment horizons (habitats) dictated by the nature of the liabilities they hold. Thus, interest rates are determined by distinct supply and demand conditions within a particular maturity segment (e.g., the short end and long end of the bond market).

**Figure 2–8** **Unbiased Expectations Theory of the Term Structure of Interest Rates**

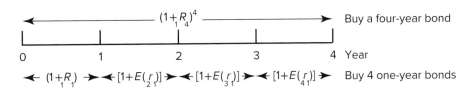

Buy a four-year bond

Buy 4 one-year bonds

rates $[E(_2r_1), E(_3r_1),$ and $E(_4r_1)]$. Note that each interest rate term has two subscripts, for example, $_1R_4$. The first subscript indicates the period in which the security is bought, so that 1 represents the purchase of a security in period 1. The second subscript indicates the maturity on the security, so that 4 represents the purchase of a security with a four-year life. Similarly, $E(_3r_1)$ is the expected return on a security with a one-year life purchased in period 3.

In equilibrium, the return to holding a four-year bond to maturity should equal the expected return to investing in four successive one-year bonds. If this equality does not hold, an arbitrage opportunity exists. For example, if the investor could earn more on the one-year bond investments, he could short (or sell) the four-year bond, use the proceeds to buy the four successive one-year bonds, and earn a guaranteed profit over the four-year investment horizon. Thus, according to the unbiased expectations theory, if future one-year rates are expected to rise each successive year into the future, then the yield curve will slope upward. Specifically, the current four-year T-bond rate will exceed the three-year bond rate, which will exceed the two-year bond rate, and so on. Similarly, if future one-year rates are expected to remain constant each successive year into the future, then the four-year bond rate will be equal to the three-year bond rate—that is, the term structure of interest rates will remain constant over the relevant time period. Specifically, the unbiased expectations theory posits that current long-term interest rates $(_1R_N)$ are geometric averages of current $(_1R_1)$ and expected *future* $E(_Nr_1)$ short-term interest rates. The mathematical equation representing this relationship is:

$$(1 + {_1R_N})^N = (1 + {_1R_1})(1 + E(_2r_1))\ldots(1 + E(_Nr_1)) \qquad \textbf{(2-5)}$$

therefore:

$$_1R_N = [(1 + {_1R_1})(1 + E(_2r_1))\ldots(1 + E(_Nr_1))]^{1/N} - 1$$

where

$_1R_N$ = Actual $N$-period rate today (i.e., the first day of year 1)
$N$ = Term to maturity, $N = 1, 2, \ldots, 4, \ldots$
$_1R_1$ = Actual current one-year rate today
$E(_ir_1)$ = Expected one-year rates for years, $i = 2, 3, 4, \ldots, N$ in the future

Notice that uppercase interest rate terms, $_1R_t$, are the actual current interest rates on securities purchased today with a maturity of $t$ years. Lowercase interest rate terms, $_tr_1$, are estimates of future one-year interest rates starting $t$ years into the future.

**EXAMPLE 2–2** **Construction of a Yield Curve Using the Unbiased Expectations Theory of the Term Structure of Interest Rates**

Suppose that the current one-year rate (one-year spot rate) and expected one-year T-bond rates over the following three years (i.e., years 2, 3, and 4, respectively) are as follows:

$$_1R_1 = 1.94\%, \quad E(_2r_1) = 3.00\%, \quad E(_3r_1) = 3.74\%, \quad E(_4r_1) = 4.10\%$$

Using the unbiased expectations theory, current (or today's) rates for one-, two-, three-, and four-year maturity Treasury securities should be:

$$_1R_1 = 1.94\%$$
$$_1R_2 = [(1 + 0.0194)(1 + 0.03)]^{1/2} - 1 = 2.47\%$$
$$_1R_3 = [(1 + 0.0194)(1 + 0.03)(1 + 0.0374)]^{1/3} - 1 = 2.89\%$$
$$_1R_4 = [(1 + 0.0194)(1 + 0.03)(1 + 0.0374)(1 + 0.041)]^{1/4} - 1 = 3.19\%$$

and the current yield curve will be upward sloping as shown:

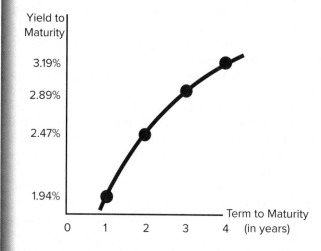

This upward-sloping yield curve reflects the market's expectation of persistently rising one-year (short-term) interest rates over the future horizon.[3]

### Liquidity Premium Theory

A weakness of the unbiased expectations theory is that it assumes that investors are equally willing to invest in short-term and long-term securities with no additional reward (in the form of higher interest rates) to compensate them for any added risk from locking in their funds in long-term securities, i.e., it assumes investors are risk neutral. However, with uncertainty about future interest rates (and future monetary policy actions) and hence about future security prices, these instruments become risky in the sense that the return over a future investment period is unknown. In other words, because of future uncertainty of returns, there is a risk in holding long-term securities, and that risk increases with the security's maturity, i.e., investors are risk averse.

The second theory, the liquidity premium theory of the term structure of interest rates, is an extension of the unbiased expectations theory. It is based on the idea that investors will hold long-term maturities only if they are offered at a premium to compensate for future uncertainty in a security's value, which increases with an asset's maturity. Specifically, in a world of uncertainty, short-term securities provide greater marketability (due to their more active secondary market) and have less price risk (due to smaller price fluctuations for a given change in interest rates) than long-term securities. As a result, investors prefer to hold shorter-term securities because they can be converted into cash with little risk of a capital loss (i.e., a fall in the price of the security below its original purchase price). Thus, investors

---

3. That is, $E(_4r_1) > E(_3r_1) > E(_2r_1) > {_1R_1}$.

**Figure 2–9** Yield Curve under the Unbiased Expectations Theory (UET) versus the Liquidity Premium Theory (LPT)

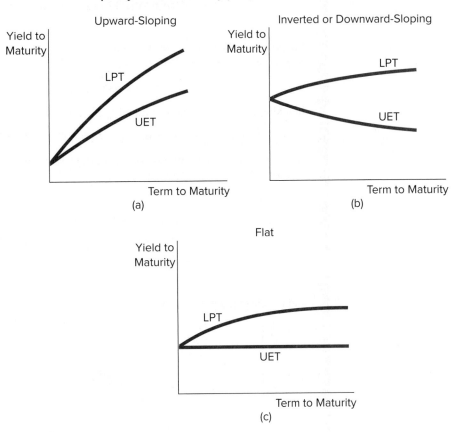

must be offered a liquidity premium to buy longer-term securities which have a higher risk of capital losses. This difference in price or liquidity risk can be directly related to the fact that longer-term securities are more sensitive to interest rate changes in the market than are shorter-term securities—see Chapter 3 for a discussion on bond interest rate sensitivity and the link to a bond's maturity or duration. Because the longer the maturity on a security the greater its risk, the liquidity premium increases as maturity increases.

The liquidity premium theory states that long-term rates are equal to geometric averages of current and expected short-term rates (as under the unbiased expectations theory), plus liquidity risk premiums that increase with the maturity of the security. Figure 2–9 illustrates the differences in the shape of the yield curve under the unbiased expectations theory versus the liquidity premium theory. For example, Panel c of Figure 2–9 shows that according to the liquidity premium theory, an upward-sloping yield curve may reflect investors' expectations that future short-term rates will be flat, but because liquidity premiums increase with maturity, the yield curve will nevertheless be upward sloping. Indeed, an upward-sloping yield curve may reflect expectations that future interest rates will rise (Panel a), be flat (Panel c), or even fall (Panel b), as long as the liquidity premium increases with maturity fast enough to produce an upward-sloping yield curve. The liquidity premium theory may be mathematically represented as:

$$_1R_N = [(1 + {}_1R_1)(1 + E({}_2r_1) + L_2) \ldots (1 + E({}_Nr_1) + L_N)]^{1/N} - 1 \qquad \textbf{(2-6)}$$

where

$L_t$ = Liquidity premium for a period $t$

$L_2 < L_3 < \ldots L_N$

**EXAMPLE 2–3**   Construction of a Yield Curve Using the Liquidity Premium Theory of the Term Structure of Interest Rates

Suppose that the current one-year rate (one-year spot rate) and expected one-year T-bond rates over the following three years (i.e., years 2, 3, and 4, respectively) are as follows:

$$_1R_1 = 1.94\%, \quad E(_2r_1) = 3.00\%, \quad E(_3r_1) = 3.74\%, \quad E(_4r_1) = 4.10\%$$

In addition, investors charge a liquidity premium on longer-term securities such that:

$$L_2 = 0.10\%, \quad L_3 = 0.20\%, \quad L_4 = 0.30\%$$

Using the liquidity premium theory, current rates for one-, two-, three-, and four-year maturity Treasury securities should be:

$$_1R_1 = 1.94\%$$
$$_1R_2 = [(1 + 0.0194)(1 + 0.03 + 0.001)]^{1/2} - 1 = 2.52\%$$
$$_1R_3 = [(1 + 0.0194)(1 + 0.03 + 0.001)(1 + 0.0374 + 0.002)]^{1/3} - 1 = 2.99\%$$
$$_1R_4 = [(1 + 0.0194)(1 + 0.03 + 0.001)(1 + 0.0374 + 0.002)(1 + 0.041 + 0.003)]^{1/4} - 1$$
$$= 3.34\%$$

and the current yield curve will be upward sloping as shown:

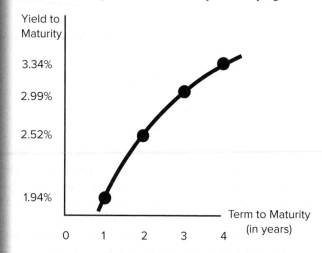

Comparing the yield curves in Example 2–2 and this example, notice that the liquidity premium in year 2 ($L_2 = 0.10\%$) produces a 0.05 percent premium on the yield to maturity on a two-year T-note, the liquidity premium for year 3 ($L_3 = 0.20\%$) produces a 0.10 percent premium on the yield to maturity on the three-year T-note, and the liquidity premium for year 4 ($L_4 = 0.30\%$) produces a 0.15 percent premium on the yield to maturity on the four-year T-note.

### Market Segmentation Theory

A weakness of both the unbiased expectations and liquidity premium theories is that they assume that investors have no preference when it comes to different maturities and the risks associated with them. The market segmentation theory argues that individual investors and FIs have specific maturity preferences, and to get them to hold securities with maturities other than their most preferred requires a higher interest rate (maturity premium). Accordingly, the market segmentation theory does not consider securities with different maturities as perfect substitutes. Rather, individual investors and FIs have preferred investment horizons (habitats) dictated by the nature of the liabilities they hold (i.e., investors have complete risk aversion for securities outside their maturity preferences). For example, banks might prefer to hold relatively short-term U.S. Treasury bonds because of the short-term nature of their deposit liabilities, while insurance companies may prefer to hold long-term U.S. Treasury bonds because of the long-term nature of their life insurance contractual liabilities. Accordingly, interest rates are determined by distinct supply and demand conditions within a particular maturity segment (e.g., the short end and long end of the bond market). The market segmentation theory assumes that investors and borrowers are generally unwilling to shift from one maturity sector to another without adequate compensation in the form of an interest rate premium. Figure 2–10 demonstrates how changes in the supply curve for short- versus long-term bond segments of the market result in changes in the shape of the yield curve. Specifically in Figure 2–10, the higher the yield on securities (the lower the price), the higher the demand for them.[4] Thus, as the *supply* of securities *decreases in the short-term* market and *increases in the long-term* market, the *slope* of the yield curve *becomes steeper.* If the *supply* of *short-term* securities had *increased* while the *supply* of *long-term* securities had *decreased,* the *yield curve would have a flatter slope* and might even have sloped downward. Indeed, the large-scale repurchases of long-term Treasury bonds (i.e., reductions in supply) by the U.S. Treasury in early 2000 has been viewed as the major cause of the inverted yield curve that appeared in February 2000. More recently, between October 2011 and June 2012 the Federal Reserve conducted its Operation Twist.

**Figure 2–10**    **Market Segmentation and Determination of the Slope of the Yield Curve**

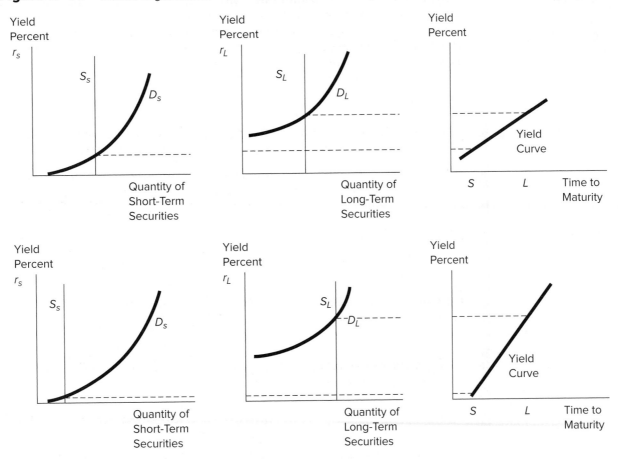

4. In general, the price and yield on a bond are inversely related. Thus, as the price of a bond falls (becomes cheaper), the demand for the bond will rise. This is the same as saying that as the yield on a bond rises, it becomes cheaper and the demand for it increases.

DO YOU UNDERSTAND:

**9.** *What the three explanations are for the shape of the yield curve? Discuss each and compare them.*

The program involved the sale of $400 billion of short-term Treasuries in exchange for long-term Treasuries. The program was designed to lower rates on long-term bonds, while keeping short-term interest rates unchanged. By intentionally lowering yields, the Fed was forcing investors to consider other investments that would help the economy more. Many argue that the policy worked. In June 2012, the yield on the 10-year Treasury fell to a 200-year low. As a result, the housing market and bank lending started to come back.

## FORECASTING INTEREST RATES

LG 2-8

As will be seen in the time value of money examples in the next section, as interest rates change, so do the values of financial securities. Accordingly, the ability to predict or forecast interest rates is critical to the profitability of financial institutions and individual investors alike. For example, if interest rates rise, the value of investment portfolios of FIs and individuals will fall, resulting in a loss of wealth. Thus, interest rate forecasts are extremely important for the financial wealth of both FIs and individuals. The discussion of the unbiased expectations theory in the previous section of this chapter indicated that the shape of the yield curve is determined by the market's current expectations of future short-term interest rates. For example, an upward-sloping yield curve suggests that the market expects future short-term interest rates to increase. Given that the yield curve represents the market's current expectations of future short-term interest rates, the unbiased expectations theory can be used to forecast (short-term) interest rates in the future (i.e., forward one-year interest rates). A **forward rate** is an expected or "implied" rate on a short-term security that is to be originated at some point in the future. Using the equations representing the unbiased expectations theory, the market's expectation of forward rates can be derived directly from existing or actual rates on securities currently traded in the spot market. In this section, we use the notation $f$, rather than $E(r)$ used in the previous section, to highlight the terminology "forward rate."

**forward rate**

*An expected rate (quoted today) on a security that originates at some point in the future.*

---

**EXAMPLE 2–4**    Calculation of Implied Forward Rates on One-Year Securities Using the Unbiased Expectations Theory

To find an implied forward rate on a one-year security to be issued one year from today, the unbiased expectations theory equation can be rewritten as follows:

$$_1R_2 = \left[(1 + {}_1R_1)(1 + [_2f_1])\right]^{1/2} - 1$$

where

$_2f_1$ = Expected one-year rate for year 2, or the implied forward one-year rate for next year

Therefore, $_2f_1$ is the market's estimate of the expected one-year rate for year 2. Solving for $_2f_1$, we get:

$$_2f_1 = [(1 + {}_1R_2)^2/(1 + {}_1R_1)] - 1$$

In general, we can find the one-year forward rate for any year, $N$ years into the future, using the following equation:[5]

$$_Nf_1 = [(1 + {}_1R_N)^N/(1 + {}_1R_N - 1)^{N-1}] - 1 \tag{2-7}$$

---

5. This formula focuses on solving for one-year rates only. However, practitioners construct the entire implied future yield curve. The general formula that allows solving for forward rates beyond the one-year maturity, $K$, is as follows:

$$_{N-K}f_K = \left[\frac{(1 + R_N)^N}{(1 + R_{N-K})^{N-K}}\right]^{1/K} - 1$$

For example, on May 4, 2016, the existing or current (spot) one-year, two-year, three-year, and four-year zero-coupon Treasury security rates were as follows:

$$_1R_1 = 0.553\%, \quad _1R_2 = 0.774\%, \quad _1R_3 = 0.905\%, \quad _1R_4 = 1.278\%$$

Using the unbiased expectations theory, one-year forward rates on zero-coupon Treasury bonds for years 2, 3, and 4 as of May 4, 2016, were:

$$_2f_1 = [(1.00774)^2/(1.00553)] - 1 = 0.995\%$$
$$_3f_1 = [(1.00905)^3/(1.00774)^2] - 1 = 1.012\%$$
$$_4f_1 = [(1.01278)^4/(1.00905)^3] - 1 = 2.405\%$$

Thus, the expected one-year rate, one year in the future, was 0.995 percent; the expected one-year rate, two years into the future, was 1.012 percent; and the expected one-year rate, three years into the future, was 2.405 percent.

## TIME VALUE OF MONEY AND INTEREST RATES[6]

**LG 2-9**

So far, we have looked at factors that determine the level of interest rates and at what causes interest rate movements over time. We finish the chapter with a look at the technical details of how interest rates affect the value of financial securities by reviewing time value of money concepts. Time value of money is a crucial tool for much of the analysis in this textbook. For example, interest rates have a direct and immediate effect on the value of virtually all financial securities—that is, interest rates affect the price or value the seller of a security receives and the buyer of a security pays in organized financial markets.

### Time Value of Money

Time value of money is the basic notion that a dollar received today is worth more than a dollar received at some future date. This is because a dollar received today can be invested and its value enhanced by an interest rate or return such that the investor receives more than a dollar in the future. The interest rate or return reflects the fact that people generally prefer to consume now rather than wait until later. To compensate them for delaying consumption (i.e., saving), they are paid a rate of interest by those who wish to consume more today than their current resources permit (users of funds). Users of funds are willing to pay this rate of interest because they plan to productively use the borrowed funds such that they will earn even more than the rate of interest promised to the savers (suppliers of the funds).

The time value of money concept can be used to convert cash flows earned over an investment horizon into a value at the end of the investment horizon: the investment's future value (*FV*). Alternatively, the time value of money concept can be used to convert the value of future cash flows into their current or present values (*PV*) (i.e., future dollars converted into their equivalent present value or current dollars). Two forms of time value of money calculations are commonly used in finance for security valuation purposes: the value of a lump sum and the value of annuity payments. A **lump sum payment** is a single cash payment received at the beginning or end of some investment horizon (e.g., $100 received at the end of five years). **Annuity** payments are a series of equal cash flows received at fixed intervals over the entire investment horizon (e.g., $100 a year received each year for five years). In actual practice, "annuity" payments can be paid more

**lump sum payment**

*A single cash flow occurs at the beginning and end of the investment horizon with no other cash flows exchanged.*

**annuity**

*A series of equal cash flows received at fixed intervals over the investment horizon.*

6. The time value of money concept is a topic that finance students probably studied in introductory financial management courses. However, an understanding of its use in the valuation of financial instruments created, traded, and held by individual investors and financial institutions is critical. Therefore, in this chapter, we review and provide a reference guide to the general relationships between interest rates and security valuation. This material can be included or dropped from the chapter reading, depending on the need for review of the material, without harming the continuity of the chapter. In Chapter 3, we use these general relationships to determine the values of specific securities (e.g., equities and bonds).

frequently than once a year—so that the term *annuity* really means a constant payment received at equal intervals throughout an investment horizon (e.g., twice, three times, ... a year). We first discuss lump sum time value of money calculations, followed by annuity calculations.

### Lump Sum Valuation

**Present Value of a Lump Sum.**   The present value function converts cash flows received over a future investment horizon into an equivalent (present) value as if they were received at the beginning of the current investment horizon. This is done by discounting future cash flows back to the present using the current market interest rate. The present value of an investment is the intrinsic value or price of the investment. The time value of money equation used to calculate this value can be represented as follows.

Present value ($PV$) of a *lump sum* received at the end of the investment horizon, or future value ($FV$):

$$PV = FV_t/(1 + r)^t \qquad\qquad (2\text{-}8)$$

where

$PV$ = Present value of cash flows

$FV_t$ = Future value of cash flows (lump sum) received in $t$ periods

$r$ = Interest rate earned per period on an investment (equals the nominal annual interest rate, $i$, divided by the number of compounding periods per year—for example, daily, weekly, monthly, quarterly, semiannually)

$t$ = Number of compounding periods in the investment horizon (equals the number of years in the investment horizon times the number of compounding periods per year)

### EXAMPLE 2–5    Calculation of Present Value of a Lump Sum

You have been offered a security investment such as a bond that will pay you $10,000 at the end of six years in exchange for a fixed payment today. If the appropriate annual interest rate on the investment is 8 percent compounded annually, the present value of this investment is computed as follows:

$$PV = FV_t/(1 + r)^t = \$10{,}000/(1 + 0.08)^6 = \$10{,}000\,(0.630170) = \$6{,}301.70$$

If the annual interest rate on the investment rises to 12 percent, the present value of this investment becomes:

$$PV = \$10{,}000/(1 + 0.12)^6 = \$10{,}000\,(0.506631) = \$5{,}066.31$$

If the annual interest rate on the investment rises to 16 percent, the present value of this investment becomes:

$$PV = \$10{,}000/(1 + 0.16)^6 = \$10{,}000\,(0.410442) = \$4{,}104.42$$

Finally, if the annual interest rate on the investment of 16 percent is compounded semiannually (that is, you will receive $t = 12\,(= 6 \times 2)$ total interest payments, each calculated as $r = 8$ percent $(= 16$ percent $\div 2)$ times the principal value in the investment, where $r$ in this case is the semiannual interest payment) rather than annually, the present value of this investment becomes:

$$PV = \$10{,}000/(1 + 0.08)^{12} = \$10{,}000\,(0.397114) = \$3{,}971.14$$

Notice from the previous examples that the *present values* of the security investment *decrease as interest rates increase.* For example, as the interest rate rose from 8 percent to

12 percent, the (present) value of the security investment fell $1,235.39 (from $6,301.70 to $5,066.31). As interest rates rose from 12 percent to 16 percent, the value of the investment fell $961.89 (from $5,066.31 to $4,104.42). This is because as interest rates increase, fewer funds need to be invested at the beginning of an investment horizon to receive a stated amount at the end of the investment horizon. This inverse relationship between the value of a financial instrument—for example, a bond—and interest rates is one of the most fundamental relationships in finance and is evident in the swings that occur in financial asset prices whenever major changes in interest rates arise.

Note also that *as interest rates increase,* the *present values* of the investment *decrease at a decreasing rate.* The fall in present value is greater when interest rates rose by 4 percent, from 12 percent to 16 percent, compared to when they rose from 8 percent to 12 percent—the inverse relationship between interest rates and the present value of security investments is neither linear nor proportional.

Finally, from this example notice that the greater the number of compounding periods per year (i.e., semiannually versus annually), the smaller the present value of a future amount.[7]

**Future Value of a Lump Sum.**   The future value of a lump sum equation translates a cash flow received at the beginning of an investment period to a terminal (future) value at the end of an investment horizon (e.g., 5 years, 6 years, 10 years, etc.). The future value (*FV*) equation can be represented as follows:

Future value (*FV*) of a lump sum received at the beginning of the investment horizon:

$$FV_t = PV(1 + r)^t \tag{2-9}$$

---

**EXAMPLE 2–6**   Calculation of Future Value of a Lump Sum

**CALCULATOR HINTS**

$N = 6$
$I = 8$
$PV = 10{,}000$
$PMT = 0$
CPT $FV = -15{,}868.74$

You plan to invest $10,000 today in exchange for a fixed payment at the end of six years. If the appropriate annual interest rate on the investment is 8 percent compounded annually, the future value of this investment is computed as follows:

$$FV = PV(1 + r)^t = \$10{,}000\,(1 + 0.08)^6 = \$10{,}000\,(1.586874) = \$15{,}868.74$$

If the annual interest rate on the investment rises to 12 percent, the future value of this investment becomes:

$$FV = \$10{,}000(1 + 0.12)^6 = \$10{,}000\,(1.973823) = \$19{,}738.23$$

If the annual interest rate on the investment rises to 16 percent, the future value of this investment becomes:

$$FV = \$10{,}000(1 + 0.16)^6 = \$10{,}000\,(2.436396) = \$24{,}363.96$$

Finally, if the annual interest rate on the investment of 16 percent is compounded semiannually rather than annually (i.e., $r = 16\%/2 = 8\%$ and $t = 6 \times 2 = 12$), the future value of this investment becomes:

$$FV = \$10{,}000(1 + 0.08)^{12} = \$10{,}000\,(2.518170) = \$25{,}181.70$$

---

7. The ultimate of compounding periods is instantaneous, or continuous, compounding over the investment horizon (period). In this case the present value formula becomes:

$$PV = FV_t[1/(1 + r/\infty)]^{n\infty} = FV_n(e^{-rn})$$

where *n* is the number of years in the investment horizon (period). Thus, in Example 2–5, if the annual interest rate on the investment is 16 percent compounded continuously, the present value of the $10,000 investment in six years is:

$$PV = \$10{,}000(e^{-0.16 \times 6}) = \$10{,}000(0.382893) = \$3{,}828.93$$

Notice that the *future value of an investment increases as interest rates increase.* As interest rates rose from 8 percent to 12 percent, the (future) value of the investment of $10,000 for six years rose by $3,869.49 (from $15,868.74 to $19,738.23). As rates rose from 12 percent to 16 percent, the (future) value of the investment rose $4,625.73 (from $19,738.23 to $24,363.96). Note also that *as interest rates increase, future values increase at an increasing rate.* The increase in future value is greater when interest rates rose by 4 percent, from 8 percent to 12 percent, compared to when they rose from 12 percent to 16 percent—the positive relationship between interest rates and the future value of security investments is neither linear nor proportional. With the compounding of interest rates, as interest rates increase, a stated amount of funds invested at the beginning of an investment horizon accumulates to an expotentially larger amount at the end of the investment horizon. By contrast, as stated earlier, as interest rates increase, the present value of an investment decreases at a decreasing rate. Finally, notice that as the number of compounding periods per year increases, the *future value* of a present amount increases.

### Annuity Valuation

**Present Value of an Annuity.**    The present value of an annuity equation converts a finite series of constant (or equal) cash flows received on the last day of equal intervals throughout the investment horizon into an equivalent (present) value as if they were received at the beginning of the investment horizon. The time value of money equation used to calculate this value is represented as follows:

Present value (*PV*) of an annuity stream (*PMT*) received in the future:

$$PV = PMT \sum_{j=1}^{t} [1/(1+r)]^{j} \qquad (2\text{-}10)$$

which can be reduced to the simpler equation:

$$PV = PMT \times \left[ \frac{1 - \dfrac{1}{(1+r)^{t}}}{r} \right]$$

where

$PMT$ = Periodic annuity payment received during an investment horizon

$\displaystyle\sum_{j=1}^{t}$ = Summation sign for addition of all terms from $j = 1$ to $j = t$.

---

**CALCULATOR HINTS**
$N = 6$
$I = 8$
$FV = 0$
$PMT = 10{,}000$
CPT $PV = -46{,}228.80$

**EXAMPLE 2–7**    **Calculation of Present Value of an Annuity**

You have been offered a bond that will pay you $10,000 on the last day of every year for the next six years in exchange for a fixed payment today. If the appropriate annual interest rate on the investment is 8 percent, the present value of this investment is computed as follows:

$$PV = PMT \times \left[ \frac{1 - \dfrac{1}{(1+r)^{t}}}{r} \right]$$

$$= \$10{,}000 \times \left[ \frac{1 - \dfrac{1}{(1+0.08)^{6}}}{0.08} \right]$$

$$= \$10{,}000\,(4.622880) = \$46{,}228.80$$

If the investment pays you \$10,000 on the last day of every quarter for the next six years (i.e., $r = 8\%/4 = 2\%$ and $t = 6 \times 4 = 24$), the present value of the annuity becomes:

$$PV = \$10,000 \times \left[ \frac{1 - \dfrac{1}{(1 + 0.02)^{24}}}{0.02} \right]$$

$$= \$10,000\,(18.913926) = \$189,139.26$$

If the annuity is paid on the first day of each quarter (referred to as an annuity due), an extra interest payment would be received for each \$10,000 payment. Thus, the time value of money equation for the present value of an annuity due becomes:

$$PV = PMT \left[ \frac{1 - \dfrac{1}{(1 + r)^{t}}}{r} \right] (1 + r)$$

The present value of this investment becomes:

$$PV = \$10,000 \left[ \frac{1 - \dfrac{1}{(1 + 0.02)^{24}}}{0.02} \right] (1 + 0.02)$$

$$= \$10,000\,(18.913926)(1.02) = \$192,922.04$$

**Future Value of an Annuity.** The future value of an annuity equation converts a series of equal cash flows received at equal intervals throughout the investment horizon into an equivalent future amount at the end of the investment horizon. The equation used to calculate this value is represented as follows:

Future value ($FV$) of an annuity payment stream received over an investment horizon:[8]

$$FV_{t} = PMT \sum_{j=0}^{t-1} (1 + r)^{j} \tag{2-11}$$

which can be reduced to the simpler equation:

$$FV_{t} = PMT \times \left[ \frac{(1 + r)^{t} - 1}{r} \right]$$

**EXAMPLE 2–8**   **Calculation of the Future Value of an Annuity**

You plan to invest \$10,000 on the last day of every year for the next six years. If the interest rate on the investment is 8 percent, the future value of your investment in six years is computed as follows:

$$FV = \$10,000 \left[ \frac{(1 + 0.08)^{6} - 1}{0.08} \right]$$

$$= \$10,000\,(7.335929) = \$73,359.29$$

8. Note that the last annuity payment occurs on the last day of the investment horizon. Thus, it earns no interest (i.e., the future value interest factor takes a power of zero). Similarly, the first annuity payment earns only five years of interest. Thus, the future value interest factor takes a power of five. Accordingly, in the future value interest factor of annuity term, $j$ runs from 0 to $t - 1$, or, in this example, $(6 - 1 =) 5$. In Example 2–7, note that the first annuity payment earns one year of interest. Thus, the present value interest factor term takes a power of one. Likewise, the last annuity payment earns six years of interest. Thus, the present value interest factor takes a power of six. Accordingly, in the present value interest factor of annuity term, $j$ runs from 1 to $t$.

If the investment pays you \$10,000 on the last day of every quarter for the next six years (i.e., $r = 8\%/4 = 2\%$ and $t = 6 \times 4 = 24$), the future value of the annuity becomes:

$$FV = \$10,000 \left[ \frac{(1 + 0.02)^{24} - 1}{0.02} \right]$$

$$= \$10,000 \, (30.421862) = \$304,218.62$$

**DO YOU UNDERSTAND:**

12. What should happen to the present value of a lump sum cash flow as interest rates increase?

13. What should happen to the future value of an annuity stream of cash flows as interest rates increase?

If the annuity is paid on the first day of each quarter (an annuity due), an extra interest payment would be earned on each \$10,000 investment. The time value of money equation for the future value of an annuity due becomes:

$$FV = PMT \left[ \frac{(1 + r)^t - 1}{r} \right] (1 + r)$$

Thus, the future value of this investment becomes:

$$FV = \$10,000 \left[ \frac{(1 + 0.02)^{24} - 1}{0.02} \right] (1 + 0.02)$$

$$= \$10,000 \, (30.421862)(1.02) = \$310,303.00$$

## SUMMARY

This chapter reviewed the determinants of nominal interest rates and their effects on security prices and values in domestic and foreign financial markets. It described the way funds flow through the financial system from lenders to borrowers and how the level of interest rates and its movements over time are determined. The chapter also introduced theories regarding the determination of the shape of the term structure of interest rates.

## QUESTIONS

1. Who are the suppliers of loanable funds? (*LG 2-1*)
2. Who are the demanders of loanable funds? (*LG 2-2*)
3. What factors cause the supply of funds curve to shift? (*LG 2-4*)
4. What factors cause the demand for funds curve to shift? (*LG 2-4*)
5. What are six factors that determine the nominal interest rate on a security? (*LG 2-6*)
6. What should happen to a security's nominal interest rate as the security's liquidity risk increases? (*LG 2-6*)
7. Discuss and compare the three explanations for the shape of the yield curve. (*LG 2-7*)

8. If we observe a one-year Treasury security rate higher than the two-year Treasury security rate, what can we infer about the one-year rate expected one year from now? (*LG 2-7*)
9. How does the liquidity premium theory of the term structure of interest rates differ from the unbiased expectations theory? In a normal economic environment, that is, an upward-sloping yield curve, what is the relationship of liquidity premiums for successive years into the future? Why? (*LG 2-7*)
10. What is a forward interest rate? (*LG 2-8*)
11. What is the relationship between present values and interest rates as interest rates increase? (*LG 2-9*)

## PROBLEMS

1. A particular security's equilibrium rate of return is 8 percent. For all securities, the inflation risk premium is 1.75 percent and the real risk-free rate is 3.5 percent. The security's liquidity risk premium is 0.25 percent and maturity risk premium is 0.85 percent. The security has no special covenants. Calculate the security's default risk premium. (*LG 2-6*)

2. You are considering an investment in 30-year bonds issued by Moore Corporation. The bonds have no special covenants. *The Wall Street Journal* reports that 1-year T-bills

are currently earning 3.25 percent. Your broker has determined the following information about economic activity and Moore Corporation bonds: (*LG 2-6*)

| | |
|---|---|
| Real risk-free rate | = 2.25% |
| Default risk premium | = 1.15% |
| Liquidity risk premium | = 0.50% |
| Maturity risk premium | = 1.75% |

a. What is the inflation premium?
b. What is the fair interest rate on Moore Corporation 30-year bonds?

3. Dakota Corporation 15-year bonds have an equilibrium rate of return of 8 percent. For all securities, the inflation premium is 1.75 percent and the real risk-free rate is 3.50 percent. The security's liquidity risk premium is 0.25 percent and maturity risk premium is 0.85 percent. The security has no special covenants. Calculate the bond's default risk premium. (*LG 2-6*)

4. A two-year Treasury security currently earns 1.94 percent. Over the next two years, the real risk-free rate is expected to be 1.00 percent per year and the inflation premium is expected to be 0.50 percent per year. Calculate the maturity risk premium on the two-year Treasury security. (*LG 2-6*)

5. Tom and Sue's Flowers Inc.'s 15-year bonds are currently yielding a return of 8.25 percent. The expected inflation premium is 2.25 percent annually and the real risk-free rate is expected to be 3.50 percent annually over the next 15 years. The default risk premium on Tom and Sue's Flowers's bonds is 0.80 percent. The maturity risk premium is 0.75 percent on 5-year securities and increases by 0.04 percent for each additional year to maturity. Calculate the liquidity risk premium on Tom and Sue's Flowers Inc.'s 15-year bonds. (*LG 2-6*)

6. Nikki G's Corporation's 10-year bonds are currently yielding a return of 6.05 percent. The expected inflation premium is 1.00 percent annually and the real risk-free rate is expected to be 2.10 percent annually over the next 10 years. The liquidity risk premium on Nikki G's bonds is 0.25 percent. The maturity risk premium is 0.10 percent on 2-year securities and increases by 0.05 percent for each additional year to maturity. Calculate the default risk premium on Nikki G's 10-year bonds. (*LG 2-6*)

7. The current one-year Treasury-bill rate is 5.2 percent and the expected one-year rate 12 months from now is 5.8 percent. According to the unbiased expectations theory, what should be the current rate for a two-year Treasury security? (*LG 2-7*)

8. Suppose that the current one-year rate (one-year spot rate) and expected one-year T-bill rates over the following three years (i.e., years 2, 3, and 4, respectively) are as follows:

$_1R_1 = 6\%, E(_2r_1) = 7\%, E(_3r_1) = 7.5\%, E(_4r_1) = 7.85\%$

Using the unbiased expectations theory, calculate the current (long-term) rates for one-, two-, three-, and four-year-maturity Treasury securities. Plot the resulting yield curve. (*LG 2-7*)

9. One-year Treasury bills currently earn 3.45 percent. You expect that one year from now, one-year Treasury bill rates will increase to 3.65 percent. If the unbiased expectations theory is correct, what should the current rate be on two-year Treasury securities? (*LG 2-7*)

10. Suppose we observe the following rates: $_1R_1 = 8\%$, $_1R_2 = 10\%$. If the unbiased expectations theory of the term structure of interest rates holds, what is the one-year interest rate expected one year from now, $E(_2r_1)$? (*LG 2-7*)

11. Suppose we observe the three-year Treasury security rate to be 12 percent, the expected one-year rate next year—$E(_2r_1)$—to be 8 percent, and the expected one-year rate the following year—$E(_3r_1)$—to be 10 percent. If the unbiased expectations theory of the term structure of interest rates holds, what is the one-year Treasury security rate? (*LG 2-7*)

12. *The Wall Street Journal* reports that the rate on four-year Treasury securities is 5.60 percent and the rate on five-year Treasury securities is 6.15 percent. According to the unbiased expectations theory, what does the market expect the one-year Treasury rate to be four years from today, $E(_5r_1)$? (*LG 2-7*)

13. A recent edition of *The Wall Street Journal* reported interest rates of 2.25 percent, 2.60 percent, 2.98 percent, and 3.25 percent for three-year, four-year, five-year, and six-year Treasury notes, respectively. According to the unbiased expectations theory of the term structure of interest rates, what are the expected one-year rates during years 4, 5, and 6? (*LG 2-7*)

14. Based on economists' forecasts and analysis, one-year Treasury bill rates and liquidity premiums for the next four years are expected to be as follows:

$_1R_1 = 5.65\%$
$E(_2R_1) = 6.75\%$     $L_2 = 0.05\%$
$E(_3R_1) = 6.85\%$     $L_3 = 0.10\%$
$E(_4R_1) = 7.15\%$     $L_4 = 0.12\%$

Using the liquidity premium theory, plot the current yield curve. Make sure you label the axes on the graph and identify the four annual rates on the curve both on the axes and on the yield curve itself. (*LG 2-7*)

15. Suppose we observe the following rates: $_1R_1 = 10\%$, $_1R_2 = 14\%$, and $E(_2r_1) = 18\%$. If the liquidity premium theory of the term structure of interest rates holds, what is the liquidity premium for year 2? (*LG 2-7*)

16. *The Wall Street Journal* reports that the rate on three-year Treasury securities is 5.25 percent and the rate on four-year Treasury securities is 5.50 percent. The one-year interest rate expected in three years, $E(_4r_1)$, is 6.10 percent. According to the liquidity premium theory, what is the liquidity premium on the four-year Treasury security, $L_4$? (*LG 2-7*)

17. If you note the following yield curve in *The Wall Street Journal*, what is the one-year forward rate for the period beginning one year from today, $_2f_1$ according to the unbiased expectations theory? (*LG 2-8*)

| Maturity | Yield |
|---|---|
| One day | 2.00% |
| One year | 5.50 |
| Two years | 6.50 |
| Three years | 9.00 |

18. You note the following yield curve in *The Wall Street Journal*. According to the unbiased expectations theory, what is the one-year forward rate for the period beginning two years from today, $_3f_1$? (*LG 2-8*)

| Maturity | Yield |
|---|---|
| One day | 2.00% |
| One year | 5.50 |
| Two years | 6.50 |
| Three years | 9.00 |

19. On March 11, 20XX, the existing or current (spot) one-year, two-year, three-year, and four-year zero-coupon Treasury security rates were as follows:

$_1R_1 = 4.75\%$,   $_1R_2 = 4.95\%$,   $_1R_3 = 5.25\%$,   $_1R_4 = 5.65\%$

Using the unbiased expectations theory, calculate the one-year forward rates on zero-coupon Treasury bonds for years two, three, and four as of March 11, 20XX. (*LG 2-8*)

20. A recent edition of *The Wall Street Journal* reported interest rates of 6 percent, 6.35 percent, 6.65 percent, and 6.75 percent for three-year, four-year, five-year, and six-year Treasury notes, respectively. According to the unbiased expectations theory, what are the expected one-year rates for years 4, 5, and 6 (i.e., what are $_4f_1$, $_5f_1$, and $_6f_1$)? (*LG 2-8*)

21. Assume the current interest rate on a one-year Treasury bond ($_1R_1$) is 4.50 percent, the current rate on a two-year Treasury bond ($_1R_2$) is 5.25 percent, and the current rate on a three-year Treasury bond ($_1R_3$) is 6.50 percent. If the unbiased expectations theory of the term structure of interest rates is correct, what is the one-year interest rate expected on Treasury bills during year 3 ($E(_3r_1)$ or $_3f_1$)? (*LG 2-8*)

22. Calculate the present value of $5,000 received five years from today if your investments pay
    a. 6 percent compounded annually
    b. 8 percent compounded annually
    c. 10 percent compounded annually
    d. 10 percent compounded semiannually
    e. 10 percent compounded quarterly

    What do your answers to these questions tell you about the relation between present values and interest rates and between present values and the number of compounding periods per year? (*LG 2-9*)

23. Calculate the future value in five years of $5,000 received today if your investments pay
    a. 6 percent compounded annually
    b. 8 percent compounded annually
    c. 10 percent compounded annually
    d. 10 percent compounded semiannually
    e. 10 percent compounded quarterly

    What do your answers to these questions tell you about the relation between future values and interest rates and between future values and the number of compounding periods per year? (*LG 2-9*)

24. Calculate the present value of the following annuity streams: (*LG 2-9*)
    a. $5,000 received each year for five years on the last day of each year if your investments pay 6 percent compounded annually.

b. $5,000 received each quarter for five years on the last day of each quarter if your investments pay 6 percent compounded quarterly.
c. $5,000 received each year for five years on the first day of each year if your investments pay 6 percent compounded annually.
d. $5,000 received each quarter for five years on the first day of each quarter if your investments pay 6 percent compounded quarterly.

25. Calculate the future value of the following annuity streams: (*LG 2-9*)
    a. $5,000 received each year for five years on the last day of each year if your investments pay 6 percent compounded annually.
    b. $5,000 received each quarter for five years on the last day of each quarter if your investments pay 6 percent compounded quarterly.
    c. $5,000 received each year for five years on the first day of each year if your investments pay 6 percent compounded annually.
    d. $5,000 received each quarter for five years on the first day of each quarter if your investments pay 6 percent compounded quarterly.

26. Compute the future values of the following first assuming that payments are made on the last day of the period and then assuming payments are made on the first day of the period: (*LG 2-9*)

| Payment | Years | Interest Rate | Future Value (Payment made on last day of period) | Future Value (Payment made on first day of period) |
|---|---|---|---|---|
| $   123 | 13 | 13% | | |
| 4,555 | 8 | 8 | | |
| 74,484 | 5 | 10 | | |
| 167,332 | 9 | 1 | | |

27. Compute the present values of the following first assuming that payments are made on the last day of the period and then assuming payments are made on the first day of the period: (*LG 2-9*)

| Payment | Years | Interest Rate | Present Value (Payment made on last day of period) | Present Value (Payment made on first day of period) |
|---|---|---|---|---|
| $  678.09 | 7 | 13% | | |
| 7,968.26 | 13 | 6 | | |
| 20,322.93 | 23 | 4 | | |
| 69,712.54 | 4 | 31 | | |

28. If you deposit $500 in a bank account that earns 6 percent per year, how much total interest will you have earned after the third year? (*LG 2-9*)

29. How much money would you have to deposit today in order to have $2,000 in four years if the discount rate is 8 percent per year? (*LG 2-9*)

**30.** If an ounce of gold, valued at $1,200, increases at a rate of 7.5 percent per year, how long will it take to be valued at $2,000? (*LG 2-9*)

**31.** You can save $1,000 per year for the next six years in an account earning 10 percent per year. How much will you have at the end of the sixth year if you make the first deposit today? (*LG 2-9*)

**32.** What are the monthly payments (principal and interest) on a 15-year home mortgage for an $180,000 loan when interest rates are fixed at 8 percent? (*LG 2-9*)

---

## SEARCH THE SITE

Go to the U.S. Treasury website and find the latest information available on the size of the U.S. national debt. Go to **www.treasurydirect.gov**. Under "Government," click on "Public Debt Reports." Click on "Debt to the Penny." This will bring up the relevant tables. For example, on May 4, 2016, the size of the national debt was $19.21 trillion.

### Questions

1. What is the most recent dollar value of the U.S. national debt?
2. Calculate the percentage change in the U.S. national debt since May 4, 2016.

# chapter

# Interest Rates and Security Valuation

## Learning Goals

**LG 3-1**    *Understand the differences in the required rate of return, the expected rate of return, and the realized rate of return.*

**LG 3-2**    *Calculate bond values.*

**LG 3-3**    *Calculate equity values.*

**LG 3-4**    *Appreciate how security prices are affected by interest rate changes.*

**LG 3-5**    *Understand how the maturity and coupon rate on a security affect its price sensitivity to interest rate changes.*

**LG 3-6**    *Know what duration is.*

**LG 3-7**    *Understand how maturity, yield to maturity, and coupon rate affect the duration of a security.*

**LG 3-8**    *Understand the economic meaning of duration.*

## INTEREST RATES AS A DETERMINANT OF FINANCIAL SECURITY VALUES: CHAPTER OVERVIEW

In Chapter 2, we reviewed the basic concepts of time value of money and how time value of money equations can be used to convert cash flows received or paid over an investment horizon into either a present value or future value. Of particular importance was the fact that interest rate levels, and changes in interest rate levels, affect security values. We also reviewed factors that determine the level of interest rates, changes in interest rates, and interest rate differences among securities (e.g., default risk, callability).

With this understanding of how and why interest rates change, in this chapter we apply time value of money principles to the valuation of specific financial securities, paying particular attention to the change in a security's value when interest rates change. We examine how characteristics specific to a financial security (e.g., coupon rate and remaining time to maturity) also influence a financial security's price.[1] We conclude the chapter with an analysis of the duration of a security. Duration, which measures the weighted-average time to maturity of an asset or liability, using the present values of the cash flows as weights, also has economic meaning as the sensitivity of an asset or liability's value or price to a small interest rate change. The valuation and duration models reviewed in this chapter are used by traders to determine whether to transact in the various financial markets we discuss in Chapters 5 through 10.

# VARIOUS INTEREST RATE MEASURES

**LG 3-1**

In Chapter 2, we presented a general discussion of interest rates and how they are determined. The term *interest rates* can actually have many different meanings depending on the time frame used for analysis and the type of security being analyzed. In this chapter, we start off by defining different interest rate measures employed in the valuation of financial securities by market participants. These definitions are summarized in Table 3–1. In the body of the chapter, we apply these rates to the valuation of bonds (bond markets and their operations are discussed in detail in Chapter 6) and the valuation of stocks (stock markets and their operations are discussed in Chapter 8).

## Coupon Rate

**coupon rate**

*Interest rate used to calculate the annual cash flow the bond issuer promises to pay the bond holder.*

One variation on the meaning of the term *interest rate* specific to debt instruments is the **coupon rate** paid on a bond. As discussed in detail in the next section, the coupon rate on a bond instrument is the annual (or periodic) cash flow that the bond issuer contractually promises to pay the bond holder. This coupon rate is only one component of the overall return (required, expected, or realized rate of return) the bond holder earns on a bond, however. As discussed below, required, expected, or realized rates of return incorporate not only the coupon payments but all cash flows on a bond investment, including full and partial repayments of principal by the issuer.

## Required Rate of Return

Market participants use time value of money equations to calculate the fair present value of a financial security over an investment horizon. As we discussed in Chapter 2 and will see later in this chapter, this process involves the discounting of all projected cash flows[2]

**TABLE 3–1**  **Various Interest Rate Measures**

**Coupon rate**—interest rate on a bond instrument used to calculate the annual cash flow the bond issuer promises to pay the bond holder.

**Required rate of return**—interest rate an investor should receive on a security given its risk. Required rate of return is used to calculate the fair present value on a security.

**Expected rate of return**—interest rate an investor expects to receive on a security if he or she buys the security at its current market price, receives all expected payments, and sells the security at the end of his or her investment horizon.

**Realized rate of return**—actual interest rate earned on an investment in a financial security. Realized rate of return is a historical (ex post) measure of the interest rate.

---

1. Security valuation is a topic that finance students probably studied in introductory financial management courses. However, these models are critical tools for traders of financial securities and managers of financial institutions. Therefore, in this chapter we review and provide a reference guide to the general pricing relationships. This material can be included or dropped from the chapter reading, depending on the need for review of the material, without harming the continuity of the chapter.

2. The projected cash flows used in these equations may be those promised by the security issuer or expected cash flows estimated by the security purchaser (or some other analyst) from a probability distribution of the possible cash flows received on the security. In either case, the cash flows received are not ex ante known with perfect certainty because of default and other risks.

**required rate of return**

*The interest rate an investor should receive on a security, given its risk.*

(*CFs*) on the security at an appropriate interest rate. (For easy reference to the notation used in this chapter, we list and define all variables used in this chapter at the end of the chapter.) The interest rate used to find the fair present value of a financial security is called the **required rate of return** (*r*). This interest rate is a function of the various risks associated with a security (discussed in Chapter 2) and is thus the interest rate the investor *should* receive on the security given its risk (default risk, liquidity risk, etc.). The required rate of return is thus an ex ante (before the fact) measure of the interest rate on a security. The *present value* (*PV*) is determined by the following formula:

$$PV = \frac{CF_1}{(1+r)^1} + \frac{CF_2}{(1+r)^2} + \frac{CF_3}{(1+r)^3} + \ldots + \frac{CF_n}{(1+r)^n} = \sum_{t=1}^{n} \frac{CF_t}{(1+r)^t}$$

where

$r$ = Required rate of return
$CF_t$ = Cash flow projected in period $t$ ($t = 1, \ldots, n$)
$n$ = Number of periods in the investment horizon

Once a *PV* is calculated, market participants then compare this present value with the *current market price* ($\bar{P}$) at which the security is trading in a financial market. If the current market price of the security ($\bar{P}$) is less than its fair value (*PV*), the security is currently undervalued. The market participant would want to buy more of this security at its current price. If the current market price of the security is greater than its present value, the security is overvalued. The market participant would not want to buy this security at its current price. If the present value of the security equals its current market price, the security is said to be fairly priced given its risk characteristics. In this case, *PV* equals $\bar{P}$.

---

**EXAMPLE 3–1**   **Application of Required Rate of Return**

A Walmart bond you purchased two years ago for $890 is now selling for $925. The bond paid $100 per year in coupon interest on the last day of each year (the last payment made today). You intend to hold the bond for four more years and project that you will be able to sell it at the end of year 4 for $960. You also project that the bond will continue paying $100 in interest per year. Given the risk associated with the bond, its required rate of return (*r*) over the next four years is 11.25 percent. Accordingly, the bond's fair present value is:

**CALCULATOR HINTS**
$N = 4$
$I = 11.25$
$PMT = 100$
$FV = 960$
$CPT\ PV = 935.31$

$$PV = \frac{100}{(1+0.1125)^1} + \frac{100}{(1+0.1125)^2} + \frac{100}{(1+0.1125)^3} + \frac{100+960}{(1+0.1125)^4}$$

$$= \$935.31$$

Given the current selling price of the Walmart bond, $925, relative to the fair present value, $935.31, this bond is currently undervalued.

---

**expected rate of return**

*The interest rate an investor would expect to earn on a security if he or she were to buy the security at its current market price, receive all promised or expected payments on the security, and sell the security at the end of his or her investment horizon.*

### Expected Rate of Return

The **expected rate of return**, *E*(*r*), on a financial security is the interest rate a market participant *expects to* earn by buying the security at its *current market price* ($\bar{P}$), receiving all projected cash flow payments (*CFs*) on the security, and selling the security at the end of the participant's investment horizon. Thus, the expected rate of return is also an ex ante measure of the interest rate on a security. However, the expected rate of return on an investment is based on the current market price rather than fair present value. As discussed above, these may or may not be equal.

Again, time value of money equations are used to calculate the expected rate of return on a security. In this case, the current market price of the security is set equal to the present value of all projected cash flows received on the security over the investment horizon. The

**TABLE 3-2   The Relation between Required Rate of Return and Expected Rate of Return**

| | |
|---|---|
| $E(r) \geq r$ or $\overline{P} \leq PV$ | The projected cash flows received on the security are greater than or equal to those required to compensate for the risk incurred from investing in the security. Thus, buy this security. |
| $E(r) < r$ or $\overline{P} > PV$ | The projected cash flows received on the security are less than is required to compensate for the risk incurred from investing in the security. Thus, do *not* buy this security. |

expected rate of return is the discount rate in the present value equation that just makes the present value of projected cash flows equal to its current market price $(\overline{P})$[3] That is:

$$\overline{P} = \frac{CF_1}{[1 + E(r)]^1} + \frac{CF_2}{[1 + E(r)]^2} + \frac{CF_3}{[1 + E(r)]^3} + \cdots + \frac{CF_n}{[1 + E(r)]^n}$$

where

$E(r)$ = Expected rate of return

$CF_t$ = Cash flow projected in period $t$ $(t = 1, \ldots, n)$

$n$ = Number of periods in the investment horizon

Once an expected rate of return, $E(r)$, on a financial security is calculated, the market participant compares this expected rate of return to its required rate of return $(r)$. If the expected rate of return is greater than the required rate of return, the projected cash flows on the security are greater than is required to compensate for the risk incurred from investing in the security. Thus, the market participant would want to buy more of this security. If the expected rate of return is less than the required rate of return, the projected cash flows from the security are less than those required to compensate for the risk involved. Thus, the market participant would not want to invest in the security.[4] We summarize these relationships in Table 3–2.

---

**EXAMPLE 3-2   Application of Expected Rate of Return**

**CALCULATOR HINTS**
$N = 4$
$PMT = 100$
$FV = 960$
$PV = -925$
CPT $I = 11.607\%$

Refer to information in Example 3–1 describing a Walmart bond you purchased two years ago for $890. Using the current market price of $925, the expected rate of return on the bond over the next four years is calculated as follows:

$$925 = \frac{100}{[1 + E(r)]^1} + \frac{100}{[1 + E(r)]^2} + \frac{100}{[1 + E(r)]^3} + \frac{100 + 960}{[1 + E(r)]^4}$$

$$\Rightarrow Er = 11.607\%$$

Given that the required return on the bond is 11.25 percent, the projected cash flows on the bond are greater than is required to compensate you for the risk on the bond.

---

### Required versus Expected Rates of Return: The Role of Efficient Markets

We have defined two ex ante (before the fact) measures of interest rates. The *required* rate of return is used to calculate a *fair* present value of a financial security, while the *expected* rate of return is a discount rate used in conjunction with the *current* market price of a

---

3. We are also assuming that any cash flows on the investment can be reinvested to earn the same expected rate of return.

4. Note also that by implication, if $E(r) > r$, then the market price of a security $(\overline{P})$ is less than its fair present value $(PV)$ and vice versa if $E(r) < r$.

security. As long as financial markets are efficient (see below), the current market price of a security tends to equal its fair price present value. This is the case most of the time. However, when an event occurs that unexpectedly changes interest rates or a characteristic of a financial security (e.g., an unexpected dividend increase, an unexpected decrease in default risk), the current market price of a security can temporarily diverge from its fair present value. When investors determine a security is undervalued (i.e., its current market price is less than its fair present value), demand for the security increases, as does its price. Conversely, when investors determine a security is overvalued (i.e., its current market price is greater than its fair present value), they will sell the security, resulting in a price drop. The speed with which financial security prices adjust to unexpected news, so as to maintain equality with the fair present value of the security, is referred to as **market efficiency.** We examine the three forms of market efficiency (weak form, semistrong form, and strong form) in Chapter 8.

**market efficiency**

*The process by which financial security prices move to a new equilibrium when interest rates or a security-specific characteristic changes.*

### Realized Rate of Return

Required and expected rates of return are interest rate concepts pertaining to the returns expected or required just prior to the investment being made. Once made, however, the market participant is concerned with how well the financial security actually performs. The **realized rate of return** $(\bar{r})$ on a financial security is the interest rate *actually* earned on an investment in a financial security. The realized rate of return is thus a historical interest rate of return—it is an ex post (after the fact) measure of the interest rate on the security.

**realized rate of return**

*The actual interest rate earned on an investment in a financial security.*

To calculate a realized rate of return $(\bar{r})$, all cash flows actually paid or received are incorporated in time value of money equations to solve for the realized rate of return. By setting the price actually paid for the security $(\bar{P})$ equal to the present value of the realized cash flows $(RCF_1, RCF_2, \ldots, RCF_n)$, the realized rate of return is the discount rate that just equates the purchase price to the present value of the realized cash flows. That is:

$$\bar{P} = \frac{RCF_1}{(1 + \bar{r})^1} + \frac{RCF_2}{(1 + \bar{r})^2} + \ldots + \frac{RCF_n}{(1 + \bar{r})^n}$$

where

$RCF_t$ = Realized cash flow in period $t$ $(t = 1, \ldots, n)$

$\bar{r}$ = Realized rate of return on a security

If the realized rate of return $(\bar{r})$ is greater than the required rate of return $(r)$, the market participant actually earned more than was needed to be compensated for the ex ante or expected risk of investing in the security. If the realized rate of return is less than the required rate of return, the market participant actually earned less than the interest rate required to compensate for the risk involved.

---

**DO YOU UNDERSTAND:**

1.  The difference between a required rate of return and an expected rate of return?

2.  The difference between the coupon rate on a bond and the realized rate of return on a bond?

---

**EXAMPLE 3–3**  **Application of Realized Rate of Return**

Consider again the Walmart bond investment described in Examples 3–1 and 3–2. Using your original purchase price, $890, and the current market price on this bond, the realized rate of return you have earned on this bond over the last two years is calculated as follows:

$$890 = \frac{100}{(1 + \bar{r})^1} + \frac{100 + 925}{(1 + \bar{r})^2}$$

$$\Rightarrow \bar{r} = 13.08\%$$

**CALCULATOR HINTS**

$N = 2$

$PMT = 100$

$FV = 925$

$PV = -890$

$CPT\ I = 13.08\%$

# BOND VALUATION

The valuation of a bond instrument employs time value of money concepts. The fair value of a bond reflects the present value of all cash flows promised or projected to be received on that bond discounted at the required rate of return ($r_b$). Similarly, the expected rate of return, $E(r_b)$, is the interest rate that equates the current market price of the bond with the present value of all promised cash flows received over the life of the bond. Finally, a realized rate of return ($\bar{r}_b$) on a bond is the actual return earned on a bond investment that has already taken place. Promised cash flows on bonds come from two sources: (1) interest or coupon payments paid over the life of the bond and (2) a lump sum payment (face or par value) when a bond matures.

**LG 3-2**

## Bond Valuation Formula Used to Calculate Fair Present Values

**coupon bonds**

*Bonds that pay interest based on a stated coupon rate. The interest, or coupon, payments per year are generally constant over the life of the bond.*

**zero-coupon bonds**

*Bonds that do not pay interest.*

Most bonds pay a stated coupon rate of interest to the holders of the bonds. These bonds are called **coupon bonds.** The interest, or coupon, payments per year, INT, are generally constant (fixed) over the life of the bond.[5] Thus, the fixed interest payment is essentially an annuity paid to the bond holder periodically (normally semiannually) over the life of the bond. Bonds that do not pay coupon interest are called **zero-coupon bonds.** For these bonds, INT is zero. In addition to coupon payments, the face or par value of the bond, $M$, is a lump sum payment received by the bond holder when the bond matures. Face value is generally set at $1,000 in the U.S. bond market. When new bonds are issued, the coupon rate on the new bonds is typically set at the current required rate of return. As discussed below, this results in the original sale of the bond occurring at the par value.

Using time value of money formulas, and assuming that the bond issuer makes its promised semiannual coupon and principal payments, the present value of a bond, $V_b$, can be written as:[6]

$$V_b = \frac{INT/2}{(1 + r_b/2)^1} + \frac{INT/2}{(1 + r_b/2)^2} + \ldots + \frac{INT/2}{(1 + r_b/2)^{2T}} + \frac{M}{(1 + r_b/2)^{2T}}$$

$$= \frac{INT}{2} \sum_{t=1}^{2T} \left(\frac{1}{1 + r_b/2}\right)^t + \frac{M}{(1 + r_b/2)^{2T}}$$

$$= \frac{INT}{(2)} \left[\frac{1 - \dfrac{1}{(1 + r_b/2)^{2T}}}{r_b/2}\right] + M\left[\frac{1}{(1 + r_b/2)^{2T}}\right]$$

where

$V_b$ = Present value of the bond

$M$ = Par or face value of the bond

$INT$ = Annual interest (or coupon) payment on the bond; equals the par value of the bond times the (percentage) coupon rate

$T$ = Number of years until the bond matures

$r_b$ = Annual interest rate used to discount cash flows on the bond

---

5. Variable rate bonds pay interest that is indexed to some broad interest rate measure (such as Treasury bill rates) and thus experience variable coupon payments. Income bonds pay interest only if the issuer has sufficient earnings to make the promised payments. Index (or purchasing power) bonds pay interest based on an inflation index. Each of these types of bonds, therefore, can have variable interest payments.

6. More generally, for bonds that pay interest other than semiannually:

$$V_b = \frac{INT}{m}\left[\frac{1 - \dfrac{1}{(1 + r_b/m)^{mT}}}{r_b/m}\right] + M\left[\frac{1}{(1 + r_b/m)^{mT}}\right]$$

where $m$ = Number of times per year interest is paid.

**EXAMPLE 3–4** Calculation of the Fair Value of a Coupon Bond

You are considering the purchase of a $1,000 face value bond issued by ExxonMobil. The bond pays 10 percent coupon interest per year, with the coupon paid semiannually (i.e., $50 [= 1,000(0.10)/2] over the first half of the year and $50 over the second half of the year). The bond matures in 12 years (i.e., the bond pays interest (12 × 2 =) 24 times before it matures). If the required rate of return ($r_b$) on this bond is 8 percent (i.e., the periodic discount rate is (8%/2 = 4 percent), the market value of the bond is calculated as follows:

$$V_b = \frac{1,000(0.10)}{2} \left[ \frac{1 - \dfrac{1}{[1 + (0.08/2)]^{2(12)}}}{0.08/2} \right] + 1,000/[1 + (0.08/2)]^{2(12)}$$

$$= 50(15.24696) + 1,000(0.39012) = \$1,152.47$$

or an investor would be willing to pay no more than $1,152.47 for this bond.

If the required rate of return on this bond is 10 percent, the market value of the bond is calculated as follows:

$$V_b = \frac{1,000(0.10)}{2} \left[ \frac{1 - \dfrac{1}{[1 + (0.10/2)]^{2(12)}}}{0.10/2} \right] + 1,000/[1 + (0.10/2)]^{2(12)}$$

$$= 50(13.79864) + 1,000(0.31007) = \$1,000.00$$

or an investor would be willing to pay no more than $1,000.00 for this bond.

If the required rate of return on this bond is 12 percent, the market value of the bond is calculated as follows:

$$V_b = \frac{1,000(0.10)}{2} \left[ \frac{1 - \dfrac{1}{[1 + (0.12/2)]^{2(12)}}}{0.12/2} \right] + 1,000/[1 + (0.12/2)]^{2(12)}$$

$$= 50(12.55036) + 1,000(0.24698) = \$874.50$$

or an investor would be willing to pay no more than $874.50 for this bond.

**bond**

*Long-term debt obligation issued by corporations and government units.*

**premium bond**

*A bond in which the present value of the bond is greater than its face value.*

**discount bond**

*A bond in which the present value of the bond is less than its face value.*

**par bond**

*A bond in which the present value of the bond is equal to its face value.*

In the preceding example, when the required rate of return ($r_b$) on the bond is 8 percent, the present value of the bond, $1,152.47, is greater than its face value of $1,000. When the bond's coupon rate is greater than the required rate of return (10 percent versus 8 percent in our example), the **bond** should sell at a **premium.** To achieve the required rate of return, the bond holder takes a loss on the difference between the purchase price of the bond and the face value received at maturity. When the bond's required rate of return is 12 percent, its present value is less than its face value and the bond should sell at a **discount.** This occurs because the coupon rate on the bond is below the required rate of return. To achieve the required rate of return, the bond holder experiences a gain on the difference between the purchase price of the bond and the face value received at maturity. Finally, when the bond's required rate of return is 10 percent, its present value is equal to its face value and the bond should sell at **par.** This occurs because the coupon rate on the bond is equal to the required rate of return on the bond. To achieve the required rate of return on the bond, the bond holder experiences neither a gain nor a loss on the difference between the purchase price of the bond and the face value received at maturity. We summarize the scenarios for premium, discount,[7] and par bonds in Table 3–3.

---

7. The term *discount bond* is also used to denote a zero-coupon bond.

**TABLE 3–3  Description of a Premium, Discount, and Par Bond**

**Premium bond**—when the *coupon rate* on a bond is greater than the *required rate of return* on the bond, the *fair present value* is greater than the *face value* of the bond.

When the *coupon rate* on a bond is greater than the *yield to maturity* on the bond, the *current market price* is greater than the *face value* of the bond.

**Discount bond**—when the *coupon rate* on a bond is less than the *required rate of return* on the bond, the *fair present value* is less than the *face value* of the bond.

When the *coupon rate* on a bond is less than the *yield to maturity* on the bond, the *current market price* is less than the *face value* of the bond.

**Par bond**—when the *coupon rate* on a bond is equal to the *required rate of return* on the bond, the *fair present value* is equal to the *face value* of the bond.

When the *coupon rate* on a bond is equal to the *yield to maturity* on the bond, the *current market price* is equal to the *face value* of the bond.

The designation as a premium, discount, or par bond does not help in the decision to buy or sell a bond. These terms are simply descriptive designations regarding the relationship between the present value of the bond and its face value. Rather, investors make the decision to buy or sell by comparing the bond's present value to its current market price. As we noted above, the present value of the bond will equal the bond's price only in an efficient market where prices instantaneously adjust to new information about the security's value.

Bond issuers usually set a bond's coupon rate close to the required rate of return at the time of issuance, which forces new bonds to sell close to par. As time goes by, a bond's required rate of return may change due to the arrival of new information (e.g., changes in future expected inflation or the issuer's credit risk). As a result, a bond may become a premium or a discount bond, and its price may oscillate above and below par throughout the bond's life.

### Bond Valuation Formula Used to Calculate Yield to Maturity

**yield to maturity**

*The return or yield the bond holder will earn on the bond if he or she buys it at its current market price, receives all coupon and principal payments as promised, and holds the bond until maturity.*

The present value formulas can also be used to find the expected rate of return, $E(r_b)$, or, assuming all promised coupon and principal payments are made as promised, what is often called the **yield to maturity (ytm)** on a bond (i.e., the return the bond holder will earn on the bond if he or she buys the bond at its current market price, receives all coupon and principal payments as promised, and holds the bond until maturity). The yield to maturity calculation implicitly assumes that all coupon payments periodically received by the bond holder can be reinvested at the same rate—that is, reinvested at the calculated yield to maturity.[8]

Rewriting the bond valuation formula, where $V_b$ is the current market price that has to be paid to buy the bond, we can solve for the yield to maturity (*ytm*) on a bond as follows—where we write *ytm* instead of $E(r_b)$:

$$V_b = \frac{INT/2}{(1 + ytm/2)^1} + \frac{INT/2}{(1 + ytm/2)^2} + \ldots + \frac{INT/2}{(1 + ytm/2)^{2T}} + \frac{M}{(1 + ytm/2)^{2T}}$$

$$= \frac{INT}{2} \left[ \frac{1 - \dfrac{1}{(1 + ytm/2)^{2T}}}{ytm/2} \right] + M\left[1 + (ytm/2)\right]^{2T}$$

---

8. As discussed in Appendix 3A to this chapter (available through Connect or your course instructor), if coupon payments are reinvested at less (more) than this rate, the yield to maturity will be lower (higher) than that calculated in this section. This concept will be key to understanding interest rate risk discussed later in the text (Chapters 22 and 23).

**CALCULATOR HINTS**

$N = 15(2) = 30$

$PV = -931.176$

$PMT = 110/2 = 55$

$FV = 1000$

CPT $I = 6.0$ @ MONTHS

$6.0 \times = 12.0$ @ YEAR

## EXAMPLE 3–5    Calculation of the Yield to Maturity on a Coupon Bond

You are considering the purchase of a $1,000 face value bond that pays 11 percent coupon interest per year, paid semiannually (i.e., $55 [= $1,000(0.11)/2] per semiannual period). The bond matures in 15 years and has a face value of $1,000. If the current market price of the bond is $931.176, the yield to maturity, or $E(r_b)$ is calculated as follows:

$$931.176 = \frac{1,000(0.11)}{2}\left[\frac{1 - \dfrac{1}{(1 + ytm/2)^{2(15)}}}{ytm/2}\right] + 1,000/(1 + ytm/2)^{2(15)}$$

Solving for *ytm*, the yield to maturity (or expected rate of return) on the bond is 12 percent.[9] Equivalently, you would be willing to buy the bond only if the required rate of return ($r$) was no more than 12 percent (i.e., the yield to maturity is greater than or equal to the required return on the bond).

**DO YOU UNDERSTAND:**

3. The difference between a zero-coupon bond and a coupon bond?

4. What the differences are among a discount bond, a premium bond, and a par bond?

5. How the difference between the yield to maturity on a bond and the coupon rate on the bond will cause the bond to sell at a premium or a discount?

LG 3-3

## EQUITY VALUATION

The valuation process for an equity instrument (such as preferred or common stock) involves finding the present value of an infinite series of cash flows on the equity discounted at an appropriate interest rate. Cash flows from holding equity come from dividends paid out by the firm over the life of the stock, which in expectation can be viewed as infinite since a firm (and thus the dividends it pays) has no defined maturity or life. Even if an equity holder decides not to hold the stock forever, he or she can sell it to someone else who in a fair and efficient market is willing to pay the present value of the remaining (expected) dividends to the seller at the time of sale. Dividends on equity are that portion of a firm's earnings paid out to the stockholders. Those earnings retained are normally reinvested to produce future income and future dividends for the firm and its stockholders. Thus, conceptually, the fair price paid for investing in stocks is the present value of its current and future dividends.[10] Growth in dividends occurs primarily because of growth in the firm's earnings, which is, in turn, a function of the profitability of the firm's investments and the percentage of these profits paid out as dividends rather than being reinvested in the firm. Thus, earnings growth, dividend growth, and stock value (price) will generally be highly correlated.

We begin by defining the variables we use to value an equity:

$Div_t$ = Dividend paid to stockholders at the end of the year $t$

$P_t$ = Price of a firm's common stock at the end of the year $t$

$P_0$ = Current price of a firm's common stock

$r_s$ = Interest rate used to discount cash flows on an investment in a stock

As described above, time value of money equations can be used to evaluate a stock from several different perspectives. For example, the realized rate of return ($\bar{r}_s$) is the appropriate interest rate (discount rate) to apply to cash flows when evaluating the historical performance of an equity.

---

9. The yield to maturity is the nominal return on the bond. Its effective annual return is calculated as:

$$EAR = (1 + ytm/2)^2 - 1 = (1 + 0.12/2)^2 - 1 = 12.36\%$$

10. For firms that pay no dividends can be valued using a firm's free cash flows (FCF) (cash flows available for distribution to investors after the company has made all the investments in fixed assets and working capital necessary to sustain ongoing operations) discounted at the weighted average cost of capital. Such that the value of the firm is equal to:

$$V = \sum_{t=1}^{\infty} \frac{FCF_t}{(1 + WACC)^t} = \frac{FCF_{t+1}}{WACC - g}$$

The fair price of each share of stock would then be equal to $V$/number of shares of common stock outstanding.

## EXAMPLE 3-6   Calculation of Realized Rate of Return on a Stock Investment

Suppose you owned stock in General Monsanto for the last two years. You originally bought the stock two years ago for $25 ($P_{-2}$) and just sold it for $35 ($P_0$). The stock paid an annual dividend of $1($Div$) on the last day of each of the past two years. Your realized rate of return on the General Monsanto stock investment can be calculated using the following time value of money equation:

$$P_{-2} = Div\left[\frac{1 - \frac{1}{(1 + \bar{r}_s)^2}}{\bar{r}_s}\right] + P_0/(1 + \bar{r}_s)^2$$

or

$$25 = 1\left[\frac{1 - \frac{1}{(1 + \bar{r}_s)^2}}{\bar{r}_s}\right] + 35/(1 + \bar{r}_s)^2$$

Solving for $\bar{r}_s$ your annual realized rate of return on this investment was 22.02 percent.

$$25 = 1(1.4912) + 35(0.6716)$$

The expected rate of return, $E(r_s)$, is the appropriate interest rate when analyzing the expected future return on stocks, assuming the investor buys the stock at its current market price, receives all promised payments, and sells the stock at the end of his or her investment horizon.

## EXAMPLE 3-7   Calculation of Expected Rate of Return on a Stock Investment

You are considering the purchase of stock in Hewlett-Packard (HP). You expect to own the stock for the next three years. The current market price of the stock is $32 ($P_0$) and you expect to sell it for $45 in three years' time ($P_3$). You also expect the stock to pay an annual dividend ($Div$) of $1.50 on the last day of each of the next three years. Your expected return on the HP stock investment can be calculated using the following time value of money equation:

$$P_0 = Div\left[\frac{1 - \frac{1}{[1 + E(r_s)]^3}}{E(r_s)}\right] + P_3/[1 + E(r_s)]^3$$

or

$$32 = 1.50\left[\frac{1 - \frac{1}{[1 + E(r_s)]^3}}{E(r_s)}\right] + 45/[1 + E(r_s)]^3$$

Solving for $E(r_s)$, your annual expected rate of return on this investment is 16.25 percent.

Finally, the required rate of return ($r_s$) is the appropriate interest rate when analyzing the fair value of a stock investment over its whole lifetime. The fair value of a stock reflects the present value of all relevant (but uncertain) cash flows to be received by an investor discounted at the required rate of return ($r_s$)—the interest rate or return that should be earned on the investment given its risk.

Present value methodology applies time value of money to evaluate a stock's cash flows over its life as follows:

$$P_0 = \frac{Div_1}{(1 + r_s)^1} + \frac{Div_2}{(1 + r_s)^2} + \ldots + \frac{Div_\infty}{(1 + r_s)^\infty}$$

The price or value of a stock is equal to the present value of its future dividends ($Div_t$), whose values are uncertain. This requires an infinite number of future dividend values to be estimated, which makes the equation above difficult to use for stock valuation and $r_s$ calculation in practice. Accordingly, assumptions are normally made regarding the expected pattern of the uncertain flow of dividends over the life of the stock. Three assumptions that are commonly used are (1) zero growth in dividends over the (infinite) life of the stock, (2) a constant growth rate in dividends over the (infinite) life of the stock, and (3) nonconstant growth in dividends over the (infinite) life of the stock.

### Zero Growth in Dividends

Zero growth in dividends means that dividends on a stock are expected to remain at a constant level forever. Thus, $Div_0 = Div_1 = Div_2 = \ldots = Div_\infty = Div$. Accordingly, the equity valuation formula can be written as follows:

$$P_0 = \frac{Div_1}{(1 + r_s)^1} + \frac{Div_2}{(1 + r_s)^2} + \ldots + \frac{Div_\infty}{(1 + r_s)^\infty} = Div \sum_{t=1}^{\infty} \left( \frac{1}{1 + r_s} \right)^t$$

where

$Div_0$ = Current (time 0) value of dividends
$Div_t$ = Value of dividends at time $t = 1, 2, \ldots, \infty$

or[11]

$$P_0 = Div/r_s$$

This formula can be generalized as follows:

$$P_t = Div/r_s$$

Companies that issue preferred stock usually pay investors dividends that exhibit zero growth through time. The value of a stock with zero growth in dividends is equal to the (current) dividend divided by the return on the stock. If the required rate of return ($r_s$) is applied to the formula, the price we solve for is the fair market price. If the expected return $E(r_s)$ is applied to the formula, the price we solve for is the current market price. Furthermore, the formula can be rearranged to determine a return on the stock if it were purchased at a price, $P_0$.

$$r_s = Div/P_0$$

If the fair present value is applied to this formula, the return we solve for is the required rate of return ($r_s$). If the current market price is applied to the formula, the price we solve for is the expected return $E(r_s)$. Recall from above, in efficient markets the required rate of return equals the expected rate of return. Thus, the current market price on a security equals its fair present value.

11. Remember that, in the limit:

$$\sum_{t=1}^{\infty} \left( \frac{1}{1+x} \right)^t = \left( \frac{1}{1+x} \right)^1 + \left( \frac{1}{1+x} \right)^2 + \ldots + \left( \frac{1}{1+x} \right)^\infty = \frac{1}{x}$$

Thus:

$$\sum_{t=1}^{\infty} \left( \frac{1}{1 + xr_s} \right)^t = \frac{1}{r_s}$$

---

**EXAMPLE 3–8**  Calculation of Stock Price with Zero Growth in Dividends

A preferred stock you are evaluating is expected to pay a constant dividend of $5 per year each year into the future. The required rate of return, $r_s$, on the stock is 12 percent. The fair value (or price) of this stock is calculated as follows:

$$P_0 = 5/0.12 = \$41.67$$

---

### Constant Growth in Dividends

Constant growth in dividends means that dividends on a stock are expected to grow at a constant rate, $g$, each year into the future. Thus, $Div_1 = Div_0(1 + g)^1$, $Div_2 = Div_0(1 + g)^2$, $\ldots, Div_\infty = Div_0(1 + g)^\infty$. Accordingly, the equity valuation formula can now be written as follows:

$$P_0 = \frac{Div_0(1 + g)^1}{(1 + r_s)^1} + \frac{Div_0(1 + g)^2}{(1 + r_s)^2} + \ldots + \frac{Div_0(1 + g)^\infty}{(1 + r_s)^\infty} = Div_0 \sum_{t=1}^{\infty} \left[\frac{(1 + g)}{(1 + r_s)}\right]^t$$

or[12]

$$P_0 = \frac{Div_0(1 + g)^1}{r_s - g} = \frac{Div_1}{r_s - g}$$

This formula can be generalized as follows:

$$P_t = \frac{Div_0(1 + g)^t}{r_s - g} = \frac{Div_{t+1}}{r_s - g}$$

If the required rate of return ($r_s$) is applied to the formula, the price we solve for is the fair present value. If the expected return, $E(r_s)$, is applied to the formula, the price we solve for is the current market price. The equity valuation formula can also be rearranged to determine a rate of return on the stock if it were purchased at a price $P_0$:

$$r_s = \frac{Div_0(1 + g)}{P_0} + g = \frac{Div_1}{P_0} + g$$

If the fair present value is applied to the formula, the return we solve for is the required rate of return ($r_s$). If the current market price is applied to the formula, the price we solve for is the expected return $E(r_s)$.

---

**EXAMPLE 3–9**  Calculation of Stock Price with Constant Growth in Dividends

You are evaluating J.P. Morgan Chase (JPM) stock. The stock paid a dividend at the end of last year of $3.50. Dividends have grown at a constant rate of 2 percent per year over the last 20 years, and this constant growth rate is expected to continue into the future. The

---

12. Remember that in the limit:

$$\sum_{t=1}^{\infty} \left(\frac{1 + g}{1 + r_s}\right)^t = \sum_{t=1}^{\infty} \left(\frac{1}{1 + \frac{r_s - g}{1 + g}}\right)^t = \frac{1 + g}{r_s - g}$$

required rate of return ($r_s$) on the stock is 10 percent. The fair present value (or price) of JPM stock is calculated as follows:

$$P_0 = \frac{3.50(1 + 0.02)}{0.10 - 0.02} = \$44.625$$

As an investor, you would be willing to pay no more than $44.625 for this stock.

---

**EXAMPLE 3–10**   Calculation of the Expected Rate of Return, $E(r_s)$, on a Stock with Constant Growth in Dividends

You are evaluating Bank of America (BOA) stock. The stock paid a dividend at the end of last year of $4.80. Dividends have grown at a constant rate of 1.75 percent per year over the last 15 years, and this constant growth rate is expected to continue into the future. The stock is currently selling at a price of $52 per share. The expected rate of return on BOA stock is calculated as follows:

$$E(r_s) = \frac{4.80(1 + 0.0175)}{52} + 0.0175 = 11.14\%$$

---

### Supernormal (or Nonconstant) Growth in Dividends

Firms often experience periods of supernormal or nonconstant dividend growth, after which dividend growth settles at some constant rate. The stock value for a firm experiencing supernormal growth in dividends is, like firms with zero or constant dividend growth, equal to the present value of the firm's expected future dividends. However, in this case, dividends during the period of supernormal (nonconstant) growth must be evaluated individually. The constant growth in dividends model can then be adapted to find the present value of dividends following the supernormal growth period.

To find the present value of a stock experiencing supernormal or nonconstant dividend growth, we calculate the present value of dividends during the two different growth periods. A three-step process is used as follows:

**Step 1:**   Find the present value of the dividends during the period of supernormal (nonconstant) growth.

**Step 2:**   Find the price of the stock at the end of the supernormal (nonconstant) growth period (when constant growth in dividends begins) using the constant growth in dividends model. Then discount this price to a present value.

**Step 3:**   Add the two components of the stock price together.

---

**EXAMPLE 3–11**   Calculation of Stock Price with Supernormal or Nonconstant Growth in Dividends

You are evaluating Home Depot (HD) stock. The stock is expected to experience supernormal growth in dividends of 10 percent, $g_s$, over the next five years. Following this period, dividends are expected to grow at a constant rate of 4 percent, $g$. The stock paid a dividend of $4 last year, and the required rate of return on the stock is 15 percent. The fair present value of HD stock is calculated as follows:

**Step 1:**   Find the present value of the dividends during the period of supernormal growth.

| Year | Dividends $[Div_0 (1 + g_s)^t]$ | $1/(1 + 0.15)^t$ | Present Value |
|------|------|------|------|
| 1 | $4(1 + 0.1)^1 = 4.400$ | 0.8696 | 3.826 |
| 2 | $4(1 + 0.1)^2 = 4.840$ | 0.7561 | 3.659 |
| 3 | $4(1 + 0.1)^3 = 5.324$ | 0.6575 | 3.500 |
| 4 | $4(1 + 0.1)^4 = 5.856$ | 0.5718 | 3.349 |
| 5 | $4(1 + 0.1)^5 = 6.442$ | 0.4972 | 3.203 |

Present value of dividends during supernormal growth period      $17.537

**DO YOU UNDERSTAND:**

6. How stock valuation differs from bond valuation?

7. The difference between constant growth in dividends and supernormal growth in dividends?

**Step 2:** Find the present value of dividends after the period of supernormal growth.

    a. Find stock value at beginning of constant growth period:

$$P_5 = \frac{Div_6}{r_s - g} = \frac{Div_0(1 + g_s)^5(1 + g)^1}{r_s - g} = \frac{4(1 + 0.1)^5(1 + 0.04)^1}{0.15 - 0.04} = \$60.906$$

    b. Find present value of constant growth dividends:

$$P_0 = P_5/(1 + 0.15)^5 = 60.906(0.4972) = \$30.283$$

**Step 3:** Find present value of the HD stock = Value during supernormal growth period + Value during normal growth period:

$$\$17.537 + \$30.283 = \$47.820$$

## IMPACT OF INTEREST RATE CHANGES ON SECURITY VALUES

**LG 3-4**

As already discussed in this chapter and in Chapter 2, the variability of financial security prices depends on interest rates and the characteristics of the security. Specifically, factors that affect financial security prices include interest rate changes, the time remaining to maturity, and the cash flows received prior to and at maturity. We evaluate next the impact of each of these factors as they affect bond prices. In the discussion, the interest rate used in the pricing formula is the required rate of return on a bond, and thus the price we refer to is the fair value of the bond. However, all relations apply equally if the interest rate used in the pricing formula is the expected rate of return on a bond and thus the price is the current market price of the bond. The impact on equity prices is similar. Table 3–4 summarizes the major relationships we will be discussing.

Refer back to Example 3–4. Notice in this example that the present values of the cash flows on bonds decreased as interest rates increased. Specifically, when the required rate of return increased from 8 percent to 10 percent, the fair present value of the bond fell from $1,152.47 to $1,000, or by 13.23 percent [i.e., $(1,000 - 1,152.47)/1,152.47 = 0.1323 = 13.23\%$]. Similarly, when the required rate of return increased from 10 percent to 12 percent,

**TABLE 3–4**    **Summary of Factors That Affect Security Prices and Price Volatility when Interest Rates Change**

**Interest rate**—there is a negative relation between interest rate changes and present value (or price) changes on financial securities.

As interest rates increase, security prices decrease at a decreasing rate.

**Time remaining to maturity**—the shorter the time to maturity for a security, the closer the price is to the face value of the security.

The longer the time to maturity for a security, the larger the price change of the security for a given interest rate change.

The maturity effect described above increases at a decreasing rate.

**Coupon rate**—the higher a security's coupon rate, the smaller the price change on the security for a given change in interest rates.

**Figure 3–1** Relation between Interest Rates and Bond Values

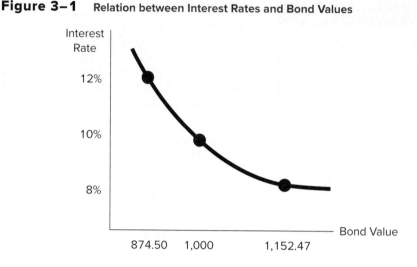

the fair present value of the bond fell from $1,000 to $874.50, or by 12.55 percent [(874.50 − 1,000)/1,000]. This is the inverse relationship between present values and interest rates we discussed in Chapter 2. While the examples refer to the relation between fair values and required rates of return, the inverse relation also exists between current market prices and expected rates of return—as yields on bonds increase, the current market prices of bonds decrease. We illustrate this inverse relation between interest rates on bonds and the present value of bonds in Figure 3–1.

Notice too from the earlier example that the inverse relationship between bond prices and the required rate of return is not linear. Rather, the percentage change in the present value of a bond to a given change in the required rate of return is smaller when interest rates are higher. When the required rate of return on the bond increased from 8 percent to 10 percent (a 2 percent increase), the fair present value on the bond decreased by 13.23 percent. However, another 2 percent increase in the required rate of return (from 10 percent to 12 percent) resulted in a fair present value decrease of only 12.55 percent. The same nonlinear relationship exists for current market prices and yields to maturity. Thus, as interest rates increase, present values of bonds (and bond prices) decrease at a decreasing rate. This is illustrated in Figure 3–1.

The relationship between interest rates and security values is important for all types of investors. Financial institutions (FIs) such as commercial banks, thrifts, and insurance companies are affected because the vast majority of the assets and liabilities held by these firms are financial securities (e.g., loans, deposits, investment securities). When required rates of return rise (fall) on these securities, the fair present values of the FI's asset and liability portfolios decrease (increase) by possibly different amounts, which in turn affects the fair present value of the FI's equity (the difference between the fair present value of an FI's assets and liabilities). We examine the measurement and management of an FI's interest rate risk in more detail in Chapter 22.

In the next two sections we look at how the maturity of, and coupon rate on, a security affects the size of the value changes for a given change in interest rates.

---

**DO YOU UNDERSTAND:**

8. *What happens to the fair present value of a bond when the required rate of return on the bond increases?*

9. *What happens to the fair present value of a bond when the required rate of return on the bond decreases?*

---

## IMPACT OF MATURITY ON SECURITY VALUES

**LG 3-5**

A bond's **price sensitivity** is measured by the percentage change in its present value for a given change in interest rates. If interest rate changes are measured using required rates of return, fair present value is the price sensitivity being measured. If interest rate changes are measured using expected rates of return, current market price is the price sensitivity being measured. The larger the percentage change in the bond's value for a given interest

**price sensitivity**

*The percentage change in a bond's present value for a given change in interest rates.*

rate change, the larger the bond's price sensitivity. An important factor that affects the degree to which the price of a bond changes (or the price sensitivity of a bond changes) as interest rates change is the time remaining to maturity on the bond. Specifically, as is explained below, the shorter the time remaining to maturity, the closer a bond's price is to its face value. Also, the further a bond is from maturity, the more sensitive the price of the bond as interest rates change. Finally, the relationship between bond price sensitivity and maturity is not linear. As the time remaining to maturity on a bond increases, price sensitivity increases but at a decreasing rate. Table 3–5 presents the bond information we will be using to illustrate these relationships. In Table 3–5, we first list the fair present values of the bonds analyzed in Example 3–4. We then repeat the present value calculations using three bonds with identical characteristics except for the time to maturity: 12 years versus 14 years versus 16 years.

### Maturity and Security Prices

Table 3–5 lists the present values of 10 percent (compounded semiannually) coupon bonds with a $1,000 face value and 12 years, 14 years, and 16 years, respectively, remaining to maturity. We calculate the fair present value of these bonds using an 8 percent, 10 percent, and 12 percent required rate of return. Notice that for each of these bonds, the closer the bond is to maturity, the closer the fair present value of the bond is to the $1,000 face value. This is true regardless of whether the bond is a premium, discount, or par bond. For example, at an 8 percent required rate of return, the 12-year, 14-year, and 16-year bonds have present values of $1,152.47, $1,166.63, and $1,178.74, respectively. The intuition behind this is that nobody would pay much more than the face value of the bond and any remaining (in this case semiannual) coupon payments just prior to maturity since these are the only cash flows left to be paid on the bond. Thus, the time value effect is reduced as the maturity of the bond approaches. Many people call this effect the pull to par—bond prices and fair values approach their par values (e.g., $1,000) as time to maturity declines towards zero.

### Maturity and Security Price Sensitivity to Changes in Interest Rates

The Percentage Price Change columns in Table 3–5 provide data to examine the effect time to maturity has on bond price sensitivity to interest rate changes. From these data we see that the longer the time remaining to maturity on a bond, the more sensitive are bond prices to a given change in interest rates. (Note again that all bonds in Table 3–5 have a 10 percent coupon rate and a $1,000 face value.) For example, the fair present value of the 12-year bond falls 13.23 percent [i.e., ($1,000 − $1,152.47)/$1,152.47 = −0.1323 = −13.23%] as the required rate of return increases from 8 percent to 10 percent. The same 2 percent increase (from 8 percent to 10 percent) in the required rate of return produces

**TABLE 3–5**  The Impact of Time to Maturity on the Relation between a Bond's Fair Present Value and Its Required Rate of Return

| Required Rate of Return | 12 Years to Maturity | | | 14 Years to Maturity | | | 16 Years to Maturity | | |
|---|---|---|---|---|---|---|---|---|---|
| | Fair Price* | Price Change | Percentage Price Change | Fair Price* | Price Change | Percentage Price Change | Fair Price* | Price Change | Percentage Price Change |
| 8% | $1,152.47 | | | $1,166.63 | | | $1,178.74 | | |
| | | −$152.47 | −13.23% | | −$166.63 | −14.28% | | −$178.74 | −15.16% |
| 10% | 1,000.00 | | | 1,000.00 | | | 1,000.00 | | |
| | | − 125.50 | −12.55 | | −134.06 | −13.41 | | −140.84 | −14.08 |
| 12% | 874.50 | | | 865.94 | | | 859.16 | | |

*The bond pays interest semiannually, and has a face value of $1,000.

**Figure 3–2**    The Impact of a Bond's Maturity on Its Price Sensitivity

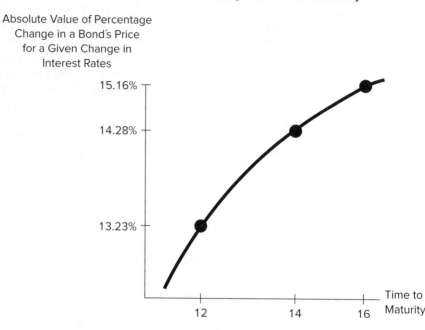

a larger 14.28 percent drop in the fair present value of the 14-year bond, and the 16-year bond's fair present value drops 15.16 percent. This same trend is demonstrated when the required rate of return increases from 10 percent to 12 percent—the longer the bond's maturity, the greater the percentage decrease in the bond's fair present value.

The same relationship occurs when analyzing expected rates of return (or yields to maturity) and the current market price of the bond—the longer the time to maturity on a bond, the larger the change in the current market price of a bond for a given change in yield to maturity.

**DO YOU UNDERSTAND:**

10. *What happens to a bond's price as it approaches maturity?*

11. *What happens to a bond's price sensitivity for a given change in interest rates as its time to maturity increases? decreases?*

**Incremental Changes in Maturity and Security Price Sensitivity to Changes in Interest Rates.**   A final relationship we can examine from Table 3–5 is that between incremental changes in time remaining to maturity and incremental changes in security price sensitivity to a given change in interest rates. Specifically, notice that the maturity effect described above is not linear. For example, a 2 percent increase in the required rate of return (from 8 percent to 10 percent) on the 12-year bond produces a 13.23 percent [i.e., ($1,000 − $1,152.47)/$1,152.47 = −0.1323 = −13.23%] decrease in the bond's fair present value. The same 2 percent increase (from 8 percent to 10 percent) in the required rate of return on the 14-year bond produces a 14.28 percent decrease in the fair present value. The difference, as we move from a 12-year to a 14-year maturity, is 1.05 percent (14.28% − 13.23%). Increasing the time to maturity two more years (from 14 years to 16 years) produces an increase in price sensitivity of 0.88 percent [−14.28% − (−15.16%)]. While price sensitivity for a given increase in interest rates increases with maturity, the increase is nonlinear (decreasing) in maturity. We illustrate this relationship in Figure 3–2, as the required rate of return increases from 8 percent to 10 percent.

## IMPACT OF COUPON RATES ON SECURITY VALUES

**LG 3-5**    Another factor that affects the degree to which the price sensitivity of a bond changes as interest rates change is the bond's coupon rate. Specifically, the higher the bond's coupon rate, the higher its present value at any given interest rate. Also, the higher the bond's coupon rate, the smaller the price changes on the bond for a given change in interest rates.

**TABLE 3–6** The Impact of Coupon Rate on the Relation between a Bond's Fair Present Value and Its Required Rate of Return

| | 10 Percent Coupon Bond | | | 12 Percent Coupon Bond | | |
|---|---|---|---|---|---|---|
| Required Rate of Return | Fair Price* | Price Change | Percentage Price Change | Fair Price* | Price Change | Percentage Price Change |
| 8% | $1,152.47 | | | $1,304.94 | | |
| | | −$152.47 | −13.23% | | −$166.95 | −12.79% |
| 10% | 1,000.00 | | | 1,137.99 | | |
| | | − 125.50 | −12.55 | | − 137.99 | −12.13 |
| 12% | 874.50 | | | 1,000.00 | | |

*The bond pays interest semiannually, has 12 years remaining to maturity, and has a face value of $1,000.

These relationships hold when evaluating either required rates of return and the resulting fair present value of the bond or expected rates of return and the current market price of the bond. To understand these relationships better, consider again the bonds in Example 3–4. Table 3–6 summarizes the bond values and value changes as interest rates change.

### Coupon Rate and Security Price

In Table 3–6, we first list the fair present values of the bonds analyzed in Example 3–4. We then repeat the present value calculations using a bond with identical characteristics except for the coupon rate: 10 percent versus 12 percent. Notice that the fair present value of the 10 percent coupon bond is lower than that of the 12 percent coupon bond at every required rate of return. For example, when the required rate of return is 8 percent, the fair value of the 10 percent coupon bond is $1,152.47 and that of the 12 percent coupon bond is $1,304.94.

**LG 3-5**

### Coupon Rate and Security Price Sensitivity to Changes in Interest Rates

Table 3–6 also demonstrates the effect a bond's coupon rate has on its price sensitivity to a given change in the required rate of return. The intuition behind this relation is as follows. The higher (lower) the coupon rate on the bond, the larger (smaller) is the portion of the required rate of return paid to the bond holder in the form of coupon payments. Any security that returns a greater (smaller) proportion of an investment sooner is more (less) valuable and less (more) price volatile.

To see this, notice in Table 3–6 that the higher the bond's coupon rate, the smaller the bond's price sensitivity for any given change in interest rates. For example, for the 10 percent coupon bond, a 2 percent increase in the required rate of return (from 8 percent to 10 percent) results in a 13.23 percent decrease in the bond's fair present value. A further 2 percent increase in the required rate of return (from 10 percent to 12 percent) results in a smaller 12.55 percent decrease in the fair present value.

For the 12 percent coupon bond, notice that the 2 percent increase in the required rate of return (from 8 percent to 10 percent) results in a 12.79 percent decrease in the bond's fair present value, while an increase in the required rate of return from 10 percent to 12 percent results in a lower 12.13 percent decrease in the bond's fair present value. Thus, price sensitivity on a bond is negatively related to the level of the coupon rate on a bond. The higher the coupon rate on the bond, the smaller the decrease in the bond's fair present value for a given increase in the required rate of return on the bond.

We illustrate this relationship in Figure 3–3. The high coupon-paying bond is less susceptible to interest rate changes than the low coupon-paying bond. This is represented in Figure 3–3 by the slope of the line representing the relation between interest rates and bond prices. The sensitivity of bond prices is smaller (the slope of the line is flatter) for high-coupon bonds than for low-coupon bonds.

**DO YOU UNDERSTAND:**

12. *Whether a high or low coupon rate bond experiences a larger price change if interest rates increase?*

13. *Whether a high or low coupon rate bond experiences a larger price change if interest rates decrease?*

**Figure 3–3**   The Impact of a Bond's Coupon Rate on Its Price Sensitivity

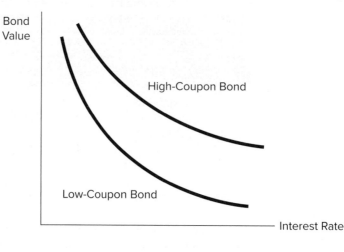

## DURATION

LG 3-6

**duration**

*The weighted-average time to maturity on an investment using the relative present values of the cash flows as weights.*

**elasticity**

*The percentage change in the price of a bond for a given change in interest rates.*

The estimation of the effect of maturity and coupon rates on the sensitivity of bond prices to changes in interest rates, as discussed in the previous section, is complex and using these relationships as the basis for decision making is difficult in dealing with multiple bonds. Duration, on the other hand, provides a simple measure that allows for a straightforward calculation of a bond's price sensitivity to changes in interest rates. In this section, we show that the price sensitivity of a bond, or the percentage change in the bond's value, for a given change in interest rates (either required rate of return or yield to maturity) can be more directly measured by a concept called duration (or Macaulay's duration). We also show that duration produces an accurate measure of the price sensitivity of a bond to interest rate changes for relatively small changes in interest rates. The duration measure is a less accurate measure of price sensitivity the larger the change in interest rates. **Duration** is the *weighted-average* time to maturity on a financial security *using the relative present values of the cash flows as weights*. On a time value of money basis, duration measures the weighted average of when cash flows are received on a security. In addition to being a measure of the average life of an asset or liability, duration also has *economic* meaning as the sensitivity, or **elasticity,** of that asset or liability's value to small interest rate changes (either required rate of return or yield to maturity). Duration describes the percentage price, or present value, change of a financial security for a given (small) change in interest rates. That is, rather than calculating present value changes resulting from interest rate changes, as we did in the previous sections, the duration of a financial security can be used to directly calculate the price change. Thus, for investors and financial managers duration is a tool that can be used to estimate the change in the value of a portfolio of securities or even firm value for a given change in interest rates.

In this section, we present the basic arithmetic needed to calculate the duration of an asset or liability. Then we analyze the economic meaning of the number we calculate for duration and explain why duration, as a measure of price sensitivity to changes in interest rates, is most accurate only for small changes in interest rates. Appendix 3A to this chapter (available through Connect or your course instructor) looks at how duration can be used to immunize an asset or liability against interest rate risk.

### A Simple Illustration of Duration

Duration is a measure that incorporates the time of arrival of all cash flows on an asset or liability along with the asset or liability's maturity date. To see this, consider a bond with one year remaining to maturity, a $1,000 face value, an 8 percent coupon rate (paid

**Figure 3–4** Promised Cash Flows on the One-Year Bond

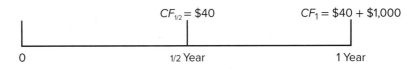

semiannually), and an interest rate (either required rate of return or yield to maturity) of 10 percent. The promised cash flows from this bond are illustrated in Figure 3–4. The bond holder receives the promised cash flows ($CF$) from the bond issuer at the end of one-half year and at the end of one year.

$CF_{1/2}$ is the $40 promised payment of (semiannual) coupon interest ($1,000 \times 8\% \times \frac{1}{2}$) received after six months. $CF_1$ is the promised cash flow at the end of year 1; it is equal to the second $40 promised (semiannual) coupon payment plus the $1,000 promised payment of face value. To compare the relative sizes of these two cash flow payments—since duration measures the weighted-average time to maturity of a bond—we should put them in the same dimensions, because $1 of principal or interest received at the end of one year is worth less to an investor in terms of time value of money than is $1 of principal or interest received at the end of six months. Assuming that the current rate of return (either required or expected) is 10 percent per year, we calculate the present values ($PV$) of the two cash flows ($CF$) as:

$$CF_{1/2} = \$40 \qquad PV_{1/2} = \$40/(1.05) = \$38.10$$
$$CF_1 = \$1,040 \qquad PV_1 = \$1,040(1.05)^2 = \$943.31$$
$$PV_{1/2} + PV_1 = \$981.41$$

Note that since $CF_{1/2}$, the cash flow received at the end of one-half year, is received earlier, it is discounted at $(1 + R/2)$ (where $R$ is the current rate of return on the bond); this discount factor is smaller than the discount rate applied to the cash flow received at the end of the year $(1 + R/2)^2$. Figure 3–5 summarizes the $PV$s of the cash flows from the bond.

The bond holder receives some cash flows at one-half year and some at one year (see Figure 3–5). Intuitively, duration is the weighted-average maturity on the portfolio of zero-coupon bonds, one that has payments at one-half year and at the end of the year (year 1) in this example. Specifically, duration analysis weights the time at which cash flows are received by the relative importance in *present value terms* of the cash flows arriving at each point in time. In present value terms, the relative importance of the cash flows arriving at time $t = \frac{1}{2}$ year and time $t = 1$ year are as follows:

| Time ($t$) | Weight ($X$) | | |
|---|---|---|---|
| ½ year | $X_{1/2} = \dfrac{PV_{1/2}}{PV_{1/2} + PV_1} = \dfrac{38.10}{981.41} = 0.0388 = 3.88\%$ | | |
| 1 year | $X_1 = \dfrac{PV_1}{PV_{1/2} + PV_1} = \dfrac{943.31}{981.41} = 0.9612 = 96.12\%$ | | |
| | | 1.0 | 100% |

**Figure 3–5** Present Value of the Cash Flows from the Bond

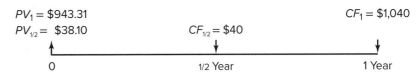

In present value terms, the bond holder receives 3.88 percent of the cash flows on the bond with the first coupon payment at the end of six months ($t_{1/2}$) and 96.12 percent with the second payment of coupon plus face value at the end of the year ($t_1$). By definition, the sum of the (present value) cash flow weights must equal 1:

$$X_{1/2} + X_1 = 1$$
$$0.0388 + 0.9612 = 1$$

We can now calculate the duration ($D$), or the weighted-average time to maturity of the bond, using the present value of its cash flows as weights:

$$D_L = X_{1/2} \times (t_{1/2}) + X_1 \times (t_1)$$
$$= 0.0388 \times \left(\frac{1}{2}\right) + 0.9612 \times (1) = 0.9806 \; years$$

Thus, although the maturity of the bond is one year, its duration or average life in a cash flow sense is only 0.9806 years. Duration is less than maturity because in present value terms, 3.88 percent of the cash flows are received during the year.

### A General Formula for Duration

You can calculate the duration for any fixed-income security that pays interest annually using the following formula:

$$D = \frac{\displaystyle\sum_{t=1}^{N} \frac{CF_t \times t}{(1+r)^t}}{\displaystyle\sum_{t=1}^{N} \frac{CF_t}{(1+r)^t}} = \frac{\displaystyle\sum_{t=1}^{N} PV_t \times t}{\displaystyle\sum_{t=1}^{N} PV_t}$$

where

$D$ = Duration measured in years

$t$ = 1 to $T$, the period in which a cash flow is received

$N$ = Number of period to maturity

$CF_t$ = Cash flow received on the security *at end of period t*

$r$ = Current required rate of return ($r$) or yield to maturity (*ytm*) on the investment

$PV_t$ = Present value of the cash flow received at the end of the period $t$

For bonds that pay interest semiannually, the duration equation becomes:[13]

$$D = \frac{\displaystyle\sum_{t=1/2}^{N} \frac{CF_t \times t}{(1+r/2)^{2t}}}{\displaystyle\sum_{t=1/2}^{N} \frac{CF_t}{(1+r/2)^{2t}}}$$

where $t = \frac{1}{2}, 1, 1\frac{1}{2}, \ldots, N$.

Notice that the denominator of the duration equation is the present value of the cash flows on the security. The numerator is the present value of each cash flow received on the security multiplied or weighted by the length of time required to receive the cash flow. To help you fully understand this formula, we look at some examples next.

---

13. In general, the duration equation is written as:

$$D = \frac{\displaystyle\sum_{t=1/m}^{N} \frac{CF_t \times t}{(1+r/m)^{mt}}}{\displaystyle\sum_{t=1/m}^{N} \frac{CF_t}{(1+r/m)^{mt}}}$$

where $m$ = number of times per year interest is paid.

---

**EXAMPLE 3–12**   The Duration of a Four-Year Bond Paying
Annual Interest

Suppose that you have a bond that offers a coupon rate of 10 percent paid annually. The face value of the bond is $1,000, it matures in four years, its current yield to maturity ($r_b$) is 8 percent, and its current price is $1,066.24. See Table 3–7 for the calculation of its duration. As the calculation indicates, the duration, or weighted-average time to maturity, on this bond is 3.50 years. In other words, on a time value of money basis, the initial investment of $1,066.24 is recovered after 3.50 years.

---

Most bonds pay interest semiannually rather than annually as in Example 3–12. Thus, we next look at the duration on a bond that pays interest semiannually.

---

**EXAMPLE 3–13**   The Duration of a Four-Year Bond Paying
Semiannual Interest

Suppose that you have a bond that offers a coupon rate of 10 percent paid semiannually (or 5 percent paid every 6 months). The face value of the bond is $1,000, it matures in four years, its current rate of return ($r_b$) is 8 percent, and its current price is $1,067.34. See Table 3–8 for the calculation of its duration. As the calculation indicates, the duration, or weighted-average time to maturity, on this bond is 3.42 years. In other words, on a time value of money basis, the initial investment of $1,067.34 is recovered after 3.42 years.

Table 3–9 shows that if the annual coupon rate is lowered to 6 percent, the duration of the bond rises to 3.60 years. Since 6 percent annual coupon payments are smaller than 10 percent coupon payments, it takes longer to recover the initial investment with the 6 percent coupon bond. In Table 3–10, duration is calculated for the original 10 percent coupon bond, assuming that its rate of return ($r_b$) increases from 8 percent to 10 percent. Now duration falls from 3.42 years (in Table 3–8) to 3.39 years. The higher the rate of return on the bond, the more the investor earns on reinvested coupons and the shorter the time needed to recover his or her initial investment. Finally, as the maturity on a bond decreases, in this case to 3 years in Table 3–11, duration falls to 2.67 years (i.e., the shorter the maturity on the bond, the more quickly the initial investment is recovered).

---

**TABLE 3–7**   Duration of a Four-Year Bond with 10 Percent Coupon Paid Annually
and 8 Percent Yield

| $t$ | $CF_t$ | $\dfrac{1}{(1+8\%)^t}$ | $\dfrac{CF_t}{(1+8\%)^t}$ | $\dfrac{CF_t \times t}{(1+8\%)^t}$ |
|---|---|---|---|---|
| 1 | 100 | 0.9259 | 92.59 | 92.59 |
| 2 | 100 | 0.8573 | 85.73 | 171.47 |
| 3 | 100 | 0.7938 | 79.38 | 238.15 |
| 4 | 1,100 | 0.7350 | 808.53 | 3,234.13 |
| | | | 1,066.24 | 3,736.34 |

$$\frac{3,736.34}{1,066.24} = 3.50 \text{ years}$$

**TABLE 3–8** Duration of a Four-Year Bond with 10 Percent Coupon Paid Semiannually and 8 Percent Rate of Return

| $t$ | $CF_t$ | $\dfrac{1}{(1+4\%)^{2t}}$ | $\dfrac{CF_t}{(1+4\%)^{2t}}$ | $\dfrac{CF_t \times t}{(1+4\%)^{2t}}$ |
|---|---|---|---|---|
| ½ | 50 | 0.9615 | 48.08 | 24.04 |
| 1 | 50 | 0.9246 | 46.23 | 46.23 |
| 1½ | 50 | 0.8890 | 44.45 | 66.67 |
| 2 | 50 | 0.8548 | 42.74 | 85.48 |
| 2½ | 50 | 0.8219 | 41.10 | 102.75 |
| 3 | 50 | 0.7903 | 39.52 | 118.56 |
| 3½ | 50 | 0.7599 | 38.00 | 133.00 |
| 4 | 1,050 | 0.7307 | 767.22 | 3,068.88 |
| | | | 1,067.34 | 3,645.61 |

$$D = \frac{3,645.61}{1,067.34} = 3.42 \; years$$

**TABLE 3–9** Duration of a Four-Year Bond with 6 Percent Coupon Paid Semiannually and 8 Percent Rate of Return

| $t$ | $CF_t$ | $\dfrac{1}{(1+4\%)^{2t}}$ | $\dfrac{CF_t}{(1+4\%)^{2t}}$ | $\dfrac{CF_t \times t}{(1+4\%)^{2t}}$ |
|---|---|---|---|---|
| ½ | 30 | 0.9615 | 28.84 | 14.42 |
| 1 | 30 | 0.9246 | 27.74 | 27.74 |
| 1½ | 30 | 0.8890 | 26.67 | 40.00 |
| 2 | 30 | 0.8548 | 25.64 | 51.28 |
| 2½ | 30 | 0.8219 | 24.66 | 61.65 |
| 3 | 30 | 0.7903 | 23.71 | 71.13 |
| 3½ | 30 | 0.7599 | 22.80 | 79.80 |
| 4 | 1,030 | 0.7307 | 752.62 | 3,010.48 |
| | | | 932.68 | 3,356.50 |

$$D = \frac{3,356.50}{932.62} = 3.60 \; years$$

**TABLE 3–10** Duration of a Four-Year Bond with 10 Percent Coupon Paid Semiannually and 10 Percent Rate of Return

| $t$ | $CF_t$ | $\dfrac{1}{(1+5\%)^{2t}}$ | $\dfrac{CF_t}{(1+5\%)^{2t}}$ | $\dfrac{CF_t \times t}{(1+5\%)^{2t}}$ |
|---|---|---|---|---|
| ½ | 50 | 0.9524 | 47.62 | 23.81 |
| 1 | 50 | 0.9070 | 45.35 | 45.35 |
| 1½ | 50 | 0.8638 | 43.19 | 64.78 |
| 2 | 50 | 0.8227 | 41.14 | 82.28 |
| 2½ | 50 | 0.7835 | 39.18 | 97.95 |
| 3 | 50 | 0.7462 | 37.31 | 111.93 |
| 3½ | 50 | 0.7107 | 35.53 | 124.36 |
| 4 | 1,050 | 0.6768 | 710.68 | 2,842.72 |
| | | | 1,000.00 | 3,393.18 |

$$D = \frac{3,393.18}{1,000.00} = 3.39 \; years$$

**TABLE 3–11**   Duration of a Three-Year Bond with 10 Percent Coupon Paid
Semiannually and 8 Percent Rate of Return

| $t$ | $CF_t$ | $\dfrac{1}{(1+4\%)^{2t}}$ | $\dfrac{CF_t}{(1+4\%)^{2t}}$ | $\dfrac{CF_t \times t}{(1+4\%)^{2t}}$ |
|---|---|---|---|---|
| ½ | 50 | 0.9615 | 48.08 | 24.04 |
| 1 | 50 | 0.9246 | 46.23 | 46.23 |
| 1½ | 50 | 0.8890 | 44.45 | 66.67 |
| 2 | 50 | 0.8548 | 42.74 | 85.48 |
| 2½ | 50 | 0.8219 | 41.10 | 102.75 |
| 3 | 1,050 | 0.7903 | 829.82 | 2,489.46 |
| | | | 1,052.42 | 2,814.63 |

$$D = \frac{2,814.63}{1,052.42} = 2.67 \; years$$

**The Duration of a Zero-Coupon Bond.**   Zero-coupon bonds sell at a discount from face value and pay their face value (e.g., $1,000) on maturity. These bonds have no intervening cash flows, such as coupon payments, between issue and maturity. The current price that an investor is willing to pay for such a bond, assuming semiannual compounding of interest, is equal to the present value of the single, fixed (face value) payment on the bond that is received on maturity (here, $1,000):

$$P = 1,000/(1 + r_b/2)^{2T_{zc}}$$

where

$r_b$ = Required semiannually compounded rate of return or yield

$T_{zc}$ = Number of years to maturity

$P$ = Price

Because the only cash flow received on these securities is the final payment at maturity (time $T_{zc}$), the following must be true:

$$D_{zc} = T_{zc}$$

That is, the duration of a zero-coupon bond equals its maturity. Note that it is only for zero-coupon bonds that duration and maturity are equal. Indeed, for any bond that pays some cash flows prior to maturity, its duration will always be less than its maturity.

---

**EXAMPLE 3–14**   The Duration of a Zero-Coupon Bond

Suppose that you have a zero-coupon bond with a face value of $1,000, a maturity of four years, and a current rate of return of 8 percent compounded semiannually. Since the bond pays no interest, the duration equation consists of only one term—cash flow at the end of year 4:

| $t$ | $CF_4$ | $\dfrac{1}{(1+8\%/2)^{2\times4}}$ | $\dfrac{CF_4}{(1+8\%/2)^{2\times4}}$ | $\dfrac{CF_4 \times 4}{(1+8\%/2)^{2\times4}}$ |
|---|---|---|---|---|
| 4 | $1,000 | 0.7307 | 730 | 2,923 |

$$D = 2,923/730 = 4 \; years$$

or duration equals the maturity of the zero-coupon bond.

**TABLE 3–12**   Features of Duration

> 1. The higher the coupon or promised interest payment on a security, the shorter is its duration.
> 2. The higher the rate of return on a security, the shorter is its duration.
> 3. Duration increases with maturity at a decreasing rate.

**LG 3-7**

## Features of Duration

The preceding examples suggest several important features of duration relating to the time remaining to maturity, rate of return, and coupon interest of the underlying bond being analyzed. These features are summarized in Table 3–12.

**Duration and Coupon Interest.**   A comparison of Tables 3–8 and 3–9 indicates that the higher the coupon or promised interest payment on the bond, the shorter its duration. This is due to the fact that the larger the coupon or promised interest payment, the more quickly investors receive cash flows on a bond and the higher are the present value weights of those cash flows in the duration calculation. On a time value of money basis, the investor recoups his or her initial investment faster when coupon payments are higher.

**Duration and Rate of Return.**   A comparison of Tables 3–8 and 3–10 also indicates that duration decreases as the rate of return on the bond increases. This makes intuitive sense since the higher the rate of return on the bond, the lower the present value cost of waiting to receive the later cash flows on the bond. Higher rates of return discount later cash flows more heavily, and the relative importance, or weights, of those later cash flows decline when compared to cash flows received earlier.

**Duration and Maturity.**   A comparison of Tables 3–8, 3–11, and 3–13 indicates that duration increases with the maturity of a bond, but at a *decreasing* rate. As maturity of a 10 percent coupon bond decreases from four years to three years (Tables 3–8 and 3–11), duration decreases by 0.75 year, from 3.42 years to 2.67 years. Decreasing maturity for an additional year, from three years to two years (Tables 3–11 and 3–13), decreases duration by 0.81 year, from 2.67 years to 1.86 years. Notice too that for a coupon bond, the longer the maturity on the bond the larger the discrepancy between maturity and duration. Specifically, the two-year maturity bond has a duration of 1.86 years (0.14 year less than its maturity), while the three-year maturity bond has a duration of 2.67 years (0.33 year less than its maturity), and the four-year maturity bond has a duration of 3.42 years (0.58 year less than its maturity). Figure 3–6 illustrates this relation between duration and maturity for our 10 percent coupon (paid semiannually), 8 percent rate of return bond. The In the News box describes how this relation between maturity and duration can result in potentially large losses when bonds are purchased during a period of falling interest rates.

**TABLE 3–13**   Duration of a Two-Year Bond with 10 Percent Coupon Paid Semiannually and 8 Percent Rate of Return

| $t$ | $CF_t$ | $\dfrac{1}{(1+4\%)^{2t}}$ | $\dfrac{CF_t}{(1+4\%)^{2t}}$ | $\dfrac{CF_t \times t}{(1+4\%)^{2t}}$ |
|---|---|---|---|---|
| ½ | 50 | 0.9615 | 48.08 | 24.04 |
| 1 | 50 | 0.9246 | 46.23 | 46.23 |
| 1½ | 50 | 0.8890 | 44.45 | 66.67 |
| 2 | 1,050 | 0.8548 | 897.54 | 1,795.08 |
| | | | 1,036.30 | 1,932.02 |

$$D = \frac{1,932.02}{1,036.30} = 1.86 \; years$$

# IN THE NEWS

## Duration Risk in Bond Markets

Investors looking for big returns in government bonds could have found them in 2015 with bonds issued by Japan. With global interest rates extraordinarily low, and borrowers issuing long-term debt, duration shot up. Duration implies risk. As discussed in the chapter, a one percentage-point change in interest rates implies a change in the bond's price equal to the duration. A bond with a duration of 25 years will rise in price by 25 percent if interest rates fall by one percentage point and fall 25 percent in price if rates rise by one percentage point.

Japanese debt is a prime example and highlights a quiet risk in bond markets in an era of low and even negative interest rates: duration. In 2015, Japan issued 40-year bonds with a coupon of 1.4 percent. Rates fell in Japan and bond prices rose 34 percent. However, the long maturity is troublesome given that as durations got longer, interest rate risk increased. If rates rise in the next few years, a bond yielding 0.49 percent becomes unattractive, and an investor must take a potentially large loss to sell it.

Usually, to account for duration risk, the yield curve is relatively steep. Thus, to compensate an investor for facing considerable uncertainty, bonds with long maturities have considerably higher yields. However, in Japan yield curves in 2015 were flattening. Investors who usually would have bought shorter maturity government bonds in Japan purchased longer-term maturities. However, the yield on 40-year Japanese bonds declined from above 2 percent in late 2012 to around 1.5 percent at the end of 2015. At the beginning of 2016, it fell to below 0.5 percent.

Few are predicting a turnaround in Japanese rates any time soon. However, 40 years is a long time to wait, and if and when rates turn up, investors holding these long-term bonds could be forced to take heavy losses—even though Japan's government debt is regarded as some of the world's safest.

**LG 3-8**

### Economic Meaning of Duration

So far we have calculated duration for a number of different bonds. In addition to being a measure of the average life of a bond, duration is also a direct measure of its price sensitivity to changes in interest rates, or elasticity.[14] In other words, the larger the numerical value of duration ($D$), the more sensitive the price of that bond ($\Delta P/P$) to (small) changes

**Figure 3–6** Discrepancy between Maturity and Duration on a Coupon Bond

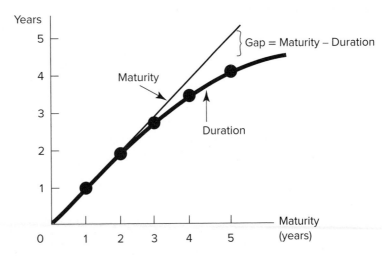

---

14. In Chapter 22, we also make the direct link between duration and the price sensitivity of an asset or liability or of an FI's entire portfolio (i.e., its duration gap). We show how duration can be used to immunize a security or portfolio of securities against interest rate risk.

or shocks in interest rates $\Delta r_b/(1 + r_b)$. The specific relationship between these factors for securities with annual compounding of interest is represented as:[15]

$$\frac{\Delta P/P}{\Delta r_b/(1 + r_b)} = -D$$

For securities with semiannual receipt (compounding) of interest, it is represented as:

$$\frac{\Delta P/P}{\Delta r_b/(1 + r_b/2)} = -D$$

The economic interpretation of this equation is that the number $D$ is the elasticity, or sensitivity, of the bond's price to small interest rate (either required rate of return or yield to maturity) changes. The negative sign in front of the $D$ indicates the inverse relationship between interest rate changes and price changes. That is, $-D$ describes the percentage value *decrease*—capital loss—on the security ($\Delta P/P$) for any given (discounted) small *increase* in interest rates [$\Delta r_b/(1 + r_b)$], where $\Delta r_b$ is the change in interest rates and $1 + r_b$ is 1 plus the *current* (or beginning) level of interest rates.

The definition of duration can be rearranged in another useful way for interpretation regarding price sensitivity:

$$\frac{\Delta P}{P} = -D\left[\frac{\Delta r_b}{1 + r_b}\right]$$

or

$$\frac{\Delta P}{P} = -D\left[\frac{\Delta r_b}{1 + r_b/2}\right]$$

for annual and semiannual compounding of interest, respectively. This equation shows that for *small changes* in interest rates, bond prices move *in an inversely proportional* manner according to the size of $D$. Clearly, for any given change in interest rates, long duration securities suffer a larger capital loss (or receive a higher capital gain) should interest rates rise (fall) than do short duration securities.[16]

The duration equation can be rearranged, combining $D$ and $(1 + r_b)$ into a single variable $D/(1 + r_b)$, to produce what practitioners call **modified duration** (*MD*). For annual compounding of interest:

**modified duration**

*Duration divided by 1 plus the initial interest rate.*

$$\frac{\Delta P}{P} = -MD \times \Delta r_b$$

where

$$MD = \frac{D}{1 + r_b}$$

For semiannual compounding of interest:

$$\frac{\Delta P}{P} = -MD \times \Delta r_b$$

---

15. In what follows, we use the $\Delta$ (change) notation instead of $d$ (derivative notation) to recognize that interest rate changes tend to be discrete rather then infinitesimally small. For example, in real-world financial markets the smallest observed rate change is usually one basis point, or 1/100 of 1 percent.

16. By implication, gains and losses under the duration model are *symmetric*. That is, if we repeated the above examples but allowed interest rates to decrease by one basis point annually (or ½ basis point semiannually), the percentage increase in the price of the bond ($\Delta P/P$) would be proportionate with $D$. Further, the capital gains would be a mirror image of the capital losses for an equal (small) decrease in interest rates.

where

$$MD = \frac{D}{1 + r_b/2}$$

This form is more intuitive than the Macaulay's duration because we multiply *MD* by the simple change in interest rates rather than the discounted change in interest rates as in the general duration equation. Thus, the modified duration is a more direct measure of bond price elasticity. Next, we use duration to measure the price sensitivity of different bonds to small changes in interest rates.

---

## EXAMPLE 3–15  Four-Year Bond

Consider a four-year bond with a 10 percent coupon paid semiannually (or 5 percent paid every 6 months) and an 8 percent rate of return ($r_b$). According to calculations in Table 3–8, the bond's duration is $D = 3.42$ years. Suppose that the rate of return increases by 10 basis points (1/10 of 1 percent) from 8 to 8.10 percent. Then, using the semiannual compounding version of the duration model shown above, the percentage change in the bond's price is:

$$\frac{\Delta P}{P} = -(3.42)\left[\frac{0.001}{1.04}\right]$$

$$= -0.00329$$

or

$$= -0.329\%$$

The bond price had been \$1,067.34, which was the present value of a four-year bond with a 10 percent coupon and an 8 percent rate of return. However, the duration model predicts that the price of this bond will fall by 0.329 percent, or by \$3.51, to \$1,063.83 after the increase in the rate of return on the bond of 10 basis points.[17]

With a lower coupon rate of 6 percent, as shown in Table 3–8, the bond's duration, *D*, is 3.60 and the bond price changes by:

$$\frac{\Delta P}{P} = -(3.60)\left(\frac{0.001}{1.04}\right) = -0.00346$$

or

$$= -0.346\%$$

for a 10-basis-point increase in the rate of return. The bond's price drops by 0.346 percent, or by \$3.23, from \$932.68 (reported in Table 3–8) to \$929.45. Notice again that, all else held constant, the higher the coupon rate on the bond, the shorter the duration of the bond and the smaller the percentage decrease in the bond's price for a given increase in interest rates.

---

### Large Interest Rate Changes and Duration

It needs to be stressed here that duration accurately measures the price sensitivity of financial securities only for *small* changes in interest rates of the order of one or a few basis points (a basis point is equal to one-hundredth of 1 percent). Suppose, however, that interest rate shocks are much larger, of the order of 2 percent or 200 basis points or more. While such large changes in interest rates are not common, this might happen in a financial

---

17. That is, a price fall of 0.329 percent in this case translates into a dollar fall of \$3.51. To calculate the dollar change in value, we can rewrite the equation as $\Delta P = (P)(-D)((\Delta r_b)/(1 + r_b/2)) = (\$1,067.34)(-3.42)(0.001/1.04) = \$3.51$.

**convexity**

*The degree of curvature of the price–interest rate curve around some interest rate level.*

crisis or if the central bank (see Chapter 4) suddenly changes its monetary policy strategy. In this case, duration becomes a less accurate predictor of how much the prices of bonds will change, and therefore, a less accurate measure of the price sensitivity of a bond to changes in interest rates. Figure 3–7 is a graphic representation of the reason for this. Note the difference in the change in a bond's price due to interest rate changes according to the proportional duration measure (*D*), and the "true relationship," using the time value of money equations of Chapter 2 (and discussed earlier in this chapter) to calculate the exact present value change of a bond's price in response to interest rate changes.

Specifically, duration predicts that the relationship between an interest rate change and a security's price change will be proportional to the security's *D* (duration). By precisely calculating the exact or true change in the security's price using time value of money calculations, however, we would find that for large interest rate increases, duration overpredicts the *fall* in the security's price, and for large interest rate decreases, it underpredicts the *increase* in the security's price. Thus, duration misestimates the change in the value of a security following a large change (either positive or negative) in interest rates. Further, the duration model predicts symmetric effects for rate increases and decreases on a bond's price. As Figure 3–7 shows, in actuality, the *capital loss effect* of large rate increases tends to be smaller than the *capital gain effect* of large rate decreases. This is the result of a bond's price–interest rate relationship exhibiting a property called **convexity** rather than *linearity,* as assumed by the simple duration model. Intuitively, this is because the sensitivity of the bond's price to a change in interest rates depends on the *level* from which interest rates change (i.e., 6 percent, 8 percent, 10 percent, 12 percent). In particular, the higher the level of interest rates, the smaller a bond's price sensitivity to interest rate changes.

---

**EXAMPLE 3–16**    **Calculation of the Change in a Security's Price Using the Duration versus the Time Value of Money Formula**

To see the importance of accounting for the effects of convexity in assessing the impact of large interest rate changes, consider the four-year, $1,000 face value bond with a 10 percent coupon paid semiannually and an 8 percent rate of return. In Table 3–8 we found this bond has a duration of 3.42 years, and its current price is $1,067.34. We represent this as point *A* in Figure 3–8. If rates rise from 8 percent to 10 percent, the duration model predicts that the bond price will fall by 6.577 percent; that is:

$$\frac{\Delta P}{P} = -3.42(0.02/1.04) = -6.577\%$$

or from a price of $1,067.34 to $997.14 (see point *B* in Figure 3–8). However, using time value of money formulas to calculate the exact change in the bond's price after a rise in rates to 10 percent, we find its true value is:

$$V_b = 50\left[\frac{1 - \dfrac{1}{[1 + (0.10/2)]^{2(4)}}}{0.10/2}\right] + 1{,}000/[1 + (0.10/2)]^{2(4)} = \$1{,}000$$

This is point *C* in Figure 3–8. As you can see, the true or actual fall in price is less than the duration predicted fall by $2.86. The reason for this is the natural convexity to the price–interest rate curve as interest rates rise.

Reversing the experiment reveals that the duration model would predict the bond's price to rise by 6.577 percent if yields were to fall from 8 percent to 6 percent, resulting in a predicted price of $1,137.54 (see point *D* in Figure 3–8). By comparison, the true or actual change in price can be computed, using time value of money formulas and a 6 percent rate of return, as $1,140.39 (see point E in Figure 3–8). The duration model has underpredicted the true bond price increase by $2.85 ($1,140.39 − $1,137.54).

**Figure 3–7**   Duration Estimated versus True Bond Price

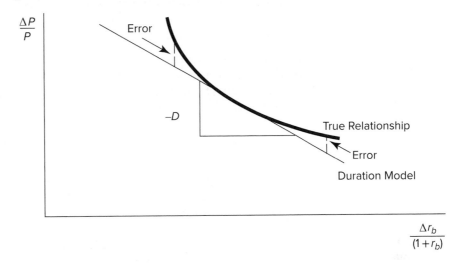

**Figure 3–8**   Price–Interest Rate Curve for the Four-Year 10 Percent Coupon Bond

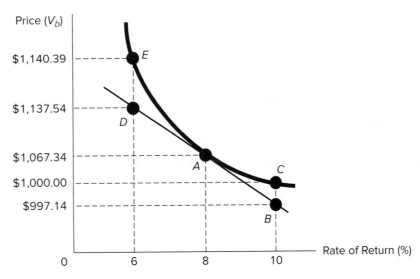

An important question for managers of financial institutions and individual savers is whether the error in the duration equation is big enough to be concerned about. This depends on the size of the interest rate change and the size of the portfolio under management. Clearly, for a large portfolio the error will also be large.

Note that convexity is a desirable feature for an investor or FI manager to capture in a portfolio of assets. Buying a bond or a portfolio of assets that exhibits a lot of convexity or curvature in the price–interest rate relationship is similar to buying partial interest rate risk insurance. Specifically, high convexity means that for equally large changes of interest rates up and down (e.g., plus or minus 2 percent), the capital gain effect of a rate decrease more than offsets the capital loss effect of a rate increase.

So far, we have established the following three characteristics of convexity:

1. Convexity is desirable. The greater the convexity of a security or portfolio of securities, the more insurance or interest rate protection an investor or FI manager has against rate increases and the greater the potential gains after interest rate falls.
2. Convexity diminishes the error in duration as an investment criterion. The larger the interest rate changes and the more convex a fixed-income security or portfolio, the greater the error the investor or FI manager faces in using just duration (and duration matching) to immunize exposure to interest rate shocks.
3. All fixed-income securities are convex. That is, as interest rates change, bond prices change at a nonconstant rate.

To illustrate the third characteristic, we can take the four-year, 10 percent coupon, 8 percent rate of return bond and look at two extreme price–interest rate scenarios. What is the price on the bond if rates fall to zero, and what is its price if rates rise to some very large number such as infinity? Where $r_b = 0$:

$$V_b = \frac{50}{(1+0)^1} + \frac{50}{(1+0)^2} + \ldots + \frac{1,050}{(1+0)^8} = \$1,400$$

The price is just the simple undiscounted sum of the coupon values and the face value of the bond. Since interest rates can never go below zero, \$1,400 is the maximum possible price for the bond. Where $r_b = \infty$:

$$V_b = \frac{50}{(1+\infty)^1} + \frac{50}{(1+\infty)^2} + \ldots + \frac{1,050}{(1+\infty)^8} = \$0$$

As interest rates go to infinity, the bond price falls asymptotically toward zero, but by definition a bond's price can never be negative. Thus, zero must be the minimum bond price (see Figure 3–9). In Appendix 3B to this chapter (available through Connect or your course instructor) we look at how to measure convexity and how this measure of convexity can be incorporated into the duration model to adjust for or offset the error in the prediction of security price changes for a given change in interest rates.

**Figure 3–9**    The Natural Convexity of Bonds

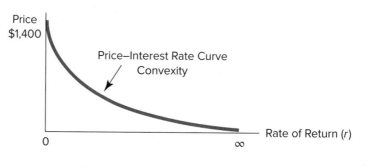

## SUMMARY

This chapter applied the time value of money formulas presented in Chapter 2 to the valuation of financial securities such as bonds and equities. With respect to bonds, we included a detailed examination of how changes in interest rates, coupon rates, and time to maturity affect their price and price sensitivity. We also presented a measure of bond price sensitivity to interest rate changes, called duration. We showed how the value of duration is affected by various bond characteristics, such as coupon rates, interest rates, and time to maturity.

## CHAPTER NOTATION

$r$ = required rate of return

$CF_t$ = cash flow received on a security at end of period $t$

$n$ = number of periods in the investment horizon

$PV$ = present value of a security

$E(r)$ = expected rate of return

$P$ or $\bar{P}$ = current market price for a security

$RCF_t$ = realized cash flow in period $t$

$\bar{r}$ = realized rate of return

$V_b$ = the price on a bond

$M$ = par or face value of a bond

$INT$ = annual interest payment on a bond

$T$ = number of years until a bond matures

$r_b$ = annual interest rate used to discount cash flows on a bond

$r_s$ = interest rate used to discount cash flows on equity

$Div_t$ = dividend paid at the end of year $t$

$g$ = constant growth rate in dividends each year

$D$ = duration on a security measured in years

$N$ = last period in which the cash flow is received or number of periods to maturity

$MD$ = modified duration = $D/(1 + r)$

## QUESTIONS

1. What is the difference between a required rate of return and an expected rate of return? (*LG 3-1*)

2. What is the relation between the expected rate of return and the required rate of return as they pertain to the fair market price and the current market price of a security? (*LG 3-1*)

3. What is the difference between a zero-coupon bond and a coupon bond? (*LG 3-2*)

4. For each of the following situations, identify whether a bond would be considered a premium bond, a discount bond, or a par bond. (*LG 3-2*)
   a. A bond's current market price is greater than its face value.
   b. A bond's coupon rate is equal to its yield to maturity.
   c. A bond's coupon rate is less than its required rate of return.
   d. A bond's coupon rate is less than its yield to maturity.
   e. A bond's coupon rate is greater than its yield to maturity.
   f. A bond's fair present value is less than its face value.

5. How does equity valuation differ from bond valuation? (*LG 3-3*)

6. What happens to the fair present value of a bond when the required rate of return on the bond increases? (*LG 3-4*)

7. All else equal, which bond's price is more affected by a change in interest rates, a short-term bond or a long-term bond? Why? (*LG 3-5*)

8. All else equal, which bond's price is more affected by a change in interest rates, a bond with a large coupon or a small coupon? Why? (*LG 3-5*)

9. How is duration related to the price elasticity of a fixed-income security? What is the relationship between duration and the price of a fixed-income security? (*LG 3-6*)

10. What is the relation between the coupon rate on a bond and its duration? (*LG 3-7*)

11. Which has the longest duration: a 30-year, 8 percent yield to maturity, 5 percent coupon bond or a 30-year, 10 percent yield to maturity, 5 percent coupon bond? (*LG 3-7*)

12. What is the economic meaning of duration? (*LG 3-8*)

## PROBLEMS

1. You bought a bond five years ago for $935 per bond. The bond is now selling for $980. It also paid $75 in interest per year, which you reinvested in the bond. Calculate the realized rate of return earned on this bond. (*LG 3-1*)

2. Refer again to the bond information in Problem 1. You expect to hold the bond for three more years, then sell it for $990. If the bond is expected to continue paying $75 per year over the next three years, what is the expected rate of return on the bond during this period? (*LG 3-1*)

3. Johnson Motors's bonds have 10 years remaining to maturity. Interest is paid annually, the bonds have a $1,000 par value, and the coupon rate is 8 percent. The bonds have a yield to maturity of 9 percent. What is the current market price of these bonds? (*LG 3-2*)

**4.** **eXcel**  **Using a Spreadsheet to Calculate Bond Values.** What is the value of a $1,000 bond with a 12-year maturity and an 8 percent coupon rate (paid semiannually) if the required rate of return is 5 percent, 6 percent, 8 percent, and 10 percent? (*LG 3-2*)

| Face Value | Number of Payments | Periodic Coupon Payment, $ | Required Return ⇒ | The Bond Value Will Be |
|---|---|---|---|---|
| $1,000 | 12 × 2 = 24 | 1,000(0.08)/2 = 40 | 5% | $1,268.27 |
| 1,000 | 24 | 40 | 6 | 1,169.36 |
| 1,000 | 24 | 40 | 8 | 1,000.00 |
| 1,000 | 24 | 40 | 10 | 862.01 |

**5.** A 10-year, 12 percent semiannual coupon bond, with a par value of $1,000 sells for $1,100. What is the bond's yield to maturity? (*LG 3-2*)

**6.** **eXcel**  **Using a Spreadsheet to Calculate Yield to Maturity.** What is the yield to maturity on the following bonds; all have a maturity of 10 years, a face value of $1,000, and a coupon rate of 9 percent (paid semiannually). The bonds' current market values are $945.50, $987.50, $1,090.00, and $1,225.875, respectively. (*LG 3-2*)

| Market Value | Number of Payments | Periodic Coupon Payment, $ | Face Value ⇒ | The Yield to Maturity Will Be |
|---|---|---|---|---|
| 945.50 | 10 × 2 = 20 | 1,000(0.09)/2 = 45 | $1,000 | 9.87% |
| 987.50 | 20 | 45 | 1,000 | 9.19 |
| 1,090.00 | 20 | 45 | 1,000 | 7.69 |
| 1,225.875 | 20 | 45 | 1,000 | 5.97 |

**7.** BSW Corporation has a bond issue outstanding with an annual coupon rate of 7 percent paid quarterly and four years remaining until maturity. The par value of the bond is $1,000. Determine the fair present value of the bond if market conditions justify a 14 percent, compounded quarterly, required rate of return. (*LG 3-2*)

**8.** You have just been offered a bond for $863.73. The coupon rate is 8 percent payable annually, and the yield to maturity on new issues with the same degree of risk are 10 percent. You want to know how many more interest payments you will receive, but the party selling the bond cannot remember. If the par value is $1,000, how many interest payments remain? (*LG 3-2*)

**9.** A bond you are evaluating has a 10 percent coupon rate (compounded semiannually), a $1,000 face value, and is 10 years from maturity. (*LG 3-4*)
   **a.** If the required rate of return on the bond is 6 percent, what is its fair present value?
   **b.** If the required rate of return on the bond is 8 percent, what is its fair present value?
   **c.** What do your answers to parts (a) and (b) say about the relation between required rates of return and fair values of bonds?

**10.** Calculate the yield to maturity on the following bonds: (*LG 3-2*)
   **a.** A 9 percent coupon (paid semiannually) bond, with a $1,000 face value and 15 years remaining to maturity. The bond is selling at $985.

   **b.** An 8 percent coupon (paid quarterly) bond, with a $1,000 face value and 10 years remaining to maturity. The bond is selling at $915.
   **c.** An 11 percent coupon (paid annually) bond, with a $1,000 face value and 6 years remaining to maturity. The bond is selling at $1,065.

**11.** Calculate the fair present values of the following bonds, all of which pay interest semiannually, have a face value of $1,000, have 12 years remaining to maturity, and have a required rate of return of 10 percent. (*LG 3-5*)
   **a.** The bond has a 6 percent coupon rate.
   **b.** The bond has a 8 percent coupon rate.
   **c.** The bond has a 10 percent coupon rate.
   **d.** What do your answers to parts (a) through (c) say about the relation between coupon rates and present values?

**12.** Repeat parts (a) through (c) of Problem 11 using a required rate of return on the bond of 8 percent. What do your calculations imply about the relation between the coupon rates and bond price volatility? (*LG 3-5*)

**13.** Calculate the fair present value of the following bonds, all of which have a 10 percent coupon rate (paid semiannually), face value of $1,000, and a required rate of return of 8 percent. (*LG 3-5*)
   **a.** The bond has 10 years remaining to maturity.
   **b.** The bond has 15 years remaining to maturity.
   **c.** The bond has 20 years remaining to maturity.
   **d.** What do your answers to parts (a) through (c) say about the relation between time to maturity and present values?

**14.** Repeat parts (a) through (c) of Problem 13 using a required rate of return on the bond of 11 percent. What do your calculations imply about the relation between time to maturity and bond price volatility? (*LG 3-5*)

**15.** A $1,000 par value bond with five years left to maturity pays an interest payment semiannually with a 6 percent coupon rate and is priced to have a 5 percent yield to maturity. If interest rates surprisingly increase by 0.5 percent, by how much will the bond's price change? (*LG 3-4*)

**16.** A $1,000 par value bond with seven years left to maturity has a 9 percent coupon rate (paid semiannually) and is selling for $945.80. What is its yield to maturity? (*LG 3-2*)

**17.** Calculate the fair present value on a stock that pays $5 in dividends per year (with no growth) and has a required rate of return of 10 percent. (*LG 3-3*)

**18.** A preferred stock from Duquesne Light Company (DQU-PRA) pays $2.10 in annual dividends. If the required rate of return on the preferred stock is 5.4 percent, what is the fair present value of the stock? (*LG 3-3*)

**19.** A preferred stock from Hecla Mining Co. (HLPRB) pays $3.50 in annual dividends. If the required rate of return on the preferred stock is 6.8 percent, what is the fair present value of the stock? (*LG 3-3*)

**20.** Financial analysts forecast Safeco Corp. (SAF) growth for the future to be 10 percent. Safeco's recent dividend was $1.20. What is the fair present value of Safeco stock if the required rate of return is 12 percent? (*LG 3-3*)

**21.** Financial analysts forecast L Brands (LB) growth for the future to be 12.5 percent. LB's most recent dividend was

$0.60. What is the fair present value of L Brands's stock if the required rate of return is 14.5 percent? (*LG 3-3*)

22. A stock you are evaluating just paid an annual dividend of $2.50. Dividends have grown at a constant rate of 1.5 percent over the last 15 years and you expect this to continue. (*LG 3-3*)

    a. If the required rate of return on the stock is 12 percent, what is its fair present value?

    b. If the required rate of return on the stock is 15 percent, what should the fair value be four years from today?

23. You are considering the purchase of a stock that is currently selling at $64 per share. You expect the stock to pay $4.50 in dividends next year. (*LG 3-3*)

    a. If dividends are expected to grow at a constant rate of 3 percent per year, what is your expected rate of return on this stock?

    b. If dividends are expected to grow at a constant rate of 5 percent per year, what is your expected rate of return on this stock?

    c. What do your answers to parts (a) and (b) say about the impact of dividend growth rates on the expected rate of return on stocks?

24. A stock you are evaluating is expected to experience supernormal growth in dividends of 8 percent over the next six years. Following this period, dividends are expected to grow at a constant rate of 3 percent. The stock paid a dividend of $5.50 last year and the required rate of return on the stock is 10 percent. Calculate the stock's fair present value. (*LG 3-3*)

25. Ecolap Inc. (ECL) recently paid a $0.46 dividend. The dividend is expected to grow at a 14.5 percent rate. At a current stock price of $44.12, what return are shareholders expecting? (*LG 3-3*)

26. Paychex Inc. (PAYX) recently paid a $0.84 dividend. The dividend is expected to grow at a 15 percent rate. At a current stock price of $40.11, what return are shareholders expecting? (*LG 3-3*)

27. Consider a firm with a 9.5 percent growth rate of dividends expected in the future. The current year's dividend was $1.32. What is the fair present value of the stock if the required rate of return is 13 percent? (*LG 3-3*)

28. A company recently paid a $0.35 dividend. The dividend is expected to grow at a 10.5 percent rate. At a current stock price of $24.25, what return are shareholders expecting? (*LG 3-3*)

29. a. What is the duration of a two-year bond that pays an annual coupon of 10 percent and has a current yield to maturity of 12 percent? Use $1,000 as the face value. (*LG 3-6*)

    b. What is the duration of a two-year zero-coupon bond that is yielding 11.5 percent? Use $1,000 as the face value.

    c. Given these answers, how does duration differ from maturity?

30. Consider the following two banks:

    Bank 1 has assets composed solely of a 10-year, 12 percent coupon, $1 million loan with a 12 percent yield to maturity. It is financed with a 10-year, 10 percent coupon, $1 million CD with a 10 percent yield to maturity.

    Bank 2 has assets composed solely of a 7-year, 12 percent, zero-coupon bond with a current value of

$894,006.20 and a maturity value of $1,976,362.88. It is financed with a 10-year, 8.275 percent coupon, $1,000,000 face value CD with a yield to maturity of 10 percent.

   All securities except the zero-coupon bond pay interest annually. (*LG 3-4*)

   a. If interest rates rise by 1 percent (100 basis points), how do the values of the assets and liabilities of each bank change?

   b. What accounts for the differences between the two banks' accounts?

31. Two bonds are available for purchase in the financial markets. The first bond is a two-year, $1,000 bond that pays an annual coupon of 10 percent. The second bond is a two-year, $1,000, zero-coupon bond. (*LG 3-7*)

    a. What is the duration of the coupon bond if the current yield to maturity is 8 percent? 10 percent? 12 percent?

    b. How does the change in the current yield to maturity affect the duration of this coupon bond?

    c. Calculate the duration of the zero-coupon bond with a yield to maturity of 8 percent, 10 percent, and 12 percent.

    d. How does the change in the yield to maturity affect the duration of the zero-coupon bond?

    e. Why does the change in the yield to maturity affect the coupon bond differently than it affects the zero-coupon bond?

32. What is the duration of a five-year, $1,000 Treasury bond with a 10 percent semiannual coupon selling at par? Selling with a yield to maturity of 12 percent? 14 percent? What can you conclude about the relationship between duration and yield to maturity? Plot the relationship. Why does this relationship exist? (*LG 3-7*)

33. Consider a 12-year, 12 percent annual coupon bond with a required rate of return of 10 percent. The bond has a face value of $1,000. (*LG 3-4*)

    a. What is the fair present value of the bond?

    b. If the required rate of return rises to 11 percent, what is the fair present value of the bond?

    c. What has been the percentage change in the fair present value?

    d. Repeat parts (a), (b), and (c) for a 16-year bond.

    e. What do the respective changes in bond values indicate?

34. Consider a five-year, 15 percent annual coupon bond with a face value of $1,000. The bond is trading at a rate of 12 percent. (*LG 3-4*)

    a. What is the price of the bond?

    b. If the rate of interest increases 1 percent, what will be the bond's new price?

    c. Using your answers to parts (a) and (b), what is the percentage change in the bond's price as a result of the 1 percent increase in interest rates?

    d. Repeat parts (b) and (c) assuming a 1 percent decrease in interest rates.

    e. What do the differences in your answers indicate about the price–interest rate relationships of fixed-rate assets?

35. Consider the following. (*LG 3-7*)

    a. What is the duration of a five-year Treasury bond with a 10 percent semiannual coupon selling at par?

**b.** What is the duration of the above bond if the yield to maturity (ytm) increases to 14 percent? What if the ytm increases to 16 percent?

**c.** What can you conclude about the relationship between duration and yield to maturity?

**36.** Consider the following. (*LG 3-7*)

**a.** What is the duration of a four-year Treasury bond with a 10 percent semiannual coupon selling at par?

**b.** What is the duration of a three-year Treasury bond with a 10 percent semiannual coupon selling at par?

**c.** What is the duration of a two-year Treasury bond with a 10 percent semiannual coupon selling at par?

**d.** Using these results, what conclusions can you draw about the relationship between duration and maturity?

**37.** What is the duration of a zero-coupon bond that has eight years to maturity? What is the duration if the maturity increases to 10 years? If it increases to 12 years? (*LG 3-7*)

**38.** Suppose that you purchase a bond that matures in five years and pays a 13.76 percent annual coupon rate. The bond is priced to yield 10 percent. (*LG 3-6*)

**a.** Show that the duration is equal to four years.

**b.** Show that if interest rates rise to 11 percent next year and your investment horizon is four years from today, you will still earn a 10 percent yield on your investment.

**39.** An insurance company is analyzing the following three bonds, each with five years to maturity, annual interest payments, and is using duration as its measure of interest rate risk: (*LG 3-6*)

**a.** \$10,000 par value, coupon rate = 8%, $r_b = 0.10$

**b.** \$10,000 par value, coupon rate = 10%, $r_b = 0.10$

**c.** \$10,000 par value, coupon rate = 12%, $r_b = 0.10$

What is the duration of each of the three bonds?

**40.** MLK Bank has an asset portfolio that consists of \$100 million of 30-year, 8 percent annual coupon, \$1,000 bonds that sell at par. (*LG 3-4, LG 3-6*)

**a.** What will be the bonds' new prices if market yields change immediately by ± 0.10 percent? What will be the new prices if market yields change immediately by ± 2.00 percent?

**b.** The duration of these bonds is 12.1608 years. What are the predicted bond prices in each of the four cases using the duration rule? What is the amount of error between the duration prediction and the actual market values?

**41.** You have discovered that when the required rate of return on a bond you own fell by 0.50 percent from 9.75 percent to 9.25 percent, the fair present value rose from \$975 to \$995. The bond pays interest annually. What is the duration of this bond? (*LG 3-8*)

---

# SEARCH THE SITE

Go to the Federal Reserve Board's website and get the latest rates on 10-year T-bond and Aaa- and Baa-rated corporate bonds using the following steps. Go to **www.federalreserve.gov**. Click on "Economic Research and Data." Click on "Selected Interest Rates: –H.15." Click on the most recent date. This will bring the file onto your computer that contains the relevant data.

## Questions

1. Calculate the percentage change in the 10-year T-bond and Aaa- and Baa-rated corporate bonds since June 2016.
2. Calculate the current spread of Aaa- and Baa-rated corporate bonds over the 10-year T-bond rate. How have these spreads changed over the last two years?

---

# APPENDIX 3A: Duration and Immunization

# APPENDIX 3B: More on Convexity

# Appendixes 3A and 3B are available through Connect or your course instructor.

# The Federal Reserve System, Monetary Policy, and Interest Rates

## Learning Goals

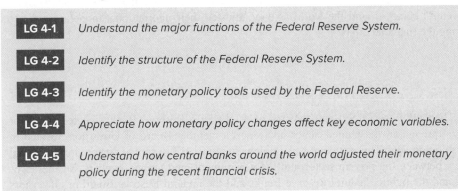

**LG 4-1**　*Understand the major functions of the Federal Reserve System.*

**LG 4-2**　*Identify the structure of the Federal Reserve System.*

**LG 4-3**　*Identify the monetary policy tools used by the Federal Reserve.*

**LG 4-4**　*Appreciate how monetary policy changes affect key economic variables.*

**LG 4-5**　*Understand how central banks around the world adjusted their monetary policy during the recent financial crisis.*

## MAJOR DUTIES AND RESPONSIBILITIES OF THE FEDERAL RESERVE SYSTEM: CHAPTER OVERVIEW

**Central banks** determine, implement, and control the monetary policy in their home countries. The Federal Reserve (the Fed) is the central bank of the United States. Founded by Congress under the Federal Reserve Act in 1913, the Fed's original duties were to provide the nation with a safer, more flexible, and more stable monetary and financial system. This was needed following a number of banking crises and panics that had occurred in the first decade of the 20th century (particularly 1907)[1] and the last decades of the 19th century. As time passed, additional legislation, including the Banking Act of 1935, the Full Employment Act of 1946, and the Full Employment and Balanced Growth Act of 1978 (also called the Humphrey-Hawkins Act), revised and supplemented the original purposes and objectives of the Federal Reserve System. These objectives included economic growth

1. The Panic of 1907 was a financial crisis that hit the United States at the turn of the 20th century while the country was in the midst of an economic recession. The New York Stock Exchange index fell by 50 percent in less than a year, and a severe drop in market liquidity by banks resulted in numerous bank runs; bank, corporate, and municipal bankruptcies; and a near collapse of the U.S. financial system.

**central banks**

*Banks that determine, implement, and control the monetary policy in their home countries.*

in line with the economy's potential to expand, a high level of employment, stable prices, and moderate long-term interest rates.

The Federal Reserve System is an independent central bank in that its decisions do not have to be ratified by the president or another member of the executive branch of the U.S. government. The system is, however, subject to oversight by the U.S. Congress under its authority to coin money. Further, the Federal Reserve is required to work within the framework of the overall objectives of economic and financial policies established by the U.S. government.

The Federal Reserve System has evolved into one of the most powerful economic bodies in the world and was critical in implementing policies to address the worldwide financial crisis in 2008–2009. Even the hint of a change in interest rate policy by the Fed can have an impact on markets around the world. Its duties incorporate four major functions: (1) conducting monetary policy; (2) supervising and regulating depository institutions; (3) maintaining the stability of the financial system; and (4) providing payment and other financial services to the U.S. government, the public, financial institutions, and foreign official institutions.

In this chapter, we present an overview of the Federal Reserve System. We start with a basic description, highlighting its organization and structure. We then examine the monetary policy tools available to the Fed and how the Fed uses these tools to influence the U.S. money supply and interest rates both domestically and internationally. As part of the discussion, the chapter highlights actions taken by the Fed during the recent financial crisis (e.g., expanding its role as a lender of last resort and purchaser/guarantor of distressed assets of banks and other FIs). Finally, we look at the independent and coordinated efforts of central banks around the world as they adjusted their international monetary policies during the financial crisis.

## STRUCTURE OF THE FEDERAL RESERVE SYSTEM

**LG 4-2**

The Federal Reserve System consists of 12 Federal Reserve Banks located in major cities throughout the United States and a seven-member Board of Governors located in Washington, DC. This structure was implemented in 1913 to spread power along regional lines, between the private sector and the government, and among bankers, businesspeople, and the public. Federal Reserve Banks and the Federal Reserve Board of Governors together comprise and operate the Federal Open Market Committee (FOMC), which is responsible for the formulation and implementation of monetary policy.

www.federalreserve.gov

### Organization of the Federal Reserve System

www.newyorkfed.org

The Federal Reserve System is divided into 12 Federal Reserve districts that are the "operating arms" of the central banking system (see Figure 4–1). Each district has one main Federal Reserve Bank, some of which also have branches in other cities within the district (identified in Figure 4–1). In addition to carrying out the functions for the central banking system as a whole, each Reserve bank acts as a depository institution for the banks in its district. In terms of total assets, the 3 largest Federal Reserve Banks are the New York, San Francisco, and Richmond banks. Together these 3 banks hold over 65 percent of the total assets (discussed later) of the Federal Reserve System. The Federal Reserve Bank of New York (FRBNY) is generally considered the most important of the Federal Reserve Banks because so many of the largest U.S. and international banks are located in the New York district. Further, the Federal Reserve's Trading Desk, which (as discussed below) carries out all the open market purchases for the Federal Reserve, is located at the FRBNY.

Federal Reserve Banks operate under the general supervision of the Board of Governors of the Federal Reserve based in Washington, DC. Each Federal Reserve Bank has its own nine-member board of directors that oversees its operations: six are elected by member banks in the district (three are professional bankers and three are businesspeople) and

**Figure 4–1**   **Federal Reserve Districts**

☆ Board of Governors of the Federal Reserve System, Washington, DC

○ Federal Reserve Bank city

▲ Federal Reserve Branch city, by District

| | Buffalo | | Little Rock, Louisville, Memphis |
|---|---|---|---|
| | Cincinnati, Pittsburgh | | Helena |
| | Baltimore, Charlotte | | Denver, Oklahoma City, Omaha |
| | Birmingham, Jacksonville, | | El Paso, Houston, San Antonio |
| | Miami, Nashville, | | Los Angeles, Portland, |
| | New Orleans | | Salt Lake City, Seattle |
| | Detroit | | |

**Source:** Federal Reserve Board website, "The Structure of the Federal Reserve System," May 2016. www.federalreserve.gov

three are appointed by the Federal Reserve Board of Governors (directors in this group are prohibited from being employees, officers, or stockholders of a member bank). These nine directors are responsible for appointing the president of their Federal Reserve Bank.

Nationally chartered banks, those chartered by the federal government through the Office of the Comptroller of the Currency (OCC),[2] are required to become members of the Federal Reserve System (FRS). State-chartered banks (those not chartered by the OCC) can also elect to become FRS members if they meet the standards set by the FRS.[3] The primary advantage of FRS membership is direct access to the federal funds wire transfer network for interbank borrowing and lending of reserves (discussed below). Commercial banks that become members of the FRS are required to buy stock in their Federal Reserve district bank. Thus, Federal Reserve Banks are quasipublic (part private, part government) entities owned by member commercial banks in their district. Their stock, however, is not publicly traded and pays a predetermined dividend (at a maximum rate of 6 percent annually). Approximately 34 percent of all U.S. banks (holding over 84 percent of the total assets in the U.S. banking system) are currently members of the Federal Reserve System.

**www.occc.treas.gov**

2. The Office of the Comptroller of the Currency (OCC) charters, regulates, and supervises national banks in the United States to ensure a safe, sound, and competitive banking system (see Chapters 11 and 13).

3. These state-chartered banks are called state-chartered member banks. State-chartered banks that are not members of the FRS are called state-chartered nonmember banks (see Chapter 11).

Federal Reserve Banks operate as nonprofit organizations. They generate income primarily from three sources: (1) interest earned on government securities acquired in the course of Federal Reserve open market transactions (see below), (2) interest earned on reserves that banks are required to deposit at the Fed (see reserve requirements below), and (3) fees from the provision of payment and other services to member depository institutions.

## Board of Governors of the Federal Reserve System

The Board of Governors of the Federal Reserve (also called the Federal Reserve Board) is a seven-member board headquartered in Washington, DC. Each member is appointed by the president of the United States and must be confirmed by the Senate. Board members serve a nonrenewable 14-year term.[4] Board members are often individuals with PhD degrees in economics and/or an extensive background in economic research and political service, particularly in the area of banking. Board members' terms are staggered so that one term expires every other January. The president designates two members of the board to be the chair and vice chair for four-year terms. The board usually meets several times per week. As they carry out their duties, members routinely confer with officials of other government agencies, representatives of banking industry groups, officials of central banks of other countries, members of Congress, and academics.

The primary responsibilities of the Federal Reserve Board are the formulation and conduct of monetary policy and the supervision and regulation of banks. All seven board members sit on the Federal Open Market Committee, which makes key decisions affecting the availability of money and credit in the economy (see below). For example, the Federal Reserve Board, through the FOMC, can and usually does set money supply and interest rate targets. The Federal Reserve Board also sets bank reserve requirements (discussed in Chapter 13) and reviews and approves the discount rates (see below) set by the 12 Federal Reserve Banks.

The Federal Reserve Board also has primary responsibility for the supervision and regulation of (1) all bank holding companies (their nonbank subsidiaries and their foreign subsidiaries), (2) state-chartered banks that are members of the Federal Reserve System (state-chartered member banks), and (3) Edge Act and agreement corporations (through which U.S. banks conduct foreign operations).[5] The Fed also shares supervisory and regulatory responsibilities with state and other federal supervisors (e.g., the OCC, the FDIC), including overseeing both the operations of foreign banking organizations in the United States and the establishment, examination, and termination of branches, commercial lending subsidiaries, and representative offices of foreign banks in the United States. The board approves member bank mergers and acquisitions and specifies permissible nonbank activities of bank holding companies. The board is also responsible for the development and administration of regulations governing the fair provision of consumer credit (e.g., the Truth in Lending Act, the Equal Credit Opportunity Act). Finally, the Wall Street Reform and Consumer Protection Act of 2010 provided unprecedented powers to the Federal Reserve, putting it in charge of monitoring any of the country's biggest financial firms—those considered critical to the health of the financial system as a whole.

**www.occ.treas.gov**

**www.fdic.gov**

The chair of the Federal Reserve Board, currently Janet Yellen, often advises the president of the United States on economic policy and serves as the spokesperson for the Federal Reserve System in Congress and to the public. All board members share the duties of conferring with officials of other government agencies, representatives of banking industry groups, officials of the central banks of other countries, and members of Congress.

---

4. The length of the term is intended to limit the president's control over the Fed and thus to reduce political pressure on board members; the nonrenewable nature of an appointment prevents any incentives for governors to take actions that may not be in the best interests of the economy yet may improve their chances of being reappointed.

5. An Edge Act corporation is a subsidiary of a federally chartered domestic bank holding company that generally specializes in financing international transactions. An agreement corporation operates like an Edge Act but is a subsidiary of a state-chartered domestic bank. Created by the Edge Act of 1919, Edge Act corporations are exempt from certain U.S. bank regulations, thus allowing U.S. banks to compete against foreign banks on an even level. For example, Edge Act corporations are exempt from prohibitions on investing in equities of foreign corporations. Ordinarily, U.S. banks are not allowed to undertake such investments.

*Federal Open Market Committee*

**Federal Open Market
Committee (FOMC)**

*The major monetary
policy-making body of the
Federal Reserve System.*

The **Federal Open Market Committee (FOMC)** is the major monetary policy-making body of the Federal Reserve System. As alluded to earlier, the FOMC consists of the seven members of the Federal Reserve Board of Governors, the president of the Federal Reserve Bank of New York, and the presidents of four other Federal Reserve Banks (on a rotating basis). The chair of the Board of Governors is also the chair of the FOMC. The FOMC is required to meet at least four times each year in Washington, DC. However, eight regularly scheduled meetings have been held each year since 1980.

The main responsibilities of the FOMC are to formulate policies to promote full employment, economic growth, price stability, and a sustainable pattern of international trade. The FOMC seeks to accomplish this by setting guidelines regarding open market operations. **Open market operations**—the purchase and sale of U.S. government and federal agency securities—is the main policy tool that the Fed uses to achieve its monetary targets (although the operations themselves are normally carried out by traders at the Federal Reserve Bank of New York, as discussed below). The FOMC also sets ranges for the growth of the monetary aggregates, sets the federal funds rate (see below), and directs operations of the Federal Reserve in foreign exchange markets (see Chapter 9). In addition, although reserve requirements and the discount rate are not specifically set by the FOMC, their levels are monitored and guided by the FOMC. Associated with each meeting of the FOMC is the release of the Beige Book. The Beige Book summarizes information on current economic conditions by Federal Reserve district. Information included in the Beige Book is drawn from reports from bank directors, interviews with key business leaders, economists, market experts, and other sources. Meetings of the FOMC are some of the most closely watched economic meetings in the world. As the FOMC formulates and implements monetary policy, its actions affect not only the U.S. economy, but economies worldwide.

**open market
operations**

*Purchases and sales of
U.S. government and fed-
eral agency securities by
the Federal Reserve.*

*Functions Performed by Federal Reserve Banks*

As part of the Federal Reserve System, Federal Reserve Banks (FRBs) perform multiple functions. These include assistance in the conduct of monetary policy; supervision and regulation of member banks and other large financial institutions; consumer protection; and the provision of services such as new currency issue, check clearing, wire transfer, and research services to the federal government, member banks, or the general public. We summarize these functions in Table 4–1. The In the News box in this section describes how the Federal Reserve provided extraordinary services in many of these areas in response to the recent financial crisis.

**TABLE 4–1**   **Functions Performed by the Federal Reserve Banks**

**Assistance in the conduct of monetary policy**—Federal Reserve Bank presidents serve on the Federal Open Market Committee (FOMC). FRBs set and change discount rates.

**Supervision and regulation**—FRBs have supervisory and regulatory authority over the activities of banks and other large financial institutions located in their district.

**Consumer protection and community affairs**—FRBs write regulations to implement many of the major consumer protection laws and establish programs to promote community development and fair and impartial access to credit.

**Government services**—FRBs serve as the commercial bank for the U.S. Treasury.

**New currency issue**—FRBs are responsible for the collection and replacement of damaged currency from circulation.

**Check clearing**—FRBs process, route, and transfer funds from one bank to another as checks clear through the Federal Reserve System.

**Wire transfer services**—FRBs and their member banks are linked electronically through the Federal Reserve Communications System.

**Research services**—each FRB has a staff of professional economists who gather, analyze, and interpret economic data and developments in the banking sector in their district and economywide.

## The Financial Crisis: Toward an Explanation and Policy Response

In the first half of 2007, as the extent of declining home prices became apparent, banks and other financial market participants started to reassess the value of mortgages and mortgage-backed securities that they owned, especially those in the subprime segment of the housing market. The autumn of 2007 saw increasing strains in a number of market segments, including asset-backed commercial paper, and banks also began to exhibit a reluctance to lend to one another for terms much longer than overnight. This reluctance was reflected in a dramatic rise in the London Interbank Offered Rate (LIBOR) at most maturities greater than overnight. LIBOR is a measure of the rates at which international banks make dollar loans to one another. Since that initial disruption, financial markets have remained in a state of high volatility, with many interest rate spreads at historically high levels.

In response to this turbulence, the Fed and the federal government have taken a series of dramatic steps. As 2007 came to a close, the Federal Reserve Board announced the creation of a Term Auction Facility (TAF), in which fixed amounts of term funds are auctioned to depository institutions against any collateral eligible for discount window loans. So while the TAF substituted an auction mechanism for the usual fixed interest rate, this facility can be seen essentially as an extension of more conventional discount window lending. In March 2008, the New York Fed provided term financing to facilitate the purchase of Bear Stearns by J.P. Morgan Chase through the creation of a facility that took a set of risky assets

off the company's balance sheet. That month, the board also announced the creation of the Term Securities Lending Facility (TSLF), swapping Treasury securities on its balance sheet for less liquid private securities held in the private sector, and the Primary Dealer Credit Facility (PDCF). These actions, particularly the latter, represented a significant expansion of the federal financial safety net by making available a greater amount of central bank credit, at prices unavailable in the market, to institutions (the primary dealers) beyond those banks that typically borrow at the discount window. . . .

In the fall of 2008, financial markets worldwide experienced another round of heightened volatility and historic changes: Lehman Brothers filed for Chapter 11 bankruptcy protection; investment banking companies Goldman Sachs and Morgan Stanley successfully submitted applications to become bank holding companies; Bank of America purchased Merrill Lynch; Wells Fargo acquired Wachovia; PNC Financial Services Group purchased National City Corporation; and the American International Group received significant financial assistance from the Federal Reserve and the Treasury Department. On the policy front, the Federal Reserve announced the creation of several new lending facilities—including the Asset-Backed Commercial Paper Money Market Mutual Fund Liquidity Facility (AMLF), the Commercial Paper Funding Facility (CPFF), the Money Market Investor Funding Facility (MMIFF), and the Term Asset-Backed Securities Loan Facility (TALF), the last of which became operational in March

2009. The TALF was designed to support the issuance of asset-backed securities collateralized by student loans, auto loans, credit card loans, and loans guaranteed by the Small Business Administration, while also expanding the TAF and the TSLF. The creation of these programs resulted in a tremendous expansion of the Federal Reserve's balance sheet. Furthermore, Congress passed the Troubled Asset Relief Program (TARP) to be administered by the Treasury Department. And in February 2009, the president signed the American Recovery and Reinvestment Act, a fiscal stimulus program of roughly $789 billion. . . .

Much of the public policy response to turmoil in financial markets over the two years took the form of expanded lending by the Fed and central banks in other countries. The extension of credit to financial institutions has long been one of the tools available to a central bank for managing the supply of money—specifically, bank reserves—to the economy. Indeed, discount window lending by the 12 Reserve Banks was the primary means for affecting the money supply at the time the Fed was created. Over time, open market operations, in which the Fed buys and sells securities in transactions with market participants, have become the main tool for managing the money supply. Lending has become a relatively little-used tool, mainly accessed by banks with occasional unexpected flows into or out of their Fed reserve accounts late in the day. If such banks were to seek funding in the market, they would likely have to pay above-normal rates for a short-term (overnight) loan.

*continued*

## The Financial Crisis: Toward an Explanation and Policy Response

In this way, the discount window became a tool for dampening day-to-day fluctuations in the federal funds rate. In 2006, average weekly lending by the Reserve Banks through the discount window was $59 million.

Since the outset of the widespread market disruptions in the summer of 2007, the Fed has changed the terms of its lending to banks and created new lending facilities. In the first three quarters of 2008, weekly Fed lending

averaged $132.2 billion, and in the fourth quarter of the year, that figure rose to $847.8 billion.

**Source:** Aaron Steelman and John A. Weinberg, *Federal Reserve Bank of Richmond Annual Report 2008,* April 2009.

---

**discount rate**

*The interest rate on loans made by Federal Reserve Banks to financial institutions.*

**discount window**

*The facility through which Federal Reserve Banks issue loans to financial institutions.*

**Assistance in the Conduct of Monetary Policy.** As mentioned, a primary responsibility of the Federal Reserve System is to influence the monetary (and financial) conditions in U.S. financial markets and thus the economy. Federal Reserve Banks conduct monetary policy in several ways. For example, as discussed previously, 5 of the 12 Federal Reserve Bank presidents serve on the Federal Open Market Committee (FOMC), which determines monetary policy with respect to the open market sale and purchase of government securities and, therefore, interest rates. The Boards of Directors of each Federal Reserve Bank set and change the **discount rate** (the interest rate on loans made by Federal Reserve Banks to financial institutions). These loans are transacted through each Federal Reserve Bank's **discount window** and involve the discounting of eligible short-term securities in return for cash loans. Federal Reserve Bank Boards also have discretion in deciding which banks qualify for discount window loans. As discussed above, any discount rate change must be reviewed by the Board of Governors of the Federal Reserve. For example, in an attempt to stimulate the U.S. economy and prevent a severe economic recession, the Federal Reserve approved 11 decreases in the discount (and federal funds) rate in 2001.

In the spring of 2008, in an attempt to avoid a deep recession and rescue a failing financial system, the Federal Reserve took a series of unprecedented steps in the conduct of monetary policy. First, Federal Reserve Banks cut interest rates sharply, including one cut on a Sunday night in March 2008 (see below). Second, the Federal Reserve Bank of New York brokered the sale of Bear Stearns, the then fifth-largest investment bank in the United States, to J.P. Morgan Chase. Without this deal, Bear Stearns was highly likely to fail (and along with it other investment banks in similar situations as Bear Stearns). To get J.P. Morgan Chase to purchase Bear Stearns, the Fed agreed to take any losses in Bear Stearns's investment portfolio up to $29 billion. Similarly, in September 2008 AIG (one of the world's largest insurance companies) met with Federal Reserve officials to ask for desperately needed cash. Concerned about how the firm's failure would impact the U.S. financial system, the Federal Reserve agreed to lend $40 billion to AIG to prevent its failure. The financial crisis saw the Fed's widening regulatory arm moving beyond depository institutions to other types of financial institutions. Third, for the first time Federal Reserve Banks lent directly to Wall Street investment banks. In the first three days, securities firms borrowed an average of $31.3 billion per day from the Fed.

While the Federal Reserve's conduct of monetary policy is primarily designed to affect the U.S. economy, in our ever increasing global economy, any policy changes made by the Fed also influence, and are influenced by, international developments. For example, as discussed below and in Chapter 9, the Fed's monetary policy actions affect the U.S. dollar for foreign currency exchange rates. A change in the foreign exchange value of the dollar affects the foreign currency price of U.S. goods bought and sold on world markets as well as the dollar price of foreign goods purchased by U.S. citizens. These transactions, in turn, affect output and price levels in the U.S. economy. Therefore, it is essential that the Federal Reserve and the FOMC incorporate information about and analysis of international transactions, movements in foreign exchange rates, and other international developments as well as U.S. domestic influences when formulating appropriate monetary policy.

**Supervision and Regulation.**   Each Federal Reserve Bank has supervisory and regulatory authority over the activities of state-chartered member banks and bank holding companies located in their districts. These activities include (1) the conduct of examinations and inspections of member banks, bank holding companies, and foreign bank offices by teams of bank examiners; (2) the authority to issue warnings (e.g., cease and desist orders should some banking activity be viewed as unsafe or unsound); and (3) the authority to approve various bank and bank holding company applications for expanded activities (e.g., mergers and acquisitions). Further, in the area of bank supervision and regulation, innovations in international banking require continual assessments of, and occasional modifications in, the Federal Reserve's procedures and regulations.

Notably, after March 2008, as the Fed stepped in to save investment bank Bear Stearns from failure, politicians proposed an expanded role for the Fed as the main supervisor for all financial institutions. In July 2010, the U.S. Congress passed the Wall Street Reform and Consumer Protection Act, which called for the Fed to supervise the most complex financial companies in the United States and gave regulators (including the Fed) authority to seize and break up any troubled financial firm whose collapse might cause widespread economic damage. Thus, the Fed's supervision and regulation duties have spread to include commercial banks as well as other types of financial institutions.

**Consumer Protection and Community Affairs.**   The U.S. Congress has assigned the Federal Reserve, through FRBs, with the responsibility to implement federal laws intended to protect consumers in credit and other financial transactions. These responsibilities include writing and interpreting regulations to carry out many of the major consumer protection laws; reviewing bank compliance with the regulations; investigating complaints from the public about state member banks' compliance with consumer protection laws; addressing issues of state and federal jurisdiction; testifying before Congress on consumer protection issues; and conducting community development activities. Further, community affairs offices at FRBs engage in a wide variety of activities to help financial institutions, community-based organizations, government entities, and the public understand and address financial services issues that affect low- and moderate-income people and geographic regions.

**Government Services.**   As discussed, the Federal Reserve serves as the commercial bank for the U.S. Treasury (U.S. government). Each year government agencies and departments deposit and withdraw billions of dollars from U.S. Treasury operating accounts held by Federal Reserve Banks. For example, it is the Federal Reserve Banks that receive deposits relating to federal unemployment taxes, individual income taxes withheld by payroll deduction, and so on. Further, some of these deposits are not protected by deposit insurance and must be fully collateralized at all times. It is the Federal Reserve Banks that hold collateral put up by government agencies. Finally, Federal Reserve Banks are responsible for the operation of the U.S. savings bond scheme, the issuance of Treasury securities, and other government-sponsored securities (e.g., Fannie Mae, Freddie Mac—see Chapter 7). Federal Reserve Banks issue and redeem savings bonds and Treasury securities, deliver government securities to investors, provide for a wire transfer system for these securities (the Fedwire), and make periodic payments of interest and principal on these securities.

**New Currency Issue.**   Federal Reserve Banks are responsible for the collection and replacement of currency (paper and coin) from circulation. They also distribute new currency to meet the public's need for cash. For example, at the end of 1999 the Fed increased the printing of currency to meet the estimated $697 billion demand for currency resulting from the Y2K scare, in which it was feared that computers worldwide (incapable of recognizing the year 2000) would cease to function on January 1, 2000. Afraid that bank accounts would be lost, depositors withdrew funds in record amounts. More recently, beginning in 2011, there was talk of the Treasury minting a $1 trillion platinum coin as a way of addressing the U.S. debt ceiling crisis. A few, otherwise intended, sentences in the 1997 Omnibus Consolidated Appropriations Act allowed such a minting as long as the coin was platinum. Advocates argued that minting the $1 trillion coin to pay off some of the national debt was a better option than the continued fighting by political leaders over raising the U.S. debt ceiling. However, talk of this solution was relatively short-lived, as in January 2013 the Federal Reserve announced that if the Treasury did mint the coin and present it for payment, the Fed would not accept it.

**Check Clearing.**   The Federal Reserve System operates a central check clearing system for U.S. banks, routing interbank checks to depository institutions on which they are written and transferring the appropriate funds from one bank to another. All depository institutions have accounts with the Federal Reserve Bank in their district for this purpose. Table 4–2 shows the number and value of checks collected by the Federal Reserve Banks from 1920 through 2015.

The number of checks cleared through the system peaked in 1990, with 18.60 billion checks cleared. For several reasons, this fell to 5.45 billion by 2015. Industry consolidation and greater use of electronic products has resulted in a reduction in the number of checks written and thus cleared through the Federal Reserve System. Further, in October 2004, the Check 21 Act, enacted by the Congress and the Federal Reserve, allowed banks to destroy checks after taking a digital image that is then processed electronically. The act begins the process of moving to a paperless environment. Check 21 authorizes the use of a substitute check (Image Replacement Document) for settlement. The new law is designed to encourage the adoption of electronic check imaging. It was prompted partly by the September 11 attacks, which grounded the cargo airplanes that flew 42 billion checks a year around the United States, threatening to disrupt the financial system. The switch to electronic processing of checks has saved as much as $3 billion a year for the banking industry. For customers, the implications are mixed. Because checks are processed much more quickly, check writers have lost the "float" of several days between the time checks are deposited and when they are debited from the account.

**Wire Transfer Services.**   The Federal Reserve Banks and their member banks are linked electronically through the Federal Reserve Communications System. This network allows these institutions to transfer funds and securities nationwide in a matter of minutes. Two electronic (wire) transfer systems are operated by the Federal Reserve: Fedwire and the Automated Clearinghouse (ACH). Fedwire is a network linking more than 7,300 domestic banks with the Federal Reserve System. Banks use this network to make deposit and loan payments, to transfer book entry securities among themselves, and to act as payment agents on behalf of

**TABLE 4–2**   Number and Value of Checks and Electronic Transactions Processed by the Federal Reserve

| | Checks Cleared | | Fedwire Transactions Processed | | ACH Transactions Processed | |
|---|---|---|---|---|---|---|
| Year | Number (in billions) | Value (in trillions of dollars) | Number (in billions) | Value (in trillions of dollars) | Number (in billions) | Value (in trillions of dollars) |
| 1920 | 0.42 | $ 0.15 | 0.5 | $ 0.03 | n.a. | n.a. |
| 1930 | 0.91 | 0.32 | 2.0 | 0.20 | n.a. | n.a. |
| 1940 | 1.18 | 0.28 | 0.8 | 0.09 | n.a. | n.a. |
| 1950 | 1.96 | 0.86 | 1.0 | 0.51 | n.a. | n.a. |
| 1960 | 3.42 | 1.15 | 3.0 | 2.43 | n.a. | n.a. |
| 1970 | 7.16 | 3.33 | 7.0 | 12.33 | n.a. | n.a. |
| 1980 | 15.72 | 8.04 | 43.0 | 78.59 | 227 | $ 0.29 |
| 1990 | 18.60 | 12.52 | 62.6 | 199.07 | 1,435 | 4.66 |
| 2000 | 16.99 | 13.85 | 108.3 | 379.76 | 4,651 | 14.02 |
| 2005 | 12.23 | 15.68 | 132.4 | 518.50 | 8,303 | 15.96 |
| 2010 | 7.71 | 8.81 | 125.1 | 608.32 | 11,455 | 21.37 |
| 2015 | 5.45 | 8.11 | 142.8 | 834.60 | 13,856 | 25.62 |

large corporate customers.[6] Fedwire transfers are typically large dollar payments (averaging $5.85 million per transaction). The ACH was developed jointly by the private sector and the Federal Reserve System in the early 1970s and has evolved as a nationwide method to electronically process credit and debit transfers of funds. Table 4–2 shows the number and dollar value of Fedwire and ACH transactions processed by Federal Reserve Banks from 1920 through 2015. In contrast to the falling volume of checks cleared by the Federal Reserve, electronic Fedwire and ACH transactions processed have grown significantly in recent years.

**Research Services.**   Each Federal Reserve Bank has a staff of professional economists who gather, analyze, and interpret economic data and developments in the banking sector as well as the overall economy. These research projects are often used in the conduct of monetary policy by the Federal Reserve. Research papers are freely accessible to the public, are of very high quality, and are quite readable. This makes them one of the best resources for economists, investors, FI managers, and any other individual interested in the operations and performance of the financial system.

### Balance Sheet of the Federal Reserve

Table 4–3 shows the balance sheet for the Federal Reserve System for various years from 2007 through 2016. The conduct of monetary policy by the Federal Reserve involves changes in the assets and liabilities of the Federal Reserve System, which are reflected in the Federal Reserve System's balance sheet.

**TABLE 4–3**   **Balance Sheet of the Federal Reserve** *(in billions of dollars)*

| Assets | 2007 | 2008 | 2010 | 2013 | 2016 | Percentage of Total, 2016 |
|---|---|---|---|---|---|---|
| U.S. official reserve assets | $   34.2 | $   35.7 | $   37.0 | $   34.5 | $   30.5 | 0.7% |
| SDR certificates | 2.2 | 2.2 | 5.2 | 5.2 | 5.2 | 0.1 |
| Treasury currency | 38.7 | 38.7 | 43.5 | 45.0 | 47.6 | 1.0 |
| Federal Reserve float | −0.0 | −1.5 | −1.4 | −0.6 | −0.0 | −0.0 |
| Interbank loans | 48.6 | 559.7 | 0.2 | 0.0 | 0.1 | 0.0 |
| Security repurchase agreements | 46.5 | 80.0 | 0.0 | 0.0 | 0.0 | 0.0 |
| U.S. Treasury securities | 740.6 | 475.9 | 1,021.5 | 1,796.0 | 2,461.6 | 54.2 |
| U.S. government agency securities | 0.0 | 19.7 | 1,139.6 | 1,143.4 | 1,780.4 | 39.2 |
| Miscellaneous assets | 40.5 | 1,060.2 | 207.6 | 220.3 | 216.8 | 4.8 |
| Total assets | $ 951.3 | $2,270.6 | $2,453.2 | $3,243.8 | $4,542.2 | 100.0% |

| Liabilities and Equity | 2007 | 2008 | 2010 | 2013 | 2016 | |
|---|---|---|---|---|---|---|
| Depository institution reserves | $   20.8 | $   860.0 | $   968.1 | $1,790.4 | $1,977.2 | 43.5% |
| Vault cash of commercial banks | 55.0 | 57.7 | 52.7 | 59.7 | 74.2 | 1.6 |
| Deposits due to federal government | 16.4 | 365.7 | 340.9 | 79.4 | 333.7 | 7.4 |
| Deposits due to government agencies | 1.7 | 21.1 | 13.5 | 20.2 | 31.1 | 0.7 |
| Currency outside banks | 773.9 | 832.2 | 930.0 | 1,117.3 | 1,350.8 | 29.7 |
| Security repurchase agreements | 44.0 | 88.4 | 59.7 | 105.5 | 712.4 | 15.7 |
| Miscellaneous liabilities | 2.5 | 3.4 | 35.3 | 16.2 | 23.3 | 0.5 |
| Federal Reserve Bank stock | 18.5 | 21.1 | 26.5 | 27.6 | 29.5 | 0.7 |
| Equity | 18.5 | 21.0 | 26.5 | 27.5 | 10.0 | 0.2 |
| Total liabilities and equity | $951.3 | $2,270.6 | $2,453.2 | $3,243.8 | $4,542.2 | 100.0% |

**Source:** Federal Reserve Board, "Flow of Fund Accounts," *Monetary Authority,* June 2016, p. L.109. www.federalreserve.gov

6. A second major wire transfer service is the Clearing House Interbank Payments System (CHIPS). CHIPS operates as a private network, independent of the Federal Reserve. At the core of the CHIPS system are approximately 50 large U.S. and foreign banks acting as correspondent banks for smaller domestic and international banks in clearing mostly international transactions in dollars.

**reserves**

*Depository institutions' vault cash plus reserves deposited at Federal Reserve Banks.*

**monetary base**

*Currency in circulation and reserves (depository institution reserves and vault cash of commercial banks) held by the Federal Reserve. Also referred to as money base.*

**required reserves**

*Reserves the Federal Reserve requires banks to hold.*

**excess reserves**

*Additional reserves banks choose to hold.*

**Liabilities.** The major liabilities on the Fed's balance sheet are currency in circulation and **reserves** (depository institution reserve balances in accounts at Federal Reserve Banks plus vault cash on hand at commercial banks). Their sum is often referred to as the Fed's **monetary base** or **money base.** We can represent these as follows:

**Reserves**—depository institution reserve balances at the Fed plus vault cash.
**Money base**—currency in circulation plus reserves.

For example, in March 2016 the monetary base totaled $3.90 trillion, of which $2.46 trillion was reserves and $1.44 trillion was currency in circulation. As we show below, changes in these accounts are the major determinants of the size of the nation's money supply—increases (decreases) in either or both of these balances (e.g., currency in circulation or reserves) will lead to an increase (decrease) in the money supply (see below for a definition of the U.S. money supply).

**Reserve Deposits.** The largest liability on the Federal Reserve's balance sheet (43.5 percent of total liabilities and equity) is depository institution reserves. All banks hold reserve accounts at their local Federal Reserve Bank. These reserve holdings are used to settle accounts between depository institutions when checks and wire transfers are cleared (see above). Reserve accounts also influence the size of the money supply (as described below).

Total reserves can be classified into two categories: (1) **required reserves** (reserves that the Fed requires banks to hold by law) and (2) **excess reserves** (additional reserves over and above required reserves) that banks choose to hold themselves. Required reserves are reserves banks must hold by law to back a portion of their customer transaction accounts (deposits). For example, the Federal Reserve currently requires up to 10 cents of every dollar of transaction deposit accounts at U.S. commercial banks to be backed with reserves (see Chapter 13). Thus, required reserves expand or contract with the level of transaction deposits and with the required reserve ratio set by the Federal Reserve Board. Because these deposits earn little interest, banks try to keep excess reserves to a minimum. Excess reserves, on the other hand, may be lent by banks to other banks that do not have sufficient reserves on hand to meet their required levels.

As the Federal Reserve implements monetary policy, it uses the market for excess reserves. For example, in the fall of 2008, the Federal Reserve implemented several measures to provide liquidity to financial markets that had frozen up as a result of the financial crisis. The liquidity facilities introduced by the Federal Reserve in response to the crisis created a large quantity of excess reserves at depository institutions (DIs). Specifically, in October 2008 the Federal Reserve began paying interest on excess reserves for the first time.[7] Further, during the financial crisis, the Fed set the interest rate it paid on excess reserves equal to its target for the federal funds rate (see below). This policy essentially removed the opportunity cost of holding reserves. That is, the interest banks earned by holding excess reserves was approximately equal to what was previously earned by lending to other FIs. As a result, banks drastically increased their holdings of excess reserves at Federal Reserve Banks. Because the U.S. economy was slow to recover from the financial crisis, the Fed kept the fed funds rate at historic lows into 2016. Thus, banks continued to hold large amounts of excess reserves. Note in Table 4–3 that depository institution reserves were 43.5 percent of total liabilities and equity of the Fed in 2016, up from 37.9 percent in 2008. This in turn was up from 2.2 percent in 2007, prior to the start of the financial crisis.

Some observers claim that the large increase in excess reserves implied that many of the policies introduced by the Federal Reserve in response to the financial crisis were ineffective. Rather than promoting the flow of credit to firms and households, critics argued that the increase in excess reserves indicated that the money lent to banks and other FIs

7. On October 1, 2008, the Board of Governors amended its rules governing the payment of interest on *excess* reserves so that the interest rate on excess balances was set at 25 basis points.

by the Federal Reserve in late 2008 and 2009 was simply sitting idle in banks' reserve accounts. Many asked why banks were choosing to hold so many reserves instead of lending them out, and some claimed that banks' lending of their excess reserves was crucial for resolving the credit crisis. In this case, the Fed's lending policy generated a large quantity of excess reserves without changing banks' incentives to lend to firms and households. Thus, the total level of reserves in the banking system is determined almost entirely by the actions of the central bank and is not necessarily affected by private banks' lending decisions.

**Currency Outside Banks.** The second-largest liability, in terms of percentage of total liabilities and equity, of the Federal Reserve System is currency in circulation (29.7 percent of total liabilities and equity in 2016). At the top of each Federal Reserve note ($1 bill, $5 bill, $10 bill, etc.) is the seal of the Federal Reserve Bank that issued it. Federal Reserve notes are basically IOUs from the issuing Federal Reserve Bank to the bearer. In the United States, Federal Reserve notes are recognized as the principal medium of exchange and therefore function as money (see Chapter 1).

**Assets.** The major assets on the Federal Reserve's balance sheet are Treasury and government agency (i.e., Fannie Mae, Freddie Mac) securities, Treasury currency, and gold and foreign exchange. While interbank loans (loans to domestic banks) are quite a small portion of the Federal Reserve's assets, they play an important role in implementing monetary policy (see below).

**Treasury Securities.** Treasury securities (54.2 percent of total assets in 2016) are the largest asset on the Fed's balance sheet. They represent the Fed's holdings of securities issued by the U.S. Treasury (U.S. government). The Fed's open market operations involve the buying and selling of these securities. An increase (decrease) in Treasury securities held by the Fed leads to an increase (decrease) in the money supply.

**U.S. Government Agency Securities.** U.S. government agency securities are the second-largest asset account on the Fed's balance sheet (39.2 percent of total assets in 2016). However, in 2007 this account was 0.0 percent of total assets. This account grew as the Fed took steps to improve credit market liquidity and support the mortgage and housing markets during the financial crisis by buying mortgage-backed securities (MBS) backed by Fannie Mae, Freddie Mac, and Ginnie Mae. Under the MBS purchase program, the FOMC called for the purchase of up to $1.25 trillion of agency MBS. The purchase activity began on January 5, 2009, and continued through 2016. Thus, the Fed expanded its role as purchaser/guarantor of assets in the financial markets.

**Gold and Foreign Exchange and Treasury Currency.** The Federal Reserve holds Treasury gold certificates that are redeemable at the U.S. Treasury for gold. The Fed also holds small amounts of Treasury-issued coinage and foreign-denominated assets to assist in foreign currency transactions or currency swap agreements with the central banks of other nations.

**Interbank Loans.** As mentioned earlier, depository institutions in need of additional funds can borrow at the Federal Reserve's discount window (discussed in detail below). The interest rate or discount rate charged on these loans is often lower than other interest rates in the short-term money markets (see Chapter 5). As we discuss below, in January 2003 the Fed implemented changes to its discount window lending policy that increased the cost of discount window borrowing but eased the requirements on which depository institutions can borrow. As part of this change, the discount window rate was increased so that it would be higher than the fed funds rate. As a result, (discount) interbank loans are normally a relatively small portion of the Fed's total assets.

---

**DO YOU UNDERSTAND:**

1. What the main functions of Federal Reserve Banks are?

2. What the main responsibilities of the Federal Reserve Board are?

3. How the FOMC implements monetary policy?

4. What the main assets and liabilities of the Federal Reserve are?

**Miscellaneous Assets.** Generally, miscellaneous assets are a small portion of the Fed's total assets (e.g., 4.8 percent in 2016). However, during the financial crisis, the Fed undertook a number of measures to support various sectors of the financial markets. For example, as mentioned above (and below), during the financial crisis, the Fed provided AIG with a loan to prevent its failure; lent funds (for the first time ever) through its discount window to brokers and dealers; and committed over $1 trillion of loans to support the commercial paper market. These temporary programs were recorded as miscellaneous assets and, as a result, this item rose to 46.7 percent of total assets in 2008.

## MONETARY POLICY TOOLS

**LG 4-3**

In the previous section of this chapter, we referred briefly to tools or instruments that the Federal Reserve uses to implement its monetary policy. These included open market operations, the discount rate, and reserve requirements. In this section, we explore the tools or instruments used by the Fed to implement its monetary policy strategy.[8] Figure 4–2 illustrates the monetary policy implementation process that we will be discussing in more detail below. Regardless of the tool the Federal Reserve uses to implement monetary policy, the major link by which monetary policy impacts the macroeconomy occurs through the Federal Reserve influencing the market for bank reserves (required and excess reserves held as depository institution reserve balances in accounts at Federal Reserve Banks plus the vault cash on hand of commercial banks). Specifically, the Federal Reserve's monetary policy seeks to influence either the demand for, or supply of, excess reserves at depository institutions and in turn the money supply and the level of interest rates. As we describe in the next section, a change in excess reserves resulting from the implementation of monetary policy triggers a sequence of events that affect such economic factors as short-term interest rates, long-term interest rates, foreign exchange rates, the amount of money and credit in the economy, and ultimately the levels of employment, output, and prices. Some of the specific economic variables the Federal Reserve works to affect as it implements monetary policy are listed in Table 4–4. These economic variables are referred to as the index of leading indicators. A leading indicator is a measurable economic factor that changes before the economy starts to follow a particular pattern or trend, and, as such, can be used to predict future economic trends.

**Figure 4–2** **Federal Reserve Monetary Policy Activities**

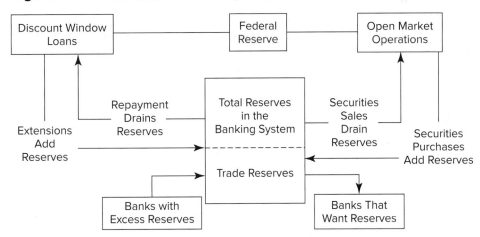

**Source:** Federal Reserve Board website, "Purposes & Functions." www.federalreserve.gov

8. In addition to the tools described here, the Fed (as well as the Federal Deposit Insurance Corporation and the Office of the Comptroller of the Currency) can indirectly affect the money supply by signaling to bankers to tighten or loosen credit availability. Further, changes in other types of regulations such as capital requirements can affect the money supply. Finally, the U.S. Congress and the U.S. Treasury can use fiscal policy (the use of government expenditure and revenue collection through taxation) to affect the level of aggregate demand in the economy to achieve economic objectives.

**TABLE 4–4**    **List of Leading Economic Indicators**

Average number of weekly hours worked by manufacturing workers
Average number of initial applications for unemployment insurance
Number of manufacturers' new orders for consumer goods and materials
Speed of delivery of new merchandise to vendors from suppliers
Number of new orders for capital goods unrelated to defense
Number of new building permits for residential buildings
S&P 500 stock index
Inflation-adjusted monetary supply (M2)
Spread between long- and short-term interest rates
Consumer sentiment

**fed funds rate**

*The interest rate on short-term funds transferred between financial institutions, usually for a period of one day.*

Depository institutions trade excess reserves held at their local Federal Reserve Banks among themselves. Banks with excess reserves—whose reserves exceed their required reserves—have an incentive to lend these funds (generally overnight) to banks in need of reserves since excess reserves held in the vault or on deposit at the Federal Reserve earn little or no interest. The rate of interest (or price) on these interbank transactions is a benchmark interest rate, called the federal funds rate or **fed funds rate,** which is used in the United States to guide monetary policy. The fed funds rate is a function of the supply and demand for federal funds among banks and the effects of the Fed's trading through the FOMC.

Further, the Financial Services Regulatory Relief Act of 2006 authorized the Federal Reserve to pay interest on reserve balances held by depository institutions effective October 1, 2011. Because of the severity of the financial crisis and the need by the Fed to have as many tools available to fight off the crisis, the Emergency Economic Stabilization Act of 2008 moved the effective date to October 1, 2008. The interest rate on required reserves (IORR) is determined by the Fed and is intended to eliminate effectively the implicit tax that reserve requirements used to impose on depository institutions (see Chapter 13). The interest rate on excess reserves (IOER) is also determined by the board and gives the Federal Reserve an additional tool for the conduct of monetary policy. Specifically, during monetary policy normalization, the Federal Reserve intends to move the federal funds rate into the target range set by the FOMC primarily by adjusting the IOER rate. As indicated in the minutes of the March 2015 FOMC meeting, the Federal Reserve intends to set the IOER rate equal to the top of the target range for the federal funds rate. Thus, as of December 2015, both the IORR and the IOER rates were set at 0.50 percent.

In implementing monetary policy, the Federal Reserve can take one of two basic approaches to affect the market for banks' excess reserves: (1) it can target the quantity of reserves in the market based on the FOMC's objectives for the growth in the monetary base (the sum of currency in circulation and reserves) and, in turn, the money supply (see below); or (2) it can target the interest rate on those reserves (the fed funds rate). The actual approach used by the Federal Reserve has varied according to considerations such as the need to combat inflation or the desire to encourage sustainable economic growth (we discuss the various approaches below). Since 1993, the FOMC has implemented monetary policy mainly by targeting interest rates (mainly using the fed funds rate as a target).

As mentioned earlier, to reduce the effects of an economic slowdown in the United States, the Fed decreased the fed funds rate 11 times in 2001. This was done to soften the effects of the collapse of the dot-com bubble and the September 2001 terrorist attacks, as well as to combat the perceived risk of deflation. Even into August 2003 the FOMC took the unusual step of foreshadowing its future policy course by announcing that the historically low interest rates could be maintained for a considerable period. Although the FOMC did not specify the length of the considerable period, it was not until the summer of 2004 that the Fed increased the fed funds rate (initially by 0.25 percent). It has been argued that this lowering of interest rates was a contributing factor to the rise in housing prices. From 2000 to 2003, the Federal Reserve lowered the fed funds target from 6.5 percent to

## Fed Cuts Rates to Record Low

In an effort to prevent a worsening recession, in December of 2008 the U.S. Federal Reserve made the unprecedented decision to cut its benchmark interest rates to as low as zero. According to a Fed spokesperson, "The Federal Reserve will employ all available tools to promote the resumption of sustainable economic growth and to preserve price stability." In a historic move, the Fed lowered its target for the benchmark federal funds rates from 1.0 percent to a record low range of zero to 0.25 percent.

The Fed also mentioned that it was considering additional ways to support and boost the faltering economy, including expanding a plan to purchase large amounts of debt issued or guaranteed by government-sponsored mortgage agencies and purchasing longer-term U.S. Treasury debt. According to the Fed, "The focus of the committee's policy going forward will be to support the functioning of financial markets and stimulate the economy through open market operations and other measures that sustain the size of the Federal Reserve's balance sheet at a high level."

In an article from Reuters, Michael Woolfolk, senior currency strategist at the Bank of New York-Mellon in New York, said, "It's a highly unorthodox and creative step. We think it's the best possible move for the U.S. consumer and for the financial market." Even with a large and varied number of new initiatives planned to encourage lending by banks, as of late 2008, U.S. authorities had been unable to stop the recession from worsening. They increased their efforts after the increased economic disruption and confusion that accompanied the failure of Lehman Brothers in September of 2008.

In the fall of 2008, the Fed also injected huge amounts of money into credit markets, increasing the size of its balance sheet from $887 billion to $2.2 trillion over just three months. According to Ian Shephardson, chief U.S. economist for High Frequency Economics in Valhalla, New York, the decision "is a reflection of an utterly desolate economic picture, which will persist for the foreseeable future as the wrenching adjustment in household finances continues."

**Source:** Mark Felsenthal, "Fed Cuts Rates to Record Low," *Reuters,* December 16, 2008, http://www.reuters.com/article/us-usa-fed-preview-idUSN1550484520081216.

1.0 percent. The Fed believed that interest rates could be lowered safely primarily because the rate of inflation was low. However, some have argued that the Fed's interest rate policy during the early 2000s was misguided, because measured inflation in those years was below true inflation, which led to a monetary policy that contributed to the housing bubble. Low interest rates and the increased liquidity provided by the central bank resulted in a rapid expansion in mortgage financing as demand for residential mortgages rose dramatically, especially among those who had previously been excluded from participating in the market because of their poor credit ratings.

The Fed then raised the fed funds rate significantly between July 2004 and August 2006; it increased the rate by 0.25 percent for 17 straight meetings. As a result, the fed funds rate rose from a 46-year low of 1 percent in July 2004 to 5.25 percent in August 2006. This contributed to an increase in one-year and five-year adjustable-rate mortgage (ARM) rates and triggered resets of rates on existing ARMs, making ARM interest payments more expensive for homeowners. This also may have contributed to the deflating of the housing bubble, as asset prices generally move inversely to interest rates and it became riskier to speculate in housing.

Then, on December 16, 2008, as the U.S. economy faced a severe financial crisis and fell into its deepest recession since the Great Depression, the Fed, in a historic move, unexpectedly announced that it would drop its target fed funds rate to a range between 0 and one-quarter of 1 percent and lowered its discount window rate (see below) to one-half percent, the lowest level since the 1940s (see the In the News box in this section). The overall reduction in the federal funds rate between late 2007 and December 2008 was dramatic, going from 5.26 percent in September 2007 to a range of 0 percent to 0.25 percent as of December 16, 2008. The rate remained at these historically low levels into 2010, and in June 2010 the Fed announced that the fed funds rate would remain at these levels for an "extended period." It was not until the spring and summer of 2013 that the Fed mentioned the end of these low interest rates and the tightening of monetary policy. And even then, the Fed repeatedly stated that the end of its monetary easing actions would not come until the very slow economic growth picked up. It was not until December 2015 that the Fed eventually raised interest rates (for the first time in 10 years).

### Open Market Operations

www.newyorkfed.org

**Federal Reserve Board Trading Desk**

*Unit of the Federal Reserve Bank of New York through which open market operations are conducted.*

**policy directive**

*Statement sent to the Federal Reserve Board Trading Desk from the FOMC that specifies the daily amount of open market purchases or sales to transact.*

As mentioned earlier, open market operations are the Federal Reserves's purchases or sales of securities in the U.S. Treasury securities market. When a targeted monetary aggregate or interest rate level is determined by the FOMC, it is forwarded to the **Federal Reserve Board Trading Desk** at the Federal Reserve Bank of New York (FRBNY) through a statement called the **policy directive.** The manager of the Trading Desk uses the policy directive to instruct traders on the daily amount of open market purchases or sales to transact. These transactions take place on an over-the-counter market in which traders are linked to each other electronically (see Chapter 5).

To determine a day's activity for open market operations, the staff at the FRBNY begins each day with a review of developments in the fed funds market since the previous day and a determination of the actual amount of reserves in the banking system the previous day. The staff also reviews forecasts of short-term factors that may affect the supply and demand of reserves on that day. With this information, the staff decides the level of transactions needed to obtain the desired fed funds rate. The process is completed with a daily conference call to the Monetary Affairs Division at the Board of Governors and one of the four voting Reserve Bank presidents (outside of New York) to discuss the FRBNY plans for the day's open market operations. Once a plan is approved, the Trading Desk is instructed to execute the day's transactions.

Open market operations are particularly important because they are the primary determinant of changes in bank excess reserves in the banking system and thus directly impact the size of the money supply and/or the level of interest rates (e.g., the fed funds rate). When the Federal Reserve purchases securities, it pays for the securities by either writing a check on itself or directly transferring funds (by wire transfer) into the seller's account. Either way, the Fed credits the reserve deposit account of the bank that sells it (the Fed) the securities. This transaction increases the bank's excess reserve levels. When the Fed sells securities, it either collects checks received as payment or receives wire transfers of funds from these agents (such as banks) using funds from their accounts at the Federal Reserve Banks to purchase securities. This reduces the balance of the reserve account of a bank that purchases securities. Thus, when the Federal Reserve sells (purchases) securities in the open market, it decreases (increases) banks' (reserve account) deposits at the Fed.

---

**EXAMPLE 4–1**    **Purchases of Securities by the Federal Reserve**

Suppose the FOMC instructs the FRBNY Trading Desk to purchase $500 million of Treasury securities. Traders at the FRBNY call primary government securities dealers of major commercial and investment banks (such as Goldman Sachs and Morgan Stanley),[9] who provide a list of securities they have available for sale, including the denomination, maturity, and the price on each security. FRBNY traders seek to purchase the target number of securities (at the desired maturities and lowest possible price) until they have purchased the $500 million. The FRBNY then notifies its government bond department to receive and pay the sellers for the securities it has purchased. The securities dealer sellers (such as

---

9. As of June 2016, there were 23 primary securities dealers trading, on average, $0.82 trillion of securities per day.

banks) in turn deposit these payments in their accounts held at their local Federal Reserve Bank. As a result of these purchases, the Treasury securities account balance of the Federal Reserve System is increased by $500 million and the total reserve accounts maintained by these banks and dealers at the Fed are increased by $500 million. We illustrate these changes to the Federal Reserve's balance sheet in Table 4–5. In addition, there is also an impact on commercial bank balance sheets. Total reserves (assets) of commercial banks will increase by $500 million due to the purchase of securities by the Fed, and demand deposits (liabilities) of the securities dealers (those who sold the securities) at their banks will increase by $500 million.[10] We also show the changes to commercial banks' balance sheets in Table 4–5.

Note the Federal Reserve's purchase of Treasury securities has increased the total supply of bank reserves in the financial system. This in turn increases the ability of banks to make new loans and create new deposits. For example, in March 2009 the Federal Reserve announced that it would buy $300 billion of long-term Treasury securities over the next six months in order to try and get credit flowing to the financial markets. This program was eventually referred to as the Fed's Quantitative Easing 1 (QE1) program. The Fed generally conducts open market operations using short-term Treasury bills (to set the fed funds rate) and generally does not intervene in long-term Treasury markets (allowing the market to set long-term rates). In fact, the Fed had not purchased long-term Treasury securities since the 1960s. In November 2010, the Fed followed up its QE1 program with QE2, in which it purchased $600 billion of long-term Treasury securities between November 2010 and June 2011. In September 2012 the Fed announced the beginning of QE3, an open-ended program involving the purchase of $40 billion of Treasury securities per month. QE3 ended in October 2014. The results of the QE programs can be seen on the Federal Reserve's balance sheet in Table 4–3. Treasury securities totaled $2.46 trillion in 2016, up from $741 billion in 2007, while depository institution reserves were $1.98 trillion in 2016, up from $21 billion in 2007. The message to the financial markets from these actions was that the Fed was willing to do whatever was necessary to stabilize the economy until it had sufficiently recovered from the financial crisis.

**TABLE 4–5**  Purchase of Securities in the Open Market

| Change in Federal Reserve's Balance Sheet | | | |
|---|---|---|---|
| **Assets** | | **Liabilities** | |
| Treasury securities | + $500m | Reserve account of securities dealers' banks | + $500m |

| Change in Commercial Bank Balance Sheets | | | |
|---|---|---|---|
| **Assets** | | **Liabilities** | |
| Reserve accounts at Federal Reserve | + $500m | Securities dealers' demand deposit accounts at banks | + $500m |

## EXAMPLE 4–2    Sale of Securities by the Federal Reserve

Suppose the FOMC instructs the FRBNY Trading Desk to sell $500 million of securities. Traders at the FRBNY call government securities dealers who provide a list of securities they are willing to buy, including the price on each security. FRBNY traders sell

---

10. In reality, not all of the $500 million will generally be deposited in demand deposit accounts of commercial banks, and commercial banks will not generally hold all of the $500 million in reserve accounts of Federal Reserve Banks. We relax these simplifying assumptions and look at the effect on total reserves and the monetary base later in the chapter.

securities to these dealers at the highest prices possible until they have sold $500 million. The FRBNY then notifies its government bond department to deliver the securities to, and receive payment from, the buying security dealers. The securities dealers pay for these securities by drawing on their deposit accounts at their commercial banks. As a result of this sale, the Treasury securities account balance for the Federal Reserve System is decreased by $500 million (reflecting the sale of $500 million in Treasury securities) and the reserve accounts maintained at the Fed by commercial banks that handle these securities transactions for the dealers are decreased by $500 million. The changes to the Federal Reserve's balance sheet in this case would have the opposite sign (negative) as those illustrated in Table 4–5. In addition, total reserves of commercial banks have decreased by $500 million due to the purchase of securities from the Fed, and demand deposits of the securities dealers at their banks have decreased by $500 million (reflecting the payments for the securities by the securities dealers). Commercial banks' balance sheet changes would have the opposite sign as those illustrated in Table 4–5 for a purchase of securities.

Note that the Federal Reserve's sale of Treasury or other government securities has decreased the total supply of bank reserves in the financial system. This in turn decreases the ability of banks to make loans and create new deposits.

While the Federal Reserve conducts most of its open market operations using Treasury securities, other government securities can be used as well. For example, in addition to the purchase of Treasury securities, the QE programs of the Federal Reserve also involved the purchase of over $1 trillion Fannie Mae and Freddie Mac mortgage-backed securities and bonds. The purchase of these securities is evident on the Fed's balance sheet in Table 4–3. In 2016, the Fed's holding of U.S. government agency securities was $1.78 trillion, up from $0 in 2007. Treasury securities are used most, however, because the secondary market for such securities is highly liquid and there is an established group of primary dealers who also trade extensively in the secondary market. Thus, the Treasury securities market can absorb a large number of buy and sell transactions without experiencing significant price fluctuations.

### The Discount Rate

The discount rate is the second monetary policy tool or instrument used by the Federal Reserve to control the level of bank reserves (and thus the money supply or interest rates). As defined previously, the discount rate is the rate of interest Federal Reserve Banks charge on loans to financial institutions in their district. The Federal Reserve can influence the level and price of reserves by changing the discount rate it charges on these loans.

Specifically, changing the discount rate signals to the market and the economy that the Federal Reserve would like to see higher or lower rates in the economy. Thus, the discount rate is like a signal of the FOMC's intentions regarding the tenor of monetary policy. For example, raising the discount rate signals that the Fed would like to see a tightening of monetary conditions and higher interest rates in general (and a relatively lower amount of borrowing). Lowering the discount rate signals a desire to see more expansionary monetary conditions and lower interest rates in general.

For two reasons, the Federal Reserve has rarely used the discount rate as a monetary policy tool. First, it is difficult for the Fed to predict changes in bank discount window borrowing when the discount rate changes. There is no guarantee that banks will borrow more (less) at the discount window in response to a decrease (increase) in the discount rate. Thus, the exact direct effect of a discount rate change on the money supply is often uncertain. The In the News box in this section demonstrates how in August 2007, the Fed's lowering of the discount rate to calm financial markets battered by deteriorating conditions in the mortgage and other debt markets resulted in little effect on the borrowing by banks. However, the Fed's lowering of the fed funds rate less than a month later resulted in a surge in discount window borrowing.

Second, because of its "signaling" importance, a discount rate change often has great effects on the financial markets. For example, the unexpected decrease in the Fed's discount rate (to 0.50 percent) on December 16, 2008, resulted in a 359.61 point increase in the Dow Jones Industrial Average, one of the largest one-day point gains in the history of the Dow and one of a handful of up days during the height of the financial crisis. Moreover, virtually all interest rates respond in the same direction (if not the same amount) to the discount rate change. For example, Figure 4–3 shows the correlation in four major U.S. interest rates (discount rate, prime rate [the rate banks charge to large corporations for short-term loans], three-month CD rate, and three-month T-bill rate) from 1990 through June 2016.

In general, discount rate changes are used only when the Fed wants to send a strong message to financial markets to show that it is serious about wanting to implement new monetary policy targets. For example, Federal Reserve Board members commented that the December 16, 2008, discount rate change was taken in light of a deterioration in labor market conditions and a decline in consumer spending, business investment, and industrial production. Further, financial markets remained quite strained and credit conditions tight. The board commented that overall, the outlook for economic activity had weakened further. Thus, this drop in the discount rate was intended to signal the Fed's strong and persistent intention to allow the money supply to increase and to stimulate economic growth. The discount rate stayed at this historical low until February 2010, when the Fed raised the rate to 0.75 percent.

Historically, discount window lending was limited to depository institutions (DIs) with severe liquidity needs. The discount window rate, which was set below the fed funds rate, was charged on loans to depository institutions only under emergency or special liquidity

**Figure 4–3**   Various U.S. Interest Rates

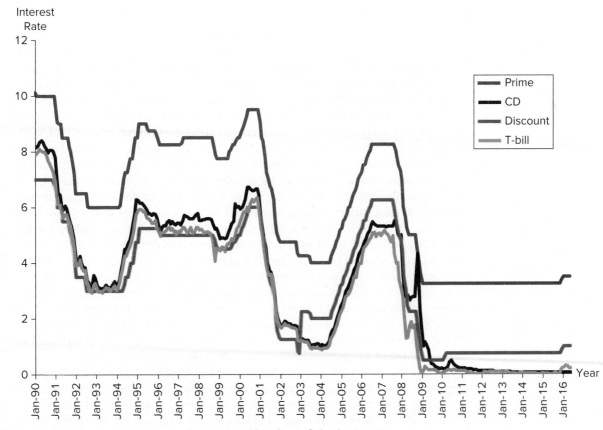

## Top Four Banks Tap Fed Discount Window

In August of 2007, top banks in the United States, including Citigroup and Bank of America, borrowed $2 billion from the U.S. Federal Reserve. This rare move was designed to stabilize and reassure U.S. markets and change the perceived stigma around receiving assistance from the central bank. Traditionally, borrowing funds from the Fed can be perceived as a sign of financial weakness, but three large banks, J.P. Morgan Chase & Co, Bank of America, and Wachovia Corp. claim that they made the choice in the interest of helping the financial system. According to Reuters, "All four banks have emphasized that they have access to other, cheaper funds."

After the transactions occurred, U.S. shares rose, though bank stocks'

performance continued to be mixed because of persistent concerns about worsening mortgage and mortgage backed securities markets. Nevertheless, the banks' choice to borrow from the Fed signaled credit markets may be starting to heal. Other banks may also start to follow the lead of their larger counterparts. Robert Albertson, chief strategist at Sandler O'Neill in New York, says, "The psychology is, if a bank needs to borrow from the discount window, and they think there's a stigma attached to it, they can say, 'Citi has done it, too.'"

Traditionally, banks tend to hesitate to borrow funds from the Fed's discount window. In the past, it has been seen as a sign that a bank is in distress. Discount window borrowing

also often resulted in additional regulation and oversight. Borrowing from the Fed no longer requires additional federal supervision, but "the stigma remains," according to Richard DeKaser, chief economist at National City Corp. in Cleveland.

Across the world, central banks are adapting to the financial crisis by pumping liquidity into the global economy. The losses in the U.S. subprime mortgage market continue to make credit difficult to obtain in a range of markets such as commercial paper and junk bonds.

**Source:** Dan Wilchins, "Top Four Banks Tap Fed Discount Window," *Reuters*, August 22, 2007, http://www.reuters. com/article/us-banks-federalreserve- idUSN2243173420070822.

situations (see Figure 4–3, 1990–2002). However, in January 2003 the Fed implemented changes to its discount window lending that increased the cost of borrowing but eased the terms. Specifically, three lending programs are now offered through the Fed's discount window. Primary credit is available to generally sound depository institutions on a very short-term basis, typically overnight, at a rate above the Federal Open Market Committee's target rate for federal funds. Primary credit may be used for any purpose, including financing the sale of fed funds. Primary credit may be extended for periods of up to a few weeks to depository institutions in generally sound financial condition that cannot obtain temporary funds in the financial markets at reasonable terms. Secondary credit is available to depository institutions that are not eligible for primary credit. It is extended on a very short-term basis, typically overnight, at a rate that is above the primary credit rate. Secondary credit is available to meet backup liquidity needs when its use is consistent with a timely return to a reliance on market sources of funding or the orderly resolution of a troubled institution. Secondary credit may not be used to fund an expansion of the borrower's assets. The Federal Reserve's seasonal credit program is designed to assist small depository institutions in managing significant seasonal swings in their loans and deposits. Seasonal credit is available to depository institutions that can demonstrate a clear pattern of recurring intrayearly swings in funding needs. Eligible institutions are usually located in agricultural or tourist areas. Under the seasonal program, borrowers may obtain longer-term funds from the discount window during periods of seasonal need so that they can carry fewer liquid assets during the rest of the year and make more funds available for local lending.

With the change, discount window loans to healthy banks would be priced at 1 percent above the fed funds rate rather than below, as it generally was in the period preceding January 2003. Note in Figure 4–3 the jump in the discount window rate in January 2003. Loans to troubled banks would cost 1.5 percent above the fed funds rate. The changes were intended not to change the Fed's use of the discount window to implement monetary policy, but to significantly increase the discount rate while making it easier to get a discount window loan. By increasing banks' use of the discount window as a source of funding, the Fed hoped to reduce volatility in the fed funds market as well. The change also allowed healthy banks to borrow from the Fed regardless of the availability of private funds. Previously, the Fed required borrowers to prove they could not get funds from the private sector, which put a stigma on discount window borrowing. With the changes, the Fed lends to all banks, but the subsidy of below fed fund rate borrowing is gone.

The Fed took additional unprecedented steps, expanding the usual function of the discount window, to address the financial crisis. While the discount window had traditionally been available only to DIs, in the spring of 2008 (as Bear Stearns nearly failed) investment banks gained access to the discount window through the Primary Dealer Credit Facility (PDCF). In the first three days, securities firms borrowed an average of $31.3 billion per day from the Fed. The largest expansion of the discount window's availability to all FIs occurred in the wake of the Lehman Brothers's failure, as a series of actions were taken in response to the increasingly fragile state of financial markets.

During the financial crisis, the Fed also significantly reduced the spread (premium) between the discount rate and the federal funds target to just one-quarter of a point, bringing the discount rate down to one-half percent. With lower rates at the Fed's discount window and interbank liquidity scarce as many lenders cut back their lending, more financial institutions chose to borrow at the discount window. The magnitude and diversity of nontraditional lending programs and initiatives developed during the crisis were unprecedented in Federal Reserve history. The lending programs were all designed to "unfreeze" and stabilize various parts of the credit markets, with the overall goal that parties receiving credit via these new Fed programs would, in turn, provide funding to creditworthy individuals and firms.

### Reserve Requirements (Reserve Ratios)

The third monetary policy tool available to the Federal Reserve to achieve its monetary targets is depository institution reserve requirements. As defined previously, reserve requirements determine the minimum amount of reserve assets (vault cash plus bank deposits at Federal Reserve Banks) that depository institutions must maintain by law to back transaction deposit accounts (e.g., demand deposits and interest-bearing checking accounts) held as liabilities on their balance sheets. This requirement is usually set as a ratio of transaction accounts—for example, 10 percent (see Chapter 13 for a detailed description of the process used by depository institutions to calculate required reserves). A decrease in the reserve requirement ratio means that depository institutions may hold fewer reserves (vault cash plus reserve deposits at the Fed) against their transaction accounts (deposits). Consequently, they are able to lend out a greater percentage of their deposits, thus increasing credit availability in the economy. As new loans are issued and used to finance consumption and investment expenditures, some of these funds spent will return to depository institutions as new deposits by those receiving them in return for supplying consumer and investment goods to bank borrowers. In turn, these new deposits, after deducting the appropriate reserve requirement, can be used by banks to create additional loans, and so on. This process continues until the banks' deposits have grown sufficiently large such that banks willingly hold their *current* reserve balances at the new lower reserve ratio. Thus, a decrease in the reserve requirement results in a multiplier increase in the supply of bank deposits and thus the money supply. The multiplier effect can be written as follows:

Change in bank deposits = (1/New reserve requirement)

× Increase in reserves created by reserve requirement change

Conversely, an increase in the reserve requirement ratio means that depository institutions must hold more reserves against the transaction accounts (deposits) on their balance sheet. Consequently, they are able to lend out a smaller percentage of their deposits than before, thus decreasing credit availability and lending, and eventually, leading to a multiple contraction in deposits and a decrease in the money supply. Now the multiplier effect is written as:

Change in bank deposits = (1/New reserve requirement)

× Decrease in reserves created by reserve requirement change

---

**EXAMPLE 4–3** **Increasing the Money Supply by Lowering Banks' Reserve Requirements on Transaction Accounts**

City Bank currently has $400 million in transaction deposits on its balance sheet. The current reserve requirement, set by the Federal Reserve, is 10 percent. Thus, City Bank must have reserve assets of at least $40 million ($400 million × 0.10) to back its deposits. In this simple framework, the remaining $360 million of deposits can be used to extend loans to borrowers. Table 4–6, Panel A, illustrates the Federal Reserve's and City Bank's balance sheets, assuming City Bank holds all of its reserves at the Fed (i.e., City Bank has no vault cash).

If the Federal Reserve decreases the reserve requirement from 10 percent to 5 percent, City Bank's minimum reserve requirement decreases by $20 million, from $40 million to $20 million ($400 million × 0.05). City Bank can now use $20 million of its reserves at its local Federal Reserve Bank (since these are now excess reserves that earn little interest) to make new loans. Suppose, for simplicity, that City Bank is the only commercial bank (in practice, the multiplier effect described below will work the same except that deposit growth will be spread over a number of banks). Those who borrow the $20 million from the bank will spend the funds on consumption and investment goods and services and those who produce and sell these goods and services will redeposit the $20 million in funds received from their sale at their bank (assumed here to be City Bank). We illustrate this redeposit of funds in Figure 4–4. As a result of these transaction deposits, City Bank's balance sheet changes to $420 million (shown in Panel B of Table 4–6). Because of the $20 million increase in transaction account deposits, City Bank now must increase its reserves held at the Federal Reserve Bank by $1 million ($20 million × 0.05) but still has $19 million in excess reserves with which to make more new loans from the additional deposits of $20 million (see row 2 in Figure 4–4).

Assuming City Bank continues to issue new loans and that borrowers continue to spend the funds from their loans, and those receiving the loanable funds (in exchange for the sale of goods and services) redeposit those funds in transaction deposits at City Bank, City Bank's balance sheet will continue to grow until there are no excess reserves held by City Bank (Panel C in Table 4–6). The resulting change in City Bank's deposits will be:

Change in bank deposits = (1/0.05) × (40m − 20m) = $400m

For this to happen, City Bank must willingly hold the $40 million it has as reserves. This requires City Bank's balance sheet (and its deposits) to double in size as a result of the reserve requirement decrease from 10 percent to 5 percent (i.e., $800 million deposits × 0.05 = $40 million).

---

While the deposit multiplier effect has been illustrated here using the example of a change in reserve requirements, it also holds when other monetary policy tools or instruments are changed as well (e.g., open market operations). For example, suppose the FOMC instructs the FRBNY Trading Desk to purchase $200 million in U.S. Treasury securities. If the reserve requirement is set at 10 percent, the $200 million open market purchase will result in an increase in bank reserves of $200 million, and ultimately, via the multiplier (1/0.1), an increase in bank deposits and the money supply of $2 billion:

1/0.1 × $200 million = $2,000 million = $2 billion

We have made some critical assumptions about the behavior of banks and borrowers to simplify our illustration of the impact of a change in open market operations and reserve requirements on bank deposits and the money supply. In Example 4–3 we assume that City Bank is the only bank, that it converts all (100 percent) of its excess reserves into loans, that all (100 percent) of these funds are spent by borrowers, and that all are returned to City Bank as "new" transaction deposits. If these assumptions are relaxed, the overall impact of a decrease in the reserve requirement ratio, or increase in excess reserves from an open market purchase, on the amount of bank deposits and the money supply will be smaller than illustrated, albeit still a multiplier similar to that above, and the precise effect of a change in the reserve base on the money supply is less certain. For example, in Example 4–3, if only 90 percent of any funds lent by City Bank are returned to the bank in the form of transaction deposits and 10 percent is held in cash, then the resulting change in City Bank's deposits will be:

**TABLE 4–6**  Lowering the Reserve Requirement

**Panel A: Initial Balance Sheets**

**Federal Reserve Bank**

| Assets | | Liabilities | |
|---|---|---|---|
| Securities | $ 40m | Reserve accounts | $ 40m |

**City Bank**

| Assets | | Liabilities | |
|---|---|---|---|
| Loans | $ 360m | Transaction deposits | $400m |
| Reserve deposits at Fed (10% of deposits) | 40m | | |

**Panel B: Balance Sheet Immediately after Decrease in Reserve Requirement**

**Federal Reserve Bank**

| Assets | | Liabilities | |
|---|---|---|---|
| Securities | $ 21m | Reserve accounts | $ 21m |

**City Bank**

| Assets | | Liabilities | |
|---|---|---|---|
| Loans | $ 380m | Transaction deposits | $420m |
| Reserve deposits at Fed (5% of deposits) | 21m | | |
| Cash (from liquidated reserves) | 19m | | |

**Panel C: Balance Sheet after All Changes Resulting from Decrease in Reserve Requirement**

**Federal Reserve Bank**

| Assets | | Liabilities | |
|---|---|---|---|
| Securities | $ 40m | Reserve accounts | $ 40m |

**City Bank**

| Assets | | Liabilities | |
|---|---|---|---|
| Loans | $ 760m | Transaction deposits | $800m |
| Reserve deposits at Fed (5% of deposits) | 40m | | |

**Figure 4–4**   Deposit Growth Multiplier

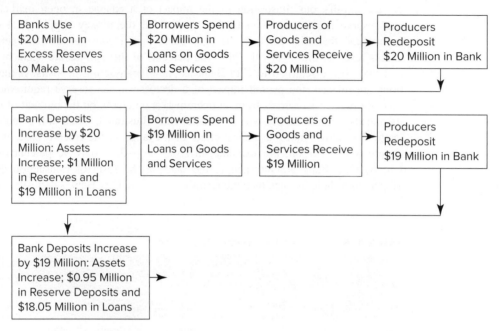

$$\text{Change in bank deposits} = [1/(\text{New reserve requirement} + c)]$$
$$\times \text{Change in reserves created by reserve requirement change}$$

where $c$ = the public's cash-to-deposit ratio or preference for holding cash outside banks relative to bank deposits = 0.1 (or 10/100). Thus, City Bank's change in deposits = [1/(0.05 + 0.1)] × (40m – 20m) = \$133.33 million.

Nevertheless, as long as some portion of the excess reserves created by the decrease in the reserve requirement are converted into loans and some portion of these loans after being spent are returned to the banking system in the form of transaction deposits, a decrease in reserve requirements will result in a multiple (that is, greater than one) increase in bank deposits, the money supply, and credit availability.

Conversely, if the Federal Reserve increases reserve requirement ratios, depository institutions must convert some of the loans on their balance sheets back into reserves held at their local Federal Reserve Bank. The overall result is that an increase in the reserve requirements will result in a multiple decline in credit availability, bank deposits, and the money supply (i.e., the multiplier effect described above will be reversed). Again, the overall effect on the money supply is not fully predictable.

Because changes in reserve requirements can result in unpredictable changes in the money supply (depending on the amount of excess reserves held by banks, the willingness of banks to make loans rather than hold other assets such as securities, and the predictability of the public's willingness to redeposit funds lent at banks instead of holding cash—that is, whether they have a stable cash-deposit ratio or not), the reserve requirement is very rarely used by the Federal Reserve as a monetary policy tool.

## DO YOU UNDERSTAND:

5. *What the major policy tools used by the Federal Reserve to influence the economy are?*

6. *What the impact is on credit availability and the money supply if the Federal Reserve purchases securities?*

7. *Why the Federal Reserve is unique in its ability to change the money supply through monetary policy tools?*

## THE FEDERAL RESERVE, THE MONEY SUPPLY, AND INTEREST RATES

LG 4-4

As we introduced this chapter, we stated that the Federal Reserve takes steps to influence monetary conditions—the money supply, credit availability, interest rates, and ultimately security prices—so it can promote price stability (low inflation) and other macroeconomic objectives. We illustrate this process in Figure 4–5. Historically, the Fed has sought to influence the economy by directly targeting the quantity of bank reserves in the market

**Figure 4–5** The Process of Monetary Policy Implementation

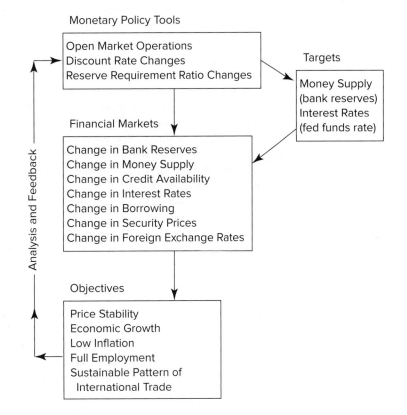

based on the FOMC's objectives for growth in the monetary base, and in turn the money supply or interest rates. In this section, we take a look at the ultimate impact of monetary policy changes on key economic variables. We also look at the Fed's choice of whether to target the money supply or interest rates in order to best achieve its overall macroeconomic objectives.

### Effects of Monetary Tools on Various Economic Variables

The examples in the previous section illustrated how the Federal Reserve and bank balance sheets change as a result of monetary policy changes. Table 4–7 goes one step further and looks at how the money supply, credit availability, interest rates, and security prices are affected by these monetary policy actions. To do this, we categorize monetary policy tool changes into expansionary activities versus contractionary activities.

**TABLE 4–7** The Impact of Monetary Policy on Various Economic Variables

| | Expansionary Activities (open market purchases of securities, discount rate decreases, reserve requirement ratio decreases) | Contractionary Activities (open market sales of securities, discount rate increases, reserve requirement ratio increases) |
|---|---|---|
| Impact on: | | |
| Reserves | ↑ | ↓ |
| Money supply | ↑ | ↓ |
| Credit availability | ↑ | ↓ |
| Interest rates | ↓ | ↑ |
| Security prices | ↑ | ↓ |

**Expansionary Activities.**   We described earlier the three monetary policy tools that the Fed can use to increase the money supply: open market purchases of securities, discount rate decreases, and reserve requirement ratio decreases. All else held constant, when the Federal Reserve purchases securities in the open market, the reserve accounts of banks increase. When the Fed lowers the discount rate, this generally results in a lowering of interest rates in the economy. Finally, a decrease in the reserve requirements, all else constant, results in an increase in bank reserves.

In two of the three cases (open market operations and reserve requirement changes), an increase in reserves results in an increase in bank deposits and the money supply. One immediate effect of this is that interest rates fall and security prices start to rise (see Chapters 2 and 3). In the third case (a discount rate change), the impact of a lowering of interest rates is more direct. Lower interest rates encourage borrowing from banks. Economic agents spend more when they can get cheaper funds. Households, businesses, and governments are more likely to invest in fixed assets (e.g., housing, plant, and equipment). Households increase their purchases of durable goods (e.g., automobiles, appliances). State and local government spending increases (e.g., new road construction, school improvements). Finally, lower domestic interest rates relative to foreign rates can result in a drop in the (foreign) exchange value of the dollar relative to other currencies.[11] As the dollar's (foreign) exchange value drops, U.S. goods become relatively cheaper compared to foreign goods. Eventually, U.S. exports increase. The increase in spending from all of these market participants results in economic expansion, stimulates additional real production, and may cause the inflation rate (defined in Chapter 2) to rise. Ideally, the expansionary policies of the Fed are meant to be conducive to real economic expansion (economic growth, full employment, sustainable international trade) without price inflation. However, when the Fed undertakes expansionary activities, the resulting increase in demand for goods and services tends to push wages and other costs higher and can lead to inflation. Indeed, price stabilization (low inflation) can be viewed as a primary policy objective of the Fed.

**Contractionary Activities.**   We also described three monetary policy tools that the Fed can use in a contractionary fashion: open market sales of securities, discount rate increases, and reserve requirement ratio increases. All else constant, when the Federal Reserve sells securities in the open market, reserve accounts of banks decrease. When the Fed raises the discount rate, interest rates generally increase in the open market, making borrowing more expensive. Finally, an increase in the reserve requirement ratio, all else constant, results in a decrease in excess reserves for all banks and limits the availability of funds for additional loans.

In all three cases, interest rates will tend to rise. Higher interest rates discourage credit availability and borrowing. Economic participants spend less when funds are expensive. Households, businesses, and governments are less likely to invest in fixed assets. Households decrease their purchases of durable goods. State and local government spending decreases. Finally, an increase in domestic interest rates relative to foreign rates may result in an increase in the (foreign) exchange value (rate) of the dollar. As the dollar's exchange rate increases, U.S. goods become relatively expensive compared to foreign goods. Eventually, U.S. exports decrease.

### Money Supply versus Interest Rate Targeting

Table 4–8 shows how the Federal Reserve has varied between its use of the money supply and interest rates as the target variable used to control economic activity in the United States. Panel a of Figure 4–6 illustrates the targeting of money supply, while Panel b of Figure 4–6 shows the targeting of interest rates. For example, letting the demand curve for money be represented as $M_D$ in Panel a of Figure 4–6, suppose the FOMC sets the target

---

11. See the discussion of the interest rate parity theorem in Chapter 9.

**TABLE 4–8**    **Federal Reserve Monetary Policy Targets**

| Target | Years |
|---|---|
| Fed funds rate targeted using bank reserves to achieve target | 1970–October 1979 |
| Nonborrowed reserves targeted | October 1979–October 1982 |
| Borrowed reserves targeted | October 1982–July 1993 |
| Fed funds rate targeted (rate announced) | July 1993–present |

money supply (currency and bank reserves) at a level that is consistent with 5 percent growth, line $M_S$ in Panel a of Figure 4–6. At this $M_S$ level, the FOMC expects the equilibrium interest rate to be $i^*$. However, unexpected increases or decreases in production, or changes in inflation, may cause the demand curve for money to shift up and to the right, $M_D'$, or down and to the left, $M_D''$. Accordingly, interest rates will fluctuate between $i'$ and $i''$. Thus, targeting the money supply can lead to periods of relatively high volatility in interest rates.

**Figure 4–6**    **Targeting Money Supply versus Interest Rates**

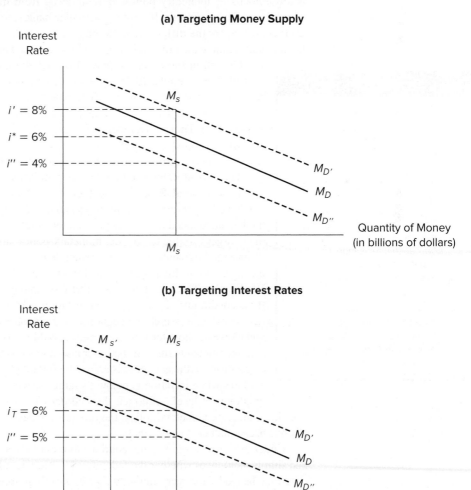

**Source:** Bank for International Settlements, *BIS Papers,* No. 48, July 2009. www.bis.org

In Panel b of Figure 4–6, suppose instead the FOMC targets the interest rate, $i_T = 6$ percent. If the demand for money falls, to $M_D''$, interest rates will fall to $i'' = 5$ percent with no intervention by the Fed. In order to maintain the target interest rate, the FOMC has to conduct monetary policy actions (such as open market sales of U.S. securities) to lower bank reserves and the money supply (to $M_S'$). This reduction in the money supply will maintain the target interest rate at $i_T = 6$ percent. As should be obvious from these graphs and the discussion, the Federal Reserve can successfully target *only one of these two variables* (money supply or interest rates) at any one moment. If the money supply is the target variable used to implement monetary policy, interest rates must be allowed to fluctuate relatively freely. By contrast, if an interest rate (such as the fed funds rate) is the target, then bank reserves and the money supply must be allowed to fluctuate relatively freely.

In the 1970s, the Fed, and then chairs Arthur Burns and G. William Miller, implemented its monetary policy strategy by targeting the federal funds rate. However, during the 1970s interest rates rose dramatically (Figure 4–7). The Fed responded to these interest rate increases by increasing the money supply, which led to historically high levels of inflation (e.g., over 10 percent in the summer of 1979). With rapidly rising inflation, Paul Volcker (chair of the Federal Reserve Board from 1979 to 1987) felt that interest rate targets were not doing an appropriate job in constraining the demand for money (and the inflationary side of the economy). Thus, on October 6, 1979, the Fed chose to completely refocus its monetary policy, moving away from interest rate targets toward targeting the money supply itself, and in particular bank reserves—so-called nonborrowed reserves, which are the difference between total reserves and reserves borrowed through the discount window (see the earlier discussion in this chapter).

Growth in the money supply, however, did not turn out to be any easier to control. For example, the Fed missed its money supply growth rate targets in each of the first three years in which reserve targeting was used. Further, in contrast to expectations, volatility in the money supply growth rate grew as well (Figure 4–7). Thus, in October 1982, the Federal Reserve abandoned its policy of targeting nonborrowed reserves for a policy of targeting borrowed reserves (those reserves banks borrow from the Fed's discount window).

The borrowed reserve targeting system lasted from October 1982 until 1993, when the Federal Reserve, and then chair Alan Greenspan, announced that it would no longer target bank reserves and money supply growth at all. At this time, the Fed announced that it would use interest rates—the federal funds rate—as the main target variable to conduct monetary policy (initially setting the target rate at a constant 3 percent). A guiding principle used by the Fed to set short-term interest rates during this period is the Taylor rule, a formula developed by economist John Taylor. The rule states that short-term interest rates should be determined by three conditions: (1) where actual inflation is relative to the Fed's targeted level, (2) the extent to which the economy is above or below its full employment level, and (3) what short-term interest rates should be to achieve full employment. The rule recommends that the Fed increase interest rates when inflation is above its target or when the economy is above the full employment level and decrease interest rates when inflation is below its target or when the economy is below the full employment level. Although the Fed does not follow the Taylor rule unequivocally in conducting monetary policy, the rule closely describes how monetary policy actually has been conducted since 1993.

Under the current regime, and contrary to previous tradition such as in the 1970s, the Fed simply announces whether the federal funds rate target has been increased, decreased, or left unchanged after every monthly FOMC meeting—previously, the federal funds rate change had kept secret. This announcement is watched very closely by financial market participants who react quickly to any change in the fed funds rate target. As a result of this regime, there has been relatively small volatility in interest rates since the late 1980s (see Figure 4–7).

**DO YOU UNDERSTAND:**

8. What actions the Federal Reserve can take to promote economic expansion? Describe how each affects money supply, credit availability, interest rates, and security prices.

9. What actions the Federal Reserve can take to contract the U.S. economy? Describe how each affects money supply, credit availability, interest rates, and security prices.

10. Why the simultaneous targeting of the money supply and interest rates is sometimes impossible to achieve?

**Figure 4–7**   Federal Funds Rates and Annualized Money Supply Growth Rates, 1977–2016

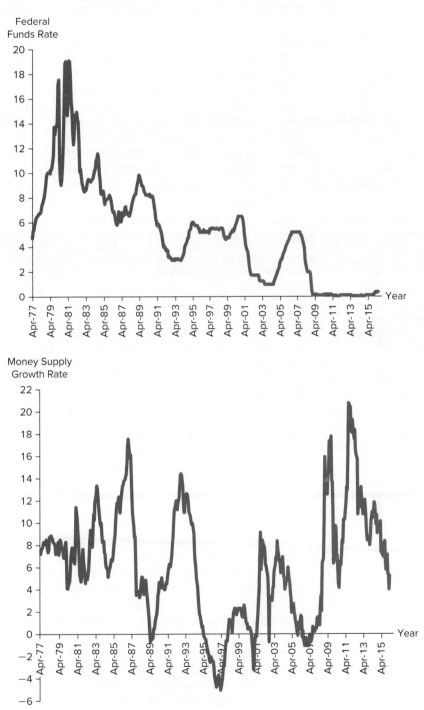

**Source:** Federal Reserve Board website, "Research and Data," June 2016. www.federalreserve.gov

In addition, following its meeting in January 2012, the FOMC issued a statement announcing that it would adopt a strategy of inflation targeting. The FOMC noted in its statement that inflation at the rate of 2 percent is most consistent over the longer run with the Federal Reserve's statutory mandate. By communicating an inflation goal the Fed hoped to clearly keep longer-term inflation expectations firmly anchored, thereby fostering price

## Minutes of the Federal Open Market Committee

At the March 2016 FOMC meeting, participants generally expected that, under appropriate monetary policy, growth in real gross domestic product (GDP) would be at or somewhat above their individual estimates of the longer-run growth rate in 2016 and 2017 and would converge toward the longer-run rate in 2018 (see table). All participants projected that by the end of the current year, the unemployment rate would decline to, or fall below, their individual estimates of the longer-run normal unemployment rate—that is, their projected unemployment gaps would be zero or negative—and that these zero or negative gaps would persist through 2018, even though many participants reduced their estimates of the longer-run normal rate. All participants projected that inflation, as measured by the four-quarter change in the price index for personal consumption expenditures (PCE), would pick up in 2016 and 2017 from the very low rate seen in 2015. Participants generally projected inflation to be either at or just slightly below the committee's 2 percent objective by the end of 2018.

**Economic Projections of Federal Reserve Board Members and Federal Reserve Bank Presidents, March 2016** *(percentage)*

| | Median | | | | Central Tendency | | | | Range | | | |
|---|---|---|---|---|---|---|---|---|---|---|---|---|
| Variable | 2016 | 2017 | 2018 | Longer | 2016 | 2017 | 2018 | Longer | 2016 | 2017 | 2018 | Longer |
| Change in real GDP | 2.2 | 2.1 | 2.0 | 2.0 | 2.1–2.3 | 2.0–2.3 | 1.8–2.1 | 1.8–2.1 | 1.9–2.5 | 1.7–2.3 | 1.8–2.3 | 1.8–2.4 |
| December projection | 2.4 | 2.2 | 2.0 | 2.0 | 2.3–2.5 | 2.0–2.3 | 1.8–2.2 | 1.8–2.2 | 2.0–2.7 | 1.8–2.5 | 1.7–2.4 | 1.8–2.3 |
| Unemployment rate | 4.7 | 4.6 | 4.5 | 4.8 | 4.6–4.8 | 4.5–4.7 | 4.5–5.0 | 4.7–5.0 | 4.5–4.9 | 4.3–4.9 | 4.3–5.0 | 4.7–5.8 |
| December projection | 4.7 | 4.7 | 4.7 | 4.9 | 4.6–4.8 | 4.6–4.8 | 4.6–5.0 | 4.8–5.0 | 4.3–4.9 | 4.5–5.0 | 4.5–5.3 | 4.7–5.8 |
| PCE inflation | 1.2 | 1.9 | 2.0 | 2.0 | 1.0–1.6 | 1.7–2.0 | 1.9–2.0 | 2.0 | 1.0–1.6 | 1.6–2.0 | 1.8–2.0 | 2.0 |
| December projection | 1.6 | 1.9 | 2.0 | 2.0 | 1.2–1.7 | 1.8–2.0 | 1.9–2.0 | 2.0 | 1.2–2.1 | 1.7–2.0 | 1.7–2.1 | 2.0 |
| Core PCE inflation | 1.6 | 1.8 | 2.0 | | 1.4–1.7 | 1.7–2.0 | 1.9–2.0 | | 1.4–2.1 | 1.6–2.0 | 1.8–2.0 | |
| December projection | 1.6 | 1.9 | 2.0 | | 1.5–1.7 | 1.7–2.0 | 1.9–2.0 | | 1.4–2.1 | 1.6–2.0 | 1.7–2.1 | 2.0 |
| Memo: Projected appropriate policy path | | | | | | | | | | | | |
| Federal funds rate | 0.9 | 1.9 | 3.0 | 3.3 | 0.9–1.4 | 1.6–2.4 | 2.5–3.3 | 3.0–3.5 | 0.6–1.4 | 1.6–2.8 | 2.1–3.9 | 3.0–4.0 |
| December projection | 1.4 | 2.4 | 3.3 | 3.5 | 0.9–1.4 | 1.9–3.0 | 2.9–3.5 | 3.3–3.5 | 0.9–2.1 | 1.9–3.4 | 2.1–3.9 | 3.0–4.0 |

stability and moderate long-term interest rates and enhancing the FOMC's ability to promote maximum employment.

Finally, in 2013 the Fed altered the purpose of its Summary of Economic Projections (SEP). Historically, the SEP contained information on FOMC meeting participants' forecasts of the unemployment rate, the change in real GDP, inflation, and core inflation rate at different points in time under appropriate monetary policy. However, since January 2012 the Fed started to disclose its members' views on the future path of the target interest rate under appropriate monetary policy as well. For example, in conjunction with the FOMC meeting held on March 16, 2016, meeting participants submitted their projections of the most likely outcomes for real output growth, the unemployment rate, inflation, and the federal funds rate for each year from 2016 to 2018 and over the longer run. The Industry Perspectives box shows the SEP for March 16, 2016. Each participant's projection is based on information available at the time of the meeting together with his or her assessment of appropriate monetary policy and assumptions about the factors likely to affect economic outcomes. The longer-run projections represent each participant's assessment of the value to which each variable would be expected to converge, over time, under "appropriate monetary policy" and in the absence of further shocks to the economy. *Appropriate monetary policy* is defined as the future path of policy that each participant deems most likely to foster outcomes for economic activity and inflation that best satisfy his or her individual interpretation of the Federal Reserve's objectives of maximum employment and stable prices.

# INTERNATIONAL MONETARY POLICIES AND STRATEGIES

Central banks guide the monetary policy in virtually all countries. For example, the European Central Bank (ECB) is the central bank for the European Union, while the Bank of England is the central bank of the United Kingdom. Like the Federal Reserve, these are independent central banks whose decisions do not need to be ratified by the government. In contrast, the People's Bank of China, the Reserve Bank of India, and the Central Bank of Brazil are less independent in that the government imposes direct political control over the operations of these central banks. Independence of a central bank generally means that the bank is free from pressure from politicians who may attempt to enhance economic activity in the short term (e.g., around election time) at the expense of long-term economic growth. Therefore, independent central banks operate with more credibility.

Regardless of their independence, in the increasingly global economy, central banks around the world must work not only to guide the monetary policy of their individual countries, but also to coordinate their efforts with those of other central banks. In this section, we look at how central banks around the world took independent as well as coordinated actions as they set their monetary policy during the financial crisis. For example, as news spread

**LG 4-5**

that Lehman Brothers would not survive, FIs around the world moved to disentangle trades made with Lehman. The Dow fell more than 500 points, the largest drop in over seven years. By Wednesday, September 17, 2008, tension had mounted around the world. Stock markets saw huge swings in value as investors tried to sort out who might survive (markets from Russia to Europe were forced to suspend trading as stock prices plunged).

As the U.S. government debated a rescue plan, the financial crisis continued to spread worldwide. During the last week of September and the first week of October 2008, the German government guaranteed all consumer bank deposits and arranged a bailout of Hypo Real Estate, the country's second-largest commercial property lender. The United Kingdom nationalized mortgage lender Bradford & Bingley (the country's eighth-largest mortgage lender) and raised deposit guarantees from $62,220 to $88,890 per account. Ireland guaranteed the deposits and debt of its six major financial institutions. Iceland rescued its third-largest bank with an $860 million purchase of 75 percent of the bank's stock and a few days later seized the country's entire banking system. The Netherlands, Belgium, and Luxembourg central governments together agreed to inject $16.37 billion into Fortis NV (Europe's first ever cross-border financial services company) to keep it afloat. However, five days later this deal fell apart and the bank was split up. The Dutch government bought all assets located in the Netherlands for approximately $23 billion. The central bank in India stepped in to stop a run on the country's second-largest bank, ICICI Bank, by promising to pump in cash. Central banks in Asia injected cash into their banking systems as banks' reluctance to lend to each other and a run on Bank of East Asia Ltd. led the Hong Kong Monetary Authority to inject liquidity into its banking system. South Korean authorities offered loans and debt guarantees to help small and midsized businesses with short-term funding. Table 4–9 lists some other systemwide support programs (e.g., on October 12, Australia committed an unspecified amount of funds to guarantee the country's bank liabilities) and bank-specific actions (e.g., on September 30, the ECB and the French government pledged $3 billion to recapitalize Dexia, one of France's largest banks) taken by central governments during the heat of the crisis. All of these actions were a result of the spread of the U.S. financial market crisis to world financial markets.

## Systemwide Rescue Programs Employed during the Financial Crisis

While the previously mentioned actions by central banks represent steps taken by individual countries, they were just part of a coordinated effort by major countries to ease the monetary conditions brought about by the financial crisis and avoid a deep worldwide recession. At the heart of the efforts were 11 countries, which accounted for the bulk of the rescue programs: Australia, Canada, France, Germany, Italy, Japan, the Netherlands, Spain, Switzerland, the United Kingdom, and the United States. The central banks in these countries took substantive actions targeted at the balance sheets of financial institutions in their

**TABLE 4–9** Central Bank Actions, September 2008–June 2009

| Date of Announcement | Country/ Institution | Type of Action | Type of Measure | Currency | Amount (inBillions)* | Description |
|---|---|---|---|---|---|---|
| 16 Sep 2008 | AIG | SAA | CI | USD | 85 | Emergency credit line to AIG from the NY Fed, in exchange for which the US Treasury gets a 79.9% equity interest. |
| 29 Sep 2008 | Fortis | SAA | CI | EUR | 4 | The Dutch government purchases 49% of the Dutch activity of Fortis Group (jointly with Belgium and Luxembourg). |
| 30 Sep 2008 | Dexia | SAA | CI | EUR | 3 | The French government recapitalizes Dexia, replacing top management positions (jointly with Belgium and Luxembourg). |
| 03 Oct 2008 | Fortis | SAA | CI | EUR | 13 | The Dutch government completes the nationalization of the Dutch arm of Fortis Group. |
| | US | PRO | AP | USD | 700 | Emergency Economic Stabilization Act, containing a commitment for up to $700 billion to purchase bad assets from banks (TARP). |
| 06 Oct 2008 | Hypo Real Estate | SAA | DG | EUR | 50 | First round of help for HRE. |
| 08 Oct 2008 | IT | PRO | CI | EUR | Unspecified | Italy approves a law granting the government the possibility to recapitalize distressed banks. |
| | GB | PRO | CI | GBP | 50 | The United Kingdom adopts a comprehensive rescue plan, including CI and DG measures. |
| | | PRO | DG | GBP | 250 | |
| 09 Oct 2008 | NL | PRO | CI | EUR | 20 | The government announces that public funds can be used for bank recapitalization, of which €20 billion immediately available. |
| 10 Oct 2008 | CA | PRO | DG | CAD | Unspecified | The government announces a scheme to guarantee bank liabilities. |
| 12 Oct 2008 | AU | PRO | DG | AUD | Unspecified | The government announces a scheme to guarantee bank liabilities. |
| 13 Oct 2008 | FR | PRO | CI | EUR | 40 | Over the weekend, euro area countries agree on a concerted action plan to preserve banking stability; as a follow-up national governments approve schemes including CI, DG and AP. |
| | | PRO | DG | EUR | 265 | |
| | DE | PRO | DG | EUR | 400 | |
| | | PRO | CI&AP | EUR | 80 | |
| | IT | PRO | DG | EUR | Unspecified | |
| | ES | PRO | DG | EUR | 100 | |
| | | PRO | CI | EUR | Unspecified | |
| | US | PRO | CI | USD | 250 | The government announces that up to $250 billion of TARP funds, originally earmarked to buy bad assets, will instead be used to recapitalize banks (Capital Purchase Program). |
| 14 Oct 2008 | NL | PRO | DG | EUR | 200 | Debt guarantee scheme approved. |
| | US | PRO | DG | USD | 2,250 | Debt guarantee scheme approved. |
| 16 Oct 2008 | UBS | SAA | AP | USD | 54 | The Swiss government recapitalizes UBS and the SNB sets up a vehicle to remove up to $60 billion worth of illiquid assets from UBS's balance sheet, on which the bank will bear the first $6 billion loss. |
| | | | CI | CHF | 6 | |
| 05 Nov 2008 | CH | PRO | DG | CHF | Unspecified | The government announces that it will—if needed—provide a guarantee on bank liabilities. |
| 10 Nov 2008 | AIG | SAA | AP | USD | 47 | Second round of help to AIG, including purchase of illiquid assets and capital injection via preferred shares (partly replacing the $85 billion credit line). |
| | | | CI | USD | 15 | |
| 13 Nov 2008 | Hypo Real Estate | SAA | DG | EUR | 20 | The government provides a guarantee on loans to HRE worth €20 billion (partly replacing the first round of measures). |
| 23 Nov 2008 | Citigroup | SAA | AG | USD | 262 | The Treasury subscribes $20 billion preferred shares and ring-fences troubled assets worth up to $306 billion (later reduced to $301 billion—on which Citigroup bears a first loss). |
| | | | CI | USD | 20 | |
| 28 Nov 2008 | IT | PRO | CI | EUR | Unspecified | The government approves a law to inject capital into sound banks. |
| 17 Dec 2008 | JP | PRO | CI | JPY | 12,000 | A law is approved increasing the available funds for recapitalization of banks from JPY 2 trillion to 12 trillion. |
| 16 Jan 2009 | Bank of America | SAA | AG | USD | 97 | The Treasury subscribes $20 billion of preferred shares and ring-fences troubled assets worth up to $118 billion (on which BoA bears a first loss). |
| | | | CI | USD | 20 | |
| 19 Jan 2009 | GB | PRO | AG | GBP | Unspecified | A new plan is announced by the government, including the possibility for financial institutions to ring-fence selected portfolios of illiquid assets through a government backstop insurance. |
| 26 Jan 2009 | ING | SAA | AG | EUR | 28 | The Dutch government provides a backup facility to cover the risks of the bank's securitized mortgage portfolio worth €35.1billion (of which ING bears a 20% loss). |
| 03 Feb 2009 | JP | PRO | AP | JPY | 1,000 | Japan reintroduces a previously abandoned programme to purchase stocks from banks' balance sheets will resume. |
| 10 Feb 2009 | US | PRO | CI | USD | Unspecified | The Obama administration announces a new plan, including the Capital Assistance Program (stress tests and capital injections) and the Public–Private Investment Program (to remove legacy assets from banks' balance sheets; committed resources have been later quantified in $75–100 billion). |
| | | PRO | AP | USD | Unspecified | |
| 02 Mar 2009 | AIG | SAA | CI | USD | 30 | Third round of help to AIG: the Treasury commits to a further $30 billion equity line, converts part of earlier preferred stock investments into instruments more closely resembling equity and restructures parts of AIG activities. |
| 17 Mar 2009 | JP | PRO | CI | JPY | 1,000 | The Bank of Japan announces a framework for providing subordinated loans to banks. |
| 13 May 2009 | DE | PRO | AG | EUR | 200 | Facility for banks to transfer toxic assets to a SPV, in exchange for government-guaranteed bonds. |
| 09 Jun 2009 | US | PRO | CI | USD | −68 | The US Treasury allows 10 big banks to pay back funds received under the Capital Purchase Program. |

SAA = standalone action; PRO = programme  CI = capital injection or emergency loan; DG = debt guarantee; AP = asset purchase; AG = asset guarantee.

*Indicates the size of government exposure for the various interventions

**Source:** Bank for International Settlements, *BIS Papers*, No. 48, July 2009. www.bis.org

**Figure 4–8** Deposit Insurance Coverage for Commercial Banks in Various Countries (USD equivalents, at current exchange rates, as of mid-September and early December 2008)

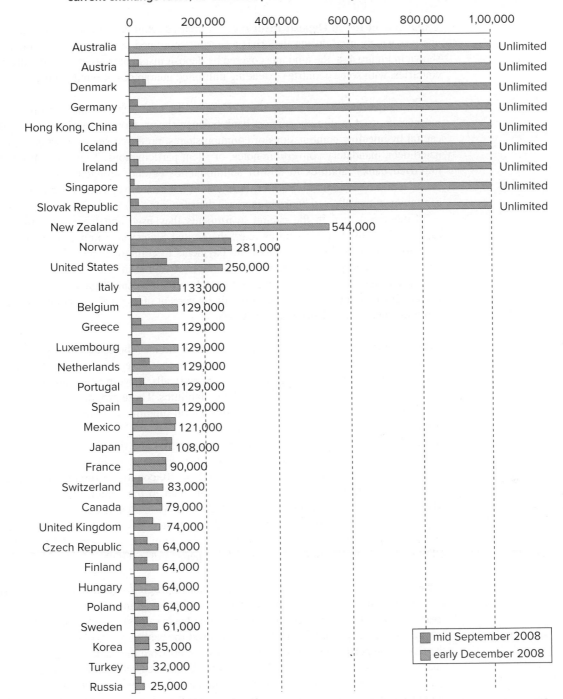

**Source:** "Financial Crisis: Deposit Insurance and Financial Safety Net Aspects," Organization for Economic Co-operation and Development working paper, December 2008. www.oecd.org

countries. The programs can be categorized into four general areas: expansion of retail deposit insurance, capital injections, debt guarantees, and asset purchases/guarantees.[12] Figure 4–8 summarizes deposit insurance coverage in various countries before versus after the start of the financial crisis, and Table 4–10 provides a more detailed overview of the

12. For a detailed summary of each of these, see *BIS Quarterly Review,* December 2008, www.bis.org.

commitments and outlays associated with capital injections, debt guarantees, and asset purchases/guarantees made by various countries.

**Expansion of Retail Deposit Insurance**    Increased retail bank deposit insurance coverage was widely used during the crisis to ensure continued access to deposit funding. As shown in Figure 4–8, the amounts covered by deposit insurance varied substantially across countries, with some countries extending unlimited guarantees of retail deposits.

**Capital Injections**    Direct injections of capital by central governments were the main mechanism used to directly support bank balance sheets. Governments increased banks' capital by injecting combinations of common shares, preferred shares, warrants, subordinated debt, mandatory convertible notes, or silent participations. These capital injections improved banks' abilities to absorb additional losses and strengthened protection for banks' uninsured creditors. Further, because they relieved balance sheet constraints, the capital injections allowed banks to increase their lending.

Countries varied in the capital instruments they used and the conditions of their capital injections. Some countries (e.g., the United States) also imposed restrictions on executive compensation and/or dividend payments to common stockholders. As seen in Table 4–10, countries also varied in the amounts of capital injected into the banking system. The Netherlands made commitments totaling 6.2 percent of the country's GDP, the United Kingdom made commitments worth 3.4 percent of its GDP, and Switzerland made commitments worth 1.1 percent of its GDP.

**Debt Guarantees**    As financial markets froze, so did the wholesale funding market used by banks to support lending activities. In response to these events, governments announced state guarantees on bank wholesale debt. Specifically, governments provided explicit guarantees against default on uninsured bank liabilities. These programs allowed banks to maintain access to reasonably priced, medium-term funding. They also reduced liquidity risk and lowered overall borrowing costs for banks.

Countries varied in the range of liabilities covered and the fee structures associated with these programs (e.g., some charged a flat fee, while others linked fees to bank credit default swap spreads). Further, as seen in Table 4–10, countries committed significantly larger amounts to the debt guarantee programs than to the capital injection programs. Many countries (e.g., Australia, Canada, Italy, and Switzerland) committed unspecified amounts for debt guarantees, the Netherlands committed an amount totaling 33.6 percent of the country's GDP, the United Kingdom made commitments worth 17.2 percent of its GDP, and Spain made commitments worth 9.1 percent of its GDP.

**Asset Purchases or Guarantees**    Asset purchase programs removed distressed assets from bank balance sheets. Thus, bank liquidity was improved and capital relief was provided (particularly if purchase prices were higher than book values). Asset guarantee programs left the distressed assets with the banks. However, the central banks assumed part or all of the risk of the portfolio of distressed or illiquid assets from the banks. Asset purchase and guarantee programs were not used extensively. A main reason for this is that it was difficult to determine the price at which the central bank would purchase the distressed assets. A purchase price set too close to par effectively amounted to a covert recapitalization of the bank. Further, there was a debate regarding the range of eligible assets. To have a significant and immediate impact on market confidence, the programs would have to cover all distressed assets, which would require large programs. As seen in Table 4–10, the United Kingdom used asset guarantees extensively (commitments amounted to 33.4 percent of the country's GDP). Beyond this, Germany committed an unspecified amount for asset purchases and an amount totaling 8.0 percent of the country's GDP for asset guarantees, while the United States committed 1.0 percent of its GDP for asset purchases and an amount totaling 2.5 percent of the country's GDP for asset guarantees.

**DO YOU UNDERSTAND:**

11. *The monetary policy measures taken by central banks to address the recent worldwide financial crisis? What were they?*

**TABLE 4–10   Summary of Central Bank Programs**

| Euro billions and percentage points | | Capital injections — Euro bn | Capital — % of GDP (2008) | Capital — % of banking sector assets (end 2008) | Debt guarantees (1) — Euro bn | Debt — % of GDP (2008) | Debt — % of banking sector assets (end 2008) | Asset purchase — Euro bn | Asset purchase — % of GDP (2008) | Asset purchase — % of banking sector assets (end 2008) | Asset guarantees (1) — Euro bn | Asset guar. — % of GDP (2008) | Asset guar. — % of banking sector assets (end 2008) | Total — Euro billions | Total — % of GDP | Total — % of banking sector assets (end 2008) |
|---|---|---|---|---|---|---|---|---|---|---|---|---|---|---|---|---|
| Australia | Commitments | – | – | – | UNS | UNS | UNS | – | – | – | – | – | – | UNS | UNS | UNS |
| | Outlays | – | – | – | 62 | 10.4 | 4.6 | – | – | – | – | – | – | 62 | 10.4 | 4.6 |
| Canada | Commitments | – | – | – | UNS | UNS | UNS | – | – | – | – | – | – | UNS | UNS | UNS |
| | Outlays | – | – | – | 0 | 0 | 0 | – | – | – | – | – | – | – | – | – |
| France | Commitments | 43 | 2.2 | 0.6 | 320 | 16.4 | 4.2 | – | – | – | 5 | 0.2 | 0.1 | 368 | 18.9 | 4.8 |
| | Outlays | 28 | 1.4 | 0.4 | 72 | 3.7 | 0.9 | – | – | – | 5 | 0.2 | 0.1 | 104 | 5.3 | 1.4 |
| Germany (2) | Commitments | 80 | 3.2 | 1.0 | 420 | 16.9 | 5.3 | UNS | UNS | UNS | 200 | 8.0 | 2.5 | 700 | 28.1 | 8.9 |
| | Outlays | 22 | 0.9 | 0.3 | 129 | 5.2 | 1.6 | 0 | 0 | 0 | 0 | 0 | 0 | 151 | 6.1 | 1.9 |
| Italy (3) | Commitments | 20 | 1.3 | 0.5 | UNS | UNS | UNS | – | – | – | – | – | – | UNS | UNS | UNS |
| | Outlays | 10 | 0.6 | 0.3 | 0 | 0 | 0 | – | – | – | – | – | – | 10 | 0.6 | 0.3 |
| Japan | Commitments | 105 | 2.5 | 1.7 | – | – | – | 8 | 0.2 | 0.1 | – | – | – | 113 | 2.7 | 0.9 |
| | Outlays | 3 | 0.1 | 0.0 | – | – | – | 0 | 0.0 | 0.0 | – | – | – | 3 | 0.1 | 0.0 |
| Netherlands | Commitments | 37 | 6.2 | 1.7 | 200 | 33.6 | 9.0 | – | – | – | 28 | 4.7 | 1.3 | 265 | 44.6 | 11.9 |
| | Outlays | 31 | 5.1 | 1.4 | 40 | 6.8 | 1.8 | – | – | – | 28 | 4.7 | 1.3 | 99 | 16.6 | 4.4 |
| Spain | Commitments | UNS | UNS | UNS | 100 | 9.1 | 3.0 | – | – | – | – | – | – | UNS | UNS | UNS |
| | Outlays | 0 | 0 | 0 | 31 | 2.8 | 0.9 | – | – | – | – | – | – | 31 | 2.8 | 0.9 |
| Switzerland | Commitments | 4 | 1.1 | 0.2 | UNS | UNS | UNS | 27 | 7.6 | 1.3 | – | – | – | UNS | UNS | UNS |
| | Outlays | 4 | 1.1 | 0.2 | 0 | 0 | 0 | 27 | 7.6 | 1.3 | – | – | – | 31 | 8.7 | 1.5 |
| United Kingdom | Commitments | 54 | 3.4 | 0.7 | 269 | 17.2 | 3.4 | – | – | – | 523 | 33.4 | 6.7 | 845 | 54.0 | 10.8 |
| | Outlays | 54 | 3.4 | 0.7 | 113 | 7.2 | 1.4 | – | – | – | 523 | 33.4 | 6.7 | 690 | 44.1 | 8.8 |
| United States (4) | Commitments | 335 | 3.0 | 3.4 | 1,760 | 15.7 | 18.0 | 115 | 1.0 | 1.3 | 281 | 2.5 | 2.9 | 2,491 | 22.3 | 25.5 |
| | Outlays | 237 | 2.1 | 2.4 | 271 | 2.4 | 2.8 | 36 | 0.3 | 0.4 | 281 | 2.5 | 2.9 | 825 | 7.4 | 8.4 |
| **Total commitments (5)** | | **677** | **2.6** | **1.1** | **3,131** | **11.8** | **5.2** | **150** | **0.6** | **0.3** | **1,036** | **3.9** | | **4,994** | **18.8** | **8.3** |
| **Total outlays** | | **387** | **1.5** | **0.6** | **719** | **2.7** | **1.2** | **64** | **0.2** | **0.1** | **836** | **3.2** | | **2,006** | **7.6** | **3.3** |

Note: As of 10 June 2009 unless otherwise specified. UNS = unspecified amount; "—" = no programme/action. Banking sector assets are consolidated data of: for Australia, banks, credit unions, building societies and corporations; for Canada, chartered banks; for Japan, depository corporations (banks and collectively managed trusts); for Switzerland, all domestic banks; for the five euro area countries and the United Kingdom, monetary financial institutions; and for the United States, commercial banks. (1) Outlays indicate the value of liabilities/assets actually under government guarantee. Debt guarantee outlays comprise only bonds publicly issued up to 29 May, except for Australia, where they indicate average daily outstanding amounts of both deposits and wholesale funding in May 2009; and for the United States, where they include all outstanding FDIC-guaranteed liabilities as of 31 May. (2) Part of the €60 billion set aside for recapitalization can be used also for asset purchase. (3) The commitment for capital injection indicates the upper bound of the global budget for the measure as approved by the European Commission; outlays include the intended (publicly announced) requests for funds not yet finalized. (4) Figures exclude the capital injections to Freddie Mac and the Fannie Mae and the $700 billion TARP commitment to buy illiquid assets (later modified for other purposes); capital injection outlays are net of funds already repaid by the time of writing. (5) Unspecified commitments are proxied by actual outlays.

**Source:** Bank for International Settlements, *BIS Papers*, No. 48, July 2009. www.bis.org

### Challenges Remain after the Crisis

While the worst of the financial crisis subsided in the United States in the last half of 2009, throughout the spring of 2010 Greece struggled with a severe debt crisis. Early on, the European Central Bank (ECB) and some of the healthier European countries tried to step in and assist the debt-ridden country. Specifically, in March 2010 the ECB, Germany, and France began formulating a plan to bail out Greece with as much as $41 billion in aid. However, in late April, Greek bond prices dropped dramatically as traders determined that a debt default was inevitable, even if the country received a massive bailout. The selloff was the result of still more bad news for Greece, which showed that the 2009 budget deficit was worse than had been previously reported. As a result, politicians in Germany began to voice opposition to a Greek bailout. Further, Moody's Investors Service downgraded Greece's debt rating and warned that additional cuts could be on the way. However, the ECB stated that it would continue to support Greece regardless of the country's credit rating.

The problems in the Greek bond market then spread to other European nations with fiscal problems, such as Portugal, Spain, and Italy. As a result, in May the ECB, Euro-zone countries, and the International Monetary Fund, seeking to halt a widening European debt crisis that had now threatened the stability of the euro, agreed to extend to Greece an unprecedented $147 billion rescue in return for huge budget cuts. Additional rescue packages and promises of further austerity measures intended to cut the burgeoning Greek deficit occurred through 2012. Yet the European debt crisis continued. While Greece had not yet missed a bond payment, in March the International Swaps and Derivatives Association (ISDA)[13] declared that Greece had undergone a "restructuring credit event" which triggered insurance policy payments. The restructuring event was a forced swap of old debt held by some of its private bond holders for new debt. The swap forced a 74 percent haircut on those creditors that held out, triggering the effective default.

At one point, Greece seemed unable to form a government and the leader of one party rejected the country's bailout commitments. It seemed increasingly conceivable that Greece might have to leave the Euro zone. Economists estimated that a Greek exit from the Euro zone would cost the European Union $1 trillion, or about 5 percent of the Union's annual economic output. Yet, the leaders of EU countries, particularly Germany and France, continued to work to keep Greek reform on track and the EU together. Further, the ECB stated that it would do whatever it took to protect the euro; the ECB prepared to move forcefully into bond markets in tandem with Europe's rescue funds and concentrated on buying shorter-term debt. Through June 2012, the cost of bailouts required to do so totaled over $480 billion and, while calmer, the crisis in the EU was not over as Spain and Italy required bailouts as well. Fear arose that, in their efforts to keep the European Union together and the euro intact, sound countries would be drawn into their own crises as they were called upon to bail out unhealthy countries.

The situation in Greece and the European Union stabilized after 2012. However, a major debt payment was due from Greece to its creditors on June 30, 2015, a payment required to continue to receive rescue funds from the EU. Knowing that they could not make the payment, Greek officials met with Euro-zone leaders in an attempt to get a better deal. Greece, however, was unwilling to agree to more spending cuts and other concessions requested by the EU and talks broke down. Greece would be the first developed country to default on its debt and faced the real possibility that it would be forced to leave the European Union. With its financial system near collapse and a debt payment due to the ECB on July 20, Greece was forced to continue negotiations with its creditors. A deal was reached on July 13 that essentially required Greece to surrender to all of its creditors' demands including tax increases, pension reform, and the creation of a fund (under European supervision) that would hold some €50 billion in state-owned

---

13. The ISDA is the trade group that oversees the market for credit default swaps. Credit default swaps are essentially insurance policies against bond defaults (see Chapter 10).

assets earmarked to be privatized or liquidated (with the proceeds to be used to pay off Greece's debt and help recapitalize its banks).

Underscoring both the importance and limits of monetary policy in a global economy, in the mid-2010s, beleaguered by painfully slow growth and anxious financial markets well after the financial crisis that began in 2008, central banks around the world went to new lengths to boost their economies. For example, in early 2016 the Bank of Japan (BOJ) set its key short-term interest rate below zero. Specifically, the BOJ charged a 0.10 percentage point penalty on excess reserves that banks keep on deposit at the BOJ. In theory, the increasingly radical steps would encourage Japan's commercial banks to circulate more money in the economy, where it can be used for investment and growth. The move followed three years of aggressive monetary easing by the BOJ, in which the central bank purchased ¥80 trillion ($660.8 billion) in government bonds a year, an amount equal to one-fifth of the size of Japan's economy. As a result, by 2016 the BOJ owned nearly one-third of the Japanese government bond market and 43 percent of Tokyo's exchange-traded stock fund market.

The move by the BOJ came a week after the European Central Bank indicated that it was ready to begin additional monetary stimulus. The central bank, trying to stimulate growth and hold off deflation in the wake of the global financial crisis, announced it would be lowering rates and buying increasing amounts of assets to get cash into their economies. The ECB set negative interest rates on some bank reserves in 2014. But the announcement indicated that the ECB would cut rates even further into negative territory in coming months. Economists predicted that Canada, Australia, Norway, and even China would also set their policy rates negative should macroeconomic conditions turn out even weaker than expected.

Negative rates have had powerful effects, in particular by driving down currencies, which helped boost inflation and exports. However, this comes at the expense of other countries to some extent. These countries often respond with easier money policies of their own. For example, between 2014 and 2016, China authorized six interest rate cuts and several reductions in required bank reserves and approved hundreds of infrastructure projects aimed at halting its economic downturn. But even with these efforts, China's economic slowdown has proved deeper than expected. In 2015, the economy grew by 6.9 percent, its slowest pace in 25 years. The People's Bank of China's decision to devalue the yuan in January 2016 was driven in part by the need to lower its own interest rates to stimulate growth. Going full circle, the lower yuan, in turn, put pressure on China's trading partners, including Japan, to ease monetary policy.

Challenges to central banks became even bigger in June 2016 when the people of the United Kingdom voted to leave the EU after 43 years (Brexit). The shock from the UK's surprise vote to leave the EU swept across global markets, triggering steep drops in stock markets and the British pound, and a flight into safe assets such as U.S. bonds and gold. The pound fell more than 11 percent to its lowest point since 1985. The DJIA dropped 610.32 points, or 3.4 percent. The Stoxx Europe 600 index fell 7 percent, its steepest drop since 2008, while Japan's Nikkei Stock Average declined 7.9 percent. Bonds also sold off sharply, pushing UK government borrowing costs sharply higher as traders and investors grappled with the market implications of Brexit. The UK had its credit rating outlook cut to "negative" by the ratings agency Moody's. Less than an hour after the markets opened in London, the governor of the Bank of England stood in front of television cameras to announce that the central bank had earmarked £250 billion (about $344 billion) to release as needed for stability. The Bank of England faces an extraordinarily tricky situation as it attempts to navigate Brexit. It simultaneously must plan for a possible recession caused by Brexit uncertainty and for higher inflation because of the drop in the currency value and outflow of capital. It can fight one of those problems, but it cannot fight both at once. So a decline in business confidence and a rise in uncertainty, paired with limited responses by central banks, makes a recession a major risk in Britain and something of a risk in the rest of Europe and the United States. The vote to leave raised the prospect of sustained anxiety in the global economy as investors struggle to surmise what is happening.

## SUMMARY

This chapter described the Federal Reserve System in the United States. The Federal Reserve is the central bank charged with conducting monetary policy, supervising and regulating depository institutions, maintaining the stability of the financial system, and providing specific financial services to the U.S. government, the public, and financial institutions. We reviewed the structure under which the Fed provides these functions, the monetary policy tools it uses, and the impact of monetary policy changes on money supply, credit availability, interest rates, security prices, and foreign exchange rates.

## QUESTIONS

1. Describe the functions performed by Federal Reserve Banks. (*LG 4-1*)

2. Define the discount rate and the discount window. (*LG 4-2*)

3. Describe the structure of the Board of Governors of the Federal Reserve System. (*LG 4-2*)

4. What are the primary responsibilities of the Federal Reserve Board? (*LG 4-1*)

5. What are the primary responsibilities of the Federal Open Market Committee? (*LG 4-2*)

6. What are the major liabilities of the Federal Reserve System? Describe each. (*LG 4-2*)

7. Why did reserve deposits increase to the point that this account represented the largest liability account on the Federal Reserve's balance sheet in the late 2000s? (*LG 4-2*)

8. What are the major assets of the Federal Reserve System? Describe each. (*LG 4-2*)

9. Why did U.S. government agency securities go from nothing to being the largest asset account on the Federal Reserve's balance sheet in the late 2000s? (*LG 4-2*)

10. What are the tools used by the Federal Reserve to implement monetary policy? (*LG 4-3*)

11. Explain how a decrease in the discount rate affects credit availability and the money supply. (*LG 4-3*)

12. Why does the Federal Reserve rarely use the discount rate to implement its monetary policy? (*LG 4-3*)

13. What changes did the Fed implement to its discount window lending policy in the early 2000s? in the late 2000s? (*LG 4-3*)

14. Which of the monetary tools available to the Federal Reserve is most often used? Why? (*LG 4-3*)

15. Describe how expansionary activities conducted by the Federal Reserve impact the money supply, credit availability, interest rates, and security prices. Do the same for contractionary activities. (*LG 4-4*)

16. Summarize the monetary policy measures taken by central banks to address the worldwide financial crisis. (*LG 4-5*)

## PROBLEMS

1. Suppose the Federal Reserve instructs the Trading Desk to purchase $1 billion of securities. Show the result of this transaction on the balance sheets of the Federal Reserve System and commercial banks. (*LG 4-3*)

2. Suppose the Federal Reserve instructs the Trading Desk to sell $850 million of securities. Show the result of this transaction on the balance sheets of the Federal Reserve System and commercial banks. (*LG 4-3*)

3. Bank Three currently has $600 million in transaction deposits on its balance sheet. The Federal Reserve has currently set the reserve requirement at 10 percent of transaction deposits. (*LG 4-3*)
   a. If the Federal Reserve decreases the reserve requirement to 8 percent, show the balance sheet of Bank Three and the Federal Reserve System just before and after the full effect of the reserve requirement change. Assume Bank Three withdraws all excess reserves and gives out loans and that borrowers eventually return all of these funds to Bank Three in the form of transaction deposits.
   b. Redo part (a) using a 12 percent reserve requirement.

4. BSW Bank currently has $150 million in transaction deposits on its balance sheet. The Federal Reserve has currently set the reserve requirement at 10 percent of transaction deposits. (*LG 4-3*)
   a. If the Federal Reserve decreases the reserve requirement to 6 percent, show the balance sheet of BSW and the Federal Reserve System just before and after the full effect of the reserve requirement change. Assume BSW withdraws all excess reserves and gives out loans and that borrowers eventually return all of these funds to BSW in the form of transaction deposits.
   b. Redo part (a) using a 14 percent reserve requirement.

5. National Bank currently has $500 million in transaction deposits on its balance sheet. The current reserve requirement is 10 percent, but the Federal Reserve is decreasing this requirement to 8 percent. (*LG 4-3*)
   a. Show the balance sheet of the Federal Reserve and National Bank if National Bank converts all excess reserves to loans, but borrowers return only 50 percent of these funds to National Bank as transaction deposits.
   b. Show the balance sheet of the Federal Reserve and National Bank if National Bank converts 75 percent of its excess reserves to loans and borrowers return 60 percent of these funds to National Bank as transaction deposits.

6. MHM Bank currently has $250 million in transaction deposits on its balance sheet. The current reserve requirement is 10 percent, but the Federal Reserve is increasing this requirement to 12 percent. (*LG 4-3*)

    a. Show the balance sheet of the Federal Reserve and MHM Bank if MHM Bank converts all excess reserves to loans, but borrowers return only 80 percent of these funds to MHM Bank as transaction deposits.

    b. Show the balance sheet of the Federal Reserve and MHM Bank if MHM Bank converts 85 percent of its excess reserves to loans and borrowers return 90 percent of these funds to MHM Bank as transaction deposits.

7. The FOMC has instructed the FRBNY Trading Desk to purchase $500 million in U.S. Treasury securities. The Federal Reserve has currently set the reserve requirement at 5 percent of transaction deposits. Assume U.S. banks withdraw all excess reserves and give out loans. (*LG 4-3*)

    a. Assume also that borrowers eventually return all of these funds to their banks in the form of transaction deposits. What is the full effect of this purchase on bank deposits and the money supply?

    b. What is the full effect of this purchase on bank deposits and the money supply if borrowers return only 95 percent of these funds to their banks in the form of transaction deposits?

8. The FOMC has instructed the FRBNY Trading Desk to purchase $750 million in U.S. Treasury securities. The Federal Reserve has currently set the reserve requirement at 10 percent of transaction deposits. Assume U.S. banks withdraw all excess reserves and give out loans. (*LG 4-3*)

    a. Assume also that borrowers eventually return all of these funds to their banks in the form of transaction deposits. What is the full effect of this purchase on bank deposits and the money supply?

    b. What is the full effect of this purchase on bank deposits and the money supply if borrowers return only 90 percent of these funds to their banks in the form of transaction deposits?

9. Marly Bank currently has $650 million in transaction deposits on its balance sheet. The current reserve requirement is 10 percent, but the Federal Reserve is decreasing this requirement to 9 percent. (*LG 4-3*)

    a. Show the balance sheet of the Federal Reserve and Marly Bank if Marly Bank converts all excess reserves to loans, but borrowers return only 60 percent of these funds to National Bank as transaction deposits.

    b. Show the balance sheet of the Federal Reserve and Marly Bank if Marly Bank converts 90 percent of its excess reserves to loans and borrowers return 75 percent of these funds to Marly Bank as transaction deposits.

10. Brown Bank currently has $350 million in transaction deposits on its balance sheet. The current reserve requirement is 10 percent, but the Federal Reserve is increasing this requirement to 11 percent. (*LG 4-3*)

    a. Show the balance sheet of the Federal Reserve and Brown Bank if Brown Bank converts all excess reserves to loans, but borrowers return only 50 percent of these funds to Brown Bank as transaction deposits.

    b. Show the balance sheet of the Federal Reserve and Brown Bank if National Bank converts 75 percent of its excess reserves to loans and borrowers return 60 percent of these funds to Brown Bank as transaction deposits.

# SEARCH THE SITE

Go to the Federal Reserve Board website and find the latest information available on the prime rate, the discount rate, and the three-month T-bill rate using the following steps. Go to **www.federalreserve.gov**. Under "Select Statistical Releases," click on "Selected Interest Rates." Click on the most recent date. The data will be in this file on your computer screen.

## Questions

1. What are the current levels for each of these interest rates?
2. Calculate the percentage change in each of these rates since June 2016.

# chapter

# Money Markets

## Learning Goals

**LG 5-1**    *Define money markets.*

**LG 5-2**    *Identify the major types of money market securities.*

**LG 5-3**    *Examine the process used to issue Treasury securities.*

**LG 5-4**    *List the main participants in money markets.*

**LG 5-5**    *Examine the extent to which foreign investors participate in U.S. money markets.*

## DEFINITION OF MONEY MARKETS: CHAPTER OVERVIEW

**LG 5-1**    In **money markets,** short-term debt instruments (those with an original maturity of one year or less) are issued by economic agents that require short-term funds (e.g., corporations that need to purchase inventory for increased production in September, the sales of which will not occur until December) and are purchased by economic agents that have excess short-term funds (e.g., individuals who receive a paycheck yet have few bills due for two months). Once issued, money market instruments trade in active secondary markets. Capital markets serve a similar function for market participants with excess funds to invest for periods of time longer than one year and/or who wish to borrow for periods longer than one year. Market participants who concentrate their investments in capital market instruments also tend to invest in some money market securities so as to meet their short-term liquidity needs. The secondary markets for money market instruments are extremely important, as they serve to reallocate the (relatively) fixed amounts of liquid funds available in the market at any particular time.

Money markets played a major role in the financial crisis of 2008–2009. As mortgage and mortgage-backed securities (MBS) markets started to experience large losses, money markets froze and banks stopped lending to each other at anything but high overnight rates. The overnight London Interbank Offered Rate (LIBOR, a benchmark rate that reflects the rate at which banks lend to one another) more than doubled, rising from 2.57 percent on September 29, 2008, to an all-time high of 6.88 percent on September 30, 2008. Further, commercial paper markets, short-term debt used to finance companies' day-to-day operations, shrank by $52.1 billion (from $1.7 trillion in size) in less than a one-week period in mid-September 2008.

**money markets**

*Markets that trade debt securities or instruments with maturities of less than one year.*

In this chapter, we present an overview of money markets. We define and review the various money market instruments that exist, the new issue and secondary market trading process for each, and the market participants trading these securities. We also look at international money markets and instruments, taking a particularly close look at the Euro markets.

## MONEY MARKETS

 LG 5-1

The need for money markets arises because the immediate cash needs of individuals, corporations, and governments do not necessarily coincide with their receipts of cash. For example, the federal government collects taxes quarterly. However, its operating and other expenses occur daily. Similarly, corporations' daily patterns of receipts from sales do not necessarily occur with the same pattern as their daily expenses (e.g., wages and other disbursements). Because excessive holdings of cash balances involve a cost in the form of forgone interest, called **opportunity cost,** those economic units with excess cash usually keep such balances to the minimum needed to meet their day-to-day transaction requirements. Consequently, holders of cash invest "excess" cash funds in financial securities that can be quickly and relatively costlessly converted back to cash when needed with little risk of loss of value over the short investment horizon. Money markets are efficient in performing this service in that they enable large amounts of money to be transferred from suppliers of funds to users of funds for short periods of time both quickly and at low cost to the transacting parties. A money market instrument provides an investment opportunity that generates a higher rate of interest (return) than holding cash (which yields zero interest), but it is also very liquid and (because of its short maturity) has relatively low default risk.

**opportunity cost**

*The forgone interest cost from the holding of cash balances when they are received.*

Notice, from the description above, that money markets and money market securities or instruments have three basic characteristics. First, money market instruments are generally sold in large denominations (often in units of $1 million to $10 million). Most money market participants want or need to borrow large amounts of cash, so that transactions costs are low relative to the interest paid. The size of these initial transactions prohibits most individual investors from investing directly in money market securities. Rather, individuals generally invest in money market securities indirectly, with the help of financial institutions such as money market mutual funds.

**default risk**

*The risk of late or non-payment of principal or interest.*

Second, money market instruments have low **default risk;** the risk of late or nonpayment of principal and/or interest is generally small. Since cash lent in the money markets must be available for a quick return to the lender, money market instruments can generally be issued only by high-quality borrowers with little risk of default.

Finally, money market securities must have an original maturity of one year or less. Recall from Chapter 3 that the longer the maturity of a debt security, the greater is its interest rate risk and the higher is its required rate of return. Given that adverse price movements resulting from interest rate changes are smaller for short-term securities, the short-term maturity of money market instruments helps lower the risk that interest rate changes will significantly affect the security's market value and price.

### DO YOU UNDERSTAND:

1. *What the three characteristics common to money market securities are?*

2. *Why it is difficult for individual investors to be involved in the initial sale of a money market security?*

## YIELDS ON MONEY MARKET SECURITIES

For many of the money market securities discussed below, returns are measured and quoted in a manner that does not allow them to be evaluated using the time value of money equations. For example, some securities interest rates or returns are based on a 360-day year, while others are based on a 365-day year. It is therefore inappropriate to compare annual interest rates on the various money market securities as well as on short-term and long-term securities without adjusting their interest rates for differences in the securities' characteristics.

### Bond Equivalent Yields

The bond equivalent yield, $i_{be}$, is the quoted nominal, or stated, yield on a security. From Chapters 2 and 3, the bond equivalent yield is the rate used to calculate the present value of an investment. For money market securities, the bond equivalent yield is the product of the periodic rate and the number of periods in a year. It is calculated as follows:

$$i_{be} = \left[ \frac{(P_f - P_0)}{P_0} \right] \times \frac{365}{n}$$

where

$P_f$ = Face value

$P_0$ = Purchase price of the security

$n$ = Number of days until maturity

### Effective Annual Return

The bond equivalent yield is a quoted nominal or stated rate earned on an investment over a one-year period. The bond equivalent yield does not consider the effects of compounding of interest during a less than one year investment horizon. If interest is paid or compounded more than once per year, the true annual rate earned is the effective annual return on an investment. The bond equivalent yield on money market securities with a maturity of less than one year can be converted to an effective annual interest return (*EAR*) using the following equation:[1]

$$EAR = \left( 1 + \frac{i_{be}}{365/n} \right)^{365/n} - 1$$

---

### EXAMPLE 5–1   Calculation of EAR on a Money Market Security

Suppose you can invest in a money market security that matures in 75 days and offers a 3 percent nominal annual interest rate (i.e., bond equivalent yield). The effective annual interest return on this security is:

$$EAR = \left( 1 + \frac{0.03}{365/75} \right)^{365/75} - 1 = 3.036\%$$

---

### Discount Yields

Some money market instruments (e.g., Treasury bills and commercial paper) are bought and sold on a discount basis. That is, instead of directly received interest payments over the investment horizon, the return on these securities results from the purchase of the security at a discount from its face value ($P_0$) and the receipt of face value ($P_f$) at maturity, as we show in the following time line.

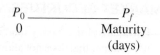

$$
\begin{array}{ll}
P_0 \rule{3cm}{0.4pt} & P_f \\
0 & \text{Maturity} \\
& \text{(days)}
\end{array}
$$

---

1. This equation assumes that as these short-term securities mature they can be reinvested for the remainder of the year at the same interest rate.

Further, yields on these securities use a 360-day year rather than a 365-day year. Interest rates on discount securities, or discount yields ($i_d$), are quoted on a discount basis using the following equation:

$$i_d = \frac{P_f - P_0}{P_f} \times \frac{360}{n}$$

There are several features of a discount yield that make it difficult to compare with bond equivalent yields on other (nondiscount) securities—for example, U.S. Treasury bonds. Notice the discount yield uses the terminal price, or the security's face value ($P_f$), as the base price in calculating an annualized interest rate. By contrast, bond equivalent yields are based on the purchase price ($P_0$) of a security. Further, and as already mentioned, discount yields generally use a 360-day rather than a 365-day year to compute interest returns. Prior to the advent of calculators and computers, it was quicker and easier for investors and traders to compute discount yields using a 360-day year. Similarly, manual calculations of discount yields were simpler using the face value (a nice round number) as the base number rather than the purchase price (which can take many values). Thus, these became the convention for calculating discount yields. Although these features mean that the discount yield is a measure of return that is incorrect, convention has not changed, even as calculators and computers have become commonplace. An appropriate comparison of interest rates on discount securities versus nondiscount securities, adjusting for both the base price and days in the year differences, requires converting a discount yield into a bond equivalent yield in the following manner:

$$i_{be} = i_d \times \frac{P_f}{P_0} \times \frac{365}{360}$$

---

**EXAMPLE 5–2**  Comparison of Discount Yield, Bond Equivalent Yield, and EAR

Suppose you can purchase a $1 million Treasury bill that is currently selling on a discount basis (i.e., with no explicit interest payments) at 98½ percent of its face value. The T-bill is 140 days from maturity (when the $1 million will be paid). Depending on the setting in which you are interested, any one of the following three yields or interest rates could be appropriate:

Discount yield: $i_d$ = [($1m. − $985,000)/$1m.](360/140) = 3.857%

Bond equivalent yield: $i_{be}$ = [($1m. − $985,000)/$985,000](365/140) = 3.970%

EAR: $EAR = [1 + 0.03970/(365/140)]^{365/140} − 1 = 4.019\%$

---

### Single-Payment Yields

Some money market securities (e.g., negotiable CDs and fed funds) pay interest only once during their lives: at maturity. Thus, the single-payment security holder receives a terminal payment consisting of interest plus the face value of the security, as we show in the following time line. Such securities are special cases of the pure discount securities that only pay the face value on maturity.

Invest $1      Receive $1 + Interest

0                Maturity (days)

Further, quoted nominal interest rates on single-payment securities (or single-payment yield, $i_{sp}$) normally assume a 360-day year. In order to compare interest rates on these securities with others, such as U.S. Treasury bonds, that pay interest based on a 365-day year, the nominal interest rate must be converted to a bond equivalent yield in the following manner:

$$i_{be} = i_{sp}(365/360)$$

Further, allowing for interest rate compounding, the EAR for single-payment securities must utilize the bond equivalent yield as follows:

$$EAR = \left[1 + \frac{i_{sp}(365/360)}{365/n}\right]^{365/n} - 1$$

or,

$$EAR = [1 + i_{be}/(365/n)]^{365/n} - 1$$

---

**EXAMPLE 5–3**   Comparison of Single-Payment Yield, Bond Equivalent Yield, and EAR

Suppose you can purchase a $1 million negotiable CD that is currently 105 days from maturity. The CD has a quoted annual interest rate of 4.16 percent for a 360-day year. The bond equivalent yield is calculated as:

$$i_{be} = 4.16\%(365/360) = 4.218\%$$

The EAR on the CD is calculated as:

$$EAR = [1 + (0.04218)/(365/105)]^{365/105} - 1 = 4.282\%$$

---

**DO YOU UNDERSTAND:**

3.  *What characteristics of a discount yield prevent it from being directly compared to a bond equivalent yield?*

Table 5–1 lists various money market instruments and their quoted interest rates, as reported in *The Wall Street Journal* for May 16, 2016. Current market rates (as well as data on stocks, bonds, foreign exchange, and other securities) can also be found at Bloomberg's website, www.bloomberg.com/markets/rates/index.html. As we proceed with the discussion of the various money market instruments, pay particular attention to the convention used to state returns in the various money markets. For example, Treasury bill rates are stated as discount yields and use a 360-day year. Commercial paper and banker's acceptance yields are also quoted as discount yields. Federal funds, repurchase agreements, and negotiable certificates of deposit are stated on a single-payment yield basis. Differences in the convention used to calculate yields must be considered particularly when comparing returns across various securities.

## MONEY MARKET SECURITIES

**LG 5-2**

A variety of money market securities are issued by corporations and government units to obtain short-term funds. These securities include Treasury bills, federal funds, repurchase agreements, commercial paper, negotiable certificates of deposit, and banker's acceptances. In this section, we look at the characteristics of each of these. Table 5–2 defines each of the money market securities, and Table 5–3 lists the amounts of each outstanding and the interest rate on each of these instruments in 1990 and 2016. As noted in previous chapters, in the late 2000s, as the U.S. economy faced a severe financial crisis and fell into its deepest recession since the Great Depression, in a historic move the Fed unexpectedly announced that it would drop its target fed funds rate to a range between zero

**TABLE 5–1** Various U.S. Money Market Security Rates

# Money Rates

May 16, 2016

Key annual interest rates paid to borrow or lend money in U.S. and international markets. Rates below are a guide to general levels but don't always represent actual transactions.

| | Latest | Week ago | —52-WEEK—<br>High | Low | | Latest | Week ago | —52-WEEK—<br>High | Low |
|---|---|---|---|---|---|---|---|---|---|
| **Prime rates** | | | | | **Commercial paper** | | | | |
| U.S. | **3.50** | 3.50 | 3.50 | 3.25 | **Nonfinancial** | | | | |
| Canada | **2.70** | 2.70 | 2.85 | 2.70 | One month | **0.34** | 0.35 | 0.36 | 0.08 |
| Euro zone | **0.00** | 0.00 | 0.05 | 0.00 | Two month | **0.41** | 0.40 | 0.42 | 0.08 |
| Japan | **1.475** | 1.475 | 1.475 | 1.475 | Three month | **0.48** | 0.46 | 0.49 | 0.09 |
| Switzerland | **0.50** | 0.50 | 0.50 | 0.50 | **Financial** | | | | |
| Britain | **0.50** | 0.50 | 0.50 | 0.50 | One month | **0.37** | 0.40 | 0.42 | 0.09 |
| Australia | **1.75** | 1.75 | 2.00 | 1.75 | Two month | **0.46** | 0.48 | 0.49 | 0.12 |
| | | | | | Three month | **0.54** | 0.57 | 0.59 | 0.15 |
| **Overnight repurchase** | | | | | | | | | |
| U.S. | **0.44** | 0.44 | 0.54 | 0.07 | **London interbank offered rate, or Libor** | | | | |
| **U.S. government rates** | | | | | One month | **0.43620** | 0.43865 | 0.44185 | 0.18300 |
| | | | | | Three month | **0.62610** | 0.62960 | 0.64195 | 0.27600 |
| **Discount** | | | | | Six month | **0.90640** | 0.90540 | 0.91740 | 0.41425 |
| | **1.00** | 1.00 | 1.00 | 0.75 | One year | **1.23265** | 1.22715 | 1.24470 | 0.72510 |
| **Federal funds** | | | | | | | | | |
| Effective rate | **0.41** | 0.40 | 0.41 | 0.06 | | | | | |
| Target rate | **0.25–0.50** | 0.25–0.50 | 0.25–0.50 | 0–0.25 | | | | | |
| High | **0.5625** | 0.5625 | 0.5900 | 0.3100 | | | | | |
| Low | **0.3000** | 0.3400 | 0.3600 | 0.0200 | | | | | |
| Bid | **0.3600** | 0.3700 | 0.5500 | 0.0400 | | | | | |
| Offer | **0.3800** | 0.5000 | 0.5600 | 0.0800 | | | | | |
| **Treasury bill auction** | | | | | | | | | |
| 4 weeks | **0.245** | 0.170 | 0.295 | 0.000 | | | | | |
| 13 weeks | **0.275** | 0.240 | 0.350 | 0.000 | | | | | |
| 26 weeks | **0.370** | 0.380 | 0.585 | 0.065 | | | | | |
| **Banker's acceptances** | | | | | | | | | |
| 30 days | **0.40** | – | – | – | | | | | |
| 60 days | **0.50** | – | – | – | | | | | |
| 90 days | **0.58** | – | – | – | | | | | |
| 180 days | **0.88** | – | – | – | | | | | |

**Source:** *The Wall Street Journal Online*, May 17, 2016. www.wsj.com

and one-quarter of 1 percent and lowered its discount window rate to one-half percent, the lowest level since the 1940s. The lowering of the fed funds and discount window rates filtered through to affect all money market rates, dropping them to historic lows as well (as seen in Table 5–3). Interest rates remained at these lows through 2015.

**TABLE 5–2** Money Market Instruments

**Treasury bills**—short-term obligations issued by the U.S. government.

**Federal funds**—short-term funds transferred between financial institutions usually for no more than one day.

**Repurchase agreements**—agreements involving the sale of securities by one party to another with a promise to repurchase the securities at a specified date and price.

**Commercial paper**—short-term unsecured promissory notes issued by a company to raise short-term cash.

**Negotiable certificates of deposit**—bank-issued time deposits that specify an interest rate and maturity date and are negotiable (saleable on a secondary market).

**Banker's acceptances**—time drafts payable to a seller of goods, with payment guaranteed by a bank.

**TABLE 5–3   Money Market Instruments Outstanding, 1990 and 2016**
*(in billions of dollars)*

|  | Amount Outstanding | | Yield | |
|---|---|---|---|---|
|  | **1990** | **2016** | **1990** | **2016** |
| Treasury bills | $454 | $1,527 | 7.73% | 0.24% |
| Federal funds and | | | | |
| repurchase agreements | 351 | 3,749 | 8.29 | 0.41 |
| Commercial paper | 558 | 941 | 8.25 | 0.41 |
| Negotiable certificates | | | | |
| of deposit | 547 | 1,865 | 8.23 | 0.08 |
| Banker's acceptances | 52 | 0 | 8.00 | 0.50 |

**Sources:** Federal Reserve Board website, June 1990 and June 2016, various tables. www.federalreserve.gov

### Treasury Bills

**Treasury bills (T-bills)**

*Short-term obligations of the U.S. government issued to cover government budget deficits and to refinance maturing government debt.*

**www.federalreserve.gov**

**Treasury bills (T-bills)** are short-term obligations of the U.S. government issued to cover current government budget shortfalls (deficits)[2] and to refinance maturing government debt. As discussed in Chapter 4, Treasury bill purchases and sales are also a main tool used by the Federal Reserve to implement monetary policy. For example, in the late 2000s, to stimulate the economy and increase the amount of funding available in the economy, the Fed purchased large amounts of Treasury bills. In 2016 there were over $1.6 trillion of Treasury bills outstanding, up from $1 trillion in 2007. T-bills are sold through an auction process (described below). Original maturities are 4, 13, 26, and 52 weeks, and they are issued in denominations of multiples of $100. The minimum allowable denomination for a T-bill bid is $100. A typical purchase in the newly issued T-bill market is a round lot of $5 million. However, existing T-bills can be bought and sold in an active secondary market through government securities dealers who purchase Treasury bills from the U.S. government and resell them to investors. Thus, investors wanting to purchase smaller amounts of T-bills can do so through a dealer for a fee.

Because they are backed by the U.S. government, T-bills are virtually default risk free. In fact, T-bills are often referred to as *the* risk-free asset in the United States. Further, because of their short-term nature and active secondary market, T-bills have little interest rate risk and liquidity risk.

**LG 5-3**

**Treasury bill auctions**

*The formal process by which the U.S. Treasury sells new issues of Treasury bills.*

**The New Issue and Secondary Market Trading Process for Treasury Bills.**   The U.S. Treasury has a formal process by which it sells new issues of Treasury bills through its regular **Treasury bill auctions.** Every week (usually on a Thursday), the amount of new T-bills the Treasury will offer for sale is announced. Bids may be submitted by government securities dealers, financial and nonfinancial corporations, and individuals and must be received by a Federal Reserve Bank (over the Internet [through TreasuryDirect[3]], by phone, or by paper form) by the deadline of 1 p.m. on the Monday following the auction announcement. Allocations and prices are announced the following morning (Tuesday), and the T-bills are delivered on the Thursday following the auction.

Submitted bids can be either competitive bids or noncompetitive bids. As of 1998, all successful bidders (both competitive and noncompetitive) are awarded securities at the same price, which is the price equal to the lowest price of the competitive bids accepted (as will be explained below). Prior to this, Treasury security auctions were discriminatory auctions in that different successful bidders paid different prices (their

---

2. The excess of U.S. government expenditures minus revenues.
3. TreasuryDirect, operated by the Office of the U.S. Treasury, allows investors to buy and sell Treasury securities directly from the Treasury Department.

www.ustreas.gov

bid prices). Appendix 5A to this chapter (available through Connect or your course instructor) discusses the reasons behind the change and the benefits to the U.S. Treasury from a single price auction.

Competitive bids specify the amount of par value of bills desired (the minimum is $100) and the discount yield (in increments of 0.005%), rather than the price. The amount of non-competitive bids is subtracted from the total face value of the auctioned bills, with the remainder to be allocated to competitive bidders. Competitive bids are then ranked from the lowest discount yield (highest price) to the highest yield (lowest price). The cut-off yield (the yield of the last accepted bid) is the highest accepted discount yield. It is known as the *stop-out yield* or *stop-out rate* of the auction. It determines the price per $100 that every successful bidder pays. All bids with yields above the stop-out yields are rejected. If the amount of competitive bids at the stop-out yield exceeds the amount of bills remaining to be allocated after the superior bids have been allocated, the bids at the stop-out rate are distributed on a pro-rata basis. For example, if the bids at the stop-out yield total $5 billion of par value, but there is only $3 billion of par value remaining after satisfying noncompetitive bids and competitive bids with lower yields (higher prices), then the bidders whose yield turned out to be the stop-out yield will receive 60 percent of their desired allocations ($3 billion/$5 billion). This proportion is reported as "allotted at high" in the U.S. Treasury auction result announcements. Bidders cannot submit negative yields in T-bill auctions but may submit a yield of zero, which means that they are willing to pay face value and earn no income from the bills.

Competitive bids are generally used by large investors and government securities dealers and make up the majority of the auction market. Table 5–4 shows the results of the Treasury auction of 13- and 26-week Treasury bills on May 16, 2016. At this auction, 27.04 percent and 25.01 percent of the submitted bids were accepted for the 13- and 26-week T-bills, respectively. Figure 5–1 illustrates the T-bill auction for the 26-week T-bills. The highest accepted bid on the 26-week T-bills was 99.823056 percent of the face value of the T-bills. Bids were filled at prices below the high. The lowest accepted bid price was 99.812944 percent. The median accepted bid price was 99.818000 percent. All bidders who submitted prices *above* 99.812944 percent (categories 1 through 5 in Figure 5–1) were awarded in full (winning bids) at a price of 99.812944 percent. Thus, those who submitted a bid at a price greater than 99.812944 percent paid less than their bid price yet received their full allocation of T-bills requested. Bidders who submitted a price below 99.812944 percent (categories 7 and beyond in Figure 5–1) received no allocation of the auctioned T-bills. Finally, of the bidders whose yield turned out to be the stop-out yield (i.e., the price submitted was exactly 99.812944 percent, category C in Figure 5–1), 5.56 percent received their desired allocations (the "allotted at high").

Noncompetitive bids are limited to $5 million; they specify only the desired amount of the face value of the bills. Noncompetitive bids usually represent a small portion of total Treasury bills auctioned. If the amount of noncompetitive bids exceeds the amount of bills auctioned, all noncompetitive bids are satisfied on a pro-rata basis, all competitive bids

**TABLE 5–4**   Treasury Auction Results, May 16, 2016

|  | 13-Week Treasury Bill Auction | 26-Week Treasury Bill Auction |
|---|---|---|
| Bids tendered (in billions) | $114.7 | $103.9 |
| Bids accepted (in billions) | $31.0 | $26.0 |
| Noncompetitive bids (in billions) | $0.5 | $0.6 |
| Price | 99.930486% | 99.812944% |
| High price | 99.987766% | 99.823056% |
| Low price | 99.930486% | 99.812944% |
| Median price | 99.934278% | 99.818000% |
| Allotted at high | 28.58% | 5.56% |

**Source:**  Department of Treasury website, TreasuryDirect, May 17, 2016. www.ustreas.gov

**Figure 5–1**   **Treasury Auction Results**

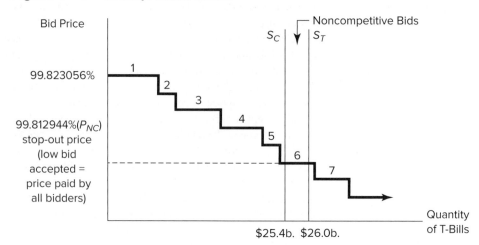

are rejected, and the price of the bills is set at par, reflecting a yield at zero. Noncompetitive bids allow small investors to participate in the T-bill auction market without incurring large risks. That is, small investors who are unfamiliar with money market interest rate movements can use a noncompetitive bid to avoid bidding a price too low to receive any of the T-bills or bidding too high and paying more than the "fair" market price. Notice, from Table 5–4, that 1.34 percent ($0.5b./$31.0b.) and 2.29 percent ($0.6b./$26.0b.), respectively, of the accepted bids at the May 16, 2016 Treasury auction were noncompetitive for 13- and 26-week T-bills. This resulted in a supply of T-bills available to competitive bidders ($S_C$) that is lower than the total supply ($S_T$) because of the preferential bidding status of noncompetitive bidders (i.e., noncompetitive bidders always receive a 100 percent allocation of their bids).

The secondary market for T-bills is the largest of any U.S. money market security. At the heart of this market are those securities dealers designated as primary government securities dealers by the Federal Reserve Bank of New York (consisting of 23 financial institutions) who purchase the majority of the T-bills sold competitively at auction and who create an active secondary market. In addition, there are many (approximately 500) smaller dealers who directly trade in the secondary market. Primary dealers make a market for T-bills by buying and selling securities for their own account and by trading for their customers, including depository institutions, insurance companies, pension funds, and so on. T-bill transactions by primary dealers averaged $820 billion per day in 2016. The T-bill market is decentralized, with most trading transacted over the telephone. Brokers keep track of the market via closed circuit television screens located in the trading rooms of the primary dealers. These television screens display bid and asked prices available at any point in time. Treasury markets are generally open from 9:00 a.m. to 3:30 p.m. EST.

Secondary market T-bill transactions between primary government securities dealers are conducted over the Federal Reserve's wire transfer service—Fedwire (see Chapter 4)—and are recorded via the Federal Reserve's book-entry system.[4] We illustrate a transaction in Figure 5–2. For example, if J.P. Morgan Chase wants to sell $10 million of T-bills to Bank of New York Mellon, J.P. Morgan Chase would instruct its district Federal Reserve Bank—the Federal Reserve Bank of New York (FRBNY)—to electronically transfer the (book-entry) T-bills, via the Fedwire, from its account to Bank of New York Mellon (also in the district of the FRBNY). The transaction would be recorded in the Fed's book-entry system with no physical transfer of paper necessary. An individual wanting to purchase $50,000 of T-bills in the secondary market must contact his or her bank or broker. A bank or broker that is not a primary government securities dealer or a secondary market dealer must contact (via phone, fax, or wire) one of these dealers (e.g., J.P. Morgan Chase) to

---

4. With a book-entry system, no physical documentation of ownership exists. Rather, ownership of Treasury securities is accounted for electronically by computer records.

**Figure 5–2** Secondary Market Treasury Bill Transaction

Transaction between primary government securities dealers:

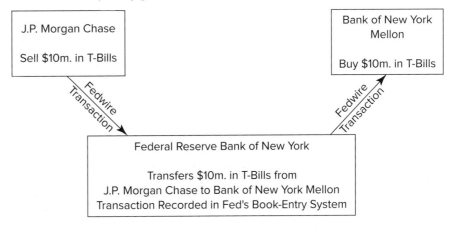

Purchase by an individual:

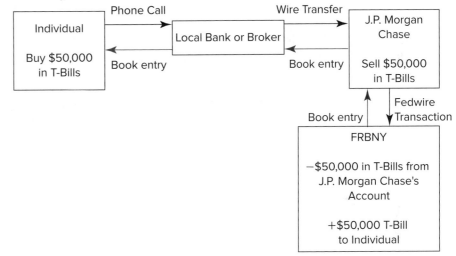

complete the transaction. The T-bill dealer will instruct its local Federal Reserve Bank to increase (credit) its T-bill account at the Fed. In exchange for the investor's $50,000, these securities are subsequently recorded in the dealer's book-entry system as an issue held for the investor. T-bill dealers maintain records identifying owners of all Treasury securities held in its account in the book-entry system.

**Treasury Bill Yields.**   As we discussed previously, Treasury bills are sold on a discount basis. Rather than directly paying interest on T-bills (the coupon rate is zero), the government issues T-bills at a discount from their par (or face) value. The return comes from the difference between the purchase price paid for the T-bill and the face value received at maturity. During the financial crisis, investors worldwide, searching for a safe haven for their funds, invested huge amounts of funds in U.S. Treasury securities. The amount of money invested in Treasury bills was so large that the yield on the three-month Treasury bill went below zero for the first time ever. Investors were essentially paying the U.S. government to borrow money.

Table 5–5 lists T-bill rates as quoted in *The Wall Street Journal* for trading on May 16, 2016. Column 1 in the quote lists the maturity date of the T-bill. Column 2, labeled *Bid,* is the discount yield (defined below) on the T-bill given the current selling price available to T-bill holders (i.e., the price dealers are willing to pay T-bill holders to purchase their T-bills for them). Column 3, labeled *Asked,* is the discount yield based on the current purchase price set by dealers that is available to investors (i.e., potential T-bill buyers) and is calculated from the settlement date, one day after the quote date. The percentage difference in the ask and bid yields is known as the spread. The spread is essentially the profit the dealers make in return for conducting the trade for investors. It is part of the transaction cost incurred by investors for the trade. Column 4, labeled *Chg,* is the change in the asked (discount) yield from the previous day's closing yield. Finally, the last column (column 5), labeled *Asked Yield,* is the asked discount yield converted to a bond equivalent yield. As discussed above, the discount yield (*d*) on a T-bill is calculated as follows:

$$i_{\text{T-bill}, d} = \frac{P_f - P_0}{P_f} \times \frac{360}{n}$$

---

### EXAMPLE 5–4    Calculating a Treasury Bill Asked Discount Yield

Suppose that you purchase the T-bill maturing on September 15, 2016, for \$9,991.362. The T-bill matures 122 days after the settlement date, May 17, 2016, and has a face value of \$10,000. The T-bill's asked discount yield is reported as:

$$i_{\text{T-bill}, d} = \frac{\$10,000 - \$9,991.362}{\$10,000} \times \frac{360}{122} = 0.255\%$$

Thus, 0.255 percent is the asked discount yield on this T-bill reported in Table 5–5.

---

As described above, the discount yield differs from a true rate of return (or bond equivalent yield) for two reasons: (1) the base price used is the face value of the T-bill and not the purchase price of the T-bill, and (2) a 360-day year rather than a 365-day year is used. The bond equivalent yield uses a 365-day year and the purchase price, rather than the face value of the T-bill, as the base price. Thus, the formula for a bond equivalent yield on a T-bill, $i_{\text{T-bill}, be}$, is:

$$i_{\text{T-bill}, be} = \frac{P_f - P_0}{P_0} \times \frac{365}{n}$$

For example, the bond equivalent yield (or asked yield reported in Table 5–5) in Example 5–4 is calculated as:

$$i_{\text{T-bill}, be} = \frac{\$10,000 - \$9,991.362}{\$9,991.362} \times \frac{365}{122} = 0.02587\%$$

Finally, the *EAR* on the T-bill is calculated as:

$$EAR = \left(1 + \frac{0.002587}{365/122}\right)^{365/122} - 1 = 0.02589\%$$

A Treasury bill's price (such as that used in the examples previously) can be calculated from the quote reported in the financial press (e.g., *The Wall Street Journal*) by rearranging the yield equations listed above. Specifically, for the asked discount yield, the required market ask price would be:

$$P_0 = P_f - \left(i_{\text{T-bill}, d} \times \frac{n}{360} \times P_f\right)$$

and for the bond equivalent yield:

$$P_0 = P_f / \left[1 + \left(i_{\text{T-bill}, be} \times \frac{n}{360}\right)\right]$$

**TABLE 5–5**   Treasury Bill Rates

| Monday, May 16, 2016 |
|---|
| Treasury bill bid and ask data are representative over-the-counter quotations as of 3 p.m. Eastern time quoted as a discount to face value. Treasury bill yields are to maturity and based on the asked quote. |

| Maturity | Bid | Asked | Chg | Asked Yield |
|---|---|---|---|---|
| 5/19/2016 | 0.168 | 0.158 | −0.030 | 0.160 |
| 5/26/2016 | 0.173 | 0.163 | −0.055 | 0.165 |
| 6/2/2016 | 0.203 | 0.193 | −0.038 | 0.196 |
| 6/9/2016 | 0.195 | 0.185 | −0.038 | 0.188 |
| 6/16/2016 | 0.193 | 0.183 | 0.028 | 0.186 |
| 6/23/2016 | 0.203 | 0.193 | −0.010 | 0.196 |
| 6/30/2016 | 0.210 | 0.200 | −0.010 | 0.203 |
| 7/7/2016 | 0.208 | 0.198 | −0.015 | 0.201 |
| 7/14/2016 | 0.215 | 0.205 | −0.020 | 0.209 |
| 7/21/2016 | 0.233 | 0.223 | −0.023 | 0.226 |
| 7/28/2016 | 0.245 | 0.235 | −0.008 | 0.239 |
| 8/4/2016 | 0.255 | 0.245 | −0.005 | 0.249 |
| 8/11/2016 | 0.255 | 0.245 | −0.020 | 0.249 |
| 8/18/2016 | 0.255 | 0.245 | −0.018 | 0.249 |
| 8/25/2016 | 0.265 | 0.255 | 0.005 | 0.259 |
| 9/1/2016 | 0.258 | 0.248 | −0.015 | 0.252 |
| 9/8/2016 | 0.255 | 0.245 | −0.015 | 0.249 |
| **9/15/2016** | **0.263** | **0.253** | **0.003** | **0.255** |
| 9/22/2016 | 0.278 | 0.268 | −0.018 | 0.272 |
| 9/29/2016 | 0.280 | 0.270 | −0.013 | 0.274 |
| 10/6/2016 | 0.303 | 0.293 | −0.013 | 0.297 |
| 10/13/2016 | 0.308 | 0.298 | −0.005 | 0.303 |
| 10/20/2016 | 0.323 | 0.313 | −0.025 | 0.317 |
| 10/27/2016 | 0.320 | 0.310 | −0.025 | 0.315 |
| **11/3/2016** | **0.338** | **0.328** | **−0.025** | **0.333** |
| 11/10/2016 | 0.345 | 0.335 | −0.025 | 0.341 |
| 12/8/2016 | 0.350 | 0.340 | −0.005 | 0.346 |
| 1/5/2017 | 0.338 | 0.328 | −0.005 | 0.334 |
| 2/2/2017 | 0.428 | 0.418 | 0.003 | 0.426 |
| 3/2/2017 | 0.460 | 0.450 | −0.010 | 0.458 |
| 3/30/2017 | 0.485 | 0.475 | −0.013 | 0.484 |
| 4/27/2017 | 0.523 | 0.513 | −0.010 | 0.522 |

**Source:** *The Wall Street Journal Online*, May 17, 2016. www.wsj.com

---

**EXAMPLE 5–5**   Calculation of Treasury Bill Price from a *Wall Street Journal* Quote

From Table 5–5, the asked (or discount) yield on the T-bill maturing on November 3, 2016 (or 171 days from the settlement date, May 17, 2016), is 0.328 percent. The T-bill price for these T-bills is calculated as:

$$P_0 = \$10,000 - \left( 0.00328 \times \frac{171}{360} \times \$10,000 \right) = 9,984.42$$

or using the asked yield (or the bond equivalent yield) on the T-bill, 0.333 percent:

$$P_0 = \$10,000 / \left[ 1 + \left( 0.00333 \times \frac{171}{365} \right) \right] = \$9,984.423$$

## Federal Funds

**federal funds
(fed funds)**

*Short-term funds transferred between financial institutions, usually for a period of one day.*

**federal funds rate**

*The interest rate for borrowing fed funds.*

**Federal funds (fed funds)** are short-term loans between financial institutions, usually for a period of one day. For example, commercial banks trade fed funds in the form of excess reserves held at their local Federal Reserve Bank. That is, one commercial bank may be short of reserves, requiring it to borrow excess reserves from another bank that has a surplus. The institution that borrows fed funds incurs a liability on its balance sheet, "federal funds purchased," while the institution that lends the fed funds records an asset, "federal funds sold." The overnight (or one day) interest rate in the interbank lending market is the **federal funds rate.** The fed funds rate is a function of the supply and demand for federal funds among financial institutions and the effects of the Federal Reserve's trading through the FOMC (as discussed in Chapter 4).

One of the primary risks of the interbank lending system is that the borrowing bank does not have to pledge collateral for the funds it receives, which are usually in millions of dollars. While the Fed has the ability to use open market operations to influence the interest rates banks charge each other and can introduce new capital to encourage banks to lend, the interbank loans are conducted with little scrutiny between parties. The financial crisis of 2008–2009 produced unprecedented and persistent strains in interbank lending and exposed problems produced by banks that were heavily leveraged with fed funds. The financial crisis created a huge demand for liquid assets across the entire financial system. Rather than lend excess funds in the interbank market, banks preferred to hold onto liquid assets just in case their own needs might increase. Banks also grew concerned about the risks of borrowing banks and became increasingly unwilling to lend, even at very high interest rates, as the level of confidence in the banking system plunged. Interbank loans fell to $153 billion in June 2010 from a peak of $494 billion in September 2008, the month that Lehman Brothers declared bankruptcy. Unable to borrow in the interbank market, U.S. banks turned to the Fed for short-term borrowing, and the Fed obliged. At the height of the financial crisis, the Fed unexpectedly announced that it would drop its target fed funds rate to a range between zero and one-quarter of 1 percent. (The rate remained at these historically low levels until December 2015.) Eventually, unprecedented actions by the Fed to add liquidity and guarantee bank debt were able to counter the record strains in the interbank market. However, the financial crisis made it painfully clear that financial institutions cannot always count on being able to borrow at a low cost when needed.

**Federal Funds Yields.**   Federal funds (fed funds) are single-payment loans—they pay interest only once, at maturity. Further, fed funds transactions take the form of short-term (mostly overnight) *unsecured* loans. Quoted interest rates on fed funds, $i_{ff,\,sp}$, assume a 360-day year. Therefore, to compare interest rates on fed funds with other securities such as Treasury bills, the quoted fed funds interest rate must be converted into a bond equivalent rate or yield, $i_{ff,\,be}$.

---

**EXAMPLE 5–6**   Conversion of Federal Funds Rate of Interest to a Bond Equivalent Rate

From Table 5–1, the overnight fed funds rate on May 16, 2016, was 0.41 percent. The conversion of the fed funds rate to a bond equivalent rate is calculated as follows:

$$i_{ff,\,be} = i_{ff,\,sp}\,(365/360)$$
$$= 0.41\%\,(365/360) = 0.41569\%$$

Remembering that fed funds are generally lent for one day, the *EAR* on the fed funds can then be calculated as:

$$EAR = \left(1 + \frac{0.0041569}{365/1}\right)^{365/1} - 1 = 0.41656\%$$

In addition to being the cost of unsecured, overnight, interbank borrowing, the federal funds rate is of particular importance because, as was discussed in Chapter 4, it is a focus or target rate in the conduct of monetary policy.

**Trading in the Federal Funds Market.** The fed funds market is a highly liquid and flexible source of funding for commercial banks and savings banks. Commercial banks, especially the largest commercial banks, conduct the vast majority of transactions in the fed funds market. Fed funds transactions are created by banks borrowing and lending excess reserves held at their Federal Reserve Bank (see Chapter 4), using Fedwire, the Federal Reserve's wire transfer network, to complete the transaction. Banks with excess reserves lend fed funds, while banks with deficient reserves borrow fed funds.

Federal funds transactions can be initiated by either the lending or the borrowing bank, with negotiations between any pair of commercial banks taking place directly over the telephone. Alternatively, trades can be arranged through fed funds brokers (such as ICAP and Tullett Prebon), who charge a small fee for bringing the two parties to the fed funds transaction together.[5]

**correspondent banks**

*Banks with reciprocal accounts and agreements.*

Figure 5–3 illustrates a fed funds transaction. For example, a bank that finds itself with $75 million in excess reserves (e.g., J.P. Morgan Chase) can call its **correspondent banks** (banks with which it has reciprocal accounts and agreements)[6] to see if they need overnight reserves. The bank will then sell its excess reserves to those correspondent banks that offer the highest rates for these fed funds (e.g., Bank of America). When a transaction is agreed upon, the lending bank (J.P. Morgan Chase) instructs its district Federal Reserve Bank (e.g., the FRBNY) to transfer the $75 million in excess reserves to the borrowing bank's (Bank of America) reserve account at its Federal Reserve Bank (e.g., the Federal Reserve Bank of San Francisco). The Federal Reserve System's wire transfer network, Fedwire, is used to complete the transfer of funds. The next day, the funds are transferred back, via Fedwire, from the borrowing bank to the lending bank's reserve account at the Federal Reserve Bank plus one day's interest.[7] Overnight fed funds loans will likely be based on an oral agreement between the two parties and are generally unsecured loans.

## Repurchase Agreements

**repurchase agreement (repo or RP)**

*An agreement involving the sale of securities by one party to another with a promise to repurchase the securities at a specified price and on a specified date.*

A **repurchase agreement (repo or RP)** is an agreement involving the sale of securities by one party to another with a promise to repurchase the securities at a specified price and on a specified date in the future. Thus, a repurchase agreement is essentially a collateralized fed funds loan, with the collateral (held by the repo seller) taking the form of securities. One-day maturity repos are called *overnight repos* and repos with longer maturities are called *term repos*. The securities used most often as collateral in repos are U.S. Treasury securities (e.g., T-bills) and government agency securities (e.g., Fannie Mae). Collateral pledged in a repurchase agreement has a "haircut" applied, which means the loan is slightly smaller than the market value of securities pledged. This haircut reflects the underlying risk of the collateral and protects the repo buyer against a change in the value of the collateral. Haircuts are specific to classes of collateral. For example, a U.S. Treasury bill might have one haircut rate, while a government agency security might have another

---

5. Brokerage fees are often as low as 50 cents per $1 million transacted.
6. Correspondent bank relations are discussed in more detail in Chapter 12.
7. Increasingly, participants in the fed funds markets do not hold balances at the Federal Reserve (e.g., commercial banks that do not belong to the Federal Reserve System). In this case, the fed funds transaction is settled in immediately available funds–fed funds on deposit at the lending bank that may be transferred or withdrawn with no delay. A federal funds broker, typically a commercial bank, matches up institutions using a telecommunications network that links federal funds brokers with participating institutions. Upon maturity of the fed funds loan, the borrowing bank's fed funds demand deposit account at the lending bank is debited for the total value of the loan and the borrowing bank pays the lending bank an interest payment for the use of the fed funds. Most of these fed funds transactions are for more than $5 million (they averaged around $40 million in the 2010s) and usually have a one- to seven-day maturity.

**Figure 5–3**   **Federal Funds Transaction**

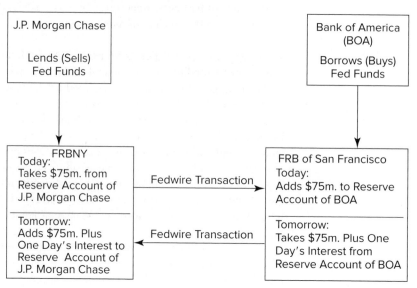

**reverse repurchase agreement (reverse repo)**

*An agreement involving the purchase of securities by one party from another with the promise to sell them back.*

haircut rate. A **reverse repurchase agreement (reverse repo)** is the lender's position in the repo transaction (i.e., an agreement involving the purchase (buying) of securities by one party from another with the promise to sell them back at a given date in the future).

Most repos have very short terms to maturity (generally from 1 to 14 days), but there is a growing market for longer-term one- to three-month repos. Repos with a maturity of less than one week generally involve denominations of $25 million or more. Longer-term repos are more often in denominations of $10 million.

Many commercial firms, with idle funds in their deposit accounts at banks, use repos as a way to earn a small return until these funds are needed. In this case the firm uses its idle funds to buy T-bills from its bank. The bank then agrees to repurchase the T-bills in the future at a higher price. Banks generally pay no interest on corporate checking accounts. Thus, a repo is a way for a bank to allow its valued corporate customers to earn some interest on their balances. Other securities, such as mortgage-backed securities, may be used as repo collateral as well.

**The Trading Process for Repurchase Agreements.**   Repurchase agreements are arranged either directly between two parties or with the help of brokers and dealers. Figure 5–4 illustrates a $75 million repurchase agreement of Treasury bonds arranged directly between two parties (e.g., J.P. Morgan Chase and Bank of America). The repo buyer, J.P. Morgan Chase, arranges to purchase fed funds from the repo seller, Bank of America, with an agreement that the seller will repurchase the fed funds within a stated period of time—one day. The repo is collateralized with T-bonds. In most repurchase agreements, the repo buyer acquires title to the securities for the term of the agreement.

Once the transaction is agreed upon, the repo buyer, J.P. Morgan Chase, instructs its district Federal Reserve Bank (the FRBNY) to transfer $75 million in excess reserves, via Fedwire, to the repo seller's reserve account. The repo seller, Bank of America, instructs its district Federal Reserve Bank (the FRB of San Francisco) to transfer $75 million from its T-bond account via securities Fedwire to the repo buyer's T-bond account. Upon maturity of the repo (one day in this example), these transactions are reversed. In addition, the repo seller transfers additional funds (representing one day's interest) from its reserve account to the reserve account of the repo buyer.

**Repurchase Agreement Yields.**   Because Treasury securities back most repurchase agreements, they are low credit risk investments and have lower interest rates than

**Figure 5–4** A Repurchase Agreement Transaction

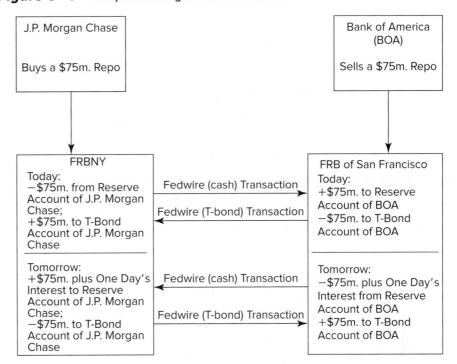

uncollateralized fed funds.[8] The yield on repurchase agreements is calculated as the annualized percentage difference between the initial selling price of the securities and the contracted (re)purchase price (the selling price plus interest paid on the repurchase agreement), using a 360-day year. Specifically:

$$i_{repo,\,sp} = \frac{P_f - P_0}{P_0} \times \frac{360}{n}$$

where

$P_f$ = Repurchase price of the securities (equals the selling price plus interest paid on the repurchase agreement)
$P_0$ = Selling price of the securities
$n$ = Number of days until the repo matures

---

**EXAMPLE 5–7** Calculation of a Yield on a Repurchase Agreement

Suppose a bank enters a reverse repurchase agreement in which it agrees to buy fed funds from one of its correspondent banks at a price of $10,000,000, with the promise to sell these funds back at a price of $10,000,291.67 ($10,000,000 plus interest of $291.67) after five days. The yield on this repo to the bank is calculated as follows:

$$i_{repo,\,sp} = \frac{\$10,000,291.67 - \$10,000,000}{\$10,000,000} \times \frac{360}{5} = 0.21\%$$

---

8. There is a one-day interest rate risk that may impact credit risk if interest rates suddenly rise so that the market value of the collateral backing the repo falls. To avoid the risk many repo transactions require a securities "haircut" to be imposed at the time of the transaction–more securities are used to back the cash part of the transaction. For example, Bank A may send $100 million in cash to Bank B. In turn, Bank B sends $105 million in securities as collateral to back the cash loan from Bank A.

Because of their common use as a source of overnight funding and the fact that repos are essentially collateralized fed fund transactions, the Federal Reserve generally classifies federal funds and repurchase agreements together in its statistical data. Together, these amounted to more than $3.7 trillion outstanding in 2016 (see Table 5–3). Some notable differences exist, however, between repurchase agreements and fed funds. For example, repurchase agreements are less liquid than fed funds since they can only be arranged after an agreed upon type of collateral is posted (i.e., repos are hard to arrange at the close of the banking day, whereas fed funds can be arranged at very short notice, even a few minutes). Further, nonbanks are more frequent users of repurchase agreements.

## Commercial Paper

**commercial paper**

*An unsecured short-term promissory note issued by a company to raise short-term cash, often to finance working capital requirements.*

**www.sec.gov**

**Commercial paper** is an unsecured short-term promissory note issued by a corporation to raise short-term cash, often to finance working capital requirements. Commercial paper is one of the largest (in terms of dollar value outstanding) of the money market instruments, with almost $1.0 trillion outstanding as of 2016. One reason for such large amounts of commercial paper outstanding is that companies with strong credit ratings can generally borrow money at a lower interest rate by issuing commercial paper than by directly borrowing (via loans) from banks. Indeed, although business loans were the major asset on bank balance sheets between 1965 and 1990, they have dropped in importance since 1990. This trend reflects the growth of the commercial paper market. Figure 5–5 illustrates the difference between the commercial paper rate and the prime rate for borrowing from banks from 1973 through 2016.[9] Notice that in the 1990s and 2000s, the spread between the prime rate and commercial paper rate increased relative to the 1970s and 1980s.

Commercial paper is generally sold in denominations of $100,000, $250,000, $500,000, and $1 million. Maturities generally range from 1 to 270 days—the most common maturities are between 20 and 45 days. This 270-day maximum is due to a

**Figure 5–5**    **Commercial Paper and Prime Rate, 1973–2016**

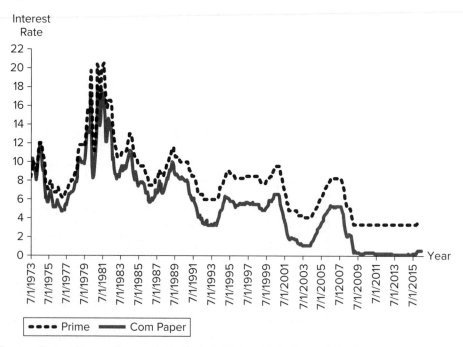

**Source:** Federal Reserve Board website, "Selected Interest Rates." www.federalreserve.gov

9. It should be noted, however, that the best borrowers from banks can borrow below prime. Prime rate in today's banking world is viewed as a rate to be charged to an average borrower—best borrowers pay prime rate minus some spread.

Securities and Exchange Commission (SEC) rule that securities with a maturity of more than 270 days must go through the time-consuming and costly registration process to become a public debt offering (i.e., a corporate bond). As a result, at maturity most commercial paper is rolled over into new issues of commercial paper (again avoiding the SEC registration process). Commercial paper can be sold directly by the issuers to a buyer such as a mutual fund (a direct placement) or can be sold indirectly by dealers in the commercial paper market. The dollar value outstanding (in thousands of dollars) via each method of issue from 1991 through 2016 is reported in Figure 5–6. Notice that dealer placements of commercial paper dominated the market except for between 2010 and 2013. Further, the total dollar value of commercial paper outstanding decreased significantly after the financial crisis. We discuss reasons for these trends below.

www.standardandpoors
.com

Commercial paper is generally held by investors from the time of issue until maturity. Thus, there is no active secondary market for commercial paper.[10] Because commercial paper is not actively traded and because it is also unsecured debt, the credit rating of the issuing company is of particular importance in determining the marketability of a commercial paper issue. Credit ratings provide potential investors with information regarding the ability of the issuing firm to repay the borrowed funds, as promised, and to compare the commercial paper issues of different companies. Several credit rating firms rate commercial paper issues (e.g., Standard & Poor's, Moody's, and Fitch IBCA, Inc.). Standard & Poor's rates commercial paper from A-1 for highest-quality issues to D for lowest-quality issues, while Moody's rates commercial paper from P-1 for highest-quality issues to "not rated" for lowest-quality issues. Virtually all companies that issue commercial paper obtain ratings from at least one rating services company, and most obtain two rating evaluations.

www.moodys.com

Commercial paper issuers with lower than prime credit ratings often back their commercial paper issues with a letter of credit obtained from a commercial bank. In these cases, the bank agrees to make the promised payment on the commercial paper if the issuer cannot pay off the debt on maturity. Thus, a letter of credit backing commercial paper effectively substitutes the credit rating of the issuer with the credit rating of the bank. This reduces the risk to the purchasers of the paper and results in a lower interest rate (and higher credit rating) on the commercial paper. In other cases, an issuer arranges a line of credit with a bank (a loan commitment) and draws on this line if it has insufficient funds to meet the repayment of the commercial paper issue at maturity.

In the early 2000s, the slowdown in the U.S. economy resulted in ratings downgrades for some of the largest commercial paper issuers. For example, the downgrade of General Motors and Ford from a tier-one to tier-two commercial paper issuer had a huge impact on the commercial paper markets. The result is that these commercial paper issuers were forced to give up the cost advantage of commercial paper and to move to the long-term debt markets to ensure they would have access to cash. The decrease in the number of eligible commercial paper issuers in the early 2000s resulted in a decrease in the size of the commercial paper market for the first time in 40 years (see Figure 5–6).

The mid-2000s saw a huge rise in the use of asset-backed commercial paper (ABCP). In July 2007, $1.19 trillion of the total $2.16 trillion commercial paper outstanding was ABCP. ABCP is collateralized by other financial assets of the issuer. The financial assets that serve as collateral for ABCP are ordinarily a mix of many different assets, which are jointly judged to have a low risk of bankruptcy by a ratings agency. In the mid-2000s, the collateralized assets were mainly mortgage-backed securities. However, in 2007–2008 many of these mortgage-backed securities performed more poorly than expected. Billions of dollars of asset-backed commercial paper were tainted because some of the proceeds were used to buy investments tied to U.S. subprime mortgages. Issuers found buyers much

---

10. This is partly because any dealer that issues (underwrites) commercial paper of a given company will generally buy back that commercial paper should a buyer wish to sell it. Thus, in general, underwriters act as counterparties in any secondary market trade.

**Figure 5–6**    Direct versus Dealer Placements of Commercial Paper

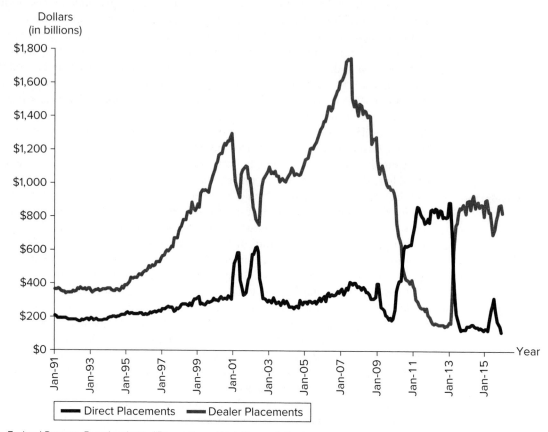

Source: Federal Reserve Board website, "Research and Data." www.federalreserve.gov

less willing to purchase ABCP. The result was another big drop in the dollar value of the commercial paper markets. In May 2016, just $256 billion of ABCP was outstanding (of the total $1,116 billion commercial paper market).

In addition, on September 16, 2008 (one day after Lehman Brothers filed for bankruptcy), Reserve Primary Fund, the oldest money market fund in the United States, saw its shares fall to 97 cents (below the $1.00 book value) after writing off debt issued by Lehman Brothers. Resulting investor anxiety about Reserve Primary Fund spread to other funds, and money market mutual fund withdrawals skyrocketed. Fund investors pulled out a record $144.5 billion during the week ending Wednesday, September 17 (redemptions during the week of September 10 totaled just $7.1 billion), as investors worried about the safety of even these safest investments. Money market mutual funds participate heavily in the commercial paper market. As investors pulled their money from these funds, the commercial paper market shrank by $52.1 billion for the week (through Wednesday). These outflows severely undermined the stability of short-term funding markets, upon which many financial institutions and large corporations rely heavily to meet their short-term borrowing needs. In response, the Federal Reserve Board announced the creation of the Commercial Paper Funding Facility (CPFF), a facility that complemented the Federal Reserve's existing credit facilities, to help provide liquidity to short-term funding markets. Under the plan, the Federal Reserve stepped in to purchase commercial paper and other short-term debt.

Even as markets stabilized after the financial crisis, outstanding values of financial and nonfinancial commercial paper continued to fall: from over $2.16 trillion at its peak in July 2007, the commercial paper market fell to $1.76 trillion in July 2008, $1.21 trillion in July 2009, and just $0.99 trillion in July 2013. Reasons for this continued fall include a combination of related factors. First, negative and low positive economic growth experienced for years after the financial crisis produced lower demand for funds and thus less of a need to issue commercial paper. Second, financial and nonfinancial firms held record amounts of cash reserves after the financial crisis and thus did not need to borrow as much in the short-term commercial paper markets. Finally, long-term debt rates were at historical lows after the financial crisis. As a result, many corporations increased their issuance of longer-term debt so as to lock in their financing costs at these low rates for many years: the financial crisis showed how risky rolling over short-term borrowings can be. Further, given the increased risk, direct placement of commercial paper became more difficult. Thus, dealer placement of commercial paper dominated the placement market. These changes can be seen in Figure 5–6.

The better the credit rating on a commercial paper issue, the lower the interest rate on the issue. The spread between the interest rate on medium grade commercial paper and prime grade commercial paper is shown in Figure 5–7. During the 1990s, the spread was generally on the order of 0.22 percent (22 basis points) per year. From June 2001 through June 2003, as the economy slowed, the spread increased to an average of 0.38 percent per year. In the mid-2000s, the spread was at times close to zero. However, as credit markets deteriorated in the summer of 2007 spreads again increased. For example, in August 2007, the spreads surged to 1.25 percent. The situation worsened throughout the financial crisis. Figure 5–7 shows that the cost of commercial paper funding skyrocketed for the medium-grade commercial paper following the collapse of Lehman Brothers in the fall of 2008. When the spread between prime versus medium-grade commercial paper hit 1.60 percent in 2007, the market was shocked. However, this became minor when the spread increased to an eight-month high of 3.42 percent in September 2008 after the U.S. House of Representatives rejected a plan to rescue banks and then rose to 4.85 percent in late 2008. Usually the spread between prime and medium-grade commercial paper reflects a concern for default on the riskier paper. But during the financial crisis the spread also reflected a lack of liquidity in the system: credit markets were essentially locked up waiting for the federal government to present some type of solution or bailout. While the Federal Reserve was

**Figure 5–7**    **Rates on Prime versus Medium-Grade Commercial Paper, 1997–2016**

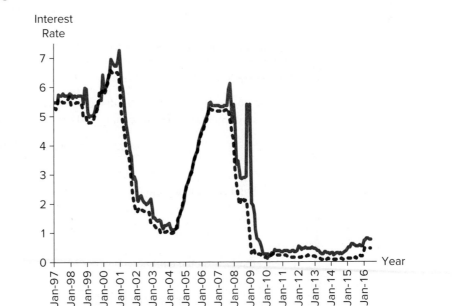

**Source:** Federal Reserve Board website, "Research and Data." www.federalreserve.gov

able to bring commercial paper rates down during the crisis, the commercial paper market has yet to recover.

**The Trading Process for Commercial Paper.**   Commercial paper is sold to investors either directly (about 12 percent of all issues in 2016—see Figure 5–6), using the issuer's own sales force (e.g., GMAC), or indirectly through brokers and dealers, such as major bank subsidiaries that specialize in investment banking activities and investment banks underwriting the issues. Commercial paper underwritten and issued through brokers and dealers is more expensive to the issuer, usually increasing the cost of the issue by one-tenth to one-eighth of a percent, reflecting an underwriting cost. In return, the dealer guarantees, through a firm commitment underwriting, the sale of the whole issue. To help achieve this goal, the dealer contacts prospective buyers of the commercial paper, determines the appropriate discount rate on the commercial paper, and relays any special requests for the commercial paper in terms of specific quantities and maturities to the issuer. When a company issues commercial paper through a dealer, a request made at the beginning of the day by a potential investor (such as a money market mutual fund) for a particular maturity is often completed by the end of the day.

When commercial paper is issued directly from an issuer to a buyer, the company saves the cost of the dealer (and the underwriting services), but must find appropriate investors and determine the discount rate on the paper that will place the complete issue. When the firm decides how much commercial paper it wants to issue, it posts offering rates to potential buyers based on its own estimates of investor demand. The firm then monitors the flow of money during the day and adjusts its commercial paper rates depending on investor demand.

**Commercial Paper Yields.**   Like Treasury bills, yields on commercial paper are quoted on a discount basis—the discount return to commercial paper holders is the annualized percentage difference between the price paid for the paper and the par value using a 360-day year. Specifically:

$$i_{cp,\,d} = \frac{P_f - P_0}{P_f} \times \frac{360}{n}$$

and when converted to a bond equivalent yield:

$$i_{cp,\,be} = \frac{P_f - P_0}{P_0} \times \frac{365}{n}$$

---

### EXAMPLE 5–8   Calculation of the Yield on Commercial Paper

Suppose an investor purchases 95-day commercial paper with a par value of $1,000,000 for a price of $990,023. The discount yield ($d$) on the commercial paper is calculated as:

$$i_{cp,\,d} = \frac{\$1,000,000 - \$990,023}{\$1,000,000} \times \frac{360}{95} = 0.3702\%$$

and the bond equivalent yield (*be*) is:

$$i_{cp,\,be} = \frac{\$1,000,000 - \$990,023}{\$990,023} \times \frac{365}{95} = 0.3757\%$$

Finally, the *EAR* on the commercial paper is:

$$EAR = \left(1 + \frac{0.003757}{365/95}\right)^{365/95} - 1 = 0.3763\%$$

## *Negotiable Certificates of Deposit*

**negotiable certificate of deposit (CD)**

*A bank-issued, fixed maturity, interest-bearing time deposit that specifies an interest rate and maturity date and is negotiable.*

**bearer instrument**

*An instrument in which the holder at maturity receives the principal and interest.*

A **negotiable certificate of deposit (CD)** is a bank-issued time deposit that specifies an interest rate and maturity date and is negotiable (i.e., salable) in the secondary market. As of 2016, there were over $1.86 trillion of negotiable CDs outstanding. A negotiable CD is a **bearer instrument**—whoever holds the CD when it matures receives the principal and interest. A negotiable CD can be traded any number of times in secondary markets; therefore, the original buyer is not necessarily the owner at maturity.[11] Negotiable CDs have denominations that range from $100,000 to $10 million; $1 million is the most common denomination. The large denominations make negotiable CDs too large for most individuals to buy. However, negotiable CDs are often purchased by money market mutual funds (see Chapter 17), which pool funds of individual investors and allow this group to indirectly purchase negotiable CDs. Negotiable CD maturities range from two weeks to one year, with most having a maturity of one to four months.

While CDs have been used by banks since the early 1900s, they were not issued in a negotiable form until the early 1960s. Because of rising interest rates in the 1950s and significant interest rate penalties charged on the early withdrawal of funds invested in CDs, large CDs became unattractive to deposit holders. The result was a significant drop in deposits at banks (disintermediation). In 1961, First National City Bank of New York (now known as Citigroup) issued the first negotiable CD, and money market dealers agreed to make a secondary market in them. These negotiable CDs were well received and helped banks regain many of their lost deposits. Indeed, the success of negotiable CDs helped bank managers focus more actively on managing the liability side of their portfolios (see Chapter 21).

**The Trading Process for Negotiable Certificates of Deposit.** Banks issuing negotiable CDs post a daily set of rates for the most popular maturities of their negotiable CDs, normally 1, 2, 3, 6, and 12 months. Then, subject to its funding needs, the bank tries to sell as many CDs to investors who are likely to hold them as investments rather than sell them to the secondary market.

In some cases, the bank and the CD investor directly negotiate a rate, the maturity, and the size of the CD. Once this is done, the issuing bank delivers the CD to a custodian bank specified by the investor. The custodian bank verifies the CD, debits the amount to the investor's account, and credits the amount to the issuing bank. This is done through the Fedwire system by transferring fed funds from the custodian bank's reserve account at the Fed to the issuing bank's reserve account.

The secondary market for negotiable CDs allows investors to buy existing negotiable CDs rather than new issues. While it is not a very active market, the secondary market for negotiable CDs is made up of a linked network of approximately 15 brokers and dealers using telephones to transact. The secondary market is predominantly located in New York City, along with most of the brokers and dealers.

The mechanics of the secondary market are similar to those of the primary market for negotiable CDs. Certificates are physically transported between traders or their custodian banks. The custodian bank verifies the certificate and records the deposit in the investor's account. Most transactions executed in the morning are settled the same day. Most transactions executed later in the day are settled the next business day.

**Negotiable CD Yields.** Negotiable CD rates are negotiated between the bank and the CD buyer. Large, well-known banks can offer CDs at slightly lower rates than smaller, less well-known banks. This is due partly to the lower perceived default risk and greater

---

11. By contrast, retail CDs with face values under $100,000 are not traded. Thus, a negotiable CD is more "liquid" to an investor than a retail CD or time deposit.

marketability of well-known banks and partly to the belief that larger banks are often "too big to fail"—regulators will bail out troubled large banks and protect large depositors beyond the explicit ($250,000) deposit cap under the current FDIC insurance program (see Chapter 13). As mentioned earlier, negotiable CDs are single-payment securities. Thus, interest rates on negotiable CDs are generally quoted using a 360-day year.

---

**EXAMPLE 5–9**    Calculation of the Secondary Market Yield on a Negotiable CD

A bank has issued a six-month, $1 million negotiable CD with a 0.72 percent quoted annual interest rate ($i_{CD, sp}$). The bond equivalent yield on the CD is:

$$i_{CD, be} = 0.72\%(365/360) = 0.73\%$$

Thus, at maturity (in 6 months) the CD holder will receive:

$$FV = \$1m.(1 + 0.0073/2) = \$1,003,650$$

in exchange for $1 million deposited in the bank today. Further, the *EAR* on the CD is:

$$EAR = \left(1 + \frac{0.0073}{2}\right)^2 - 1 = 0.7313\%$$

Immediately after the CD is issued, the secondary market price on the $1 million CD falls to $999,651. As a result, the secondary market bond equivalent yield on the $1 million face value CD increases as follows:

$$1,003,650/(1 + i_{CD. be}/2) = \$999,651$$
$$\Rightarrow i_{CD, be} = 0.8001\%$$

The single-payment yield increases to:

$$i_{CD. sp} = 0.8001\%(360/365) = 0.7891\%$$

and the *EAR* becomes:

$$EAR = (1 + 0.008001/2)^2 - 1 = 0.8017\%$$

---

### Banker's Acceptances

**banker's acceptance**

*A time draft payable to a seller of goods, with payment guaranteed by a bank.*

A **banker's acceptance** is a time draft payable to a seller of goods, with payment guaranteed by a bank. Banker's acceptances make up an increasingly small part of the money markets. There were less than $1 billion banker's acceptances outstanding in 2016. Time drafts issued by a bank are orders for the bank to pay a specified amount of money to the bearer of the time draft on a given date.

**The Trading Process for Banker's Acceptances.**    Many banker's acceptances arise from international trade transactions and the underlying letters of credit (or time drafts) that are used to finance trade in goods that have yet to be shipped from a foreign exporter (seller) to a domestic importer (buyer). Foreign exporters often prefer that banks act as guarantors for payment before sending goods to domestic importers, particularly when the foreign supplier has not previously done business with the domestic importer on a regular basis.

In the United States, a majority of all acceptances are originated in New York, Chicago, and San Francisco. The U.S. bank insures the international transaction by stamping "Accepted" on a time draft written against the letter of credit between the exporter and the importer, signifying its obligation to pay the foreign exporter (or its bank) on a specified date should the importer fail to pay for the goods. Foreign exporters can then hold the banker's acceptance (the accepted time draft written against the letter of credit) until the date specified on the letter of credit. If they have an immediate need for cash, they can sell the acceptance before that date at a discount from the face value to a buyer in the money market (e.g., a bank). In this case, the ultimate bearer will receive the face value of the banker's acceptance on maturity. We describe this process in more detail in Appendix 5B to this chapter (available through Connect or your course instructor).

Because banker's acceptances are payable to the bearer at maturity, they can be and are traded in secondary markets. Maturities on banker's acceptances traded in secondary markets range from 30 to 270 days. Denominations of banker's acceptances are determined by the size of the original transaction (between the domestic importer and the foreign exporter). Once in the secondary markets, however, banker's acceptances are often bundled and traded in round lots, mainly of $100,000 and $500,000.

Only the largest U.S. banks are active in the banker's acceptance market. Because the risk of default is very low (essentially an investor is buying a security that is fully backed by commercial bank guarantees), interest rates on banker's acceptances are low. Specifically, there is a form of double protection underlying banker's acceptances that reduces their default risk. Since both the importer and the importer's bank must default on the transaction before the investor is subject to risk, the investor is also protected by the value of the goods imported to which he or she now has a debtor's claim—the goods underlying the transaction can be viewed as collateral. Like T-bills and commercial paper, banker's acceptances are sold on a discounted basis.

### Comparison of Money Market Securities

Having reviewed the different money market securities, it should be obvious that the different securities have a number of characteristics in common: large denominations, low default risk, and short maturities. It should also be noted that these securities are quite different in terms of their liquidity. For example, Treasury bills have an extensive secondary market. Thus, these money market securities can be converted into cash quickly and with little loss in value. Commercial paper, on the other hand, has no organized secondary market. These securities cannot be converted into cash quickly unless resold to the original dealer/underwriter, and conversion may involve a relatively higher cost. Federal funds also have no secondary market trading, since they are typically overnight loan transactions and are not intended as investments to be held beyond very short horizons (thus, the lack of a secondary market is inconsequential). Indeed, longer-horizon holders simply roll over their holdings. Bank negotiable CDs also can be traded on secondary markets, but in recent years trading has been relatively inactive, as most negotiable CDs are being bought by "buy and hold" oriented money market mutual funds, as are banker's acceptances.

---

**DO YOU UNDERSTAND:**

4. How Treasury bills are first issued?

5. What federal funds are?

6. What the two types of federal funds transactions are? Describe each.

7. What securities are mainly used as collateral in repurchase agreements?

8. Why the negotiable CD market was created?

9. What the process is by which a banker's acceptance is created?

---

## MONEY MARKET PARTICIPANTS

The major money market participants are the U.S. Treasury, the Federal Reserve, commercial banks, money market mutual funds, brokers and dealers, corporations, other financial institutions such as insurance companies, and individuals. Table 5–6 summarizes the role (issuer or investor) each of these participants plays in the markets for the various money market securities.

**TABLE 5–6**   Money Market Participants

| Instrument | Principal Issuer | Principal Investor |
|---|---|---|
| Treasury bills | U.S. Treasury | Federal Reserve System<br>Commercial banks<br>Mutual funds<br>Brokers and dealers<br>Other financial institutions<br>Corporations<br>Individuals |
| Federal funds | Commercial banks | Commercial banks |
| Repurchase agreements | Federal Reserve System<br>Commercial banks<br>Brokers and dealers<br>Other financial institutions | Federal Reserve System<br>Commercial banks<br>Mutual funds<br>Brokers and dealers<br>Other financial institutions<br>Corporations |
| Commercial paper | Commercial banks<br>Other financial institutions<br>Corporations | Brokers and dealers<br>Mutual funds<br>Corporations<br>Other financial institutions<br>Individuals |
| Negotiable CDs | Commercial banks | Brokers and dealers<br>Mutual funds<br>Corporations<br>Other financial institutions<br>Individuals |
| Banker's acceptances | Commercial banks | Commercial banks<br>Brokers and dealers<br>Corporations |

### The U.S. Treasury

www.ustreas.gov

The U.S. Treasury raises significant amounts of funds in the money market when it issues T-bills. T-bills are the most actively traded of the money market securities. T-bills allow the U.S. government to raise money to meet unavoidable short-term expenditure needs prior to the receipt of tax revenues. Tax receipts are generally concentrated around quarterly dates, but government expenditures are more evenly distributed over the year.

### The Federal Reserve

www.federalreserve.gov

The Federal Reserve is a key (arguably the most important) participant in the money markets. The Federal Reserve holds T-bills (as well as T-notes and T-bonds) to conduct open market transactions—purchasing T-bills when it wants to increase the money supply and selling T-bills when it wants to decrease the money supply. The Federal Reserve often uses repurchase agreements and reverse repos to temporarily smooth interest rates and the money supply. Moreover, the Fed targets the federal funds rate as part of its overall monetary policy strategy, which can in turn affect other money market rates. Finally, the Fed operates the discount window, which it can use to influence the supply of bank reserves to commercial banks and ultimately the demand for and supply of fed funds and repos.

### Commercial Banks

Commercial banks are the most diverse group of participants in the money markets. As Table 5–6 shows, banks participate as issuers and/or investors of almost all money market instruments discussed above. For example, banks are the major issuers of negotiable CDs, banker's acceptances, federal funds, and repurchase agreements.

The importance of banks in the money markets is driven in part by their need to meet reserve requirements imposed by regulation. For example, during periods of economic expansion, heavy loan demand can produce reserve deficiencies for banks (i.e., their actual reserve holdings are pushed below the minimums required by regulation). Additional reserves can be obtained by borrowing fed funds from other banks, engaging in a repurchase agreement, selling negotiable CDs, or selling commercial paper.[12] Conversely, during contractionary periods, many banks have excess reserves that they can use to purchase Treasury securities, trade fed funds, engage in reverse repos, and so on.

### Money Market Mutual Funds

Money market mutual funds purchase large amounts of money market securities and sell shares in these pools based on the value of their underlying (money market) securities (see Chapter 17). In doing so, money market mutual funds allow small investors to invest in money market instruments. In 2016 money market mutual funds had $1.4 trillion invested in short-term financial securities—such as repurchase agreements, negotiable CDs, open market paper (mostly commercial paper), and U.S. government securities. Money market mutual funds provide an alternative investment opportunity to interest-bearing deposits at commercial banks.[13]

### Brokers and Dealers

Brokers' and dealers' services are important to the smooth functioning of money markets. We have alluded to various categories of brokers and dealers in this chapter. First are the 23 primary government security dealers. This group of participants plays a key role in marketing new issues of Treasury bills (and other Treasury securities). Primary government securities dealers also make the market in Treasury bills, buying securities from the Federal Reserve when they are issued and selling them in the secondary market. Secondary market transactions in the T-bill markets are transacted in the trading rooms of these primary dealers. These dealers also assist the Federal Reserve when it uses the repo market to temporarily increase or decrease the supply of bank reserves available.

The second group of brokers and dealers are money and security brokers. Some of the major brokers in this group are ICAP, Liberty, Martin Holdings, RMJ Securities, Tullett Prebon, and Tradeweb. When government securities dealers trade with each other, they often use this group of brokers as intermediaries. These brokers also play a major role in linking buyers and sellers in the fed funds market and assist secondary trading in other money market securities as well. These brokers never trade for their own account, and they keep the names of dealers involved in trades they handle confidential.

The third group of brokers and dealers are the thousands of brokers and dealers who act as intermediaries in the money markets by linking buyers and sellers of money market securities (see Chapter 16). These brokers and dealers often act as the intermediaries for

---

12. Only bank holding companies such as Citigroup can issue commercial paper. However, funds so borrowed can be lent (downstreamed) to bank subsidiaries such as Citibank. Currently, the Federal Reserve imposes reserve requirements on such transactions.
13. Indeed, the short maturity of these asset holdings is an objective of these funds so as to retain the deposit-like nature of their liabilities (called shares). The major difference between deposits and money market mutual fund (MMMF) shares is that interest-bearing deposits (below $250,000) are fully insured by the FDIC, whereas MMMF shares are not. Moreover, because of bank regulatory costs (such as reserve requirements, capital adequacy requirements, and deposit insurance premiums), bank deposits generally offer lower interest rates or returns than noninsured money market mutual funds. Thus, the net gain in switching to a money market mutual fund is a higher return in exchange for the loss of FDIC deposit insurance coverage. Many investors appeared willing to give up FDIC insurance coverage to obtain additional returns in the late 1990s and 2000s.

smaller investors who do not have sufficient funds to invest in primary issues of money market securities or who simply want to invest in the money markets.

### Corporations

Nonfinancial and financial corporations raise large amounts of funds in the money markets, primarily in the form of commercial paper. Because corporate cash inflows rarely equal their cash outflows, they often invest their excess cash funds in money market securities, especially T-bills, repos, commercial paper, negotiable CDs, and banker's acceptances.

### Other Financial Institutions

Because their liability payments are relatively unpredictable, property-casualty (PC) insurance companies, and to a lesser extent life insurance companies, must maintain large balances of liquid assets (see Chapter 15). To accomplish this, insurance companies invest heavily in highly liquid money market securities, especially T-bills, repos, commercial paper, and negotiable CDs.

Since finance companies are not banks and cannot issue deposits, they raise large amounts of funds in the money markets (see Chapter 14), especially through the issuance of commercial paper.

### Individuals

Individual investors participate in the money markets through direct investments in these securities (e.g., negotiable CDs) or through investments in money market mutual funds, which contain a mix of all types of money market securities.

> **DO YOU UNDERSTAND:**
>
> **10.** Who the major money market participants are?
>
> **11.** Which money market securities commercial banks issue?
>
> **12.** What services brokers and dealers provide for money market participants?

## INTERNATIONAL ASPECTS OF MONEY MARKETS

**LG 5-5**

While U.S. money markets are the largest and most active in the world, money markets across the world have been growing in size and importance. Two forms of growth include (1) U.S. money market securities bought and sold by foreign investors and (2) foreign money market securities. As a result of the growth in money markets worldwide, the flow of funds across borders in various countries has grown as international investors move their funds to money markets offering the most attractive yields. Table 5–7 lists the total amounts of various U.S. money market securities held by foreign investors from 1994 through 2016. Figure 5–8 shows the U.S. dollar equivalent amounts of money market instruments held by commercial banks worldwide traded in international money markets as of 2016, by the currency of issue and type of instrument issued.

**TABLE 5–7**  Foreign Investments in U.S. Money Market Instruments
*(in billions of dollars)*

|  | 1994 | 1997 | 2000 | 2004 | 2007 | 2010 | 2013 | 2016 |
|---|---|---|---|---|---|---|---|---|
| Treasury securities* | $633 | $1,252 | $1,222 | $1,814 | $2,376 | $4,467 | $5,794 | $6,118 |
| Repurchase agreements | 47 | 91 | 91 | 665 | 1,109 | −46 | 707 | 717 |
| Negotiable CDs | 56 | 74 | 107 | 149 | 208 | 247 | 445 | 453 |
| Open market paper† | 25 | 78 | 111 | 230 | 278 | 191 | 101 | 103 |

*Includes Treasury bills, notes, and bonds.
†Commercial paper and banker's acceptances.
**Source:** Federal Reserve Board website, "Financial Accounts of the United States." www.federalreserve.gov

**Figure 5–8** Worldwide Money Market Instruments Outstanding

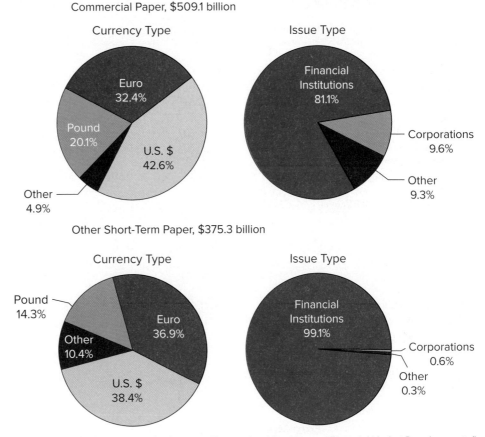

Commercial Paper, $509.1 billion

Currency Type

Euro 32.4%
Pound 20.1%
U.S. $ 42.6%
Other 4.9%

Issue Type

Financial Institutions 81.1%
Corporations 9.6%
Other 9.3%

Other Short-Term Paper, $375.3 billion

Currency Type

Pound 14.3%
Other 10.4%
Euro 36.9%
U.S. $ 38.4%

Issue Type

Financial Institutions 99.1%
Corporations 0.6%
Other 0.3%

**Source:** Bank for International Settlements, "International Banking and Financial Market Developments," *Quarterly Review,* March 2016. www.bis.org

Table 5–8 shows the variation in central bank interest rates (discount rates for lender of last resort loans) in several countries in 2007, 2010, and 2016.

Note from Table 5–7 that foreign investments in U.S. money market securities increased from 1994 through 2007 (before the financial crisis). During the crisis, only foreign investments in Treasury securities increased significantly (from $2.376 trillion in 2007 to $4.467 trillion in 2010). In contrast, foreign investments in repos decreased significantly (from $1.109 trillion in 2007 to −$0.460 trillion in 2010), as did investments in open market paper (from $0.278 trillion in 2007 to $0.191 trillion in 2010). During the financial crisis, investors worldwide, searching for a safe haven for their funds, invested huge amounts of funds in U.S. Treasury securities, while reducing investments in other money market (and capital market) securities. These trends reversed by the mid-2010s. For example, foreign investments in negotiable CDs rose to $0.453 trillion by 2016, surpassing pre-crisis levels. In addition, while central banks varied in the level of interest rates they set, all countries reduced their interest rates to historic lows during the financial crisis as they took steps to stimulate their local economies (see Table 5–8). For example, the United Kingdom lowered its repurchase rate from 5.75 percent in 2007, prior to the crisis, to 0.50 percent in 2010, during the crisis. Japan, whose economy was relatively weak in 2007, set its discount rate at 0.75 percent in 2007 and lowered it even further, to 0.10 percent, during the crisis. The low rates existed even into 2016 when the central banks of Sweden, Switzerland, and Japan all set interest rates below zero.

**DO YOU UNDERSTAND:**

13. *What the major U.S. money market securities held by foreign investors are?*

**TABLE 5–8**   Selected Central Bank Interest Rates

| Country/Interest Rate | 2007 Rate | | 2010 Rate | | 2016 Rate | |
|---|---|---|---|---|---|---|
| | Percentage per Year | Applicable From | Percentage per Year | Applicable From | Percentage per Year | Applicable From |
| 1. EU countries | | | | | | |
| Euro area | 5 | June '07 | 1.00 | May '09 | 0.00 | Mar '16 |
| Denmark | | | | | | |
| Discount rate | 4 | June '07 | 0.75 | Jan. '10 | 0.00 | July '12 |
| Sweden | | | | | | |
| Deposit rate | 3 | Sept. '07 | −0.25 | Aug. '09 | −1.25 | Feb '16 |
| Repurchase rate | 3.75 | Sept. '07 | 0.50 | July '10 | −0.50 | Feb '16 |
| United Kingdom | | | | | | |
| Repurchase rate* | 5.75 | July '07 | 0.50 | Mar. '09 | 0.50 | Mar. '09 |
| 2. Switzerland | | | | | | |
| Three-month LIBOR target | 2.25–3.25 | Sept. '07 | 0.25 | Mar. '09 | −1.25 to −0.25 | Jan '15 |
| 3. Non-European countries | | | | | | |
| Canada† | | | | | | |
| Discount rate | 4.5 | July '07 | 0.50 | June '10 | 0.50 | July '15 |
| Japan | | | | | | |
| Discount rate | 0.75 | Feb. '07 | 0.10 | Nov. '08 | −0.10 | Jan '16 |
| United States | | | | | | |
| Federal funds rate‡ | 5.75 | Sept. '07 | 0.25 | Dec. '08 | 0.50 | Dec '15 |

*Bank of England key rate.
†Bank of Canada's ceiling rate for call money.
‡Rate targeted for interbank trade in central bank money.
**Source:** Authors' research.

### Euro Money Markets

Because of the importance of the U.S. dollar relative to other currencies, many international financial contracts call for payment in U.S. dollars—the U.S. dollar is still the major international medium of exchange (64 percent of the world's currency reserves are held in U.S. dollars). As a result, foreign governments and businesses have historically held a store of funds (deposits) denominated in dollars outside of the United States. Further, U.S. corporations conducting international trade often hold U.S. dollar deposits in foreign banks overseas to facilitate expenditures and purchases. These dollar-denominated deposits held offshore in U.S. bank branches overseas and in other (foreign) banks are called Eurodollar deposits (Eurodollar CDs) and the market in which they trade is called the **Eurodollar market.** Eurodollars may be held by governments, corporations, and individuals from anywhere in the world and are not directly subject to U.S. bank regulations, such as reserve requirements and deposit insurance premiums (or protection). As a result, the rate paid on Eurodollar CDs is generally higher than that paid on U.S.–domiciled CDs (see below). As an alternative to the Eurodollar market, companies can also obtain short-term funding by issuing Eurocommercial paper. Eurocommercial paper is issued in Europe but can be held by investors inside or outside of Europe.

**Eurodollar market**

*The market in which Eurodollars trade.*

**The Eurodollar Market.**   Large banks in London organized the interbank Eurodollar market. This market is now used by banks around the world as a source of overnight funding. The term *Eurodollar market* is something of a misnomer because the markets have no true physical location. Rather, the Eurodollar market is simply a market in which dollars held outside the United States (so-called Eurodollars) are tracked among multinational banks, including the offices of U.S. banks abroad, such as Citigroup's branch in London or its subsidiary in London. For example, a company in Italy needing U.S. dollars for a foreign trade transaction might ask Citigroup's subsidiary in London to borrow these dollars on the Eurodollar market. Alternatively, a Greek bank needing U.S. dollar funding may raise the required funds by issuing a Eurodollar CD. Most Eurodollar transactions take place in London. However, with the UK's 2016 referendum (so-called Brexit) in which citizens voted to leave the European Union, the role that London banks will play in the Eurodollar market is now in doubt. As it leaves the EU, the UK's ability to trade and interact with the remaining EU nations is no longer without restrictions and must be negotiated as the UK "divorces" itself from the EU. Thus, international banks may decide to leave London for another country in the EU in to conduct these financial transactions.

**London Interbank Offered Rate (LIBOR)**

*The rate paid on Eurodollars.*

The rate offered for sale on Eurodollar funds is known as the **London Interbank Offered Rate (LIBOR).** Funds traded in the Eurodollar market are often used as an alternative to fed funds as a source of overnight funding for banks.[14] Initially, most short-term adjustable-rate business loans were tied to the U.S. fed funds rate. However, the tremendous growth of the Eurodollar market has resulted in the LIBOR becoming the standard rate by which loan rates are now priced. For example, the commercial paper market in the United States now quotes rates as a spread over the LIBOR rate rather than over the fed funds or Treasury bill rate. As alternative sources of overnight funding, the LIBOR and the U.S. federal funds rate tend to be very closely related. Should rates in one of these markets (e.g., the LIBOR market) decrease relative to the other (e.g., the fed funds market), overnight borrowers will borrow in the LIBOR market rather than the fed funds market. As a result, the LIBOR will increase with this increased demand and the fed funds rate will decrease with the decline in demand. This will make the difference between the two rates quite small, although not equal, as is discussed below. The ease of transacting in both markets makes it virtually costless to use one market versus the other.

The fed funds rate and LIBOR between 1997 and 2016 are plotted in Figure 5–9. While they are close substitutes for overnight funding, the fed funds rate is generally lower than the LIBOR. This difference is due to the low-risk nature of U.S. bank deposits versus foreign bank deposits. U.S. bank deposits are covered by deposit insurance up to certain levels. Moreover, there is a perception that large U.S. banks and large U.S. bank depositors are implicitly insured via TBTF guarantees. Such guarantees lower U.S. bank risk and thus the cost of borrowing in the fed funds market. Foreign banks have no such explicit or implicit guarantees. Further, remember from Chapter 4 that the Federal Reserve sets the fed funds rate as it implements monetary policy. Thus, the fed funds rate is affected not just by the demand for interbank lending, but also by the Fed's actions. Note from Figure 5–9 that the fed funds rate sometimes exceeds the LIBOR rate. As noted previously, the increased demand for Eurodollars relative to fed funds as a source of overnight funding has, at times, outweighed the effect of the deposit insurance and "too big to fail" (or TBTF) guarantees. The result is that the fed funds rate has, at times, risen above the LIBOR rate.

Note, too, from Figure 5–9 that during the financial crisis the LIBOR rate spiked significantly, while the fed funds rate did not. The first spike occurred in the summer of 2007. In June and July, two Bear Stearns hedge funds required assistance, and Countrywide, one of the largest subprime mortgage originators, announced unexpectedly large losses. Then in August 2007, the asset-backed securities market dried up when several issuers failed to provide liquidity to support funding of securitized assets financed with short-term commercial paper. In response to the decline in asset values and an increase in concerns about bank solvency, the interbank market began to freeze. To prevent trouble in the financial markets, the Fed kept the fed funds rate low. The result was that the LIBOR rate rose especially sharply, while the fed funds rate did not. For example, the spread between the LIBOR and fed funds rates was 0.07 percent in May 2007, 0.50 percent in August 2007, and 0.75 percent in December 2007.

Conditions improved following the bailout of Bear Stearns. The cost of funds to banks fell, as did the spread between the LIBOR and fed funds rates. In the summer of 2008, however, mortgage foreclosures continued to rise, leading to further downgrades of mortgage-backed securities by the credit rating agencies and the acceleration of losses to holders of those securities. Losses on mortgages and mortgage-backed securities eventually led to

---

14. Also, the rate paid by banks buying these funds is the London Interbank Bid Rate (LIBID). The spread between LIBOR and LIBID is small, rarely exceeding 12.5 basis points.

**Figure 5–9**    Overnight Interest Rates, 1997–2016

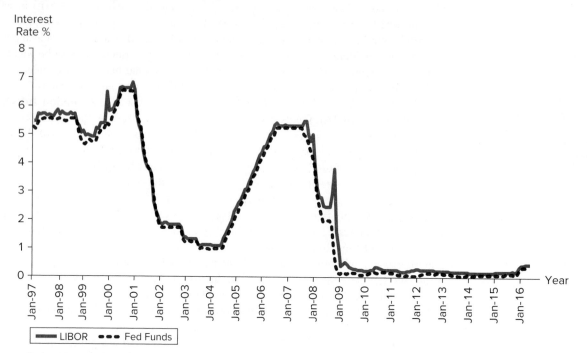

**Sources:** Federal Reserve Board website, "Research and Data"; and authors' research.

the failure of several financial institutions, most notably during the week of September 15, 2008, in which both AIG (technically) and Lehman Brothers failed. The demise of AIG and Lehman massively increased the demand for funding liquidity across the whole financial system. Panic soon spread globally and overnight borrowing rates jumped. However, the Fed again stepped in and lowered the fed funds rate (to between 0 and 0.25 percent) and expanded insurance on bank deposits. Public capital was also injected into all of the large banks in an attempt to allay fears about insolvency. The result was a huge spike in the spread between the LIBOR and fed funds rates. At the height of the crisis, the spread jumped to about 3 percent.

One of the more grievous actions by some global investment banks during the financial crisis was the manipulation of the LIBOR. LIBOR is the average of the interest rates submitted by major banks in the United States, Europe, and the United Kingdom in a variety of major currencies such as the dollar, euro, and yen. The scandal arose when it was discovered that banks had been manipulating the LIBOR rate so as to make either profits on its derivative positions (such as interest rate swaps) or to make the bank look stronger for reputational reasons. It is estimated that the banks involved made at least $75 billion on the manipulations. The In the News box in this chapter looks at allegations associated with the manipulation of the LIBOR during the financial crisis. The scandal became widely public in June 2012 when British investment bank Barclays agreed to pay $450 million to settle allegations by U.S. and British authorities that some of its traders attempted to manipulate LIBOR rates to increase the bank's profits and reduce concerns about its stability during the financial crisis.

Concerns were also raised about the failure of British and U.S. regulators to stop the manipulation of LIBOR when there was evidence that both were aware of it. In July 2012, a former trader stated that LIBOR manipulation had been occurring since at least 1991. In July 2012, the Federal Reserve Bank of New York released documents dated as far back as 2007 showing that it knew that banks were misreporting their borrowing costs when setting LIBOR. Yet, no action was taken. Similarly, documents from the Bank of England indicated that the bank knew as early as November 2007 that the LIBOR rate was being manipulated. It was not until June 2012 that Barclays became the first bank to agree to settle LIBOR manipulation allegations. In late 2012, eight global financial institutions, including J.P. Morgan Chase and Deutsche Bank, were fined $2.32 billion by the European Union regulators for alleged collusion in fixing the

# IN THE NEWS

LIBOR rate. In December 2012, UBS agreed to pay about $1.5 billion to settle charges that it manipulated LIBOR. Also in December, the U.S. Justice Department charged Tom Hayes, a former UBS and Citigroup trader, with conspiracy to commit fraud by manipulating the LIBOR (in June 2013, he was charged with eight counts of fraud as part of the UK investigation). In February 2013, the Royal Bank of Scotland also decided to settle at a cost of $610 million. In early 2013, Deutsche Bank stated that it had set aside money to cover potential fines associated with its role in the manipulation of the LIBOR. While several big banks pleaded guilty to and accepted penalties for manipulating LIBOR, the first criminal conviction of an individual occurred in August 2015. Former bank trader Tom Hayes was sentenced to 14 years in prison after a London jury convicted him of trying to fraudulently rig the LIBOR. The unanimous jury verdict delivered one of the harshest penalties against a banker since the financial crisis. Finally, in 2016 U.S. and British regulators fined six major global banks (Barclays, J.P. Morgan Chase, Citigroup, the Royal Bank of Scotland, UBS, and Bank of America) a total of nearly $6 billion for rigging the foreign exchange market and LIBOR interest rates. Foreign exchange traders from the banks had met in online chatroom groups, one brazenly named "the Cartel" and another "Mafia," to set rates that cheated customers while adding to their own profits.

Since its inception in the 1980s, LIBOR was managed by the British Bankers' Association (a London-based trade group whose members are some of the world's biggest banks). As a result of the LIBOR scandal, British authorities started looking for a new owner for LIBOR in 2012. In July 2013, the British government announced that LIBOR would be sold to NYSE Euronext which was, in turn, acquired by the Intercontinental Exchange in 2014. While ownership of LIBOR would be based in the United States, responsibility for regulating it would remain in the United Kingdom.

Whereas money markets in the United States stabilized after the financial crisis, European markets continued to face gridlock as the Euro zone dealt with debt crises in Greece,

Italy, Spain, Portugal, and even Cypress. A fall in confidence worsened after Cyprus needed a bailout in 2013, reigniting fears about the euro and its banks. Interbank funding across borders within the Euro zone dropped by a third. Even in Germany, cross-border interbank funding dropped 11.2 percent between March 2012 and March 2013. To prevent a complete economic collapse, the European Central Bank (ECB) provided banks with an alternative source of funding by creating more than €1 trillion of liquidity. Further, the ECB became the intermediary for many of the money market transactions. For example, the subsidiary of a Spanish bank in Germany (which was not allowed to transfer funds to its holding company in Spain) would deposit its surplus funds at the Bundesbank. The Spanish holding company would then access the ECB's lending facilities to obtain the funding it needed. The freeze in the European interbank market resulted in the ECB becoming the de facto clearer of the interbank market.

**Eurodollar certificates of deposit (CDs)**

*Dollar-denominated deposits in non-U.S. banks.*

**Eurodollar Certificates of Deposit.** **Eurodollar certificates of deposit (CDs)** are U.S. dollar–denominated CDs in foreign banks. Maturities on Eurodollar CDs are less than one year, and most have a maturity of one week to six months. Because these securities are deposited in non-U.S. banks, Eurodollar CDs are not subject to reserve requirements in the same manner as U.S. deposits (although the reserve requirement on U.S. CDs was set to zero at the beginning of 1991).

Figure 5–10 shows the difference between three-month Eurodollar and U.S. bank–issued CDs from 1971 through 2016. As can be seen in this figure, prior to the 1990s, the Eurodollar CD paid consistently higher interest rates than U.S. CDs. In the 1990s, after the reserve requirement on CDs was set to zero, it is difficult to distinguish the Eurodollar CD rate from the U.S. CD rate. Indeed, in 2007, the average rate paid on three-month Eurodollar CDs was 5.52 percent and on three-month U.S. CDs the average rate paid was 5.49 percent. Note, however, that during the financial crisis, Eurodollar CD rates rose above U.S. CD rates. In October 2008, the Eurodollar CD rate (5.31 percent) was 0.99 percent higher than the U.S. CD rate (4.32 percent). This difference was again due to the low-risk nature of U.S. bank deposits relative to foreign bank deposits. This trend continued through 2016.

**Figure 5–10**   Three-Month U.S. Bank–Issued versus Eurodollar CD Rates, 1971–2016

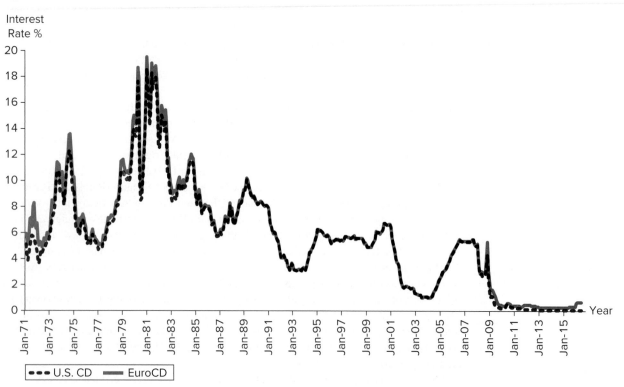

**Source:** Federal Reserve Board website, "Research and Data." www.federalreserve.com

**TABLE 5–9**  Eurocommercial Paper Outstanding, 1995–2016 *(in billions of U.S. dollars)*

| | | | | | Amount Outstanding | | | |
|---|---|---|---|---|---|---|---|---|
| | 1995 | 1998 | 2001 | 2004 | June 2008 | March 2010 | June 2010 | March 2016 |
| **Eurocommercial paper** | $87 | $133 | $243 | $415 | $807 | $595 | $521 | $509 |
| Currency type | | | | | | | | |
|   U.S. dollar | 56 | 78 | 103 | 113 | 208 | 183 | 159 | 217 |
|   Euro-area currencies* | 9 | 24 | 80 | 209 | 405 | 295 | 259 | 165 |
|   Japanese yen | 2 | 4 | 14 | 4 | 19 | 5 | 5 | 0 |
|   Pound sterling | n.a. | n.a. | 29 | 62 | 122 | 79 | 68 | 102 |
|   Other currencies | 20 | 27 | 17 | 27 | 53 | 33 | 30 | 25 |
| Issuer nationality | | | | | | | | |
|   Germany | 9 | 14 | 61 | 109 | 94 | 60 | 53 | 73 |
|   United Kingdom | 5 | 9 | 26 | 49 | 225 | 149 | 120 | 122 |
|   United States | 14 | 20 | 30 | 51 | 63 | 40 | 53 | 15 |
|   Japan | 12 | 18 | 7 | 17 | 1 | 2 | 1 | 2 |
|   Other developed countries | 36 | 56 | 92 | 176 | 377 | 317 | 277 | 219 |
|   Other | 11 | 16 | 27 | 13 | 47 | 27 | 17 | 78 |

*The BIS used the deutsche mark in 1995.
**Sources:** Bank for International Settlements, "International Banking and Financial Market Developments," *Quarterly Review,* various issues. www.bis.org

**Eurocommercial paper (Euro-CP)**

*Eurosecurities issued in Europe by dealers of commercial paper without involving a bank.*

**DO YOU UNDERSTAND:**

**14.** *What the relation is between the federal funds rate and the LIBOR?*

**15.** *Which currencies most international money market instruments are issued in?*

**16.** *What the differences are between a Eurodollar CD and Eurocommercial paper?*

**Eurocommercial Paper.** **Eurocommercial paper (Euro-CP)** is issued in Europe by dealers of commercial paper without involving a bank. The Eurocommercial paper rate is generally about one-half to 1 percent above the LIBOR rate. Foreign commercial paper markets are new and small relative to U.S. commercial paper markets. Eurocommercial paper is issued in local currencies as well as in U.S. dollars. Table 5–9 lists the amount of Eurocommercial paper outstanding in the international money markets from 1995 through 2016 by currency and nationality of issuer. Notice that with the introduction of the European Currency Unit in 1999, Eurocommercial paper denominated in euro-area currencies increased significantly. By 2010, 49.7 percent of all Euro-commercial paper outstanding was denominated in euros. In comparison, UK (British pound sterling) paper comprised 13.1 percent of all Eurocommercial paper outstanding, while U.S dollar–denominated paper fell to 30.5 percent of the total. Projections are that the Euro money market will only continue to grow. However, the European crisis resulted in a drop in the amount of Eurocommercial paper denominated in euro-area currencies. In 2016, just 32.4 percent of all Eurocommercial paper outstanding was denominated in euros, while pound sterling paper comprised 20.0 percent and U.S. dollar–denominated paper rose to 42.6 percent of the total.

## SUMMARY

In this chapter, we reviewed money markets, which are markets that trade debt securities with original maturities of one year or less. The need for money markets arises because cash receipts do not always coincide with cash expenditures for individuals, corporations, and government units. Because holding cash involves an opportunity cost, holders of excess cash invest these funds in money market securities. We looked at the various money market securities available to short-term investors and the major borrowers and issuers of each. We also outlined the processes by which each of these securities are issued and traded in secondary markets. We concluded the chapter by examining international issues involving money markets, taking a particular look at Euro money markets.

## QUESTIONS

1. What are the three characteristics common to money market securities? *(LG 5-1)*

2. What is the difference between a discount yield and a bond equivalent yield? Which yield is used for Treasury bill quotes? *(LG 5-1)*

3. Why can discount yields not generally be compared to yields on other (nondiscount) securities? *(LG 5-1)*

4. What is the difference between a single-payment yield and a bond equivalent yield? *(LG 5-1)*

5. Describe the T-bill auction process. *(LG 5-3)*

6. What is the difference between a competitive bid and a non-competitive bid in a T-bill auction? *(LG 5-3)*

7. How are T-bills traded in secondary markets? *(LG 5-2)*

8. What are federal funds? How are they recorded on the balance sheets of commercial banks? *(LG 5-2)*

9. Describe the two types of fed funds transactions. *(LG 5-2)*

10. What is the primary risk of trading in the fed funds markets? How did this risk come into play during the financial crisis of 2008–2009? *(LG 5-2)*

11. What is the difference between a repurchase agreement and a reverse repurchase agreement? *(LG 5-2)*

12. Describe the trading process for repurchase agreements. *(LG 5-2)*

13. Why do commercial paper issues have an original maturity of 270 days or less? *(LG 5-2)*

14. Why do commercial paper issuers almost always obtain a rating of their issues? *(LG 5-2)*

15. What factors caused the amount of outstanding commercial paper to increase from 1992 through 2000 and in the mid-2000s? What factors caused the amount of outstanding commercial paper to decrease from 2000 through 2004 and from 2007 through 2013? *(LG 5-2)*

16. What is the process through which negotiable CDs are issued? *(LG 5-2)*

17. Describe the process by which a banker's acceptance is created. *(LG 5-2)*

18. Who are the major issuers of and investors in money market securities? *(LG 5-4)*

19. Describe the issues regarding the validity of the LIBOR rate before and during the financial crisis. *(LG 5-5)*

20. What are Eurodollar CDs and Eurocommercial paper? *(LG 5-5)*

## PROBLEMS

1. What is the discount yield, bond equivalent yield, and effective annual return on a $1 million Treasury bill that currently sells at 99.375 percent of its face value and is 65 days from maturity? *(LG 5-2)*

2. What is the discount yield, bond equivalent yield, and effective annual return on a $5 million commercial paper issue that currently sells at 98.625 percent of its face value and is 136 days from maturity? *(LG 5-1)*

3. Calculate the bond equivalent yield and effective annual return on a negotiable CD that is 115 days from maturity and has a quoted nominal yield of 6.56 percent. *(LG 5-2)*

4. Calculate the bond equivalent yield and effective annual return on fed funds that are 3 days from maturity and have a quoted yield of 0.25 percent. *(LG 5-1)*

5. You would like to purchase a Treasury bill that has a $10,000 face value and is 68 days from maturity. The current price of the Treasury bill is $9,875. Calculate the discount yield on this Treasury bill. *(LG 5-2)*

6. Suppose you purchase a T-bill that is 125 days from maturity for $9,765. The T-bill has a face value of $10,000. *(LG 5-2)*
   a. Calculate the T-bill's quoted discount yield.
   b. Calculate the T-bill's bond equivalent yield.

7. You can purchase a T-bill that is 95 days from maturity for $9,965. The T-bill has a face value of $10,000. *(LG 5-2)*
   a. Calculate the T-bill's quoted yield.
   b. Calculate the T-bill's bond equivalent yield.
   c. Calculate the T-bill's EAR.

8. Refer to Table 5–5. *(LG 5-2)*
   a. Calculate the ask price of the T-bill maturing on September 1, 2016, as of May 16, 2016.
   b. Calculate the bid price of the T-bill maturing on November 10, 2016, as of May 16, 2016.

9. **eXcel**  **Using a Spreadsheet to Calculate T-bill Prices:** What is the bid price of a $10,000 face value T-bill with a bid rate of 2.23 percent if there are 10, 25, 50, 100, and 250 days to maturity? *(LG 5-2)*

| Face Value | Bid Rate | Days to Maturity | ⇒ | The Answer Will Be |
|---|---|---|---|---|
| $10,000 | 2.23% | 10 | | $9,993.81 |
| 10,000 | 2.23 | 25 | | 9,984.51 |
| 10,000 | 2.23 | 50 | | 9,969.03 |
| 10,000 | 2.23 | 100 | | 9,938.06 |
| 10,000 | 2.23 | 250 | | 9,845.14 |

10. A T-bill that is 225 days from maturity is selling for $98,850. The T-bill has a face value of $100,000. *(LG 5-2)*
    a. Calculate the discount yield, bond equivalent yield, and EAR on the T-bill.
    b. Calculate the discount yield, bond equivalent yield, and EAR on the T-bill if it matures in 300 days.

11. **eXcel**  **Using a Spreadsheet to Calculate T-bill Yield:** What is the quoted yield of a $10,000 face value T-bill with a market price of $8,885 if there are 10, 25, 50, 100, and 250 days to maturity? *(LG 5-2)*

| Face Value | Market Price | Days to Maturity | ⇒ | The Answer Will Be |
|---|---|---|---|---|
| $10,000 | $8,885 | 10 | | 4.014% |
| 10,000 | 8,885 | 25 | | 1.606 |
| 10,000 | 8,885 | 50 | | 0.803 |
| 10,000 | 8,885 | 100 | | 0.401 |
| 10,000 | 8,885 | 250 | | 0.161 |

12. If the overnight fed funds rate is quoted as 0.75 percent, what is the bond equivalent rate? Calculate the bond equivalent rate on fed funds if the quoted rate is 1.00 percent. *(LG 5-2)*

13. The overnight fed funds rate on May 20, 2016, was 0.37 percent. Compute the bond equivalent rate and the effective annual return on the fed funds as of May 20, 2016. *(LG 5-2)*

14. Suppose a bank enters a repurchase agreement in which it agrees to buy Treasury securities from a correspondent bank at a price of $24,995,000, with the promise to buy them back at a price of $25,000,000. *(LG 5-2)*
    a. Calculate the yield on the repo if it has a 7-day maturity.
    b. Calculate the yield on the repo if it has a 21-day maturity.

15. Calculate the bond equivalent yields and the equivalent annual returns for the repurchase agreements described in Problem 14. *(LG 5-2)*

16. You can buy commercial paper of a major U.S. corporation for $498,000. The paper has a face value of $500,000 and is 45 days from maturity. Calculate the discount yield and bond equivalent yield on the commercial paper. *(LG 5-2)*

17. Suppose an investor purchases 125-day commercial paper with a par value of $1,000,000 for a price of $995,235. Calculate the discount yield, bond equivalent yield, and the equivalent annual return on the commercial paper. *(LG 5-2)*

18. A bank has issued a six-month, $2 million negotiable CD with a 0.52 percent quoted annual interest rate ($i_{CD,\ sp}$). *(LG 5-2)*
    a. Calculate the bond equivalent yield and the EAR on the CD.
    b. How much will the negotiable CD holder receive at maturity?
    c. Immediately after the CD is issued, the secondary market price on the $2 million CD falls to $1,998,750. Calculate the new secondary market quoted yield, the bond equivalent yield, and the EAR on the $2 million face value CD.

19. A bank has issued a six-month, $5 million negotiable CD with a 0.35 percent quoted annual interest rate ($i_{CD,\ sp}$). *(LG 5-2)*
    a. Calculate the bond equivalent yield and the EAR on the CD.
    b. How much will the negotiable CD holder receive at maturity?
    c. Immediately after the CD is issued, the secondary market price on the $5 million CD falls to $4,994,500. Calculate the new secondary market quoted yield, the bond equivalent yield, and the EAR on the $5 million face value CD.

20. You have just purchased a three-month, $500,000 negotiable CD, which will pay a 5.5 percent annual interest rate. *(LG 5-2)*
    a. If the market rate on the CD rises to 6 percent, what is its current market value?
    b. If the market rate on the CD falls to 5.25 percent, what is its current market value?

# SEARCH THE SITE

Go to the Bureau of Public Debt website at **www.treasurydirect.gov** and find the latest information on 13-week and 26-week Treasury bill auctions using the following steps.

Under "Financial Institutions," click on "Auction Announcements and Results." Click on "Bill." Click on "Term: 13-Week." Under the column, "Competitive Results," click on "PDF." This will bring the file onto your computer that contains the relevant data. This will bring up the relevant information. Repeat the process, clicking on "Term: 26-week."

## Questions

1. What are the high, low, and median prices on the most recent issues?
2. What is the dollar value of tendered and accepted bids for the most recent issues?
3. What is the dollar value of noncompetitive bids on the most recent issues?

## SEARCH THE SITE

Go to the Federal Reserve website at **www.federalreserve.gov** and find the most recent information on prime versus commercial paper rates using the following steps. Click on "Selected Interest Rates" and then on the most recent date. This will bring up the relevant data ("Commercial Paper, Nonfinancial, 3-Month" and "Bank prime loan").

**Questions**

1. By how much have the prime rate and commercial paper rate changed since May 2016?
2. Calculate the average spread between the prime rate and the commercial paper rate over the last year. How does this compare to the spread seen in the fall of 2008?

**APPENDIX 5A: Single versus Discriminating Price Treasury Auctions**

**APPENDIX 5B: Creation of a Banker's Acceptance**

Appendixes 5A and 5B are available through Connect or your course instructor.

# Bond Markets

## Learning Goals

| | |
|---|---|
| **LG 6-1** | *Describe the major bond markets.* |
| **LG 6-2** | *Identify the characteristics of the various bond market securities.* |
| **LG 6-3** | *List the major bond market participants.* |
| **LG 6-4** | *Describe the types of securities traded in international bond markets.* |

## DEFINITION OF BOND MARKETS: CHAPTER OVERVIEW

Equity (stocks) and debt (notes, bonds, and mortgages) instruments with maturities of more than one year trade in **capital markets.** In the next several chapters, we look at characteristics of the different capital markets, starting in this chapter with bond markets.[1] In Chapter 7, we look at the mortgage markets (e.g., mortgage-backed securities), and in Chapter 8, we describe equity markets. In this chapter, we look at bond markets.

    **Bonds** are long-term debt obligations issued by corporations and government units. Proceeds from a bond issue are used to raise funds to support long-term operations of the issuer (e.g., for capital expenditure projects). In return for the investor's funds, bond issuers promise to pay a specified amount in the future on the maturity of the bond (the face value) plus coupon interest on the borrowed funds (the coupon rate times the face value of the bond). If the terms of the repayment are not met by the bond issuer, the bond holder (investor) has a claim on the assets of the bond issuer.

    **Bond markets** are markets in which bonds are issued and traded. They are used to assist in the transfer of funds from individuals, corporations, and government units with excess funds to corporations and government units in need of long-term debt funding. Bond markets are traditionally classified into three types: (1) Treasury notes and bonds, (2) municipal bonds, and (3) corporate bonds. Figure 6–1 shows the distribution of each type outstanding in 1994 and 2016. In Chapter 3, we applied time value of money principles

**LG 6-1**

---

1. Although both notes and bonds are issued by agents such as the U.S. government, their characteristics (e.g., coupon rate) other than maturity are generally the same. In this chapter, the term *bond* will mean bonds and notes in general, except where we distinguish notes by their special maturity features. For example, U.S. Treasury notes have maturities of over one year and up to 10 years. U.S. Treasury bonds have maturities from over 10 years at the time of issue.

**capital markets**

*Markets that trade debt (bonds and mortgages) and equity (stocks) instruments with maturities of more than one year.*

**bond**

*Long-term debt obligation issued by corporations and government units.*

**bond markets**

*Markets in which bonds are issued and traded.*

**Figure 6–1**    Bond Market Instruments Outstanding, 1994–2016

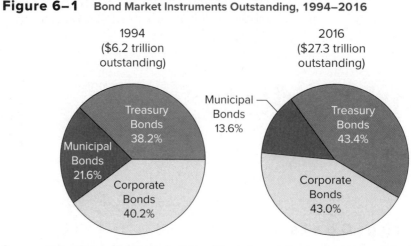

Sources: Federal Reserve Board website, "Flow of Funds Accounts," various issues. www.federalreserve.gov

to the valuation and duration of bonds, paying particular attention to the change in a bond's value when interest rates change. We also examined how characteristics specific to a bond (e.g., coupon rate and remaining time to maturity) influence its price. In this chapter, we look at the characteristics of the various bond securities (including the trading process in bond markets), the participants in the bond markets, and international bond markets and securities.

# BOND MARKET SECURITIES

**LG 6-2**

Government units and corporations are the major bond security issuers. Figure 6–1 shows that the dollar amount of bond securities outstanding by these groups has increased from $6.2 trillion in 1994 to $27.3 trillion in 2016. Much of this increase occurred between 2007 and 2016 during the depths of the financial crisis as bond markets grew by more than $10 trillion. Historically low rates on debt during this period were a major reason for the boom in bond markets. In this section, we look at the bond market securities issued by each of these groups: Treasury notes and bonds, municipal bonds, and corporate bonds.

## Treasury Notes and Bonds

**Treasury notes (T-notes) and bonds (T-bonds)**

*Long-term securities issued by the U.S. Treasury to finance the national debt and other federal government expenditures.*

**Treasury notes (T-notes) and bonds (T-bonds)** are issued by the U.S. Treasury to finance the national debt and other federal government expenditures ($11.8 trillion outstanding in 2016). The national debt (*ND*) reflects the historical accumulation of annual federal government deficits or expenditures (*G*) minus taxes (*T*) over the last 200-plus years, as follows:

$$ND_t = \sum_{t=1}^{N}(G_t - T_t)$$

www.ustreas.gov

Figure 6–2 shows the composition of the U.S. national debt from 1994 through 2016. Notice that over this period, approximately 40 to 50 percent of the U.S. national debt consisted of Treasury notes and bonds. Notice also that as the U.S. economy boomed in the late 1990s and the U.S. budget deficit shrank, the amount of public debt outstanding in the form of U.S. Treasury securities decreased from a year-end high of $3.10 trillion in 1994 (52.5 percent of the U.S. gross domestic product [GDP]) to $2.97 trillion in 2000 (29.8 percent of GDP). While the amount of Treasury securities grew through the 2000s, so did economic growth. The level of outstanding U.S. Treasury securities grew to $4.7 trillion

**Figure 6–2** Composition of the U.S. National Debt

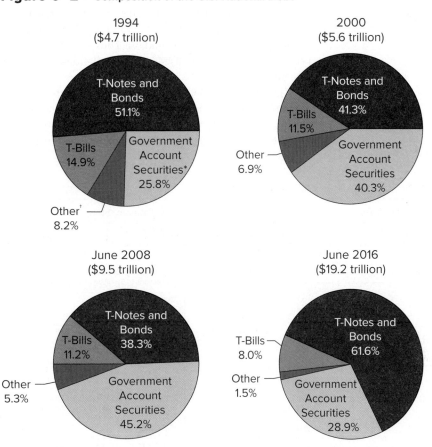

*Includes securities held by government trust funds, revolving funds, and special funds such as Social Security and government pension funds.
†Includes U.S. savings securities, dollar-denominated foreign government securities issued by the U.S. Treasury directly to foreign governments, and other.
**Sources:** U.S. Treasury Department, *Treasury Bulletin,* various issues. www.ustreas.gov

by June 2008 (32.9 percent of GDP). During the financial crisis, the U.S. government used Treasury securities in its attempts to stimulate the economy (see Chapter 4) and the national debt ballooned to $16.7 trillion—$11.4 trillion of which was Treasury securities (representing 71.3 percent of GDP).

Like T-bills, T-notes and bonds are backed by the full faith and credit of the U.S. government and are, therefore, default risk free. As a result, T-notes and bonds pay relatively low rates of interest (yields to maturity) to investors. T-notes and bonds, however, are not completely risk free. Given their longer maturity (i.e., duration), these instruments experience wider price fluctuations than do money market instruments as interest rates change (and thus are subject to interest rate risk—see Chapter 22). Further, many of the older issued bonds and notes—"off the run" issues—may be less liquid than newly issued bonds and notes—"on the run" issues—in which case they may bear an additional premium for illiquidity risk.

In contrast to T-bills, which are sold on a discount basis from face value (see Chapter 5), T-notes and T-bonds pay coupon interest (semiannually). Further, T-bills have an original maturity of one year or less. Treasury notes have original maturities from over 1 to 10 years, while T-bonds have original maturities from over 10 years. T-notes and bonds are issued in minimum denominations of $100, or in multiples of $100. The Treasury issues two types of notes and bonds: fixed principal and inflation-indexed. While both types pay interest twice a year, the principal value used to determine the percentage interest payment (coupon) on inflation-indexed bonds is adjusted to reflect inflation (measured by the consumer price index). Thus, the semiannual coupon payments and the final principal payment are based on the inflation-adjusted principal value of the security (see below).

Like T-bills, once issued T-notes and T-bonds trade in very active secondary markets. Table 6–1 presents part of a T-note and T-bond (including Treasury STRIPS—see below) closing price/interest yield quote sheet from *The Wall Street Journal* for trading on May 23, 2016. Column 1 is the date the note or bond matures. Column 2 in the table lists the

**TABLE 6–1**   **Treasury Note and Bond Quote**

| Treasury Notes & Bonds | | | | | |
|---|---|---|---|---|---|
| Monday, May 23, 2016 | | | | | |
| Treasury note and bond data are representative over-the-counter quotations as of 3pm Eastern time. For notes and bonds callable prior to maturity, yields are computed to the earliest call date for issues quoted above par and to the maturity date for issues below par. | | | | | |
| Maturity | Coupon | Bid | Asked | Chg | Asked yield |
| 5/31/2016 | 0.375 | 100.0000 | 100.0156 | 0.0078 | −0.441 |
| 6/15/2016 | 0.500 | 100.0078 | 100.0234 | 0.0078 | 0.110 |
| 6/30/2016 | 0.500 | 100.0078 | 100.0234 | unch. | 0.269 |
| 7/15/2016 | 0.625 | 100.0391 | 100.0547 | 0.0156 | 0.242 |
| 7/31/2016 | 0.500 | 100.0234 | 100.0391 | unch. | 0.291 |
| 8/15/2016 | 0.625 | 100.0547 | 100.0703 | 0.0078 | 0.316 |
| 8/31/2016 | 0.500 | 100.0391 | 100.0547 | 0.0234 | 0.296 |
| 9/15/2016 | 0.875 | 100.1250 | 100.1406 | −0.0156 | 0.420 |
| 9/30/2016 | 0.500 | 100.0469 | 100.0625 | 0.0234 | 0.322 |
| 10/15/2016 | 1.000 | 100.0547 | 100.0703 | −0.0234 | 0.446 |
| 11/15/2016 | 0.625 | 100.0547 | 100.0703 | 0.0078 | 0.477 |
| 2/15/2017 | 0.625 | 100.0156 | 100.0313 | unch. | 0.582 |
| **2/28/2017** | **0.875** | **100.1641** | **100.1797** | **−0.0313** | **0.640** |
| 3/15/2017 | 0.750 | 100.0859 | 100.1016 | −0.0078 | 0.624 |
| 3/31/2017 | 1.000 | 100.2813 | 100.2969 | −0.0078 | 0.650 |
| 4/30/2017 | 0.500 | 99.8203 | 99.8359 | 0.0156 | 0.676 |
| 4/30/2017 | 0.875 | 100.1641 | 100.1797 | −0.0078 | 0.682 |
| 5/15/2017 | 0.875 | 100.1563 | 100.1719 | −0.0078 | 0.698 |
| 5/31/2017 | 0.625 | 99.8828 | 99.8984 | 0.0078 | 0.725 |
| 6/15/2017 | 0.875 | 100.1250 | 100.1406 | −0.0234 | 0.742 |
| 6/30/2017 | 0.750 | 99.9844 | 100.0000 | −0.0078 | 0.750 |
| 7/31/2017 | 0.625 | 99.7891 | 99.8047 | −0.0391 | 0.790 |
| 9/30/2017 | 1.875 | 101.3906 | 101.4063 | −0.0156 | 0.827 |
| 10/15/2017 | 0.875 | 100.0469 | 100.0625 | −0.0156 | 0.830 |
| 10/31/2017 | 1.875 | 101.4609 | 101.4766 | unch. | 0.837 |
| 11/15/2017 | 0.875 | 100.0234 | 100.0391 | −0.0078 | 0.848 |
| 11/15/2017 | 4.250 | 104.9766 | 104.9922 | −0.0234 | 0.839 |
| **11/30/2017** | **0.625** | **99.6406** | **99.6828** | **−0.0156** | **0.853** |
| 11/30/2017 | 0.875 | 100.0234 | 100.0318 | −0.0156 | 0.849 |
| 12/31/2017 | 1.000 | 100.2109 | 100.2266 | −0.0078 | 0.857 |
| 2/15/2019 | 2.750 | 104.7109 | 104.7266 | −0.0234 | 0.989 |
| 2/28/2019 | 1.375 | 100.9297 | 100.9453 | −0.0156 | 1.028 |
| 2/28/2019 | 1.500 | 101.2813 | 101.2969 | −0.0313 | 1.024 |
| 3/15/2019 | 1.000 | 99.8984 | 99.9141 | −0.0078 | 1.031 |
| 3/31/2019 | 1.500 | 101.3281 | 101.3438 | −0.0156 | 1.021 |
| 3/31/2019 | 1.625 | 101.6250 | 101.6406 | −0.0234 | 1.040 |
| 5/15/2020 | 3.500 | 108.6953 | 108.7109 | −0.0234 | 1.247 |
| 5/31/2020 | 1.375 | 100.4766 | 100.4922 | −0.0234 | 1.249 |
| 5/31/2020 | 1.500 | 100.9141 | 100.9297 | −0.0313 | 1.262 |
| 6/30/2020 | 1.625 | 101.3594 | 101.3750 | −0.0078 | 1.280 |
| 6/30/2020 | 1.875 | 102.4141 | 102.4297 | −0.0078 | 1.265 |
| 7/31/2020 | 2.000 | 102.8750 | 102.8906 | −0.0234 | 1.288 |
| 8/15/2020 | 2.625 | 105.4375 | 105.4531 | −0.0156 | 1.295 |
| 5/15/2023 | 1.750 | 100.6875 | 100.7031 | 0.0703 | 1.643 |
| 8/15/2023 | 2.500 | 105.7500 | 105.7656 | 0.0547 | 1.650 |
| 11/15/2023 | 2.750 | 107.5234 | 107.5391 | 0.0703 | 1.673 |
| 2/15/2024 | 2.750 | 107.5781 | 107.5938 | 0.0703 | 1.697 |
| 5/15/2024 | 2.500 | 105.7656 | 105.7813 | 0.1094 | 1.721 |
| 8/15/2024 | 2.375 | 104.7656 | 104.7813 | 0.1016 | 1.748 |
| 11/15/2024 | 2.250 | 103.7422 | 103.7578 | 0.1172 | 1.771 |
| 5/15/2045 | 3.000 | 107.6875 | 107.7188 | 0.1094 | 2.618 |
| 11/15/2045 | 3.000 | 107.6563 | 107.6875 | 0.0938 | 2.624 |
| 2/15/2046 | 2.500 | 97.2109 | 97.2422 | 0.0938 | 2.634 |
| 5/15/2046 | 2.500 | 97.2656 | 97.2969 | 0.1250 | 2.631 |

| U.S. Treasury Strips | | | | |
|---|---|---|---|---|
| Monday, May 23, 2016 | | | | |
| U.S. zero-coupon STRIPS allow investors to hold the interest and principal components of eligible Treasury notes and bonds as separate securities. STRIPS offer no interest payment; investors receive payment only at maturity. Quotes are as of 3 p.m. Eastern time based on transactions of $1 million or more. Yields calculated on the ask quote. | | | | |
| Maturity | Bid | Asked | Chg | Asked yield |
| **Treasury Bond, Stripped Principal** | | | | |
| 2016 Aug 15 | 99.896 | 99.899 | −0.002 | 0.44 |
| 2016 Nov 15 | 99.748 | 99.752 | −0.004 | 0.52 |
| **2017 May 15** | **99.234** | **99.244** | **−0.010** | **0.78** |
| 2018 Nov 15 | 97.764 | 97.788 | −0.018 | 0.90 |
| 2019 Feb 15 | 97.420 | 97.447 | −0.019 | 0.95 |
| 2019 Aug 15 | 96.522 | 96.553 | −0.023 | 1.09 |
| 2022 Nov 15 | 90.261 | 90.319 | 0.021 | 1.58 |
| 2023 Feb 15 | 89.752 | 89.812 | 0.052 | 1.60 |
| 2023 Aug 15 | 88.683 | 88.746 | 0.039 | 1.66 |
| 2024 Nov 15 | 86.080 | 86.153 | 0.066 | 1.77 |
| 2029 Aug 15 | 75.932 | 76.031 | 0.125 | 2.08 |
| 2030 May 15 | 74.786 | 74.889 | 0.130 | 2.08 |
| 2031 Feb 15 | 73.491 | 73.598 | 0.134 | 2.09 |
| 2044 Feb 15 | 47.378 | 47.508 | 0.063 | 2.70 |
| 2044 May 15 | 46.675 | 46.804 | 0.063 | 2.73 |
| 2044 Nov 15 | 45.689 | 45.818 | 0.030 | 2.76 |
| 2045 Feb 15 | 45.309 | 45.437 | 0.063 | 2.77 |
| 2045 May 15 | 44.969 | 45.097 | 0.063 | 2.77 |
| 2045 Nov 15 | 44.256 | 44.385 | 0.063 | 2.78 |
| 2046 Feb 15 | 44.077 | 44.207 | 0.063 | 2.77 |
| 2046 May 15 | 43.907 | 44.037 | 0.063 | 2.76 |
| **Treasury Note, Stripped Principal** | | | | |
| 2016 Aug 31 | 99.874 | 99.876 | −0.002 | 0.46 |
| 2016 Nov 30 | 99.704 | 99.708 | −0.005 | 0.56 |
| 2017 Aug 15 | 98.980 | 98.992 | −0.012 | 0.83 |
| 2017 Nov 30 | 98.779 | 98.794 | −0.017 | 0.80 |
| 2018 Aug 31 | 97.918 | 97.940 | −0.019 | 0.92 |
| 2018 Nov 30 | 97.769 | 97.794 | −0.025 | 0.89 |
| 2022 May 15 | 91.080 | 91.134 | 0.020 | 1.56 |
| 2025 Nov 15 | 83.742 | 83.820 | 0.072 | 1.87 |
| 2026 May 15 | 82.949 | 83.289 | 0.069 | 1.84 |
| **Stripped Coupon Interest** | | | | |
| 2016 Jun 15 | 99.980 | 99.981 | unch. | 0.32 |
| 2016 Nov 15 | 99.730 | 99.735 | −0.004 | 0.56 |
| 2019 May 31 | 96.611 | 96.640 | −0.020 | 1.13 |
| 2019 Nov 30 | 95.893 | 95.927 | −0.005 | 1.18 |
| 2024 May 15 | 86.487 | 86.556 | 0.042 | 1.82 |
| 2024 Nov 15 | 85.307 | 85.378 | 0.067 | 1.87 |
| 2025 Feb 15 | 84.721 | 84.794 | 0.087 | 1.90 |
| 2025 May 15 | 84.080 | 84.155 | 0.088 | 1.93 |
| 2025 Aug 15 | 83.575 | 83.651 | 0.089 | 1.94 |
| 2035 May 15 | 62.664 | 62.782 | 0.146 | 2.47 |
| 2035 Nov 15 | 61.612 | 61.731 | 0.118 | 2.49 |
| 2036 Feb 15 | 61.316 | 61.435 | 0.119 | 2.48 |
| 2036 May 15 | 60.737 | 60.857 | 0.120 | 2.50 |
| 2036 Aug 15 | 60.181 | 60.301 | 0.120 | 2.52 |
| 2036 Nov 15 | 59.633 | 59.753 | 0.120 | 2.53 |
| 2044 Nov 15 | 45.338 | 45.465 | 0.031 | 2.79 |
| 2045 May 15 | 44.808 | 44.937 | 0.062 | 2.78 |
| 2045 Aug 15 | 44.528 | 44.657 | 0.063 | 2.78 |
| 2045 Nov 15 | 44.128 | 44.256 | 0.063 | 2.79 |
| 2046 May 15 | 43.907 | 44.037 | 0.063 | 2.76 |

**Source:** *The Wall Street Journal Online,* May 24, 2016. www.wsj.com

coupon rate on the Treasury security. Note that coupon rates are set at intervals of 0.125 (or ⅛ of 1) percent. Column 3, labeled *Bid,* is the close of the day selling price (in percentage terms) available to T-note and bond holders (i.e., the price dealers are willing to pay T-note and bond holders for their Treasury securities). Prices are quoted as percentages of the face value on the Treasury security. For example, using a face value of $1,000, the bid price on the 0.875 percent coupon, February 2017 T-note was $1,001.641 (100.1641% × $1,000). Column 4, labeled *Asked,* is the close of the day purchase price available to investors. Column 5, labeled *Chg,* is the change in the asked price from the previous day's close—that is, the February 2017 T-note's price was 0.0313 percent lower than the previous day's close (100.2110 percent). Finally, the last column, labeled *Asked Yield,* is the asked price converted into a yield to maturity on the T-note or T-bond. This yield is calculated using the yield to maturity formulas found in Chapter 3—it is the interest rate or yield (using semiannual compounding) that makes the price of the security just equal to the present value of the expected coupon and face value cash flows on the bond (where this yield is the single discount rate that makes this equality hold).

**STRIPS**

*A Treasury security in which the periodic interest payment is separated from the final principal payment.*

**www.ml.com**

**STRIPS.** In 1985, the Treasury began issuing 10-year notes and 30-year bonds[2] to financial institutions using a book-entry system under a program titled Separate Trading of Registered Interest and Principal Securities (STRIPS). A **STRIPS** is a Treasury security in which periodic coupon interest payments can be separated from each other and from the final principal payment. As illustrated in Figure 6–3, a STRIPS effectively creates two sets of securities—one set for each semiannual interest payment and one for the final principal payment. Each of the components of the STRIPS are often referred to as "Treasury zero bonds" or "Treasury zero-coupon bonds" because investors in the individual components receive only the single stripped payments (e.g., the third semiannual coupon) in which they invest. Investors needing a lump sum payment in the distant future (e.g., life insurers) would prefer to hold the principal portion of the STRIPS. Investors wanting nearer-term cash flows (e.g., commercial banks) would prefer the interest portions of the STRIPS. Also, some state lotteries invest the present value of large lottery prizes in STRIPS to be sure that funds are available to meet required annual payments to lottery winners. Pension funds purchase STRIPS to match payment cash flows received on their assets (STRIPS) with those required on their liabilities (pension contract payments).

STRIPS were created by the U.S. Treasury in response to the separate trading of Treasury security principal and interest that had been developed by securities firms. Specifically, in the early 1980s, Merrill Lynch introduced Treasury Investment Growth Receipts (TIGRs). Merrill Lynch purchased Treasury securities, stripped them into one security representing the principal component only and a separate security for each coupon payment, and put these individual securities up for resale. The Treasury's creation of the STRIPS was meant to offer a competitive product to the market.

**Figure 6–3**   **Creation of a Treasury STRIP**

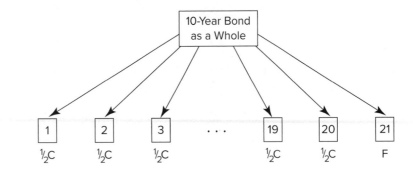

2. The U.S. Treasury stopped issuing 30-year bonds between 2001 and 2006.

The U.S. Treasury does not issue STRIPS directly to investors. Rather, stripped Treasury notes and bonds may be purchased only through financial institutions and government securities brokers and dealers, who create the STRIPS components after purchasing the original T-notes or T-bonds (whole) in Treasury auctions (see below). After the STRIPS components have been created, by requesting that the Treasury separate each coupon and face value payment on each bond and recording them as separate securities in its book-entry computer system, they can be sold individually in the secondary markets.[3]

---

### EXAMPLE 6–1  Creation of a STRIPS

Suppose the Treasury issues a five-year T-note with a par value of $10,000 and an 8 percent coupon rate (paid semiannually, or $400 is paid to the holder every six months for the next five years) to Citigroup. Citigroup decides to convert the bond into a set of stripped securities by requesting the Treasury to separate the coupons and face value of the note into separate securities on its computer system (basically giving each coupon and face value a separate I.D. or CUSIP number). This means that Citigroup can then sell 11 different securities: 10 securities associated with each of the semiannual coupon payments of $400 and one that pays $10,000 (the face or principal value) in five years to outside investors. We show the value of each of these securities in Table 6–2, assuming the yield to maturity on each of the stripped securities is 7.90 percent and is the same as the bond sold "whole."

Notice that the total present value of the 11 different securities involved with the STRIPS is the same as that of the original T-note before it is stripped, $10,040.65. However, in general, the bank (Citigroup) will try to sell the 11 stripped securities for a greater total present value than the bond as a whole. The reason for this is that many investors desire particular maturity zero-coupon bonds to meet investment goals and needs. Such goals and needs (such as duration targets—see below) are often harder to achieve through buying whole T-notes or T-bonds. Consequently, investors are willing to pay a higher price and thus accept a yield lower than 7.90 percent on the stripped investments. As a result, the total price Citigroup would get from selling the 11 STRIPS would exceed $10,040.65.

---

**TABLE 6–2**  Present Value of STRIPS Components of a Five-Year T-Note with an 8 Percent Coupon Rate and 7.90 Percent Yield to Maturity

| Maturity on Security (in years) | Cash Flow Received at Maturity | Present Value of Cash Flow at 7.90 Percent |
|---|---|---|
| 0.5 | $ 400 | $ 384.80 |
| 1.0 | 400 | 370.18 |
| 1.5 | 400 | 356.11 |
| 2.0 | 400 | 342.58 |
| 2.5 | 400 | 329.56 |
| 3.0 | 400 | 317.04 |
| 3.5 | 400 | 304.99 |
| 4.0 | 400 | 293.40 |
| 4.5 | 400 | 282.25 |
| 5.0 | 400 | 271.53 |
| 5.0 | 10,000 | 6,788.21 |
| Total | | $10,040.65 |

3. Once a bond is stripped, if an investor purchases each coupon and face value component at a later time, he or she can ask the Treasury to reconstitute the original bond on its computer system. Thus, the Treasury STRIPS program is highly flexible and STRIPS can be reconstituted as whole bonds.

As mentioned previously, STRIPS are attractive investments to investors desiring particular maturity zero-coupon bonds to meet investment goals and needs. For example, STRIPS are used as investment securities for individual retirement accounts, Keogh plans, and pension funds. Frequently, managers of these types of financial institutions face the problem of structuring their asset investments so they can pay a given cash amount to policyholders in some future period. The classic example of this is an insurance policy that pays the holder some lump sum when the holder reaches retirement age. The risk to the life insurance company manager is that interest rates on the funds generated from investing the holder's premiums could fall. Thus, the accumulated returns on the premiums invested might not meet the target or promised amount. In effect, the insurance company would be forced to draw down its reserves and net worth to meet its payout commitments. (See Chapter 15 for a discussion of this risk.) To immunize or protect itself against interest rate risk, the insurer can invest in Treasury zero-coupon bonds (or STRIPS).

---

**EXAMPLE 6–2**   Using a STRIPS to Immunize against Interest Rate Risk

Suppose that it is 2019 and an insurer must make a guaranteed payment to an investor in five years, 2024. For simplicity, we assume that this target guaranteed payment is $1,480,000, a lump sum policy payout on retirement, equivalent to investing $1,000,000 at a semianually compounded rate of 8 percent over five years.

To immunize or protect itself against interest rate risk, the insurer needs to determine which investments would produce a cash flow of exactly $1,480,000 in five years, regardless of what happens to interest rates in the immediate future. By investing in a five-year maturity (and duration) Treasury zero-coupon bond (or STRIPS), the insurance company would produce a $1,480,000 cash flow in five years, no matter what happens to interest rates in the immediate future.

Given a $1,000 face value and an 8 percent yield and assuming annual compounding, the current price per five-year STRIPS is $675.56 per bond:

$$P = 675.56 = \frac{1,000}{(1 + 0.08/2)^{2 \times 5}}$$

If the insurer buys 1,480 of these bonds at a total cost of $1,000,000 in 2019, these investments would produce $1,480,000 on maturity in five years. The reason is that the duration of this bond portfolio exactly matches the target horizon for the insurer's future liability to its policyholders. Intuitively, since the STRIPS pays no intervening cash flows or coupons, future changes in interest rates have no reinvestment income effect. Thus, the return would be unaffected by intervening interest rate changes.

---

Most T-note and T-bond issues are eligible for the STRIPS program. The components of a STRIPS are sold with minimum face values of $100 and in increasing multiples of $100 (e.g., $200, $300). Thus, the par amount of the securities must be an amount that will produce semiannual coupon payments of $100 or a multiple of $100. The original Treasury note and bond issues that are eligible for the STRIPS program are usually limited to those with large par values.

The T-note and T-bond quote list in Table 6–1 includes a portion of the Treasury STRIPS that traded on May 23, 2016. The quote first lists principal value stripped from Treasury bonds, second is the principal value stripped from Treasury notes, and finally the coupon payments stripped from both Treasury bonds and Treasury notes. Look at the row for Treasury bond, stripped principal, maturing in May 2017. The first column of the quote lists the date the STRIPS matures (e.g., 2017 May 15). Columns 2 and 3 list the bid and asked prices for the STRIPS. Like the quote for other Treasury securities (discussed above), the bid is the close of the day selling price (in percentage terms) available to STRIPS holders (i.e., the price dealers are willing to pay T-note and bond holders for their Treasury securities). Prices are quoted as percentages of the face value on the Treasury security. The asked price is the close of the day purchase price available to investors. Column 4, labeled Chg, is the change in the asked price from the previous day's close. Finally, the last column, labeled *Asked Yield,* is the asked price converted into a yield to maturity on the STRIPS. This yield is calculated using the yield to maturity formulas found in Chapter 3. That is, it is the interest rate or yield (using semiannual compounding to correspond with the semiannual coupon payments that are "stripped" from each other and the final principal payment) that makes the price of the security just equal to the present value of the expected coupon or face value cash flows on the STRIPS.

---

### EXAMPLE 6–3    Calculation of Yield on a STRIPS

**CALCULATOR HINTS**

$N = 97534247(2) =$
$1.95068493$
$PV = -99.244$
$PMT = 0$
$FV = 100$
$CPT\ I = 0.38978627$
$0.38978627 \times 2 = 0.78\%$

For the principal STRIPS maturing in May 2017 (reported in Table 6–1), the asked price at the close on Monday, May 23, 2016 (or present value), is 99.244 percent. Settlement occurs one business day after purchase, so you receive actual ownership on Wednesday, May 24, 2016. When the STRIPS matures, on May 15, 2017 (in 0.97534247 year), the STRIPS holder will receive 100 percent of the face value (or future value). Using semiannual compounding, the yield to maturity (*ytm*), or asked yield is calculated as:

$$100\% = 99.244\%(1 + ytm/2)^{2 \times 97534247}$$

Solving for *ytm,* we get:

$$ytm = 0.78\%$$

---

**Treasury Note and Bond Yields.**    Treasury note and bond yields to maturities and prices are calculated using the bond valuation formulas presented in Chapter 3. The general bond valuation formula is:

$$V_b = \frac{INT}{m} \sum_{t=1}^{mN} \left( \frac{1}{1 + \dfrac{r_b}{m}} \right)^t + \frac{M}{\left(1 + \dfrac{r_b}{m}\right)^{mN}}$$

$$= \frac{INT}{m} \left[ \frac{1 - \dfrac{1}{\left(1 + \dfrac{r_b}{m}\right)^{mN}}}{\dfrac{r_b}{m}} \right] + M \left[ \frac{1}{\left(1 + \dfrac{r_b}{m}\right)^{mN}} \right]$$

where

$V_b$ = Present value of the bond
$M$ = Par or face value of the bond
$INT$ = Annual interest (or coupon) payment on the bond equals the par value times the coupon rate
$N$ = Number of years until the bond matures
$m$ = Number of times per year interest is paid
$r_b$ = Interest rate used to discount cash flows on the bond

The bond value calculated from this general formula is the price (also referred to as the *clean price)* quoted in the financial press.

---

**EXAMPLE 6–4**   Calculation of a T-Note Price from a *Wall Street Journal Online* Quote

In Table 6–1, look at the T-note outstanding on Monday, May 23, 2016 (or a settlement date of Wednesday, May 24, 2016), with a maturity on November 30, 2017 (i.e., they were 1.52328767 years from maturity). The T-note had a coupon rate of 0.625 percent and an asked yield of 0.853 percent. Using the bond valuation formula, the asked price on the bond should have been:

**CALCULATOR HINTS**

$N = 1.52328767(2) =$
3.04657534
$I = 0.853/2 = 0.4265$
$PMT = 0.625/2 = 0.3125$
$FV = 100$
$CPT\ PV = 99.6828$

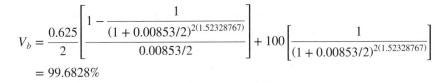

$$V_b = \frac{0.625}{2}\left[\frac{1 - \dfrac{1}{(1 + 0.00853/2)^{2(1.52328767)}}}{0.00853/2}\right] + 100\left[\frac{1}{(1 + 0.00853/2)^{2(1.52328767)}}\right]$$

$$= 99.6828\%$$

The asked quote reported in *The Wall Street Journal Online* was indeed 99.6858.

---

*Accrued Interest.*   When an investor buys a T-note or T-bond between coupon payments, the buyer must compensate the seller for that portion of the coupon payment accrued between the last coupon payment and the settlement day (normally, settlement takes place 1 day after a trade), while the seller was still the owner of the security. This amount is called **accrued interest.** Accrued interest on a T-note or T-bond is based on the actual number of days the bond was held by the seller since the last coupon payment:

**accrued interest**

*That portion of the coupon payment accrued between the last coupon payment and the settlement day.*

$$\text{Accrued interest} = \frac{INT}{2} \times \frac{\text{Actual number of days since last coupon payment}}{\text{Actual number of days in coupon period}}$$

At settlement, the buyer must pay the seller the purchase price of the T-note or T-bond plus accrued interest. The sum of these two is often called the *full price* or *dirty price* of the security. The price without the accrued interest added on is called the *clean price.*[4] In the United States, it is market practice that newspapers list bond quotes on a clean price basis. Then, when a bond trade is settled, the accrued interest is added to the value based on the clean price of the bond. Thus, bond price quotes are typically the clean prices, but buyers of bonds pay the dirty, or full, price.

---

**EXAMPLE 6–5**   Calculation of Accrued Interest and Yield to Maturity on a Bond

On August 5, 2019, you purchase a $10,000 T-note that matures on May 15, 2025 (settlement occurs one day after purchase, so you receive actual ownership of the bond on August 6, 2019). The coupon rate on the T-note is 5.875 percent and the current price quoted on the bond in the financial press is 101.3437. The last coupon payment occurred on May 15, 2019 (82 days before settlement), and the next coupon payment will be paid on November 15, 2019 (102 days from settlement). We illustrate this time line in Figure 6–4.

The accrued interest due to the seller from the buyer at settlement is calculated as:

$$(5.875\%/2) \times 82/184 = 1.3251\%$$

---

4. Remember that coupons are paid semiannually. Thus, the bond buyer receives the full payment of the coupon even though he or she did not own the bond during the full coupon period. The technicalities of the trading process work such that the buyer pays the seller the accrued portion of the coupon payment at the time of purchase and then gets this amount back on the first coupon payment date. The buyer gets the full coupon payment, but part of this payment is just the return of the accrued interest paid at purchase. It is not part of the quote (i.e., the clean price).

of the face value of the bond, or $130.91. The dirty price of this transaction, or the full price paid by the bond buyer, is:

$$\text{Clean price} + \text{Accrued interest} = \text{Dirty price}$$
$$101.3437\% + 1.3091\% = 102.6528\%$$

of the face value of the bond, or $10,265.28 per $10,000 face value bond.

Notice that as the purchase date approaches the coupon interest payment date, the accrued interest due to the seller from the buyer increases. Just before a coupon payment date the buyer pays the seller fractionally less than the full coupon payment. However, as the accrued interest portion of the dirty price of the note increases, the clean price of the note decreases to offset this, keeping the overall price of the note to the buyer constant. This is illustrated in Figure 6–5.

**Treasury Inflation Protected Securities (TIPS).**   In January 1997, the U.S. Treasury began issuing inflation-indexed bonds called Treasury Inflation Protected Securities (TIPS), which provide returns tied to the inflation rate. By 2016, the outstanding value of TIPS was over $1.2 trillion. Like the fixed-coupon bonds issued by the Treasury, the coupon rate on TIPS is determined by the auction process described below. However, unlike the fixed-principal bonds, the principal value of a TIPS bond can increase (or decrease) every six months by the amount of U.S. inflation (or deflation) as measured by the percentage change in the consumer price index (CPI). This principal is called the inflation-adjusted principal. TIPS bonds are used by investors who wish to earn a rate of return on their investments that keeps up with the inflation rate over time.

**Figure 6–4**    Time Line Used to Determine Accrued Interest on a Bond

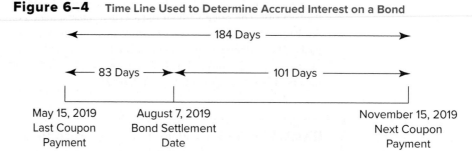

| 184 Days |
| 83 Days | 101 Days |

May 15, 2019          August 7, 2019                          November 15, 2019
Last Coupon          Bond Settlement                          Next Coupon
Payment                      Date                                      Payment

**Figure 6–5**    Dirty Price of Treasury Note

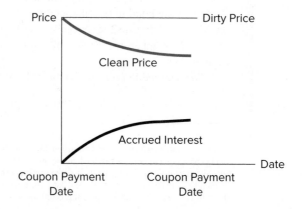

Price                                                  Dirty Price

Clean Price

Accrued Interest

                                                                    Date
Coupon Payment                    Coupon Payment
        Date                                  Date

**EXAMPLE 6–6**   Calculation of Inflation-Adjusted Principal Values and Coupon Payments on TIPS

To see how TIPS bonds work, consider an investor who, on January 1, 2019, purchases a TIPS bond with an original principal of $100,000, a 4 percent annual (or 2 percent semi-annual) coupon rate, and 10 years to maturity. The inflation-adjusted principal at the end of the first six months, on June 30, 2019, is found by multiplying the original par value ($100,000) by the semiannual inflation rate. Thus, if the semiannual inflation rate during the first six months is 0.5 percent, the principal amount used to determine the first coupon payment is adjusted upward by 0.5 percent:

$$\$100,000 \times 1.005 = \$100,500$$

Therefore, the first coupon payment, paid on June 30, 2019, is calculated as:

$$\$100,500 \times 2.0\% = \$2,010$$

The inflation-adjusted principal at the beginning of the second six months is $100,500. Suppose that the semiannual inflation rate for the second six-month period is 1 percent. Then the inflation-adjusted principal at the end of the second six months (on December 31, 2019), and the principal amount used to determine the second coupon payment, is adjusted upward by 1 percent:

$$\$100,500 \times 1.01 = \$101,505$$

The coupon payment to the investor for the second six-month period is the inflation-adjusted principal on this coupon payment date ($101,505) times the semiannual coupon rate (2 percent). Or on December 31, 2019, the investor receives a coupon payment of:

$$\$101,505 \times 2.0\% = \$2,030.10$$

The TIPS yield may be viewed as a real yield, and the spread between the yields of TIPS and non-TIPS of the same maturity is the market's consensus estimate of average annual inflation over the period. While TIPS may appear attractive to investors fearing inflation, the yields are lower. Further, the periodic principal adjustments are taxable as interest. Thus, while TIPS may provide a large payoff at maturity (due to an increase in the principal value) they may end up being negative cash-flow securities for taxable investors in some periods. Consequently, TIPS may not be an appropriate investment for someone looking for significant current income.

**Primary and Secondary Market Trading in Treasury Notes and Bonds.**   As in primary market T-bill sales, the U.S. Treasury sells T-notes and T-bonds through competitive and noncompetitive Treasury auctions (see Chapter 5). Table 6–3 shows a recent auction pattern for new T-note and T-bond issues. The Treasury issues a press release about a week before each auction announcing the details of the auction, including the auction date, the amount to be sold, and other details about the securities to be issued (see the In the News box).

**TABLE 6–3**   Auction Pattern for Treasury Notes and Bonds

| Security | Purchase Minimum | General Auction Schedule |
|---|---|---|
| 2-year note | $100 | Monthly |
| 3-year note | $100 | Monthly |
| 5-year note | $100 | Monthly |
| 7-year note | $100 | Monthly |
| 10-year note | $100 | February, May, August, November |
| 30-year bond | $100 | February, May, August, November |

**Source:** U.S. Treasury website, TreasuryDirect. www.treasurydirect.gov

## Treasury Offers 10-Year Notes

# TREASURY NEWS

Department of the Treasury • Bureau of the Fiscal Service

Embargoed Until 08:30 A.M.
May 04, 2016

CONTACT: Treasury Securities Services
202-504-3550

### TREASURY OFFERING ANNOUNCEMENT[1]

| | |
|---|---|
| Term and Type of Security | 10-Year Note |
| Offering Amount | $23,000,000,000 |
| Currently Outstanding | $0 |
| CUSIP Number | 912828R36 |
| Auction Date | May 11, 2016 |
| Original Issue Date | May 16, 2016 |
| Issue Date | May 16, 2016 |
| Maturity Date | May 15, 2026 |
| Dated Date | May 15, 2016 |
| Series | C-2026 |
| Yield | Determined at Auction |
| Interest Rate | Determined at Auction |
| Interest Payment Dates | November 15 and May 15 |
| Accrued Interest from 05/15/2016 to 05/15/2016 | Determined at Auction |
| Premium or Discount | Determined at Auction |
| | |
| Minimum Amount Required for STRIPS | $100 |
| Corpus CUSIP Number | 9128202R7 |
| Additional TINT(s) Due Date(s) and | None |
| CUSIP Number(s) | None |
| | |
| Maximum Award | $8,050,000,000 |
| Maximum Recognized Bid at a Single Yield | $8,050,000,000 |
| NLP Reporting Threshold | $8,050,000,000 |
| NLP Exclusion Amount | $0 |
| | |
| Minimum Bid Amount and Multiples | $100 |
| Competitive Bid Yield Increments[2] | 0.001% |
| Maximum Noncompetitive Award | $5,000,000 |
| Eligible for Holding in TreasuryDirect® | Yes |
| Estimated Amount of Maturing Coupon Securities Held by the Public | $60,093,000,000 |
| Maturing Date | May 15, 2016 |
| SOMA Holdings Maturing | $14,021,000,000 |
| SOMA Amounts Included in Offering Amount | No |
| FIMA Amounts Included in Offering Amount[3] | Yes |
| | |
| Noncompetitive Closing Time | 12:00 Noon ET |
| Competitive Closing Time | 1:00 p.m. ET |

[1]Governed by the Terms and Conditions set forth in The Uniform Offering Circular for the Sale and Issue of Marketable Book-Entry Treasury Bills, Notes, and Bonds (31 CFR Part 356, as amended), and this offering announcement.

[2]Must be expressed as a yield with three decimals (e.g., 7.123%).

[3]FIMA up to $1,000 million in noncompetitive bids from Foreign and International Monetary Authority not to exceed $100 million per account.

**Source:** U.S. Treasury website, Treasury Direct, May 24, 2016. www.treasurydirect.gov

www.treasurydirect.gov

Bids may be submitted by government securities dealers, businesses, and individuals through the TreasuryDirect website until noon Eastern time for noncompetitive bids and 1 p.m. Eastern time for competitive bids on the day of the auction. Bidders submit the yield to maturities they are willing to accept (in increments of 0.001 percent). Awards are announced the following day. The auction is a single-price auction—all bidders pay the same price, which is the price associated with the highest of the competitive yields bid. At each auction, first noncompetitive bids are filled. Next, competitive bids are ranked from the lowest to highest yield (a bidder willing to accept the lowest yield is willing to pay the highest price). The stop-out yield of the auction is the highest accepted yield. The bids at the stop-out yield are filled on a pro-rata basis, and all the bids above the stop-out yield are rejected.[5]

5. Similar to Treasury bill auctions (discussed in Chapter 5), this single-price auction process went into effect in 1998. Prior to this, the Treasury used a discriminatory auction process.

So far, the procedure described is the same as the one for T-bill auctions. The differences arise because notes and bonds are coupon-bearing instruments. The coupon rate of the auctioned notes or bonds is the stop-out yield rounded down to the nearest 1/8 percent (unless it already falls on 1/8 percent). Recall that coupon rates are set in increments of one-eighth of 1 percent. The security's price is set for the yield to maturity to equal the auction's stop-out yield. Because the coupon rate is the stop-out yield rounded down, the coupon rate is usually below the stop-out yield, meaning that the price is usually slightly below par. This process helps ensure that successful bidders will not pay more than the par value of the requested bonds.[6] In Treasury auction result announcements, the stop-out yield is called "high yield" and the coupon rate is called "interest rate." Negative yields cannot be bid in the auctions for non-inflation-protected Treasuries, but are allowed (and have happened) in TIPS auctions. A negative yield on TIPS implies that investors are willing to accept a negative real return on their investment. TIPS first traded with a negative yield in late 2010. Remember that the yield on a TIPS bond is equal to the Treasury bond yield minus the rate of expected inflation. As was the case in late 2010, when non-inflation-protected Treasury bonds trade at yields below the expected inflation rate, TIPS yields became negative.

Table 6–4 shows the results of the 10-year T-note auction of May 11, 2016. At this auction, 37.27 percent (or $23,000,026,900) of the submitted bids ($61,704,731,400) were accepted. Further, 0.14 percent ($31,051,400) of the accepted bids at the May 11, 2016, Treasury auction were noncompetitive. Figure 6–6 illustrates the auction results for the 10-year T-notes. The lowest yield bid on the 10-year T-notes was 1.600 percent (or a high price of 100.2301774 percent of the face value of the T-notes). Bids were filled at yields above the low (prices below the high). The highest yield bid was 1.71 percent (or a low price of 99.2217501 percent).[7] At this price, all $23,000,026,900 in 10-year T-notes offered were sold. All bidders who submitted yields below 1.71 percent (prices above 99.2217501 percent, categories 1 through 5 in Figure 6–6) were awarded in full (winning bids) at the low price (i.e., 99.2217501 percent). Bidders who submitted a yield above 1.71 percent (price below 99.2217501 percent categories 7 and beyond in Figure 6–6) received no allocation of the auctioned T-notes. A portion, but not all, of the bids submitted at 99.2217501 were filled (category 6 in Figure 6–6). These bids are filled pro rata at this price. For example, if total bids in category 6 were $100 million, but only $25 million in notes remained to be allocated to competitive bidders (given the $S_C$ supply curve in Figure 6–6), each bidder would receive 25 percent of his or her bid quantity at this price. All of the $31,051,400 noncompetitive bids were filled at a price of 99.2217501 percent (which is equal to the low price paid by the winning competitive bidders).

Most secondary market trading of Treasury notes and bonds occurs directly through broker and dealer trades (see Chapters 5 and 16). For example, according to the Federal Reserve Bank of New York, the average daily trading volume in T-note and T-bond issues for the week ended May 11, 2016, was $374.61 billion. The Treasury quotes in Table 6–1 show just a small number of the Treasury securities that traded on May 23, 2016. The full quote listed in *The Wall Street Journal Online* shows the hundreds of different Treasury securities that trade daily.

**municipal bonds**

*Securities issued by state and local (e.g., county, city, school) governments.*

## Municipal Bonds

**Municipal bonds** are securities issued by state and local (e.g., county, city, school) governments ($3.7 trillion outstanding in 2016) either to fund temporary imbalances

---

6. However, there is one exception to this procedure. If the stop-out rate of a T-note or T-bond auction is below 0.125 percent, the annual coupon rate is set at 0.125 percent and the price that all successful bidders pay will be above par. This rule was enacted in April 2011; before then, the coupon rate would be set at zero.

7. Note: The stop-out yield of the auction is 1.71 percent (the highest accepted yield). The annual coupon rate of the auction bonds is 1.625 percent (1.710 percent rounded down to the nearest 1/8 percent). For this 10-year T-note, the price every successful bidder paid per $100 of par is $99.2217501 ($N = 10 \times 2 = 20$; $I = 1.71/2 = 0.855$; $PMT = 1.625/2 = 0.8125$, $FV = 100$; thus, $CPT\ PV = 99.2217501$).

**TABLE 6–4**   Announcement of Treasury Auction Results, May 11, 2016

# TREASURY NEWS

Department of the Treasury • Bureau of the Fiscal Service

| For Immediate Release | CONTACT: | Treasury Securities Services |
| May 11, 2016 | | 202-504-3550 |

**TREASURY AUCTION RESULTS**

| | |
|---|---:|
| Term and Type of Security | 10-Year Note |
| CUSIP Number | 912828R36 |
| Series | C-2026 |
| | |
| Interest Rate | 1-5/8% |
| High Yield[1] | 1.710% |
| Allotted at High | 30.57% |
| Price | 99.221906 |
| Accrued Interest per $1,000 | $0.04416 |
| | |
| Median Yield[2] | 1.680% |
| Low Yield[3] | 1.600% |
| | |
| Issue Date | May 16, 2016 |
| Maturity Date | May 15, 2026 |
| Original Issue Date | May 16, 2016 |
| Dated Date | May 15, 2016 |

| | Tendered | Accepted |
|---|---:|---:|
| Competitive | $61,673,680,000 | $22,968,975,500 |
| Noncompetitive | $31,051,400 | $31,051,400 |
| FIMA (Noncompetitive) | $0 | $0 |
| **Subtotal[4]** | **$61,704,731,400** | **$23,000,026,900[5]** |
| SOMA | $5,201,456,300 | $5,201,456,300 |
| **Total** | **$64,761,788,800** | **$28,201,483,200** |

| | Tendered | Accepted |
|---|---:|---:|
| Primary Dealer[6] | $38,851,900,000 | $3,832,496,000 |
| Direct Bidder[7] | $3,655,000,000 | $2,708,000,000 |
| Indirect Bidder[8] | $19,166,780,000 | $16,878,479,500 |
| **Total Competitive** | **$61,673,680,000** | **$22,968,975,500** |

[1]All tenders at lower yields were accepted in full.

[2]50% of the amount of accepted competitive tenders was tendered at or below that yield.

[3]5% of the amount of accepted competitive tenders was tendered at or below that yield.

[4]Bid-to-Cover Ratio: $61,704,731,400/$23,000,026,900 = 2.68.

[5]Awards to TreasuryDirect = $15,883,400.

[6]Primary dealers as submitters bidding for their own house accounts.

[7]Non-Primary dealer submitters bidding for their own house accounts.

[8]Customers placing competitive bids through a direct submitter, including Foreign and International Monetary Authorities placing bids through the Federal Reserve Bank of New York.

**Source:** U.S. Treasury website, TreasuryDirect, May 24, 2016. www.treasurydirect.gov

between operating expenditures and receipts or to finance long-term capital outlays for activities such as school construction, public utility construction, or transportation systems. Tax receipts or revenues generated from a project are the source of repayment on municipal bonds.

Municipal bonds are attractive to household investors since interest payments on municipal bonds (but not capital gains) are exempt from federal income taxes and most state and local income taxes (in contrast, interest payments on Treasury securities are exempt only from state and local income taxes). As a result, the interest borrowing cost to the state or local government is lower, because investors are willing to accept lower interest rates on municipal bonds relative to comparable taxable bonds such as corporate

**Figure 6–6** Treasury Auction Results

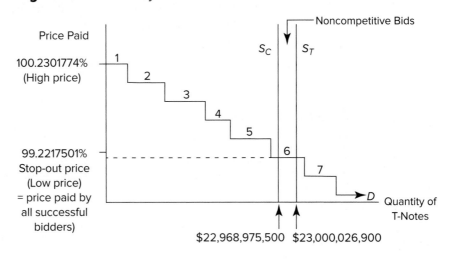

bonds. Further, many municipal bonds are insured by a third party. Bond insurance ensures payment to bond holders in the event that the issuer defaults on a payment. Generally, the insurance company assuring a bond has a higher credit rating than the issuer. As a result, the bond issue will have the credit rating of the insurance company. This helps improve the credit ratings of bond issuers and lowers interest rates on bonds backed by insurance substantially. Bond insurance also increases the liquidity of bonds because it is easier to sell an insured bond on the market.

**Municipal Bond Yields.** To compare returns from tax-exempt municipal bonds with those on fully taxable corporate bonds, the after-tax (or equivalent tax-exempt) yield on a taxable bond can be calculated as follows:

$$r_a = r_b(1 - t)$$

where

$r_a$ = After-tax (equivalent tax-exempt) yield on a taxable corporate bond
$r_b$ = Before-tax yield on a taxable bond
$t$ = Marginal income tax rate of the bond holder (i.e., the sum of his or her marginal federal, state, and local taxes)[8]

---

**EXAMPLE 6–7** Comparison of a Municipal Bond and a Fully Taxable Corporate Bond Rate

Suppose you can invest in taxable corporate bonds that are yielding a 10 percent annual interest rate or municipal bonds. If your marginal tax rate is 28 percent (i.e., the sum of federal, local, and state taxes on the last dollar of interest income), the after-tax or equivalent tax-exempt yield on the taxable bond is:

$$10\% \, (1 - 0.28) = 7.2\%$$

Thus, the comparable yield on municipal bonds of similar risk would be 7.2 percent.

---

8. Treasury securities are not exempt from federal taxes but are exempt from state and local income taxes. Thus, the after-tax yield on a Treasury security is calculated as:

$$r_a = r_b(1 - t_f)$$

where $t_f$ = the marginal federal tax rate.

Alternatively, the yield on a tax-exempt municipal bond can be used to determine the tax equivalent yield for a taxable security that would cause an investor to be just indifferent between the taxable and tax-exempt bonds of the same default and liquidity risks. Rearranging the equation above,

$$r_b = r_a/(1 - t)$$

---

**EXAMPLE 6–8**    Conversion of a Municipal Bond Rate to a Tax Equivalent Rate

You are considering an investment in a municipal bond that has a yield of $r_a = 6.5$ percent annually. If your marginal tax rate ($t$) is 21 percent, the tax equivalent yield on this bond ($r_b$) is:

$$8.223\% = 6.5\%/(1 - 0.21)$$

---

**general obligation (GO) bonds**

*Bonds backed by the full faith and credit of the issuer.*

Two types of municipal bonds exist: general obligation bonds and revenue bonds. Table 6–5 shows the amount of both issued in 1990 through 2016. **General obligation (GO) bonds** are backed by the full faith and credit of the issuer—that is, the state or local government promises to use all of its financial resources (e.g., its taxation powers) to repay the bond. GO bonds generally have neither specific assets pledged as collateral backing the bond nor a specific revenue stream identified as a source of repayment of the bond's principal and interest. Because the taxing authority of the government issuer is promised to ensure repayment, the issuance of new GO bonds generally requires local taxpayer approval. Possibly because of this requirement, and taxpayers' reluctance to have their taxes increased, general obligation bonds represent a small portion of municipal bonds issued (44.0 percent in 2016).

**revenue bonds**

*Bonds sold to finance a specific revenue-generating project, backed by cash flows from that project.*

**Revenue bonds** are sold to finance a specific revenue-generating project and are backed by cash flows from that project. For example, a revenue bond may be issued to finance an extension of a state highway. To help pay off the interest and principal on that bond, tolls collected from the use of the highway may be pledged as collateral. If revenue from the project is insufficient to pay interest and retire the bonds on maturity as promised—perhaps because motorists are reluctant to use the highway and pay the tolls—general tax revenues may not be used to meet these payments. Instead, the revenue bond goes into default and bond holders are not paid. Thus, revenue bonds are generally riskier than GO bonds.

Municipal bonds are typically issued in minimum denominations of $5,000. Although trading in these bonds is less active than that of Treasury bonds, a secondary market exists for municipal bonds. Table 6–6 lists a portion of a municipal bond quote sheet from *The Wall Street Journal Online* on May 23, 2016. Column 1 lists the (local) government issuer. Column 2 lists the coupon rate (generally paid semiannually) on the bond issue. Column 3, labeled *Maturity,* is the maturity date of the bond issue. Column 4, labeled *Price,* is the

**TABLE 6–5**    General Obligation and Revenue Bonds Issued, 1990 through 2016
*(in millions of dollars)*

|  | 1990 | 2001 | 2007 | 2010 | 2011 | 2013 | 2016* |
|---|---|---|---|---|---|---|---|
| General obligation bonds | $39,610 | $100,519 | $130,497 | $137,529 | $95,970 | $116,215 | $56,767 |
| Revenue bonds | 81,295 | 170,047 | 295,779 | 323,249 | 224,201 | 197,706 | 72,242 |

*Through March.
**Source:** Federal Reserve Board website, "New Security Issues." www.federalreserve.gov

**TABLE 6–6**   Municipal Bond Quote

### Tax Exempt Bonds
Monday, May 23, 2016

| Issue | Coupon | Mat. | Price | YTM |
|---|---|---|---|---|
| Building Aid Revenue Bonds, Fiscal 2016 | 4.000 | 07-15-45 | 109 2/7 | 3.49 |
| California (State) various purpose gener | 5.000 | 11-01-43 | 119 3/4 | 3.83 |
| California (State) various purpose GO bo | 5.000 | 04-01-42 | 117 1/6 | 3.96 |
| California St Pub Wks lease revenue Seri | 5.000 | 11-01-38 | 120 | 3.68 |
| Colorado Hlth Facs Auth rev bds Ser 13 A | 5.000 | 01-01-44 | 115 1/5 | 4.09 |
| Delaware River Port Auth PA Revenue Bond | 5.000 | 01-01-37 | 118 | 3.77 |
| Health Facilities Revenue Bonds | 4.000 | 11-15-45 | 106 2/3 | 3.63 |
| Health Facilities Revenue Bonds, Series | 4.000 | 12-01-44 | 104 1/9 | 3.76 |
| Illinois (State) GOs Series 2013 | 5.500 | 07-01-38 | 111 | 4.69 |
| Lehigh Co Auth PA wtr & swr rev bds Ser | 5.000 | 12-01-43 | 115 1/2 | 2.72 |
| Metro Transp Auth NY transp rev bonds Se | 5.000 | 11-15-43 | 118 2/3 | 3.89 |
| Metro Transp Auth NY transp rev Ser 2013 | 5.000 | 11-15-38 | 119 3/8 | 3.72 |
| Missouri St Hlth & Ed hospital rev Ser 2 | 4.000 | 11-15-42 | 105 5/9 | 3.67 |
| Rochester MN health care facs rev bds Se | 4.000 | 11-15-41 | 106 6/7 | 3.58 |
| San Antonio Pub Facs Corp TX impro & ref | 4.000 | 09-15-42 | 106 3/8 | 3.62 |
| South Carolina Public Service Authr even | 5.500 | 12-01-53 | 117 1/2 | 4.53 |
| South Carolina Public Service Authr even | 5.000 | 12-01-48 | 114 1/3 | 4.03 |
| The City Of New York GO Bonds, Fiscal 20 | 4.000 | 03-01-39 | 109 5/7 | 3.40 |
| Transportation Program Bonds, Series 201 | 4.250 | 06-15-44 | 102 | 4.12 |
| Water and Sewer system second GN resolut | 4.000 | 06-15-34 | 111 4/9 | 3.16 |

bond price in percentage terms (i.e., 119 ¾ = 119.75 percent of the face value). Column 5, *YTM,* is the yield to maturity on the municipal bond based on the current selling price available to the municipal bond holder. As discussed above, these yields are not taxed at the federal, state, or local levels and thus are not comparable to corporate bond yields.

Municipal bonds are not default risk free. Defaults on municipal bonds peaked in 1990 at $1.4 billion, due mainly to a major economic recession in the United States. As the economy grew in the 1990s and early and mid-2000s, these defaults subsided. However, defaults on municipal debt increased dramatically during the recent financial crisis, from $329 million in 2007 to $8.2 billion in 2008, $7.3 billion in 2009, $2.9 billion in 2010, $6.5 billion in 2011, and $4.8 billion in 2012. Defaults totaled only $278 million in the first quarter of 2013. However, they then soared to $6.68 billion as in June 2013. Detroit announced that it had suspended payments on its unsecured debt and the city declared bankruptcy, the largest U.S. city to ever do so. Even into 2014 defaults continued to rise, to $9.02 billion for the year. Municipal defaults stabilized in 2015. However, in May 2016 Puerto Rico defaulted on a $270 million payment due on its municipal debt. This was just the start as, at the time, Puerto Rico had over $70 billion in municipal debt outstanding. A payment of $1.9 billion was due in July 2016, for which Puerto Rico announced it did not have the funds to pay.

Unlike Treasury securities, for which the federal government (in the worst case) can raise taxes or print money to make promised payments, state and local governments are limited to their local tax and revenue base as sources of funds for municipal bond repayment. Note from Table 6–5 that during the financial crisis, this resulted in a sharp decrease in the amount of municipal debt outstanding. General obligation bonds issuances decreased from $130.5 billion in 2007 to $96.0 billion in 2011, while revenue bonds issuances fell from $295.8 billion to $224.2 billion.

**The Trading Process for Municipal Bonds.**   The initial (primary market) sale for municipal bonds (and corporate bonds, discussed below) occurs either through a public offering, using an investment bank serving as a security underwriter, or through a private placement to a small group of investors (often financial institutions). Generally, when a large state or local governmental unit issues municipals to the public, many investment banks are interested in underwriting the bonds and the municipals can generally be sold in a national market. Total dollar volume of these new issues was $399.597 billion in 2015, up significantly from $318,478 billion in the first five months of 2014.

**firm commitment underwriting**

*The issue of securities by an investment bank in which the investment bank guarantees the issuer a price for newly issued securities by buying the whole issue at a fixed price from the issuer. It then seeks to resell these securities to suppliers of funds (investors) at a higher price.*

**www.bondbuyer.com**

*Firm Commitment Underwriting.*   Public offerings of municipal (and corporate, see below) bonds are most often made through an investment banking firm (see Chapter 16) serving as the underwriter. Normally, the investment bank facilitates this transfer using a **firm commitment underwriting,** illustrated in Figure 6–7. The investment bank guarantees the municipality (or corporation for a corporate bond) a price for newly issued bonds by buying the whole issue at a fixed price from the municipal issuer (the bid price). The investment bank then seeks to resell these securities to suppliers of funds (investors) at a higher price (the offer price). As a result, the investment bank takes a risk that it may not be able to resell the securities to investors at a higher price. This may occur if prices of municipal bonds suddenly fall due to an unexpected change in interest rates or negative information being released about the creditworthiness of the issuing municipality. If this occurs, the investment bank takes a loss on its underwriting of the security. However, the municipal issuer is protected by being able to sell the whole issue.

The investment bank can purchase the bonds through competitive bidding against other investment banks or through direct negotiation with the issuer. In a competitive sale, the issuer invites bids from a number of underwriters. The investment bank that submits the highest bid to the issuer wins the bid. The underwriter may use a syndicate of other underwriters and investment banks to distribute (sell) the issue to the public. Most state and local governments require a competitive municipal bond issue to be announced in a trade publication, such as the *Bond Buyer.* With a negotiated sale, the investment bank obtains the exclusive right to originate, underwrite, and distribute the new bonds through a one-on-one negotiation process. With a negotiated sale, the investment bank provides the origination and advising services to the issuers. Most states require that GO bonds be issued through competitive bids.

**best-efforts offering**

*The issue of securities in which the investment bank does not guarantee a price to the issuer and acts more as a placing or distribution agent on a fee basis related to its success in placing the issue.*

*Best-Efforts Offering.*   Some municipal (and corporate) securities are offered on a **best-efforts** basis, in which the investment bank does not guarantee a firm price to the issuer (as with a firm commitment offering) and acts more as a placing or distribution agent for a fee. With best-efforts offerings, the investment bank incurs no risk of mispricing the security since it seeks to sell the bonds at the price it can get in the market. In return the investment bank receives a fee. Further, the investment bank offers the securities at a price originally set by the municipality. Thus, the investment bank does not incur the expense of establishing the market price for the customer. Often, knowing that the investment bank has not put any of its own funds into the issue, investors in best-efforts issues are not willing to pay as much for the bonds as with a firm commitment issue.

**private placement**

*A security issue placed with one or a few large institutional buyers.*

*Private Placement.*   In a **private placement,** a municipality (or corporation), sometimes with the help of an investment bank, seeks to find a large institutional buyer or group of buyers (usually fewer than 10) to purchase the whole issue. To protect smaller individual investors against a lack of disclosure, the Security and Exchange Act of 1934 requires publicly traded securities to be registered with the Securities and Exchange Commission (SEC). Private placements, on the other hand, can be unregistered and can be resold only to large, financially sophisticated investors (see below). These large investors supposedly possess the resources and expertise to analyze a security's risk.

Privately placed bonds (and stocks) have traditionally been among the most illiquid securities in the bond market, with only the very largest financial institutions or institutional

**Figure 6–7**   **Firm Commitment Underwriting of a Municipal or Corporate Bond Issue**

investors being able or willing to buy and hold them in the absence of an active secondary market. In April 1990, however, the Securities and Exchange Commission amended its Regulation 144A. This allowed large investors to begin trading these privately placed securities among themselves even though, in general, privately placed securities do not satisfy the stringent disclosure and informational requirements that the SEC imposes on approved publicly registered issues. Rule 144A private placements may now be underwritten by investment banks on a firm commitment basis. Of the total $57.5 billion in private placements in 2015, $52.2 billion (91 percent) were Rule 144A placements. Bank of America Merrill Lynch was the lead underwriter of private placements in 2015 (underwriting $11.1 billion, 19.4 percent of the total placements).

Issuers of privately placed bonds tend to be less well known (e.g., medium-sized municipalities and corporations). As a result of a lack of information on these issues, and the resulting possibility of greater risk, interest rates paid to holders of privately placed bonds tend to be higher than on publicly placed bond issues. Although Rule 144A has improved the liquidity of privately placed bonds, this market is still less liquid than the public placement market. Another result of the increased attention to this market by investment banks is that the interest premiums paid by borrowers of privately placed issues over public issues have decreased.

Although the SEC defines large investors as those with assets of $1 million or more or income above $200,000 per year in the last two years ($300,000 for families)—which excludes all but the very wealthiest household savers—it is reasonable to ask how long this size restriction will remain. As they become more sophisticated and the costs of information acquisition fall, savers will increasingly demand access to the private placement market. In such a world, savers would have a choice not only between the secondary securities from financial institutions and the primary securities publicly offered by municipalities and corporations but also between publicly offered (registered) securities and privately offered (unregistered) securities.

*Secondary Market Trading.* The secondary market for municipal bonds is thin (i.e., trades are relatively infrequent). Thin trading is mainly a result of a lack of information on bond issuers, as well as special features (such as covenants) that are built into those bonds' contracts. Information on municipal bond issuers (particularly of smaller government units) is generally more costly to obtain and evaluate, although this is in part offset by bond rating agencies (see below). In a similar fashion, bond rating agencies generate information about corporate and sovereign (country) borrowers as well.

### Corporate Bonds

**corporate bonds**

*Long-term bonds issued by corporations.*

**Corporate bonds** are long-term bonds issued by corporations ($11.7 trillion outstanding in 2016, some 43.0 percent of all outstanding long-term bonds). The minimum denomination on publicly traded corporate bonds (which, in contrast to privately placed corporate bonds, require SEC registration) is $1,000, and coupon-paying corporate bonds generally pay interest semiannually.

**bond indenture**

*The legal contract that specifies the rights and obligations of the bond issuer and the bond holders.*

The **bond indenture** is the legal contract that specifies the rights and obligations of the bond issuer (corporate or government) and the bond holders. The bond indenture contains a number of covenants associated with a bond issue. These bond covenants describe rules and restrictions placed on the bond issuer and bond holders. As described below, these covenants include rights for the bond issuer, such as the ability to call the bond issue, and restrictions, such as limits on the ability of the issuer to increase dividends paid to equity holders. By legally documenting the rights and obligations of all parties involved in a bond issue, the bond indenture helps lower the risk (and therefore the interest cost) of the bond issue. All matters pertaining to the bond issuer's performance regarding any debt covenants as well as bond repayments are overseen by a trustee (frequently a bank trust department) who is appointed as the bond holders' representative or "monitor." The signature of a trustee on the bond is a guarantee of the bond's authenticity. The trustee also acts as the transfer agent for the bonds when ownership changes as a result of secondary market sales and when interest payments are made from the bond issuer to the bond holder. The trustee also informs the bond holders if the firm is no longer meeting the terms of the indenture. In this case, the trustee initiates any legal action on behalf of the bond holders against the issuing firm. In the event of a subsequent reorganization or liquidation of the bond issuer, the trustee continues to act on behalf of the bond holders to protect their principal.

Table 6–7 presents a portion of a bond market quote sheet from the Financial Industry Regulatory Authority (FINRA) website for May 23, 2016. Quotes are listed by dollar volume of trading, from highest to lowest. Look at the sixth quote posted in Table 6–7. Column 1 of the quote lists the issuer, Anadarko Pete. Column 2 lists the bond's ticker symbol (e.g., APC.HM). Column 3 lists the coupon rate (6.375 percent). Column 4 lists the maturity date (September 15, 2017). Column 5 lists the bond's Moody's, S&P, and Fitch bond rating (Ba1/BBB/BBB) (see below). Columns 6 and 7 list the High (106.13171 percent) and Low (105.25 percent) prices at which the bonds traded on May 23, 2016. Column 8, labeled *Last,* is the closing price (in percent) of the bond on May 23 (105.375 percent). Column 9, labeled *Change,* is the change (−0.083000 percent) in the closing price from the previous day's close. Column 10, labeled *Yield %,* is the yield to maturity (see Chapter 3) on the bond (2.157 percent) using the Last price.

**Bond Characteristics.**   Corporate bonds have many different characteristics that differentiate one issue from another. We list and briefly define these characteristics in Table 6–8, and we describe them in detail below. Many of these characteristics apply to other bond types as well.

*Bearer versus Registered Bonds.*   Corporate bonds can be bearer bonds or registered bonds. With **bearer bonds,** coupons are attached to the bond and the holder (bearer) at the time of the coupon payment gets the relevant coupon paid on presentation to the issuer (i.e., gets the bond coupon "clipped"). With a **registered bond,** the bond holder's (or owner's) identification information is kept in an electronic record by the issuer and the coupon payments are mailed or wire-transferred to the bank account of the registered owner. Because of the lack of security with bearer bonds, they have largely been replaced by registered bonds in the United States.

*Term versus Serial Bonds.*   Most corporate bonds are **term bonds,** meaning that the entire issue matures on a single date. Some corporate bonds (and most municipal bonds), on the other hand, are **serial bonds,** meaning that the issue contains many maturity dates, with a portion of the issue being paid off on each date. For economic reasons, many issuers like to avoid

---

**bearer bonds**

*Bonds with coupons attached to the bond. The holder presents the coupons to the issuer for payments of interest when they come due.*

**registered bond**

*A bond in which the owner is recorded by the issuer and the coupon payments are mailed to the registered owner.*

**term bonds**

*Bonds in which the entire issue matures on a single date.*

**serial bonds**

*Bonds that mature on a series of dates, with a portion of the issue paid off on each.*

---

**TABLE 6–7   Corporate Bond Market Quote**

| Most Active Investment Grade Bonds | | | | | | | | | |
|---|---|---|---|---|---|---|---|---|---|
| (1)<br>Issuer Name | (2)<br>Symbol | (3)<br>Coupon | (4)<br>Maturity | (5)<br>Moody's/S&P/<br>Fitch | (6)<br>High | (7)<br>Low | (8)<br>Last | (9)<br>Change | (10)<br>Yield % |
| CHEVRON CORP NEW | CVX4362390 | 2.954% | 05/16/2026 | Aa2// | 102.00410 | 99.61400 | 100.00510 | 0.057100 | 2.953 |
| HSBC HLDGS PLC | HBC4365146 | 3.900% | 05/25/2026 | A1// | 102.00000 | 99.77800 | 99.95900 | 0.113000 | 3.905 |
| ASTRAZENECA PLC | AZN.GD | 5.900% | 09/15/2017 | A3//A | 106.25000 | 104.35700 | 105.97900 | −0.021000 | 1.291 |
| SOUTHERN CO | SO4365693 | 4.400% | 07/01/2046 | Baa2//A− | 100.24100 | 99.71200 | 99.94400 | 0.116000 | 4.403 |
| AMERICAN INTL GROUP | AIG4338112 | 3.300% | 03/01/2021 | Baa1//BBB+ | 103.63400 | 102.05200 | 102.17200 | −0.319000 | 2.801 |
| **ANADARKO PETE CORP** | **APC.HM** | **6.375%** | **09/15/2017** | **Ba1/BBB/BBB** | **106.13171** | **105.25000** | **105.37500** | **−0.083000** | **2.157** |
| BNP PARIBAS / BNP | BNPQF3900102 | 2.375% | 09/14/2017 | A1// | 101.38600 | 101.05000 | 101.05000 | −0.143000 | 1.553 |
| VALE OVERSEAS LTD | VALE3676238 | 5.625% | 09/15/2019 | Ba3//BBB | 101.25000 | 99.00000 | 101.25000 | 2.250000 | 5.205 |
| WALGREENS BOOTS | WAG4182655 | 3.800% | 11/18/2024 | Baa2/BBB/BBB | 105.35190 | 102.33200 | 102.59800 | −0.262000 | 3.435 |
| STRYKER CORP | SYK4341754 | 3.500% | 03/15/2026 | Baa1// | 105.36200 | 103.25800 | 103.54600 | −0.332000 | 3.069 |

**Sources:**  FINRA TRACE Corporate Bond Data, May 24, 2016, FINRA. www.finra.org; http://finra-markets.morningstar.com/BondCenter/TRACEMarketAggregateStats.jsp

**TABLE 6–8** Bond Characteristics

**Bearer bonds**—bonds on which coupons are attached. The bond holder presents the coupons to the issuer for payments of interest when they come due.

**Registered bonds**—with a registered bond, the owner's identification information is recorded by the issuer and the coupon payments are mailed to the registered owner.

**Term bonds**—bonds in which the entire issue matures on a single date.

**Serial bonds**—bonds that mature on a series of dates, with a portion of the issue paid off on each.

**Mortgage bonds**—bonds that are issued to finance specific projects that are pledged as collateral for the bond issue.

**Equipment trust certificates**—bonds collateralized with tangible non–real estate property (e.g., railcars and airplanes).

**Debentures**—bonds backed solely by the general credit of the issuing firm and unsecured by specific assets or collateral.

**Subordinated debentures**—unsecured debentures that are junior in their rights to mortgage bonds and regular debentures.

**Convertible bonds**—bonds that may be exchanged for another security of the issuing firm at the discretion of the bond holder.

**Stock warrants**—bonds that give the bond holder an opportunity to purchase common stock at a specified price up to a specified date.

**Callable bonds**—bonds that allow the issuer to force the bond holder to sell the bond back to the issuer at a price above the par value (at the call price).

**Sinking fund provisions**—bonds that include a requirement that the issuer retire a certain amount of the bond issue each year.

**mortgage bonds**

*Bonds issued to finance specific projects, which are pledged as collateral for the bond issue.*

**debentures**

*Bonds backed solely by the general credit worthiness of the issuing firm, unsecured by specific assets or collateral.*

**subordinated debentures**

*Bonds that are unsecured and are junior in their rights to mortgage bonds and regular debentures.*

**convertible bonds**

*Bonds that may be exchanged for another security of the issuing firm at the discretion of the bond holder.*

a "crisis at maturity." Rather than having to pay off one very large principal sum at a given time in the future (as with a term issue), many issuers like to stretch out the period over which principal payments are made—especially if the corporation's earnings are quite volatile.

*Mortgage Bonds.* Corporations issue **mortgage bonds** to finance specific projects that are pledged as collateral for the bond issue. Thus, mortgage bond issues are secured debt issues.[9] Bond holders may legally take title to the collateral to obtain payment on the bonds if the issuer of a mortgage bond defaults. Because mortgage bonds are backed with a claim to specific assets of the corporate issuer, they are less risky investments than unsecured bonds. As a result, mortgage bonds have lower yields to bond holders than unsecured bonds. *Equipment trust certificates* are bonds collateralized with tangible (movable) non–real estate property such as railcars and airplanes.

*Debentures and Subordinated Debentures.* Bonds backed solely by the general creditworthiness of the issuing firm, unsecured by specific assets or collateral, are called **debentures**. Debenture holders generally receive their promised payments only after the secured debt holders, such as mortgage bond holders, have been paid. **Subordinated debentures** are also unsecured, and they are junior in their rights to mortgage bonds and regular debentures. In the event of a default, subordinated debenture holders receive a cash distribution only after all nonsubordinated debt has been repaid in full. As a result, subordinated bonds are the riskiest type of bond and generally have higher yields than nonsubordinated bonds. In many cases, these bonds are termed *high-yield* or *junk bonds* because of their below investment grade credit ratings (see the following).

*Convertible Bonds.* **Convertible bonds** are bonds that may be exchanged for another security of the issuing firm (e.g., common stock) at the discretion of the bond holder. If

9. Open-end mortgage bonds allow the firm to issue additional bonds in the future, using the same assets as collateral and giving the same priority of claim against those assets. Closed-end mortgage bonds prohibit the firm from issuing additional bonds using the same assets as collateral and giving the same priority of claim against those assets.

the market value of the securities the bond holder receives with conversion exceeds the market value of the bond, the bond holder can return the bonds to the issuer in exchange for the new securities and make a profit. As a result, conversion is an attractive option or feature to bond holders. Thus, convertible bonds are hybrid securities involving elements of both debt and equity. They give the bond holder an investment opportunity (an option) that is not available with nonconvertible bonds. As a result, the yield on a convertible bond is usually lower (generally, 2 to 5 percentage points) than that on a nonconvertible bond:

$$r_{cvb} = r_{ncvb} - op_{cvb}$$

where

$r_{cvb}$ = Yield on a convertible bond
$r_{ncvb}$ = Yield on a nonconvertible bond
$op_{cvb}$ = Value of the conversion option to the bond holder

---

## EXAMPLE 6–9    Analysis of a Convertible Bond

In May 2016, Tesla Motors had a convertible bond issue outstanding. Each bond, with a face value of $1,000, could be converted into common shares at a rate of 2.7788 shares of stock per $1,000 face value bond (the conversion rate), or $359.87 per share. In May 2016, Tesla's common stock was trading (on the NASDAQ) at $217.87 per share. While this might look like conversion would not be very profitable, Tesla's convertible bonds were trading at 90.897 percent of the face value of the bond, or $908.97.

To determine whether or not it is profitable to convert the bonds into common stock in Tesla, the conversion value of each bond can be calculated as:

$$\text{Conversion value} = \frac{\text{Current market price of common}}{\text{stock received on conversion}} \times \text{Conversion rate}$$

If a bond holder were to convert Tesla bonds into stock, each bond (worth $908.97) could be exchanged for 2.7788 shares of stock worth $217.87. The conversion value of the bonds is:

$$\$217.87 \times 2.7788 = \$605.417$$

Thus, a convertible bondholder would have no incentive to convert his or her Tesla convertible bonds into its common stock equivalent.

---

Figure 6–8 illustrates the value of a convertible bond as a function of the issuing firm's asset value. The horizontal axis plots the firm's value, which establishes an upper bound for the value of the convertible bond (since it cannot trade for more than the value of the firm's assets). Thus, the value of the issuing firm line that bisects the figure at a 45° angle also represents the issuing firm's value and sets an upper bound for the value of the convertible bond. In addition, the figure plots the values of the firm's convertible and nonconvertible bonds. At low firm values, the values of both bonds drop off as bankruptcy becomes more likely. Note that the nonconvertible bond's value does not increase at higher firm asset values since bond holders receive only their promised payments and no more. However, the convertible bond values rise directly with the firm's asset value. Specifically, at low firm asset values the convertible bond value acts more like a nonconvertible bond, trading at only a slight premium over the nonconvertible bond. When the issuing firm's value is high, however, the convertible will act more like a stock, selling for only a slight premium over the conversion value. In the middle range, the convertible bond will trade as a hybrid security, acting partly like a bond and partly like a stock.

**Figure 6–8**    Value of a Convertible Bond

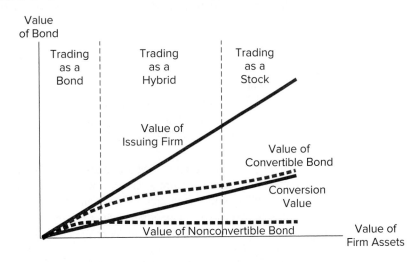

Most convertible bond issues are set up so that it is not initially profitable to convert to stock. Usually the stock price must increase 15 to 20 percent before it becomes profitable to convert the bond to the new security.

**stock warrants**

*Bonds issued with stock warrants attached giving the bond holder an opportunity to purchase common stock at a specified price up to a specified date.*

*Stock Warrants.*    Bonds can also be issued with **stock warrants** attached. Similar to convertible bonds, bonds issued with stock warrants attached give the bond holder an opportunity to detach the warrants to purchase common stock at a prespecified price up to a prespecified date. In this case, however, if the bond holder decides to purchase the stock (by returning or exercising the warrant), the bond holder does not have to return the underlying bond to the issuer (as with a convertible bond). Instead, he or she keeps the bond and pays for additional stock at a price specified in the warrant. Bond holders will exercise their warrants if the market value of the stock is greater than the price at which the stock can be purchased through the warrant. Further, the bond holder may sell the warrant rather then exercise it, while maintaining ownership of the underlying bond. Risky firms commonly attach stock warrants to their bonds to increase the bonds' marketability. Rather than paying extremely high interest rates or accepting very restrictive bond covenants, the firm attaches stock warrants to the bonds in order to get investors to buy them.

**call provision**

*A provision on a bond issue that allows the issuer to force the bond holder to sell the bond back to the issuer at a price above the par value (or at the call price).*

**call premium**

*The difference between the call price and the face value on the bond.*

*Callable Bonds.*    Many corporate bond issues include a **call provision,** which allows the issuer to require the bond holder to sell the bond back to the issuer at a given (call) price—usually set above the par value of the bond. The difference between the call price and the face value on the bond is the **call premium.** Many callable bond issues have a deferred call provision in which the right to call the bond is deferred for a period of time after the bond is issued (generally 10 years). Bonds are usually called in when interest rates drop (and bond prices rise) so that the issuer can gain by calling in the old bonds (with higher coupon rates) and issuing new bonds (with lower coupon rates). Thus, the call feature facilitates refinancing of the debt if/when interest rates fall during the life of the bond.

For example, in 2016, ACCO Brands Corp. had a $500,000 callable debt issue outstanding. The face value of each bond was $1,000. The issue, with a maturity date of April 30, 2020, was callable as a whole or in part not less than 30 days nor more than 60 days following April 30 of each year at a redemption price of 103.38 percent beginning April 30, 2017, and thereafter at prices declining annually to 100 percent on or after April 30, 2019. Note that as the bond approaches maturity, the call premium declines. The closer the bond is to maturity, the smaller the premium required for forcing bond holders to give up the bonds early.

A call provision is an unattractive feature to bond holders, since the bond holder may be forced to return the bond to the issuer before he or she is ready to end the investment and the investor can only reinvest the funds at a lower interest rate. As a result, callable bonds have higher yields (generally between 0.05 and 0.25 percent) than comparable noncallable bonds:

$$r_{ncb} = r_{cb} - op_{cb}$$

where

$r_{ncb}$ = Yield on a noncallable bond
$r_{cb}$ = Yield on a callable bond
$op_{cb}$ = Value of the issuer's option to call the debt early

**sinking fund provision**

*A requirement that the issuer retire a certain amount of the bond issue each year.*

*Sinking Fund Provisions.*   Many bonds have a **sinking fund provision,** which is a requirement that the issuer retire a certain amount of the bond issue early over a number of years, especially as the bond approaches maturity. The bond issuer provides the funds to the trustee by making frequent payments to a sinking fund. This sinking fund accumulates in value and is eventually used to retire the entire bond issue at maturity or to periodically retire a specified dollar amount of bonds either by purchasing them in the open market or by randomly calling bonds to be retired. In this case, the selected bonds are called and redeemed. Once the bonds are called they cease to earn interest. The bond holders must surrender their bonds to receive their principal.[10] For example, in 2016 State of Illinois had a sinking fund debenture issue outstanding that required that the state put an amount each year from 2032 through 2038 (as listed in Table 6–9) into a sinking fund, so that all of the $348 billion principal on the bonds would be accumulated before maturity.

Since it reduces the probability of default at the maturity date, a sinking fund provision is an attractive feature to bond holders. Thus, bonds with a sinking fund provision are less risky to the bond holder and generally have lower yields than comparable bonds without a sinking fund provision. Some sinking fund bonds, however, are redeemed at par or market value, whichever is less, which creates price risk for the holder (if a bond is redeemed at par when its straight value is above par).

**The Trading Process for Corporate Bonds**   Primary sales of corporate bond issues occur through either a public sale (issue) or a private placement in a manner identical to that discussed for municipal bonds (see above). In 2015 a total of $1.6 trillion and in the first three months of 2016 a total of $350 billion of corporate debt was issued in the United States.

There are two secondary markets that trade corporate bonds: the exchange market (e.g., NYSE Bonds) and the over-the-counter (OTC) market. The major exchange for corporate bonds is the New York Stock Exchange Bonds Trading Platform. Most of the trading on the NYSE's bond market is completed through its NYSE Arca all-electronic trading system, which provides investors with the ability to readily obtain transparent pricing and

**TABLE 6–9**   Sinking Fund Installments: State of Illinois Sinking Fund Bonds Due 2038

| Year | Principal Amount | Year | Principal Amount |
|------|------------------|------|------------------|
| 2032 | $52,000,000 | 2036 | $52,000,000 |
| 2033 | 36,000,000 | 2037 | 52,000,000 |
| 2034 | 52,000,000 | 2038 | 52,000,000 |
| 2035 | 52,000,000 | | |

**Source:** Reuters, News Release, 2016.

10. If the bond holder does not turn the bonds in for redemption, they continue to be outstanding and are obligations of the issuer. However, the issuer's obligation is limited to refunding only the principal, since interest payments stopped on the call date.

trading information. The system includes the bonds of all NYSE-listed companies and their subsidiaries without the companies having to list each bond issued. However, only a small amount of bond trading volume occurs on organized exchanges. The average daily dollar value of bond trading totaled $29.3 billion in 2016 in a market with $11.7 trillion of bonds outstanding.

Most bonds are traded OTC among major bond dealers such as Morgan Stanley Wealth Management and UBS Paine Webber. Some mutual funds, such as Fidelity and Vanguard, make both primary and secondary markets in bonds and facilitate the participation of individual investors in these markets. Virtually all large trades are carried out on the OTC market, even for bonds listed on an exchange, such as the NYSE bond market. As a result, prices reported on the exchanges (like those in Table 6–7) are generally considered to be inexact estimates of prices associated with large transactions. Thus, in contrast to Treasury securities, secondary market trading of corporate bonds can involve a significant degree of liquidity risk.

### Bond Ratings and Interest Rate Spreads

As mentioned earlier, the inability of investors to get information pertaining to the risk, especially default risk, on bonds, at a reasonable cost, can result in thinly traded markets. In Chapter 3, we examined the impact of interest rate risk (i.e., interest rate changes) on bond prices. Specifically, we demonstrated that bonds with longer maturities (durations) and low coupon rates experience larger price changes for a given change in interest rates than bonds with short maturities and high coupon rates (i.e., bonds with longer maturities and lower coupon rates are subject to greater interest rate risk). Just as important, bond investors also need to measure the degree of default risk on a bond.

Large bond investors, traders, and managers often evaluate default risk by conducting their own analysis of the issuer, including an assessment of the bond issuer's financial ratios (see Chapter 20) and security prices. Small investors are not generally capable of generating the same extensive information and thus frequently rely on bond ratings provided by the bond rating agencies. The three major bond rating agencies are Moody's, Standard & Poor's (S&P), and Fitch Ratings. Each of these companies rank bonds based on the perceived probability of issuer default and assign a rating based on a letter grade. Table 6–10 summarizes these rating systems and provides a brief definition of each. The highest credit quality (lowest default risk) that rating agencies assign is a triple-A (Aaa for Moody's and AAA for S&P and Fitch). Bonds with a triple-A rating have the lowest interest spread over similar maturity Treasury securities (see below). As the assessed default risk increases, Moody's, S&P, and Fitch lower the credit rating assigned on a bond issue, and the interest spread over similar maturity Treasuries paid to bond holders generally increases.[11]

As a practical matter, a bond needs to be rated if it is to be used as an investment vehicle by certain institutional investors. Bonds rated Baa or better by Moody's and BBB or better by S&P and Fitch are considered to be investment grade bonds. Financial institutions (e.g., banks, insurance companies) are generally prohibited by state and federal law from purchasing anything but investment grade bond securities.[12] Bonds rated below Baa by Moody's and BBB by S&P and Fitch are considered to be speculative grade bonds and are often termed **junk bonds,** or high-yield bonds. A bond downgraded from investment grade status (e.g., BBB) to junk bond status (e.g., B) is called a "fallen angel." The issuance of speculative bonds was rare prior to the economic downturn of the late 1970s. Given the risk involved with speculative bonds and the ready availability of investment grade bonds, investment banks had a difficult time marketing the more speculative bonds

www.moodys.com

www.standardandpoors
.com

www.fitchratings.com

**junk bond**

*Bond rated as speculative or less than investment grade (below Baa by Moody's and BBB by S&P and Fitch) by bond-rating agencies.*

---

11. Note that the three companies sometimes disagree on ratings (recently differences occur about 15 percent of the time). When this occurs, a bond is said to have a "split" rating.

12. For example, the Financial Institutions Reform, Recovery, and Enforcement Act of 1989 rescinded the ability of savings associations to purchase and hold below-investment-grade bonds (see Chapter 13).

**TABLE 6–10**   Bond Credit Ratings

| Explanation | Moody's | S&P | Fitch |
|---|---|---|---|
| Best quality; smallest degree of risk | Aaa | AAA | AAA |
| High quality; slightly more long-term | Aa1 | AA+ | AA+ |
|    risk than top rating | Aa2 | AA | AA |
| | Aa3 | AA– | AA– |
| Upper medium grade; possible impairment | A1 | A+ | A+ |
|    in the future | A2 | A | A |
| | A3 | A– | A– |
| Medium grade; lacks outstanding investment | Baa1 | BBB+ | BBB+ |
|    characteristics | Baa2 | BBB | BBB |
| | Baa3 | BBB– | BBB– |
| Speculative issues; protection may be | Ba1 | BB+ | BB+ |
|    very moderate | Ba2 | BB | BB |
| | Ba3 | BB– | BB– |
| Very speculative; may have small assurance | B1 | B+ | B+ |
|    of interest and principal payments | B2 | B | B |
| | B3 | B– | B– |
| Issues in poor standing; may be in default | Caa | CCC | CCC |
| Speculative in a high degree; with marked shortcomings | Ca | CC | CC |
| Lowest quality; poor prospects of attaining real | C | C | C |
|    investment standing | | | |
| Payment default | | D | D |

**Sources:** Websites for Moody's, Standard & Poor's, and Fitch Ratings. www.moodys.com; www.standardandpoors.com; www.fitchratings.com

to primary bond market investors. The market grew significantly in the late 1990s, with smaller and medium-sized firms, unqualified to issue investment grade debt securities, issuing long-term debt in this market. For example, in 1990, $503.3 million in corporate "high-yield" straight debt was issued. In 2007, $137.3 billion was issued. This fell to just $37.2 billion in 2008. However, as the credit quality of corporations deteriorated during the financial crisis, the issuance of high-yield debt increased, peaking at $362.2 billion in 2012. By 2015 high-yield debt issuance fell back to $252.3 billion and to $32.9 billion in the first three months of 2016.

Rating agencies consider several factors in determining and assigning credit ratings on bond issues. For example, a financial analysis is conducted of the issuer's operations and its needs, its position in the industry, and its overall financial strength and ability to pay the required interest and principal on the bonds. Rating agencies analyze the issuer's liquidity, profitability, debt capacity, and more recently its corporate governance structure (following the passage of the Sarbanes-Oxley Act in 2002—see Chapter 8). Then for each particular issue, rating agencies evaluate the nature and provisions of the debt issue (e.g., the covenants and callability of the bond) and the protection afforded by, and relative position of, the debt issue in the event of bankruptcy, reorganization, or other arrangements under the laws of bankruptcy and other laws affecting creditors' rights.

In recent years rating agencies have been criticized as slow to react. One example of this was the failure to downgrade Enron (one of the largest corporate bankruptcy in U.S. history) in the months leading up to its failure in 2001. More recent is the failure of rating agencies to downgrade ratings on mortgage-backed securities. Throughout the financial crisis, major credit rating firms were criticized for putting top ratings on these securities, which ultimately collapsed in value and led to billions of dollars of losses for investors who had relied on the ratings to signal which securities were safe to buy. Further, because rating agencies, in particular Moody's, Standard & Poor's, and Fitch, are for-profit companies, their incentives were criticized for being misaligned. Specifically, conflicts of interest arose because the rating agencies are paid by the investment companies issuing the securities—an arrangement that came under fire as a disincentive for the agencies to be vigilant on behalf of investors. As a result of these criticisms, the Wall Street Reform and Consumer Protection Act, passed in July 2010, included a provision that allows investors to sue credit rating firms for "knowing or reckless" failure, establishes an oversight office within the SEC with the ability to fine credit raters, and empowers the SEC to deregister firms that give too many incorrect ratings over time. Almost three years later, in February 2013, the U.S. Justice Department sued S&P, alleging the firm ignored its own standards to rate mortgage bonds that imploded in the financial crisis, cost investors billions, and nearly brought down the world's financial systems. A week later 13 state attorneys general also filed lawsuits against S&P, alleging the firm presented its ratings as based on objective and independent analysis, when they were actually inflated to cater to banking clients.

In Chapter 2, we examined other factors (in addition to default risk) that affect interest rates on individual bonds. These factors included liquidity risk, special provisions written into the bond contract (e.g., callability, sinking fund provisions), and the term to maturity of the bond. In addition to these factors that are unique to each bond, interest rates on all bonds are affected by inflation and the real risk-free rate (typically measured using Treasury rates). The interest rate spread on a bond contains information on how these other factors, along with default risk, affect the rate of return on a bond. The interest rate spread (or just spread) is the difference between the rate of return on a bond and the return on a similar maturity Treasury security. The spread measures the return premium a bond earns to compensate not just for default risk, but also for liquidity risk and any special provisions on the bond. Thus, a spread is considered by many investors to be a more comprehensive and more current source of information regarding the overall risk of a bond than Moody's, S&P, and Fitch credit ratings. Given the added factors incorporated into bond spreads, it is possible for spreads and credit ratings to sometimes appear to conflict with each other. Consider a bond issued by a company that is financially sound but trades very infrequently. The credit rating (which captures mainly default risk) may be high, which would imply that the interest rate and thus the spread on the bond would be low. However, the spread also incorporates liquidity risk, which is high in this case and results in a higher interest rate and a higher spread on the bond.

Figure 6–9 shows the rates on 10-year Treasury securities versus Aaa-rated and Baa-rated bonds from 1980 through 2016. The average spread over this period on Aaa-rated bonds and Baa-rated bonds was 1.23 percent and 2.32 percent, respectively. Note the sharp

**Figure 6–9**   Rates on Treasury Bonds, Aaa-Rated Bonds, and Baa-Rated Bonds

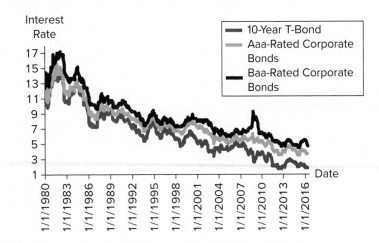

**Source:** Federal Reserve Board website, "Research and Data." www.federalreserve.gov

increase in the spread in late 2008 and early 2009, rising to as much as 2.63 percent on Aaa-rated bonds and 6.01 percent on Baa-rated bonds in November 2008. During the financial crisis, investors worldwide, searching for a safe haven for their funds, invested huge amounts of funds in U.S. Treasury securities. The amount of money invested in these securities was so large that the yields dropped significantly. At the same time, default and liquidity risk on corporate bonds increased as the U.S. economy experienced a strong recession. The result was an increase in the interest rate spreads (risk premiums) on corporate bonds.

## Bond Market Indexes

Table 6–11 lists major bond market indexes as of May 24, 2016. Data in this table give investors general information on returns of bonds from various types of issuers (e.g., Treasuries, municipals, and corporate bonds) and various maturities. The indexes are those managed by major investment banks (e.g., Barclays, Merrill Lynch) and reflect both the monthly capital gain and loss on bonds in the index plus any interest (coupon) income earned. Changes in the values of these broad market indexes can be used by bond traders to evaluate changes in the investment attractiveness of bonds of different types and maturities.

**TABLE 6–11**   Major Bond Market Indexes

# Tracking Bond Benchmarks

Tuesday, May 24, 2016

Closing index values, return on investment and yields paid to investors compared with 52-week highs and lows for different types of bonds. **Preliminary data and data shown as "n.a." will update around 12 p.m. the following business day.**

| Index | Close | % Chg | YTD total return | 52-wk % Chg | YIELD (%), 52-WEEK RANGE Latest | Low | High | SPREAD, 52-WEEK RANGE Latest | Low | High |
|---|---|---|---|---|---|---|---|---|---|---|
| **Hourly Treasury Indexes Barclays Capital** | | | | | | | | | | |
| Composite (Price Return) | 1473.33 | −0.06 | 1.69 | 3.20 | 1,400 | 1.190 | 2.130 | ... | ... | ... |
| Composite (Total Return) | 13983.39 | −0.06 | 2.63 | 5.61 | 1,400 | 1.190 | 2.130 | ... | ... | ... |
| Intermediate (Price Return) | 1291.91 | −0.05 | 1.00 | 2.66 | 1,230 | 1.000 | 1.990 | ... | ... | ... |
| Intermediate (Total Return) | 11506.26 | −0.04 | 1.83 | 4.84 | 1,230 | 1.000 | 1.990 | ... | ... | ... |
| Long-Term (Price Return) | 2318.77 | −0.14 | 6.15 | 6.51 | 2,420 | 2.260 | 3.090 | ... | ... | ... |
| Long-Term (Total Return) | 27992.54 | −0.13 | 7.79 | 10.45 | 2,420 | 2.260 | 3.090 | ... | ... | ... |
| **U.S. Corporate Indexes Barclays Capital** | | | | | | | | | | |
| U.S. Corporate | 2592.45 | −0.10 | 4.78 | 3.98 | 3,200 | 3.040 | 3.710 | n.a. | 131.00 | 215.00 |
| Intermediate | 2498.30 | −0.03 | 3.23 | 2.96 | 2,620 | 2.430 | 3.120 | n.a. | 105.00 | 188.00 |
| Long term | 3423.53 | −0.27 | 8.41 | 6.35 | 4,540 | 4.390 | 5.130 | n.a. | 191.00 | 279.00 |
| Double-A-rated (AA) | 542.69 | −0.05 | 3.93 | 4.69 | 2,360 | 2.220 | 2.700 | n.a. | 76.00 | 121.00 |
| Triple-B-rated (Baa) | 650.24 | −0.13 | 5.31 | 2.78 | 3,700 | 3.540 | 4.450 | n.a. | 169.00 | 283.00 |
| **High Yield Bonds Merrill Lynch** | | | | | | | | | | |
| High Yield Constrained* | 355.71 | 0.26 | 7.55 | −1.33 | 7,599 | 5.947 | 10.099 | 613.00 | 446.00 | 887.00 |
| Triple-C-rated (CCC) | 319.59 | 0.45 | 14.42 | −6.66 | 16.071 | 10.507 | 21.753 | 1482.00 | 931.00 | 2076.00 |
| High Yield 100 | 2487.59 | 0.23 | 4.78 | −3.72 | 6,420 | 5.342 | 8.696 | 500.00 | 399.00 | 741.00 |
| Europe High Yield Constrained | 272.05 | 0.13 | 3.38 | 0.38 | 4,434 | 3.921 | 6.500 | 466.00 | 379.00 | 639.00 |
| Global High Yield Constrained | 324.53 | 0.21 | 6.80 | −0.21 | 7,168 | 5.899 | 9.437 | 607.00 | 469.00 | 859.00 |
| **U.S. Corporate Debt S&P Dow Jones Indices** | | | | | | | | | | |
| U.S. Issued High Yield | 112.76 | 0.23 | 7.49 | −0.72 | 7,236 | 5.874 | 9.624 | 595.58 | 449.48 | 1025.61 |
| U.S. Issued Investment Grade | 110.39 | −0.06 | 4.70 | 3.51 | 3,023 | 2.875 | 3.504 | 145.55 | 124.99 | 203.47 |
| **Tax-Exempt Merrill Lynch** | | | | | | | | | | |
| Muni Master | 511.05 | −0.09 | 2.29 | 5.61 | 1,535 | 1.440 | 2.099 | 0.00 | −9.00 | 7.00 |
| 7-12 years | 356.96 | −0.11 | 2.43 | 6.20 | 1,575 | 1.398 | 2.144 | 8.00 | −1.00 | 16.00 |
| 12-22 years | 397.42 | −0.08 | 2.86 | 7.40 | 1,893 | 1.823 | 2.636 | −14.00 | −36.00 | −4.00 |
| 22-plus years | 381.83 | −0.08 | 4.03 | 9.02 | 2,406 | 2.356 | 3.351 | −3.00 | −15.00 | 14.00 |
| Bond Buyer 6% Muni | 131.88 | −0.12 | 3.61 | 7.19 | 3,900 | 3.870 | 4.500 | ... | ... | ... |

**Source:** *The Wall Street Journal Online,* May 25, 2016. www.wsj.com

## BOND MARKET PARTICIPANTS

**LG 6-3**

Bond markets bring together suppliers and demanders of long-term funds. We have just seen that the major issuers of debt market securities are federal, state, and local governments and corporations. The major purchasers of capital market securities are households, businesses, government units, and foreign investors. In 2007, China held $388 billion of U.S. Treasury securities. As a result, China is deeply dependent on the success of the U.S. economy. However, threatened with sanctions on its imports to the United States in summer 2007, China stated that it would liquidate its holdings of U.S. Treasury securities and send the U.S. economy into a downward spiral, a so-called nuclear option. Further, such a large holding of U.S. Treasury securities by one country, threatening to ruin the U.S. economy, threatened the position of the dollar as a reserve currency. Just the threat of such action by China resulted in Russia, Switzerland, and several other countries reducing their dollar holdings. Despite these threats, China had increased its holdings of Treasury securities to $1.32 trillion by 2013. In mid-2015 Japan reclaimed its position as the largest investor in U.S. Treasury securities. U.S. debt offered the highest yields relative to other countries, which provided Japan with the incentive to increase its holdings. Holdings of U.S. Treasuries remained at high levels until late 2015 when China's central bank (as well as the Bank of Japan) started to sell its holdings of U.S. Treasury securities to prop up its own currencies. During the financial crisis, these countries bought hundreds of billions of dollars of debt issued by the U.S. Treasury as a chance to build up their foreign reserves. After years of building up savings, the U.S. Treasury security sales were a sign of how aggressively central banks were willing to act to keep their economy afloat amid global weakness.

Figure 6–10 shows the percentage of each type of bond security held by the major groups. Notice that financial firms, called Business Financial (e.g., banks, insurance companies, mutual funds), are the major suppliers of funds for two of the three types of bonds. Financial firms hold 29.83 percent of all Treasury securities, 56.04 percent of municipal bonds, and 69.35 percent of the corporate bonds outstanding. In addition to their direct investment reported in Figure 6–10, households often deposit excess funds in financial firms (such as mutual bond funds and pension funds) that use these funds to purchase bond market securities. Thus, much of the business and financial holdings of bond securities shown in Figure 6–10 reflects indirect investments of households in the bond market.

---

**DO YOU UNDERSTAND:**

8. *Who the major purchasers of bond market securities are?*

---

**Figure 6–10**    **Bond Market Securities Held by Various Groups of Market Participants, 2016**

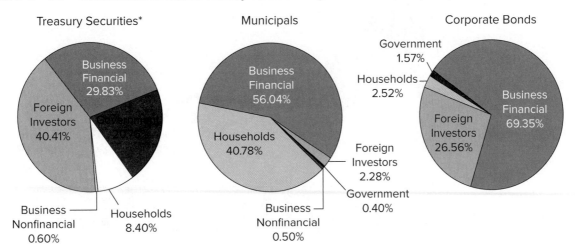

*Includes Treasury bills, notes, and bonds.

**Source:** Federal Reserve Board website, "Financial Accounts of the United States." www.federalreserve.gov

## COMPARISON OF BOND MARKET SECURITIES

**www.stlouisfed.org**

**www.bloomberg.com**

Figure 6–11 shows the yield to maturity on various types of bonds (e.g., 10-year Treasury bonds, municipal bonds, and high-grade corporate bonds) from 1980 through 2016. While the general trends in yields were quite similar over this period (i.e., yield changes are highly correlated), yield spreads among bonds can vary as default risk, tax status, and marketability change. For example, yield spread differences can change when characteristics of a particular type of bond are perceived to be more or less favorable to the bond holder (e.g., relative changes in yield spreads can result when the default risk increases for a firm that has one bond issue with a sinking fund provision and another issue without a sinking fund provision). Economic conditions can also cause bond yield spreads to vary over time. This is particularly true during periods of slow economic growth (e.g., 1982, 1989–1991, and 2008–2016, as discussed previously), as investors require higher default risk premiums. The St. Louis Federal Reserve Bank offers free online access to its database (called FRED) of U.S. economic and financial data, including daily U.S. interest rates, monetary business indicators, exchange rates, balance of payments, and regional economic data. Also, Bloomberg has free online access to current bond yields of all types and characteristics discussed in this chapter.

> ### DO YOU UNDERSTAND:
>
> **9.** *What events can cause yield spreads on bond securities to change?*

## INTERNATIONAL ASPECTS OF BOND MARKETS

**LG 6-4**

International bond markets are those markets that trade bonds that are underwritten by an international syndicate, offer bonds to investors in different countries, issue bonds outside the jurisdiction of any single country, and offer bonds in unregistered form. For investors, adding international bonds to a fixed-income portfolio can be a way to diversify risk in a domestically based portfolio. International sovereign bonds have historically exhibited low correlation in returns with U.S. and international stocks. This is particularly true during times of extreme stock market stress. However, during times of foreign turmoil, such as the 2009–2013 European sovereign debt crisis, the costs of international debt can be too high

**Figure 6–11**   **Yields on Bond Market Securities, 1980–2016**

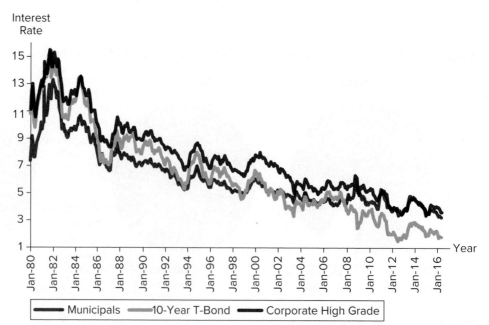

**Source:** Federal Reserve Board website, "Research and Data." www.federalreserve.gov

(i.e., the returns can be too low) and the diversification benefits not worthwhile. Further, changes in the dollar/foreign currency exchange rate must be considered when investing in international bonds. If the dollar goes up (down) in value during the period of investment, international bonds will lose (gain) value (see Chapter 9).

For bond issuers, the existence of sophisticated international bond markets increases the available financing options and range of assets. Further, competition from international markets motivates domestic markets to implement improvements in market infrastructure, investor protection, and tax distortions that hinder domestic market development. However, international bond market placements can also increase risk for an issuer. For example, they may cause sudden shifts in capital flows and result in a concentration of liquidity away from the domestic market. If liquidity tends to concentrate in offshore bond markets, there are likely to be significant costs for bond issuers connected to reduced liquidity onshore, less scope for development of a lower-grade market in domestic currency, more limited availability of collateral for domestic markets, and restricted access for domestic investors.

The rapid growth in international bond markets in recent years can be seen in Table 6–12, which lists the dollar volume of new issues of international bond securities from 1994 through 2015. In just 14 years (from 1994 through 2007) new issues grew from $253.6 billion (in 1994) to 3,002.5 billion (in 2007). Much of this growth was driven by investors' demand for international securities and international portfolio diversification (e.g., the growth of specialized U.S. mutual funds that invest in offshore bond issues). The majority of the growth was from debt issued by developed countries (e.g., the U.S. and Europe). New debt issues in "Other countries" fell from $115.9 billion in 1997 to $56.5 billion in 2000 before rising to $193.5 billion in 2007. Finally, notice that the world-wide financial crisis resulted in a significant decrease in net issues of debt securities. Net issues dropped from its peak of $3,002.5 billion in 2007 (before the financial crisis) to $2,329.2 billion in 2009 (during the crisis) and $1,506.7 billion in 2010 (after the worst of the U.S. financial crisis had past, but as the European debt crisis took hold). This decreasing trend continued as just $704.9 billion of new debt was issued worldwide in 2012. Like the growth in debt prior to the crisis, the decrease in new debt issues came mainly from developed countries, where new debt issues decreased from $2,784.5 billion in 2007 to $2,072.5 billion in 2009 and just $1,187.1 billion in 2010. Showing the collapse in this market, net debt issues in 2012 were –$37.8 billion (i.e., more debt was retired/defaulted than issued) before finally rising to $887.8 billion in 2015.

Table 6–13 lists the values of international debt outstanding by currency and type (e.g., floating-rate, straight fixed-rate, and equity-related debt) from 1995 through 2016. In March 2016, international bonds and notes outstanding totaled $20.67 trillion, compared

**TABLE 6–12** International Debt Securities Issued, 1994–2015 *(in billions of U.S. dollars)*

|  | 1994 | 1997 | 2000 | 2007 | 2009 | 2010 | 2012 | 2015 |
|---|---|---|---|---|---|---|---|---|
| Total net issues | $253.6 | $519.9 | $1,138.2 | $3,002.5 | $2,329.2 | $1,506.7 | $704.9 | $887.8 |
| Money market instruments | 3.3 | 19.6 | 122.0 | 198.7 | –237.5 | 12.1 | 20.3 | 48.8 |
| Bonds and notes | 250.3 | 500.3 | 1,016.2 | 2,803.8 | 2,566.7 | 1,494.6 | 684.7 | 839.0 |
| Developed countries | 205.5 | 389.1 | 1,065.6 | 2,784.5 | 2,072.5 | 1,187.1 | –37.8 | 494.8 |
| Offshore centers | 7.2 | 14.9 | 16.1 | 24.5 | 21.5 | 13.8 | 62.9 | 23.4 |
| Other countries | 32.5 | 115.9 | 56.5 | 193.5 | 235.1 | 305.8 | 679.8 | 369.6 |
| International institutions | 8.5 | 35.1 | 22.4 | 38.1 | 1,330.5 | 93.2 | 287.4 | 95.2 |
| Financial institutions | 136.1 | 346.5 | 622.3 | 2,592.6 | 322.7 | 583.5 | 85.7 | 500.0 |
| Public sector | 103.1 | 68.0 | 221.5 | 88.2 | 101.9 | 260.3 | 38.8 | –21.4 |
| Corporate issuers | 14.4 | 70.3 | 272.0 | 283.6 | 574.1 | 569.7 | 293.0 | 314.0 |

**Sources:** Bank for International Settlements, *Quarterly Review,* various issues. www.bis.org

**TABLE 6–13**   International Bonds and Notes Outstanding, 1995–2016 *(in billions of U.S. dollars)*

| Type; Sector and Currency | 1995 | 1997 | 2000 | 2004 | 2007 | 2010 | 2013 | 2016[†] |
|---|---|---|---|---|---|---|---|---|
| **Total Issues** | $2,209.3 | $3,347.6 | $5,907.7 | $13,264.3 | $21,635.4 | $26,750.8 | $21,895.0 | $20,666.7 |
| **Floating Rate** | **326.2** | **732.5** | **1,521.0** | **3,668.8** | **7,210.2** | **7,871.0** | **5,975.5** | **5,170.6** |
| U.S. dollar | 181.5 | 436.6 | 788.5 | 1,131.0 | 2,071.9 | 2,164.0 | 1,568.9 | 1,592.0 |
| Euro | 44.2 | 62.8 | 499.0 | 2,073.6 | 4,190.6 | 4,300.8 | 3,239.3 | 2,555.4 |
| Japanese yen | 27.0 | 73.4 | 93.2 | 111.8 | 128.4 | 195.1 | 89.5 | 66.5 |
| Pound sterling | n.a. | n.a. | 116.9 | 264.6 | 581.1 | 934.9 | 811.5 | 753.4 |
| Other currencies | 73.6 | 159.7 | 23.9 | 87.8 | 238.2 | 276.2 | 266.3 | 203.3 |
| Financial institutions | 203.2 | 522.2 | 1,171.4 | 3,413.1 | 6,822.3 | 7,484.2 | 5,611.1 | 4,816.2 |
| Government and state agencies | 61.9 | 83.1 | 113.8 | 111.3 | 115.7 | 155.9 | 91.2 | 71.9 |
| International institutions | 18.4 | 28.5 | 21.3 | 29.9 | 25.0 | 61.5 | 128.9 | 135.1 |
| Corporate issuers | 42.8 | 98.7 | 214.5 | 114.1 | 247.2 | 169.4 | 144.3 | 147.4 |
| **Straight Fixed Rate** | **1,712.4** | **2,445.8** | **4,151.7** | **9,225.0** | **14,026.1** | **18,394.4** | **15,542.8** | **15,081.9** |
| U.S. dollar | 490.8 | 871.4 | 1,963.5 | 3,593.4 | 5,327.1 | 8,090.8 | 6,085.7 | 6,975.2 |
| Euro | 214.4 | 267.1 | 1,198.0 | 4,005.3 | 6,224.3 | 7,382.8 | 6,584.2 | 5,450.1 |
| Japanese yen | 315.4 | 392.4 | 398.2 | 381.4 | 409.2 | 514.1 | 364.2 | 302.5 |
| Pound sterling | n.a. | n.a. | 329.9 | 708.5 | 1,122.7 | 1,128.2 | 1,226.7 | 1,227.6 |
| Other currencies | 691.9 | 914.9 | 262.1 | 536.4 | 942.8 | 1,278.5 | 1,282.1 | 1,120.5 |
| Financial institutions | 501.4 | 923.2 | 1,573.4 | 6,189.0 | 9,891.9 | 12,228.8 | 10,138.8 | 9,865.8 |
| Government and state agencies | 492.8 | 647.8 | 1,105.2 | 1,236.0 | 1,733.1 | 2,232.0 | 1,561.2 | 1,486.3 |
| International institutions | 268.3 | 292.6 | 354.0 | 520.1 | 618.4 | 820.2 | 1,330.5 | 1,315.7 |
| Corporate issuers | 449.3 | 582.2 | 1,119.1 | 1,279.8 | 1,782.6 | 3,114.0 | 2,512.3 | 2,594.0 |
| **Equity Related*** | **170.7** | **169.3** | **235.0** | **370.5** | **399.2** | **485.4** | **376.6** | **414.3** |
| U.S. dollar | 83.1 | 97.4 | 123.7 | 145.0 | 159.7 | 244.4 | 203.4 | 248.8 |
| Euro | 10.7 | 7.2 | 74.2 | 143.5 | 135.0 | 107.2 | 83.2 | 80.6 |
| Japanese yen | 7.4 | 14.7 | 16.4 | 45.7 | 50.6 | 52.9 | 31.5 | 33.2 |
| Pound sterling | n.a. | n.a. | 8.8 | 12.2 | 9.3 | 8.6 | 7.4 | 6.9 |
| Other currencies | 69.5 | 50.0 | 11.9 | 24.1 | 44.6 | 72.3 | 51.2 | 44.8 |
| Financial institutions | 32.5 | 43.1 | 66.4 | 171.5 | 210.5 | 222.8 | 160.0 | 152.7 |
| Government and state agencies | 0.4 | 4.0 | 4.9 | 5.3 | 1.9 | 1.0 | 2.9 | 1.5 |
| International institutions | — | 0.1 | 0.2 | — | — | — | — | — |
| Corporate issuers | 137.7 | 122.1 | 163.5 | 193.7 | 186.8 | 261.6 | 213.7 | 260.1 |

[†]*As of March.

*Convertible bonds and bonds with equity warrants.

**Sources:** Bank for International Settlements, *Quarterly Review,* various issues. www.bis.org

to $2.21 trillion in 1995. Straight fixed-rate securities dominate the market, mainly because of the strong demand for dollar and some euro currency assets and historically low interest rates in developed countries. Floating-rate notes were second in size, partly as a result of interest rate uncertainty in the late 1990s and 2000s.

Notice that prior to 2004 a majority of international debt instruments were denominated in U.S. dollars. For example, in December 2000, some 51.8 percent of the floating-rate debt, 47.3 percent of the straight fixed-rate debt, and 52.6 percent of the equity-related debt was denominated in U.S. dollars. The U.S. dollar was the currency of choice as an international medium of exchange and store of value. However, euro-denominated debt outstanding surpassed the U.S. dollar as the main currency in which international debt is denominated. In 2013, 54.2 percent of floating-rate debt, 42.4 percent of straight fixed-rate debt, and 22.1 percent of equity-related debt outstanding was issued in euros. Thus, since its introduction, the euro has surpassed the Japanese yen and the U.S. dollar as the lead currency with which debt issues are denominated. This trend has occurred despite a severe sovereign debt crisis in Europe. However, as the U.S. economy recovered while Europe continued to slump, the trend began to reverse. In the first quarter of 2016, 49.4 percent of floating-rate debt, 46.2 percent of straight fixed-rate debt, and

**Figure 6–12**    Distribution of International Bonds Outstanding by Type of Issuer, March 2016

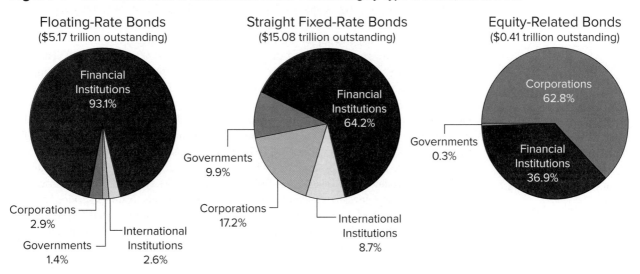

**Source:** Bank for International Settlements, *Quarterly Review,* June 2016. www.bis.org

60.1 percent of equity-related debt outstanding was issued in U.S. dollars. Notice too from Table 6–13 that the markets for emerging-country bonds (other currencies) have recovered from the Asian crisis of the late 1990s and early 2000s. Fear of losses on holdings of these emerging market bonds sparked a wide selloff in the emerging markets in the late 1990s and early 2000s.[13]

Figure 6–12 illustrates the distribution of international bonds by type of issuer (e.g., financial institutions, governments) as of 2016. Financial institutions issue the vast majority of floating-rate bonds (93.1 percent) and most of the straight fixed-rate bonds (64.2 percent). Financial institutions had been hampered in 1998 by concerns over their exposures to lower-rated countries. However, the stabilization of market conditions in 1999 and the 2000s made it easier for U.S. and European financial institutions to issue new debt securities. Public-sector issues were largely accounted for by U.S. financing agencies and a few emerging market issues. Financial institutions and corporations, as might be expected, issue the majority of the equity-related bonds (36.9 percent and 62.8 percent, respectively).

---

**DO YOU UNDERSTAND:**

10. *The major currencies in which international bonds are denominated?*

11. *What group of market participants is the major issuer of international debt?*

---

### Eurobonds, Foreign Bonds, and Sovereign Bonds

International bonds can also be classified into three main groups: Eurobonds, foreign bonds, and sovereign bonds.

**Eurobonds.**    Eurobonds are long-term bonds issued and sold outside the country of the currency in which they are denominated (e.g., dollar-denominated bonds issued in Europe or Asia). Perhaps confusingly, the term *Euro* simply implies the bond is issued outside the country in whose currency the bond is denominated. Thus, "Euro" bonds are issued in countries outside of Europe and in currencies other than the euro. Indeed, the majority of issues are still in U.S. dollars and can be issued in virtually any region of the world. Eurobonds were first sold in 1963 as a way to avoid taxes and regulation. U.S. corporations were limited by regulations on the amount of funds they could borrow domestically (in the United States) to finance overseas operations, while foreign issues in the United States were subject to a special 30 percent tax on their coupon interest. In 1963, these

---

13. For example, Argentina had severe economic and financial problems in the early 2000s that culminated in an $82 billion default in government bonds in 2002.

corporations created the Eurobond, by which bonds were denominated in various currencies and were not directly subject to U.S. regulation. Even when these regulations were abandoned, access to a new and less-regulated market by investors and corporations created sufficient demand and supply for the market to continue to grow.

Eurobonds are generally issued in denominations of $5,000 and $10,000. They pay interest annually using a 360-day year (floating-rate Eurobonds generally pay interest every six months on the basis of a spread over some stated rate, usually the LIBOR rate). Eurobonds are generally *bearer* bonds and are traded in the over-the-counter markets, mainly in London and Luxembourg. Historically, they have been of interest to smaller investors who want to shield the ownership of securities from the tax authorities. The classic investor is the "Belgian dentist" who would cross the border to Luxembourg on the coupon date to collect his coupons without the knowledge of the Belgian tax authority. However, today small investors—of the Belgian dentist type—are overshadowed in importance by large investors such as mutual and pension funds. Ratings services such as Moody's and Standard & Poor's generally rate Eurobonds. Equity-related Eurobonds are convertible bonds (bonds convertible into equity) or bonds with equity warrants attached.

Eurobonds are placed in primary markets by investment banks. Often, a syndicate of investment banks works together to place the Eurobonds. Most Eurobonds are issued via firm commitment offerings, although the spreads in this market are much larger than for domestic bonds because of the need to distribute the bonds across a wide investor base often covering many countries. Thus, the underwriters bear the risk associated with the initial sale of the bonds. The Eurobond issuer chooses the currency in which the bond issue will be denominated. The promised payments of interest and principal must then be paid in this currency. Thus, the choice of currency, and particularly the level and volatility in the interest rates of the country of the currency, affect the overall cost of the Eurobond to the bond issuer and the rate of return to the bond holder.

The full introduction of the euro in 2002 has certainly changed the structure of the Eurobond market. Most obvious is that Eurobonds denominated in the individual European currencies no longer exist but rather are denominated in a single currency, the euro. Further, liquidity created by the consolidation of European currencies allows for the demand and size of euro-denominated Eurobond issues to increase. Such growth was exhibited early in the life of the euro (or the European currency unit [ECU] prior to 2002) as the volume of new Euro debt issues in the first and second quarter of 1999 rose 32 percent and 43 percent, respectively, from the same periods in 1998. In January 1999, a record $415 billion in long-term Eurobonds were issued. In 2000 and 2001, a total of $989.1 billion long-term Eurobonds were issued, and in 2007 over $1.2 trillion of long-term Eurobonds were issued. The worldwide financial crisis and then the European debt crisis severely impacted the growth of the Eurobond markets. New issuances of long-term Eurobonds fell to $947.0 billion in 2008, $322.0 billion in 2010, $76.0 billion in 2012, and $87.2 billion in 2015.

**Foreign Bonds.**   Foreign bonds are long-term bonds issued by firms and governments outside of the issuer's home country and are usually denominated in the currency of the country in which they are issued rather than in their own domestic currency—for example, a Japanese company issuing a dollar-denominated public bond rather than a yen-denominated bond in the United States. Foreign bonds were issued long before Eurobonds and, as a result, are frequently called traditional international bonds. Countries sometimes name their foreign bonds to denote the country of origin. For example, foreign bonds issued in the United States are called Yankee bonds, foreign bonds issued in Japan are called Samurai bonds, and foreign bonds issued in the United Kingdom are called Bulldog bonds.

**Sovereign Bonds.**   **Sovereign bonds** are government-issued debt. Sovereign bonds have historically been issued in foreign currencies, in either U.S. dollars or euros. Lesser developed country (LDC) sovereign debt tends to have a lower credit rating than other sovereign debt because of the increased economic and political risks. Where most developed countries are either AAA- or AA-rated, most LDC issuance is rated below investment

www.moodys.com

www.standardandpoors
.com

**sovereign bonds**

*Government-issued,
foreign currency-
denominated debt.*

grade, although a few countries that have seen significant improvements have been upgraded to BBB or A ratings, and a handful of lower income countries have reached ratings levels equivalent to more developed countries. Accordingly, sovereign bonds require higher interest spreads. For example, sovereign bonds are uncollateralized and their price or value reflects the credit risk rating of the country issuing the bonds. The $2.8 billion June 1997 issue by Brazil of 30-year dollar-denominated bonds (rated BB grade by Standard & Poor's) was sold at a yield spread of nearly 4 percent over U.S. Treasuries at the time of issue. In July 2001, Argentinian sovereign bonds were trading at spreads of over 15 percent above U.S. Treasury rates, with the J.P. Morgan Emerging Market Bond Index showing a spread of nearly 10 percent over U.S. Treasuries. This reflected the serious economic problems in Argentina and the contagious effects these were having on other sovereign bond markets. More recently, in September 2008, fears of the global economic crisis and falling commodity prices hit emerging markets particularly hard: the sovereign debt spread jumped from 165 to over 587 basis points in Mexico; from 200 to over 586 basis points in Brazil; from 69 to over 322 basis points in Chile; from over 29 to more than 600 basis points in Colombia; and from 942 and 873 basis points to over 4,019 and 2,325 basis points in Argentina and Venezuela, respectively. By the week of October 24, 2008, spreads had tripled since early August 2008. However, it should also be noted that credit default spreads on 10-year U.S. Treasury debt rose to a record 29.2 basis points. Clearly, developed countries were not immune to the crisis.

Problems with sovereign bonds continued into 2009 and 2010. For example, in November 2009, Dubai World, the finance arm of Dubai, asked creditors for a six-month delay on interest payments due on $60 billion of the country's debt. In the mid- and late 2000s, Dubai became a center of investment and development, much of it funded by burgeoning oil wealth from neighboring countries. But during the financial crisis, the Middle East nation was hard hit by a falling real estate market. Further, throughout the spring of 2010 Greece struggled with a severe debt crisis. Early on, some of the healthier European countries tried to step in and assist the debt-ridden country. Specifically, in March 2010, a plan led by Germany and France to bail out Greece with as much as $41 billion in aid began to take shape. However, in late April, Greek bond prices dropped dramatically as traders began betting a debt default was inevitable, even if the country received a massive bailout. The selloff was the result of still more bad news for Greece, which showed that the 2009 budget deficit was worse than had been previously reported. As a result, politicians in Germany began to voice opposition to a Greek bailout. Further, Moody's Investors Service downgraded Greece's debt rating and warned that additional cuts could be on the way.

The problems in the Greek bond market then spread to other European nations with fiscal problems, such as Portugal, Spain, and Italy. As a result, in May, Euro-zone countries and the International Monetary Fund, seeking to halt a widening European debt crisis that had threatened the stability of the euro, agreed to extend Greece an unprecedented $147 billion rescue in return for huge budget cuts. Additional rescue packages and promises of further austerity measures intended to cut the burgeoning Greek deficit occurred through 2012. Yet the European debt crisis continued. While Greece had not yet missed a bond payment, in March the International Swaps and Derivatives Association (ISDA) declared that Greece had undergone a "restructuring credit event" which triggered insurance policy payments. The restructuring event was a forced swap of old debt held by some of its private bond holders for new debt. The swap forced a 74 percent haircut on those creditors that held out, triggering the effective default.

At one point, Greece seemed unable to form a government, and the leader of one party rejected the country's bailout commitments. It seemed increasingly conceivable that Greece might have to leave the Euro zone. Economists estimated that a Greek exit from the Euro zone would cost the European Union $1 trillion, or about 5 percent of the Union's annual economic output. Yet, the leaders of EU countries, particularly Germany and France, continued to work to keep Greek reform on track and the EU together. Further, the European Central Bank (ECB) stated that it would do whatever it took to protect the euro; the ECB prepared to move forcefully into bond markets in tandem with Europe's rescue funds and concentrated on buying shorter-term debt. Through June 2012, the cost of bailouts required to do so totaled over $480 billion and, while calmer, the crisis in the EU was not over as Spain and Italy required bailouts as well. Some feared that keeping the European Union together and the euro intact might actually draw sound countries into a crisis as they bailed out unhealthy countries to prevent them from leaving the currency union. Even into 2013 the Euro-zone crisis continued, becoming Europe's longest economic slump of the post–WWII era. Continued government austerity, minimal bank lending, and high levels of household debt hampered growth in most countries. However, in June a closely watched purchasing managers survey for the Euro zone rose to a 15-month high of 48.9. This and other evidence that overall economic activity in the 17-country bloc could stabilize led the European Central Bank to project that growth would return by year-end 2013.

Under the doctrine of sovereign-immunity, the repayment of sovereign debt cannot be forced by the creditors and it is thus subject to compulsory rescheduling, interest rate reduction, or even repudiation. The only protection available to creditors is the threat of the loss of credibility and a lowering of the country's international standing (the sovereign debt rating of the country, which may make it much more difficult to borrow in the future).

Sovereign debt markets were rocked again in June 2016 when the people of the United Kingdom voted to leave the European Union (EU) after 43 years (dubbed Brexit). The shock from the UK's surprise vote to leave the EU swept across global markets, triggering steep drops in stock markets and the British pound, and a flight into safe assets such as U.S. bonds and gold. The pound fell more than 11 percent to its lowest point since 1985. The DJIA dropped 610.32 points, or 3.4 percent. The Stoxx Europe 600 index fell 7 percent, its steepest drop since 2008, while Japan's Nikkei Stock Average declined 7.9 percent. Bonds also sold off sharply, pushing UK government borrowing costs sharply higher, as traders and investors grappled with the market implications of Brexit. The UK had its credit rating outlook cut to "negative" by the ratings agency Moody's.

---

**DO YOU UNDERSTAND:**

12. *What Eurobonds are?*
13. *What sovereign bonds are?*

---

## SUMMARY

This chapter looked at the domestic and international bond markets. We defined and discussed the three types of bonds available to long-term debt investors: Treasury notes and bonds, municipal bonds, and corporate bonds. We also reviewed the process through which bonds trade in both primary and secondary bond markets. International bond markets have grown dramatically in recent years. We documented and offered some reasons for this growth. We concluded the chapter with a description of the different types of international bonds: the traditional foreign bonds, the relatively new Eurobonds, and sovereign bonds.

## QUESTIONS

1. What are capital markets, and how do bond markets fit into the definition of capital markets? (*LG 6-1*)

2. What are the differences among T-bills, T-notes, and T-bonds? (*LG 6-2*)

3. What is a STRIPS? Who would invest in a STRIPS? (*LG 6-2*)

4. What are the advantages and disadvantages of investing in TIPS bonds? (*LG 6-2*)

5. Describe the process through which T-notes and T-bonds are issued in the primary markets. (*LG 6-2*)

6. What is the difference between general obligation bonds and revenue bonds? (*LG 6-2*)

7. Why would a municipal bond issuer want to purchase third-party insurance on the bond payments? (*LG 6-2*)

8. How does a firm commitment underwriting differ from a best-efforts underwriting? (*LG 6-2*)

9. What is a bond indenture? (*LG 6-2*)

10. What is the difference between bearer bonds and registered bonds? (*LG 6-2*)

11. What is the difference between term bonds and serial bonds? (*LG 6-2*)

12. Which type of bond—a mortgage bond, a debenture, or a subordinated debenture—generally has the (*LG 6-2*)
    a. Highest cost to the bond issuer?
    b. Least risk to the bond holder?
    c. Highest yield to the bond holder?

13. What is a convertible bond? Is a convertible bond more or less attractive to a bond holder than a nonconvertible bond? (*LG 6-2*)

14. What is a callable bond? Is a call provision more or less attractive to a bond holder than a noncallable bond? (*LG 6-2*)

15. Explain the meaning of a sinking fund provision on a bond issue. (*LG 6-2*)

16. What is the difference between an investment grade bond and a junk bond? (*LG 6-2*)

17. What happens to the fair present value of a bond when the required rate of return on the bond increases? (*LG 6-2*)

18. All else equal, which bond's price is more affected by a change in interest rates, a short-term bond or a longer-term bond? Why? (*LG 6-2*)

19. Discuss the issues surrounding credit rating firms during the financial crisis. (*LG 6-2*)

20. How do bond ratings and interest rate spreads on bonds differ? Which measure is considered by many investors to be a more comprehensive measure of risk? Why? (*LG 6-2*)

21. Describe the major bond market participants. (*LG 6-3*)

22. What is the difference between a Eurobond and a foreign bond? (*LG 6-4*)

23. What are sovereign bonds? (*LG 6-4*)

24. How did sovereign bonds perform during the 2000s? (*LG 6-4*)

## PROBLEMS

1. Refer to the T-note and T-bond quotes in Table 6–1. (*LG 6-2*)
   a. What is the asking price on the 2.750 percent November 2023 T-bond if the face value of the bond is $10,000?
   b. What is the bid price on the 0.500 percent August 2016 T-note if the face value of the bond is $10,000?

2. Refer again to Table 6–1. (*LG 6-2*)
   a. Verify the asked price on the 0.875 percent November 30, 2017 T-note for Monday, May 23, 2016. The asked yield on the note is 0.849 percent and the note matures on November 30, 2017. Settlement occurs one business day after purchase (i.e., you would take possession of the note on Wednesday, May 24, 2016).
   b. Verify the asked yield on the 0.625 percent July 31, 2017 T-note for May 23, 2016. The asked price is 99.8047 and the note matures on July 31, 2017.

3. Refer to Table 6–1. (*LG 6-2*)
   a. Verify the May 23, 2016, asked yield of 1.09 percent on the Treasury bond, stripped principal STRIPS maturing August 2019. Use a one-day settlement period from the date of purchase (i.e., ownership occurs on Wednesday, May 24, 2016). The STRIPS matures on August 15, 2019.
   b. Verify the asked price (99.709) on the Treasury note, stripped principal STRIPS maturing in November 2016 (i.e., the STRIPS matures on November 30, 2016).

4. On October 5, 2019, you purchase a $10,000 T-note that matures on August 15, 2031 (settlement occurs one day after purchase, so you receive actual ownership of the bond on October 6, 2019). The coupon rate on the T-note is 4.375 percent and the current price quoted on the bond is 105.250 percent. The last coupon payment occurred on May 15, 2019 (144 days before settlement), and the next coupon payment will be paid on November 15, 2019 (40 days from settlement). (*LG 6-2*)
   a. Calculate the accrued interest due to the seller from the buyer at settlement.
   b. Calculate the dirty price of this transaction.

5. On July 10, 2019, you purchase a $10,000 T-note that matures on December 31, 2028 (settlement occurs one day after purchase, so you receive actual ownership of the bond on July 11, 2019). The coupon rate on the T-note is 2.125 percent and the current price quoted on the bond is 98.250 percent. The last coupon payment occurred on June 30, 2019 (11 days before settlement), and the next coupon payment will be paid on December 31, 2019 (173 days from settlement). (*LG 6-2*)
   a. Calculate the accrued interest due to the seller from the buyer at settlement.
   b. Calculate the dirty price of this transaction.

6. Consider an investor who, on January 1, 2019, purchases a TIPS bond with an original principal of $100,000, an 8 percent annual (or 4 percent semiannual) coupon rate, and 10 years to maturity. (*LG 6-2*)
   a. If the semiannual inflation rate during the first six months is 0.3 percent, calculate the principal amount used to determine the first coupon payment and the first coupon payment (paid on June 30, 2019).
   b. From your answer to part (a), calculate the inflation-adjusted principal at the beginning of the second six months.
   c. Suppose that the semiannual inflation rate for the second six-month period is 1 percent. Calculate the inflation-adjusted principal at the end of the second six months (on December 31, 2019) and the coupon payment to the investor for the second six-month period. What is the inflation-adjusted principal on this coupon payment date?

7. Consider an investor who, on January 1, 2020, purchases a TIPS bond with an original principal of $100,000, an 4.50 percent annual (or 2.25 percent semiannual) coupon rate, and 5 years to maturity. (*LG 6-2*)
   a. If the semiannual inflation rate during the first six months is 1.25 percent, calculate the principal amount used to determine the first coupon payment and the first coupon payment (paid on June 30, 2020).

   **b.** From your answer to part (a), calculate the inflation-adjusted principal at the beginning of the second six months.

   **c.** Suppose that the semiannual inflation rate for the second six-month period is 0.5 percent. Calculate the inflation-adjusted principal at the end of the second six months (on December 31, 2020) and the coupon payment to the investor for the second six-month period. What is the inflation-adjusted principal on this coupon payment date?

8. You can invest in taxable bonds that are paying a yield of 9.50 percent or a municipal bond paying a yield of 7.75 percent. If your marginal tax rate is 21 percent, which security bond should you buy? (*LG 6-2*)

9. A municipal bond you are considering as an investment currently pays a yield of 6.75 percent. (*LG 6-2*)

   **a.** Calculate the tax equivalent yield if your marginal tax rate is 28 percent.

   **b.** Calculate the tax equivalent yield if your marginal tax rate is 21 percent.

10. Refer to Table 6–6. (*LG 6-2*)

   **a.** On May 23, 2016, what were the coupon rate, price, and yield on municipal bonds issued by the Delaware River Port Authority?

   **b.** What was the yield to maturity, on May 23, 2016, on State of California bonds maturing on November 1, 2043?

11. Refer to Table 6–6. Verify the yield to maturity of 4.69 percent on the State of Illinois municipal bonds. Settlement occurs two days after purchase, so actual ownership of the bond occurs on May 25, 2016. (*LG 6-2*)

12. Use the bond pricing formula and Table 6–6 to calculate the number of years (to the nearest 1/1000th of a year) between the May 25, 2016, settlement date and the maturity date on the City of New York general obligation bonds maturing on March 1, 2039. The YTM, 3.40 percent, is rounded from 3.40083577 percent. (*LG 6-2*)

13. Refer to Table 6–7. (*LG 6-2*)

   **a.** What was the closing price on the Chevron 2.954 percent coupon bonds on Monday, May 23, 2016?

   **b.** What was the S&P bond rating on Walgreens 3.800 percent coupon bonds maturing in 2024 on May 23, 2016?

   **c.** What was the closing price on Stryker 3.500 percent bonds on Friday, May 20, 2016?

14. Refer to Table 6–7. Verify the yield of 4.403 percent on the Southern bonds with a coupon of 4.400 percent and a maturity date of July 1, 2046. Settlement occurs two days after purchase, so actual ownership of the bond occurs on May 25, 2016. (*LG 6-2*)

15. A $1,000 face value corporate bond with a 6.5 percent coupon (paid semiannually) has 15 years left to maturity. It has had a credit rating of BBB and a yield to maturity of 7.2 percent. The firm has recently gotten into some trouble and

the rating agency is downgrading the bonds to BB. The new appropriate discount rate will be 8.5 percent. What will be the change in the bond's price in dollars and percentage terms? (*LG 6-2*)

16. A client in the 33 percent marginal tax bracket is comparing a municipal bond that offers a 4.50 percent yield to maturity and a similar risk corporate bond that offers a 6.45 percent yield. Which bond will give the client more profit after taxes? (*LG 6-2*)

17. A $1,000 face value corporate bond with a 6.75 percent coupon (paid semiannually) has 10 years left to maturity. It has had a credit rating of BB and a yield to maturity of 8.2 percent. The firm recently became more financially stable and the rating agency is upgrading the bonds to BBB. The new appropriate discount rate will be 7.1 percent. What will be the change in the bond's price in dollars and percentage terms? (*LG 6-2*)

18. **eXcel** **Using a Spreadsheet to Calculate Bond Values:** What is the bond quote for a $1,000 face value bond with an 8 percent coupon rate (paid semiannually) and a required return of 7.5 percent if the bond is 6.48574, 8.47148, 10.519, and 14.87875 years from maturity? (*LG 6-2*)

| Face Value | Total Payments | Periodic Coupon Payment | Required Return | The Bond Value Will Be |
|---|---|---|---|---|
| 100% | 6.48574 × 2 = 12.97148 | 8%/2 = 4% | 7.5% | 102.531% |
| 100 | 8.47148 × 2 = 16.94296 | 4 | 7.5 | 103.094 |
| 100 | 10.519 × 2 = 21.0380 | 4 | 7.5 | 103.594 |
| 100 | 14.87875 × 2 = 29.7575 | 4 | 7.5 | 104.437 |

19. Hilton Hotels Corp. has a convertible bond issue outstanding. Each bond, with a face value of $1,000, can be converted into common shares at a rate of 61.2983 shares of stock per $1,000 face value bond (the conversion rate), or $16.316 per share. Hilton's common stock is trading (on the NYSE) at $15.90 per share and the bonds are trading at $975. (*LG 6-2*)

   **a.** Calculate the conversion value of each bond.

   **b.** Determine if it is currently profitable for bond holders to convert their bonds into shares of Hilton Hotels common stock.

20. Gentherm Inc. has a convertible bond issue outstanding. Each bond, with a face value of $1,000, can be converted into common shares at a rate of 42.25 shares of stock per $1,000 face value bond (the conversion rate), or $19.85 per share. Gentherm's common stock is trading (on the NYSE) at $19.85 per share and the bonds are trading at $1,025. (*LG 6-2*)

   **a.** Calculate the conversion value of each bond.

   **b.** Determine if it is currently profitable for bond holders to convert their bonds into shares of Gentherm common stock.

## SEARCH THE SITE

Go to *The Wall Street Journal*'s website at **www.wsj.com** and find the most recent data on Treasury security trading using the following steps. Under "Markets," click on "Bonds." In the section "Quotes & Trading Statistics," click on "Treasury Quotes." This will bring up the most recent Treasury data.

**Questions**

1. Find a Treasury note that is maturing 1 year from the current date. What is the ask price on this Treasury security? What is the asked yield?
2. Find a Treasury bond that is maturing in 20 years from the current date. What is the coupon rate on this Treasury bond? What is the bid price on this bond?

# chapter

# 7

# Mortgage Markets

## Learning Goals

**LG 7-1**    *Distinguish between a mortgage and a mortgage-backed security.*

**LG 7-2**    *Describe the main types of mortgages issued by financial institutions.*

**LG 7-3**    *Identify the major characteristics of a mortgage.*

**LG 7-4**    *Examine how a mortgage amortization schedule is determined.*

**LG 7-5**    *Describe some of the new innovations in mortgage financing.*

**LG 7-6**    *Define a mortgage sale.*

**LG 7-7**    *Define a pass-through security.*

**LG 7-8**    *Define a collateralized mortgage obligation.*

**LG 7-9**    *List the major mortgage holders in the United States.*

**LG 7-10**    *Describe the trends in the international securitization of mortgages.*

## MORTGAGES AND MORTGAGE-BACKED SECURITIES: CHAPTER OVERVIEW

**Mortgages** are loans to individuals or businesses to purchase a home, land, or other real property. The property purchased with the loan serves as collateral backing the loan. As of March 2016, there were $13.8 trillion of primary mortgages outstanding, held by various financial institutions such as banks and mortgage companies. Figure 7–1 lists the major categories of mortgages and the amount of each outstanding in 1995 and 2016. Home mortgages (one to four families) are the largest loan category (72.3 percent of all mortgages in 2016), followed by commercial mortgages (used to finance specific projects that are pledged as collateral for the mortgage—18.2 percent), multifamily dwellings (8.0 percent), and farms (1.5 percent).

    Many mortgages, particularly residential mortgages, are subsequently **securitized** by the mortgage holder—they are packaged and sold as assets backing a publicly traded or privately held debt instrument. Securitization allows financial institutions' (FIs') asset portfolios to become more liquid, reduces interest rate risk and credit risk, provides FIs

**Figure 7–1**  Mortgage Loans Outstanding

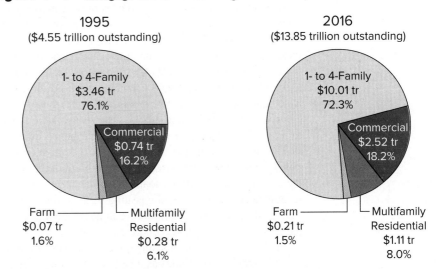

**1995**
($4.55 trillion outstanding)

1- to 4-Family
$3.46 tr
76.1%

Commercial
$0.74 tr
16.2%

Farm
$0.07 tr
1.6%

Multifamily
Residential
$0.28 tr
6.1%

**2016**
($13.85 trillion outstanding)

1- to 4-Family
$10.01 tr
72.3%

Commercial
$2.52 tr
18.2%

Farm
$0.21 tr
1.5%

Multifamily
Residential
$1.11 tr
8.0%

**Source:** Federal Reserve Board website, "Flow of Fund Accounts," July 2016. www.federalreserve.gov

**LG 7-1**

**mortgages**

*Loans to individuals or businesses to purchase a home, land, or other real property.*

**securitized**

*Securities packaged and sold as assets backing a publicly traded or privately held debt instrument.*

with a source of fee income, and helps reduce the effects of regulatory constraints such as capital requirements, reserve requirements, and deposit insurance premiums on FI profits (see Chapter 13). Currently, approximately 60 percent of home mortgages are securitized.

We examine mortgage markets separately from bond and stock markets for several reasons. First, mortgages are backed by a specific piece of real property. If the borrower defaults on a mortgage, the financial institution can take ownership of the property. Only mortgage bonds are backed by a specific piece of property that allows the lender to take ownership in the event of a default. All other corporate bonds and stock give the holder a general claim to a borrower's assets. Second, there is no set size or denomination for primary mortgages. Rather, the size of each mortgage depends on the borrower's needs and ability to repay. Bonds generally have a denomination of $1,000 or a multiple of $1,000 per bond, and shares of stock are generally issued in (par value) denominations of $1 per share. Third, primary mortgages generally involve a single investor (e.g., a bank or mortgage company). Bond and stock issues, on the other hand, are generally held by many (sometimes thousands of) investors. Finally, the typical issuers in the mortgage market (individuals) are quite different from issuers (corporations and governments) in other financial markets. Because primary mortgage borrowers are often individuals, information on these borrowers is less extensive and unaudited. Bonds and stocks issued by publicly traded corporations and governments are subject to extensive rules and regulations regarding information availability and reliability.

The mortgage markets are something of a bellwether for the bond and stock markets, as well as the overall economy. Indeed, at the very heart of the recent financial crisis were losses associated with mortgages and off-balance-sheet mortgage-backed securities, so-called toxic assets, created and held by FIs. The roots of the financial crisis go back to the early 2000s, particularly after the terrorist attacks of 9/11, when the U.S. economy experienced a boom ("bubble") in the housing markets. The immediate response by regulators to the terrorist attacks was to create stability in the financial markets by providing liquidity to FIs. For example, the Federal Reserve lowered the short-term interest rate that banks and other financial institutions pay in the federal funds market and even made lender of last resort funds available to nonbank FIs such as investment banks. Perhaps not surprisingly, low interest rates and the increased liquidity provided by the central banks resulted in a rapid expansion in mortgage financing. Demand for residential mortgages rose dramatically. As the demand for mortgage debt grew, especially among those who had previously been excluded from participating in the market because of their poor credit ratings, FIs began lowering their credit quality cut-off points. Moreover, to boost their earnings in the market now popularly known as the "subprime market," banks and other mortgage lenders often offered relatively low "teaser" rates on adjustable rate mortgages (i.e., exceptionally low initial interest rates which, if market rates rose in the future, were subject to substantial increases after expiration of the initial rate period two or three year later).

Historically, banks (and other depository institutions) held these loans on their balance sheets. Under this traditional originate-and-hold model, banks might have been reluctant to so aggressively pursue low credit quality borrowers for fear that the loans would default. However, in the 1990s and 2000s, asset securitization and loan syndication allowed banks to retain little or no part of the loans, and hence little or none of the default risk on the loans that they originated. As a result, the incentive for banks to monitor the mortgage borrower's default risk decreased dramatically. As long as the borrower did not default within the first few months after a loan's issuance and the loans were sold or securitized without recourse back to the bank, the issuing bank could ignore longer-term credit risk concerns. The result was a deterioration in credit quality, while at the same time there was a dramatic increase in consumer and corporate leverage.

Eventually, in 2006, housing prices started to fall. At the same time, the Federal Reserve started to raise interest rates as it began to fear inflation. Since many of the subprime mortgages that originated in the 2001–2005 period had adjustable rates, the cost of meeting mortgage commitments rose to unsustainable levels for many low-income households. The confluence of falling house prices, rising interest rates, and rising mortgage costs led to a wave of mortgage defaults in the subprime market and foreclosures that only reinforced the downward trend in housing prices. The number of subprime mortgages more than 60 days behind on their payments was 17.1 percent in June 2007 and over 20 percent by August 2007. As this happened, the poor quality of the collateral and credit quality underlying subprime mortgage pools became apparent, with default rates far exceeding those apparently anticipated by the rating agencies in setting their initial subprime mortgage securitizations ratings. In 2007, the percentage of subprime mortgage-backed securities delinquent by 90 days or more was 10.09 percent, substantially higher than the 5.37 percent rate in May 2005. The financial crisis began.

In this chapter, we look at characteristics and operations of the mortgage and mortgage-backed securities markets. We look at different types of mortgages and the determination of mortgage payments. (We look at the processes used by financial institutions to evaluate mortgage loan applicants in Chapter 20.) We also discuss the agencies owned or sponsored by the U.S. government that help securitize mortgage pools. We briefly describe the major forms of mortgage-backed securities and discuss the process of securitization. More complete details of the securitization process are provided in Chapter 24. We conclude the chapter with a look at international investors in mortgages and mortgage-backed securities markets, as well as trends in international securitization of mortgage assets.

# PRIMARY MORTGAGE MARKET

**LG 7-2**

Four basic categories of mortgages are issued by financial institutions: home, multifamily dwelling, commercial, and farm. Home mortgages ($10.01 trillion outstanding in 2016) are used to purchase one- to four-family dwellings. Multifamily dwelling mortgages ($1.11 trillion outstanding) are used to finance the purchase of apartment complexes, townhouses, and condominiums. Commercial mortgages ($2.52 trillion outstanding) are used to finance the purchase of real estate for business purposes (e.g., office buildings, shopping malls). Farm mortgages ($0.21 trillion outstanding) are used to finance the purchase of farms. As seen in Figure 7–1, while all four areas have experienced tremendous growth, the historically low mortgage rates in the 1990s and 2000s have particularly spurred growth in the single-family home area (189 percent growth from 1995 through 2016), commercial business mortgages (241 percent growth), and multifamily residential mortgages (296 percent growth).

## Mortgage Characteristics

As mentioned previously, mortgages are unique as capital market instruments because the characteristics (such as size, fees, and interest rate) of each mortgage held by a financial institution can differ. A mortgage contract between a financial institution and a borrower must specify all of the characteristics of the mortgage agreement. When a financial institution receives a mortgage application, it must determine whether the applicant qualifies for a loan. (We describe this process in Chapter 20.) Because most financial institutions sell or securitize their mortgage loans in the secondary mortgage market (discussed below), the guidelines set by the secondary market buyer for acceptability, as well as the guidelines set by the financial institution, are used to determine whether or not a mortgage borrower is qualified. Further, the characteristics of loans to be securitized will generally be more standardized than those that are not to be securitized. When mortgages are not securitized, the financial institution can be more flexible with the acceptance/rejection guidelines it uses and mortgage characteristics will be more varied.

**lien**

*A public record attached to the title of the property that gives the financial institution the right to sell the property if the mortgage borrower defaults.*

**Collateral.** As mentioned in the introduction, all mortgage loans are backed by a specific piece of property that serves as collateral to the mortgage loan. As part of the mortgage agreement, the financial institution will place a **lien** against a property that remains in place until the loan is fully paid off. A lien is a public record attached to the title of the property that gives the financial institution the right to sell the property if the mortgage borrower defaults or falls into arrears on his or her payments. The mortgage is secured by the lien—that is, until the loan is paid off, no one can buy the property and obtain clear title to it. If someone tries to purchase the property, the financial institution can file notice of the lien at the public recorder's office to stop the transaction.

**down payment**

*A portion of the purchase price of the property a financial institution requires the mortgage borrower to pay up front.*

**Down Payment.** As part of any mortgage agreement, a financial institution requires the mortgage borrower to pay a portion of the purchase price of the property (a **down payment**) at the closing (the day the mortgage is issued). The balance of the purchase price is the face value of the mortgage (or the loan proceeds). A down payment decreases the probability that the borrower will default on the mortgage. A mortgage borrower who makes a large down payment invests more personal wealth into the home and, therefore, is less likely to walk away from the house should property values fall, leaving the mortgage unpaid. However, the drop in real estate values during the recent financial crisis caused many mortgage borrowers to walk away from their homes and mortgages, as well as many mortgage lenders to fail.

The size of the down payment depends on the financial situation of the borrower. Generally, a 20 percent down payment is required (i.e., the loan-to-value ratio may be no more than 80 percent). Borrowers that put up less than 20 percent are required to purchase **private mortgage insurance (PMI).** (Technically, the insurance is purchased by the lender (the financial institution) but paid for by the borrower, generally as part of the monthly payment.) In the event of default, the PMI issuer (such as Radian Group, Inc.) guarantees to pay the financial institution a portion (generally between 12 percent and 35 percent) of the difference between the value of the property and the balance remaining on the mortgage. As payments are made on the mortgage, or if the value of the property increases, a mortgage borrower can eventually request that the PMI requirement be removed. Every financial institution differs in its requirements for removing the PMI payment from a mortgage. However, in most cases financial institutions require a waiting period of one to two years after the loan's origination date, proof through an approved appraiser that the loan-to-value ratio is less than 80 percent, on-time payments during the waiting period, and a letter from the borrower requesting that the PMI be removed from the loan.

**private mortgage insurance (PMI)**

*Insurance contract purchased by a mortgage borrower guaranteeing to pay the financial institution the difference between the value of the property and the balance remaining on the mortgage.*

**federally insured mortgages**

*Mortgages originated by financial institutions, with repayment guaranteed by either the Federal Housing Administration (FHA) or the Veterans Administration (VA).*

**Insured versus Conventional Mortgages.** Mortgages are classified as either federally insured or conventional. **Federally insured mortgages** are originated by financial institutions, but repayment is guaranteed (for a fee of 0.5 percent of the loan amount) by either the Federal Housing Administration (FHA) or the Veterans Administration (VA). In order to qualify, FHA and VA mortgage loan applicants must meet specific requirements set by these government agencies (e.g., VA-insured loans are available only to individuals who served and were honorably discharged from military service in the United States). Further, the maximum size of the mortgage is limited (the limit varies by state and is based on the cost of housing). For example, in 2016, FHA loan limits on single-family homes ranged from $271,050 to $625,500, depending on location and cost of living. FHA or VA mortgages require either a very low or zero down payment. (FHA mortgages require as little as a 3 percent down payment.)

**conventional mortgages**

*Mortgages issued by financial institutions that are not federally insured.*

**Conventional mortgages** are mortgages held by financial institutions and are not federally insured (but as already discussed, they generally are required to be privately insured if the borrower's down payment is less than 20 percent of the property's value). Secondary market mortgage buyers will not generally purchase conventional mortgages that are not privately insured and that have a loan-to-value ratio of greater than 80 percent.

**Mortgage Maturities.**   A mortgage generally has an original maturity of either 15 or 30 years. Until recently, the 30-year mortgage was the one most frequently used. However, the 15-year mortgage has grown in popularity. Mortgage borrowers are attracted to the 15-year mortgage because of the potential saving in total interest paid (see below). However, because the mortgage is paid off in half the time, monthly mortgage payments are higher on a 15-year than on a 30-year mortgage. Financial institutions find the 15-year mortgage attractive because of the lower degree of interest rate risk on a 15-year relative to a 30-year mortgage. To attract mortgage borrowers to the 15-year maturity mortgage, financial institutions generally charge a lower interest rate on a 15-year mortgage than a 30-year mortgage.

**amortized**

*A mortgage is amortized when the fixed principal and interest payments fully pay off the mortgage by its maturity date.*

**balloon payment mortgage**

*Mortgage that requires a fixed monthly interest payment for a three- to five-year period. Full payment of the mortgage principal (the balloon payment) is then required at the end of the period.*

Most mortgages allow the borrower to prepay all or part of the mortgage principal early without penalty. In general, the monthly payment is set at a fixed level to repay interest and principal on the mortgage by the maturity date (i.e., the mortgage is fully **amortized**). We illustrate this payment pattern for a 15-year fixed-rate mortgage in Figure 7–2. However, other mortgages have variable interest rates and thus payments that vary (see below).

In addition to 15- and 30-year fixed-rate and variable-rate mortgages, financial institutions sometimes offer **balloon payment mortgages.** A balloon payment mortgage requires a fixed monthly interest payment (and, sometimes, principal payments) for a three- to five-year period. Full payment of the mortgage principal (the balloon payment) is then required at the end of the period, as illustrated for a five-year balloon payment mortgage in Figure 7–2. Because they normally consist of interest only, the monthly payments prior to maturity are lower than those on an amortized loan (i.e., a loan that requires periodic repayments of principal and interest). Generally, because few borrowers save enough funds to pay off the

**Figure 7–2**    **Fixed-Rate versus Balloon Payment Mortgage**

A 15-year fixed-rate mortgage: *PMT* consists of principal and interest

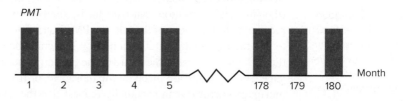

A 5-year balloon payment mortgage: *PMT* consists of interest only; *PRIN* represents the full payment of the principal at the end of the mortgage period

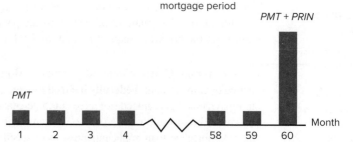

mortgage in three to five years, the mortgage principal is refinanced at the current mortgage interest rate at the end of the balloon loan period (refinancing at maturity is not, however, guaranteed). Thus, with a balloon mortgage the financial institution essentially provides a long-term mortgage in which it can periodically revise the mortgage's characteristics.

**Interest Rates.**   Possibly the most important characteristic identified in a mortgage contract is the interest rate on the mortgage. Mortgage borrowers often decide how much to borrow and from whom solely by looking at the quoted mortgage rates of several financial institutions. In turn, financial institutions base their quoted mortgage rates on several factors. First, they use the market rate at which they obtain funds (e.g., the fed funds rate, Treasury bond rate, or the rate on certificates of deposit). The market rate on available funds is the base rate used to determine mortgage rates. Figure 7–3 illustrates the trend in 30-year fixed-rate mortgage rates and 10-year Treasury bond rates from 1980 through 2016. Note the declining trend in mortgage (and T-bond) rates over the period. During the last week of June 2016, the average rate on a 30-year fixed-rate mortgage was 3.54 percent, up only slightly from 3.31 percent in November 2012, an all-time record low. The average rate on a 15-year fixed-rate mortgage was 2.74 percent, down from 3.66 percent in September 2013. Once the base mortgage rate is determined, the rate on a specific mortgage is then adjusted for other factors (e.g., whether the mortgage specifies a fixed or variable (adjustable) rate of interest and whether the loan specifies discount points and other fees), as discussed below.

*Fixed versus Adjustable-Rate Mortgages.*   Mortgage contracts specify whether a fixed or variable rate of interest will be paid by the borrower. A **fixed-rate mortgage** locks in the borrower's interest rate and thus required monthly payments over the life of the mortgage, regardless of how market rates change. In contrast, the interest rate on an **adjustable-rate mortgage (ARM)** is tied to some market interest rate or interest rate index. Thus, the required monthly payments can change over the life of the mortgage. ARMs generally limit the change in the interest rate allowed each year and during the life of the mortgage (called *caps*). For example, an ARM might adjust the interest rate based on the average Treasury bill rate plus 1.5 percent, with caps of 1.5 percent per year and 4 percent over the life of the mortgage.

Figure 7–4 shows the percentage of ARMs relative to all mortgages closed and 30-year mortgage rates from 1987 through 2016. Notice that mortgage borrowers generally prefer fixed-rate loans to ARMs when interest rates in the economy are low. If interest rates rise, ARMs may cause borrowers to be unable to meet the promised payments on the mortgage. In contrast, most mortgage lenders prefer ARMs when interest rates are low. When interest rates eventually rise, ARM payments on their mortgage assets will rise. Since deposit rates and other liability rates too will be rising, it will be easier for

www.research.stlouisfed
.org/fred2
www.bloomberg.com

**fixed-rate mortgage**

*A mortgage that locks in the borrower's interest rate and thus the required monthly payment over the life of the mortgage, regardless of how market rates change.*

**adjustable-rate mortgage (ARM)**

*A mortgage in which the interest rate is tied to some market interest rate. Thus, the required monthly payments can change over the life of the mortgage.*

**Figure 7–3**   **30-Year Mortgage versus 10-Year Treasury Rates**

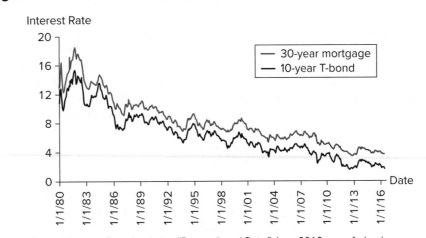

**Source:** Federal Reserve Board website, "Research and Data," June 2016. www.federalreserve.gov

**Figure 7–4**   ARMs' Share of Total Loans Closed, 1987–2016

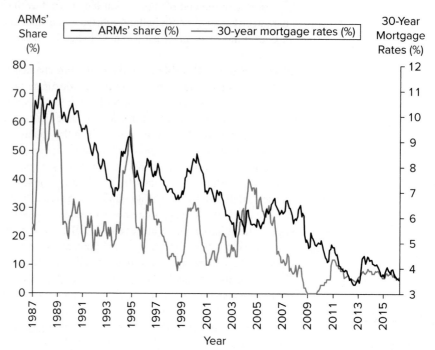

**Sources:** Federal Housing Finance Agency and Federal Reserve Board websites, June 2016. www.fhfa .gov and www.federalreserve.gov

financial institutions to pay the higher interest rates to their depositors when they issue ARMs. However, higher interest payments mean mortgage borrowers may have trouble making their payments. Thus, default risk increases. Such was the case during the recent financial crisis. As the general level of interest rates in the economy rose, rates on ARMs increased to the point that many borrowers had trouble meeting their payments. The result (as discussed earlier) was a record number of foreclosures. Thus, while ARMs reduce a financial institution's interest rate risk, they also increase its default risk.

Note from Figure 7–4 the behavior of the share of ARMs to fixed-rate mortgages over the period 2001 through 2003 and 2008 through 2016—when interest rates fell. Notice that borrowers' preferences for fixed-rate mortgages prevailed over this period, as a consistently low percentage of total mortgages closed were ARMs (between 2001 and 2003 the percentage of ARMs to total mortgages issued averaged only 14.8 percent). During the height of the financial crisis (late 2008–early 2009), as interest rates were dropping to historic lows, virtually no ARMs were issued.

**discount points**

*Interest payments made when the loan is issued (at closing). One discount point paid up front is equal to 1 percent of the principal value of the mortgage.*

*Discount Points.*   **Discount points** (often just called *points*) are fees or payments made when a mortgage loan is issued (at closing). One discount point paid up front is equal to 1 percent of the principal value of the mortgage. For example, if the borrower pays 2 points up front on a $100,000 mortgage, he or she must pay $2,000 at the closing of the mortgage. While the mortgage principal is $100,000, the borrower effectively has received $98,000. In exchange for points paid up front, the financial institution reduces the interest rate used to determine the monthly payments on the mortgage. The borrower determines whether the reduced interest payments over the life of the loan outweigh the up-front fee through points. This decision depends on the period of time the borrower expects to hold the mortgage (see below).

*Other Fees.*   In addition to interest, mortgage contracts generally require the borrower to pay an assortment of fees to cover the mortgage issuer's costs of processing the mortgage. These include such items as:

> *Application fee.* Covers the issuer's initial costs of processing the mortgage application and obtaining a credit report.

*Title search.* Confirms the borrower's legal ownership of the mortgaged property and ensures there are no outstanding claims against the property.

*Title insurance.* Protects the lender against an error in the title search.

*Appraisal fee.* Covers the cost of an independent appraisal of the value of the mortgaged property.

*Loan origination fee.* Covers the remaining costs to the mortgage issuer for processing the mortgage application and completing the loan.

*Closing agent and review fees.* Cover the costs of the closing agent who actually closes the mortgage.

*Other costs.* Any other fees, such as VA loan guarantees, or FHA or private mortgage insurance.

Figure 7–5 presents a sample closing statement in which the various fees are reported and the payment required by the borrower at closing is determined.

### Figure 7–5    Mortgage Closing Statement

Borrower(s): Manuel Goodperson, Manuela Goodperson
Lender: Starpointe Savings Bank Peasant Run Plaza Warre
Property: 321 Main St. Watchung, NJ 07060

Date: 02/05/2019

| Type of Mortgage FHA ( )  GI ( )  Convent. ( ) | | | Amount of Loan | $106,400.00 |
| Additional Funds made available by: $ | | | | |
| | | | Total A | $106,400.00 |

| PAYMENTS to Lender (to establish escrow reserve) | | | | |
|---|---|---|---|---|
| Taxes | 3 months @ | $   172.50 | $ | 517.50 |
| Insurance | 3 months @ | $     28.92 | $ | 86.76 |
| Mortgage Insurance Premium | 2 months @ | $     69.16 | $ | 138.32 |
| 0.00 | | | $ | |
| 0.00 | | | $ | |
| Flood Ins. | | | $ | 44.08 |
| | | Total B | $ | 786.66 |
| OTHER PAYMENTS to Lender | | | | |
| Application Fee | | | $ | 54.00 |
| Appraisal Fee | | | $ | 500.00 |
| Credit Report Fee | | | $ | |
| Mortgage Origination Fee | | | $ | 564.00 |
| Points Paid by the Seller(s) | | | $ | |
| Processing Fee | | | $ | |
| Interest on Loan to | | | $ | 629.66 |
| | | | $ | |
| | | | $ | |
| | | | $ | |
| | | Total C | $ | 1,747.66 |
| PAYMENTS to Others | | | | |
| Current Taxes & Assessments | | | $ | |
| Title Search & Examination | | | $ | |
| Survey | | | $ | 415.00 |
| Title Insurance Policies | | | $ | 932.00 |
| Hazard Insurance | | | $ | |
| Recording Fees | | | $ | 8.11 |
| Attorney Fees | | | $ | 750.00 |
| Realty Transfer Fee or Tax | | | $ | |
| Broker's Commission | | | $ | |
| Mortgage Cancellation Fee | | | $ | |
| Pay off of Mortgage Loan(s) | | | $ | 1,000.00 |
| Balance due to Seller(s) | | | $ | 104,482.00 |
| | | | $ | |
| | | | $ | |
| | | | $ | |
| | | Total D | $ | 107,587.11 |
| | | Total B, C, and D | | $110,121.43 |
| Overpayment returned to Borrower (A less total B, C, and D) | | | | $ −3,721.43 |

0 Year Mortgage @ % per year monthly payment payable day of each month commencing 02/05/2016

| Principal & Interest | $ | |
| 1/12 Taxes (Estimated) | $ | |
| 1/12 Insurance | $ | |
| 1/12 Mortgage Insurance Premium | $ | |
| Total | $ | |

This statement has been examined by us and explained to our complete satisfaction. We have been given a copy of this statement. We authorize and direct that the closing attorney distribute the funds as set forth above.

Borrower Manuel Goodperson

Closing Attorney
Larry Lawyer, Esq

Borrower Manuela Goodperson

*Mortgage Refinancing.* Mortgage refinancing occurs when a mortgage borrower takes out a new mortgage and uses the proceeds obtained to pay off the current mortgage. Mortgage refinancing involves many of the same details and steps involved in applying for a new mortgage and can involve many of the same fees and expenses. Mortgages are most often refinanced when a current mortgage has an interest rate that is higher than the current interest rate. As coupon rates on new mortgages fall, the incentive for mortgage borrowers to pay off old, high coupon rate mortgages and refinance at lower rates increases. Figure 7–6 shows the percentage of mortgage originations that involved refinancings and 30-year mortgage rates from 1990 through 2016. Notice that as mortgage rates fall, the percentage of mortgages that are refinancings increases. For example, as mortgage rates fell in the early 2010s, refinancings increased to over 80 percent of all mortgages originated.

By refinancing the mortgage at a lower interest rate, the borrower pays less each month—even if the new mortgage is for the same amount as the current mortgage. Traditionally, the decision to refinance involves balancing the savings of a lower monthly payment against the costs (fees) of refinancing. That is, refinancing adds transaction and recontracting costs. Origination costs or points for new mortgages, along with the cost of appraisals and credit checks, frequently arise as well. An often-cited rule of thumb is that the interest rate for a new mortgage should be 2 percentage points below the rate on the current mortgage for refinancing to make financial sense.

## Mortgage Amortization

**LG 7-4**

**amortization schedule**

*Schedule showing how the monthly mortgage payments are split between principal and interest.*

The fixed monthly payment made by a mortgage borrower generally consists partly of repayment of the principal borrowed and partly of the interest on the outstanding (remaining) balance of the mortgage. In other words, these fixed payments fully amortize (pay off) the mortgage by its maturity date. During the early years of the mortgage, most of the fixed monthly payment represents interest on the outstanding principal and a small amount represents a payoff of the outstanding principal. As the mortgage approaches maturity, most of the payment represents a payoff of the outstanding principal and a small amount represents interest. An **amortization schedule** shows how the fixed monthly payments are split between principal and interest.

**Figure 7–6**   Mortgage Refinancings as a Percentage of All Mortgages Originated, 1990–2016

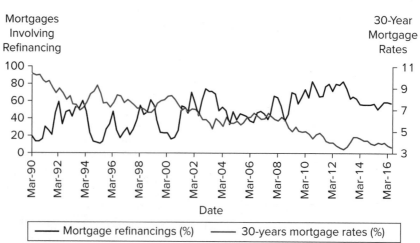

**Source:** Mortgage Bankers Association website, July 2016. www.mbaa.org

---

**EXAMPLE 7-1**   Calculation of Monthly Mortgage Payments

You plan to purchase a house for $150,000 using a 30-year mortgage obtained from your local bank. The mortgage rate offered to you is 8 percent with zero points. In order to forgo the purchase of private mortgage insurance, you will make a down payment of 20 percent of the purchase price ($30,000 = 0.20 × $150,000) at closing and borrow $120,000 through the mortgage.

The monthly payments on this mortgage are calculated using the time value of money formulas presented in Chapter 2. Specifically, the amount borrowed through the mortgage represents a present value of the principal, and the monthly payments represent a monthly annuity payment. The equation used to calculate your fixed monthly mortgage payments to pay off the $120,000 mortgage at an 8 percent annual (8%/12 = 0.6667% monthly) interest rate over 30 years (or 30 × 12 = 360 payments) is as follows:

$$PV = PMT \sum_{j=1}^{t} \left(\tfrac{1}{1+r}\right)^{j}$$

$$= PMT\left[\left(1 - [1/(1 + r)^{t}]\right)/r\right]$$

where

$PV$ = Principal amount borrowed through the mortgage

$PMT$ = Monthly mortgage payment

$r$ = Monthly interest rate on the mortgage (equals the nominal annual interest rate, $i$, divided by 12 [months per year])

$t$ = Number of months (payments) over the life of the mortgage

For the mortgage in this example:

$$\$120,000 = PMT\left[\left(1 - [1/(1 + 0.006667)^{360}]\right)/0.006667\right]$$

or:

$$PMT = \$120,000/\left[\left(1 - [1/(1 + 0.006667)^{360}]\right)/0.006667\right]$$

Therefore:

$$PMT = \$120,000/136.2835 = \$880.52$$

Thus, your monthly payment is $880.52.

---

We now construct the amortization schedule for this mortgage.

---

**EXAMPLE 7-2**   Construction of an Amortization Schedule

Using the monthly payment calculated on the mortgage in Example 7–1, we construct a partial amortization schedule in Table 7–1. Column 1 is the month in the 360-month loan period. Column 2 is the balance of the mortgage outstanding at the beginning of each month. Column 3 is the monthly payment on the mortgage, calculated in Example 7–1. Column 4, Interest, is the portion of the monthly payment that represents the pure interest payment based on the loan balance outstanding at the beginning of the month (beginning loan balance × 8%/12). Column 5, Principal, is the portion of the monthly payment that represents the repayment of the mortgage's principal (monthly payment – monthly interest, or in this example for month 1, $880.52 – $800 = $80.52). Column 6 is the balance of the mortgage principal outstanding at the end of the month (beginning loan balance [column 2] – principal [column 5]).[1] This value becomes the beginning balance in the next month. The full amortization schedule is shown in Appendix 7A to the chapter (available through Connect or your course instructor).

Notice that the total payments made by the mortgage borrower over the 30-year life of the mortgage are $316,987.20. Of this amount, $120,000 is repayment of the original principal. Thus, the borrower pays a total of $196,978.20 in interest over the life of the mortgage. Figure 7–7 illustrates the proportion of each payment that is interest versus principal. Notice that during the early years the majority of each payment is interest and very little goes toward the repayment of principal. As the mortgage approaches maturity the majority of each payment is principal and very little goes to paying interest.

**TABLE 7–1**    Amortization Schedule for a 30-Year Mortgage

| (1) Month | (2) Beginning Loan Balance | (3) Payment | (4) Interest | (5) Principal | (6) Ending Loan Balance |
|---|---|---|---|---|---|
| 1 | $120,000.00 | $ 880.52 | $ 800.00 | $ 80.52 | $119,919.48 |
| 2 | 119,919.48 | 880.52 | 799.46 | 81.06 | 119,838.42 |
| • | • | • | • | • | • |
| • | • | • | • | • | • |
| 119 | 105,623.54 | 880.52 | 704.16 | 176.36 | 105,447.18 |
| 120 (10 years) | 105,447.18 | 880.52 | 702.98 | 177.54 | 105,269.64 |
| • | • | • | • | • | • |
| • | • | • | • | • | • |
| 239 | 73,359.08 | 880.52 | 489.06 | 391.46 | 72,967.62 |
| 240 (20 years) | 72,967.62 | 880.52 | 486.45 | 394.07 | 72,573.55 |
| • | • | • | • | • | • |
| • | • | • | • | • | • |
| 359 | 1,743.58 | 880.52 | 11.63 | 868.89 | 874.69 |
| 360 (30 years) | 874.69 | 880.52 | 5.83 | 874.69 | 0 |
| Total | | $316,987.20 | $196,987.20 | $120,000.00 | |

**Figure 7–7**    Amortization of a 30-Year Mortgage

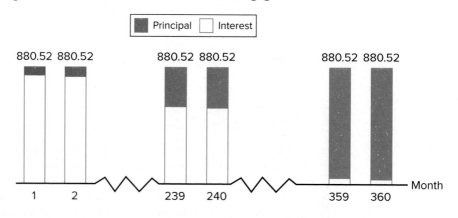

1. The loan balance remaining for any period, $x$, can also be calculated as:

$$(\{1 - [1/(1 + r)^{(30(12)-x)}]\}/r)/(\{1 - [(1 + r)^{30(12)}]\}/r) \times \text{Original principal}$$

For example, with 120 payments remaining on the loan, the ending loan balance is:

$$(\{1 - [1/(1 + 0.006667)^{30(12)-120}]\}/0.006667)/(\{1 - [1/(1 + 0.006667)^{(30)12}]\}/0.006667) \times \$120,000 = \$105,269.64$$

As discussed, an advantage of a 15-year mortgage to a mortgage borrower is that the total interest paid on a 15-year mortgage is smaller than that paid on a 30-year mortgage. This is due to the shorter time frame in which payments are made on the loan and the lower interest rates that are offered by mortgage issuers to entice borrowers to choose the shorter maturity mortgages.

---

**EXAMPLE 7–3**  **Comparison of Interest Paid on a 15-Year versus a 30-Year Mortgage**

Using the information in Example 7–1 but changing the loan maturity to 15 years (180 months) and the mortgage rate to 7.25 percent, the monthly payment on the $120,000 mortgage loan is:

$$\$120,000 = PMT[(1 - [1/(1 + 0.00604167)^{180}])/0.00604167]$$

or:

$$PMT = \$120,000/[(1 - 1/(1 + 0.00604167)^{180}])/0.00604167]$$

Therefore:

$$PMT = \$120,000/109.545477 = \$1,095.44$$

Solving for *PMT,* the monthly mortgage payment is $1,095.44. Table 7–2 shows the corresponding loan amortization schedule.

Total payments on the 15-year mortgage are $197,179.20, of which $77,179.20 is interest. This compares to interest of $196,987.20 on the 30-year mortgage (a difference of $119,808.00, disregarding time value of money). The mortgage borrower's interest payments are reduced significantly with the 15-year mortgage relative to the 30-year mortgage. However, the borrower must pay $1,095.44 per month with the 15-year mortgage compared to $880.52 with the 30-year mortgage, a difference of $214.92 per month. This may be difficult if the borrower's income level is not very high.

---

**TABLE 7–2**  Amortization Schedule for a 15-Year Mortgage

| Month | Beginning Loan Balance | Payment | Interest | Principal | Ending Loan Balance |
|---|---|---|---|---|---|
| 1 | $120,000.00 | $ 1,095.44 | $ 725.00 | $ 370.44 | $119,629.56 |
| 2 | 119,629.56 | 1,095.44 | 722.76 | 372.68 | 119,256.88 |
| • | • | • | • | • | • |
| • | • | • | • | • | • |
| 59 | 94,360.69 | 1,095.44 | 570.10 | 525.34 | 93,835.35 |
| 60 (5 years) | 93,835.35 | 1,095.44 | 566.92 | 528.52 | 93,306.83 |
| • | • | • | • | • | • |
| 119 | 56,505.45 | 1,095.44 | 341.39 | 754.05 | 55,751.40 |
| 120 (10 years) | 55,751.40 | 1,095.44 | 336.83 | 758.61 | 54,992.79 |
| • | • | • | • | • | • |
| 179 | 2,169.86 | 1,095.44 | 13.11 | 1,082.33 | 1,087.53 |
| 180 (15 years) | 1,087.53 | 1,095.44 | 6.57 | 1,087.53 | 0 |
| Total | | $197,179.20 | $77,179.20 | $120,000.00 | |

Another factor that affects the amortization of a loan is whether the borrower pays discount points up front in exchange for a reduced interest rate and, consequently, reduced monthly payments.

**EXAMPLE 7–4**    Analyzing the Choice between Points and Monthly Payments of Interest

You plan to purchase a house for $150,000 using a 30-year mortgage obtained from your local bank. You will make a down payment of 20 percent of the purchase price, in this case, equal to $30,000. Thus, the mortgage loan amount will be $120,000. Your bank offers you the following two options for payment:

**Option 1:** Mortgage rate of 8 percent (or 8%/12 = 0.6667% per month) and zero points.

**Option 2:** Mortgage rate of 7.75 percent (or 7.75%/12 = 0.6458% per month) and 2 points ($2,400 = $120,000 × 0.02).

If option 2 is chosen, you receive $117,600 at closing ($120,000 – $2,400), although the mortgage principal is $120,000.

To determine the best option, we first calculate the monthly payments for both options as follows:

**Option 1:** $120,000 = $PMT[(1 + [1/(1 + 0.006667)^{360}])/0.006667] \rightarrow PMT = \$880.52$
**Option 2:** $120,00 = $PMT[(1 + [1/(1 + 0.006458)^{360}])/0.006458] \rightarrow PMT = \$859.69$

In exchange for $2,400 up front, option 2 reduces your monthly mortgage payments by $20.83. The amortization schedules for the two loans are given in Appendix 7A to the chapter (available through Connect or your course instructor). The present value of these savings (evaluated at 7.75 percent) over the 30 years is:

$$PV = \$20.83 \,[(1 - [1/(1 + 0.006458)^{360}])/0.006458] = \$2,906.54$$

Option 2 is the better choice. The present value of the monthly savings, $2,906.54, is greater than the points paid up front, $2,400.

Suppose, however, you plan on paying off the loan in 10 years (120 months) even though the mortgage has a 30-year maturity. Since option 2 (the mortgage with points) has a lower interest rate, the principal remaining each month prior to maturity is lower. The lower interest rate means that a larger amount of each month's payment can go to pay off the principal on the mortgage. At 120 months, the principal balance remaining on option 1 (the no points mortgage) is $105,269.26, while the principal remaining on option 2 (the points mortgage) is $104,720.52 (see Appendix 7A). The difference in principal balance to be paid after 120 months ($548.74) must also be included in the calculation. Now the monthly savings from option 2 have a present value of:

$$PV = \$20.83 \,[(1 - [1/(1 + 0.006458)^{120}])/0.006458] + \$548.74/(1 + 0.006458)^{120}$$
$$= \$1,989.12$$

Option 1 becomes the better deal. The present value of the monthly savings, $1,989.12, is less than the points paid up front, $2,400.

The indifference point (the number of years) between the two options would be the point where the difference in interest payments ($25.00),[2] equals the up-front payment, $2,400. As mentioned above, the lower interest rate on option 2 results in the remaining principal being lower each month prior to maturity of the mortgage and thus, a lower pay-off amount on early payoff by the mortgage borrower. Thus, we use the difference in interest payments (rather than the difference in total payments, $20.83) to identify the indifference point between the two mortgages. To find the point at which you are indifferent between the two options, you solve the following equation:

$$\$2,400 = \$25 \,[(1 - [1/(1 + 0.006458)^{x}])/0.006458]$$

---

2. As can be seen in the amortization schedules for the two loans (in Appendix 7A, available through Connect or your course instructor), the difference in the interest portion of the monthly mortgage payments is pennies around $25.00 during the first 18 years of the mortgage. Thus, to simplify the math we use a $25 annuity payment in our calculations.

Solving for *X* gives 150 months, or 12.5 years. Thus, if you plan on paying off the mortgage in 12.5 years or less, option 1 is the better deal. If you plan on paying off the mortgage in more than 12.5 years, option 2 is preferred.

Notice that the choice of points (and lower monthly payments) versus no points (and higher monthly payments) depends on how long the mortgage borrower takes to pay off the mortgage. Specifically, the longer the borrower takes to pay off the mortgage, the more likely he or she is to choose points and a lower mortgage rate. Thus, by offering points, the mortgage lender decreases the probability that the mortgage borrower will prepay the mortgage—paying the mortgage off early reduces the present value of the monthly savings to the mortgage borrower.

### Other Types of Mortgages

New methods of creative financing have been developed by financial institutions to attract mortgage borrowers. These include jumbo mortgages, subprime mortgages, Alt-As, option ARMs, second mortgages, and reverse-annuity mortgages.

**jumbo mortgages**

*Mortgages that exceed the conventional mortgage conforming limits.*

**Jumbo Mortgages.** **Jumbo mortgages** are those mortgages that exceed the conventional mortgage conforming limits. Limits are set by the two government-sponsored enterprises, Fannie Mae and Freddie Mac (discussed below), and are based on the maximum value of any individual mortgage they will purchase from a mortgage lender. In 2016, the general limit was $417,000 for most of the United States (the limit is set higher in high cost areas of the country). Because the large size and the inability to sell jumbo mortgages to Fannie Mae or Freddie Mac creates more risk for mortgage lenders, interest rates on jumbo mortgages are generally higher than on conforming mortgages. Typically, the spread in interest rates on jumbo versus conventional mortgages is about 0.25 to 0.50 percent. However, during periods of high economywide risk (e.g., during the late 2000s), the spread can be greater than 1.50 percent. Further, to reduce the risk of these loans, lenders will often require a higher down payment on jumbo mortgages than conventional mortgages.

**subprime mortgages**

*Mortgages to borrowers who have weakened credit histories.*

**Subprime Mortgages.** **Subprime mortgages** are mortgages to borrowers who do not qualify for prime mortgages because of weakened credit histories, including payment delinquencies and possibly more severe problems such as charge-offs, judgments, and bankruptcies. Subprime borrowers may also display reduced repayment capacity as measured by credit scores, debt-to-income ratios, or other criteria that may encompass borrowers with incomplete credit histories. Subprime mortgages have a higher rate of default than prime mortgage loans and are thus riskier loans for the mortgage lender. As a result, these mortgages have higher interest rates than prime mortgages. Although the majority of home loans are not subprime mortgages, their numbers grew rapidly in the mid-2000s. Subprime mortgages accounted for 9 percent of all mortgage originations from 1996 through 2004 and rose to about 21 percent from 2004 through 2006. As mentioned earlier, the huge growth in subprime mortgages was a major instigator of the recent financial crisis.

**Alt-A mortgages**

*Mortgages that are considered riskier than a prime mortgage and less risky than a subprime mortgage.*

**Alt-A Mortgages.** **Alt-A mortgages** short for Alternative A-paper, are mortgages that are considered riskier than a prime mortgage and less risky than a subprime mortgage. Typically, Alt-A mortgages are characterized by borrowers with less than full documentation, lower credit scores, higher loan-to-value ratios, and more investment properties than prime mortgage borrowers, but more extensive documentation, higher credit scores, lower loan-to-value ratios, and fewer investment properties than subprime mortgage borrowers. Therefore, Alt-A interest rates, which are determined by credit risk, tend to be between those of prime and subprime home loans. As a result of their less-than-prime credit qualities, Alt-A loans do not meet the standard of conforming mortgages for sale to Fannie Mae and Freddie Mac.

During the recent financial crisis, Alt-A mortgages came under particular scrutiny. One problem associated with Alt-A loans is the lack of necessary proof or documentation needed to be approved for a loan. Thus, some lenders suggested that borrowers skew their incomes or assets in order to qualify for a larger loan. As housing prices fell and the U.S. economy entered a recession, borrowers proved unable to afford their payments. The mortgage lenders, however, still collected a hefty profit, which led to intense scrutiny of their lending practices. As of 2008, there was strong evidence that the securities backing Alt-A mortgages suffered from the same weaknesses as the securities backing subprime mortgages.

**option ARMs**

*Adjustable rate mortgages that offer the borrower several monthly payment options.*

**Option ARMs.**   **Option ARMs,** also called pick-a-payment or pay-option ARMs, are 15- or 30-year adjustable rate mortgages that offer the borrower several monthly payment options. The four major types of payment options include: minimum payment, interest-only payment, a 30-year fully amortizing payment, and a 15-year fully amortizing payment.

*Minimum Payment Option.*   The minimum payment is the lowest of the four payment options and carries the most risk. With these option ARMs, the monthly payment is set for 12 months at an initial interest rate. After that, the payment changes annually, and a payment cap limits how much it can increase or decrease each year (generally 7.5 percent). If the minimum payment is continued after the end of the initial interest rate period, which usually holds only for the first 1 to 3 months, it may not be enough to pay all of the interest charged on the loan for the previous month. In this case, the unpaid interest is added to the principal balance. This is called negative amortization, and it means that the amount owed increases and the borrower is charged additional interest at the rate on the loan times the new, larger principal balance.

The minimum payment on most option ARM programs is 1 percent fully amortized. Every time the borrower makes the minimum payment, the difference between the minimum payment and the interest-only payment (see below) is tacked onto the balance of the loan. A borrower can pay the minimum payment until the loan balance reaches 110 to 115 percent of the original loan balance. This allows the typical borrower to pay the minimum payment for roughly the first five years of the life of the loan. After the loan balance reaches 110 to 115 percent, the borrower loses the minimum payment option, leaving the three remaining payment options.

*Interest-Only Payment.*   An interest-only option ARM requires the borrower to pay only the interest on the loan during the initial period of the loan. During this period, no principal must be repaid. After the interest-only period, the mortgage must amortize so that the mortgage will be paid off by the end of its original term. This means that monthly payments must increase substantially after the initial interest-only period lapses. The length of the interest-only period varies with each mortgage type. The interest-only payment may change every month based on changes in the ARM index used to determine the loan interest rate. After 10 years from the start of the loan, the interest-only option typically goes away as well, and the borrower must pay using one of the two remaining payment options. Interest-only payment option ARMs carry a great deal of payment-shock risk. Not only do the payments have the potential to increase because of an increasing fully indexed interest rate, but the expiration of the interest-only payment means that payments will increase when the mortgage becomes a fully amortizing loan.

*30-Year Fully Amortizing Payment.*   With 30-year fully amortizing option ARMs, the borrower pays both principal and interest on the loan. By making this payment each month, the borrower is ensured that all interest and principal payments are fully paid on schedule, based on a 30-year term. The payment is calculated each month based on the prior month's fully indexed rate, loan balance, and remaining loan term.

*15-Year Fully Amortizing Payment.*   This option ARM is similar to the 30-year fully amortizing payment option ARM, with a full principal and interest payment, but with a larger amount of principal paid each month. This amount includes all of the interest charged on the loan for the previous month plus principal to pay off the loan based on a 15-year (instead of a 30-year) term. The payment amount may change from month to month based on changes in the index value used to determine the fully indexed rate. Choosing the 15-year fully amortizing payment puts the mortgage on an accelerated amortization schedule.

**second mortgages**

*Loans secured by a piece of real estate already used to secure a first mortgage.*

**home equity loans**

*Loans that let customers borrow on a line of credit secured with a second mortgage on their homes.*

**reverse-annuity mortgage (RAM)**

*A mortgage for which a mortgage borrower receives regular monthly payments from a financial institution rather than making them. When the RAM matures (or the borrower dies), the borrower (or the estate of the borrower) sells the property to retire the debt.*

**Second Mortgages.** **Second mortgages** are loans secured by a piece of real estate already used to secure a first mortgage. Should a default occur, the second mortgage holder is paid only after the first mortgage is paid off. As a result, interest rates on second mortgages are generally higher than on first mortgages.

About 15 percent of all primary mortgage holders also have second mortgages. Second mortgages provide mortgage borrowers with a way to use the equity they have built up in their homes as collateral on another mortgage, thus allowing mortgage borrowers to raise funds without having to sell their homes. Financial institutions often offer **home equity loans** that let customers borrow on a line of credit secured with a second mortgage on their homes. The dollar value of home equity loans issued by U.S. depository institutions and outstanding in March 2016 was $458 billion, compared to a total of $10.01 trillion in total home mortgage loans. Further, the rate of interest financial institutions charged on home equity loans was 4.93 percent compared to 2.89 percent on 15-year fixed-rate first mortgage loans.

Interest on all mortgages (first, second, and home equity) secured by residential real estate is tax deductible. Interest on other types of individual loans—such as consumer loans—is not eligible for a tax deduction.

**Reverse-Annuity Mortgages.** With a **reverse-annuity mortgage (RAM),** a mortgage borrower receives regular monthly payments from a financial institution rather than making them. When the RAM matures (or the borrower dies), the borrower (or the borrower's estate) sells the property to retire the debt. RAMs were designed as a way for retired people to live on the equity they have built up in their homes without the necessity of selling the homes. Maturities on RAMs are generally set such that the borrower will likely die prior to maturity.

As the U.S. population ages, RAMs are growing in popularity. Because so many people retire asset-rich and income-poor, RAMs present a way for seniors to unlock some of the value tied up in their home to boost their income. Funds received from a RAM may be used for any purpose, including meeting housing expenses (such as taxes, insurance, and maintenance expenses), as well as other living expenses. RAMs provide a way for retired homeowners to maintain financial independence as well as ownership of their home, but they are more costly than more conventional types of mortgages. Thus, RAMs are attractive mainly to older homeowners who have accumulated substantial equity in their homes.

**DO YOU UNDERSTAND:**

1. What the function of a lien placed on a mortgage contract is?

2. When private mortgage insurance is required for a mortgage?

3. What the difference is between a federally insured mortgage and a conventional mortgage?

4. What the typical mortgage maturity is?

5. What jumbo mortgages are?

## SECONDARY MORTGAGE MARKETS

Through one of two mechanisms, financial institutions can remove mortgages from their balance sheets, placing them for trading in secondary mortgage markets. First, they can pool their recently originated mortgages together and sell them in the secondary mortgage market. Second, financial institutions can issue mortgage-backed securities, creating securities that are backed by their newly originated mortgages (i.e., securitization of mortgages). In 2016, over 60 percent of all residential mortgages were sold or securitized in this fashion. The sale/securitization of mortgages in the secondary mortgage markets reduces the liquidity risk, interest rate risk, and credit risk experienced by the originating financial institution compared to keeping the mortgage in its asset portfolio. For example, depository institutions obtain the majority of their funds from short-term deposits. Holding long-term fixed-rate mortgages in their asset portfolios subjects them to interest rate risk, particularly if interest rates are expected to increase (see Chapter 22). Moreover, selling/securitizing mortgages can generate fee income for the mortgage-originating financial institution and help reduce the effects of regulatory constraints (see Chapter 13).

Many financial institutions such as mortgage companies prefer to concentrate on the servicing of mortgages rather than the long-term financing of them, which occurs if they are kept on the balance sheet. The loan originator may also act as a servicer, collecting payments from mortgage borrowers and passing the required interest and principal payments through to the secondary market investor. The servicer also keeps the formal records of all transactions pertaining to the mortgage. In return for these services, the financial institution collects a monthly fee. Mortgage servicers generally charge fees ranging from 1/4 to 1/2 percent of the mortgage balance.

In this section, we introduce and provide an overview of the secondary mortgage markets, including a discussion of the crucial role they played in the financial crisis of the late 2000s. We look at these markets in more detail, including how financial institutions can use these markets to hedge credit risk on their balance sheets, in Chapter 24.

### History and Background of Secondary Mortgage Markets

The mortgage market is unique in that the U.S. government is deliberately involved in the development of its secondary markets. The secondary mortgage markets were created by the federal government to help boost U.S. economic activity during the Great Depression. As borrowers defaulted on mortgages, banks and thrifts found themselves strapped for cash. To create liquidity in the mortgage markets and to raise levels of home ownership and the availability of affordable housing, in 1938 the government established the Federal National Mortgage Association (FNMA, or Fannie Mae) to buy mortgages from depository institutions so they could lend to other mortgage borrowers. FNMA's mandate was to act as a secondary mortgage market facility that could purchase, hold, and sell mortgage loans. The government also established the Federal Housing Administration (FHA) and the Veterans Administration (VA) to insure certain mortgages against default risk (described earlier). This made it easier to sell/securitize mortgages. Financial institutions originated the mortgages and secondary market buyers did not have to be as concerned with a borrower's credit history or the value of collateral backing the mortgage since they had a federal government guarantee protecting them against default risk. Fannie Mae grew very large over the years. To remove Fannie Mae's growing debt portfolio from the government balance sheet, in 1968 Fannie Mae was converted into a publicly traded company owned by investors.

Further, by the late 1960s, fewer veterans were obtaining guaranteed VA loans. As a result, the secondary market for mortgages declined. To encourage continued expansion in the housing market and to promote competition for FNMA (which was functioning as a virtual monopoly), the U.S. government created the Government National Mortgage Association (GNMA, or Ginnie Mae) and the Federal Home Loan Mortgage Corporation (FHLMC, or Freddie Mac). Like FNMA, GNMA and FHLMC provide direct or indirect guarantees that allow for the creation of mortgage-backed securities (we provide a detailed description of each agency below). Also like FNMA, FHLMC became quite large and was converted to a public company in 1989, removing the debt from the balance sheet of the federal government. Thus, while GNMA is a government-owned enterprise, FNMA and FHLMC are government-sponsored enterprises **(GSEs).**

As secondary mortgage markets have evolved, a wide variety of mortgage-backed securities have been developed to allow primary mortgage lenders to securitize their mortgages and to allow a thriving secondary market for mortgages to develop. The organizations involved in the secondary mortgage markets (e.g., GNMA, FNMA) differ in the types of mortgages included in the mortgage pools, security guarantees (or insurance), and payment patterns on the securities.

www.fanniemae.com

www.hud.gov
www.va.com

www.ginniemae.gov
www.freddiemac.com

**GSEs**

*Government-sponsored enterprises such as Fannie Mae or Freddie Mac.*

**correspondent banking**

*A relationship between a small bank and a large bank in which the large bank provides a number of deposit, lending, and other services.*

**mortgage sale**

*Sale of a mortgage originated by a bank with or without recourse to an outside buyer.*

**recourse**

*The ability of a loan buyer to sell the loan back to the originator should it go bad.*

## Mortgage Sales

Financial institutions have sold mortgages and commercial real estate loans among themselves for more than 100 years. In fact, a large part of **correspondent banking** involves small banks making loans that are too big for them to hold on their balance sheets—either for lending concentration risk or capital adequacy reasons—and selling parts of these loans to large banks with whom they have had a long-term deposit and lending correspondent relationship. In turn, large banks often sell parts of their loans, called *participations,* to smaller banks.

A **mortgage sale** occurs when a financial institution originates a mortgage and sells it with or without recourse to an outside buyer. If the mortgage is sold without recourse, the financial institution not only removes it from its balance sheet but also has no explicit liability if the mortgage eventually goes bad. Thus, the buyer of the mortgage (not the financial institution that originated the loan) bears all the credit risk.[3] If, however, the mortgage is sold with **recourse,** under certain conditions the buyer can return the mortgage to the selling financial institution. Therefore, the financial institution retains a contingent credit risk liability. In practice, most mortgage sales are without recourse. Mortgage sales usually involve no creation of new types of securities, such as those described below. We discuss loan sales in more detail in Chapter 24.

A major reason that financial institutions sell loans is to manage their credit risk better (see Chapter 20). Mortgage sales remove assets (and credit risk) from the balance sheet and allow a financial institution to achieve better asset diversification. Additionally, mortgage sales allow financial institutions to improve their liquidity risk and interest rate risk situations. Other than risk management, however, financial institutions are encouraged to sell loans for a number of other economic (generation of fee income) and regulatory reasons (including reducing the cost of reserve requirements and reducing the cost of holding required capital against mortgages). The benefits of loan sales are discussed in detail in Chapter 24.

A wide array of potential buyers and sellers of mortgage loans exist. The five major buyers of primary mortgage loans are investment banks, vulture funds, domestic banks, foreign banks, insurance companies and pension funds, closed-end bank loan mutual funds, and nonfinancial corporations. The major sellers of mortgage loans are money center banks, small regional or community banks, foreign banks, investment banks, hedge funds, and the U.S. government. We discuss the motivations of each in Chapter 24.

## Mortgage-Backed Securities

In this section, we introduce the three major types of mortgage-backed securities—the pass-through security, the collateralized mortgage obligation (CMO), and the mortgage-backed bond. In Chapter 24, we provide a detailed analysis of these securities and the processes by which these mortgage-backed securities are created and used to reduce credit, interest rate, and liquidity risk for an FI. Pass-through securities and CMOs are securitized mortgages. Securitization of mortgages involves the pooling of a group of mortgages with similar characteristics, the removal of these mortgages from the balance sheet, and the subsequent sale of interests in the mortgage pool to secondary market investors. Securitization of mortgages results in the creation of mortgage-backed securities (e.g., government agency securities, collateralized mortgage obligations), which can be traded in secondary mortgage markets. For example, there were $7.81 trillion in outstanding mortgage securitization pools in 2016.

Mortgage-backed securities allow mortgage issuers to separate the credit risk exposure from the lending process itself. That is, FIs can assess the creditworthiness of loan applicants, originate loans, fund loans, and even monitor and service loans without retaining exposure to loss from credit events, such as default or missed payments. This moves banks away from the traditional "originate and hold" banking model, in which the originating

---

3. However, the buyer's credit risk is reduced if the mortgage is federally insured against default risk.

## Goldman Reaches $5 Billion Settlement over Mortgage-Backed Securities

In January 2016, Goldman Sachs agreed to pay more than $5 billion, the largest regulatory penalty in its history. In settling with the Justice Department and a collection of other state and federal entities, Goldman resolved claims stemming from the Wall Street firm's sale of mortgage bonds heading into the financial crisis. It joined a list of other big banks in moving past one of the biggest, and most costly, legal problems of the crisis era. The government had earlier won multibillion-dollar settlements from J.P. Morgan Chase, Bank of America, and Citigroup. Crisis-related settlements by banks, mortgage firms, brokerages and others total at least $181.1 billion.

The investigations examined how Wall Street sold bonds tied to residential mortgages, and whether banks deceived investors by misrepresenting the quality of underlying loans. The government's inquiry into Goldman related to mortgage-backed securities the firm packaged and sold between 2005 and 2007, when the housing market was booming and investor demand for related bonds was strong.

The latest settlement is just one of several that Goldman has paid in relation to the crisis. Goldman agreed to pay $1.2 billion in penalties to the Federal Housing Finance Agency in 2014 to settle claims that it failed to disclose the risks on mortgage bonds it sold. In 2010, the firm agreed to pay $550 million to settle a Securities and Exchange Commission complaint stemming from its handling of a complex mortgage-linked deal. In February 2015, Morgan Stanley reached a preliminary accord with the Justice Department in which the firm agreed to pay $2.6 billion. That month, Goldman said in a regulatory filing that it had been informed by U.S. officials in December 2014 that it might face a civil lawsuit stemming from the government's mortgage-bond probe. In May, the firm said it was in talks with U.S. and state authorities to resolve those claims. In the settlement, Goldman agreed to pay to the Justice Department a $2.385 billion civil monetary penalty. Goldman must also provide $1.8 billion in consumer relief through debt forgiveness to borrowers, the construction and financing of affordable housing, and other programs.

bank retains the loan and the risk exposure, until the loan is paid off. Rather, mortgage securitization and loan syndication allows banks to retain little or no part of the loans, and hence little or no part of the default risk on loans that they originate: bank have moved to the originate-to-distribute model of banking. Thus, as long as the borrower does not default within the first months after a loan's issuance and the loans are sold or securitized without recourse back to the bank, the issuing bank can ignore longer term credit risk concerns. This decoupling of the risk from the lending activity allows the market to efficiently transfer risk across counterparties. However, it also loosens the incentives to carefully perform each of the steps of the lending process. This loosening of incentives was an important factor leading to the global financial crisis of 2008–2009, which witnessed the after-effects of poor loan underwriting, shoddy documentation and due diligence, failure to monitor borrower activity, and fraudulent activity on the part of both lenders and borrowers. The result was a deterioration in credit quality at the same time as there was a dramatic increase in consumer and corporate leverage. Eventually, in 2006, housing prices started to fall. At the same time, the Federal Reserve started to raise interest rates as it began to fear inflation. Since many of the subprime mortgages that originated in the 2001–2005 period had adjustable rates, the cost of meeting mortgage commitments rose to unsustainable levels for many low-income households. The result of these events was a wave of mortgage defaults in the subprime market and foreclosures that only reinforced the downward trend in housing prices. As this happened, the poor quality of the collateral and credit quality underlying subprime mortgage pools became apparent, with default rates far exceeding those apparently anticipated by the rating agencies who set their initial subprime mortgage securitizations ratings. The financial crisis began.

Although bank regulators attempt to examine the off-balance-sheet activities of banks so as to ascertain their safety and soundness, these activities receive far less scrutiny than on-balance-sheet activities (i.e., traditional lending and deposit taking). To the extent that counterparty credit risk was not fully disclosed to, or monitored by, regulators, the increased use of these innovations transferred risk in ways that were not necessarily scrutinized or understood. It was in this context of increased risk and inadequate regulation that the credit crisis developed. The After the Crisis box illustrates how, even into 2016, federal securities regulators pursued legal charges against financial institutions over alleged mortgage-backed securities violations. See Chapter 24 for more discussion of this topic.

**LG 7-7**

**pass-through mortgage securities**

*Mortgage-backed securities that "pass through" promised payments of principal and interest on pools of mortgages created by financial institutions to secondary market participants holding interests in the pools.*

www.ginniemae.gov

**Pass-Through Securities.**   Financial institutions frequently pool the mortgages and other assets they originate and offer investors an interest in the pool in the form of *pass-through certificates or securities.* **Pass-through mortgage securities** "pass through" promised payments of principal and interest on pools of mortgages created by financial institutions to secondary market investors (mortgage-backed security bond holders) holding an interest in these pools. After a financial institution accepts mortgages, it pools them and sells interests in these pools to pass-through security holders. Each pass-through mortgage security represents a fractional ownership share in a mortgage pool. Thus, a 1 percent owner of a pass-through mortgage security issue is entitled to a 1 percent share of the principal and interest payments made over the life of the mortgages underlying the pool of securities. The originating financial institutions (e.g., bank or mortgage company) or a third-party servicer receives principal and interest payments from the mortgage holder and passes these payments (minus a servicing fee) through to the pass-through security holders. This is a simplification of the process. In actual practice, the mortgages are generally first sold (placed) in a "special purpose vehicle" (SPV) off the balance sheet, and it is this SPV that issues the bonds backed by the mortgages. The details of how pass-through securities are created and operated are provided in Chapter 24. There we also explain how FIs can use these securities to hedge credit, liquidity, and interest rate risk.

Three agencies, either government-owned or government-sponsored enterprises (GSEs), are directly involved in the creation of mortgage-backed pass-through securities. Informally, they are known as Ginnie Mae (GNMA), Fannie Mae (FNMA), and Freddie Mac (FHLMC). Private mortgage issuers, such as banks and thrifts, also purchase mortgage pools, but they do not conform to government-related issuer standards. Table 7–3 reports the amount of mortgage-backed pass-through securities outstanding for each from 1995 through the first quarter of 2016. Note the tremendous growth in these securities between 1995 and 2008, and the subsequent drop from 2010 to 2016. As we discuss in Chapter 10, part of the Wall Street Reform and Consumer Protection Act, passed in 2010 in response to the financial crisis, is the Volcker Rule which prohibits U.S. depository institutions (DIs) from engaging in proprietary trading (i.e., trading as a principal for the trading account of the bank). This includes any transaction to purchase or sell derivatives such as mortgage-backed securities. Thus, only the investment banking arm of the business is allowed to conduct such trading. The Volcker Rule was implemented in April 2014 and banks had until July 21, 2015, to be in compliance. The result has been a reduction in mortgage-backed securities held off-balance-sheet by these financial institutions.

**TABLE 7–3**   Government-Related Mortgage-Backed Pass-Through Securities Outstanding *(in trillions of dollars)*

|  | 1995 | 2000 | 2005 | 2008* | 2010 | 2012 | 2016** |
|---|---|---|---|---|---|---|---|
| GNMA | $0.47 | $0.61 | $0.40 | $0.51 | $1.10 | $1.37 | $1.67 |
| FNMA | 0.58 | 1.06 | 1.83 | 2.44 | 3.02 | 3.00 | 3.03 |
| FHLMC | 0.52 | 0.82 | 1.31 | 1.80 | 1.90 | 1.74 | 1.88 |
| Private mortgage issuers | 0.29 | 0.74 | 2.14 | 2.79 | 1.92 | 1.49 | 0.90 |
| Total | $1.86 | $3.23 | $5.68 | $7.54 | $7.94 | $7.60 | $7.48 |

*Second quarter.
**First quarter.
**Source:** Federal Reserve Board website. www.federalreserve.gov

*GNMA*    The Government National Mortgage Association (GNMA), or Ginnie Mae, began operations in 1968 when it split off from the Federal National Mortgage Association (FNMA), discussed below. GNMA is a government-owned agency with two major functions: sponsoring mortgage-backed securities programs of financial institutions such as banks, thrifts, and mortgage bankers and acting as a guarantor to investors in mortgage-backed securities regarding the timely pass-through of principal and interest payments from the financial institution or mortgage servicer to the bond holder. In other words, GNMA provides **timing insurance.** In acting as a sponsor and payment-timing guarantor, GNMA supports only those pools of mortgage loans whose default or credit risk is insured by one of four government agencies: the Federal Housing Administration (FHA), the Veterans Administration (VA), the Department of Housing and Urban Development's Office of Indian and Public Housing, and the USDA Rural Development. Mortgage loans insured by these agencies target groups that might otherwise be disadvantaged in the housing market, such as low-income families, young families, and veterans. As such, the maximum mortgage under the GNMA securitization program is capped. The cap was generally $417,000 for a single-family home in 2016. Higher cost areas of the country have a higher limit; the high cost limit in 2016 was $625,000.

**timing insurance**

*A service provided by a sponsor of pass-through securities (such as GNMA) guaranteeing the bond holder interest and principal payments at the calendar date promised.*

GNMA securities are issued in minimum denominations of $25,000. The minimum pool size for GNMA single-family mortgages is $1 million. Once a pool of mortgages is packaged by a financial institution in accordance with GNMA specifications, pass-through securities can be issued. Cash flows of interest and principal received from the original mortgages are used to pay the promised payments on the GNMA securities. The mortgages from the pool are used as collateral, guaranteeing the promised payments to the GNMA holders. GNMA requires that all of the mortgages in a pool used to back a particular GNMA pass-through security issue have the same interest rate. Secondary market purchasers of GNMA pass-through securities generally receive 0.50 percent less than the rate on the underlying mortgages. The 0.50 percent is divided between the financial institution that services the mortgages and GNMA, which charges a fee for the provision of its timing insurance.

www.fanniemae.com

*FNMA.*    Originally created in 1938, the Federal National Mortgage Association (FNMA, or Fannie Mae) is the oldest of the three mortgage-backed security-sponsoring agencies. While, since 1968, FNMA has operated as a private corporation owned by shareholders, in the minds of many investors, it has had implicit government backing, which makes it equivalent to a government-owned enterprise. Indeed, the fact that FNMA has historically had a secured line of credit available from the U.S. Treasury should it need funds in an emergency supports this view. Further, and as discussed in more detail below, on September 7, 2008, the Federal Housing Finance Agency (FHFA) placed Fannie Mae (and Freddie Mac, as discussed below) in conservatorship. As conservator, the FHFA was given full powers to control the assets and operations of the firms. Dividends to common and preferred shareholders were suspended, but the U.S. Treasury put in place a set of financing agreements to ensure that the GSEs would continue to meet their obligations to bond holders. This means that the U.S. taxpayer basically was the guarantor behind about $5 trillion of GSE debt. This step was taken because a default by either Fannie Mae or Freddie Mac, both of which had been battered by the downturn in housing and credit markets, could have caused severe disruptions in global financial markets, made home mortgages more difficult and expensive to obtain, and had negative repercussions throughout the economy.

FNMA is a more active agency than GNMA in creating pass-through securities. GNMA merely sponsors such programs and guarantees the timing of payments from financial institution servicers to GNMA investors. FNMA actually helps create pass-throughs by buying and holding mortgages on its balance sheet. It also issues bonds directly to finance those purchases. Specifically, FNMA creates mortgage-backed securities (MBSs) by purchasing packages of mortgage loans from banks and thrifts. It finances such purchases by selling MBSs to outside investors such as life insurers or pension funds. In addition, FNMA engages in swap transactions by which it swaps MBSs with a bank or thrift for original mortgages. Since FNMA guarantees securities in regard to the full and timely payment of interest and principal, the financial institution receiving the MBSs can then resell them in the capital market or can hold them in its own portfolio. Unlike GNMA, FNMA securitizes conventional mortgage loans, as well as FHA/VA insured loans, as long as the conventional loans have acceptable loan-to-value or collateral ratios not normally exceeding 80 percent. Conventional loans with high loan-to-value ratios usually require that the mortgages be insured with private mortgage insurance (see earlier discussion) before they are accepted into FNMA securitization pools.

**www.freddiemac.com**    *FHLMC.*   The Federal Home Loan Mortgage Corporation (FHLMC), or Freddie Mac (FMAC), performs a similar function to that of FNMA except that its major securitization role has historically involved thrifts. Like FNMA, FHLMC is a stockholder-owned corporation, yet it is currently in conservatorship with the FHFA. Further, like FNMA, it buys mortgage pools from financial institutions and swaps MBSs for loans. FHLMC also sponsors conventional mortgage pools and mortgages that are not federally insured as well as FHA/VA mortgage pools and guarantees timely payment of interest and ultimate payment of principal on the securities it issues.

*Private Mortgage Pass-Through Issuers.*   Private mortgage pass-through issuers (such as commercial banks, thrifts, and private conduits) purchase nonconforming mortgages (e.g., mortgages that exceed the size limit set by government agencies, such as the $417,000 cap set by the FHA), pool them, and sell pass-through securities on which the mortgage collateral does not meet the standards of a government-related mortgage issuer. There are a limited number of private conduits—GE Capital Mortgages, Chase Mortgage Finance, and Citigroup/Citibank Housing. Private mortgage pass-through securities must be registered with the SEC and are generally rated by a rating agency (such as Moody's) in a manner similar to corporate bonds.

*Mortgage-Backed Pass-Through Quotes.*   Table 7–4 presents a quote sheet for mortgage-backed pass-through securities traded on June 21, 2016. The quote lists the trades by issuer

**TABLE 7–4**   Pass-Through Securities Quote Sheet

| (1) | | (2) | (3) | (4) | (5) | (6) | (7) | (8) |
|---|---|---|---|---|---|---|---|---|
| **Mortgage-Backed Securities** | | | | | | | | |
| **Tuesday, June 21, 2016** | | | | | | | | |
| **Indicative, not guaranteed; from Bear Stearns Cos./Street SoftwareTechnology Inc.** | | | | | | | | |
| | | **Price (Pts-32ds)** | **Price Change (32ds)** | **Avg Life (Years)** | **Spread to Avg Life (Bps)** | **Spread Change** | **PSA (Prepay Spread)** | **Yield to Maturity***  |
| **30-Year** | | | | | | | | |
| FMAC GOLD | 4.0% | 106-24 | −02 | 3.6 | 97 | 1 | 448 | 1.95 |
| FMAC GOLD | 4.5% | 108-28 | −02 | 3.8 | 92 | — | 368 | 1.92 |
| FMAC GOLD | 5.0% | 110-09 | — | 3.4 | 75 | −1 | 393 | 1.69 |
| FNMA | 4.0% | 106-29 | −03 | 3.7 | 93 | 1 | 440 | 1.92 |
| FNMA | 4.5% | 108-31 | −02 | 3.8 | 86 | −1 | 371 | 1.86 |
| FNMA | 5.0% | 110-29 | — | 3.4 | 57 | −1 | 391 | 1.51 |
| GNMA† | 4.0% | 107-04 | −01 | 3.8 | 91 | −1 | 350 | 1.91 |
| GNMA† | 4.5% | 109-30 | +01 | 3.6 | 56 | −2 | 362 | 1.53 |
| GNMA† | 5.0% | 110-29 | +06 | 3.5 | 64 | −7 | 382 | 1.60 |
| **15-Year** | | | | | | | | |
| FMAC GOLD | 4.0% | 103-18 | — | 1.6 | 95 | 2 | 299 | 1.61 |
| FNMA | 4.0% | 103-21 | — | 1.6 | 85 | 2 | 300 | 1.52 |
| GNMA† | 4.0% | 103-25 | — | 2.6 | 159 | — | 269 | 2.42 |

*Extrapolated from benchmarks based on projections from Bear Stearns prepayment model, assuming interest rates remain unchanged.
†Government guaranteed.

**Source:** *The Wall Street Journal Online*, June 21, 2016. www.wsj.com

(e.g., GNMA, FNMA). Column 1 of the quote lists the sponsor of the issue (e.g., FMAC, FNMA, GNMA), the mortgage coupons on the mortgages in each pool (e.g., 4.0%), and information about the maximum delay between the receipt of interest by the servicer/sponsor and the actual payment of interest to bond holders. The "GOLD" next to FMAC indicates a maximum stated delay of 55 days. The current market price of a bond is shown in column 2, with the daily price change in column 3. Both prices are in percentages, and the number after the dash is in 32nds (*e.g.*, $106{-}24 = 106^{24}/_{32}$). Column 4 shows the average life of the bond reflecting the prepayment patterns of homeowners in the pool as estimated by one investment bank (Bear Stearns). Notice these pools of 15- and 30-year mortgages have an expected weighted-average life[4] of no more than 3.8 years. The fifth column in the quote is a measure of the yield spread of the mortgage-backed security over a Treasury bond with the same average life, and column 6 reports the spread change for the day. Column 7 is a measure of the estimated prepayment speed. The prepayment speeds are shown relative to those normally occurring on pass-through securities as estimated by the Public Securities Association (PSA) (now a part of the Securities Industry and Financial Markets Association, or SIFMA). Thus, 448 PSA (prepayment speed) means that these MBS mortgage holders are prepaying about 4.5 times quicker than the speed that normally would be expected. This is because interest rates on new mortgages in June 2016 were well below historic levels. We discuss prepayment risk and prepayment speeds as estimated by the PSA in greater detail in Chapter 24. Finally, the last column (8) is the yield to maturity on the mortgage-backed pass-through security. This yield is calculated using the yield to maturity formulas found in Chapter 3, given the contractual income, principal cash flows, and the expected prepayment pattern (based on projections made by Bear Stearns's prepayment model, see Chapter 24).

**Government Sponsorship and Oversight of FNMA and Freddie Mac.** Together FNMA and FHLMC represent a huge presence in the financial system as they have over 60 percent of the single-family mortgage pools in the United States. Some regulators and politicians have argued that these two government-sponsored enterprises have gained too much of a market share. In the early 2000s, their credit losses increased as did their debt-to-equity ratios. Debt to equity for these two agencies ranged from 30 to 97 percent, depending on the assumptions made about off-balance-sheet exposures.

Also, in the early 2000s, these two agencies came under fire for several reasons. First, in September 2002, Fannie Mae was criticized for allowing a sharp increase in interest rate risk to exist on its balance sheet. The Office of Federal Housing Enterprise Oversight (OFHEO), a main regulator of Fannie Mae, required Fannie Mae to submit weekly reports to the OFHEO on the company's exposure to interest rate risk. The OFHEO also instructed Fannie Mae to keep regulators apprised of any challenges associated with returning its interest rate risk measure to more acceptable levels and warned that additional action would be taken if there were adverse developments with Fannie Mae management's effectiveness in lowering interest rate risk. In October 2003, Fannie Mae and Freddie Mac came under new criticism for allegedly overcharging lenders for services they provided. The overcharges came in the fees that the companies collect from banks, thrifts, and other lenders for guaranteeing repayment of their mortgages. The overcharges hurt mortgage lenders, squeezing their profit margins, and perhaps home buyers, too, as lenders increased mortgage interest rates to recover the increased fees. Later that same month, Fannie Mae announced that it miscalculated the value of its mortgages, forcing it to make a $1.1 billion restatement of its stockholders' equity. Earlier in the year, Freddie Mac announced a $4.5 billion misstatement of its earnings. While both were claimed to be computational errors, the episodes reinforced fears that Fannie Mae and Freddie Mac lack the necessary skills to operate their

---

4. The weighted-average life of these securities is not the same as duration, which measures the weighted-average time to maturity based on the relative present values of cash flows as weights. Rather, the weighted-average life is a significant simplification of the duration measure that seeks to concentrate on the expected timing of repayments of principal; that is, it is the weighted-average time over which principal repayments will be received. (See Chapter 24 for a detailed discussion.)

massive and complex businesses, which some investors and political critics worried could pose a risk to the nation's financial system if not properly managed. Finally, in February 2004, then Federal Reserve chair Alan Greenspan stated that Fannie Mae and Freddie Mac pose very serious risks to the U.S. financial system and urged Congress to curb their growth sooner rather than later.

Underlying the concerns about the actions of these two GSEs was the widespread perception among investors that neither would be allowed to fail if they got into trouble. This perception created a subsidy for the agencies and allowed them to borrow more cheaply than other firms with similar balance sheets. The fear was that the two agencies used their implicit federal backing to assume more risk and finance expansion through increased debt. Such actions created a source of systemic risk for the U.S. financial system. These fears and concerns became reality during the financial crisis. The turmoil in the housing and credit markets that began in 2007 put extreme financial pressure on Fannie Mae and Freddie Mac. The value of their mortgage assets fell, but the debt they issued to purchase those assets remained on their balance sheets. To maintain a positive net worth in the face of falling asset values, financial firms have several options to raise capital, none of which were readily available to Fannie or Freddie. If they sold assets, they would depress the prices of mortgage loans and MBSs even further, worsening both their own balance sheet positions and those of many other financial firms. They could not use retained earnings to increase capital because their operations had not earned a profit since 2006. Finally, rapidly falling share prices made it difficult to raise capital by selling new common stock.

GSE status, however, enabled them to continue to fund their operations by selling debt securities, because the market believed that Fannie and Freddie debt was implicitly guaranteed by the government. In July 2008, however, Fannie and Freddie's share prices fell sharply, resulting in the possibility that market participants might refuse to extend credit to Fannie and Freddie under any terms. Even though Fannie and Freddie maintained access to the debt markets (albeit at higher than usual interest rates), their inability to raise new capital cast doubts on their long-term viability. As a result, the federal government concluded that "the companies cannot continue to operate safely and soundly and fulfill their critical public mission, without significant action" to address their financial weaknesses.

The Housing and Economic Recovery Act of 2008, enacted July 30, 2008, gave the authority for the government's takeover of the GSEs. The act created a new GSE regulator, the Federal Housing Finance Agency (FHFA), with the authority to take control of either GSE to restore it to a sound financial condition. The act also gave the Treasury emergency authority to purchase an unlimited amount of GSE debt or equity securities if necessary to provide stability to the financial markets, prevent disruptions in the availability of mortgage finance, and protect taxpayers. On September 7, 2008, the FHFA established a conservatorship for both Fannie and Freddie. As conservator, the FHFA took over the assets and assumed all the powers of the shareholders, directors, and officers. The government lent the two GSEs $188 billion and received the right to acquire almost 80 percent of each company's stock. Stockholders' voting rights were suspended during the conservatorship, and both firms replaced their CEOs. Dividends on common and preferred stock were suspended, although the shares continued to trade. (However, in June 2010, the NYSE, through the FHFA, notified Fannie and Freddie that they no longer met NYSE listing standards. The FHFA ordered the two GSEs to transfer trading of their common and preferred shares from the NYSE to the over-the-counter market.) The FHFA stated that the conservatorship would end when the FHFA finds that a safe and solvent condition has been restored.

The takeover of Fannie and Freddie, and specifically the commitment to meet all of the firms' obligations to debt holders, exposes the U.S. government to a potentially large financial risk. At the time the FHFA took over, debt issued or guaranteed by the GSEs totaled more than $5 trillion. The risks of not acting, however, clearly appeared intolerable to the government. A failure or default by either Fannie or Freddie would have severely disrupted financial markets around the world. If the GSE portfolios of mortgage loans and MBSs had been liquidated, prices would have plunged even further, the secondary market for mortgages would have been decimated, and the supply of new mortgage credit would have been severely restricted.

In February 2011, the Obama administration recommended phasing out the GSEs and gradually reducing the government's involvement in the mortgage market. In the proposal, any dismantling of Fannie and Freddie would happen gradually to avoid a shake-up in the mortgage markets. Steps to reduce the government role in the mortgage market likely would raise borrowing costs for home buyers, adding pressure on the still-fragile U.S. housing markets. Consequently, the implementation of the proposal would take years and would be driven by the pace of the housing market's recovery.

Complicating these efforts, as the U.S. economy and housing market slowly recovered, so did the GSEs. In 2012, Fannie Mae and Freddie Mac reported net income of $17.2 billion and $11.0 billion, respectively, the best year ever for both companies. By mid-2016 the companies' stocks were trading at $2.04 and $1.87, respectively, up from $0.97 to $0.98 at the beginning of the year. The two GSEs had repaid $66 billion of the loans received in 2008 to the U.S. Treasury and the government projected a total of $238 billion in revenues due to the government from the two, a $50 billion profit. The GSEs were making money and expected to remain profitable. The prospect of steady profits confounded legislative efforts to shrink the federal role in securitizing home loans.

LG 7-8

**collateralized mortgage obligation (CMO)**

*A mortgage-backed bond issued in multiple classes or tranches.*

**tranche**

*A bond holder class associated with a CMO.*

**Collateralized Mortgage Obligations.**   Although pass-throughs are still the primary mechanism for securitization, the **collateralized mortgage obligation (CMO)** is a second vehicle for securitizing financial institution assets that is increasingly used. Innovated in 1983 by FHLMC and First Boston, the CMO is a device for making mortgage-backed securities more attractive to certain types or classes of investors. The CMO does this by repackaging the cash flows from mortgages and pass-through securities in a different fashion.

A pass-through security gives each investor a pro rata share of any interest and principal cash flows on a mortgage pool. By contrast, a CMO can be viewed as a multiclass pass-through with a number of different bond holder classes or **tranches.** Unlike a pass-through, which has no guaranteed annual coupon, each bond holder class in a CMO has a different guaranteed coupon (paid semiannually) just as a regular T-bond. More importantly, the allocation of any excess cash flows over and above the guaranteed coupon payments due to increased mortgage prepayments goes toward retiring the principal outstanding of only one class of bond holders, leaving all other classes prepayment-protected for a period of time.[5] CMOs give investors greater control over the maturity of the mortgage-backed securities they buy. By comparison, for pass-throughs, the mortgage-backed security holder has a highly uncertain maturity date due to the risk of very rapid prepayments (called *prepayment risk*) by the mortgagees. We provide a detailed analysis of CMOs and the process by which they are created in Chapter 24.

**mortgage-backed bonds (MBBs)**

*Bonds collateralized by a pool of assets. Also called asset-backed bond.*

**asset-backed bond**

*Bond collateralized by a pool of assets. Also called mortgage-backed bond.*

**Mortgage-Backed Bond.**   **Mortgage-backed bonds (MBBs),** also called **asset-backed bonds,** are the third type of mortgage-backed security. These bonds differ from pass-throughs and CMOs in two key dimensions. First, while pass-throughs and CMOs help financial institutions remove mortgages from their balance sheets, mortgages backing MBBs normally remain on the balance sheet. Second, pass-throughs and CMOs have a direct link between the cash flows on the underlying mortgages and the cash flows on the bond instrument issued. By contrast, the relationship for MBBs is one of collateralization rather than securitization; the cash flows on the mortgages backing the bond are not necessarily directly connected to interest and principal payments on the MBB.

Essentially, a financial institution issues an MBB to raise long-term low-cost funds. MBB holders have a first claim to a segment of the financial institution's mortgage assets. Practically speaking, the financial institution segregates a group of mortgage assets on

---

5. Some CMOs, however, are issued with planned amortization class (PAC) bonds. PAC bonds offer a fixed principal redemption schedule that is met as long as prepayments on the underlying mortgages remain within a certain range. PACs are designed to protect CMO investors against prepayment risk. See the discussion in Chapter 24.

its balance sheet and pledges this group of assets as collateral against the MBB issue. A trustee normally monitors the segregation of assets and ensures that the market value of the collateral exceeds the principal owed to MBB holders. Financial institutions back most

MBB issues by excess collateral. This excess collateral backing of the bond, in addition to the priority rights of the bond holders, generally ensures the sale of these bonds with a high investment grade credit rating (BBB or better). In contrast, the financial institution, when evaluated as a whole, could be rated as BB or even lower. A high credit rating results in lower coupon payments than would be required if significant default risk had lowered the credit rating.

Weighed against the benefits of MBB issuance are a number of costs. The first cost is that MBBs tie up mortgages on the financial institution's balance sheet for a long time. This decreases the asset portfolio's liquidity. Second, balance sheet illiquidity is enhanced by the need to overcollateralize MBBs to ensure a high-quality credit risk rating for the issue. Third, by keeping the mortgages on the balance sheet, the financial institution continues to be liable for capital adequacy and reserve requirement taxes. Because of these costs, MBBs are the least used of the three basic vehicles of securitization. In Chapter 24, we provide a more detailed analysis of MBBs.

## PARTICIPANTS IN THE MORTGAGE MARKETS

**LG 7-9** In this chapter, we have demonstrated that financial institutions are critical in the operations of both the primary and secondary mortgage markets. Some financial institutions (e.g., banks, savings institutions) contribute mainly to the primary mortgage markets. Others (e.g., mortgage companies) contribute to both the primary and secondary markets. Figure 7–8 shows the distribution of mortgages outstanding in 1992, 2007, and 2016 by type of mortgage holder—the ultimate investor. Notice in Figure 7–8 the growth in the importance of mortgage securitization pools over the period (40.42 percent of all mortgages outstanding in 1992 versus 55.35 percent in 2007 and 56.40 percent in 2016). By contrast, mortgages held by life insurance companies, households, businesses, and the federal government have fallen as a percentage of the total pool of mortgages outstanding (5.95 percent

**Figure 7–8** Mortgages Outstanding by Type of Holder, 1992, 2007, and 2016

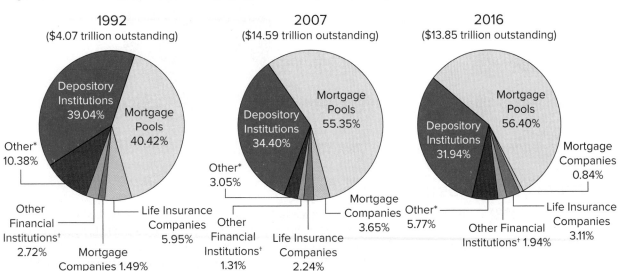

*Includes households, businesses, state and local governments, and the federal government.
†Includes other insurance companies, pension funds, and REITs.
**Source:** Federal Reserve Board website, "Flow of Fund Accounts," July 2016. www.federalreserve.gov

for life insurance companies in 1992 versus 2.24 percent in 2007 and 3.11 percent in 2016; 10.38 percent for households, businesses, and government in 1992 versus 3.05 percent in 2007 and 5.77 percent in 2016).

Notice that the actual holdings of mortgages by specialized mortgage companies (such as Sierra Pacific Mortgage Company and Blue Water Mortgage Corp. of New Hampshire) are small (1.49 percent in 1992, 3.65 percent in 2007, and 0.84 percent in 2016). Mortgage companies, or mortgage bankers, are financial institutions[6] that originate mortgages and collect payments on them. Unlike banks or thrifts, mortgage companies typically do not hold on to the mortgages they originate. Instead, they sell the mortgages they originate but continue to service the mortgages by collecting payments and keeping records on each loan. Mortgage companies earn income to cover the costs of originating and servicing the mortgages from the servicing fees they charge the ultimate buyers of mortgages. Figure 7–9 shows the distribution of issuers of GNMA securities by type of originating financial institution. Mortgage companies issued 71 percent of all GNMA securities in 2016. What should be evident from this figure is that, despite originating such a large volume in the mortgage market, the reason for the small investments in mortgages by mortgage companies (as seen in Figure 7–8) is that, while mortgage companies are major *originators* of home mortgages, they generally do not *hold* the mortgage loans in their asset portfolios for a long period of time. Rather, mortgage companies *sell* or *securitize* most of the mortgages they originate in the secondary market.

From these two figures, it should be evident that securitization allows institutional investors (insurance companies, pension plans, mutual funds, hedge funds) to lend indirectly to households through purchases of mortgage-backed securities. Further, it should be noted that in 2011, the three largest banks—Wells Fargo, J.P. Morgan Chase, and Bank of America—accounted for 68 percent of GNMA's mortgage-backed securities business. Today, nonbank mortgage lenders are responsible for 71 percent of GNMA MBS issuance. Banks have reduced their GNMA issuance in part due to pressure from the Justice Department and the Department of Housing and Urban Development to enter into major settlements for allegedly careless underwriting of FHA-insured loans.

**DO YOU UNDERSTAND:**

9. *Who the major holders of mortgages are in the United States?*

10. *Why mortgage companies hold such a small portion of the mortgage market on their balance sheets?*

**Figure 7–9**   Issuers of Ginnie Mae Securities

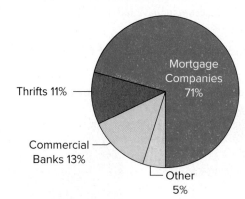

**Source:** Ginnie Mae website, July 2016. www.ginniemae.gov

## INTERNATIONAL TRENDS IN SECURITIZATION

LG 7-10

International investors participate in U.S. mortgage and mortgage-backed securities markets. Table 7–5 lists the dollar value of primary mortgages issued and held by foreign banking offices in the United States between 1992 and 2016. Notice that the value of mortgages held by foreign banks has decreased over this period by 43 percent (from $51.6 billion in 1992 to $29.7 billion in 2013, before rebounding to $56.0 billion in 2016.). This compares

---

6. Most of these mortgage companies are finance companies, which are discussed in Chapter 14.

**TABLE 7–5** Foreign Investments in U.S. Mortgage Markets *(in billions of dollars)*

|  | 1992 | 1995 | 2000 | 2004 | 2007 | 2013 | 2016 |
|---|---|---|---|---|---|---|---|
| Mortgages held by foreign banking offices in the United States | $51.6 | $35.1 | $17.1 | $16.9 | $39.0 | $29.7 | $56.0 |

**Sources:** Federal Reserve Board website, "Flow of Fund Accounts," various issues. www.federalreserve.gov

**DO YOU UNDERSTAND:**

11. *What the international trends in securitization of assets have been?*

to primary mortgages issued and held by domestic entities of $13.85 trillion in 2016 (see Figure 7–8)—foreign bank offices issue and hold less than 0.40 percent of the total primary mortgage market in the United States.

While they have not evolved to the level of U.S. mortgage markets, securitization vehicles have also been developed for mortgages in countries other than the United States. After the United States, Europe is the world's second-largest and most developed securitization market. Although a form of securitization has been in existence in Europe in the German and Danish mortgage markets since the 1700s, securitization as we currently know it emerged outside the United States only in the mid-1980s. The original growth of "modern" securitization in Europe was largely based on the activities of a small number of centralized lenders in the booming UK residential mortgage market of the late 1980s.

Germany is one of the countries that moved toward making widespread use of securitization in its mortgage markets. Thus, like the United States, Germany relies heavily on capital markets to fund new mortgages, rather than relying simply on deposits at banks and other lending institutions. The German secondary mortgage market appears, in fact, to be a very well developed one, having served the country for close to 200 years. But there ends the historical similarity with the United States. In Germany, the capital markets have traditionally funded mortgages through bonds known as *Pfandbriefe,* which are conceptually distinct from mortgage-backed bonds. The *Pfandbriefe* are covered bonds, which function similarly to securitization *only* in that they help raise money from private investors. Otherwise, they differ significantly in their structure.

Since mid-1993, the number of European originators of securitized assets has continued to grow, as have the types of assets that can be securitized and the investor base. Further, securitization costs have fallen, and legislative and regulatory changes in European countries have supported this market's growth. The volume of European securitizations skyrocketed in 1996 and 1997, when European countries securitized a total of $41.5 billion assets. Despite the world economic crisis in 1998, the European securitization market fell only slightly to $38.4 billion. More than $22 billion of securitized vehicles were issued in just the first half of 1999 alone, including $3.5 billion in international deals from Japan. Japan and Europe accounted for $16 billion of the first quarter total. Latin America and the emerging markets (still struggling with economic crises) lagged behind, with issues totaling $7.0 billion.

Table 7–6 reports the value of securitized mortgage issuances in the United States, Europe, and the rest of the world from 2002 to 2016. The European securitization market topped $90.6 billion in 2002 (3.88 percent of the size of mortgage securitizations in the United States), $698.4 billion in 2007 (31.68 percent of the issuances in the United States), and $970.5 billion in 2008 (69.14 percent of the issuances in the United States). European securitizations fell to $432.7 billion in 2009 (21.20 percent of the size of mortgage securitizations in the United States), and to just $213.8 billion in 2015 (12.60 percent of the issuances in the United States). The United Kingdom was the biggest European issuer of mortgage-backed securities in 2015, with over 21 percent of the European market. However, with the UK's 2016 referendum (so-called Brexit) in which citizens voted to leave the European Union, the role that London banks will play in the mortgage-backed securitization market is now in doubt. As it leaves the EU, the UK's ability to trade and interact with the remaining EU nations is no longer without restrictions and

**TABLE 7–6**  Global Securitized Asset Issuance *(in billions of dollars)*

| Year | United States | Europe | Rest of the World | Total |
|------|--------------:|-------:|------------------:|------:|
| 2002 | $2,337.8 | $ 90.6 | $ 42.4 | $2,470.8 |
| 2003 | 3,172.6 | 166.4 | 57.3 | 3,396.3 |
| 2004 | 1,916.6 | 203.1 | 80.1 | 2,199.8 |
| 2005 | 2,230.5 | 301.1 | 97.6 | 2,629.2 |
| 2006 | 2,110.3 | 448.4 | 121.8 | 2,680.5 |
| 2007 | 2,204.3 | 698.4 | 132.9 | 3,035.6 |
| 2008 | 1,403.6 | 970.5 | 118.9 | 2,493.0 |
| 2009 | 2,041.1 | 432.7 | 96.0 | 2,569.8 |
| 2010 | 1,975.7 | 421.2 | 87.1 | 2,484.0 |
| 2011 | 1,660.2 | 394.0 | 94.0 | 2,148.2 |
| 2012 | 2,157.2 | 253.4 | 81.4 | 2,492.0 |
| 2013 | 2,087.8 | 180.8 | 123.2 | 2,391.8 |
| 2014 | 1,347.7 | 217.0 | 110.5 | 1,675.2 |
| 2015 | 1,690.2 | 213.8 | 88.3 | 1,992.3 |
| 2016* | 348.4 | 56.9 | 15.9 | 421.2 |

*Through March.

**Source:** SIFMA website, July 2016. www.sifma.org

must be negotiated as the UK "divorces" itself from the EU. Thus, international banks may decide to leave London for another country in the EU to conduct these financial transactions. In Europe, the factors driving the securitization market include the conversion to a single currency (a factor driving many European markets at the beginning of the 21st century), the effects of globalization of all markets, and the spread of U.S.-style financial securities.

Notice that European mortgage securitization peaked in 2008, then fell dramatically in 2009. This is because, quickly after it hit the United States, the financial crisis spread worldwide. As the crisis spread, banks worldwide saw losses driven by their portfolios of securitized exposures to the subprime mortgage market. Losses were magnified by illiquidity in the markets for those instruments. As with U.S. banks, this led to substantial losses in their marked to market valuations of the securitized mortgages. In Europe, the general picture of bank performance in 2008 was similar to that in the United States. That is, net income fell sharply at all banks. The largest banks in the Netherlands, Switzerland, and the United Kingdom had net losses for the year. Banks in Ireland, Spain, and the United Kingdom were especially hard hit as they had large investments in "toxic" mortgages and mortgage-backed securities, both U.S. and domestic. Because they focused on domestic retail banking, French and Italian banks were less affected by losses on mortgage-backed securities. Continental European banks, in contrast to UK banks, partially cushioned losses through an increase in their net interest margins.

Synthetic securitizations are a far more common form of mortgage financing in countries outside the United States. *Synthetic securitization* refers to structured transactions in which banks use credit derivatives to transfer the credit risk of a specified pool of assets to third parties, such as insurance companies, other banks, and unregulated entities. Synthetic securitization can replicate the economic risk transfer characteristics of a traditional securitization without actually removing the portfolio of assets from the originating bank's balance sheet. There are numerous reasons for preferring synthetic securitization. The reasons can depend on the regulatory climate of the country in question, as well as the goals of the mortgage originator and arranger. Reasons to prefer synthetic securitization might include the complexity and prohibitive cost of a traditional securitization transaction as well as its potentially unfavorable tax implications. The important point to remember in a synthetic securitization is that the owner of the assets remains the owner and does not actually pass legal title to other investors, unlike in a traditional securitization.

## SUMMARY

In this chapter, we examined the primary and secondary mortgage markets. For several reasons, mortgages are analyzed separately from other capital market securities (e.g., bonds and stocks). We identified several characteristics associated with mortgages and various categories of primary mortgage markets. We also provided an overview of the secondary mortgage markets. The sale and securitization of mortgages allows financial institutions to reduce interest rate risk exposure experienced when mortgages are left in the asset portfolios for the entire life of the mortgage. We look at the details of the securitization process in a risk-return framework in Chapter 24.

## QUESTIONS

1. Why are mortgage markets studied as a separate capital market? (*LG 7-1*)

2. What are the four major categories of mortgages and what percentage of the overall market does each entail? (*LG 7-2*)

3. What is the purpose of putting a lien against a piece of property? (*LG 7-3*)

4. Explain the difference between a federally insured mortgage and a conventional mortgage. (*LG 7-3*)

5. Explain the difference between a fixed-rate mortgage and an adjustable-rate mortgage. Include a discussion of mortgage borrowers' versus mortgage lenders' preferences for each. (*LG 7-3*)

6. What are the benefits and drawbacks to a mortgage borrower when refinancing a mortgage? (*LG 7-3*)

7. What are "points" on a mortgage? What factors does a mortgage borrower need to consider when deciding whether or not to take points on a mortgage? (*LG 7-3*)

8. What is a jumbo mortgage? (*LG 7-5*)

9. What is a subprime mortgage? What instrumental role did these mortgages play in the recent financial crisis? (*LG 7-5*)

10. What is an option ARM? What are the different options available with this type of mortgage? (*LG 7-5*)

11. How did the U.S. secondary mortgage markets evolve? (*LG 7-1*)

12. What is a mortgage sale? How does a mortgage sale differ from the securitization of a mortgage? (*LG 7-6*)

13. How did mortgage-backed securities contribute to the recent financial crisis? (*LG 7-1*)

14. What is a pass-through security? (*LG 7-7*)

15. What is the Government National Mortgage Association? How does this organization play a role in secondary mortgage markets? (*LG 7-7*)

16. What is the Federal National Mortgage Association? How does this organization play a role in secondary mortgage markets? (*LG 7-7*)

17. How has the U.S. government's sponsorship of FNMA and FHLMC affected their operations? Describe the problems these two GSEs have experienced over the last 15 years. (*LG 7-9*)

18. Describe a collateralized mortgage obligation. How is a CMO created? (*LG 7-8*)

19. What is a mortgage-backed bond? Why do financial institutions issue MBBs? (*LG 7-1*)

20. Who are the major participants in the mortgage markets? (*LG 7-9*)

## PROBLEMS

1. You plan to purchase a $100,000 house using a 30-year mortgage obtained from your local credit union. The mortgage rate offered to you is 8.25 percent. You will make a down payment of 20 percent of the purchase price. (*LG 7-4*)
   a. Calculate your monthly payments on this mortgage.
   b. Calculate the amount of interest and, separately, principal paid in the 25th payment.
   c. Calculate the amount of interest and, separately, principal paid in the 225th payment.
   d. Calculate the amount of interest paid over the life of this mortgage.

2. You plan to purchase a $175,000 house using a 15-year mortgage obtained from your local bank. The mortgage rate offered to you is 7.75 percent. You will make a down payment of 20 percent of the purchase price. (*LG 7-4*)
   a. Calculate your monthly payments on this mortgage.
   b. Calculate the amount of interest and, separately, principal paid in the 60th payment.

   c. Calculate the amount of interest and, separately, principal paid in the 180th payment.
   d. Calculate the amount of interest paid over the life of this mortgage.

3. You plan to purchase an $80,000 house using a 15-year mortgage obtained from your local bank. The mortgage rate offered to you is 8.00 percent. You will make a down payment of 20 percent of the purchase price. (*LG 7-4*)
   a. Calculate your monthly payments on this mortgage.
   b. Calculate the amount of interest and, separately, principal paid in the 127th payment.
   c. Calculate the amount of interest and, separately, principal paid in the 159th payment.
   d. Calculate the amount of interest paid over the life of this mortgage.

4. You plan to purchase a $150,000 house using a 15-year mortgage obtained from your local credit union. The mortgage

rate offered to you is 5.25 percent. You will make a down payment of 20 percent of the purchase price. (*LG 7-4*)

**a.** Calculate your monthly payments on this mortgage.

**b.** Construct the amortization schedule for the first six payments.

**5.** You plan to purchase a $200,000 house using a 30-year mortgage obtained from your local credit union. The mortgage rate offered to you is 6.50 percent. You will make a down payment of 20 percent of the purchase price. (*LG 7-4*)

**a.** Calculate your monthly payments on this mortgage.

**b.** Construct the amortization schedule for the first six payments.

**6.** **eXcel** **Using a Spreadsheet to Calculate Mortgage Payments:** What is the monthly payment on a $150,000, 15-year mortgage if the mortgage rate is 5.75 percent? 6.25 percent? 7.5 percent? 9 percent? (*LG 7-4*)

| Present Value | Periods | Interest Rate | ⇒ | The Payment Will Be |
|---|---|---|---|---|
| $150,000 | 15 × 12 | 5.75%/12 | | $1,245.62 |
| 150,000 | 15 × 12 | 6.25%/12 | | 1,286.13 |
| 150,000 | 15 × 12 | 7.50%/12 | | 1,390.52 |
| 150,000 | 15 × 12 | 9.00%/12 | | 1,521.40 |

**7.** **eXcel** **Using a Spreadsheet to Calculate Mortgage Payments:** What is the monthly payment on a $150,000, 30-year mortgage if the mortgage rate is 5.75 percent? 6.25 percent? 7.5 percent? 9 percent? (*LG 7-4*)

| Present Value | Periods | Interest Rate | ⇒ | The Payment Will Be |
|---|---|---|---|---|
| $150,000 | 30 × 12 | 5.75%/12 | | $ 875.36 |
| 150,000 | 30 × 12 | 6.25%/12 | | 923.58 |
| 150,000 | 30 × 12 | 7.50%/12 | | 1,048.82 |
| 150,000 | 30 × 12 | 9.00%/12 | | 1,206.93 |

**8.** You plan to purchase a $200,000 house using either a 30-year mortgage obtained from your local savings bank with a rate of 7.25 percent, or a 15-year mortgage with a rate of 6.50 percent. You will make a down payment of 20 percent of the purchase price. (*LG 7-3*)

**a.** Calculate the amount of interest and, separately, principal paid on each mortgage. What is the difference in interest paid?

**b.** Calculate your monthly payments on the two mortgages. What is the difference in the monthly payment on the two mortgages?

**9.** You plan to purchase a $240,000 house using either a 30-year mortgage obtained from your local bank with a rate of 5.75 percent, or a 15-year mortgage with a rate of 5.00 percent. You will make a down payment of 20 percent of the purchase price. (*LG 7-3*)

**a.** Calculate the amount of interest and, separately, principal paid on each mortgage. What is the difference in interest paid?

**b.** Calculate your monthly payments on the two mortgages. What is the difference in the monthly payment on the two mortgages?

**10.** You plan to purchase a house for $115,000 using a 30-year mortgage obtained from your local bank. You will make a down payment of 20 percent of the purchase price. You will not pay off the mortgage early. (*LG 7-3*)

**a.** Your bank offers you the following two options for payment:
**Option 1:** Mortgage rate of 9 percent and zero points.
**Option 2:** Mortgage rate of 8.85 percent and 2 points.
Which option should you choose?

**b.** Your bank offers you the following two options for payment:
**Option 1:** Mortgage rate of 10.25 percent and 1 point.
**Option 2:** Mortgage rate of 10 percent and 2.5 points.
Which option should you choose?

**11.** You plan to purchase a house for $195,000 using a 30-year mortgage obtained from your local bank. You will make a down payment of 20 percent of the purchase price. You will not pay off the mortgage early. (*LG 7-3*)

**a.** Your bank offers you the following two options for payment:
**Option 1:** Mortgage rate of 5.5 percent and zero points.
**Option 2:** Mortgage rate of 5.35 percent and 1.5 points.
Which option should you choose?

**b.** Your bank offers you the following two options for payments:
**Option 1:** Mortgage rate of 5.35 percent and 1 point.
**Option 2:** Mortgage rate of 5.25 percent and 2 points.
Which option should you choose?

**12.** You plan to purchase a house for $175,000 using a 15-year mortgage obtained from your local bank. You will make a down payment of 25 percent of the purchase price. You will not pay off the mortgage early. (*LG 7-3*)

**a.** Your bank offers you the following two options for payment:
**Option 1:** Mortgage rate of 5 percent and zero points.
**Option 2:** Mortgage rate of 4.75 percent and 2 points.
Which option should you choose?

**b.** Your bank offers you the following two options for payments:
**Option 1:** Mortgage rate of 4.85 percent and 2 points.
**Option 2:** Mortgage rate of 4.68 percent and 3 points.
Which option should you choose?

**13.** You plan to purchase a $220,000 house using a 15-year mortgage obtained from your bank. The mortgage rate offered to you is 4.75 percent. You will make a down payment of 20 percent of the purchase price. (*LG 7-4*)

**a.** Calculate your monthly payments on this mortgage.

**b.** Construct the amortization schedule for the mortgage. How much total interest is paid on this mortgage?

**14.** You plan to purchase a $300,000 house using a 15-year mortgage obtained from your bank. The mortgage rate offered to you is 4.50 percent. You will make a down payment of 20 percent of the purchase price. (*LG 7-4*)

**a.** Calculate your monthly payments on this mortgage.

**b.** Construct the amortization schedule for the mortgage. How much total interest is paid on this mortgage?

## SEARCH THE SITE

Go to the Federal Reserve Board's website at **www.federalreserve.gov** and find the most recent data on Mortgage Loans Outstanding.

Click on "Financial Accounts of the United States." Click on the most recent date. Click on "Level Tables." This downloads a file onto your computer that contains the relevant data in Table 217.

**Questions**

1. What is the current dollar value of mortgage loans outstanding? How has this value changed since 2016 as reported in Figure 7–1?
2. Calculate the percentage of mortgage loans outstanding comprised of 1- to 4-family, multifamily residential, commercial, and farm loans.

## APPENDIX 7A: Amortization Schedules for 30-Year Mortgage in Example 7–2 and No-Points versus Points Mortgages in Example 7–4

This appendix is available through Connect or your course instructor.

chapter

8

# Stock Markets

## Learning Goals

| | |
|---|---|
| **LG 8-1** | *Identify the major characteristics of common stock.* |
| **LG 8-2** | *Identify the major characteristics of preferred stock.* |
| **LG 8-3** | *Examine the process by which common stock is issued in primary stock markets.* |
| **LG 8-4** | *Describe the major secondary stock markets.* |
| **LG 8-5** | *Examine the process by which a trade takes place in the stock markets.* |
| **LG 8-6** | *Identify the major stock market indexes.* |
| **LG 8-7** | *Know who the major stock market participants are.* |
| **LG 8-8** | *Explain the three forms of market efficiency.* |
| **LG 8-9** | *Describe the major characteristics of international stock markets.* |

## THE STOCK MARKETS: CHAPTER OVERVIEW

Stock markets allow suppliers of funds to efficiently and cheaply get equity funds to public corporations (users of funds). In exchange, the fund users (firms) give the fund suppliers ownership rights in the firm as well as cash flows in the form of dividends. Thus, corporate stock or equity serves as a source of financing for firms, in addition to debt financing or retained earnings financing. In the 1990s, the market value of corporate stock outstanding increased faster than any other type of financial security. Figure 8–1 shows the market value of corporate stock outstanding in the United States in 1994, 2007, and 2016 by type of issuer. Notice that from 1994 through 2013, stock values increased 463 percent, compared to 340 percent growth in bond values (see Figure 6–1) and 204 percent growth in primary mortgage market values (see Figure 7–1). However, stock prices fell precipitously during the financial crisis of 2008–2009. At the end of the third quarter 2007, U.S. stock market values peaked at $26.4 trillion before falling to $13.9 trillion in March 2009, a loss of 47.3 percent in less than 1½ years. Stock prices recovered along with the economy in the last half of 2009 and 2010, doubling in value from March 2009 to March 2010. However, it took until March 5, 2013, for the Dow Jones Industrial Average (DJIA) to surpass its pre-crisis high of 14,164.53, closing at 14,253.77 for the day. To date, the average's all-time record close stands at 21,529, seen on June 19, 2017.

**Figure 8–1** Market Value of Common Stock Outstanding, by Type of Issuer

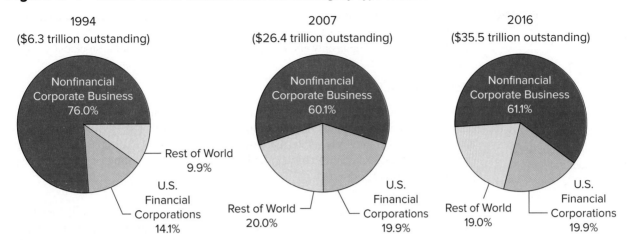

1994
($6.3 trillion outstanding)

Nonfinancial Corporate Business 76.0%
Rest of World 9.9%
U.S. Financial Corporations 14.1%

2007
($26.4 trillion outstanding)

Nonfinancial Corporate Business 60.1%
Rest of World 20.0%
U.S. Financial Corporations 19.9%

2016
($35.5 trillion outstanding)

Nonfinancial Corporate Business 61.1%
Rest of World 19.0%
U.S. Financial Corporations 19.9%

**Sources:** Federal Reserve Board website, "Flow of Fund Accounts," various issues. www.federalreserve.gov

Legally, holders of a corporation's common stock or equity have an ownership stake in the issuing firm that reflects the percentage of the corporation's stock they hold. Specifically, corporate stockholders have the right to a share in the issuing firm's profits, as in dividend payments, after the payment of interest to bond holders and taxes. They also have a residual claim on the firm's assets if the company fails or is dissolved after all debt and tax liabilities are paid. Bond holders, on the other hand, are creditors of the issuing firm. They have no direct ownership interest in the firm, but they have a superior claim to the firm's earnings and assets relative to that of stockholders.

Common stockholders have voting privileges on major issues in the firm, such as the election of the board of directors. It is the board of directors, through the firm managers, who oversee the day-to-day operations of the firm. The board is charged with ensuring that the firm is being run so as to maximize the value of the firm (i.e., the value of its equity and debt claims). Thus, while stockholders have no direct control over a firm's day-to-day operations, they do decide on who will oversee these operations and they can replace the board when they feel the firm is not being run efficiently from a value-maximizing perspective.

The secondary market for corporate stock is the most closely watched and reported of all financial security markets. Daily television and newspaper reports include recaps of the movements in stock market values (both in the United States and abroad). This is because stock market movements are sometimes seen as predictors of economic activity and performance. This is also because corporate stocks may be the most widely held of all financial securities. Most individuals own stocks either directly or indirectly through pension fund and mutual fund investments, and thus their economic wealth fluctuates closely with that of the stock market.

In this chapter, we present a description of equity or stock securities and the markets in which they trade. We begin with a description of the different types of corporate stock. We next look at how they are sold to the public and then traded: first in primary markets (the original sale) and then in secondary markets (the markets for resale). We also review the major stock market indexes. We look at the participants in stock markets and other issues relating to those markets (such as the link between stock market indexes and overall economic activity, the efficiency of the stock market, and regulations covering stock market operations). We conclude the chapter with an examination of international participation in U.S. stock markets and some characteristics of foreign stock markets.

# ₊TOCK MARKET SECURITIES

LG 8-1

Two types of corporate stock exist: common stock and preferred stock. While all public corporations issue common stock, many do not offer preferred stock. The market value of preferred stock outstanding is only about 1 percent of the value of common stock outstanding.

## Common Stock

**common stock**

*The fundamental ownership claim in a public or private corporation.*

**Common stock** is the fundamental ownership claim in a public or private corporation. Many characteristics of common stock differentiate it from other types of financial securities (e.g., bonds, mortgages, preferred stock). These include (1) discretionary dividend payments, (2) residual claim status, (3) limited liability, and (4) voting rights. These characteristics are described next.

**Dividends.**   While common stockholders can potentially receive unlimited dividend payments if the firm is highly profitable, they have no special or guaranteed dividend rights. The payment and size of dividends are determined by the board of directors of the issuing firm (who are elected by the common stockholders). Unlike interest payments on debt, a corporation does not default if it misses a dividend payment to common stockholders. Thus, common stockholders have no legal recourse if dividends are not received, even if a company is highly profitable and chooses to use these profits to reinvest in new projects and firm growth. In fact, many firms pay no dividends, but instead reinvest all of their net earnings in the firm. For example, in 2016, 101 of the firms listed in the S&P 500 Index (see below) paid no dividends.

Another drawback with common stock dividends, from an investor's viewpoint, is that they are taxed twice—once at the firm level (at the corporate tax rate, by virtue of the fact that dividend payments are not tax deductible from the firm's profits or net earnings) and once at the personal level (at the personal income tax rate). Investors can partially avoid this double taxation effect by holding stocks in growth firms that reinvest most of their earnings to finance growth rather than paying larger dividends. Generally, earnings growth leads to stock price increases. Thus, stockholders can sell their stock for a profit and pay capital gains taxes rather than ordinary income taxes on dividend income. Under current tax laws, capital gains tax rates are lower than ordinary income tax rates. For example, in the 2010s, ordinary income tax rates ranged from 15 percent to 39 percent of an individual's taxable income. Long-term (a 12-month or longer investment horizon) capital gains tax rates were capped at 20 percent.

The return to a stockholder over a period $t - 1$ to $t$ can be written as:

$$R_t = \frac{P_t - P_{t-1}}{P_{t-1}} + \frac{D_t}{P_{t-1}}$$

where

$P_t$ = Stock price at time $t$

$D_t$ = Dividends paid over time $t - 1$ to $t$

$\dfrac{P_t - P_{t-1}}{P_{t-1}}$ = Capital gain over time $t - 1$ to $t$

$\dfrac{D_t}{P_{t-1}}$ = Return from dividends over time $t - 1$ to $t$

In the context of the return equation, the reinvestment of earnings (rather than payment of dividends) affects both return components: capital gains and dividends. By reinvesting earnings (rather than paying dividends), the dividend component of returns, $D_t/P_{t-1}$, decreases. However, the reinvestment of earnings generally results in a relatively larger increase in the capital gains component, $(P_t - P_{t-1})/P_{t-1}$.

---

**EXAMPLE 8–1**  Payment of Dividends versus Reinvestment of Earnings

A corporation has after- (corporate) tax earnings that would allow a $2 dividend per share to be paid to its stockholders. If these dividends are paid, the firm will be unable to invest in new projects, and its stock price, currently $50 per share, probably will not change. The return to the firm's stockholders in this case is:

$$R_t = \frac{\$50 - \$50}{\$50} + \frac{\$2}{\$50} = 4\%$$

Suppose a stockholder bought the stock at the beginning of the year (at $50) and sold it at the end of the year (at $50). The stockholder's ordinary income tax rate is 30 percent and the capital gains tax rate is 20 percent. (The capital gains tax rate depends on several things, including the holding period of the investment, the investor's income level, and any tax-code changes made during the holding period.) The return to the stockholder in this case is all in the form of ordinary income (dividends). Thus, the after-tax rate of return to the stockholder is $4\%(1 - 0.30) = 2.8\%$.

Alternatively, rather than pay dividends, the firm can use the earnings to invest in new projects that will increase the overall value of the firm such that the stock price will rise to $52 per share. The return to the firm's stockholders in this case is:

$$R_t = \frac{\$52 - \$50}{\$50} + \frac{\$0}{\$50} = 4\%$$

Further, the return to the stockholder is all in the form of capital gains and is taxed at a rate of 20 percent. Thus, the after-tax rate of return to the stockholder is $4\% (1 - 0.20) = 3.2\%$.

---

**residual claim**

*In the event of liquidation, common stockholders have the lowest priority in terms of any cash distribution.*

**Residual Claim.**   Common stockholders have the lowest priority claim on a corporation's assets in the event of bankruptcy—they have a **residual claim.** Only after all senior claims are paid (i.e., payments owed to creditors such as the firm's employees, bond holders, the government (taxes), and preferred stockholders) are common stockholders entitled to what assets of the firm are left. For example, the bankruptcy of Lehman Brothers in 2008 left its shareholders with nothing. The residual claim feature associated with common stock makes it riskier than bonds as an investible asset.

**limited liability**

*No matter what financial difficulties the issuing corporation encounters, neither it nor its creditors can seek repayment from the firm's common stockholders. This implies that common stockholders' losses are limited to the original amount of their investment.*

**Limited Liability.**   One of the most important characteristics of common stock is its limited liability feature. Legally, **limited liability** implies that common stockholder losses are limited to the amount of their original investment in the firm if the company's asset value falls to less than the value of the debt it owes. That is, the common stockholders' personal wealth held outside their ownership claims in the firm are unaffected by bankruptcy of the corporation—even if the losses of the firm exceed its total common stock ownership claims. In contrast, sole proprietorship or partnership stock interests mean the stockholders may be liable for the firm's debts out of their total private wealth holdings if the company gets into financial difficulties and its losses exceed the stockholders' ownership claims in the firm. This is the case of "unlimited" liability.

**Voting Rights.**   A fundamental privilege assigned to common stock is voting rights. While common stockholders do not exercise control over the firm's daily activities (these activities are overseen by managers hired to act in the best interests of the firm's common stockholders and bond holders), they do exercise control over the firm's activities indirectly through the election of the board of directors. Stockholders also vote on major changes pertaining to the firm (e.g., mergers and dividend changes). For example, in February 2016, diagnostics company Alere was forced to delay a proposed $5.8 billion acquisition by Abbott. A shareholder lawsuit accused Alere of misleading investors by stating that its financial reporting failed to follow generally accepted accounting principles. The plaintiffs, a group of individual investors, cited a federal probe into the company's accounting for overseas sales arguing that Alere had not adhered to those principles. The lawsuit said Alere failed to disclose "material adverse facts" about the company that eventually threw its merger with Abbott into doubt. Alere's shares dropped about 18 percent to $40.51 after Abbott CEO Miles White declined to respond directly when asked whether he would reaffirm Abbott's commitment to the Alere deal. The deal had been approved by the boards of both companies but was subject to approval by Alere shareholders.

**dual-class firms**

*Two classes of common stock are outstanding, with differential voting and/or dividend rights assigned to each class.*

The typical voting rights arrangement is to assign one vote per share of common stock. However, some corporations are organized as **dual-class firms,** in which two classes of common stock are outstanding, with different voting and/or dividend rights assigned to each class. For example, inferior voting rights have been assigned by (1) limiting the number of votes per share on one class relative to another (e.g., Berkshire Hathaway Class B shares are entitled to 1/10,000th vote per share, while Class A shares are entitled to one vote per share), (2) limiting the fraction of the board of directors that one class can elect relative to another (e.g., Reinsurance Group of America Class B common stock has the right to elect at least 80 percent of the members of the board of directors, while the holders of Class A common stock have the right to elect no more than 20 percent of the members of the board), or (3) a combination of these two (e.g., the Molson Coors Brewing Company allows holders of Class B common stock the right to elect three directors to the Molson Coors board of directors and the right to one vote per share on other specified transactional actions, while the right to vote for all other activities remains exclusively with Class A common stock). To offset the reduced voting rights, inferior class shares are often assigned higher dividend rights. For example, no dividends are paid on the Class B common shares of Berkshire Hathaway unless equal or greater dividends are paid on the Class A stock. Dual-class firms have often been used in corporations owned and controlled by a single family or group turning to the public market to raise capital through the issue of new shares. To retain voting control over the firm, the family or group issues the dual classes of stock, keeping the high voting stock for themselves and selling the limited voting shares to the public. In all other respects the shares of the two classes are often identical. Because dual classes of stock have often been used by a small group (i.e., family managers) to entrench themselves in the firm, dual-class firms are controversial.

**cumulative voting**

*All directors up for election are voted on at the same time. The number of votes assigned to each stockholder equals the number of shares held multiplied by the number of directors to be elected.*

Shareholders exercise their voting rights, electing the board of directors by casting votes at the issuing firm's annual meeting or by mailing in a proxy vote (see below). Two methods of electing a board of directors are generally used: cumulative voting and straight voting. Cumulative voting is required by law in some states (e.g., Arizona and Illinois) and is authorized in others. With **cumulative voting,** all directors up for election, as nominated by the shareholders and selected by a committee of the board, are voted on at the same time. The number of votes assigned to each stockholder equals the number of shares held multiplied by the number of directors to be elected. A shareholder may assign all of his or her votes to a single candidate for the board or may spread them over more than one candidate. The candidates with the highest number of total votes are then elected to the board. Cumulative voting permits minority stockholders to have some real say in the election of the board of directors, since less than a majority of the votes can affect the outcome.

---

**EXAMPLE 8–2**   Cumulative Voting of a Board of Directors

Suppose a firm has 1 million shares of common stock outstanding and three directors up for election. With cumulative voting, the total number of votes each shareholder may cast equals the number of shares owned multiplied by the number of directors to be elected. Thus, the total number of votes available is 3,000,000 (= 1 million shares outstanding × 3 directors).

If there are four candidates for the three board positions, the three candidates with the highest number of votes will be elected to the board and the candidate with the fewest total votes will not be elected. In this example, the minimum number of votes needed to ensure election is one-fourth of the 3 million votes available, or 750,000 votes. If one candidate receives 750,000, the remaining votes together total 2,250,000. No matter how these votes are spread over the remaining three director candidates, it is mathematically impossible for *each* of the three to receive *more than* 750,000. This would require more than $3 \times 750,000$ votes, or more than the 2,250,000 votes that remain.

For example, if candidate 1 receives 750,000 votes, and votes for the other three candidates are spread as follows:

$$\text{Candidate 2} = 2 \text{ million votes}$$
$$\text{Candidate 3} = 150,000 \text{ votes}$$
$$\text{Candidate 4} = 100,000 \text{ votes}$$

for a total of 3 million votes cast, candidates 1, 2, and 3 are elected to the board. Alternatively, votes for the other three candidates can be spread as:

$$\text{Candidate 3} = 751,000 \text{ votes}$$
$$\text{Candidate 2} = 750,000 \text{ votes}$$
$$\text{Candidate 4} = 749,000 \text{ votes}$$

Again, candidates 1, 2, and 3 are elected. Indeed, any distribution of the remaining 2,250,000 votes will ensure that candidate 1 is one of the top three vote getters and will be elected to the board. The number of shares needed to elect $p$ directors, $N_p$, is

$$N_p = [(P \times \text{Number of votes available})/(\text{Number of directors to be elected} + 1)] + 1$$

or, in our example, to ensure the election of candidates 1 and 2, a stockholder would need

$$N_p = [(2 \times 3,000,000)/(3 + 1)] + 1 = 1,500,001 \text{ shares}$$

and these would be split as 750,001 for candidate 1 and 750,000 for candidate 2.

With straight voting, the vote on the board of directors occurs one director at a time. Thus, the number of votes eligible for each director is the number of shares outstanding. Straight voting results in a situation in which an owner of over half the voting shares can elect the entire board of directors. The state of Delaware allows only straight voting of directors, unless a company specifically affirmatively "opts in" to cumulative voting in its certificate of incorporation. Because of the advantages of straight voting to large stockholders (often corporate insiders or institutional investors), over 50 percent of all publicly traded corporations are incorporated in Delaware.

**proxy**

*A voting ballot sent by a corporation to its stockholders. When returned to the issuing firm, a proxy allows stockholders to vote by absentee ballot or authorizes representatives of the stockholders to vote on their behalf.*

**Proxy Votes.** Most shareholders do not attend annual meetings. Most corporations anticipate this and routinely mail proxies to their stockholders prior to the annual meeting. A completed **proxy** returned to the issuing firm allows stockholders to vote by absentee ballot or authorize representatives of the stockholders to vote on their behalf. It is estimated that, on average, less than 30 percent of the total possible votes are cast at corporate meetings. However, use of the Internet may increase this number in the future. By the 2010s, virtually all U.S. firms were putting proxy statements online and allowing votes to be cast via the Internet. The entire documentation delivery process can be electronically automated with the use of services such as Computershare or Automatic Data Processing's (ADP's) ProxyVote. Official documentation is delivered in electronic form to shareholders, who log onto the system with a control number or personal identification number and vote for or against the resolutions presented.

**LG 8-2**

### Preferred Stock

**preferred stock**

*A hybrid security that has characteristics of both bonds and common stock.*

**Preferred stock** is a hybrid security that has characteristics of both bonds and common stock. Preferred stock is similar to common stock in that it represents an ownership interest in the issuing firm, but like a bond it pays a fixed periodic (dividend) payment. Preferred stock is senior to common stock but junior to bonds. Therefore, preferred stockholders are paid only when profits have been generated and all debt holders have been paid (but before common stockholders are paid). Like common stock, if the issuing firm does not have sufficient profits to pay the preferred stock dividends, preferred stockholders cannot force the firm into bankruptcy. Further, if the issuing firm goes bankrupt, preferred stockholders are paid their claim only after all creditors have been paid, but before common stockholders are paid.

Corporations find preferred stock beneficial as a source of funds because, unlike coupon interest on a bond issue, dividends on preferred stock can be missed without fear of bankruptcy proceedings. Additionally, preferred stock is beneficial to an issuing firm's debt holders. Funds raised through a preferred stock issue can be used by the firm to fund the purchase of assets that will produce income needed to pay debt holders before preferred stockholders can be paid.

However, preferred stock also has its drawbacks for corporations. The first drawback is that, if a preferred dividend payment is missed, new investors may be reluctant to make investments in the firm. Thus, firms are generally unable to raise any new capital until all missed dividend payments are paid on preferred stock. In addition, preferred stockholders must be paid a rate of return consistent with the risk associated with preferred stock (i.e., dividend payments may be delayed). Therefore, preferred stock may be a costlier source of funding for the issuing firm than bonds.[1]

A second drawback of preferred stock from the issuing firm's viewpoint is that, unlike coupon interest paid on corporate bonds, dividends paid on preferred stock are not a tax-deductible expense—preferred dividends are paid out of after-tax earnings. This raises the cost of preferred stock relative to bonds for a firm's shareholders. Specifically, this difference in the tax treatment between coupon interest on debt and preferred stock dividends affects the net profit available to common stockholders of the firm.

Dividends on preferred stock are generally fixed (paid quarterly) and are expressed either as a dollar amount or a percentage of the face or par value of the preferred stock.

---

**EXAMPLE 8–3**   Calculation of Preferred Stock Dividends

Suppose you own a preferred stock that promises to pay an annual dividend of 5 percent of the par (face) value of the stock (received in quarterly installments). If the par value of the stock is $100, the preferred stockholder will receive:

$$\text{Annual dividends} = \$100 \times 0.05 = \$5$$

or:

$$\text{Quarterly dividend} = \$5 \div 4 = \$1.25$$

at the end of each quarter.

Alternatively, the preferred stock could promise to pay an annual dividend of $5 per year in quarterly installments.

---

**nonparticipating preferred stock**

*Preferred stock in which the dividend is fixed regardless of any increase or decrease in the issuing firm's profits.*

Preferred stockholders generally do not have voting rights in the firm. An exception to this rule may exist if the issuing firm has missed a promised dividend payment. For example, preferred stock in Pitney Bowes, Inc. has no voting rights except when dividends are in arrears for six quarterly payments. In this case, preferred stockholders can elect one-third of the board of directors. Further, most preferred stock may be converted to common stock in the firm at any time the investor chooses.

Typically, preferred stock is nonparticipating and cumulative. **Nonparticipating preferred stock** means that the preferred stock dividend is fixed regardless of any increase

---

1. Nevertheless, the cost of preferred stock is lowered because *corporate* investors in preferred stock can shelter up to 70 percent of their dividends against taxes. Some of these tax savings may be "passed back" to the issuing firm in the form of lower required gross dividends. Thus, debt may or may not be a lower-cost vehicle for the issuing firm, depending on the value of this tax shield to corporate investors.

**cumulative preferred stock**

*Preferred stock in which missed dividend payments go into arrears and must be made up before any common stock dividends can be paid.*

**participating preferred stock**

*Preferred stock in which actual dividends paid in any year may be greater than the promised dividends.*

**noncumulative preferred stock**

*Preferred stock in which dividend payments do not go into arrears and are never paid.*

or decrease in the issuing firm's profits. **Cumulative preferred stock** means that any missed dividend payments go into arrears and *must* be made up before *any* common stock dividends can be paid. For example, during the peak of the financial crisis in late 2008, the federal government instituted the Capital Purchase Program (CPP), a component of the Troubled Asset Relief Program (TARP). The CPP involved the U.S. Treasury's investment in hundreds of financial institutions. In return, the U.S. Treasury received shares of preferred stock. The preferred stock carried a 5 percent cumulative dividend rate for the first five years and then reset to a 9 percent dividend.

In contrast, **participating preferred stock** means that actual dividends paid in any year may be greater than the promised dividends. In some cases, if the issuing firm has an exceptionally profitable year, preferred stockholders may receive some of the high profits in the form of an extra dividend payment. In others, the participating preferred stock pays and changes dividends along the same lines as common stock dividends. Participating preferred stock is frequently used by private equity investors and venture capital firms. In a deal with participating preferred stock, preferred stockholders receive the full return of their investment before any other money is paid out, and then also participate in the distribution of the remaining proceeds, up to an agreed-upon multiple (often two or three times) of the investment. If **preferred stock** is **noncumulative,** missed dividend payments do not go into arrears and are never paid. For example, Doral Financial Corp.'s noncumulative preferred stock entitles stockholders to monthly dividends based on an annual rate of $0.151 per share. In 2009, Doral suspended dividend payments on the preferred stock. The dividends did not go into arrears. Noncumulative preferred stock is generally unattractive to prospective preferred stockholders. Thus, noncumulative preferred stock generally has some other special features (e.g., voting rights) to make up for this drawback.

---

**DO YOU UNDERSTAND:**

1. *What common stock is?*
2. *What some of the drawbacks are of dividends paid on common stock from the stockholder's point of view?*
3. *What the difference is between cumulative voting and straight voting of the board of directors?*
4. *What preferred stock is? How preferred stock is similar to common stock and bonds?*

---

## PRIMARY AND SECONDARY STOCK MARKETS

Before common stock can be issued by a corporation, shares must be authorized by a majority vote of both the board of directors and the firm's existing common stockholders. Once authorized, new shares of stock are distributed to existing and new investors through a primary market sale with the help of investment banks. Once issued, the stocks are traded in secondary stock markets (such as the NYSE or NASDAQ—see below).

In this section, we examine the process involved with the primary sale of corporate stock. We also describe the secondary markets, the process by which stocks trade in these markets, and the indexes that are used to summarize secondary stock market value changes.

### Primary Stock Markets

**LG 8-3**

**primary stock markets**

*Markets in which corporations raise funds through new issues of securities.*

**Primary stock markets** are markets in which corporations raise funds through *new* issues of stocks. The new stock securities are sold to initial investors (suppliers of funds) in exchange for funds (money) that the issuer (user of funds) needs. As illustrated in Figure 8–2, most primary market transactions go through investment banks (e.g., Morgan Stanley or Bank of America Merrill Lynch—see Chapter 16), which serve as the intermediary between the issuing corporations (fund users) and ultimate investors (fund suppliers) in securities.

**Figure 8–2**   **Primary Market Stock Transaction**

**net proceeds**

*The price at which the investment bank purchases the stock from the issuer.*

**gross proceeds**

*The price at which the investment bank resells the stock to investors.*

**underwriter's spread**

*The difference between the gross proceeds and the net proceeds.*

**syndicate**

*The process of distributing securities through a group of investment banks.*

**originating houses**

*The lead banks in the syndicate, which negotiate with the issuing company on behalf of the syndicate.*

Like the primary sale of bonds (discussed in Chapter 6), the investment bank can conduct a primary market sale of stock using a firm commitment underwriting (where the investment bank guarantees the corporation a price for newly issued securities by buying the whole issue at a fixed price from the corporate issuer) or a best efforts underwriting basis (where the underwriter does not guarantee a price to the issuer and acts more as a placing or distribution agent for a fee). In a firm commitment underwriting, the investment bank purchases the stock from the issuer for a guaranteed price (called the **net proceeds**) and resells it to investors at a higher price (called the **gross proceeds**). The difference between the gross proceeds and the net proceeds (called the **underwriter's spread**) is compensation for the expenses and risks incurred by the investment bank with the issue. We discuss these costs in more detail in Chapter 16.

Often an investment bank will bring in a number of other investment banks to help sell and distribute a new issue—called a **syndicate.** For example, in Figure 8–3, the stock issue announcement of 10,344,827 shares of common stock in Acadia Pharmaceuticals lists the syndicate of seven investment banks involved in the initial issue. The investment banks are listed according to their degree of participation in the sale of new shares. The lead banks in the syndicate (e.g., Merrill Lynch and J.P. Morgan Securities), which directly negotiate with the issuing company on behalf of the syndicate, are the **originating houses.** Once an issue is arranged and its terms set, each member of the syndicate is assigned a given number of shares in the issue for which it is responsible for selling. Shares of stock issued through a syndicate of investment banks spread the risk associated with the sale of the stock among several investment banks. A syndicate also results in a larger pool of potential outside investors, increasing the probability of a successful sale and widening the scope of the investor base.

A primary market sale may be a first-time issue by a private firm going public (i.e., allowing its equity, some of which was held privately by managers and venture capital

**Figure 8–3**   **Stock Issue Announcement**

**Acadia Pharmaceuticals, Inc.** (NASDAQ: ACAD)

Underwriting Agreement dated January 6, 2016

Underwriters:   Merrill Lynch, Pierce, Fenner & Smith
                J.P. Morgan Securities LLC

Title, Purchase Price and Description of Securities:

| | |
|---|---|
| Title: | Common Stock |
| Number of Securities to be sold by the Selling Stockholders: | 10,344,827 |
| Price per Security to Public (include accrued dividends, if any): | $29.00 |
| Price per Security to each Underwriter: | $27.26 |

Closing Date, Time and Location:   9:00 a.m. New York time, on January 12, 2016 at Merrill Lynch, One Bryant Park, New York, New York 10036

SCHEDULE A

| Underwriters | Number of Firm Shares |
|---|---|
| Merrill Lynch, Pierce, Fenner & Smith | 3,103,449 |
| J.P. Morgan Securities LLC | 3,103,449 |
| Cowen and Company, LLC | 2,068,965 |
| JMP Securities LLC | 620,689 |
| Needham & Company, LLC | 620,689 |
| H.C. Wainwright & Co., LLC | 413,793 |
| Ladenburg Thalmann & Co. Inc. | 413,793 |
| Total | 10,344,827 |

**initial public offering (IPO)**

*The first public issue of a financial instrument by a firm.*

**seasoned offering**

*The sale of additional securities by a firm whose securities are currently publicly traded.*

**preemptive rights**

*A right of existing stockholders in which new shares must be offered to existing shareholders first in such a way that they can maintain their proportional ownership in the corporation.*

investors, to be *publicly* traded in stock markets for the first time). These first-time issues are also referred to as **initial public offerings (IPOs)** discussed in Chapter 16. For example, in 2016, MGM Growth Properties raised $1.05 billion in the biggest IPO offering of common stock in the United States that year. The financial crisis of 2008–2009 resulted in a large decline in IPO activity. Indeed, the U.S. IPO market virtually seized up, with a record-setting stretch of inactivity that began in August 2008 and ended in November 2008, and only 20 IPOs for all of 2008. Alternatively, a primary market sale may be a **seasoned offering,** in which the firm already has shares of the stock trading in the secondary markets. In both cases, the issuer receives the proceeds of the sale and the primary market investors receive the securities. Like the primary sales of corporate bond issues, corporate stocks may initially be issued through either a public sale (where the stock issue is offered to the general investing public) or a private placement (where stock is sold privately to a limited number of large investors).

**Preemptive Rights.** Corporate law in some states, and some corporate charters, gives shareholders **preemptive rights** to the new shares of stock when they are issued. This means that before a seasoned offering of stock can be sold to outsiders, the new shares must first be offered to existing shareholders in such a way that they can maintain their proportional ownership in the corporation. A "rights offering" generally allows existing stockholders to purchase shares at a price slightly below the market price. Stockholders can then exercise their rights (buying the allotted shares in the new stock) or sell them. The result can be a low-cost distribution of new shares for a firm (i.e., the issuing firm avoids the expense of an underwritten offering).

---

### EXAMPLE 8–4 Calculation of Shares Purchased through a Rights Offering

Suppose you own 1,000 shares of common stock in a firm with 1 million total shares outstanding. The firm announces its plan to sell an additional 500,000 shares through a rights offering. Thus, each shareholder will be sent 0.5 right for each share of stock owned. One right can then be exchanged for one share of common stock in the new issue.

Your current ownership interest is 0.1 percent (1,000/1 million) prior to the rights offering and you receive 500 rights (1,000 × 0.5) allowing you to purchase 500 of the new shares. If you exercise your rights (buy the 500 shares), your ownership interest in the firm after the rights offering is still 0.1 percent [(1,000 + 500)/(1 million + 500,000)]. Thus, the rights offering ensures that every investor can maintain his or her fractional ownership interest in the firm.

Suppose the market value of the common stock is $40 before the rights offering, or the total market value of the firm is $40 million ($40 × 1 million), and the 500,000 new shares are offered to current stockholders at a 10 percent discount, or for $36 per share. The firm receives $18 million ($36 × 500,000). The market value of the firm after the rights offering is $58 million (the original $40 million plus the $18 million from the new shares), or $38.67 per share ($58 million ÷ 1.5 million).

Your 1,000 shares are worth $40,000 ($40 × 1,000) before the rights offering, and you can purchase 500 additional shares for $18,000 ($36 × 500). Thus, your total investment in the firm after the rights offering is $58,000, or $38.67 per share ($58,000 ÷ 1,500).

Suppose you decide not to exercise your preemptive right. Since each right allows a stockholder to buy a new share for $36 per share when the shares are worth $38.67, the value of one right should be $2.67. Should you sell your rights rather than exercise them, you maintain your original 1,000 shares of stock. These have a value after the rights offering of $38,667 (1,000 × 38.67). You could also sell your rights to other investors for $1,333 (500 × $2.67). As a result, you have a total wealth level of $40,000—you have lost no wealth.

In 2016, S&W Seed Company (SANW) announced a rights offering to its common stockholders intended to raise $10.375 million in new stock at a subscription price of $4.15 per share—that is, to issue 2.5 million new shares of common stock. Each subscription right allowed shareholders to purchase 0.0937646 of a share of S&W Seed's stock. S&W Seed common stock traded between $4.10 and $4.32 per share during the period of the rights offering. Thus, right holders could purchase new shares in S&W Seed at a discount of as much as $0.17 per share from the market price of the stock. These rights could be sold by S&W Seed common stockholders to other investors. Rights are similar to options in that they give the holder the option, but not the obligation, to buy the stock at a fixed price (see Chapter 10). The rights holder has the option of buying the new shares at the stated price, selling the rights to other investors, or letting the rights expire at the end of the offering period unused.

**Registration.**    In a public sale of stock, once the issuing firm and the investment bank have agreed on the details of the stock issue, the investment bank must get SEC approval in accordance with the Securities and Exchange Act of 1934. Registration of a stock can be a lengthy process. We illustrate the process in Figure 8–4. The process starts with the preparation of the registration statement to be filed with the SEC. The registration statement includes information on the nature of the issuer's business, the key provisions and features of the security to be issued, the risks involved with the security, and background on the management. The focus of the registration statement is on full information disclosure about the firm and the securities issued to the public at large. At the same time that the issuer and its investment bank prepare the registration statement to be filed with the SEC, they prepare a preliminary version of the public offering's prospectus called the **red herring prospectus.** The red herring prospectus is similar to the registration statement but is distributed to potential equity buyers. It is a preliminary version of the official or final prospectus that will be printed upon SEC registration of the issue and makes up the bulk of the registration statement. Firms use the feedback provided from the distribution of the red herring prospectus to help set the price on the new shares to ensure the sale of the full issue.

After submission of the registration statement, the SEC has 20 days to request additional information or changes to the registration statement. It generally takes about 20 days for the SEC to declare whether or not a registration statement is effective. First-time or infrequent issuers can sometimes wait up to several months for SEC registration, especially if the SEC keeps requesting additional information and revised red herring prospectuses. However, companies that know the registration process well can generally obtain registration in a few days. This period of review is called the waiting period.

Once the SEC is satisfied with the registration statement, it registers the issue. At this point, the issuer (along with its investment bankers) sets the final selling price on the shares, prints the official prospectus describing the issue, and sends it to all potential buyers of the issue. Upon issuance of the prospectus (generally the day following SEC registration), the shares can be sold.

**red herring prospectus**

*A preliminary version of the prospectus describing a new security issue distributed to potential buyers prior to the security's registration.*

**Figure 8–4**    **Getting Shares of Stock to the Investing Public**

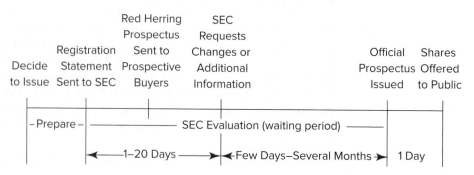

The period of time between the company's filing of the registration statement with the SEC and the selling of shares is referred to as the "quiet period." Historically, the issuing company could send no written communication to the public during the quiet period other than information regarding the normal course of business. Once a company registered with the SEC for a public offering it could engage in oral communication only. That meant the company executives could go on so-called roadshows to solicit investors or have brokers call potential investors to discuss the offering. But they could not provide any written communication, such as faxes or letters, or give interviews about the company's offering. These rules, adopted in 1933, did not foresee new technology, such as the Internet and e-mail. Moreover, these outdated rules may have hurt investors by giving them too little information. Thus, in December 2005, the SEC enacted a rule change giving large companies (market capitalization of at least $700 million or with at least $1 billion in debt) more freedom to communicate with investors during the quiet period. Specifically, these companies are now allowed to communicate with investors at any time prior to a public offering through e-mail, letters, or even TV ads, as long as the information is also filed with the SEC. Such communication was previously prohibited.

Further, in December 2005, the SEC enacted an overhaul in the issuing process for stock IPOs that facilitated greater use of the Internet to disseminate information to the markets. Although the use of the Internet was not forbidden by the SEC, prior rules put issuers in legal jeopardy if they departed from the formal written prospectuses and face-to-face roadshows. Under the new rules, the SEC formally allows Internet broadcasts of roadshows. Retail investors can view roadshow presentations while the company is on the road at www.retailroadshow.com. These online broadcasts are open to all investors, not just the chosen few invited to previously closed-door presentations. In fact, the rules encourage broad Internet roadshow dissemination, giving investment banks that open them to the public a break from certain filing requirements. Furthermore, issuers and investment bankers are able to forgo sending final offering prospectuses to IPO investors. Under the SEC's new rules, issuers still have to distribute preliminary (red herring) prospectuses to potential investors. But realizing that most investors get offering documents electronically anyway, the SEC wanted to allow issuers to e-mail investors when a stock price is set, tell them their allocations, and point out that a formal prospectus would soon be filed with the SEC.

In order to reduce the time and cost of registration, yet still protect the public by requiring issuers to disclose information about the firm and the security to be issued, the SEC passed a rule in 1982 allowing for "shelf registration." As illustrated in Figure 8–5, **shelf registration** allows firms that plan to offer multiple issues of stock over a two-year period to submit one registration statement as described above (called a master registration statement). The registration statement summarizes the firm's financing plans for the two-year period. Thus, the securities are shelved for up to two years until the firm is ready to issue them. Once the issuer and its investment bank decide to issue shares during the two-year shelf registration period, they prepare and file a short form statement with the SEC. Upon SEC approval, the shares can be priced and offered to the public usually within one or two days of deciding to take the shares "off the shelf."

**www.sec.gov**

**shelf registration**

*Allows firms that plan to offer multiple issues of stock over a two-year period to submit one registration statement summarizing the firm's financing plans for the period.*

**Figure 8–5**    Getting Shelf Registrations to the Investing Public

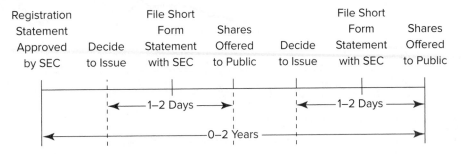

Thus, shelf registration allows firms to get stocks into the market quickly (e.g., in one or two days) if they feel conditions (especially the price they can get for the new stock) are right, without the time lag generally associated with full SEC registration. For example, in June 2016, Tonix Pharmaceuticals Corp. announced a public offering of up to $10 million worth of shares of its common stock under its shelf registration filed with the SEC in August 2014.

**LG 8-4**

### Secondary Stock Markets

**secondary stock markets**

*The markets in which stocks, once issued, are traded (i.e., rebought and resold).*

**Secondary stock markets** are the markets in which stocks, once issued, are traded—that is, bought and sold by investors. The New York Stock Exchange (NYSE) and the National Association of Securities Dealers Automated Quotation (NASDAQ) system are well-known examples of secondary markets in stocks. When a transaction occurs in a secondary stock market, funds are exchanged, usually with the help of a securities broker or firm acting as an intermediary between the buyer and the seller of the stock. The original issuer of the stock is not involved in this transfer of stocks or funds. In this section, we look at the major secondary stock markets, the process by which a trade occurs, and the major stock market indexes.

**www.nyse.com**

**Stock Exchanges.**    The two major U.S. stock markets are the New York Stock Exchange Euronext (NYSE Euronext) and the National Association of Securities Dealers Automated Quotation (NASDAQ) system. Prior to its acquisition by the NYSE in 2008, the American Stock Exchange (AMEX) was a third major stock exchange. Figures 8–6 and 8–7 present data comparing the three stock markets. Figure 8–6 shows dollar volume of trading in each market from 1979 through 2016; Figure 8–7 shows the number of companies listed in each market from 1975 through 2016. Obvious from these trading volume and listing figures is that, while historically the NYSE was the premier stock market, the NASDAQ has become a strong second market. Other smaller stock exchanges include the Chicago Stock Exchange, the Philadelphia Stock Exchange (also called the NASDAQ OMX PHLX), and the Boston Stock Exchange (now the NASDAQ OMX BX). These account for no more than 5 percent of daily U.S. stock market volume.

**www.nasdaq.com**

**The New York Stock Exchange.**    Worldwide, the New York Stock Exchange Euronext (NYSE Euronext) is the most well known of all the organized exchanges. The exchange was created by the merger of NYSE Group, Inc. and Euronext N.V. (which was created from the mergers of the Paris Bourse, the Brussels Exchange, and the Amsterdam Exchange in 2000) on April 4, 2007. NYSE Euronext, which merged six cash equities exchanges in five

**Figure 8–6**    Dollar Volume of Trading on the NYSE, AMEX,* and NASDAQ

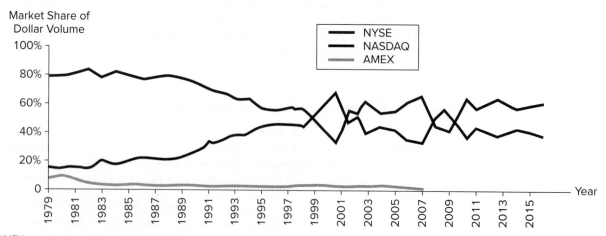

*AMEX was purchased by the NYSE in 2008.
**Source:** World Federation of Exchanges website. www.world-exchanges.org

**Figure 8–7**   Number of Companies Listed on the NYSE, AMEX,* and NASDAQ

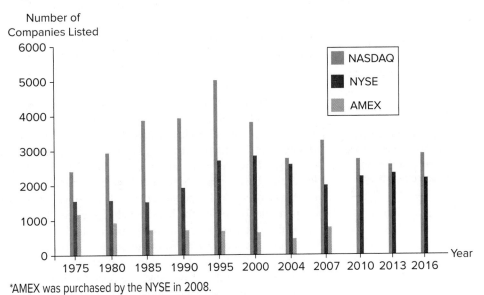

*AMEX was purchased by the NYSE in 2008.
**Source:** World Federation of Exchanges website. www.world-exchanges.org

countries and six derivatives exchanges, is the world leader for listings, trading in cash equities, equity and interest rate derivatives, bonds, and the distribution of market data. The merger was the largest of its kind and the first to create a truly global stock market. Prior to this merger, in May 2006 the NYSE went public, allowing shares of the world's largest stock exchange to trade for the first time. The offering followed the NYSE's merger with publicly traded electronic exchange operator Archipelago Holdings. NYSE Euronext operates four equity markets in the United States: NYSE, NYSE Arca, NYSE MKT, and ArcaEdge. The NYSE (the largest and most well known of the four) and the NYSE Arca markets are both registered securities exchanges for the listing and trading of equities, fixed-income products (primarily corporate bonds), and structured products such as electronically traded funds (ETFs). The American Stock Exchange was renamed NYSE Amex after its acquisition and then NYSE MKT in 2012. This market focuses on the listing and trading of smaller companies. Finally, ArcaEdge trades include over-the-counter (OTC) and pink sheet stocks (stocks that trade very inactively because of their low price or limited geographic interest). Over 2,350 different stocks are listed and traded on the NYSE Euronext. The daily average dollar volume of trading in 2016 was $46 billion on over 59 billion shares traded.

As discussed in Chapter 5, as a result of the LIBOR scandal, in July 2013 the British government announced that LIBOR would be sold to NYSE Euronext. Since its inception in the 1980s, LIBOR was managed by the British Bankers' Association (a London-based trade group whose members are some of the world's biggest banks). While ownership of LIBOR would be based in the United States, responsibility for regulating it would remain in the United Kingdom. Also in 2013, the European Commission gave unconditional approval to IntercontinentalExchange (ICE) to buy NYSE Euronext for $8.2 billion. This followed votes by stockholders of both organizations approving the sale. ICE, a leader in the development of electronic trading, announced that it would operate dual headquarters in Atlanta and New York, stressed that it has no current plans to shut down the NYSE's famous trading floor, and said that it would keep the NYSE Euronext name and continue to operate the company's trading floor at the corner of Wall and Broad Streets in Lower Manhattan. The combined ICE-NYSE Euronext would is the third-largest exchange group globally, behind Hong Kong Exchanges and Clearing and the CME Group.

LG 8-5

**trading post**

*A specific place on the floor of the exchange where transactions on the NYSE occur.*

**specialists**

*Exchange members who have an obligation to keep the market going, maintaining liquidity in their assigned stock at all times.*

*The Trading Process.*     All transactions occurring on the NYSE occur at a specific place on the floor of the exchange (called a **trading post**)—see Figure 8–8. Each stock is assigned a special market maker (a **specialist**). The market maker is like a monopolist with the power to arrange the market for the stock. In return, the specialist has an affirmative obligation to stabilize the order flow and prices for the stock in times when the market becomes turbulent (e.g., when there is a large imbalance of sell orders, the specialist has an obligation to buy the stock to stabilize the price).

Because of the large amount of capital needed to serve the market-making function, specialists often organize themselves as firms (e.g., Dermott W. Clancy, Spear, Leeds, and Kellogg Specialists, Inc.). Specialist firms on the NYSE range in size from 2 to over 20 members. Specialist firms may be designated to serve as the market maker for more than one stock. However, only one specialist is assigned to each stock listed on the exchange. In general, because specialists are obligated to establish the fair market price of a stock and must even occasionally step in and stabilize a stock's price, underwriters/investment banks (responsible for getting the best available price for their customers' new issues) are rarely allowed by the Exchange to become specialists.

Three types of transactions can occur at a given post: (1) brokers trade on behalf of customers at the "market" price (market order), (2) limit orders are left with a specialist to be executed, and (3) specialists transact for their own account. These types of trades are discussed in more detail below. As of December 2005, trading licenses are needed to make trades on the floor of the New York Stock Exchange. These trading licenses are made available by means of a Dutch auction through a process called the Stock Exchange Auction Trading System (SEATS). Only a member organization of NYSE is eligible to bid for one of the 1,400 available trading licenses. Each trading license entitles its member organization holder to have physical and electronic access to the trading facilities of the NYSE market. Trading licenses are sold at an auction and are good for one calendar year only.

Generally, as illustrated in Figure 8–9, when individuals want to transact (e.g., purchase) on the NYSE, they contact their broker (such as Wells Fargo Securities). The broker then sends the order to its representative at the exchange (called a commission broker) or to a floor broker (working for themselves) to conduct the trade with the appropriate designated market maker (DMM) in the stock (e.g., Citadel Securities, LLC). Large brokerage firms generally own several "trading licenses" on the floor filled by their commission brokers trading orders for the firm's clients or its own accounts. One of the DMM's jobs is to execute orders for floor and commission brokers. However, these brokers can transact at a post with others without DMM participation. DMMs participate in only about 10 percent of all shares

**Figure 8–8**   **New York Stock Exchange Trading Post**

A: Post information display
B: Flat-panel display screen
C: Point-of-sale workstation
D: Broker
E: Broker
F: Designated market maker (DMM)
G: DMM trading assistant

A Typical Trading Post

**Source:** The New York Stock Exchange website, April 2016. www.nyse.com

**Figure 8–9** Purchase of a Stock on the NYSE

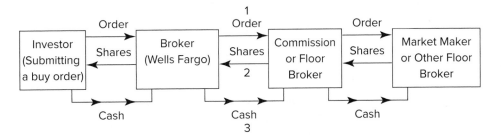

traded. Also, orders are increasingly coming from the public using online (Internet) trading, bypassing the commission broker and going directly to the floor broker (see Chapter 16). Once the transaction is completed (generally in less than 15 minutes), the investor's broker is contacted and the trade is confirmed. Generally, the transaction is settled in three days (so-called settlement at T + 3)—that is, the investor has three days to pay for the stock and the floor or commission broker has three days to deliver the stock to the investor's broker.

The vast majority of orders sent to floor or commission brokers are of two types: market orders or limit orders. A **market order** is an order for the broker and the DMM to transact at the best price available when the order reaches the post. The floor or commission broker will go to the post and conduct the trade. Before 2005, the best price meant that brokers were required to enter only their very best bid and offer prices for a stock at a specified time into a public electronic database of stock quotes. In 2004, the SEC proposed an overhaul of the rules that radically altered the way the best price would be established: Brokers seeking the best price on a trade would have to enter all their bids and offers for a stock into the public database. This would enable other brokers who wanted to fill orders, including large block trades, to "sweep" all markets for the best price and to simultaneously execute trades in the same stock across different markets. The so-called intermarket sweep would allow brokers to pick off the best prices among all accessible quotes. So a customer (like an individual investor) who wants to buy shares of stock could get chunks of that order filled at the best price across various markets. The change introduces more computerization into the trading process and reduces the amount of NYSE trading conducted via the auction system overseen by specialist firms.

A **limit order** is an order to transact only at a specified price (the limit price). When a floor or commission broker receives a limit order, he or she will stand by the post with the order if the current price is near the limit price. When the current price is not near the limit price, a floor or commission broker does not want to stand at the post for hours (and even days) waiting for the current price to equal the limit price on this single limit order. In this case, the floor broker enters the limit order on the **order book** of the DMM at the post. The DMM, who is at the post at all times when the market is open, will monitor the current price of the stock and conduct the trade when, and if, it equals the limit price. Some limit orders are submitted with time limits. If the order is not filled by the time date for expiration, it is deleted from the market maker's book.[2] The third type of trade is that of a DMM trading for his or her own account.

Figure 8–10 illustrates the link between a market order and a limit order. When a market order is placed, the transaction occurs at the current market price, $97.75 per share, determined by the intersection of investors' aggregate supply (S) of and demand (D) for the stock. If the limit order price (e.g., $97.625 per share) differs from the current market price, the order is placed on the DMM's book. If supply and/or demand conditions change (e.g., the demand curve in Figure 8–10 falls to D') such that the market price falls to $97.625 per share, the DMM completes the limit order and notifies the floor broker who submitted the order.[3]

**market order**

*An order to transact at the best price available when the order reaches the post.*

**limit order**

*An order to transact at a specified price.*

**order book**

*A DMM's record of unexecuted limit orders.*

---

2. Similar to a limit order, a stop order is an order to sell a stock when its price falls to a particular point.

3. Many other types of orders may be made as well. A complete list of order types available on the NYSE can be found at the NYSE website, www.nyse.com.

**Figure 8–10**    **Price on a Market Order versus a Limit Order**

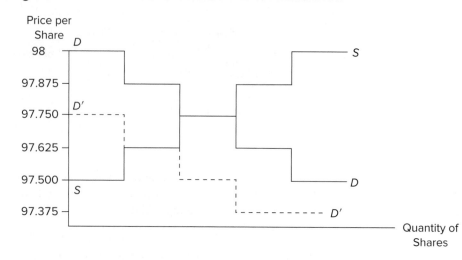

*Program Trading.*    The NYSE has defined *program trading* as the simultaneous buying and selling of a portfolio of at least 15 different stocks valued at more than $1 million, using computer programs to initiate the trades. For example, program trading can be used to create portfolio insurance. A program trader can take a long position in a portfolio of stocks and a short position in a stock index futures contract (see Chapter 10). Should the market value of the stock portfolio fall, these losses are partly offset by the position in the futures contract. The timing of these trades is determined by the computer program.

Program trading has been criticized for its impact on stock market prices and increased volatility. For example, on May 6, 2010, the financial markets experienced a brief but severe drop in prices, falling 998 points (more than 5 percent) in a matter of minutes, only to recover a short time later. The original focus was that computer trading, coupled with the market's complex trading systems, triggered the free fall that appeared to have begun with an order to sell a single stock, Procter & Gamble. A few days later, the fall was attributed to a $7.5 million hedge fund trade placed for 50,000 option contracts in the Chicago options trading pits. Another potential culprit was a so-called fat finger error, when a Citigroup trader accidentally entered a sell billion-sized trade when he or she meant to enter a million-sized trade. Regulators eventually found no evidence that the fall was caused by erroneous (fat finger) orders, computer hacking, or terrorist activity. Rather, the "flash crash" was attributed to trading by a little-known mutual fund—Asset Strategy Fund—located in Kansas City. A fund trader triggered the fall with the sale of $4.1 billion of futures contracts linked to the S&P 500 Index. The trader used a computer algorithm that tied the sale to the market's overall volume. Trading volume soared on May 6 and the sell order was executed. While similar trades had taken several hours to execute, this trade was executed in 20 minutes. Regardless of how this historic drop started, it was exacerbated by computer trading. The initial trade triggered a pyramiding effect from computerized trading programs designed to sell when the market moves lower.

As a result of the potential for increased volatility created by program trading, the New York Stock Exchange introduced trading curbs (or circuit breakers) on trading. Circuit breakers are limitations placed on trading when the Dow Jones Industrial Average (DJIA) falls significantly. Circuit breakers are an imposed halt in trading that gives buyers and sellers time to assimilate incoming information and make investment choices. Circuit breakers promote investor confidence by giving investors time to make informed choices during periods of high market volatility. For example, the circuit breakers for the third quarter of 2016 are shown in Figure 8–11.

Also as a result of the flash crash, circuit breakers, termed in this case *limit up–limit down* (LULD) rules, were instituted for individual stocks. Figure 8–12 shows the rules put

**Figure 8–11**    Circuit-Breaker Levels for the Third Quarter of 2016

In the event of a 7 percent decline in the S&P:

Before 3:25 p.m.          After 3:25 p.m.
15–MIN. HALT              NO HALT

In the event of a 13 percent decline in the S&P.

Before 3:25 p.m.          After 3:25 p.m.
15–MIN. HALT              NO HALT

In the event of a 20 percent decline in the S&P, regardless of the time MARKET CLOSES for the day.

**Source:** New York Stock Exchange Euronext website. www.nyse.com

**Figure 8–12**    Limit Up–Limit Down Structure in Place in 2016

| Reference Price | Percentage Parameter |
|---|---|
| Tier I securities — S&P 500 and Russell 1000 stocks, and selected ETPs | |
| < $0.75, | Lesser of $0.15 and 75% |
| ≥ $0.75 and ≤ $3.00, | 20% |
| > $3.00 | 5% |
| Tier II securities — all other stocks | |
| < $0.75, | Lesser of $0.15 and 75% |
| ≥ $0.75 and ≤ $3.00, | 20% |
| > $3.00 | 10% |

in place in 2016. Phase I began in April 2013 for Tier I stocks (S&P 500, Russell 1000 stocks, and selected exchange-traded products), while phase II began in August 2013 for Tier II stocks (all other stocks). The LULD band structure is based on percentages away from a "reference price." Specifically, trading is halted (put in a "limit state") if the stock price moves outside the price band, as follows:

Price band = (Reference price) ± [(Reference price) × (Percentage parameter)]

The reference price is the mean price of reported transactions over the past 5 minutes. If no trades have occurred in the previous 5 minutes, the previous reference price will remain. The first reference price of the day is set as the opening price on the stock's primary listing exchange. When a stock is outside the applicable LULD band, trading is halted for 15 seconds. For example, an S&P 500 stock with a reference price of $5.00 would see trading halted if its price moved outside a range of $4.75—$5.25 ($5.00 ± 0.05 × $5.00).

Trading may begin after the halt if the entire size of all limit state quotations is executed or canceled within 15 seconds of entering the limit state. If the market does not exit the limit state within 15 seconds, then the primary listing market for the security will declare a 5 minute trading pause. During a trading pause, no trades in the security can be executed, but all bids and offers may be displayed. Percentage parameters are doubled during the first 15 and last 25 minutes of trading.

In the late 1980s, about 15 million shares were traded per day on the NYSE as program trades. In 2016, almost 20 percent of the average daily volume involved program trading. The most active program traders are investment banks (e.g., Morgan Stanley, Barclays Capital) conducting trades for their own accounts or those of their customers (e.g., insurance companies, hedge funds, pension funds). Much of this program trading involves index funds (e.g., Vanguard's 500 Index Fund, which seeks to replicate the S&P 500 Index—see below) and futures contracts on various indexes (e.g., S&P 500 Index futures—see Chapter 10). Investment in these index funds grew in the 1980s through the 2000s as a result of the relatively poor performance (in terms of returns) of specialized mutual funds (see Chapter 17) and the strong performance in the major indexes.

*Controversial Trading Practices.*    With the advent of powerful, high-speed computers and with traders' search for ever-increasing ways to trade, some controversial trading practices have arisen.

**flash trading**

*For a fee, traders are allowed to see incoming buy or sell orders milliseconds earlier than general market traders.*

**Flash trading** is a controversial practice in which, for a fee, traders are allowed to see incoming buy or sell orders milliseconds earlier than general market traders. With this very slight advance notice of market orders, these traders can conduct rapid statistical analysis (with the help of powerful computers) and carry out high-frequency trading (trades involving very short holding periods) ahead of the public market. Exchanges claim that the flash trading benefits all traders by creating more market liquidity and the opportunity for price improvement. Critics contend that flash trading creates a market in which certain traders can unfairly exploit others. The Wall Street Reform and Consumer Protection Act of 2010 gave the Commodity Futures Trading Commission (CFTC) expanded powers to investigate and prosecute disruptive trading practices, including those by high-speed flash traders. For example, in 2013 the CFTC investigated whether high-frequency traders are routinely distorting stock and futures markets by illegally acting as buyer and seller in the same transactions. Such transactions, known as *wash trades,* are banned by U.S. law because they can feed false information into the market and be used to manipulate prices. CFTC examiners have found that several hundred thousand potential wash trades occur daily on futures exchanges. Regulators are also requiring exchanges to improve their oversight of high-speed trading in the wake of computer-driven glitches in 2012, including the case of Knight Capital Group, which incurred losses of more than $450 million when a high-speed trading algorithm malfunctioned.

**naked access**

*Allows some traders to rapidly buy and sell stocks directly on exchanges using a broker's computer code without exchanges or regulators always knowing who is making the trades.*

**Naked access** trading allows some traders and others to rapidly buy and sell stocks directly on exchanges using a broker's computer code without exchanges or regulators always knowing who is making the trades. The firms, usually high-frequency traders, are then able to shave microseconds from the time it takes to trade. A report says that 38 percent of all U.S. stock trading is now done by firms that have "naked sponsored access" to markets. The SEC, fearing that a firm trading anonymously in this way could trigger destabilizing losses and threaten market stability if its rapid-fire trades go awry, banned naked access trading in late 2010.

**dark pools of liquidity**

*Trading networks that provide liquidity but that do not display trades on order books.*

**Dark pools of liquidity** are trading networks (e.g., crossing networks[4]) that provide liquidity but that do not display trades on order books. This is useful for traders such as institutional traders who wish to buy and sell large numbers of shares without revealing their trades to the overall market. Dark pool trading offers institutional investors many of

---

4. A *crossing network* is an alternative trading system (ATS) that anonymously matches buy and sell orders electronically for execution. The order is either anonymously placed into a black box or flagged to other participants of the crossing network.

the efficiencies associated with trading on the NYSE or NASDAQ, but it does not require that they show their transactions to others. Dark pool trades are recorded to a national database. However, they are recorded as over-the-counter transactions. Thus, detailed information about the volume and type of transaction is left to the trading network to report to its clients if they so desire. In 2016, nearly 42 percent of daily stock trading was processed through dark pools, up from 3 percent in 2008. Dark pool trading has been criticized as unfair. With dark pool trading, traders who use trading strategies based on liquidity do not have access to all trading information.

As a result of these unfair advantages and the new powers given to regulators (through the Wall Street Reform and Consumer Protection Act), in 2013 the SEC approved a plan for new rules requiring dark pools to disclose and detail trading activity on their platforms. Specifically, the SEC called for dark pools and other alternative trading systems to provide more information on how they work. The new rules require such systems to file detailed information about their operations including trading by broker dealer operators on the ATS, which could pose conflicts of interest. What regulators have focused on are the promises the dark pool operators have made to customers about how their orders are being handled and whether high-speed trading firms have the opportunity to trade against those orders. For example, in January 2016 the SEC announced that Barclays Capital and Credit Suisse Securities agreed to settle separate cases finding that they violated federal securities laws while operating dark pools. Barclays agreed to settle the charges by admitting wrongdoing and paying $35 million penalties to the SEC and the New York Attorney General (NYAG) for a total of $70 million. Credit Suisse agreed to settle the charges by paying a $30 million penalty to the SEC, a $30 million penalty to the NYAG, and $24.3 million in disgorgement and prejudgment interest to the SEC for a total of $84.3 million.

*Stock Market Quote.*   Table 8–1 presents a small part of a NYSE stock quote list from *The Wall Street Journal Online* summarizing trading on July 7, 2016. Column 1 lists the name of the corporation and Column 2 its ticker symbol (e.g., Aaron's, Inc. and AAN, respectively). When trades are recorded on a stock, the ticker symbol is used rather than the company name. Columns 3 through 6 of the stock quote list the open, high, low, and closing price, respectively, on the stock for trading on July 7, 2016. Column 7, Net Chg, is the dollar change in the closing price from the previous day's closing price [e.g., Aaron's, Inc. closed at $22.84 ($22.70 + $0.14) on July 6, 2016]. Column 8 lists the change from the previous day's close in percentage terms (e.g., −0.14/22.84 = −0.61 percent). Column 9, Vol, lists the day's trading volume (e.g., 667,029 shares of Aaron's, Inc. traded on July 7, 2016). Columns 10 and 11, 52 Week High and 52 Week Low, show the high and low closing prices on the listed stocks over the previous (from July 7, 2016) 52 weeks. Column 12, Div, is the annual dividend per share based on the most recent dividend payment (e.g., Aaron's,

**TABLE 8–1   Stock Market Quote, July 7, 2016**

| (1)<br>Name | (2)<br>Symbol | (3)<br>Open | (4)<br>High | (5)<br>Low | (6)<br>Close | (7)<br>Net<br>Chg | (8)<br>%Chg | (9)<br>Volume | (10)<br>52 Week<br>High | (11)<br>52 Week<br>Low | (12)<br>Div | (13)<br>Yield | (14)<br>P/E | (15)<br>YTD<br>%Chg |
|---|---|---|---|---|---|---|---|---|---|---|---|---|---|---|
| AAR Corp. | AIR | 22.98 | 23.15 | 22.50 | 22.72 | −0.15 | −0.66 | 79,163 | 32.76 | 18.36 | 0.30 | 1.32 | 16.20 | −13.58 |
| Aaron's Inc. | **AAN** | **22.86** | **23.21** | **22.55** | **22.70** | **−0.14** | **−0.61** | **667,029** | **40.80** | **20.24** | **0.10** | **0.44** | **12.14** | **1.38** |
| Abbott Laboratories | ABT | 40.83 | 41.57 | 40.80 | 41.36 | 0.53 | 1.30 | 17,396,628 | 51.74 | 36.00 | 1.04 | 2.51 | 25.73 | −7.90 |
| Abercrombie & Fitch | ANF | 18.08 | 18.39 | 18.05 | 18.22 | 0.13 | 0.72 | 1,878,642 | 32.83 | 15.42 | 0.80 | 4.39 | 21.44 | −32.52 |
| ACCO Brands | ACCO | 10.27 | 10.45 | 10.16 | 10.20 | −0.06 | −0.58 | 425,836 | 10.75 | 5.47 | ... | ... | 11.59 | 43.06 |
| E.I. DuPont de Nemours | DD | 61.91 | 62.85 | 61.75 | 61.92 | 0.07 | 0.11 | 3,394,283 | 75.72 | 47.11 | ... | ... | 25.91 | −7.03 |
| Eli Lilly | LLY | 79.83 | 80.05 | 78.64 | 79.32 | −0.70 | −0.87 | 3,481,348 | 92.85 | 67.88 | 2.04 | 2.57 | 36.85 | −5.86 |
| El Paso Electric | EE | 47.50 | 47.50 | 46.38 | 46.46 | −1.09 | −2.29 | 180,068 | 48.05 | 33.90 | 1.24 | 2.67 | 25.81 | 20.68 |
| McDonald's | MCD | 120.89 | 121.24 | 120.41 | 120.92 | 0.29 | 0.24 | 3,549,634 | 131.96 | 87.50 | 3.56 | 2.94 | 23.25 | 2.35 |
| McKesson | MCK | 191.88 | 193.60 | 190.08 | 191.20 | −0.68 | −0.35 | 1,233,179 | 236.86 | 148.29 | 1.12 | 0.59 | 19.73 | −3.06 |
| Merck & Co | MRK | 58.89 | 59.02 | 58.29 | 58.78 | −0.38 | −0.64 | 8,973,018 | 60.07 | 45.69 | 1.84 | 3.13 | 36.06 | 11.28 |
| Waste Management | WM | 67.30 | 67.63 | 66.88 | 67.29 | 0.08 | 0.12 | 1,503,043 | 70.50 | 47.07 | 1.64 | 2.44 | 26.60 | 26.08 |
| Webster Financial | WBS | 32.88 | 33.67 | 32.88 | 33.43 | 0.55 | 1.67 | 743,866 | 40.72 | 30.09 | 1.00 | 2.99 | 15.55 | −10.11 |
| Weight Watchers International | WTW | 11.50 | 11.86 | 11.36 | 11.50 | −0.02 | −0.17 | 864,155 | 28.05 | 3.75 | ... | ... | 22.12 | −49.56 |
| Wells Fargo | WFC | 46.58 | 47.22 | 46.44 | 46.80 | 0.15 | 0.32 | 17,523,922 | 58.77 | 44.50 | 1.52 | 3.25 | 11.41 | −13.91 |

**Source:** *The Wall Street Journal Online,* July 8, 2016. www.wsj.com

Inc. paid dividends of $0.10 per share on its common stock in 2016). Column 13, Yield, is the dividend yield on the stock [equal to the annual dividends per year divided by the closing stock price (e.g., for Aaron's, Inc. $0.10/22.70 = 0.44$ percent). Column 14 is the firm's P/E ratio—the ratio of the company's closing price to earnings per share over the previous year (e.g., Aaron's, Inc.'s P/E ratio is reported to be 12.14; Aaron's price—the numerator of the P/E ratio—is reported as $22.70; thus, Aaron's earnings per share—the denominator of the P/E ratio—over the period July 2015 through July 2016 must have been $1.87 per share: $E = P \div P/E = \$22.70/12.14$. The P/E ratio is used by traders as an indicator of the relative value of the stock. Looking at the inverse of the P/E ratio (E/P), traders can estimate the number of years (based on the firm's current earnings) that it will take to recoup their investment in the stock (the payback period). High P/E ratio stocks reflect the market's expectation of growth in earnings. Should earnings expectations fail to materialize, these stocks will see a price drop. Low P/E ratio stocks generally have low earnings growth expectations. Finally, Column 15 reports the year-to-date percentage change in the stock price (e.g., Aaron's, Inc.'s stock price of $22.70 at the close of trading on July 7, 2016, was 1.38 percent higher than the closing price on July 7, 2015).

**LG 8-4**

www.nasdaq.com

**The NASDAQ and OTC Market.**   Securities not sold on one of the organized exchanges such as the NYSE Euronext are traded over the counter (OTC). Unlike the centralized NYSE Euronext exchanges, the over-the-counter markets do not have a physical trading floor. Rather, transactions are completed via an electronic market. The NASDAQ (National Association of Securities Dealers Automated Quotation) market, owned by the NASDAQ OMX Group, Inc., was the world's first electronic stock market. The NASDAQ system provides continuous trading for the most active stocks traded over the counter. Indeed, as seen in Figures 8–6 and 8–7, the NASDAQ currently has more firms listed than the NYSE. Further, during the tech boom in the late 1990s, the dollar volume of trading on the NASDAQ exceeded that on the NYSE. As the tech boom crashed in the early 2000s, however, the NYSE again saw the greatest dollar and share volume of trading. In 2008–2009, during the financial crisis, the dollar value of trading on the NASDAQ again exceeded that on the NYSE. Trading totaled $33.10 trillion on the NASDAQ and $30.92 trillion on the NYSE in 2008 and (hurt by the financial crisis) $28.95 trillion on the NASDAQ and $17.78 trillion on the NYSE in 2009. However as markets recovered, the NASDAQ fell back to trading levels below that of the NYSE. Through May 2016, trading totaled $4.92 trillion on the NASDAQ and $7.43 trillion on the NYSE.

The NASDAQ market is primarily a dealer market, in which dealers are the market makers who stand ready to buy or sell particular securities. Unlike the NYSE, many dealers, in some cases more than 20, will make a market for a single stock—that is, quote a bid (buy) and ask (sell) price. There are no limits on the number of stocks a NASDAQ market maker can trade or on the number of market makers in a particular stock. A NASDAQ broker or dealer may also be a member of an organized exchange (e.g., the NYSE). Moreover, the original underwriter of a new issue can also become the dealer in the secondary market—unlike the NYSE, which seeks a separation between underwriters and dealers. Anyone who meets the fairly low capital requirements for market makers on the NASDAQ can register to be a broker-dealer.

An individual wanting to make a trade contacts his or her broker. The broker then contacts a dealer in the particular security to conduct the transaction. In contrast to the NYSE, the NASDAQ structure of dealers and brokers results in the NASDAQ being a negotiated market (e.g., quotes from several dealers are usually obtained before a transaction is made). When a request for a trade is received, a dealer will use the NASDAQ electronic communications network (ECN) to find the dealers providing the inside quotes—the lowest ask and the highest bid. The dealer may also request the quotes of every market maker in the stock. The dealer initiating the trade will then contact the dealer offering the best price and execute the order. The dealer will confirm the transaction with the investor's broker and the customer will be charged that quote plus a commission for the broker's services. Like exchange trading, online (Internet) trading services now allow investors to trade directly with a securities dealer without going through a personal broker.

Because of a lack of liquidity in the NASDAQ market after the 1987 market crash and the negative impact this had on the ability of small traders to transact in this market, NASDAQ implemented a mandatory system, the Small Order Execution System (SOES), to provide automatic order execution for individual traders with orders of less than or equal to 1,000 shares. Market makers must accept SOES orders, which means small investors and traders are provided with excellent liquidity. The SOES allows small investors and traders to compete on a level playing field for access to NASDAQ orders and execution.

**penny stocks**

*Stocks that trade for less than $5 per share.*

For very small firms, NASDAQ maintains an electronic "OTC bulletin board," which is not part of the NASDAQ market but is a means for brokers and dealers to get and post current price quotes over a computer network. These smaller firms are mainly **penny stocks,** which are stocks traded for less than $5 per share[5] and generally issued by high-risk firms with short or erratic histories of revenues and earnings. Roughly 30,000 stocks trade on this OTC market. However, this market is not a formal exchange. There are no membership requirements for trading or listing requirements for securities. Thousands of brokers register with the SEC as dealers in these OTC securities, quoting prices at which they are willing to buy or sell securities. A broker executes a trade by contacting a dealer listing an attractive quote. The smallest stocks are listed on "pink sheets" distributed through the National Association of Securities Dealers. These OTC quotations of stock are recorded manually and published daily on pink sheets by which dealers communicate their interest in trading at various prices.

**Choice of Market Listing.**    Firms listed with the NYSE Euronext market must meet the listing requirements of the exchange. The requirements are extensive and can be found at the websites of the exchanges. The basic qualifications are based on such characteristics as firm market value, earnings, total assets, number of shares outstanding, number of shareholders, and trading volume. There are several reasons that NYSE listing is attractive to a firm: improved marketability of the firm's stock (making it more valuable); publicity for the firm, which could result in increased sales; and improved access to the financial markets, as firms find it easier to bring new issues of listed stock to the market. A NYSE-listed firm may also have its securities listed on regional exchanges.

Firms that do not meet the requirements for NYSE Euronext exchange listings trade on the NASDAQ. Thus, most NASDAQ firms are smaller, of regional interest, or unable to meet the listing requirements of the organized exchanges. Many NASDAQ companies are newly registered public issues with only a brief history of trading. Over time, many of these apply for NYSE listing. Not all companies eligible to be listed on the NYSE actually do so. Some companies—for example, Microsoft—believe that the benefits of exchange listing (improved marketability, publicity) are not significant. Others prefer not to release the financial information required by the exchanges for listing.

**Electronic Communications Networks and Online Trading.**    The major stock markets currently open at 9:30 a.m. eastern time and close at 4:00 p.m. eastern time. Extended-hours trading involves any securities transaction that occurs outside these regular trading hours. Almost all extended-hours trading is processed through computerized alternative trading systems (ATSs), also known as electronic communications networks (ECNs) such as NYSE Arca (owned by the NYSE Euronext) and Instinet (owned by NASDAQ). Newer ECNs include BATS (Better Alternative Trading System, founded in Kansas in June 2005, which is now the third-largest exchange in the world, based on volume, behind the NYSE and the NASDAQ) and IEX Group Inc. (which won SEC approval as the United States' 13th national stock exchange in June 2016 and which is the first new stock exchange that uses a "speed bump" that slows the speed of trading by 350 millionths of a second; a delay is just long enough to protect investors from predatory high-speed trading that can front-run the orders of slower investors). ECNs are computerized systems that automatically

www.instinet.com

www.batstrading.com

www.iextrading.com

---

5. This is the formal SEC value assigned to a penny stock. Many investors refer to penny stocks as those that trade at less than $1 per share.

match orders between buyers and sellers and serve as an alternative to traditional market making and floor trading. They are also the major vehicles for extended-hours trading. ECNs account for approximately one-third of all transactions and almost all extended-hours trading.

As a result of the increased availability of computer technology to individual as well as professional traders in the 1990s, online stock trading via the Internet became one of the biggest growth areas for financial services firms in the late 1990s and into the 2000s. For example, the number of people living in U.S. households that used an online investing/stock trading service within the last 12 months increased from 3 million in 1997 to over 14 million in 2015. Online trading is an area of stock trading that is not likely to go away. The Internet will continue to produce opportunities for investors to communicate with their financial advisors and enact trades without incurring the cost of an office visit. For example, the top-level accounts offered by E*Trade now enable customers to view all of their E*Trade accounts. A client with multiple brokerage accounts as well as bank accounts can view balances for all of these accounts. Customers can also see, in real time, the value of each account, the total value of all accounts together, and how account values have changed. However, with increased trading via high-speed flash trading, naked access, and dark pool trading, the ability for individual traders to "beat the market," even when executing trades via the Internet, is becoming increasingly difficult.

**LG 8-6**

## Stock Market Indexes

www.dowjones.com

www.nyse.com

www.standardandpoors.com

A stock market index is the composite value of a group of secondary market–traded stocks. Movements in a stock market index provide investors with information on movements of a broader range of secondary market securities. Table 8–2 shows a listing of some major stock market indexes as of July 7, 2016. Figure 8–13 shows the trends in some of these indexes (the Dow Jones Industrial Average [DJIA], the NYSE Composite Index, the S&P Composite Index, the NASDAQ Composite Index, and the Wilshire 5000 Index) from 1989 through 2016. Notice that movements in these indexes are highly correlated over the 27-year period. Indeed, notice that after a 6-year period of unprecedented growth (1995–2000) for all of these indexes, the early 2000s and the downturn in the U.S. economy produced little growth of these indexes. As the U.S. economy picked up through the first

**TABLE 8-2**   Major Stock Market Indexes

**Thursday, July 7, 2016**

| | DAILY | | | | | YTD | 52 WEEK | | % | 3-yr |
| Index | High | Low | Close | Chg | % Chg | % Chg | High | Low | Chg | % Chg* |
|---|---|---|---|---|---|---|---|---|---|---|
| **Dow Jones** | | | | | | | | | | |
| Industrial Average | 17984.95 | 17816.65 | 17895.88 | −22.74 | −0.13 | 2.7 | 18120.25 | 15660.18 | 2.0 | 5.7 |
| Transportation Average | 7550.30 | 7458.39 | 7492.56 | 34.53 | 0.46 | −0.2 | 8437.15 | 6625.53 | −7.0 | 6.0 |
| Utility Average | 722.07 | 708.41 | 710.20 | −13.31 | −1.84 | 22.9 | 723.51 | 541.97 | 25.1 | 14.2 |
| **Nasdaq Stock Market** | | | | | | | | | | |
| Composite | 4889.01 | 4853.68 | 4876.81 | 17.65 | 0.36 | −2.6 | 5218.86 | 4266.84 | −0.9 | 11.9 |
| Nasdaq 100 | 4468.31 | 4438.80 | 4459.58 | 14.88 | 0.33 | −2.9 | 4719.05 | 3947.80 | 2.5 | 14.6 |
| **Standard & Poor's** | | | | | | | | | | |
| 500 Index | 2109.08 | 2089.39 | 2097.90 | −1.83 | −0.09 | 2.6 | 2128.28 | 1829.08 | 2.3 | 8.7 |
| MidCap 400 | 1502.10 | 1487.03 | 1492.60 | 2.58 | 0.17 | 6.7 | 1525.14 | 1238.82 | 0.3 | 8.0 |
| SmallCap 600 | 710.08 | 701.96 | 705.56 | 1.25 | 0.18 | 5.0 | 728.07 | 588.26 | −0.5 | 7.5 |
| **New York Stock Exchange** | | | | | | | | | | |
| Composite | 10495.27 | 10373.47 | 10413.97 | −27.61 | −0.26 | 2.7 | 11024.87 | 9029.88 | −2.6 | 4.2 |
| **Other U.S Indexes** | | | | | | | | | | |
| Russell 2000 | 1156.89 | 1143.42 | 1149.76 | 2.42 | 0.21 | 1.2 | 1273.33 | 953.72 | −6.8 | 4.6 |
| PHLX Gold/Silver† | 105.82 | 103.21 | 103.84 | −3.02 | −2.82 | 129.2 | 106.86 | 38.84 | 74.0 | 6.3 |
| CBOE Volatility | 15.98 | 14.33 | 14.76 | −0.20 | −1.34 | −18.9 | 40.74 | 11.95 | −26.1 | −0.3 |
| Value Line | 460.64 | 455.24 | 457.10 | 0.62 | 0.14 | 2.5 | 504.10 | 383.82 | −7.0 | 2.2 |

*Three-year returns are annualized.

†Philadelphia Stock Exchange.

**Source:** *The Wall Street Journal Online,* July 8, 2016. www.wsj.com

**Figure 8–13**  DJIA, NYSE Composite Index, S&P Composite Index, NASDAQ Composite Index, and Wilshire 5000 Index Values

**Sources:** Dow Jones, the New York Stock Exchange, Standard & Poor's, NASDAQ, and Wilshire websites, various dates

www.nasdaq.com

www.wilshire.com

decade of the 2000s, however, all four indexes grew steadily. Finally, notice that all of the indexes experienced large losses in value during the financial crisis of 2008–2009. The DJIA closed at an all-time high of 14,164.53 on October 9, 2007. As of mid-March 2009, the DJIA had fallen in value 53.8 percent in less than 1½ years, larger than the decline during the market crash of 1929 when it fell 49 percent. Similarly, the NYSE, S&P 500, NASDAQ Composite, and Wilshire 5000 indexes all also fell over 50 percent during this period. However, stock prices recovered along with the economy in the last half of 2009 and into 2010, with the DJIA rising 71.1 percent between March 2009 and April 2010. In the spring of 2013, the DJIA surpassed the 2007 high, closing at 14,164.53 on March 5. By the summer of 2017, the DJIA was trading at record highs of 21,500.

**The Dow Jones Industrial Average.**  The Dow Jones Industrial Average (the DJIA or the Dow) is the most widely reported stock market index. The Dow was first published in 1896 as an index of 12 industrial stocks. In 1928, the Dow was expanded to include the values of 30 large (in terms of sales and total assets) corporations selected by the editors of *The Wall Street Journal* (owned by Dow Jones & Company). In choosing companies to be included in the DJIA, the editors look for the largest companies with a history of successful growth and with interest among stock investors. The composition of the DJIA was most recently revised in March 2015, when AT&T was replaced by Apple. Table 8–3 lists the 30 NYSE and NASDAQ corporations included in the DJIA. Dow Jones and Company has also established and publishes indexes of 20 transportation companies, 15 utility companies, and a composite index consisting of all 65 companies in the industrial, transportation, and utility indexes. Because the DJIA includes only 30 companies, critics charge that the index fails to reflect the movement of hundreds of other stock prices. But the 30 securities included in the DJIA are chosen to be representative of the broad stock market. The companies are the major firms in their industries and the stocks are widely held by both individuals and institutions.

Dow indexes are *price-weighted averages,* meaning that the stock *prices* of the companies in the indexes are added together and divided by an adjusted value (or divisor), as follows:

$$\sum_{i=1}^{30} P_{it}/\text{Divisor}$$

where

$P_{it}$ = Price of each stock in the Dow index on day $t$

The divisor was set at 30 in 1928, but due to stock splits, stock dividends, and changes in the 30 firms included in the index, this value dropped to 0.14602128057775 by July 2016.

**The NYSE Composite Index.**  In 1966, the NYSE established the NYSE Composite Index to provide a comprehensive measure of the performance of the overall NYSE market. The index consists of all common stocks listed on the NYSE. In addition to the composite index, NYSE stocks are divided into four subgroups: industrial, transportation, utility, and financial companies. The indexed value of each group is also reported daily.

The NYSE is a *value-weighted index,* meaning that the *current market values* (stock price × number of shares outstanding) of all stocks in the index are added together and divided by their value on a base date. Any changes in the stocks included in the index are incorporated by adjusting the base value of the index. To modernize and align the index methodology with those used in other indexes, the NYSE revised its NYSE Composite Index in January 2003. At this time the composite was recalculated to reflect a new base value of 5,000 rather than the original base value of 50 set in December 1965.

**The Standard & Poor's 500 Index.**  Standard & Poor's established the S&P 500 Index (a value-weighted index) consisting of the stocks of the top 500 of the largest U.S. corporations listed on the NYSE and the NASDAQ. The NYSE stocks included in the S&P 500 Index account for over 80 percent of the total market value of all stocks listed on the

**TABLE 8–3**  Dow Jones Industrial Average Companies

| | |
|---|---|
| American Express | J.P. Morgan Chase |
| Apple | McDonald's |
| Boeing | Merck |
| Caterpillar | Microsoft |
| Chevron | Minnesota Mining & Manufacturing (3M) |
| Cisco Systems | Nike |
| Coca-Cola | Pfizer |
| DuPont | Procter & Gamble |
| ExxonMobil | Travelers Companies |
| General Electric | United Health Group |
| Goldman Sachs | United Technologies |
| Home Depot | Verizon Communications |
| IBM | Visa |
| Intel | Walmart |
| Johnson & Johnson | Walt Disney |

**Source:** Dow Jones & Company website, July 2016. www.dowjones.com

NYSE. Thus, movements in the S&P 500 Index are highly correlated with those of the NYSE Composite Index (the correlation between the two indexes was 0.98 from 1989 through June 2016—see Figure 8–13). Standard & Poor's also reports subindexes consisting of industrials and utilities in the S&P 500 Index.

**The NASDAQ Composite Index.** Established in 1971, the NASDAQ Composite Index (a value-weighted index) consists of three categories of NASDAQ companies: industrials, banks, and insurance companies. All stocks traded through the NASDAQ in these three industries are included. NASDAQ also reports separate indexes based on industrials, banks, insurance companies, computers, and telecommunications companies.

**The Wilshire 5000 Index.** The Wilshire 5000 Index was created in 1974 (when computers made the daily computation of such a large index possible) to track the value of the entire stock market. It is the broadest stock market index and possibly the most accurate reflection of the overall stock market. The Wilshire 5000 Index contains virtually every stock that meets three criteria: the firm is headquartered in the United States; the stock is actively traded in a U.S.-based stock market; and the stock has widely available price information (which rules out the smaller OTC stocks from inclusion). Though the index started with 5,000 firms, because of firm delistings, privatizations, and acquisitions it currently includes just 3,618 stocks. Like the NYSE Composite Index, the S&P 500 Index, and the NASDAQ Composite Index, the Wilshire 5000 Index is a value-weighted index. The Wilshire 5000 Index has the advantage that it is the best index to track the path of the U.S. stock market. Since it includes essentially every public firm, it is highly representative of the overall market. However, because it is so diverse, determining which sectors or asset classes (technology, industrial, small-cap, large-cap, etc.) are moving the market is impossible.

---

**EXAMPLE 8–5** Price-Weighted versus Value-Weighted Indexes

Suppose a stock index contains the stock of four firms: W, X, Y, and Z. The stock prices for the four companies are $50, $25, $60, and $5, respectively, and the firms have 100 million, 400 million, 200 million, and 50 million shares outstanding, respectively. If the index is price-weighted, its initial value, *PWI,* is calculated as:

$$PWI = \sum_{i=1}^{4} P_{it}/4$$
$$= (\$50 + \$25 + \$60 + \$5)/4$$
$$= 140/4$$
$$= 35$$

If the index is value-weighted, its initial value, *VWI,* is:

$$VWI = \sum_{i=1}^{4} (P_{it} \times \text{Number of shares outstanding})/4$$
$$= [(\$50 \times 100m) + (\$25 \times 400m) + (\$60 \times 200m) + (\$5 \times 50m)]/4$$
$$= \$6,812.5 \text{ million}$$

If the next day, share prices change to $55, $24, $62, and $6, respectively, the price-weighted index value changes to:

$$PWI = \sum_{i=1}^{4} P_{it}/4$$
$$= (\$55 + \$24 + \$62 + \$6)/4$$
$$= 147/4$$
$$= 36.75$$

and the percentage change in the index is $(36.75 - 35)/35 = 5$ percent. The value-weighted index is now:

$$VWI = \sum_{i=1}^{4}(P_{it} \times \text{Number of shares outstanding})/4$$
$$= [(\$55 \times 100m) + (\$24 \times 400m) + (\$62 \times 200m) + (\$6 \times 50m)]/4$$
$$= \$6,950 \text{ million}$$

and the percentage change in this index is $(6,950 - 6,812.5)/6,812.5 = 2.02$ percent.

If, after the market closes, company W undergoes a two-for-one split, its stock price falls to $\$55/2 = \$27.50$ and the number of shares increases to 200 million. The prices now sum to \$119.50. At the same time the divisor on the price-weighted index adjusts such that:

$$\text{Divisor} = 119.5/36.75$$
$$= 3.2517$$

Thus, the value of the price-weighted index remains at:

$$PWI = \sum_{i=1}^{4}P_{it}/3.2517$$
$$= (\$27.50 + \$24 + \$62 + \$6)/3.2517$$
$$= 119.5/3.2517$$
$$= 36.75$$

Further, the value-weighted index remains unchanged at \$6,950 million. Both indexes are unaffected by the stock split. Apparent from this example, however, is that the firms included in the index and the weighting process used affect the values of the reported changes in the overall stock market.

## STOCK MARKET PARTICIPANTS

**LG 8-7**

Table 8–4 shows the holdings of corporate stock from 1994 through 2016 by type of holder. Households are the single largest holders of corporate stock (holding 39.0 percent of all corporate stock outstanding in 2016). Mutual funds and foreign investors (rest of world) are also prominent in the stock markets (holding 24.2 percent and 15.7 percent of the \$35.5 trillion in corporate stock outstanding, respectively). Households indirectly invest in corporate stock through investments in mutual funds and pension funds. Together, these holdings totaled approximately 80 percent in 2016. Notice the drop in corporate stock held by the various groups before (third quarter 2007) versus after (first quarter 2010) the worst of the financial crisis. Holdings of stock by households dropped 21.9 percent, private pension funds dropped 32.2 percent, public pension funds fell 19.1 percent, mutual funds fell 18.0, closed-end funds decreased 38.0 percent, and brokers and dealers dropped 50.0 percent. While some of these changes are due to the general decrease in common stock prices, they are also due to investors switching their investments to safer securities during the financial crisis.

As a result of the tremendous increase in stock values in the 1990s, most individuals in the United States either directly own corporate stock or indirectly own stock via investments in mutual funds and pension funds. Figure 8–14 shows the percentage of Americans with investments in the stock market from 1998 through 2016. Ownership peaked at 65 percent in 2007 as stock markets reached record highs. As the stock market plummeted in value during the financial crisis, so did ownership. Although the stock market recovered

**TABLE 8–4**   Holders of Corporate Stock *(in billions of dollars)*

| | 1994 | 1997 | 2000 | 2004 | 2007* | 2010† | 2013 | 2016† | Percentage of 2016 Total |
|---|---|---|---|---|---|---|---|---|---|
| Household sector | $3,294.2 | $6,144.1 | $8,140.2 | $7,516.9 | $9,975.0 | $7,793.3 | $12,851.9 | $13,851.6 | 39.0% |
| State and local governments | 10.6 | 78.4 | 93.2 | 87.8 | 111.4 | 117.2 | 162.2 | 184.6 | 0.5 |
| Rest of world | 352.8 | 837.3 | 1,483.0 | 1,904.6 | 2,822.0 | 2,628.3 | 5,204.4 | 5,564.4 | 15.7 |
| Federal government | 0.0 | 0.0 | 0.0 | 0.0 | 0.0 | 67.3 | 35.1 | 33.4 | 0.1 |
| Monetary authority | 0.0 | 0.0 | 0.0 | 0.0 | 0.0 | 25.4 | 0.0 | 0.0 | 0.0 |
| Depository institutions | 13.3 | 25.9 | 43.3 | 57.5 | 68.6 | 56.5 | 101.3 | 93.6 | 0.2 |
| Life insurance companies | 231.4 | 539.7 | 891.9 | 1,053.9 | 1,505.1 | 1,334.0 | 298.5 | 310.4 | 0.9 |
| Property-casualty insurance companies | 111.7 | 184.3 | 191.4 | 196.6 | 248.5 | 232.7 | 310.4 | 316.2 | 0.9 |
| Private pension funds | 1,013.7 | 1,603.7 | 1,970.6 | 2,338.5 | 2,829.0 | 1,918.1 | 2,243.8 | 2,222.8 | 6.3 |
| Public pension funds | 527.9 | 1,081.2 | 1,355.3 | 1,660.8 | 2,210.5 | 1,789.0 | 2,379.2 | 2,329.1 | 6.5 |
| Mutual funds | 709.6 | 2,018.7 | 3,226.9 | 3,693.6 | 5,701.3 | 4,363.7 | 8,227.3 | 8,584.3 | 24.2 |
| Closed-end funds | 31.9 | 49.6 | 36.5 | 81.8 | 153.6 | 94.6 | 114.2 | 97.5 | 0.3 |
| Exchange-traded funds | 0.4 | 6.7 | 65.6 | 219.0 | 521.9 | 687.2 | 1,427.3 | 1,771.0 | 5.0 |
| Brokers and dealers | 20.1 | 51.9 | 77.2 | 129.1 | 220.6 | 109.4 | 172.4 | 136.8 | 0.4 |
| Finance companies | 0.0 | 0.0 | 0.0 | 0.0 | 0.0 | 25.4 | 0.0 | 0.0 | 0.0 |

*As of the end of the third quarter.
†As of the end of the first quarter.

**Sources:** Federal Reserve Board website, various issues. www.federalreserve.gov

**Figure 8–14**   Percentage of Americans Invested in the Stock Market

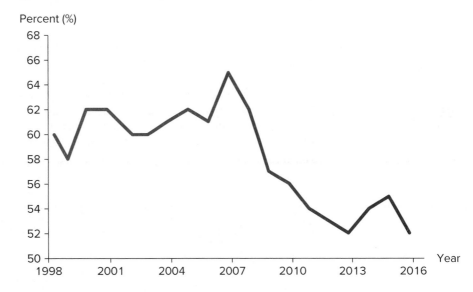

**DO YOU UNDERSTAND:**

8. *Who the major holders of stock are?*

9. *What age group of individual investors is the most active in the stock market?*

in 2010–2016, individual investors did not reenter the market, and it fell to a low of 52 percent in April 2016. Despite an improving economy overall, unemployment remained above 6.0 percent throughout much of this period (not falling below 5.0 percent until January 2016), a level still too high to support wide-ranging stock ownership.

Table 8–5 reports characteristics of adult investors in the stock markets in April 2007 and 2016. Note that in every category, percentages have dropped over this period. Older investors are the most active. In 2016, 62 percent of individuals 35 to 54 years old are invested, compared to just 38 percent of those 18 to

**TABLE 8–5**    Profiles of Adult Stockholders

|  | April 2007 | April 2016 | Change |
|---|---|---|---|
| **Age:** | | | |
| 18–34 years | 52% | 38% | −14% |
| 35–54 years | 73 | 62 | −11 |
| 55 and older | 65 | 56 | −9 |
| | | | |
| **Income:** | | | |
| $75,000 and over | 90 | 79 | −11 |
| $30,000–$74,999 | 72 | 50 | −22 |
| Less than $30,000 | 28 | 23 | −5 |

34 years old. These numbers are down from 2007 when 73 percent and 62 percent, respectively, were invested in the stock market. The higher the income, the higher the percentage of individuals investing in stocks. In 2016, 79 percent of individuals earning $75,000 and over were invested in stocks, while just 23 percent of individuals earning less than $30,000 were invested.

## OTHER ISSUES PERTAINING TO STOCK MARKETS

### Economic Indicators

In Chapter 3 we used time value of money equations to determine the fair value of a stock. Specifically, we saw that the fair value of a stock today ($P_0$) could be represented as:

$$P_0 = \frac{D_1}{(1 + r_s)^1} + \frac{D_2}{(1 + r_s)^2} + \dots + \frac{D_\infty}{(1 + r_s)^\infty}$$

The present value of a stock today is the discounted (at a rate $r_s$) sum of the expected future dividends ($D_t$) to be paid on the stock. As expected future dividends increase (decrease), stock prices should increase (decrease). Appendix 8A to this chapter (available through Connect or your course instructor) reviews the capital asset pricing model, which is used to determine an appropriate interest rate at which to discount these dividends.

To the extent that today's stock values reflect expected future dividends, stock market indexes might be used to forecast future economic activity. An increase (decrease) in stock market indexes today potentially signals the market's expectation of higher (lower) corporate dividends and profits and, in turn, higher (lower) economic growth. To the extent that the market's assessment of expected dividends is correct, stock market indexes can be predictors of economic activity. Indeed, stock prices are one of the 10 variables included in the index of leading economic indicators used by the Federal Reserve as it formulates economic policy (see Chapter 4).[6]

www.federalreserve.gov

Figure 8–15 shows the relation between stock market movements (using the DJIA) and economic cycles in the United States. Notice some recessionary periods (represented in by the shaded bars) were indeed preceded by a decline in stock market index values; other recessionary periods were not preceded by a decline in stock market index values. Figure 8–15 suggests that stock market movements are not consistently accurate predictors of economic activity. In fact, of the 14 major stock market predicted recessions since 1942, only 8 actually occurred.

---

6. The other indicators include average weekly hours of manufacturing production workers; average weekly initial claims for unemployment insurance; manufacturers' new orders, consumer goods and materials; vendor performance, slower diffusion index; manufacturers' new orders, nondefense capital goods; building permits for new private housing units; money supply; interest rate spread, 10-year Treasury bonds less fed funds; and index of consumer expectations. These data, tabulated by the National Bureau of Economic Research (NBER), are available in the *Survey of Current Business*.

**Figure 8–15**  The Relation between Stock Market Movements and Economic Activity

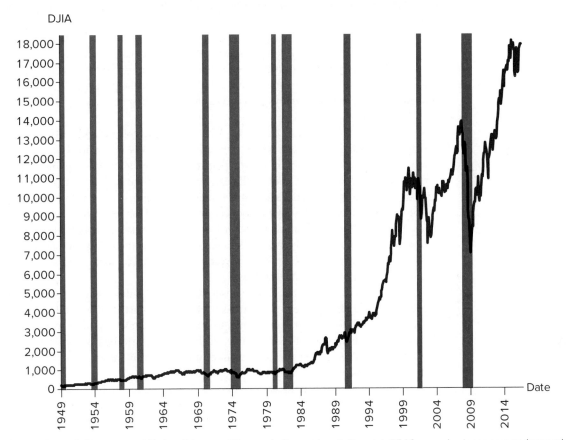

**Sources:** Dow Jones & Company and National Bureau of Economic Research websites, July 2016. www.dowjones.com and www.nber.org

LG 8-8

## Market Efficiency

As discussed previously (and in Chapter 3), theoretically, the *current* market price of a stock equals the present value of its expected future dividends (or the *fair* market or intrinsic value of the security). However, when an event occurs that unexpectedly changes interest rates or a characteristic of the company (e.g., an unexpected dividend increase or decrease in default risk), the current market price of a stock can temporarily diverge from its fair present value. When market traders determine that a stock is undervalued (i.e., the current price of the stock is less than its fair present value), they will purchase the stock, thus driving its price up. Conversely, when market traders determine that a stock is overvalued (i.e., its current price is greater than its fair present value), they will sell the stock, resulting in a price decline.

The degree to which financial security prices adjust to "news" and the degree (and speed) with which stock prices reflect information about the firm and factors that affect firm value is referred to as **market efficiency.**[7] Three measures (weak form, semistrong form, and strong form market efficiency) are commonly used to measure the degree of stock market efficiency. The measures differ in the type of information or news (e.g., public versus private, historic versus nonhistoric) that is impounded into stock prices.

**market efficiency**

*The speed with which financial security prices adjust to unexpected news pertaining to interest rates or a stock-specific characteristic.*

**Weak Form Market Efficiency.**  According to the weak form of market efficiency, current stock prices reflect all historic price and volume information about a company. Old news and trends are already impounded in historic prices and are of no use in predicting

---

7. While we discuss market efficiency in the context of stock markets, it also applies to the speed with which any security's price changes in response to new information.

today's or future stock prices. Thus, weak form market efficiency concludes that investors cannot make more than the fair (required) return using information based on historic price movements.

Empirical research on weak form market efficiency generally confirms that markets are weak form efficient. Evidence suggests that successive price changes are generally random and that the correlation between stock prices from one day to the next is virtually zero. Thus, historical price and volume trends are of no help in predicting future price movements (and technical analysis has no value as a trading strategy).

**Semistrong Form Market Efficiency.**   The semistrong form market efficiency hypothesis focuses on the speed with which public information is impounded into stock prices. According to the concept of semistrong form market efficiency, as public information arrives about a company, it is immediately impounded into its stock price. For example, semistrong form market efficiency states that a common stock's value should respond immediately to unexpected news announcements by the firm regarding its future earnings. Thus, if an investor calls his or her broker just as the earnings news is released, that investor cannot earn an abnormal return. Prices have already (immediately) adjusted. According to semistrong form market efficiency, investors cannot make more than the fair (required) return by trading on public news releases.

Since historical information is a subset of all public information, if semistrong form market efficiency holds, weak form market efficiency must hold as well. However, it is possible for weak form market efficiency to hold when semistrong form market efficiency does not. This implies that investors can earn abnormal returns by trading on current public news releases. The quicker the stock market impounds this information, the smaller any abnormal returns will be.

Semistrong form market efficiency has been examined by testing how security prices react to unexpected news releases or announcement "events" (see Appendix 8B, Event Study Tests, available through Connect or your course instructor). Some specific announcements that have been tested include macroeconomic events such as interest rate changes and firm-specific announcements such as earnings and dividend changes, stock splits, brokerage house buy and sell recommendations, and mergers and acquisitions. Financial markets have generally been found to immediately reflect information from news announcements.

**Strong Form Market Efficiency.**   The strong form of market efficiency states that stock prices fully reflect all information about the firm, both public and private. Thus, according to strong form market efficiency, even learning private information about the firm is of no help in earning more than the required rate of return. As individuals[8] get private information about a firm, the market has already reacted to it and has fully adjusted the firm's common stock price to its new equilibrium level. Thus, strong form market efficiency implies that there is no set of information that allows investors to make more than the fair (required) rate of return on a stock.

If strong form market efficiency holds, semistrong form market efficiency must hold as well. However, semistrong form market efficiency can hold when strong form market efficiency does not. This implies that private information can be used to produce abnormal returns, but as soon as the private or inside information is publicly released, abnormal returns are unobtainable.

Because private information is not observable, testing for strong form market efficiency is difficult. As a result, there are few studies testing its validity. The limited empirical tests of strong form market efficiency examine information available to insiders.

---

8. How institutional investors factor into efficient markets raises questions. Many consider institutional investors to have private information that results from better analysis of public information and greater resources. Obviously, whether these institutions can expect to discover the private information and thus expect to earn abnormal returns in the long run is an issue. Indeed, whether the information set of institutions belongs in the semistrong or strong form group is arguable.

## Pro Golfer Agrees to Repay Trading Profits

The Securities and Exchange Commission today announced insider trading charges against a professional sports gambler who allegedly made $40 million based on illegal stock tips from a corporate insider who owed him money.

The SEC alleges that sports gambler William "Billy" Walters of Las Vegas was owed money by Thomas C. Davis, then–board member of Dean Foods Company. According to the SEC complaint, Davis regularly shared inside information about Dean Foods with Walters in advance of market-moving events using prepaid cell phones and other methods in an effort to avoid detection. The SEC further alleges that while Walters made millions of dollars insider trading using the confidential information, he provided Davis with almost $1 million and other benefits to help Davis address his financial debts.

The SEC complaint also alleges that professional golfer Phil Mickelson

traded Dean Foods's securities at Walters's urging and then used his almost $1 million of trading profits to help repay his own gambling debt to Walters. Walters and Davis are charged with insider trading, and Mickelson is named as a relief defendant. Relief defendants are not accused of wrongdoing but are named in SEC complaints for the purposes of recovering alleged ill-gotten gains in their possession from schemes perpetrated by others, said Andrew Ceresney, director of the SEC's Enforcement Division. "Additionally, Mickelson will repay the money he made from his trading in Dean Foods because he should not be allowed to profit from Walters's illegal conduct."

According to the SEC's complaint filed in federal court in Manhattan:

- In July 2012, Walters called Mickelson, who had placed bets with Walters and owed him money at the time. While Walters was in possession of material nonpublic

information about Dean Foods, he urged Mickelson to trade in Dean Foods stock.
- Mickelson bought Dean Foods stock the next trading day in three brokerage accounts he controlled. About one week later, Dean Foods's stock price jumped 40 percent following public announcements about the White-Wave spin-off and strong second-quarter earnings.
- Mickelson then sold his shares for more than $931,000 in profits. He repaid his debt to Walters in September 2012 in part with the trading proceeds.

Mickelson neither admitted nor denied the allegations in the SEC's complaint and agreed to pay full disgorgement of his trading profits totaling $931,738.12 plus interest of $105,291.69.

**Source:** SEC Press Release, May 19, 2016, Securities and Exchange Commission. www.sec.gov

Generally, studies have found that corporate insiders (e.g., directors, officers, and chairs) do earn abnormal returns from trading and that the more informed the insider, the more often abnormal returns are earned. Therefore, information possessed by corporate insiders can be used in trading to earn abnormal returns.

Because private information can be used to earn abnormal returns, laws prohibit investors from trading on the basis of private information (insider trading), although they can trade, like any investor, based on publicly available information about the firm. For example, in October 2011, Galleon Group LLC cofounder Raj Rajaratnam was sentenced to 11 years in prison, the longest-ever term imposed in an insider-trading case. Galleon Group was one of the largest hedge fund management firms in the world before announcing its closure in October 2009. The firm was at the center of a 2009 insider trading scandal that resulted in investors pulling capital from the firm rapidly. Twenty people, including Rajaratnam, were criminally charged in what federal authorities called the biggest prosecution of alleged hedge fund insider trading in the United States. Prosecutors said they had evidence from wiretaps, trading records, and cooperating witnesses to prove widespread trafficking in illegal insider information, including an insider trading operation that paid sources for nonpublic information that netted the hedge fund more than $20 million. More recently, the In the News box describes how an insider trading scandal landed pro golfer Phil Mickelson in trouble with the SEC.

To try to ensure that insider trading does not occur, publicly traded companies are required to file monthly reports with the Securities and Exchange Commission reporting every purchase and sale of the company's securities by officers and directors of the company. Even with this information, identifying trades driven by private (inside) as opposed to public information is often hard.

### Stock Market Regulations

**www.sec.gov**

Stock markets and stock market participants are subject to regulations imposed by the SEC as well as the exchanges on which stocks are traded. The main emphasis of SEC regulations is on full and fair disclosure of information on securities issues to actual and potential investors. The two major regulations that were created to prevent unfair and unethical trading practices on security exchanges are the Securities Act of 1933 and the Securities Exchange Act of 1934. The 1933 act required listed companies to file a registration statement and to issue a prospectus that details the recent financial history of the company when issuing new stock. The 1934 act established the SEC as the main administrative agency responsible for the oversight of secondary stock markets by giving the SEC the authority to monitor the stock market exchanges and administer the provisions of the 1933 act. SEC regulations are not intended to protect investors against poor investment choices but rather to ensure that investors have full and accurate information available when making their investment decisions.

For example, in the early 2000s, a number of securities firms received tremendous publicity concerning conflicts of interest between analysts' research recommendations on buying or not buying stocks and whether the firm played a role in underwriting the securities of the firm the analysts were recommending. After an investigation by the New York State's attorney general, Merrill Lynch agreed to pay a fine of $100 million and to follow procedures more clearly separating analysts' recommendations (and their compensation) from the underwriting activities of the firm. Major Wall Street firms were also investigated. This investigation was triggered by the dramatic collapse of many new technology stocks while analysts were still making recommendations to buy or hold them.

Subsequent to these investigations, the SEC instituted rules requiring Wall Street analysts to vouch that their stock picks have not been influenced by investment banking colleagues and to disclose details of their compensation that would flag investors to any possible conflicts. Evidence that analysts have falsely attested to the independence of their work could be used to institute enforcement actions. Violators could face a wide array of sanctions, including fines and penalties such as a suspension or a bar from the securities industry. In addition, the SEC proposed that top officials from all public companies sign off on financial statements.

Along with these changes instituted by the SEC, the U.S. Congress passed the Sarbanes-Oxley Act in July 2002. This act created an independent auditing oversight board under the SEC, increased penalties for corporate wrongdoers, forced faster and more extensive financial disclosure, and created avenues of recourse for aggrieved shareholders. Further, in 2002 the NYSE took actions intended to heighten corporate governance standards on domestic NYSE-listed companies. Key changes included requirements on companies to have a majority of independent directors, to adopt corporate governance guidelines and codes of ethics and business conduct, to have shareholders' approval of all equity-based compensation plans, and to have CEOs annually certify information given to investors. The goal of the legislation was to prevent deceptive accounting and management practices and to bring stability to jittery stock markets battered in the summer of 2002 by the corporate governance scandals of Enron, Global Crossings, Tyco, WorldCom, and others.

The SEC came under fire during the financial crisis for its failure to uncover Bernie Madoff's Ponzi scheme. The SEC apparently had evidence as early as 1994 (in relation to another case) that Madoff, a former chair of the NASDAQ stock market who was a member of SEC advisory committees, was conducting illegal activities. Further, Harry Markopolos, who worked for a rival company of Bernard L. Madoff Investment Securities, had written to the SEC in May 1999 informing it of Madoff's Ponzi scheme. Markopolos examined the options markets that Madoff told investors he used to produce his steady stream of returns and concluded that Madoff's results were impossible. On May 19, 2006, when the SEC questioned Madoff under oath, he falsely described how he would buy and sell stock and options contracts in Europe on behalf of his clients. The SEC asked Madoff: "Is there any documentation generated?" Madoff said yes, but the SEC failed to pursue this further. Eventually, the SEC recommended closing the investigation "because those violations were not so serious as to warrant an enforcement action." Making things worse for the SEC, Madoff's family had close ties with the SEC. Madoff's sons, brother, and niece worked with or advised the SEC on various matters. Madoff's niece is married to a former SEC attorney who was part of a team that examined Madoff's securities brokerage operation in 1999 and 2004. Neither review resulted in an action against Madoff. In the end, it was not the SEC that discovered Madoff's Ponzi scheme. Because of large redemption claims that his clients filed during the financial crisis, Madoff's Ponzi scheme began to collapse. Madoff admitted to his sons what he had done and they turned him in to authorities.

<table>
<tr><td>

**DO YOU UNDERSTAND:**

**10.** *Whether movements in stock market indexes are always accurate predictors of changes in economic activity?*

**11.** *What the differences are among weak form, semistrong form, and strong form market efficiency?*

**12.** *The purpose of regulations imposed on stock market participants by the SEC?*

</td></tr>
</table>

**www.nyse.com**

**www.finra.org**

The SEC's internal watchdog, Inspector General H. David Kotz, stated that he was so concerned about the agency's failure to uncover Madoff's alleged Ponzi scheme that he expanded an inquiry called for by SEC chair Christopher Cox. However, in July 2010, nearly 18 months after Madoff's Ponzi scheme was exposed, lawmakers were still questioning how the SEC staffers who reviewed the Madoff firm and investigated fraud allegations were being punished. SEC chair Mary Schapiro told Congress during an oversight hearing that 15 of 20 enforcement attorneys and 19 of 36 examination staffers that dealt with the Madoff matter had left the agency, but the SEC was still conducting a disciplinary process. Schapiro also said the Madoff incident did change the culture of the SEC. For example, SEC examiners are now verifying custody of assets with third parties, something the SEC failed to do in its review of Madoff and something Madoff later told SEC officials he was sure would have led to his scheme's unraveling.

The SEC has delegated certain regulatory responsibilities to the markets (e.g., NYSE or NASDAQ). In these matters, the NYSE and NASDAQ are self-regulatory organizations. Specifically, the NYSE has primary responsibility for the day-to-day surveillance of trading activity. It monitors specialists to ensure adequate compliance with their obligation to make a fair and orderly market; monitors all trading to guard against unfair trading practices; monitors broker-dealer activity with respect to minimum net capital requirements, standards, and licensing; and enforces various listing and disclosure requirements. For example, in October 2007 NYSE regulators censured and fined several NYSE member firms for failure to deliver prospectuses to a large number of customers.

The Financial Industry Regulatory Authority (FINRA) is the largest independent regulator for all securities firms doing business in the United States. FINRA was formed in July 2007 as a result of the merger of the National Association of Securities Dealers (NASD) with the enforcement arm of the New York Stock Exchange. FINRA oversees all aspects of the securities business, including registering and educating industry participants, examining securities firms, writing rules, enforcing those rules and the federal securities laws, informing and educating the investing public, providing trade reporting and other industry reports, and administering the largest dispute resolution forum for investors and registered firms.

As mentioned earlier, the Wall Street Reform and Consumer Protection Act of 2010 (passed in response to the financial crisis) gave the SEC and other regulators new powers to oversee the operations of stock markets. These rules empower the SEC to disseminate a fiduciary standard for broker-dealers that provide personalized investment services, to require disclosures on broker-dealers that sell only proprietary products, to review rule changes of self-regulatory organizations that affect custody of customer securities or funds, and to facilitate the provision of simple and clear investor disclosures regarding the terms of relationships with broker-dealers and investment advisors. The new rules also require the SEC to undertake a study on conflicts of interest involving analysts.

Six years after the passage of the Wall Street Reform and Consumer Protection Act, 271 rule-making deadlines have passed. Of these, 204 (75.3 percent) have been met with finalized rules and rules have been proposed that would meet 34 (12.5 percent) more. Rules have not yet been proposed to meet 33 (12.2 percent) passed rule-making requirements. Of the 390 total rule-making requirements, 267 (68.5 percent) have been met with finalized rules and rules have been proposed that would meet 40 (10.2 percent) more. Rules have not yet been proposed to meet 83 (21.3 percent) rule-making requirements. The enormity of the act has consumed a vast amount of the SEC's resources and left many pressing issues affecting investor confidence unaddressed.

## INTERNATIONAL ASPECTS OF STOCK MARKETS

**LG 8-9**

The U.S. stock markets are the world's largest. However, with the full implementation of a common currency—the euro—in 2002, European markets grew in importance during the 2000s. Further, economic growth in Pacific Basin countries, China, and other emerging market countries has resulted in significant growth in their stock markets. Figure 8–16 shows the proportion of stock market capitalization among various countries in 1990, 2000, 2009, and 2016. The U.S. dominance in the stock markets is best seen in 2000. However, U.S. market capitalization decreased in size in 2009.

Factors behind the U.S. dominance in world stock markets changed in the mid-2000s. Strict new U.S. regulations such as Sarbanes-Oxley (discussed earlier) increased the cost of operating in the United States and resulted in a significant drop in IPOs of foreign firms

**Figure 8–16**   **Worldwide Stock Market Capitalization**

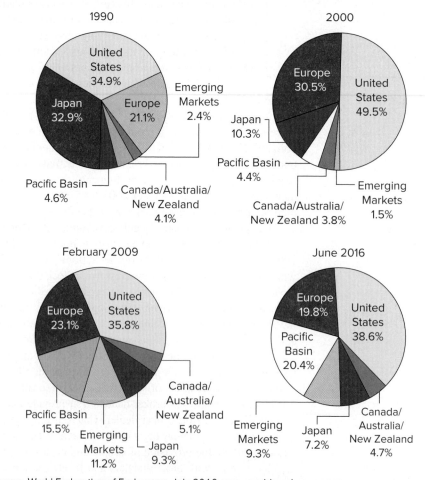

**Source:** World Federation of Exchanges, July 2016. www.world-exchanges.org

in the United States. Further, U.S. economic growth slowed from an annual rate of over 4 percent in the first two quarters of 2006 to 1¼ percent in the first quarter of 2007. A sharp downturn in the U.S. subprime housing market was a major factor for the slow U.S. growth. During this period growth strengthened in most other major countries, including the euro area, China, the United Kingdom, and Canada. Indeed, in early 2007 growth in the euro area exceeded that in the United States for the first time since 2002. Further, China's economy continued to expand.

Note also the stock market developments in Europe, the Pacific Basin, and the emerging market countries from 1990 to 2016. European markets increased their market share (from 21.1 percent in 1990 to 30.5 percent of the total in 2000). However, as the U.S. financial crisis spread and Europe then fell into a deep sovereign debt crisis in the late 2010s, European markets fell to just 23.1 percent of the world total. Issues got worse in Europe in 2016 as the United Kingdom voted to leave the European Union, sending the British and European markets down further, to 19.8 percent by June 2016. The Asian economic problems that started in 1997 reduced the value of these markets significantly (for example, Pacific Basin and emerging markets stock markets decreased from 4.6 percent and 2.4 percent in 1990 to 4.4 percent and 1.5 percent in 2000 of the worldwide stock markets, respectively). However, these regions were less affected by the financial crisis that hit the United States and Europe. Thus, they recovered and grew to 20.4 percent and 9.3 percent, respectively, in 2016.

From an investor's viewpoint, international stock markets are attractive because some risk can be eliminated (diversified away—see Chapter 20) by holding stocks issued by corporations in foreign countries. For example, while a stock issued by a corporation in one country might be reduced in value by a recessionary slowdown, increases in the value of stocks issued by a corporation in another country (that is experiencing economic growth or an appreciation in the foreign exchange rate of its currency) can offset those losses. Figure 8–17 shows the movements of major world stock markets from 2000 through 2016. While these markets generally move together, the correlation in the movements is not perfect. The Bank for International Settlements reported that correlations in stock returns between U.S. and a combination of euro area and Japanese stocks was as high as 0.93 from 2003 to 2005 and decreased to 0.63 by 2007. By 2013, correlations in stock returns were again running between 0.85 and 0.90 (see Figure 8–17).

**Figure 8–17**   Correlation of the S&P 500 with Global Stock Indexes

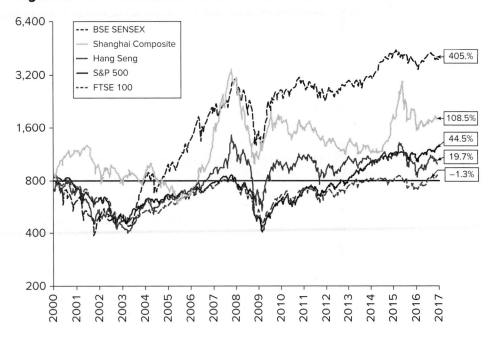

**TABLE 8–6**   Correlation of Returns on International Stock Markets 2012–2015

| Mthly Correl (Past 36M) | S&P 500 | Dow Jones | Nasdaq | Canada | Europe | UK | Australia | Japan | Hong Kong | Brazil | China | India | Russia | South Africa |
|---|---|---|---|---|---|---|---|---|---|---|---|---|---|---|
| S&P 500 | 1.000 | | | | | | | | | | | | | |
| Dow Jones | 0.967 | 1.000 | | | | | | | | | | | | |
| Nasdaq | 0.912 | 0.835 | 1.000 | | | | | | | | | | | |
| Canada | 0.588 | 0.490 | 0.544 | 1.000 | | | | | | | | | | |
| Europe | 0.596 | 0.516 | 0.595 | 0.511 | 1.000 | | | | | | | | | |
| UK | 0.732 | 0.671 | 0.656 | 0.678 | 0.731 | 1.000 | | | | | | | | |
| Australia | 0.472 | 0.416 | 0.384 | 0.497 | 0.489 | 0.612 | 1.000 | | | | | | | |
| Japan | 0.482 | 0.554 | 0.452 | 0.023 | 0.416 | 0.321 | 0.294 | 1.000 | | | | | | |
| Hong Kong | 0.424 | 0.385 | 0.381 | 0.529 | 0.368 | 0.571 | 0.528 | 0.343 | 1.000 | | | | | |
| Brazil | 0.446 | 0.372 | 0.403 | 0.621 | 0.317 | 0.327 | 0.356 | 0.174 | 0.586 | 1.000 | | | | |
| China | 0.114 | 0.172 | 0.100 | 0.247 | 0.117 | 0.196 | 0.122 | 0.285 | 0.535 | 0.280 | 1.000 | | | |
| India | 0.479 | 0.408 | 0.426 | 0.326 | 0.481 | 0.388 | 0.286 | 0.248 | 0.366 | 0.323 | (0.112) | 1.000 | | |
| Russia | 0.144 | 0.081 | 0.240 | 0.163 | 0.348 | 0.273 | 0.106 | 0.083 | 0.275 | 0.175 | (0.113) | 0.424 | 1.000 | |
| South Africa | 0.436 | 0.351 | 0.436 | 0.696 | 0.533 | 0.630 | 0.322 | 0.054 | 0.544 | 0.449 | 0.253 | 0.293 | 0.305 | 1.000 |
| MSCI EM | 0.548 | 0.504 | 0.382 | 0.711 | 0.476 | 0.599 | 0.443 | 0.163 | 0.647 | 0.626 | 0.236 | 0.456 | 0.187 | 0.632 |

Table 8–6 lists correlations among the returns in major stock indexes between 2012 and 2015. Looking at correlations between foreign stock market returns and U.S. stock market returns, you can see that all are positive. Correlations across markets vary from a high of 0.732 between the United States and the United Kingdom to a low of −0.113 between Russia and China.

---

**EXAMPLE 8–6**   **Returns from Investing in an International Portfolio of Stocks**

Suppose you owned stock in a U.S. company and a UK company. U.S. dollars were converted to British pounds last year to make the investment, and pounds were converted back to dollars as you liquidated the investment. Also suppose the exchange rate of British pounds into U.S. dollars was 1.8081 last year and is now 1.8909. Thus, the pound appreciated relative to the dollar over the investment period. The details of the two stock investments are as follows:

| | U.S. Stock | UK Stock | | U.S. Dollar Equivalent for UK Stocks |
|---|---|---|---|---|
| Purchase price, $P_{t-1}^C$ | $50 | £60 | = | $108.486 |
| Sale price, $P_t^C$ | $48 | £64 | = | $121.0176 |
| Dividends, $D_t^C$ | $1.50 | £2.50 | = | $ 4.72725 |

The return on the U.S. company's stock was:

$$R_t^{US} = \frac{\$48 - \$50}{\$50} + \frac{\$1.5}{\$50} = -1\%$$

and the return on the UK company's stock, ignoring the change in the exchange rate, was:

$$R_t^{UK} = \frac{£64 - £60}{£60} + \frac{£2.5}{£60} = 10.83\%$$

On a U.S. dollar equivalent basis the return was:

$$R_t^{UK} = \frac{\$121.0176 - \$108.486}{\$108.486} + \frac{\$4.72725}{108.486} = 15.91\%$$

> The loss on the U.S. stock, 1 percent, was offset by an increase in the value of the UK stock, reflecting both an increase in its local market value and an appreciation in the pound relative to the dollar.

While international diversification eliminates some risks, it introduces others. For example, for smaller investors, information about foreign stocks is less complete and timely than that for U.S. stocks. Further, international investments introduce foreign exchange risk (see Chapter 9) and political (or sovereign) risk (see Chapter 19). Table 8–7 shows the return on various world stock markets in U.S. dollars and in the local currency for the year May 2015–May 2016. Note the impact that foreign exchange rate changes have on these returns. For example, the return on the Buenos Aires Stock Exchange was −12.2 percent when measured in U.S. dollars and 36.0 percent when measured using the Argentine Peso.

As seen in Table 8–4 (Rest of world), in 2016 foreign investors held $5.6 trillion (or 15.7 percent) of the outstanding stock in the United States. Moreover, trading of foreign companies on U.S. stock exchanges totaled $2.5 trillion. Facilitating U.S. investment in stocks of foreign corporations is the creation of the American Depositary Receipt (ADR). An ADR is a certificate that represents ownership of a foreign stock. An ADR is typically created by a U.S. bank, which buys stock in foreign corporations in their domestic currencies and places them with a custodian. The bank then issues dollar ADRs backed by the shares of the foreign stock. Each ADR is a claim on a given number of shares of stock held by the bank. These ADRs are then traded in the United States, in dollars, on and off the organized exchanges. Global Depositary Receipts (GDRs) are similar to ADRs, but are issued worldwide.

There are currently over 3,600 ADRs of foreign corporations (such as Nokia and Petrobras) available to U.S. investors (mainly listed on the NYSE or the NASDAQ). The ADRs represented asset values of over $3.1 trillion in 2015. There are three main types of ADR issuances: Level 1, Level 2, and Level 3.

*Level 1 ADRs* are the most common and most basic of the ADRs. Level 1 ADRs are traded only on the over-the-counter (OTC) market and have the least amount of regulatory requirements as stipulated by the SEC. The companies issuing these ADRs do not have to abide by U.S. accounting (GAAP) standards, nor do they have to issue annual reports. Companies with shares trading under a Level 1 program may decide to upgrade their program to a Level 2 or Level 3 program to gain better exposure in U.S. markets.

**TABLE 8–7**  Impact of Change in Foreign Currency Exchange Rates on Market Returns

*(U.S. dollars and local currencies in millions)*

| Exchange | Currency | Value in Local Currency<br>May 2016 | in U.S. Dollars<br>May 2016 | Percentage Change since May 2015<br>(in U.S. dollars) | Percentage Change since May 2015<br>(in local currency) |
|---|---|---|---|---|---|
| Buenos Aires SE | Argentine peso | 816,261.2 | 58,654.2 | −12.2% | 36.0% |
| Colombia SE | Colombian peso | 296,356,386.0 | 98,048.8 | −21.3% | −6.4% |
| Mexican Exchange | Mexican peso | 7,204,606.5 | 389,948.3 | −17.6% | −0.6% |
| TMX Group | Canadian dollar | 2,454,982.9 | 1,879,628.6 | −11.1% | −6.9% |
| BSE India | Indian rupee | 99,286,781.7 | 1,479,132.7 | −8.3% | −3.6% |
| Japan Exchange Group—Tokyo | Japanese yen | 529,918,536.3 | 4,772,750.9 | −4.6% | −14.6% |
| National Stock Exchange India | Indian rupee | 97,405,511.5 | 1,451,106.3 | −7.6% | −2.8% |
| Johannesburg SE | South African rand | 3,074,158.0 | 3,419,911.0 | −2.2% | −4.0% |
| NYSE Euronext (Europe) | Euro | 15,496,523.3 | 982,527.6 | 3.3% | 34.8% |
| Oslo Børs | Norwegian Krone | 1,729,085.5 | 207,140.6 | −11.6% | −5.3% |
| Tel Aviv SE | Israeli new sheqel | 852,286.0 | 221,637.8 | −2.0% | −2.6% |
| Wiener Börse | Euro | 84,699.2 | 94,225.4 | −6.3% | −8.0% |

*Level 2 ADRs* can be listed on the major stock exchanges (NYSE and NASDAQ), but they have more regulatory requirements than Level 1 ADRs. Issuers of Level 2 ADRs are required to register with the SEC, to file a form 20-F (the basic equivalent to the regular 10-K filing by companies in the United States), and to file an annual report that complies with GAAP standards. Due to their listing on the NYSE and NASDAQ markets, Level 2 ADRs have much higher trading volumes than Level 1 ADRs. While listed on these exchanges, the company must meet their listing requirements. If it fails to do so, it may be delisted and forced to downgrade its ADR program.

*Level 3 ADRs* represent the most respected ADR level a foreign company can achieve in the United States markets. Like Level 2 ADRs, companies that issue Level 3 ADRs are required to register with the SEC, to file a form 20-F, and to file annual reports that comply with GAAP standards. Level 3 ADR companies, however, are allowed to issue shares directly into the U.S. markets, rather than simply allowing the indirect purchase of already created shares. Thus, the foreign company can actually issue shares in U.S. markets to raise capital. A foreign company with a Level 3 program is required to share any news that it distributes within its home country with U.S. investors. Thus, foreign companies with Level 3 programs are the easiest on which to find information.

Most ADR programs are subject to possible termination, which results in the cancellation of all the depository receipts, and a subsequent delisting from all exchanges on which they trade. The termination can be at the discretion of the foreign issuer or the depository bank, but is typically at the request of the issuer. In most cases, some type of reorganization or merger is the reason for termination of an ADR program.

The major attraction to U.S. investors is that ADRs are claims to foreign companies that trade on domestic (U.S.) exchanges *and* in dollars. Further, fees on ADRs are lower than those on many international mutual funds. Additionally, as mentioned above, investments in foreign securities help diversify a stock portfolio. However, like all international investments there are unique risks that are associated with them that are not usually present with domestic securities. For example, investors must consider country risk, foreign exchange risk, and other attributes when evaluating ADRs. Further, international companies and their underlying countries are not subject to as strict financial reporting standards as are companies in the United States. Thus, investors may experience trouble understanding financial reports, terms, and definitions due to differing accounting standards as well as language barriers.

As noted earlier, U.S. stock exchanges are regulated by the SEC on some matters and are self-regulated organizations for others. Stock market structures in Japan, Canada, Hong Kong, and Australia are similar to the U.S. structure. These exchanges are self-regulating, with the government mainly playing the role of monitor. In Canada, Hong Kong, and Australia, the exchanges determine which securities are listed and the criteria that firms must meet for membership. In Japan, the Ministry of Finance must approve all listed securities. In France, Belgium, Spain, and Italy, governments exercise the major control over the operations and activities of the exchanges. Membership on these exchanges may require government approval or licensing, and to insure against insolvency government agencies set minimum capital requirements. In Germany, Switzerland, Austria, and Sweden, the majority of the exchange trading is conducted through banks, reflecting regulatory and government policy.

Similar to the United States, stock markets in Canada, Japan, Hong Kong, and most of Europe use continuous trading. Stock markets in Germany and Austria use call-based trading, in which orders are batched for simultaneous execution at the same price and at a particular time during the day. Only the Montreal Stock Exchange uses a DMM system of trading directly similar to that of the NYSE. The Amsterdam Stock Exchange gives certain firms the DMMs' duties for small and medium-sized trades. Large trades, however, are transacted directly by the parties involved. On the Toronto Stock Exchange, market makers are similar to specialists. These traders are selected by the exchange to trade for their own accounts and to create an orderly price flow in stocks that the exchange assigns them. These traders are obligated to post bid and ask prices throughout the day and to keep their bid-ask spreads small.

**DO YOU UNDERSTAND:**

13. *What percentage of the world's capital markets are represented by U.S. stocks?*

14. *What an ADR is?*

All other continuous trading markets in the world use a competitive dealer system of trading similar to that used by NASDAQ. For example, the London International Stock Exchange allows any well-capitalized firm that follows the regulations to act as a dealer for any security. Market makers publish firm bid-ask quotes for their stocks. One difference in this market is that for a limit order, only the broker-dealer that accepts the order from a customer knows about it. The computerized trading system does not record the existence of an order. The dealer then executes the order when his or her own price reaches the requested level. The Tokyo Stock Exchange uses a variation of the competitive dealer system, in which a broker functions as an intermediary between the dealers and the brokers who are members of the exchange. The brokers cannot buy or sell for their own accounts, but can only arrange transactions among dealers, conduct trading auctions, and match buy and sell orders submitted by brokers for their clients.

## SUMMARY

In this chapter, we examined corporate stocks and stock markets. Holders of corporate (preferred and common) stock have an ownership interest in the issuing firm based on the percentage of stock held. Stock markets are the most watched and reported of the financial markets. We described the major characteristics of corporate stocks—for example, dividend rights, residual claim status, limited liability, and voting rights of stockholders. We also looked at the primary and secondary markets for stocks, including a description of the trading process. While the NYSE has historically been the major stock market exchange in the United States, we showed that the NASDAQ system is increasing in importance. We also looked at stock market indexes as predictors of future economic activity, reviewed the speed with which stock market prices adjust to new information, and described the major regulations governing stock market trading. We concluded the chapter with a brief look at international stock market activity—foreign investments in U.S. corporate stocks and U.S. investments in foreign corporate stocks.

## QUESTIONS

1. Why are stock markets the most watched and reported of the financial security markets? (*LG 8-1*)

2. What are some characteristics associated with dividends paid on common stock? (*LG 8-1*)

3. What is meant by the statement "common stockholders have a residual claim on the issuing firm's assets"? (*LG 8-1*)

4. What is a dual-class firm? Why do firms typically issue dual classes of common stock? (*LG 8-1*)

5. What is the difference between nonparticipating and participating preferred stock? (*LG 8-2*)

6. What is the difference between cumulative and noncumulative preferred stock? (*LG 8-2*)

7. Describe the registration process for a new stock issue. (*LG 8-3*)

8. What have been the trends in the growth of the major U.S. stock market exchanges? (*LG 8-4*)

9. What is a market order? What is a limit order? How are each executed? (*LG 8-5*)

10. What are circuit breakers in the context of stock market trading and volatility? (*LG 8-5*)

11. What are limit up–limit down rules? (*LG 8-5*)

12. What are flash trading, naked access, and dark pool trading? What are the benefits and drawbacks of these activities? (*LG 8-5*)

13. What are the major U.S. stock market indexes? (*LG 8-6*)

14. What is the difference between a price-weighted stock market index and a value-weighted stock market index? (*LG 8-6*)

15. Who are the major holders of corporate stock? (*LG 8-7*)

16. Are stock market indexes consistently accurate predictors of economic activity? (*LG 8-8*)

17. Describe the three forms of stock market efficiency. (*LG 8-8*)

18. Who are the major regulators of the stock markets? (*LG 8-4*)

19. Which countries or regions of the world have the largest stock markets? (*LG 8-9*)

20. What is an ADR? How is an ADR created? (*LG 8-9*)

## PROBLEMS

1. Suppose a firm has 15 million shares of common stock outstanding and six candidates are up for election to five seats on the board of directors. (*LG 8-1*)
   a. If the firm uses cumulative voting to elect its board, what is the minimum number of votes needed to ensure election to the board?
   b. If the firm uses straight voting to elect its board, what is the minimum number of votes needed to ensure election to the board?

2. Suppose a firm has 50 million shares of common stock outstanding and eight candidates are up for election to six seats on the board of directors. (*LG 8-1*)
   a. If the firm uses cumulative voting to elect its board, what is the minimum number of votes needed to ensure election to the board?
   b. If the firm uses straight voting to elect its board, what is the minimum number of votes needed to ensure election to the board?

3. Suppose you own 50,000 shares of common stock in a firm with 2.5 million total shares outstanding. The firm announces a plan to sell an additional 1 million shares through a rights offering. The market value of the stock is $35 before the rights offering and the new shares are being offered to existing shareholders at a $5 discount. (*LG 8-3*)
   a. If you exercise your preemptive rights, how many of the new shares can you purchase?
   b. What is the market value of the stock after the rights offering?
   c. What is your total investment in the firm after the rights offering? How is your investment split between original shares and new shares?
   d. If you decide not to exercise your preemptive rights, what is your investment in the firm after the rights offering? How is this split between old shares and rights?

4. Suppose you own 100,000 shares of common stock in a firm with 12.5 million total shares outstanding. The firm announces a plan to sell an additional 2.5 million shares through a rights offering. The market value of the stock is $22.50 before the rights offering and the new shares are being offered to existing shareholders at a $2.40 discount. (*LG 8-3*)
   a. If you exercise your preemptive rights, how many of the new shares can you purchase?

   b. What is the market value of the stock after the rights offering?
   c. What is your total investment in the firm after the rights offering? How is your investment split between original shares and new shares?
   d. If you decide not to exercise your preemptive rights, what is your investment in the firm after the rights offering? How is this split between old shares and rights?

5. Refer to the stock market quote in Table 8–1. (*LG 8-5*)
   a. What was the closing stock price for Abbott Laboratories on July 7, 2016?
   b. What were the high and low prices at which McDonald's traded between July 7, 2015, and July 7, 2016?
   c. What was the dividend yield on Waste Management stock as of July 7, 2016?

6. Refer to the stock market quote in Table 8–1. (*LG 8-5*)
   a. What was the closing stock price for Abercrombie & Fitch on July 6, 2016?
   b. What was the dividend yield on El Paso Electric stock as of July 7, 2016?
   c. What were the earnings per share on Wells Fargo stock for the period July 2015 through July 2016?

7. At the beginning of the year, you purchased a share of stock for $35. Over the year the dividends paid on the stock were $2.75 per share. (*LG 8-5*)
   a. Calculate the return if the price of the stock at the end of the year is $30.
   b. Calculate the return if the price of the stock at the end of the year is $40.

8. **eXcel** **Using a Spreadsheet to Calculate Stock Returns:** At the beginning of the year, you purchased a share of stock for $50. Over the year the dividends paid on the stock were $4.50 per share. Calculate the return if the price of the stock at the end of the year is $40, $48, $50, and $55. (*LG 8-5*)

| Price at Beginning of Year | Dividends | Price at End of Year ⇒ | The Return Is |
|---|---|---|---|
| $50 | $4.50 | $40 | −11.00% |
| 50 | 4.50 | 48 | 5.00 |
| 50 | 4.50 | 50 | 9.00 |
| 50 | 4.50 | 55 | 19.00 |

9. Use the information in the following stock quote to calculate McKesson's earnings per share over the last year. (*LG 8-5*)

| (1) Name | (2) Symbol | (3) Open | (4) High | (5) Low | (6) Close | (7) Net Chg | (8) % Chg | (9) Volume | (10) 52 Week High | (11) 52 Week Low | (12) Div | (13) Yield | (14) PE | (15) YTD % Chg |
|---|---|---|---|---|---|---|---|---|---|---|---|---|---|---|
| McKesson | MCK | 61.00 | 61.14 | 60.28 | 60.60 | −1.01 | −1.64 | 2,719,785 | 71.49 | 53.57 | 0.72 | 1.19 | 13.00 | −3.04 |

10. Use the information in the following stock quote to calculate Abercrombie & Fitch's earnings per share over the last year. (*LG 8-5*)

| (1) Name | (2) Symbol | (3) Open | (4) High | (5) Low | (6) Close | (7) Net Chg | (8) % Chg | (9) Volume | (10) 52 Week High | (11) 52 Week Low | (12) Div | (13) Yield | (14) PE | (15) YTD % Chg |
|---|---|---|---|---|---|---|---|---|---|---|---|---|---|---|
| Abercrombie & Fitch | ANF | 37.89 | 38.41 | 37.20 | 37.60 | −1.21 | −3.12 | 2,323,747 | 51.12 | 28.76 | 0.70 | 1.86 | 55.29 | 7.89 |

# SEARCH THE SITE

Go to the Federal Reserve Board's website and find the most recent data on the market value of common stock outstanding, by type of issue and by holder.

Go to the Federal Reserve Board's website at **www.federalreserve.gov/releases/Z1.** Click on the most recent date. Click on "Level tables." This will download a file onto your computer that will contain the data on the market value of common stock outstanding, Table L.223.

**Questions**

1. What is the market value of common stock currently outstanding? Calculate the percentage change in this value since 2016, reported in Figure 8–1.
2. What is the percentage of common stock outstanding issued by nonfinancial corporate businesses, financial corporations, and the rest of the world?

---

**APPENDIX 8A: The Capital Asset Pricing Model**

**APPENDIX 8B: Event Study Tests**

Appendixes 8A and 8B are available through Connect or your course instructor.

**chapter**

# 9

# Foreign Exchange Markets

## Learning Goals

**LG 9-1**  *Understand what foreign exchange markets and foreign exchange rates are.*

**LG 9-2**  *Understand the history of and current trends in foreign exchange markets.*

**LG 9-3**  *Identify the world's largest foreign exchange markets.*

**LG 9-4**  *Distinguish between a spot foreign exchange transaction and a forward foreign exchange transaction.*

**LG 9-5**  *Calculate return and risk on foreign exchange transactions.*

**LG 9-6**  *Describe the role of financial institutions in foreign exchange transactions.*

**LG 9-7**  *Identify the relations among interest rates, inflation, and exchange rates.*

## FOREIGN EXCHANGE MARKETS AND RISK: CHAPTER OVERVIEW

**LG 9-1**  Cash flows from the sale of products, services, or assets denominated in a foreign currency are transacted in **foreign exchange (FX) markets.** A **foreign exchange rate** is the price at which one currency (e.g., the U.S. dollar) can be exchanged for another currency (e.g., the Swiss franc) in the foreign exchange markets. These transactions expose U.S. corporations and investors to **foreign exchange risk** as the cash flows are converted into and out of U.S. dollars. Thus, in addition to understanding the operations of domestic financial markets, financial managers and investors must also understand the operations of foreign exchange markets and foreign capital markets.

Today's U.S.-based companies operate globally. It is therefore essential that financial managers understand how events and movements in financial markets in other countries affect the profitability and performance of their own companies. For example, in 2015 McDonald's net income was down 5 percent from 2014. However, excluding losses from foreign exchange movements, net income would have increased 5 percent. In 2015, more than 75 percent of McDonald's revenue came from outside the United States. Most growth going forward was expected to come from business expansion overseas rather than from within the United States. Foreign currency exchange is therefore an important factor for investors

**foreign exchange (FX) markets**

*Markets in which cash flows from the sale of products or assets denominated in a foreign currency are transacted.*

**foreign exchange rate**

*The price at which one currency can be exchanged for another currency.*

**foreign exchange risk**

*Risk that cash flows will vary as the actual amount of U.S. dollars received on a foreign investment changes due to a change in foreign exchange rates.*

**currency depreciation**

*When a country's currency falls in value relative to other currencies, meaning the country's goods become cheaper for foreign buyers and foreign goods become more expensive for foreign sellers.*

**currency appreciation**

*When a country's currency rises in value relative to other currencies, meaning that the country's goods are more expensive for foreign buyers and foreign goods are cheaper for foreign sellers.*

to consider. More broadly, extreme foreign exchange risk from a single event was evident in 2015 when banks, brokers, and individual investors lost hundreds of millions of dollars after an unexpected surge in the Swiss franc shook foreign exchange markets. The Swiss franc jumped by nearly 30 percent against the euro and 18 percent against the dollar in the minutes following the Swiss National Bank's decision to stop capping the value of the franc against the euro. Citigroup and Deutsche Bank each lost about $150 million on the franc's appreciation. Barclays expected losses to be in the tens of millions of dollars. FXCM Inc., a major U.S. retail foreign exchange broker, saw the biggest losses and had to be rescued with emergency funding of $300 million from investment firm Leucadia National Corp.

An even larger event was United Kingdom's 2016 vote to leave the European Union (called Brexit), which shocked the global economy in an unusual way. In the aftermath of the June 23 vote, the value of the British pound plummeted. The U.S. dollar and the Japanese yen surged. Unlike normal times, when at least one of those moves would signal faster growth to come, all three countries braced for foreign exchange risk-driven slowdowns in their economies. The United States and Japan worried that the strength of their currencies would hurt exports of their goods and services. The United Kingdom suddenly found itself in a similar situation to many developing nations, less concerned with how a weaker currency might boost its export sectors and more with the faltering economic prospects that caused investors to flee the pound.

In 2015, U.S. imports of foreign goods were $3.7 trillion, while exports totaled $3.3 trillion. Trades of this magnitude would not be possible without a market where investors can easily buy and sell foreign currencies. Additionally, as firms and investors increase the volume of transactions in foreign currencies, hedging foreign exchange risk has become a more important activity. Financial managers therefore must understand how events in other countries in which they operate affect cash flows received from or paid to other countries and thus their company's profitability. Foreign exchange markets are the markets in which traders of foreign currencies transact most efficiently and at the lowest cost. As a result, foreign exchange markets facilitate foreign trade, the raising of capital in foreign markets, the transfer of risk between participants, and speculation on currency values.

The actual amount of U.S. dollars received on a foreign transaction depends on the (foreign) exchange rate between the U.S. dollar and the foreign currency when the nondollar cash flow is received (and exchanged for U.S. dollars) at some future date. If the foreign **currency** declines (or **depreciates**)[1] in value relative to the U.S. dollar over the period between the time a foreign investment is made and the time it is liquidated, the dollar value of the cash flows received will fall. If the foreign **currency** rises (or **appreciates**) in value relative to the U.S. dollar, the dollar value of the cash flows received on the foreign investment increases.

In this chapter, we examine the operations of foreign exchange markets. We start with a brief look at the history of foreign exchange markets. We define and describe the spot and forward foreign exchange transaction process. We also look at how changes in a country's inflation and short-term interest rates affect the exchange rate of the country's currency. Transactions between citizens of one country (e.g., the United States) with other countries are summarized in the balance of payment accounts of that country. Balance of payment (international transactions) accounts for the United States are presented and described in Appendix 9A (available through Connect or your course instructor).

## BACKGROUND AND HISTORY OF FOREIGN EXCHANGE MARKETS

Foreign exchange markets have existed for some time as international trade and investing have resulted in the need to exchange currencies. The type of exchange rate system used to accomplish this exchange, however, has changed over time. During most of the 1800s,

---

1. Currency depreciation is most often used as the term describing the unofficial decrease in the exchange rate in a floating exchange rate system. Devaluation is a reduction in the value of a currency with respect to other monetary units. In common modern usage, it specifically implies an official lowering of the value of a country's currency within a fixed exchange rate system, by which the monetary authority formally sets a new fixed rate with respect to a foreign reference currency. Depreciation and devaluation are sometimes used interchangeably, but they always refer to values in terms of other currencies.

foreign exchange markets operated under a gold standard or system. Under the gold standard, currency issuers guaranteed to redeem notes, upon demand, in an equivalent amount of gold. Governments that employed such a fixed system of exchange, and which redeemed their notes to other governments in gold, shared a fixed-currency relationship. As a result, gold became a transportable, universal, and stable unit of valuation. Further, the United Kingdom, which at the time was the dominant international trading country, had a long-standing commitment to the gold standard. However, during the 1939–1942 period, the United Kingdom depleted much of its gold stock in purchases of munitions and weaponry from the United States and other nations to fight the Second World War. This depletion of the United Kingdom's reserve signaled to Winston Churchill (the UK prime minister at the time) that returning to a prewar-style gold standard was impractical. As a result, from 1944 to 1971 the Bretton Woods Agreement called for the exchange rate of one currency for another to be fixed within narrow bands around a specified rate with the help of government intervention. The Bretton Woods Agreement, however, led to a situation in which some currencies (such as the U.S. dollar) became overvalued and others (such as the German mark) became undervalued. The Smithsonian Agreement of 1971 sought to address this situation. Under this agreement, major countries allowed the dollar to be devalued and the boundaries between which exchange rates could fluctuate were increased from 1 percent to 2¼ percent.

In 1973, under the Smithsonian Agreement II, the exchange rate boundaries were eliminated altogether. This effectively allowed exchange rates of major currencies to float freely. This free-floating foreign exchange rate system is still partially in place. However, as discussed in Chapter 4 and below, central governments may still intervene in the foreign exchange markets directly to change the direction of exchange rate and currency movements by altering interest rates to affect the value of their currency relative to others. In 1992, 12 major European countries and Vatican City pegged their exchange rates together to create a single currency, called the euro.[2]

Until 1972, the interbank foreign exchange market was the only channel through which spot and forward (see below) foreign exchange transactions took place. The interbank market involves electronic trades between major banks (such as between J.P. Morgan Chase and HSBC) around the world. This market is over the counter (OTC) and thus has no regular trading hours, so that currencies can be bought or sold somewhere around the world 24 hours a day. Since 1972, organized markets such as the International Money Market (IMM) of the Chicago Mercantile Exchange (CME) have developed derivatives trading in foreign currency futures and options. However, the presence of such a well-developed interbank market for foreign exchange forward contracts has hampered the development of the futures market for foreign exchange trading. For example, while foreign currency trading has grown significantly since 1972, trading in the forward market continues to be much larger than the futures market (on the order of 20 times the daily volume measured by value of trades).

The major differences between the interbank foreign exchange market and organized trading on exchanges include market location, standardization of contracts, standardization of delivery dates, and differences in the way contracts are settled. While the interbank forward market is a worldwide market with no geographic boundaries, the principal futures market is the IMM in Chicago. Futures market contracts trade in the major currencies (e.g., the euro, British pound) with contracts expiring on the third Wednesday of March, June, September, and December. In contrast, forward market contracts can be entered into on any currency, with maturity stated as a given number of days for delivery of the currency in the future. The futures market (the IMM of the CME) determines the size of futures contracts on foreign currencies, and all contracts must be of these sizes. In the forward market, contract size is negotiated between the bank and the customer. Finally, less than 1 percent of all futures contracts are completed by delivery of the foreign currency. Rather, profit or loss on the futures contract is settled daily between the trader and the exchange, and many traders

---

2. The 12 countries are Austria, Belgium, Finland, France, Germany, Greece, Ireland, Italy, Luxembourg, the Netherlands, Portugal, and Spain. As of 2013, 10 additional countries (Andorra, Cyrus, Estonia, Kosovo, Malta, Monaco, Montenegro, San Marino, Slovakia, and Slovenia) have adopted the euro as their sole currency.

**Figure 9–1** Largest Global Foreign Exchange Markets

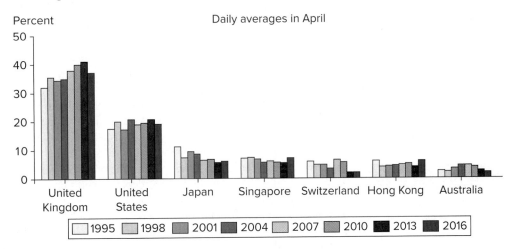

Note: Foreign exchange market turnover adjusted for local double-counting (i.e., net-gross basis).

sell their contracts prior to maturity (see Chapter 10). In contrast, delivery of the foreign currency occurs on the contract's maturity in over 90 percent of forward contracts.

**LG 9-3**

The foreign exchange markets have become among the largest of all financial markets, with turnover exceeding $4.8 trillion per day in 2015, down from $6 trillion in 2014. Figure 9–1 shows the percentage share of the major foreign exchange trading centers worldwide from 1995 through 2016. London continues to be the largest center for trading in foreign exchange (37.1 percent of worldwide trading); it handles over twice the daily volume of New York, the second-largest market (19.4 percent of all trading). However, London's status as the dominant location for foreign exchange trading and the world's principal location for trading the euro (a $2 trillion a day market) is uncertain after the United Kingdom's vote to leave the European Union. In 2015, the European Central Bank attempted to bar clearing houses outside the EU from trading the euro. The attempt failed because the UK was a member of the EU. The country now faces losing its euro business. Other connected trading activity could follow. Third-ranked Singapore handles approximately one-seventh the volume of London. Moreover, the FX market is essentially a 24-hour market, moving from Tokyo, London, and New York throughout the day. Therefore, fluctuations in exchange rates and thus FX trading risk exposure continues into the night even when some FI operations are closed.

**LG 9-2**

**The Introduction of the Euro.** The euro is the name of the European Union's single currency. It started trading on January 1, 1999, when exchange rates among the currencies of the original 12 participating countries were fixed, although domestic currencies (e.g., the Italian lira and French franc) continued to circulate. By January 1, 2002, domestic currencies started to be phased out and euro notes and coins began circulating within 12 EU countries (increased to 22 EU countries by 2013) and Vatican City. The eventual creation of the euro had its origins in the creation of the European Community (EC): a consolidation of three European communities in 1967 (the European Coal and Steel Community, the European Economic Market, and the European Atomic Energy Community). The emphasis of the EC was both political and economic. Its aim was to break down trade barriers within a common market and create a political union among the people of Europe. The Maastricht Treaty of 1993 set out stages for transition to an integrated monetary union among the EC participating countries, referred to as the European Monetary Union (EMU). Some of the main stipulations of the Maastricht Treaty included the eventual creation of a single currency (the euro), the creation of an integrated European system of central banks, and the establishment of a single European Central Bank (ECB).

While the creation of the euro has had a significant effect throughout Europe, it has also had a notable impact on the global financial system. For example, in the first decade of the 2000s, as the United States experienced an increasing national debt, rapid consumer spending, and a current account deficit big enough to bankrupt most other countries (see below), the euro increased in value by 35 percent against the U.S. dollar. Indeed, in the mid-2000s, as the dollar depreciated in value against the euro, Russia's Central Bank said it was considering replacing some of the U.S. dollars in its reserves with euros. Asian central banks hinted that they would soon do the same. The Chinese Central Bank had already substituted some of its dollars for euros. As a result of these actions, the euro was the world's second most important currency for international transactions behind the dollar and some predicted, given the combined size of the "euro-economies," that it would compete against the dollar as the premier international currency. However, in the 2010s, while the U.S. debt problems continued, Europe was in a full-blown sovereign debt crisis. The dollar strengthened against the euro as Europe's debt crisis continued to persist. Central banks turned back to the dollar over the euro. The dollar remains the unparalleled medium of exchange because it is the world's easiest currency to buy or sell. In 2016, 43.8 percent of all foreign exchange transactions were denominated in dollars, while 15.6 percent were denominated in euros.

> **DO YOU UNDERSTAND:**
>
> 1. How the Bretton Woods Agreement affected the ability of foreign exchange rates to fluctuate freely?
> 2. What the euro is?

**Dollarization.**     Following the abandonment of the gold standard and the Bretton Woods Agreement, some countries sought ways to promote global economic stability and hence their own prosperity. For many of these countries, currency stabilization was achieved by pegging the local currency to a major convertible currency. Other countries simply abandoned their local currency in favor of exclusive use of the U.S. dollar (or another major international currency, such as the euro). The use of a foreign currency in parallel to, or instead of, the local currency is referred to as **dollarization.**[3] Dollarization can occur unofficially (when private agents prefer the foreign currency over the domestic currency) or officially (when a country adopts the foreign currency as legal tender and ceases to issue the domestic currency). For example, if the U.S. dollar is the currency adopted, Federal Reserve notes become legal tender and the only form of paper money recognized by the government. There is nothing to prevent a country from unilaterally moving to an official dollarized currency. However, if the U.S. dollar is to be used as another country's official currency, the Fed has recommended that it receive advance notification of the extra notes that it would have to make available.

**dollarization**

*The use of a foreign currency in parallel to, or instead of, the local currency.*

The major advantage of dollarization is the promotion of fiscal discipline and thus greater financial stability and lower inflation. The biggest economies to have officially dollarized are Panama (since 1904), Ecuador (since 2000), and El Salvador (since 2001). The U.S. dollar, the euro, the New Zealand dollar, the Swiss franc, the Indian rupee, and the Australian dollar are the only currencies used by other countries for official dollarization. Dollarization was highly unsuccessful at helping Argentina address its financial crisis in the early 2000s and was abandoned. Prior to its economic crisis from 1999 to 2002, Argentina operated under a currency board system that maintained a 1:1 exchange rate between the dollar and the peso. Dollarization required holding sufficient dollar reserves to fully back the pesos in circulation. With the appreciation of the dollar in the late 1990s, the Argentine currency board experienced overvaluation. Argentina's exports became less competitive on the world market. In addition, Argentina had been running massive fiscal budget deficits for some years. The climbing deficit led to an increase in devaluation concerns. As a result, roughly $20 billion in capital fled the country in 2001. Peso interest rates climbed to between 40 and 60 percent, which further weakened the government's budget position. At the end of 2001, Argentina abandoned the peg to the dollar and went to a floating exchange rate for the peso.

---

3. The term is not only applied to usage of the U.S. dollar, but is used generally to refer to the use of any foreign currency as the national currency.

**The Free-Floating Yuan.**   On July 21, 2005, the Chinese government shifted away from its currency's (the yuan) peg to the U.S. dollar, stating that the value of the yuan would be determined using a "managed" floating system with reference to an unspecified basket of foreign currencies. The partial free-floating of the yuan was in part the result of pressure from Western countries whose politicians argued that China's currency regime gave it an unfair advantage in global markets due to the relative underpricing of the yuan with respect to the dollar and other currencies.[4] The undervalued yuan resulted in Chinese exports being relatively cheap, which hurt domestic manufacturing in other countries, especially the United States. Indeed, lawmakers in the U.S. Congress, worried about the loss of U.S. jobs, threatened to impose steep tariffs on Chinese goods unless China changed its foreign exchange policy. Finance ministers from the world's leading economies unanimously argued that China should let the yuan float.

Using statistical methods that take into account concurrent movements in exchange rates among the reference currencies, economists inferred that the yuan eventually became equally weighted between the dollar and the euro after Beijing de-pegged from the dollar. The yuan's 20 percent appreciation against the dollar between 2005 and 2008 mostly reflected the euro's gains against the dollar. By May 2008, as the global financial crisis unfolded and the dollar began to rebound against the euro, Beijing started to move the yuan back toward giving primary weighting to the dollar. This move kept the yuan from falling against the dollar during the global financial meltdown. Thus, China's currency policy had come full circle, virtually back to what it was in late 2005.

Throughout the financial crisis U.S. officials worried that, by keeping its currency artificially weak and thus its goods more competitive on world markets, China's failure to let the yuan float freely would slow down the U.S. and worldwide recovery from the financial crisis and the recession of 2008–2009. Beijing promised a more flexible exchange rate in June 2010, effectively ditching a two-year peg to the dollar that was enacted during the global financial crisis. But the yuan rose by only about 2 percent against the dollar in the following three months. Its appreciation sped up slightly after the U.S. House of Representatives passed a bill in September 2010 that would allow Washington to sanction countries that manipulate their currency for trade gain. Further, in October 2010, the then U.S. Treasury secretary Timothy Geithner held talks with top Chinese finance officials amid currency tensions after a pledge by finance leaders worldwide to rebalance the global economy. Additionally, in November 2010, G-20 finance ministers and central bankers promised to avoid debilitating currency devaluations, to reduce trade and financial imbalances, and to give China and other major developing countries a bigger role in managing the global economy. However, actions by the United States had little effect (particularly as the United States was accused of its own currency manipulation from 2010 through 2013 as it purchased billions in U.S. Treasury securities in its efforts to stimulate the U.S. economy) and the yuan remained weak through the end of the decade.

In the 2010s, aware of the criticisms pertaining to currency manipulation and repercussions to its economic growth, China began to respond, albeit slowly. In 2009, it began a pilot program of internationalizing its currency by allowing Hong Kong banks to trade the yuan. As a result, the number of yuan-held deposits in Hong Kong exploded, from less than 100 billion yuan in 2010 to about 600 billion yuan in 2013. In January 2011, China began allowing Americans to trade in the currency and Chinese-based companies were allowed for the first time to use the yuan for business outside the mainland. By October 2011, foreign companies were allowed to settle direct investments on the mainland using the yuan. Then in 2012, China eased the yuan's trading band against the dollar for the first time in five years—allowing the currency to fluctuate more broadly. The rapid growth in off-the-mainland yuan deposits was recognized by the Chicago Mercantile Exchange (CME). In February 2013 the CME announced it would join Hong Kong Exchanges and Clearing Limited and start trading Chinese Renmimbi (CNH) futures under contracts of up to three years.

---

4. In May 2007, the daily trading band for the yuan against the U.S. dollar was widened.

In November 2015, the International Monetary Fund (IMF) designated the Chinese yuan (also called renminbi or RMB), an IMF-accepted reserve currency, along with the U.S. dollar, Japanese yen, British pound sterling, and euro in the Special Drawing Right (SDR) basket (effective on October 1, 2016). The SDR is neither a currency nor a claim on the IMF. It was created by the 188-country organization that works to foster global monetary cooperation in 1969 to support the Bretton Woods fixed exchange rate system. It is a potential claim on the freely usable currencies of its members, and SDRs can be exchanged for freely usable currencies. For China, SDR inclusion is mostly a symbolic event. It would be the first emerging market currency added to the SDR and the first new currency added since the SDR's creation. With the inclusion, China begins to enjoy the privilege of issuing a currency that is viewed not just as an invoice currency, but as a true reserve currency by its foreign partners.

# FOREIGN EXCHANGE RATES AND TRANSACTIONS

## Foreign Exchange Rates

As mentioned earlier, a foreign exchange rate is the price at which one currency (e.g., the U.S. dollar) can be exchanged for another currency (e.g., the Swiss franc). Table 9–1 lists the exchange rates between the U.S. dollar and other currencies as of 4:00 p.m. eastern standard time on July 15, 2016. Foreign exchange rates are listed in two ways: U.S. dollars received for one unit of the foreign currency exchanged (IN US$ or USD,[5] also referred to as the *direct quote*) and foreign currency received for each U.S. dollar exchanged (PER US$, also referred to as the *indirect quote*). For example, the exchange rate of U.S. dollars for Canadian dollars (CAD) on July 15, 2016, was $0.7709 (US$/C$ or CAD/ USD), or U.S. $0.7709 could be received for each Canadian dollar exchanged. Conversely, the exchange rate of Canadian dollars for U.S. dollars was 1.2972 (C$/US$ or USD/CAD), or 1.2972 Canadian dollars could be received for each U.S. dollar exchanged.

Notice that the "IN US$" exchange rates, or the rate of U.S. dollars for the foreign currency, are simply the inverse of the "PER US$" exchange rates, or the rate of exchange of foreign currency for U.S. dollars and vice versa. For example, US$/C$ = $0.7709 = 1/(C$/US$) = 1/1.2972, and C$/US$ = 1.2972 = 1/(US$/C$) = 1/$0.7709. This is the case for both spot and forward exchange rates in Table 9–1.

## Foreign Exchange Transactions

**LG 9-4**

**spot foreign exchange transactions**

*Foreign exchange transactions involving the immediate exchange of currencies at the current (or spot) exchange rate.*

There are two types of foreign exchange rates and foreign exchange transactions: spot and forward. **Spot foreign exchange transactions** involve the immediate exchange of currencies at the current (or spot) exchange rate—see Figure 9–2. Spot transactions can be conducted through the foreign exchange division of commercial banks or a nonbank foreign currency dealer. For example, a U.S. investor wanting to buy British pounds through a local bank on July 15, 2016, essentially has the dollars transferred from his or her bank account to the dollar account of a pound seller at a rate of $1 per 0.7583 pound (or $1.3188 per pound).[6] Simultaneously, pounds are transferred from the seller's account into an account designated by the U.S. investor. If the dollar depreciates in value relative to the pound (e.g., $1 per 0.7542 pound or $1.3259 per pound), the value of the pound investment, if converted back into U.S. dollars, increases. If the dollar appreciates in value relative to the pound (e.g., $1 per 0.7599 pound or $1.3160 per pound), the value of the pound investment, if converted back into U.S. dollars, decreases.

---

5. USD is the currency code for the U.S. dollar set by the International Organization for Standardization (ISO). The ISO is an international standard-setting body composed of representatives from various national standards organizations. The ISO 4217 standard specifies the structure for a three-letter alphabetic code for the representation of currencies. The designations for the major currencies are: U.S. dollar (USD), euro (EUR), Japanese yen (JPY), British pound (GBP), Australian dollar (AUD), Canadian dollar (CAD), Swiss franc (CHF), and Hong Kong dollar (HKD).

6. In actual practice, settlement—exchange of currencies—occurs normally two days after a transaction.

**TABLE 9–1** Foreign Currency Exchange Rates

| Exchange Rates: New York Closing Snapshot<br>Friday, July 15, 2016<br>U.S.-dollar foreign-exchange rates in late New York trading | | | | | Country/Currency | IN US$ | | PER US$ | |
|---|---|---|---|---|---|---|---|---|---|
| | **IN US$** | | **PER US$** | | | Fri | Thurs | Fri | Thurs |
| **Country/Currency** | **Fri** | **Thurs** | **Fri** | **Thurs** | Thailand baht | 0.02860 | 0.02855 | 34.970 | 35.030 |
| | | | | | Vietnam dong | 0.00004482 | 0.00004488 | 22310 | 22282 |
| **Americas** | | | | | **Europe** | | | | |
| Argentina peso* | 0.0669 | 0.0679 | 14.9390 | 14.7260 | Bulgaria lev | 0.56367 | 0.56844 | 1.774 | 1.759 |
| Brazil real | 0.3050 | 0.3074 | 3.2784 | 3.2533 | Croatia kuna | 0.1471 | 0.1484 | 6.7973 | 6.7387 |
| Canada dollar | 0.7709 | 0.7758 | 1.2972 | 1.2891 | Czech Rep. koruna** | 0.04084 | 0.04114 | 24.489 | 24.309 |
| 1-month forward | 0.7709 | 0.7758 | 1.2971 | 1.2890 | Denmark krone | 0.1483 | 0.1495 | 6.7422 | 6.6888 |
| 3-months forward | 0.7710 | 0.7759 | 1.2970 | 1.2889 | Euro area euro | 1.1037 | 1.1121 | 0.9061 | 0.8992 |
| 6-months forward | 0.7711 | 0.7760 | 1.2968 | 1.2887 | 1-month forward | 1.1052 | 1.1135 | 0.9048 | 0.8980 |
| Chile peso | 0.001526 | 0.001538 | 655.10 | 650.40 | 3-months forward | 1.1079 | 1.1163 | 0.9026 | 0.8958 |
| Colombia peso | 0.0003422 | 0.0003429 | 2922.25 | 2916.55 | 6-months forward | 1.1123 | 1.1207 | 0.8990 | 0.8923 |
| Ecuador US dollar | 1 | 1 | 1 | 1 | Hungary forint | 0.00349993 | 0.00353782 | 285.72 | 282.66 |
| Mexico peso* | 0.0537 | 0.0545 | 18.6066 | 18.3528 | Iceland krona | 0.008237 | 0.008219 | 121.41 | 121.67 |
| Peru new sol | 0.3050 | 0.3049 | 3.2785 | 3.2795 | Norway krone | 0.1179 | 0.1196 | 8.4836 | 8.3631 |
| Uruguay peso† | 0.03294 | 0.03299 | 30.3600 | 30.3100 | Poland zloty | 0.2492 | 0.2522 | 4.0126 | 3.9645 |
| Venezuela bolivar | 0.1000996 | 0.10014972 | 9.9901 | 9.9851 | Romania leu | 0.2463 | 0.2479 | 4.0603 | 4.0339 |
| | | | | | Russia ruble‡ | 0.01570 | 0.01590 | 63.706 | 62.904 |
| **Asia-Pacific** | | | | | Sweden krona | 0.1164 | 0.1177 | 8.5882 | 8.4973 |
| Australian dollar | 0.7575 | 0.7632 | 1.3201 | 1.3103 | Switzerland franc | 1.0175 | 1.0195 | 0.9828 | 0.9809 |
| China yuan | 0.1494 | 0.1497 | 6.6924 | 6.6818 | 1-month forward | 1.0193 | 1.0213 | 0.9810 | 0.9791 |
| Hong Kong dollar | 0.1290 | 0.1290 | 7.7546 | 7.7543 | 3-months forward | 1.0229 | 1.0249 | 0.9776 | 0.9757 |
| India rupee | 0.01489 | 0.01496 | 67.14050 | 66.84320 | 6-months forward | 1.0286 | 1.0306 | 0.9722 | 0.9703 |
| Indonesia rupiah | 0.0000763 | 0.0000767 | 13110 | 13037 | Turkey lira** | 0.3311 | 0.3474 | 3.0198 | 2.8783 |
| Japan yen | 0.00953 | 0.00949 | 104.91 | 105.35 | Ukraine hryvnia | 0.0404 | 0.0404 | 24.7590 | 24.7535 |
| 1-month forward | 0.0095320 | 0.0094918 | 104.90991 | 105.35397 | UK pound | 1.3188 | 1.3344 | 0.7583 | 0.7494 |
| 3-months forward | 0.0095320 | 0.00949235 | 104.90980 | 105.34796 | 1-month forward | 1.3192 | 1.3348 | 0.7581 | 0.7492 |
| 6-months forward | 0.0095320 | 0.00949237 | 104.90961 | 105.34777 | 3-months forward | 1.3202 | 1.3358 | 0.7575 | 0.7486 |
| Kazakhstan tenge | 0.00295 | 0.00295 | 339.27 | 339.33 | 6-months forward | 1.3221 | 1.3377 | 0.7564 | 0.7475 |
| Macau pataca | 0.1251643 | 0.1253039 | 7.990 | 7.981 | **Middle East/Africa** | | | | |
| Malaysia ringgit | 0.2522 | 0.2542 | 3.9657 | 3.9335 | Bahrain dinar | 2.6500 | 2.6506 | 0.3774 | 0.3773 |
| New Zealand dollar | 0.7118 | 0.7199 | 1.4049 | 1.3891 | Egypt pound* | 0.1127 | 0.1126 | 8.8726 | 8.8782 |
| Pakistan rupee | 0.00955 | 0.00954 | 104.72 | 104.80 | Israel shekel | 0.2580 | 0.2597 | 3.8767 | 3.8511 |
| Philippines peso | 0.0214 | 0.0213 | 46.7930 | 46.8900 | Kuwait dinar | 3.3113 | 3.3097 | 0.3020 | 0.3021 |
| Singapore dollar | 0.7420 | 0.7450 | 1.3477 | 1.3423 | Oman sul rial | 2.59912 | 2.59663 | 0.38 | 0.39 |
| South Korea won | 0.0008784 | 0.0008831 | 1138.47 | 1132.42 | Qatar rial | 0.2748 | 0.2746 | 3.6387 | 3.6422 |
| Sri Lanka rupee | 0.0068757 | 0.0068644 | 145.44 | 145.68 | Saudia Arabia riyal | 0.2668 | 0.2666 | 3.7475 | 3.7503 |
| Taiwan dollar | 0.03130 | 0.03125 | 31.95 | 32.00 | South Africa rand | 0.0690 | 0.0703 | 14.5015 | 14.2255 |

*Floating rate. †Financial. ‡Russian Central Bank rate.
**Commercial rate. ††Special Drawing Rights (SDR); from the International Monetary Fund; based on exchange rates for U.S., British and Japanese currencies.
**Note:** Based on trading among banks of $1 million and more, as quoted at 4 P.M. ET by Thomson Reuters.
**Source:** *The Wall Street Journal Online,* July 18, 2016. www.wsj.com

The exchange rates listed in Table 9–1 all involve the exchange of U.S. dollars for the foreign currency, or vice versa. Historically, the exchange of a sum of money into a different currency required a trader to first convert the money into U.S. dollars and then convert

**Figure 9–2** Spot versus Forward Foreign Exchange Transaction

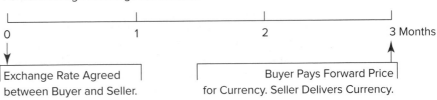

it into the desired currency. More recently, cross-currency trades allow currency traders to bypass this step of initially converting into U.S. dollars. Cross-currency trades are a pair of currencies traded in foreign exchange markets that do not involve the U.S. dollar. For example, GBP/JPY cross-exchange trading was created to allow individuals in the UK and Japan who wanted to convert their money into the other currency to do so without having to bear the cost of having to first convert into U.S. dollars. Cross-currency exchange rates for eight major countries are listed at Bloomberg's website www.bloomberg.com/markets/currencies/fxc.html.

The appreciation of a country's currency (or a rise in its value relative to other currencies) means that the country's goods are more expensive for foreign buyers and foreign goods are cheaper for foreign sellers (all else constant). Thus, when a country's currency appreciates, domestic manufacturers find it harder to sell their goods abroad and foreign manufacturers find it easier to sell their goods to domestic purchasers. Conversely, depreciation of a country's currency (or a fall in its value relative to other currencies) means the country's goods become cheaper for foreign buyers and foreign goods become more expensive for foreign sellers.

Figure 9–3 shows the pattern of spot exchange rates between the U.S. dollar and several foreign currencies from 2002 through 2016. As the figure shows, the U.S. dollar depreciated relative to the euro and a number of other floating currencies between 2003 and 2007. For example, in just the first four months of 2007, the euro for U.S. dollar exchange rate, €/US\$, fell almost 6 percent against the euro and depreciated relative to most other currencies as well. In October 2007, the dollar hit a record low against the euro, the Canadian dollar, and the Australian dollar, and it fell to a three-month low against the British pound. A main factor affecting exchange rate movements was interest rate differentials across major economies. The euro's rise in value against the U.S. dollar was due, at least in part, to the fact that the euro area had the highest interest rates and thus attracted yield-driven investment capital. In the summer of 2007, the Federal Reserve decreased interest rates to boost a weakening economy that was particularly hard hit as a result of a crumbling subprime mortgage market and a record slowdown in the overall housing market. Relatively high interest rates in the United Kingdom contributed to the appreciation of the pound against the dollar (and the yen) as well. A second factor affecting the exchange rates was a high volume of central bank intervention relative to past practice, especially in Asian countries. These actions kept upward pressure on the local currencies but helped devalue the U.S. dollar. For example, the Japanese Ministry of Finance purchased \$316 billion of U.S. assets between January 2003 and March 2004 (many times the purchases in earlier years). Chinese monetary authorities bought dollar reserves while trying to preserve the yuan's fixed exchange rate with the U.S. dollar. In India, Korea, and Taiwan, dollar reserves also rose substantially as monetary authorities tried to limit the appreciation of their currencies against the U.S. dollar. Official foreign exchange reserves held by monetary authorities worldwide increased another \$850 billion in 2006 (twice the amount held in 2005). China had the largest accumulation of foreign exchange reserves, despite moving to a more flexible exchange rate regime in 2005. Russia had the second-largest increase, followed by Brazil and India. By 2007 there was talk of a possible dollar crisis.

The financial crisis, however, brought a halt to such discussions. As can be seen in Figure 9–3, during the crisis, the dollar appreciated sharply against most foreign currencies. Notice the significant swings in the exchange rates of most foreign currencies relative to the U.S. dollar during the financial crisis. Between September 2008 and mid-2010, exchange rates have gone through three trends. During the first phase, from September 2008 to March 2009, the U.S. dollar appreciated relative to most foreign currencies (or, foreign currencies depreciated relative to the dollar) as investors sought a safe haven in U.S. Treasury securities. Such a sharp appreciation of the dollar had not been seen since 1973, when the generalized floating of currency exchange rates began. Many explanations have been given for the sharp appreciation of the dollar during the financial crisis. One explanation is that U.S. and foreign investors led a flight to quality, selling corporate bonds and mortgage-backed securities and investing in U.S. Treasury securities. Seen as a safe

**Figure 9–3** Exchange Rate of the U.S. Dollar with Various Foreign Currencies*

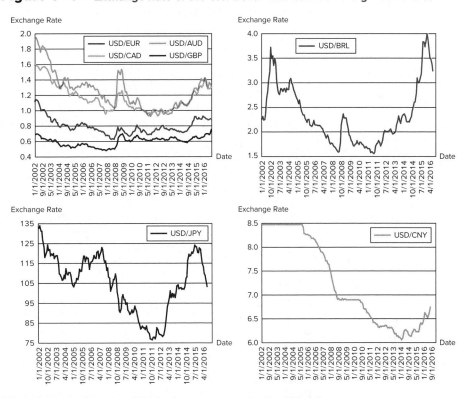

*Vertical axes are the value of the foreign currency against the U.S. dollar.

haven, U.S. Treasuries gained in value as equities plunged and credit spreads widened to record levels. This demand for U.S. Treasuries resulted in a dollar shortage and resulted in high dollar interest rates that supported the U.S. dollar. Following the crisis, however, the dollar depreciated in value almost as quickly as it had appreciated in value during the crisis.

During the second phase, from March 2009 through November 2009, much of the appreciation of the dollar relative to foreign currencies was reversed as worldwide confidence returned. In the third phase, between November 2009 and June 2010, countries (particularly those in the euro area) began to see depreciation relative to the dollar resume (the dollar appreciated relative to the euro) amid concerns about the euro, due to problems in various EU countries (such as Portugal, Ireland, Iceland, Greece, and Spain, the so-called PIIGS). From June 2010 through August 2011 worries about Europe subsided somewhat and the U.S. government struggled to pass legislation allowing an increase in the national debt ceiling that would allow the country to avoid a potential default on U.S. sovereign debt. The dollar depreciated against many foreign currencies until a debt ceiling increase was passed on August 2, 2011. Despite a rating downgrade on U.S. debt by Standard & Poor's on August 5, 2011 (resulting from the inability of the U.S. Congress to stabilize the U.S. debt deficit situation in the long term), the dollar again appreciated relative to most foreign currencies in the period after August 2011 as fears of escalating problems in Europe, including a possible dissolution of the euro, led investors to again seek a safe haven in U.S. Treasury securities. In Figure 9–3, notice the lack of movement in the exchange rate between the U.S. dollar and the Chinese yuan between 2001 and 2005 and again between 2008 and 2010. As discussed above, during these periods the Chinese government intentionally pegged the yuan to the U.S. dollar.

Finally, in Figure 9–3 note the increase in the exchange rate of the British pound and the euro for the U.S. dollar in June 2016 when the United Kingdom voted to leave the European Union. Figure 9–4 highlights these currency trends in more detail, from June 1 through mid-July 2016. On June 23, 2016, following the vote, the pound fell to its lowest

**Figure 9–4**   Exchange Rate of the British Pound and Euro for the U.S. Dollar around the Brexit Vote

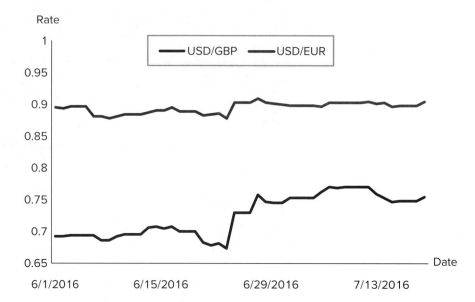

level in 30 years against the dollar. Only 24 hours earlier the pound had been rising against the dollar on the observation that bookmakers were seeing a 90 percent chance the outcome of the vote would be to remain in the EU. Given uncertainty about the impact of a Brexit on the Euro-zone economy, the euro also dropped sharply against the dollar. The vote to leave the EU began an up to two-year period of uncertainty for the UK and the EU economies and their currency. The uncertainty started with the need to choose a new leader of the Conservative Party, then to a drawn-out process of untangling the UK from the EU. Many expected the pound to fall another 10 percent over time and the euro to fall by about half that much. Further, economists saw Britain's exit from Europe as a major step backward for globalization. Such a significant secular shift had the potential to have substantial implications for growth, corporate profits, and asset prices in the medium term. All agreed that there will be significant volatility in currency rates until a greater understanding of the consequences of the UK's decision is resolved.

**forward foreign exchange transaction**

*The exchange of currencies at a specified exchange rate (or forward exchange rate) at some specified date in the future.*

A **forward foreign exchange transaction** is the exchange of currencies at a specified exchange rate (or forward exchange rate) at some specified date in the future, as illustrated in Figure 9–2. An example is an agreement today (at time 0) to exchange dollars for pounds at a given (forward) exchange rate three months into the future. Forward contracts are typically written for one-, three-, or six-month periods, but in practice they can be written over any given length of time.

Of the $5.09 trillion in average daily trading volume in the foreign exchange markets in 2016, $1.65 trillion (32.5 percent) involved spot transactions while $3.43 trillion (67.5 percent) involved forward and other transactions. This compares to 1989 where (as shown in Table 9–2) average daily trading volume was $590 billion; $317 billion

**TABLE 9–2**   Foreign Exchange Market Trading *(in billions of U.S. dollars)*

|  | 1989 | 1992 | 1995 | 1998 | 2000 | 2004 | 2007 | 2010 | 2013 | 2016 |
|---|---|---|---|---|---|---|---|---|---|---|
| Total trading | $590 | $820 | $1,190 | $1,490 | $1,200 | $1,880 | $3,210 | $3,971 | $5,345 | $5,088 |
| Spot transactions | 317 | 394 | 494 | 568 | 387 | 621 | 1,005 | 1,488 | 2,046 | 1,654 |
| Forward and other transactions | 273 | 426 | 696 | 922 | 813 | 1,259 | 2,205 | 2,483 | 3,299 | 3,434 |

**Sources:** Bank for International Settlements, Annual Report, various dates. www.bis.org

(53.7 percent) of which was spot foreign exchange transactions and $273 billion (46.3 percent) forward and other foreign exchange transactions. The main reason for this increase in the use of forward relative to spot foreign exchange transactions is the increased ability to hedge foreign exchange risk with forward foreign exchange contracts (see below).

### Return and Risk of Foreign Exchange Transactions

**LG 9-5**

This section discusses the extra dimensions of return and risk from foreign exchange transactions. The section also explores ways that financial institutions can hedge foreign exchange risk.

**Measuring Risk and Return on Foreign Exchange Transactions.** The risk involved with a spot foreign exchange transaction is that the value of the foreign currency may change relative to the U.S. dollar over a holding period. Further, foreign exchange risk is introduced by adding foreign currency assets and liabilities to a firm's balance sheet. Like domestic assets and liabilities, returns result from the contractual income from or costs paid on a security. With foreign assets and liabilities, however, returns are also affected by changes in foreign exchange rates.

---

**EXAMPLE 9–1** Foreign Exchange Risk

Suppose that on July 15, 2016, a U.S. firm plans to purchase 3 million Swiss francs' (Sf) worth of Swiss bonds from a Swiss FI in one month's time. The Swiss FI wants payment in Swiss francs. Believing that the exchange rate of U.S. dollars for Swiss francs will move against it in the next month, the U.S. firm will convert dollars into Swiss francs today. The spot exchange rate for July 15, 2016 (reported in Table 9–1), of U.S. dollars for Swiss francs (or CHF/USD) is 1.0175, or one franc costs 1.0175 in dollars. Consequently, the U.S. firm must convert:

$$\text{U.S.\$/Sf exchange rate} \times \text{Sf 3 million} =$$
$$1.0175 \times \text{Sf 3m} = \$3,052,500$$

into Swiss francs today.

One month after the conversion of dollars to Swiss francs, the Swiss bond purchase deal falls through and the U.S. firm no longer needs the Swiss francs it purchased at $1.0175 per franc. The spot exchange rate of the Swiss franc to the dollar has fallen or depreciated over the month so that the value of a franc is worth only $1.0050, or the exchange rate is $1.0050 per franc. The U.S. dollar value of 3 million Swiss francs is now only:

$$1.0050 \times \text{Sf 3 million} = \$3,015,000$$

The depreciation of the Swiss franc relative to the dollar over the month has caused the U.S. firm to suffer a $37,500 ($3,015,000 − $3,052,500) loss due to exchange rate fluctuations.

---

To avoid such a loss in the spot markets, the U.S. firm could have entered into a forward transaction, which is the exchange of currencies at a specified future date and a specified exchange rate (or forward exchange rate). Forward exchange rates for July 15, 2016, are also listed in Table 9–1. As mentioned previously, forward contracts are typically written for a one-, three-, or six-month period from the date the contract is written, although they can be written for any time period from a few days to many years. For example, if the U.S. firm had entered into a one-month forward contract selling the Swiss franc on July 15, 2016, at the same time it purchased the spot francs, the U.S. firm would have been guaranteed an exchange rate of 1.0193 U.S. dollars per Swiss franc, or 0.9810 Swiss francs per U.S. dollar, on delivering the francs to the buyer in one month's time. If the U.S. firm had sold francs one month forward at 1.0193 on July 15, 2016, it would have largely avoided the loss of $37,500 described in Example 9–1. Specifically, by selling 3 million francs forward, it would have received:

$$1.0193 \times \text{Sf 3 million} = \$3,057,900$$

at the end of the month, suggesting a small net profit of $3,057,900 − $3,052,500 = $5,400 on the combined spot and forward transactions. Essentially, by using the one-month forward contract, the U.S. firm hedges (or insures itself) against foreign currency risk in the spot market.

As discussed below, financial institutions, and particularly commercial banks, are the main participants in the foreign exchange markets. When issuing a foreign currency–denominated liability or buying a foreign currency–denominated asset an FI will do so only if the expected return is positive.

---

**EXAMPLE 9–2**     Calculating the Return on Foreign Exchange
                    Transactions of a U.S. FI

Suppose that a U.S. FI has the following assets and liabilities:

| Assets | Liabilities |
|---|---|
| $81.25 million U.S. loans (one year) in dollars | $162.5 million U.S. CDs (one year) in dollars |
| $81.25 million equivalent UK loans (one year) in pounds | |

The U.S. FI is raising all of its $162.5 million liabilities in dollars (one-year CDs), but it is investing 50 percent in U.S. dollar assets (one-year maturity loans) and 50 percent in British pound assets (one-year maturity loans).[7] In this example, the FI has matched the maturity ($M$) or duration ($D$) of its assets ($A$) and liabilities ($L$):

$$(M_A = M_L = D_A = D_L = 1 \text{ year})$$

but has mismatched the currency composition of its asset and liability portfolios. Suppose that the promised one-year U.S. dollars CD rate is 8 percent, to be paid in dollars at the end of the year, and that one-year, default risk–free loans in the United States are yielding 9 percent. The FI would have a positive spread of 1 percent from investing domestically. Suppose, however, that credit risk–free one-year loans are yielding 15 percent in the United Kingdom.

To invest $81.25 million (of the $162.5 million in CDs issued) in one-year loans in the United Kingdom, the U.S. FI engages in the following transactions:

1. At the beginning of the year, it sells $81.25 million for pounds on the spot currency markets. If the exchange rate is $1.30 to £1 (or GBP/USD = 1.30), this translates into $81.25 million/1.3 = £62.5 million.
2. It takes the £62.5 million and makes one-year UK loans at a 15 percent interest rate.
3. At the end of the year, pound revenue from these loans will be £62.5(1.15) = £71.875 million.[8]
4. It repatriates these funds back to the United States at the end of the year—that is, the U.S. FI sells the £71.875 million in the foreign exchange market at the spot exchange rate that exists at that time, the end of the year spot rate.

---

7. For simplicity, we ignore the leverage or net worth aspects of the FI's portfolio.
8. No default risk is assumed.

Suppose that the spot foreign exchange rate has not changed over the year—it remains fixed at \$1.30/£1. Then the dollar proceeds from the UK investment are:

$$£71.875 \text{ million} \times \$1.30/£1 = \$93.4375 \text{ million or as a return}$$

$$\frac{\$93.4375 \text{ million} - \$81.25 \text{ million}}{\$81.25 \text{ million}} = 15\%$$

Given this, the weighted or average return on the FI's portfolio of investments would be:

$$(0.5)(0.09) + (0.5)(0.15) = 0.12, \text{ or } 12\%$$

This exceeds the cost of the FI's CDs by 4 percent (12% − 8%).

Suppose, however, that the pound had fallen (depreciated) in value against the U.S. dollar from \$1.30/£1 at the beginning of the year to \$1.18/£1 at the end of the year, when the FI needed to repatriate the principal and interest on the loan. At an exchange rate of \$1.18/£1, the pound loan revenues at the end of the year translate into:

$$£71.875 \text{ million} \times \$1.18/£1 = \$84.8125 \text{ million}$$

or as a return on the original dollar investment of:

$$\frac{\$84.8125 - \$81.25}{\$81.25} = 0.04385 = 4.385\%$$

The weighted return on the FI's asset portfolio would be:

$$(0.5)(0.09) + (0.5)(0.04385) = 0.06692 = 6.692\%$$

In this case, the FI actually has a loss or a negative interest margin (6.692% − 8% = −1.308%) on its balance sheet investments. The reason for the loss is that the depreciation of the pound from \$1.30 to \$1.18 has offset the attractively high yield on British pound loans relative to domestic U.S. loans.

If the pound had instead appreciated (risen in value) against the dollar over the year—say, to \$1.400/£1—the U.S. FI would have generated a dollar return from its UK loans of:

$$£71.875 \text{ million} \times \$1.400 = \$100.625 \text{ million}$$

or a percentage return of 23.846 percent. The U.S. FI would receive a double benefit from investing in the United Kingdom, a high yield on the domestic British loans and an appreciation in pounds over the one-year investment period.

**Hedging Foreign Exchange Risk.**  Since a manager cannot know in advance what the pound/dollar spot exchange rate will be at the end of the year, a portfolio imbalance or investment strategy in which the bank is *net long* \$81.25 million in pounds (or £71.875 million) is risky. As we discussed, the British loans would generate a return of 23.846 percent if the pound appreciated from \$1.30/£1 to \$1.40/£1, but would produce a return of only 4.385 percent if the pound were to depreciate in value against the dollar to \$1.18.

Managers hedge to manage their exposure to currency risks, not to eliminate it. As in the case of interest rate risk exposure, it is not necessarily an optimal strategy to completely hedge away all currency risk exposure. By its very definition, hedging reduces a firm's risk by reducing the volatility of possible future returns. This narrowing of the probability distribution of returns reduces possible losses, but also reduces possible gains (i.e., it shortens both tails of the distribution). A hedge would be undesirable, therefore, if the firm wants to take a speculative position in a currency in order to benefit from some information about future currency rate movements. The hedge would reduce possible gains from the speculative position. In principle, an FI can better control the scale of its FX exposure in either of two major ways: on-balance-sheet hedging and off-balance-sheet hedging. On-balance-sheet hedging involves making changes in the on-balance-sheet assets and liabilities to protect the FI's profits from FX risk. Off-balance-sheet hedging involves no on-balance-sheet changes, but rather involves taking a position in forward or other derivative securities to hedge FX risk.

*On-Balance-Sheet Hedging.*    The following example illustrates how an FI manager can control FX exposure by making changes on the balance sheet.

---

**EXAMPLE 9–3**    Hedging on the Balance Sheet

Suppose that instead of funding the $81.25 million investment in 15 percent British loans with U.S. CDs, the FI manager funds the British loans with $81.25 million equivalent one-year pound sterling CDs at a rate of 11 percent. Now the balance sheet of the FI would be as follows:

| Assets | Liabilities |
|---|---|
| $81.25 million U.S. loans (9%) in dollars | $81.25 million U.S. CDs (8%) in dollars |
| $81.25 million equivalent UK loans (15%) in pounds | $81.25 million equivalent UK CDs (11%) in pounds |

In this situation, the FI has both a matched maturity and foreign currency asset–liability book. We might now consider the FI's profitability or spreads between the return on assets and cost of funds under two scenarios: first, when the pound depreciates in value against the dollar over the year from $1.30/£1 to $1.18/£1, and second, when the pound appreciates in value during the year from $1.30/£1 to $1.40/£1.

**1. The Depreciating Pound.**    When the pound falls in value to $1.18/£1, the return on the British loan portfolio is 4.385 percent. Consider what happens to the cost of $81.25 million in pound liabilities in dollar terms:

1. At the beginning of the year, the FI borrows $81.25 million equivalent in pound CDs for one year at a promised interest rate of 11 percent. At an exchange rate of $1.30/£1, this is a pound equivalent amount of borrowing of $81.25 million/1.30 = £62.50 million.
2. At the end of the year, the FI must pay the pound CD holders their principal and interest, £62.50 million (1.11) = £69.375 million.
3. If the pound had depreciated to $1.18/£1 over the year, the repayment in dollar terms would be $81.8625 million (= £69.375 million times $1.18/£1), or a dollar cost of funds of 0.754 percent.

Thus, at the end of the year, the following occurs:

Average return on assets:

$$(0.5)(0.9) + (0.5)(0.04385) = 0.06692 = 6.692\%$$
U.S. asset return + UK asset return = Overall return

Average cost of funds:

$$(0.5)(0.08) + (0.5)(0.00754) = 0.04377 = 4.377\%$$
U.S. cost of funds + UK cost of funds = Overall cost

Net return:

Average return on assets − Average cost of funds
$$6.692\% - 4.377\% = 2.315\%$$

**2. The Appreciating Pound.**    When the pound appreciates over the year from $1.30/£1 to $1.40/£1, the return on British loans equals 23.846 percent. Now consider the dollar cost of British one-year CDs at the end of the year when the U.S. FI must pay the principal and interest to the CD holder:

$$£69.375 \text{ million} \times \$1.40/£1 = \$97.125 \text{ million}$$

or a dollar cost of funds of 19.538 percent. Thus, at the end of the year:

Average return on assets:

$$(0.5)(0.09) + (0.5)(0.23846) = 0.16423, \text{ or } 16.423\%$$

Average cost of funds:

$$(0.5)(0.08) + (0.5)(0.19538) = 0.13769, \text{ or } 13.769\%$$

Net return:

$$16.423\% - 13.769\% = 2.654\%$$

Thus, by directly matching its foreign asset and liability book, an FI can lock in a positive return or profit spread whichever direction exchange rates change over the investment period. For example, even if domestic U.S. banking is a relatively low-profit activity (i.e., there is a low spread between the return on assets and the cost of funds), the FI could be very profitable overall. Specifically, it could lock in a large positive spread—if it exists—between deposit rates and loan rates in foreign markets. In our example, a 4 percent positive spread occurred between British one-year loan rates and deposit rates compared to only a 1 percent spread domestically.

Note that for such imbalances in domestic spreads and foreign spreads to continue over long periods of time, financial service firms would have to face significant barriers to entry into foreign markets. Specifically, if real and financial capital were free to move, FIs would increasingly withdraw from the U.S. market and reorient their operations toward the United Kingdom. Reduced competition would widen loan deposit interest spreads in the United States, and increased competition would contract UK spreads until the profit opportunities from overseas activities disappeared. If there are no real or financial barriers to international capital and goods flows, FIs can eliminate all foreign exchange rate risk exposure. Sources of foreign exchange risk exposure include international differentials in real prices, cross-country differences in the real rate of interest (perhaps, as a result of differential rates of time preference), regulatory and government intervention, and restrictions on capital movements, trade barriers, and tariffs.

**Hedging with Forwards.** Instead of matching its $81.25 million foreign asset position with $81.25 million of foreign liabilities, the FI might have chosen to remain with a currency mismatch on the balance sheet. Instead, as a lower-cost alternative, it could hedge by taking a position in the forward or other derivative markets for foreign currencies—for example, the one-year forward market for selling pounds for dollars. Any forward position taken would not appear on the balance sheet. It would appear as a contingent off-balance-sheet claim, which we describe as an item below the bottom line in Chapter 12. The role of the forward FX contract is to offset the uncertainty regarding the future spot rate on pounds at the end of the one-year investment horizon. Instead of waiting until the end of the year to transfer pounds back into dollars at an unknown spot rate, the FI can enter into a contract to sell forward its *expected* principal and interest earnings on the loan at today's known forward exchange rate for dollars/pounds, with delivery of pound funds to the buyer of the forward contract taking place at the end of the year. Essentially, by selling the expected proceeds on the pound loan forward at a known (forward FX) exchange rate today, the FI removes the future spot exchange rate uncertainty and thus the uncertainty relating to investment returns on the British loan.

## EXAMPLE 9–4  Hedging with Forwards

Consider the following transactional steps when the FI hedges its FX risk by immediately selling its expected one-year pound loan proceeds in the forward FX market:

1. The U.S. FI sells $81.25 million for pounds at the spot exchange rate today and receives $81.25 million/1.30 = £62.50 million.

2. The FI then immediately lends the £62.50 million to a British customer at 15 percent for one year.
3. The FI also sells the expected principal and interest proceeds from the pound loan forward for dollars at today's forward rate for one-year delivery. Let the current forward one-year exchange rate between dollars and pounds stand at \$1.25/£1 or at a 5 cent discount to the spot rate; as a percentage discount:

$$(\$1.25 - \$1.30)/\$1.30 = -3.846\%$$

This means that the forward buyer of the pounds promises to pay:

£62.50 million $(1.15) \times \$1.25/£ = £71.875$ million $\times \$1.25/£ = \$89.84375$ million

to the FI (the forward seller) in one year when the FI delivers the £71.875 million proceeds of the loan to the forward buyer.

4. In one year, the British borrower repays the loan to the FI plus interest in pounds (£71.875 million).
5. The FI delivers the £71.875 million to the buyer of the one-year forward contract and receives the promised \$89.84375 million.

Barring the pound borrower's default on the loan or the pound forward buyer's reneging on the forward contract, the FI knows from the very beginning of the investment period that it has locked in a guaranteed return on the British loan of:

$$\frac{\$89.84375\text{m.} - \$81.25\text{m.}}{\$81.25\text{m.}} = 0.10577, \text{ or } 10.577\%$$

Specifically, this return is fully hedged against any dollar/pound exchange rate changes over the one-year holding period of the loan investment. Given this return on British loans, the overall expected return on the FI's asset portfolio is:

$$(0.5)(0.09) + (0.5)(0.10577) = 0.09788, \text{ or } 9.788\%$$

Since the cost of funds for the FI's \$200 million U.S. CDs is an assumed 8 percent, it has been able to lock in a return spread over the year of 1.788 percent regardless of spot exchange rate fluctuations between the initial overseas (loan) investment and repatriation of the foreign loan proceeds one year later.

---

In the preceding example, it is profitable for the FI to drop domestic U.S. loans and to hedge foreign UK loans, since the hedged dollar return on foreign loans of 10.577 percent is so much higher than the 9 percent return for domestic loans. As the FI seeks to invest more in British loans, it needs to buy more spot pounds. This drives up the spot price of pounds in dollar terms to more than \$1.30/£1. In addition, the FI could sell more pounds forward (the proceeds of these pound loans) for dollars, driving the forward rate to below \$1.25/£1. The outcome would widen the dollar forward–spot exchange rate difference on pounds, making forward hedged pounds investments less attractive than before. This process would continue until the U.S. cost of FI funds just equals the forward hedged return on British loans—that is, the FI could make no further profits by borrowing in U.S. dollars and making forward contract–hedged investments in UK loans (see also the following discussion on the interest rate parity theorem). Futures and options foreign exchange contracts, as well as foreign exchange swaps, are other derivative securities that may be used to hedge foreign exchange risk. We discuss and illustrate the use of these contracts in Chapter 23.

**LG 9-6** *Role of Financial Institutions in Foreign Exchange Transactions*

Foreign exchange market transactions, like corporate bond and money market transactions, are conducted among dealers mainly over the counter (OTC) using telecommunication and computer networks. Foreign exchange traders are generally located in one large trading room at a bank or other FI where they have access to foreign exchange data and telecommunications equipment. Traders generally specialize in just a few currencies.

A major structural change in foreign exchange trading has been the growing share of electronic brokerage in the interbank markets at the expense of direct dealing (and telecommunication). The transnational nature of the electronic exchange of funds makes secure, Internet-based trading an ideal platform. Online trading portals—terminals where currency transactions are being executed—are a low-cost way of conducting spot and forward foreign exchange transactions. In the 2000s, some 85 to 95 percent of interbank trading in major currencies was conducted by using electronic brokerage. This compares to 50 percent in 1998 and 20 to 30 percent in 1995. Three companies, Thomson Reuters, BATS Global Markets, and ICAP's EBS, currently dominate the market for the provision of electronic trading platforms, software, and FX quotation systems. Electronic brokers automatically provide traders with the best prices available to them. In contrast, traders using traditional methods typically needed to contact several dealers to obtain market price information.

Since 1982, when Singapore opened its FX market, foreign exchange markets have operated 24 hours a day. When the New York market closes, trading operations in San Francisco are still open; when trading in San Francisco closes, the Hong Kong and Singapore markets open; when Tokyo and Singapore close, the Frankfurt market opens; an hour later, the London market opens; and before these markets close, the New York market reopens. The nation's largest commercial banks are major players in foreign currency trading and dealing, with large money center banks such as Citigroup and J.P. Morgan Chase also taking significant positions in foreign currency assets and liabilities. Smaller banks maintain lines of credit with these large banks for foreign exchange transactions. Table 9–3 lists the top foreign currency traders as of 2016.

Table 9–4 lists the outstanding dollar value of U.S. banks' foreign assets and liabilities for the period 1993 to March 2016. The March 2016 figure for foreign assets is $451.4 billion, with foreign liabilities of $232.2 billion. Both foreign currency liabilities and assets were growing during the mid-1990s and then fell in the late 1990s and early 2000s. The financial crises in Asia and Russia in 1997 and 1998 and in Argentina in the early 2000s are likely reasons for the decrease in foreign assets and liabilities during this period. After this period, growth accelerated rapidly as the world economy recovered. While the growth of liabilities to and asset claims on foreigners slowed during the financial crisis, levels remained stable as U.S. FIs were seen as some of the safest FIs during the crisis. Further, in many of the reported years (e.g., 2002 and 2007), U.S. banks had more liabilities to than claims (assets) on foreigners. Thus, if the dollar depreciated relative to foreign currencies,

**TABLE 9–3** Top Currency Traders by Percentage of Overall Volume

| Rank | Name | Market Share |
|------|------|--------------|
| 1 | Citigroup | 12.91% |
| 2 | J.P. Morgan Chase | 8.77 |
| 3 | UBS | 8.76 |
| 4 | Deutsche Bank | 7.86 |
| 5 | Bank of America Merrill Lynch | 6.40 |
| 6 | Barclays Capital | 5.67 |
| 7 | Goldman Sachs | 4.65 |
| 8 | HSBC | 4.56 |
| 9 | XTX Markets | 3.87 |
| 10 | Morgan Stanley | 3.19 |

**TABLE 9–4**    Liabilities to and Claims on Foreigners Reported by Banks in the United States, Payable in Foreign Currencies *(millions of dollars, end of period)*

| Item | 1993 | 1996 | 1999 | 2002 | 2004 | 2007 | 2010 | 2013 | 2016[†] |
|---|---|---|---|---|---|---|---|---|---|
| Banks' liabilities | $78,259 | $103,383 | $88,537 | $80,543 | $ 68,189 | $279,559 | $167,408 | $316,811 | $232,186 |
| Banks' claims (assets) | 62,017 | 66,018 | 67,365 | 71,724 | 129,544 | 170,113 | 341,739 | 491,083 | 451,400 |
| Claims of banks' domestic customers[*] | 12,854 | 10,978 | 20,826 | 35,923 | 32,056 | 74,693 | 82,123 | 75,608 | 74,398 |

**Note:** Data on claims exclude foreign currencies held by U.S. monetary authorities.

[*]Assets owned by customers of the reporting bank located in the United States that represents claims on foreigners held by reporting banks for the accounts of the domestic customers.

[†]As of March.

**Sources:** *Treasury Bulletin,* various issues. www.ustreas.gov

more dollars (converted into foreign currencies) would be needed to pay off the liabilities and U.S. banks would experience a loss due to foreign exchange risk. However, the reverse was true in many of the most recent years (e.g., 2010, 2013, and 2016); that is, as the dollar appreciated relative to foreign currencies, U.S. banks experienced a gain from their foreign exchange exposures.

Table 9–5 gives the categories of foreign currency positions (or investments) of all U.S. banks in five major currencies in March 2016. Columns 1 and 2 of Table 9–5 refer to the assets and liabilities denominated in foreign currencies that are held in the portfolios of U.S. banks. Columns 3 and 4 refer to foreign currency trading activities (the spot and forward foreign exchange contracts bought—a long position—and sold—a short position—in each major currency). Foreign currency trading dominates direct portfolio investments. Even though the aggregate trading positions appear very large—for example, U.S. banks bought 685,706 billion Japanese yen—their overall or net exposure positions can be relatively small (e.g., the net position in Japanese yen was ¥7,405 billion).

A financial institution's overall net foreign exchange (FX) exposure in any given currency can be measured by its net book or position exposure, which is measured in column 5 of Table 9–5 as:

$$\text{Net exposure}_i = (\text{FX assets}_i - \text{FX liabilities}_i) + (\text{FX bought}_i - \text{FX sold}_i)$$
$$= \text{Net foreign assets}_i + \text{Net FX bought}_i$$
$$= \text{Net position}_i$$

**TABLE 9–5**    Monthly U.S. Bank Positions in Foreign Currencies and Foreign Assets and Liabilities, 2016 *(in currency of denomination)*

| | (1) Assets | (2) Liabilities | (3) FX Bought[*] | (4) FX Sold[*] | (5) Net Position[†] |
|---|---|---|---|---|---|
| Canadian dollars (millions of C$) | 226,067 | 134,872 | 1,526,743 | 1,583,258 | 34,680 |
| Japanese yen (billions of ¥) | 148,749 | 138,778 | 685,706 | 688,272 | 7,405 |
| Swiss francs (millions of Sf) | 77,259 | 54,884 | 1,149,675 | 1,186,001 | −13,951 |
| British pounds (millions of £) | 719,273 | 754,868 | 2,534,914 | 2,639,397 | −140,078 |
| Euros (millions of €) | 2,086,812 | 2,036,857 | 8,416,797 | 8,573,605 | −106,853 |

[*]Includes spot, future, and forward contracts.

[†]Net position = Assets − Liabilities + FX bought − FX sold

**Source:** *Treasury Bulletin,* June 2016. www.ustreas.gov

where

$$i = i\text{th country's currency}$$

Clearly, a financial institution could match its foreign currency assets to its liabilities in a given currency and match buys and sells in its trading book in that foreign currency to reduce its foreign exchange net exposure to zero and thus avoid foreign exchange risk. It could also offset an imbalance in its foreign asset–liability portfolio by an opposing imbalance in its trading book so that its **net exposure** position in that currency would also be zero.

Notice in Table 9–5 that U.S. banks carried a positive net exposure position in two of the five major currencies in March 2016. A *positive* net exposure position implies that a U.S. financial institution is overall **net long in a currency** (i.e., the financial institution has purchased more foreign currency than it has sold). The institution will profit if the foreign currency appreciates in value against the U.S. dollar, but it also faces the risk that the foreign currency will fall in value against the U.S. dollar, the domestic currency. A *negative* net exposure position implies that a U.S. financial institution is **net short** (i.e., the financial institution has sold more foreign currency than it has purchased) in a foreign currency. The institution will profit if the foreign currency depreciates in value against the U.S. dollar, but it faces the risk that the foreign currency will rise in value against the dollar. Thus, failure to maintain a fully balanced position in any given currency exposes a U.S. financial institution to fluctuations in the exchange rate of that currency against the dollar. Indeed, the greater the volatility of foreign exchange rates given any net exposure position, the greater the fluctuations in value of a financial institution's foreign exchange portfolio (see also Chapter 19, where we discuss market risk). An FI's net position in a currency may not be completely under its own control. For example, even though an FI may feel that a particular currency will fall in value relative to the U.S. dollar, it may hold a positive net exposure in that currency because of many previous business loans issued to customers in that country. Thus, it is important that the FI manager recognize the potential for future foreign exchange losses and undertake hedging or risk management strategies like those described above (in Example 9–4) when making medium- and long-term decisions in nondomestic currencies.

We have given the foreign exchange exposures for U.S. banks only, but most large nonbank financial institutions also have some foreign exchange exposure either through asset–liability holdings or currency trading. The absolute sizes of these exposures are smaller than for major U.S. money center banks. The reasons for this are threefold: smaller asset sizes, prudent person concerns,[9] and regulations.[10] Table 9–6 shows international versus U.S.-based assets held by private pension funds from 1989 to 2016.

A financial institution's position in the foreign exchange markets generally reflects four trading activities:

1. The purchase and sale of foreign currencies to allow customers to partake in and complete international commercial trade transactions.

**net exposure**

*A financial institution's overall foreign exchange exposure in any given currency.*

**net long (short) in a currency**

*A position of holding more (fewer) assets than liabilities in a given currency.*

**TABLE 9–6** Foreign versus U.S.-Based Assets Held by Private Pension Funds
*(in billions of U.S. dollars)*

|                  | 1989      | 1999      | 2004      | 2007      | 2010      | 2013      | 2016      |
|------------------|-----------|-----------|-----------|-----------|-----------|-----------|-----------|
| Total assets     | $1,631.8  | $4,593.8  | $4,922.8  | $6,108.2  | $6,143.1  | $8,061.0  | $8,574.2  |
| Foreign assets   | 137.8     | 341.9     | 267.8     | 447.2     | 443.4     | 653.0     | 718.2     |
| U.S.-based assets| 1,494.0   | 4,251.9   | 4,655.0   | 5,661.0   | 5,669.7   | 7,408.0   | 7,856.0   |

**Sources:** Board of Governors of the Federal Reserve, *Flow of Funds Accounts,* various issues. www.federalreserve.gov

9. *Prudent person concerns,* which require financial institutions to adhere to investment and lending policies, standards, and procedures that a reasonable and prudent person would apply with respect to a portfolio of investments and loans to avoid undue risk of loss and obtain a reasonable return, are especially important for pension funds.

10. For example, New York State restricts foreign asset holdings of New York–based life insurance companies to less than 10 percent of their assets.

2. The purchase and sale of foreign currencies to allow customers (or the financial institution itself) to take positions in foreign real and financial investments.
3. The purchase and sale of foreign currencies for hedging purposes to offset customer (or financial institution) exposure in any given currency.
4. The purchase and sale of foreign currencies for speculative purposes through forecasting or anticipating future movements in foreign exchange rates.

**open position**

*An unhedged position in a particular currency.*

In the first two activities, the financial institution normally acts as an *agent* on behalf of its customers for a fee, but does not assume the foreign exchange risk itself. J.P. Morgan Chase is a dominant supplier of foreign exchange trading to retail customers in the United States. As of December 31, 2015, the aggregate value of J.P. Morgan Chase's notional or principal amounts of foreign exchange contracts totaled $9.6 trillion. In the third activity, the financial institution acts defensively as a hedger to reduce foreign exchange exposure. For example, it may take a short (sell) position in the foreign exchange of a country to offset a long (buy) position in the foreign exchange of that same country. Thus, foreign exchange risk exposure essentially relates to **open** (or speculative) **positions** taken by the FI, the fourth activity. A financial institution usually creates open positions by taking an unhedged position in a foreign currency in its foreign exchange trading with other financial institutions. The Federal Reserve estimates that 200 financial institutions are active market makers in foreign currencies in the U.S. foreign exchange market, with about 25 commercial and investment banks making a market in the five most important currencies. Financial institutions can make speculative trades directly with other financial institutions or arrange them through specialist foreign exchange brokers. The Federal Reserve Bank of New York estimates that approximately 45 percent of speculative or open position trades are accomplished through specialized brokers who receive a fee for arranging trades between financial institutions. Speculative trades can be instituted through a variety of foreign exchange instruments. Spot currency trades are the most common, with financial institutions seeking to make a profit on the difference between buy and sell prices (i.e., movements in the purchase and sale prices over time). However, financial institutions can also take speculative positions in foreign exchange forward contracts, futures, and options (see Chapter 10).

---

> ### DO YOU UNDERSTAND:
>
> 3. What the difference is between a spot and forward foreign exchange market transaction?
>
> 4. The two ways in which an FI manager can hedge foreign exchange risk?
>
> 5. What the advantages are for an FI that hedges foreign exchange risk with forward contracts (as opposed to hedging this risk on the balance sheet)?
>
> 6. What the four major foreign exchange trading activities are that financial institutions perform?

---

## INTERACTION OF INTEREST RATES, INFLATION, AND EXCHANGE RATES

**LG 9-7**

As global financial markets and financial institutions and their customers have become increasingly interlinked, so have interest rates, inflation, and foreign exchange rates. For example, higher domestic interest rates may attract foreign financial investment and impact the value of the domestic currency. In this section, we look at the effect that inflation (or the change in the price level of a given set of goods and services, defined earlier, in Chapter 2, as the variable *IP*) in one country has on its foreign currency exchange rates—purchasing power parity (PPP). We also examine the links between domestic and foreign interest rates and spot and forward foreign exchange rates—interest rate parity (IRP).

Recall from Chapter 2 that the relationship among nominal interest rates, real interest rates, and expected inflation is often referred to as the *Fisher effect,* named for the economist Irving Fisher, who identified these relationships early in the last century. The Fisher effect theorizes that nominal interest rates observed in financial markets must (1) compensate investors for any reduced purchasing power due to inflationary price changes and (2) provide an additional premium above the expected rate of inflation for forgoing present consumption due to the time value of money (which reflects the real risk-free rate), such that

$$i = \text{IP} + \text{RFR}$$

where

$$i = \text{Interest rate}$$
$$IP = \text{Inflation rate}$$
$$RFR = \text{Real risk-free rate}$$

The international Fisher effect incorporates foreign exchange rates into the relationship, assuming the appreciation or depreciation of exchange rates is proportional to differences in nominal interest rates across countries. Specifically, the expected spot rate is the current spot rate multiplied by the ratio of the foreign nominal interest rate to the domestic nominal interest rate:

$$E(S_{US\$/C\$}) = S_{US\$/C\$} \times [(1 + i_{US})/(1 + i_C)]$$

The country with the higher (lower) nominal interest rate will see its currency depreciate (appreciate). For example, suppose the spot exchange rate of U.S. dollars for Canadian dollars is 0.7709, the current nominal interest rate in the United States is 4 percent, and the nominal interest rate in Canada is 5 percent. The international Fisher effect predicts that:

$$E(S_{US\$/C\$}) = 0.7709 \times [(1 + 0.04)/(1 + 0.05)] = 0.7636$$

The international Fisher effect predicts that the U.S. dollar will appreciate to 0.7636 and the Canadian dollar will depreciate to 1.3097. Thus, investors in either currency will achieve the same average nominal rate of interest—that is, an investor in U.S. dollars will earn a lower interest rate of 4 percent but will also gain from appreciation of the U.S. dollar relative to the Canadian dollar.

### Purchasing Power Parity

One factor affecting a country's foreign currency exchange rate with another country is the relative inflation rate in each country (which, as shown below, is directly related to the relative interest rates in these countries). Specifically, in Chapter 2, we showed that:

$$i_{US} = IP_{US} + RFR_{US}$$

and

$$i_S = IP_S + RFR_S$$

where

$$i_{US} = \text{Interest rate in the United States}$$
$$i_S = \text{Interest rate in Switzerland (or another foreign country)}$$
$$IP_{US} = \text{Inflation rate in the United States}$$
$$IP_S = \text{Inflation rate in Switzerland (or another foreign country)}$$
$$RFR_{US} = \text{Real risk-free rate in the United States}$$
$$RFR_S = \text{Real risk-free rate in Switzerland (or another foreign country)}$$

Assuming real rates of interest (or rates of time preference) are equal across countries:

$$RFR_{US} = RFR_S$$

then:

$$i_{US} - i_S = IP_{US} - IP_S$$

The (nominal) interest rate spread between the United States and Switzerland reflects the difference in inflation rates between the two countries.

**purchasing power parity (PPP)**

*The theory explaining the change in foreign currency exchange rates as inflation rates in the countries change.*

As relative inflation rates (and interest rates) change, foreign currency exchange rates that are not constrained by government regulation should also adjust to account for relative differences in the price levels (inflation rates) between the two countries. One theory that explains how this adjustment takes place is the theory of **purchasing power parity (PPP).** According to PPP, foreign currency exchange rates between two countries adjust to reflect changes in each country's price levels (or inflation rates and, implicitly, interest rates) as consumers and importers switch their demands for goods from relatively high inflation (interest) rate countries to low inflation (interest) rate countries. Specifically, the PPP theorem states that the change in the exchange rate between two countries' currencies is proportional to the difference in the inflation rates in the two countries. That is:

$$IP_{US} - IP_S = \Delta S_{US/S}/S_{US/S}$$

where

$$S_{US/S} = \text{Spot exchange rate of U.S. dollars for Swiss francs (or another currency)}$$

Thus, according to PPP, the most important factor determining exchange rates is the fact that in open economies, differences in prices (and by implication, price level changes with inflation) drive trade flows and thus demand for and supplies of currencies.

---

**EXAMPLE 9–5**  **Application of Purchasing Power Parity**

Suppose that the current spot exchange rate of U.S. dollars for Russian rubles, $S_{US/R}$ (or $S_{RUB/USD}$), is 0.017 (i.e., 0.017 dollars, or 1.7 cents, can be received for 1 ruble). The price of Russian-produced goods increases by 7.5 percent (i.e., inflation in Russia, $IP_R$, is 7.5 percent) and the U.S. price index increases by 0.8 percent (i.e., inflation in the United States, $IP_{US}$, is 0.8 percent). According to PPP, the 7.5 percent rise in the price of Russian goods relative to the 0.8 percent rise in the price of U.S. goods results in a depreciation of the Russian ruble (by 6.7 percent). Specifically, the exchange rate of Russian rubles to U.S. dollars should fall over the course of the year, so that:[11]

$$\begin{array}{ccc} \text{U.S.} \\ \text{inflation rate} \end{array} - \begin{array}{c} \text{Russian} \\ \text{inflation rate} \end{array} = \dfrac{\begin{array}{c}\text{Change in spot exchange rate} \\ \text{of U.S. dollars for Russian rubles}\end{array}}{\begin{array}{c}\text{Initial spot exchange rate} \\ \text{of U.S. dollars for Russian rubles}\end{array}}$$

or

$$IP_{US} - IP_R = \Delta S_{US/R}/S_{US/R}$$

Plugging in the inflation and exchange rates, we get:

$$0.008 - 0.075 = \Delta S_{US/R}/S_{US/R} = \Delta S_{US/R}/0.017$$

or

$$-0.067 = S_{US/R}/0.017$$

and

$$\Delta S_{US/R} = -(0.067) \times 0.017 = -0.001139$$

Thus, it takes 0.01139 cents less to receive a ruble [or 1.6986 cents (1.7 cents − 0.001139 cents), or 0.016986 of $1, can be received for 1 ruble]. Over the course of the year, the Russian ruble depreciates in value by 6.7 percent against the U.S. dollar as a result of its higher inflation rate.[12]

---

**law of one price**

*An economic rule which states that, in an efficient market, identical goods and services produced in different countries should have a single price.*

The theory behind purchasing power parity is that in the long run exchange rates should move toward rates that would equalize the prices of an identical basket of goods and services in any two countries. This is also known as the **law of one price,** an economic concept which states that in an efficient market, if countries produce a good or service that

---

11. This is the relative version of the PPP theorem. There are other versions of the theory (such as absolute PPP and the law of one price). However, the version shown here is the one most commonly used.

12. A 6.7 percent fall in the ruble's value would translate into a new exchange rate of 0.016986 dollar per ruble if the original exchange rate between dollars and rubles was 0.017.

is identical to that in other countries, that good or service must have a single price, no matter where it is purchased. This is the thinking behind *The Economist*'s "Big Mac" index, proposed in 1986 as a lighthearted measure of whether currencies are at their correct level. The "basket" in the Big Mac index is a McDonald's Big Mac, which is produced locally in almost 120 countries. The Big Mac PPP is the exchange rate that would leave a burger in any country costing the same as in America. For example, in January 2016 the average price of a Big Mac in four American cities was $4.93 (including tax). In China a Big Mac cost yuan 17.60. Dividing this by the American price of $4.93 produces a dollar PPP against the yuan of yuan 3.57, compared with its spot exchange rate of yuan 6.56, suggesting that the yuan is 45.6 percent undervalued. In contrast, the Swedish krona was 6.1 percent overvalued. Interestingly, all emerging-market currencies were undervalued against the dollar. The Big Mac index was never intended as a precise forecasting tool. Burgers are not "traded" across borders as the PPP theory demands; prices are distorted by differences in the cost of nontradable goods and services, such as property rents. Yet these very failings make the Big Mac index useful, since looked at another way it can help measure countries' differing costs of living. That a Big Mac is cheap in China does not in fact prove that the yuan is being held massively below its fair value. It is quite natural for average prices to be lower in poorer countries and therefore for their currencies to appear cheap.

### Interest Rate Parity

We discussed above that foreign exchange spot market risk can be reduced by entering into forward foreign exchange contracts. Table 9–1 lists foreign exchange rates on July 15, 2016. Notice that spot rates and forward rates differ. For example, the spot exchange rate between the Canadian dollar and U.S. dollar was 0.7709 on July 15, 2016, meaning that one Canadian dollar could be exchanged on July 15, 2016, for 0.7709 U.S. dollar. The six-month forward rate between the two currencies on July 15, 2016, was 0.7711. This forward exchange rate is determined by the spot exchange rate and the interest rate differential between the two countries.

**interest rate parity theorem (IRPT)**

*The theory that the domestic interest rate should equal the foreign interest rate minus the expected appreciation of the domestic currency.*

The relationship that links spot exchange rates, interest rates, and forward exchange rates is described as the **interest rate parity theorem (IRPT).** Given that investors have an opportunity to invest in domestic or foreign markets, the IRPT implies that, by hedging in the forward exchange rate market, an investor should realize the same returns, whether investing domestically or in a foreign country—that is, the hedged dollar return on foreign investments just equals the return on domestic investments. This is consistent with the assumption of PPP that real rates of interest are equal across countries. Mathematically, the IRPT can be expressed as:

$$1 + i_{USt} = (1/S_t) \times (1 + i_{UKt}) \times F_t$$

Return on U.S. investment = Hedged return on foreign (UK) investment

where

$1 + i_{USt} = 1$ plus the interest rate on a U.S. investment maturing at time $t$

$1 + i_{UKt} = 1$ plus the interest rate on a UK investment maturing at time $t$

$S_t = \$/\pounds$ spot exchange rate at time $t$

$F_t = \$/\pounds$ forward exchange rate at time $t$

Rearranging, the IRPT can be expressed as:

$$(i_{USt} - i_{UKt})/(1 + i_{UKt}) = (F_t - S_t)/S_t$$

As can be seen, if interest rates in the United States and a foreign country are the same (i.e., $i_{USt} = i_{UKt}$) so that the left-hand side of the equation is zero, then the forward rate should equal the spot exchange rate ($F_t = S_t$) since the right-hand side of the equation must also equal zero. If U.S. interest rates are higher than foreign rates, the forward dollar value of the foreign currency will be greater than the spot dollar value, since investors can earn more over the investment horizon in the United States than in the foreign market. If U.S. interest rates are lower than foreign rates, the forward dollar value of the foreign currency will be less than the spot dollar value, since investors can earn more in foreign markets than in U.S. markets. Finally, note from the IRPT that a change in U.S. interest rates ($i_{USt}$), foreign interest rates ($i_{UKt}$), and expected exchange rates ($F_t$) affects the current exchange rate, $S_t$.

---

**EXAMPLE 9–6**   **An Example of the Interest Rate Parity Theorem**

Suppose that on July 15, 2016, a U.S. citizen has excess funds available to invest in either U.S. or British bank time deposits. It is assumed that both types of deposits are credit- or default-risk free and that the investment horizon is one month. The interest rate available on British pound one-month time deposits, $i_{UK}$, is 0.5 percent monthly. The spot exchange rate of U.S. dollars for British pounds on July 15, 2016 (from Table 9–1), is \$1.3188/£, and the one-month forward rate is \$1.3192/£. According to the IRPT, the interest rate on comparable U.S. one-month time deposits should be:

$$1 + i_{US} = (1/1.3188) \times (1 + 0.005) \times 1.3192 = 1.005305$$

or 0.5305 percent. We can rearrange this relationship as shown above as:

$$\frac{0.005305 - 0.005}{1 + 0.005} = \frac{1.3192 - 1.3188}{1.3188}$$

$$-0.000303 = -0.000303$$

Thus, the discounted spread between domestic and foreign interest rates is, in equilibrium, equal to the percentage spread between forward and spot exchange rates.

---

**DO YOU UNDERSTAND:**

7. *What the term purchasing power parity means?*

8. *What the interest rate parity condition is? How it relates to the existence or nonexistence of arbitrage opportunities?*

Suppose that, in the preceding example, the annual rate on U.S. time deposits was 0.60 percent per month (rather than 0.5305 percent). In this case, it would be profitable for the investor to put any excess funds into U.S. rather than UK time deposits. In fact, a risk-free (or arbitrage) investment opportunity now exists and will result in a flow of funds out of UK time deposits into U.S. time deposits. According to the IRPT, this flow of funds will quickly drive up the U.S. dollar for British pound spot exchange rate until the potential risk-free profit opportunities from investment in U.S. time deposits are eliminated. Thus, any arbitrage opportunity should be small and fleeting. Any long-term violations of this relationship are likely to occur only if major imperfections exist in international deposit markets, including barriers to cross-border financial flows.

## SUMMARY

In this chapter, we reviewed foreign exchange markets. Foreign exchange markets have grown to be among the largest of the world's financial markets. We reviewed the trading process in this market, paying particular attention to the role played by financial institutions in the operations of the foreign exchange market. In Appendix 9A, we look at balance of payment accounts, which summarize the trading activity of one country with all others.

## QUESTIONS

1. What are foreign exchange markets and foreign exchange rates? Why is an understanding of foreign exchange markets important to financial managers and individual investors? (*LG 9-1*)

2. If the Swiss franc is expected to depreciate relative to the U.S. dollar in the near future, would a U.S.-based FI in Bern City prefer to be net long or net short in its asset positions? Discuss. (*LG 9-1*)

3. A U.S. insurance company invests $1,000,000 in a private placement of British bonds. Each bond pays £300 in interest per year for 20 years. If the current exchange rate is £1.364/$, what is the nature of the insurance company's exchange rate risk? Specifically, what type of exchange rate movement concerns this insurance company? (*LG 9-1*)

4. How did the Bretton Woods and the Smithsonian Agreements affect the ability of foreign exchange rates to float freely? How did the elimination of exchange boundaries in 1973 affect the ability of foreign exchange rates to float freely? (*LG 9-1*)

5. How are foreign exchange markets open 24 hours per day? (*LG 9-2*)

6. What is the spot market for FX? What is the forward market for FX? What is the position of being net long in a currency? (*LG 9-4, 9-6*)

7. What motivates FI managers to hedge foreign currency exposures? What are the limitations to hedging foreign currency exposures? (*LG 9-5*)

8. What are the two primary methods of hedging FX risk for an FI? What conditions are necessary to achieve a perfect hedge through on-balance-sheet hedging? What are the advantages and disadvantages of off-balance-sheet hedging in comparison to on-balance-sheet hedging? (*LG 9-5*)

9. If international capital markets are well integrated and operate efficiently, will FIs be exposed to foreign exchange risk? What are the sources of foreign exchange risk for FIs? (*LG 9-5*)

10. What are the major foreign exchange trading activities performed by financial institutions? (*LG 9-6*)

11. What is the implication for cross-border trades if it can be shown that interest rate parity is maintained consistently across different markets and different currencies? (*LG 9-7*)

12. What is the purchasing power parity theorem? (*LG 9-7*)

13. Explain the concept of interest rate parity. What does this concept imply about the long-run profit opportunities from investing in international markets? What market conditions must prevail for the concept to be valid? (*LG 9-7*)

14. What are some reasons why interest rate parity may not hold in spite of the economic forces that should ensure the equilibrium relationship? (*LG 9-7*)

15. One form of the interest rate parity equation appears as $1 + r_{USt} = (1/S_t) \times (1 + r_{UKt}) \times F_t$ where both the spot and forward rates are expressed in terms of dollars for pounds or direct exchange rates. How would the equation be written if the exchange rates were indirect—that is, pounds for dollars? (*LG 9-7*)

16. Why has the United States held a trade deficit for most of the 1990s and 2000s? Make sure you distinguish between the imports versus exports of goods and services. (*LG 9-1*)

17. Why must the current account balance equal the value of the capital plus financial account balance (in opposite sign)? (*LG 9-1*)

## PROBLEMS

1. Refer to Table 9–1. (*LG 9-4*)
   a. What was the spot exchange rate of Canadian dollars for U.S. dollars (USD/CAD) on July 15, 2016?
   b. What was the six-month forward exchange rate of Canadian dollars for U.S. dollars (USD/CAD) on July 15, 2016?
   c. What was the three-month forward exchange rate of U.S. dollars for Japanese yen (JPY/USD) on July 15, 2016?

2. Refer to Table 9–1. (*LG 9-4*)
   a. On June 15, 2016, you purchased a British pound–denominated CD by converting $1 million to pounds at a rate of 0.7605 pound for U.S. dollars. It is now July 15, 2016. Has the U.S. dollar appreciated or depreciated in value relative to the British pound (see Table 9–1)?
   b. Using the information in part (a), what is your gain or loss on the investment in the CD? Assume no interest has been paid on the CD.

3. On July 15, 2016, you convert 500,000 U.S. dollars to Japanese yen in the spot foreign exchange market and purchase a six-month forward contract to convert yen into dollars. How much will you receive in U.S. dollars at the end of six months? Use the data in Table 9–1 for this problem. (*LG 9-4*)

4. Bank USA recently purchased $10 million worth of euro-denominated one-year CDs that pay 10 percent interest annually. The current spot rate of U.S. dollars for euros is $1.104/€1. (*LG 9-5*)
   a. Is Bank USA exposed to an appreciation or depreciation of the dollar relative to the euro?
   b. What will be the return on the one-year CD if the dollar appreciates relative to the euro such that the spot rate of U.S. dollars for euros at the end of the year is $1.004/€1?
   c. What will be the return on the one-year CD if the dollar depreciates relative to the euro such that the spot rate of U.S. dollars for euros at the end of the year is $1.204/€1?

5. Bankone issued $200 million worth of one-year CD liabilities in Brazilian reals at a rate of 6.50 percent. The exchange rate of U.S. dollars for Brazilian reals at the time of the transaction was $0.305/Br 1. (*LG 9-5*)
   a. Is Bankone exposed to an appreciation or depreciation of the U.S. dollar relative to the Brazilian real?
   b. What will be the percentage cost to Bankone on the if the dollar depreciates relative to the Brazilian re that the exchange rate of U.S. dollars for Brazil is $0.325/Br 1 at the end of the year?

**c.** What will be the percentage cost to Bankone on this CD if the dollar appreciates relative to the Brazilian real such that the exchange rate of U.S. dollars for Brazilian reals is $0.285/Br 1 at the end of the year?

6. Sun Bank USA has purchased a 16 million one-year Australian dollar loan that pays 12 percent interest annually. The spot rate of U.S. dollars for Australian dollars (AUD/USD) is $0.757/A$1. It has funded this loan by accepting a British pound (BP)–denominated deposit for the equivalent amount and maturity at an annual rate of 10 percent. The current spot rate of U.S. dollars for British pounds (GBP/USD) is $1.320/£1. (*LG 9-5*)

   **a.** What is the net interest income earned in dollars on this one-year transaction if the spot rate of U.S. dollars for Australian dollars and U.S. dollars for BPs at the end of the year are $0.715/A$1 and $1.520/£1, respectively?

   **b.** What should the spot rate of U.S. dollars for BPs be at the end of the year in order for the bank to earn a net interest income of $200,000 (disregarding any change in principal values)?

7. East Bank has purchased a 5 million one-year Swiss franc (Sf) loan that pays 6 percent interest annually. The spot rate of U.S. dollars for Swiss francs (CHF/USD) is 1.0175. It has funded this loan by accepting a Canadian dollar (C$)–denominated deposit for the equivalent amount and maturity at an annual rate of 4 percent. The current spot rate of U.S. dollars for Canadian dollars (CAD/USD) is 0.7710. (*LG 9-5*)

   **a.** What is the net interest income earned in dollars on this one-year transaction if the spot rate of U.S. dollars for Sfs and U.S. dollars for C$s at the end of the year are 1.0310 and 0.7680, respectively?

   **b.** What should the spot rate of U.S. dollars for C$s be in order for the bank to earn a net interest income of $108,000 (disregarding any change in principal values)?

8. North Bank has been borrowing in the U.S. markets and lending abroad, thereby incurring foreign exchange risk. In a recent transaction, it issued a one-year $2 million CD at 6 percent and is planning to fund a loan in British pounds at 8 percent for a 2 percent expected spread. The spot rate of U.S. dollars for British pounds is $1.32/£1. (*LG 9-5*)

   **a.** However, new information now indicates that the British pound will appreciate such that the spot rate of U.S. dollars for British pounds is $1.30/£1 by year-end. What should the bank charge on the loan to maintain the [2] percent spread?

   [**b.**] [The] bank has an opportunity to hedge using one-year [forward] contracts at 1.33 U.S. dollars for British pounds. [What is t]he spread if the bank hedges its forward foreign [exchange e]xposure?

   [**c.** How should] the loan rates be increased to maintain the [2 percent sprea]d if the bank intends to hedge its exposure [using the forward] rates?

[9. ...] [b]orrowing in the U.S. markets and [... in]curring foreign exchange risk. In [...] [issu]ed a one-year $5 million CD at [... to fu]nd a loan in yen at 6 percent [... ] The spot rate of U.S. dollars [... (*L*]*G 9-5*)

[**a.** ...] indicates that the yen [... s]pot rate of U.S. dollars for

yen is 0.009483/¥1 by year-end. What should the bank charge on the loan in order to maintain the 2 percent spread?

   **b.** The bank has an opportunity to hedge using one-year forward contracts at 0.009493 U.S. dollars for yen. What is the spread if the bank hedges its forward foreign exchange exposure?

   **c.** How should the loan rates be increased to maintain the 2 percent spread if the bank intends to hedge its exposure using the forward rates?

10. Suppose that a U.S. FI has the following assets and liabilities:

| Assets | Liabilities |
|---|---|
| $300 million U.S. loans (one year) in dollars | $500 million U.S. CDs (one year) in dollars |
| $200 million equivalent German loans (one year) in euros | |

The promised one-year U.S. CD rate is 4 percent, to be paid in dollars at the end of the year; one-year, default risk–free loans in the United States are yielding 6 percent; and default risk–free one-year loans are yielding 10 percent in Germany. The exchange rate of dollars for euros at the beginning of the year is $1.10/€1. (*LG 9-5*)

   **a.** Calculate the dollar proceeds from the German loan at the end of the year, the return on the FI's investment portfolio, and the net interest margin for the FI if the spot foreign exchange rate has not changed over the year.

   **b.** Calculate the dollar proceeds from the German loan at the end of the year, the return on the FI's investment portfolio, and the net interest margin for the FI if the spot foreign exchange rate falls to $1.00/€1 over the year.

   **c.** Calculate the dollar proceeds from the German loan at the end of the year, the return on the FI's investment portfolio, and the net interest margin for the FI if the spot foreign exchange rate rises to $1.20/€1 over the year.

11. Suppose that, instead of funding the $200 million investment in 10 percent German loans with U.S. CDs, the FI manager in Problem 10 funds the German loans with $200 million equivalent one-year euro CDs at a rate of 7 percent. Now the balance sheet of the FI would be as follows: (*LG 9-5*)

| Assets | Liabilities |
|---|---|
| $300 million U.S. loans (6%) | $300 million U.S. CDs (4%) |
| $200 million equivalent German loans (10%) in euros | $200 million equivalent German CDs (7%) in euros |

   **a.** Calculate the return on the FI's investment portfolio, the average cost of funds, and the net interest margin for the FI if the spot foreign exchange rate falls to $1.00/€1 over the year.

   **b.** Calculate the return on the FI's investment portfolio, the average cost of funds, and the net interest margin for the FI if the spot foreign exchange rate rises to $1.20/€1 over the year.

12. **eXcel** **Using a Spreadsheet to Calculate Foreign Exchange Risk:** Suppose that on January 18, 2019, a U.S. firm plans to purchase 3 million euros' (€)

worth of French bonds from a French FI in one month's time. The French FI wants payment in euros. Thus, the U.S. firm must convert dollars into euros. The spot exchange rate for January 18, 2019, of U.S. dollars for euros is 1.10, or one euro costs $1.10 in dollars. Consequently, the U.S. firm must convert:

*U.S. $/€ exchange rate* × €3 million =

$$1.10 \times €3m. = \$3,300,000$$

into euros today. One month after the conversion of dollars to euros, the French bond purchase deal falls through and the U.S. firm no longer needs the euros it purchased at $1.10 per euro. Calculate the gain/loss on the bond to the U.S. firm if the spot exchange rate of U.S. dollars for euros is 1.20, 1.10, 1.05, and 0.99 at the end of the month. (*LG 9-5*)

| Price at Beginning of Month | U.S. $ to Exchange Rate at End of Month | Price at End of Month | ⇒ The Gain/Loss Will Be |
|---|---|---|---|
| $3.3m | 1.20 | 1.20 × €3 million = $3.6m | $3.6m − $3.3m = $300,000 |
| $3.3m | 1.10 | 1.10 × €3 million = $3.3m | $3.3m − $3.3m = $0 |
| $3.3m | 1.05 | 1.05 × €3 million = $3.15m | $3.15m − $3.3m = −$150,000 |
| $3.3m | 0.99 | 0.99 × €3 million = $2.97m | $2.97m − $3.3m = −$330,000 |

13. Citibank holds $23 million in foreign exchange assets and $18 million in foreign exchange liabilities. Citibank also conducted foreign currency trading activity in which it bought $5 million in foreign exchange contracts and sold $12 million in foreign exchange contracts. (*LG 9-6*)
    a. What is Citibank's net foreign assets?
    b. What is Citibank's net foreign exchange bought?
    c. What is Citibank's net foreign exposure?

14. P.J. Chase Stanley Bank holds $75 million in foreign exchange assets and $68 million in foreign exchange liabilities. P.J. Chase Stanley also conducted foreign currency trading activity in which it bought $165 million in foreign exchange contracts and sold $128 million in foreign exchange contracts. (*LG 9-6*)
    a. What is P.J. Chase Stanley's net foreign assets?
    b. What is P.J. Chase Stanley's net foreign exchange bought?
    c. What is P.J. Chase Stanley's net foreign exposure?

15. X-IM Bank has ¥14 million in assets and ¥23 million in liabilities and has sold ¥8 million in foreign currency trading. What is the net exposure for X-IM? For what type of exchange rate movement does this exposure put the bank at risk? (*LG 9-6*)

16. The following are the foreign currency positions of an FI, expressed in the foreign currency: (*LG 9-6*)

| Currency | Assets | Liabilities | FX Bought | FX Sold |
|---|---|---|---|---|
| Swiss franc (Sf) | Sf127,500 | Sf51,000 | Sf10,200 | Sf15,300 |
| British pound (£) | £38,168 | £16,794 | £11,450 | £15,267 |
| Japanese yen (¥) | ¥7,869,885 | ¥3,147,954 | ¥1,259,181 | ¥9,233,998 |

The exchange rate of dollars for Sf is 1.02, of dollars for British pound is 1.31, and of dollars for yen is 0.00953.

The following are the foreign currency positions converted to dollars:

| Currency | Assets | Liabilities | FX Bought | FX Sold |
|---|---|---|---|---|
| Swiss franc (Sf) | $125,000 | $50,000 | $10,000 | $15,000 |
| British pound (£) | $ 50,000 | $22,000 | $15,000 | $20,000 |
| Japanese yen (¥) | $ 75,000 | $30,000 | $12,000 | $88,000 |

a. What is the FI's net exposure in Swiss francs stated in Swiss francs (Sf) and in dollars ($)?
b. What is the FI's net exposure in British pounds stated in British pounds (£) and in dollars ($)?
c. What is the FI's net exposure in Japanese yen stated in Japanese yen (¥) and in dollars ($)?
d. What is the expected loss or gain if the Sf exchange rate appreciates by 1 percent? State your answer in Swiss francs (Sf) and in dollars ($).
e. What is the expected loss or gain if the £ exchange rate appreciates by 1 percent? State your answer in British pounds (£) and in dollars ($).
f. What is the expected loss or gain if the ¥ exchange rate appreciates by 2 percent? State your answer in Japanese yen (¥) and in dollars ($).

17. Suppose that the current spot exchange rate of U.S. dollars for Australian dollars, $S_{US\$/A\$}$, is 0.757 (i.e., $0.757 can be received for 1 Australian dollar). The price of Australian-produced goods increases by 5 percent (i.e., inflation in Australia, $IP_A$, is 5 percent), and the U.S. price index increases by 3 percent (i.e., inflation in the United States, $IP_{US}$, is 3 percent). Calculate the new spot exchange rate of U.S. dollars for Australian dollars that should result from the differences in inflation rates. (*LG 9-7*)

18. If the interest rate in the United Kingdom is 8 percent, the interest rate in the United States is 10 percent, the spot exchange rate is $1.35/£1, and interest rate parity holds, what must be the one-year forward exchange rate? (*LG 9-7*)

19. Suppose all of the conditions in Problem 18 hold except that the forward rate of exchange is also $1.35/£1. How could an investor take advantage of this situation? (*LG 9-7*)

20. If a bundle of goods in Japan costs ¥4,000,000 while the same goods and services cost $40,000 in the United States, what is the current exchange rate of U.S. dollars for yen? If, over the next year, inflation is 6 percent in Japan and 10 percent in the United States, what will the goods cost next year? Will the dollar depreciate or appreciate relative to the yen over this time period? (*LG 9-7*)

21. Assume that annual interest rates are 8 percent in the United States and 4 percent in Switzerland. An FI can borrow (by issuing CDs) or lend (by purchasing CDs) at these rates. The spot rate is $1.02/Sf. (*LG 9-7*)
    a. If the forward rate is $1.08/Sf, how could the bank arbitrage using a sum of $1 million? What is the spread earned?
    b. At what forward rate is this arbitrage eliminated?

22. Assume that annual interest rates are 5 percent in the United States and 4 percent in Turkey. An FI can borrow

(by issuing CDs) or lend (by purchasing CDs) at these rates. The spot rate is $0.3310/Turkish lira (TL). (*LG 9-7*)

**a.** If the forward rate is $0.3420/TL, how could the bank arbitrage using a sum of $5 million? What is the spread earned?

**b.** At what forward rate is this arbitrage eliminated?

The following problem is related to Appendix 9A material (available through Connect or your course instructor).

23. The following table lists balance of payment current accounts for Country A. (*LG 9-1*)

**Current Accounts**

| | | |
|---|---|---|
| 1. Exports of goods, services, and income | | $168,953 |
| 2. Goods | $92,543 | |
| 3. Services | 45,689 | |

**Current Accounts**

| | | |
|---|---|---|
| 4. Income receipts on U.S. assets abroad | 30,721 | |
| 5. Imports of goods, services, and income | | −160,357 |
| 6. Goods | −93,528 | |
| 7. Services | −31,689 | |
| 8. Income payments on foreign assets in the United States | −35,140 | |

**a.** What is Country A's total current accounts?
**b.** What is Country A's balance on goods?
**c.** What is Country A's balance on services?
**d.** What is Country A's balance on investment income?

---

# SEARCH THE SITE

Go to the Financial Management service of the United States Treasury at **www.treasury.gov** and find the latest information available on the Monthly U.S. Bank Positions in Foreign Currencies and Foreign Assets and Liabilities using the following steps. Click on "Bureau of Fiscal Services." Click on "Programs & Services" and then on "Reports & Statements." Click on "Treasury Bulletin." Click on the most recent date. This will bring up the Table of Contents. Scroll down and click on "Foreign Currency Positions." This will bring up a file containing the Monthly U.S. Bank Positions in Foreign Currencies and Foreign Assets and Liabilities.

**Questions**

1. Calculate the net foreign exchange exposure of U.S. banks to the Canadian dollar, Japanese yen, Swiss franc, British pound, and the euro.
2. What do the values say about the foreign exchange exposure of U.S. banks to these currencies?

---

# SEARCH THE SITE

Go to the Oanda website at **www.fxtop.com** and find the latest information on foreign exchange rates by clicking on "Historical Rates."

**Questions**

3. Create a graph of the exchange rate of U.S. dollars for Canadian dollars (CAD/USD) from January 1, 2012, through June 1, 2017. Has the U.S. dollar appreciated or depreciated against the Canadian dollar over this period?
4. Create a graph of the exchange rate of U.S. dollars for Swiss francs (CHF/USD) from January 1, 2012, through June 1, 2017. Has the U.S. dollar appreciated or depreciated against the Swiss franc over this period?

---

# APPENDIX 9A: Balance of Payment Accounts

## This appendix is available through Connect or your course instructor.

# Derivative Securities Markets

## Learning Goals

**LG 10-1**  *Distinguish between forward and future contracts.*

**LG 10-2**  *Understand how a futures transaction is conducted.*

**LG 10-3**  *Identify information that can be found in a futures quote.*

**LG 10-4**  *Recognize what option contracts are.*

**LG 10-5**  *Examine information found in an options quote.*

**LG 10-6**  *Know the main regulators of futures and options markets.*

**LG 10-7**  *Describe how swaps work.*

**LG 10-8**  *Understand caps, floors, and collars.*

**LG 10-9**  *Identify the biggest derivative securities markets globally.*

## DERIVATIVE SECURITIES: CHAPTER OVERVIEW

A **derivative security** is a financial security whose payoff is linked to another, previously issued security. Derivative securities generally involve an agreement between two parties to exchange a standard quantity of an asset or cash flow at a predetermined price and at a specified date in the future. As the value of the underlying security to be exchanged changes, the value of the derivative security changes. Derivatives involve the buying and selling, or transference, of risk. Under normal circumstances, trading in derivatives should not adversely affect the economic system because it allows individuals who want to bear risk to take more risk, while allowing individuals who want to avoid risk to transfer that risk elsewhere. Indeed, in 2003 former Federal Reserve Board chair Alan Greenspan credited the derivative securities markets with helping the banking system maintain its strength through the economic recession in the early 2000s.

However, derivative securities' traders can experience large losses if the price of the underlying asset moves against them significantly. Indeed, at the very heart of the recent

**derivative security**

*An agreement between two parties to exchange a standard quantity of an asset at a predetermined price at a specified date in the future.*

**derivative securities markets**

*The markets in which derivative securities trade.*

www.cmegroup.com

www.federalreserve.gov

financial crisis were losses associated with off-balance-sheet derivative securities created and held by FIs. These losses resulted in the failure, acquisition, or bailout of some of the largest FIs (including investment banks Lehman Brothers, Bear Stearns, and Merrill Lynch; savings institution Washington Mutual; insurance company AIG; commercial bank Citigroup; finance company Countrywide Financial; and government-sponsored agencies Fannie Mae and Freddie Mac) and a near meltdown of the world's financial and economic systems. Losses from the falling value of subprime mortgages and off-balance-sheet securities backed by these mortgages reached over $1 trillion worldwide through 2009.

A securitized asset such as a mortgage-backed security (see Chapter 7) is a derivative security in that its value is based on the value of an underlying security (e.g., a mortgage). Option contracts are also derivatives since their value depends on the price of some underlying security (e.g., a stock) relative to a reference (or strike) price. **Derivative securities markets** are the markets in which derivative securities trade. While derivative securities have been in existence for centuries, the growth in derivative securities markets has occurred mainly since the 1970s. As major markets, therefore, the derivative securities markets are the newest of the financial security markets.

The first of the modern wave of derivatives to trade were foreign currency futures contracts. These contracts were introduced by the International Monetary Market (IMM), now a subsidiary of the CME Group, in response to the introduction of floating exchange rates between currencies of different countries following the Smithsonian Agreements of 1971 and 1973 (see Chapter 9).

The second wave of derivative security growth was with interest rate derivative securities. Their growth was mainly in response to increases in the volatility of interest rates in the late 1970s and after, as the Federal Reserve started to target nonborrowed reserves (see Chapter 4) rather than interest rates. Financial institutions such as banks and savings institutions had many rate-sensitive assets and liabilities on their balance sheets. As interest rate volatility increased, the sensitivity of the net worth (equity) of these institutions to interest rate shocks increased as well. In response, the Chicago Board of Trade (CBOT) introduced numerous short-term and long-term interest rate futures contracts in the 1970s and stock index futures and options in the 1980s. Accordingly, financial institutions are the major participants in the derivative securities markets. Financial institutions can be either users of derivative contracts for hedging (see Chapter 23); dealers that act as counterparties in trades with customers for a fee; or arbitrageurs, buying in one market (i.e., the spot market) and simultaneously selling in another market (i.e., the futures market) to make a risk-free profit when there is a mismatch between the two prices. Approximately 1,420 U.S. banks use derivatives and only four large dealer banks—J.P. Morgan Chase, Citigroup, Goldman Sachs, and Bank of America—account for some 91 percent of the derivatives that user banks hold.[1]

A third wave of derivative security innovations occurred in the 1990s and 2000s with credit derivatives (e.g., credit forwards, credit risk options, and credit swaps). For example, a credit forward is a forward agreement that hedges against an increase in default risk on a loan (a decline in the credit quality of a borrower) after the loan rate is determined and the loan is issued. Although the credit protection buyer hedges exposure to default risk, there is still counterparty credit risk in the event that the seller fails to perform his or her obligations under the terms of the contract (as was the concern in September 2008 with regard to AIG, an active credit default swap seller).[2] In March 2016, the notional value of credit derivatives held by U.S. banks was approximately $7.4 trillion, down from $13.9 trillion in 2013. As we discuss later in the chapter, part of the Wall Street Reform and Consumer Protection Act, passed in 2010 in response to the financial crisis, is the Volcker Rule which prohibits U.S. depository institutions (DIs) from engaging in proprietary trading (i.e., trading as a principal for the trading account of the bank). This includes any transaction to

---

1. See Office of the Comptroller of the Currency, "Bank Derivatives Report," First Quarter, March 2016.
2. Indeed, under the U.S. government's bailout of AIG, the largest component was to satisfy counterparty claims in AIG credit default swaps (CDSs). Under AIG CDS programs, if AIG was downgraded (e.g., from AAA to BB) then the CDS contract had to be marked to market and marking to market losses of AIG paid to the CDS counterparty. Since AIG was close to insolvent, these losses were borne by the U.S. government as part of the AIG bailout.

purchase or sell derivatives such as credit derivatives. Thus, only the investment banking arm of the business is allowed to conduct such trading. The Volcker Rule was implemented in April 2014 and banks had until July 21, 2015, to be in compliance. The result has been a reduction in credit derivatives held off-balance-sheet by these financial institutions. These derivative securities have become particularly useful for managing credit risk of emerging-market countries and credit portfolio risk in general.

The rapid growth of derivatives use by both FIs and nonfinancial firms has been controversial. In the 1990s and 2000s, critics charged that derivatives contracts contain potential losses that can materialize, particularly for banks and insurance companies that deal heavily in these instruments. As will be discussed in this chapter and the following two chapters, when employed appropriately, derivatives can be used to hedge or reduce an FI's risk. However, when misused, derivatives can increase the risk of an FI's insolvency. In the 1990s, a number of scandals involving FIs, firms, and municipalities (such as Bankers Trust and the Allied Irish Bank) led to a tightening of the accounting (reporting) requirements for derivative contracts. Specifically, beginning in 2000, the Financial Accounting Standards Board (FASB) required all derivatives to be marked to market and mandated that losses and gains be immediately transparent on FIs' and other firms' financial statements. Then in the late 2000s, billions of dollars of losses on derivative securities and the near collapse of the world's financial markets led to a call for major regulations to be imposed on the trading of derivative securities. These regulations were intended to bring many over-the-counter derivative contracts made between financial institutions under federal regulation and to empower securities and commodities regulators to police them. The result has been a significant drop in derivative securities held by commercial banks from a high of $249.3 trillion in June 2011 to $192.9 trillion in March 2016.

In this chapter, we present an overview of the derivative securities markets. We look at the markets for forwards, futures, options, swaps, and some special derivative contracts (caps, floors, and collars). We define the various derivative securities and focus on the markets themselves—their operations and trading processes. In Chapter 23, we describe in detail how these securities can be used to manage and hedge the foreign exchange, interest rate, and credit risks of financial institutions.

# FORWARDS AND FUTURES

**LG 10-1**

To present the essential nature and characteristics of forward and futures contracts and markets, we compare them with spot contracts. We define each in Table 10–1. We illustrate appropriate time lines for each of the three contracts using a bond as the underlying financial security to the derivative contract in Figure 10–1.

**spot contract**

*An agreement to transact involving the immediate exchange of assets and funds.*

## Spot Markets

A **spot contract** is an agreement between a buyer and a seller at time 0, when the seller of the asset agrees to deliver it immediately and the buyer agrees to pay for that

**TABLE 10–1**   Spot, Forward, and Futures Contracts

> **Spot contract**—agreement made between a buyer and a seller at time 0 for the seller to deliver the asset immediately and the buyer to pay for the asset immediately.
> **Forward contract**—agreement between a buyer and a seller at time 0 to exchange a nonstandardized asset for cash at some future date. The details of the asset and the price to be paid at the forward contract expiration date are set at time 0. The price of the forward contract is fixed over the life of the contract.
> **Futures contract**—agreement between a buyer and a seller at time 0 to exchange a standardized asset for cash at some future date. Each contract has a standardized expiration and transactions occur in a centralized market. The price of the futures contract changes daily as the market value of the asset underlying the futures fluctuates.

**Figure 10–1**   Contract Time Line

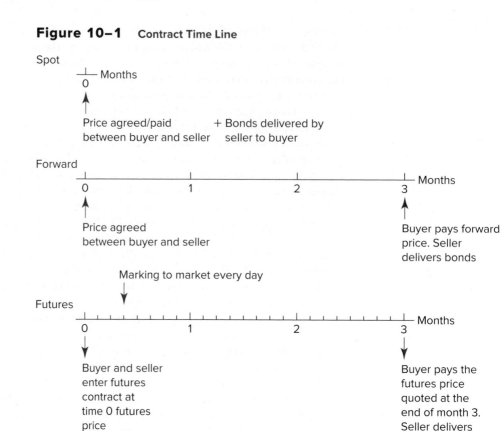

asset immediately.[3] Thus, the unique feature of a spot market is the immediate and simultaneous exchange of cash for securities, or what is often called *delivery versus payment*. A spot bond quote of $97 for a 20-year maturity bond is the price the buyer must pay the seller, per $100 of face value, for immediate (time 0) delivery of the 20-year bond.

Spot transactions occur because the buyer of the asset believes its value will increase in the immediate future (over the investor's holding period). If the value of the asset increases as expected, the investor can sell the asset at its higher price for a profit. For example, if the 20-year bond increases in value to $99 per $100 of face value, the investor can sell the bond for a profit of $2 per $100 of face value.

### Forward Markets

**Forward Contracts.**   A **forward contract** is a contractual agreement between a buyer and a seller at time 0 to exchange a prespecified asset for cash at some later date at a price set at time 0. Market participants take a position in forward contracts because the future (spot) price or interest rate on an asset is uncertain. Rather than risk that the future spot price will move against them—that the asset will become more expensive to buy in the future—forward traders pay a financial institution a fee to arrange a forward contract. Such a contract lets the market participant hedge the risk that future spot prices on an asset will move against him or her by guaranteeing a future price for the asset *today*.

For example, in a three-month forward contract to deliver $100 face value of 10-year bonds, the buyer and seller agree on a price and amount today (time 0), but the delivery (or exchange) of the 10-year bond for cash does not occur until three months into the future. If the forward price agreed to at time 0 was $98 per $100 of face value, in three

**forward contract**

*An agreement to transact involving the future exchange of a set amount of assets at a set price.*

3. Technically, in bond markets physical settlement and delivery may take place one or two days after the contractual spot agreement is made. In equity markets, delivery and cash settlement normally occur three business days after the spot contract agreement ($T + 3$ settlement).

months' time the seller delivers $100 of 10-year bonds and receives $98 from the buyer. This is the price the buyer must pay and the seller must accept no matter what happens to the spot price of 10-year bonds during the three months between the time the contract is entered into and the time the bonds are delivered for payment (i.e., whether the spot price falls to $97 or below or rises to $99 or above).

In Chapter 9, we discussed the market for forward foreign currency exchange contracts, which allows market participants to buy or sell a specified currency for a specified price at a specified date (e.g., one-month, three-month, or six-month contracts are standard). Forward contracts can also be based on a specified interest rate (e.g., LIBOR) rather than a specified asset (called forward rate agreements, or FRAs). The buyer of a FRA agrees to pay the contract rate based on some notional principal amount (e.g., $1 million)—he or she buys the notional amount at the stated interest rate. The seller of a FRA agrees to sell the funds to the buyer at the stated rate. For example, for a three-month FRA written today with a notional value of $1 million and a contract rate of 1.70 percent, the buyer of the FRA agrees to pay 1.70 percent (the current three-month LIBOR rate) to borrow $1 million starting three months from now. The seller of the FRA agrees to lend $1 million to the buyer at 1.70 percent starting three months from now. If interest rates rise in the next three months, the FRA buyer benefits from the FRA. He or she can borrow $1 million at the rate stated on the FRA (1.70 percent) rather than at the higher market rate (say, 2 percent).

Forward contracts often involve underlying assets that are nonstandardized, because the terms of each contract are negotiated individually between the buyer and the seller (e.g., a contract between Bank A to buy from Bank B, six months from now, $1 million in 30-year Treasury bonds with a coupon rate of 2.50 percent). As a result, the buyer and seller involved in a forward contract must locate and deal directly with each other in the over-the-counter market to set the terms of the contract rather than transacting the sale in a centralized market (such as a futures market exchange).

**Forward Markets.** Commercial banks (see Chapter 11) and investment banks and broker-dealers (see Chapter 16) are the major forward market participants, acting as both principals and agents. These financial institutions make a profit on the spread between the price at which they buy and sell the asset underlying the forward contracts.

Each forward contract is originally negotiated between the financial institution and the customer, and therefore the details of each (e.g., price, expiration, size, delivery date) can be unique. Most forward contracts are tailor-made contracts that are negotiated between two parties. Thus, there is a risk of default by either party. If an over-the-counter (OTC) transaction is not structured carefully, it may pass along unintended risks to participants, exposing them to higher frequency and severity of losses than if they had held an equivalent cash position. As the forward market has grown over the last decade, however, traders have begun making secondary markets in some forward contracts, communicating the buy and sell prices on the contracts over computer networks. As of March 2016, U.S. commercial banks held over $29.5 trillion of forward contracts that were listed for trading in the over-the-counter markets. The advent of this secondary market trading has resulted in an increase in the standardization of forward contracts. It has also become increasingly easy to get out of a forward position by taking an offsetting forward position in the secondary market. Secondary market activity in forward contracts has made them more attractive to firms and investors that had previously been reluctant to get locked into a forward contract until expiration. Secondary market activity has also resulted in a situation in which the differences between forward and future contracts have significantly narrowed.

In recent years credit derivative instruments have been developed to better allow financial institutions to hedge their credit risk. Credit derivatives can be used to hedge the credit risk on individual loans or a portfolio of loans. The credit derivative market, while still relatively young, has gained a reputation as an early warning signal for spotting corporate debt problems. One such credit derivative instrument is a credit forward. A credit forward is a forward agreement that hedges against an increase in default risk on a loan (a decline in the credit quality of a borrower) after the loan rate is determined and the loan is issued by a bank. Common buyers of credit forwards are banks and common sellers are insurance companies.

### Futures Markets

**futures contract**

*An agreement to transact involving the future exchange of a set amount of assets for a price that is settled daily.*

**Futures Contracts.** A **futures contract** is normally traded on an organized exchange such as the ICE (Intercontinental Exchange) Futures U.S. A futures contract, like a forward contract, is an agreement between a buyer and a seller at time 0 to exchange a standardized, prespecified asset at some later date at a price set at time 0. Thus, a futures contract is very similar to a forward contract. One difference between forwards and futures is that forward contracts are bilateral contracts subject to counterparty default risk, but the default risk on futures is significantly reduced by the futures exchange guaranteeing to indemnify counterparties against credit or default risk. Another difference relates to the contract's price, which in a forward contract is fixed over the life of the contract (e.g., $98 per $100 of face value for three months to be paid on expiration of the forward contract), whereas a futures contract is **marked to market** daily. This means that the contract's price is adjusted each day as the price of the asset underlying the futures contract changes and as the contract approaches expiration. Therefore, actual daily cash settlements occur between the buyer and seller in response to these price changes (this is called marking to market). This can be compared to a forward contract. While the value of a forward contract can change daily between when the buyer and seller agree on the deal and the maturity date of the forward contract, cash payment from buyer to seller occurs only at the end of the contract period. Marking futures contracts to market ensures that both parties to the futures contract maintain sufficient funds in their account to guarantee the eventual payoff when the contract matures. For the buyers of the futures contract, marking to market can result in unexpected payments from their account if the price of the futures contract moves against them.

**marked to market**

*Describes the prices on outstanding futures contracts that are adjusted each day to reflect current futures market conditions.*

With a futures contract, like a forward contract, a person or firm makes a commitment to deliver an asset (such as foreign exchange) at some future date. If a counterparty were to default on a futures contract, however, the exchange would assume the defaulting party's position and payment obligations. Thus, unless a systematic financial market collapse threatens an exchange itself, futures are essentially default-risk free. In addition, the default risk of a futures contract is less than that of a forward contract for at least four reasons: (1) daily marking to market of futures (so that there is no buildup of losses or gains), (2) margin requirements on futures that act as a security bond should a counterparty default, (3) price movement limits that spread extreme price fluctuations over time, and (4) default guarantees by the futures exchange itself.

**Futures Markets.** Futures trading occurs on organized exchanges—for example, the Chicago Board of Trade (CBOT) and the New York Mercantile Exchange (NYMEX), both of which are part of the CME Group.[4] Financial futures market trading was introduced in 1972 with the establishment of foreign exchange future contracts on the International Money Market (IMM). In 2016, several major exchanges existed in the United States[5] as well as abroad.[6] Table 10–2 lists the characteristics of some of the most widely traded financial futures contracts. Futures contracts also exist on commodity (e.g., corn, wheat), energy (e.g., electricity), metals (e.g., copper, gold), and other (e.g., weather) contracts as well. Figure 10–2 shows the notional value of futures and forwards held by commercial

**www.cmegroup.com**

---

4. The New York Mercantile Exchange (NYMEX) is the world's largest physical commodity futures exchange, located in New York City. The New York Mercantile Exchange handles billions of dollars' worth of energy products, metals, and other commodities (e.g., crude oil, gasoline, gold, and propane) being bought and sold on the trading floor and the overnight electronic trading computer systems. The prices quoted for transactions on the exchange are the basis for prices that people pay throughout the world. The floor of the NYMEX is regulated by the Commodity Futures Trading Commission.

5. These include the CME Group (which includes the Chicago Mercantile Exchange, the Chicago Board of Trade, the New York Mercantile Exchange, the MidAmerica Commodity Exchange, and the Kansas City Board of Trade), CBOE Holdings, and the ICE Futures U.S.

6. Some of these include the Liffe (in London, which is part of the ICE), the Singapore Exchange (SGX), the Eurex (in Germany), the National Stock Exchange (in India), the Shanghai Futures Exchange, and the Montreal Exchange (part of the TMX Group).

banks from 1992 through 2016. The terms of futures contracts (e.g., contract size, delivery month, trading hours, minimum price fluctuation, daily price limits, and process used for delivery) traded in the United States are set by the exchange and are subject to the approval of the Commodity Futures Trading Commission (CFTC), the principal regulator of futures markets. For example, the contract terms for 10-year T-note futures are listed in Table 10–3.

**TABLE 10–2** **Characteristics of Actively Traded Futures Contracts**

| Type of Futures | Contract Size | Exchange* | Open Interest |
|---|---|---|---|
| **Interest Rates** | | | |
| Treasury bonds | $100,000 | CBOT | 565,872 |
| Treasury notes | $100,000 | CBOT | 2,803,617 |
| Treasury notes—5 year | $100,000 | CBOT | 2,774,435 |
| Treasury notes—2 year | $200,000 | CBOT | 1,096,652 |
| Federal funds—30 days | $5,000,000 | CBOT | 798,818 |
| Eurodollars | $1,000,000 | CME | 10,774,413 |
| **Currency** | | | |
| Japanese yen | ¥12,500,000 | CME | 159,811 |
| Canadian dollar | C$100,000 | CME | 115,675 |
| British pound | £62,500 | CME | 244,578 |
| Swiss franc | Sfr 125,000 | CME | 45,224 |
| Australian dollar | A$ 100,000 | CME | 100,183 |
| Euro FX | Euro 125,000 | CME | 367,157 |
| **Index** | | | |
| Mini DJIA | $5 times average | CBOT | 142,984 |
| S&P 500 index | $250 times index | CME | 92,766 |
| Mini S&P index | $50 times index | CME | 2,014,809 |
| Mini Nasdaq 100 | $20 times index | CME | 287,132 |
| Mini Russell 1000 | $100 times index | ICE-US | 940 |
| Mini FTSE 100 index | £10 times index | ENXT | 51 |

*CBOT = Chicago Board of Trade; CME = Chicago Mercantile Exchange; ICE-U.S. = Intercontinental Exchange Futures U.S.; ENXT = Euronext.liffe.

**Source:** CME Group website, August 3, 2016. www.cmegroup.com

**Figure 10–2** **Forward and Futures Contracts Held by Commercial Banks, 1992–2016**

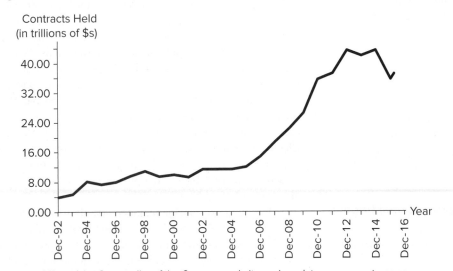

**Sources:** Office of the Comptroller of the Currency website, various dates. www.occ.treas.gov

**TABLE 10–3**   Contract Terms for 10-Year Treasury Note Futures

**Underlying unit**—one U.S. Treasury note having a face value at maturity of $100,000.

**Deliverable grades**—U.S. Treasury notes with a remaining term to maturity of at least 6½ years, but not more than 10 years, from the first day of the delivery month. The invoice price equals the futures settlement price times a conversion factor, plus accrued interest. The conversion factor is the price of the delivered note ($1 par value) to yield 6 percent.

**Price quote**—points ($1,000) and halves of 1/32 of a point. For example, 126-16 represents 126 16/32 and 126-165 represents 126 16.5/32. Par is on the basis of 100 points.

**Tick size (minimum fluctuation)**—one-half of one thirty-second (1/32) of one point ($15.625, rounded up to the nearest cent per contract), except for intermonth spreads, where the minimum price fluctuation will be one-quarter of one thirty-second of one point ($7.8125 per contract).

**Contract months**—the first three consecutive contracts in the March, June, September, and December quarterly cycle.

**Last trading day**—seventh business day preceding the last business day of the delivery month. Trading in expiring contracts closes at 12:01 p.m. on the last trading day.

**Last delivery day**—last business day of the delivery month.

**Delivery method**—Federal Reserve book-entry wire-transfer system.

**Settlement**—U.S. Treasury Futures Settlement Procedures.

**Position limits**—current position limits.

**Trading hours (all times listed are central time)**—Sunday–Friday: 5:00 p.m.–4:00 p.m. with a 60-minute break each day beginning at 4:00 p.m.

**Ticker symbol**—CME ClearPort—21; Clearing—21; CME Globex—ZN

**Exchange rule**—these contracts are listed with, and subject to, the rules and regulations of the CBOT.

**Source:** CME Group website, August 2016. www.cmegroup.com

**open-outcry auction**

*Method of futures trading where traders face each other and "cry out" their offer to buy or sell a stated number of futures contracts at a stated price.*

**floor broker**

*Exchange members who place trades from the public.*

**professional traders**

*Exchange members who trade for their own account.*

Trading on most of the largest exchanges such as the CBOT has historically taken place in trading "pits." A trading pit consists of circular steps leading down to the center of the pit. Traders for each delivery date on a futures contract informally group together in the trading pit. Futures trading occurs using an **open-outcry auction** method where traders face each other and "cry out" their offer to buy or sell a stated number of futures contracts at a stated price. However, the 2000s saw the rise in derivative trading on electronic exchanges. In 2004 Eurex, the world's largest derivatives exchange, launched a fully electronic exchange in the United States. Based in Chicago, this exchange offers futures and options on U.S. Treasury notes and 30-year Treasury bonds as well as 2-, 5-, and 10-year contracts on euro interest rate contracts. By 2016, trading volume on Eurex exceeded 1.87 billion contracts annually, including futures and options on stocks, bonds, commodities, and financial indexes. The CME Group has developed the CME Globex, which is the world's leading electronic trading platform. Customers trade on CME Globex around the globe and virtually around the clock. Further, in 2008, the ICE Futures U.S. announced that floor trading of all ICE Futures U.S. futures contracts would end at the close of trading on February 29, 2008. Effective March 1, 2008, these futures contracts now trade exclusively on the ICE electronic trading platform. Electronic trading offers advantages of high-speed trade execution, transparency in trading, and global access in the trading process. Finally, in July 2015 the CME Group closed all open-outcry trading pits except for the S&P contracts and moved all trading to electronic platforms.

Only futures exchange members are allowed to transact on futures exchanges. Trades from the public are placed with a **floor broker.** When an order is placed, a floor broker may trade with another floor broker or with a professional trader. **Professional traders** are similar to designated market makers on the stock exchanges in that they trade for their

**position traders**

*Exchange members who take a position in the futures market based on their expectations about the future direction of the prices of the underlying assets.*

**day traders**

*Exchange members who take a position within a day and liquidate it before day's end.*

**scalpers**

*Exchange members who take positions for very short periods of time, sometimes only minutes, in an attempt to profit from this active trading.*

**long position**

*A purchase of a futures contract.*

**short position**

*A sale of a futures contract.* **LG 10-3**

**clearinghouse**

*The unit that oversees trading on the exchange and guarantees all trades made by the exchange traders.*

own account. Professional traders are also referred to as position traders, day traders, or scalpers. **Position traders** take a position in the futures market based on their expectations about the future direction of prices of the underlying assets. **Day traders** generally take a position within a day and liquidate it before day's end. **Scalpers** take positions for very short periods of time, sometimes only minutes, in an attempt to profit from this active trading. Scalpers do not have an affirmative obligation to provide liquidity to futures markets but do so in expectation of earning a profit. Scalpers' profits are related to the bid-ask spread and the length of time a position is held. Specifically, it has been found that scalper trades held longer than three minutes, on average, produce losses to scalpers. Thus, this need for a quick turnover of a scalper's position enhances futures market liquidity and is therefore valuable.

Similar to trading in the stock market (see Chapter 8), futures trades may be placed as market orders (instructing the floor broker to transact at the best price available) or limit orders (instructing the floor broker to transact at a specified price). The order may be for a purchase of the futures contract in which the futures holder takes a **long position** in the futures contract, or the order may be for a sale of the futures contract in which the futures holder takes a **short position** in the futures contract.

Once a futures price is agreed upon, the two parties do not complete the deal with each other but rather (as illustrated in Figure 10–3) with the **clearinghouse** overseeing the exchange. The exchange's clearinghouse guarantees all trades made by exchange traders. The clearinghouse breaks up every trade into a buy and sell transaction and takes the opposite side of the transaction, becoming the buyer for every futures contract seller (transaction 1 in Figure 10–3) and the seller for every futures contract buyer (transaction 2 in Figure 10–3). Thus, the clearinghouse ensures that all trading obligations are met. Clearinghouses are able to perform their function as guarantor of an exchange's futures contracts by requiring all member firms to deposit sufficient funds (from customers' margin accounts) to ensure that the firm's customers will meet the terms of any futures contract entered into on the exchange.

Table 10–4 shows a futures quote from *The Wall Street Journal Online* for August 3, 2016. The three types of financial futures contracts are interest rate futures, currency futures, and equity index futures. The underlying asset on an interest rate futures contract is a bond or a short-term fixed-interest security's price or interest rate (e.g., Treasury securities, Eurodollar CDs); on a currency contract, it is an exchange rate (e.g., yen to U.S. dollar); and on an index futures contract, it is a major U.S. or foreign stock market index (e.g., the Dow Jones Industrial Average—see Chapter 8). Look at the quote for Treasury bond interest rate futures contracts. The bold heading of each quote contains information about the underlying deliverable asset (e.g., Treasury bonds) on the futures contract, the exchange on which the futures contract is traded (e.g., CBT), the face value of a contract (e.g., $100,000), and the basis for the quoted prices (e.g., pts 32nds of 100%, or 172-050 = 172 5/32 percent). Each row of the quote provides information for a specific delivery month (e.g., Sept 16 = September 2016). The first column of the quote lists the delivery month and year. The

**Figure 10–3** **Clearinghouse Function in Futures Markets**

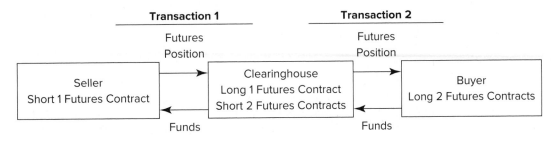

**TABLE 10–4** Futures Quote

### Interest Rate Futures

Wednesday, August 03, 2016

NOTICE TO READERS: As of 6/15/11, Lifetime High and Low values represent Year-to-date High and Low until further notice.

KEY TO EXCHANGES: CBT: Chicago Board of Trade; CME: Chicago Mercantile Exchange; CMX: Comex; DME: Dubai Mercantile Exchange;ENXT: Euronext.liffe; EUREX: EUREX; ICE-EU: ICE Futures Europe; ICE-US: ICE Futures U.S.; KC: Kansas City Board of Trade; ME: Montreal Exchange; MPLS: Minneapolis Grain Exchange; NYM: New York Mercantile Exchange, or Nymex; SGX-DT: Singapore Exchange Derivatives Trading Ltd

**Treasury Bonds** (CBT)-$100,000; pts 32nds of 100%

| | Open | High | Low | Settle | Chg | LIFETIME High | Low | Open Int |
|---|---|---|---|---|---|---|---|---|
| Sep 16 | 171-310 | 172-210 | 171-140 | **172-050** | −6.0 | 177-110 | 158-200 | 562,270 |
| Dec 16 | 170-140 | 171-040 | 170-020 | **170-230** | −6.0 | 175-190 | 159-290 | 958 |

Est vol 395,934; vol 570,038; open int, 563,228

**Treasury Notes** (CBT)-$100,000; pts 32nds of 100%

| | Open | High | Low | Settle | Chg | LIFETIME High | Low | Open Int |
|---|---|---|---|---|---|---|---|---|
| Sep 16 | 132-130 | 132-205 | 132-085 | **132-185** | +1.0 | 134-075 | 128-140 | 2,756,433 |
| Dec 16 | 131-130 | 131-220 | 131-110 | **131-205** | +1.0 | 133-095 | 130-015 | 13,059 |

Est vol 1,977,784; vol 2,791,794; open int, 2,769,492

**5 Yr. Treasury Notes** (CBT)-$100,000; pts 32nds of 100%

| | Open | High | Low | Settle | Chg | LIFETIME High | Low | Open Int |
|---|---|---|---|---|---|---|---|---|
| Sep 16 | 121-250 | 121-290 | 121-220 | **121-280** | +1.0 | 122-285 | 119-235 | 2,738,240 |
| Dec 16 | 121-270 | 121-282 | 121-237 | **121-285** | +.7 | 122-162 | 121-090 | 17,726 |

Est vol 813,686; vol 1,141,306; open int, 2,755,966

**2 Yr. Treasury Notes** (CBT)-$200,000; pts 32nds of 100%

| | Open | High | Low | Settle | Chg | LIFETIME High | Low | Open Int |
|---|---|---|---|---|---|---|---|---|
| Sep 16 | 109-145 | 109-155 | 109-135 | **109-147** | −.2 | 109-282 | 108-250 | 1,089,190 |

Est vol 317,124; vol 410,632; open int, 1,093,965

**Eurodollar** (CME)-$1,000,000; pts of 100%

| | Open | High | Low | Settle | Chg | LIFETIME High | Low | Open Int |
|---|---|---|---|---|---|---|---|---|
| Aug 16 | 99.2100 | 99.2100 | 99.1900 | **99.1975** | −.0125 | 99.4350 | 99.1100 | 162,446 |
| Sep 16 | 99.1800 | 99.1850 | 99.1550 | **99.1650** | −.0150 | 99.4100 | 98.9200 | 1,174,950 |
| Oct 16 | 99.1500 | 99.1500 | 99.1350 | **99.1400** | −.0200 | 99.3300 | 99.1050 | 36,768 |
| Dec 16 | 99.1350 | 99.1400 | 99.1050 | **99.1250** | −.0100 | 99.3800 | 98.7500 | 1,393,526 |
| Mar 17 | 99.1100 | 99.1100 | 99.0800 | **99.1000** | −.0100 | 99.3700 | 98.6000 | 1,016,815 |
| Jun 17 | 99.0750 | 99.0850 | 99.0450 | **99.0750** | −.0050 | 99.3500 | 98.4550 | 927,677 |
| Sep 17 | 99.0450 | 99.0550 | 99.0200 | **99.0500** | −.0050 | 99.3200 | 98.3250 | 816,393 |
| Dec 17 | 99.0050 | 99.0150 | 98.9750 | **99.0100** | −.0050 | 99.2700 | 98.2050 | 1,213,547 |
| Mar 18 | 98.9800 | 98.9950 | 98.9550 | **98.9900** | ... | 99.2400 | 98.1100 | 615,874 |
| Jun 18 | 98.9500 | 98.9600 | 98.9200 | **98.9550** | ... | 99.2000 | 98.0250 | 464,573 |
| Sep 18 | 98.9050 | 98.9250 | 98.8850 | **98.9200** | ... | 99.1550 | 97.9500 | 428,536 |
| Dec 18 | 98.8500 | 98.8800 | 98.8350 | **98.8750** | +.0050 | 99.1050 | 97.8700 | 534,731 |
| Mar 19 | 98.8150 | 98.8500 | 98.8050 | **98.8400** | +.0050 | 99.0650 | 97.8100 | 390,000 |
| Jun 19 | 98.7750 | 98.8100 | 98.7650 | **98.8000** | +.0050 | 99.0200 | 97.7450 | 287,696 |
| Sep 19 | 98.7300 | 98.7650 | 98.7250 | **98.7600** | +.0100 | 98.9750 | 97.6850 | 231,594 |
| Dec 19 | 98.6750 | 98.7150 | 98.6700 | **98.7100** | +.0100 | 98.9050 | 97.6250 | 224,505 |
| Mar 20 | 98.6350 | 98.6750 | 98.6300 | **98.6650** | +.0050 | 98.8600 | 97.5570 | 142,250 |
| Jun 20 | 98.5800 | 98.6250 | 98.5800 | **98.6150** | +.0050 | 98.8150 | 97.5250 | 92,368 |
| Sep 20 | 98.5300 | 98.5750 | 98.5300 | **98.5650** | +.0050 | 98.7700 | 97.4700 | 82,732 |
| Dec 20 | 98.4700 | 98.5200 | 98.4700 | **98.5100** | +.0050 | 98.7150 | 97.4200 | 90,244 |
| Mar 21 | 98.4250 | 98.4700 | 98.4250 | **98.4600** | ... | 98.6700 | 97.3750 | 53,826 |
| Jun 21 | 98.3850 | 98.4200 | 98.3700 | **98.4100** | ... | 98.6200 | 97.3300 | 47,830 |
| Sep 21 | 98.3300 | 98.3700 | 98.3200 | **98.3600** | ... | 98.5750 | 97.2900 | 21,024 |
| Dec 21 | 98.2750 | 98.3200 | 98.2650 | **98.3050** | −.0050 | 98.5200 | 97.2500 | 17,020 |
| Mar 22 | 98.2350 | 98.2750 | 98.2250 | **98.2650** | −.0050 | 98.4800 | 97.2200 | 10,521 |
| Jun 22 | 98.2000 | 98.2350 | 98.1850 | **98.2250** | −.0050 | 98.4350 | 97.1900 | 5,456 |
| Sep 22 | 98.1900 | 98.1950 | 98.1550 | **98.1850** | −.0050 | 98.3950 | 97.1600 | 5,294 |
| Dec 22 | 98.1150 | 98.1450 | 98.1100 | **98.1450** | −.0050 | 98.3500 | 97.1350 | 5,584 |
| Mar 23 | 98.1100 | 98.1150 | 98.0850 | **98.1200** | −.0050 | 98.3200 | 97.1200 | 4,537 |
| Jun 23 | 98.0800 | 98.0950 | 98.0850 | **98.0850** | −.0050 | 98.2850 | 97.1000 | 860 |
| Sep 23 | 98.0500 | 98.0500 | 98.0500 | **98.0600** | −.0050 | 98.0800 | 97.0800 | 1,253 |
| Dec 23 | 98.0150 | 98.0200 | 98.0000 | **98.0200** | −.0100 | 98.1200 | 97.1850 | 747 |

Est vol 1,617,855; vol 2,143,795; open int, 10,506,734

### Currency Futures

Wednesday, August 03, 2016

**Japanese Yen** (CME)-¥12,500,000; $ per 100¥

| | Open | High | Low | Settle | Chg | LIFETIME High | Low | Open Int |
|---|---|---|---|---|---|---|---|---|
| Sep 16 | .9927 | .9942 | .9861 | **.9903** | −.0025 | 1.0131 | .8282 | 154,625 |
| Dec 16 | .9952 | .9978 | .9899 | **.9940** | −.0025 | 1.0138 | .8305 | 1,700 |
| Mar 17 | 1.0029 | 1.0049 | .9949 | **.9980** | −.0025 | 1.0063 | .8346 | 251 |
| Jun 17 | .9730 | .9940 | .9643 | **1.0026** | −.0024 | 1.0182 | .8976 | 111 |

Est vol 92,011; vol 145,331; open int, 156,696

**Canadian Dollar** (CME)-CAD 100,000; $ per CAD

| | Open | High | Low | Settle | Chg | LIFETIME High | Low | Open Int |
|---|---|---|---|---|---|---|---|---|
| Sep 16 | .7634 | .7657 | .7608 | **.7648** | +.0006 | .8024 | .6825 | 111,397 |
| Dec 16 | .7634 | .7659 | .7612 | **.7651** | +.0007 | .8014 | .6840 | 3,805 |
| Mar 17 | .7618 | .7659 | .7618 | **.7654** | +.0006 | .7999 | .6905 | 406 |
| Jun 17 | .7574 | .7579 | .7564 | **.7657** | +.0007 | .7909 | .6917 | 147 |

Est vol 59,282; vol 80,382; open int, 115,825

**British Pound** (CME)-£62,500; $ per £

| | Open | High | Low | Settle | Chg | LIFETIME High | Low | Open Int |
|---|---|---|---|---|---|---|---|---|
| Sep 16 | 1.3364 | 1.3382 | 1.3289 | **1.3325** | −.0032 | 1.5009 | 1.2806 | 230,182 |
| Dec 16 | 1.3365 | 1.3402 | 1.3314 | **1.3348** | −.0032 | 1.5000 | 1.2827 | 1,965 |
| Mar 17 | 1.3300 | 1.3410 | 1.3243 | **1.3371** | −.0032 | 1.4735 | 1.2930 | 572 |
| Jun 17 | 1.3326 | 1.3350 | 1.3326 | **1.3397** | −.0033 | 1.5003 | 1.2950 | 526 |

Est vol 65,616; vol 95,466; open int, 233,265

**Swiss Franc** (CME)-CHF 125,000; $ per CHF

| | Open | High | Low | Settle | Chg | LIFETIME High | Low | Open Int |
|---|---|---|---|---|---|---|---|---|
| Sep 16 | 1.0396 | 1.0403 | 1.0294 | **1.0299** | −.0100 | 1.0654 | .9898 | 44,731 |
| Dec 16 | 1.0408 | 1.0458 | 1.0408 | **1.0354** | −.0100 | 1.0602 | .9964 | 102 |

Est vol 18,138; vol 14,808; open int, 44,853

**Euro** (CME)-€125,000; $ per €

| | Open | High | Low | Settle | Chg | LIFETIME High | Low | Open Int |
|---|---|---|---|---|---|---|---|---|
| Sep 16 | 1.1244 | 1.1245 | 1.1162 | **1.1167** | −.0081 | 1.1666 | 1.0804 | 370,655 |
| Dec 16 | 1.1283 | 1.1283 | 1.1208 | **1.1213** | −.0080 | 1.1701 | 1.0850 | 5,820 |
| Mar 17 | 1.1313 | 1.1315 | 1.1257 | **1.1258** | −.0080 | 1.1733 | 1.0864 | 1,332 |
| Jun 17 | 1.1332 | 1.1350 | 1.1324 | **1.1309** | −.0080 | 1.1782 | 1.1100 | 675 |

Est vol 116,941; vol 131,019; open int, 378,500

### Index Futures

Wednesday, August 03, 2016

**Mini DJ Industrial Average** (CBT)-$5 x index

| | Open | High | Low | Settle | Chg | LIFETIME High | Low | Open Int |
|---|---|---|---|---|---|---|---|---|
| Sep 16 | 18248 | 18281 | 18188 | **18269** | +21 | 18495 | 15751 | 138,900 |
| Dec 16 | 18149 | 18186 | 18103 | **18174** | +21 | 18390 | 15916 | 490 |

Est vol 106,323; vol 157,066; open int, 139,480

**S & P 500 Index** (CME)-$250 x index

| | Open | High | Low | Settle | Chg | LIFETIME High | Low | Open Int |
|---|---|---|---|---|---|---|---|---|
| Sep 16 | 2152.20 | 2158.00 | 2145.30 | **2157.00** | +4.30 | 2171.50 | 1819.80 | 93,992 |
| Dec 16 | 2140.00 | 2149.30 | 2140.00 | **2149.40** | +4.40 | 2163.10 | 1812.40 | 1,189 |

Est vol 1,781; vol 3,915; open int, 95,301

**Mini S & P 500** (CME)-$50 x index

| | Open | High | Low | Settle | Chg | LIFETIME High | Low | Open Int |
|---|---|---|---|---|---|---|---|---|
| Sep 16 | 2152.25 | 2158.25 | 2145.25 | **2157.00** | +4.25 | 2171.75 | 1807.00 | 2,902,982 |
| Dec 16 | 2144.50 | 2150.50 | 2137.75 | **2149.50** | +4.50 | 2164.25 | 1823.75 | 39,058 |
| Mar 17 | 2134.75 | 2143.00 | 2131.50 | **2142.50** | +4.25 | 2156.50 | 1802.00 | 869 |

Est vol 1,362,407; vol 1,964,515; open int, 2,943,229

**Mini Nasdaq 100** (CME)-$20 x index

| | Open | High | Low | Settle | Chg | LIFETIME High | Low | Open Int |
|---|---|---|---|---|---|---|---|---|
| Sep 16 | 4713.3 | 4729.3 | 4698.0 | **4728.3** | +14.0 | 4736.5 | 3983.0 | 283,965 |
| Dec 16 | 4698.8 | 4720.5 | 4691.3 | **4720.3** | +14.0 | 4727.8 | 3971.5 | 490 |

Est vol 168,412; vol 260,958; open int, 284,511

**Mini Russell 2000** (ICE-US)-$100 x index

| | Open | High | Low | Settle | Chg | LIFETIME High | Low | Open Int |
|---|---|---|---|---|---|---|---|---|
| Sep 16 | 1199.50 | 1211.40 | 1195.90 | **1211.00** | +11.10 | 1224.80 | 979.80 | 326,874 |
| Dec 16 | 1198.00 | 1205.00 | 1198.00 | **1206.50** | +11.10 | 1218.70 | 1006.00 | 1,013 |

Est vol 67,048; vol 84,267; open int, 328,302

**Nikkei Stock Average** (CME)-$5 x index

| | Open | High | Low | Settle | Chg | LIFETIME High | Low | Open Int |
|---|---|---|---|---|---|---|---|---|
| Sep 16 | 16155 | 16285 | 15980 | **16095** | −30 | 17795 | 14990 | 35,866 |
| Dec 16 | 16115 | 16215 | 15950 | **16060** | −20 | 16495 | 15060 | 151 |

Est vol 13,124; vol 14,927; open int, 36,017

**CBOE VOLATILITY INDEX (VX)**

| Description | Open | High | Low | Close | Settle | Chg | Contract Volume Total | Open Int |
|---|---|---|---|---|---|---|---|---|
| Aug 16 | 14.25 | 14.71 | 13.80 | 13.83 | 13.825 | −0.40 | 82857 | 210686 |
| Sep 16 | 16.60 | 17.00 | 16.25 | 16.25 | 16.275 | −0.35 | 72264 | 160339 |
| Oct 16 | 18.25 | 18.60 | 17.99 | 18.02 | 18.000 | −0.28 | 20879 | 54491 |
| Nov 16 | 18.57 | 18.85 | 18.35 | 18.35 | 18.375 | −0.20 | 10728 | 34135 |
| Dec 16 | 18.65 | 18.91 | 18.45 | 18.50 | 18.475 | −0.20 | 4716 | 29271 |
| Jan 17 | 19.60 | 19.85 | 19.50 | 19.53 | 19.525 | −0.10 | 2438 | 18575 |
| Feb 17 | 19.85 | 20.05 | 19.74 | 19.80 | 19.775 | −0.10 | 943 | 6375 |
| Mar 17 | 20.00 | 20.15 | 19.90 | 19.96 | 19.950 | −0.02 | 223 | 1835 |

**Source:** *The Wall Street Journal Online*, August 4, 2016. www.wsj.com

second through fourth columns, labeled *Open, High,* and *Low,* are the opening price, high price, and low price at which trades occurred during the day (e.g., 171-310 = 171 31/32 percent of $100,000 = $171,968.75 at the open of trading on August 3, 2016). The fifth column, labeled *Settle,* is a representative price at which a trade occurs at the end of the day.[7] If trading in a futures contract is active, the settle price is the price on the last trade of the day. If, however, the contract does not trade actively, the settlement price is determined by a committee of the exchange immediately after the market's close. The settlement price is the price used to determine the value of a trader's position at the end of each trading day. The sixth column, labeled *Chg,* is the change in the futures price quote from the previous day's settlement price. Columns 7 and 8, labeled *LIFETIME High* and *Low,* are the highest and lowest prices at which a trade has occurred over the life of the futures contract. Finally, the last column, labeled *Open Int,* is the **open interest,** or total number of futures contracts outstanding at the beginning of the day. The bottom line of the futures quote lists the estimated trading volume for the day (e.g., 395,934 contracts), the volume of trading in the contract the previous day (e.g., 570,038), and the number of contracts outstanding for that type (T-bonds), regardless of expiration month (e.g., 563,228).

**open interest**

*The total number of futures (or option) contracts outstanding at the beginning of the day.*

Table 10–4 also reports a futures quote on the CBOE Volatility Index (VIX) introduced by the CBOE in 1993. The VIX is a measure of market expectations of near-term volatility taken from S&P 500 stock index option prices. VIX futures contracts indicate investors' consensus assessment of future expected stock market volatility. VIX values greater than 30 are generally a sign of increased volatility resulting from investor fear or uncertainty, while values below 20 generally indicate less volatile, even complacent, times in the markets. VIX is considered by many to be a primary barometer of investor sentiment and market volatility.

A holder of a futures contract has two choices for liquidating his or her position: liquidate the position before the futures contract expires, or hold the futures contract to expiration. To liquidate before the expiration date, the futures holder simply calls his or her broker and requests an offsetting trade to his or her original position, an opposite position. For example, if the original transaction was a buy or long position, the trader can sell or short the same futures contract. Thus, any losses on the buy position will be exactly offset by gains on the sell position over the remaining life (time) to expiration of the contract. Generally, a vast majority (99 percent) of all futures positions are liquidated before maturity. If the futures holder keeps the futures contract to expiration, the parties will either (as specified in the futures contract) conduct a cash settlement where the traders exchange cash based on the final price of the underlying asset relative to the futures price, or the futures holder will take delivery of the underlying asset (e.g., a T-bond) from the futures seller. Multiple Treasury bonds (based on maturity of the bond) are eligible for delivery when a Treasury futures contract matures. The CBOT lists the conversion factors for all eligible securities underlying the various Treasury futures contracts at its website (for example, www.cmegroup.com/trading/interest-rates/treasury-conversion-factors.html shows the securities are eligible for delivery for various Treasury futures contracts).

Traders in futures (as well as option) markets can be either speculators, hedgers, or arbitrageurs. Speculators in futures contracts buy to profit from a price increase or sell to profit from a price decrease. Speculators buy futures contracts with the hope of later being able to sell them at a higher price. Conversely, speculators sell futures contracts with the hope of being able to buy back identical and offsetting futures contracts at a lower price. Thus, speculators put their money at risk in the hope of profiting from an anticipated price change. Hedgers take a position in a futures contract as protection against an increase or decrease in the price of a security such as a bond or stock in the future. Hedgers buy a futures contract to lock in a price now to protect against future rising securities prices. Hedgers sell a futures contract to lock in a price now to protect against a future decline in securities prices. As noted at the beginning of this chapter, arbitrageurs seek to take advantage of pricing inefficiencies for the same asset by taking a long position in one market (i.e., the spot market) and simultaneously taking a short position in another market (i.e., the futures market) to make a risk-free profit when there is a mismatch between the two prices. The arbitrageur is neither

---

7. One model that explains how futures prices are determined is the cost of carry model. This model asserts that the futures price equals the spot price on the underlying asset plus the cost of carrying the asset over the life of the futures contract. Carrying costs include any financing costs of purchasing the underlying asset (e.g., interest costs) plus any storage, insurance, and transportation costs. For financial futures the costs of storage, insurance, and transportation are negligible.

speculating on market movements nor hedging market movements. Rather, he or she is betting on the mispricing of a security that occurs in related markets.

**Profit and Loss on a Futures Transaction.**   In Table 10–4, a December 2016 Treasury bond futures contract traded on the CBOT could be bought (long) or sold (short) on August 3, 2016, for 170-230 (or 170.71875) percent of the face value of the T-bond. The minimum contract size on one of these futures is $100,000, so a position in one contract can be taken at a price of $170,718.75.

The subsequent profit or loss from a position in December 2016 T-bonds taken on August 3, 2016, is graphically described in Figure 10–4. A long position in the futures market produces a profit when the value of the underlying T-bond increases (i.e., interest rates fall between August 3, 2016, and the December expiration).[8] A short position in the futures will produce a profit when the value of the underlying T-bond decreases (i.e., interest rates rise). For example, if the T-bond futures price falls to 169-280 percent (or 169 28/32 percent = 169.875%) of the face value between August 3, 2016, and the December expiration, the long position incurs a loss of $843.75 [(169.875% − 170.71875%) × $100,000], while the short position incurs a gain of $843.75.[9]

**Margin Requirements on Futures Contracts.**   Brokerage firms require their customers to post only a portion of the value of the futures (and option) contracts, called an **initial margin,** any time they request a trade. The amount of the margin varies according to the type of contract traded and the quantity of futures contracts traded (e.g., 5 percent of the value of the underlying asset). Minimum margin levels are set by each exchange. Margin requirements for futures options traded on the CME and CBOT can be found at www.cmegroup.com/clearing/margins/. If losses on the customer's futures position occur (when their account is marked to market at the end of the trading day) and the level of the funds in the margin account drops below a stated level (called the **maintenance margin**), the customer receives a margin call. A margin call requires the customer to deposit additional funds into his or her margin account, bringing the balance back up to the initial level. The maintenance margin is generally about 75

**initial margin**

*A deposit required on futures trades to ensure that the terms of any futures contract will be met.*

**maintenance margin**

*The margin a futures trader must maintain once a futures position is taken. If losses on the customer's futures position occur and the level of the funds in the margin account drop below the maintenance margin, the customer is required to deposit additional funds into his or her margin account, bringing the balance back up to the initial margin.*

**Figure 10–4**    **Profit or Loss on a Futures Position in Treasury Bonds Taken on August 3, 2016**

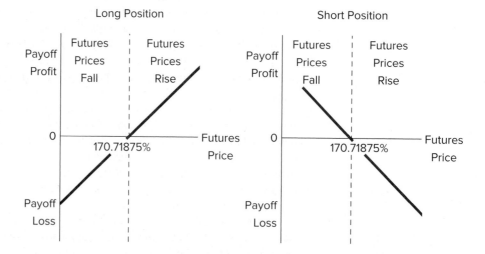

8. Notice that if rates move in an opposite direction from that expected, losses are incurred on the futures position. That is, if rates rise and futures prices drop, the long investor loses on his or her futures position. Similarly, if rates fall and futures prices rise, the short investor loses on his or her futures position.

9. It should be noted that a risk in trading of derivatives is that favorable price moves may occur after the derivative contract matures. For example, if the T-bond futures price rises to 171-170 on January 2, 2017, the December T-bond contract would have matured and yet the long futures trader would have incurred no profit.

## DO YOU UNDERSTAND:

1. *What the differences are among a spot contract, a forward contract, and a futures contract?*

2. *What the major futures exchanges in the United States are?*

3. *What position traders, day traders, and scalpers are?*

4. *When a futures trader would buy (long) a futures contract? Sell (short) a futures contract?*

percent of the initial margin. If the margin is not maintained, the broker closes out (sells) the customer's futures position. Any amount of cash received above the initial margin may be withdrawn by the customer from his or her account. Brokerage firms are responsible for ensuring that their customers maintain the required margin requirements.

Because futures traders must post and maintain only a small portion of the value of their futures position in their accounts (e.g., 2 percent of the value of the contracts), these investments are highly leveraged (called **leveraged investments**). That is, the vast majority of the investment is "borrowed" from the investor's broker. This high degree of leverage, combined with the marking to market feature of these contracts, can require the payment of large, unexpected cash flows from the investor to the broker if the price of the futures contracts moves against the investor.

**leveraged investment**

*An investment in which traders post and maintain only a small portion of the value of their futures position in their accounts. The vast majority of the investment is borrowed from the investor's broker.*

---

**EXAMPLE 10–1** The Impact of Marking to Market and Margin Requirements on Futures Investments

Suppose an investor has a $1 million long position in T-bond futures. The investor's broker requires a maintenance margin of 4 percent, or $40,000 ($1m × 0.04), which is the amount currently in the investor's account. Suppose also that the value of the futures contracts drops by $50,000 to $950,000. The investor will now be required to hold $38,000 ($950,000 × 0.04) in his account (or he has a $2,000 surplus). Further, because futures contracts are marked to market, the investor's broker will make a margin call to the investor requiring him to immediately send a check for $50,000 – $2,000, or $48,000, leaving him with an account balance of $38,000 at his broker for the $950,000 T-bond futures position.

If the next day the futures contract drops in value by another $40,000 to $910,000, the investor is now required to hold $36,400 ($910,000 × 0.40) in his account. He has $1,600 surplus ($38,000 – $36,400). But, because futures contracts are marked to market, the investor's broker will make a margin call to the investor requiring him to immediately send a check for $40,000 – $1,600, or $38,400, leaving him with an account balance of $36,400 at his broker for the $910,000 T-bond futures position.

If on day 3 the futures contract increases in value by $65,000, to $975,000, the investor is now required to hold $39,000 ($975,000 × 0.04) in his account. He has a $2,600 deficit. Marking the account to market, to maintain the appropriate margin the investor may have his broker send him a check for $65,000 – $2,600, or $62,400, leaving him with an account balance of $39,000 at his broker for the $975,000 T-bond futures position.

As this example illustrates, the marking to market feature of futures contracts can lead to unexpected cash outflows as well as cash inflows for a futures investor.

---

Chapters 22 and 23 provide more details on the use of futures contracts to manage interest rate and credit risk.

## OPTIONS

**option**

*A contract that gives the holder the right, but not the obligation, to buy or sell the underlying asset at a specified price within a specified period of time.*

An **option** is a contract that gives the holder the right, but not the obligation, to buy or sell an underlying asset at a prespecified price for a specified time period. Options are classified as either call options or put options. We discuss both of these below, highlighting their payoffs in terms of price movements on the underlying asset.

### Call Options

A **call option** gives the purchaser (or buyer) the right to buy an underlying security (e.g., a stock) at a prespecified price called the *exercise* or *strike* price (*X*). In return, the buyer of the call option must pay the writer (or seller) an up-front fee known as a *call premium (C)*.

**call option**

*An option that gives a purchaser the right, but not the obligation, to buy the underlying security from the writer of the option at a prespecified exercise price on or before a prespecified date.*

This premium is an immediate negative cash flow for the buyer of the call option. However, he or she potentially stands to make a profit should the underlying stock's price be greater than the exercise price (by an amount exceeding the premium). If the price of the underlying stock is greater than $X$ (the option is referred to as "in the money"), the buyer can exercise the option, buying the stock at $X$ and selling it immediately in the stock market at the current market price, greater than $X$. If the price of the underlying stock is less than $X$ (the option is referred to as "out of the money"), the buyer of the call would not exercise the option (i.e., buy the stock at $X$ when its market value is less than $X$). If this is the case when the option matures, the option expires unexercised. The same is true when the underlying stock price is exactly equal to $X$ when the option expires (the option is referred to as "at the money"). The call buyer incurs a cost $C$ (the call premium) for the option, and no other cash flows result.

**Buying a Call Option.** The profit or loss from buying a call option is illustrated in Figure 10–5. As Figure 10–5 shows, if, as the option expires, the price of the stock underlying the option is $S$, the buyer makes a profit of $\pi$, which is the difference between the stock's price ($S$, e.g., \$9.80) and the exercise price of the option ($X$, e.g., \$7.50) minus the call premium paid to the writer of the option ($C$, e.g., \$1.30). If the underlying stock's price is $A$ (i.e., \$8.80) as the option expires, the buyer of the call has just broken even because the net proceeds from exercising the call ($A - X = \$8.80 - \$7.50 = \$1.30$) just equal the premium payment for the call ($C$, or \$1.30 in this case).

Notice two important things about call options in Figure 10–5:

1. As the underlying stock's price rises, the call option buyer has a large profit potential. The higher the underlying stock's price at expiration, the larger the profit on the exercise of the option, that is, if $S = \$9.80$, then $\pi = \$9.80 - \$7.50 - \$1.30 = \$1.00$.
2. As the underlying stock's price falls, the call option buyer has a higher potential for losses, but they are limited to the call option premium. If the underlying stock's price at expiration is below the exercise price, $X$, the call buyer is not obligated to exercise the option. Thus, the buyer's losses are limited to the amount of the up-front premium payment ($C$, or \$1.30 in this case) made to purchase the call option.

Thus, buying a call option is an appropriate position when the underlying asset's price is expected to rise.[10]

**Figure 10–5**    **Payoff Function for the Buyer of a Call Option on a Stock**

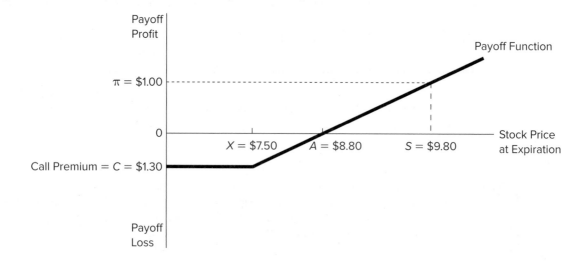

10. Traders using options get extra leverage on their investments. For example, suppose that a stock price is \$32 and an investor who feels that this price will rise buys call options with an exercise price of \$35 for \$0.50 per option. If the price does not go above \$35 during the life of the option, the investor will lose \$0.50 per option (or 100 percent of the investment). However, if the price rises to \$40, the investor will realize a profit of \$4.50 per option (or 900 percent of the original investment).

**Writing a Call Option.** The writer of a call option sells the option to the buyer (or is said to take a short position in the option). In writing a call option on a stock, the writer or seller receives an up-front fee or premium ($C$, e.g., $1.30) and must stand ready to sell the underlying stock to the purchaser of the option at the exercise price, $X$ (e.g., $7.50). Note the payoff from writing a call option on a stock in Figure 10–6.

Notice two important things about this payoff function:

1. As the underlying stock's price falls, the potential for a call option writer to receive a positive payoff (or profit) increases. If the underlying stock's price is less than the exercise price ($X$) at expiration, the call option buyer will not exercise the option. The call option writer's profit has a maximum value equal to the call premium ($C$, or $1.30 in this case) charged up front to the buyer of the option.
2. As the underlying stock's price rises, the call option writer has unlimited loss potential. If the underlying stock's price ($S$, e.g., $9.80) is greater than the exercise price ($X$, e.g., $7.50) at expiration, the call option buyer will exercise the option, forcing the option writer to buy the underlying stock at its high market price and then sell it to the call option buyer at the lower exercise price. That is, if $S = \$9.80$, then $\pi = \$1.30 - \$9.80 + \$7.50 = -\$1.00$. Since stock prices are theoretically unbounded in the upward direction, these losses could be very large.

Thus, writing a call option is an appropriate position when the underlying asset's price is expected to fall. Caution is warranted, however, because profits are limited but losses are potentially unlimited. A rise in the underlying stock's price to $S$ results in the writer of the option losing $\pi$ (in Figure 10–6).

### Put Options

**put option**

*An option that gives a purchaser the right, but not the obligation, to sell the underlying security to the writer of the option at a prespecified price on or before a prespecified date.*

A **put option** gives the option buyer the right to sell an underlying security (e.g., a stock) at a prespecified price to the writer of the put option. In return, the buyer of the put option must pay the writer (or seller) the put premium ($P$). If the underlying stock's price is less than the exercise price ($X$) (the put option is "in the money"), the buyer will buy the underlying stock in the stock market at less than $X$ and immediately sell it at $X$ by exercising the put option. If the price of the underlying stock is greater than $X$ (the put option is "out of the money"), the buyer of the put option would not exercise the option (i.e., selling the stock at $X$ when its market value is more than $X$). If this is the case when the option matures, the option expires unexercised. This is also true if the price of the underlying stock is exactly equal to $X$ when the option expires (the put option is trading "at the money"). The put option buyer incurs a cost $P$ for the option, and no other cash flows result.

**Figure 10–6** Payoff Function for the Writer of a Call Option on a Stock

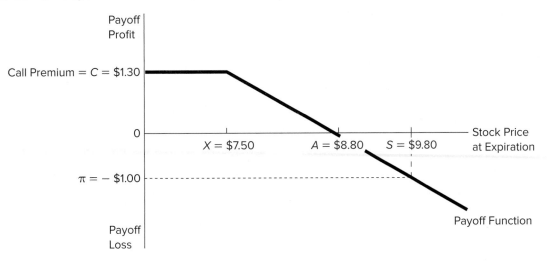

**Buying a Put Option.**   The buyer of a put option on a stock has the right (but not the obligation) to sell the underlying stock to the writer of the option at an agreed upon exercise price ($X$, e.g., \$9.00). In return for this option, the buyer of the put option pays a premium ($P$, e.g., \$0.65) to the option writer. We show the potential payoffs to the buyer of the put option in Figure 10–7. Note the following:

1. The lower the price of the underlying stock at the expiration of the option, the higher the profit to the put option buyer upon exercise. For example, if stock prices fall to $D$ (= \$7.00) in Figure 10–7, the buyer of the put option can purchase the underlying stock in the stock market at $D$ = \$7.00 and put it (sell it) back to the writer of the put option at the higher exercise price $X$ = \$9.00. As a result, after deducting the cost of the put premium, $P$ = \$0.65, the buyer makes a profit of $\pi p$ (= −\$7.00 − \$0.65 +\$9.00 = \$1.35) in Figure 10–7.
2. As the underlying stock's price rises, the probability that the buyer of a put option has a negative payoff increases. If the underlying stock's price is greater than the exercise price ($X$ = \$9.00) at expiration, the put option buyer will not exercise the option. As a result, his or her maximum loss is limited to the size of the up-front put premium ($P$ = \$0.65 in this case) paid to the put option writer.

Thus, buying a put option is an appropriate position when the price on the underlying asset is expected to fall.

**Writing a Put Option.**   The writer or seller of a put option receives a fee or premium ($P$, e.g., \$0.65) in return for standing ready to buy the underlying stock at the exercise price ($X$, e.g., \$9.00) should the buyer of the put choose to exercise the option. See the payoff function for writing a put option on a stock in Figure 10–8. Note the following:

1. When the underlying stock's price rises, the put option writer has an enhanced probability of making a profit. If the underlying stock's price is greater than the exercise price ($X$ = \$9.00) at expiration, the put option buyer will not exercise the option. The put option writer's maximum profit, however, is constrained to equal the put premium ($P$, or \$0.65 in this case).
2. When the underlying stock's price falls, the writer of the put option is exposed to potentially large losses. If the price of the underlying stock is below the exercise price (e.g., $D$ = \$7.00 in Figure 10–8), the put option buyer will exercise the option, forcing the option writer to buy the underlying stock from the option buyer at the exercise price ($X$ = \$9.00) when it is worth only $D$ = \$7.00 in the stock market (i.e., if $D$ = \$7.00, then $\pi p$ = \$0.65 − \$9.00 + \$7.00 = −\$1.35). The lower the stock's price at expiration relative to the exercise price, the greater the losses to the option writer.

**Figure 10–7**   **Payoff Function for the Buyer of a Put Option on a Stock**

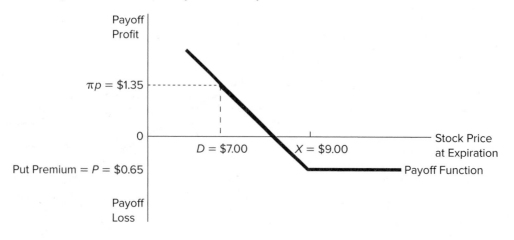

**Figure 10–8**  **Payoff Function for the Writer of a Put Option on a Stock**

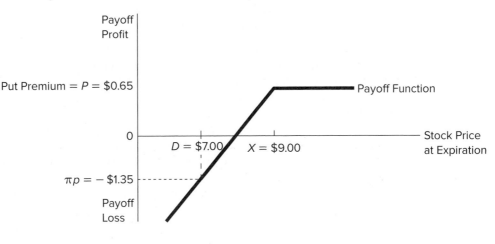

Thus, writing a put option is an appropriate position if the price on the underlying asset is expected to rise. However, profits are limited and losses are potentially large.

Notice from the above discussion that an option holder has three ways to liquidate his or her position. First, if conditions are never profitable for an exercise (the option remains "out of the money"), the option holder can let the option expire unexercised. Second, the holder can take the opposite side of the transaction. Thus, an option buyer can sell options on the underlying asset with the same exercise price and the same expiration date. Third, the option holder can exercise the option, enforcing the terms of the option. An **American option** gives the option holder the right to buy or sell the underlying asset at *any time* before and on the expiration date of the option. A **European option** (e.g., options on the S&P 500 Index) gives the option holder the right to buy or sell the underlying option *only* on the expiration date. Most options traded on exchanges in the United States and abroad are American options.

To understand the differences between futures versus options contracts, compare the profit and losses illustrated in Figure 10–4 (for a long position in futures contracts) with those in Figure 10–5 (for buying call option contracts). A long position in futures contracts produces both the potential for unlimited gains (if the underlying security increases in value) and unlimited losses (if the underlying security decreases in value). The larger the price change (up or down) on the underlying security, the larger the profit or loss for the futures investor. Further, the futures investor must eventually close out his/her position (either by liquidating the position before maturity or by holding the futures contract until maturity). Thus, the futures investor must take not only any gains that occur if the underlying security price increases, but any losses that may occur if the price of the underlying security falls. In comparison, the holder of a call option contract gains value if the price of the underlying security increases. However, if the underlying security falls in value, the call option holder is not obligated to take the losses. Because the option holder can let the option expire, the maximum loss the call option holder must take is the call option premium. Thus, like a long position in a futures contract, a call option allows the investor to gain when the value of the underlying security increases. However, unlike a futures contract, an option contract protects the investor against value losses when the price of the underlying security falls. The same is true when comparing a short position in a futures contract with a purchase of a put option.

**American option**

*An option that can be exercised at any time before and on the expiration date.*

**European option**

*An option that can be exercised only on the expiration date.*

### Option Values

The model most commonly used by practitioners and traders to price and value options is the Black–Scholes pricing model. The Black–Scholes model examines five factors that affect the price of an option:

**1.** The spot price of the underlying asset
**2.** The exercise price on the option

**3.** The option's exercise date

**4.** Price volatility of the underlying asset

**5.** The risk-free rate of interest

We show how to calculate an option's time value and, in turn, its overall value for any price of the underlying asset (at any point in time prior to maturity for a European option) using the Black–Scholes option pricing model in the appendix to this chapter (available through Connect or your course instructor). In the body of the text, we discuss these factors and the intuition behind their effect on an option's value.

Notice in the discussion above that we examined the profit and loss from exercising an option *at expiration.* The profit and loss on an option was a function of the spot price of the option's underlying asset and the exercise price on the option. The difference between the underlying asset's spot price and an option's exercise price is called the option's **intrinsic value.** For a call option, the intrinsic value is:

**intrinsic value of an option**

*The difference between an option's exercise price and the underlying asset's price.*

| | |
|---|---|
| Stock price − Exercise price | if Stock price > Exercise price (option is in the money) |
| Zero | if Stock price ≤ Exercise price (option is out of or at the money) |

For a put option, the intrinsic value is:

| | |
|---|---|
| Exercise price − Stock price | if Stock price < Exercise price (option is in the money) |
| Zero | if Stock price ≥ Exercise price (option is out of or at the money) |

At expiration, an option's value is equal to its intrinsic value.

We limit the analysis of the profit and loss on an option to exercise at expiration because research has found that it is generally not optimal to exercise a European option (or American options on stocks that do not pay dividends) before its expiration date because of its potential "time value" (see below).[11] Specifically, exercising a call option prior to expiration is only appropriate if the value of the option before expiration is continuously less than its intrinsic value, which is rarely the case.

Figure 10–9 illustrates the time value effect for a call option. For example, suppose you have a call option on a stock with an exercise price of $50.00 and an expiration in three months. The underlying stock's price is currently $60.00. The intrinsic value of the option is $10 ($60.00 − $50.00). The option is currently selling on the Chicago Board of Trade for $12.50. Thus, the value of the call option is greater than its intrinsic value by $2.50. The difference between an option's price (or premium)

**Figure 10–9**   **The Intrinsic Value versus the Before-Exercise Value of a Call Option**

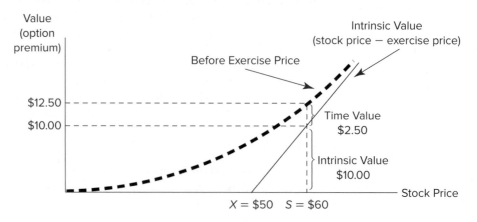

---

11.  See J. Cox and M. Rubinstein, *Options Markets* (Englewood Cliffs, NJ: Prentice-Hall, 1985).

**time value of an option**

*The difference between an option's price (or premium) and its intrinsic value.*

and its intrinsic value is called its **time value.** If you exercise the option today (prior to expiration), you receive the intrinsic value but give up the time value (which in this example is $2.50).

The time value of an option is the value associated with the probability that the intrinsic value *could* increase (if the underlying asset's price moves favorably) between the option's purchase and the option's expiration date. The time value of an option is a function of the price volatility of the underlying asset and the time until the option matures (its expiration date). As price volatility increases, the chance that the stock will go up or down in value increases. The owner of the call option benefits from price increases but has limited downside risk if the stock price decreases, since the loss of value of an option can never exceed the call premium. Thus, over any given period of time, the greater the price volatility of the underlying asset, the greater the chance the stock price will increase and the greater the time value of the option. Further, the greater the time to maturity, the greater (longer in time) the opportunity for the underlying stock price to increase; thus, the time value of the option increases.

It is this "time value" that allows an out-of-the-money option to have value and trade on the option markets. As noted above, a call option is out of the money if the exercise price is greater than the underlying stock's price, or the intrinsic value of the option is zero. This option still has "time" value and will trade at a positive price or premium if, however, investors believe that prior to the option's expiration, the stock price might increase (to a value greater than the exercise price). As an option moves toward expiration, its time value goes to zero. At any point in time, the time value of an option can be calculated by subtracting its intrinsic value (e.g., $10.00) from its current market price or premium (e.g., $12.50).

The risk-free rate of interest affects the value of an option in a less than clear-cut way. All else constant, as the risk-free rate increases, the growth rate of the stock price increases. Recall from Chapter 2 that as the risk-free rate of interest increases, the required rate (and ultimately realized rate) of return increases on all investments. The result is greater stock price growth. However, the present value of any future cash flows received by the option holder decreases. For a call option, the first effect tends to increase the price of the option, while the second effect tends to decrease the price. It can be shown that the first effect always dominates the second effect. That is, the price of a call option always increases as the risk-free rate increases. Conversely, the two effects both tend to decrease the value of a put option. Thus, the price of a put option decreases as the risk-free rate increases.

### Option Markets

www.cboe.com

The Chicago Board of Options Exchange (CBOE) opened in 1973. It was the first exchange devoted solely to the trading of stock options. In 1982, financial futures options contracts (options on financial futures contracts, e.g., Treasury bond futures contracts) started trading. Options markets have grown rapidly since the mid-1980s.

Figure 10–10 shows the notional value of option contracts held by commercial banks from 1992 through 2016. Table 10–5 lists some of the most active option contracts. The largest option exchange is the Chicago Board Options Exchange (CBOE).[12] The first option exchanges abroad were the European Options Exchange and the London International Financial Futures Exchange (now the Euronext.liffe). Options exchanges have more recently been opened in Paris, Sweden, Switzerland, Germany, and Japan. As with futures trading, many options also trade over the counter. Thus, the volume of trading in options is more than what is reported in the option quotes (see below) for the organized exchanges.

www.nyseeuronext.com

---

12. Other major exchanges are the New York Stock Exchange, the American Stock Exchange, the Pacific Stock Exchange (part of NYSE Euronext), the Financial Instrument Exchange of the ICE Futures U.S., the Philadelphia Exchange (owned by NASDAQ), and the CME Group (which includes the CBOT and CME).

**Figure 10–10** Options Contracts Held by Commercial Banks, 1992–2016

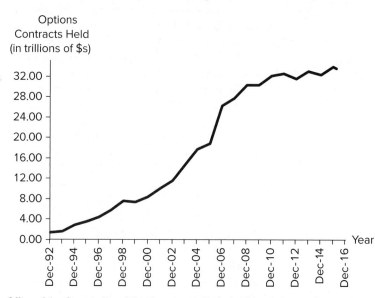

**Sources:** Office of the Comptroller of the Currency website, various dates. www.occ.treas.gov

**TABLE 10–5** Characteristics of Actively Traded Options

| Type of Option | Exchange* | Contract Traded |
| --- | --- | --- |
| Stock options | CBOE | Stock options |
| | AM | Stock options |
| | NASDAQ OMX PHLX | Stock options |
| | NASDAQ OMX BX | Stock options |
| | NY | Stock options |
| Stock index options | CBOE | Dow Jones Industrial Average |
| | CBOE | Nasdaq 100 |
| | CBOE | Russell 2000 |
| | CBOE | S&P 100 Index |
| | CBOE | S&P 500 Index |
| | AM | S&P Midcap |
| | NASDAQ OMX PHLX | Gold/Silver |
| Financial futures options: | | |
| Interest rate | CBOT | T-bonds |
| | CBOT | T-notes |
| | CBOT | T-notes—5 year |
| | CME | Eurodollar |
| Currency | CME | Japanese yen |
| | CME | Canadian dollar |
| | CME | British pound |
| | CME | Swiss franc |
| | CME | Euro FX |
| Stock index | CBOT | DJIA |
| | CME | S&P 500 Index |

*CBOE = Chicago Board Options Exchange; AM = American Exchange; NASDAQ OMX PHLX = Philadelphia Stock Exchange; NASDAQ OMX BX = Boston Stock Exchange; NY = NYSE Archipelago Exchange; CBOT = Chicago Board of Trade; CME = Chicago Mercantile Exchange.

The trading process for options is similar to that for futures contracts. An investor desiring to take an option position calls his or her broker and places an order to buy or sell a stated number of call or put option contracts with a stated expiration date and exercise price. The broker directs this order to its representative on the appropriate exchange for execution. Most trading on the largest exchanges such as the CBOE takes place in trading pits, where traders for each delivery date on an option contract informally group together. Like futures contracts, options trading generally occurs using an open-outcry auction or electronic trading method.

Only option exchange members are allowed to transact on the floor of option exchanges. Trades from the public are placed with a floor broker, professional trader, or a market maker for the particular option being traded. Option trades may be placed as market orders (instructing the floor broker to transact at the best price available) or limit orders (instructing the floor broker to transact at a specified price). Once an option price is agreed upon in a trading pit, the two parties electronically send the details of the trade to the option clearinghouse (the Options Clearing Corporation), which breaks up trades into buy and sell transactions and takes the opposite side of each transaction—becoming the seller for every option contract buyer and the buyer for every option contract seller. The broker on the floor of the options exchange confirms the transaction with the investor's broker.

In the early 2000s, the CBOE increased the speed at which orders can be placed, executed, and filled by equipping floor brokers with handheld touch-screen computers that allow them to route and execute orders more easily and efficiently. For example, when a broker selects an order from the workstation, an electronic trading card appears on the handheld computer screen. The electronic card allows the broker to work the order and enter necessary trade information (e.g., volume, price, opposing market makers). When the card (details of the transaction) is complete, the broker can execute the trade with the touch of a finger. Once the broker has submitted the trade, the system simultaneously sends a "fill" report to the customer and instantaneously transmits these data to traders worldwide.

Table 10–6 shows portions of an option quote table for August 3, 2016. Three types of options trade: stock options, stock index options, and options on futures contracts. More "exotic" or special types of options (e.g., credit options—see Chapter 23) tend to trade over the counter rather than on organized exchanges. We discuss the three major types of exchange-traded options next.

**LG 10-5**

**Stock Options.**   The underlying asset on a stock option contract is the stock of a publicly traded company. One option generally involves 100 shares of the underlying company's stock. As mentioned earlier, options on U.S. option exchanges are American options. Look at the options quotes for ExxonMobil (XOM) in Table 10–6. The first line lists the name of the company and its closing stock price for the day (e.g., $87.49). The first column is the expiration month on the option (e.g., 16 Aug = August 2016). The second column lists the strike or exercise price on the different options on ExxonMobil stock (e.g., $87 and $87.50). Note that the same stock can have many different call and put options differentiated by expiration and strike price. Further, the quote gives an indication of whether the call and put options are trading in, out of, or at the money. For example, as shown in Figure 10–11, the ExxonMobil call option with an exercise price of $85.00 is trading in the money ($85.00 is less than the current stock price, $87.49), while the call options with an exercise price of $90.00 are trading out of the money ($90.00 is greater than the current stock price, $87.49). The exact opposite holds for the put options. That is, the put option with an exercise price of $85.00 is trading out of the money ($85.00 is less than the current stock price, $87.49), while the put options with an exercise price of $90.00 are trading in the money ($90.00 is greater than the current stock price, $87.49). Columns 3 through 5 give data on (1) the call price or premium (e.g., Last Sale) of the option (e.g., $3.20, or one September 2016 call option with an exercise price of $85.00 would cost $3.20 × 100 = $320),[13] (2) volume (e.g., 22 call options traded on August 3, 2016), and (3) open interest (e.g., 536 September 2016 call options with an $85.00 strike price were outstanding at the open of trading on August 3, 2016). Columns 6 through 8 list the same type of data for put options traded.

---

13. Times 100 since each option contract is for 100 shares.

## TABLE 10–6   Option Quote, August 3, 2016

### STOCK OPTIONS
Prices at close August 3, 2016

| ExxonMobil | | | | | | Underlying stock price: $87.49 | |
| --- | --- | --- | --- | --- | --- | --- | --- |
| | | Call | | | Put | | |
| Expiration | Strike Price | Last Sale | Volume | Open Interest | Last Sale | Volume | Open Interest |
| 16 Aug | 87.00 | 1.13 | 56 | 2042 | 1.26 | 22 | 861 |
| 16 Aug | 87.50 | 0.80 | 20 | 4265 | 1.63 | 1 | 16825 |
| **16 Sep** | **85.00** | **3.20** | **22** | **536** | **1.33** | **20** | **2103** |
| 16 Sep | 87.50 | 1.67 | 20 | 4700 | 2.32 | 197 | 1561 |
| 16 Oct | 87.50 | 2.50 | 1 | 7740 | 3.10 | 7 | 3853 |
| 16 Oct | 90.00 | 1.37 | 13 | 16859 | 4.95 | 5 | 4398 |
| 17 Jan | 87.50 | 5.50 | 10 | 520 | 8.92 | 0 | 140 |
| 17 Jan | 90.00 | 4.28 | 5 | 649 | 6.50 | 0 | 507 |
| 18 Jan | 87.50 | 7.42 | 8 | 1910 | 11.66 | 0 | 1820 |
| 18 Jan | 90.00 | 6.17 | 2 | 5239 | 12.45 | 0 | 2369 |

### STOCK INDEX OPTIONS
Prices at close August 3, 2016

**DJ Industrials (DJX)** — Closing price: 183.57

| | | Call | | | Put | | |
| --- | --- | --- | --- | --- | --- | --- | --- |
| Expiration | Strike Price | Last Sale | Volume | Open Interest | Last Sale | Volume | Open Interest |
| 16 Sep | 180.00 | 4.55 | 0 | 5807 | 1.90 | 7 | 5440 |
| 16 Sep | 181.00 | 3.88 | 0 | 22 | 2.58 | 0 | 72 |
| **16 Sep** | **182.00** | **3.40** | **0** | **16** | **3.00** | **30** | **12** |
| 16 Sep | 183.00 | 2.80 | 280 | 141 | 2.75 | 280 | 485 |
| 16 Sep | 184.00 | 1.95 | 0 | 10 | 3.87 | 0 | 162 |
| 16 Sep | 185.00 | 1.52 | 10 | 1819 | 3.86 | 5 | 2084 |
| 16 Sep | 186.00 | 1.05 | 0 | 168 | 4.60 | 0 | 45 |
| 16 Dec | 175.00 | 11.53 | 0 | 5505 | 3.97 | 20 | 1768 |
| 16 Dec | 180.00 | 7.30 | 0 | 6808 | 5.35 | 20 | 7666 |
| 16 Dec | 185.00 | 4.22 | 0 | 1234 | 7.35 | 2 | 345 |
| 16 Dec | 190.00 | 1.88 | 0 | 3487 | 9.70 | 0 | 427 |
| 16 Dec | 195.00 | 0.74 | 99 | 1630 | 34.61 | 0 | 46 |
| 17 Dec | 170.00 | 20.37 | 0 | 3525 | 10.64 | 3 | 2072 |
| 17 Dec | 180.00 | 14.65 | 0 | 2104 | 14.51 | 0 | 1977 |

**S&P 500 (SPX)** — Closing price: 2166.70

| | | Call | | | Put | | |
| --- | --- | --- | --- | --- | --- | --- | --- |
| Expiration | Strike Price | Last Sale | Volume | Open Interest | Last Sale | Volume | Open Interest |
| 16 Sep | 2090.00 | 73.25 | 0 | 1 | 8.30 | 52 | 1319 |
| 16 Sep | 2100.00 | 69.30 | 2500 | 14 | 9.65 | 262 | 1600 |
| **16 Sep** | **2125.00** | **50.35** | **29** | **100** | **17.85** | **0** | **927** |
| 16 Sep | 2145.00 | 33.40 | 20 | 71 | 21.80 | 10 | 69 |
| 16 Sep | 2160.00 | 26.20 | 22 | 5773 | 22.90 | 74 | 145 |
| 16 Sep | 2175.00 | 17.20 | 1000 | 14968 | 40.98 | 0 | 1163 |
| 16 Sep | 2195.00 | 8.35 | 35 | 531 | 46.30 | 0 | 351 |
| 16 Sep | 2210.00 | 4.42 | 787 | 1384 | 64.55 | 0 | 403 |
| 16 Oct | 2125.00 | 70.10 | 10 | 4801 | 38.70 | 1463 | 9760 |
| 16 Oct | 2150.00 | 53.80 | 515 | 21719 | 45.85 | 936 | 33764 |
| 16 Oct | 2160.00 | 46.30 | 154 | 1316 | 48.00 | 43 | 2513 |
| 16 Oct | 2200.00 | 25.00 | 1004 | 16527 | 72.15 | 0 | 52 |
| 16 Oct | 2250.00 | 7.90 | 20 | 29030 | 98.20 | 4 | 24 |
| 16 Dec | 2025.00 | 166.03 | 36 | 15265 | 39.95 | 250 | 23720 |
| 16 Dec | 2125.00 | 90.10 | 11 | 12468 | 64.45 | 250 | 5689 |
| 16 Dec | 2175.00 | 59.15 | 9 | 21315 | 85.80 | 0 | 7028 |
| 16 Dec | 2200.00 | 45.05 | 1103 | 41739 | 96.60 | 1 | 6948 |

### INTEREST RATE Futures Options
For Wednesday, August 3, 2016
All prices are settlement prices. Open interest is from the previous trading day.

**30-YEAR US TREASURY BOND OPTIONS**

| Strike | Call Sep | Call Oct | Call Dec | Put Sep | Put Oct | Put Dec |
| --- | --- | --- | --- | --- | --- | --- |
| 17000 | 3'06 | 3'04 | 4'28 | 0'60 | 2'22 | 3'46 |
| 17100 | 2'28 | 2'34 | 3'60 | 1'18 | 2'52 | 4'14 |
| 17200 | 1'56 | 2'04 | 3'30 | 1'46 | 3'22 | 4'48 |
| **17300** | **1'25** | **1'43** | **3'03** | **2'15** | **3'61** | **5'21** |
| 17400 | 1'00 | 1'22 | 2'43 | 2'54 | 4'40 | 5'61 |
| 17500 | 0'45 | 1'04 | 2'21 | 3'35 | 5'22 | 6'38 |

EST. VOL 37334   VOLUME 36470   OPEN INT 228545   EST. VOL 30451   VOLUME 26297   OPEN INT 220041

### 10-YEAR US TREASURY NOTE

| Strike | Call Sep | Call Oct | Call Dec | Put Sep | Put Oct | Put Dec |
| --- | --- | --- | --- | --- | --- | --- |
| 13100 | 1'48 | 1'22 | 1'50 | 0'11 | 0'45 | 1'09 |
| 13150 | 1'22 | 1'03 | 1'33 | 0'17 | 0'58 | 1'24 |
| 13200 | 0'63 | 0'51 | 1'18 | 0'26 | 1'10 | 1'41 |
| 13250 | 0'44 | 0'38 | 1'04 | 0'39 | 1'29 | 1'59 |
| 13300 | 0'29 | 0'28 | 0'56 | 0'56 | 1'51 | 2'15 |
| 13350 | 0'18 | 0'20 | 0'46 | 1'13 | 2'11 | 2'37 |
| 13400 | 0'11 | 0'14 | 0'37 | 1'38 | 2'37 | 2'60 |
| 13450 | 0'07 | 0'10 | 0'30 | 2'02 | 3'01 | 3'21 |

EST. VOL 89481   VOLUME 106300   OPEN INT 1063053   EST. VOL 50758   VOLUME 98329   OPEN INT 936900

### 5-YEAR US TREASURY NOTE

| Strike | Call Sep | Call Oct | Call Dec | Put Sep | Put Oct | Put Dec |
| --- | --- | --- | --- | --- | --- | --- |
| 12050 | 1'275 | 1'388 | 1'475 | 0'035 | 0'105 | 0'225 |
| 12075 | 0'125 | 1'220 | 1'355 | 0'045 | 0'130 | 0'265 |
| 12100 | 0'625 | 1'095 | 1'240 | 0'065 | 0'165 | 0'310 |
| 12125 | 0'495 | 0'615 | 1'130 | 0'095 | 0'205 | 0'360 |
| 12150 | 0'375 | 0'505 | 1'030 | 0'135 | 0'255 | 0'420 |
| 12175 | 0'270 | 0'410 | 0'580 | 0'190 | 0'320 | 0'490 |
| 12200 | 0'185 | 0'330 | 0'500 | 0'265 | 0'400 | 0'570 |
| 12225 | 0'120 | 0'255 | 0'425 | 0'360 | 0'485 | 1'015 |
| 12250 | 0'075 | 0'195 | 0'355 | 0'475 | 0'585 | 1'105 |

EST. VOL 5174   VOLUME 16839   OPEN INT 191859   EST. VOL 22298   VOLUME 13207   OPEN INT 668820

### EURODOLLAR

| Strike | Call Sep | Call Dec | Call Mar | Put Sep | Put Dec | Put Mar |
| --- | --- | --- | --- | --- | --- | --- |
| 9850 | 0.6650 | 0.6275 | 0.6505 | 0.5875 | 0.5750 | 0.5900 |
| 9862 | 0.5400 | 0.5050 | 0.4850 | 0.4825 | 0.4800 | 0.4975 |
| 9875 | 0.4150 | 0.3825 | 0.3700 | 0.3875 | 0.3925 | 0.4150 |
| 9887 | 0.2925 | 0.2675 | 0.2675 | 0.3025 | 0.3150 | 0.3375 |
| 9900 | 0.1700 | 0.1620 | 0.1800 | 0.2275 | 0.2450 | 0.2700 |
| 9912 | 0.0675 | 0.0850 | 0.1100 | 0.1650 | 0.1850 | 0.2125 |
| 9925 | 0.0100 | 0.0325 | 0.0600 | 0.1150 | 0.1350 | 0.1625 |

EST. VOL 209732   VOLUME 147078   OPEN INT 10016110   EST. VOL 313719   VOLUME 317189   OPEN INT 11733652

### INDEX Futures Options
For Wednesday, August 3, 2016
All prices are settlement prices. Open interest is from the previous trading day.

**Mini-sized $5 x DJIA**

| Strike | Call Sep | Call Dec | Call Mar | Put Sep | Put Dec | Put Mar |
| --- | --- | --- | --- | --- | --- | --- |
| 18200 | 324 | 591 | 775 | 255 | 617 | 879 |
| 18250 | 292 | 561 | 746 | 276 | 637 | 899 |
| 18300 | 260 | 531 | 716 | 291 | 657 | 920 |
| 18350 | 231 | 502 | 688 | 312 | 677 | 941 |
| 18400 | 203 | 473 | 660 | 334 | 699 | 962 |
| 18450 | 178 | 446 | 632 | 358 | 721 | 985 |
| 18500 | 154 | 419 | 605 | 384 | 744 | 1007 |

EST. VOL 7   VOLUME 5   OPEN INT 1741   EST. VOL 24   VOLUME 129   OPEN INT 8430

### CME S&P 500

| Strike | Call Sep | Call Dec | Call Mar | Put Sep | Put Dec | Put Mar |
| --- | --- | --- | --- | --- | --- | --- |
| 2130 | 51.70 | 86.20 | 110.20 | 24.70 | 66.90 | 97.70 |
| 2135 | 48.10 | 82.90 | 107.10 | 26.10 | 68.50 | 99.50 |
| 2140 | 44.60 | 79.60 | 103.90 | 27.60 | 70.20 | 101.30 |
| 2145 | 41.20 | 76.40 | 100.85 | 29.20 | 72.00 | 103.20 |
| 2150 | 37.80 | 73.20 | 97.70 | 30.80 | 73.80 | 105.10 |
| 2155 | 34.50 | 70.10 | 94.60 | 32.50 | 75.70 | 106.30 |
| 2160 | 31.40 | 67.00 | 91.60 | 34.40 | 77.60 | 108.80 |
| 2165 | 28.40 | 64.00 | 88.60 | 36.40 | 79.60 | 110.95 |
| 2170 | 25.50 | 61.10 | 85.70 | 38.50 | 81.60 | 113.00 |
| 2175 | 22.80 | 58.20 | 82.85 | 40.80 | 83.70 | 115.10 |
| 2180 | 20.30 | 55.40 | 79.90 | 43.30 | 85.90 | 117.10 |

EST. VOL 6294   VOLUME 3380   OPEN INT 131784   EST. VOL 3419   VOLUME 4535   OPEN INT 80820

### CBOE MARKET VOLATILITY (VIX)

| Strike | Call Sep | Call Oct | Call Dec | Put Sep | Put Oct | Put Dec |
| --- | --- | --- | --- | --- | --- | --- |
| 10.00 | 6.40 | — | | | | 0.00 |
| 11.00 | 5.80 | 7.10 | 7.60 | 0.05 | 0.05 | 0.05 |
| 12.00 | 4.40 | 6.10 | 6.69 | 0.10 | 0.10 | 0.15 |
| 13.00 | 3.50 | 5.29 | 5.90 | 0.32 | 0.20 | 0.31 |
| 14.00 | 3.00 | 4.50 | 5.20 | 0.65 | 0.47 | 0.60 |
| 15.00 | 2.45 | — | | | | 1.15 |

EST. VOL 221,269   VOLUME 368,254   OPEN INT 4,350,790   EST. VOL 128,190   VOLUME 153,167   OPEN INT 2,223,589

### CURRENCY Futures Options
For Wednesday, August 3, 2016
All prices are settlement prices. Open interest is from the previous trading day.

**BRITISH POUND**

| Strike | Call Sep | Call Dec | Call Mar | Put Sep | Put Dec | Put Mar |
| --- | --- | --- | --- | --- | --- | --- |
| 1310 | 3.13 | 4.61 | 5.59 | 0.88 | 2.14 | 2.89 |
| 1320 | 2.45 | 3.98 | 4.96 | 1.20 | 2.50 | 3.26 |
| 1330 | 1.86 | 3.40 | 4.38 | 1.61 | 2.92 | 3.67 |
| 1340 | 1.37 | 2.87 | 3.83 | 2.12 | 3.39 | 4.12 |
| 1350 | 0.98 | 2.41 | 3.33 | 2.73 | 3.92 | 4.62 |
| 1360 | 0.68 | 2.00 | 2.88 | 3.43 | 4.51 | 5.16 |
| 1370 | 0.46 | 1.65 | 2.48 | 4.21 | 5.16 | 5.76 |

EST. VOL 4878   VOLUME 3525   OPEN INT 59879   EST. VOL 5457   VOLUME 3015   OPEN INT 60212

### CANADIAN DOLLAR

| Strike | Call Sep | Call Dec | Call Mar | Put Sep | Put Dec | Put Mar |
| --- | --- | --- | --- | --- | --- | --- |
| 7450 | 2.210 | 2.890 | 3.330 | 0.230 | 0.880 | 1.300 |
| 7500 | 1.800 | 2.540 | 3.000 | 0.320 | 1.040 | 1.470 |
| 7550 | 1.430 | 2.220 | 2.690 | 0.450 | 1.210 | 1.650 |
| 7600 | 1.100 | 1.920 | 2.390 | 0.620 | 1.420 | 1.860 |
| 7650 | 0.820 | 1.650 | 2.110 | 0.840 | 1.640 | 2.080 |
| 7700 | 0.590 | 1.400 | 1.860 | 1.110 | 1.890 | 2.320 |
| 7750 | 0.410 | 1.180 | 1.630 | 1.430 | 2.160 | 2.590 |
| 7800 | 0.280 | 0.980 | 1.420 | 1.800 | 2.460 | 2.880 |
| 7850 | 0.180 | 0.810 | 1.230 | 2.200 | 2.790 | 3.190 |

EST. VOL 1504   VOLUME 1292   OPEN INT 28500   EST. VOL 1387   VOLUME 2338   OPEN INT 36815

### EURO

| Strike | Call Sep | Call Dec | Call Mar | Put Sep | Put Dec | Put Mar |
| --- | --- | --- | --- | --- | --- | --- |
| 1095 | 0.02520 | 0.03800 | 0.04800 | 0.00350 | 0.01260 | 0.01740 |
| 1100 | 0.02130 | 0.03530 | 0.04450 | 0.00460 | 0.01410 | 0.01890 |
| 1105 | 0.01770 | 0.03190 | 0.04120 | 0.00600 | 0.01570 | 0.02050 |
| 1110 | 0.01430 | 0.02870 | 0.03790 | 0.00770 | 0.01750 | 0.02220 |
| 1115 | 0.01140 | 0.02570 | 0.03480 | 0.00970 | 0.01940 | 0.02410 |
| 1120 | 0.00880 | 0.02280 | 0.03190 | 0.01210 | 0.02160 | 0.02610 |
| 1125 | 0.00670 | 0.02020 | 0.02910 | 0.01500 | 0.02390 | 0.02830 |

EST. VOL 7581   VOLUME 12187   OPEN INT 114352   EST. VOL 11137   VOLUME 10779   OPEN INT 141828

### JAPANESE YEN

| Strike | Call Sep | Call Dec | Call Mar | Put Sep | Put Dec | Put Mar |
| --- | --- | --- | --- | --- | --- | --- |
| 9700 | 2.630 | 4.180 | 5.020 | 0.610 | 1.790 | 2.240 |
| 9750 | 2.290 | 3.880 | 4.730 | 0.770 | 1.990 | 2.440 |
| 9800 | 1.990 | 3.610 | 4.460 | 0.960 | 2.210 | 2.660 |
| 9850 | 1.710 | 3.340 | 4.190 | 1.190 | 2.450 | 2.900 |
| 9900 | 1.470 | 3.100 | 3.940 | 1.440 | 2.700 | 3.150 |
| 9950 | 1.260 | 2.870 | 3.710 | 1.730 | 2.970 | 3.410 |
| 10000 | 1.090 | 2.660 | 3.490 | 2.040 | 3.260 | 3.690 |

EST. VOL 3534   VOLUME 12670   OPEN INT 84457   EST. VOL 7197   VOLUME 15383   OPEN INT 100209

### SWISS FRANC

| Strike | Call Sep | Call Dec | Call Mar | Put Sep | Put Dec | Put Mar |
| --- | --- | --- | --- | --- | --- | --- |
| 10400 | 0.590 | 1.840 | 2.670 | 1.600 | 2.290 | 2.600 |
| 10450 | 0.460 | 1.630 | 2.450 | 1.970 | 2.590 | 2.870 |
| 10500 | 0.360 | 1.440 | 2.240 | 2.370 | 2.900 | 3.170 |
| 10550 | 0.280 | 1.280 | 2.050 | 2.790 | 3.230 | 3.470 |
| 10600 | 0.220 | 1.130 | 1.880 | 3.230 | 3.580 | 3.800 |
| 10650 | 0.180 | 1.000 | 1.720 | 3.680 | 3.950 | 4.140 |
| 10700 | 0.140 | 0.890 | 1.580 | 4.150 | 4.340 | 4.490 |

EST. VOL 25   VOLUME 89   OPEN INT 3381   EST. VOL 31   VOLUME 72   OPEN INT 5757

**Sources:** Chicago Board of Trade and CME Group websites. www.cbot.com, www.cmegroup.com

**Figure 10–11** In the Money and Out of the Money Options

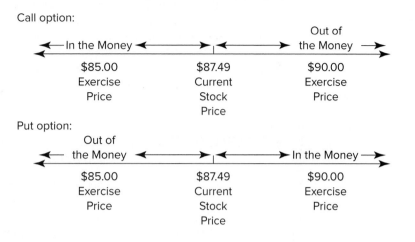

EXAMPLE 10–2 Calculating Profits and Losses on a Stock Option

You have purchased a put option on Micron Tech common stock. The option has an exercise price of $14.00 and Micron Tech's stock currently trades at $14.35. The option premium is $0.17 per contract.

Calculate your net profit on the option if Micron Tech's stock price falls to $13.25 and you exercise the option.

| | |
|---|---|
| Purchase option: | –$ 0.17 × 100 shares |
| Buy stock to exercise option: | – 13.25 × 100 shares |
| Sell stock by exercising option: | 14.00 × 100 shares |
| Net profit | $ 0.58 × 100 shares = $58 |

Calculate your net profit on the option if Micron Tech's stock price does not change over the life of the option.

| | |
|---|---|
| Purchase option: | –$0.17 × 100 shares |
| Net profit | –$0.17 × 100 shares = –$17 |

The option never moves into the money, so it would never be exercised.

**Stock Index Options.**   The underlying asset on a stock index option is the value of a major stock market index (e.g., the DJIA or the S&P 500 Index—see Chapter 8). An investor buys a call (put) option on a stock index when he or she thinks the value of the underlying stock market index will rise (fall) by the expiration date of the option. If the index does indeed rise above (fall below) the exercise price on the option, the call (put) option holder profits by an amount equal to the intrinsic value when the option expires. A difference between a stock option and a stock index option is that at expiration, the stock index option holder cannot settle the option contract with the actual purchase or sale of the underlying stock index. Rather, at expiration, stock index options are settled in cash (i.e., the option holder receives the intrinsic value if the option is in the money and nothing if the option is out of the money). Except for the S&P 500 and CBOE VIX (which are European options), stock index options are American options.

Options on stock indexes allow investors to invest indirectly in a diversified portfolio that replicates a major market index (e.g., the S&P 500 Index). If an investor thinks the S&P 500 Index will rise in the future, he or she can buy a call option on the S&P 500 Index. If the S&P 500 Index does rise, the value of the call option also rises. Thus, the investor can earn returns based directly on the S&P 500 Index without investing the large amounts of money needed to directly buy every stock in the index.

The dollar value associated with each stock index option is established by a particular multiplier—the value of a stock index option is equal to the index times its multiplier. For example, the multiplier on the S&P 500 index option is 500, on the S&P 100 index option it is 100, on the DJIA option it is 100, and on the NYSE Composite index option it is 500. Thus, if an S&P 500 index option has an exercise price of 2,100, the dollar amount involved with the exercise of this option is $2,100 \times \$500 = \$1,050,000$.

Options on stock indexes also give investors a way to hedge their existing stock portfolios.

---

### EXAMPLE 10–3     Using a Stock Index Option to Hedge a Stock Portfolio

Suppose that over the last seven years an investor's stock portfolio increased in value from $500,000 to $4.2 million. The stock portfolio was originally set up to (virtually) replicate the S&P 500 Index. The investor believes that due to expected rising interest rates in the next three months, stock market indexes (including the S&P 500 Index, currently at 2,100) will soon experience sharp declines in value and her stock portfolio will experience the same percentage drop in value. The investor has thought of liquidating her stock portfolio but is in the 20 percent capital gains tax bracket and does not want to incur such high tax payments.[14]

Instead, the investor takes a long position in (or buys) put options on the S&P 500 Index with a three-month expiration and an exercise price of 2,100. Incorporating the S&P 500 multiplier of $500, this is equivalent to a cost of $1,050,000 ($2,100 \times \$500$) per option. To hedge her $4.2 million stock portfolio, the investor would buy 4 [$4.2 million $\div$ ($2,100 \times \$500$)] put options on the S&P 500 Index.

Suppose the investor was correct in her expectations. In three months' time (as the put option on the S&P 500 Index expires), the S&P 500 Index has dropped 15 percent to 1,785, as has the value of her stock portfolio (now valued at $2.89 million). The investor has lost $510,000 in value on her stock portfolio. However, the investor can settle the put options she purchased for cash—the intrinsic value at the option's expiration is $630,000 [($2,100 - 1,785$ per option) $\times \$500 \times 4$ options].

The investor was able to take a position in the stock index option market such that any losses on her stock portfolio were offset with gains on the put option position in stock index options. We ignored transaction costs in this example (i.e., the premiums required to purchase the four put options), but they would be small relative to the losses the investor would have incurred had she not hedged her stock portfolio with stock index options.

---

Stock index option quotes (in Table 10–6) list the underlying index (e.g., DJ Industrials = DJX). The first column lists the expiration month of the option contract and the second column lists the exercise price, often listed in some submultiple of the actual value of the index (e.g., 100 = 10,000 for the DJIA). Columns 3 through 5 provide information on call options. Column 3 lists the settlement price (or premium) on the option (e.g., 3.40 means the price of one September 2016 call option with an exercise price of 100.00 is $3.40 \times 100 = \$340$). Column 4 is the trading volume (e.g., 0 = no call options traded), and Column 5 of the quote table reports the number of contracts outstanding at the beginning of the day (e.g., 100). Columns 6 through 8 list the same type of information for put options traded.

**Options on Futures Contracts.**   The underlying asset on a futures option is a futures contract (e.g., $100,000 Treasury bond futures—discussed above). The buyer of a call (put) option on a futures contract has the right to buy (sell) the underlying futures contract

---

14. To keep the focus of this example on the ability to hedge risk on a stock portfolio using a stock index option, we do not include transaction costs or taxes in the calculations.

at or before expiration. The seller of a call (put) option on a futures contract creates the obligation to sell (buy) the underlying futures contract on exercise by the option buyer. If exercised, a call (put) option holder can buy (sell) the underlying futures contracts at the exercise price. Options on futures can be more attractive to investors than options on an underlying asset when it is cheaper or more convenient to deliver futures contracts on the asset rather than the actual asset. For example, trading options on T-bond futures contracts rather than options on T-bonds ensures that a highly liquid asset will be delivered and that problems associated with accrued interest and the determination of which long-term bond to deliver are avoided. Another advantage is that price information about futures contracts (the underlying asset on the option) is generally more readily available than price information on the T-bonds themselves (T-bond price information can be obtained only by surveying bond dealers). Options are currently written on interest rate, currency, and stock index futures contracts.

Look at the first futures option quote listed in Table 10–6 (for T-bonds). The bold heading for each quote lists the type of option (e.g., on 30 YEAR US TREASURY BOND OPTIONS contracts), the face value of each option contract (e.g., $100,000), and the basis for the quote (e.g., "pts & 64ths of 100pct"). Each row in the quote then lists trading results for a specific exercise price (e.g., 17300). Column 1 lists the strike price; Columns 2 through 4 list settlement prices on call options traded, by expiration month of the option contract (e.g., September, October, and December). The last three columns list settlement prices for the various expiration put options.

**Credit Options.**   Options also have a potential use in hedging the credit risk of a financial institution. Compared to their use in hedging interest rate risk, options used to hedge credit risk are a relatively new phenomenon. Two alternative credit option derivatives exist to hedge credit risk on a balance sheet: credit spread call options and digital default options. A credit spread call option is a call option whose payoff increases as the (default) risk premium or yield spread on a specified benchmark bond of the borrower increases above some exercise spread. A financial institution concerned that the risk on a loan to that borrower will increase can purchase a credit spread call option to hedge its increased credit risk. A digital default option is an option that pays a stated amount in the event of a loan default (the extreme case of increased credit risk). In the event of a loan default, the option writer pays the financial institution the par value of the defaulted loans. If the loans are paid off in accordance with the loan agreement, however, the default option expires unexercised. As a result, the institution will suffer a maximum loss on the option equal to the premium (cost) of buying the default option from the writer (seller).

Chapter 23 provides more details on the use of option contracts to manage interest rate and credit risk.

# REGULATION OF FUTURES AND OPTIONS MARKETS

**LG 10-6**

www.cftc.gov

www.sec.gov

Derivative securities are subject to three levels of institutional regulation. First, regulators of derivatives specify "permissible activities" that institutions may engage in. Second, once permissible activities have been specified, institutions engaging in those activities are subjected to supervisory oversight. Third, regulators attempt to judge the overall integrity of each institution engaging in derivative activities by assessing the capital adequacy of the institutions and by enforcing regulations to ensure compliance with those capital requirements. The Securities and Exchange Commission (SEC) and the Commodities Futures Trading Commission (CFTC) are often viewed as "functional" regulators. The SEC regulates all securities traded on national securities exchanges, including several exchange-traded derivatives. The SEC's regulation of derivatives includes price reporting requirements, antimanipulation regulations, position limits, audit trail requirements, and margin requirements. The CFTC has exclusive jurisdiction over all exchange-traded derivative securities. It therefore regulates all national futures exchanges, as well as all futures and options contracts. The CFTC's regulations include minimum capital requirements for traders, reporting and transparency requirements, antifraud and antimanipulation regulations, and minimum standards for clearinghouse organizations.

Since January 1, 2000, the main regulator of accounting standards (the Financial Accounting Standards Board, or FASB) has required all FIs (and nonfinancial firms) to reflect the mark to market value of their derivative positions in their financial statements. This means that FIs must immediately recognize all gains and losses on such contracts and disclose those gains and losses to shareholders and regulators. Further, firms must show whether they are using derivatives to hedge risks connected to their business or whether they are just taking an open (risky) position.

The main bank regulators—the Federal Reserve, the FDIC, and the Comptroller of the Currency—also have issued uniform guidelines for banks that trade in futures and forwards. These guidelines require a bank to (1) establish internal guidelines regarding its hedging activity, (2) establish trading limits, and (3) disclose large contract positions that materially affect bank risk to shareholders and outside investors. Overall, the policy of regulators is to encourage the use of futures for hedging and discourage their use for speculation, although on a practical basis it is often difficult to distinguish between the two. Further, as we will discuss in Chapter 13, exchange-traded derivative securities such as futures contracts are not subject to risk-based capital requirements. By contrast, OTC derivative securities such as forward contracts are potentially subject to capital requirements. Indeed, the growth of the derivative securities markets was one of the major factors underlying the imposition of the Bank for International Settlements (BIS) risk-based capital requirements in January 1993 (see Chapter 13). The fear then was that in a long-term derivative security contract, an out-of-the-money counterparty—that is, a counterparty that is currently at a disadvantage in terms of cash flows—would have incentives to default on such contracts to deter current and future losses. Consequently, the BIS imposed a required capital ratio for depository institutions against their holdings of derivative securities. However, these capital requirements were not sufficient to insure the solvency of some FIs against the extreme losses experienced during the financial crisis.

Because of their lack of regulation and because of the significant negative role that over-the-counter (OTC) derivative securities played during the financial crisis, the Wall Street Reform and Consumer Protection Act of 2010 included a plan to regulate OTC derivatives. First, the plan called for most of the OTC derivatives to trade on regulated exchanges, which would guarantee trades and help cushion against potential defaults. This change would make it easier for participants to see the market prices of these securities and make the markets more transparent. Second, like exchange-traded derivatives, the previous OTC traded securities would now come under the authority of the SEC and the CFTC, while bank regulators would oversee the banks dealing in these derivatives. Thus, the changes result in OTC derivative securities being regulated in a similar fashion as exchange-traded securities. As of 2016, standards and requirements for the new trade reporting, central clearing, and platform trading rules are in force for over 90 percent of OTC transactions.

---

**DO YOU UNDERSTAND:**

5. What the difference is between a call option and a put option?

6. When an option trader would want to buy a call option on a stock?

7. When an option trader would want to buy a put option on a stock?

8. What the three types of options traded in the United States are?

9. Who the main regulators of futures and option markets are?

---

## SWAPS

**swap**   `LG 10-7`

*An agreement between two parties to exchange a series of cash flows for a specific period of time at a specified interval.*

A **swap** is an agreement between two parties (called counterparties) to exchange specified periodic cash flows in the future based on some underlying instrument or price (e.g., a fixed or floating rate on a bond or note). Like forward, futures, and option contracts, swaps allow firms to better manage their interest rate, foreign exchange, and credit risks. However, swaps also can result in large losses. At the heart of the financial crisis in 2008–2009 were derivative securities, mainly credit swaps, held by financial institutions. Specifically, in the late 2000s, FIs such as Lehman Brothers and AIG had written and also (in the case of AIG) insured billions of dollars of credit default swap (CDS) contracts. When the mortgages underlying these contracts fell drastically in value, credit swap writers found themselves unable to make good on their promised payments to the swap holders. The result was a significant increase in risk and a decrease in profits for the FIs that had purchased these swap contracts. To prevent a massive collapse of the financial system, the federal government had to step in and bail out several of these FIs.

Swaps were first developed in 1981 when IBM and the World Bank entered into a currency swap agreement. At the time, IBM had large amounts of debt denominated in Swiss franc and German deutsche mark debt. Also during this period, borrowing rates were at record highs: the U.S. prime rate at the time was 18 percent, in West Germany the prime rate was 12 percent, and in Switzerland it was 8 percent. The World Bank was looking for the cheapest source of funding its lending programs, and the West German and Swiss governments limited the amount that the World Bank could borrow. Thus, IBM and the World Bank worked out an agreement in which the World Bank borrowed dollars in the U.S. market and swapped the dollar payment obligation with IBM in exchange for taking over IBM's Swiss franc and German deutsche mark obligations. Seeing the advantages of such agreements, the swap market grew quickly.

Figure 10–12 shows the growth in the notional value of swaps outstanding from 1992 through 2016. Of the $395.5 trillion outstanding in 2016, the notional value of swap contracts outstanding by U.S. commercial banks (by far the major participant in the swap markets) was $114.8 trillion. The five generic types of swaps are interest rate swaps, currency swaps, credit risk swaps, commodity swaps, and equity swaps.[15] The asset or instrument underlying the swap may change, but the basic principle of a swap agreement is the same in that it involves the transacting parties restructuring their asset or liability cash flows in a preferred direction. In this section, we consider the role of the two major generic types of swaps—interest rate and currency. We also discuss the fastest growing type of swap—credit swaps. We look at other types of swaps and describe the ability of swaps to hedge various kinds of risk in more detail in Chapter 23.

**interest rate swap**

*An exchange of fixed-interest payments for floating-interest payments by two counterparties.*

## Interest Rate Swaps

By far the largest segment of the swap market is comprised of **interest rate swaps.** Conceptually, an interest rate swap is a succession of forward contracts on interest rates

**Figure 10–12**   **Swap Contracts Held by Commercial Banks, 1992–2016**

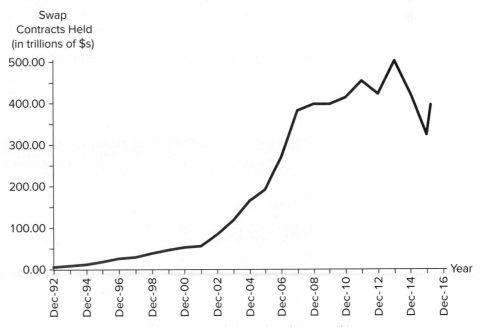

**Sources:** Bank for International Settlements website, various dates. www.bis.org

15. There are also *swaptions,* which are options to enter into a swap agreement at some preagreed contract terms (e.g., a fixed rate of 10 percent) at some time in the future in return for the payment of an up-front premium.

arranged by two parties.[16] As such, it allows the swap parties to put in place long-term protection (sometimes for as long as 15 years) against interest rate risk (see Chapter 22). The swap reduces the need to "roll over" contracts from old ones into new ones if futures or forward contracts had been relied on to achieve such long-term hedging protection.[17]

**swap buyer**

*By convention, a party that makes the fixed-rate payments in an interest rate swap transaction.*

**notional principal**

*The principal amount involved in a swap.*

**swap seller**

*By convention, a party that makes the floating-rate payments in an interest rate swap transaction.*

In a swap contract, the **swap buyer** agrees to make a number of fixed interest rate payments based on a principal contractual amount (called the **notional principal**) on periodic settlement dates to the **swap seller.** The swap seller, in turn, agrees to make floating-rate payments, tied to some interest rate, to the swap buyer on the same periodic settlement dates. In undertaking this transaction, the party that is the fixed-rate payer is seeking to transform the variable-rate nature of its liabilities into fixed-rate liabilities to better match the fixed returns earned on its assets. Meanwhile, the party that is the variable-rate payer seeks to turn its fixed-rate liabilities into variable-rate liabilities to better match the variable returns on its assets.

**Hedging Interest Rate Risk with an Interest Rate Swap.** To explain the role of a swap transaction in protecting a firm against interest rate risk, we use a simple example of an interest rate swap. Consider two financial institutions. The first is a money center bank that has raised $50 million of its funds by issuing five-year, medium-term notes with 6 percent annual fixed coupons (see Table 10–7). On the asset side of its portfolio, the bank makes commercial and industrial (C&I) loans whose rates are indexed to annual changes in the London Interbank Offered Rate (LIBOR) (say, LIBOR + 2%). FIs index most large commercial and industrial loans to either LIBOR or the federal funds rate in the money market.

As a result of having floating-rate loans and fixed-rate liabilities in its asset–liability structure, the money center bank is exposed to interest rate risk. Specifically, if interest rates decrease, the bank's interest income decreases, since the variable interest return on loans (assets) will fall relative to the fixed cost of its funds (liabilities). On the balance sheet, the money center bank could attract an additional $50 million in short-term deposits that are indexed to the LIBOR rate (say, LIBOR plus 1.5 percent) in a manner similar to its loans. The proceeds of these deposits could then be used to pay off the medium-term notes. This on-balance-sheet change would eliminate the interest rate exposure of the bank. Alternatively, to protect the bank's income against this interest rate risk, the bank could go off the balance sheet and sell an interest rate swap—that is, enter into a swap agreement to make the floating-rate payment side of a swap agreement.

The second party to the swap in this example is a savings bank that has invested $50 million in fixed interest rate (at say 8.5 percent) residential mortgage assets of long maturity. To finance this residential mortgage portfolio, the savings bank uses short-term LIBOR deposits with an average duration of one year (see Table 10–7). On maturity, these must be "rolled over" at the current LIBOR rate. Consequently, the savings bank's asset–liability deposits balance

**TABLE 10–7** Balance Sheets of Swap Participants

| Assets | | Liabilities | |
|---|---|---|---|
| **Panel A: Money Center Bank's Balance Sheet (Swap Seller)** | | | |
| C&I loans (rate indexed to LIBOR + 2%) = | $50m | Medium-term notes (coupons fixed at 6%) = | $50m |
| **Panel B: Savings Bank's Balance Sheet (Swap Buyer)** | | | |
| Fixed-rate mortgages (at 8.5%) = | $50m | Short-term LIBOR deposits (one year) = | $50m |

---

16. For example, a four-year swap with annual swap dates involves four net cash flows between the parties to a swap. This is essentially similar to arranging four forward rate agreement (FRA) contracts: a one-year, a two-year, a three-year, and a four-year contract.

17. For example, futures contracts are offered usually with a maximum maturity of two years or less.

**Figure 10–13** **A Swap Transaction**

Direct arrangement of swap:

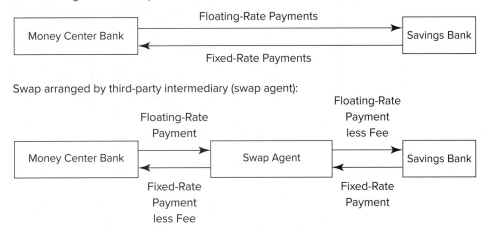

Swap arranged by third-party intermediary (swap agent):

sheet structure is the reverse of the money center bank's—if interest rates increase, the savings bank's interest expense increases. Since its assets (mortgages) are fixed rate, while its liabilities (deposits) are floating, the savings bank's net income falls. On the balance sheet, the savings bank could issue long-term notes with a maturity equal or close to that on the mortgages (at, say, 7.5 percent). The proceeds of the sale of the notes could then be used to pay off the CDs and reduce the interest rate risk. Alternatively, the savings bank could hedge this interest rate risk exposure by going off the balance sheet and buying a swap—that is, the savings bank could enter into a swap agreement to make the fixed-rate payment side of a swap agreement.

The opposing balance sheet and interest rate risk exposures of the money center bank and the savings bank provide the necessary conditions for an interest rate swap agreement between the two parties. This swap agreement can be arranged directly by the two parties themselves—for example, by direct telephone contact. However, it is likely that a third financial institution or institutions—another commercial bank or an investment bank—would act either as a broker or an agent, receiving a fee for bringing the two parties together or intermediating fully by accepting the credit risk exposure and guaranteeing the cash flows underlying the swap contract. The intermediary stage of a swap can pass through many brokers, each taking a commission. We illustrate these swap transactions in Figure 10–13. By acting as a principal as well as an agent in arranging the swap, the third party financial institution can add a credit risk premium to the fee. However, the credit risk exposure of a swap to a financial institution is somewhat less than that on a loan (see Chapter 23). Conceptually, when a third-party financial institution fully intermediates the swap, that institution is really entering into two separate swap agreements—in this example, one with the money center bank and one with the savings bank.

## EXAMPLE 10–4  Expected Cash Flows on an Interest Rate Swap

For the two financial institutions, a swap agreement might dictate that the savings bank send fixed payments of 7 percent per year of the notional $50 million value of the swap to the money center bank, each year for 5 years, to allow the money center bank to cover fully the coupon interest payments on its note issue. In return, the money center bank could send annual payments indexed to the one-year LIBOR + 1 percent, for 5 years, to help the savings bank cover the cost of refinancing its one-year renewable LIBOR deposits.[18] We depict this fixed–floating rate swap transaction in Figure 10–14. The expected net financing costs for the FIs are listed in Table 10–8.

18. These rates implicitly assume that this is the cheapest way each party can hedge its interest rate exposure. For example, LIBOR plus 1.5 percent is the lowest cost way that the money center bank can transform its fixed-rate liabilities into floating-rate liabilities.

As a result of the swap, the money center bank has transformed its five-year, fixed-rate liability notes into a variable-rate liability matching the variability of returns on its C&I loans. Further, through the interest rate swap, the money center bank effectively pays LIBOR for its financing. Had it gone to the debt market, the money center bank would have paid LIBOR plus 1.5 percent (a savings of 1.5 percent with the swap). Further, the savings bank also has transformed its variable-rate LIBOR deposits into fixed-rate payments (of 6 percent) similar to those received on its fixed-rate mortgages. Had it gone to the debt market, the savings bank would have paid 7.5 percent (a savings of 1.5 percent).

**Figure 10–14**   Fixed–Floating Rate Swap

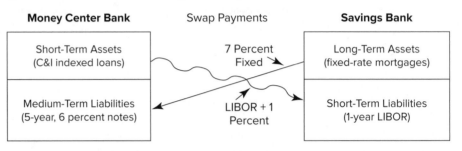

**TABLE 10–8**   Financing Cost Resulting from Interest Rate Swap *(in millions of dollars)*

|  | Money Center Bank | Savings Bank |
|---|---|---|
| Cash outflows from balance sheet financing | –6% × $50 | – (LIBOR) × $50 |
| Cash inflows from swap | 7% × $50 | (LIBOR + 1% ) × $50 |
| Cash outflows from swap | –(LIBOR + 1%) × $50 | –7% × $50 |
| Net cash flows | –(LIBOR) × $50 | –6% × $50 |
| Rate available on: | | |
| Variable-rate debt | LIBOR + 1.5% | |
| Fixed-rate debt | | 7.5% |

In analyzing this swap, the parties also must consider the actual realized cash flows on the swap. Realized cash flows on the swap depend on the actual market rates (here, LIBOR) that materialize over the life of the swap contract.

**EXAMPLE 10–5**   Realized Cash Flows on an Interest Rate Swap

Assume that the realized or actual path of interest rates (LIBOR) over the five-year life of the swap contract are as follows:

| End of Year | LIBOR |
|---|---|
| 1 | 6.5% |
| 2 | 6.5 |
| 3 | 3.0 |
| 4 | 2.0 |
| 5 | 2.0 |

Given this actual path of LIBOR, the money center bank's variable payments to the savings bank were indexed to these rates by the formula (LIBOR + 1%) × $50 million. By contrast, the fixed annual payments the savings bank made to the money center bank were the same each year: 7 percent times $50 million.

We summarize the actual or realized cash flows among the two parties over the five years in Table 10–9. The savings bank's net payments from the swap in years 1 and 2 are $0.25 million per year. The enhanced cash flow offsets the increased cost of refinancing its LIBOR deposits in a higher interest rate environment; that is, the savings bank is hedged against rising rates. By contrast, the money center bank makes net payments on the swap in years 3, 4, and 5 when rates fall; thus, it is hedged against falling rates. The positive cash flow from the swap offsets the decline in the variable returns on the money center bank's asset portfolio. Overall, the savings bank received a net dollar payment on the swap of $5.0 million in nominal dollars and the money center bank made a net payment of $5.0 million. However, as shown in Table 10–10, both FIs have completely insulated their net income against changes in interest rates. The money center bank receives income of LIBOR + 2 percent on its assets and pays LIBOR on its existing debt and the swap, or its net income is $1 million each year. The savings bank receives 8.5 percent on its assets and pays 6 percent on its existing debt and the swap, or its net income is $1.25 million each year.

**TABLE 10–9**   Realized Cash Flows on Swap Agreement *(in millions of dollars)*

| End of Year | One-Year LIBOR | One-Year LIBOR + 1 Percent | Cash Payment by Money Center Bank | Cash Payment by Savings Bank | Net Payment Made by Money Center Bank |
|---|---|---|---|---|---|
| 1 | 6.5% | 7.5% | $ 3.75 | $ 3.5 | $0.25 |
| 2 | 6.5 | 7.5 | 3.75 | 3.5 | 0.25 |
| 3 | 3.0 | 4.0 | 2.00 | 3.5 | –1.50 |
| 4 | 2.0 | 3.0 | 1.50 | 3.5 | –2.00 |
| 5 | 2.0 | 3.0 | 1.50 | 3.5 | –2.00 |
| Total | | | $12.50 | $17.5 | –$5.00 |

**TABLE 10–10**   Net Income for the FIs *(in millions of dollars)*

| Year | NI Money Center Bank (LIBOR + 2%) – LIBOR | NI Savings Bank (8.5% – 6%) |
|---|---|---|
| 1 | (8.5% – 6.5%) × $50m = $1m | (8.5% – 6%) × $50m = $1.25m |
| 2 | (8.5% – 6.5%) × $50m = $1m | (8.5% – 6%) × $50m = $1.25m |
| 3 | (5.0% – 3.0%) × $50m = $1m | (8.5% – 6%) × $50m = $1.25m |
| 4 | (4.0% – 2.0%) × $50m = $1m | (8.5% – 6%) × $50m = $1.25m |
| 5 | (4.0% – 2.0%) × $50m = $1m | (8.5% – 6%) × $50m = $1.25m |

## Currency Swaps

**currency swap**

*A swap used to hedge against exchange rate risk from mismatched currencies on assets and liabilities.*

Interest rate swaps are long-term contracts that can be used to hedge interest rate risk exposure. This section considers a simple example of how **currency swaps** can be used to immunize or hedge against exchange rate risk when firms mismatch the currencies of their assets and liabilities.

**Fixed-Fixed Currency Swaps.**   Consider a U.S. financial institution with all of its fixed-rate assets denominated in dollars. It is financing its $200 million asset portfolio with a £100 million issue of five-year, medium-term British pound notes that have a fixed annual coupon of 6 percent. By comparison, a financial institution in the United Kingdom has all its £100 million assets denominated in pounds. It is funding those assets with a $200 million issue of five-year, medium-term dollar notes with a fixed annual coupon of 6 percent.

These two financial institutions are exposed to opposing currency risks. The U.S. institution is exposed to the risk that the dollar will depreciate (decline in value) against the pound over the next five years, which would make it more costly to cover the annual coupon interest payments and the principal repayment on its pound-denominated note liabilities. On the other hand, the UK institution is exposed to the risk that the dollar will appreciate against the pound, making it more difficult to cover the dollar coupon and principal payments on its five-year, $200 million note liabilities.

These financial institutions can hedge their exposures off the balance sheet. Assume that the dollar/pound exchange rate is fixed at $2/£1. The UK and U.S. financial institutions would enter into a currency swap by which the UK institution sends annual payments in pounds to cover the coupon and principal repayments of the U.S. financial institution's pound note issue, and the U.S. financial institution sends annual dollar payments to the UK financial institution to cover the interest and principal payments on its dollar note issue.[19] We summarize this currency swap in Figure 10–15. As a result of the swap, the UK financial institution transforms its fixed-rate dollar liabilities into fixed-rate pound liabilities that better match the fixed-rate pound cash flows from its asset portfolio. Similarly, the U.S. financial institution transforms fixed-rate pound liabilities into fixed-rate dollar liabilities that better match the fixed-rate dollar cash flows on its asset portfolio. In undertaking this exchange of cash flows, the two parties normally agree on a fixed exchange rate for the cash flows at the beginning of the period. In this case, the fixed exchange rate is $2/£1. Chapter 23 explains in more detail how swaps can be used to hedge currency risk.

Note in the previous example that should the exchange rate change from the rate agreed in the swap ($2/£1), either one or the other side would be losing in the sense that a new swap might be entered into at a more favorable exchange rate to one party. Specifically, if the dollar were to appreciate against the pound over the life of the swap, the agreement would become more costly for the U.S. financial institution. If, however, the dollar depreciated, the UK financial institution would find the agreement increasingly costly over the swap's life.

### Credit Swaps

In recent years the fastest-growing types of swaps have been those developed to better allow financial institutions to hedge their credit risk, so-called credit swaps or credit default swaps. In 2000, commercial banks' total notional principal for outstanding credit derivative contracts was $426 billion. By March 2008, this amount had risen to $16.44 trillion, before falling to $13.44 trillion in 2009 during the financial crisis. By March 2016 (as explained below), the notional principal of credit derivative contracts had fallen dramatically, to $7.42 trillion. Of this 2016 amount, $7.05 trillion was credit swaps. Two types of credit swaps are total return swaps and pure credit swaps. A *total return swap* involves swapping an obligation to pay interest at a specified fixed or floating rate for payments

**Figure 10–15**   **Fixed-Fixed Pound/Dollar Currency Swap**

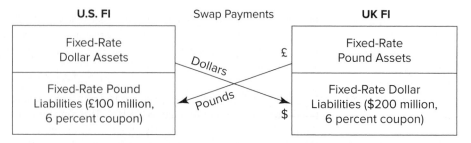

representing the total return on a loan (interest and principal value changes) of a specified amount. While total return swaps can be used to hedge credit risk exposure, they contain an element of interest rate risk as well as credit risk. For example, if the base rate on the loan changes, the net cash flows on the total return swap also will change—even though the credit risks of the underlying loans have not changed.

To strip out the "interest rate"–sensitive element of total return swaps, an alternative swap has been developed called a *pure credit swap*. In this case, the financial institution lender will send (each swap period) a fixed fee or payment (like an insurance premium) to the counterparty. If the financial institution lender's loan or loans do not default, it will receive nothing back from the counterparty. However, if the loan or loans default, the counterparty will cover the default loss by making a default payment that is often equal to the par value of the original loan minus the secondary market value of the defaulted loan. Thus, a pure credit swap is like buying credit insurance and/or a multi-period credit option.

While commercial banks have been the main buyers of credit risk protection through credit swaps, insurance companies (such as AIG) have been the net sellers of credit risk protection. Thus, they have been more willing than banks to bear credit risk. The result is that the FI bearing the credit risk of a loan is often different from the FI that issued the loan. Credit swaps are important for two reasons. First, credit risk is still more likely to cause an FI to fail than either interest rate risk or foreign exchange risk. Second, credit swaps allow FIs to maintain long-term customer lending relationships without bearing the full credit risk exposure from those relationships. Credit derivatives, such as credit default swaps, allow FIs to separate the credit risk exposure from the lending process itself. That is, FIs can assess the creditworthiness of loan applicants, originate loans, fund loans, and even monitor and service loans without retaining exposure to loss from credit events, such as default or missed payments. This decoupling of the risk from the lending activity allows the market to efficiently transfer risk across counterparties. However, it also loosens the incentives to carefully perform each of the steps of the lending process. This loosening of incentives was an important factor leading to the global financial crisis of 2008–2009, which witnessed the after-effects of poor loan underwriting, shoddy documentation and due diligence, failure to monitor borrower activity, and fraudulent activity on the part of both lenders and borrowers. Further, although the credit protection buyer hedges exposure to default risk, there is still counterparty credit risk in the event that the seller fails to perform its obligations under the terms of the contract (as was the concern in September 2008 with regard to AIG, an active credit default swap seller).[20] We look at types of credit swaps and their use as hedges of credit risk in detail in Chapter 23.

## Swap Markets

Swap transactions are generally heterogeneous in terms of maturities, indexes used to determine payments, and timing of payments—there is no standardized contract. Swap dealers (generally an FI performing this brokerage activity) exist to serve the function of taking the opposite side of each transaction in order to keep the swap market liquid by locating or matching counterparties or, in many cases, taking one side of the swap themselves. In a direct swap between two counterparties, each party must find another party having a mirror image financing requirement—for example, a financial institution in need of swapping fixed-rate payments, made quarterly for the next 10 years, on $25 million in liabilities must find a counterparty in need of swapping $25 million in floating-rate payments made quarterly for the next 10 years. Without swap dealers, the search costs of finding such counterparties to a swap can be significant.

A further advantage of swap dealers is that they generally guarantee swap payments over the life of the contract. If one of the counterparties defaults on a direct swap, the other

---

20. See footnote 2 in this chapter.

counterparty is no longer adequately hedged against risk and may have to replace the defaulted swap with a new swap at less favorable terms (replacement risk). By booking a swap with a swap dealer, a default by a counterparty will not affect the other counterparty. The swap dealer incurs any costs associated with the default (the fee or spread charged by the swap dealer to each party in a swap incorporates this default risk).[21] Commercial and investment banks have evolved as the major swap dealers, mainly because of their close ties to the financial markets and their specialized skills in assessing credit risk. Each swap market dealer manages a large "book" of swaps listing its swap positions. As a result, swap dealers can also diversify some of their risk exposure away.

**www.federalreserve.gov**

In contrast to futures and options markets, swap markets were historically governed by very little regulation—there was no central governing body overseeing swap market operations. Because commercial banks were the major swap dealers, the swap markets were subject, indirectly, to regulations imposed by the Board of Governors of the Federal Reserve, the FDIC, and other bank regulatory agencies charged with monitoring bank risk. For example, commercial banks must include swap risk exposure when calculating risk-based capital requirements (see Chapter 13). To the extent that swap activity was part of a bank's overall business, swap markets were monitored for abuses. However, despite their growing presence in the swap markets, investment banks and insurance companies were subject to few regulations on their swap dealings.

Because of the role credit swaps (and other derivative securities) played in the financial crisis, the call for stricter regulation over these securities was strong in late 2008 and early 2009. The early months of 2009 saw several fundamental changes to the way credit swaps and other over-the-counter derivative securities operate. First, the market saw the introduction of central clearinghouses; one for the United States and one for Europe. In the United States, central clearing operations (operated by InterContinental Exchange, or ICE) began in March 2009. Clearinghouses act as the central counterparty to both sides of a credit swap transaction and thus reduce counterparty risk to both buyers and sellers. Second, there was a trend toward the international standardization of credit swap contracts. Standardization prevents legal disputes in ambiguous cases where the swap payout is unclear. The Wall Street Reform and Consumer Protection Act of 2010 formalized these changes by calling for new rules to be implemented and calling for previously over-the-counter traded swaps to be traded through exchanges. As of 2016, the CFTC has completed most mandated rulemakings, establishing a regime of regulatory oversight for many new entities, including swap intermediaries known as "Swap Dealers" and "Major Swap Participants," as wells as clearinghouses and trading platforms. The SEC is also well under way in regard to its rulemaking and implementation of requirements covering security-based swaps (SBSs). Under this new regime, sufficiently liquid and standardized derivatives transactions are required to be centrally cleared, and the most liquid of those are required to be executed on platforms. Some derivatives still fall into the category of over-the-counter, which means that their terms are privately negotiated between two parties, and some will also remain uncleared. These non-centrally cleared swaps will be subject to new margin requirements based on an international standard developed by the Basel Committee on Banking Supervision and International Organization of Securities Commissions.

In August 2013, the Commodities Futures Trading Commission (CFTC) uncovered evidence that several commercial and investment banks had manipulated a benchmark for interest rate derivatives, the ISDAfix. As a result, the FIs earned millions of dollars in trading profits at the expense of companies and pension funds. The CFTC investigation found recorded telephone calls and e-mails showing that swap traders at the banks instructed ICAP Plc brokers, a New Jersey–based interdealer broker, to buy or sell as many interest rate swaps as necessary to move the ISDAfix to a specified level. By manipulating the benchmark, the banks profited on individual derivatives trades they had with

---

21. For interest rate swaps where the dealer intermediates, a different (higher) fixed rate will be set for receiving fixed-rate payments compared to paying a fixed rate.

DO YOU UNDERSTAND:

10. Which party in a swap is the swap buyer and which party is the swap seller?

11. What the difference is between an interest rate swap and a currency swap?

customers seeking to hedge against moves in interest rates. Companies and pension and mutual funds, including Calpers, the largest U.S. pension fund, and Pimco, manager of the world's largest mutual fund, use the derivatives at the center of the ISDAfix probe to hedge against losses or to speculate on interest rate fluctuations. The actions are in direct violation of the 2010 Wall Street Reform and Consumer Protection Act, which prohibits market makers from intentionally influencing the orderly execution of transactions that determine settlement prices.

Chapter 23 provides more details on the use of swaps to manage interest rate and credit risk.

## CAPS, FLOORS, AND COLLARS

**cap**

*A call option on interest rates, often with multiple exercise dates.*

LG 10-8

Caps, floors, and collars are derivative securities that have many uses, especially in helping an FI to hedge interest rate risk. Buying a **cap** means buying a call option or a succession of call options on interest rates.[22] In general, FIs purchase interest rate caps if they are exposed to losses when interest rates rise. Usually, this happens if FIs are funding assets with floating-rate liabilities such as notes indexed to the London Interbank Offered Rate (or some other floating cost of funds) and they have fixed-rate assets or they are net long in bonds. Specifically, if interest rates rise above a cap rate, which acts in a similar fashion to a strike price in an option contract, the seller of the cap—usually a bank—compensates the buyer—for example, another financial institution—in return for an up-front premium. Suppose that two firms enter a two-year cap agreement with a notional value of $1 million. The cap rate is 10 percent and payments are settled once a year based on year-end interest rates. For the interest rate movements shown in Figure 10–16, the cap writer owes the cap buyer (11% − 10%) × $1 million, or $10,000, at the end of year 1, and (12% − 10%) × $1 million, or $20,000, at the end of year 2. As a result, buying an interest rate cap is like buying insurance against an (excessive) increase in interest rates. A cap agreement can have one or many exercise dates.

**floor**

*A put option on interest rates, often with multiple exercise dates.*

Buying a **floor** is similar to buying a put option on interest rates. FIs purchase floors when they have fixed costs of debt and they have variable or floating rates (returns) on assets or they are net short in bonds. If interest rates fall below the floor rate, the seller of the floor compensates the buyer in return for an up-front premium. For example, suppose that two financial institutions enter a two-year floor agreement with a notional value

**Figure 10–16**　Hypothetical Path of Interest Rates during a Cap Agreement

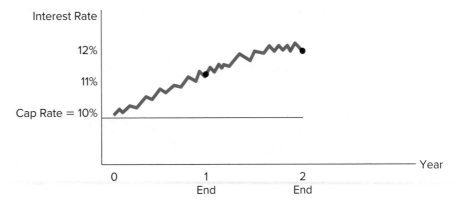

22. Note that a cap can be viewed as a call option on interest rates (as discussed here) or as a put option on bond prices, since rising interest rates mean falling bond prices. Similarly, a floor (discussed in the next paragraph) can be viewed as a put option on interest rates or a call option on bond prices. We follow market convention and discuss caps and floors as options on interest rates rather than on bond prices.

**Figure 10–17**    Hypothetical Path of Interest Rates during a Floor Agreement

of $1 million. The floor rate is 8 percent, and payments are settled once a year based on year-end rates. For the interest rate movements shown in Figure 10–17, the floor writer owes the floor buyer (8% − 7%) × $1 million, or $10,000, at the end of year 1, and (8% − 6%) × $1 million, or $20,000, at the end of year 2. As with caps, floor agreements can have one or many exercise dates.

**collar**

*A position taken simultaneously in a cap and a floor.*

A **collar** occurs when a firm takes a simultaneous position in a cap and a floor (e.g., *buying* a cap and *selling* a floor). FIs purchase collars to finance cap or floor positions or when they are concerned about excessive interest rate volatility. The idea here is that the firm wants to hedge itself against rising rates but wants to finance the cost of the cap. One way to do this is to sell a floor and use the premiums earned on the floor to pay the premium on the purchased cap. For example, suppose that a financial institution enters into a two-year collar agreement with a notional value of $1 million. The floor rate is 8 percent and the cap rate is 10 percent. Payments are settled once a year based on year-end rates. For the interest rate movements shown in Figure 10–18, the collar buyer, the financial institution, gains (11% − 10%) × $1 million, or $10,000, at the end of year 1. However, since the financial institution has written or sold a floor to another financial institution to finance the cap purchase, it pays (8% − 7%) × $1 million, or $10,000, at the end of year 2.

Many firms invested in caps and collars in the mid-2000s in expectation that interest rates would decrease. For example, in 2007 Deutsche Bank arranged a $500 million collar for Dubai Islamic Bank, which wanted to hedge a large portfolio against interest rate increases with minimal costs.

**DO YOU UNDERSTAND:**

12. What the difference is between a cap and a collar?

13. The conditions under which a firm would buy a floor?

**Figure 10–18**    Hypothetical Path of Interest Rates during a Collar Agreement

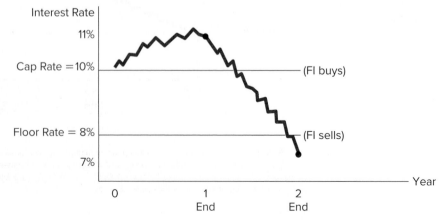

# INTERNATIONAL ASPECTS OF DERIVATIVE SECURITIES MARKETS

**LG 10-9**

Tables 10–11 and 10–12 report the amount of global over-the-counter (OTC) and exchange-traded derivative securities from 1999 through 2016. Notice global OTC trading far outweighs exchange trading. The total notional amount of outstanding OTC contracts was

**TABLE 10–11**  Amounts of Global Derivative Securities Outstanding on the OTC Market *(in billions of dollars)*

| Contract | 1999 | 2001 | 2004 | June 2008 | December 2008 | December 2010 | December 2013 | March 2016 |
|---|---|---|---|---|---|---|---|---|
| **Total Contracts** | $88,202 | $111,115 | $220,058 | $683,814 | $547,983 | $601,046 | $632,579 | $492,911 |
| Foreign Exchange Contracts | 14,344 | 16,748 | 26,997 | 62,983 | 44,200 | 57,796 | 67,358 | 70,446 |
| By currency | | | | | | | | |
| Canadian dollar | 647 | 593 | 968 | 2,226 | 1,568 | 2,421 | 3,099 | 3,038 |
| Euro | 4,667 | 6,368 | 10,312 | 25,963 | 18,583 | 21,913 | 23,797 | 23,418 |
| Japanese yen | 4,236 | 4,178 | 6,516 | 13,616 | 11,292 | 12,574 | 14,111 | 12,519 |
| Pound | 2,242 | 2,315 | 4,614 | 8,377 | 4,732 | 6,584 | 7,825 | 9,113 |
| Swiss franc | 880 | 800 | 1,344 | 3,964 | 3,034 | 4,213 | 3,812 | 3,802 |
| U.S. dollar | 12,834 | 15,410 | 24,551 | 52,152 | 37,516 | 48,741 | 57,600 | 61,297 |
| Other | 2,746 | 3,689 | 5,687 | 19,668 | 11,657 | 19,145 | 24,472 | 27,705 |
| Interest Rate Contracts | 60,091 | 77,513 | 164,626 | 458,304 | 385,896 | 465,260 | 489,703 | 384,025 |
| By currency | | | | | | | | |
| Canadian dollar | 825 | 781 | 1,298 | 3,286 | 2,631 | 4,247 | 7,507 | 7,353 |
| Euro | 20,692 | 26,185 | 63,006 | 171,877 | 146,085 | 177,831 | 187,363 | 117,849 |
| Japanese yen | 12,391 | 11,799 | 21,103 | 58,056 | 57,425 | 59,509 | 54,812 | 38,607 |
| Pound | 4,588 | 6,215 | 11,867 | 38,619 | 23,532 | 37,813 | 42,244 | 38,127 |
| Swiss franc | 1,414 | 1,362 | 2,651 | 5,253 | 4,940 | 5,114 | 5,357 | 3,749 |
| U.S. dollar | 16,510 | 27,422 | 57,827 | 149,813 | 129,898 | 151,583 | 148,676 | 138,964 |
| Other | 3,195 | 3,673 | 6,872 | 31,400 | 21,385 | 29,163 | 43,744 | 39,377 |
| Equity-Linked Contracts | 1,809 | 1,881 | 4,520 | 10,177 | 6,155 | 5,635 | 6,251 | 7,141 |
| By currency | | | | | | | | |
| U.S. equities | 516 | 376 | 867 | 2,064 | 1,403 | 1,565 | 1,936 | 2,763 |
| European equities | 1,040 | 1,353 | 2,768 | 6,134 | 3,862 | 2,793 | 2,829 | 2,839 |
| Japanese equities | 124 | 56 | 447 | 628 | 364 | 595 | 460 | 296 |
| Other equities | 129 | 97 | 438 | 1,351 | 526 | 682 | 1,026 | 1,244 |

**Sources:** Bank for International Settlements, *Quarterly Review,* various dates. www.bis.org

**TABLE 10–12**  Derivative Financial Instruments Traded on Organized Exchanges *(in billions of dollars)*

| Contract | 1999 | 2001 | 2004 | June 2008 | December 2008 | December 2010 | December 2013 | March 2016 |
|---|---|---|---|---|---|---|---|---|
| Futures | | | | | | | | |
| All markets | $8,294.2 | $ 9,633.5 | $17,661.8 | $28,631.7 | $19,478.0 | $22,312.0 | $26,012.7 | $25,443 |
| Interest rate | 7,913.9 | 9,234.0 | 17,024.8 | 26,892.1 | 18,732.3 | 21,013.4 | 24,577.4 | 25,213 |
| Currency | 36.7 | 65.6 | 84.1 | 176.0 | 95.2 | 170.2 | 230.3 | 230 |
| Equity index | 343.2 | 334.0 | 552.9 | 1,563.5 | 650.5 | 1,128.4 | 1,205.0 | n.a. |
| North America | 3,553.2 | 5,906.4 | 9,777.9 | 14,975.6 | 10,137.0 | 11,863.5 | 13,686.0 | 15,784 |
| Europe | 2,379.2 | 2,444.5 | 5,533.8 | 9,430.5 | 6,506.3 | 6,345.3 | 8,860.2 | 7,083 |
| Asia and Pacific | 2,149.8 | 1,202.0 | 2,200.7 | 3,581.7 | 2,466.5 | 3,168.6 | 2,432.3 | 1,762 |
| Other markets | 211.9 | 80.4 | 149.4 | 643.9 | 368.1 | 934.7 | 1,033.8 | 814 |
| Options | | | | | | | | |
| All markets | $5,258.7 | $14,083.7 | $31,330.3 | $55,655.0 | $38,237.3 | $45,634.6 | $33,796.2 | $47,564 |
| Interest rate | 3,755.5 | 12,492.6 | 28,335.0 | 46,898.2 | 33,978.8 | 40,930.0 | 31,019.9 | 47,410 |
| Currency | 22.4 | 27.4 | 37.2 | 190.8 | 129.3 | 144.2 | 113.9 | 153 |
| Equity index | 1,480.8 | 1,563.7 | 2,958.1 | 8,566.1 | 4,129.1 | 4,560.4 | 2,662.4 | n.a. |
| North America | 3,377.1 | 10,292.2 | 18,119.7 | 27,838.7 | 19,533.4 | 24,353.4 | 11,557.1 | 35,621 |
| Europe | 1,603.2 | 3,698.0 | 12,975.4 | 26,720.3 | 18,115.7 | 19,247.2 | 20,640.3 | 11,636 |
| Asia and Pacific | 240.7 | 62.8 | 169.6 | 463.2 | 219.4 | 383.3 | 657.6 | 13 |
| Other markets | 37.7 | 30.8 | 65.6 | 632.9 | 368.7 | 1,650.7 | 941.3 | 294 |

**Sources:** Bank for International Settlements, *Quarterly Review,* various dates. www.bis.org

$492.91 trillion in 2016 compared to exchange-traded contracts which totaled $73.01 trillion in 2016. In both markets interest rate contracts dominated: $384.02 trillion in notional value in the OTC markets and $72.62 trillion on exchanges. Notice also the impact the financial crisis had on these worldwide markets. In June 2008, total OTC derivative contracts outstanding were $683.81 trillion and contracts traded on exchanges totaled $84.29 trillion. These fell to $547.98 trillion traded in the OTC markets and $57.72 trillion traded on exchanges in December 2008, at the height of the crisis and have continued to fall as of 2016.

　　U.S. markets and currencies dominate global derivative securities markets. On organized exchanges, North American markets traded $51.40 trillion of the $23.01 trillion contracts outstanding in 2016. In the OTC markets, $61.30 trillion of the currency contracts, $138.96 trillion of the interest rate contracts, and $2.76 trillion of the equity-linked contracts were denominated in U.S. dollars. The euro and European derivative securities markets, however, are now a strong second behind, and in some areas actually exceed, the United States. In 2016 European exchange markets traded $18.72 trillion of the total $73.01 trillion contracts. In the OTC markets, $23.42 trillion of the currency contracts, $117.85 trillion of the interest rate contracts, and $2.84 trillion of the equity-linked contracts were denominated in the euro or European currencies. In fact, for every year but 2001 and 2016, more interest rate contracts on the OTC were euro-denominated than U.S. dollar–denominated. Also, in each year more equity-linked contracts on the OTC were euro-denominated than U.S. dollar–denominated.

**DO YOU UNDERSTAND:**

14. *Which are the largest derivative securities markets globally?*

15. *In which currencies most global derivative securities are denominated?*

## SUMMARY

In this chapter, we introduced the major derivative securities and the markets in which they trade. Derivative securities (forwards, futures, options, and swaps) are securities whose value depends on the value of an underlying asset but whose payoff is not guaranteed with cash flows from these assets. Derivative securities can be used as investments on which a trader hopes to directly profit or as hedge instruments used to protect the trader against risk from another asset or liability held. We examined the characteristics of the various securities and the markets in which each trade. We look at how these securities are used by financial institutions to hedge various risks in Chapter 23.

## QUESTIONS

1. What is a derivative security? (*LG 10-1, LG 10-4, LG 10-7*)

2. What are the differences among a spot contract, a forward contract, and a futures contract? (*LG 10-1*)

3. What are the functions of floor brokers and professional traders on the futures exchanges? (*LG 10-2*)

4. What is the purpose of requiring a margin on a futures or option transaction? What is the difference between an initial margin and a maintenance margin? (*LG 10-2*)

5. When is a futures or option trader in a long versus a short position in the derivative contract? (*LG 10-2*)

6. What is the meaning of a Treasury bond futures price quote of 103-13? (*LG 10-3*)

7. Refer to Table 10–4. (*LG 10-3*)

   a. If you think five-year Treasury note prices will fall between August 3, 2016, and December 2016, what type of futures position would you take?

   b. If you think inflation in Japan will increase by more than that in the United States between August 2016 and December 2016, what type of Japanese yen futures position would you take?

   c. If you think stock prices will fall between August 2016 and December 2016, what type of position would you take in the December S&P 500 Index futures contract? What happens if stock prices actually rise?

8. What is an option? How does an option differ from a forward or futures contract? (*LG 10-4*)

9. What is the difference between a call option and a put option? (*LG 10-4*)

10. What must happen to the price of the underlying T-bond futures contract for the purchaser of a call option on T-bond futures to make money? How does the writer of the call option make money? (*LG 10-4*)

11. What must happen to the price of the underlying stock for the purchaser of a put option on the stock to make money? How does the writer of the put option make money? (*LG 10-4*)

12. What are the three ways an option holder can liquidate his or her position? (*LG 10-4*)

13. What factors affect the value of an option? (*LG 10-4*)

14. Who are the major regulators of futures and options markets? (*LG 10-6*)

15. What is a swap? (*LG 10-7*)

16. What is the difference between an interest rate swap and a currency swap? (*LG 10-7*)

17. Which party is the swap buyer and which is the swap seller in an interest rate swap transaction? (*LG 10-7*)

18. A commercial bank has fixed-rate, long-term loans in its asset portfolio and variable-rate CDs in its liability portfolio. Bank managers believe interest rates will increase in the future. What side of a fixed-floating rate swap would the commercial bank need to take to protect against this interest rate risk? (*LG 10-7*)

19. An American firm has British pound–denominated accounts payable on its balance sheet. Managers believe the exchange rate of British pounds to U.S. dollars will depreciate before the accounts will be paid. What type of currency swap should the firm enter? (*LG 10-7*)

20. What are the differences between a cap, a floor, and a collar? When would a firm enter any of these derivative security positions? (*LG 10-8*)

## PROBLEMS

1. Refer to Table 10–4. (*LG 10-3*).
   a. What was the settlement price on the December 2017 Eurodollar futures contract on August 3, 2016?
   b. How many five-year Treasury note futures contracts traded on August 2, 2016?
   c. What is the face value on a Swiss franc currency futures contract on August 3, 2016?
   d. What was the settlement price on the September 2016 Mini DJIA futures contract on August 2, 2016?

2. Suppose you purchase a Treasury bond futures contract at a price of 95 percent of the face value, $100,000. (*LG 10-3*)
   a. What is your obligation when you purchase this futures contract?
   b. Assume that the Treasury bond futures price falls to 94 percent. What is your loss or gain?
   c. Assume that the Treasury bond futures price rises to 97. What is your loss or gain?

3. e**X**cel **Using a Spreadsheet to Calculate Profit and Loss on Futures Transactions:** At the beginning of the quarter, you purchased a $100,000 Treasury bond futures contract for 108-12. Calculate the profit on the futures contract if the price at the end of the quarter is 106-16, 108-20, 110-8, and 112-02. (*LG 10-2*)

| Price at Beginning of Quarter | Price at End of Quarter ⇒ | The Profit or Loss Is |
|---|---|---|
| $100,000 × 108.375 = 108,375 | $100,000 × 106.5 = 106,500 | −$ 1,875 |
| 100,000 × 108.375 = 108,375 | 100,000 × 108.625 = 108,625 | $250 |
| 100,000 × 108.375 = 108,375 | 100,000 × 110.25 = 110,250 | 1,875 |
| 100,000 × 108.375 = 108,375 | 100,000 × 112.0625 = 112,062.5 | 3,687.5 |

4. Tree Row Bank wishes to take a position in Treasury bond futures contracts, which currently have a quote of 95-040. Tree Row thinks interest rates will go up over the period of investment. (*LG 10-2*)
   a. Should the bank go long or short on the futures contracts?
   b. Calculate the net profit to Tree Row Bank if the price of the futures contracts decreases to 94-280.
   c. Calculate the net profit to Tree Row Bank if the price of the futures contracts increases to 95-210.

5. Dudley Savings Bank wishes to take a position in Treasury bond futures contracts, which currently have a quote of 105-100. Dudley Savings thinks interest rates will go down over the period of investment. (*LG 10-2*)
   a. Should the bank go long or short on the futures contracts?
   b. Calculate the net profit to Dudley Savings Bank if the price of the futures contracts increases to 105–220.
   c. Calculate the net profit to Dudley Savings Bank if the price of the futures contracts decreases to 104–280.

6. Suppose an investor has a $1 million long position in T-bond futures. The investor's broker requires a maintenance margin of 4 percent, which is the amount currently in the investor's account. (*LG 10-2*)
   a. Suppose also that the value of the futures contract drops by $50,000 to $950,000. How much will the investor be required to pay his broker to maintain his margin? What will be the value of the investor's account balance (assuming no excess) as a result of the price drop?
   b. If the futures contract drops in value the next day by another $40,000, to $910,000, how much will the investor be required to pay his broker to maintain his margin? What will be the value of the investor's account balance (assuming no excess) as a result of the price drop?
   c. If, on day 3, the futures contract increases in value by $65,000, to $975,000, how much will the investor be able to withdraw from his account to maintain his margin? What will be the value of the investor's account balance (assuming no excess) as a result of the price drop?
   d. Suppose, instead, an investor has a $1 million short position in T-bond futures and that the value of the futures contract increases by $50,000 to $1,050,000. How much will the investor be required to pay his broker to maintain his margin? What will be the value of the investor's account balance (assuming no excess) as a result of the price drop?

7. You have taken a long position in a call option on IBM common stock. The option has an exercise price of $176 and IBM's stock currently trades at $180. The option premium is $5 per contract. (*LG 10-4*)
   a. How much of the option premium is due to intrinsic value versus time value?

**b.** What is your net profit on the option if IBM's stock price increases to $190 at expiration of the option and you exercise the option?

**c.** What is your net profit if IBM's stock price decreases to $170?

8. You have written a call option on Walmart common stock. The option has an exercise price of $74, and Walmart's stock currently trades at $72. The option premium is $1.25 per contract. (*LG 10-4*)

**a.** How much of the option premium is due to intrinsic value versus time value?

**b.** What is your net profit if Walmart's stock price decreases to $70 and stays there until the option expires?

**c.** What is your net profit on the option if Walmart's stock price increases to $80 at expiration of the option and the option holder exercises the option?

9. You have purchased a put option on Pfizer common stock. The option has an exercise price of $27 and Pfizer's stock currently trades at $29. The option premium is $0.50 per contract. (*LG 10-4*)

**a.** What is your net profit on the option if Pfizer's stock price does not change over the life of the option?

**b.** What is your net profit on the option if Pfizer's stock price falls to $23 and you exercise the option?

10. You have written a put option on Diebold Inc. common stock. The option has an exercise price of $28 and Diebold's stock currently trades at $30.50. The option premium is $0.75 per contract. (*LG 10-4*)

**a.** What is your net profit if Diebold's stock price increases to $32 and stays there until the option expires?

**b.** What is your net profit on the option if Diebold's stock price decreases to $25 at expiration of the option and the option holder exercises the option?

11. Refer to Table 10–6. (*LG 10-5*)

**a.** How many ExxonMobil October 2016 $90.00 put options were outstanding at the open of trading on August 3, 2016?

**b.** What was the closing price of a 10-year Treasury note December 13300 futures call option on August 3, 2016?

**c.** What was the closing and dollar price of a December 2160 call option on the S&P 500 Stock Index futures contract on August 3, 2016?

**d.** What was the open interest on September 2016 put options (with an exercise price of 185) on the DJ Industrial Average stock index on August 3, 2016?

12. You have purchased a call option contract on Johnson & Johnson common stock. The option has an exercise price of $89.00 and J & J's stock currently trades at $90.43. The option premium is quoted at $2.17 per contract. (*LG 10-4*)

**a.** Calculate your net profit on the option contract if J & J's stock price rises to $94.00 and you exercise the option.

**b.** Calculate your net profit on the option contract if J & J's stock price falls to $89.50 and you exercise the option.

**c.** If J & J's stock price falls to $89.50 show that it is more profitable to exercise than not exercise the option you have purchased.

13. You have purchased a put option on Kimberly Clark common stock. The option has an exercise price of $95.00 and

Kimberly Clark's stock currently trades at $96.18. The option premium is $1.25 per contract. (*LG 10-4*)

**a.** Calculate your net profit on the option if Kimberly Clark's stock price falls to $93.00 and you exercise the option.

**b.** Calculate your net profit on the option if Kimberly Clark's stock price does not change over the life of the option.

14. You buy an at-the-money March call option on MMC Corp. common stock, which has a strike price of 15 and a premium of 2.83. What must happen to the price of MMC Corp. stock for you to make a profit? (*LG 10-4*)

15. A stock is currently selling for $75 per share. You could purchase a call with a strike price of $70 for $7. You could purchase a put with a strike price of $70 for $2. Calculate the intrinsic value of the call option. (*LG 10-4*)

16. An FI has purchased a $200 million cap of 9 percent at a premium of 0.65 percent of face value. A $200 million floor of 4 percent is also available at a premium of 0.69 percent of face value. (*LG 10-8*)

**a.** If interest rates rise to 10 percent, what is the amount received by the FI? What are the net savings after deducting the premium?

**b.** If the FI also purchases a floor, what are the net savings if interest rates rise to 11 percent? What are the net savings if interest rates fall to 3 percent?

**c.** If, instead, the FI sells (writes) the floor, what are the net savings if interest rates rise to 11 percent? What if they fall to 3 percent?

17. An insurance company owns $50 million of floating-rate bonds yielding LIBOR plus 1 percent. These loans are financed with $50 million of fixed-rate guaranteed investment contracts (GICs) costing 10 percent. A finance company has $50 million of auto loans with a fixed rate of 14 percent. The loans are financed with $50 million in CDs at a variable rate of LIBOR plus 4 percent. (*LG 10-7*)

**a.** What is the risk exposure of the insurance company?

**b.** What is the risk exposure of the finance company?

**c.** What would be the cash flow goals of each company if they were to enter into a swap agreement?

**d.** Which company would be the buyer and which company would be the seller in the swap?

**e.** Diagram the direction of the relevant cash flows for the swap arrangement.

18. A commercial bank has $200 million of floating-rate loans yielding the T-bill rate plus 2 percent. These loans are financed with $200 million of fixed-rate deposits costing 9 percent. A savings bank has $200 million of mortgages with a fixed rate of 13 percent. They are financed with $200 million in CDs with a variable rate of T-bill rate plus 3 percent. (*LG 10-7*)

**a.** Discuss the type of interest rate risk each institution faces.

**b.** Propose a swap that would result in each institution having the same type of asset and liability cash flows.

**c.** Show that this swap would be acceptable to both parties.

**19.** Consider the following two financial institutions:

Money Center Bank:

| Assets | | Liabilities | |
|---|---|---|---|
| C&I loans (CD rate + 4%) | $400m | Medium-term notes (4-year, 8%) | $400m |

Savings Bank:

| Assets | | Liabilities | |
|---|---|---|---|
| Fixed-rate mortgages (4-year, 9.5%) | $400m | Short-term CDs (1-year) | $400m |

Managers of the money center bank are concerned that interest rates may fall over the next four years, while managers of the savings bank are concerned that interest rates may rise over the next four years.

On the balance sheet, the money center bank could attract an additional $400 million in short-term deposits that are indexed to the CD rate (say, CD plus 2 percent) in a manner similar to its loans. The proceeds of these deposits can be used to pay off the medium-term notes. Alternatively, the bank could go off the balance sheet and sell an interest rate swap. On the balance sheet, the savings bank could issue long-term notes with a maturity equal or close to that on the mortgages (at, say, 9 percent). The proceeds of the sale of the notes can be used to pay off the CDs and reduce the interest rate risk. Alternatively, the savings bank could hedge this interest rate risk exposure by going off the balance sheet and buying a swap.

The two FIs enter a swap agreement such that the savings bank sends fixed payments of 8 percent per year of the notional $400 million value of the swap to the money center bank, each year for 4 years, to allow the money center bank to cover fully the coupon interest payments on its note issue. In return, the money center bank sends annual payments indexed to the one-year CD rate + 1 percent, for 5 years, to help the savings bank cover the cost of refinancing its one-year renewable LIBOR deposits. (*LG 10-7*)

**a.** Calculate the gain over the market rates for the money center bank and the savings bank from the swap.

**b.** Assume that the realized or actual path of CD rates over the four-year life of the swap contract is as follows:

| End of Year | CD Rate |
|---|---|
| 1 | 8.0% |
| 2 | 7.0 |
| 3 | 6.0 |
| 4 | 4.5 |

Calculate the swap payments made by the money center bank and the savings bank over the four-year swap period.

**c.** Calculate the net income for the money center bank and the savings bank over the four-year swap period.

**20.** Consider the following two financial institutions:

Bank:

| Assets | | Liabilities | |
|---|---|---|---|
| C&I loans (T-bill + 4%) | $200m | Medium-term notes (5-year, 9% fixed) | $200m |

Savings Association:

| Assets | | Liabilities | |
|---|---|---|---|
| Fixed-rate mortgages (5-year, 13% fixed) | $200m | Short-term CDs (T-bill + 3%) | $200m |

Managers of the bank are concerned that interest rates may fall over the next four years, while managers of the savings association are concerned that interest rates may rise over the next four years.

On the balance sheet, the bank could attract an additional $200 million in short-term deposits that are indexed to the T-bill rate (say, T-bill plus 2 ½ percent) in a manner similar to its loans. The proceeds of these deposits can be used to pay off the medium-term notes. Alternatively, the bank could go off the balance sheet and sell an interest rate swap. On the balance sheet, the savings association could issue long-term notes with a maturity equal or close to that on the mortgages (at, say, 11 percent). The proceeds of the sale of the notes can be used to pay off the CDs and reduce the interest rate risk. Alternatively, the savings association could hedge this interest rate risk exposure by going off the balance sheet and buying a swap.

The two FIs enter a swap agreement such that the savings association sends fixed payments of 10 percent per year of the notional $200 million value of the swap to the bank, each year for 5 years, to allow the bank to cover fully the coupon interest payments on its note issue. In return, the bank sends annual payments indexed to the one-year T-bill + 2 ¼ percent, for 5 years, to help the savings association cover the cost of refinancing its one-year renewable T-bill deposits. (*LG 10-7*)

**a.** Calculate the gain over the market rates for the bank and the savings association from the swap.

**b.** Assume that the realized or actual path of T-bill rates over the five-year life of the swap contract is as follows:

| End of Year | CD Rate |
|---|---|
| 1 | 4% |
| 2 | 3 |
| 3 | 5 |
| 4 | 6 |
| 5 | 5 |

Calculate the swap payments made by the bank and the savings association over the five-year swap period.

**c.** Calculate the net income for the bank and the savings association over the four-year swap period.

## SEARCH THE SITE

Go to the Bank for International Settlements website at **www.bis.org** and find the most recent data on the amount of derivatives traded worldwide over the counter and on organized exchanges using the following steps. Click on "Statistics" and then on "+ Derivatives statistics." First, click on "OTC derivatives—the semiannual survey" and then on "D5.1 Foreign exchange, interest rate, equity linked contracts PDF." Second, click on "Exchange-traded derivatives" and then on "D1 Exchange-traded futures and options by location of exchange PDF." This downloads a file onto your computer that contains the relevant data, in Tables 10–11 and 10–12.

**Questions**

1. By what percentage have these values changed since 2016 as reported in Tables 10–11 and 10–12?
2. What countries are currently the biggest traders of derivative securities?

---

### APPENDIX 10A: Black–Scholes Option Pricing Model

# This appendix is available through Connect or your course instructor.

# Commercial Banks

*Industry Overview*

## Learning Goals

**LG 11-1** *Define what a commercial bank is.*

**LG 11-2** *Identify the main assets held by commercial banks.*

**LG 11-3** *Identify the main liabilities held by commercial banks.*

**LG 11-4** *Understand the types of off-balance-sheet activities that commercial banks undertake.*

**LG 11-5** *Discuss which factors have motivated the significant decrease in the number of commercial banks.*

**LG 11-6** *Evaluate the performance of the commercial banking industry in recent years.*

**LG 11-7** *Know the main regulators of commercial banks.*

**LG 11-8** *List the world's biggest banks.*

## COMMERCIAL BANKS AS A SECTOR OF THE FINANCIAL INSTITUTIONS INDUSTRY: CHAPTER OVERVIEW

The largest (in dollar value of assets) FI group is commercial banks, also called *depository institutions* because a significant proportion of their funds come from customer deposits. Savings institutions and credit unions (discussed in Chapter 14) are also depository institutions. Chapters 11 through Chapter 13 describe commercial banks, their financial statements, and the regulations that govern their operations. As we examine the structure of commercial banks and their financial statements, notice a distinguishing feature between them and nonfinancial firms illustrated in Figure 11–1. Specifically, commercial banks' major assets are loans (financial assets) and their major liabilities are deposits. Just the opposite is true for nonfinancial firms, whose deposits are listed as assets on their balance sheets and whose loans are listed as liabilities. In contrast to commercial banks, nonfinancial firms' major assets are nonfinancial (tangible) assets such as buildings and

**Figure 11–1** Differences in Balance Sheets of Commercial Banks and Nonfinancial Firms

| Commercial Banks | | Nonfinancial Firms | |
|---|---|---|---|
| Assets | Liabilities and Equity | Assets | Liabilities and Equity |
| Loans | Deposits | Deposits | Loans |
| Other financial assets | | Other financial assets | |
| Other nonfinancial assets | Other liabilities and equity | Other nonfinancial assets | Other liabilities and equity |

**Figure 11–2** Interaction between Commercial Banks and Nonfinancial Firms

machinery. Indeed, as illustrated in Figure 11–2, commercial banks provide loans to, and accept deposits from, nonfinancial firms (and individuals), while nonfinancial firms provide deposits to, and obtain loans from, commercial banks.

During the recent financial crisis, several nondepository financial institutions (e.g., investment banks Goldman Sachs and Morgan Stanley and finance company GMAC) requested and were allowed to convert to bank holding companies. The change was recognition that their models of finance and investing had become too risky and the FIs needed the cushion of bank deposits that kept some of the bigger commercial banks like J.P. Morgan Chase relatively safe during the crisis. By becoming bank holding companies, the firms agreed to significantly tighter regulations and much closer supervision by bank examiners from government agencies rather than only the Securities and Exchange Commission. The new charters required the FIs to be subject to more disclosure, hold higher capital reserves, and take less risk. However, the new bank holding companies also gained access to the full array of the Federal Reserve lending facilities, something the failed investment bank Lehman Brothers did not have.

As we discussed in Chapter 1, depository institutions, and commercial banks in particular, perform several services that are essential to the efficient functioning of the financial markets in the United States. For example, because deposits are a significant component of the money supply, commercial banks play a key role in the transmission of monetary policy for the central bank to the rest of the economy. Further, commercial banks are special in that the efficiency with which they provide payment services directly benefits the economy. Finally, commercial banks offer maturity intermediation services to the economy. Specifically, by maturity mismatching, commercial banks can produce new types of contracts such as long-term mortgage loans to households while still raising funds with short-term liability contracts such as deposits. Because of the vital nature of the services they provide, commercial banks are regulated to protect against a disruption in the provision of these services and the cost this would impose on the economy and society at large. Our attention in this chapter focuses on (1) the size, structure, and composition of the commercial banking industry; (2) its balance sheets and recent trends; (3) the industry's recent performance; and (4) its regulators.

## DEFINITION OF A COMMERCIAL BANK

**LG 11-1**

Commercial banks represent the largest group of depository institutions measured by asset size. They perform functions similar to those of savings institutions and credit unions—they accept deposits (liabilities) and make loans (assets). As we discuss in more detail in Chapter 14, commercial banks are distinguishable from savings institutions and credit unions, however, in the size and composition of their loans and deposits. Specifically, while deposits are the major source of funding, commercial bank liabilities usually include several types of *non*deposit sources of funds (such as subordinated notes and debentures). Moreover, their loans are broader in range, including consumer, commercial, international, and real estate loans. Commercial banks are regulated separately from savings institutions and credit unions. Within the banking industry, the structure and composition of assets and liabilities also vary significantly for banks of different asset sizes.

### DO YOU UNDERSTAND:

1. *What the three categories of depository institutions are?*
2. *What distinguishes a commercial bank from nonfinancial firms?*

## BALANCE SHEETS AND RECENT TRENDS

Chapter 12 provides a detailed discussion of the financial statements (balance sheets and income statements) of commercial banks and how financial statements are used by regulators, stockholders, depositors, and creditors to evaluate bank performance. In this chapter, we present a brief introduction to the commercial bank industry balance sheets and their recent performance, highlighting trends in each.

### Assets

**LG 11-2**

Consider the aggregate balance sheet (in Table 11–1) and the percentage distributions (in Figure 11–3) for all U.S. commercial banks as of 2016. Cash assets ($1,798.7 billion in 2016) represent 11.8 percent of total assets, and other assets (premises, equipment, other real estate owned, $1,183.8 billion in 2016) are 7.8 percent of total assets. The majority of the assets held by commercial banks are loans. Total loans amounted to $8,161.2 billion, or 53.7 percent of total assets, and fell into four broad classes: business or commercial and industrial loans; commercial and residential real estate loans; individual loans, such as consumer loans for auto purchases and credit card loans; and all other loans, such as loans to emerging-market countries.[1]

Investment securities consist of items such as interest-bearing deposits purchased from other FIs, federal funds sold to other banks, repurchase agreements (RPs or repos), U.S. Treasury and agency securities, municipal securities issued by states and political subdivisions, mortgage-backed securities, and other debt and equity securities. In 2016, the investment portfolio totaled $4,059.1 billion, or 26.7 percent of total assets. U.S. government securities such as U.S. Treasury bonds totaled $2,123.8 billion, with other securities making up the remainder. Investment securities generate interest income for the bank and are also used for trading and liquidity management purposes. Many investment securities held by banks are highly liquid, have low default risk, and can usually be traded in secondary markets (see Chapter 12).

While loans are the main revenue-generating assets for banks, investment securities provide banks with liquidity. Unlike manufacturing companies, commercial banks and other financial institutions are exposed to high levels of liquidity risk. Liquidity risk is the risk that arises when a financial institution's liability holders such as depositors demand cash for the financial claims they hold with the financial institution. Because of the extensive levels of deposits held by banks (see below), they must hold significant amounts of cash and investment securities to make sure they can meet the demand from their liability holders if and when they liquidate the claims they hold.

---

1. The reserve for loan and lease losses is a contra-asset account representing an estimate by the bank's management of the percentage of gross loans (and leases) that will have to be "charged-off" due to future defaults (see Chapter 12).

**TABLE 11–1**   Balance Sheet *(all U.S. commercial banks, in billions of dollars)*

**Assets**

| | | |
|---|---:|---:|
| Total cash assets | | $ 1,798.7 |
| U.S. government securities | $2,123.8 | |
| Federal funds and repurchase agreements | 379.3 | |
| Other | 1,556.0 | |
| Investment securities | | 4,059.1 |
| Commercial and industrial | $1,849.2 | |
| Real estate | 3,965.8 | |
| Individual | 1,343.5 | |
| All other | 1,115.9 | |
| Less: Reserve for loan losses | 111.3 | |
| Unearned income | 1.9 | |
| Total loans | | 8,161.2 |
| Other assets | | 1,183.8 |
| Total assets | | $15,202.8 |

**Liabilities and Equity**

| | | |
|---|---:|---:|
| Transaction accounts | $1,797.2 | |
| Nontransaction accounts | 9,771.6 | |
| Total deposits | | $11,568.8 |
| Borrowings | | 1,574.9 |
| Other liabilities | | 339.4 |
| Total liabilities | | $13,483.1 |
| Equity | | $ 1,719.7 |

**Source:** Federal Deposit Insurance Corporation, *Statistics on Banking,* First Quarter 2016. www.fdic.gov

A major inference we can draw from this asset structure (and the importance of loans in this asset structure) is that the major risks faced by modern commercial bank managers are credit or default risk, liquidity risk, interest rate risk, and, ultimately, insolvency risk (see Chapters 19 through 24). Because commercial banks are highly leveraged and therefore hold little equity (see below) compared to total assets, even a relatively small amount of loan defaults can wipe out the equity of a bank, leaving it insolvent. Losses such as those due to defaults are charged off against the equity (stockholders' stake) in a bank. Additions

**Figure 11–3**   Distribution of Commercial Bank Assets, Liabilities, and Equity, 2016

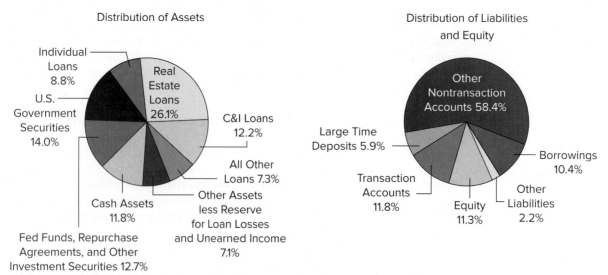

**Source:** Federal Deposit Insurance Corporation, *Quarterly Banking Profile,* First Quarter 2016. www.fdic.gov

to the reserve for loan and lease losses account (and, in turn, the expense account "provisions for losses on loans and leases") to meet *expected* defaults reduce retained earnings and, thus, reduce equity of the bank (see Chapter 12). *Unexpected* defaults (e.g., due to a sudden major recession) are meant to be written off against the remainder of the bank's equity (e.g., its retained earnings and funds raised from share offerings). We look at recent loan performance below. Loan sales and securitization—the packaging and selling of loans and other assets backed by loans or other securities issued by the FI—are mechanisms that FIs have used to hedge their credit risk exposure. In addition, loan sales and securitization have allowed FI asset portfolios to become more liquid and have provided an important source of fee income (with FIs acting as servicing agents for the assets sold). We look at these activities in detail in Chapter 24.

Loans and investment securities continue to be the primary assets of the banking industry. Commercial loans are relatively more important for the larger banks, while consumer loans, small business loans, and residential mortgages are more important for small banks. Each of these types of loans creates credit and, to varying extents, liquidity risks for the banks. The security portfolio normally is a source of liquidity and interest rate risk, especially with the increased use of various types of mortgage-backed securities and structured notes. In certain environments, each of these risks can create operational and performance problems for a bank. Figure 11–4 shows broad trends over the 1951–2016 period in the four principal earning asset areas of commercial banks: business loans (or commercial and industrial loans, C&I), securities, mortgages, and consumer loans. Although business loans were the major asset on bank balance sheets between 1965 and 1987, they have dropped in importance (as a proportion of the balance sheet) since 1987. The major reason for this has been the rise in nonbank loan substitutes, especially commercial paper. As discussed in Chapter 5, commercial paper is a short-term debt instrument issued by corporations either directly or via an underwriter to institutional investors in the financial markets, such as money market mutual funds. By using commercial paper, a corporation can sidestep banks and the loan market to raise funds, often at rates below those that banks charge.[2] Moreover, since only the largest corporations can access the commercial paper market, banks are often left with a pool of increasingly smaller and riskier borrowers in the commercial and industrial (C&I) loan market. This makes credit risk evaluation more important today than ever before.

**Figure 11–4**  Portfolio Shift: U.S. Commercial Banks' Financial Assets

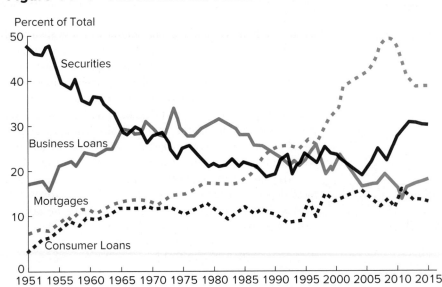

**Sources:** Federal Deposit Insurance Corporation, *Statistics on Banking,* various issues. www.fdic.gov

---

2. This is because, unlike banks, commercial paper issuers do not have to pay the regulatory "costs" associated with capital requirements that are imposed by bank regulators on loans.

As business loans have decreased, mortgages have increased in importance. These trends reflect a number of long-term and temporary influences. Important long-term influences have been, as mentioned above, the growth of the commercial paper market (see Chapter 5) and the public bond markets (see Chapter 6), which have become competitive and alternative funding sources to commercial bank loans for major corporations. Another factor has been the securitization of mortgage loans (see Chapters 7 and 24), which entails the pooling and packaging of mortgage loans for sale in the form of bonds. A more temporary influence was the so-called credit crunch and decline in the demand for business loans as a result of the economic downturn and recession in 1989–1992 and 2001–2002. The financial crisis and the recession of 2008–2009 resulted in a reduction in all areas of lending and an increase in banks' holdings of less risky securities investments (e.g., Treasury securities, federal funds, and U.S. government agency securities).

### Liabilities

**LG 11-3**

Commercial banks have two major sources of funds (other than the equity provided by owners and stockholders): (1) deposits and (2) borrowed or other liability funds. As noted previously, a major difference between banks and other firms is their high leverage or debt-to-assets ratio. For example, banks had an average ratio of equity to assets of 11.3 percent in 2016; this implies that 88.7 percent of assets were funded by debt, either deposits or borrowed funds.

Note that in Table 11–1, which shows the aggregate balance sheet of U.S. banks, in 2016, deposits amounted to $11,568.8 billion (76.1 percent of total assets) and borrowings and other liabilities were $1,574.9 and $339.4 billion (10.4 percent and 2.2 percent of total assets), respectively. Of the total stock of deposits, transaction accounts represented 15.5 percent of total deposits (and 11.8 percent of total assets), or $1,797.2 billion. **Transaction accounts** are checkable deposits that are either demand deposits or **NOW accounts** (negotiable order of withdrawal accounts). Since their introduction in 1980, NOW accounts have dominated the transaction accounts of banks. Nevertheless, since limitations are imposed on the ability of corporations to hold such accounts, demand deposits are still held. NOW accounts may be held only by individuals, sole proprietorships, nonprofit organizations, governmental units, and pension funds. Historically, demand deposits were prohibited from paying interest. Thus, businesses could not earn interest on their bank demand deposits. However, as of July 2011, the federal prohibition against the payment of interest on demand deposits, including business checking accounts, was repealed.

**transaction accounts**

*The sum of noninterest-bearing demand deposits and interest-bearing checking accounts.*

**NOW account**

*An interest-bearing checking account.*

The second major segment of deposits is retail or household savings and time deposits, normally individual account holdings of less than $100,000. Important components of bank retail savings accounts are small nontransaction accounts, which include passbook savings accounts and retail time deposits. Small nontransaction accounts compose 76.7 percent of total deposits (and 58.4 percent of total assets). However, this disguises an important trend in the supply of these deposits to banks. Specifically, the amount held of retail savings and time deposits has been falling in recent years, largely as a result of competition from money market mutual funds. These funds pay a competitive rate of interest based on wholesale money market rates by pooling and investing funds (see Chapter 17) while requiring relatively small-denomination investments.

The third major segment of deposit funds is large time deposits ($100,000 or more);[3] these deposits amounted to $895.0 billion, or approximately 7.7 percent of total deposits (and 5.9 percent of total assets) in 2016. These are primarily **negotiable certificates of deposit (CDs)** (deposit claims with promised interest rates and fixed maturities of at least 14 days) that can be resold to outside investors in an organized secondary market. As such, they are usually distinguished from retail time deposits by their negotiability and secondary market liquidity.

**negotiable certificates of deposit (CDs)**

*Fixed-maturity interest-bearing deposits with face values of $100,000 or more that can be resold in the secondary market.*

Nondeposit liabilities comprise borrowings and other liabilities that total 12.6 percent of total assets, or $1,914.3 billion. These categories include a broad array of instruments,

---

3. $100,000 was the cap for explicit coverage under FDIC-provided deposit insurance. This was increased to $250,000 during the recent financial crisis. We discuss this in more detail in Chapter 13.

such as purchases of federal funds (bank reserves) on the interbank market and repurchase agreements (temporary swaps of securities for federal funds) at the short end of the maturity spectrum, to the issuance of notes and bonds at the longer end (see Chapters 5 and 6). We discuss commercial banks' use of each of these in Chapter 12.

Overall, the liability structure of banks' balance sheets tends to reflect a shorter maturity structure than that of their asset portfolio. Further, relatively more liquid instruments such as deposits and interbank borrowings are used to fund relatively less liquid assets such as loans. Thus, interest rate risk—or maturity mismatch risk—and liquidity risk are key exposure concerns for bank managers (see Chapters 19 through 24).

### Equity

Commercial bank equity capital (11.3 percent of total liabilities and equity in 2016) consists mainly of common and preferred stock (listed at par value), surplus or additional paid-in capital, and retained earnings. Regulators require banks to hold a minimum level of equity capital to act as a buffer against losses from their on- and off-balance-sheet activities (see Chapter 13). Because of the relatively low cost of deposit funding, banks tend to hold equity close to the minimum levels set by regulators. As we discuss in Chapters 13 and 22 , this impacts banks' exposure to risk and their ability to grow—both on and off the balance sheet—over time.

Part of the Troubled Asset Relief Program (TARP) of 2008–2009 was the Capital Purchase Program, which was intended to encourage U.S. financial institutions to build capital to increase the flow of financing to U.S. businesses and consumers and to support the U.S. economy. Under the program, the Treasury purchased over $200 billion of senior preferred equity. The senior preferred shares rank senior to common stock should the bank be closed. In addition to capital injections received as part of the Capital Purchase Program, TARP provided additional emergency funding to Citigroup ($25 billion) and Bank of America ($20 billion). Through the summer of 2016, $245 billion of TARP capital injections had been allocated to depository institutions (DIs), of which $239.4 billion had been paid back plus a return of $35.7 billion in dividends and assessments to the government. The After the Crisis box describes the TARP Capital Purchase Program.

As part of the 2010 Wall Street Reform and Consumer Protection Act, the largest banks are subject to annual stress tests, designed to ensure that the banks are properly capitalized. Scenarios used as part of the stress tests range from mild to calamitous, with the most extreme including a 5 percent decline in gross domestic product, an unemployment rate of 12 percent, and a volatile stock market that loses half its value. The original stress test was announced in late February 2009 when the Obama administration announced that it would conduct a "stress test" of the 19 largest U.S. DIs, which would measure the ability of these DIs to withstand a protracted economic slump (an unemployment rate above 10 percent and home prices dropping another 25 percent). Results of the stress test showed that 10 of the 19 DIs needed to raise a total of $74.6 billion in capital. Within a month of the May 7, 2009, release of the results the DIs had raised $149.45 billion of capital. As part of the 2016 stress tests, the worst-case scenario includes a deep and prolonged global recession accompanied by a period of heightened corporate financial stress and negative yields for short-term U.S. Treasury securities. In this scenario, the unemployment rate increases to 10 percent, the level of real GDP falls 6.25 percent, housing prices decline 25 percent, the annualized rate of change in the consumer price index (CPI) rises to 1.25 percent, equity prices fall approximately 50 percent, and equity market volatility increases sharply.

### Off-Balance-Sheet Activities

**LG 11-4**

The balance sheet itself does not reflect the total scope of bank activities. Banks conduct many fee-related activities off the balance sheet. Off-balance-sheet (OBS) activities are becoming increasingly important, in terms of their dollar value and the income they generate for banks—especially as the ability of banks to attract high-quality loan applicants and deposits becomes ever more difficult. OBS activities include issuing various types of guarantees (such as letters of credit), which often have a strong insurance underwriting element,

## The TARP Program

In the wake of Lehman Brothers's bankruptcy, the U.S. Congress passed the Emergency Economic Stabilization Act (EESA) of 2008 to "restore the liquidity and stability to the financial system." The act authorized the Treasury Department to establish the Troubled Asset Relief Program (TARP) and to spend up to $700 billion to "bail out" the U.S. financial system. In the original plan presented by then-secretary of the treasury Henry Paulson, the government would use TARP funds to buy distressed assets in financial institutions. On October 14, 2008, Paulson announced a revision in TARP implementation in which the Treasury directly injected $250 billion of TARP funds (through the Capital Purchase Program [CPP]) into the U.S. banking system through the purchase of senior preferred stock and warrants in qualifying financial institutions (QFIs). The first $125 billion was to be invested in nine large, systemically important bank holding companies. The remaining $125 billion was to be made available for other banks. The amount of CPP capital that a QFI could apply for was restricted to between 1 percent and 3 percent of the QFI's risk-weighted assets. The Treasury was paid a 5 percent dividend on the preferred stock in the first five years and a 9 percent dividend thereafter. Over 700 of the approximate 8,300 depository institutions were accepted into CPP, receiving $245 billion in capital infusions. The largest investment was $25 billion and the smallest was $301,000.

To apply for CPP investments, banks were asked to submit their applications to their primary federal regulator: the Federal Reserve (the Fed), the Federal Deposit Insurance Corporation (FDIC), the Office of the Comptroller of the Currency (OCC), or the Office of Thrift Supervision (OTS). Based on recommendations from federal banking regulators, the Treasury made the final decision on whether or not to make the capital purchase. Many institutions decided to apply, while others opted out. Some were asked by federal regulators not to apply. A large number of banks withdrew their applications. However, because the Treasury did not release details of the applicant list to the public, it is not known how many banks withdrew their TARP applications voluntarily despite being qualified and how many withdrew because they did not meet the requirements and were encouraged to withdraw by the banking regulators. The application period for publicly held financial institutions to participate in CPP closed on November 14, 2008. The final investment under the CPP was made in December 2009.

To encourage banks to participate in CPP, the Treasury made the terms of CPP investments quite attractive. In the first nine CPP transactions, the Treasury paid $125 billion for financial claims worth only $89–$112 billion (these banks held over half of the banking industry's assets). The Congressional Oversight Panel issued an evaluation report on February 6, 2009, concluding that "[for] all capital purchases made in 2008 under TARP, the Treasury paid $254 billion, for which it received assets worth approximately $176 billion, a shortfall of $78 billion."

The attractive terms of CPP induced thousands of applicants, among which only about 700 financial institutions received any TARP funds.

The Capital Purchase Program is often characterized as a program for "big banks." Indeed, $163.5 billion of all CPP funds were allotted to the largest 19 banks. Further, many believe that small institutions were not able to and did not participate in the program. In fact, because of financial obligations associated with CPP, federal regulators did not initially allow temporarily unhealthy community banks to participate in CPP because such institutions would risk the Treasury's investment. However, on May 13, 2009, Treasury Secretary Timothy Geithner announced that the Treasury would reopen the application window for participation in the CPP to banks with total assets under $500 million and increase the amount that could be invested from 3 percent of risk-weighted assets to 5 percent of risk-weighted assets. In the end, smaller financial institutions made up the vast majority of participants in the CPP. By the time it closed on December 31, 2009, of the 707 applications approved and funded by the Treasury through the CPP, over half were institutions with less than $500 million in assets.

As the TARP CPP program progressed, many, particularly healthy, banks realized that the costs of participating in TARP were higher than had been expected. As public outrage swelled over the rapidly growing cost of "bailing out" financial institutions, the Obama administration and lawmakers attached more and more restrictions on banks that

*continued*

received TARP funds. For example, with the acceptance of TARP funds, banks were told to put off evictions and modify mortgages for distressed homeowners, let shareholders vote on executive pay packages, slash dividends, and withdraw job offers to foreign citizens. Some bankers stated that conditions of the TARP program had become so onerous that they wanted to return the bailout money as soon as regulators set up a process to accept the repayments. For example, just three months after receiving TARP funds, Signature Bank of New York announced that because of new executive pay restrictions assessed as a part of the acceptance of TARP funds, it notified the Treasury that it intended to return the $120 million it had received. As a result, many banks, particularly those that were sufficiently healthy, repaid their TARP funds quickly.

As of August 2013, banks had repaid $272 billion through principal and interest payment—representing a $27 billion positive return to taxpayers so far. In late 2008 few would have predicted that TARP would end up with a profit.

**Source:** Authors' research

and making future commitments to lend. Both services generate additional fee income for banks. Off-balance-sheet activities also involve engaging in derivative transactions—futures, forwards, options, and swaps.

Under current accounting standards, such activities are not shown on the current balance sheet. Rather, an item or activity is an **off-balance-sheet (OBS) asset** if, when a contingent event occurs, the item or activity moves onto the asset side of the balance sheet or an income item is realized on the income statement. Conversely, an item or activity is an **off-balance-sheet (OBS) liability** if, when a contingent event occurs, the item or activity moves onto the liability side of the balance sheet or an expense item is realized on the income statement.

By undertaking off-balance-sheet activities, banks hope to earn additional fee income to complement declining margins or spreads on their traditional lending business. At the same time, they can avoid regulatory costs or "taxes" since reserve requirements and deposit insurance premiums are not levied on off-balance-sheet activities (see Chapter 13). Thus, banks have both earnings and regulatory "tax-avoidance" incentives to undertake activities off their balance sheets.

Off-balance-sheet activities, however, can involve risks that add to the overall insolvency exposure of a financial intermediary (FI). Indeed, at the very heart of the financial crisis were losses associated with off-balance-sheet mortgage-backed securities created and held by FIs. These losses resulted in the failure, acquisition, or bailout of some of the largest FIs and a near meltdown of the world's financial and economic systems. Thus, off-balance-sheet activities and instruments have risk-reducing as well as risk-increasing attributes, and, when used appropriately, they can reduce or hedge an FI's interest rate, credit, and foreign exchange risks.

We show the notional, or face, value of bank OBS activities and their distribution and growth for 1992 to 2016 in Table 11–2. Notice the relative growth in the notional dollar value of OBS activities in Table 11–2. The notional value of OBS activities at commercial banks was $10,075.8 billion in 1992 compared to $3,476.4 billion of on-balance-sheet activities. By 2013, the notional value of OBS bank activities was $239,752.7 billion (compared to the $13,362.6 billion value of on-balance-sheet activities) before falling to $203,687.9 billion in 2016. It should be noted that the notional or face value of OBS activities does not accurately reflect the risk to the bank undertaking such activities. The potential for the bank to gain or lose on the contract is based on the possible change in the market value of the contract over the life of the contract rather than the notional or face value of the contract, normally less than 3 percent of the notional value of an OBS contract.

The use of derivative contracts accelerated during the 1992–2013 period and accounted for much of the growth in OBS activity. Along with the growth in the notional value of OBS activities, banks have seen significant growth in the percentage of their total operating income

**off-balance-sheet (OBS) asset**

*When an event occurs, this item moves onto the asset side of the balance sheet or income is realized on the income statement.*

**off-balance-sheet (OBS) liability**

*When an event occurs, this item moves onto the liability side of the balance sheet or an expense is realized on the income statement.*

**TABLE 11–2**  Aggregate Volume of Off-Balance-Sheet Commitments and Contingencies by U.S. Commercial Banks  *(in billions of dollars)*

| | 1992 | 2004 | 2007 | 2010 | 2013 | 2016 | Distribution 2016 | Percentage Increase from 1992 through 2016 |
|---|---|---|---|---|---|---|---|---|
| Commitments to lend | $ 1,272.0 | $ 5,686.4 | $ 7,236.9 | $ 5,113.5 | $ 5,344.6 | $ 6,356.6 | 3.1% | 399.7% |
| Future and forward contracts (excludes FX) | | | | | | | | |
| On commodities and equities | 26.3 | 123.7 | 251.2 | 245.3 | 332.5 | 259.9 | 0.1 | 888.2 |
| On interest rates | 1,738.1 | 6,923.0 | 9,116.9 | 23,987.0 | 31,216.0 | 22,011.1 | 10.8 | 1,166.4 |
| Notional amount of credit derivatives | 8.6 | 1,909.3 | 15,862.8 | 14,150.8 | 13,900.8 | 7,417.1 | 3.6 | 86,145.3 |
| Standby contracts and other option contracts | | | | | | | | |
| Option contracts on interest rates | 1,012.7 | 15,340.8 | 20,984.4 | 27,015.4 | 25,871.0 | 25,137.4 | 12.3 | 2,382.2 |
| Option contracts on foreign exchange | 494.8 | 1,627.2 | 4,024.7 | 3,336.0 | 5,617.1 | 6,219.8 | 3.1 | 1,157.0 |
| Option contracts on commodities | 60.3 | 1,020.2 | 2,715.9 | 1,723.7 | 2,249.2 | 2,190.3 | 1.1 | 3,532.3 |
| Commitments to buy FX (includes $U.S.), spot, and forward | 3,015.5 | 4,969.2 | 10,057.9 | 12,316.2 | 15,046.1 | 17,415.0 | 8.5 | 477.5 |
| Standby LCs and foreign office guarantees | 162.5 | 391.3 | 1,139.6 | 525.3 | 594.8 | 531.9 | 0.3 | 227.3 |
| (amount of these items sold to others via participations) | (14.9) | (66.5) | (220.5) | (89.4) | (148.1) | (185.3) | | |
| Commercial LCs | 28.1 | 29.5 | 29.7 | 27.7 | 23.5 | 15.7 | 0.0 | −44.1 |
| Participations in acceptances | 1.0 | 0.9 | 0.1 | 0.1 | 0.0 | 0.0 | 0.0 | −100.0 |
| Securities borrowed or lent | 107.2 | 1,073.1 | 2,052.2 | 1,029.5 | 984.3 | 1,225.6 | 0.6 | 1,043.3 |
| Other significant commitments and contingencies | 25.7 | 44.0 | 173.1 | 168.2 | 240.3 | 122.2 | 0.1 | 375.5 |
| Notional value of all outstanding swaps | 2,122.0 | 52,909.2 | 103,091.1 | 149,319.6 | 138,332.5 | 114,785.3 | 56.4 | 5,309.3 |
| Total | $10,200.3 | $92,047.8 | $176,763.5 | $238,958.3 | $239,752.7 | $203,687.9 | 100% | 1,896.9 |
| Total assets (on-balance-sheet items) | $ 3,476.4 | $ 8,244.4 | $ 11,176.1 | $ 12,065.5 | $ 13,362.6 | $ 15,202.8 | | 337.3 |

FX = Foreign exchange; LC = Letter of credit.

**Sources:**  FDIC, *Statistics on Banking,* various issues. www.fdic.gov

(interest income plus noninterest income) coming from these off-balance-sheet activities. Indeed, the percentage of noninterest income to total operating income has increased from 22.66 percent in 1979 to 46.56 percent in 2013. As we discuss in detail in Chapter 23, the significant growth in derivative securities activities by commercial banks has been a direct response to the increased interest rate risk, credit risk, and foreign exchange risk exposures they have faced, both domestically and internationally. In particular, these contracts offer banks a way to hedge these risks without having to make extensive changes on the balance sheet. However, these assets and liabilities also introduce unique risks that must be managed. During the recent financial crisis, as mortgage borrowers defaulted on their mortgages, financial institutions that held these "toxic" mortgages and "toxic" credit derivatives (in the form of mortgage-backed securities) started announcing huge losses on them. Losses from the falling value of OBS securities reached over $1 trillion worldwide through 2009.

TARP gave the U.S. Treasury funds to buy "toxic" mortgages and other securities from financial institutions. However, the TARP plan was slow to be instituted and not all FIs chose to participate in the program. Better capitalized FIs wanted to hold on to their troubled OBS securities rather than sell them and record losses. Despite this, investors impounded the values of these toxic securities into the market prices of FIs that held them. As a result, early 2009 saw a plunge in the market values of financial institutions. Banks such as Citigroup, Bank of America, and J.P. Morgan Chase traded at less than book value as investors had little confidence in the value of their assets. As a result, a new plan, announced on February 10, 2009, involved a number of initiatives, including offering federal insurance to banks against losses on bad assets. In addition, the Treasury, working with the Federal Reserve, FDIC, and private investors, created the Public-Private Investment Fund (PPIF) to acquire real estate–related OBS assets. By selling to PPIF, financial institutions could reduce balance sheet risk, support new lending, and help improve overall market functioning. The PPIF facility was initially funded at $500 billion with plans to expand the program to up to $1.25 trillion over time. After several months of discussion, in July 2009, the government had selected nine financial firms to manage a scaled-down program, investing $30 billion to start the fund. The selected firms had 12 weeks to raise $500 million of capital each from private investors willing to invest in FIs' toxic assets. The total investment would be matched by the federal government. The purchase of $1.25 trillion in OBS mortgage-backed securities was completed in March 2010.

Although the simple notional dollar value of OBS items overestimates their risk exposure amounts, the increase in these activities between 1992 and 2013 was still nothing short of phenomenal. Indeed, this phenomenal increase and the potential for losses from them pushed regulators into imposing capital requirements on such activities and into explicitly recognizing an FI's solvency risk exposure from pursuing such activities. We describe these capital requirements in Chapter 13. Further, as a result of the role derivatives played in the recent financial crisis, the 2010 Wall Street Reform and Consumer Protection Act has called for a revamping of the U.S. financial regulatory system that includes extending regulatory oversight to unregulated OTC derivative securities. The regulation requires that all over-the-counter derivatives contracts be subject to regulation, and that all derivatives dealers be subject to supervision. It also empowers regulators to enforce rules against manipulation and abuse. Additionally, part of the Wall Street Reform and Consumer Protection Act is the Volcker Rule which prohibits U.S. depository institutions (DIs) from engaging in proprietary trading (i.e., trading as a principal for the trading account of the bank). Proprietary trading of bank holding company capital is banned in the bank and all subsidiaries, including investment banks. This includes any transaction to purchase or sell derivatives (hedging is allowed under certain restrictions). Nonproprietary trading (i.e., of client's money) is permitted anywhere in the bank holding company. The Volcker Rule was implemented in April 2014 and banks had until July 21, 2015, to be in compliance. The result has been a reduction in derivative securities held off-balance-sheet by these financial institutions and a reduction in overall OBS activities to $203,687.9 billion by 2016.

### Other Fee-Generating Activities

Commercial banks engage in other fee-generating activities that cannot be easily identified from analyzing their on- and off-balance-sheet accounts. Two of these include trust services and correspondent banking.

**Trust Services.**  The trust department of a commercial bank holds and manages assets for individuals or corporations. Only the largest banks have sufficient staff to offer trust services. Individual trusts represent about one-half of all trust assets managed by commercial

**DO YOU UNDERSTAND:**

3. *What major assets commercial banks hold?*

4. *What the major sources of funding for commercial banks are?*

5. *What OBS assets and liabilities are?*

6. *What other types of fee-generating activities banks participate in?*

banks. These trusts include estate assets and assets delegated to bank trust departments by less financially sophisticated investors. Pension fund assets are the second largest group of assets managed by the trust departments of commercial banks. The banks manage the pension funds, act as trustees for any bonds held by the pension funds, and act as a transfer and disbursement agent for the pension funds. We discuss pension funds in more detail in Chapter 18.

**Correspondent Banking.**   Correspondent banking is the provision of banking services to other banks that do not have the staff resources to perform the services themselves. These services include check clearing and collection, foreign exchange trading, hedging services, and participation in large loan and security issuances. Correspondent banking services are generally sold as a package of services. Payment for the services is generally in the form of non-interest-bearing deposits held at the bank offering the correspondent services (see Chapter 12).

## SIZE, STRUCTURE, AND COMPOSITION OF THE INDUSTRY

**LG 11-5**

As of 2016, the United States had 5,289 commercial banks. Even though this may seem to be a large number, in fact the number of banks has been decreasing. For example, in 1984, the number of banks was 14,483.[4] Figure 11–5 illustrates the number of bank mergers, bank failures, and new charters for the period 1980 through 2016. Notice that much of the change in the size, structure, and composition of this industry is the result of mergers and acquisitions. As we discuss in Chapter 13, strict regulations imposed on commercial banks over much of the last century limited geographical diversification opportunities. As a result, commercial bank operational areas were often narrow (and specialized) and the number of commercial banks was large. It was not until the 1980s and 1990s that regulators (such as the Federal Reserve or state banking authorities) allowed banks to merge with other banks across state lines (interstate mergers), and it has only been since 1994 that Congress has passed legislation (the Reigle-Neal Act) easing branching by banks across state lines. Finally, it has only been since 1987 that banks have possessed powers to underwrite corporate securities. (Full authority to enter the investment banking [and insurance] business was received only with the passage of the Financial Services Modernization Act in 1999.) We discuss the impact that changing regulations have had on the ability of commercial banks to merge and branch in Chapter 13.

**Figure 11–5**   **Structural Changes in the Number of Commercial Banks, 1980–2016**

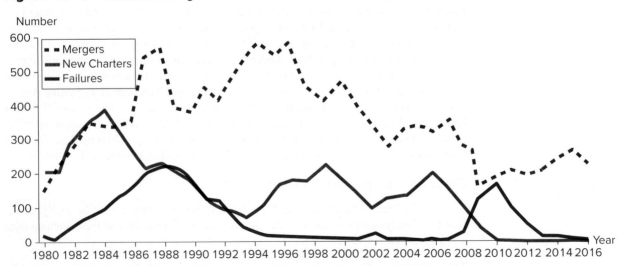

**Sources:** Federal Deposit Insurance Corporation, *Quarterly Banking Profile*, various issues. www.fdic.gov

4. However, during this period the number of offices has risen, from 60,000 in 1984 to over 93,200 in 2016.

These changes were not all one way. In mid-2005, Walmart filed an application with the FDIC to open a Utah-based "nonbank" bank,[5] stating that it wanted to use the bank to reduce the costs of processing electronic payments. Target, the retail chain, made a similar banking license application stating that it would use the "bank" to issue business credit cards. Target's application was approved in 2005. However, Walmart's application led to an unprecedented wave of opposition from regulators, the banking industry, and others, leading to the FDIC holding its first public hearings on an application. In July 2006, the FDIC declared a six-month moratorium on approving any new ILC licenses, saying it wanted to provide time to assess developments in the sector, including any need to improve regulatory oversight. In October 2006, a bill was introduced before the U.S. Congress that would keep Walmart and other retailers out of the banking sector. Specifically, the bill would prohibit nonfinancial firms from owning industrial banks or ILCs, thus barring Walmart from obtaining ILC charters. At the end of 2006, the FDIC was considering an extension of its moratorium, a move that would give Congress time to move forward with the bill. However, in March 2007, Walmart announced that it was withdrawing its application to open a bank.

**shadow banking**

*Activities of nonfinancial services firms that perform banking services.*

More recently, activities of nonfinancial service firms that perform banking services have been termed **shadow banking.** In the shadow banking system, savers place their funds with money market mutual and similar funds, which invest these funds in the liabilities of shadow banks. Borrowers get loans and leases from shadow banks rather than from banks. Like the traditional banking system, the shadow banking system intermediates the flow of funds between net savers and net borrowers. However, instead of the bank serving as the intermediary, it is the nonbank financial service firm, or shadow bank, that intermediates. Further, unlike the traditional banking system, where the complete credit intermediation is performed by a single bank, in the shadow banking system it is performed through a series of steps involving many nonbank financial service firms. Finally, shadow banks face significantly reduced regulation than traditional banks.

Because of the specialized nature involved in the credit intermediation process performed by shadow banks, these nonbank financial service firms can often perform the process more cost efficiently than traditional banks. Further, because of the lower costs and lack of regulatory controls, shadow banks can take on risks that traditional banks either cannot or are unwilling to take. Thus, the shadow banking system allows credit to be available that might not otherwise be generated through the traditional banking system. The 2010 Wall Street Reform and Consumer Protection Act called for regulators to be given broad authority to monitor and regulate nonbank financial firms that pose risks to the financial system. As of 2016, U.S. regulators had outlined a process to identify nonbank financial service firms that should receive increased oversight. However, these shadow banks remain unregulated by the federal government.

### Bank Size and Concentration

**community bank**

*A bank that specializes in retail or consumer banking.*

**retail banking**

*Consumer-oriented banking, such as providing residential and consumer loans and accepting smaller deposits.*

Interestingly, a comparison of asset concentration by bank size (see Figure 11–6) indicates that the recent consolidation in banking appears to have reduced the asset share of the smallest banks (under \$1 billion) from 36.6 percent in 1984 to 7.1 percent in 2016. These small or **community banks**—with less than \$1 billion in asset size—tend to specialize in **retail banking,** or consumer banking, such as providing residential mortgages and consumer loans and accessing the local deposit base. Clearly, this group of banks is decreasing both in number and importance.

The relative asset share of the largest banks (over \$1 billion in size), on the other hand, increased from 63.4 percent in 1984 to 92.9 percent in 2016. The largest 10 U.S.

5. These nonbank banks are called industrial loan corporations (ILCs). Located in the state of Utah, ILCs provide loans to low-quality, high-interest-rate corporations that banks avoid. While headquartered in Utah, ILCs can operate in nearly all 50 states by direct mail and other, electronic means. ILCs are regulated by the state of Utah and deposits of ILCs are insured by the Federal Deposit Insurance Corporation. Yet ILCs are regulated by neither the Federal Reserve nor the Office of the Comptroller of the Currency. By operating in Utah, nonbank companies can behave like commercial banks without being regulated like them.

**Figure 11–6** U.S. Bank Asset Concentration, 1984 versus 2016

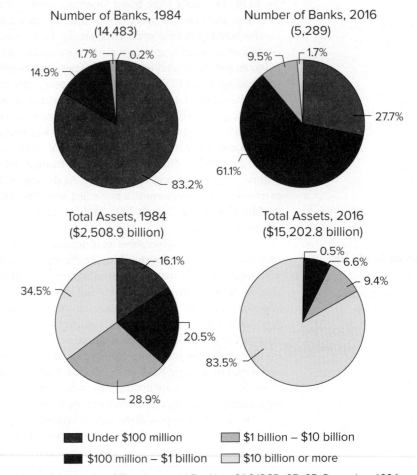

Number of Banks, 1984
(14,483)

1.7%    0.2%
14.9%
83.2%

Number of Banks, 2016
(5,289)

9.5%    1.7%
27.7%
61.1%

Total Assets, 1984
($2,508.9 billion)

16.1%
34.5%
20.5%
28.9%

Total Assets, 2016
($15,202.8 billion)

0.5%
6.6%
9.4%
83.5%

■ Under $100 million        ▨ $1 billion – $10 billion

■ $100 million – $1 billion    ☐ $10 billion or more

**Sources:** General Accounting Office, *Interstate Banking,* GAO/GGD, 95–35, December 1994, p. 101; and FDIC *Quarterly Banking Profile,* First Quarter 2016. www.fdic.gov

banks as of 2016 are listed in Table 11–3. The ranking is by size of assets devoted to banking services. The table also lists the assets at the holding company level. Many of these large depository institutions (e.g., J.P. Morgan Chase and Bank of America) operate in other financial service areas (e.g., investment banking and security brokerage) as well. Thus, assets held at the holding company level can be much larger than those devoted to

**TABLE 11–3** Top 10 U.S. Banks Listed by Total Asset Size 2016 *(in billions of dollars)*

| Bank | Banking Assets | Holding Company Assets |
|------|---------------|------------------------|
| 1. J.P. Morgan Chase | $2,015.8 | $2,466.1 |
| 2. Wells Fargo | 1,694.2 | 1,889.2 |
| 3. Bank of America | 1,676.7 | 2,189.8 |
| 4. Citigroup | 1,342.6 | 1,818.8 |
| 5. U.S. Bancorp | 423.2 | 438.5 |
| 6. Capital One | 370.7 | 339.2 |
| 7. PNC Financial | 350.6 | 361.5 |
| 8. Bank of New York Mellon | 301.9 | 372.4 |
| 9. TD Bank | 273.4 | 276.3 |
| 10. HSBC North America | 198.9 | 295.5 |

**Source:** Federal Reserve Board website, National Information Center. August 2016. www .federalreserve.gov

banking services only. Notice that several of these large depository institutions manage assets of over $1 trillion. The majority of banks in the two largest size classes are often either **regional or superregional banks.** Regional or superregional banks range in size from several billion dollars to several hundred billion dollars in assets. The banks normally are headquartered in larger regional cities and often have offices and branches in locations throughout large portions of the United States. They engage in a more complete array of **wholesale banking,** or commercial banking, activities encompassing consumer and residential lending as well as commercial and industrial lending (C&I loans), both regionally and nationally. Although these banks provide lending products to large corporate customers, many of the regional banks have developed sophisticated electronic and branching services for consumer and residential customers. Regional and superregional banks utilize retail deposit bases for funding, but also develop relationships with large corporate customers and international money centers. These banks have access to the markets for purchased funds, such as the interbank or **federal funds market,** to finance their lending and investment activities. Some of the biggest banks are often classified as being **money center banks.** U.S.-based money center banks include the Bank of New York Mellon, Deutsche Bank (through its U.S. acquisition of Bankers Trust), Citigroup, J.P. Morgan Chase, and HSBC North America (formerly Republic NY Corporation).[6]

It is important to note that asset or lending size does not necessarily make a bank a money center bank. For example, Bank of America Corporation, with $2,189.8 billion in assets in 2016, is not a money center bank, but HSBC North America (with only $295.5 billion in assets) is a money center bank. Classification as a money center bank is based in part on location of the bank and in part on the bank's heavy reliance on nondeposit or borrowed sources of funds. Specifically, a money center bank is a bank located in a major financial center (e.g., New York) that heavily relies on both national and international money markets for its source of funds. In fact, because of its extensive retail branch network, Bank of America tends to be a net supplier of funds on the interbank market (federal funds market).[7] By contrast, money center banks have fewer retail branches and rely heavily on wholesale and borrowed funds as sources of funds. Money center banks are also major participants in foreign currency markets and are therefore subject to foreign exchange risk (see Chapter 9).

## Bank Size and Activities

Bank size has traditionally affected the types of activities and financial performance of commercial banks. Small banks generally concentrate on the retail side of the business—making loans and issuing deposits to consumers and small businesses. In contrast, large banks engage in both retail and wholesale banking and often concentrate on the wholesale side of the business. Further, small banks generally hold fewer off-balance-sheet assets and liabilities than large banks. For example, while small banks issue some loan commitments and letters of credit, they rarely hold derivative securities. Large banks' relatively easy access to purchased funds and capital markets compared to small banks' access is a reason for many of these differences. For example, with easier access to capital markets, large banks operate with lower amounts of equity capital than do small banks. Also, large banks tend to use more purchased funds (such as fed funds) and have fewer core deposits (deposits such as demand deposits that are stable over short periods of time, see Chapter 12) than do small banks. At the same time, large banks lend to larger corporations. This means that their **interest rate spreads** (i.e., the difference between their lending rates and deposit rates) and **net interest margins** (i.e., interest income minus interest expense divided by earning assets) have usually been narrower than those of smaller regional banks, which are more sheltered from competition in highly localized markets and lend to smaller, less sophisticated customers.

**regional or superregional banks**

*A bank that engages in a complete array of wholesale commercial banking activities.*

**wholesale banking**

*Commercial-oriented banking, such as providing commercial and industrial loans funded with purchased funds.*

**federal funds market**

*An interbank market for short-term borrowing and lending of bank reserves.*

**money center bank**

*A bank that relies heavily on nondeposit or borrowed sources of funds.*

**interest rate spread**

*The difference between lending and deposit rates.*

**net interest margin**

*Interest income minus interest expense divided by earning assets.*

---

6. Bankers Trust was purchased by Deutsche Bank (a German bank) in 1998. The Bankers Trust name, however, has been retained for U.S. operations. Republic NY Corporation was purchased by HSBC (a British bank) in 1999. Republic NY Bank was renamed HSBC North America.
7. In 2016, Bank of America had over 4,700 branches nationwide.

In addition, large banks tend to pay higher salaries and invest more in buildings and premises than small banks do. They also tend to diversify their operations and services more than small banks do. Large banks generate more noninterest income (i.e., fees, trading account, derivative security, and foreign trading income) than small banks. Although large banks tend to hold less equity, they do not necessarily return more on their assets. However, as the barriers to regional competition and expansion in banking fell in the early and mid-2000s, the largest banks generally improved their return on equity (ROE) and return on asset (ROA) performance relative to small banks (see Figure 11–7).[8] Notice also from Figure 11–7 that both the ROAs and the ROEs of banks of all sizes dropped significantly during the financial crisis of 2008–2009. As the economy recovered in 2010–2016, ROA and ROE returned closer to their pre-crisis levels. The recovery occurred quicker for bigger banks that received more government assistance and monitoring throughout the crisis. The biggest banks' ROAs and ROEs returned to positive by 2009, while the smaller banks' ROAs and ROEs remained negative until 2010. We discuss the banking industry's performance next. We cover the impact of size on bank financial statements and performance in more detail in Chapter 12.

## INDUSTRY PERFORMANCE

**LG 11-6**

Table 11–4 presents selected performance ratios for the commercial banking industry for 1989 through March 2016. With the economic expansion in the U.S. economy and falling interest rates throughout most of the 1990s, U.S. commercial banks flourished. In 1999 commercial bank earnings were a record $71.6 billion. More than two-thirds of all U.S. banks reported an ROA of 1 percent or higher, and the average ROA for all banks was 1.31 percent, up from 1.19 percent for the year 1998. With the economic downturn in the early 2000s, bank performance deteriorated slightly. For example, commercial banks' string of eight consecutive years of record earnings ended in 2000 as their net income fell to $71.2 billion. Banks' provision for loan losses rose to $9.5 billion in the fourth quarter of 2000, an increase of $3.4 billion (54.7 percent) from the level of a year earlier. This was the largest quarterly loss provision since the fourth quarter of 1991. Finally, the average ROA was 1.19 percent in 2000, down from 1.31 percent in 1999.

This downturn was short-lived, however. In 2001, net income of $74.3 billion easily surpassed the old record of $71.6 billion and net income rose further to $106.3 billion in 2003. Moreover, in 2003, both ROA and ROE reached all-time highs of 1.40 percent and 15.34 percent, respectively. The two main sources of earnings strength in 2003 were higher noninterest income (up $18.9 billion, 10.3 percent) and lower loan-loss provisions (down $14.2 billion, or 27.6 percent). The greatest improvement in profitability occurred at large institutions, whose earnings had been depressed in the early 2000s by credit losses on loans to corporate borrowers and by weakness in market-sensitive noninterest income. Only 5.7 percent of all institutions were unprofitable in 2003, the lowest proportion since 1997. In 2004, a combination of continued strength in consumer loan demand and growing demand for commercial loans added to the growth of earnings. The third quarter of 2004 saw the sixth time in seven quarters that industry earnings set a new record. Further, at the end of September **noncurrent loans** fell to their lowest level since the end of 2000.

**noncurrent loans**

*Loans past due 90 days or more and loans that are not accruing interest because of problems of the borrower.*

Several explanations have been offered for the strong performance of commercial banks during the early 2000s. First, the Federal Reserve cut interest rates 13 times during this period. Lower interest rates made debt cheaper to service and kept many households and small firms borrowing. Second, lower interest rates made home purchasing more affordable. Thus, the housing market boomed throughout the period. Third, the development of new financial instruments such as credit derivatives and mortgage-backed

---

8. ROA is calculated as net income divided by the book value of total assets for the bank. ROE is calculated as net income divided by common equity of the bank and measures the return to the bank's common stockholders. We discuss ROA and ROE in more detail in Chapter 12.

**Figure 11–7**    **ROA and ROE on Different-Sized Banks, 1990–2016**

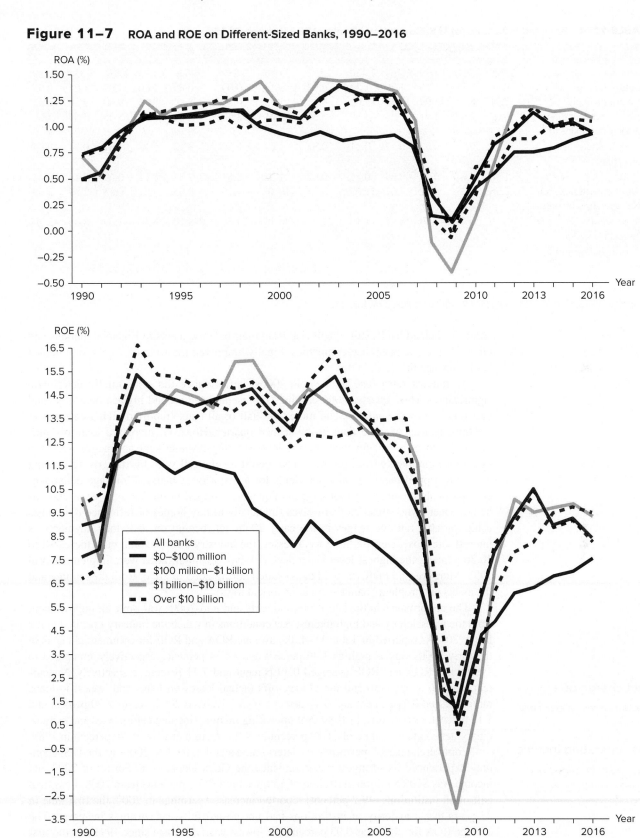

**Sources:** Federal Deposit Insurance Corporation, *Quarterly Banking Profile,* various issues. www.fdic.gov

**TABLE 11–4** Selected Indicators for U.S. Commercial Banks, 1989 through 2016

| | 1989 | 1999 | 2001 | 2003 | 2006 | 2007 | 2008 | 2009 | 2010 | 2012 | 2013 | 2015 | 2016* |
|---|---|---|---|---|---|---|---|---|---|---|---|---|---|
| Number of institutions | 12,709 | 8,580 | 8,079 | 7,769 | 7,450 | 7,283 | 7,086 | 6,839 | 6,530 | 6,096 | 5,876 | 5,338 | 5,289 |
| Return on assets (%) | 0.49 | 1.31 | 1.15 | 1.40 | 1.33 | 0.93 | 0.13 | 0.09 | 0.65 | 1.00 | 1.07 | 1.04 | 0.95 |
| Return on equity (%) | 7.71 | 15.31 | 13.09 | 15.34 | 13.02 | 9.12 | 1.33 | 0.85 | 5.86 | 8.92 | 9.60 | 9.26 | 8.43 |
| Net interest margin (%) | 4.02 | 4.07 | 3.91 | 3.83 | 3.39 | 3.35 | 3.21 | 3.50 | 3.81 | 3.42 | 3.25 | 3.04 | 3.06 |
| Noncurrent loans to total assets (%) | 2.30 | 0.63 | 0.92 | 0.77 | 0.51 | 0.87 | 1.84 | 3.36 | 3.12 | 2.18 | 1.62 | 0.94 | 0.94 |
| Net charge-offs to loans (%) | 1.16 | 0.61 | 0.95 | 0.89 | 0.41 | 0.62 | 1.32 | 2.57 | 2.67 | 1.11 | 0.69 | 0.43 | 0.44 |
| Asset growth rate (%) | 5.38 | 5.37 | 4.91 | 7.42 | 11.63 | 10.75 | 10.15 | −3.76 | 2.05 | 5.87 | 2.13 | 2.89 | 3.30 |
| Net operating income growth (%) | −38.70 | 20.42 | −1.89 | 14.92 | 11.19 | −21.21 | −80.48 | −22.55 | 1,088.10 | 26.30 | 13.69 | 8.06 | −2.79 |
| Number of failed/assisted institutions | 206 | 7 | 3 | 3 | 0 | 2 | 20 | 120 | 139 | 41 | 23 | 8 | 1 |

*Through March.

**Sources:** FDIC, *Quarterly Banking Profile,* various dates. www.fdic.gov

securities helped banks shift credit risk from their balance sheets to financial markets and other FIs such as insurance companies. Finally, improved information technology helped banks manage their risk better.

As interest rates rose in the mid-2000s, performance did not initially deteriorate significantly. Third quarter 2006 earnings represented the second highest quarterly total ever reported by the industry and more than half of all banks reported higher earnings in the third quarter of 2006 than in the second quarter. However, increased loan-loss provisions, reduced servicing income, and lower trading revenue kept net income reported by commercial banks from setting a new record for the full year. Further, rising funding costs outstripped increases in asset yields for a majority of banks. Mortgage delinquencies, particularly subprime mortgage delinquencies, surged in the last quarter of 2006 as home owners who stretched themselves financially to buy homes or refinance mortgages using variable rate mortgages in the early 2000s fell behind on their loan payments as interest rates rose. Despite these weaknesses, the industry's core capital ratio increased to 10.36 percent, the highest level since new, risk-based capital ratios were implemented in 1993. Moreover, no FDIC-insured banks failed during 2005 or 2006. Both the number and the assets of "problem" banks were at historical lows.

The performance in the late 1990s and early and mid-2000s was quite an improvement from the recessionary and high interest rate conditions in which the industry operated in the late 1980s. As reported in Table 11–4, the average ROA and ROE for commercial banks in the early 2000s was as high as 1.40 percent and 15.34 percent, respectively, compared to 1989 when ROA and ROE averaged 0.49 percent and 7.71 percent, respectively. Noncurrent loans to assets ratio and **net charge-offs** (actual losses on loans and leases) to loans ratio averaged 0.51 percent and 0.41 percent, respectively, in 2006, versus 2.30 percent and 1.16 percent, respectively, in 1989. **Net operating income** (income before taxes and extraordinary items) grew at a rate of 11.19 percent in 2006 versus a drop of 38.70 percent in 1989.

Commercial banks' performance deteriorated again in the late 2000s as the U.S. economy experienced its strongest recession since the Great Depression. For all of 2007, net income was $105.5 billion, a decline of $39.8 billion (27.4 percent) from 2006. Less than half of all institutions (49.2 percent) reported increased earnings in 2007, the first time in 23 years that a majority of institutions had not posted full-year earnings increases. The average ROA for 2007 was 0.93 percent, the lowest yearly average since 1991 and the first time in 15 years that the industry's annual ROA had been below 1 percent. The ROA for 2008 was 0.13 percent, the lowest since 1987. Almost one in four institutions (23.6 percent) was unprofitable in 2008, and nearly two out of every three institutions (62.8 percent) reported lower full-year earnings than in 2007.

**net charge-offs**

*Actual losses on loans and leases.*

**net operating income**

*Income before taxes and extraordinary items.*

As the economy improved in the second half of 2009, so did commercial bank performance. While loan-loss provisions continued to surge, growth in operating revenues, combined with appreciation in securities values, helped the industry post a net profit. Commercial banks earned $2.8 billion in net income in the third quarter of 2009, more than three times the $879 million from 2008. However, the industry was still feeling the effects of the long recession. Provisions for loan and lease losses totaled $62.5 billion, the third consecutive quarter that industry provisions had exceeded $60 billion. Net charge-offs continued to rise, for an eleventh consecutive quarter. Commercial banks charged off $50.8 billion in the third quarter of 2009, an increase of $22.6 billion (80.5 percent) over the third quarter of 2008. As a result, the full year 2009 ROA and ROE fell to 0.09 and 0.85 percent, respectively. Further, 120 commercial banks failed in 2009. This was the largest number of failures since 1992.

As the economy continued to slowly recover in 2010 through 2016, so did bank performance. The 2010 industry ROA and ROE increased to 0.65 percent and 5.86 percent, respectively. By 2015, industry ROA and ROE increased to 1.04 percent and 9.26 percent, respectively. Full-year earnings totaled $163.7 billion, an increase of $11.4 billion over 2014. Over 60 percent of all banks reported higher net income in 2015. Net operating income increased $14.9 billion in 2015, as net interest income rose by $9.4 billion and noninterest income increased by $5.5 billion. Total noninterest expenses were $5.5 billion lower than in 2014. However, on a negative note, loan-loss provisions showed an increase for the first time in six years, rising by $7.2 billion. The number of insured institutions on the FDIC's "Problem List" declined from 203 to 183 during the quarter and there were only eight bank failures.

Performance deteriorated slightly in 2016 as ROA and ROE fell to 0.95 percent and 8.43 percent, respectively. Higher expenses for loan losses and lower noninterest income from trading and asset servicing contributed to a $765 million decline in quarterly earnings in the first quarter. Most of the year-over-year drop in net income was concentrated among the largest banks. More than half of all banks—61.4 percent—reported higher quarterly earnings compared with first quarter 2015. Banks set aside $12.5 billion in provisions for loan losses in the first quarter, a year-over-year increase of $4.2 billion. This was the largest quarterly increase since fourth quarter 2012. Further, the amount of loan balances that were noncurrent—90 days or more past due or in nonaccrual status—rose by $3.3 billion during the first three months of 2016. This was the first quarterly increase in total noncurrent loan balances in 24 quarters (driven by a $9.3 billion increase in noncurrent C&I loans) and was the largest quarterly increase in noncurrent C&I loans since first quarter 1987.

---

**DO YOU UNDERSTAND:**

9. *What the trend in bank performance has been in the commercial banking industry over the last 30 years?*

---

## REGULATORS

**LG 11-7**

Chapter 13 provides a detailed description of the regulations governing commercial banks and their impact on the banking industry. This section briefly describes the regulators who develop, implement, and monitor these regulations. Unlike other countries that have one or sometimes two regulators, U.S. banks may be subject to the supervision and regulations of as many as four separate regulators. These regulators provide the common rules and regulations under which banks operate. They also monitor banks to ensure they abide by the regulations imposed. As discussed in Chapter 4, it is the regulators' job to, among other things, ensure the safety and soundness of the banking system. The key commercial bank regulators are the Federal Deposit Insurance Corporation (FDIC), the Office of the Comptroller of the Currency (OCC), the Federal Reserve System (FRS), and state bank regulators. The next sections discuss the principal role that each plays.

### Federal Deposit Insurance Corporation

**www.fdic.gov**

Established in 1933, the Federal Deposit Insurance Corporation (FDIC) insures the deposits of commercial banks. In so doing, it levies insurance premiums on banks, manages the deposit insurance fund (which is generated from those premiums and their reinvestment), and conducts bank examinations. In addition, when an insured bank is closed, the FDIC acts as the receiver and liquidator, although the closure decision itself is technically made by the bank's chartering or licensing agency (see below). Because of problems in the thrift industry and the insolvency of the savings association insurance fund (FSLIC) in 1989 (see Chapter 13), the FDIC now manages the insurance fund for both commercial banks and savings associations; the fund is called the Depositors Insurance Fund or DIF. The number of FDIC-insured banks and the division between nationally and state-chartered banks is shown in Figure 11–8.

To see how deposit insurance protects commercial banks from depositor runs, consider the case of Bear Stearns, an investment bank. In the summer of 2007, two Bear Stearns hedge funds suffered heavy losses on investments in the subprime mortgage market. The two funds filed for bankruptcy in the fall of 2007. Bear Stearns's market value was hurt badly by these losses. The losses became so great that by March 2008 Bear Stearns was struggling to finance its day-to-day operations. Lacking any kind of federal insurance of its liabilities, rumors of Bear Stearns's liquidity crisis became a reality as investors began quickly selling off their stock and draining what little liquid assets the firm had left. These events resulted in the first major run on a U.S. FI since the Great Depression. In contrast, during the financial crisis, investors looking for a "safe haven" for their money deposited funds in FDIC-insured depository institutions.

### Office of the Comptroller of the Currency

www.occ.treas.gov

The Office of the Comptroller of the Currency (OCC) is the oldest U.S. bank regulatory agency. Established in 1863, it is organized as a subagency of the U.S. Treasury. Its primary function is to charter national banks as well as to close them. In addition, the OCC examines national banks and has the power to approve or disapprove their merger applications. Instead of seeking a national charter, however, banks can seek to be chartered by 1 of 50 individual state bank regulatory agencies.

Historically, state-chartered banks have been subject to fewer regulations and restrictions on their activities than national banks. This lack of regulatory oversight was a major reason many banks chose not to be nationally chartered. Many more recent regulations (such as the Depository Institutions Deregulation and Monetary Control Act of 1980)

**Figure 11–8**    **Bank Regulators**

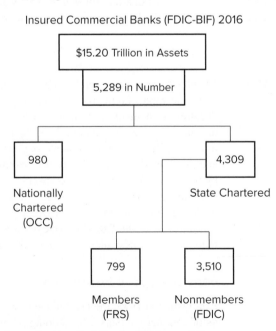

Insured Commercial Banks (FDIC-BIF) 2016

$15.20 Trillion in Assets

5,289 in Number

980 — Nationally Chartered (OCC)

4,309 — State Chartered

799 — Members (FRS)

3,510 — Nonmembers (FDIC)

**Source:** FDIC, *Statistics on Banking,* First Quarter 2016. www.fdic.gov

attempted to level the restrictions imposed on federal and state-chartered banks (see Chapter 13). Not all discrepancies, however, were changed and state chartered banks are still generally less heavily regulated than nationally chartered banks. The choice of being a nationally chartered or state-chartered bank lies at the foundation of the **dual banking system** in the United States. Most large banks, such as Citibank, choose national charters, but others have state charters. For example, Morgan Guaranty, the money center bank subsidiary of J.P. Morgan Chase, is chartered as a state bank under State of New York law. In 2016, 980 banks were *nationally* chartered and 4,309 were *state* chartered, representing 68.5 percent and 31.5 percent, respectively, of all commercial bank assets.

### Federal Reserve System

In addition to being concerned with the conduct of monetary policy, the Federal Reserve, as this country's central bank, also has regulatory power over some banks and, where relevant, their holding company parents. All 980 nationally chartered banks shown in Figure 11–8 are automatically members of the Federal Reserve System (FRS). In addition, 799 of the state-chartered banks have also chosen to become members. Since 1980, all banks have had to meet the same non-interest-bearing reserve requirements whether they are members of the FRS or not. The primary advantage of FRS membership is direct access to the federal funds wire transfer network for nationwide interbank borrowing and lending of reserves. Finally, many banks are often owned and controlled by parent **holding companies**— for example, Citigroup is the parent holding company of Citibank (a national bank). Because the holding company's management can influence decisions taken by a bank subsidiary and thus influence its risk exposure, the FRS regulates and examines bank holding companies as well as the banks themselves.

### State Authorities

As mentioned previously, banks may choose to be state chartered rather than nationally chartered. State-chartered commercial banks are regulated by state agencies. State authorities perform functions similar to those the OCC performs for national banks.

## GLOBAL ISSUES

**LG 11-8**

For the reasons discussed in earlier chapters, financial institutions are of central importance to the development and integration of markets globally. However, U.S. financial institutions must now compete not only with other domestic financial institutions for a share of these markets, but increasingly with foreign financial institutions. Total assets of banks that report data to the Bank for International Settlements were $80.2 trillion in 2016. Only 17.3 percent of this amount represented assets of U.S. banks. Table 11–5 lists the 20 largest banks in the world, measured by total assets, as of June 2016. Chinese banks dominate the list as 4 of the top 5 banks are headquartered in China. Only 4 of the top 20 banks are U.S. banks. Table 11–6 lists foreign bank offices' assets and liabilities held in the United States from 1992 through 2016. Total foreign bank assets over this period increased from $509.3 billion to $850.9 billion in 2001, and then fell to $664.1 billion in 2004 before increasing to $1,624.5 billion in 2008. Foreign bank assets fell again during the recent financial crisis to a low of $1,300.2 in 2009, but increased to a historic high of $2,093.4 billion by 2014 and $2,040.7 in 2016.

### Advantages and Disadvantages of International Expansion

International expansion has six major advantages.

**Risk Diversification.** As with domestic geographic expansions, an FI's international activities potentially enhance its opportunity to diversify the risk of its earnings flows.

---

**dual banking system**

*The coexistence of both nationally and state-chartered banks, as in the United States.*

www.federalreserve.gov

**holding company**

*A parent company that owns a controlling interest in a subsidiary bank or other FI.*

**DO YOU UNDERSTAND:**

10. *Who the major regulators of commercial banks are?*

11. *Which of all commercial banks the OCC regulates?*

**TABLE 11-5** The 20 Largest (in Total Assets) Banks in the World *(in billions of dollars)*

| Bank | Country | Total Assets |
|---|---|---|
| **1.** Industrial Commercial Bank of China | China | $3,422 |
| **2.** China Construction Bank Corp. | China | 2,827 |
| **3.** Agricultural Bank of China | China | 2,741 |
| **4.** Mitsibushi UJF Financial Group | Japan | 2,649 |
| **5.** Bank of China | China | 2,591 |
| **6.** HSBC Holdings | United Kingdom | 2,410 |
| **7.** J.P. Morgan Chase | United States | 2,352 |
| **8.** BNP Paribas | France | 2,168 |
| **9.** Bank of America | United States | 2,147 |
| **10.** Crédit Agricole | France | 1,847 |
| **11.** Wells Fargo | United States | 1,788 |
| **12.** Deutsche Bank | Germany | 1,771 |
| **13.** Citigroup | United States | 1,731 |
| **14.** Mizuho Financial Group | Japan | 1,718 |
| **15.** Barclays Bank | United Kingdom | 1,672 |
| **16.** Sumitomo Mitsui Financial | Japan | 1,657 |
| **17.** Banco Santander | Spain | 1,457 |
| **18.** Société Generale | France | 1,450 |
| **19.** Groupe BPCE | France | 1,268 |
| **20.** Royal Bank of Scotland | United Kingdom | 1,217 |

**Source:** Authors' research.

**TABLE 11-6** Foreign Bank Offices' Assets and Liabilities Held in the United States *(in billions of dollars)*

| | 1992 | 1996 | 2001 | 2004 | 2007 | 2008 | 2009 | 2010 | 2012 | 2014 | 2016* |
|---|---|---|---|---|---|---|---|---|---|---|---|
| Financial assets | $509.3 | $714.8 | $850.9 | $664.1 | $1,048.8 | $1,624.5 | $1,300.2 | $1,336.7 | $1,967.0 | $2,093.4 | $2,040.7 |
| Financial liabilities | 519.3 | 731.9 | 883.9 | 680.3 | 1,067.5 | 1,639.3 | 1,316.2 | 1,354.1 | 1,991.6 | 2,205.2 | 2,111.3 |

*As of June.
**Sources:** Federal Reserve Board, "Flow of Funds Accounts," Statistical Releases, various issues. www.federalreserve.gov

Often domestic earnings flows from financial services are strongly linked to the state of the domestic economy. Therefore, the less integrated the economies of the world are, the greater is the potential for earnings diversification through international expansions.

**Economies of Scale.** To the extent that economies of scale exist, an FI can potentially lower its average operating costs by expanding its activities beyond domestic boundaries.

**Innovations.** An FI can generate extra returns from new product innovations if it can sell such services internationally rather than just domestically. For example, consider complex financial innovations, such as securitization, caps, floors, and options, that FIs have innovated in the United States and sold to new foreign markets with few domestic competitors until recently.

**Funds Source.** International expansion allows an FI to search for the cheapest and most available sources of funds. This is extremely important with the very thin profit margins in domestic and international wholesale banking. It also reduces the risk of fund shortages (credit rationing) in any one market.

**Customer Relationships.** International expansions also allow an FI to maintain contact with and service the needs of domestic multinational corporations. Indeed, one of the fundamental factors determining the growth of FIs in foreign countries has been the parallel growth of foreign direct investment and foreign trade by globally oriented multinational corporations from the FI's home country.

**Regulatory Avoidance.**   To the extent that domestic regulations such as activity restrictions and reserve requirements impose constraints or taxes on the operations of an FI, seeking low-regulatory, low-tax countries can allow an FI to lower its net regulatory burden and increase its potential net profitability.

In contrast, international expansion has three major disadvantages.

**Information/Monitoring Costs.**   Although global expansions allow an FI the potential to better diversify its geographic risk, the absolute level of exposure in certain areas such as lending can be high, especially if the FI fails to diversify in an optimal fashion. For example, the FI may fail to choose a loan portfolio combination on its efficient portfolio frontier (see Chapter 20). Foreign activities may also be riskier for the simple reason that monitoring and information collection costs are often higher in foreign markets. For example, Japanese and German accounting standards differ significantly from the generally accepted accounting principles (GAAP) that U.S. firms use. In addition, language, legal, and cultural issues can impose additional transaction costs on international activities. Finally, because the regulatory environment is controlled locally and regulation imposes a different array of net costs in each market, a truly global FI must master the various rules and regulations in each market.

**Nationalization/Expropriation.**   To the extent that an FI expands by establishing a local presence through investing in fixed assets such as branches or subsidiaries, it faces the political risk that a change in government may lead to the nationalization of those fixed assets. If foreign FI depositors take losses following a nationalization, they may seek legal recourse from the FI in U.S. courts rather than from the nationalizing government. For example, the resolution of the outstanding claims of depositors in Citicorp's branches in Vietnam following the Communist takeover and expropriation of those branches took many years.

**Fixed Costs.**   The fixed costs of establishing foreign organizations may be extremely high. For example, a U.S. FI seeking an organizational presence in the London banking market faces real estate prices significantly higher than in New York. Such relative costs can be even higher if an FI chooses to enter by buying an existing UK bank rather than establishing a new operation, because of the cost of acquiring UK equities (i.e., paying an acquisition premium). These relative cost considerations become even more important if the expected volume of business to be generated, and thus the revenue flows, from foreign entry are uncertain.

### Global Banking Performance

After it hit the United States, the financial crisis of 2008–2009 quickly spread worldwide. As the crisis spread, banks worldwide saw losses driven by their portfolios of structured finance products and securitized exposures to the subprime mortgage market. Losses were magnified by illiquidity in the markets for those instruments. As with U.S. banks, this led to substantial losses in their market valuations. In Europe, the general picture of bank performance in 2008 was similar to that in the United States. That is, net income fell sharply at all banks. The largest banks in the Netherlands, Switzerland, and the United Kingdom had net losses for the year. Banks in Ireland, Spain, and the United Kingdom were especially hard hit as they had large investments in mortgages and mortgage-backed securities, both U.S. and domestic. Because they focused on domestic retail banking, French and Italian banks were less affected by losses on mortgage-backed securities. Continental European banks, in contrast to UK banks, partially cushioned losses through an increase in their net interest margins.

A number of European banks averted outright bankruptcy thanks to direct support from their central banks and national governments. During the last week of September and the first week of October 2008, the German government guaranteed all consumer bank deposits and arranged a bailout of Hypo Real Estate, the country's second-largest commercial property lender. The United Kingdom nationalized mortgage lender Bradford & Bingley (the country's eighth-largest mortgage lender) and raised deposit guarantees from $62,220 to $88,890 per account. Ireland guaranteed the deposits and debt of its six major financial institutions. Iceland rescued its third-largest bank with an $860 million purchase of 75 percent of the bank's stock and a few days later seized the country's entire banking system. The Netherlands, Belgium, and Luxembourg central governments together agreed to inject $16.37 billion into Fortis NV (Europe's first ever cross-border financial services company) to keep it afloat. However, five days later this deal fell apart and the bank was split up. The central bank in India stepped in to stop a run on the country's second-largest bank, ICICI Bank, by promising to pump in cash. Central banks in Asia injected cash into their banking systems as banks' reluctance to lend to each other led the Hong Kong Monetary Authority to inject liquidity into its banking system after rumors led to a run on Bank of East Asia Ltd. South Korean authorities offered loans and debt guarantees to help small and midsized businesses with short-term funding. The United Kingdom, Belgium, Canada, Italy, and Ireland were just a few of the countries to pass an economic stimulus plan and/or bank bailout plan. The Bank of England lowered its target interest rate to a record low of 1 percent hoping to help the British economy out of a recession. The Bank of Canada, Bank of Japan, and Swiss National Bank also lowered their main interest rates to 1 percent or below. All of these actions were a result of the spread of the U.S. financial market crisis to world financial markets.

As a result of the worldwide economic slowdown experienced in the later stages of the crisis, bank losses became more closely connected to macroeconomic performance. Countries across the world saw companies scrambling for credit and cutting their growth plans. Additionally, consumers worldwide reduced their spending. Even China's booming economy slowed more than had been predicted, from 10.1 percent in the second quarter of 2008 to 9 percent in the third quarter. This was the first time since 2002 that China's growth was below 10 percent and dimmed hopes that Chinese demand could help keep world economies growing. In late October 2008, the global crisis hit the Persian Gulf as Kuwait's central bank intervened to rescue Gulf Bank, the first bank rescue in the oil rich region. Until this time, the area had been relatively immune to the world financial crisis. However, plummeting oil prices (which had dropped over 50 percent between July and October 2008) left the area's economies vulnerable. In this period, the majority of bank losses were more directly linked to a surge in borrower defaults and to anticipated defaults as evidenced by the increase in the amount and relative importance of loan loss provision expenses.

International banks' balance sheets continued to shrink during the first half of 2009 (although at a much slower pace than in the preceding six months) and, as in the United States, they began to recover in the latter half of the year. In the fall of 2009, a steady stream of mostly positive macroeconomic news reassured investors that the global economy had turned around, but investor confidence remained fragile. For example, in late November 2009, security prices worldwide dropped sharply as investors reacted to news that government-owned Dubai World had asked for a delay in some payments on its debt. Further, throughout the spring of 2010 Greece struggled with a severe debt crisis. Early on, some of the healthier European countries tried to step in and assist the debt-ridden country. Specifically, in March 2010 a plan led by Germany and France to bail out Greece with as much as $41 billion in aid began to take shape. However, in late April Greek bond prices dropped dramatically as traders began betting a debt default was inevitable, even if the country received a massive bailout. The selloff was the result of still more bad news for Greece, which showed that the 2009 budget deficit was worse than had been previously reported. As a result, politicians in Germany began to voice opposition to a Greek bailout. Further, Moody's Investors Service downgraded Greece's debt rating and warned that additional cuts could be on the way. Greece's debt created heavy losses across the Greek banking sector. A run on Greek banks ensued. Initially, between €100 and €500 million per day was being withdrawn from Greek banks. At its peak, the run on Greek banks produced deposit withdrawals as high as €750 million a day, nearly 0.5 percent of the entire €170 billion deposit base in the Greek banking system.

Problems in the Greek banking system then spread to other European nations with fiscal problems, such as Portugal, Spain, and Italy. The risk of a full-blown banking crisis arose in Spain, where the debt rating of 16 banks and four regions were downgraded by Moody's Investors Service. Throughout Europe, some of the biggest banks announced billions of euros lost from write-downs on Greek loans. In 2011, Crédit Agricole reported a record quarterly net loss of €3.07 billion ($4.06 billion U.S.) after a €220 million charge on its Greek debt. Great Britain's Royal Bank of Scotland revalued its Greek bonds at a 79 percent loss—or £1.1 billion ($1.7 billion U.S.)—for 2011. Germany's Commerzbank's fourth quarter 2011 earnings decreased by €700 million due to losses on Greek sovereign debt. The bank needed to find €5.3 billion to meet the stricter new capital requirements set by Europe's banking regulator. Bailed-out Franco-Belgian bank Dexia warned it risked going out of business due to losses of €11.6 billion from its breakup and exposure to Greek debt and other toxic assets such as U.S. mortgage-backed securities. Even U.S. banks were affected by the European crisis. In late 2010, U.S. banks had sovereign risk exposure to Greece totaling $43.1 billion. In addition, exposures to Ireland, Portugal, and Spain totaled $113.9 billion, $47.1 billion, and $187.5 billion, respectively. Worldwide, bank exposure to these four countries totaled $2,512.3 billion. Default by a small country like Greece cascaded into something that threatened the world's financial system.

Worried about the effect a Greek debt crisis might have on the European Union, other European countries tried to step in and assist Greece. On May 9, 2010, in return for huge budget cuts, Europe's finance ministers and the International Monetary Fund approved a rescue package worth $147 billion and a "safety net" of $1 trillion aimed at ensuring financial stability across Europe. Through the rest of 2010 and into 2012, Euro-zone leaders agreed on more measures designed to prevent the collapse of Greece and other member economies. In return, Greece continued to offer additional austerity reforms and agreed to reduce its budget deficits. At times, the extent of these reforms and budget cuts led to worker strikes and protests (some of which turned violent), as well as changes in Greek political leadership. In December 2011, the leaders of France and Germany agreed on a new fiscal pact that they said would help prevent another debt crisis. Then French President Nicolas Sarkozy outlined the basic elements of the plan to increase budget discipline after meeting with German Chancellor Angela Merkel in Paris. The pact, which involved amending or rewriting the treaties that govern the European Union, was presented in detail at a meeting of European leaders and approved.

These efforts by the EU and reforms enacted by the Greek and other European country governments appear to have worked. On December 18, 2012, Standard & Poor's raised its rating on Greek debt by six notches, to B minus from selective default. S&P cited a strong and clear commitment from members of the Euro zone to keep Greece in the common currency bloc as the main reason for the upgrade. After the bailout, the market price of Greek debt rose: Some hedge funds made huge profits by betting on this bailout effect.

The situation in Greece and the European Union stabilized after 2012. However, a major debt payment was due from Greece to its creditors on June 30, 2015, a payment required to continue to receive rescue funds from the EU. Knowing that they could not make the payment, Greek officials met with Euro-zone leaders in an attempt to get a better deal. Greece, however, was unwilling to agree to more spending cuts and other concessions requested by the EU and talks broke down. Greece would be the first developed country to default on its debt and faced the real possibility that it would be forced to leave the EU. With its financial system near collapse and a debt payment due to the ECB on July 20, Greece was forced to continue negotiations with its creditors. A deal was reached on July 13 that essentially required Greece to surrender to all of its creditors' demands, including tax increases, pension reform, and the creation of a fund (under European supervision) that would hold some €50 billion in state-owned assets earmarked to be privatized or liquidated (with the proceeds to be used to pay off Greece's debt and help recapitalize its banks).

While the situation in Greece settled somewhat in the mid-2010s, the European bank system was rocked again in June 2016 when the people of the United Kingdom voted to leave the EU after 43 years (dubbed Brexit). The UK's vote to leave the EU shook the region, precipitating an immediate political crisis in Britain. Although the outcome of Brexit is not clear, only countries that pay into the EU budget, and permit free movement of people from within the EU, currently benefit to any degree from flexible entry into the EU's financial services single market. The UK must negotiate access to EU markets in financial services. Brexit would therefore challenge London's role as the venue of choice for global firms to conduct their European banking business. Brexit may impact the location, liquidity, and cost of financial services in Europe if it undermines London's competitive position as a banking center. Most large European banks have major operations in London which would be costly to relocate. Only a small number of banking centers elsewhere may benefit. The most likely beneficiaries in the EU are Paris, Frankfurt, Amsterdam, and Dublin. But they cannot replicate overnight the advantages of London's ability to support financial services, including skilled staff, legal services, and market infrastructure. Businesses in Europe would lose due to higher bank charges, poorer products, and less liquidity. European corporates would, for example, find it more inconvenient and costly to raise capital in London, which currently provides a one-stop shop.

---

### DO YOU UNDERSTAND:

**12.** *What the major advantages of international expansion to an FI are?*

**13.** *What the major disadvantages of international expansion to an FI are?*

---

## SUMMARY

This chapter provided an overview of the major activities of commercial banks and recent trends in the banking industry. Commercial banks rely heavily on deposits to fund their activities, although borrowed funds are becoming increasingly important for the largest institutions. Historically, commercial banks have concentrated on commercial or business lending and on investing in securities. Differences between the asset and liability portfolios of commercial banks and other financial institutions, however, are being eroded due to competitive forces, consolidation, and regulation. Indeed, in the 2000s, the largest group of assets in commercial bank portfolios were mortgage related. The chapter examined recent financial statements for the commercial banking industry, as well as industry trends in size and activities. Finally, the chapter provided an overview of this industry's performance over the last decade and discussed several global issues in commercial banking.

## QUESTIONS

1. What is meant by the term *depository institution?* How does a depository institution differ from an industrial corporation? (*LG 11-1*)

2. What are the major sources of funds for commercial banks in the United States? What are the major uses of funds for commercial banks in the United States? For each of your answers, specify where the item appears on the balance sheet of a typical commercial bank. (*LG 11-2, LG 11-3*)

3. What are the principal types of financial assets for commercial banks? How has the relative importance of these assets changed over the past several decades? What are some of the forces that have caused these changes? What are the primary types of risk associated with these types of assets? (*LG 11-2*)

4. Why do commercial banks hold investment securities? (*LG 11-2*)

5. What are the principal liabilities for commercial banks? What does this liability structure tell us about the maturity of the liabilities of banks? What types of risks does this liability structure entail for commercial banks? (*LG 11-3*)

6. What type of transaction accounts do commercial banks issue? Which type of accounts have dominated the transaction accounts of banks? (*LG 11-3*)

7. What are the three major segments of deposit funding? How are these segments changing over time? Why? What strategic impact do these changes have on the profitable operation of a bank? (*LG 11-3*)

8. How does the liability maturity structure of a bank's balance sheet compare with the maturity structure of the asset portfolio? What risks are created or intensified by these differences? (*LG 11-2, LG 11-3*)

9. What is meant by an off-balance-sheet activity? What are some of the forces responsible for them? (*LG 11-4*)

10. How does one distinguish between an off-balance-sheet asset and an off-balance-sheet liability? (*LG 11-4*)

11. What types of activities are normally classified as off-balance-sheet (OBS) activities? (*LG 11-4*)
    a. How does an OBS activity move onto the balance sheet as an asset or liability?
    b. What are the benefits of OBS activities to a bank?
    c. What are the risks of OBS activities to a bank?

12. What are the main off-balance-sheet activities undertaken by commercial banks? (*LG 11-4*)

13. The following balance sheet accounts (in millions of dollars) have been taken from the annual report for a U.S. bank. Arrange the accounts in balance sheet order and determine the value of total assets. Based on the balance sheet structure, would you classify this bank as a community bank, regional bank, or a money center bank? (*LG 11-6*)

| | | | |
|---|---|---|---|
| Premises | $1,078 | Net loans | $29,981 |
| Savings deposits | 3,292 | Short-term borrowing | 2,080 |
| Cash | 2,660 | Other liabilities | 778 |
| NOW accounts | 12,816 | Equity | 3,272 |
| Long-term debt | 1,191 | Investment securities | 5,334 |
| Other assets | 1,633 | Demand deposits | 5,939 |
| | | Certificates of deposit | |
| Intangible assets | 758 | (under $100,000) | 9,853 |
| Other time deposits | 2,333 | Federal funds sold | 110 |

14. What has been the recent trend in the number of commercial banks in the United States? What factors account for this trend? (*LG 11-5*)

15. What challenges have been made to the commercial banking industry by nonbanks? (*LG 11-5*)

16. What is a money center bank and a regional bank? (*LG 11-5*)

17. What are the differences between community banks, regional banks, and money center banks? Contrast the business activities, locations, and markets of each of these bank groups. (*LG 11-6*)

18. How do small bank activities differ from large bank activities? (*LG 11-5*)

19. Compare and contrast the profitability ratios (ROE and ROA) of banks with assets below and above $100 million in Figure 11–7 from 1990 through 2016. What conclusions can you derive from those numbers? (*LG 11-6*)

20. How has the performance of the commercial banking industry changed in the last 30 years? (*LG 11-6*)

21. Which commercial banks are experiencing the highest profitability? Which commercial banks are experiencing the lowest profitability? (*LG 11-6*)

22. Who are the major regulators of commercial banks? Which banks does each agency regulate? (*LG 11-7*)

23. What are the major functions performed by the FDIC? (*LG 11-7*)

24. What are the main advantages of being a member of the Federal Reserve System? (*LG 11-7*)

25. For each of the following banking organizations, identify which regulatory agencies (OCC, FRB, FDIC, or state banking commission) may have some regulatory supervision responsibility. (*LG 11-7*)
    a. State-chartered, nonmember, non–holding company bank
    b. State-chartered, nonmember, holding company bank
    c. State-chartered member bank
    d. Nationally chartered non–holding company bank
    e. Nationally chartered holding company bank

26. What are the advantages and disadvantages of international expansion? (*LG 11-8*)

# SEARCH THE SITE

Go to the Federal Deposit Insurance Corporation website at **www.fdic.gov** and find the latest balance sheet information available for commercial banks. Click on "Analysts." Click on "Statistics on Banking." Under "Standard Report#1," click on "Run Report." This will download a file onto your computer that will contain the most recent balance sheet information for commercial banks.

## Questions

1. Calculate the percentage change in total assets for the commercial bank industry since 2016 reported in Table 11–1.

2. Calculate the percentage of investment securities to total assets, loans to total assets, deposits to total assets, and equity to total assets. How have these changed since 2016?

# chapter

# Commercial Banks' Financial Statements and Analysis

## Learning Goals

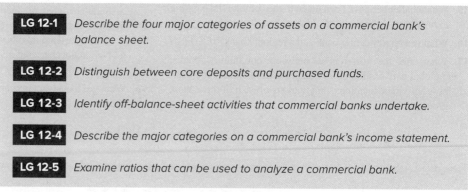

**LG 12-1**   *Describe the four major categories of assets on a commercial bank's balance sheet.*

**LG 12-2**   *Distinguish between core deposits and purchased funds.*

**LG 12-3**   *Identify off-balance-sheet activities that commercial banks undertake.*

**LG 12-4**   *Describe the major categories on a commercial bank's income statement.*

**LG 12-5**   *Examine ratios that can be used to analyze a commercial bank.*

## WHY EVALUATE THE PERFORMANCE OF COMMERCIAL BANKS? CHAPTER OVERVIEW

Unlike other private corporations, commercial banks (CBs) are unique in the special services they perform (e.g., assistance in the implementation of monetary policy) and the level of regulatory attention they receive (see Chapters 1 and 13). As a result, CBs are unique in the types of assets and liabilities they hold. Like any for-profit corporation, however, the ultimate measure of a CB's performance is the value of its common equity to its shareholders. This chapter discusses the financial statements of these institutions. Managers, stockholders, depositors, regulators, and other parties use performance, earnings, and other measures obtained from financial statements to evaluate commercial banks. For example, the In The News box looks at how regulators use financial statement data to evaluate the overall safety and soundness of a bank. As we proceed through the chapter, notice the extent to which regulators' evaluation of the overall safety and soundness of a bank (or their assignment of a so-called CAMELS rating) depends on financial statement data. Given the extensive level of regulation and the accompanying requirements for public availability of financial information, the financial statements of commercial banks are ideal candidates to use in examining the performance of depository institutions.

## The CAMELS Evaluation Components

The Uniform Financial Institutions Rating System (UFIRS) was adopted by the Federal Financial Institutions Examination Council (FFIEC) on November 13, 1979. Under the 1997 revision of the UFIRS, each financial institution is assigned a composite rating based on an evaluation and rating of six essential components of an institution's financial condition and operations that are summarized in a composite "CAMELS" rating. The acronym CAMELS stands for Capital Adequacy, Asset Quality, Management, Earnings, Liquidity, and Sensitivity to Market Risk.

An institution's *Capital Adequacy* is evaluated in relation to the volume of risk assets; the volume of marginal and inferior quality assets; the bank's growth experience, plan, and prospects; and the strength of management. Consideration is also given to an institution's capital ratios relative to its peer group, its earnings retention, its dividend policies, and its access to capital markets or other appropriate sources of financial assistance.

*Asset Quality* is evaluated by the level, distribution, and severity of adversely classified assets; the level and distribution of nonaccrual and reduced-rate assets; the adequacy of the allowance for loan losses; and management's demonstrated ability to administer and collect problem credits. In addition, examiners evaluate the volume of concentrations of credit, trends in asset quality, volume of out-of-territory loans, level and severity of other real estate held, and the bank's underwriting standards.

*Management* is evaluated against virtually all factors considered necessary to operate the bank within accepted banking practices and in a safe and sound manner. Thus, management is evaluated in relation to technical competence; leadership and administrative ability; compliance with banking regulations and statutes; adequacy of, and compliance with, internal policies and controls; and whether the board has a plan covering management succession. The assessment of management also takes into account the quality of internal controls, operating procedures, and all lending, investment, and other operating policies. Finally, examiners review and assess the composition, experience level, abilities, and involvement of the officers, directors, and shareholders.

*Earnings* are evaluated with respect to their ability to cover losses and provide adequate capital protection; trends; peer group comparisons; the quality and composition of net income; and the degree of reliance on interest-sensitive funds. Consideration is also given to the bank's dividend payout ratio, the rate of growth of retained earnings, and the adequacy of bank capital. The adequacy of provisions to the allowance for loan losses, and the extent which extraordinary items, securities transactions, and tax effects contribute to net income, are also assessed.

*Liquidity* is evaluated in relation to the volatility of deposits, the frequency and level of borrowings, the use of brokered deposits, technical competence relative to the structure of liabilities, the availability of assets readily convertible into cash, and access to money markets or other ready sources of funds. The overall effectiveness of asset–liability management is considered, as well as the adequacy of, and compliance with, established liquidity policies. The nature, volume, and anticipated use of credit commitments are also factors that are weighed.

The *Sensitivity to Market Risk* component reflects the degree to which changes in interest rates, foreign exchange rates, commodity prices, or equity prices can adversely affect a financial institution's earnings or economic capital. When evaluating this component, consideration should be given to: management's ability to identify, measure, monitor, and control market risk; the institution's size; the nature and complexity of its activities; and the adequacy of its capital and earnings in relation to its level of market risk exposure.

CAMELS ratings range from 1 to 5.

**Composite "1"**—Institutions in this group are basically sound in every respect.

**Composite "2"**—Institutions in this group are fundamentally sound but may reflect modest weaknesses correctable in the normal course of business.

**Composite "3"**—Institutions in this category exhibit financial, operational, or compliance weaknesses ranging from moderately severe to unsatisfactory.

**Composite "4"**—Institutions in this group have an immoderate volume of serious financial weaknesses or a combination of other conditions that are unsatisfactory.

**Composite "5"**—This category is reserved for institutions with an extremely high immediate or near term probability of failure.

**Source:** Federal Deposit Insurance Corporation, *DOS Manual of Examination Policies,* October 2016. www.fdic.gov

This chapter uses commercial banks to illustrate a return on equity (ROE) framework as a method of evaluating depository institutions' profitability. The ROE framework decomposes this frequently used measure of profitability into its various component parts to identify existing or potential financial management and risk exposure problems. All financial institutions, and particularly commercial banks, are engaging in an increased level of off-balance-sheet (OBS) activities. These activities produce income (and sometimes losses) for the FI that are reported on the income statement. This chapter also summarizes off-balance-sheet activities (and the risks involved with such activities), which are discussed in more detail in Chapters 19 and 23. Finally, the fact that bank size and/or niche (i.e., the financial market segment the bank specializes in servicing) may affect the evaluation of financial statements is also highlighted.

## FINANCIAL STATEMENTS OF COMMERCIAL BANKS

**report of condition**

*Balance sheet of a commercial bank reporting information at a single point in time.*

**report of income**

*Income statement of a commercial bank reporting revenues, expenses, net profit or loss, and cash dividends over a period of time.*

**www.ffiec.gov**

**www.hbtbank.com**

Financial information on commercial banks is reported in two basic documents. The **report of condition** (or balance sheet) presents financial information on a bank's assets, liabilities, and equity capital. The balance sheet reports a bank's condition at a single point in time. The **report of income** (or the income statement) presents the major categories of revenues and expenses (or costs) and the net profit or loss for a bank over a period of time. Financial statements of commercial banks must be submitted to regulators and stockholders at the end of each calendar quarter—March, June, September, and December. The Federal Financial Institutions Examination Council (FFIEC), based in Washington, DC, prescribes uniform principles, standards, and report forms for depository institutions.[1]

To evaluate the performance of commercial banks, we use two financial services institutions of varying sizes and market niches: Heartland Bank and Trust Company and Bank of America Corporation. Excel spreadsheets of the financial statements and financial ratios discussed in this chapter are available through Connect or your course instructor.

Heartland Bank and Trust Company is a privately owned community bank operating in 39 communities in central northern Illinois. In 2016, Heartland had $2.45 billion in total assets, 57 offices, and 67 ATMs. Heartland is a full-service commercial lender focused on supporting local farms, businesses, municipalities, and nonprofit entities. As one of the largest community banks in central Illinois, the bank has the necessary capital and expertise to successfully back large-scale projects, from $100,000 business loans to multimillion-dollar municipal bond transactions. The bank offers farm management services, including one-on-one consulting intended to improve customers' farmland productivity and asset value. The bank also assists with land transactions; for example, the licensed real estate employees of the bank offer unique knowledge and expertise with markets throughout Illinois to help achieve the best price per acre. Heartland is widely recognized as one of the strongest and most progressive banks in the area, yet it is also a financial institution that is focused on customer and community support. The bank launched new Online Bill Pay features in March 2015 to make paying bills easier and more convenient for its customers. During the fall of 2015, the bank joined forces with Apple to introduce Apple Pay for its customers, a simple, secure way for debit card customers to complete in-store and mobile app purchases. Heartland Bank and Trust Company also offers comprehensive wealth management solutions to individuals, foundations, corporate trusts, and qualified retirement plan sponsors.

Bank of America Corporation (BOA) is a financial services holding company,[2] headquartered in Charlotte, North Carolina, with holding company assets of $2,188.63 billion

---

1. The financial statements reported by banks use book value accounting concepts; that is, assets, liabilities, and equity accounts are generally reported at their original cost or book value. An alternative accounting method frequently discussed for use by banks is market value accounting. We discuss the issues, consequences of, and current status of the use of market value accounting in Chapter 22.

2. The U.S. Congress passed the Financial Services Modernization Act of 1999, which opened the door for the creation of full-service financial institutions in the United States. A financial services holding company can engage in banking activities, insurance activities, and securities activities. Thus, while we examine financial institutions by functional area, the financial services holding company (which combines many activities in a single financial institution) has become the dominant form of financial institution in terms of total assets (see Chapter 13).

and bank assets of $1,676.74 billion as of 2016. BOA operates nationally and internationally with more than 4,700 offices in the United States and offices in over 20 countries supporting approximately 53 million clients. As of 2016, the bank's client base included 96 percent of the U.S. Fortune 1,000 and 81 percent of the Global Fortune 500. The bank offers products in many business lines, including retail and wholesale banking, investment and trust management, and credit card company business. Bank of America has created one of the nation's largest ATM networks, with 16,000 ATMs serving more than 32 million active users. It is one of the nation's largest debit card issuers, the nation's leading small business lender, and a world-leading institution in number of relationships, investment banking, treasury management, syndications, secured and unsecured credit, and leasing to middle-market U.S. companies. BOA leads the world in global distribution of fixed-income, currency, and energy commodity products and derivatives, as well as being one of the largest equity trading operations.

### Balance Sheet Structure

**www.fdic.gov**

Table 12–1 presents 2016 balance sheet information for the two commercial banks (hereafter called *banks*). As stated in Chapter 11, many banks are owned by parent bank holding companies. One-bank holding companies control only one subsidiary commercial bank. Multiple-bank holding companies control two or more subsidiary commercial banks (see Chapter 13). The financial statements reported in this chapter are for the consolidated multiple-bank holding company, which includes the parent holding company plus bank subsidiaries. These data are taken from the Federal Deposit Insurance Corporation call reports, available at the FDIC website. Pay particular attention to the fact that, unlike manufacturing corporations, the majority of a commercial bank's assets are financial assets rather than physical or fixed assets (such as buildings or machines). Additionally, a relatively large portion of a commercial bank's liabilities are short-term deposits and borrowings. In general, banks have higher leverage than manufacturing corporations do.

**LG 12-1**

**Assets.** A bank's assets are grouped into four major subcategories: (1) cash and due from depository institutions, (2) investment securities, (3) loans and leases, and (4) other assets. Investment securities and loans and leases are the bank's earning assets. Cash and due from depository institutions (item 5 in Table 12–1) consists of vault cash, deposits at the Federal Reserve (the central bank), deposits at other financial institutions, and cash items in the process of collection. None of these items generates much income for the bank, but each is held because it performs a specific function.

*Cash and Due from Depository Institutions.* Vault cash (item 1) is composed of the currency and coin needed to meet customer withdrawals. Deposits at the Federal Reserve (item 2) are used primarily to meet legal reserve requirements (see Chapter 13), to assist in check clearing, wire transfers, and the purchase or sale of Treasury securities. Deposits at other financial institutions (item 3) are primarily used to purchase services from those institutions. These banks generally purchase services such as check collection, check processing, fed funds trading, and investment advice from **correspondent banks** (see below). Cash items in the process of collection (item 4) are checks written against accounts at other institutions that have been deposited at the bank. Credit is given to the depositor of these checks only after they clear.

**correspondent bank**

*A bank that provides services to another commercial bank.*

*Investment Securities.* Investment securities (item 11 in Table 12–1) consist of federal funds sold, repurchase agreements (RPs or repos), U.S. Treasury and agency securities, securities issued by states and political subdivisions (municipals), mortgage-backed securities, and other debt and equity securities. These securities generate some income for the

**TABLE 12–1**   Balance Sheet for Two Commercial Banks *(in millions of dollars)*

| | Heartland Bank and Trust | Bank of America |
|---|---|---|
| **Assets** | | |
| 1. Vault cash | $ 15.37 | $ 10,784 |
| 2. Deposits at Federal Reserve | 93.98 | 127,024 |
| 3. Deposits at other financial institutions | 6.70 | 28,141 |
| 4. Cash items in process of collection | 0.02 | 7,130 |
| 5. *Cash and due from depository institutions* | $ 116.07 | $ 173,079 |
| 6. Federal funds sold and RPs | 0.00 | 19,340 |
| 7. U.S. Treasury and U.S. agency securities | 57.83 | 50,625 |
| 8. Securities issued by states and political subdivisions | 242.71 | 13,115 |
| 9. Mortgage-backed securities | 220.70 | 298,029 |
| 10. Other debt and equity securities | 56.06 | 16,598 |
| 11. *Investment securities* | $ 577.30 | $ 397,707 |
| 12. Commercial and industrial loans | 307.26 | 239,581 |
| 13. Loans secured by real estate | 1,239.50 | 335,760 |
| 14. Consumer loans | 8.87 | 173,132 |
| 15. Other loans | 100.90 | 127,968 |
| 16. Leases | 0.03 | 22,339 |
| 17. Gross loans and leases | $1,656.56 | $ 898,780 |
| 18. Less: Unearned income | 0.00 | 0 |
| 19. Reserve for loan and lease losses | 15.66 | 11,929 |
| 20. *Net loans and leases* | $1,640.90 | $ 886,851 |
| 21. Trading assets | 0.00 | 75,057 |
| 22. Premises and fixed assets | 48.95 | 8,803 |
| 23. Other real estate owned | 11.61 | 392 |
| 24. Intangible assets | 24.53 | 60,634 |
| 25. Other | 29.00 | 74,220 |
| 26. *Other assets* | $ 114.09 | $ 219,106 |
| 27. **Total assets** | $2,448.36 | $1,676,743 |
| **Liabilities and Equity Capital** | | |
| 28. Demand deposits | $ 311.14 | $ 156,109 |
| 29. NOW accounts | 141.97 | 28,961 |
| 30. MMDAs | 431.34 | 477,983 |
| 31. Other savings deposits | 844.46 | 504,760 |
| 32. Deposits in foreign offices | 0.00 | 83,953 |
| 33. Retail CDs | 271.56 | 29,967 |
| 34. Core deposits | $2,000.47 | $1,281,733 |
| 35. Wholesale CDs | 109.71 | 34,955 |
| 36. *Total deposits* | $2,110.18 | $1,316,688 |
| 37. Federal funds purchased and RPs | 39.83 | 29,675 |
| 38. Other borrowed funds | 1.14 | 89,060 |
| 39. Subordinated notes and debentures | 0.00 | 6,270 |
| 40. Other liabilities | 39.27 | 23,775 |
| 41. *Total liabilities* | $2,190.42 | $1,465,468 |
| 42. Preferred stock | 0.00 | 0 |
| 43. Common stock | 5.00 | 3,042 |
| 44. Surplus and paid-in capital | 67.50 | 171,745 |
| 45. Retained earnings | 185.44 | 36,488 |
| 46. *Total equity capital* | $ 257.94 | $ 211,275 |
| 47. **Total liabilities and equity capital** | $2,448.36 | $1,676,743 |

**Source:**  Values are taken from the 2016 FDIC report of condition data tapes and are available at the Federal Deposit Insurance Corporation website. www.fdic.gov

bank and are used for liquidity risk management purposes. Investment securities are highly liquid,[3] have low default risk, and can usually be traded in secondary markets. Banks generally maintain significant amounts of these securities to ensure that they can easily meet liquidity needs that arise unexpectedly. However, because the revenue generated from investment securities is low compared to that from loans and leases, many (particularly larger) banks attempt to minimize the amount of investment securities they hold.

Short-maturity (less than one year to maturity) investments include federal funds sold and repurchase agreements (item 6), and U.S. Treasury bills and agency securities (item 7). Returns on these investments vary directly with changes in market interest rates. Although banks with excess cash reserves invest some of this in interest-earning liquid assets such as T-bills and short-term securities, they have the option to lend excess reserves for short intervals to other banks seeking increased short-term funding. The interbank market for excess reserves is called the federal funds (fed funds) market. In the United States, federal funds are short-term uncollateralized loans made by one bank to another; more than 90 percent of such transactions have maturities of one day. Repurchase agreements (RPs or repos) can be viewed as collateralized federal funds transactions. In a federal funds transaction, the bank with excess reserves sells fed funds for one day to the purchasing bank. The next day, the purchasing bank returns the fed funds plus one day's interest, reflecting the fed funds rate. Since credit risk exposure exists for the selling bank, because the purchasing bank may be unable to repay the fed funds the next day, the seller may seek collateral backing for the one-day fed funds loan. In an RP transaction, the funds-selling bank receives government securities as collateral from the funds-purchasing bank—that is, the funds-purchasing bank temporarily exchanges securities for cash. The next day, this transaction is reversed—the funds purchasing bank sends back the fed funds it borrowed plus interest (the RP rate); it receives in return (or repurchases) its securities used as collateral in the transaction.

Long-maturity investments such as U.S. Treasury bonds and U.S. agency securities (item 7), municipals (item 8), mortgage-backed securities (item 9), and most other securities (item 10) usually offer somewhat higher expected returns than short-maturity investments since they are subject to greater interest rate risk exposure—see Chapter 22. U.S. Treasury securities and Government National Mortgage Association (agency) bonds are fully backed by the U.S. government and thus carry no default risk. Other U.S. government agency securities, such as those of the Federal National Mortgage Association and the Federal Home Loan Mortgage Corporation, are not directly backed by the full faith and credit of the U.S. government and therefore carry some default risk (see Chapter 7). Municipal securities held by commercial banks are generally high-rated, investment-grade (i.e., low-risk) securities, issued by municipalities as either general obligation or revenue bonds.[4] Interest paid on municipals is exempt from federal income tax obligations. Mortgage-backed securities include items such as collateralized mortgage obligations and mortgage-backed bonds (see Chapter 7). Other investment securities include investment-grade corporate bonds, foreign debt securities, and securities such as U.S. Treasury securities and municipals held for short-term trading purposes. These trading account securities earn interest for the bank and generate capital gains or losses from changes in the market values of these securities.[5]

www.ginniemae.gov

www.fanniemae.com

www.freddiemac.com

*Loans and Leases.*   Loans and leases (items 12–16 in Table 12–1) are the major asset items on a bank's balance sheet and generate the largest flow of revenue income. However, these

3. Not all of a bank's investment securities can be sold immediately. Some securities, such as U.S. Treasury securities and municipals, can be pledged against certain types of borrowing by the bank and, therefore, must remain on the bank's books until the debt obligation is removed or another security is pledged as collateral.

4. Payments of principal and interest on general obligation bonds are backed by the full faith, credit, and taxing authority of the issuer. Payments of principal and interest on revenue bonds are backed only by the revenues generated from the facility or project that the proceeds of the bonds are financing.

5. Investment securities included in the bank's trading portfolio and designated as *trading securities* or *available-for-sale securities* are listed on the balance sheet at their *market value*. All other items on the balance sheet are listed at their *book values*.

items are also the least liquid asset items and the major sources of credit and liquidity risk for most banks. Loans are categorized as commercial and industrial (C&I) loans (item 12), loans secured by real estate (item 13), individual or consumer loans (item 14), and other loans (item 15). Leases (item 16) are used as alternatives to loans when the bank, as owner of a physical asset, allows a customer to use an asset in return for periodic lease payments.

*Commercial and Industrial Loans.*   C&I loans are used to finance a firm's capital needs, equipment purchases, and plant expansion. They can be made in quite small amounts such as $100,000 to small businesses or in packages as large as $10 million or more to major corporations. Commercial loans can be made at either fixed rates or floating rates of interest. The interest rate on a fixed-rate loan is set at the beginning of the contract period. This rate remains in force over the loan contract period no matter what happens to market rates. The interest rate on a floating-rate loan can be adjusted periodically according to a formula so that the interest rate risk is transferred in large part from the bank to the borrower. As might be expected, longer-term loans are more likely to be made under floating-rate contracts than are relatively short-term loans. In addition, commercial loans can be made for periods as short as a few weeks to as long as eight years or more. Traditionally, short-term commercial loans (those with an original maturity of one year or less) are used to finance firms' working capital needs and other short-term funding needs, while long-term commercial loans are used to finance credit needs that extend beyond one year, such as the purchase of real assets (machinery), new venture start-up costs, and permanent increases in working capital. Commercial loans can be secured or unsecured. A *secured loan* (or asset-backed loan) is backed by specific assets of the borrower, while an *unsecured loan* (or junior debt) gives the lender only a general claim on the assets of the borrower should default occur.

*Real Estate Loans.*   Real estate loans are primarily mortgage loans and some revolving home equity loans (see Chapter 7). For banks (as well as savings institutions), residential mortgages are the largest component of the real estate loan portfolio. Until recently, however, commercial real estate mortgages had been the fastest-growing component of real estate loans. Residential mortgages are very long-term loans with an average maturity of approximately 20 years. As with C&I loans, the characteristics of residential mortgage loans differ widely. As discussed in Chapter 7, these include the size of the loan, the loan-to-value ratio, and the maturity of the mortgage. Other important characteristics are the mortgage interest (or commitment) rate and fees and charges on the loan, such as commissions, discounts, and points paid by the borrower or the seller to obtain the loan. In addition, the mortgage rate differs according to whether the mortgage has a fixed rate or a floating rate, also called an *adjustable rate.*

*Consumer Loans.*   A third major category of loans is the individual or consumer loan—for example, personal and auto loans. Commercial banks, finance companies, retailers, savings banks, and gas companies also provide consumer loan financing through credit cards such as Visa, MasterCard, and proprietary credit cards issued by companies such as Sears and AT&T.

*Other Loans.*   Other loans include a wide variety of borrowers and types such as loans to nonbank financial institutions, state and local governments, foreign banks, and sovereign governments.

Each loan category entails a wide variety of characteristics that must be evaluated to determine the risk involved, whether the bank should grant the loan, and, if so, at what price. We discuss the evaluation methods in Chapter 20.

*Unearned Income and Allowance for Loan and Lease Losses.*   Unearned income (item 18) and the allowance (reserve) for loan and lease losses (item 19) are contra-asset accounts that are deducted from gross loans and leases (item 17) on the balance sheet to create net loans and leases (item 20). Unearned income is the amount of income that the bank has received on a loan from a customer but has not yet recorded as income on the income statement. Over the life of the loan, the bank earns (or accrues) interest income and accordingly transfers it out of unearned income into interest income. The allowance for loan and lease losses is an estimate by the bank's management of the amount of the gross loans (and leases) that will not be repaid to the bank. Although the maximum amount of the reserve is influenced by tax laws, the bank's management actually sets the level based on loan growth and recent loan loss experience. The allowance for loan losses is an accumulated reserve that is adjusted each period as management recognizes the possibility of additional bad loans and makes appropriate provisions for such losses. Actual losses are then deducted from, and recoveries are added to (referred to as **net write-offs**), their accumulated loan and lease loss reserve balance.

**net write-offs**

*Actual loan losses less loan recoveries.*

Investment securities plus net loans and leases are the **earning assets** of a depository institution. It is these items on the balance sheet that generate interest income and some of the noninterest income described below.

**earning assets**

*Investment securities plus net loans and leases.*

*Other Assets.* Other assets on the bank's balance sheet (item 26) consist of items such as trading assets (item 21, a separate account managed by banks that buy [underwrite] U.S. government securities and other securities for their own trading account or for resale at a profit to other banks and to the public, rather than for investment in the bank's own investment portfolio), premises and fixed assets (item 22), other real estate owned (collateral seized on defaulted loans—item 23), intangible assets (i.e., goodwill and mortgage servicing rights—item 24), and other (i.e., deferred taxes, prepaid expenses, and mortgage servicing fees receivable—item 25). These accounts are generally a small part of the bank's overall assets.

**Liabilities.** A bank's liabilities consist of various types of deposit accounts and other borrowings used to fund the investments and loans on the asset side of the balance sheet. Liabilities vary in terms of their maturity, interest payments, check-writing privileges, and deposit insurance coverage.

*Deposits.* Demand deposits (item 28) are transaction accounts held by individuals, corporations, partnerships, and governments that generally pay no explicit interest. Corporations are prohibited from using deposits other than demand deposits (e.g., NOW accounts) for transaction account purposes. This group therefore constitutes the major holders of demand deposits. Since 1980, all banks in the United States have been able to offer checkable deposits that pay interest and are withdrawable on demand; they are called *negotiable order of withdrawal accounts,* or **NOW accounts**[6] (item 29). The major distinction between these instruments and traditional demand deposits is that these instruments require the depositor to maintain a minimum account balance to earn interest. If the minimum balance falls below some level, such as $500, the account formally converts to a status equivalent to a demand deposit and earns no interest. Also, there are restrictions on corporations holding NOW accounts.

**NOW accounts**

*Negotiable order of withdrawal accounts are similar to demand deposits but pay interest when a minimum balance is maintained.*

**MMDAs**

*Money market deposit accounts with retail savings accounts and some limited checking account features.*

Money market deposit accounts or **MMDAs** (item 30) are an additional liability instrument that banks can use. To make banks competitive with the money market mutual funds offered by groups such as Vanguard and Fidelity, the MMDAs they offer must be liquid. In the United States, MMDAs are checkable but subject to restrictions on the number of checks written on each account per month, the number of preauthorized automatic transfers per month, and the minimum denomination of the amount of each check. In addition, MMDAs impose minimum balance requirements on depositors. The Federal Reserve does not require banks to hold cash reserves against MMDAs. Accordingly, banks generally pay higher rates on MMDAs than on NOW accounts. **Other savings deposits** (item 31) are all savings accounts other than MMDAs (i.e., regular passbook accounts)

**other savings deposits**

*All savings accounts other than MMDAs.*

6. Super-NOW accounts have very similar features to NOW accounts, but require a larger minimum balance.

with no set maturity and no check-writing privileges. Like MMDAs, savings accounts currently carry zero reserve requirements.

Some banks separate foreign from domestic deposits on the balance sheet (item 32). Foreign deposits are not explicitly covered by FDIC-provided deposit insurance guarantees (see Chapter 13). These deposits are generally large and held by corporations with a high level of international transactions and activities.

The major categories of time deposits are retail certificates of deposit (CDs) and wholesale CDs. **Retail CDs** (item 33) are fixed-maturity instruments with face values under $100,000. Although the size, maturity, and rates on these CDs are negotiable, most banks issue standardized retail CDs. **Wholesale CDs** (item 35) (discussed also in Chapter 5) were created by banks in the early 1960s as a contractual mechanism to allow depositors to liquidate their position in these CDs by selling them in the secondary market rather than having to hold them to maturity or requesting that the bank cash in the deposit early (which involves a penalty cost for the depositor). Thus, a depositor can sell a relatively liquid instrument without causing adverse liquidity risk exposure for the bank. Consequently, the unique feature of wholesale CDs is not so much their large minimum denomination size of $100,000 or more but the fact that they are **negotiable instruments**. That is, they can be resold by title assignment in a secondary market to other investors. This means, for example, that if IBM had bought a $1 million three-month CD from J.P. Morgan Chase, but for unexpected liquidity reasons needed funds after only one month passed, it could sell this CD to another outside investor in the secondary market. This does not impose any obligation on J.P. Morgan Chase in terms of an early funds withdrawal request. Wholesale CDs obtained through a brokerage or investment house rather than directly from a customer are referred to as **brokered deposits**.[7] CDs held in foreign offices and denominated in dollars are referred to as *Eurodollar deposits* (see Chapter 5).

*Borrowed Funds.*    The liabilities described previously are all deposit liabilities, reflecting deposit contracts issued by banks in return for cash. However, banks not only fund their assets by issuing deposits, but borrow in various markets for purchased funds. Since the funds generated from these purchases are not deposits, they are subject to neither reserve requirements (as with demand deposits and NOW accounts) nor deposit insurance premium payments to the FDIC (as with all the domestic deposits described earlier). The largest market available for purchased funds is the federal funds market (item 37). As we discussed earlier, a bank with excess reserves can sell them in the fed funds market, recording them as an asset on the balance sheet. The bank that purchases fed funds shows them as a liability on its balance sheet. As with the fed funds market, the RP market (item 37) is a highly liquid and flexible source of funds for banks needing to increase their liabilities and to offset deposit withdrawals. Moreover, like fed funds, these transactions can be rolled over each day if the counterparty is willing. The major difference in flexibility of liability management for fed funds and RPs is that a fed funds transaction can be entered into at virtually any time in the banking day. In general, it is difficult to transact an RP borrowing late in the day since the bank sending the fed funds must be satisfied with the type and quality of the securities' collateral proposed by the borrowing bank. Although this collateral is normally T-bills, T-notes, T-bonds, and mortgage-backed securities, the maturities and other features, such as callability or coupons, may be unattractive to the fund seller.

Fed funds and RPs have been the major sources of borrowed funds, but banks have utilized other borrowing (item 38) sources to supplement their flexibility in liability management. Four of these sources are banker's acceptances (BAs), commercial paper, medium-term notes, and discount window loans. Banks often convert off-balance-sheet letters of credit into on-balance-sheet BAs by discounting the letter of credit when the holder presents it for acceptance (see Chapter 5). In addition, these BAs may be resold to

---

**retail CDs**

*Time deposits with a face value below $100,000.*

**wholesale CDs**

*Time deposits with a face value of $100,000 or more.*

**negotiable instrument**

*An instrument whose ownership can be transferred in the secondary market.*

**brokered deposits**

*Wholesale CDs obtained through a brokerage house.*

---

7.  These are often purchased in $100,000 increments. For example, a broker may receive $1 million from an investor and break this up into 10 lots of $100,000 CDs that are placed (brokered out) at 10 different banks. Thus, effectively, the full $1 million is covered by FDIC deposit insurance.

money market investors. As a result, BA sales to the secondary market are an additional funding source. Although a bank subsidiary itself cannot issue commercial paper, its parent holding company can—that is, Citigroup can issue commercial paper but Citibank cannot. This provides banks owned by holding companies—most of the largest banks in the United States—with an additional funding source, since the holding company can "downstream" funds generated from its commercial paper sales to its bank subsidiary. Finally, banks facing temporary liquidity crunches can borrow from the central bank's discount window at the discount rate. Since this rate is not market determined and usually lies below government security rates, it offers a very attractive borrowing opportunity to a bank with deficient reserves as the reserve maintenance period comes to an end (see Chapter 13).

A number of banks in search of stable sources of funds with low withdrawal risk have begun to issue subordinated notes and debentures (item 39), often in the five- to seven-year range. These notes are especially attractive because they are subject to neither reserve requirements nor deposit insurance premiums, and some can serve as (Tier II) capital for the bank to satisfy Federal Reserve regulations regarding minimum capital requirements (see Chapter 13).

**core deposits**

*Deposits of the bank that are stable over short periods of time and thus provide a long-term funding source to a bank.*

**purchased funds**

*Rate-sensitive funding sources of the bank.*

Some banks separate core deposits from purchased funds on their balance sheets. The stable deposits of the bank are referred to as **core deposits** (item 34). These deposits are not expected to be withdrawn over short periods of time and are therefore a more permanent source of funding for the bank. Core deposits are also the cheapest funds banks can use to finance their assets. Because they are both a stable and low-cost source of funding, core deposits are the most frequently used source of funding by commercial banks. Core deposits generally are defined as demand deposits, NOW accounts, MMDAs, other savings accounts, and retail CDs. **Purchased funds** are more expensive and/or volatile sources of funds because they are highly rate sensitive—these funds are more likely to be immediately withdrawn or replaced as rates on competitive instruments change. Further, interest rates on these funds, at any point in time, are generally higher than rates on core deposits. Purchased funds are generally defined as brokered deposits, wholesale CDs, deposits at foreign offices, fed funds purchased, RPs, and subordinated notes and debentures.

*Other Liabilities.* Banks also list other liabilities (item 40) that do not require interest to be paid. These items consist of accrued interest, deferred taxes, dividends payable, minority interests in consolidated subsidies, and other miscellaneous claims.

**Equity Capital.** The bank's equity capital (item 46) consists mainly of preferred (item 42) and common (item 43) stock (listed at par value), surplus and additional paid-in capital (item 44), and retained earnings (item 45). Regulations require banks to hold a minimum level of equity capital to act as a buffer against losses from their on- and off-balance-sheet assets (see Chapter 13).

### Off-Balance-Sheet Assets and Liabilities

Off-balance-sheet (OBS) items are *contingent* assets and liabilities that *may* affect the future status of a financial institution's balance sheet. OBS activities are less obvious and often invisible to financial statement readers because they usually appear "below the bottom line," frequently as footnotes to accounts. As part of the quarterly financial reports submitted to regulators, schedule L lists the notional dollar size of OBS activities of banks. We briefly summarized the OBS activities of commercial banks in Chapter 11. In this chapter, we introduce the items as they appear off the FI's balance sheet.

Although OBS activities are now an important source of fee income for many FIs, they have the potential to produce positive as well as negative *future* cash flows. Some OBS activities can involve risks that add to the institution's overall risk exposure; others can hedge or reduce the institution's interest rate, credit, and foreign exchange risks. A depository institution's performance and solvency are also affected by the management of these items. Off-balance-sheet activities can be grouped into four major categories: loan

**loan commitment**

*Contractual commitment to loan to a firm a certain maximum amount at given interest rate terms.*

**up-front fee**

*The fee charged for making funds available through a loan commitment.*

**commitment fee**

*The fee charged on the unused component of a loan commitment.*

**commercial letters of credit (LCs)**

*Contingent guarantees sold by an FI to underwrite the trade or commercial performance of the buyers of the guarantees.*

**standby letters of credit (SLCs)**

*Guarantees issued to cover contingencies that are potentially more severe and less predictable than contingencies covered under trade-related or commercial letters of credit.*

commitments, letters of credit, loans sold, and derivative securities. The OBS activities for Heartland Bank and Trust and Bank of America are reported in Table 12–2.

**Loan Commitments.**   These days, most commercial and industrial loans are made by firms that take down (or borrow against) prenegotiated lines of credit or loan commitments rather than borrow cash immediately in the form of spot loans. A **loan commitment** agreement (item 1 in Table 12–2) is a contractual commitment by a bank or another FI (such as an insurance company) to loan to a customer a certain maximum amount (say, $10 million) at given interest rate terms (say, 12 percent). The loan commitment agreement also defines the length of time over which the borrower has the option to take down this loan. In return for making this loan commitment, the bank may charge an **up-front fee** (or facility fee) of, say, 1/8 percent of the commitment size, or $12,500 in this example. In addition, the bank must stand ready to supply the full $10 million at any time over the commitment period—for example, one year. Meanwhile, the borrower has a valuable option to take down any amount between $0 and $10 million over the commitment period. The bank may also charge the borrower a **commitment fee** on any unused commitment balances at the end of the period. In this example, if the borrower takes down only $8 million over the year and the fee on *unused* commitments is 1/4 percent, the bank generates additional revenue of 1/4 percent times $2 million, or $5,000.

Note that only when the borrower actually draws on the commitment do the loans made under the commitment appear on the balance sheet. Thus, only when the $8 million loan is taken down exactly halfway through the one-year commitment period (i.e., six months later) does the balance sheet show the creation of a new $8 million loan. We illustrate the transaction in Figure 12–1. When the $10 million commitment is made at time 0, nothing shows on the balance sheet. Nevertheless, the bank must stand ready to supply the full $10 million in loans on any day within the one-year commitment period—at time 0 a new contingent claim on the resources of the bank is created. At time 6 months, when the $8 million is drawn down, the balance sheet will reflect this as an $8 million loan.

**Commercial Letters of Credit and Standby Letters of Credit.**   In selling **commercial letters of credit (LCs)** (item 2 in Table 12–2) and **standby letters of credit (SLCs)** (item 3) for fees, banks add to their contingent future liabilities. Commercial letters of credit are widely used in both domestic and international trade. For example, they ease

**TABLE 12–2**  Off-Balance-Sheet Activities for Two Commercial Banks
*(in millions of dollars)*

| | Heartland Bank and Trust | Bank of America |
|---|---|---|
| **Commitments and Contingencies** | | |
| 1. Loan commitments | $396.49 | $   812,278 |
| 2. Commercial letters of credit | 0.00 | 1,756 |
| 3. Standby letters of credit | 9.21 | 47,511 |
| 4. Loans sold | 5.42 | 24,695 |
| **Notional Amounts for Derivatives*** | | |
| 5. Forwards and futures | $ 23.56 | $ 9,169,744 |
| 6. Options | 0.00 | 2,047,803 |
| 7. Interest rate swaps | 205.71 | 14,061,372 |
| 8. Credit derivatives | 0.00 | 1,653,695 |
| 9. Total | $640.39 | $27,818,854 |

**Source:** Values are taken from the 2016 FDIC Report of Condition data tapes available at the Federal Deposit Insurance Corporation website. www.fdic.gov
* Notional amounts reflect the face value of the contracts entered into.

**Figure 12–1** Loan Commitment Transaction

| 0 | 6 Months | 1 Year |
|---|---|---|
| $10m. Loan Commitment Agreement Begins Off Balance Sheet; No Change Made On Balance Sheet. | Take Down $8m. of Loan Commitment; Loans Increase by $8m. On Balance Sheet; $2m. Commitment Remains Off Balance Sheet. | Loan Commitment Period Ends and Is Removed Off Balance Sheet; No Change On Balance Sheet. |

the shipment of grain between a farmer in Iowa and a purchaser in New Orleans or the shipment of goods between a U.S. importer and a foreign exporter. The bank's role is to provide a formal guarantee that payment for goods shipped or sold will be forthcoming regardless of whether the buyer of the goods defaults on payment.

Standby letters of credit perform an insurance function similar to commercial and trade letters of credit. The structure and type of risk covered differ, however. FIs may issue SLCs to cover contingencies that are potentially more severe, less predictable or frequent, and not necessarily trade related. These contingencies include performance bond guarantees by which an FI may guarantee that a real estate development will be completed in some interval of time. Alternatively, the FI may offer default guarantees to back an issue of commercial paper or municipal revenue bonds to allow issuers to achieve a higher credit rating and a lower funding cost than otherwise would be possible.

Both LCs and SLCs are essentially *guarantees* to underwrite performance that a depository institution sells to the buyers of the guarantees (such as a corporation). In economic terms, the depository institution that sells LCs and SLCs is selling insurance against the frequency or severity of some particular future event occurring. Further, similar to the different lines of insurance sold by property-casualty insurers, LC and SLC contracts differ as to the severity and frequency of their risk exposures.

**loans sold**

*Loans originated by the bank and then sold to other investors that can be returned to the originating institution.*

**recourse**

*The ability to put an asset or loan back to the seller should the credit quality of that asset deteriorate.*

**Loans Sold.** **Loans sold** (item 4 in Table 12–2) are loans that a bank has originated and then sold to other investors that may be returned (sold with **recourse**) to the originating institution in the future if the credit quality of the loans deteriorates. We discuss the types of loans that banks sell, their incentives to sell, and the way in which they can sell them in more detail in Chapter 24. Banks and other FIs increasingly originate loans on their balance sheets, but rather than holding the loans to maturity, they quickly sell them to outside investors. These outside investors include other banks, insurance companies, mutual funds, or even corporations. In acting as loan originators and loan sellers, banks are operating more as loan brokers than as traditional asset transformers (see Chapters 1 and 11).

When an outside party buys a loan with absolutely no recourse to the seller of the loan should the loan eventually go bad, loan sales have no OBS contingent liability implications for banks. Specifically, *no recourse* means that if the loan the bank sells should go bad, the buyer of the loan must bear the full risk of loss. In particular, the buyer cannot go back to the seller or originating bank to seek payment on the bad loan. Suppose that the loan is sold with recourse. Then, loan sales present a long-term off-balance-sheet or contingent credit risk to the seller. Essentially, the buyer of the loan holds an option to put the loan back to the seller, which the buyer can exercise should the credit quality of the purchased loan materially deteriorate. In reality, the recourse or nonrecourse nature of loan sales is often ambiguous. For example, some have argued that banks generally are willing to repurchase bad no-recourse loans to preserve their reputations with their customers. Obviously, reputation concerns may extend the size of a selling bank's contingent liabilities from OBS activities.

**derivative securities**

*Futures, forward, swap, and option positions taken by the FI for hedging or other purposes.*

**Derivative Contracts.**   **Derivative securities** (items 5 to 8 in Table 12–2) are the futures, forward, swap, and option positions taken by a bank for hedging and other purposes (see Chapters 10 and 23). We discussed the tremendous growth of derivative securities activity in Chapter 11. Banks can be either users of derivative contracts for hedging (see Chapter 10 and 23) and other purposes or dealers that act as intermediaries in trades with customers for a fee. It has been estimated that some 1,420 U.S. banks use derivatives and that four large dealer banks—J.P. Morgan Chase, Citigroup, Goldman Sachs, and Bank of America—account for some 91 percent of the derivatives that user banks hold.[8]

Counterparty, or contingent credit, risk is likely to be present when banks expand their positions in futures, forward, swap, and option contracts. This risk relates to the fact that the counterparty to one of these contracts may default on payment obligations, leaving the bank unhedged and having to replace the contract at today's interest rates, prices, or exchange rates, which may be relatively unfavorable. In addition, such defaults are most likely to occur when the counterparty is losing heavily on the contract and the bank is in the money on the contract. This type of default risk is much more serious for forward contracts than for futures contracts. This is because forward contracts are nonstandard contracts entered into bilaterally by negotiating parties, such as two banks, and all cash flows are required to be paid at one time (on contract maturity). Thus, they are essentially over-the-counter (OTC) arrangements with no external guarantees should one or the other party default on the contract (see Chapter 10). By contrast, futures contracts are standardized contracts guaranteed by organized exchanges such as the New York Mercantile Exchange (NYMEX). Futures contracts, like forward contracts, make commitments to deliver foreign exchange (or some other asset) at some future date. If a counterparty were to default on a futures contract, however, the exchange would assume the defaulting party's position and payment obligations.

Option contracts can also be traded over the counter (OTC) or bought/sold on organized exchanges. If the options are standardized options traded on exchanges, such as bond options, they are virtually default risk free.[9] If they are specialized options purchased OTC, such as interest rate caps (see Chapter 10), some elements of default risk exist.[10] Similarly, swaps are OTC instruments normally susceptible to default risk (see Chapter 10).[11] In general, default risk on OTC contracts increases with the time to maturity of the contract and the fluctuation of underlying prices, interest rates, or exchange rates.[12]

### Other Fee-Generating Activities

Commercial banks engage in other fee-generating activities that cannot be easily identified from analyzing their on- and off-balance-sheet accounts. These include trust services, processing services, and correspondent banking.

**Trust Services.**   The trust department of a commercial bank holds and manages assets for individuals or corporations. Only the largest banks have sufficient staff to offer trust services. Individual trusts represent about one-half of all trust assets managed by commercial banks. These trusts include estate assets and assets delegated to bank trust departments by less financially sophisticated investors. Pension fund assets are the second largest group of assets managed by the trust departments of commercial banks. The banks manage the pension funds, act as trustees for any bonds held by the pension funds, and act as transfer and disbursement agents for the pension funds.

---

8. See *OCC Bank Derivative Report,* First Quarter 2016, and Chapter 10.
9. Note that the options still can be subject to interest rate risk; see the discussion in Chapter 23.
10. Under an interest rate cap, the seller, in return for a fee, promises to compensate the buyer should interest rates rise above a certain level. If rates rise much more than expected, the cap seller may have an incentive to default to truncate the losses. Thus, selling a cap is similar to a bank's selling interest rate risk insurance (see Chapter 10 for more details).
11. In a swap, two parties contract to exchange interest rate payments or foreign exchange payments. If interest rates (or foreign exchange rates) move a good deal, one party can face considerable future loss exposure, creating incentives to default.
12. Reputational considerations and the need for future access to markets for hedging deter the incentive to default (see Chapter 23 as well). However, most empirical evidence suggests that derivative contracts have reduced FI risk.

**Processing Services.** Commercial banks have traditionally provided financial data processing services for their business customers. These services include managing a customer's accounts receivable and accounts payable. Similarly, bank cash management services include the provision of lockbox services where customers of a firm send payments to a post office box managed by a bank, which opens, processes, collects, and deposits checks within a very short time (sometimes as short as one hour) in the business customer's account. Banks also provide personalized services for both large and small companies, including moving funds from savings accounts that earn interest to transactions accounts that do not earn interest as firms need to make payments. The larger commercial banks have broadened their range of business services to include management consulting, data processing, and information systems or other technological services. Information systems and software marketed by commercial banks assist clients in collecting, analyzing, and reporting data effectively and efficiently.

**Correspondent Banking.** Correspondent banking is the provision of banking services to other banks that do not have the staff resources to perform the service themselves. These services include check clearing and collection, foreign exchange trading, hedging services, and participation in large loan and security issuances. Correspondent banking services are generally sold as a package of services. Payment for the services is generally in the form of non-interest-bearing deposits held at the bank offering the correspondent services.

---

**LG 12-4**

## Income Statement

See Table 12–3 for the report of income or income statement for Heartland Bank and Trust and Bank of America for 2016. The report of income identifies the interest income and expenses, net interest income, provision for loan losses, noninterest income and expenses, income before taxes and extraordinary items, and net income for the banks earned from the on- and off-balance-sheet activities described earelier. As we discuss the income statement, notice the direct relationship between it and the balance sheet (both on and off balance sheet). The composition of an FI's assets and liabilities, combined with the interest rates earned or paid on them, directly determines the interest income and expense on the income statement. In addition, because the assets and liabilities of FIs are mainly financial, most of the income and expense items reported on the income statement are interest rate related (rather than reflecting sales prices and cost of goods sold, as seen with manufacturing corporations).

**Interest Income.** The income statement for a commercial bank first shows the sources of interest income (item 14). Interest and fee income on loans and leases (item 6 in Table 12–3) is the largest interest income-producing category. Subcategories are often listed on the income statement (items 1–4) for each category of loan listed earlier. Most banks also list income on leases (item 5) as a separate item. Interest on investment securities held (item 13) is also included as interest income. These too may be listed by subcategories (items 7–12) described earlier. Interest income is recorded on an accrued basis (see earlier discussion). Thus, loans on which interest payments are past due can still be recorded as generating income for a bank.[13] Interest income is taxable, except for that on municipal securities and tax-exempt income from direct lease financing. Tax-exempt interest can be converted to a taxable equivalent basis as follows:

$$\text{Taxable equivalent interest income} = \frac{\text{Interest income}}{1 - \text{Bank's tax rate}}$$

**Interest Expenses.** Interest expense (item 24) is the second major category on a bank's income statement. Items listed here come directly from the liability section of the balance

---

13. A bank can recognize income for at least 90 days after the due date of the interest payment.

**TABLE 12–3**　Income Statement for Two Commercial Banks *(in millions of dollars)*

| | Heartland Bank and Trust | Bank of America |
|---|---|---|
| **Interest Income** | | |
| 1. Income on C&I loans | $ 18.44 | $ 5,468 |
| 2. Income on real estate loans | 61.41 | 11,576 |
| 3. Income on consumer loans | 0.75 | 11,292 |
| 4. Income on other loans | 4.24 | 5,204 |
| 5. Income on leases | 0.00 | 852 |
| 6. Interest and fees on loans and leases | $ 84.84 | $34,392 |
| 7. Interest on deposits at other institutions | 0.32 | 680 |
| 8. Interest on fed funds and RPs | 0.00 | 156 |
| 9. Interest on U.S. Treasury and agency securities | 0.86 | 320 |
| 10. Interest on securities issued by states and political subdivisions | 5.94 | 452 |
| 11. Interest on mortgage-backed securities | 4.14 | 3,346 |
| 12. Interest on municipals and other debt and equity securities | 1.96 | 1,480 |
| 13. Interest income on investment securities | $ 13.22 | $ 6,524 |
| 14. *Total interest income* | $ 98.06 | $40,916 |
| **Interest Expense** | | |
| 15. Interest on NOW accounts | $ 0.09 | $ 96 |
| 16. Interest on MMDA accounts and other savings | 1.10 | 272 |
| 17. Interest on foreign deposits | 0.00 | 332 |
| 18. Interest on retail CDs | 1.22 | 112 |
| 19. Interest on wholesale CDs | 0.48 | 108 |
| 20. Interest on deposit accounts | $ 2.89 | $ 920 |
| 21. Interest on fed funds and RPs | 0.04 | 192 |
| 22. Interest on other borrowed funds | 0.22 | 748 |
| 23. Interest on subordinated notes and debentures | 0.00 | 88 |
| 24. Total interest expense | $ 3.15 | $ 1,948 |
| 25. *Net interest income* | $ 94.91 | $38,968 |
| 26. *Provision for loan losses* | ($ 0.03) | $ 4,116 |
| **Noninterest Income** | | |
| 27. Income from fiduciary activities | $ 4.43 | $ 1,768 |
| 28. Service charges on deposit accounts | 6.72 | 5,308 |
| 29. Trading revenue | 0.00 | 2,540 |
| 30. Fees from investment banking and security brokerage | 0.94 | 1,328 |
| 31. Fees from insurance | 0.02 | 28 |
| 32. Net servicing fees | 0.39 | (1,124) |
| 33. Net gain (loss) from sale of loans and investment securities | 5.13 | 2,064 |
| 34. Other noninterest income | 9.45 | 13,792 |
| 35. *Total noninterest income* | $ 27.08 | $25,704 |
| **Noninterest Expense** | | |
| 36. Salaries and employee benefits | $ 42.45 | $18,652 |
| 37. Expenses of premises and fixed assets | 8.48 | 4,828 |
| 38. Other noninterest expense | 16.23 | 14,660 |
| 39. *Total noninterest expense* | $ 67.16 | $38,140 |
| 40. Income before taxes and extraordinary items | $ 54.86 | $22,416 |
| 41. Applicable income taxes | 0.73 | 7,204 |
| 42. Extraordinary items | 0.00 | 0 |
| 43. **Net income** | $ 54.13 | $15,212 |

**Source:** Values are taken from the 2016 FDIC Report of Condition data tapes available at the Federal Deposit Insurance Corporation website. www.fdic.gov

sheet: interest on deposits (item 20) (NOW accounts (item 15), MMDAs and other savings (item 16), foreign deposits (item 17), retail CDs (item 18), and wholesale CDs (item 19)), and interest on fed funds and RPs (item 21), and other borrowed funds (item 22). Interest on subordinated notes and debentures (item 23) is generally reported as a separate item.

**Net Interest Income.**   Total interest income minus total interest expense is listed next on the income statement as net interest income (item 25). Net interest income is an important tool in assessing the bank's ability to generate profits and control interest rate risk (see below).

**Provision for Loan Losses.**   The provision for loan losses (item 26) is a noncash, tax-deductible expense. The provision for loan losses is the current period's allocation to the allowance for loan losses listed on the balance sheet. This item represents the bank management's prediction of loans at risk of default for the period. While the loans remain on the bank's balance sheet, the expected losses from any bad loans affect net income and equity on the income statement and balance sheet, respectively. For example, during the financial crisis Bank of America increased its loan loss reserve (recording a provision for loan losses) by $13.4 billion in the second quarter of 2009. This loan-loss provision expense was recorded in recognition of expected losses on mortgages and loans tied to the financial crisis. As a result, Bank of America's earnings per share fell 54 percent.

As mentioned earlier, the size of the provision is determined by management, and in the United States it is subject to a maximum allowable tax-deductible amount set by the Internal Revenue Service. Currently, banks do not have to record a provision until there are signs of a loss on a loan. However, a key reform emerging from the financial crisis is a rule that would require banks to look ahead and record a provision for loan loss on the day a loan is made. The rules for recording provisions were faulted as being too little, too late during the financial crisis. Many banks were battered by defaults on loans for which no provision had been set aside. As a remedy, banking regulators have called for the timelier recording of provisions. Critics, however, warn that the proposed changes will make earnings more volatile as banks must continuously adjust their expectations for losses. FASB officials estimated some U.S. banks would require a 50 percent increase in reserves under the proposed change. The rules were approved in June 2016. Banks that are publicly traded have to adopt the FASB's change beginning in 2020 and privately held banks in 2021.

---

**EXAMPLE 12–1**   **The Relationship between Allowance for Loan Losses, Provision for Loan Losses, and Loan Balances**

At the beginning of the month, a bank has $1 million in its loan portfolio and $50,000 in the allowance for loan losses (see Panel a of Figure 12–2). During the month, management estimates that an additional $5,000 of loans will not be paid as promised. Accordingly, the bank records an expense to loan loss provision (which reduces net income and thus retained earnings and equity of the bank) and increases the allowance for loan losses to $55,000 on the balance sheet (see Panel b in Figure 12–2). Notice that the loan is still listed as an asset on the bank's balance sheet at this time. After another month, management feels there is no chance of recovering the loan and writes the $5,000 loan off its books. At this time, loans are reduced by $5,000 as is the allowance for loan losses (see Panel c in Figure 12–2). Notice when the loan is considered unrecoverable and actually removed from the balance sheet, there is no impact on the bank's income or equity value.

---

**Noninterest Income.**   Noninterest income (item 35) includes all other income received by the bank as a result of its on- and off-balance-sheet activities and is becoming increasingly important as the ability to attract core deposits and high-quality loan applicants becomes

**Figure 12–2**    The Relationship between Allowance for Loan Losses, Provision for Loan Losses, and Loan Balances

(a) Beginning of Month 1

| Assets | | Liabilities and Equity | |
|---|---|---|---|
| Securities | $ 250,000 | Deposits | $ 700,000 |
| Gross Loans | 1,000,000 | Common Stock | 200,000 |
| Less: Allowance | | Ret. Earnings | 300,000 |
| for Loan Losses | $ 50,000 | Total Equity | 500,000 |
| Net Loans | $ 950,000 | Total | $1,200,000 |
| Total Assets | $1,200,000 | | |

(b) End of Month 1

| Assets | | Liabilities and Equity | |
|---|---|---|---|
| Securities | $ 250,000 | Deposits | $ 700,000 |
| Gross Loans | 1,000,000 | Common Stock | 200,000 |
| Less: Allowance | | Ret. Earnings | 295,000 |
| for Loan Losses | $ 55,000 | Total Equity | 495,000 |
| Net Loans | $ 945,000 | Total | $1,195,000 |
| Total Assets | $1,195,000 | | |

(c) End of Month 2

| Assets | | Liabilities and Equity | |
|---|---|---|---|
| Securities | $ 250,000 | Deposits | $ 700,000 |
| Gross Loans | 995,000 | Common Stock | 200,000 |
| Less: Allowance | | Ret. Earnings | 295,000 |
| for Loan Losses | $ 50,000 | Total Equity | 495,000 |
| Net Loans | $ 945,000 | Total | $1,195,000 |
| Total Assets | $1,195,000 | | |

more difficult. Included in this category is income from fiduciary activities (for example, earnings from operating a trust department—item 27), service charges on deposit accounts (item 28), trading revenues (gains [losses] and fees from trading marketable instruments and OBS derivative instruments—item 29), fees from other-than-banking activities such fees from investment banking and security brokerage (item 30), fees from insurance (item 31), servicing fees from mortgages, credit cards, and other assets (item 32), gains and losses from the sale of loans and investment securities (item 33), and other noninterest income (fee income from OBS loan commitments and letters of credit, ATM fees, money order, cashier's check, and travelers' check fees, data processing revenue, and revenue from one-time transactions such as sales of real estate owned, loans, premises, and fixed assets—item 34).

**total operating income**

*The sum of the interest income and noninterest income.*

The sum of interest income and noninterest income is referred to as the bank's **total operating income** or *total revenue.* Total operating income for a bank is equivalent to total sales in a manufacturing firm and represents the bank's income received from all sources.

**Noninterest Expense.**   Noninterest expense (item 39) items consist mainly of personnel expenses and are generally large relative to noninterest income. Items in this category include salaries and employee benefits (item 36), expenses of premises and fixed assets (i.e., utilities and depreciation—item 37), and other operating expenses (e.g., deposit insurance premiums and expenses of one-time transactions such as losses on the sale of real estate, loans, and premises—item 38). For almost all banks, noninterest expense is greater than noninterest income. Thus, noninterest expense is sometimes referred to as the "burden" of the bank.

**Income before Taxes and Extraordinary Items.** Net interest income minus provisions for loan losses plus noninterest income minus noninterest expense produces the operating profit or income before taxes and extraordinary items for the bank (item 40).

**Income Taxes.** All federal, state, local, and foreign income taxes due from the bank are listed next on the income statement (item 41). Some of this amount may have been paid to the Internal Revenue Service (IRS) and the remainder is recorded as a liability (deferred taxes) to be paid to the IRS later.

**Extraordinary Items.** Extraordinary items and other adjustments (item 42) are events or transactions that are both unusual and infrequent. This includes such things as effects of changes in accounting rules, corrections of accounting errors made in previous years, and equity capital adjustments (losses from a major disaster such as an earthquake in an area where earthquakes are not expected to occur in the foreseeable future).

**Net Income.** Income before taxes and extraordinary items minus income taxes plus (or minus) extraordinary items results in the net income for the bank (item 43). Net income is the *bottom line* on the income statement.

## DO YOU UNDERSTAND:

1. What a DI's CAMELS rating measures?

2. What the trade-offs are in holding a large proportion of short-term securities, such as T-bills, versus long-term securities, such as loans?

3. What the trade-offs are in issuing short-term deposit accounts (core deposits), such as demand deposits and retail CDs, versus long-term deposits and other funding sources (borrowed funds), such as wholesale CDs and long-term debt?

4. What the major difference is between a commercial letter of credit and a standby letter of credit?

5. What counterparty risk in a forward contract means?

6. Which is riskier for a bank, loan sales with recourse or loan sales without recourse?

7. What the nature of the relationship is between balance sheet and income statement items?

8. How paying a lower rate for new deposits than for other liabilities affects a bank's income statement

## Direct Relationship between the Income Statement and the Balance Sheet

As mentioned earlier, banks' financial statements are directly related (more so than for nonfinancial companies). That is, the items on the income statement are determined by the balance sheet assets and liabilities along with the interest rates on each item. This direct relationship between the two financial statements can be seen by depicting the income statement as follows:

$$NI = \sum_{n=1}^{N} r_n A_n - \sum_{m=1}^{M} r_m L_m - P + NII - NIE - T$$

where

$NI$ = Bank's net income
$A_n$ = Dollar value of the bank's $n$th asset
$L_m$ = Dollar value of the bank's $m$th liability
$r_n$ = Rate earned on the bank's $n$th asset
$r_m$ = Rate paid on the bank's $m$th liability
$P$ = Provision for loan losses
$NII$ = Noninterest income earned by the bank, including income from off-balance-sheet activities
$NIE$ = Noninterest expenses incurred by the bank
$T$ = Bank's taxes and extraordinary items
$N$ = Number of assets the bank holds
$M$ = Number of liabilities the bank holds

Net income is the direct result of (1) the amount and mix of assets and liabilities held by the bank taken from the balance sheet and (2) the interest rate on each of them. For example, increasing the dollar value of an asset, all else constant, results in a direct increase in the bank's net income equal to the size of the increase times the rate of interest on the asset. Likewise, decreasing the rate paid on a liability, all else constant, directly increases net income by the size of the rate decrease times the dollar value of the liability on the balance sheet. Finally, changing the mix of assets or liabilities on the balance sheet has a direct effect on net income equal to the size of the rate difference times the dollar value of the asset or liability being changed. For example, suppose that a bank has the following net income:

$$NI = 0.046(1m.) + 0.06(3m.) - 0.035(3m.) - 0.0475(1m.) = \$73,500$$

The bank replaces $500,000 of assets currently yielding 4.60 percent with assets yielding 6 percent. As a result, net income increases by $7,000 [(6% − 4.6%) × $500,000], or

$$NI = 0.046(0.5m.) + 0.06(3.5m.) - 0.035(3m) - 0.0475(1m.) = \$80,500$$

## FINANCIAL STATEMENT ANALYSIS USING A RETURN ON EQUITY FRAMEWORK

**time series analysis**

*Analysis of financial statements over a period of time.*

**cross-sectional analysis**

*Analysis of financial statements comparing one firm with others.*

www.ffiec.gov/UBPR.htm

In the early and mid-2000s, the commercial banking industry experienced a period of record profits. The financial crisis brought about an abrupt reversal of this trend. During periods of falling profits and even during periods of record profits, many banks have weak and inefficient areas that need to be addressed. One way to identify weaknesses and problem areas is by analyzing financial statements. In particular, an analysis of selected accounting ratios—ratio analysis—allows a bank manager to evaluate the bank's current performance, the change in its performance over time (**time series analysis** of ratios over a period of time), and its performance relative to that of competitor banks (**cross-sectional analysis** of ratios across a group of firms).

Analyzing ratio trends over time, along with absolute ratio levels, gives managers, analysts, and investors information about whether a firm's financial condition is improving or deteriorating. For example, ratio analysis may reveal that a bank's capital-to-assets ratio is decreasing. This suggests that capital is decreasing as a source of financing the assets of the bank and that deposits and purchased funds are being increasingly used to finance the bank's assets. If this increase is the result of a deliberate policy to decrease capital and use cheaper sources of asset financing, the decreased capital ratio is good for the bank. Managers and investors should be concerned, on the other hand, if a decreased capital-to-asset ratio is the result of declining profits.

Looking at one bank's financial ratios, even through time, gives managers, analysts, and investors only a limited picture of bank performance. Ratio analysis almost always includes a comparison of one bank's ratios relative to the ratios of other firms in the industry, or cross-sectional analysis. Key to cross-sectional analysis is identifying similar banks in that they compete in the same markets, have similar sized assets, and operate in a similar manner to the bank being analyzed. Since no two banks are identical, obtaining such a comparison group is no easy task. Thus, the choice of companies to use in cross-sectional analysis is at best subjective. A tool available to assist in cross-sectional analysis is the Uniform Bank Performance Report (UBPR) maintained by the Federal Financial Institutions Examination Council. The UBPR summarizes the performance of banks for various peer groups (banks similar in size and economic environment), for various size groups, and by state.

Figure 12–3 summarizes the return on equity (ROE) framework.[14] The ROE framework starts with the most frequently used measure of profitability, ROE, and then breaks it down to identify strengths and weaknesses in a bank's performance. The resulting breakdown provides a convenient and systematic method to identify strengths and weaknesses of a bank's profitability. Identification of strengths and weaknesses, and the reasons for them, provides an excellent tool for bank managers as they look for ways to improve profitability. Table 12–4 summarizes the role of ROE and the first two levels of the ROE framework (from Figure 12–3) in analyzing an FI's performance.

---

14. The ROE framework is similar to the DuPont analysis that managers of nonfinancial institutions frequently use.

The remainder of this chapter applies the ROE framework to our two banks: Heartland Bank and Trust and Bank of America. All of the ratios discussed as part of the ROE breakdown are reported in Tables 12–5 through 12–7. We refer to these ratios by number (1 through 127). In addition, Figure 12–3 lists these ratios (by ratio number) as they fit into the ROE framework.

**LG 12-5**

### Return on Equity and Its Components

ROE (ratio 1 in Table 12–5) is defined as:

$$\text{ROE} = \frac{\text{Net income}}{\text{Total equity capital}}$$

It measures the amount of net income after taxes earned for each dollar of equity capital contributed by the bank's stockholders. Taking these data from the financial statements for Heartland Bank and Trust and Bank of America, the banks' ROEs for 2016 were:[15]

|  | **Heartland** | **Bank of America** |
|---|---|---|
| ROE | $\frac{54.13}{257.94} = 20.99\%$ | $\frac{15,212}{211,275} = 7.20\%$ |

Generally, bank stockholders prefer ROE to be high. It is possible, however, that an increase in ROE indicates increased risk. For example, ROE increases if total equity capital decreases relative to net income. A large drop in equity capital may result in a violation of minimum regulatory capital standards and an increased risk of insolvency for the bank (see Chapters 13 and 22). An increase in ROE may simply result from an increase in a bank's leverage—an increase in its debt-to-equity ratio.

To identify potential problems, ROE (ratio 1) can be decomposed into two component parts, as follows:

$$\text{ROE} = \frac{\text{Net income}}{\text{Total assets}} \times \frac{\text{Total assets}}{\text{Total equity capital}}$$

$$= \text{ROA} \times \text{EM}$$

where

ROA (ratio 2) = Return on assets (a measure of profitability linked to the asset size of the bank)

EM (ratio 3) = Equity multiplier (a measure of leverage)

ROA determines the net income produced per dollar of assets. EM measures the dollar value of assets funded with each dollar of equity capital (the higher this ratio, the more leverage or debt the bank is using to fund its assets). The values of these ratios for our two banks in 2016 were:

|  | **Heartland** | **Bank of America** |
|---|---|---|
| ROA | $\frac{54.13}{2,448.36} = 2.21\%$ | $\frac{15,212}{1,676,743} = 0.91\%$ |
| EM | $\frac{2,448.36}{257.94} = 9.49$ times | $\frac{1,676,743}{211,275} = 7.94$ times |

15. We are using quarter-end balance sheet data to calculate ratios. The use of these data may bias ratios in that they are data for one day in the year, whereas income statement data cover the full year. To avoid this bias, average values for balance sheet data are often used to calculate ratios.

**Figure 12–3**   Classification of Ratios Listed in Tables 12–5 through 12–7

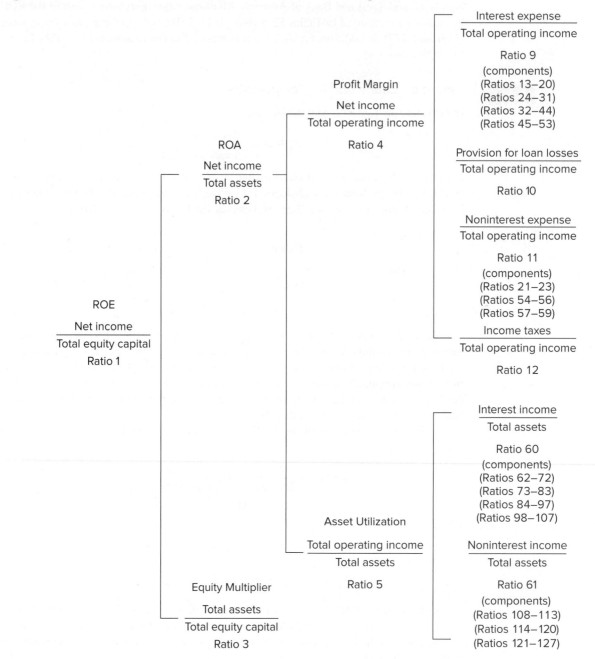

**Note:** Ratios 6–8 are discussed in the section "Other Ratios" later in the chapter.

**TABLE 12–4**   Role of ROE, ROA, EM, PM, and AU in Analyzing Financial Institution Performance

**Return on equity (ROE)**—measures overall profitability of the FI per dollar of equity.
**Return on assets (ROA)**—measures profit generated relative to the FI's assets.
**Equity multiplier (EM)**—measures the extent to which assets of the FI are funded with equity relative to debt.
**Profit margin (PM)**—measures the ability to pay expenses and generate net income from interest and noninterest income.
**Asset utilization (AU)**—measures the amount of interest and noninterest income generated per dollar of total assets.

**TABLE 12–5**  Overall Performance Ratios for Two Commercial Banks

| Ratio | Heartland Bank and Trust | Bank of America |
|---|---|---|
| **1.** ROE | 20.99% | 7.20% |
| **2.** ROA | 2.21% | 0.91% |
| **3.** Equity multiplier | 9.49× | 7.94× |
| **4.** Profit margin | 43.26% | 22.83% |
| **5.** Asset utilization | 5.11% | 3.97% |
| **6.** Net interest margin | 4.28% | 3.03% |
| **7.** Spread | 4.25% | 3.03% |
| **8.** Overhead efficiency | 40.32% | 67.39% |

High values for these ratios produce high ROEs, but, as noted, managers should be concerned about the source of high ROEs. For example, an increase in ROE due to an increase in the EM means that the bank's leverage, and therefore its solvency risk, has increased.

### Return on Assets and Its Components

A further breakdown of a bank's profitability is that of dividing ROA (ratio 2 in Table 12–5) into its profit margin (PM) and asset utilization (AU) ratio components:

$$\text{ROA} = \frac{\text{Net income}}{\text{Total operating income}} \times \frac{\text{Total operating income}}{\text{Total assets}}$$

$$= \text{PM} \times \text{AU}$$

where

PM (ratio 4) = Net income generated per dollar of total operating (interest and noninterest) income

AU (ratio 5) = Amount of interest and noninterest income generated per dollar of total assets

For our two banks, these are as follows:

| | Heartland | Bank of America |
|---|---|---|
| PM | $\dfrac{54.13}{98.06 + 27.08} = 43.26\%$ | $\dfrac{15{,}212}{40{,}916 + 25{,}704} = 22.83\%$ |
| AU | $\dfrac{98.06 + 27.08}{2{,}448.36} = 5.11\%$ | $\dfrac{40{,}916 + 25{,}704}{1{,}676{,}743} = 3.97\%$ |

Again, high values for these ratios produce high ROAs and ROEs. PM measures the bank's ability to control expenses. The better the expense control, the more profitable the bank. AU measures the bank's ability to generate income from its assets. The more income generated per dollar of assets, the more profitable the bank. Again, bank managers should be aware that high values of these ratios may indicate underlying problems. For example, PM increases if the bank experiences a drop in salaries and benefits. However, if this expense decreases because the most highly skilled employees are leaving the bank, the increase in PM and in ROA is associated with a potential "labor quality" problem. Thus, it is often prudent to break these ratios down further.

**Profit Margin.**  As stated, PM measures a bank's ability to control expenses and thus its ability to produce net income from its operating income (or revenue). A breakdown of PM, therefore, can isolate the various expense items listed on the income statement as follows (ratios used to decompose the profit margin are listed in Table 12–6):

$$\text{Interest expense ratio (ratio 9)} = \frac{\text{Interest expense}}{\text{Total operating income}}$$

$$\text{Provision for loan loss ratio (ratio 10)} = \frac{\text{Provision for loan losses}}{\text{Total operating income}}$$

$$\text{Noninterest expense ratio (ratio 11)} = \frac{\text{Noninterest expense}}{\text{Total operating income}}$$

$$\text{Tax ratio (ratio 12)} = \frac{\text{Income taxes}}{\text{Total operating income}}$$

These ratios measure the proportion of total operating income that goes to pay the particular expense item. The values of these ratios for Heartland Bank and Trust and Bank of America are as follows:

|  | **Heartland** | **Bank of America** |
|---|---|---|
| Interest expense ratio | $\dfrac{3.15}{98.06 + 27.08} = 2.52\%$ | $\dfrac{1,948}{40,916 + 25,704} = 2.92\%$ |
| Provision for loan loss ratio | $\dfrac{-0.03}{98.06 + 27.08} = -0.02\%$ | $\dfrac{4,116}{40,916 + 25,704} = 6.18\%$ |
| Noninterest expense ratio | $\dfrac{67.16}{98.06 + 27.08} = 53.67\%$ | $\dfrac{38,140}{40,916 + 25,704} = 57.25\%$ |
| Tax ratio | $\dfrac{0.73}{98.06 + 27.08} = 0.58\%$ | $\dfrac{7,204}{40,916 + 25,704} = 10.81\%$ |

The sum of the numerators of these four ratios subtracted from the denominator (total operating income) is the bank's net income.[16] Thus, the lower any of these ratios, the higher the bank's profitability (PM). As mentioned, however, although a low value for any of these ratios produces an increase in the bank's profit, it may be indicative of a problem situation in the bank. Thus, an even more detailed breakdown of these ratios may be warranted. For example, the interest expense ratio can be broken down according to the various interest expense-generating liabilities (ratios 13–20 in Table 12–6; e.g., interest on NOW accounts/total operating income). Additionally, the noninterest expense ratio may be broken down according to its components (ratios 21–23—e.g., salaries and employee benefits/total operating income). These ratios allow for a more detailed examination of the generation of the bank's expenses.

A different method to evaluate the bank's expense management is to calculate such ratios as deposit yields (ratios 24–31; e.g., interest expense on NOW accounts/dollar value of NOW accounts) or size of investment (e.g., dollar value of NOW accounts/total assets—ratios 32–44—or dollar value of NOW accounts/total interest-bearing liabilities—ratios 45–53). The noninterest expense items can be evaluated using component percentages (ratios 54–56; e.g., salaries and employee benefits/noninterest income) or size of expense (ratios 57–59; e.g., salaries and employee benefits/total assets).

**Asset Utilization.**   The AU ratio measures the extent to which the bank's assets generate revenue. The breakdown of the AU ratio separates the total revenue generated into interest

---

16. For example, for Bank of America, the denominator of each of the four ratios ($40,916 + $25,704 = $66,620) less the sum of the numerators of the four ratios ($1,948 + $4,116 + $38,140 + $7,204 = $51,408) is $15,212, which is the net income reported for Bank of America in Table 12–3.

**TABLE 12–6**  Decomposition of Profit Margin for Two Commercial Banks

| Ratio | Heartland Bank and Trust | Bank of America |
|---|---|---|
| **Profit Margin Components** | | |
| 9. Interest expense ratio | 2.52% | 2.92% |
| 10. Provision for loan loss ratio | −0.02 | 6.18 |
| 11. Noninterest expense ratio | 53.67 | 57.25 |
| 12. Tax ratio | 0.58 | 10.81 |
| **Interest Expenses as a Percentage of Total Operating Income** | | |
| 13. NOW accounts | 0.07% | 0.14% |
| 14. MMDAs and other savings | 0.88 | 0.41 |
| 15. Foreign deposits | — | 0.50 |
| 16. Retail CDs | 0.98 | 0.17 |
| 17. Wholesale CDs | 0.39 | 0.16 |
| 18. Fed funds and RPs | 0.03 | 0.29 |
| 19. Other borrowed funds | 0.17 | 1.12 |
| 20. Subordinated notes and debentures | — | 0.13 |
| **Noninterest Expense as a Percentage of Total Operating Income** | | |
| 21. Salaries and employee benefits | 33.92% | 28.00% |
| 22. Expenses of premises and fixed assets | 6.78 | 7.25 |
| 23. Other noninterest expenses | 12.87 | 22.01 |
| **Liability Yields** | | |
| 24. NOW accounts | 0.06% | 0.33% |
| 25. MMDAs and other savings | 0.09 | 0.03 |
| 26. Foreign deposits | — | 0.40 |
| 27. Retail CDs | 0.45 | 0.37 |
| 28. Wholesale CDs | 0.44 | 0.31 |
| 29. Fed funds and RPs | 0.11 | 0.65 |
| 30. Other borrowed funds | 18.90 | 0.84 |
| 31. Subordinated notes and debentures | — | 1.40 |
| **Liability Accounts as a Percentage of Total Assets** | | |
| 32. Demand deposits | 12.71% | 9.31% |
| 33. NOW accounts | 5.80 | 1.73 |
| 34. MMDAs | 17.62 | 28.51 |
| 35. Other savings | 34.49 | 30.10 |
| 36. Foreign deposits | — | 5.01 |
| 37. Retail CDs | 11.09 | 1.79 |
| 38. Core deposits | 81.71 | 76.44 |
| 39. Wholesale CDs | 4.48 | 2.08 |
| 40. Fed funds and RPs | 1.63 | 1.77 |
| 41. Other borrowed funds | 0.05 | 5.31 |
| 42. Subordinated notes and debentures | — | 0.37 |
| 43. Purchased funds | 6.15 | 9.54 |
| 44. Other liabilities | 1.60 | 1.42 |
| **Liability Items as a Percentage of Interest-Bearing Liabilities** | | |
| 45. NOW accounts | 6.60% | 2.01% |
| 46. MMDAs | 20.05 | 33.15 |
| 47. Other savings | 39.26 | 35.01 |
| 48. Foreign deposits | — | 5.82 |
| 49. Retail CDs | 12.62 | 2.08 |
| 50. Wholesale CDs | 5.10 | 2.42 |
| 51. Fed funds and RPs | 1.85 | 2.06 |
| 52. Other borrowed funds | 0.05 | 6.18 |
| 53. Subordinated notes and debentures | — | 0.43 |
| **Noninterest Expense as a Percentage of Noninterest Income** | | |
| 54. Salaries and employee benefits | 156.74% | 72.56% |
| 55. Expenses of premises and equipment | 31.33 | 18.78 |
| 56. Other noninterest expense | 59.94 | 57.03 |
| **Noninterest Expense as a Percentage of Total Assets** | | |
| 57. Salaries and employee benefits | 1.73% | 1.11% |
| 58. Expenses of premises and equipment | 0.35 | 0.29 |
| 59. Other noninterest expense | 0.66 | 0.87 |

income and noninterest income as follows (ratios used to decompose asset utilization are listed in Table 12–7):

$$\text{Asset utilization ratio} = \frac{\text{Total operating income}}{\text{Total assets}} = \frac{\text{Interest}}{\text{income ratio}} + \frac{\text{Noninterest}}{\text{income ratio}}$$

where

$$\text{Interest income ratio (ratio 60)} = \frac{\text{Interest income}}{\text{Total assets}}$$

$$\text{Noninterest income ratio (ratio 61)} = \frac{\text{Noninterest income}}{\text{Total assets}}$$

which measure the bank's ability to generate interest income and noninterest income, respectively. For the banks represented in Tables 12–1 and 12–3, the values of these ratios are as follows:

|  | Heartland | Bank of America |
|---|---|---|
| Interest income ratio | $\frac{98.06}{2,448.36} = 4.01\%$ | $\frac{40,916}{1,676,743} = 2.44\%$ |
| Noninterest income ratio | $\frac{27.08}{2,448.36} = 1.11\%$ | $\frac{25,704}{1,676,743} = 1.53\%$ |

**TABLE 12–7**   Decomposition of Asset Utilization for Two Commercial Banks

| Ratio | Heartland Bank and Trust | Bank of America |
|---|---|---|
| **Asset Utilization Breakdown** | | |
| **60.** Interest income ratio | 4.01% | 2.44% |
| **61.** Noninterest income ratio | 1.11 | 1.53 |
| **Interest Income as a Percentage of Total Assets** | | |
| **62.** C&I loans | 0.75% | 0.33% |
| **63.** Real estate loans | 2.51 | 0.69 |
| **64.** Consumer loans | 0.03 | 0.67 |
| **65.** Other loans | 0.17 | 0.31 |
| **66.** Leases | 0.00 | 0.05 |
| **67.** Deposits at other institutions | 0.01 | 0.04 |
| **68.** Fed funds and RPs | 0.00 | 0.01 |
| **69.** U.S. Treasury and agencies | 0.03 | 0.02 |
| **70.** Securities issued by states and political subdivisions | 0.24 | 0.03 |
| **71.** Mortgage-backed securities | 0.17 | 0.20 |
| **72.** Other debt and equity securities | 0.08 | 0.09 |
| **Asset Yields** | | |
| **73.** C&I loans | 6.00% | 2.28% |
| **74.** Real estate loans | 4.95 | 3.45 |
| **75.** Consumer loans | 8.43 | 6.52 |
| **76.** Other loans | 4.21 | 4.07 |
| **77.** Leases | 16.00 | 3.81 |
| **78.** Deposits at other institutions | 4.83 | 2.42 |
| **79.** Fed funds and RPs | 0.00 | 0.81 |
| **80.** U.S. Treasury and agencies | 1.48 | 0.63 |
| **81.** Securities issued by states and political subdivisions | 2.45 | 3.45 |
| **82.** Mortgage-backed securities | 1.88 | 1.15 |
| **83.** Other debt and equity securities | 3.50 | 8.92 |
| **Asset Items as a Percentage of Total Assets** | | |
| **84.** Cash and balances due from institutions | 4.74% | 10.32% |
| **85.** C&I loans | 12.55 | 14.29 |

(*continued*)

**TABLE 12–7** Decomposition of Asset Utilization for Two Commercial Banks *(Continued)*

| Ratio | Heartland Bank and Trust | Bank of America |
|---|---|---|
| 86. Real estate loans | 50.63% | 20.02% |
| 87. Consumer loans | 0.36 | 10.33 |
| 88. Other loans | 4.12 | 7.63 |
| 89. Leases | 0.00 | 1.33 |
| 90. Net loans and leases | 67.02 | 52.89 |
| 91. Fed funds and RPs | 0.00 | 1.15 |
| 92. U.S. Treasury and agencies | 2.36 | 3.02 |
| 93. Securities issued by states and political subdivisions | 9.91 | 0.78 |
| 94. Mortgage-backed securities | 9.01 | 17.77 |
| 95. Other debt and equity securities | 2.29 | 0.99 |
| 96. Total investment securities | 23.58 | 23.72 |
| 97. Other assets | 4.66 | 13.07 |
| **Asset Items as a Percentage of Earning Assets** | | |
| 98. C&I loans | 13.75% | 18.48% |
| 99. Real estate loans | 55.49 | 25.90 |
| 100. Consumer loans | 0.40 | 13.35 |
| 101. Other loans | 4.52 | 9.87 |
| 102. Leases | 0.00 | 1.72 |
| 103. Fed funds and RPs | 0.00 | 1.49 |
| 104. U.S. Treasury and agencies | 2.59 | 3.90 |
| 105. Securities issued by states and political subdivisions | 10.87 | 1.01 |
| 106. Mortgage-backed securities | 9.88 | 22.99 |
| 107. Other debt and equity securities | 2.51 | 1.29 |
| **Off-Balance-Sheet Items as a Percentage of Total Assets** | | |
| 108. Loan commitments | 16.19% | 48.44% |
| 109. Commercial letters of credit | 0.00 | 0.10 |
| 110. Standby letters of credit | 0.38 | 2.83 |
| 111. Loans sold | 0.22 | 1.47 |
| 112. Derivative securities | 9.36 | 1606.25 |
| 113. Total off-balance-sheet items | 26.16 | 1659.10 |
| **Noninterest Income as a Percentage of Total Assets** | | |
| 114. Fiduciary activities | 0.18% | 0.11% |
| 115. Service charges | 0.27 | 0.32 |
| 116. Trading revenue | 0.00 | 0.15 |
| 117. Fees from nonbanking services | 0.04 | 0.08 |
| 118. Net servicing fees | 0.02 | −0.07 |
| 119. Net gain (loss) from sale of investment securities | 0.21 | 0.12 |
| 120. Other noninterest income | 0.39 | 0.82 |
| **Noninterest Income as a Percentage of Total Noninterest Income** | | |
| 121. Fiduciary activities | 16.37% | 6.88% |
| 122. Service charges | 24.82 | 20.65 |
| 123. Trading revenue | 0.00 | 9.88 |
| 124. Fees from nonbanking services | 3.53 | 5.28 |
| 125. Net servicing fees | 1.45 | −4.37 |
| 126. Net gain (loss) from sale of investment securities | 18.94 | 8.03 |
| 127. Other noninterest income | 34.90 | 53.66 |

The interest income and noninterest income ratios are not necessarily independent. For example, the bank's ability to generate loans affects both interest income and, through fees and service charges, noninterest income. High values for these ratios signify the efficient use of bank resources to generate income and are thus generally positive for the bank. But some problematic situations that result in high ratio values could exist. For example, a bank that replaces low-risk, low-return loans with high-risk, high-return loans will experience an increase in its interest income ratio. However, high-risk loans have a higher default probability, which could result in the ultimate loss of both interest and principal payments. Further breakdown of these ratios is therefore a valuable tool in the financial performance evaluation process.

The interest income ratio can be broken down using the various components of interest income (ratios 62–72; e.g., income on C&I loans/total assets); or by using asset yields (ratios 73–83; e.g., income on C&I loans/dollar value of C&I loans); or by using size of investment (e.g., dollar value of C&I loans/total assets—ratios 84–97—or dollar value of C&I loans/total earning assets—ratios 98–107). Off-balance-sheet activities can also be measured in terms of the size of the notional values they create in relation to bank assets (ratios 108–113—e.g., loan commitments/total assets). The noninterest income ratio can also be subdivided into the various subcategories (e.g., income from fiduciary activities/total assets—ratios 114–120—or income from fiduciary activities/noninterest income—ratios 121–127).

### Other Ratios

A number of other profit measures are commonly used to evaluate bank performance. Three of these are (1) the net interest margin, (2) the spread (ratio), and (3) overhead efficiency.

**net interest margin**

*Interest income minus interest expense divided by earning assets.*

**Net Interest Margin.**   **Net interest margin** (ratio 6 in Table 12–5) measures the net return on the bank's earning assets (investment securities and loans and leases) and is defined as follows:

$$\text{Net interest margin} = \frac{\text{Net interest income}}{\text{Earning assets}} = \frac{\text{Interest income} - \text{Interest expense}}{\text{Investment securities} + \text{Net loans and leases}}$$

Generally, the higher this ratio, the better. Suppose, however, that the preceding scenario (replacement of low-risk, low-return loans with high-risk, high-return loans) is the reason for the increase. This situation can increase risk for the bank. It highlights the fact that looking at returns without looking at risk can be misleading and potentially dangerous in terms of bank solvency and long-run profitability.

**spread**

*The difference between lending and borrowing rates.*

**The Spread.**   The **spread** (ratio 7 in Table 12–5) measures the difference between the average yield on earning assets and the average cost of interest-bearing liabilities and is thus another measure of return on the bank's assets. The spread is defined as:

$$\text{Spread} = \frac{\text{Interest income} - \text{Interest income}}{\text{Earning assets}} - \frac{\text{Interest expense}}{\text{Interest-bearing liabilities}}$$

The higher the spread, the more profitable the bank, but again, the source of a high spread and the potential risk implications should be considered.

**Overhead Efficiency.**   **Overhead efficiency** (ratio 8 in Table 12–5) measures the bank's ability to generate noninterest income to cover noninterest expenses. It is represented as:

$$\text{Overhead efficiency} = \frac{\text{Noninterest income}}{\text{Noninterest expense}}$$

In general, the higher this ratio, the better. However, because of the high levels of noninterest expense relative to noninterest income, overhead efficiency is rarely higher than 1 (or in percentage terms, 100 percent). Further, low operating expenses (and thus low noninterest expenses) can also indicate increased risk if the institution is not investing in the most efficient technology or its back office systems are poorly supported. The values of these ratios for the two banks are as follows:

**DO YOU UNDERSTAND:**

9.  Why a high value of ROE may signal a risk problem for a bank?
10. What ratios ROA can be broken down into?
11. What the spread measure means?

**overhead efficiency**

*A bank's ability to generate noninterest income to cover noninterest expense.*

| | Heartland | Bank of America |
|---|---|---|
| Net interest margin | $\dfrac{94.91}{507.30 + 1,640.90} = 4.28\%$ | $\dfrac{38,968}{397,707 + 886,851} = 3.03\%$ |
| Spread | $\dfrac{98.06}{2,218.20} - \dfrac{3.15}{1,840.01} = 4.25\%$ | $\dfrac{40,916}{1,284,558} - \dfrac{1,948}{1,285,584} = 3.03\%$ |
| Overhead efficiency | $\dfrac{27.08}{67.16} = 40.32\%$ | $\dfrac{25,704}{38,140} = 67.39\%$ |

# IMPACT OF MARKET NICHE AND BANK SIZE ON FINANCIAL STATEMENT ANALYSIS

## Impact of a Bank's Market Niche

As mentioned earlier, based on 2016 data, Heartland Bank and Trust is a profitable and efficient community bank that invests mainly in agriculture, real estate loans, and low-cost funding methods. Bank of America, on the other hand, operates with a larger and more balanced portfolio of assets and liabilities across both wholesale and retail banking. Keeping the more specialized market niche of Heartland Bank and Trust in mind, let us make a comparative financial analysis using the ROE framework and the banks' 2016 financial statements.

**ROE and Its Components.** As stated, the ROE (ratio 1) of 20.99 percent for Heartland Bank and Trust (HBT) was higher than the 7.20 percent ROE reported for Bank of America (BOA). The breakdown of ROE indicates that HBT's greater profitability was due to its ROA of 2.21 percent compared with that of 0.91 percent for BOA (ratio 2). However, HBT's equity multiplier or leverage (ratio 3) was higher than that of BOA. HBT's EM of 9.49× translated to an equity-to-asset ratio (= 1/EM) of 10.53 percent, and BOA's EM of 7.94× translated to an equity-to-asset ratio of 12.59 percent. Thus, although both banks appeared to be well capitalized, HBT had less equity.

The more focused orientation of HBT relative to BOA can best be seen by looking at the composition of the asset, and particularly the loan, portfolios (ratios 84 through 97 in Table 12–7) and the liabilities (ratios 32 through 44 in Table 12–6) of the two banks. HBT held 50.63 percent of its total assets in the form of real estate loans. Thus, consistent with its niche, a large majority of HBT's assets were tied up in real estate–related assets. BOA, on the other hand, had its asset investments more evenly distributed: 14.29 percent in C&I loans, 20.02 percent in real estate loans, 10.33 percent in consumer loans, and 7.63 percent in other loans.

On the liability side of the balance sheet, HBT issued mainly retail-oriented deposits: demand deposits were 12.77 percent, MMDAs were 17.62 percent, other savings were 34.49 percent, and retail CDs were 11.09 percent of total assets. BOA again used a broader array of deposits: demand deposits were 9.31 percent, MMDAs were 28.57 percent, other savings were 30.10 percent, foreign deposits were 5.01 percent, and retail CDs were 1.79 percent of total assets. HBT has specialized its service in the retail area, while BOA offers a broader spectrum of financial services.

## Impact of Size on Financial Statement Analysis

Bank size has traditionally affected the financial ratios of commercial banks, resulting in significant differences across size groups. Large banks' relatively easy access to purchased funds and capital markets compared to small banks' access is a reason for many of these differences. For example, large banks with easier access to capital markets generally operate with lower amounts of equity capital than do small banks. Also, large banks generally use more purchased funds (such as fed funds and RPs) and fewer core deposits than do small banks. Large banks tend to put more into salaries, premises, and other expenses than small banks, and they tend to diversify their operations and services more than small banks. Large banks also generate more noninterest income (i.e., trading account, derivative security, and foreign trading income) than small banks and when risky loans pay off, they earn more interest income. As a result, although large banks tend to hold less equity than small banks, large banks do not necessarily return more on their assets. A study by the Federal Reserve Bank of St. Louis reported that ROA consistently increased for banks grouped by size up to $15 billion in total assets, but decreased for banks with more than $15 billion.

Examining ratios for the relatively large Bank of America (BOA) compared to the smaller Heartland Bank and Trust (HBT), we see only some of these size-related effects on accounting ratios. Looking at ROA (ratio 2 in Table 12–5), HBT is the more profitable overall of the two banks. Notice that HBT is producing the higher income per dollar of total operating income (ratio 4; PM for HBT = 43.26 percent and for BOA = 22.83 percent). Further, BOA is producing lower operating income per dollar of assets (AU for BOA = 3.97 percent and for HBT = 5.11 percent). The generation of total operating income in the form of interest income (ratio 60 in Table 12–7) is smaller for BOA (interest income ratio for BOA = 2.44 percent and for HBT = 4.01 percent). We do see that BOA generates more noninterest income (1.53 percent of total assets) than HBT (1.11 percent of total assets; see ratio 61 in Table 12–7). This is likely due to BOA's relatively large amount of off-balance-sheet activities (which is typical of large banks compared with small banks). Indeed, the notional or face value of BOA's OBS activities is 1,659.10 percent of its assets on balance sheet compared to HBT's 26.16 percent (see ratios 108 through 113 in Table 12–7). Notice, too, that BOA's other assets (ratio 97 in Table 12–7) are 13.07 percent of total assets, compared with 4.66 percent for HBT. BOA also uses more purchased funds to total assets than HBT (9.54 percent versus 6.15 percent, respectively) and fewer core deposits (76.44 percent versus 81.71 percent, respectively) (see ratios 43 and 38 in Table 12–6). Finally and atypically, notice that BOA is financing its assets with more equity than HBT. The equity multiplier (ratio 3 in Table 12–5) for BOA, 7.94×, translates to an equity ratio of 12.59 percent, while that for HBT, 9.49×, translates to an equity ratio of 10.53 percent. Also uncharacteristically, BOA's ROE (ratio 1 in Table 12–5) is smaller than that of HBT (7.20 percent versus 20.99 percent).

**DO YOU UNDERSTAND:**

**12.** How a bank's choice of market niche affects its financial ratios?

**13.** How a bank's asset size affects its financial ratios?

## SUMMARY

This chapter analyzed the financial statements of commercial banks. The assets, liabilities, and equity capital were described as they appear in the balance sheet. The financial statements of other FIs such as savings banks and credit unions take a similar form. The income and expenses were described as they appear in the income statement. From the items on the financial statements, the profitability of two banks was analyzed using a return on equity (ROE) framework. What might appear as a favorable sign of profitability and performance can sometimes, in fact, indicate risk problems that management should address. Many problems and areas of managerial concern can be identified by performing a detailed breakdown of the financial ratios of banks. Thus, both profitability and risk management are interlinked and should be of concern to managers. The various risks to which FIs are exposed are examined in more detail in the next several chapters.

## QUESTIONS

1. How does a bank's report of condition differ from its report of income? (*LG 12-1, LG 12-4*)
2. What does it mean when a bank has a CAMELS rating of 2? Of 4? (*LG 12-1*)
3. Match these three types of cash balances with the functions that they serve: (*LG 12-1*)

a. Vault cash
b. Deposits at the Federal Reserve
c. Deposits at other FIs
   (1) Used to meet legal reserve requirements
   (2) Used to purchase services
   (3) Used to meet customer withdrawals

4. Classify the following accounts into one of the following categories: (*LG 12-1, LG 12-2, LG 12-3, LG 12-4*)
   a. Assets
   b. Liabilities
   c. Equity
   d. Revenue
   e. Expense
   f. Off-balance-sheet activities
      (1) Service fees charged on deposit accounts
      (2) Retail CDs
      (3) Surplus and paid-in capital
      (4) Loan commitments
      (5) Consumer loans
      (6) Federal funds sold
      (7) Swaps
      (8) Interest on municipals
      (9) Interest on NOW accounts
      (10) NOW accounts
      (11) Commercial letters of credit
      (12) Leases
      (13) Retained earnings
      (14) Provision for loan losses
      (15) Interest on U.S. Treasury securities

5. If we examine a typical bank's asset portion of the balance sheet, how are the assets arranged in terms of expected return and liquidity? (*LG 12-1*)

6. Repurchase agreements are listed as both assets and liabilities in Table 12–1. How can an account be both an asset and a liability? (*LG 12-1, LG 12-2*)

7. How does a NOW account differ from a demand deposit? (*LG 12-2*)

8. How does a retail CD differ from a wholesale CD? (*LG 12-2*)

9. How do core deposits differ from purchased funds? (*LG 12-2*)

10. What are the major categories of off-balance-sheet activities? (*LG 12-3*)

11. How does a bank's annual net income compare with its annual cash flow? (*LG 12-4*)

12. How might the use of an end-of-the-year balance sheet bias the calculation of certain ratios? (*LG 12-5*)

13. How does the asset utilization ratio for a bank compare to that of a retail company? How do the equity multipliers compare? (*LG 12-5*)

14. What is the likely relationship between the interest income ratio and the noninterest income ratio? (*LG 12-5*)

15. A security analyst calculates the following ratios for two banks. How should the analyst evaluate the financial health of the two banks? (*LG 12-5*)

| | Bank A | Bank B |
|---|---|---|
| Return on equity | 22% | 24% |
| Return on assets | 2% | 1.5% |
| Equity multiplier | 11× | 16× |
| Profit margin | 15% | 14% |
| Asset utilization | 13% | 11% |
| Spread | 3% | 3% |
| Interest expense ratio | 35% | 40% |
| Provision for loan-loss ratio | 1% | 4% |

16. If a bank's asset utilization ratio increases, what will happen to its return on equity, all else constant? (*LG 12-5*)

17. A bank has an ROA of 1.0 percent. The industry average ROA is 1.5 percent. How can ratio analysis help the firm's managers identify the reasons for this difference? (*LG 12-5*)

18. What is the difference between the net interest margin and the spread?

19. How does a bank's choice of market niche affect its financial ratios? (*LG 12-5*)

20. How does a bank's asset size affect its financial ratios? (*LG 12-5*)

## PROBLEMS

1. A bank is considering two securities: a 30-year Treasury bond yielding 7 percent and a 30-year municipal bond yielding 5 percent. If the bank's tax rate is 30 percent, which bond offers the higher tax equivalent yield? (*LG 12-4*)

2. A bank is considering an investment in a municipal security that offers a yield of 6 percent. What is this security's tax equivalent yield if the bank's tax rate is 35 percent? (*LG 12-4*)

3. The financial statements for First National Bank (FNB) are shown below: (*LG 12-5*)

**Balance Sheet First National Bank**

| Assets | | Liabilities and Equity | |
|---|---|---|---|
| Cash | $ 450 | Demand deposits | $ 5,510 |
| Demand deposits from other FIs | 1,350 | Small time deposits | 10,800 |
| Investments | 4,050 | Jumbo CDs | 3,200 |
| Federal funds sold | 2,025 | Federal funds purchased | 2,250 |
| Loans | 15,525 | Equity | 2,200 |

**Balance Sheet First National Bank**

| Assets | | Liabilities and Equity | |
|---|---|---|---|
| Reserve for loan losses | (1,125) | | |
| Premises | 1,685 | | |
| | | Total | |
| Total assets | $23,960 | liabilities/equity | $23,960 |

**Income Statement First National Bank**

| | |
|---|---|
| Interest income | $2,600 |
| Interest expense | 1,650 |
| Provision for loan losses | 180 |
| Noninterest income | 140 |
| Noninterest expense | 420 |
| Taxes | 90 |

a. Calculate the dollar value of FNB's earning assets.
b. Calculate FNB's ROA.
c. Calculate FNB's asset utilization ratio.
d. Calculate FNB's spread.

**4.** The financial statements for BSW National Bank (BSWNB) are shown below: (*LG 12-5*)

**Balance Sheet BSW National Bank**

| Assets | | | Liabilities and Equity | | |
|---|---|---|---|---|---|
| Cash and due from banks | $ | 936 | Demand deposits | | $ 5,040 |
| Investments | | 3,100 | Small time deposits | | 4,020 |
| Federal funds sold | | 1,664 | Jumbo CDs | | 4,680 |
| Loans (less reserve for loan losses of 2,400) | | 9,120 | Federal funds purchased | | 312 |
| Premises | | 780 | Equity | | 1,548 |
| | | | Total | | |
| Total assets | | $15,600 | liabilities/equity | | $15,600 |

**Income Statement BSW National Bank**

| | |
|---|---|
| Interest income | $1,150 |
| Interest expense | 475 |
| Provision for loan losses | 150 |
| Noninterest income | 260 |
| Noninterest expense | 525 |
| Taxes | 60 |

**a.** What is the dollar value of earning assets held by BSWNB?

**b.** What is the dollar value of interest-bearing liabilities held by BSWNB?

**c.** What is BSWNB's total operating income?

**d.** Calculate BSWNB's asset utilization ratio.

**e.** Calculate BSWNB's net interest margin.

**5.** A bank has a balance sheet as shown below. At the beginning of the month, the bank has $15,141,000 in its loan portfolio and $183,000 in the allowance for loan losses. During the month, management estimates that an additional $5,200 of loans will not be paid as promised. After another month, management feels there is no chance of recovering the loan and writes the $5,200 loan off its books. Assuming no other changes, show the bank's balance sheet at the end of Month 1 and Month 2. (*LG 12-4*)

| Assets | | Liabilities and Equity | |
|---|---|---|---|
| Securities | $ 960,000 | Deposits | $17,088,000 |
| Gross loans | 15,141,000 | Common stock | 500,000 |
| Less: Allowance for loan losses | $ 183,000 | Ret. earnings | 1,612,000 |
| | | Total equity | 2,112,000 |
| Net loans | 1,000 | Total | $19,200,000 |
| Other assets | 3,282,000 | | |
| Total assets | $19,200,000 | | |

**6.** The financial statements for MHM Bank (MHM) are shown below: (*LG 12-5*)

**a.** Calculate the dollar value of MHM's earning assets.

**b.** Calculate the dollar value of MHM's interest-bearing liabilities.

**c.** Calculate MHM's spread.

**d.** Calculate MHM's interest expense ratio.

**Balance Sheet MHM Bank**

| Assets | | | Liabilities and Equity | | |
|---|---|---|---|---|---|
| Cash and due from banks | $ 1,920 | | Demand deposits | | $10,620 |
| Demand deposits at other FIs | 1,100 | | Small time deposits | | 10,350 |
| Investments | 6,080 | | Jumbo CDs | | 7,670 |
| Federal funds sold | 2,990 | | Federal funds purchased | | 470 |
| Loans (less reserve for loan losses of 2,400) | 20,040 | | Other liabilities | | 2,000 |
| Premises | 2,270 | | Equity | | 3,290 |
| | | | Total | | |
| Total assets | $34,400 | | liabilities/equity | | $34,400 |

**Income Statement MHM Bank**

| | |
|---|---|
| Interest income | $4,048 |
| Interest expense | 2,024 |
| Provision for loan losses | 100 |
| Noninterest income | 700 |
| Noninterest expense | 975 |
| Taxes | 235 |

**7.** The financial statements for THE Bank are shown below: (*LG 12-5*)

**Balance Sheet THE Bank**

| Assets | | | Liabilities and Equity | | |
|---|---|---|---|---|---|
| Cash | $ | 200 | Demand deposits | | $ 2,450 |
| Demand deposits from other FIs | | 600 | Small time deposits | | 4,800 |
| Investments | | 1,800 | Jumbo CDs | | 1,425 |
| Federal funds sold | | 900 | Federal funds purchased | | 1,000 |
| Loans | | 6,900 | Equity | | 975 |
| Reserve for loan losses | | (500) | | | |
| Premises | | 750 | | | |
| | | | Total | | |
| Total assets | | $10,650 | liabilities/equity | | $10,650 |

**Income Statement THE Bank**

| | |
|---|---|
| Interest income | $2,450 |
| Interest expense | 1,630 |
| Provision for loan losses | 80 |
| Noninterest income | 240 |
| Noninterest expense | 410 |
| Taxes | 40 |

**a.** Calculate THE Bank's earning assets.

**b.** Calculate THE Bank's ROA.

**c.** Calculate THE Bank's total operating income.

**d.** Calculate THE Bank's spread.

**8.** Smallville Bank has the following balance sheet, rates earned on its assets, and rates paid on its liabilities.

**Balance Sheet (in thousands)**

| Assets | | Rate Earned (%) |
|---|---|---|
| Cash and due from banks | $ 6,000 | 0 |
| Investment securities | 22,000 | 8 |
| Repurchase agreements | 12,000 | 6 |
| Loans less allowance for losses | 80,000 | 10 |
| Fixed assets | 10,000 | 0 |
| Other earning assets | 4,000 | 9 |
| Total assets | $134,000 | |

| Liabilities and Equity | | Rate Paid (%) |
|---|---|---|
| Demand deposits | $ 9,000 | 0 |
| NOW accounts | 69,000 | 5 |
| Retail CDs | 18,000 | 7 |
| Subordinated debentures | 14,000 | 8 |
| Total liabilities | 110,000 | |
| Common stock | 10,000 | |
| Paid-in capital surplus | 3,000 | |
| Retained earnings | 11,000 | |
| Total liabilities and equity | $134,000 | |

If the bank earns $120,000 in noninterest income, incurs $80,000 in noninterest expenses, and pays $2,500,000 in taxes, what is its net income? (*LG 12-5*)

**9.** Community Bank has the following balance sheet, rates earned on its assets, and rates paid on its liabilities. (*LG 12-4*)

**Balance Sheet (in thousands)**

| Assets | | Rate Earned (%) |
|---|---|---|
| Cash and due from banks | $ 7,900 | 0 |
| Investment securities | 29,600 | 1.50 |
| Repurchase agreements | 15,960 | 1.15 |
| Loans less allowance for losses | 106,400 | 7.25 |
| Fixed assets | 13,500 | 0 |
| Other assets | 5,320 | 0 |
| Total assets | $178,680 | |

| Liabilities and Equity | | Rate Paid (%) |
|---|---|---|
| Demand deposits | $ 27,490 | 0 |
| NOW accounts | 90,700 | 0.50 |
| Retail CDs | 23,940 | 1.20 |
| Subordinated debentures | 15,000 | 5.50 |
| Total liabilities | 157,130 | |
| Common stock | 5,000 | |
| Paid-in capital surplus | 5,000 | |
| Retained earnings | 11,550 | |
| Total liabilities and equity | $178,680 | |

If the bank earns $159,000 in noninterest income, incurs $306,000 in noninterest expenses, and pays $3,320,000 in taxes, what is its net income?

**10.** Megalopolis Bank has the following balance sheet and income statement. (*LG 12-5*)

**Balance Sheet (in millions)**

| Assets | | Liabilities and Equity | |
|---|---|---|---|
| Cash and due from banks | $ 9,000 | Demand deposits | $ 19,000 |
| Investment securities | 23,000 | NOW accounts | 89,000 |
| Repurchase agreements | 42,000 | Retail CDs | 28,000 |
| Loans | 90,000 | Debentures | 19,000 |
| Fixed assets | 15,000 | Total liabilities | $155,000 |
| Other assets | 4,000 | Common stock | 12,000 |
| Total assets | $183,000 | Paid-in capital | 4,000 |
| | | Retained earnings | 12,000 |
| | | Total liabilities and equity | $183,000 |

**Income Statement**

| | |
|---|---|
| Interest on fees and loans | $ 9,000 |
| Interest on investment securities | 4,000 |
| Interest on repurchase agreements | 6,000 |
| Interest on deposits in banks | 1,000 |
| Total interest income | $20,000 |
| Interest on deposits | $ 9,000 |
| Interest on debentures | 2,000 |
| Total interest expense | $11,000 |
| Net interest income | $ 9,000 |
| Provision for loan losses | 2,000 |
| Noninterest income | 2,000 |
| Noninterest expenses | 1,000 |
| Income before taxes | $ 8,000 |
| Taxes | 3,000 |
| Net income | $ 5,000 |

For Megalopolis, calculate:
 **a.** Return on equity
 **b.** Return on assets
 **c.** Asset utilization
 **d.** Equity multiplier
 **e.** Profit margin
 **f.** Interest expense ratio
 **g.** Provision for loan loss ratio
 **h.** Noninterest expense ratio
 **i.** Tax ratio

**11.** Dudley Bank has the following balance sheet and income statement. (*LG 12-5*)

**Balance Sheet (in millions)**

| Assets | | Liabilities and Equity | |
|---|---|---|---|
| Cash and due from banks | $ 7,500 | Demand deposits | $ 15,500 |

**Balance Sheet (in millions)**

| Assets | | Liabilities and Equity | |
|---|---|---|---|
| Repurchase agreements | 13,000 | NOW accounts | 35,625 |
| Other investment securities | 34,050 | Retail CDs | 57,000 |
| Loans | 70,500 | Debentures | 14,250 |
| Fixed assets | 9,250 | Total liabilities | $122,375 |
| Other assets | 3,200 | Common stock | 5,000 |
| Total assets | $137,500 | Paid-in capital | 4,000 |
| | | Retained earnings | 6,125 |
| | | Total liabilities and equity | $137,500 |

**Income Statement**

| | |
|---|---|
| Interest on fees and loans | $6,715 |
| Interest on repurchase agreements | 143 |
| Interest on other investment securities | 1,705 |
| Interest on deposits in banks | 60 |
| Total interest income | $8,623 |
| Interest on deposits | 3,018 |
| Interest on debentures | 1,140 |
| Total interest expense | $4,158 |
| Net interest income | $4,465 |
| Provision for loan losses | 200 |
| Noninterest income | 950 |
| Noninterest expenses | 1,720 |
| Income before taxes | $3,495 |
| Taxes | 1,220 |
| Net income | $2,275 |

For Dudley Bank, calculate:
   a. Return on equity
   b. Return on assets
   c. Asset utilization
   d. Equity multiplier
   e. Profit margin
   f. Interest expense ratio
   g. Provision for loan loss ratio
   h. Noninterest expense ratio
   i. Tax ratio
   j. Overhead efficiency

12. Anytown Bank has the following ratios: (*LG 12-5*)
   a. Profit margin: 21%
   b. Asset utilization: 11%
   c. Equity multiplier: 12×

   Calculate Anytown's ROE and ROA.

13. Everytown Bank has the following ratios: (*LG 12-5*)
   a. Profit margin: 5%
   b. Asset utilization: 20%
   c. Equity multiplier: 7.75×

   Calculate Everytown's ROE and ROA.

14. You have been asked to analyze First Union Bank. You have only the following information on the bank at year-end 2018: Net income is $250,000, total debt is $2.5 million, and the bank's debt ratio is 55 percent. What is First Union Bank's ROE for 2018? (*LG 12-5*)

15. Financial Fitness Bank reported a debt-to-equity ratio of 1.75× at the end of 2018. If the firm's total assets at year-end were $25 million, how much of its assets are financed with debt? How much with equity? (*LG 12-5*)

# SEARCH THE SITE

Go to the FDIC's website at **www.fdic.gov**. Find the most recent Balance Sheet and Income Statement for Bank of America using following steps. Click on "Analysts," then on "Statistics on Depository Institutions (SDI)." Click on BankFind." Enter "Bank of America" in the Bank Name box. Click on the Bank of America subsidiaries listed. Click on "Financials," then on ". . . more Financials." Under "ID Report Selections:" select the financial statement for "Assets and Liabilities" and then "Income and Expense." This will download the most recent Balance Sheet and Income Statement.

## Questions

1. What is the most recent value of total deposits for Bank of America? How has this changed since 2016 as reported in Table 12–1?

2. What is the most recent value of total interest income for Bank of America? How has this changed since 2016 as reported in Table 12–3?

3. From the most recent balance sheet and income statement, calculate the interest income, noninterest income, provision for loan loss, and tax ratios. Which ratio has changed the most since 2016 as reported in Table 12–5?

# Regulation of Commercial Banks

## Learning Goals

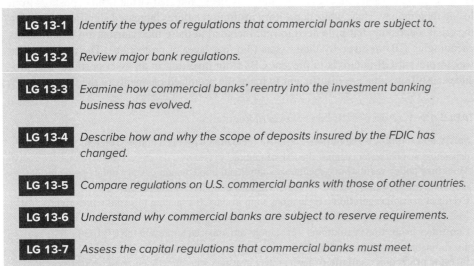

**LG 13-1** *Identify the types of regulations that commercial banks are subject to.*

**LG 13-2** *Review major bank regulations.*

**LG 13-3** *Examine how commercial banks' reentry into the investment banking business has evolved.*

**LG 13-4** *Describe how and why the scope of deposits insured by the FDIC has changed.*

**LG 13-5** *Compare regulations on U.S. commercial banks with those of other countries.*

**LG 13-6** *Understand why commercial banks are subject to reserve requirements.*

**LG 13-7** *Assess the capital regulations that commercial banks must meet.*

## SPECIALNESS AND REGULATION: CHAPTER OVERVIEW

Chapter 1 showed that FIs are special because they provide vital services to various important sectors of the economy, such as information services, liquidity services, and price-risk reduction services. Failure to provide these services or a breakdown in their efficient provision can be costly to both the ultimate providers (households) and users (firms) of funds. The financial crisis of the late 2000s is a prime example of how such a breakdown in the provision of financial services can cripple financial markets worldwide and bring the world economy into a deep recession. Because of the vital nature of the services they provide, commercial banks (CBs) are regulated at the federal level (and sometimes at the state level) to protect against a disruption in the provision of these services and the cost this would impose on the economy and society at large. In this chapter, we provide an overview of the regulations imposed on CBs. We first discuss the history of commercial banks' regulation and then review the specific balance sheet regulations under which commercial banks operate. We also highlight differences in regulations imposed on domestic versus international commercial banks.

# TYPES OF REGULATIONS AND THE REGULATORS

**LG 13-1**

Six types of regulations seek to enhance the net social benefits of commercial banks' services to the economy: (1) safety and soundness regulation, (2) monetary policy regulation, (3) credit allocation regulation, (4) consumer protection regulation, (5) investor protection regulation, and (6) entry and chartering regulation. These regulations are summarized in Table 13–1. Regulations can be imposed at the federal or the state level and occasionally at the international level, as in the case of bank capital requirements.

## Safety and Soundness Regulation

To protect depositors and borrowers against the risk of CB failure—for example, due to a lack of diversification in asset portfolios—regulators have developed layers of protective mechanisms that balance a CB's profitability against its solvency, liquidity, and other types of risk (see Chapter 19). They are illustrated in Figure 13–1. These mechanisms are intended to ensure the safety and soundness of the CB and thus to maintain the credibility of the CB in the eyes of its borrowers and lenders. Indeed, even during the worst of the financial crisis, deposit runs at banks, savings institutions, and credit unions did not occur. This is because the safety and soundness regulations in place protected virtually all depositors from losing their money. Thus, while depository institution failures increased significantly during the crisis, depositors felt little need to run. Included in these mechanisms are requirements encouraging CBs to diversify their assets (the first layer of protection). The most obvious way to prevent CB failure is to prevent CBs from investing in an asset portfolio that produces cash flows that are insufficient to make the promised payments to the CB's liability

**TABLE 13–1**   **Areas of CB Specialness in Regulation**

**Safety and soundness regulation**—layers of regulation have been imposed on CBs to protect depositors and borrowers against the risk of failure.
**Monetary policy regulation**—regulators control and implement monetary policy by requiring minimum levels of cash reserves to be held against commercial bank deposits.
**Credit allocation regulation**—regulations support the CB's lending to socially important sectors such as housing and farming.
**Consumer protection regulation**—regulations are imposed to prevent the CB from discriminating unfairly in lending.
**Investor protection regulation**—laws protect investors who directly purchase securities and/or indirectly purchase securities by investing in mutual or pension funds managed directly or indirectly by CBs (as well as other FIs).
**Entry and chartering regulation**—entry and activity regulations limit the number of CBs in any given financial services sector, thus impacting the charter values of CBs operating in that sector.

**Figure 13–1**   **Layers of Regulation**

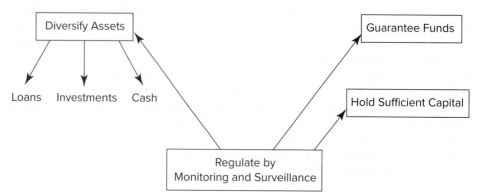

holders. Thus, banks are prohibited from making loans exceeding 15 percent of their own equity capital funds to any one company or borrower. A bank that has 10 percent of its assets funded by its own capital (and therefore 90 percent by liabilities) can lend no more than 1.5 percent of its assets to any one borrower (i.e., 15 percent of 10 percent). Although these regulations may result in lower profitability, they also lower credit and liquidity risk and ultimately lower the risk of insolvency.

The second layer of protection concerns the minimum level of stockholder capital or equity funds that the owners of a CB need to contribute to the funding of its operations. For example, bank (and thrift) regulators are concerned with the minimum ratio of capital to (risk) assets. The higher the proportion of capital contributed by owners, the greater the protection against insolvency risk for liability claimholders such as depositors. This occurs because losses on the asset portfolio due, for example, to loan defaults are legally borne by the stockholders first and then, only after the equity holders' claims are totally wiped out, by outside liability holders. For example, in 2008 the near failure of Washington Mutual and its subsequent purchase by J.P. Morgan Chase left Washington Mutual equity holders with very little. Consequently, CB regulators can directly affect the degree of risk exposure faced by nonequity claimholders in CBs (such as depositors) by varying the minimum amount of equity capital required to operate and keep a bank open (see discussions below). Indeed, part of the Troubled Asset Relief Program (TARP) of 2008–2009 was the Capital Purchase Program (CPP). The goal of the CPP was to encourage U.S. financial institutions to build capital to increase the flow of financing to U.S. businesses and consumers and to support the U.S. economy. Further, regulators acted quickly to ensure the largest depository institutions (DIs) had sufficient capital to withstand large losses during the financial crisis of 2008–2009.

The third layer of protection is the provision of guarantee funds such as the Depositors Insurance Fund (DIF) for banks. Deposit insurance mitigates a rational incentive depositors otherwise have to withdraw their funds at the first hint of trouble. By protecting CB depositors when a CB collapses and owners' equity or net worth is wiped out, a demand for regulation of insured institutions is created so as to protect the funds' (and taxpayers') resources. For example, the Federal Deposit Insurance Corporation (FDIC) monitors and regulates participants in the DIF in return for providing explicit deposit guarantees of up to $250,000 per depositor per bank. Major reforms of FDIC insurance of CB deposits have recently been adopted. We discuss these below.

**www.fdic.gov**

The fourth layer of regulation involves monitoring and surveillance. Regulators subject all CBs to varying degrees of monitoring and surveillance. This involves on-site examination of the CB by regulators as well as the CB's production of accounting statements and reports on a timely basis for off-site evaluation. Just as savers appoint CBs as delegated monitors to evaluate the behavior and actions of ultimate borrowers, society (through policy and appointments determined by the U.S. government) assigns regulators to monitor the behavior and performance of CBs. Many of the regulatory changes proposed in reaction to the financial crisis included significant increases in the monitoring and surveillance of any financial institution whose failure could have serious systemic effects.

**net regulatory burden**

*The difference between the private costs of regulations and the private benefits for the producers of financial services.*

Finally, note that regulation is not without costs for those regulated. For example, regulators may require CBs to have more equity capital than private owners believe is in their own best interests. Similarly, producing the information requested by regulators is costly for CBs because it involves the time of managers, lawyers, and accountants. Again, the socially optimal amount of information may differ from a CB's privately optimal amount. Although regulation may be socially beneficial, it imposes private costs, or a regulatory burden, on individual CB owners and managers. Consequently, regulation attempts to enhance the social welfare benefits and mitigate the social costs of providing CB services. The difference between the private benefits to a CB from being regulated—such as insurance fund guarantees—and the private costs it faces from adhering to regulation—such as examinations—is called its **net regulatory burden.** The higher the net regulatory burden on CBs, the smaller are the benefits of being regulated compared to the costs of adhering to regulations from a private (CB) owner's perspective.

In July 2010, President Obama signed into law the 2010 Wall Street Reform and Consumer Protection Act, which sought to prevent a repeat of the market meltdown of 2008 and promote the safety and soundness of the financial system. Touted as the most extensive proposal for the overhaul of financial rules since the Great Depression, this bill proposed a sweeping revision of the nation's financial system and the rules that govern it. The bill set forth reforms to meet five key objectives:

1. *Promote robust supervision and regulation of financial firms* by establishing (a) a new Financial Services Oversight Council of financial regulators (chaired by the Treasury and including the heads of the principal federal financial regulators as members) to identify emerging systemic risks and improve interagency cooperation; (b) a new authority for the Federal Reserve to supervise all firms that could pose a threat to financial stability, even those that do not own banks; (c) stronger capital and other prudential standards for all financial firms, and even higher standards for large, interconnected firms; (d) a new National Bank Supervisor to supervise all federally chartered banks; (e) the elimination of the federal thrift charter for thrifts not dedicated to mortgage lending and other loopholes that allowed some depository institutions to avoid bank holding company regulation by the Federal Reserve; and (f) the registration of advisors of hedge funds and other private pools of capital with the Securities and Exchange Commission (SEC).

2. *Establish comprehensive supervision of financial markets* by establishing (a) the regulation of securitization markets, including new requirements for market transparency, stronger regulation of credit rating agencies, and a requirement that issuers and originators retain a financial interest in securitized loans; (b) comprehensive regulation of all over-the-counter derivatives; and (c) new authority for the Federal Reserve to oversee payment, clearing, and settlement systems.

3. *Protect consumers and investors from financial abuse* by establishing (a) a new Consumer Financial Protection Bureau to protect consumers across the financial sector from unfair, deceptive, and abusive practices; (b) stronger regulations to improve the transparency, fairness, and appropriateness of consumer and investor products and services; and (c) a level playing field and higher standards for providers of consumer financial products and services, whether or not they are part of a bank.

4. *Provide the government with the tools it needs to manage financial crises* by establishing (a) a new regime to resolve crises involving nonbank financial institutions whose failure could have serious systemic effects and (b) revisions to the Federal Reserve's emergency lending authority to improve accountability.

5. *Raise international regulatory standards and improve international cooperation* by establishing international reforms to support efforts in the United States, including strengthening the capital framework, improving oversight of global financial markets, coordinating the supervision of internationally active firms, and enhancing crisis management tools.

Regulators have utilized the new authority given to them. For example, as part of the increased authority given to the Federal Reserve in the 2010 Wall Street Reform and Consumer Protection Act, the Fed proposed in late 2011 that net credit exposures between any two of the nation's six largest financial firms would be limited to 10 percent of the company's regulatory capital. Other financial firms would be subject to the 25 percent limit required by the 2010 act. The proposed Fed rule aims to reduce the interconnectedness of financial institutions in the U.S. financial system and reduce the ability of any single financial firm to damage the financial system and the broader economy—as happened when Lehman Brothers was allowed to fail. As a result of the new rules, big U.S. banks could be forced to return to a more traditional banking model that revolves around deposit taking and making loans. This could result in smaller capital markets and less securities lending.

However, not all powers provided by the act are available to regulators. Six years after the passage of the Wall Street Reform and Consumer Protection Act, only about 70 percent of the rules required by the act had been written into law. As of July 2016, of the 390 total rulemaking requirements, 274 (70.3 percent) had been met with finalized rules, 36 (9.2 percent) had been proposed that would meet requirements, and 80 (20.5 percent) had yet seen a proposal to meet rulemaking requirements. The enormity of the act has taken up a vast amount of regulators' resources and has left many pressing issues unaddressed.

### Monetary Policy Regulation

Another motivation for regulation concerns the special role that banks play in the transmission of monetary policy from the Federal Reserve (the central bank) to the rest of the economy. The central bank directly controls only the quantity of notes and coin in the economy—called **outside money**—whereas the bulk of the money supply is bank deposits—called **inside money.** Regulators commonly impose a minimum level of required cash reserves to be held against deposits, or inside money (discussed below). Some argue that imposing such reserve requirements makes the control of the money supply and its transmission more predictable. Such reserves add to a CB's net regulatory burden if they are more than the institution believes are necessary for its own liquidity purposes. In general, all CBs would choose to hold some cash reserves—even noninterest bearing—to meet the liquidity and transaction needs of their customers directly. For well-managed CBs, however, this optimal level is normally low, especially if the central bank (or other regulatory body) pays little or no interest on required reserves. As a result, CBs often view required reserves as similar to a tax and as a positive cost of undertaking financial intermediation.

### Credit Allocation Regulation

Credit allocation regulation supports the CB's lending to socially important sectors such as housing and farming. These regulations may require a CB to hold a minimum amount of assets in one particular sector of the economy or to set maximum interest rates, prices, or fees to subsidize certain sectors. An example of asset restrictions includes the qualified thrift lender (QTL) test, which requires savings institutions to hold 65 percent of their assets in residential mortgage-related assets to retain a thrift charter. Examples of interest rate restrictions are the usury laws that many states set on the maximum rates that can be charged on mortgages and/or consumer loans and regulations (now abolished) such as the Federal Reserve Bank's Regulation Q maximums on time and savings deposit interest rates.

Such price and quantity restrictions may have justification on social welfare grounds—especially if society has a preference for strong (and subsidized) housing and farming sectors. However, they can also be harmful to FIs that have to bear the private costs of meeting many of these regulations. To the extent that the net private costs of such restrictions are positive, they add to the costs and reduce the efficiency with which FIs undertake intermediation.

### Consumer Protection Regulation

Congress passed the Community Reinvestment Act (CRA) in 1977 and the Home Mortgage Disclosure Act (HMDA) in 1975 to prevent discrimination by lending institutions. HMDA is especially concerned about discrimination on the basis of age, race, sex, or income. Since 1990, examinations for bank compliance with the CRA have become increasingly rigorous. Institutions have been required to disclose publicly their CRA ratings (from outstanding to substantial noncompliance). Since 1992, CBs have had to submit reports to regulators summarizing their lending on a geographic basis, showing the relationship between the demographic area to which they are lending and the demographic data (such as income and percentage of minority population) for that location. Commercial banks also must now report to their chief federal regulator the reasons that they granted or denied credit. Many analysts believed that community and consumer protection laws were imposing a considerable net regulatory burden on CBs without offsetting social benefits that enhance equal access to mortgage and lending markets. In 1995 CRA regulations were revised to make assessments more performance based, more objective, and less burdensome for covered institutions.

A new Consumer Financial Protection Bureau (CFPB) to protect consumers across the financial sector from unfair, deceptive, and abusive practices was part of the financial services overhaul bill passed by the U.S. Congress in July 2010. An example of the CFPB oversight

**www.federalreserve.gov**

**outside money**

*That part of the money supply directly produced by the government or central bank, such as notes and coin.*

**inside money**

*That part of the money supply produced by the private banking system.*

occurred in September 2016 when Wells Fargo Bank was ordered to pay $185 million in fines and penalties (the largest penalty the CFPB has ever imposed) to settle what the CFPB called "the widespread illegal practice of secretly opening unauthorized deposit and credit card accounts." Investigators found that Wells Fargo employees opened deposit and credit card accounts without consent from consumers. Employees would then transfer funds from the consumers' legitimate accounts temporarily into the new, unauthorized accounts. Wells Fargo employees even went as far as secretly creating PINs and false e-mail and phone addresses for unauthorized deposit accounts. This widespread practice gave the employees credit for opening the new accounts, allowing them to earn additional compensation and to meet the bank's sales goals. Consumers, in turn, were sometimes harmed when the bank charged them for insufficient funds or overdraft fees because the money was not in their original accounts. The unauthorized credit cards also came with annual fees and other charges. The CFPB said that Wells Fargo employees applied for roughly 565,000 credit cards and 1.5 million deposit accounts that may have not been authorized by consumers.

Further, a new credit card reform bill, effective in 2010, put unprecedented restrictions on the actions that may be taken by all credit card issuers against credit card holders. Included in the bill were limits on allowable interest rate increases during the first year, limits on fees and penalties credit card companies may charge, protection against arbitrary interest rate increases, provisions giving credit card holders sufficient time to pay their bills, and the abolition of universal default (a practice in which a credit card issuer would raise the interest rate on a customer's account in response to the customer's actions related to other accounts; for example, missing a payment on a utility bill would result in an increase in a credit card rate).

### Investor Protection Regulation

A considerable number of laws protect investors who use commercial banks directly to purchase securities and/or indirectly to access securities markets through investing in mutual or pension funds managed by CBs. Various laws protect investors against abuses such as insider trading, lack of disclosure, outright malfeasance, and breach of fiduciary responsibilities. Important legislation affecting investment banks and mutual funds includes the Securities Acts of 1933 and 1934, the Investment Company Act of 1940, and the Wall Street Reform and Consumer Protection Act of 2010. Since CBs are increasingly moving into offering investment banking and mutual fund services following the passage of the Financial Services Modernization Act in 1999, these restrictions will increasingly impact their profits. As with consumer protection legislation, compliance with these acts can impose a net regulatory burden on CBs.

An example of investor protection occurred in 2016, when the Labor Department issued new conflict-of-interest rules that require financial advisors handling individual retirement and 401(k) accounts to act in the best interests of their clients. Prior to the passage of this rule, financial advisors were generally required only to recommend "suitable" investments, which meant that they could direct a client toward a more expensive mutual fund that paid a higher commission when an otherwise identical, cheaper fund would have been an equal or better alternative. The government move was expected to encourage a shift of retirement funds into lower-cost investments. It was estimated that conflicts of interest embedded in the way many investment professionals did business cost investors about $17 billion a year, leading to annual returns that were about 1 percentage point lower.

### Entry and Chartering Regulation

Entry into the commercial banking industry is regulated, as are activities once a CB has been established. Increasing or decreasing the cost of entry into a financial sector affects the profitability of firms already competing in that industry. Thus, the industries heavily protected against new entrants by high direct costs (e.g., through capital requirements) and high indirect costs (e.g., by restricting the type of individuals who can establish CBs) of entry produce larger profits for existing firms than those in which entry is relatively easy.

In addition, regulations define the scope of permitted activities under a given charter. For example, current regulations allow commercial banks to perform activities traditionally performed only by insurance companies and investment banks. The broader the set of financial service activities permitted under a charter, the more valuable that charter is likely to be. Thus, barriers to entry and regulations pertaining to the scope of permitted activities affect a CB's *charter value* and the size of its net regulatory burden.

### Regulators

Regulators are responsible for ensuring that CBs are operating in accordance with the regulations discussed above and that the vital services provided by these institutions are carried out safely in a sound and efficient manner. While (like auditors) regulators must analyze and evaluate the business of the CBs they monitor, they do so with special attention to a CB's ability to provide social benefits to the overall economy. Unlike other countries that have one or sometimes two regulators, U.S. commercial banks may be subject to the supervision and regulations of as many as four separate regulators. The key regulators for commercial banks were discussed in Chapter 11. They include the Federal Deposit Insurance Corporation (FDIC), the Office of the Comptroller of the Currency (OCC), the Federal Reserve (FR), and state bank regulators. Appendix 13C to this chapter (available through Connect or your course instructor) lists the regulators that oversee the various activities of commercial banks (as well as savings institutions and credit unions [discussed in Chapter 14]).

In the sections that follow, we describe four facets of the regulatory structure: (1) regulation of the overall operations, (2) regulation of product and geographic expansion, (3) the provision and regulation of deposit insurance, and (4) balance sheet regulations (reserve requirements and capital regulations).

---

**DO YOU UNDERSTAND:**

1. The six major types of regulation CBs face?
2. What the layers of protection provided by safety and soundness regulations are? Describe each.
3. What the difference is between inside and outside money?
4. Who the key regulators of commercial banks are?

www.fdic.gov

www.occ.treas.gov

www.federalreserve.gov

---

## REGULATION OF PRODUCT AND GEOGRAPHIC EXPANSION

**LG 13-2**

Historically, commercial banks have been among the most regulated firms in the United States. Because of the inherent special nature of banking and banking contracts, regulators have imposed numerous restrictions on their products and geographic activities. Table 13–2 lists the major laws, from the McFadden Act of 1927 to the Wall Street Reform and Consumer Protection Act of 2010, and briefly describes the key features of each act.

### Product Segmentation in the U.S. Commercial Banking Industry

The U.S. financial system has traditionally been segmented along product lines. Regulatory barriers and restrictions have often inhibited a commercial bank's ability to operate in some areas of the financial services industry and expand its product set beyond some limited range. Commercial banks operating in the United States can be compared with those operating in Germany, Switzerland, and the United Kingdom, where a more **universal FI** structure allows individual financial services organizations to offer a far broader range of banking, insurance, securities, and other financial services products.

**universal FI**

*An FI that can engage in a broad range of financial service activities.*

**LG 13-3**

**commercial banking**

*Banking activity of deposit taking and lending.*

**investment banking**

*Banking activity of underwriting, issuing, and distributing securities.*

**Commercial and Investment Banking Activities.** The United States has experienced several phases of regulating the links between the commercial and investment banking industries. Simply defined, **commercial banking** is the activity of deposit taking and commercial lending; **investment banking** is the activity of underwriting, issuing, and distributing (via public or private placement) securities.

After the 1929 stock market crash, the United States entered a major recession, and approximately 10,000 banks failed between 1930 and 1933. A commission of inquiry (the Pecora Commission) established in 1932 began investigating the causes of the crash. Its findings included concerns about the riskiness and conflicts of interest that arise when

**TABLE 13–2**   Major Bank Laws, Major Features

### 1927: The McFadden Act

1. Made branching of nationally chartered banks subject to the same branching regulations as state-chartered banks.
2. Liberalized national banks' securities underwriting activities, which previously had to be conducted through state-chartered affiliates.

### 1933: The Banking Act of 1933

1. The Glass-Steagall Act generally prohibited commercial banks from underwriting securities with four exceptions:
   a. Municipal general obligation bonds.
   b. U.S. government bonds.
   c. Private placements.
   d. Real estate loans.
2. The act established the FDIC to insure bank deposits.
3. The Glass-Steagall Act prohibited banks from paying interest on demand deposits.

### 1956: The Bank Holding Company Act

1. Restricted the banking and nonbanking acquisition activities of multibank holding companies.
2. Empowered the Federal Reserve to regulate multibank holding companies by:
   a. Determining permissible activities.
   b. Exercising supervisory authority.
   c. Exercising chartering authority.
   d. Conducting bank examinations.

### 1970: Amendments to the Bank Holding Company Act of 1956

1. Extended the BHC Act of 1956 to one-bank holding companies.
2. Restricted permissible BHC activities to those "closely related to banking."

### 1978: International Banking Act

1. Regulated foreign bank branches and agencies in the United States.
2. Subjected foreign banks to the McFadden and Glass-Steagall Acts.
3. Gave foreign banks access to Fedwire, the discount window, and deposit insurance.

### 1980: Depository Institutions Deregulation and Monetary Control Act (DIDMCA)

1. Set a six-year phaseout for Regulation Q interest rate ceilings on small time and savings deposits.
2. Authorized NOW accounts nationwide.
3. Introduced uniform reserve requirements for state-chartered and nationally chartered banks.
4. Increased the ceiling on deposit insurance coverage from $40,000 to $100,000.
5. Allowed federally chartered thrifts to make consumer and commercial loans (subject to size restrictions).

### 1982: Garn–St. Germain Depository Institutions Act (DIA)

1. Introduced money market deposit accounts (MMDAs) and super NOW accounts as interest rate–bearing savings accounts with limited check-writing features.
2. Allowed federally chartered thrifts more extensive lending powers and demand deposit–taking powers.
3. Allowed sound commercial banks to acquire failed savings institutions.
4. Reaffirmed limitations on bank powers to underwrite and distribute insurance.

### 1987: Competitive Equality in Banking Act (CEBA)

1. Redefined the definition of a *bank* to limit the growth of nonbank banks.
2. Sought to recapitalize the Federal Savings and Loan Insurance Corporation (FSLIC).

### 1989: Financial Institutions Reform, Recovery, and Enforcement Act (FIRREA)

1. Limited savings banks' investments in nonresidential real estate, required divestiture of junk bond holdings (by 1994), and imposed a restrictive asset test for qualifications as a savings institution (the qualified thrift lender [QTL] test).
2. Equalized the capital requirements of thrifts and banks.
3. Replaced the FSLIC with the FDIC-SAIF.
4. Replaced the Federal Home Loan Bank Board as the charterer of federal savings and loans with the Office of Thrift Supervision (OTS), an agency of the Treasury.
5. Created the Resolution Trust Corporation (RTC) to resolve failed and failing savings institutions.

*continued*

**TABLE 13-2**  **Major Bank Laws, Major Features** (*Continued*)

**1991: Federal Deposit Insurance Corporation Improvement Act (FDICIA)**

1. Introduced prompt corrective action (PCA), requiring mandatory interventions by regulators whenever a bank's capital falls.
2. Introduced risk-based deposit insurance premiums beginning in 1993.
3. Limited the use of too-big-to-fail bailouts by federal regulators for large banks.
4. Extended federal regulation over foreign bank branches and agencies in the Foreign Bank Supervision and Enhancement Act (FBSEA).

**1994: Riegle-Neal Interstate Banking and Branching Efficiency Act**

1. Permitted bank holding companies to acquire banks in other states, starting September 1995.
2. Invalidated the laws of states that allowed interstate banking only on a regional or reciprocal basis.
3. Beginning in June 1997, bank holding companies were permitted to convert out-of-state subsidiary banks into branches of a single interstate bank.
4. Newly chartered branches also permitted interstate if allowed by state law.

**1999: Financial Services Modernization Act**

1. Eliminated restrictions on banks, insurance companies, and securities firms entering into each others' areas of business. Allowed for the creation of a financial services holding company.
2. Provided for state regulation of insurance.
3. Streamlined bank holding company supervision, with the Federal Reserve as the umbrella holding company supervisor.
4. Prohibited FDIC assistance to affiliates and subsidiaries of banks and savings institutions.
5. Provided for national treatment of foreign banks engaging in activities authorized under the act.

**2010: Wall Street Reform and Consumer Protection Act**

1. Created the Financial Services Oversight Council that would look out for systemic risks at large FIs.
2. Gave the government power to break up FIs that pose a systemic risk to the financial system.
3. Created the Consumer Financial Protection Bureau to regulate products such as credit cards and mortgages.
4. Allowed Congress to order the Government Accountability Office to audit Federal Reserve activities.
5. Gave shareholders the right to a nonbinding proxy vote on corporate pay packages.
6. Required some over-the-counter derivatives be traded through clearinghouses to provide transparency of the value of trades.

commercial and investment banking activities are linked (affiliated) in one organization. This resulted in new legislation, the 1933 Banking Act, or the Glass-Steagall Act. The Glass-Steagall Act sought to impose a rigid separation (or nonaffiliation) between commercial banking—taking deposits and making commercial loans—and investment banking—underwriting, issuing, and distributing stocks, bonds, and other securities. The act defined three major exemptions to this separation. First, banks were allowed to continue to underwrite new issues of Treasury bills, notes, and bonds. Second, banks were allowed to continue underwriting municipal general obligation (GO) bonds.[1] Third, banks were allowed to continue engaging in private placements (see Chapter 6) of all types of bonds and equities, corporate and noncorporate.

For most of the 1933–1963 period, commercial banks and investment banks generally appeared to be willing to abide by both the letter and spirit of the Glass-Steagall Act. Between 1963 and 1987, however, banks challenged restrictions on their municipal *revenue* bond underwriting activities, commercial paper underwriting activities, discount brokerage activities, and advising activities, including open- and closed-end mutual funds, the underwriting of mortgage-backed securities, and selling annuities.[2] In most cases, the courts eventually permitted these activities for commercial banks.

With this onslaught, and the de facto erosion of the Glass-Steagall Act by legal interpretation, the Federal Reserve Board in April 1987 allowed commercial bank

1. A municipal general obligation bond is a bond issued by a state, city, or local government whose interest and principal payments are backed by the full faith and credit of that local government—that is, its full tax and revenue base (see Chapter 6).
2. Municipal revenue bonds are riskier than municipal GO bonds since their interest and principal are guaranteed only by the revenue from the projects they finance. One example is the revenue from road tolls of a bond funding the construction of a new section of highway (see Chapter 6).

**Section 20 affiliate**

*A securities subsidiary of a bank holding company through which a banking organization can engage in investment banking activities.*

holding companies such as J. P. Morgan & Company (now J.P. Morgan Chase), the parent of Morgan Guarantee Trust Company (a commercial bank), to establish separate **Section 20** securities **affiliates** as investment banks. Through these Section 20 affiliates, banks began to conduct all their "ineligible" or "gray area" securities activities, such as commercial paper underwriting, mortgage-backed securities underwriting, and municipal revenue bond underwriting.[3] Note the organizational structure of Citigroup Corp., its bank, and its Section 20 subsidiary (or investment bank) Smith Barney in Figure 13–2. These Section 20 subsidiaries did not violate Section 20 of the Glass-Steagall Act, which restricted affiliations of commercial banks and investment banks, since the revenue generated from securities underwriting activities amounted to less than 5 percent (increased later to 10 percent and then 25 percent) of the total revenues generated.[4] As a result of more recent regulations, discussed next, Section 20 subsidiaries are now virtually nonexistent.

Significant changes occurred in 1997 as the Federal Reserve and the Office of the Comptroller of the Currency (OCC) took actions to expand bank holding companies' permitted activities. In particular, the Federal Reserve allowed commercial banks to acquire directly existing investment banks rather than establish completely new Section 20 investment banking subsidiaries. The result was a number of mergers and acquisitions between commercial and investment banks in 1997 through 2000. Two of the largest mergers prior to those completed during the financial crisis (see below) included Citicorp's $83 billion merger with Travelers Group (which owned Smith Barney and Salomon Brothers) in April 1998 and Bank of New York's 2007 purchase of Mellon Financial for $16.5 billion. In each case, the banks stated that one motivation for their acquisition was the desire to establish a presence in the securities business since laws separating investment and commercial banking were changing. Also noted as a motivation in these acquisitions was the opportunity to expand business lines, take advantage of economies of scale and scope to reduce overall costs, and merge the customer bases of the respective commercial and investment banks involved in the acquisition.[5]

**Figure 13–2** Bank Holding Company and Its Bank and Section 20 Subsidiary

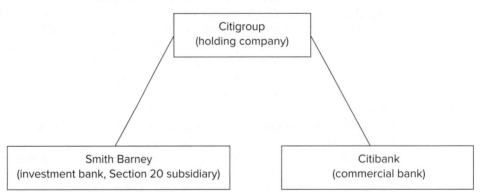

3. In 1989 corporate bonds and in 1990 corporate equities were added to the permitted list.
4. Legally, as long as less than 50 percent of the affiliate's revenues could be attributable to "ineligible activities," it could not be argued that the affiliate was "principally engaged in such activities." Therefore, an affiliate could not be viewed as violating Section 20 of the Glass-Steagall Act of 1933.
5. The erosion of the product barriers between the commercial and investment banking industries has not been all one way. Large investment banks such as Merrill Lynch have increasingly sought to offer banking products. For example, in the late 1970s, Merrill Lynch created the cash management account (CMA), which allowed investors to own a money market mutual fund with check-writing privileges into which bond and stock sale proceeds could be swept on a daily basis. This account allows the investor to earn interest on cash held in a brokerage account. In addition, investment banks have been major participants as traders and investors in the secondary market for loans to less-developed countries and other loans.

In 1999, after years of "homemade" deregulation by banks and securities firms, the U.S. Congress passed the Financial Services Modernization Act (FSMA), which repealed the Glass-Steagall barriers between commercial banking and investment banking. The bill, touted as the biggest change in the regulation of financial institutions in nearly 70 years, allowed for the creation of a "financial services holding company" that could engage in banking activities *and* securities underwriting. The bill also allowed large national banks to place certain activities, including some securities underwritings, in direct bank subsidiaries regulated by the Office of the Comptroller of the Currency. Thus, after nearly 70 years of partial or complete separation between investment banking and commercial banking, the Financial Services Modernization Act of 1999 opened the door for the creation of full-service financial institutions in the United States similar to those that existed in the United States pre-1933 and that exist in many other countries today.

www.occ.treas.gov

After passage of the FSMA, the two industries came together to a degree. Commercial banks like Bank of America and Wachovia tried to build up their own investment-banking operations, but they did not have much success in eating into the core franchises of the then five big independent investment banks: Merrill Lynch, Goldman Sachs, Morgan Stanley, Lehman Brothers, and Bear Stearns. Generally, the investment banks, which were not subject to regulation by the Federal Reserve and did not have to adhere to as strict capital requirements, remained the major investment banking financial institutions. However, the financial crisis changed the landscape dramatically. In March 2008, the Federal Reserve helped J. P. Morgan acquire Bear Stearns as the investment bank faced bankruptcy. This was seen as a controversial decision and cost the Federal Reserve $30 billion. However, the Fed defended the move as essential. In September 2008, Lehman Brothers was allowed to fail and Merrill Lynch was purchased by Bank of America.

Of the five major independent investment banks that existed a year earlier, only two—Goldman Sachs and Morgan Stanley—remained. Even Goldman Sachs and Morgan Stanley were facing a severe liquidity crisis during the weekend of September 20–21, 2008. To address the crisis, one week after the closure of Lehman Brothers and the sale of Merrill Lynch to Bank of America, the Federal Reserve granted a request by the last two major investment banks to change their status to bank holding companies. By becoming bank holding companies, the firms agreed to significantly tighter regulations and much closer supervision by bank examiners from several government agencies rather than only the Securities and Exchange Commission. With the conversion, the investment banks would look more like commercial banks, with more disclosure, higher capital reserves, and less risk taking. In exchange for subjecting themselves to more regulation, the companies would have access to the full array of the Federal Reserve's lending facilities. For example, as bank holding companies, Morgan and Goldman would have greater access to the discount window of the Federal Reserve, which banks can use to borrow money from the central bank. While they were allowed to draw on temporary Fed lending facilities early in the financial crisis, they could not borrow against the same wide array of collateral that commercial banks could. Further, as commercial banks, Morgan and Goldman had enhanced potential access to TARP money. These events on Wall Street—the failure or sale of three of the five largest independent investment banks and the conversion of the two remaining firms from investment banks to commercial banks—effectively turned back the clock to the 1920s, when investment banks and commercial banks functioned under the same corporate umbrella.

As part of the increased authority given to the Federal Reserve in the 2010, part of the Wall Street Reform and Consumer Protection Act is the Volcker Rule which prohibits U.S. depository institutions (DIs) from engaging in proprietary trading (i.e., trading as a principal for the trading account of the bank). Thus, only the investment banking arm of the business is allowed to conduct such trading. The Volcker Rule was implemented in

April 2014 and banks had until July 21, 2015, to be in compliance. The result of the new rules is that big U.S. banks could be forced to return to a more traditional banking model that revolves around deposit taking and making loans. This could result in smaller capital markets and less securities lending. Indeed, since the implementation of the Volcker Rule, dealers regulated by the rule have decreased their corporate bond market-making activities. While dealers not affected by the Volcker Rule have stepped in to provide liquidity, the net effect is a less liquid corporate bond market.[6]

**Banking and Insurance.**   Certain insurance products—for example, credit life insurance, mortgage insurance, and auto insurance—tend to have natural synergistic links to bank lending. However, a distinction should be made between a bank selling insurance as an agent by selling other FIs' policies for a fee and a bank acting as an insurance underwriter and bearing the direct risk of underwriting losses itself. In general, the risks of insurance agency activities are quite low in loss potential when compared to insurance underwriting.

Prior to the Financial Services Modernization Act of 1999, banks were under stringent restrictions when selling and underwriting almost every type of insurance. Further, the Bank Holding Company Act of 1956 and the Garn–St. Germain Depository Institutions Act of 1982 severely restricted insurance companies' ability to own, or to be affiliated with, full-service banks. A great challenge to these restrictions on bank–insurance company affiliations came from the 1998 merger between Citicorp and Travelers to create the largest financial services conglomerate in the United States. The primary activity of Travelers was insurance (life and property–casualty), while the primary activity of Citicorp was banking (both also were engaged in securities activities: Citicorp through its Section 20 subsidiary and Travelers through its earlier acquisition of Smith Barney and Salomon Brothers). The Federal Reserve gave initial approval in September 1998. Under the Bank Holding Company Act, the Federal Reserve had up to five years to formally approve the merger.

The Financial Services Modernization Act of 1999 completely changed the landscape for insurance activities as it allowed bank holding companies to open insurance underwriting affiliates and insurance companies to open commercial bank (or savings institutions) as well as securities firm affiliates through the creation of a financial service holding company. With the passage of this act banks no longer have to fight legal battles to overcome restrictions on their ability to sell insurance. The insurance industry also applauded the act, as it forced banks that underwrite and sell insurance to operate under the same set of state regulations (pertaining to their insurance lines) as insurance companies operating in that state. Under the new act, a financial services holding company that engages in commercial banking, investment banking, and insurance activities is functionally regulated. This means that the holding company's banking activities are regulated by bank regulators (such as the Federal Reserve, FDIC, OCC), its securities activities are regulated by the SEC, and its insurance activities are regulated by up to 50 state insurance regulators. Further, in July 2010, the Wall Street Reform and Consumer Protection Act established a new office at the Treasury (the Office of National Insurance) that monitors the insurance industry and helps decide if an insurer is big enough to warrant tighter oversight. The act also established a Financial Stability Oversight Council that has authority to review both banks and nonbank companies, including insurance companies, to see if they pose a threat to the overall financial system.

**Commercial Banking and Commerce.**   Although the direct holdings of other firms' equity by national banks has been constrained since 1863, the restrictions on the commercial activities of bank holding companies are a more recent phenomena. In particular, the 1970 amendments to the 1956 Bank Holding Company Act required bank holding companies to divest themselves of nonbank-related subsidiaries over a 10-year period

---

6. See Bao, O'Hara, and Zhou, "The Volcker Rule and Market-Making in Times of Stress," SSRN working paper. http://ssrn.com/abstract=2836714

following the amendment.[7] The 1956 Bank Holding Company Act also effectively restricted acquisitions of banks by commercial firms (as was true for insurance companies before 1999). The major vehicle for a commercial firm's entry into commercial banking has been through **nonbank banks** (such as Ener-Bank USA owned by Home Depot) or nonbank financial service firms that offer banking-type services by divesting a subsidiary "bank" of its commercial loans and/or its demand deposits (as well as any deposit insurance coverage).

**nonbank bank**

*A bank divested of its commercial loans and/or its demand deposits.*

The Financial Services Modernization Act of 1999 changed restrictions on ownership limits imposed on financial services holding companies. Commercial banks belonging to a financial service holding company can now take a controlling interest in a nonfinancial enterprise provided that two conditions are met. First, the investment cannot be made for an indefinite period of time. The act did not provide an explicit time limit, but simply states that the investment can be "held for a period of time to enable the sale or disposition thereof on a reasonable basis consistent with the financial viability of the [investment]." Second, the bank cannot become actively involved in the management of the corporation in which it invests. Nevertheless, corporate stocks or equities are still conspicuously absent from most bank balance sheets (see Chapter 12).

**Nonbank Financial Service Firms and Banking.**   In comparison with the barriers separating banking and either securities, insurance, or commercial sector activities, the barriers among nonbank financial service firms and banking are generally much weaker. Indeed, the erosion of product barriers between commercial banks and other financial institution services firms has not been all one way. Nonbank financial service firms increasingly offer traditional banking services. For example, money market mutual funds offer checking account–like deposit services, annuities are financial products issued by insurance companies that offer many of the features of CDs, and finance companies and industrial loan corporations (see Chapter 11) provide commercial, real estate, and consumer loans that compete directly with the same services offered by commercial banks. These financial institutions provide credit, maturity, and liquidity intermediation without access to central bank liquidity provisions or deposit insurance.[8] Their activities occur beyond the reach of existing state and federal monitoring and regulation.

**shadow banking**

*Activities of nonfinancial services firms that perform banking services.*

**DO YOU UNDERSTAND:**

5. The rationale for the passage of the Glass-Steagall Act in 1933? What permissible underwriting activities did it identify for commercial banks?

6. Why a 5 percent rather than a 50 percent maximum ceiling was originally imposed on the revenues earned from the eligible underwriting activities of a Section 20 subsidiary?

7. Why a bank that currently specializes in making consumer loans, but makes no commercial loans, qualifies as a nonbank bank?

8. What a shadow bank is?

9. How the Financial Services Modernization Act of 1999 has opened the doors for the establishment of full-service financial institutions in the United States?

More recently the activities of nonfinancial service firms that perform banking services have been termed **shadow banking.** Beyond the examples listed previously, new participants in the shadow banking system include structured investment vehicles (SIVs), special purpose vehicles (SPVs), asset-backed paper vehicles, asset-backed commercial paper (ABCP) conduits, limited-purpose finance companies, and credit hedge funds. A recent report from the U.S. Financial Stability Board (FSB) put assets of shadow banks worldwide at $75 trillion. Based on the FSB data, total assets of these nonbank financial intermediaries amount to approximately 120 percent of global GDP and approximately 56 percent of total bank assets. The United States has the largest exposure of any reporting country ($24 trillion), followed by the United Kingdom ($9 trillion). Despite government restrictions, China's shadow banking system is third in size ($4.5 trillion) and has been growing about 34 percent annually in recent years.

In the shadow banking system, savers place their funds with money market mutual and similar funds, which invest these funds in the liabilities of shadow banks. Borrowers get loans and leases from shadow banks such as finance companies rather than from banks. Like the traditional banking system, the shadow banking system intermediates the flow of funds between net savers and net borrowers. However, instead of the bank serving as the intermediary, it is the nonbank financial service firm, or shadow bank, that intermediates. Further, unlike

---

7. The Bank Holding Company Act defines *control* as a holding company's equity stake in a subsidiary bank or affiliate that exceeds 25 percent.

8. However, to show the banking-like nature of money market mutual fund deposits, the government provided a 100 percent guarantee on the safety of those deposits for one year following the Lehman Brothers failure in the fall of 2008.

the traditional banking system, where the complete credit intermediation is performed by a single bank, in the shadow banking system it is performed through a series of steps involving many nonbank financial service firms. For example, and as discussed in more detail in Chapter 24, the lending process might involve (1) loan originations performed by a finance company, (2) the purchase and warehousing of these loans conducted by single and multiple SIVs funded through asset-backed commercial paper (ABCP), and (3) the purchase of ABCP by money market mutual funds. Thus, the shadow banking system decomposes the traditional process of deposit-funded, hold-to-maturity lending conducted by banks into a more complex, wholesale-funded, securitization-based lending process that involves multiple shadow banks which are not regulated by a specific regulatory body.

As of 2016, these shadow banks continue to be unregulated by the federal government. The 2010 Wall Street Reform and Consumer Protection Act called for regulators to be given broad authority to monitor and regulate nonbank financial firms that pose risks to the financial system. As of 2016, U.S. regulators had outlined a process to identify nonbank financial services firms that should receive increased oversight. The designated firms come under the supervision of the Federal Reserve and must comply with new rules, such as more stringent capital, risk management, and leverage standards. When implemented, the process is one tool by which the 2010 act will enable regulators to extend oversight and regulation to the shadow banking system.

### Geographic Expansion in the U.S. Commercial Banking Industry

**de novo office**

*A newly established office.*

Geographic expansions can have a number of dimensions. In particular, they can be (1) domestic, (2) within a state or region, or (3) international (participating in a foreign market). Expansions can also be carried out by opening a new office or branch or by acquiring another bank. Historically, in the United States, the ability of commercial banks to expand domestically has been constrained by regulation. By comparison, no special regulations inhibit the ability of commercial firms such as General Motors, IBM, or Walmart from establishing new or **de novo offices,** factories, or stores anywhere in the country. Nor are such companies generally prohibited from acquiring other firms—as long as they are not banks. Commercial banks have faced a complex and changing network of rules and regulations covering geographic expansions. Such regulations may inhibit expansions, but they may also create potential opportunities to increase a commercial bank's returns. In particular, regulations may create locally uncompetitive markets with high economic rents that new entrants can potentially exploit. Thus, for the most innovative commercial banks, regulation can provide profit opportunities as well as costs. As a result, regulation acts both as an inhibitor and an incentive to engage in geographic expansions.

**Regulatory Factors Impacting Geographic Expansion.**

**unit bank**

*A bank with a single office.*

*Restrictions on Intrastate Banking by Commercial Banks.*   For most of the 1900s, most U.S. banks were **unit banks** with a single office. Improving communications and customer needs resulted in a rush to branching. This movement ran into increasing opposition from the smallest unit banks and the largest money center banks. The smallest unit banks perceived a competitive threat to their retail business from the larger branching banks; money center banks feared a loss of valuable correspondent business such as check-clearing and other payment services. As a result, several states restricted banks' ability to branch within the state. Indeed, some states prohibited intrastate (or within-state) branching per se, effectively constraining a bank to unit bank status. Over the years and in a very piecemeal fashion, states liberalized their restrictions on within-state branching. By 1994, only one state (Iowa) had not deregulated intrastate banking.

*Restrictions on Interstate Banking by Commercial Banks.*   The defining piece of legislation affecting interstate branching up until 1994 was the McFadden Act, passed in 1927 and amended in 1933. The McFadden Act and its amendments restricted nationally chartered banks' branching abilities to the same extent allowed to state-chartered banks, which essentially prevented all U.S. banks from branching across state lines. Given the McFadden prohibition on interstate branching, bank organizations expanding across state lines between 1927 and 1956 relied on establishing subsidiaries rather than branches. Some of the largest banking organizations established **multibank holding companies (MBHCs)** for this purpose. An MBHC is a parent company that acquires more than one bank as a direct subsidiary (e.g., First Interstate).

In 1956, Congress recognized the potential loophole to interstate banking posed by the MBHC movement and passed the Douglas Amendment to the Bank Holding Company Act. This act permitted MBHCs to acquire bank subsidiaries only to the extent allowed by the laws of the state in which the proposed bank target resided. Because states prohibited out-of-state bank acquisitions, this temporarily curtailed the growth of the MBHC movement.

Maine took the first step in eroding interstate banking restrictions in 1978 by passing a law that exploited a loophole in the Douglas amendments of 1956. To increase employment in and growth of its financial services industry, Maine passed a law allowing banks from any other state to enter and acquire local banks even if the banks in Maine could not engage in such acquisitions in other states. This nationwide nonreciprocal bank acquisition law led to a rapid acquisition of Maine's banking assets by out-of-state bank holding companies. Indeed, by 1988, some 85 percent of bank assets in Maine were held by out-of-state banking organizations such as Citicorp (now Citigroup). In the early 1980s other states in New England sought to follow Maine's example by enacting their own **interstate banking pacts.** By 1994, all states but Hawaii had passed some form of interstate banking law or pact.

*Riegle-Neal Interstate Banking and Branching Efficiency Act of 1994.* It has long been recognized that the expansion of nationwide banking through multibank holding companies is potentially far more expensive than through branching. Separate corporations and boards of directors must be established for each bank in an MBHC, and it is hard to achieve the same level of economic and financial integration and synergies as is possible with branches. Moreover, most major banking competitor countries outside of the United States, such as Japan, Germany, France, and the United Kingdom, have nationwide branching.

In the fall of 1994, the U.S. Congress passed the Riegle-Neal Banking and Branching Efficiency Act that allowed U.S. and foreign banks to branch interstate by consolidating out-of-state bank subsidiaries into a branch network and/or by acquiring banks or individual branches of banks through acquisition or merger. The effective date for these new branching powers was June 1, 1997. Although the act was silent on the ability of banks to establish de novo branches in other states—essentially leaving it to individual states to pass laws allowing de novo branching—under the Riegle-Neal Act a New York bank such as Citibank may purchase, as an example, a single branch of Bank of America in San Francisco. The result of the Riegle-Neal Act is that full interstate banking is a reality in the United States. The relaxation of the branching restrictions, along with recognition of the potential cost, revenue, and risk benefits from geographic expansions, are major reasons for the recent merger wave (and increased consolidation) in U.S. banking (see Chapter 11).

## BANK AND SAVINGS INSTITUTION GUARANTEE FUNDS

A key component of the regulatory structure of CBs is deposit insurance and financial guarantees provided to depositors of CBs by regulators. Because the insurance fund that covers deposits of CBs also covers deposits of savings institutions (discussed in Chapter 14), this section discusses the deposit insurance funds as they pertain to both CBs and savings institutions.[9]

**multibank holding company (MBHC)**

*A parent banking organization that owns a number of individual bank subsidiaries.*

**interstate banking pact**

*An agreement among states describing the conditions for entrance of out-of-state banks by acquisition.*

### DO YOU UNDERSTAND:

10. The reason for the passage of the Douglas Amendment to the Bank Holding Company Act?

11. How the Riegle-Neal Act affected the geographic expansion opportunities of banks?

---

9. In addition to deposit insurance, central banks, such as the Federal Reserve, provide a discount window facility to meet banks' short-term nonpermanent liquidity needs. We discuss the discount window as a mechanism used to ease banks' liquidity problems in Chapter 21.

### The Federal Deposit Insurance Corporation (FDIC)

**www.fdic.gov**

The Federal Deposit Insurance Corporation (FDIC) was created in 1933 in the wake of the banking panics of 1930–1933 to maintain the stability of, and public confidence in, the U.S. financial system. Over the period 1933–1979, the FDIC insurance system seemed to work well, failures were few (see Figure 13–3), and the FDIC insurance fund grew in size. During the October 1979 to October 1982 period, however, the Federal Reserve radically changed its monetary policy strategy by targeting bank reserves rather than interest rates in an attempt to lower the underlying rate of inflation (see Chapter 4). The Fed's restrictive monetary policy action led to a sudden and dramatic rise in interest rates, with rates on T-bills rising as high as 16 percent. This increase in short-term rates and the cost of funds had two effects. First, depository institutions faced negative interest spreads or net interest margins (i.e., interest income minus interest expense divided by earning assets) in funding much of their fixed-rate long-term residential mortgage portfolios over this period. Second, they had to pay more competitive interest rates on savings deposits to prevent **disintermediation** and the reinvestment of these funds in money market mutual fund accounts. Their ability to do this was constrained by the Federal Reserve's Regulation Q ceilings, which at the time limited the rates that depository institutions (DIs) could pay on traditional passbook savings account and retail time deposits.[10]

**disintermediation**

*The withdrawal of deposits from depository institutions and their reinvestment elsewhere.*

Partly to overcome the effects of rising interest rates and disintermediation on the DIs, Congress passed regulations that expanded depository institutions' deposit-taking and asset investment powers. For many DIs, the new powers created safer and more diversified institutions. For a small but significant group whose earnings and shareholders' capital were being eroded in traditional lines of business, however, it meant the opportunity to take more risks in an attempt to return to profitability. As discussed below, this risk-taking or moral hazard behavior was accentuated by the policies of depository institution insurers. They chose not to close capital-depleted, economically insolvent DIs (a policy of **regulator forbearance**) and to maintain deposit insurance premium assessments independent of the risk of the institution. As a result, beginning in 1980, the number of bank failures increased, with more than 1,039 in the decade ending in 1990 (peaking at 221 in 1988). This number of failures was actually higher than that in the entire 1933–1979 period. Moreover, the

**regulator forbearance**

*A policy of not closing economically insolvent depository institutions, but allowing them to continue in operation.*

**Figure 13–3**   **Number of Failed Banks by Year, 1934–2016**

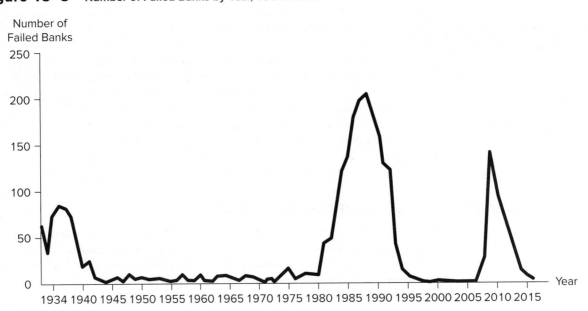

**Sources:** FDIC annual reports and *Statistics on Banking.* www.fdic.gov

10. Regulation Q restrictions on deposit interest rates were fully dropped in 1986.

costs of each of these failures were often larger than those of the mainly small bank failures that occurred in the 1933–1979 period. As the number and costs of these failures mounted in the 1980s, the FDIC fund was rapidly drained. In response to this crisis, Congress passed the FDIC Improvement Act (FDICIA) in December 1991 to restructure the bank insurance fund and to prevent its potential insolvency.

After 1991 there was a dramatic turnaround in the fund's finances and a drop in DI failures—partially in response to record profit levels in DIs. Specifically, in 2007 there were 3 DI failures; in 2005 and 2006 there were no DI failures. As of March 2008, the FDIC's Depositors Insurance Fund (DIF) had reserves of $52.8 billion. However, the financial market crisis hit the banking industry very badly. In 2008, 26 DIs failed (at a cost to the FDIC of $15.7 billion), in 2009 an additional 140 failures occurred (at a cost of over $36.4 billion), in 2010, 157 failures occurred (at a cost of $22.4 billion), and in 2011, 92 failures occurred (at a cost of $7.2 billion). Thus, during the worst of the financial crisis (2008–2011), 414 DIs failed at a total cost to the FDIC of $81.7 billion. By September 2009, the FDIC's DIF reserves had fallen to −$8.2 billion, less than zero for only the second time since its founding in 1933. The deficit peaked in the first quarter of 2010 at −$20.86 billion. However, unlike the near bankruptcy of the FDIC in 1991, the negative balance in the FDIC's DI insurance fund did not result in talk of the insurer's possible failure. Rather, the FDIC and the federal government took several steps to ensure the fund would have sufficient resources to deal with any and all DI failures. To address the falling balance in the fund, the FDIC levied one special assessment in early 2009 and a second in the fall of 2009, in addition to raising the rates banks were charged for deposit insurance (see below). Further, the agency took the unprecedented step of requiring banks to prepay $45 billion of insurance premiums by the end of 2009. The premiums covered the fourth quarter of 2009 and all of 2010 through 2012. Finally, the FDIC was given approval to tap $500 billion in additional funding from the Treasury Department through the end of 2010. The actions of regulators (and the end of the crisis) proved successful as only 92 banks failed in 2011 (costing $6.89 billion) and 51 banks in 2012 (at a cost of $2.78 billion). By 2015, just 8 banks failed and through June 2016, 3 banks failed. Further, FDIC reserves became positive ($3.9 billion) in the first quarter of 2011 and rose to $77.9 billion by June 2016.

## *The Demise of the Federal Savings and Loan Insurance Corporation (FSLIC)*

The Federal Savings and Loan Insurance Corporation (FSLIC) insured the deposits of savings institutions from 1934 to 1989. Like the FDIC, this insurance fund was in relatively good shape until the end of the 1970s. Beginning in 1980, its resources began to be depleted as more and more savings institutions failed. Between 1980 and 1988, 581 savings institutions failed at an estimated cost of $42.3 billion. By 1989, the FSLIC fund had been depleted and the present value of its liabilities exceeded that of its assets. Lacking the resources to close or resolve failing savings institutions, the FSLIC followed a policy of forbearance (or leniency) toward remaining weak and failing savings institutions. This meant that it allowed many badly run savings institutions to stay open and continue to accumulate losses. In August 1989, Congress passed the Financial Institutions Reform, Recovery, and Enforcement Act (FIRREA), largely in response to the deepening crisis in the savings institution industry and the growing insolvency of the FSLIC. This act restructured the savings association fund and transferred its management to the FDIC. At that time, the FSLIC ceased to exist. At the same time, the restructured savings association insurance fund was renamed the Savings Association Insurance Fund (SAIF) and the restructured bank insurance fund was renamed the Bank Insurance Fund (BIF). (In March 2006, the FDIC merged the BIF and the SAIF to form the Depositors Insurance Fund [DIF]. Currently, the FDIC manages the DIF, which provides deposit insurance for both commercial banks and savings institutions). See Figure 13–4 for the organizational structure of the FDIC and the number of commercial banks and savings institutions insured by the DIF.

**Figure 13–4**   The Structure of the FDIC–DIF in 2016

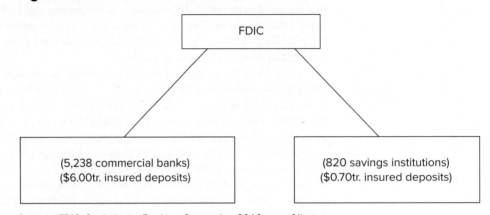

**Source:** FDIC, *Statistics on Banking,* September 2016. www.fdic.gov

### Reform of Deposit Insurance

On January 1, 1993, the FDIC introduced a risk-based deposit insurance program. Under this program, which applied equally to all deposit-insured institutions, a bank's or thrift's risk would be ranked along a capital adequacy dimension and a supervisory dimension (the depository institution's CAMELS rating, see Chapter 12). Each dimension had three categories, so a bank or thrift was placed in any one of nine cells. The best DIs, those in cell 1, which were well-capitalized and had healthy supervisory ratings, paid an annual insurance premium of 23 cents per $100 of deposits, while the worst DIs paid 31 cents. Although the 8-cent differential in insurance premiums between the safest and the riskiest CBs was a first step in risk-based pricing, it was considered to be so small that it did not effectively limit DIs' risk-taking incentives. The average assessment rate in 1993 was 23.2 cents per $100 of deposits.

The improving solvency position of the FDIC (and of the banks and thrifts it insures) resulted in a considerable reduction in insurance premiums. In 1996 (for BIF-insured DIs) and 1997 (for SAIF-insured DIs) the fee structure for deposit insurance was changed so that the healthiest institutions paid 0 cents per $100 of deposits, while the riskiest paid 27 cents per $100 of deposits. As a result, by December 2005, 94.6 percent of all BIF-insured DIs and 93.9 percent of all SAIF-insured DIs paid the statutory minimum premium, and the average assessment rate was less than 0.1 cent per $100 of deposits.

Despite the apparent strong health of the deposit insurance funds, in the early 2000s, the FDIC identified several weaknesses with the current system of deposit insurance that it felt needed to be corrected. Among these was that the current system did not effectively price risk. Specifically, regulations restricted the FDIC from charging premiums to well-capitalized and highly rated DIs as long as the insurance fund reserves were above 1.25 percent of insured deposits. As a result, and as stated earlier, over 90 percent of all insured DIs did not pay deposit insurance premiums in the late 1990s and early 2000s. The FDIC argued that it should charge regular premiums for risk regardless of the reserve levels of the fund. In February 2006, then president Bush signed the Federal Deposit Insurance Reform Act of 2005 into law. Under the act, beginning in January 2007, the FDIC began calculating deposit insurance premiums based on a more aggressive, risk-based system. Further, under the Federal Deposit Insurance Reform Act, if the reserve ratio drops below 1.15 percent—or the FDIC expects it to do so within six months—the FDIC must, within 90 days, establish and implement a plan to restore the DIF to 1.15 percent within five years. Such was the case in March 2008 when the FDIC reserve ratio dropped to 1.19 percent. At this point the FDIC was certain that the reserve ratio would drop below 1.15 by the end of the next quarter. Accordingly, the FDIC developed and implemented (on

**DO YOU UNDERSTAND:**

12.  *What events led Congress to pass the FDICIA?*

13.  *What events brought about the demise of the FSLIC?*

14.  *How the 2008–2009 financial crisis affected the FDIC deposit insurance fund solvency?*

15.  *What the main purpose of the FDIC Reform Act of 2005 was?*

April 1, 2009) a restoration plan for the DIF which would restore the DIF reserve ratio to 1.15 percent. The details of the approach, including the 2009 restoration plan and the 2011 and 2015 adjustment to the plan, are described in Appendix 13A to this chapter.

### LG 13-5 | *Non–U.S. Deposit Insurance Systems*

Most European countries have historically operated without explicit deposit insurance programs. Despite this, European countries have not seen the 1930s type of bank run and panic experienced in the United States. This is because European governments have often given implicit deposit guarantees at no cost to the largest banks in their countries. This has been possible as the result of the higher degree of concentration of deposits among the largest banks in European countries. However, deposit insurance systems are being increasingly adopted worldwide. One view of this trend toward implementation of explicit deposit programs is that governments are now simply collecting premiums as a fee to offset an obligation (implicit deposit insurance) that they previously offered for free.

Many of these systems offer quite different degrees of protection to depositors compared to the U.S. system. For example, in response to the single banking and capital market in Europe, the European Union (EU) has established a single deposit insurance system covering all EU-located banks. This insures deposit accounts up to 50,000 euros. However, depositors are subject to a 10 percent deductible (loss) to create incentives for them to monitor banks. The idea underlying the EU plan is to create a level playing field for banks across all European Union countries. Appendix 13D (available through Connect or your course instructor) shows a list of countries that offer (and do not offer) explicit deposit insurance schemes.

## BALANCE SHEET REGULATIONS

A further form of regulation of CBs pertains to various assets and liabilities on their balance sheets.

### LG 13-6 | *Regulations on Commercial Bank Liquidity*

Holding relatively small amounts of liquid assets exposes a CB to increased illiquidity and insolvency risk. Excessive illiquidity can result in a CB's inability to meet required payments on liability claims (such as deposit withdrawals) and, at the extreme, its insolvency. Moreover, it can even lead to contagious effects that negatively impact other CBs. Consequently, regulators impose minimum liquid asset reserve requirements on CBs. In general, these requirements differ in nature and scope for various CBs. The requirements depend on the illiquidity risk exposure perceived for the CB's type and other regulatory objectives that relate to minimum liquid asset requirements (see Chapter 4). Currently, in accordance with Federal Reserve Regulation D of the Federal Reserve Act of 1913, banks in the United States are required to hold the following "target" minimum reserves against net transaction accounts (transaction accounts minus demand deposit balances due from U.S. commercial banks and cash items in process of collection):[11]

| | |
|---|---|
| Less than $15.2 million | 0% |
| $15.2 million–$110.2 million | 3 |
| More than $110.2 million | 10 |

In Appendix 13B we discuss the details of how to calculate the minimum reserve requirement for a bank.

---

11. The Garn–St. Germain Commercial Banks Act of 1982 requires that $2 million of reservable liabilities of each commercial bank be subject to a zero percent reserve requirement. Each year, the Federal Reserve adjusts the amount of reservable liabilities subject to this zero percent reserve requirement for the succeeding calendar year by 80 percent of the percentage increase in the total reservable liabilities of all depository institutions, measured on an annual basis as of June 30. As of 2016, these were the requirements.

During the financial crisis, many DIs struggled to maintain adequate liquidity. Indeed, extraordinary levels of liquidity assistance were required from central banks in order to maintain the financial system. Even with this extensive support, a number of DIs failed or were forced into mergers. Recognizing the need for DIs to improve their liquidity risk management and control their liquidity risk exposure, the Bank for International Settlement's (BIS) Basel Committee on Banking Supervision developed two new regulatory standards for liquidity risk supervision. The standards are intended to "enhance tools, metrics, and benchmarks that supervisors can use to assess the resilience of banks' liquidity cushions and constrain any weakening in liquidity maturity profiles, diversity of funding sources, and stress testing practices." The two new liquidity ratios to be maintained by DIs are the *liquidity coverage ratio* and the *net stable funds ratio*. We discuss these ratios in detail in Chapter 21.

**LG 13-7**

## Regulations on Capital Adequacy (Leverage)

The FDIC Improvement Act (FDICIA) of 1991 required that banks and thrifts adopt risk-based capital requirements. Consistent with this act, U.S. DI regulators formally agreed with other member countries of the Bank for International Settlements (BIS) to implement new risk-based capital ratios for all depository institutions under their jurisdiction. The BIS phased in and fully implemented these risk-based capital ratios on January 1, 1993, under what has become known as the **Basel Agreement** (or Basle; now called *Basel I*). The 1993 Basel Agreement explicitly incorporated the different credit risks of assets (both on and off the balance sheet) into capital adequacy measures. This was followed with a revision in 1998 in which market risk was incorporated into risk-based capital in the form of an add-on to the 8 percent ratio for credit risk exposure. In 2001, the BIS issued a consultative document, "The New Basel Capital Accord," that proposed the incorporation of operational risk into capital requirements and updated the credit risk assessments in the 1993 agreement.

**Basel Agreement**

*The requirement to impose risk-based capital ratios on banks in major industrialized countries.*

The new Basel Accord or Agreement (called *Basel II*) of 2006 allowed for a range of options for addressing both credit and operational risk.[12] Two options related to the measurement of credit risk. The first was the Standardized Approach and the second was an Internal Ratings–Based (IRB) Approach. The Standardized Approach was similar to that of the 1993 agreement, but was more risk sensitive. Under the IRB Approach, DIs were allowed to use their internal estimates of borrower creditworthiness to assess credit risk in their portfolios (using their own internal rating systems and credit scoring models) subject to strict methodological and disclosure standards, as well as explicit approval by the DI's supervising regulator.

The financial crisis of 2008–2009 revealed weaknesses with Basel II. For example, ratings of credit risk on various securities, such as credit default swaps, were conducted by private companies without the supervision or review by official regulatory agencies. Further, the Basel II capital adequacy formula for credit risk was procyclical. Thus, as the financial crisis developed, the probability of borrower default and loss on default both increased, which meant that regulatory capital requirements increased. However, during the crisis, banks were unable to raise the required capital and thus had to turn to central banks for capital injections and liquidity support.

In response to these issues, Basel 2.5 was passed in 2009 (effective in 2013) and Basel III was passed in 2010 (fully effective in 2019). Basel 2.5 updated capital requirements on market risk from banks' trading operations. The goal of Basel III is to raise the quality, consistency, and transparency of the capital base of banks to withstand credit risk and to strengthen the risk coverage of the capital framework. Under Basel III, advanced (IRB) approaches may be used by institutions that have consolidated assets of $250 billion or more or consolidated on-balance-sheet foreign exposures of $10 billion or

---

12. See Basel Committee on Banking Supervision, "The New Basel Capital Accord," January 2001; and "International Convergence of Capital Measurement and Capital Standards," June 2006. www.bis.org

more (approximately 20 of the largest U.S. banking organizations). All other depository institutions must use the Standardized Approach for calculating capital adequacy.

Under Basel III, depository institutions must calculate and monitor four capital ratios: common equity Tier I (CET1) risk-based capital ratio, Tier I risk-based capital ratio, total risk–based capital ratio, and Tier I leverage ratio. A DI's capital adequacy is assessed according to where its capital ratios place in one of five target zones.

$$
\begin{aligned}
\textbf{Common equity Tier I} \quad &= \quad \text{Common equity Tier I capital/Credit} \\
\textbf{risk-based capital ratio} \quad &\quad \text{risk–adjusted assets} \\[6pt]
\textbf{Tier I risk-based capital ratio} \quad &= \quad \text{Tier I capital (Common equity Tier I} \\
&\quad \text{capital + Additional Tier I capital)/} \\
&\quad \text{Credit risk–adjusted assets} \\[6pt]
\textbf{Total risk–based capital ratio} \quad &= \quad \text{Total capital (Tier I + Tier II)/Credit} \\
&\quad \text{risk–adjusted assets} \\[6pt]
\textbf{Tier I leverage ratio} \quad &= \quad \text{Tier I capital/Total exposure}
\end{aligned}
$$

The calculation of these capital adequacy measures is quite complex. Their major innovation is to distinguish among the different credit risks of assets on the balance sheet and to identify the credit risk inherent in instruments off the balance sheet by using a risk-adjusted assets denominator in these capital adequacy ratios. In a very rough fashion, these capital ratios mark to market a DI's on- and off-balance-sheet positions to reflect its credit risk. Further, additional capital charges must be held against market risk and operational risk. To be adequately capitalized, a DI must meet the following requirements: (1) hold a minimum ratio of common equity Tier I capital to credit risk–adjusted assets of 4.5 percent, (2) maintain a ratio of Tier I capital to credit risk–adjusted assets of 6 percent, (3) hold a ratio of total capital to credit risk–adjusted assets of 8 percent, and (4) maintain a ratio of Tier I leverage ratio of 4 percent.

In addition to their use in defining adequately capitalized DIs, these capital ratios also define well capitalized, undercapitalized, significantly undercapitalized, and critically undercapitalized as part of the prompt corrective action program under the FDICIA. These five zones—specified in Table 13–3—assess capital adequacy and the actions regulators are mandated to take and those they have the discretion to take. Since December 18, 1992, under the FDICIA legislation, regulators must take specific actions—**prompt corrective action (PCA)**—when a DI falls outside the zone 1, or well-capitalized, category. Table 13–4

---

**common equity Tier I risk-based capital ratio**

*The ratio of the common equity Tier I capital to the risk-adjusted assets of the DI.*

**Tier I risk-based capital ratio**

*The ratio of the Tier I capital to the risk-adjusted assets of the DI.*

**total risk–based capital ratio**

*The ratio of the total capital to the risk-adjusted assets of the DI.*

**Tier I leverage ratio**

*The ratio of the Tier I capital to the DI's total exposure.*

**prompt corrective action**

*Mandatory actions to be taken by regulators as a DI's capital ratio falls.*

---

**TABLE 13–3** Specifications of Capital Categories for Prompt Corrective Action

| Zone | (1) Common Equity Tier I Risk-Based Ratio | | (2) Tier I Risk-Based Ratio | | (3) Total Risk–Based Ratio | | (4) Tier I Leverage Ratio | | Capital Directive/Other |
|---|---|---|---|---|---|---|---|---|---|
| 1. Well capitalized | 6.5% or above | and | 8% or above | and | 10% or above | and | 5% or above | and | Not subject to a capital directive to meet a specific level for any capital measure |
| 2. Adequately capitalized | 4.5% or above | and | 6% or above | and | 8% or above | and | 4% or above | and | Does not meet the definition of well capitalized |
| 3. Undercapitalized | Under 4.5% | or | Under 6% | or | Under 8% | or | Under 4% | | |
| 4. Significantly undercapitalized | Under 3% | or | Under 6% | or | Under 8% | or | Under 4% | | |
| 5. Critically undercapitalized | Tangible equity/Total assets ≤2% | | | | | | | | |

**TABLE 13–4** Summary of Prompt Corrective Action Provisions of the Federal Deposit Insurance Corporation Improvement Act of 1991 *(in millions of dollars)*

| Zone | Mandatory Provisions | Discretionary Provisions |
|---|---|---|
| 1. Well capitalized | | |
| 2. Adequately capitalized | 1. Prohibit brokered deposits, except with FDIC approval | |
| 3. Undercapitalized | 1. Suspend dividends and management fees<br>2. Require capital restoration plan<br>3. Restrict asset growth<br>4. Require approval for acquisitions<br>5. Prohibit brokered deposits | 1. Order recapitalization<br>2. Restrict interaffiliate transactions<br>3. Restrict deposit interest rates<br>4. Restrict certain other activities<br>5. Allow any other action that would better carry out prompt corrective action |
| 4. Significantly undercapitalized | 1. Same as for Zone 3<br>2. Order recapitalization*<br>3. Restrict interaffiliate transactions*<br>4. Restrict deposit interest rates*<br>5. Restrict pay of officers | 1. Enforce any Zone 3 discretionary actions<br>2. Appoint conservatorship or receivership if bank fails to submit or implement plan or recapitalize pursuant to order<br>3. Enforce any other Zone 5 provision, if such action is necessary to carry out prompt corrective action |
| 5. Critically undercapitalized | 1. Same as for Zone 4<br>2. Appoint receiver/conservator within 90 days*<br>3. Appoint receiver if still in Zone 5 four quarters after becoming critically undercapitalized<br>4. Suspend payments on subordinated debt*<br>5. Restrict certain other activities | |

*Not required if primary supervisor determines action would not serve purpose of prompt corrective action or if certain other conditions are met.

**Source:** Federal Reserve Board of Governors, Press Release, September 2016. www.federalreserve.gov

summarizes these regulatory actions. Most important, a receiver must be appointed when a DI's tangible equity (Tier I + Non–Tier I perpetual preferred stock) to total assets ratio falls to 2 percent or less. That is, receivership is mandatory even before the book value ratio falls to 0 percent. Between 1994 and June 2008, less than 0.5 percent of depository institution industry assets were classified as critically undercapitalized. This compares with 31.3 percent critically undercapitalized in the fourth quarter of 1990 (i.e., during the 1989–1991 recession) and 2.25 percent in June 2009 (during the much deeper recession in the late 2000s).

The idea behind the mandatory and discretionary sets of actions to be taken by regulators for each of the capital adequacy zones is to enforce minimum capital requirements and limit the ability of regulators to show forbearance to the worst capitalized DIs. For example, regulators acted quickly to ensure the largest DIs had sufficient capital to withstand large losses during the financial crisis of 2008–2009. In late February 2009, the Obama administration announced that it would conduct a "stress test" of the 19 largest U.S. FIs that would measure the ability of those FIs to withstand a protracted economic slump—an unemployment rate above 10 percent and home prices dropping another 25 percent. (This stress test focused more on leverage and tangible capital than on risk-based capital, discussed below.) Results of the stress test (reported in Table 13–5) showed that 10 of the 19 FIs needed to raise a total of $74.6 billion in capital. Within a month of the May 7, 2009, release of the results, the FIs had raised $149.45 billion of capital.

In addition to this initial stress test, as part of the 2010 Wall Street Reform and Consumer Protection Act, the largest banks are subject to annual stress tests conducted by the Federal Reserve, called the Comprehensive Capital Analysis and Review (CCAR). The annual review is designed to ensure that the banks are properly capitalized. Scenarios used

**TABLE 13–5**  Stress Test Results for the 19 Largest U.S. DIs *(in billions of dollars)*

| Bank | Total Assets | Worst-Case Loss Estimate | Capital Needed | Capital Raised* |
|------|-------------:|-------------------------:|---------------:|----------------:|
| Bank of America | $1,600.0 | $136.6 | $33.9 | $30.30 |
| Wells Fargo | 1,100.0 | 86.1 | 13.7 | 8.60 |
| GMAC | 172.7 | 9.2 | 11.5 | 3.50 |
| Citigroup | 996.2 | 104.7 | 5.5 | 70.00 |
| Regions Financial | 116.3 | 9.2 | 2.5 | 2.09 |
| SunTrust | 162.0 | 11.8 | 2.2 | 2.08 |
| Morgan Stanley | 310.6 | 19.7 | 1.8 | 8.00 |
| KeyCorp | 106.7 | 6.7 | 1.8 | 1.30 |
| Fifth Third Bancorp | 112.6 | 9.1 | 1.1 | 0.75 |
| PNC | 250.9 | 18.8 | 0.6 | 0.60 |
| J. P. Morgan Chase | 1,300.0 | 97.4 | 0.0 | 5.00 |
| Goldman Sachs | 444.8 | 17.8 | 0.0 | 7.65 |
| MetLife | 326.4 | 9.6 | 0.0 | 0.00 |
| U.S. Bancorp | 230.6 | 15.7 | 0.0 | 2.40 |
| Bank of New York Mellon | 115.8 | 5.4 | 0.0 | 1.20 |
| State Street | 69.6 | 8.2 | 0.0 | 2.23 |
| Capital One Financial | 131.8 | 13.4 | 0.0 | 1.55 |
| BB&T | 109.8 | 8.7 | 0.0 | 1.70 |
| American Express | 104.4 | 11.2 | 0.0 | 0.50 |

*As of June 4, 2009.

as part of the stress test range from baseline to severely adverse, with the most extreme including deep and prolonged global recession in which U.S. real GDP falls 6¼ percent below the pre-recession peak, the unemployment rate increases to 10 percent, consumer price inflation rises to 1¼ percent, equity prices fall 50 percent, equity market volatility increases to levels experienced in 2008, housing prices drop 25 percent, and the euro area, United Kingdom, and Japan experience severe recessions. The 2016 stress tests found 30 of the 33 of the biggest U.S. banks tested had enough capital to continue lending during a severe economic shock and received a nonobjection to their submitted capital plans. However, Morgan Stanley received a conditional nonobjection to its submitted capital plan, meaning that the bank was required to resubmit its capital plan within six months to address deficiencies observed in the submitted plan. However, the firm was allowed to continue with its planned distributions until the Federal Reserve made a determination on the resubmitted capital plan. The final 2 banks, Deutsche Bank and Santander Holdings USA, received an objection to their capital plan, meaning these banks could only make capital distributions that are expressly permitted by the Federal Reserve.

**Capital.**  In the measurement of a DI's capital adequacy, its capital is the standard by which each of these risks is measured. Under Basel III, a DI's capital is divided into common equity Tier I (CET1), additional Tier I, and Tier II. CET1 is primary or core capital of the DI; Tier I capital is the primary capital of the DI plus additional capital elements; and Tier II capital is supplementary capital. The total capital that the DI holds is defined as the sum of Tier I and Tier II capital. The definitions of CET1, additional Tier I capital, and Tier II supplementary capital are listed in Appendix 13E to this chapter (available through Connect or your course instructor).

**credit risk–adjusted assets**

*On- and off-balance-sheet assets whose values are adjusted for approximate credit risk.*

**Credit Risk–Adjusted Assets.**  Under Basel III capital adequacy rules, risk-adjusted assets represent the denominator of the risk-based capital ratios. Two components make up **credit risk–adjusted assets:** (1) credit risk–adjusted on-balance-sheet assets, and (2) credit risk–adjusted off-balance-sheet assets. In Appendix 13E to the chapter (available through Connect or your course instructor), we discuss the details of how to calculate a CB's risk-based capital ratios.

*Capital Conservation Buffer.* In addition to revising the minimum capital ratio requirements for credit risk, Basel III introduced a capital conservation buffer designed to ensure that DIs build up a capital surplus, or buffer, outside periods of financial stress that can be drawn down as losses are incurred during periods of financial stress. The buffer requirements provide incentives for DIs to build up a capital surplus (e.g., by reducing discretionary distributions of earnings [reduced dividends, share buybacks, and staff bonuses]) to reduce the risk that their capital levels could fall below the minimum requirements during periods of stress. The capital conservation buffer must be composed of CET1 capital and is held separately from the minimum risk–based capital requirements.

Under Basel III, a DI would need to hold a capital conservation buffer of greater than 2.5 percent of total risk–weighted assets to avoid being subject to limitations on capital distributions and discretionary bonus payments to executive officers. If a DI's capital buffer falls below 2.5 percent, constraints on earnings payouts (e.g., dividends, share buybacks, and "bonus" payments) will be imposed.

*Countercyclical Capital Buffer.* Basel III also introduced a countercyclical capital buffer that may be declared by any country experiencing excess aggregate credit growth. The countercyclical capital buffer can vary between 0 percent and 2.5 percent of risk-weighted assets. This buffer must be met with CET1 capital, and DIs are given 12 months to adjust to the buffer level. Like the capital conservation buffer, if a DI's capital levels fall below the set countercyclical capital buffer, restrictions on earnings payouts will be applied.

The countercyclical capital buffer aims to protect the banking system and reduce systemic exposures to economic downturns. Losses can be particularly large when a downturn is preceded by a period of excess credit growth. The accumulation of a capital buffer during an expansionary phase increases the ability of the banking system to remain healthy during periods of declining asset prices and losses from weakening credit conditions. By assessing a countercyclical buffer when credit markets are overheated, accumulated capital buffers can absorb any abnormal losses that a DI might experience when the credit cycle turns. Consequently, even after these losses are realized, DIs should remain healthy and able to access funding, meet obligations, and continue to serve as credit intermediaries.

*Global Systemically Important Banks.* As part of Basel III, the BIS imposed an additional common equity Tier I surcharge ("loss absorbency requirement") on global systemically important banks (G-SIBs): banking groups whose distress or disorderly failure would cause significant disruption to the wider financial system and economic activity. The basic idea is that because G-SIBs are too-big-to-fail banks (that would have to be bailed out by central governments and taxpayers), they need to lower their risk by increasing their tangible capital requirements even more than other banks. The surcharge ranges from 1 percent to 3.5 percent to be held over and above the 7 percent minimum CET1 plus conservation buffer requirement. Thus, to have no payment limitations, a G-SIB that is assigned a surcharge of 1.5 percent much have a CET1 ratio of 8.5 percent (= 4.5 percent required to be adequately capitalized + 2.5 percent capital conservation buffer + 1.5 percent surcharge). The surcharge may be larger under exceptional circumstances. For example, in 2015 J.P. Morgan Chase was required to hold a surcharge of 4.5 percent because of its extreme size, complexity, and entanglements with other big financial institutions. The purpose of the additional capital requirement is twofold: (1) to reduce the probability of failure of a G-SIB by increasing its going-concern loss absorbency and (2) to reduce the extent or impact of the failure of a G-SIB on the financial system by improving global recovery and resolution frameworks.

G-SIBs are identified using a methodology developed by the BIS based on an indicator measurement approach that identifies factors that cause international contagion. The indicators were selected to capture the systemic impact of a bank's failure, rather than the probability that the bank will fail. Using this methodology, the BIS designated 27 banks as G-SIBs. Three additional banks were added to this initial list based on the home supervisor's judgment, resulting in 30 G-SIBs

**DO YOU UNDERSTAND:**

16. *Why regulators impose reserve requirements on depository institutions?*

17. *What the major features of the Basel III capital requirements are?*

18. *What four capital ratios DIs must calculate and monitor under Basel III?*

19. *What actions regulators must take under prompt corrective action (PCA)?*

**TABLE 13–6**   Global Systematically Important Banks

| Capital Surcharge | Bank | Country |
| --- | --- | --- |
| 3.5% | n.a. | |
| 2.5% | HSBC | United Kingdom |
| | J.P. Morgan Chase | United States |
| 2.0% | Barclays | United Kingdom |
| | BNP Paribas | France |
| | Citigroup | United States |
| | Deutsche Bank | Germany |
| 1.5% | Bank of America | United States |
| | Credit Suisse | Switzerland |
| | Goldman Sachs | United States |
| | Mitsubishi UFJ FG | Japan |
| | Morgan Stanley | United States |
| 1.0% | Agricultural Bank of China | China |
| | Bank of China | China |
| | Bank of New York Mellon | United States |
| | China Construction Bank | China |
| | Groupe BPCE | France |
| | Groupe Crédit Agricole | France |
| | Industrial and Commerce Bank of China | China |
| | ING Bank | Netherlands |
| | Mizuho FG | Japan |
| | Nordea | Sweden |
| | Royal Bank of Scotland | United Kingdom |
| | Santander | Spain |
| | Société Générale | France |
| | Standard Chartered | United Kingdom |
| | State Street Bank | United States |
| | Sumitomo Mitsui FG | Japan |
| | UBS | Switzerland |
| | Unicredit Group | Italy |
| | Wells Fargo | United States |

headquartered in 11 countries. Table 13–6 provides a list of the 30 G-SIBs and the capital surcharge for each as of 2016. The number of G-SIBs can change over time, reflecting changes in the systemic importance of banks. The sample of banks to be assessed will be reviewed every three years, and the BIS also anticipates eventually expanding the surcharge to a wider group of financial institutions, including insurance companies and other nonbank financial institutions.[13]

## FOREIGN VERSUS DOMESTIC REGULATION OF COMMERCIAL BANKS

As discussed earlier in this chapter, many of the product and geographic expansion barriers on U.S. commercial banks have recently been lowered. Despite the loosening of regulations, however, U.S. CBs are still subject to stricter regulations than CBs in many foreign countries.

### Product Diversification Activities

With the passage of the Financial Services Modernization Act of 1999, the range of nonbank product activities that U.S. banks are permitted to engage in is now more comparable to bank activities allowed in the major industrialized countries.

13. For example, in June 2013, the U.S. Financial Stability Oversight Council proposed the designation of nonbanks AIG, Prudential Financial, and General Electric Capital Corp. as systemically important FIs.

**LG 13-5**

## Global or International Expansion Activities

U.S. CBs have expanded into foreign countries through branches and subsidiaries; this has been reciprocated by the increased entrance of foreign CBs into U.S. financial service markets.

**Regulations of U.S. Banks in Foreign Countries.**   Although some U.S. banking organizations such as Citigroup and J.P. Morgan Chase have had foreign offices since the beginning of the 20th century, the major phase of expansion began in the early 1960s following passage of the Overseas Direct Investment Control Act of 1964. This law restricted U.S. banks' ability to lend to U.S. corporations that wanted to make foreign investments. This law was eventually repealed, but it created incentives for U.S. banks to establish foreign offices to service the funding and other business needs of their U.S. clients in other countries. This offshore funding and lending in dollars created the beginning of a market we

**Eurodollar transaction**

*Any transaction involving dollars that takes place outside the United States.*

now call the *Eurodollar market*. The term **Eurodollar transaction** denotes any transaction involving dollars that takes place outside the United States. For example, a banking transaction booked externally to the boundaries of the United States, often through an overseas branch or subsidiary, qualifies as a Eurodollar.[14]

As a result of these changes, U.S. banks have been accelerating their foreign business in recent years. U.S. bank claims held outside the country have risen from $320.1 billion in 1990 to $3,252.0 billion in 2010 before declining to $2,672.6 billion in 2013 (see Table 13–7). By 2016, claims held outside the United States had risen back to $2,841.9 billion, still below 2010 levels. Interestingly, a major segment has been "offshore banking"—issuing loans and accepting deposits. The U.S. bank claims held in the United Kingdom (reported in Table 13–7) reflect its importance as the center of the Eurodollar market, which is the market for dollar loans and deposits made and held outside the United States.

Political risk concerns among savers in emerging market countries have led to enormous outflows of dollars from those countries, often to U.S. branches and subsidiaries in the Cayman Islands and the Bahamas, which have very stringent bank secrecy rules. Because of the secrecy rules in some foreign countries and the possibility that these rules may result in money laundering and the financing of terrorist activities, the U.S. government enacted the USA Patriot Act of 2001, which amended the Bank Secrecy Act in establishing standards for screening customers who open accounts at financial institutions. Title III of the act prohibits U.S. banks from providing banking services to foreign banks that have no physical presence in any country (so-called shell banks). The bill also added foreign corruption offenses to the list of crimes that can trigger a U.S. money-laundering prosecution. Also, federal authorities have the power to subpoena the records of a foreign bank's U.S. correspondent account. Further, the bill makes a depositor's funds in a foreign

**TABLE 13–7**   **U.S. Bank Claims Held Outside the United States***

|  | 1990 | 1995 | 2000 | 2005 | 2010 | 2013 | 2016** |
|---|---|---|---|---|---|---|---|
| Total | $320.1 | $551.7 | $904.6 | $1,864.8 | $3,252.0 | $2,764.2 | $2,841.9 |
| United Kingdom | 60.9 | 82.4 | 144.9 | 487.5 | 998.5 | 813.0 | 731.1 |
| Offshore banking centers[†] | 44.7 | 99.0 | 369.1 | 606.5 | 1,149.6 | 612.4 | 697.6 |

*Billions of dollars held by U.S. offices and foreign branches of U.S. banks (including U.S. banks that are subsidiaries of foreign banks).
**As of June.
[†]Includes Bahamas, Bermuda, and Cayman Islands.
**Sources:** *Federal Reserve Bulletin,* Table 3.18, various issues; and Federal Financial Institutions Examination Council. www.federalreserve.gov; www.ffiec.gov

14. That is, the definition of a Eurodollar transaction is more general than "a transaction booked in Europe." In fact, any deposit in dollars taken externally to the United States normally qualifies as a Eurodollar transaction.

bank's U.S. correspondent account subject to the same civil forfeiture rules that apply to depositors' funds in other U.S. accounts. Finally, the act requires U.S. banks to improve their due diligence review in order to guard against money laundering.

**Regulation of Foreign Banks in the United States.**   Prior to 1978, foreign branches and agencies entering the United States were primarily licensed at the state level. As such, their entry, regulation, and oversight were almost totally confined to the state level. Beginning in 1978 with the passage of the International Banking Act (IBA) and the 1991 passage of the Foreign Bank Supervision Enhancement Act (FBSEA), federal regulators have exerted increasing control over foreign banks operating in the United States.

*The International Banking Act of 1978.*   Before the passage in 1978 of the IBA, foreign agencies and branches entering the United States with state licenses had some competitive advantages and disadvantages relative to most domestic banks. The unequal treatment of domestic and foreign banks regarding federal regulation and the lobbying by domestic banks regarding the unfairness of this situation provided the impetus for Congress to pass the IBA in 1978. The fundamental regulatory philosophy underlying the IBA was one of **national treatment,** a philosophy that attempted to create a level playing field for domestic and foreign banks in U.S. banking markets. As a result of this act, foreign banks were required to hold Federal Reserve–specified reserve requirements if their worldwide assets exceeded $1 billion, and they became subject to Federal Reserve examinations as well as both the McFadden and Glass-Steagall Acts.

**national treatment**

*Regulation of foreign banks in the same fashion as domestic banks, or the creation of a level playing field.*

*The Foreign Bank Supervision Enhancement Act (FBSEA) of 1991.*   Along with the growth of foreign bank assets in the United States came concerns about foreign banks' rapidly increasing share of U.S. banking markets and about the weakness of regulatory oversight of many of these institutions. Three events focused attention on the weaknesses of foreign bank regulation. The first event was the collapse of the Bank of Credit and Commerce International (BCCI), which had a highly complex international organization structure based in the Middle East, the Cayman Islands, and Luxembourg and had undisclosed ownership stakes in two large U.S. banks. BCCI was not subject to any consolidated supervision by a home country regulator. This quickly became apparent after its collapse, when massive fraud, insider lending abuses, and money-laundering operations were discovered. The second event was the issuance of more than $1 billion in unauthorized letters of credit to Saddam Hussein's Iraq by the Atlanta agency of an Italian bank, Banca Nazionale del Lavoro. The third event was the unauthorized taking of deposit funds by the U.S. representative office of the Greek National Mortgage Bank of New York.

These events and related concerns led to the passage of the FBSEA in 1991. The objective of this act was to extend federal regulatory authority over foreign banking organizations in the United States, especially when these organizations had entered using state licenses. The act's five main features have significantly enhanced the powers of federal bank regulators over foreign banks in the United States:

1. **Entry**—under FBSEA, a foreign banking organization must now have the Fed's approval to establish a subsidiary, branch, agency, or representative office in the United States. The approval applies to both a new entry and an entry by acquisition. To secure Fed approval, the organization must meet a number of standards, two of which are mandatory. First, the foreign bank must be subject to comprehensive supervision on a consolidated basis by a home country regulator. Second, that regulator must furnish all the information that the Federal Reserve requires to evaluate the application. Both standards attempt to avoid the lack of disclosure and lack of centralized supervision associated with BCCI's failure.
2. **Closure**—FBSEA also gives the Federal Reserve authority to close a foreign bank if its home country supervision is inadequate, if it violates U.S. laws, or if it engages in unsound and unsafe banking practices.

3. **Examination**—the Federal Reserve has the power to examine each office of a foreign bank, including its representative offices. Further, each branch or agency must be examined at least once a year.

4. **Deposit taking**—only foreign subsidiaries with access to FDIC insurance can take retail deposits under $250,000. This effectively rolls back the provision of the IBA that gave foreign branches and agencies access to FDIC insurance.

5. **Activity powers**—beginning December 19, 1992, state-licensed branches and agencies of foreign banks were not allowed to engage in any activity that was not permitted to a federal branch.

Overall, the FBSEA considerably increased the Federal Reserve's authority over foreign banks and added to the regulatory burden or costs of entry into the United States for foreign banks. This has made the post-FBSEA U.S. banking market much less attractive to foreign banks than it was over the period 1980–1992.

## SUMMARY

Commercial banks provide services that are vital to all sectors of the economy. Failure to efficiently provide these services can be costly to both the suppliers and users of funds. Consequently, CBs are regulated to protect against a breakdown in the provision of CB services. In this chapter, we reviewed the regulations imposed on CBs. We provided an overview of historic and current regulations on CBs' product offerings and geographic expansion opportunities. The recent loosening of regulations in these areas has resulted in the emergence of many large U.S. CBs as globally oriented universal banks. We also described regulations on the asset and liability portfolios of CBs. The chapter concluded with a look at foreign CB regulations and the regulation of foreign CBs in the United States.

## QUESTIONS

1. What forms of protection and regulation are imposed by regulators of CBs to ensure their safety and soundness? (*LG 13-1*)

2. How has the separation of commercial banking and investment banking activities evolved through time? How does this differ from banking activities in other countries? (*LG 13-2, LG 13-3*)

3. A Section 20 subsidiary of a major U.S. bank is planning to underwrite corporate securities and expects to generate $5 million in revenues. It currently underwrites U.S. Treasury securities and general obligation municipal bonds and earns annual fees of $40 million. (*LG 13-3*)
   a. Is the bank in compliance with the laws regulating Section 20 subsidiaries?
   b. If it plans to increase underwriting of corporate securities and generate $11 million in revenues, is it in compliance? Would it have been in compliance prior to passage of the Financial Services Modernization Act of 1999?

4. What insurance activities are permitted for U.S. commercial bank holding companies? (*LG 13-2*)

5. What is shadow banking? How does the shadow banking system differ from the traditional banking system? (*LG 13-2*)

6. What are the provisions on interstate banking in the Riegle-Neal Interstate Banking and Branching Efficiency Act of 1994? (*LG 13-2*)

7. What changes did the Federal Deposit Insurance Reform Act of 2005 make to the deposit insurance premium calculations? (*LG 13-4*)

8. Why are commercial banks subject to reserve requirements? (*LG 13-6*)

9. What is the Basel Agreement? (*LG 13-7*)

10. What is the major feature in the estimation of credit risk under the Basel capital requirements? (*LG 13-7*)

11. What is the difference between Basel I, Basel II, and Basel III? (*LG 13-7*)

12. What is the significance of prompt corrective action as specified by the FDICIA legislation? (*LG 13-7*)

13. Under Basel III, what four capital ratios must DIs calculate and monitor? (*LG 13-7*)

14. How is the Tier I leverage ratio for an FI defined under Basel III? (*LG 13-7*)

15. Identify the five zones of capital adequacy and explain the mandatory regulatory actions corresponding to each zone. (*LG 13-7*)

16. What are the definitional differences between Common Equity Tier I, Tier I, and Tier II capital? (*LG 13-7*)

17. What components are used in the calculation of credit risk–adjusted assets? (*LG 13-7*)

18. How have the International Banking Act of 1978 and the FDICIA of 1991 been detrimental to foreign banks in the United States? (*LG 13-5*)

19. What are some of the main features of the Foreign Bank Supervision Enhancement Act of 1991? (*LG 13-5*)

*The following questions are related to Appendix 13A, 13B, and 13E material.*

20. What changes did the Federal Deposit Insurance Reform Act of 2005 make to the deposit insurance assessment scheme for DIs? (*LG 13-4*)

21. Under the Federal Deposit Insurance Reform Act of 2005, how is a Category I deposit insurance premium determined? (*LG 13-4*)

22. Webb Bank has a composite CAMELS rating of 2, a total risk–based capital ratio of 10.2 percent, a Tier I risk-based capital ratio of 7.2 percent, a CET1 capital ratio of 6.4 percent, and a leverage ratio of 4.8 percent. Assuming the DIF reserve ratio is 1.20 percent, what deposit insurance risk category does the bank fall into, and what is the bank's deposit insurance assessment rate? (*LG 13-4*)

23. Under Basel III, how are residential one- to four-family mortgages assigned to a credit risk class? (*LG 13-7*)

24. Under Basel III, how are risk weights for sovereign exposures determined? (*LG 13-7*)

25. What is the capital conservation buffer? What is the countercyclical capital buffer? (*LG 13-7*)

26. If the reserve computation period extends from May 18 through May 31, what is the corresponding reserve maintenance period? What accounts for the difference? (*LG 13-4*)

## PROBLEMS

*The following problems are related to Appendix 13A, 13B, and 13E material.*

1. Two depository institutions have composite CAMELS ratings of 1 or 2 and are "well capitalized." Thus, each institution falls into the FDIC Risk Category I deposit insurance assessment scheme. Further, the institutions have the following financial ratios and CAMELS ratings:

|  | Institution A | Institution B |
|---|---|---|
| Tier I leverage ratio (%) | 8.25 | 8.50 |
| Net income before taxes/ risk-weighted assets (%) | 2.15 | 1.85 |
| Nonperforming loans and leases/gross assets (%) | 0.25 | 0.55 |
| Other real estate–owned/ gross assets (%) | 0.54 | 0.75 |
| Brokered deposits/total assets (%) | 1.05 | 3.75 |
| One year asset growth | 5.66 | 7.75 |
| **Loans as a Percentage of Total Assets:** | | |
| Construction and Development | 0.00 | 0.00 |
| Commercial and Industrial | 11.35 | 15.66 |
| Leases | 0.45 | 1.05 |
| Other Consumer | 16.50 | 16.80 |
| Loans to Foreign Government | 0.00 | 0.60 |
| Real Estate Loans Residual | 0.00 | 0.00 |
| Multifamily Residential | 0.50 | 1.25 |
| Nonfarm Nonresidential | 0.00 | 0.00 |
| 1–4 Family Residential | 38.85 | 40.15 |
| Loans to Depository Banks | 0.00 | 2.80 |
| Agricultural Real Estate | 4.55 | 0.00 |
| Agricultural | 7.40 | 0.00 |
| **CAMELS Components:** | | |
| C | 1 | 1 |
| A | 2 | 2 |
| M | 1 | 2 |
| E | 2 | 3 |
| L | 1 | 1 |
| S | 2 | 1 |

The DIF reserve ratio is currently 1.30 percent. Calculate the initial deposit insurance assessment for each institution.

2. Two depository institutions have composite CAMELS ratings of 1 or 2 and are "well capitalized." Thus, each institution falls into the FDIC Risk Category I deposit insurance assessment scheme. Institution A has average total assets of $750 million and average Tier I equity of $75 million. Institution B has average total assets of $1 billion and average Tier I equity of $110 million. Institution A has no unsecured debt or brokered deposits. Institution B has no unsecured debt and an asset growth rate over the last four years of 8 percent. Further, the institutions have the following financial ratios and CAMELS ratings:

|  | Institution A | Institution B |
|---|---|---|
| Tier I leverage ratio (%) | 9.80 | 8.45 |
| Net income before taxes/ risk-weighted assets (%) | 2.00 | 1.65 |
| Nonperforming loans and leases/gross assets (%) | 0.35 | 0.90 |
| Other real estate–owned/ gross assets (%) | 0.42 | 0.90 |
| Brokered deposits/total assets (%) | 2.20 | 0.75 |
| One year asset growth | 4.35 | 6.80 |
| **Loans as a Percentage of Total Assets:** | | |
| Construction and Development | 0.00 | 0.00 |
| Commercial and Industrial | 10.56 | 18.68 |
| Leases | 0.65 | 2.15 |
| Other Consumer | 17.55 | 18.95 |
| Loans to Foreign Government | 0.00 | 0.60 |
| Real Estate Loans Residual | 0.00 | 0.00 |
| Multifamily Residential | 0.00 | 1.10 |
| Nonfarm Nonresidential | 0.00 | 0.00 |
| 1–4 Family Residential | 41.10 | 33.54 |
| Loans to Depository Banks | 0.00 | 0.50 |
| Agricultural Real Estate | 1.10 | 0.35 |
| Agricultural | 0.40 | 0.40 |

|                      | Institution A | Institution B |
|----------------------|:-------------:|:-------------:|
| **CAMELS Components:** |               |               |
| C                    | 1             | 2             |
| A                    | 1             | 1             |
| M                    | 1             | 1             |
| E                    | 2             | 1             |
| L                    | 1             | 3             |
| S                    | 2             | 3             |

The DIF reserve ratio is currently 1.30 percent. Calculate the deposit insurance assessment and the dollar value of the deposit insurance premium for each institution.

3. City Bank has estimated that its average daily net transaction accounts balance over the recent 14-day computation period was $225 million. The average daily balance with the Fed over the 14-day maintenance period was $8 million, and the average daily balance of vault cash over the two-week computation period was $5 million. (*LG 13-4*)

    a. Under the rules effective in 2016, what is the amount of average daily reserves required to be held during the reserve maintenance period for these demand deposit balances?

    b. What is the average daily balance of reserves held by the bank over the maintenance period? By what amount were the average reserves held higher or lower than the required reserves?

    c. If the bank had transferred $35 million of its deposits every Friday over the two-week computation period to one of its off-shore facilities, what would be the revised average daily reserve requirement?

4. The average daily net transaction accounts of a local bank during the most recent reserve computation period is $325 million. The amount of average daily reserves at the Fed during the reserve maintenance period is $24.60 million, and the average daily vault cash corresponding to the maintenance period is $4.3 million. (*LG 13-4*)

    a. Under the rules effective in 2016, what is the average daily reserve balance required to be held by the bank during the maintenance period?

    b. Is the bank in compliance with the reserve requirements?

5. The following net transaction accounts have been documented by a bank for the computation of its reserve requirements (in millions). (*LG 13-4*)

|                          | Tuesday 11th | Wednesday 12th | Thursday 13th | Friday 14th | Monday 17th |
|--------------------------|:------------:|:--------------:|:-------------:|:-----------:|:-----------:|
| Net transaction accounts | $300         | $250           | $280          | $260        | $280        |

|                          | Tuesday 18th | Wednesday 19th | Thursday 20th | Friday 21st | Monday 24th |
|--------------------------|:------------:|:--------------:|:-------------:|:-----------:|:-----------:|
| Net transaction accounts | $300         | $270           | $260          | $250        | $240        |

The average daily reserves at the Fed for the 14-day reserve maintenance period have been $22.7 million per day, and the average vault cash for the computation period has been estimated to be $2 million per day.

    a. What is the amount of the average daily required reserves to be held by the bank during the maintenance period?

    b. Is the bank in compliance with the requirements?

6. National Bank has the following balance sheet (in millions) and has no off-balance-sheet activities. (*LG 13-7*)

| Assets              |        | Liabilities and Equity |        |
|---------------------|-------:|------------------------|-------:|
| Cash                | $   20 | Deposits               | $  980 |
| Treasury bills      |     40 | Subordinated debentures |    25 |
| Residential mortgages (category 1; loan-to-value ratio = 70%) |    600 | Common stock           |     45 |
|                     |        | Retained earnings      |     40 |
| Business loans      |    430 | Total liabilities and equity | $1,090 |
| Total assets        | $1,090 |                        |        |

    a. What is the CET1 risk-based ratio?

    b. What is the Tier I risk-based capital ratio?

    c. What is the total risk–based capital ratio?

    d. What is the Tier I leverage ratio?

    e. In what capital risk category would National Bank be placed?

7. What is the capital conservation buffer? How would this buffer affect your answers in Problem 6? (*LG 13-7*)

8. Onshore Bank has $20 million in assets, with risk-adjusted assets of $10 million. CET1 capital is $500,000, additional Tier I capital is $50,000, and Tier II capital is $400,000. How will each of the following transactions affect the value of the CET1, Tier I, and total capital ratios? What will the new value of each ratio be? (*LG 13-7*)

The current value of the CET1 ratio is 5 percent, the Tier I ratio is 5.5 percent, and the total ratio is 9 percent.

    a. The bank repurchases $100,000 of common stock with cash.

    b. The bank issues $2 million of CDs and uses the proceeds to issue category 1 mortgage loans with a loan-to-value ratio of 80 percent.

    c. The bank receives $500,000 in deposits and invests them in T-bills.

    d. The bank issues $800,000 in common stock and lends it to help finance a new shopping mall.

    e. The bank issues $1 million in nonqualifying perpetual preferred stock and purchases general obligation municipal bonds.

    f. Homeowners pay back $4 million of mortgages with loan-to-value ratios of 40 percent and the bank uses the proceeds to build new ATMs.

9. Third Bank has the following balance sheet (in millions), with the risk weights in parentheses. (*LG 13-7*)

| Assets | | Liabilities and Equity | |
|---|---|---|---|
| Cash (0%) | $ 21 | Deposits | $176 |
| OECD interbank | | Subordinated debt | |
| deposits (20%) | 25 | (5 years) | 2 |
| Mortgage loans (50%) | 70 | Cumulative preferred | |
| | | stock | 2 |
| Consumer loans (100%) | 70 | Equity | 5 |
| Reserve for loan losses | (1) | Total liabilities and | |
| Total assets | $185 | equity | $185 |

The cumulative preferred stock is qualifying and perpetual. In addition, the bank has $30 million in performance-related standby letters of credit (SLCs) to a public corporation, $40 million in two-year forward FX contracts that are currently in the money by $1 million, and $300 million in six-year interest rate swaps that are currently out of the money by $2 million. Credit conversion factors follow:

| | |
|---|---|
| Performance-related standby letters of credit | 50% |
| 1- to 5-year foreign exchange contracts | 5 |
| 1- to 5-year interest rate swaps | 0.5 |
| 5- to 10-year interest rate swaps | 1.5 |

a. What are the risk-adjusted on-balance-sheet assets of the bank as defined under the Basel Accord?

b. To be adequately capitalized, what are the CET1, Tier I, and total capital required for both off- and on-balance-sheet assets?

c. Disregarding the capital conservation buffer, does the bank have enough capital to meet the Basel requirements? If not, what minimum CET1, additional Tier 1, or total capital does it need to meet the requirement?

d. Does the bank have enough capital to meet the Basel requirements, including the capital conservation buffer requirement? If not, what minimum CET1, additional Tier 1, or total capital does it need to meet the requirement?

10. Third Fifth Bank has the following balance sheet (in millions), with the risk weights in parentheses. (*LG 13-7*)

| Assets | | Liabilities and Equity | |
|---|---|---|---|
| Cash (0%) | $ 21 | Deposits | $133 |
| Mortgage loans (50%) | 50 | Subordinated debt | |
| | | (>5 years) | 1 |
| Consumer loans (100%) | 70 | Equity | 6 |
| Reserve for loan losses | (1) | Total liabilities and | |
| Total assets | $140 | equity | $140 |

In addition, the bank has $20 million in commercial direct-credit substitute standby letters of credit to a public corporation and $40 million in 10-year FX forward contracts that are in the money by $1 million.

a. What are the risk-adjusted on-balance-sheet assets of the bank as defined under the Basel III?

b. What is the CET1, Tier I, and total capital required for both off- and on-balance-sheet assets?

c. Disregarding the capital conservation buffer, does the bank have sufficient capital to meet the Basel requirements? How much in excess? How much short?

d. Does the bank have enough capital to meet the Basel requirements, including the capital conservation buffer

requirement? If not, what minimum CET1, additional Tier 1, or total capital does it need to meet the requirement?

11. What is the contribution to the asset base of the following items under the Basel III requirements? (*LG 13-7*)

a. $10 million cash reserves.

b. $50 million 91-day U.S. Treasury bills.

c. $25 million cash items in the process of collection.

d. $5 million UK government bonds, OECD CRD rated 1.

e. $5 million French short-term government bonds, OECD CRD rated 2.

f. $1 million general obligation bonds.

g. $40 million repurchase agreements (against U.S. Treasuries).

h. $2 million loan to foreign bank, OECD rated 3.

i. $500 million 1–4 family home mortgages, category 1, loan-to-value ratio 80 percent.

j. $10 million 1–4 family home mortgages, category 2, loan-to-value ratio 95 percent.

k. $5 million 1–4 family home mortgages, 100 days past due.

l. $500 million commercial and industrial loans, AAA rated.

m. $500 million commercial and industrial loans, B- rated.

n. $100,000 performance-related standby letters of credit to a AAA rated corporation.

o. $100,000 performance-related standby letters of credit to a municipality issuing general obligation bonds.

p. $7 million commercial letter of credit to a foreign bank, OECD CRC rated 2.

q. $3 million five-year loan commitment to a foreign government, OECD CRC rated 1.

r. $8 million bankers' acceptance conveyed to a U.S. AA rated corporation.

s. $17 million three-year loan commitment to a private agent.

t. $17 million three-month loan commitment to a private agent.

u. $30 million standby letter of credit to back an A rated corporate issue of commercial paper.

v. $4 million five-year interest rate swap with no current exposure.

w. $6 million two-year currency swap with $500,000 current exposure.

*The following information is for problems 12–16. Consider a bank's balance sheet as follows.*

A bank's balance sheet information is shown below (in $000).

| On-Balance-Sheet Items | Face Value |
|---|---|
| Cash | $ 121,600 |
| Short-term government securities (<92 days) | 5,400 |
| Long-term government securities (>92 days) | 414,400 |
| Federal Reserve stock | 9,800 |
| Repos secured by federal agencies | 159,000 |
| Claims on U.S. depository institutions | 937,900 |
| Loans to foreign banks, OECD CRC rated 2 | 1,640,000 |
| General obligation municipals | 170,000 |
| Claims on or guaranteed by federal agencies | 26,500 |
| Municipal revenue bonds | 112,900 |
| Residential mortgages, category 1, loan-to-value ratio 75% | 5,000,000 |
| Commercial loans | 4,667,669 |
| Loans to sovereigns, OECD CRC rated 3 | 11,600 |
| Premises and equipment | 455,000 |

| Off-Balance-Sheet Items: | Conversion Factor (%) | Face Value |
|---|---|---|
| **U.S. Government Counterparty** | | |
| Loan commitments: | | |
| <1 year | 20 | $      300 |
| 1–5 year | 50 | 1,140 |
| Standby letters of credit: | | |
| Performance-related | 50 | 200 |
| Direct-credit substitute | 100 | 100 |
| **U.S. Depository Institutions Counterparty** | | |
| Loan commitments: | | |
| <1 year | 20 | 100 |
| >1 year | 50 | 3,000 |
| Standby letters of credit: | | |
| Performance-related | 50 | 200 |
| Direct-credit substitute | 100 | 56,400 |
| Commercial letters of credit | 20 | 400 |
| **State and Local Government Counterparty** (revenue municipals) | | |
| Loan commitments: | | |
| >1 year | 50 | 100 |
| Standby letters of credit: | | |
| Performance-related | 50 | 135,400 |
| **Corporate Customer Counterparty** | | |
| Loan commitments: | | |
| <1 year | 20 | 3,212,400 |
| >1 year | 50 | 3,046,278 |
| Standby letters of credit: | | |
| Performance-related | 50 | 101,543 |
| Direct-credit substitute | 100 | 490,900 |
| Commercial letters of credit | 20 | 78,978 |
| **Sovereign Counterparty** | | |
| Loan commitments, OECD CRC rated 1: | | |
| <1 year | 20 | 110,500 |
| >1 year | 50 | 1,225,400 |

| Off-Balance-Sheet Items: | Conversion Factor (%) | Face Value |
|---|---|---|
| **Sovereign Counterparty** | | |
| Loan commitments, OECD CRC rated 2: | | |
| <1 year | 20 | 85,000 |
| >1 year | 50 | 115,500 |
| **Sovereign Counterparty** | | |
| Loan commitments, OECD CRC rated 7: | | |
| >1 year | 50 | 30,000 |
| Interest rate market contracts (current exposure assumed to be zero): | | |
| <1 year (notional amount) | 0 | 2,000 |
| >1–5 year (notional amount) | 0.5 | 5,000 |

12. What is the bank's risk-adjusted asset base? (*LG 13-7*)

13. To be adequately capitalized, what are the bank's CET1, Tier I, and total risk–based capital requirements under Basel III? (*LG 13-7*)

14. Using the Tier I leverage-ratio requirement, what is the bank's minimum regulatory capital requirement to keep it in the adequately capitalized zone? (*LG 13-7*)

15. Disregarding the capital conservation buffer, what is the bank's capital adequacy level (under Basel III) if the par value of its equity is $225,000, surplus value of equity is $200,000, retained earnings is $565,545, qualifying perpetual preferred stock is $50,000, subordinate debt is $50,000, and loan loss reserve is $85,000? Does the bank meet Basel (CET1, Tier I, and Tier II) adequately capitalized standards? Does the bank comply with the well-capitalized leverage ratio requirement? (*LG 13-7*)

16. Does the bank have enough capital to meet the Basel requirements, including the capital conservation buffer requirement? (*LG 13-7*)

# SEARCH THE SITE

Go to the FDIC website at **www.fdic.gov**. Find the most recent reserve balance and reserve ratios held by DIF using the following steps. Once at the website, click on "Analysts." Click on "FDIC Quarterly Banking Profile." Click on "Quarterly Banking Profile." Under "Report Date:" select the most recent date, then click on "Access QBP." Click on "Deposit Insurance Fund Trends." Then click on "Table I-C Insurance Fund Balances and Selected Indicators." This will bring up a file that contains the relevant data.

## Questions

1. How have these values changed since 2016 as reported in the chapter?
2. What is the total reserve funds held by DIF and the reserve ratio?

# APPENDIX 13A: Calculating Deposit Insurance Premium Assessments

The Federal Deposit Insurance Reform Act of 2005 instituted a deposit insurance premium scheme, effective January 1, 2007, and revised in April 2009, April 2011, and September 2015, that combined examination ratings and financial ratios. The changes instituted in September 2015 would take effect beginning the assessment period after the DIF reserve ratio first meets or exceeds 1.15 percent. The reserve ratio increased to 1.17 percent in the second quarter of 2016 from 1.13 percent in the prior quarter. The rates will remain in effect unless and until the reserve ratio meets or exceeds 2 percent. The new rules consolidate the existing nine risk categories into four, named Risk Categories I through IV as listed in Table 13–8. Risk Category I contains all well-capitalized institutions in Supervisory Group A (generally those with CAMELS composite ratings of 1 or 2). Risk Category II contains all institutions in Supervisory Groups A and B (generally those with CAMELS composite ratings of 1, 2, or 3), except those in Risk Category I and undercapitalized institutions. Risk Category III contains all undercapitalized institutions in Supervisory Groups A and B and institutions in Supervisory Group C (generally those with CAMELS composite ratings of 4 or 5) that are not undercapitalized. Risk Category IV contains all undercapitalized institutions in Supervisory Group C. Once a risk category is determined, the assessment rate for the category is multiplied by the institution's assessment base. The assessment rates are set by the FDIC and are a function of the size of the FDIC reserve ratio, as shown in Panel B of Table 13–8. For example, if the reserve ratio exceeds 1.15 percent, but is less than 2 percent, Risk Category I institutions pay between 3 and 7 basis points on the assessment base. The assessment base is the FI's average consolidated total assets less the average tangible equity (Tier I capital).

A well-capitalized institution is one that satisfies each of the following capital ratio standards: total risk–based ratio, 10.0 percent or greater; Tier I risk-based ratio, 8.0 percent or greater; CET1 capital ratio of 6.5 percent or greater; and Tier I leverage ratio, 5.0 percent or greater (as defined in Appendix 13E to this chapter, available through Connect or your course instructor). An adequately capitalized institution is one that does not satisfy the standards of well capitalized, but satisfies each of the following capital ratio standards: total risk–based ratio, 8.0 percent or greater; Tier I risk-based ratio, 6.0 percent or greater;

**TABLE 13–8** New Risk Categories and Initial Assessment Rates for FDIC Insurance *(assessment rates are in basis points)*

**Panel A: Risk category**

| Capital Group | Supervisory Group | | |
|---|---|---|---|
| | A | B | C |
| Well capitalized | I | II | III |
| Adequately capitalized | II | II | III |
| Undercapitalized | III | III | IV |

**Panel B: Annual assessment rate**

| Reserve Ratio | Risk Category | | | | |
|---|---|---|---|---|---|
| | I | | II | III | IV |
| | Minimum | Maximum | | | |
| Less than 1.15 percent | 5 | 9 | 14 | 23 | 35 |
| Between 1.15 percent and 2 percent | 3 | 7 | 12 | 19 | 30 |
| Between 2 percent and 2.5 percent | 2 | 6 | 10 | 17 | 28 |
| 2.5 percent or greater | 1 | 5 | 9 | 15 | 25 |

**Source:** FDIC, *Federal Register,* May 2016. www.fdic.gov

CET1 capital ratio of 4.5 percent or greater; and Tier I leverage ratio, 4.0 percent or greater. An undercapitalized institution is one that does not qualify as either well capitalized or adequately capitalized.

Within Risk Category I, the final rule combines CAMELS component ratings with financial ratios to determine an institution's assessment rate. For Risk Category I institutions, each of eight financial ratios component ratings will be multiplied by a corresponding pricing multiplier, as listed in Table 13–9. The eight financial ratios are: Tier I leverage ratio; net income before taxes/risk-weighted assets; nonperforming loans and leases/gross assets; other real estate–owned/gross assets; brokered deposits/total assets; one year asset growth;[15] loan mix index; and the weighted-average CAMELS component rating. The loan mix index is a measure of the extent to which a bank's total assets include higher-risk categories of loans. Each category of loan in a bank's loan portfolio is divided by the bank's total assets to determine the percentage of the bank's assets represented by that category of loan. Each percentage is then multiplied by that category of loan's historical weighted average industrywide charge-off rate since 2001. The products are then summed to determine the loan mix index value for that bank. Table 13–10 lists the weighted average charge-off rate for each category of loan, as calculated by the FDIC through the end of 2014. The weighted average of CAMELS component ratings is created by multiplying each component by a stated percentage, as listed in Table 13–11, and adding the products. The sum of these products will be added to or subtracted from a uniform amount, set at 7.352 as of September 2016. The resulting sum will equal an institution's initial assessment rate.

Large and highly complex institutions use a slightly different numeric to calculate the assessment rates. The scorecard for these institutions focuses more on the risk of the institution and differentiates risk during periods of good economic conditions and during periods of stress and downturns. The models also better take into account the losses the FDIC

**TABLE 13–9**   FDIC Insurance Premium Price Multipliers for Financial Ratios

| Risk Measures | Pricing Multipliers |
| --- | --- |
| Tier I leverage ratio | (1.264) |
| Net income before taxes/risk-weighted assets | (0.720) |
| Nonperforming loans and leases/gross assets | 0.942 |
| Other real estate–owned/gross assets | 0.533 |
| Brokered deposit ratio | 0.264 |
| One-year asset growth rate | 0.061 |
| Loan mix index | 0.081 |
| Weighted average CAMELS component rating | 1.519 |

**Source:** FDIC, *Federal Register,* May 20, 2016. www.fdic.gov

**TABLE 13–10**   Loan Mix Index Weighted Average Charge-Off Rates

| | |
| --- | --- |
| Construction and Development | 4.50 |
| Commercial and Industrial | 1.60 |
| Leases | 1.50 |
| Other Consumer | 1.46 |
| Loans to Foreign Government | 1.34 |
| Real Estate Loans Residual | 1.02 |
| Multifamily Residential | 0.88 |
| Nonfarm Nonresidential | 0.73 |
| 1–4 Family Residential | 0.70 |
| Loans to Depository Banks | 0.58 |
| Agricultural Real Estate | 0.24 |
| Agricultural | 0.24 |

**Source:** FDIC, *Federal Register,* May 20, 2016. www.fdic.gov

15. If asset growth in the previous year is negative, then the value is set to zero.

**TABLE 13–11    CAMELS Component Weights**

| CAMELS Component | Weight |
|---|---|
| C | 25% |
| A | 20 |
| M | 25 |
| E | 10 |
| L | 10 |
| S | 10 |

Source: FDIC, *Federal Register,* May 20, 2016. www.fdic.gov

may incur if a large institution fails. A large institution is an institution with assets of at least $10 billion as of December 2006 that is not classified as a highly complex institution (approximately 50 of the 5,200-plus institutions in 2016). A highly complex institution (approximately 40 institutions in 2016) is defined by the FDIC as (1) an insured depository institution (excluding a credit card bank) with greater than $50 billion in total assets that is wholly owned by a parent company with more than $500 billion in total assets, or wholly owned by one or more intermediate parent companies that are wholly owned by a holding company with more than $500 billion in assets; or (2) a processing bank and trust company with greater than $10 billion in total assets, provided that the information required to calculate assessment rates as a highly complex institution is readily available to the FDIC.

---

**EXAMPLE 13–1    Calculating Insurance Assessment Rates for Depository Institutions**

Three depository institutions have composite CAMELS ratings of 1 or 2 and are "well capitalized." Thus, each institution falls into the FDIC Risk Category I deposit insurance assessment scheme. Further, the three institutions have the following financial ratios and CAMELS ratings:

| | Institution 1 | Institution 2 | Institution 3 |
|---|---|---|---|
| Tier I leverage ratio (%) | 9.800 | 8.570 | 9.040 |
| Net income before taxes/risk-weighted assets (%) | 1.500 | 1.951 | 2.602 |
| Nonperforming loans and leases/gross assets (%) | 0.200 | 0.400 | 1.500 |
| Other real estate–owned/ gross assets (%) | 0.280 | 0.320 | 1.250 |
| Brokered deposits/total assets (%) | 0.250 | 2.560 | 1.500 |
| One year asset growth | 6.150 | 5.660 | 8.750 |
| Weighted average CAMELS component ratings | 1.200 | 1.450 | 2.100 |
| **Loans as a Percentage of Total Assets:** | | | |
| Construction and Development | 0.00 | 0.00 | 0.55 |
| Commercial and Industrial | 10.24 | 11.20 | 17.66 |
| Leases | 0.25 | 0.55 | 0.85 |
| Other Consumer | 15.61 | 18.11 | 20.55 |
| Loans to Foreign Government | 0.00 | 0.25 | 1.66 |
| Real Estate Loans Residual | 0.00 | 0.00 | 0.10 |
| Multifamily Residential | 0.85 | 1.05 | 1.55 |
| Nonfarm Nonresidential | 0.00 | 0.00 | 0.00 |
| 1–4 Family Residential | 44.25 | 34.55 | 32.75 |
| Loans to Depository Banks | 0.00 | 1.12 | 1.55 |
| Agricultural Real Estate | 2.26 | 1.66 | 0.55 |
| Agricultural | 3.69 | 0.75 | 0.25 |

The DIF reserve ratio is currently 1.20 percent. To determine the deposit insurance assessment for each institution, we set up the following tables (Excel files for these calculations are available through Connect or your course instructor):

**Loans Mix Index:**

| (1) | (2) | (3) | (4) | (5) | (6) | (7) | (8) |
|---|---|---|---|---|---|---|---|
| | | Institution A | | Institution B | | Institution C | |
| | Weighted Charge-Off Rate Percentage | Loan Category as a Percentage of Total Assets | Product of Two Columns | Loan Category as a Percentage of Total Assets | Product of Two Columns | Loan Category as a Percentage of Total Assets | Product of Two Columns |
| Construction and Development | 4.50 | 0.00 | 0.000 | 0.00 | 0.000 | 0.55 | 2.475 |
| Commercial and Industrial | 1.60 | 10.24 | 16.384 | 11.20 | 17.920 | 17.66 | 28.256 |
| Leases | 1.50 | 0.25 | 0.375 | 0.55 | 0.825 | 0.85 | 1.275 |
| Other Consumer | 1.46 | 15.61 | 22.791 | 18.11 | 26.441 | 20.55 | 30.003 |
| Loans to Foreign Government | 1.34 | 0.00 | 0.000 | 0.25 | 0.335 | 1.66 | 2.224 |
| Real Estate Loans Residual | 1.02 | 0.00 | 0.000 | 0.00 | 0.000 | 0.10 | 0.102 |
| Multifamily Residential | 0.88 | 0.85 | 0.748 | 1.05 | 0.924 | 1.55 | 1.364 |
| Nonfarm Nonresidential | 0.73 | 0.00 | 0.000 | 0.00 | 0.000 | 0.00 | 0.000 |
| 1–4 Family Residential | 0.70 | 44.25 | 30.975 | 34.55 | 24.185 | 32.75 | 22.925 |
| Loans to Depository Banks | 0.58 | 0.00 | 0.000 | 1.12 | 0.650 | 1.55 | 0.899 |
| Agricultural Real Estate | 0.24 | 2.26 | 0.542 | 1.66 | 0.398 | 0.55 | 0.132 |
| Agricultural | 0.24 | 3.69 | 0.886 | 0.75 | 0.180 | 0.25 | 0.060 |
| | | SUM (Loan Mix Index) | 72.701 | | 71.858 | | 89.715 |

**Base Assessment Rates for Three Institutions**

| (1) | (2) | (3) | (4) | (5) | (6) | (7) | (8) |
|---|---|---|---|---|---|---|---|
| | | Institution A | | Institution B | | Institution C | |
| | Pricing Multiplier | Risk Measure Value | Contribution to Assessment Rate | Risk Measure Value | Contribution to Assessment Rate | Risk Measure Value | Contribution to Assessment Rate |
| Uniform amount | | | 7.352 | | 7.352 | | 7.352 |
| Tier I leverage ratio (%) | (1.264) | 9.800 | (12.387) | 8.57 | (10.833) | 9.040 | (11.427) |
| Net income before taxes/ risk-weighted assets (%) | (0.720) | 1.500 | (1.080) | 1.951 | (1.405) | 2.602 | (1.873) |
| Nonperforming loans and leases/gross assets (%) | 0.942 | 0.200 | 0.188 | 0.400 | 0.377 | 1.500 | 1.413 |
| Other real estate–owned/ gross assets (%) | 0.533 | 0.280 | 0.149 | 0.320 | 0.171 | 1.250 | 0.666 |

**Base Assessment Rates for Three Institutions**

| | (1) | (2) | (3) | (4) | (5) | (6) | (7) | (8) |
|---|---|---|---|---|---|---|---|---|
| | | | Institution A | | Institution B | | Institution C | |
| | | Pricing Multiplier | Risk Measure Value | Contribution to Assessment Rate | Risk Measure Value | Contribution to Assessment Rate | Risk Measure Value | Contribution to Assessment Rate |
| Brokered deposits/ total assets (%) | | 0.264 | 0.250 | 0.066 | 2.560 | 0.676 | 1.500 | 0.396 |
| One year asset growth (%) | | 0.061 | 6.150 | 0.375 | 5.660 | 0.345 | 8.750 | 0.534 |
| Loan mix index | | 0.081 | 72.701 | 5.889 | 71.858 | 5.821 | 89.715 | 7.267 |
| Weighted average CAMELS component ratings | | 1.519 | 1.200 | 1.823 | 1.450 | 2.202 | 2.100 | 3.190 |
| Sum of contributions | | | | 2.375 | | 4.706 | | 7.518 |
| Assessment rate | | | | 3.000 | | 4.706 | | 7.000 |

The assessment rate for the three institutions in the table is calculated by multiplying the pricing multipliers (see Tables 13–9 and 13–10), listed in Column 2 above, by the risk measure values (Columns 3, 5, or 7) to produce each measure's contribution to the assessment rate. The sum of the products (Column 4, 6, or 8) plus the uniform amount, 7.352, gives the initial assessment rate. For Institution A, this sum is 2.375. However, Table 13–9 lists the minimum assessment rate for Category I banks of 3 basis points. For Institution C the sum is 7.518. However, Table 13–8 lists the maximum assessment rate of 7 basis points.

After applying all possible adjustments and using a DIF reserve ratio between 1.15 percent and 2 percent, minimum and maximum total base assessment rates for each risk category are set as listed in Table 13–12. The unsecured debt adjustment is determined by multiplying an institution's long-term unsecured debt as a percent of domestic deposits. The base assessment also may increase depending on the ratio of secured liabilities to domestic deposits (secured liability adjustment). Finally, for institutions in Categories II, III, and IV, the assessment rate may increase based on the amount of brokered deposits to domestic deposits.

**TABLE 13–12**  Total Base Assessment Rates

| | Risk Category I* | Risk Category II* | Risk Category III* | Risk Category IV* |
|---|---|---|---|---|
| Initial base assessment rate | 3–7 | 12 | 19 | 30 |
| Unsecured debt adjustment | −3.5–0 | −5–0 | −5–0 | −5–0 |
| Brokered deposit adjustment | | 0–10 | 0–10 | 0–10 |
| Total base assessment rate | 1.5–7 | 7–22 | 14–29 | 25–40 |

*All amounts for all risk categories are in basis points annually. Total base rates that are not the minimum or mazimum rate will vary among these rates.

# APPENDIX 13B: Calculating Minimum Required Reserves at U.S. Depository Institutions

This appendix presents a detailed example of U.S. bank liquidity management under the current minimum reserve requirements imposed by the Federal Reserve. Many of the issues and trade-offs are readily generalizable, however, to any FI facing liability withdrawal risk under conditions in which regulators impose minimum liquid asset reserve ratios. The issues involved in the optimal management of a liquid asset portfolio are illustrated using problems faced by the money desk manager in charge of a U.S. bank's cash reserve position. In the context of U.S. bank regulation, we concentrate on a bank's management of its **cash reserves,** defined as vault cash and cash deposits held at the Federal Reserve.

**cash reserves**

*Vault cash and cash deposits held at the Federal Reserve.*

**transaction accounts**

*Deposits that permit the account holders to make multiple withdrawals.*

**Transaction accounts** include all deposits on which an account holder may make withdrawals by negotiable or transferable instruments and may make more than three monthly telephone or preauthorized fund transfers for the purpose of making payments to third parties (for example, demand deposits, NOW accounts, and share draft accounts—offered by credit unions). Historically, U.S. banks also had to hold reserves against time deposits and personal savings deposits (including money market deposit accounts—MMDAs). However, this was reduced from 3 percent to 0 percent at the beginning of 1991. Transaction account balances are reduced by demand deposit balances due from U.S. depository institutions (used primarily to purchase services from those institutions, such as check collection, check processing, and fed funds trading) and cash items in process of collection (checks written against accounts at other institutions that have been deposited at the bank). Credit is given to the depositor of these checks only after they clear to obtain net transaction accounts.

To calculate the target amount of reserves and to determine whether the bank is holding too many or too few reserves, the bank reserve manager requires two additional pieces of information to manage the position. First, which period's deposits does the manager use to compute the bank's reserve requirement? Second, over which period or periods must the bank maintain the target reserve requirement just computed? The U.S. system is complicated by the fact that the period for which the bank manager computes the required reserve target differs from the period during which the reserve target is maintained or achieved. We describe the computation and maintenance periods for bank reserves next.

**reserve computation period**

*Period over which required reserves are calculated.*

### Computation Period

For the purposes of bank reserve management, a U.S. bank reserve manager must think of the year as being divided into two-week periods. The **reserve computation period** always begins on a Tuesday and ends on a Monday 14 days later.

---

**EXAMPLE 13–2**   Computation of Daily Average Required Reserves

Consider ABC Bank's reserve manager, who wants to assess the bank's minimum cash reserve requirement target. The manager knows the bank's net transaction accounts balance at the close of the banking day on each of the 14 days over the period Tuesday, June 30, to Monday, July 13. Consider the realized net transaction account positions of ABC Bank in Table 13–13.

The minimum daily average reserves that a bank must maintain is computed as a percentage of the daily average net transaction accounts held by the bank over the two-week computation period, where Friday's balances are carried over for Saturday and Sunday. The minimum daily average for ABC Bank to hold against the daily average of $1,350.70 million in net transaction accounts is calculated as follows (amounts in millions):

Daily average net
transaction accounts × Reserve percentage = Daily average reserves required

| | | |
|---|---|---|
| $15.2 | 0% | $ 0.000 |
| $110.2–$15.2 | 3 | 2.850 |
| $1,350.7–$110.2 | 10 | 124.050 |
| Minimum average reserves to be held | | $126.900 |

Note that the daily average target in Example 13–2 is calculated by taking a 14-day average of net transaction accounts even though the bank is closed for 4 of the 14 days (two Saturdays and two Sundays). Effectively, Friday's deposit figures count three times compared to those of other days in the business week. This means that the bank manager who can engage in a strategy in which deposits are lower on Fridays can, on average, lower the bank's reserve requirements. This may be important if required liquid asset reserve holdings are above the optimal level from the bank's perspective to handle liquidity drains due to expected and unexpected deposit withdrawals.

One strategy employed in the past was for a bank to send deposits out of the country (e.g., transfer them to a foreign subsidiary) on a Friday, when a reduction in deposits effectively counts for 3/14 of the two-week period, and to bring them back on the following Monday, when an increase counts for only 1/14 of the two-week period. This action effectively reduced the average demand deposits on the balance sheet of the bank over the 14-day period by 2/14 times the amount sent out of the country and, thus, reduced the amount of reserves it needed to hold. Analysts term this the **weekend game.**

**weekend game**

*Name given to the policy of lowering deposit balances on Fridays, since that day's figures count three times for reserve accounting purposes.*

Note that the $126.900 million figure is a minimum reserve target. The bank manager may hold excess cash reserves above this minimum level if the privately optimal or prudent level for the bank exceeds the regulatory specified minimum level because this bank is especially exposed to deposit withdrawal risk. In addition, the bank manager may hold some buffer reserves in the form of government securities that can quickly be turned into cash if deposit withdrawals are unusually high or to preempt the early stages of a bank run.

**TABLE 13–13**  Net Transaction Accounts and Vault Cash Balances of ABC Bank
*(in millions of dollars)*

| | Transaction Accounts | Less Demand Balances Due from U.S. Depository Institutions | Less Cash Items in Process of Collection | Net Transaction Accounts | Vault Cash |
|---|---|---|---|---|---|
| Tuesday, June 30 | $ 1,850 | $ 240 | $ 140 | $ 1,470 | $ 30 |
| Wednesday, July 1 | 1,820 | 235 | 135 | 1,450 | 28 |
| Thursday, July 2 | 1,770 | 250 | 120 | 1,400 | 24 |
| Friday, July 3 | 1,610 | 260 | 100 | 1,250 | 21 |
| Saturday, July 4 | 1,610 | 260 | 100 | 1,250 | 21 |
| Sunday, July 5 | 1,610 | 260 | 100 | 1,250 | 21 |
| Monday, July 6 | 1,655 | 250 | 125 | 1,280 | 24 |
| Tuesday, July 7 | 1,650 | 230 | 130 | 1,290 | 26 |
| Wednesday, July 8 | 1,690 | 240 | 130 | 1,320 | 25 |
| Thursday, July 9 | 1,770 | 275 | 135 | 1,360 | 25 |
| Friday, July 10 | 1,820 | 280 | 140 | 1,400 | 27 |
| Saturday, July 11 | 1,820 | 280 | 140 | 1,400 | 27 |
| Sunday, July 12 | 1,820 | 280 | 140 | 1,400 | 27 |
| Monday, July 13 | 1,785 | 260 | 135 | 1,390 | 29 |
| Total | $24,280 | $3,600 | $1,770 | $ 18,910 | $ 355 |
| Daily average net transaction accounts | | | | $1,350.7 | $25.357 |

### Maintenance Period

We have computed a daily average minimum cash reserve requirement for ABC Bank, but have yet to delineate the exact period over which the bank manager must maintain this $126.900 million daily average reserve target. Reserves may be held either as vault cash or as deposits held by the bank at the Federal Reserve. Under the current set of regulations, the average daily vault cash held during the reserve computation period (June 30 through July 13 in our example) is deducted from the institution's required reserves to determine the reserve balance to be maintained at the Federal Reserve. In addition, a lag of 30 days exists between the beginning of the reserve computation period and the beginning of the **reserve maintenance period** (over which deposits at the Federal Reserve Bank must meet or exceed the required reserve target). For ABC Bank, this reserve maintenance period is from July 30 through August 12 (see Figure 13–5). Thus, the bank's reserve manager knows the value of its target reserves with perfect certainty throughout the reserve maintenance period. However, the reserve manager still has a challenge in maintaining sufficient reserves at the Fed to hit the reserve target, while still minimizing these low interest rate balances and maintaining the liquidity position of the bank.

The reserve manager also knows the vault cash component of the reserve target, since this is based on the average vault cash held by the bank over the reserve computation period, as reported in Table 13–13. The daily balances in deposits at the Federal Reserve for ABC Bank for the 14-day reserve maintenance period from July 30 through August 12 are shown in Table 13–14. Since the average daily balance in vault cash during the reserve computation period is shown (in Table 13–13) at $25.357 million, the average daily target

**reserve maintenance period**

*Period over which deposits at the Federal Reserve Bank must meet or exceed the required reserve target.*

**Figure 13–5** Lagged Reserve Requirements

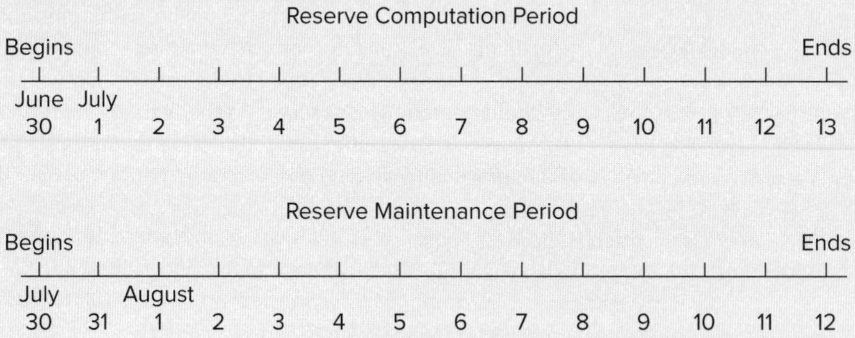

Reserve Computation Period

| Begins | | | | | | | | | | | | | Ends |

| June | July | | | | | | | | | | | | |
| 30 | 1 | 2 | 3 | 4 | 5 | 6 | 7 | 8 | 9 | 10 | 11 | 12 | 13 |

Reserve Maintenance Period

| Begins | | | | | | | | | | | | | Ends |

| July | | August | | | | | | | | | | | |
| 30 | 31 | 1 | 2 | 3 | 4 | 5 | 6 | 7 | 8 | 9 | 10 | 11 | 12 |

**TABLE 13–14** ABC Bank's Daily Reserve Position over the July 30–August 12
Reserve Maintenance Period *(in millions of dollars)*

| Date | Deposits at the Federal Reserve |
| --- | --- |
| Thursday, July 30 | $ 98 |
| Friday, July 31 | 100 |
| Saturday, August 1 | 100 |
| Sunday, August 2 | 100 |
| Monday, August 3 | 98 |
| Tuesday, August 4 | 91 |
| Wednesday, August 5 | 102 |
| Thursday, August 6 | 101 |
| Friday, August 7 | 99 |
| Saturday, August 8 | 99 |
| Sunday, August 9 | 99 |
| Monday, August 10 | 107 |
| Tuesday, August 11 | 124 |
| Wednesday, August 12 | 103.602 |
| Total | $1,421.602 |
| Daily average | $ 101.543 |

balance for deposits at the Federal Reserve are $101.543 million (i.e., $25.357 million + $101.543 million = $126.900 million). Essentially, since the vault cash component of the reserve target is based on vault cash held over the reserve computation period, the bank's active target during the maintenance period itself is its reserve position at the Fed (in this case, it seeks to hold an average of $101.543 million per day over the 14-day maintenance period).

**lagged reserve accounting system**

*An accounting system in which the reserve computation and reserve maintenance periods do not overlap.*

**contemporaneous reserve accounting system**

*An accounting system in which the reserve computation and reserve maintenance periods overlap.*

As discussed earlier, currently the reserve maintenance period for meeting the reserve target begins 30 days after the start of the reserve computation period—the reserve maintenance period does not begin until 17 days after the end of the computation period. Regulators introduced this **lagged reserve accounting system** to make it easier for bank reserve managers to calculate their required reserve balances and to increase the accuracy of information on aggregate required reserve balances. Prior to July 1998, regulators used a **contemporaneous reserve accounting system** in which the two-week reserve maintenance period for meeting the reserve target began only two days (as opposed to the current 30 days) after the start of the reserve computation period. This contemporaneous reserve system resulted in only a two-day window during which required reserves were known with certainty—in the previous example, the reserve maintenance period would have been from Thursday, July 2, through Wednesday, July 15, for a reserve computation period beginning Tuesday, June 30, and ending Monday, July 13.

## APPENDIX 13C: Primary Regulators of Depository Institutions

## APPENDIX 13D: Deposit Insurance Coverage for Commercial Banks in Various Countries

## APPENDIX 13E: Calculating Risk-Based Capital Ratios

# Appendixes 13C, 13D, and 13E are available through Connect or your course instructor.

chapter

**14**

# Other Lending Institutions

*Savings Institutions, Credit Unions, and Finance Companies*

### Learning Goals

| | |
|---|---|
| **LG 14-1** | *Recognize the differences among a savings institution, a credit union, and a finance company.* |
| **LG 14-2** | *Identify the main assets and liabilities held by savings institutions.* |
| **LG 14-3** | *Know who regulates savings institutions.* |
| **LG 14-4** | *Discuss how savings institutions performed in the 2000s.* |
| **LG 14-5** | *Describe how credit unions are different from other depository institutions.* |
| **LG 14-6** | *Identify the main assets and liabilities held by credit unions.* |
| **LG 14-7** | *Define the major types of finance companies.* |
| **LG 14-8** | *Identify the major assets and liabilities held by finance companies.* |
| **LG 14-9** | *Examine the extent to which finance companies are regulated.* |

### OTHER LENDING INSTITUTIONS: CHAPTER OVERVIEW

Like commercial banks, the main financial service provided by savings institutions, credit unions, and finance companies is lending. Savings institutions (SIs) were created in the early 1800s in response to commercial banks' concentration on serving the needs of business (commercial) enterprises rather than the needs of individuals requiring borrowed funds to purchase homes. Thus, the first SIs pooled individual savings and invested them mainly in mortgages and other securities. While today's SIs generally perform services similar to commercial banks, they are still grouped separately because they provide important residential mortgage lending and other financial services to households. That is, savings institutions concentrate primarily on residential mortgage lending. However, these institutions

LG 14-1

have recently operated in a slightly more diversified way, with a large concentration of residential mortgage assets but holding commercial loans, corporate bonds, and corporate stock as well. Credit unions are nonprofit depository institutions mutually organized and owned by their members (depositors). Credit unions have historically focused on consumer loans funded with member deposits. Savings institutions and credit unions together are often referred to as *thrifts*.

The primary function of finance companies is also to make loans to both individuals and businesses. Finance companies provide such services as consumer lending, business lending, and mortgage financing. Some finance company loans (e.g., commercial and auto loans) are similar to commercial bank loans, but others are aimed at relatively specialized areas such as high-risk (low credit quality) loans to small businesses and consumers. As we discuss in the chapter, finance companies are often willing to lend to riskier customers than are commercial banks and thrifts, and they sometimes offer rates well below those offered by depository institutions. Thus, they compete directly with depository institutions for loan customers. However, unlike banks and thrifts, finance companies do not accept deposits; instead, they rely on short- and long-term debt for funding.

The first major finance company was originated during the Depression when General Electric Corp. created General Electric Capital Corp. (GECC) to finance appliance sales to cash-strapped customers unable to obtain installment credit from banks. By the late 1950s, banks had become more willing to make installment loans, so finance companies began looking outside their parent companies for business. In 2012, GE Capital's consumer finance and banking businesses provided millions of customers with credit card, personal, auto financing, and real estate loans. GE Capital Consumer Lending's assets totaled $121 billion, while GE Energy Financial Services's assets totaled $15 billion. In a move that redefined GE Capital, in August 2012 the company announced that it would spin off its consumer lending business, including the unit that issues credit cards to over 55 million customers. At the time, the consumer lending division accounted for $50 billion of GE Capital's $274 billion loan portfolio. Under the GE Capital Exit Plan, GE retained only certain GECC businesses, principally its vertical financing businesses—GE Capital Aviation Services (GECAS), Energy Financial Services (EFS), and Industrial Finance—that directly relate to GE's core industrial domain and other operations, including Working Capital Solutions and insurance activities (together referred to as GE Capital Verticals or Verticals). As a result, in 2016 GE Capital Energy Financial Services invested in oil and gas infrastructure, including approximately 47,000 miles of pipelines and downstream oil and gas sectors such as storage and terminal. The division also invested more than $12 billion in renewable energy, with a focus on wind and solar power generation. GE Capital Aviation provided services to more than 245 customers in over 75 countries. The division maintained a warehouse of over 100,000 certified aviation parts for trade around the world. GE Capital Industrial Finance serves customers in health care, transportation, distributed power, marine industries, and municipalities around the world. For example, this division is a premier provider of capital and services to the health care industry, with investments in more than 30 subsectors including senior housing, hospitals, pharmaceuticals, and medical devices.[1]

This chapter discusses the size, structure, and composition of the savings institution, credit union, and finance company industries, the services they provide, their competitive and financial position, and their regulation.

## SAVINGS INSTITUTIONS

### Size, Structure, and Composition of the Industry

Savings institutions comprise two groups of depository institutions: savings associations and savings banks. Historically, the industry consisted of only savings associations (referred to as savings and loan [S&L] associations). However, in the 1980s, federally

---

1. See GECC's website, www.gecapital.com

chartered savings banks appeared in the United States.[2] These two types of institutions have the same regulators and regulations as the traditional savings and loans. Together they are referred to as savings institutions.

**The S&L Crisis of 1982–1992**   Savings institutions are specialized institutions that make long-term residential mortgage loans, usually funded with the short-term deposits of small savers. In the mid-1980s, real estate and land prices in Texas and the Southwest collapsed. This was followed by economic downturns in the Northeast and Western states of the United States. Many borrowers with mortgage loans issued by savings institutions in these areas defaulted. In other words, the risks incurred by many of these institutions did not pay off. This risk-taking behavior was accentuated by the policies of the federal insurer of savings associations' deposits, the FSLIC. It chose not to close capital-depleted, economically insolvent savings institutions (a policy of **regulatory forbearance**) and to maintain deposit insurance premium assessments independent of the risk taken by the institution (see Chapter 13). As a result, an alarming number (1,248) of savings institution failures occurred in the 1982–1992 period (peaking at 316 in 1989), alongside a rapid decline in asset growth of the industry. Figure 14–1 shows the number of failures, mergers, and new charters of savings institutions from 1984 through 2016. Notice the large number of failures from 1987 through 1992 and the decline in the number of new charters.

In the 1980s, the large number of savings institution failures depleted the resources of the Federal Savings and Loan Insurance Corporation (FSLIC) to such an extent that by 1989 it was massively insolvent. For example, between 1980 and 1988, 514 savings institutions failed, at an estimated cost of $42.3 billion. Moreover, between 1989 and 1992 an additional 734 savings institutions failed, at a cost of $78 billion. As a result, Congress

**regulatory forbearance**

*A policy not to close economically insolvent FIs, allowing them to continue in operation.*

**Figure 14–1**   Structural Changes in the Number of Savings Institutions, 1984–2016

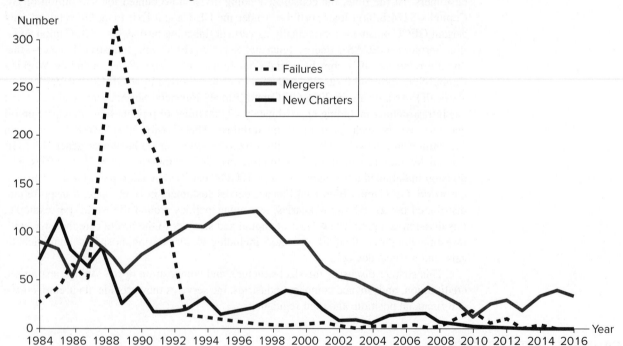

**Sources:** Federal Deposit Insurance Corporation, *Quarterly Banking Profile,* various years; and *Historical Statistics,* various years. www.fdic.gov

2. The term *savings association* has replaced S&L to capture the change in the structure of the industry. In 1978, the Federal Home Loan Bank Board (FHLBB), at the time the main regulator of savings associations, began chartering federal savings banks insured by the Federal Savings and Loan Insurance Corporation (FSLIC). In 1982, the FHLBB allowed S&Ls to convert to federal savings banks with bank (rather than S&L) names. As more and more S&Ls converted to savings banks, the title associated with this sector of the thrift industry was revised to reflect this change.

passed the Financial Institutions Reform, Recovery, and Enforcement Act (FIRREA) of 1989. This legislation abolished the FSLIC and created a new Savings Association Insurance Fund (SAIF) under the management of the FDIC (with the help of a $100 billion infusion of funds by the U.S. government). FIRREA also replaced the Federal Home Loan Bank Board with the Office of Thrift Supervision (OTS) as the main regulator of federally chartered savings institutions. In addition, the act created the Resolution Trust Corporation (RTC) to close and liquidate the most insolvent savings institutions. FIRREA also strengthened the capital requirements of savings institutions and constrained their non-mortgage-related asset investment powers under a revised qualified thrift lender test, or **QTL test** (discussed below). Following FIRREA, Congress further enacted the Federal Deposit Insurance Corporation Improvement Act (FDICIA). The FDICIA of 1991 introduced risk-based deposit insurance premiums (starting in 1993) in an attempt to limit excessive risk taking by savings institution managers. It also introduced a prompt corrective action (PCA) policy, enabling regulators to close thrifts and banks faster (see Chapter 13).

As a result of closing weak savings institutions and strengthening their capital requirements, the industry is now significantly smaller in terms of both numbers and asset size. Specifically, the number of savings institutions decreased from 3,677 in 1989 to 2,262 in 1993 (by 38 percent) and assets decreased from $1.427 trillion to $1.001 trillion (by 30 percent) over the same period. By 2016, the number of savings institutions continued to decrease to 820 and the industry's assets had slightly increased to $1.108 trillion.

### *Balance Sheets and Recent Trends*

**LG 14-2**

Even in its new smaller state, the future viability of the savings institution industry in traditional mortgage lending areas is a matter of debate. This is due partly to intense competition for mortgages from other financial institutions such as commercial banks and specialized mortgage bankers. It is also due to the securitization of mortgages into mortgage-backed security pools by government-sponsored enterprises, which we discuss in Chapters 7 and 24.[3] In addition, long-term mortgage lending exposes FIs to significant credit, interest rate, and liquidity risks.

The largest U.S. savings institution as of 2016 was Charles Schwab Bank (with total assets of $154 billion), followed by USAA Federal Savings Bank (total assets $76 billion), and Synchrony Bank (total assets $65 billion). Recall from Chapter 11 that the top four commercial banks each had assets of over $1 trillion in 2016. Thus, the savings institution industry is much smaller in size and market power than the commercial banking industry. Table 14–1 shows the balance sheet for the savings institution industry in 2016. On this balance sheet, mortgages (41.64 percent) and mortgage-backed securities (securitized pools of mortgages, 20.93 percent) represent 62.57 percent of total assets. This compares to 37.29 percent in commercial banks. As noted earlier, FIRREA uses the QTL test to establish a minimum holding of 65 percent in mortgage-related assets for savings institutions.[4] In addition to mortgage-related assets, credit card loans are includable as part of QTL. In 2016, savings institutions' credit card loans totaled 7.43 percent of total assets, bringing QTL qualifying assets to a total of 70 percent of total assets. Figure 14–2 shows the distribution of mortgage-related assets for savings institutions in 2016. Commercial loans and consumer loans amounted to just 5.79 percent and 11.52 percent of savings institution assets, respectively, compared to 12.16 percent and 8.84 percent at commercial banks (see Tables 14–1 and 11–1). Finally, savings institutions are required to hold cash and investment securities for liquidity purposes and to meet regulator-imposed reserve requirements (see Chapter 13). In 2016, cash and investment securities (U.S. Treasury securities and federal agency obligations; federal funds and repos; and bonds, notes, debentures, and other securities) holdings amounted to 14.73 percent of total assets compared to 38.53 percent at commercial banks.

**QTL test**

*Qualified thrift lender test that sets a floor on the mortgage-related assets that thrifts can hold (currently, 65 percent).*

3. The major enterprises are GNMA, FNMA, and FHLMC.

4. Failure to meet the 65 percent QTL test results in the loss of certain tax advantages and the ability to obtain Federal Home Loan Bank advances (loans).

**Figure 14–2**    Real Estate Assets as a Percentage of Total
Real Estate Assets at Savings Institutions

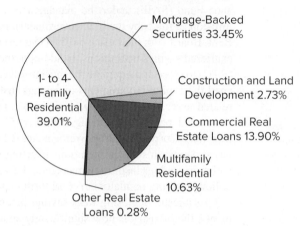

**Source:** Federal Deposit Insurance Corporation, *Quarterly Banking Profile,* Second Quarter 2016. www.fdic.gov

**TABLE 14–1**    Assets and Liabilities of Savings Institutions, 2016

|  | Billions of Dollars | Percentage |
|---|---|---|
| Cash and due from | $    84.75 | 7.65% |
| U.S. Treasury and federal agency obligations | 40.77 | 3.68 |
| Federal funds and repos | 1.21 | 0.11 |
| Bonds, corporate stock, and other securities | 36.50 | 3.29 |
| Mortgage loans | 461.55 | 41.64 |
| MBS (includes CMOs, POs, IOs) | 232.00 | 20.93 |
| Commercial loans | 64.16 | 5.79 |
| Credit card loans | 82.29 | 7.43 |
| Other consumer loans | 45.34 | 4.09 |
| Other loans and financing leases | 20.61 | 1.86 |
| Less: Allowance for loan losses and unearned income | 9.76 | 0.88 |
| Other assets | 48.92 | 4.41 |
| Total assets | $1,108.34 | 100.00% |
| Total deposits | $   867.85 | 78.30% |
| Federal funds and repos | 8.95 | 0.81 |
| Other borrowed money | 91.99 | 8.30 |
| Other liabilities | 16.52 | 1.49 |
| Total liabilities | 985.31 | 88.90% |
| Net worth | 123.03 | 11.10 |
| Total liabilities and net worth | $1,108.34 | 100.00% |
| Number of institutions | 820 | |

**Source:** FDIC, *Statistics on Banking,* Second Quarter 2016. www.fdic.gov

On the liability side of the balance sheet, transaction accounts (equivalent to those at commercial banks), and small time and savings deposits are the predominant source of funds, with total deposits accounting for 78.30 percent of total liabilities and net worth. This compares to 76.10 percent at commercial banks. The second most important source of funds is borrowing from the 12 Federal Home Loan Banks (FHLBs),[5] which the institutions themselves own. Because of their size and government-sponsored status, FHLBs have access to the wholesale capital market for notes and bonds and can relend

5. The Federal Home Loan Bank System, established in 1932, consists of 12 regional Federal Home Loan Banks (set up similar to the Federal Reserve Bank system) that borrow funds in the national capital markets and use these funds to make loans to savings institutions that are members of the Federal Home Loan Bank.

www.ots.treas.gov

**mutual organization**

*An institution in which the liability holders are also the owners—for example, in a mutual savings bank, depositors also own the bank.*

---

**DO YOU UNDERSTAND:**

1. Why the savings institution industry was created?

2. Why the performance of savings institutions deteriorated in the 1980s?

3. What was done to rescue the savings institution industry in the 1980s?

4. What the major assets and liabilities of savings institutions are?

---

the funds borrowed in these markets to savings institutions at a small markup over wholesale cost. Other borrowed funds also include repurchase agreements and direct federal fund borrowings.

Finally, net worth is the book value of the equity holders' capital contribution; it amounted to 11.10 percent in 2016. This compares to 11.31 percent at commercial banks. Historically, most savings institutions were established as **mutual organizations** (in which the depositors are the legal owners of the institution and no stock is issued). As a mutual organization, member deposits represent the equity of the savings institution. Since they have no stockholders, and thus no demand for equity investment returns, mutual organizations are generally less risky than stock-chartered organizations—mutual savings institution managers can concentrate on low-risk investments and the prevention of failure rather than higher-risk investments needed to produce higher required returns on stockholders' investments. However, through time many savings institutions have switched from mutual to stock charters (in which the holders of the stock or equity are the legal owners of the institution rather than depositors as under the mutual charter). This is mainly because stock ownership allows savings institutions to attract capital investment from outside stockholders beyond levels achievable at a mutual institution. As of 2016, 53.0 percent of all savings institutions were stock chartered, comprising 87.3 percent of industry assets.

### Regulators

The main regulators of savings institutions are the Office of the Comptroller of the Currency (OCC), the FDIC, and state regulators.

**The Office of the Comptroller of the Currency (OCC).** In 1989, FIRREA established the Office of Thrift Supervision (OTS). This office chartered and examined all *federal* savings institutions. It also supervised the holding companies of savings institutions. During the 2008–2009 financial crisis the U.S. Congress determined that the performance of savings bank regulators was relatively weak compared to commercial bank regulators. Further, a Government Accountability Office report noted that some of the savings institutions regulated by the OTS were primarily operating in areas other than those traditionally engaged in by thrifts (i.e., insurance, securities, and commercial activities). To address these concerns, the Wall Street Reform and Consumer Protection Act of 2010 mandated the consolidation of the Office of Thrift Supervision and the Office of the Comptroller of the Currency. As a result, the OTS became part of the OCC on July 21, 2011, and on October 19, 2011, the OTS ceased to exist. Thus, the OCC now regulates both national banks and federal savings institutions. Additionally, while the bill did not eliminate the charter for savings institutions dedicated to mortgage lending, it did subject savings institution holding companies to supervision by the Federal Reserve.

www.occ.gov

www.fdic.gov

**The FDIC.** Also established in 1989 under FIRREA and in the wake of the FSLIC insolvency, the FDIC oversaw and managed the Savings Association Insurance Fund (SAIF). In 1996, as part of a plan to recapitalize the SAIF, commercial banks were required to pay for part of the burden. In return, Congress promised to eventually merge bank and thrift charters (and hence insurance funds) into one. In January 2007, the FDIC merged the SAIF and the Bank Insurance Fund (BIF) to form the Deposit Insurance Fund (DIF). Thus, savings institutions now operate under the same regulatory structure that applies to commercial banks.

---

**DO YOU UNDERSTAND:**

5. Who the regulators of savings institutions are?

---

**Other Regulators.** State-chartered savings institutions are regulated by state agencies—for example, the Office of Banks and Real Estate in Illinois—rather than the OCC.

### Savings Institution Recent Performance

Like commercial banks, savings institutions experienced record profits in the mid- to late 1990s as interest rates (and thus the cost of funds to savings institutions) remained low and the U.S. economy (and thus the demand for loans) prospered. The result was an increase in the spread between interest income and interest expense for savings institutions and consequently an increase in net income. In 1999, savings institutions reported $10.7 billion in net income and an annualized ROA of 1.00 percent. Only the $10.8 billion of net income reported in 1998 exceeded these results. Asset quality improvements were widespread during 1999, providing the most favorable net operating income that the industry had ever reported. However, the downturn in the U.S. economy resulted in a decline in savings institutions' profitability in 2000. Specifically, their ROA and ROE ratios fell slightly in 2000 to 0.92 percent and 11.14 percent, respectively, from their 1999 levels. Despite an economic recession, this downturn was short-lived. Both ROA and ROE increased to record levels each year from 2001 through 2003. One reason for this trend was that in the early 2000s, the industry's net interest margins rose; the cost of funding earning assets declined by 2.70 percent, while the yield on earning assets declined by only 2.35 percent. A flat (and at times even downward sloping) yield curve increased funding costs and contributed to decreased margins in the mid-2000s. The average ROA declined to 1.15 percent in 2005 and 0.99 percent in 2006, while ROE decreased to 10.40 percent in 2005 and 8.68 percent in 2006.

In the late 2000s, as the U.S. economy experienced its strongest recession since the Great Depression, savings institutions' performance deteriorated. For all of 2007, net income was $6.0 billion, down $11.1 billion from 2006. The average ROA for the year was 0.13 percent, the lowest yearly average since 1989. In 2008, net income was −$8.6 billion. This was the first negative earnings year since 1991. The ROA for the year was −0.72 percent. However, only five savings institutions failed or were assisted during the year. In this group was Washington Mutual, the largest savings institution, with over $300 billion in assets. Like commercial banks, as the economy improved in the second half of 2009 through 2013, so did savings institutions' performance. Savings institutions earned $1.4 billion in net income in the third quarter of 2009, up from −$18.3 million in the second quarter. This trend continued into 2010 as savings institutions earned $8.3 billion for the year. ROA and ROE for the industry were 0.65 percent and 5.76 percent, respectively, up from 0.14 percent and 1.31 percent, respectively, in 2009. By 2016, the industry ROA was 1.31 percent and ROE was 11.83 percent. Further, no savings institutions failed in 2016. Table 14–2 presents several performance ratios for the industry from 1989 through 2016.

Also like commercial banks, the savings institution industry experienced substantial consolidation in the 1990s and 2000s. Figure 14–3 shows the industry

**DO YOU UNDERSTAND:**

6. The recent performance of savings institutions?

7. The ways that profit trends for savings institutions have been similar to those of commercial banks in the 1990s and 2000s?

**TABLE 14–2**   Selected Indicators for U.S. Savings Institutions, 1989–2016

|  | 1989 | 1999 | 2000 | 2003 | 2005 | 2006 | 2007 | 2008 | 2009 | 2010 | 2013 | 2016 |
|---|---|---|---|---|---|---|---|---|---|---|---|---|
| Number of institutions | 3,086 | 1,642 | 1,590 | 1,411 | 1,307 | 1,279 | 1,251 | 1,219 | 1,173 | 1,128 | 936 | 820 |
| Return on assets (%) | −0.39 | 1.00 | 0.92 | 1.28 | 1.15 | 0.99 | 0.13 | −0.72 | 0.14 | 0.65 | 1.08 | 1.31 |
| Return on equity (%) | −8.06 | 11.73 | 11.14 | 13.66 | 10.40 | 8.68 | 1.08 | −7.75 | 1.31 | 5.76 | 9.07 | 11.83 |
| Noncurrent assets plus other real estate owned to assets (%) | 2.78 | 0.58 | 0.56 | 0.62 | 0.57 | 0.63 | 1.46 | 2.40 | 3.00 | 3.04 | 1.74 | 1.12 |
| Asset growth rate (%) | −11.14 | 5.60 | 6.41 | 8.47 | 8.64 | −3.70 | 4.97 | −17.53 | −17.50 | −0.84 | −0.68 | 3.23 |
| Net operating income growth (%) | −58.95 | 16.70 | 3.55 | 23.03 | 8.03 | −9.84 | −81.68 | −456.82 | 120.44 | 273.16 | 2.50 | 16.62 |
| Number of failed institutions | 331 | 1 | 1 | 0 | 0 | 0 | 1 | 5 | 20 | 18 | 1 | 0 |

**Sources:** FDIC, *Quarterly Banking Profile,* various issues; and *Historical Statistics,* 1989. www.fdic.gov

**Figure 14–3**   U.S. Savings Institution Asset Concentration, 1992 versus 2016

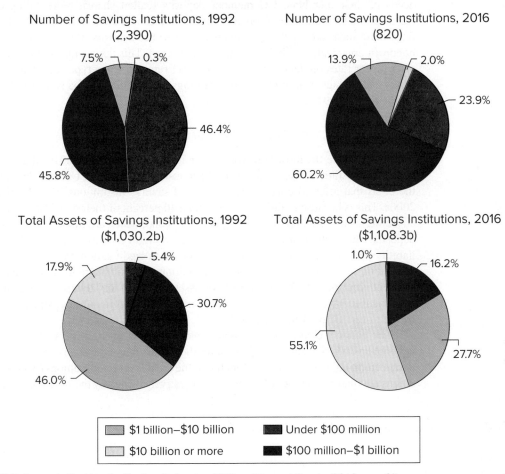

Number of Savings Institutions, 1992
(2,390)

7.5%   0.3%
46.4%
45.8%

Number of Savings Institutions, 2016
(820)

13.9%   2.0%
23.9%
60.2%

Total Assets of Savings Institutions, 1992
($1,030.2b)

5.4%
17.9%
30.7%
46.0%

Total Assets of Savings Institutions, 2016
($1,108.3b)

1.0%   16.2%
55.1%
27.7%

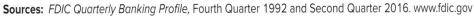

| | |
|---|---|
| ▦ $1 billion–$10 billion | ◼ Under $100 million |
| ▢ $10 billion or more | ◼ $100 million–$1 billion |

**Sources:** *FDIC Quarterly Banking Profile,* Fourth Quarter 1992 and Second Quarter 2016. www.fdic.gov

consolidation in number and asset size over the period 1992–2016. Over this period, the biggest savings institutions (over $10 billion) grew in number from 0.3 percent to 2.0 percent of the industry and their control of industry assets grew from 17.9 percent to 55.1 percent.

## CREDIT UNIONS

**LG 14-5**

Credit unions (CUs) are nonprofit depository institutions mutually organized and owned by their members (depositors). They were established in the United States in the early 1900s as self-help organizations. The first credit unions were organized in the Northeast, initially in Massachusetts. Members paid an entrance fee and put up funds to purchase at least one deposit share. Members were expected to deposit their savings in the CU, and these funds were lent only to other members.

This limit in the customer base of CUs continues today as, unlike commercial banks and savings institutions, CUs are prohibited from serving the general public. Rather, in organizing a credit union, members are required to have a common bond of occupation (e.g., police CUs); association (e.g., university-affiliated CUs); or cover a well-defined neighborhood, community, or rural district. CUs may, however, have multiple groups with more than one type of membership. Each credit union decides the common bond requirements (i.e., which groups it will serve) with the approval of the appropriate regulator (see below). To join a credit union an individual must then be a member of the approved group(s).

The primary objective of credit unions is to satisfy the depository and borrowing needs of their members. CU member deposits (called shares, representing ownership stakes in the CU) are used to provide loans to other members in need of funds. Earnings from these loans are used to pay interest on member deposits. Because credit unions are nonprofit organizations, their earnings are not taxed. This tax-exempt status allows CUs to offer higher rates on deposits and charge lower rates on some types of loans compared to banks and savings institutions, whose earnings are taxable. This is shown in Figure 14–4 for the period 1991–2016.

### Size, Structure, and Composition of the Industry

Credit unions are the most numerous of the institutions (6,105 in 2016) that compose the depository institutions segment of the FI industry. Moreover, CUs were less affected by the crisis that affected commercial banks and savings institutions in the 1980s and late 2000s. This is because traditionally more than 40 percent of their assets have been in small consumer loans, often for amounts less than $10,000, which are funded mainly by member deposits. This combination of relatively matched credit risk and maturity in the asset and liability portfolios left credit unions less exposed to credit and interest rate risk than commercial banks and savings institutions. In addition, CUs tend to hold large amounts of government securities (14.7 percent of their assets in 2016) and relatively small amounts of residential mortgages. CUs' lending activities are funded mainly by deposits contributed by their over 107.6 million members.

The nation's credit union system consists of three distinct tiers: the top tier at the national level (U.S. Central Credit Union); the middle tier at the state or regional level (corporate credit unions); and the bottom tier at the local level (credit unions). Corporate credit unions are financial institutions that are cooperatively owned by their member credit unions.

**Figure 14–4**    Credit Union versus Bank Interest Rates

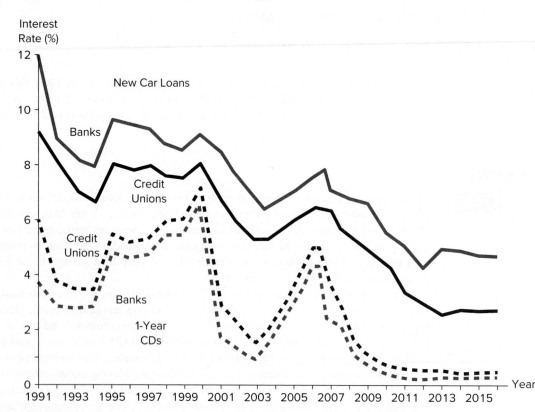

**Sources:** Federal Reserve Board and National Credit Union Administration, various dates. www.federalreserve.gov and www.ncua.gov

The 12 corporate credit unions serve their members primarily by investing and lending excess funds (unloaned deposits) that member credit unions place with them. Additional services provided by corporate credit unions include automated settlement, securities safe-keeping, data processing, accounting, and payment services. As of 2016, credit unions had over $96.6 billion (7.7 percent of total assets) invested in corporate credit unions. The U.S. Central Credit Union serves as a "corporate's corporate"—providing investment and liquidity services to corporate credit unions. The Central Credit Union acts as the main provider of liquidity for corporate credit unions. It invests their surplus funds and provides financial services and operational support.

In recent years, to attract and keep customers, CUs have expanded their services to compete with commercial banks and savings institutions. For example, CUs now offer mortgages, credit lines, and mobile banking. Some credit unions also offer business and commercial loans to their employer groups. In 2016, business loans represented 4.9 percent of the industry's lending.

As CUs have expanded in membership, size, and services, bankers claim that CUs unfairly compete with small banks that have historically been the major lender in small towns and local communities. In 1997, the banking industry filed two lawsuits in its push to restrict the growing competitive threat from credit unions. The first lawsuit (filed by four North Carolina banks and the American Bankers Association) challenged an occupation-based credit union's (the AT&T Family Credit Union based in North Carolina) ability to accept members from companies unrelated to the firm that originally sponsored the credit union. In the second lawsuit, the American Bankers Association asked the courts to bar the federal government from allowing occupation-based credit unions to convert to community-based charters. Bankers argued in both lawsuits that such actions, broadening the membership base of credit unions, would further exploit an unfair advantage allowed through the credit union tax-exempt status. In February 1998, the Supreme Court sided with the banks in its decision that credit unions could no longer accept members that were not a part of the "common bond" of membership. In April 1998, however, the U.S. House of Representatives overwhelmingly passed a bill that allowed all existing members to keep their credit union accounts. The bill was passed by the Senate in July 1998 and signed into law by the president in August 1998. This legislation allowed CUs not only to keep their existing members but also to accept new groups of members—including small businesses and low-income communities—that were not considered part of the "common bond" of membership by the Supreme Court ruling.

Credit unions provide a public service by offering loans to those who might not otherwise have access to credit through commercial banks and savings institutions: low- and moderate-income individuals within a specific group—the credit union's common bond. Further, credit union profits are distributed back to members in the form of better rates on deposits and loans as well as lower and fewer fees on services. It is these services that have justified credit unions' tax-exempt status. However, throughout the 2000s, many credit unions pursued regional charters and expanded their fields of membership. The result has been a blurring of credit unions' common bond membership. Consequently, credit unions have become more like banks, but with tax-exempt status. As credit unions have grown in size, some are again questioning their protected status. Indeed, in a recent report from the President's Economic Recovery Advisory Board, elimination of the credit union tax exemption was included in a list of recommendations addressing the nation's budget deficit. Yet, despite the renewed discussion, credit unions continue to operate as nonprofit, tax-exempt depository institutions.

In another hit to commercial banks, credit unions saw record increases in membership in late 2011 and early 2012, with most of the increase coming from commercial bank customers. For the year ending June 30, 2012, credit union membership increased by nearly 2.2 million new members: almost twice the 1.2 million average annual growth experienced in similar 12-month periods over the previous 10 years and four times greater than the 550,000 new members over that same period the prior year. Much of the growth in membership occurred as a part of nationwide campaigns, such as Bank Transfer Day on November 5, 2011, that encouraged consumers to leave their "big" banks for credit unions and community banks, which tend to incur fewer fees. Among the catalysts for these campaigns was Bank of America's plan to impose a monthly fee for debit card use. That plan was scrapped in response to consumers' strong negative reactions.

### Balance Sheets and Recent Trends

**LG 14-6**

As of 2016, 6,105 credit unions had assets of $1,254.6 billion. This compares to $192.8 billion in assets in 1988. Individually, credit unions tend to be very small, with an average asset size of $205.5 million in 2016, compared to $2,874.4 million for banks. The total assets of all credit unions are smaller than the largest U.S. banking organization(s). For example, in 2016, J.P. Morgan Chase had $2,466.1 billion in total assets, Bank of America had $2,189.8 billion, Wells Fargo had $1,889.2 billion, and Citigroup had $1,818.8. This compares to total credit union assets of $1,254.6 billion in 2016. The largest U.S. credit union as of 2016 was Navy Federal Credit Union (with total assets of $73.3 billion), followed by State Employees' Credit Union (total assets $31.8 billion), and PenFed Federal Credit Union (total assets $19.5 billion).

Table 14–3 shows the breakdown of financial assets and liabilities for credit unions as of 2016. Given their emphasis on retail or consumer lending, discussed earlier, 29.3 percent of CU assets are in the form of small consumer loans (compared to 11.5 percent at savings institutions and 8.8 percent at commercial banks) and another 28.6 percent are in the form of home mortgages (compared to 41.6 percent at savings institutions and 26.1 percent at commercial banks). Together these member loans compose 57.9 percent of total assets. Figure 14–5 provides more detail on the composition of the loan portfolio for all CUs. Because of the common bond requirement on credit union customers, few business or commercial loans are issued by CUs.

**TABLE 14–3**   Assets and Liabilities of Credit Unions, 2016

|  | **Billions of Dollars** | **Percentage** |
|---|---|---|
| **Assets** | | |
| Cash and equivalents | $  101.3 | 8.1% |
| Investment securities | | |
|     U.S. government securities | | |
|         Treasury | 11.7 | 0.9 |
|         Agency | 172.6 | 13.8 |
|     Mortgage-backed securities | 53.8 | 4.3 |
|     Other investment securities | 38.3 | 3.0 |
| Total investment securities | $  276.4 | 22.0% |
| Loans | | |
|     Home mortgages | 358.4 | 28.6 |
|     Consumer loans | 367.9 | 29.3 |
|     Business loans | 61.8 | 4.9 |
|     Other | 35.3 | 2.8 |
|     (Allowance for loan losses) | (7.5) | (0.6) |
| Total loans | $  815.9 | 65.0 |
| Other assets | 61.0 | 4.9 |
| Total assets | $1,254.6 | 100.0% |
| **Liabilities and Equity** | | |
| Share drafts | $  154.6 | 12.3% |
| Small time and savings | 814.2 | 64.9 |
| Large time | 90.1 | 7.2 |
| Shares/deposits | $1,058.9 | 84.4% |
| Other loans and advances | 47.2 | 3.7 |
| Miscellaneous liabilities | 13.4 | 1.1 |
| Total liabilities | $1,119.5 | 89.2% |
| Total ownership shares | $  135.1 | 10.8% |

**Source:** National Credit Union Administration, Second Quarter 2016. www.ncua.gov

**Figure 14–5**   **Composition of Credit Union Loan Portfolio**

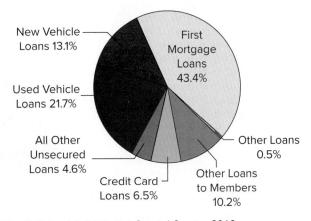

New Vehicle Loans 13.1%

Used Vehicle Loans 21.7%

All Other Unsecured Loans 4.6%

Credit Card Loans 6.5%

Other Loans to Members 10.2%

Other Loans 0.5%

First Mortgage Loans 43.4%

**Source:** National Credit Union Administration, Second Quarter, 2016. www.ncua.gov

Credit unions also invest heavily in investment securities (22.0 percent of total assets in 2016 compared to 7.1 percent at savings institutions and 26.7 percent at commercial banks). Figure 14–6 shows that 66.6 percent of the investment portfolio of CUs is in U.S. government Treasury securities or federal agency securities, while investments in other FIs (such as deposits of banks) totaled 22.2 percent of their investment portfolios. Their investment portfolio composition, along with cash holdings and reserves at the Fed (8.1 percent of total assets), allows credit unions ample liquidity to meet their daily cash needs—such as share (deposit) withdrawals. Some CUs have also increased their off-balance-sheet activities. Specifically, unused loan commitments, including credit card limits and home equity lines of credit, totaled over $195 billion in 2016.

Credit union funding comes mainly from member deposits (84.4 percent of total funding in 2016 compared to 78.3 percent for savings institutions and 76.1 percent for commercial banks). Figure 14–7 presents the distribution of these deposits in 2016. Regular share accounts (similar to passbook savings accounts at other depository institutions, but so named to designate the deposit holders' ownership status) accounted for 35.3 percent of all CU deposits, followed by money market deposit accounts (22.7 percent of deposits), certificates of deposit (18.5 percent), and share draft transaction accounts (similar to NOW accounts at other depository institutions—see Chapter 11) (14.6 percent of deposits). Credit unions hold lower levels of equity than other depository institutions. Since CUs are not stockholder owned, this equity is basically the accumulation of past earnings from

**Figure 14–6**   **Composition of Credit Union Investment Portfolio**

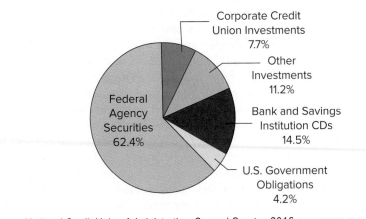

Corporate Credit Union Investments 7.7%

Other Investments 11.2%

Bank and Savings Institution CDs 14.5%

U.S. Government Obligations 4.2%

Federal Agency Securities 62.4%

**Source:** National Credit Union Administration, Second Quarter, 2016. www.ncua.gov

**Figure 14–7**  Composition of Credit Union Deposits

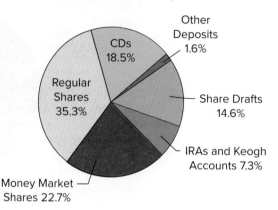

**Source:** National Credit Union Administration, Second Quarter, 2016. www.ncua.gov

CU activities that is "owned" collectively by member depositors. As will be discussed in Chapters 19 and 22, this equity protects a CU against losses on its loan portfolio as well as other financial and operating risks. In 2016, CUs' capital-to-assets ratio was 10.8 percent compared to 11.1 percent for savings institutions and 11.3 percent for commercial banks.

### Regulators

www.ncua.gov

Like commercial banks and savings institutions, credit unions can be federally or state chartered. As of 2016, 62.5 percent of the 6,105 CUs were federally chartered and subject to National Credit Union Administration (NCUA) regulation, accounting for 52.9 percent of the total membership and 52.0 percent of total assets. The NCUA is an independent federal agency that charters, supervises, examines, and insures the nation's credit unions. In addition, through its insurance fund (the National Credit Union Share Insurance Fund, or NCUSIF), the NCUA provides deposit insurance guarantees of up to $250,000 for insured state and federal credit unions. Currently, the NCUSIF covers 98 percent of all credit union deposits. The fund's reserves come entirely from premiums paid by member credit unions.

### Industry Performance

Like other depository institutions, the credit union industry has grown in asset size in the 1990s and 2000s. Asset growth from 1999 to 2016 was more than 5.4 percent annually. In addition, CU membership increased from 77.5 million to over 107.6 million over the 1999–2016 period. Asset growth was especially pronounced among the largest CUs (with assets of over $100 million) as their assets increased by almost 20 percent annually from 1999 through 2016. Figure 14–8 shows the trend in ROA for CUs from 1993 through 2016. ROA for the industry was 0.75 in the first six months of 2016. Larger CUs generally outperform small CUs. For example, the largest credit unions experienced an ROA of 0.88 percent in 2016, while ROA for the smallest credit unions was 0.09 percent. Smaller CUs generally have a smaller and less diversified customer base and have higher overhead expenses per dollar of assets. Thus, their ROAs have been hurt.

Given the mutual-ownership status of this industry, however, growth in ROA (or profits) is not necessarily the primary goal of CUs. Rather, as long as capital or equity levels are sufficient to protect a CU against unexpected losses on its credit portfolio as well as other financial and operational risks, this nonprofit industry has a primary goal of serving the deposit and lending needs of its members. This contrasts with the emphasis placed on profitability by stockholder-owned commercial banks and savings institutions.

---

**DO YOU UNDERSTAND:**

8. How credit unions differ from commercial banks and savings institutions?

9. Why credit unions have prospered in recent years in comparison to savings institutions?

10. How the credit union industry is organized?

11. Why commercial banks and savings institutions claim that credit unions have an unfair advantage in providing bank services?

12. The main assets and liabilities credit unions hold?

**Figure 14–8**    Return on Assets for Credit Unions, 1993–2016

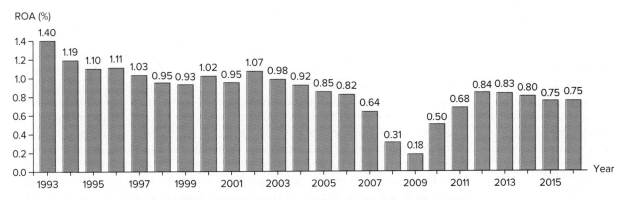

**Sources:** National Credit Union Administration, *Midyear Statistics and Year End Statistics,* various years. www.ncua.gov

While local credit unions as a whole survived the financial crisis more profitably than commercial banks and savings institutions, corporate credit unions did not. As mentioned earlier, corporate credit unions serve their members by investing and lending excess funds that member credit unions place with them. Like commercial banks, in the early- and mid-2000s, corporate credit unions faced increasingly tough business conditions that strained their financial position. To generate earnings, some corporate credit unions invested in riskier securities, such as mortgage-related and asset-backed securities. The National Credit Union Administration (NCUA) allowed corporate credit unions to invest in these higher risk securities. As the financial crisis hit, corporate credit unions that invested in higher risk securities started experiencing large losses on them. These corporate credit unions reported $18 billion in unrealized losses on securities, as of November 2008.

As information about the financial conditions of these corporate credit unions became public, local credit unions reduced their exposure to the corporates. Between March 31, 2008, and September 30, 2008, local credit unions' deposits in corporate credit unions fell by nearly 49 percent, from $44.7 billion to $22.9 billion. In addition to the resulting demand for funds that this withdrawal of deposits produced, these corporate credit unions had accumulated $50 billion in toxic mortgage-backed securities. The corporate credit union system started to collapse. Without action, losses on these problem assets would have caused the entire credit union industry to break down.

As a first step in its effort to resolve the crisis, in March 2009 the NCUA placed two corporates, U.S. Central and WesCorp, into conservatorship. Further, the NCUA purchased many of the toxic assets of the corporates. As of the third quarter 2010, the NCUA held roughly 70 percent of the assets of the corporate credit union system, which included $50 billion in toxic assets. The NCUA also took several actions to address long-term issues surrounding corporate credit unions. Capital standards were increased and minimum retained earnings levels were established. Further, prompt corrective action requirements were increased. Investments in private label residential mortgage-backed securities and subordinated securities were prohibited, and concentration limits were set on investments. Ultimately, five of the largest corporate credit unions in the United States (Constitution Corporate, Members of United Corporate, Western Corporate, Southwest Corporate, and U.S. Central Corporate) were declared insolvent. The NCUA joined the U.S. Department of Justice and other governmental plaintiffs in litigation against several financial institutions, alleging they sold faulty mortgage-backed securities to four corporate credit unions. A number of settlement agreements were reached and the NCUA was the first federal financial institutions regulator to recover losses from investments in these securities on behalf of failed financial institutions. As of September 2016, the NCUA's recoveries from various financial institutions will reach $4.3 billion.

# FINANCE COMPANIES

## Size, Structure, and Composition of the Industry

In 2016, the finance company industry assets stood at $1,820.6 billion (see Table 14–4). The three major types of finance companies are (1) sales finance institutions, (2) personal credit institutions, and (3) business credit institutions. **Sales finance institutions** (e.g., Ford Motor Credit and Sears Roebuck Acceptance Corp.) specialize in making loans to customers of a specific retailer or manufacturer. Because sales finance institutions can frequently process loans faster and more conveniently (generally at the location of purchase) than depository institutions, this sector of the industry competes directly with depository institutions for consumer loans. **Personal credit institutions** (e.g., Household Finance Corp. and AIG American General) specialize in making installment and other loans to consumers. Personal credit institutions will make loans to customers with low income or a bad credit history, in contrast to depository institutions, which find these customers too risky to lend to. These institutions compensate for the additional risk by charging higher interest rates than depository institutions and/or accepting collateral (e.g., used cars) that depository institutions do not find acceptable. **Business credit institutions** (e.g., CIT Group and U.S. Bancorp Equipment Finance) provide financing to corporations, especially through equipment leasing and **factoring,** in which the finance company purchases accounts receivable from corporate customers at a discount from face value and the finance company assumes the responsibility for collecting the accounts receivable. As a result, the corporate customer no longer has the worry of whether the accounts receivable may be delayed and thus receives cash for sales faster than the time it takes customers to pay their bills. Many large finance companies perform all three services.

The industry is quite concentrated; the 20 largest firms account for more than 65 percent of its assets. In addition, many of the largest finance companies such as Ford Motor Credit tend to be wholly owned or captive subsidiaries of major manufacturing companies. A major role of a **captive finance company** is to provide financing for the purchase of products manufactured by the parent, as Ford Motor Credit does for Ford Motor Company cars. Captive finance companies serve as an efficient marketing tool by providing consumer financing to customers of the parent company immediately at the time of purchase. They can also be used to finance distribution or dealer inventories until a sale occurs.

**sales finance institutions**

*Finance companies specializing in loans to customers of a particular retailer or manufacturer.*

**personal credit institutions**

*Finance companies specializing in installment and other loans to consumers.*

**business credit institutions**

*Finance companies specializing in business loans.*

**factoring**

*The process of purchasing accounts receivable from corporations (often at a discount), usually with no recourse to the seller should the receivables go bad.*

**captive finance company**

*A finance company wholly owned by a parent corporation.*

www.credit.ford.com

www.hsbcusa.com

www.aigag.com

www.citgroup.com

**TABLE 14–4**  Assets and Liabilities of U.S. Finance Companies (June 30, 2016)

|  | Billions of Dollars | Percentage of Total Assets |
|---|---|---|
| **Assets** | | |
| Accounts receivable gross.................................. | $1,414.7 | 77.7% |
| Consumer...................................................... | 887.5 | 48.8 |
| Business....................................................... | 410.3 | 22.5 |
| Real estate................................................... | 116.9 | 6.4 |
| Less reserves for unearned income.................. | (23.5) | (1.3) |
| Less reserves for losses.................................... | (18.3) | (1.0) |
| Accounts receivable net.................................... | $1,372.9 | 76.5% |
| All other.......................................................... | 447.7 | 24.6 |
| Total assets..................................................... | $1,820.6 | 100.0% |
| **Liabilities and Capital** | | |
| Bank loans...................................................... | $  152.4 | 8.4% |
| Commercial paper............................................ | 113.4 | 6.2 |
| Debt due to parent.......................................... | 146.7 | 8.1 |
| Notes, bonds, debentures ............................... | 956.1 | 52.5 |
| All other liabilities.......................................... | 203.0 | 11.1 |
| Capital, surplus, and undivided profits............. | 248.9 | 13.7 |
| Total liabilities and capital............................... | $1,820.5 | 100.0% |

**Source:** *Federal Reserve Bulletin,* 2016. www.federalreserve.gov

**DO YOU UNDERSTAND:**

13. *What the three major types of finance companies are? What types of customers does each serve?*

14. *What a captive finance company is?*

Table 14–5 lists some of the top finance companies (in terms of receivables, or loans outstanding) as of 2016. Citigroup's credit card unit is one of the largest finance companies with receivables totaling $146.0 billion. Notice that some of the largest finance companies (such as Citigroup and Bank of America) are actually subsidiaries of commercial bank (or financial services) holding companies. Thus, while Citibank cannot make high-risk, high-interest-rate loans due to bank regulations that restrict credit risk, it can indirectly make these loans through its finance company subsidiary. Notice too that GECC is number 8 on the list with $24.1 billion in receivables. Prior to 2014, GECC was the largest finance company, with as much as $285.0 billion in receivables. Synchrony Financial, number 11 on the list, is one of the GECC spin-off companies, specializing in personal credit such as credit cards for Walmart.

LG 14-8

## Balance Sheets and Recent Trends

**Assets.** Finance companies provide three basic types of loans: real estate, consumer, and business. The assets and liabilities of finance companies in 2016 are presented in Table 14–4. Business and consumer loans (called *accounts receivable*) are major assets held by finance companies; they represent 71.3 percent of total assets. In 1975, 92.3 percent of total assets were consumer and business loans (see Figure 14–9). Compared to depository institutions, which hold a large percentage of longer-term real estate loans, finance companies historically held shorter-term consumer and business loans. Over the last 40 years, however, finance companies have replaced consumer and business loans with increasing amounts of real estate loans and other assets, although these loans have not become dominant, as is the case with many depository institutions. Real estate loans are 6.4 percent of total assets of finance companies.

Table 14–6 presents information concerning the industry's loans from 1994 through 2016 for consumer, real estate, and business lending. In recent years, the fastest-growing areas of asset activity have been in the nonconsumer finance areas, especially leasing and business lending. In 2016, consumer loans constituted 63.2 percent of all finance company loans, mortgages represented 7.9 percent, and business loans comprised 28.9 percent. This compares to commercial banks with 16.2 percent of their loans in consumer loans, 47.9 percent in mortgages, 22.4 percent in business loans, and 13.5 percent in other loans (e.g., loans to foreign governments).

*Consumer Loans.* Consumer loans include motor vehicle loans and leases and other consumer loans. Motor vehicle loans and leases are traditionally the major type of consumer loan (62.7 percent of the consumer loan portfolio in 2016). Table 14–7 data indicate that finance companies historically charged higher rates for automobile loans than did

**TABLE 14–5** The Largest Finance Companies

| Company Name | Total Receivables (in billions) |
|---|---|
| **1.** Ally Financial | $112.7 |
| **2.** American Express | 47.5 |
| **3.** Bank of America (credit card business) | 97.5 |
| **4.** CIT Financial | 32.7 |
| **5.** Citigroup (credit card business) | 146.0 |
| **6.** Discover Financial | 71.9 |
| **7.** Ford Motor Credit Company | 101.3 |
| **8.** General Electric Capital Corp. | 24.1 |
| **9.** HSBC Finance | 79.8 |
| **10.** J.P. Morgan Chase (credit card business) | 131.6 |
| **11.** Synchrony Financial | 68.3 |

**Source:** Authors' research.

**TABLE 14–6** Finance Company Loans Outstanding from 1994–2016 *(in billions of dollars)*

| | 1994 | 2000 | 2004 | 2007 | 2010 | 2013 | 2016 | Percentage of Total, 2016 |
|---|---|---|---|---|---|---|---|---|
| Consumer | $248.0 | $ 468.3 | $ 572.5 | $ 891.1 | $ 827.7 | $ 841.4 | $ 897.8 | 63.2% |
| Motor vehicle loans | 70.2 | 141.6 | 231.2 | 261.5 | 277.4 | 305.5 | 335.1 | 23.6 |
| Motor vehicle leases | 67.5 | 108.2 | 62.4 | 122.9 | 111.8 | 156.9 | 223.6 | 15.8 |
| Revolving* | 25.9 | 37.6 | 47.4 | 86.0 | 81.5 | 67.6 | 51.7 | 3.6 |
| Other[†] | 38.4 | 40.7 | 84.6 | 236.5 | 346.1 | 302.6 | 278.5 | 19.6 |
| Securitized assets | | | | | | | | |
| Motor vehicle loans | 32.8 | 97.1 | 110.2 | 110.7 | 1.8 | 2.1 | 4.3 | 0.3 |
| Motor vehicle leases | 2.2 | 6.6 | 4.8 | 3.1 | 0.0 | 0.0 | 0.0 | 0.0 |
| Revolving | n.a. | 19.6 | 22.3 | 25.6 | 0.0 | 0.0 | 0.0 | 0.0 |
| Other | 11.2 | 17.1 | 9.6 | 44.7 | 9.1 | 6.7 | 4.6 | 0.3 |
| Real estate | $ 66.9 | $ 198.9 | $ 273.7 | $ 572.4 | $ 317.8 | $ 170.7 | $ 111.8 | 7.9% |
| One- to four-family | n.a. | 130.6 | 188.5 | 472.7 | 169.6 | 125.2 | 84.8 | 6.0 |
| Other | n.a. | 41.7 | 48.3 | 59.1 | 74.0 | 45.5 | 27.1 | 1.9 |
| Securitized real estate assets[‡] | | | | | | | | |
| One- to four-family | n.a. | 24.7 | 34.3 | 34.9 | 74.1 | 0.0 | 0.0 | 0.0 |
| Other | n.a. | 1.9 | 2.7 | 5.6 | 0.1 | 0.0 | 0.0 | 0.0 |
| Business | $298.6 | $ 525.0 | $ 565.0 | $ 602.2 | $ 372.7 | $ 396.1 | $ 410.5 | 28.9% |
| Motor vehicles | 62.0 | 75.5 | 89.8 | 105.7 | 113.9 | 134.5 | 154.1 | 10.9 |
| Retail loans | 18.5 | 18.3 | 19.6 | 16.4 | 18.2 | 25.7 | 26.7 | 1.9 |
| Wholesale loans[§] | 35.2 | 39.7 | 44.0 | 56.9 | 69.4 | 80.7 | 96.4 | 6.8 |
| Leases | 8.3 | 17.6 | 26.2 | 32.4 | 26.3 | 28.1 | 31.0 | 2.2 |
| Equipment | 166.7 | 283.5 | 263.2 | 328.2 | 178.7 | 176.3 | 156.3 | 11.0 |
| Loans | 48.9 | 70.2 | 70.1 | 111.4 | 104.5 | 110.7 | 115.3 | 8.1 |
| Leases | 117.8 | 213.3 | 193.1 | 216.9 | 74.2 | 65.6 | 41.0 | 2.9 |
| Other business receivables[‖] | 46.2 | 99.4 | 116.2 | 89.0 | 80.2 | 85.3 | 100.1 | 7.0 |
| Securitized assets[‡] | 23.7 | 66.5 | 95.9 | 79.3 | 0.0 | 0.0 | 0.0 | 0.0 |
| Total | $613.5 | $1,192.2 | $1,411.2 | $2,065.6 | $1,518.2 | $1,408.2 | $1,420.1 | 100% |

*Excludes revolving credit reported as held by depository institutions that are subsidiaries of finance companies.

[†]Includes personal cash loans, mobile home loans, and loans to purchase other types of consumer goods such as appliances, apparel, boats, and recreation vehicles.

[‡]Outstanding balances of pools on which securities have been issued; these balances are no longer carried on the balance sheets of the loan originator.

[§]Credit arising from transactions between manufacturers and dealers—that is, floor plan financing.

[‖]Includes loans on commercial accounts receivable, factored commercial accounts, and receivable dealer capital; small loans used primarily for business or farm purposes; and wholesale and lease paper for mobile homes, campers, and travel trailers.

[‡]Outstanding balances of pools on which securities have been issued; these balances are no longer carried on the balance sheets of the loan originator.

**Sources:** Federal Reserve Board, *Flow of Funds Accounts,* various issues. www.federalreserve.gov

**Figure 14–9** Finance Company Assets, 1975 versus 2016

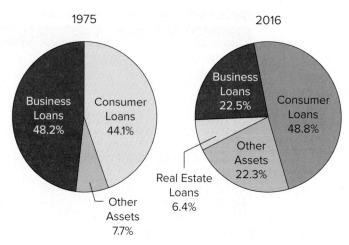

commercial banks. In 1994 and 1996, auto finance companies charged interest rates that were 1.67 and 0.79 percent higher than those of commercial banks. Because new car sales by U.S. firms in 1997 through 1999 were lower than normal, finance companies owned by the major auto manufacturers slashed the interest rates charged on new car loans (some as low as 0.9 percent) over this period. Moreover, after the terrorist attacks in September 2001 the major auto manufacturers lowered new car rates to 0.0 percent in an attempt to boost sales. Some of these 0.0 percent rates continued to be offered into 2005 as the general level of interest rates remained low. The 2008–2009 financial crisis saw a resurection of 0.0 percent car loan rates as auto manufacturers tried to boost slumping car sales. Notice that the difference between new car loans at commercial banks and finance companies continued to widen throughout the early 2000s. By 2003 finance companies were charging more than 3.53 percent less on new car loans than commercial banks, mainly due to the zero interest rates offered by the major auto manufacturers' captive finance company loans to new car buyers. It was not until 2013 that the historical trend returned as finance companies charged an average rate on new car loans that was 0.24 percent higher than commercial banks. Other than for new auto loans, these types of low rates are rare. Other consumer loans include personal cash loans, mobile home loans, and loans to purchase other types of consumer goods such as appliances, apparel, general merchandise, and recreation vehicles.

Finance companies generally charge higher rates for consumer loans because they generally attract riskier customers than commercial banks. In fact, customers who seek individual (or business) loans from finance companies are often those who have been refused loans at banks or thrifts.[6] It is, in fact, possible for individuals to obtain a mortgage from a **subprime lender** finance company (a finance company that lends to high-risk customers) even with a bankruptcy in their credit records. Banks rarely make such loans. Most finance companies that offer these mortgages, however, charge rates commensurate with the higher risk, and a few **loan shark** finance companies prey on desperate consumers, charging exorbitant rates as high as 30 percent or more per year. These predatory lenders often target disadvantaged borrowers who are not aware of the risks they are undertaking with these loans. Predatory lending by loan sharks often leads to the bankruptcy of disadvantaged borrowers.

Another case of a subprime lender is the payday lender. *Payday lenders* provide short-term cash advances that are often due when borrowers receive their next paycheck. The payday lending industry originated from check cashing outlets in the early 1990s and exploded in the 2000s as demand for short-term loans rose. By 2016, an estimated 12 million Americans used payday loans. Industry lending volume topped $46 billion and revenues exceeded $11 billion. While the number of payday stores declined slightly from 2007 to 2016, there were still 16,000 payday stores open in 2016. A typical borrower takes out a two-week loan and pays $15 for every $100 borrowed, or the equivalent of a 390 percent annual interest rate. The typical customer earns between $25,000 and $50,000 per year. As of the second quarter of 2016, payday lender Cash America International had $134.7 million in payday loans on its balance sheet and charged $21.8 million in interest and fees. Critics claim that rates are exorbitant and often trap financially strapped borrowers in a cycle of paying additional fees to renew the same amount of principal. Lenders

**subprime lender**

*A finance company that lends to high-risk customers.*

**loan sharks**

*Subprime lenders that charge unfairly exorbitant rates to desperate, subprime borrowers.*

**TABLE 14–7** Consumer Credit Interest Rates for 1994–2016

| Type | 1994 | 1996 | 1997 | 2003 | 2007 | 2010 | 2012 | 2013 | 2016 |
|---|---|---|---|---|---|---|---|---|---|
| Commercial bank new car | 8.12% | 9.05% | 9.02% | 6.93% | 7.77% | 6.21% | 4.82% | 4.46% | 4.15% |
| Auto finance company new car | 9.79 | 9.84 | 7.12 | 3.40 | 4.87 | 4.26 | 4.60 | 4.70 | 5.00 |
| Difference in commercial bank versus finance company rate | 1.67 | 0.79 | −1.90 | −3.53 | −2.90 | −1.95 | −0.22 | 0.24 | 0.85 |

**Sources:** Federal Reserve Board, *Flow of Funds Accounts,* various issues. www.federalreserve.gov

6. We look at the analysis of borrower (credit) risk in Chapter 20.

argue that the high rates are necessary to cover costs, offset higher default rates, and still earn a profit.

The payday loan industry is regulated at the state level. As of 2016, 15 states had effectively banned payday lending. When not explicitly banned, laws that prohibit payday lending are usually in the form of usury limits. Some payday lenders have succeeded in getting around usury laws in some states by forming relationships with nationally chartered banks based in a different state with no usury ceiling (such as South Dakota or Delaware). As federal banking regulators became aware of this practice, they began prohibiting these partnerships between commercial banks and payday lenders. The FDIC still allows its member banks to participate in payday lending, but it did issue guidelines in March 2005 that are meant to discourage long-term debt cycles by transitioning to a longer-term loan after six payday loan renewals.

In June 2016, the Consumer Financial Protection Bureau proposed new rules that would completely change how payday lenders do business: preventing them from burdening customers with unpayable debts. The rules would require lenders to check their customers' credit and verify that they can afford to repay their loans while still covering basic living expenses. They would also make it harder for borrowers to take out one loan after another, as is now common with payday lending. If borrowers wanted to roll over their debt, or take out a new short-term loan within 30 days of paying off a different one, they would have to show that their personal financial circumstances had "significantly improved." After three successive payday loans, the customer would be required to take a 30-day "cooling off period," during which they could not borrow any more. Finally, the new regulations would prevent lenders from charging customers excessive penalty fees. The proposed regulations are designed to prevent the recipients of payday loans from overborrowing. Successfully implemented, these rules would end payday lending as it currently operates.

*Mortgages.*     Residential and commercial mortgages have become a major component in finance companies' asset portfolios, although they did not generally offer mortgages prior to 1979 (see Figure 14–9). Finance companies, which are not subject to as extensive a set of regulations as are banks, are often willing to issue mortgages to riskier borrowers than commercial banks. They compensate for the additional risk by charging higher interest rates. Mortgages include all loans secured by liens on any type of real estate (see Chapter 7). The mortgages in the loan portfolio can be first mortgages or second mortgages in the form of home equity loans. **Home equity loans** allow customers to borrow on a line of credit secured with a second mortgage on their home. Home equity loans have become very profitable for finance companies since the Tax Reform Act of 1986 was passed, disallowing the tax deductibility of consumers' interest payments other than those made on home mortgages. Also, the bad debt expense and administrative costs of home equity loans are lower than on other finance company loans, and as a result they have become a very attractive product to finance companies.

Finance companies' mortgage portfolios also include **securitized mortgage assets.** Securitization of mortgages involves the pooling of a group of mortgages with similar characteristics, the removal of those mortgages from the balance sheet, and the subsequent sale of cash flows from the mortgage pool to secondary market investors in return for their purchase of bonds (mortgage-backed securities—see Chapters 7 and 24). Thus, securitization of mortgages results in the creation of mortgage-backed securities (e.g., government agency securities, collateralized mortgage obligations), which can be traded in secondary mortgage markets.

In addition to income from securitizing mortgage assets, finance companies earn income when they continue to service the original mortgages. **Mortgage servicing** is a fee-related business whereby, after mortgages are securitized, the flow of mortgage repayments (interest and principal) has to be collected and passed on (by the mortgage servicer) to investors in either whole mortgage loan packages or securitization vehicles such as pass-through securities (see Chapters 7 and 24). In undertaking this intermediation activity, the

**home equity loans**

*Loans that let customers borrow on a line of credit secured with a second mortgage on their home.*

**securitized mortgage assets**

*Mortgages packaged and used as assets backing secondary market securities.*

**mortgage servicing**

*A fee-related business whereby the flow of mortgage repayments is collected and passed on to investors in whole mortgage loan packages or securitization vehicles.*

servicer charges a fee. As discussed below, in 2007–2008 a sharp rise in late payments and defaults by subprime and even relatively strong credit mortgage and home equity loan borrowers caused large losses for mortgage lenders and mortgage-backed securities investors and, ultimately, was the root cause of the financial crisis of 2008–2009.

*Business Loans.* Business loans represent 28.9 percent of the loan portfolio of finance companies. Finance companies have several advantages over commercial banks in offering loan services to small-business customers. First, they are not subject to regulations that restrict the type of products and services they can offer (discussed later). Second, because finance companies do not accept deposits, they have no bank-type regulators monitoring their behavior.[7] Third, being (in many cases) subsidiaries of corporate-sector holding companies, finance companies often have substantial industry and product expertise. Fourth—as mentioned with consumer loans—finance companies are more willing to accept risky customers than are commercial banks. Fifth, finance companies generally have lower overheads than banks (e.g., they do not need expensive tellers/branches for deposit taking).

The major subcategories of business loans are retail and wholesale motor vehicle loans and leases (37.5 percent of all business loans in 2016), equipment loans (38.1 percent), and other business loans (24.4 percent). Motor vehicle loans consist of retail loans that assist in transactions between the retail seller of the good and the ultimate consumer (i.e., cars purchased by individuals and passenger car fleets purchased by a business for use by its employees). Wholesale loans are loan agreements between parties other than the companies' consumers. For example, Ford Motor Credit Company (FMCC) provides wholesale financing to Ford Motor Company dealers for inventory floor plans in which FMCC pays for Ford dealers' auto inventories received from Ford. FMCC puts a lien on each car on the showroom floor. While the dealer pays periodic interest on the floor plan loan, it is not until the car is sold that the dealer pays for the car.

Business-lending activities of finance companies also include equipment loans, with the finance company either owning or leasing the equipment directly to its industrial customer or providing the financial backing for a working capital loan or a loan to purchase or remodel the customer's facility. Finance companies often prefer to lease equipment rather than sell and finance the purchase of equipment. One reason for this is that repossession of the equipment in the event of default is less complicated when the finance company retains its title (by leasing). Further, a lease agreement generally requires no down payment, making a lease more attractive to the business customer. Finally, when the finance company retains ownership of the equipment (by leasing), it receives a tax deduction in the form of depreciation expense on the equipment. Other business loans include loans to businesses to finance or purchase accounts receivable at a discount (factoring), small farm loans, and wholesale loans and leases for mobile homes, campers, and trailers.

**Liabilities and Equity.** As mentioned earlier, unlike commercial banks and thrifts, finance companies cannot accept deposits. Rather, to finance assets, finance companies rely primarily on bank loans, short-term commercial paper, and other debt instruments (longer-term notes and bonds). As data in Table 14–4 indicate, in 2016 bank loans amounted to $152.4 billion (8.4 percent of total assets), commercial paper was $113.4 billion (6.2 percent), and other debt (due to parent holding companies and notes, bonds, and debentures) totaled $1,102.8 billion (60.6 percent). Debt due to parent includes all short- and long-term debt owed to the parent company of the finance company (e.g., debt Ford Motor Credit Corp. owes to Ford Motor Corp.). If the finance company subsidiary has a bad year and cannot make promised payments on its debt, the parent company is less likely than external fund providers to initiate legal proceedings against the finance company. However, given its large percentage funding, the parent to a finance

---

**DO YOU UNDERSTAND:**

15. *How the major assets held by finance companies have changed in the last 35 years?*

16. *How subprime lender finance company customers differ from consumer loan customers at commercial banks?*

17. *What advantages finance companies offer over commercial banks to small-business customers?*

---

7. Finance companies do, of course, have market participants observing their work and monitoring their activities.

company is susceptible to large losses of its own if the finance company subsidiary has a bad year. Total capital comprised $248.9 billion (13.7 percent of total assets). In comparison, commercial banks financed 76.1 percent of their assets with deposits, 10.4 percent with other interest-bearing liabilities, 2.2 percent with non-interest-bearing liabilities, and 11.3 percent with equity.

### Industry Performance

In the early 2000s, the outlook for the finance company industry as a whole was quite bright. Interest rates remained near historical lows. Mortgage refinancing grew. Loan demand among lower- and middle-income consumers was strong. The largest finance companies—those that lend to less risky individual and business customers and with few subprime borrowers (e.g., HSBC Finance)—experienced strong profits and loan growth.

In the mid- and late 2000s, problems for industry participants that specialized in loans to relatively lower-quality customers created large losses in the industry and a problem for the U.S. economy as a whole. As home prices began to fall in 2005 through 2007 and borrowers faced rising interest rates, more people defaulted on their mortgages. At the end of 2006, the percentage of subprime mortgage loans on which payments were at least 60 days late was 14 percent, up from 6 percent in early 2005. With delinquencies and defaults by borrowers rising, finance companies experienced large losses. The results were sharply lower equity values for finance companies. For example, Countrywide Financial, the country's leading mortgage lender, lost over half its market value in the summer and fall of 2007 as it announced continued losses in its subprime mortgage portfolio. Only a $2 billion equity investment by Bank of America in 2007 and then an acquisition offer in 2008 kept this finance company alive. In March 2008, the FBI announced a probe of Countrywide for possible securities fraud. The inquiry involved whether company officials made misrepresentations about the company's financial position and the quality of its mortgage loans in securities filings.

This crash in the subprime mortgage market led to serious problems for the U.S. and worldwide economies as a whole. As noted earlier, the crisis resulted in the failure of Countrywide Financial and the forced conversion of GMAC Financial Services to a bank holding company in order to prevent its failure. Another notable failure was that of CIT Group, which filed for Chapter 11 bankruptcy in November 2009. In 2008, CIT was a lender to nearly 1 million mostly small and midsized businesses. As the financial crisis hit, many of its borrowers became delinquent or defaulted on their loans. While CIT's failure would not have affected financial markets to the same extent as the failure of a large commercial bank such as Citigroup, it could have hurt the flow of credit to many businesses to which banks traditionally do not lend. As a result, in December 2008 the Federal Reserve approved CIT Group as a bank holding company, clearing a key hurdle for the firm to bolster its resources with loans and support from the government's financial rescue fund. However, as the financial crisis wore on, losses mounted and CIT was forced to file for bankruptcy protection. At the time of bankruptcy, CIT had assets of $71 billion and liabilities of $65 billion. The bankruptcy eliminated $10 billion of this debt, including $2.3 billion extended to CIT in 2008 as part of the taxpayer bailout of the finance company. The bankruptcy of CIT Group was one of the largest filings ever of a U.S. company—trailing only the likes of Lehman Brothers, Washington Mutual, and General Motors.

As was true with depository institutions, as the U.S. economy improved in the late 2000s and early 2010s, the finance company industry improved as well. In the mid-2010s, industry median ROE rose to 9.33 percent, up from 6.61 percent during the height of the crisis. For business credit institutions ROE rose to 13.73 percent, up from 5.31 percent during the height of the crisis. Further, industry assets were $1.82 trillion in the mid-2010s, up from $1.59 trillion during the crisis. However, financial crisis issues remained even into 2016. Industry receivables stood at $1.43 trillion in the mid-2010s, down from $1.93 trillion during the crisis, while industry employment was 562,400 in the mid-2010s, down from 715,900 as the financial crisis began.

LG 14-9

## Regulation

The Federal Reserve defines a finance company as a firm whose primary assets are loans to individuals and businesses.[8] Finance companies, like depository institutions, are financial intermediaries that borrow funds so as to profit on the difference between the rates paid on borrowed funds and those charged on loans. Also like depository institutions, finance companies may be subject to state-imposed usury ceilings on the maximum loan rates assigned to individual customers and are regulated to the extent to which they can collect on delinquent loans (e.g., the legal mechanisms to be followed, such as Chapter 7 and 11 bankruptcy regulations). However, because finance companies do not accept deposits, they are not subject to extensive oversight by federal and state regulators, as are banks or thrifts—even though they offer services that compete directly with those of depository institutions (e.g., consumer installment loans and mortgages). The lack of regulatory oversight for these companies enables them to offer a wide scope of "bank-like" services and yet avoid the expense of regulatory compliance and the same "net regulatory burden" imposed on banks and thrifts (see Chapter 13).

However, because of the impact that nonbank FIs, including finance companies, had on the U.S. economy during the financial crisis and as a result of the need for the Federal Reserve to rescue several nonbank FIs, regulators proposed that nonbank FIs receive more oversight. At the height of the financial crisis the Fed stepped in to rescue numerous finance companies, including GMAC (now Ally Financial), GE Capital, and CIT Group. Additionally, credit lenders American Express and Discover Financial (as well as investment banks Goldman Sachs and Morgan Stanley) were granted charters to become bank holding companies in 2008. For example, GE Capital's exposure to the 2008–2009 financial crisis resulted in General Electric Corp.'s market value falling by more than half during 2008 (GE Capital accounted for about half of GE's sales and profit). To reassure investors and help GE Capital compete with banks that already had government protection behind their debt, on November 12, 2008, the FDIC approved GE Capital's application for designation as an eligible entity under the FDIC's Temporary Liquidity Guarantee Program (TLGP). Granting this finance company access to the FDIC program was possible because GE Capital also owns a federal savings bank and an industrial loan company, both of which qualified for FDIC assistance. The terms of these agreements included, among other things, a requirement that GE and GE Capital reimburse the FDIC for any amounts paid by the FDIC to holders of debt guaranteed by the FDIC. December 24, 2008, was a key turning point in GMAC's history when it was approved as a bank holding company by the Federal Reserve Board under the Bank Holding Company Act. GMAC had been hit with huge losses in both its mortgage and auto loan businesses during the financial crisis. Its mortgage unit, Residential Capital, had suffered significant losses on home loans it made during the housing boom of the early and mid-2000s. The company lost $8 billion in 2007–2008. In light of the impact that GMAC's losses were having on the financial markets, and to help ensure the survival of the company, federal regulators permitted the financing arm of General Motors (renamed Ally Financial) to become a bank holding company.

As a result, as part of the Wall Street Reform and Consumer Protection Act of 2010, the federal government was provided with the tools it needed to manage financial crises by establishing (1) a new regime to resolve nonbank financial institutions whose failure could have serious systemic effects and (2) revisions to the Federal Reserve's emergency lending authority to improve accountability. The act also proposed robust supervision and regulation of all financial firms by establishing (1) a new Financial Services Oversight Council of financial regulators (chaired by the Treasury and including the heads of the principal federal financial regulators as members) to identify emerging systemic risks and improve interagency cooperation; (2) a new authority for the Federal Reserve to supervise all firms that could pose a threat to

---

8. In contrast, a bank is defined as an institution that both accepts deposits *and* makes loans.

financial stability, even those that do not own banks; and (3) stronger capital and other prudential standards for all financial firms and even higher standards for large, interconnected firms.

By 2016, some of these companies realized the burden of increased regulation was extensive and took steps to get out from under them. For example, to escape stricter regulations, in June 2016 GE Capital signed agreements for the sale of about $180 billion of businesses and closed about $156 billion of those transactions. The company had $500 billion in assets at the end of 2014. The goal was to sell around $260 billion in total assets by the end of 2017. Because GE Capital had shrunk and restructured the business, the U.S. Financial Stability Oversight Council removed GE Capital's designation as a "systemically important" financial institution, a label that had required the company to submit to stricter rules and supervision by the Federal Reserve. GE's case marked the first time the oversight council has removed a "systemically important" designation since the tag was created under the 2010 Wall Street Reform and Consumer Protection Act.

Since finance companies are heavy borrowers in the capital markets and do not enjoy the same regulatory "safety net" as banks, they need to signal their safety and solvency to investors. Such signals are usually sent by holding much higher equity or capital-to-assets ratios—and therefore, lower leverage ratios—than banks. For example, the 2016 aggregate balance sheet for finance companies (Table 14–4) shows a capital-to-assets ratio of 13.7 percent. This compares to the capital-to-assets ratio of 11.3 percent for commercial banks. Larger captive finance companies also use default protection guarantees from their parent companies and/or other guarantees, such as letters of credit or lines of credit purchased for a fee from high-quality commercial or investment banks, as additional protection against insolvency risk and as a device to increase their ability to raise additional funds in the capital and money markets. Thus, this group will tend to operate with lower capital-to-assets ratios than smaller finance companies. Given that regulatory oversight of this industry is relatively light, having sufficient capital and access to financial guarantees are critical to their continued ability to raise funds. Thus, finance companies operate more like nonfinancial, nonregulated companies than the other types of financial institutions examined in this text.

## GLOBAL ISSUES

In contrast to savings institutions in the United States, which must have at least 65 percent of their assets in the form of mortgages (or they lose their charter), savings institutions and cooperative banks (similar to credit unions in the U.S.) in Europe were created in the 19th century to channel individuals' savings into the continent's commercial industry. Savings institutions also served as an instrument for providing basic banking services to the poor. The majority of savings institutions in Europe are mutuals (owned by local officials, religious organizations, unions, and deposit holders) rather than stock-owned depository institutions. In the late 2000s, deregulation, liberalization, and privatization changed the role of these FIs. These institutions were regarded as old-fashioned, outdated, and inefficient. In some European countries, savings banks and cooperative banks completely disappeared as specific groups of financial institutions; in others, they changed so much that it was difficult to distinguish between these institutions and commercial banks. However, the problems in and the failures of commercial banks during the financial crisis changed the way that savings and cooperative banks were viewed. Indeed, many policymakers and regulators adopted policy initiatives to try to make all banks behave a bit more like the savings banks and cooperative banks.

There are two features that all savings banks in Europe have in common: (1) their focus on savings and savings mobilization and (2) their clear regional and even local focus. Cooperative banks are regional banks. They adhere to the regional principle; they are parts of dense networks that foster within-group cooperation, and they also have a dual objective. Savings banks play the dominant important role in some countries such as Spain and Germany, while cooperative banks dominate in others such as France. In some countries, both banking groups play an important role (e.g., in Austria and in Germany). In other countries, one of the two banking groups clearly dominates the other one.

While commercial banks are the most important source of credit supply in many foreign countries, particularly emerging market economies, nonbank financial institutions (finance companies, credit unions, and building societies) not only account for a substantial part of the outstanding credit by all financial institutions, but their relative importance has been increasing over the past decade. Specialized consumer finance agencies operate throughout western Europe, Canada, Australia, Japan, and some Latin American countries. For example, from 1994 to the 2010s, the percentage of aggregate credit issued by nonbank financial institutions increased from 22 percent to 35 percent in Latin America and from 4 percent to 15 percent in central Europe. In Thailand, nonbank financial institutions, particularly those specializing in credit card lending, gained market share. This trend also occurred in Mexico, where specialized mortgage institutions now dominate low-income mortgage lending. Large sales finance companies specialize in financing purchases of particular commodities and remain closely associated with specific manufacturers. Some also extend credit for wholesale purchases by retail dealers.

While the financial crisis affected the operations of finance companies, they still remained a major part of the financial sector in countries worldwide. For example, in New Zealand the financial crisis led to the consolidation, collapse, and restructuring of many of the country's finance companies. Further, in Russia significant finance company staff reductions occurred during the financial crisis. Because regulations in most foreign countries are not as restrictive as those in the United States, finance companies in foreign countries are generally subsidiaries of commercial banks or industrial firms. For those finance companies owned by commercial banks, as the bank goes, so does the finance company. Some of the major multinational business financing companies include Alliance Leicester Commercial Bank (part of Santander Group, United Kingdom), Commercial Lifeline (United Kingdom), Finance Eai (Australia), Five Arrows Commercial Finance (Australia), Lloyds TSB (United Kingdom), Lombard (United Kingdom), and SME Commercial Finance (Australia).

## SUMMARY

This chapter provided an overview of the major activities of savings institutions, credit unions, and finance companies. Savings institutions and credit unions rely heavily on deposits to fund loans, whereas finance companies do not accept deposits but fund themselves mainly with commercial paper and long-term security issues. Historically, while commercial banks have concentrated on commercial or business lending and on investing in securities, savings institutions have concentrated on mortgage lending and credit unions on consumer lending. Finance companies also compete directly with depository institutions for high-quality (prime) loan customers. Further, this industry services those subprime (high-risk) borrowers deemed too risky for depository institutions. These differences are being eroded due to competitive forces, regulation, and the changing nature of financial and business technology, so that the types of interest rate, credit, liquidity, and operational risks faced by commercial banks, savings institutions, credit unions, and finance companies are becoming increasingly similar.

## QUESTIONS

1. How do the balance sheets of savings institutions differ from those of commercial banks? How do their sizes compare? (*LG 14-1*)

2. What were the reasons for the crisis of the savings institutions industry in the mid-1980s? (*LG 14-1*)

3. What two major pieces of legislation were adopted in the late 1980s and early 1990s to ameliorate the thrift crisis? Explain. (*LG 14-1*)

4. What are the main assets and liabilities held by savings institutions? (*LG 14-2*)

5. What regulatory agencies oversee deposit insurance services to savings institutions? (*LG 14-3*)

6. What does it mean when a savings institution is a mutual organization? (*LG 14-1*)

7. How has the savings institution industry performed over the last several decades? (*LG 14-4*)

8. How do credit unions differ from savings institutions? (*LG 14-1*)

9. How and why is credit union membership limited? (*LG 14-5*)

10. Why were credit unions less affected by the sharp increase in interest rates in the late 1970s and early 1980s than the savings institution industry? (*LG 14-5*)

11. Describe the three-tier system that makes up the credit union industry. (*LG 14-5*)

12. How does the size of the credit union industry compare to the commercial banking industry? (*LG 14-5*)

13. What are the main assets and liabilities held by credit unions? (*LG 14-6*)

14. Who are the regulators of credit unions? (*LG 14-6*)

15. Why did commercial banks pursue legal action against the credit union industry in the late 1990s? What was the result of this legal action? (*LG 14-5*)

16. What was Bank Transfer Day? (*LG 14-5*)

17. How have local credit unions performed over the last several decades? (*LG 14-5*)

18. How did the corporate credit unions perform during the financial crisis? (*LG 14-5*)

19. What are the three types of finance companies and how do they differ from commercial banks? (*LG 14-7*)

20. How does the amount of equity as a percentage of assets compare for finance companies and commercial banks? What accounts for the difference? (*LG 14-8*)

21. What are the major assets and liabilities held by finance companies? (*LG 14-8*)

22. What has been the fastest-growing area of asset business for finance companies? (*LG 14-8*)

23. Why was the reported rate on motor vehicle loans historically higher for a finance company than a commercial bank? Why did this change in 1997? (*LG 14-8*)

24. What advantages do finance companies have over banks in offering services to small-business customers? (*LG 14-8*)

25. Why are finance companies less regulated than commercial banks? (*LG 14-9*)

26. Why have finance companies begun to offer more mortgage and home equity loans? (*LG 14-7*)

27. What is a wholesale motor vehicle loan? (*LG 14-8*)

28. What signal does a low debt-to-assets ratio for a finance company send to the capital markets? (*LG 14-8*)

---

## SEARCH THE SITE

Go to the FDIC website at **www.fdic.gov.** Find the most recent breakdown of U.S. savings institution asset concentrations using the following steps. Click on "Analysts." From there click on "FDIC Quarterly Banking Profile." In the "Report Date:" box, click on the most recent date, then click on "Access QBP." Click on "◆ Savings Institution Section." Then click on "TABLE III-B. 20XX, FDIC-Insured Savings Institutions." This will bring up the files that contain the relevant data.

### Questions

1. How has the number of savings institutions and the dollar value of assets held by savings institutions changed since 2016 as reported in Figure 14–3?

2. Calculate the percentage of total industry assets held by savings institutions with asset size under $100 million, between $100 million and $1 billion, between $1 billion and $10 billion, and over $10 billion.

# SEARCH THE SITE

Go to the Credit Union National Association website at **www.cuna.org** to collect the most recent information on the number of credit unions, assets of credit unions, and membership in credit unions using the following steps. Under "Research & Strategy," click on "CREDIT UNION DATA & STATISTICS." Click on "Monthly Credit Union Estimates." This will download a file onto your computer that will contain the necessary data.

**Question**

1. How have these data changed since 2016?

**chapter**

# Insurance Companies

## Learning Goals

**LG 15-1**   *Describe the two types of insurance companies.*

**LG 15-2**   *Review the four basic lines of business performed by life insurance companies.*

**LG 15-3**   *Identify the major assets and liabilities of life insurance companies.*

**LG 15-4**   *Classify the major regulations governing life insurance companies.*

**LG 15-5**   *Analyze the major lines of business performed by property–casualty insurance companies.*

**LG 15-6**   *Identify the main asset and liability items on property–casualty insurance company balance sheets.*

**LG 15-7**   *Recognize the main regulators of property–casualty insurance companies.*

**LG 15-8**   *Describe the major trends occurring in the global insurance market.*

---

**LG 15-1**   **TWO CATEGORIES OF INSURANCE COMPANIES: CHAPTER OVERVIEW**

Insurance services offered by financial institutions (FIs) compensate individuals and corporations (policyholders) if a prespecified adverse event occurs, in exchange for premiums paid to the insurer by the policyholder. The insurance provider can act either as an insurance underwriter or an insurance broker. An insurance underwriter assesses the risk of an applicant for coverage or for a policy. An insurance broker simply sells insurance contracts for coverage or for a policy. Thus, a broker acts more as an intermediary between the insurance underwriter and the applicant. Insurance services are classified into two major groups: (1) life and (2) property–casualty. Life insurance provides protection in the event of untimely death, illnesses, and retirement. Property–casualty insurance protects against personal injury and liability due to accidents, theft, fire, and other catastrophes. Many FIs (e.g., MetLife and Allstate) offer both life and property–casualty services. Further, many FIs that offer insurance services also sell a variety of investment products in a similar fashion to other financial service firms, such as mutual funds (Chapter 17) and commercial banks (Chapter 11).

The 2008–2009 financial crisis showed just how much risk insurance companies can present to FIs and the global financial system. Specifically, as the subprime mortgage market began to fail in the summer of 2008, subprime mortgage pools that FIs bought ended up falling precipitously in value as defaults and foreclosures rose on the underlying mortgage pools. Many credit default swaps (CDSs) were written on these subprime mortgage securities, basically acting as insurance on the debt. As mortgage security losses started to rise, buyers of the CDS contracts wanted to be paid for these losses. Insurance company American International Group (AIG) was a major issuer of these CDS securities. When mortgage-backed securities started to fall in value, AIG had to make good on billions of dollars of credit default swaps. Soon it became clear that AIG was not going to be able to cover its credit default swap market losses. The result was a significant increase in the risk exposure of banks, investment banks, and insurance companies that had purchased AIG CDS insurance contracts. Indeed, the reason the federal government stepped in and bailed out AIG was that the insurer was a dominant player in the CDS market. Had AIG defaulted, every FI that had bought a CDS contract from the company would have suffered substantial losses.

This chapter discusses the main features of insurance companies by concentrating on (1) the size, structure, and composition of the industry in which they operate; (2) their balance sheets and recent trends; and (3) regulations. We also look at global competition and trends in this industry.

# LIFE INSURANCE COMPANIES

Life insurance allows individuals and their beneficiaries to protect against losses in income through premature death or retirement. By pooling risks, life insurance transfers income-related uncertainties from the insured individual to a group.

## Size, Structure, and Composition of the Industry

In 2015, the United States had approximately 872 life insurance companies, compared to over 2,300 in 1988. The aggregate assets of life insurance companies were $6.47 trillion at the beginning of 2016, compared to $1.12 trillion in 1988. The four largest life insurers in terms of total assets (listed in Table 15–1) wrote 30.5 percent of the industry's over $681 billion premiums in 2015. Interestingly, many of these insurance policies are sold through commercial banks. For example, in 2015 commercial banks sold over 17 percent of all annuity contracts. Although not to the extent seen in the banking industry, the life insurance industry has experienced major mergers in recent years (e.g., Centene and HealthNet, and the pending mergers of Anthem and Cigna and Aetna and Humana) as competition within the industry and with other FIs has increased. Like consolidation in commercial banking, the consolidation of the insurance industry has mainly occurred to take advantage of economies of scale and scope and other synergies (see Chapter 11).

**TABLE 15–1**  Largest Life Insurers

| Rank | Insurance Company | Assets (in billions) |
|------|-------------------|----------------------|
| 1. | Metropolitan Life | $607.6 |
| 2. | Prudential of America Group | 541.3 |
| 3. | New York Life Group | 287.8 |
| 4. | TIAA Group | 280.5 |
| 5. | American International Group | 270.6 |
| 6. | John Hancock Group | 253.4 |
| 7. | Northwestern Mutual Group | 238.6 |
| 8. | Lincoln Financial Group | 228.2 |
| 9. | Mass Mutual Group | 222.2 |
| 10. | Aegon USA Group | 207.8 |

**Sources:** *Best's Review,* July 2016. www.ambest.com; and authors' research.

Life insurance allows individuals to protect themselves and their beneficiaries against the risk of loss of income in the event of death or retirement. By pooling the risks of individual customers, life insurance companies can diversify away some of the customer-specific risk and offer insurance services at a cost (premium) lower than any individual could achieve saving funds on his or her own. Thus, life insurance companies transfer income-related uncertainties such as those due to retirement from the individual to a group. Although life insurance may be their core activity area, modern life insurance companies also sell annuity contracts (primarily savings contracts that involve the liquidation of those funds saved over a period of time), manage pension plans (tax-deferred savings plans), and provide accident and health insurance. Figure 15–1 shows the distribution of premiums written for the various lines of insurance in 2016. We discuss these different activity lines below.

In return for insurance premiums, insurance companies accept or underwrite the risk that the prespecified event will occur. The major part of the insurance company underwriting process is deciding which requests for insurance (or risks) they should accept and which ones they should reject. Further, for those risks they accept, they must decide how much they should charge for the insurance. For example, an insurance company would not want to provide life insurance to someone with terminal cancer. Alternatively, the insurer may decide to insure a smoker but charge a higher premium than is charged to a non-smoker. Further, an increased probability of a major pandemic, such as the possibility that the bird flu could mutate to become highly lethal to humans, might cause insurance companies to increase life and health insurance premiums charged to all insured groups. Thus, the underwriting process is critical to an insurance company's profitability and survival.

One problem faced by life insurance companies (as well as property–casualty insurers) is the **adverse selection problem.** Adverse selection is the problem that customers who apply for insurance policies are more likely to be those most in need of insurance (i.e., someone with chronic health problems is more likely to purchase a life insurance policy than someone in perfect health). Thus, in calculating the probability of having to pay out on an insurance contract and, in turn, determining the insurance premium to charge, insurance companies' use of health (and other) statistics representing the overall population may not be appropriate (since the insurance company's pool of customers is likely to be more prone to health problems than the overall population). Insurance companies deal with the adverse selection problem by establishing different pools of the population based on health and related characteristics (such as income). By altering the pool used to determine the probability of losses to a particular customer's health characteristics, the insurance company can more accurately determine the probability of having to pay out on a policy and can adjust the insurance premium accordingly.

Actuaries have traditionally worked in life insurance to reduce the risks associated with underwriting and selling life insurance. With traditional life insurance, actuarial science focuses on the analysis of mortality, the production of life tables, and the application

**adverse selection problem**

*The problem that customers who apply for insurance policies are more likely to be those most in need of coverage.*

**Figure 15–1**    Distribution of Premiums Written on Various Life Insurance Lines

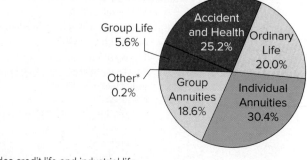

*Includes credit life and industrial life.

**Source:** Insurance Information Institute website, 2016. www.iii.org

of time value of money to produce life insurance, annuities, and endowment policies. In health insurance, actuarial science focuses on the analyses of rates of disability, morbidity, mortality, fertility, and other contingencies.

As the various types of insurance policies and services offered are described below, notice that some policies (such as universal life policies and annuities) provide not only insurance features but also savings components. For example, universal life policy payouts are a function of the interest earned on the investment of the policyholder's premiums.[1] Similarly, annuities offer the policyholder a fixed or variable payment each period (generally monthly) for life or over some predetermined future horizon.

**LG 15-2**

**Life Insurance.** The four basic classes or lines of life insurance are distinguished by the manner in which they are sold or marketed to purchasers. These classes are (1) ordinary life, (2) group life, (3) credit life, and (4) other activities. Of the life insurance policies in force in the United States, ordinary life accounts for 77.8 percent, group life for 21.6 percent, and credit life for less than 1 percent of the over $175.1 billion in premiums written.

*Ordinary Life.* Ordinary life insurance policies are marketed on an individual basis, usually in units of $1,000; policyholders make periodic premium payments in return for insurance coverage. Despite the enormous variety of contractual forms, there are essentially five basic contractual types. The first three are traditional forms of ordinary life insurance, and the last two are newer contracts that originated in the 1970s and 1980s when competition for savings from other segments of the financial services industry, such as mutual funds, increased. The three traditional contractual forms are term life, whole life, and endowment life. The two newer forms are variable life and universal life. The key features of each of these contractual forms are identified as follows:

- **Term Life.** This policy is the closest to pure life insurance; it has no savings element attached. Essentially, as long as premium payments are up to date, an individual's beneficiary receives a payout at the time of the individual's death during the coverage period. If the insured individual lives beyond the term of the contract, the contract expires along with any rights to benefits. The term of coverage can vary from as little as 1 year to 40 years or more.
- **Whole Life.** This policy protects the individual over an entire lifetime rather than for a specified coverage period. In return for periodic or level premiums, the individual's beneficiaries receive the face value of the life insurance contract on death. Thus, if the policyholder continues premium payments, the insurance company is certain to make a payment—unlike term insurance, where a payment is made only if death occurs during the coverage period. In the early years of the contract, premiums are larger than those for term life contracts and in the later years they are smaller. The overpayment in the early years creates a cash value for whole life contracts that insured individuals can borrow against (at a stated rate paid to the insurance company).
- **Endowment Life.** This type of policy combines a pure (term) insurance element with a savings element. It guarantees a payout to the beneficiaries of the policy if death occurs during some endowment period (e.g., prior to reaching retirement age). An insured person who lives to the endowment date receives the face amount of the policy.
- **Variable Life.** Unlike traditional policies that promise to pay the insured the fixed or face amount of a policy should a contingency arise, variable life insurance invests fixed premium payments in mutual funds of stocks, bonds, and money market instruments. Usually, policyholders can choose mutual fund investments to reflect their risk

---

1. The universal life policyholder buys a policy in which the underlying investments will build cash value over time. The policyholder funds the policy for a certain number of years and the growth in the cash value eventually negates the need for additional premiums. At retirement the policyholder can withdraw cash as a tax-free loan for retirement. The loans are never repaid and the only result is that the death benefit is reduced. Among the limitations of this strategy are that the underlying investments may perform below expectations, the policyholder may not be able to fund the policy at the expected level, and the policyholder might withdraw too much cash from the policy, thus triggering a taxable event.

preferences. Thus, variable life provides an alternative way to build savings compared to the more traditional policies such as whole life because the value of the policy increases (or decreases) with the asset returns of the mutual fund in which premiums are invested.

- **Universal Life and Variable Universal Life.** A universal life policy allows the insured to change both the premium amounts and the maturity of the life insurance contract, unlike traditional policies that maintain premiums at a given level over a fixed contract period. In addition, for some contracts, insurers invest premiums in money, equity, or bond mutual funds—as in variable life insurance—so that the savings or investment component of the contract reflects market returns. In this case, the policy is called *variable universal life.*

---

### EXAMPLE 15-1    Differences in Various Types of Ordinary Life Insurance Contracts

An individual wants to purchase ordinary life insurance, but she is unsure of the differences between the various types of contracts. She contacts a local insurance agent to compare and contrast them. He summarizes them as follows:

**Term Life:** Contract expires, no savings (policyholder gets nothing if he or she is alive when the contract expires), beneficiary receives face value on death during contract period.
**Whole Life:** No expiration, beneficiary receives face value on death, policyholder can borrow against cash value of contract.
**Endowment Life:** Contract expires, policyholder gets face value of contract on expiration if still alive, beneficiary receives face value on death during contract period.
**Variable Life:** No expiration, premiums invested in mutual funds, beneficiary receives variable amount on death (a function of the return on the underlying investments).
**Universal Life:** No expiration, premiums can vary, premiums invested in mutual funds, beneficiary receives variable amount on death (a function of premiums invested and the return on the underlying investments).

---

*Group Life Insurance.*   Group life insurance covers a large number of insured persons under a single policy. Usually issued to corporate employers, these policies may be either *contributory* (where both the employer and employee cover a share of the employee's cost of the insurance) or *noncontributory* (where the employee does not contribute to the cost of the insurance; rather the cost is paid entirely by the employer) for the employees themselves. The principal advantage of group life over ordinary life policies involves cost economies. These occur as the result of mass administration of plans, lower costs for evaluating individuals through medical screening and other rating systems, and reduced selling and commission costs.

*Credit Life.*   Credit life insurance protects lenders against a borrower's death prior to the repayment of a debt contract such as a mortgage or car loan. Usually, the face amount of the insurance policy reflects the outstanding principal and interest on the loan. As mentioned above, credit life policies represent less than 1 percent of the total market. Their cost per unit of coverage is usually much higher than other methods of covering these liabilities in the event of unexpected death. Thus, they are a rarely used type of life insurance.

*Other Life Insurer Activities.*   Three other major activities of life insurance companies are the sale of annuities, private pension plans, and accident and health insurance.

*Annuities.*   Annuities represent the reverse of life insurance principles. While life insurance involves different contractual methods to *build up* a fund and the eventual payout of a *lump sum* to the beneficiary, annuities involve different methods of *liquidating* a fund over a *long period* of time, such as paying out a fund's proceeds to the beneficiary. As with life insurance contracts, many different types of annuity contracts have been developed. Specifically, they can be sold to an individual or group and on either a fixed or variable basis by being linked to the return on some underlying investment portfolio. Individuals can purchase annuities with a single payment or payments spread over a number of years. Life insurance and annuity products can be used to create a steady stream of cash disbursements and payments to avoid paying or receiving a single lump sum cash amount. That is, a life insurance policy (whole life or universal life) requires regular premium payments that entitle the beneficiary to the receipt of a single lump sum payment. Upon receipt of such a lump sum, a single annuity could be obtained that would generate regular cash payments until the value of the insurance policy is depleted. Payments may be structured to begin immediately, or they can be *deferred* (e.g., to start at retirement). These payments may cease at death or continue to be paid to beneficiaries for a number of years after death. Any interest earned on annuities is tax deferred (i.e., taxes are not paid until the annuity payments are actually made to the beneficiary). In contrast to individual retirement accounts, or IRAs (see Chapter 18), annual annuity contributions are not capped and are not affected by the policyholder's income level. Thus, annuities have become popular with individuals as a mechanism used to save for retirement. Annuity sales in 2015 topped $236.7 billion ($133.0 billion of which were variable annuities), compared to $26.1 billion in 1996.

---

**EXAMPLE 15–2** Calculation of the Fair Value of an Annuity Policy

Suppose that a person wants to purchase an annuity today that would pay $15,000 after taxes per year until the end of that person's life. The insurance company expects the person to live for 25 more years and can invest the amount received for the annuity at a guaranteed interest rate of 5 percent.[2] The fair price for the annuity policy today can be calculated as follows:

$$\text{Fair value} = \frac{15,000}{1+r} + \frac{15,000}{(1+r)^2} + \cdots + \frac{15,000}{(1+r)^{25}}$$

$$= 15,000 \left[ \frac{1}{1+r} + \frac{1}{(1+r)^2} + \cdots + \frac{1}{(1+r)^{25}} \right]$$

$$= 15,000 \left[ \frac{1 - \dfrac{1}{(1+0.05)^{25}}}{0.05} \right]$$

$$= 15,000 [14.0939]$$

$$= \$211,409$$

Thus, the cost of purchasing this annuity today would be $211,409.

---

*Private Pension Funds.* Insurance companies offer many alternative pension plans to private employers in an effort to attract this business away from other financial service companies such as commercial banks and securities firms. Some of their innovative pension plans are based on guaranteed investment contracts (GICs). With such plans, the insurer guarantees not only the rate of interest credited to a pension plan over some given period—for example, five years—but also the annuity rates on beneficiaries' contracts. Other plans include immediate participation and separate account plans that follow more aggressive investment strategies than traditional life insurance contracts, such as investing premiums in special-purpose equity mutual funds. In 2016, life insurance companies were managing over $3.6 trillion in pension fund assets, equal to 41 percent of all private pension plans.

---

2. One possible way to do this would be for the insurer to buy a 25-year maturity zero-coupon Treasury bond that has an annual discount yield of 5 percent.

*Accident and Health Insurance.* While life insurance protects against mortality risk, accident and health insurance protects against morbidity or ill-health risk. More than $171 billion in accident health premiums were written by life and health companies in 2015. The major activity line is group insurance, which provides health insurance coverage to corporate employees. Life insurance companies write more than 50 percent of all health insurance premiums. In many respects, insurers in accident and health lines face loss exposures that are more similar to those faced by property–casualty insurers, as opposed to traditional life insurers (see the section on property–casualty insurance, which follows shortly).

**LG 15-3**    *Balance Sheets and Recent Trends*

**Assets.** Because of the long-term nature of their liabilities (resulting from the long-term nature of life insurance policyholders' claims) and the need to generate competitive returns on the savings elements of life insurance products, life insurance companies concentrate their asset investments at the longer end of the maturity spectrum (e.g., corporate bonds, equities, and government securities). Table 15–2 shows the distribution of life insurance assets. As you can see, in 2016, 10.8 percent of assets were invested in government securities, 67.6 percent in corporate bonds and stocks, and 6.8 percent in mortgages (commercial and home mort-

**policy loans**

*Loans made by an insurance company to its policyholders using their policies as collateral.*

gages), with other loans—including **policy loans** (i.e., loans made to policyholders using their policies as collateral)—and miscellaneous assets comprising the remaining assets. Although depository institutions are the major issuers of new mortgages (sometimes keeping the mortgages on their books and sometimes selling them to secondary market investors), insurance companies hold mortgages as investment securities. That is, they purchase many mortgages in the secondary markets (see Chapters 7 and 24). The major trend has been a long-term increase in the proportion of bonds and equities[3] and a decline in the proportion of mortgages on life insurers' balance sheets. Thus, insurance company managers must be able to measure and manage the credit risk, interest rate risk, and other risks associated with these securities.

**TABLE 15–2**    **Life Insurance Company Assets** *(distribution of assets of U.S. life insurance companies)*

| | | | Corporate Securities | | | | |
|---|---|---|---|---|---|---|---|
| Year | Total Assets (in billions) | Government Securities | Bonds | Stocks | Mortgages | Policy Loans | Miscellaneous Assets* |
| 1917 | $    5.9 | 9.6% | 33.2% | 1.4% | 34.0% | 13.6% | 5.2% |
| 1920 | 7.3 | 18.4 | 26.7 | 1.0 | 33.4 | 11.7 | 6.5 |
| 1930 | 18.9 | 8.0 | 26.0 | 2.8 | 40.2 | 14.9 | 5.2 |
| 1940 | 30.8 | 27.5 | 28.1 | 2.0 | 19.4 | 10.0 | 6.3 |
| 1950 | 64.0 | 25.2 | 36.3 | 3.3 | 25.1 | 3.8 | 4.1 |
| 1960 | 119.6 | 9.9 | 39.1 | 4.2 | 34.9 | 4.4 | 4.4 |
| 1970 | 207.3 | 5.3 | 35.3 | 7.4 | 35.9 | 7.8 | 5.3 |
| 1980 | 479.2 | 6.9 | 37.5 | 9.9 | 27.4 | 8.6 | 6.6 |
| 1990 | 1,408.2 | 15.0 | 41.4 | 9.1 | 19.2 | 4.4 | 7.8 |
| 2000 | 3,133.9 | 9.3 | 39.1 | 31.5 | 7.5 | 3.2 | 9.4 |
| 2007 | 4,949.7 | 10.0 | 37.6 | 33.4 | 6.6 | 2.9 | 9.5 |
| 2008 | 4,515.5 | 11.5 | 40.3 | 24.9 | 7.6 | 3.6 | 12.1 |
| 2009 | 4,823.9 | 12.0 | 39.9 | 28.0 | 6.8 | 2.9 | 10.4 |
| 2010 | 5,176.3 | 12.5 | 39.2 | 30.1 | 6.1 | 2.7 | 9.4 |
| 2013 | 5,731.9 | 11.6 | 38.2 | 31.8 | 6.0 | 2.6 | 9.8 |
| 2016 | 6,511.9 | 10.8 | 37.5 | 30.1 | 6.8 | 2.5 | 12.3 |

*Includes cash, checkable deposits, and money market funds.
**Note:** Beginning with 1962, these data include the assets of separate accounts.
**Sources:** *Federal Reserve Bulletin,* various issues. www.federalreserve.gov

3. The need for a more certain stream of cash flows to pay off policies is a major reason for the investment in bonds. The bull market of the 1990s is a major reason for the large percentage of assets invested in equities. The large drop in equity prices during the 2008–2009 financial crisis explains the reduction in the percentage of stocks held by insurance companies in the late 2000s.

**TABLE 15–3**   **Life Insurance Industry Balance Sheet** *(in billions of dollars)*

|  |  | Percentage of Total |
|---|---|---|
| **Assets** |  |  |
| Bonds | $2,833.4 | 43.8% |
| Preferred stock | 9.9 | 0.1 |
| Common stock | 79.1 | 1.2 |
| Mortgage loans | 414.8 | 6.4 |
| Real estate | 24.0 | 0.4 |
| Contract loans | 129.7 | 2.0 |
| Cash and short-term investments | 104.0 | 1.6 |
| Other invested assets | 231.5 | 3.6 |
| Premiums due | 30.9 | 0.5 |
| Accrued investment income | 36.9 | 0.6 |
| Separate account assets | 2,437.8 | 37.6 |
| Other assets | 141.6 | 2.2 |
| Total assets | $6,473.6 | 100.0% |
| **Liabilities and Capital/Surplus** |  |  |
| Net policy reserves | $2,853.9 | 44.1% |
| Policy claims | 44.1 | 0.7 |
| Deposit-type contracts | 281.5 | 4.3 |
| Other liabilities | 477.8 | 7.4 |
| Separate account business | 2,435.5 | 37.6 |
| Total capital and surplus | 380.8 | 5.9 |
| Total liabilities and capital/surplus | $6,473.6 | 100.0% |

**Source:** *Best's Aggregates & Averages, Life-Health* (Oldwick, NJ: A.M. Best Company, 2016), p. 84. www.ambest.com

**policy reserves**

*A liability item for insurers that reflects their expected payment commitments on existing policy contracts.*

**surrender value of a policy**

*The cash value of a policy received from the insurer if a policyholder surrenders the policy prior to maturity; normally, only a portion of the contract's face value.*

**separate account**

*Annuity program sponsored by life insurance companies in which the payoff on the policy is linked to the assets in which policy premiums are invested.*

**Liabilities.**   The aggregate balance sheet for the life insurance industry at the beginning of 2016 is presented in Table 15–3. Looking at the liability side of the balance sheet, we see that $2.9 trillion, or 44.1 percent, of total liabilities and capital reflect net **policy reserves.** These reserves are based on actuarial assumptions regarding an insurer's expected future liability or commitment to pay out on present contracts, including death benefits and maturing endowment policies (lump sum or otherwise), as well as the cash **surrender value of policies** (i.e., the cash value paid to the policyholder if the policy is "surrendered" by the policyholder before it matures). Even though the actuarial assumptions underlying policy reserves are normally very conservative, unexpected fluctuations in future payouts can occur; that is, life insurance underwriting is risky. For example, mortality rates—and life insurance payouts—might unexpectedly increase over those defined by historically based mortality tables because of a catastrophic epidemic, such as AIDS or widespread influenza. To meet unexpected future losses, a life insurer holds a capital and surplus reserve fund with which to meet such losses. The capital and surplus reserves of life insurers in 2016 totaled $380.8 billion, or 5.9 percent of their total liabilities and capital.[4]

**Separate account** business was 37.6 percent of total liabilities and capital in 2016. Separate account funds are invested and held separately from the insurance company's other assets. These funds may be invested without regard to the usual restrictions (e.g., they may be invested in all stocks or all bonds). (Note that many of the stocks and bonds represented in Table 15–2 [totaling 67.6 percent of total assets] are included under "Separate accounts assets" in Table 15–3.) The returns on life insurance policies written as part of separate account business depend, then, on the return on the funds invested in separate account assets. Another important life insurer liability, guaranteed investment contracts

---

4. An additional line of defense against unexpected underwriting losses is the insurer's investment income from its asset portfolio plus any new premium income flows. Consequently, falling asset values (e.g., due to a stock market decline) can threaten the solvency and safety of firms in the insurance industry.

or GICs (4.3 percent of total liabilities and capital), are short- and medium-term debt instruments sold by insurance companies to fund their pension plan business (see deposit-type contracts in Table 15–3).

**Recent Trends.**    Insurance companies earn profits by taking in more premium and interest income than they pay out in policy payments. Firms can increase their spread between premium income and policy payouts in two ways. The first way is to decrease future required payouts for any given level of premium payments. This can be accomplished by reducing the risk of the insured pool (provided the policyholders do not demand premium rebates that fully reflect lower expected future payouts). The second way is to increase the profitability of interest income on net policy reserves. Since insurance liabilities typically are long term, the insurance company has long periods of time to invest premium payments in interest-earning asset portfolios. The higher the yield on the insurance company's investments, the greater the difference between the premium income stream and the policy payouts (except in the case of variable life insurance) and the greater the insurance company's profitability.

The life insurance industry was very profitable in the early and mid-2000s, with over $500 billion in premiums and annuities recorded in 2004 through 2006. Net income topped $34 billion in 2006, up 6.5 percent from 2005. The credit markets continued to be strong and capital levels for the industry remained high. However, the 2008–2009 financial crisis took a toll on this industry. The value of stocks and bonds in insurers' asset portfolios dropped as the financial markets deteriorated. Further, losses were experienced on life insurers' positions in commercial mortgage-backed securities, commercial loans, and lower grade corporate debt as bond default rates increased and mortgage markets froze. Lower equity market values also reduced asset-based fees earned from balances on equity-linked products, such as variable annuities. As a result, life insurers with large proportions of separate account assets to total revenue-generating assets were particularly hard hit with declining earnings from equities. Furthermore, as investors fled to the safety of government bonds during the financial crisis, government bond yields (which are generally a significant source of investment income for life insurers) fell. These events resulted in huge losses in 2008 for the industry. Realized and unrealized capital losses from bonds, preferred stocks, and common stocks topped $35 billion, representing more than an 875 percent drop from 2007. Net investment income also fell by 3.5 percent in 2008 from 2007. The result was that net after-tax income for the year was −$51.8 billion, $83.7 billion less than in 2007.

In late 2008/early 2009, insurance company reserves began to dwindle to dangerous levels. Further, the falling value of their assets made it harder for insurers to raise capital. At this point the Treasury Department decided to extend bailout funds to a number of struggling life insurance companies, the most notable being $127 billion to AIG (including $45 billion from TARP, $77 billion to purchase collateralized debt and mortgage-backed securities, and a $44 billion bridge loan). Other life insurers receiving Troubled Asset Relief Program (TARP) funds included Hartford Financial Services Group, Prudential Financial, Lincoln National, and Allstate.

Events associated with the financial crisis continued to be felt in 2009. Premium income fell by $120 billion (19 percent) from 2008 levels, while net realized capital for the industry fell by $28.7 billion. However, late 2009 saw some improvements for the life insurance industry. Overall, the industry saw an increase in total assets, and net income returned to a positive $21.1 billion. Further, the industry continued to pay dividends of $15.0 billion in 2009. Premiums continued to recover in 2010 through 2016 as annuity and most types of life insurance premiums increased. The 2012 premiums of $684.9 billion surpassed the $625.2 billion pre-crisis (2007) levels. Premiums written fell slightly to $681.1 billion by 2015. Further, net income increased to $28.0 billion in 2010 and $40.3 billion in 2015, the highest levels in over 15 years. However, challenges remain for the industry. Interest rates remain at historical lows, which increases the risk of spread compression for existing contracts and hampers the sale of new fixed annuity and universal life insurance contracts. Further, equity markets remain volatile and new regulations (see below) could adversely affect profits.

## McCarran–Ferguson Act of 1945

*Regulation confirming the primacy of state over federal regulation of insurance companies.*

**www.naic.org**

### Regulation

An important piece of legislation affecting the regulation of life insurance companies is the **McCarran–Ferguson Act of 1945,** which confirms the primacy of state over federal regulation of insurance companies. Thus, unlike the depository institutions discussed in Chapters 11 through 13, which can be chartered at either the federal or state levels, a life insurer is chartered entirely at the state level. In addition to chartering, state insurance commissions supervise and examine insurance companies using a coordinated examination system developed by the National Association of Insurance Commissioners (NAIC). Regulations cover areas such as insurance premiums, insurer licensing, sales practices, commission charges, and the types of assets in which insurers may invest.

In 2009, the U.S. Congress considered establishing an optional federal insurance charter. Support for such a charter increased when the existing state-by-state regulatory system failed to prevent insurance giant AIG's problems from becoming a systemic risk to the national economy. Those in favor of an optional federal insurance charter noted that under the current state-by-state system, insurers face obstacles such as inconsistent regulations, barriers to innovation, conflicting agent licensing, and education requirements. The Wall Street Reform and Consumer Protection Act of 2010 established the Federal Insurance Office (FIO), an entity that reports to Congress and the president on the status of the insurance industry. While the industry continues to be regulated by the states, the FIO has the authority to monitor the insurance industry, identify regulatory gaps or systemic risk, deal with international insurance matters, and monitor the extent to which underserved communities have access to affordable insurance products. The Wall Street Reform and Consumer Protection Act also called for the establishment of the Financial Stability Oversight Council (FSOC), which is charged with identifying any financial institution (including insurance companies) that presents a systemic risk to the economy and subjecting such institutions to greater regulation.

Also the result of the Wall Street Reform and Consumer Protection Act, the Federal Reserve has become a major supervisor of insurance firms. The Fed extended much of its authority over the insurance industry through the designation of three of the largest insurers (AIG, Prudential Financial, and MetLife) as "systemically important financial institutions." However, with the closure of the Office of Thrift Supervision in 2011, the Fed also supervises 14 insurance companies that own savings institutions. In total, the Fed supervises about one-third of U.S. insurance industry assets. This increased oversight by the Fed has incited concern among insurance companies and state regulators that the Fed will enact onerous capital rules and supervise insurance firms like banks. Promoting the concerns are cases like that of MetLife that failed the Fed's "stress tests" in 2012 despite the firm's protests the Fed misunderstood its business model. In 2015, MetLife sued the U.S. government to overturn its designation as a nonbank systemically important financial institution. The insurer argued that its failure would not pose a risk to the financial system. MetLife further argued that, because it is harder for a customer to pull money from an insurance contract than it is for a depositor to withdraw money from a bank deposit account during a crisis, the insurance industry is safer than banking. Not counting on the courts to agree, in 2016 MetLife announced that it would divest a large piece of its life insurance unit: a unit that had been the core of the company's business for decades. However, shortly after this, a federal judge ruled that MetLife did not deserve to be labeled too big to fail and as such was allowed to shed its designation as a systemically important financial institution and the increased regulatory oversight that went along with that designation.

## insurance guarantee fund

*A fund of required contributions from within-state insurance companies, used to compensate insurance company policyholders in the event of failure.*

**http://www.dfs.ny.gov**

In addition to supervision and examination, states also promote life **insurance guarantee funds.** Unlike banks and thrifts, life insurers have no access to a federal guarantee fund (although, as mentioned earlier, during the financial crisis the federal government took the unprecedented step of bailing out several major insurance companies). These state guarantee funds differ in a number of important ways from deposit insurance. First, although these programs are sponsored by state insurance regulators, they are actually run and administered by the private insurance companies themselves.

Second, unlike the Depositors Insurance Fund (DIF), in which the FDIC has established a permanent reserve fund by requiring banks to pay annual premiums in excess of payouts to resolve failures (see Chapter 13), no such permanent guarantee fund exists for the insurance industry—with the sole exception of the property–casualty and life guarantee funds in the state of New York. This means that contributions are paid into the guarantee fund by surviving firms in a state only after an insurance company has actually failed.

Third, the size of the required contributions that surviving insurers make to protect policyholders in failed insurance companies differs widely from state to state. In those states that have guarantee funds, each surviving insurer is normally levied a pro rata amount, according to the size of its statewide premium income. This amount either helps pay off small policyholders after the assets of the failed insurer have been liquidated or acts as a cash injection to make the acquisition of a failed insurer attractive. The definition of small policyholders varies among states, ranging from $100,000 to $500,000.

Finally, because no permanent fund exists and the annual pro rata payments to meet payouts to failed insurer policyholders are often legally capped, a delay usually occurs before small policyholders receive the cash surrender values of their policies or other payment obligations from the guarantee fund. This contrasts with deposit insurance, which normally provides insured depositors immediate coverage of their claims up to $250,000.

<table><tr><td>**DO YOU UNDERSTAND:**

1. The difference between a life insurance contract and an annuity contract?

2. What the different forms of ordinary life insurance are?

3. Why life insurance companies invest in long-term assets?

4. What the major source of life insurance underwriting risk is?

5. Who the main regulators of the life insurance industry are?</td></tr></table>

## PROPERTY–CASUALTY INSURANCE COMPANIES

### Size, Structure, and Composition of the Industry

Currently, some 2,544 companies sell property–casualty (P&C) insurance, and approximately half of these firms write P&C business in all or most of the United States. The U.S. P&C insurance industry is quite concentrated. Collectively, the top 10 firms have a 50 percent share of the overall P&C market measured by premiums written, and the top 200 firms make up over 95 percent of the industry premiums written. In 2016, the top firm (State Farm) wrote 11.3 percent of all P&C insurance premiums, while the second-ranked insurer, Berkshire Hathaway, wrote 6.8 percent of all premiums (i.e., a joint total of 18.1 percent of premiums). In contrast, in 1985 the top two firms wrote 14.5 percent of the total industry insurance premiums. Thus, the industry leaders appear to be increasing their share of this financial services sector. The total assets of the P&C industry as of the beginning of 2016 were $1.8 trillion, or less than a third of the size of the life insurance industry's assets. While the P&C industry is small when measured by total assets, it is vital to the economic system and the management of risk.

**LG 15-5**

**P&C Insurance.**  Property insurance involves insurance coverages related to the loss of real and personal property. Casualty—or perhaps more accurately, liability—insurance offers protection against legal liability exposures. However, distinctions between the two broad areas of property and liability insurance are becoming increasingly blurred. This is due to the tendency of P&C insurers to offer multiple activity line coverages combining features of property and liability insurance into single policy packages—for example, homeowners multiple peril insurance. The following describes the key features of the main P&C lines. Note, however, that some P&C activity lines (e.g., auto insurance) are marketed as one product to individuals and another to commercial firms, while other lines (e.g., boiler and machinery insurance targeted at commercial purchasers) are marketed to one specific group. To understand the importance of each line in premium income (so-called **premiums written**) and losses incurred in 2015, review Table 15–4. The following data show the P&C lines (and their changing importance to the P&C industry):

**premiums written**

*The entire amount of premiums on insurance contracts written.*

- **Fire Insurance and Allied Lines** protect against the perils of fire, lightning, and removal of property damaged in a fire (4.3 percent of all premiums written in 2015 versus 16.6 percent in 1960).

**TABLE 15–4** **Property and Casualty Insurance** *(industry underwriting by lines)*

| Line | Premiums Written* | Percentage of Total Premiums Written | Losses Incurred[†] |
|---|---|---|---|
| Fire | $ 13.0 | 2.2% | 43.4% |
| Allied lines | 12.2 | 2.1 | 40.1 |
| Homeowners MP | 89.2 | 15.1 | 50.1 |
| Commercial MP—nonliability | 25.3 | 4.3 | 45.2 |
| Private passenger auto PD | 80.4 | 13.6 | 64.9 |
| Private passenger auto liability | 119.5 | 20.2 | 71.1 |
| Commercial auto PD | 7.5 | 1.3 | 60.7 |
| Commercial auto liability | 23.8 | 4.0 | 67.4 |
| Commercial MP—liability | 14.4 | 2.4 | 44.9 |
| Other liability | 62.3 | 10.5 | 56.6 |
| Product liability | 3.7 | 0.6 | 45.4 |
| Multiple peril (MP) crop | 9.8 | 1.7 | 72.4 |
| Farm owners MP | 4.1 | 0.7 | 50.8 |
| Mortgage guarantee | 4.9 | 0.8 | 28.9 |
| Ocean marine | 3.8 | 0.6 | 45.4 |
| Inland marine | 20.5 | 3.5 | 47.5 |
| Financial guarantee | 0.5 | 0.1 | −11.8 |
| Medical professional liability | 9.4 | 1.6 | 44.0 |
| Earthquake | 2.9 | 0.5 | −0.2 |
| Federal flood | 2.9 | 0.5 | 30.5 |
| Group accident and health | 4.4 | 0.7 | 63.9 |
| Individual accident and health | 1.8 | 0.3 | 120.3 |
| Workers' compensation | 57.6 | 9.7 | 58.7 |
| Warranty | 2.8 | 0.5 | 53.2 |
| Aircraft | 1.6 | 0.3 | 45.4 |
| Credit | 1.9 | 0.3 | 37.6 |
| Surety | 5.7 | 1.0 | 18.2 |
| Boiler and machinery | 1.8 | 0.3 | 32.4 |
| Fidelity | 1.2 | 0.2 | 39.9 |
| Burglary and theft | 0.3 | 0.0 | 23.2 |
| Other lines | 2.3 | 0.4 | 63.8 |
| Totals | $591.2 | 100.0% | 57.3% |

*In billions.
[†]To premiums earned.
**Source:** *Best's Review,* July 2016, p. 74. Copyrighted by A.M. Best Company. www.ambest.com

- **Homeowners Multiple Peril (MP) Insurance** protects against multiple perils of damage to a personal dwelling and personal property (e.g., fire, lightning, windstorm, hail, explosion, theft, weight of ice or snow) as well as liability coverage against the financial consequences of legal liability resulting from injury to others. Thus, it combines features of both property and liability insurance (15.1 percent of all premiums written in 2015; 5.2 percent in 1960).

- **Commercial Multiple Peril Insurance** protects commercial firms against perils similar to homeowners multiple peril insurance (4.3 percent of all premiums written in 2015; 0.4 percent in 1960).

- **Automobile Liability and Physical Damage (PD) Insurance** provides protection against (1) losses resulting from legal liability due to the ownership or use of the vehicle (auto liability) and (2) theft or damage to vehicles (auto physical damage) (39.1 percent of all premiums written in 2015; 43.0 percent in 1960).

- **Liability Insurance (other than auto)** provides protection to either individuals or commercial firms against non-automobile-related legal liability. For commercial firms, this includes protection against liabilities relating to their business operations (other than personal injury to employees covered by workers' compensation insurance) and product liability hazards (13.5 percent of all premiums written in 2015; 6.6 percent in 1960).

## Balance Sheets and Recent Trends

**The Balance Sheet and Underwriting Risk.**    The balance sheet of P&C firms in 2016 is shown in Table 15–5. Similar to life insurance companies, P&C insurers invest the majority of their assets in long-term securities, although the proportion held in common stock is lower than that of life insurance companies. Overall the maturity of their assets (and liabilities) tends to be shorter than that for life insurance companies. Bonds ($982.9 billion), preferred stock ($14.0 billion), and common stock ($338.7 billion) represented 71.7 percent of total assets in 2016. Looking at their liabilities, we can see that a major component is the loss reserves and loss adjustment expenses item ($641.4 billion). Loss reserves are funds set aside to meet expected losses from *underwriting* the P&C lines described previously (e.g., the payments made to settle the claims on the insurance policies). Loss adjustment expenses are the expected administrative and related costs of adjusting (settling) these claims (e.g., the costs associated with sending an adjuster to evaluate the amount of payment to be made to settle the claim). This item represents 34.4 percent of total liabilities and capital. **Unearned premiums** (set-aside reserves that contain the portion of a premium that has been paid at the start of the coverage period and therefore before insurance coverage has been provided) are also a major liability and are equal to 13.2 percent of total liabilities and capital.

> **unearned premiums**
>
> *Reserves set aside that contain the portion of a premium that has been paid before insurance coverage has been provided.*

To understand how and why the loss reserve—which is the largest liability component—on the balance sheet is established, we need to understand the risks of underwriting P&C insurance. In particular, P&C underwriting risk results when the premiums generated on a given insurance line are insufficient to cover (1) the claims (losses) incurred insuring the risk and (2) the administrative expenses of providing that insurance coverage (legal expenses, commissions, taxes, etc.), after taking into account (3) the investment income generated between the time when the premiums are received to the time when losses are covered. Thus, underwriting risk may result from (1) unexpected increases in loss rates (or loss risk), (2) unexpected increases in expenses (or expense risk), and/or (3) unexpected

**TABLE 15–5**    Property–Casualty Industry Balance Sheet *(in billions of dollars)*

|  |  |  | Percentage of Total |
|---|---|---|---|
| **Assets** |  |  |  |
| Invested assets | | $1,581.5 | 84.9% |
| Bonds | $982.9 | | 52.7% |
| Preferred stocks | 14.0 | | 0.8 |
| Common stocks | 338.7 | | 18.2 |
| Real estate investment | 24.2 | | 1.3 |
| Cash and short-term investments | 91.9 | | 4.9 |
| Other invested assets | 129.8 | | 7.0 |
| Net deferred taxes | | 27.4 | 1.5 |
| Reinsurance | | 43.0 | 2.3 |
| Premium balance | | 157.7 | 8.4 |
| Accrued interest | | 9.5 | 0.5 |
| All other assets | | 44.5 | 2.4 |
| Total assets | | $1,863.6 | 100.0% |
| **Liabilities and Capital/Surplus** |  |  |  |
| Losses and loss adjustment expenses | | $641.4 | 34.4% |
| Unearned premiums | | 246.5 | 13.2 |
| Other liabilities | | 269.7 | 13.5 |
| Policyholders' surplus | | 706.0 | 37.9 |
| Capital and assigned surplus | $270.7 | | 14.5 |
| Surplus notes | 13.0 | | 0.7 |
| Unassigned surplus | 422.3 | | 22.7 |
| Total liabilities and capital/surplus | | $1,863.6 | 100.0% |

**Source:** *Best's Aggregates & Averages, Property–Casualty* (Oldwick, NJ: A.M. Best Company, 2016), p. 140. www.ambest.com

decreases in investment yields or returns (investment yield/return risk). Next, we look more carefully at each of these three areas of P&C underwriting risk.

*Loss Risk.* The key feature of claims loss risk is the actuarial *predictability* of losses relative to premiums earned. This predictability depends on a number of characteristics or features of the perils insured, specifically:

- **Property versus Liability.** In general, the maximum levels of losses are more predictable for property lines than for liability lines. For example, the monetary value of the loss or damage to an auto is relatively easy to calculate, but the upper limit on the losses to which an insurer might be exposed in a product liability line—for example, asbestos damage to workers' health under other liability insurance—might be difficult if not impossible to estimate.
- **Severity versus Frequency.** In general, loss rates are more predictable on low-severity, high-frequency lines than on high-severity, low-frequency lines. For example, losses in fire, auto, and homeowners peril lines tend to be expected to occur with high frequency and to be independently distributed across any pool of insured customers. Thus, only a limited number of customers are affected by any single event. Furthermore, the dollar loss of each event in the insured pool tends to be relatively small. Applying the law of large numbers, the expected loss potential of such lines—the **frequency of loss** times the extent of the damage (**severity of loss**)—may be estimable within quite small probability bounds. Other lines, such as earthquake, hurricane, and financial guarantee insurance, tend to insure very low-probability (frequency) events. Here, many policyholders in the insured pool are affected by any single event (i.e., their risks are correlated) and the severity of the loss could be potentially enormous. This means that estimating expected loss rates (frequency times severity) is extremely difficult in these coverage areas. For example, even with the new federal terrorism insurance program introduced in 2002, coverage for high-profile buildings in big cities, as well as other properties considered potential targets, remains expensive. Under the 2002 federal program, the government is responsible for 90 percent of insurance industry losses that arise from any future terrorist incidents that exceed a minimum amount. The government's losses are capped at $100 billion per year. Each insurer has a maximum amount it must pay before federal aid kicks in. In 2017, the amount was 17 percent of each company's commercial property–casualty premiums. In 2020, the amount will be 20 percent. The result is that in some cases, the cost of terrorism insurance has been reduced significantly since the new law took effect. But those buildings viewed as target risks will continue to have much higher premiums than properties outside major cities. This higher uncertainty of losses forces P&C firms to invest in more *short-term assets* and hold a larger percentage of capital and reserves than life insurance firms do.
- **Long Tail versus Short Tail.** Some liability lines suffer from a long-tail risk exposure phenomenon that makes estimation of expected losses difficult. This **long-tail loss** arises in policies for which the insured event occurs during a coverage period but a claim is not filed or made until many years later. The delay in the filing of a claim is in accordance with the terms of the insurance contract and often occurs because the detrimental consequences of the event are not known for a period of time after the event actually occurs. Losses incurred but not reported have caused insurers significant problems in lines such as medical malpractice and other liability insurance where product damage suits (e.g., the Dalkon shield case and asbestos cases) have been filed many years after the event occurred and the coverage period has expired.[5] For example, in 2002 Halliburton, a major U.S. corporation, agreed to pay $4 billion in cash and stock, and to seek bankruptcy protection for a subsidiary, to settle more than 300,000

**frequency of loss**
*The probability that a loss will occur.*

**severity of loss**
*The size of a loss.*

**long-tail loss**
*A loss for which a claim is made some time after a policy was written.*

---

5. In some product liability cases, such as those involving asbestos, the nature of the risk being covered was not fully understood at the time many of the policies were written. For example, in the 1940s manufacturers began using asbestos as an insulator and fire retardant in products such as insulation and floor tiles. Thirty years later it was learned that exposure to asbestos could cause cancer.

asbestos claims. To resolve its growing asbestos liability, Halliburton considered a novel step that put one of its biggest subsidiaries into bankruptcy courts, while allowing Halliburton to hold on to the rest of its businesses. Questions still remain about how much insurance companies will be required to reimburse Halliburton for the cost of asbestos case settlements and when. The company had only $1.6 billion of expected insurance on its books for asbestos claims. If Halliburton is successful in putting just one of its subsidiaries (and not the entire firm) into bankruptcy, it could set a precedent for many companies, such as Honeywell International and Dow Chemical, which were also trying to contain their asbestos risk in subsidiaries.

- **Product Inflation versus Social Inflation.** Loss rates on all P&C property policies are adversely affected by unexpected increases in inflation. Inflation generally has an adverse effect on the cost of providing benefits that have been purchased by the insured, particularly if the policy is written in terms of the replacement cost of the asset and the premiums are not adjusted for inflation. In addition, the investment value of bonds and other fixed-rate assets of insurers from which claims proceeds are derived may decrease in value from unexpected inflation. Such increases were triggered, for example, by the oil price shocks of 1973, 1978, and 2008. However, in addition to a systematic unexpected inflation risk in each line, line-specific inflation risks may also exist. The inflation risk of property lines is likely to reflect the approximate underlying inflation risk of the economy. Liability lines, however, may be subject to social inflation, as reflected by juries' willingness to award punitive and other damages at rates far above the underlying rate of inflation. Such social inflation has been particularly prevalent in commercial liability and medical malpractice insurance and has been directly attributed by some analysts to faults in the U.S. civil litigation system. Using the predicted losses, insurance companies calculate a pure premium on each line of insurance equal to the frequency of loss times the average predicted loss. Policyholders are then charged a gross premium equal to the pure premium plus a loading fee to capture the expected profit for the insurer (see below).

*Reinsurance.*    An alternative to managing risk on a P&C insurer's balance sheet is to purchase reinsurance from a reinsurance company. Reinsurance is essentially insurance for insurance companies. Note from Table 15–5 that reinsurance (the payment that may be collected under reinsurance contracts) represented 2.3 percent of total assets in 2016. It is a way for primary insurance companies to protect against unforeseen or extraordinary losses. Depending on the contract, reinsurance can enable the insurer to improve its capital position, expand its business, limit losses, and stabilize cash flows, among other things. In addition, the reinsurer, drawing information from many primary insurers, will usually have a far larger pool of data for assessing risks. Reinsurance takes a variety of forms. It may represent a layer of risk, such as losses within certain limits, say $5 million to $10 million, that will be paid by the reinsurer to the primary insurance company for which a premium is paid, or a sharing of both losses and profits for certain types of business. Reinsurance is an international business. About 75 percent of the reinsurance business that comes from U.S. insurance companies is written by non-U.S. reinsurers such as Munich Re. Some investment banks are now setting up reinsurers as part of a move to develop alternative risk-financing deals such as catastrophe bonds. Insurers and reinsurers also typically issue catastrophe bonds. The bonds pay high interest rates and diversify an investor's portfolio because natural disasters occur randomly and are not associated with (are independent of) economic factors. Depending on how the bond is structured, if losses reach the threshold specified in the bond offering, the investor may lose all or part of the principal or interest. For example, a deep-discount or zero-coupon catastrophe bond would pay $100(1 - \alpha)$ on maturity, where $\alpha$ is the loss rate due to the catastrophe. Thus, Munich Re issued a $250 million catastrophe bond in 2018 where $\alpha$ (the loss rate) reflected losses incurred on all reinsurer policies over a 24-hour period should an event (such as a flood or hurricane) occur and losses exceed a certain threshold. The required yield on these bonds reflected the risk-free rate plus a premium reflecting investors' expectations regarding the probability of the event's occurring.

**loss ratio**

*A measure of pure losses incurred to premiums earned.*

**premiums earned**

*Premiums received and earned on insurance contracts because time has passed with no claim filed.*

*Measuring Loss Risk.*    The **loss ratio** measures the actual losses incurred on a specific policy line. It measures the ratio of losses incurred to **premiums earned** (premiums received and earned on insurance contracts because time has passed without a claim being filed). Thus, a loss ratio of less than 100 means that premiums earned were sufficient to cover losses incurred on that line. Aggregate loss ratios for the period 1951 to June 2016 are shown in Table 15–6 and Figure 15–2. Notice the steady increase in industry loss ratios over the period, increasing from the 60 percent range in the 1950s to the 70 and 80 percent range in the 1980s through the early 2010s. For example, in 2012 the aggregate loss ratio on all P&C lines was 74.5 percent. A turnaround started in 2013, as the loss ratio dropped to 67.4 and values stayed below 70 through 2015 when the loss ratio was 69.8. Over the first six months of 2016, the loss ratio rose back to 71.9. This measure includes loss adjustment expenses (LAE)—see below—as well as "pure" losses. The (pure) loss ratio, net of LAE, in 2015 was 57.3 percent (see Table 15–4), down from 63.6 in 2012.

*Expense Risk.*    The two major sources of expense risk to P&C insurers are (1) loss adjustment expenses (LAE) and (2) commissions and other expenses. LAE relate to the costs surrounding the loss settlement process. For example, many P&C insurers employ adjusters who determine the liability of an insurer and the size of an adjustment or settlement to make. The other major area of expense involves the commission costs paid to insurance brokers and sales agents and other operating expenses related to the acquisition of business. As mentioned, the loss ratio reported in Table 15–6 and Figure 15–2 includes LAE.

**TABLE 15–6**    **Property–Casualty Industry Underwriting Ratios**

| Year | Loss Ratio* | Expense Ratio[†] | Combined Ratio | Dividends to Policyholders[‡] | Combined Ratio after Dividends |
|------|-------------|------------------|----------------|-------------------------------|--------------------------------|
| 1951 | 60.3 | 34.0 | 94.3 | 2.6 | 96.9 |
| 1960 | 63.8 | 32.2 | 96.0 | 2.2 | 98.2 |
| 1970 | 70.8 | 27.6 | 98.4 | 1.7 | 100.1 |
| 1980 | 74.9 | 26.5 | 101.4 | 1.7 | 103.1 |
| 1985 | 88.7 | 25.9 | 114.6 | 1.6 | 116.2 |
| 1995 | 78.8 | 26.2 | 105.0 | 1.4 | 106.4 |
| 1997 | 72.8 | 27.1 | 99.9 | 1.7 | 101.6 |
| 2000 | 81.4 | 27.8 | 109.2 | 1.3 | 110.5 |
| 2001 | 88.4 | 26.9 | 115.3 | 0.7 | 116.0 |
| 2002 | 81.1 | 25.6 | 106.7 | 0.5 | 107.2 |
| 2003 | 74.7 | 24.9 | 99.6 | 0.5 | 100.1 |
| 2004 | 73.3 | 25.0 | 98.3 | 0.4 | 98.7 |
| 2005 | 74.8 | 25.5 | 100.3 | 0.6 | 100.9 |
| 2006 | 66.2 | 25.4 | 91.6 | 0.8 | 92.4 |
| 2007 | 68.0 | 27.1 | 95.1 | 0.5 | 95.6 |
| 2008 | 77.4 | 27.2 | 104.6 | 0.5 | 105.1 |
| 2009 | 73.2 | 27.3 | 100.5 | 0.5 | 101.0 |
| 2010 | 73.5 | 28.4 | 101.9 | 0.5 | 102.4 |
| 2011 | 79.4 | 29.8 | 107.8 | 0.4 | 108.2 |
| 2012 | 74.5 | 28.2 | 102.7 | 0.5 | 103.2 |
| 2013 | 67.4 | 28.3 | 95.7 | 0.6 | 96.3 |
| 2014 | 68.6 | 27.9 | 96.5 | 0.5 | 97.0 |
| 2015 | 69.8 | 27.8 | 97.6 | 0.7 | 98.3 |
| 2016 | 71.9 | 27.6 | 99.5 | 0.5 | 100.0 |

*Losses and adjustment expenses incurred to premiums earned.

[†]Expenses incurred (before federal income taxes) to premiums written.

[‡]Dividends to policyholders to premiums earned.

**Sources:** *Best's Aggregates & Averages, Property–Casualty* (Oldwick, NJ: A.M. Best Company, 1994), p. 158; and *Best's Review,* various issues. Copyrighted by A.M. Best Company. Used with permission. www.ambest.com

**Figure 15–2**   Property–Casualty Industry Underwriting Ratios

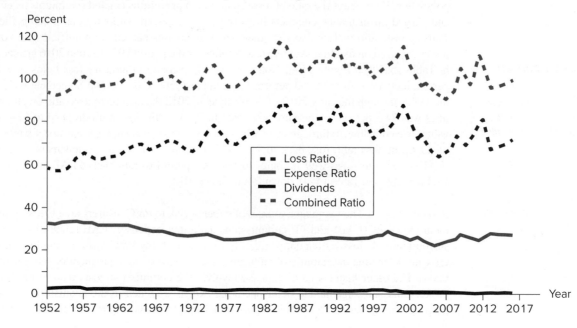

The expense ratio reported in Table 15–6 includes the commission and other expenses for P&C insurers during the 1951–2016 (June) period. Notice in this table that, in contrast to the increasing trend in the loss ratio, the expense ratio decreased over the period shown. Despite this trend, expenses continued to account for a significant portion of the overall costs of operations. In 2015, for example, commission and other expenses amounted to 27.8 percent of premiums written. Clearly, sharp rises in commissions and other operating costs can rapidly render an insurance line unprofitable.

A common measure of the overall underwriting profitability of a line, which includes the loss, loss adjustment expenses, and expense ratios, is the **combined ratio.** Technically, the combined ratio is equal to the loss ratio plus the ratios of LAE to premiums written and commissions and other expenses to premiums written. The combined ratio after dividends adds dividends paid to policyholders as a portion of premiums earned to the combined ratio. If the combined ratio is less than 100 percent, premiums alone are sufficient to cover both losses and expenses related to the line. As seen in Table 15–6, this was the case from 2013 to 2016. The combined ratio before dividends was 95.7, 96.5, 97.6, and 99.5, respectively, over this period.

---

**EXAMPLE 15–3**   Calculation of P&C Line Loss and Expense Ratios

A property–casualty insurer brings in $8.72 million in premiums on its private passenger auto physical damage (PD) line of insurance. The line's losses amount to $5,859,840 and expenses are $2,485,200. The insurer's dividend ratio is 5 percent. Calculate the line's loss ratio, expense ratio, and combined ratio after dividends.

$$\text{Loss ratio} = \$5,859,840/\$8,720,000 = 67.2\%$$
$$\text{Expense ratio} = \$2,485,200/\$8,720,000 = 28.5\%$$
$$\text{Combined ratio} = 67.2\% + 28.5\% + 5.0\% = 100.7\%$$

---

If premiums are insufficient and the combined ratio exceeds 100 percent, the P&C insurer must rely on investment income on premiums for overall profitability. For example, in 2001 the combined ratio after dividend payments was 116.0 percent, indicating that premiums alone were insufficient to cover the costs of losses and expenses related to writing P&C insurance. Conversely, in 2004 a drop in losses incurred on premiums written resulted in a combined ratio after dividends of 98.7 percent, the first year premiums covered losses since 1979. Table 15–6 presents the combined ratio and its components for the P&C industry for the years 1951–2016 (June). We see that the trend over much of this period was toward decreased profitability. The industry's premiums generally covered losses and expenses through the 1970s. Then, until 2004, premiums were unable to cover losses and expenses (i.e., combined ratios were consistently higher than 100 percent). The mid-2000s saw a return to increased profitability for the insurance industry, which was reversed in the late 2000s.

*Investment Yield/Return Risk.* As discussed previously, when the combined ratio is more than 100 percent, overall profitability can be ensured only by a sufficient investment return on premiums earned. That is, P&C firms invest premiums in assets between the time they receive the premiums and the time they make payments to meet claims. For example, in 2016 net investment income to premiums earned (or the P&C insurers' investment yield) was 8.5 percent. As a result, the overall average profitability (or **operating ratio**) of P&C insurers was 91.5 percent. It was equal to the combined ratio after dividends (100.0, see Table 15–6) minus the investment yield (8.5). Since the operating ratio was less than 100 percent, P&C insurers were profitable overall in 2016. Net returns on investments can have a big impact on industry profitability. For example, in 2012 P&C insurers' investment yield was 10.5 percent. As a result, the operating ratio of P&C insurers was 92.7 (the combined ratio after dividends [103.2] minus the investment yield [10.5]). While the combined ratio after dividends corresponds to net losses, the high investment yield resulted in an operating ratio that was less than 100. That is, P&C insurers were profitable in 2012. However, lower net returns on investments (e.g., 2.8 percent rather than 10.5 percent) would have meant that underwriting P&C insurance was marginally unprofitable (i.e., the operating ratio of insurers in this case would have been 100.4). Further, in 2001, even though net investment income to premiums earned was 14.0 percent, the overall average profitability of P&C insurers (the operating ratio) was 102 percent, meaning that underwriting P&C insurance was unprofitable. As discussed further below, 2001 was the first full year net loss experienced by the P&C industry in the post-1950 period. Thus, the behavior of interest rates and default rates on P&C insurers' investments is crucial to the P&C insurers' overall profitability. That is, measuring and managing credit and interest rate risk are key concerns of P&C managers, as they are for all FI managers.

**operating ratio**

*A measure of the overall profitability of a P&C insurer; equals the combined ratio minus the investment yield.*

---

### EXAMPLE 15–4   Calculation of P&C Company Overall Profitability

Suppose that an insurance company's loss ratio is 79.8 percent, its expense ratio is 27.9 percent, and the company pays 2 percent of its premiums earned to policyholders as dividends. The combined ratio (after dividends) for this insurance company is equal to:

$$\text{Loss ratio} + \text{Expense ratio} + \text{Dividend ratio} = \text{Combined ratio after dividends}$$
$$79.8 \quad + \quad 27.9 \quad + \quad 2.0 \quad = \quad 109.7$$

Thus, expected losses on all P&C lines, expenses, and dividends exceeded premiums earned by 9.7 percent. As a result, without considering investment income, the P&C insurer is not profitable.

Suppose, however, that the company's investment portfolio yielded 12 percent. The operating ratio and overall profitability of the P&C insurer would then be:

$$\text{Operating ratio} = \text{Combined ratio after dividends} - \text{Investment yield}$$
$$= 109.7 \text{ percent} \quad\quad - 12.0 \text{ percent}$$
$$= 97.7 \text{ percent}$$

As can be seen, the high investment returns (12 percent) make the P&C insurer profitable overall.

Given the importance of investment returns to P&C insurers' profitability, combined with the need for a predictable stream of cash flows to meet required payouts on their insurance policies, the balance sheet in Table 15–5 indicates that bonds—both treasury and corporate—dominate the asset portfolios of P&C insurers. For example, bonds represented 52.7 percent of total assets and 62.1 percent ($982.9b/$1,581.5b) of financial assets (invested assets) in 2016.

Finally, if losses, LAE, and other expenses are higher and investment yields are lower than expected, resulting in operating losses, P&C insurers carry a significant amount of surplus reserves (policyholder surplus) to reduce the risk of insolvency. In 2016, the ratio of policyholder surplus to assets was 37.9 percent.

**Recent Trends**   While catastrophes should be random, much of the period 1985–2016 was characterized by a number of catastrophes of historically high severity. This is shown in Figure 15–3. In the terminology of P&C insurers, the industry was in the trough of an **underwriting cycle**—that is, underwriting conditions were difficult. These cycles are characterized by periods of rising premiums leading to increased profitability. Following a period of solid but not spectacular rates of return, the industry enters a down phase in which premiums soften as the supply of insurance products increases. As a result, most of the period 1985–2016 was not entirely profitable for the P&C industry. In particular, the combined ratio (the measure of loss plus expense risk) was 116.2 in 1985, 115.7 in 1992, and 116.0 in 2001. (Remember that a combined ratio higher than 100 is bad in that it means that losses, expenses, and dividends totaled *more* than premiums earned.) The major reason for these losses was a succession of catastrophes including Hurricane Hugo in 1989, the San Francisco earthquake in 1991, the Oakland fires of 1991, and the almost $20 billion in losses incurred in Florida as a result of Hurricane Andrew in 1991.

In 1993, the industry showed signs of improvement, with the combined ratio after dividends falling to 106.9. In 1994, however, the ratio rose again to 108.4, partly as a result of the Northridge earthquake, with estimated losses of $7 billion to $10 billion. A drop in disaster-related losses caused the industry ratio to fall back to 101.6 in 1997. However, major losses associated with El Nino (e.g., Hurricane Georges and Midwest storms) drove the combined ratio after dividends back to 105.6 in 1998. The combined ratio after dividends increased even further to 107.9 in 1999 and 110.5 in 2000. Part of these increases is attributable to an increase in amounts paid on asbestos claims. In 1999, $3.4 billion was paid out on these claims, the largest payout ever. The Insurance Services Office Inc. estimates that the combined ratio for 1999, 107.9, would have been one percentage point lower without these claims.

The year 2001 saw yet another blow to the insurance industry and the world with terrorist attacks on the World Trade Center and the Pentagon. Estimates of the costs of these attacks to insurance companies were as high as $40 billion. It was estimated that only 10 percent of the September 11 losses were reported in 2001, and yet the losses attributed to the terrorist attacks added an estimated 4 percentage points to the combined ratio after dividends of 116.0. Because of the tremendous impact these attacks had on the health of the U.S. insurance industry, the Bush administration proposed that the U.S. government pay the majority of the losses of the insurance industry due to the attacks. The proposal capped insurers' liabilities at 10 percent of claims over $1 billion (the federal government would pay the other 90 percent) for as many as three years after a terrorist-related event. Despite this bailout of the industry, many insurers did not survive 2001 and those that did were forced to increase premiums significantly.

After several tumultuous years, 2003 saw profitability in the P&C industry improve. The combined ratio after dividends was 100.1, down sharply from 107.2 in 2002, and much better than most analysts and industry experts expected. The 2003 results were the best since 1979, when the combined ratio was 100.6. In 2004 Florida and the East Coast were hit with several major hurricanes, including Hurricanes Charley, Frances, Ivan, and Jeanne (the estimated losses from these four hurricanes were over $25 billion). Yet, these were the only major catastrophes to occur in 2004. As a result, the industry saw its first

**underwriting cycle**

*A pattern that the profits in the P&C industry tend to follow.*

**www.iso.com**

**Figure 15-3**   U.S. Catastrophes, 1949–2016

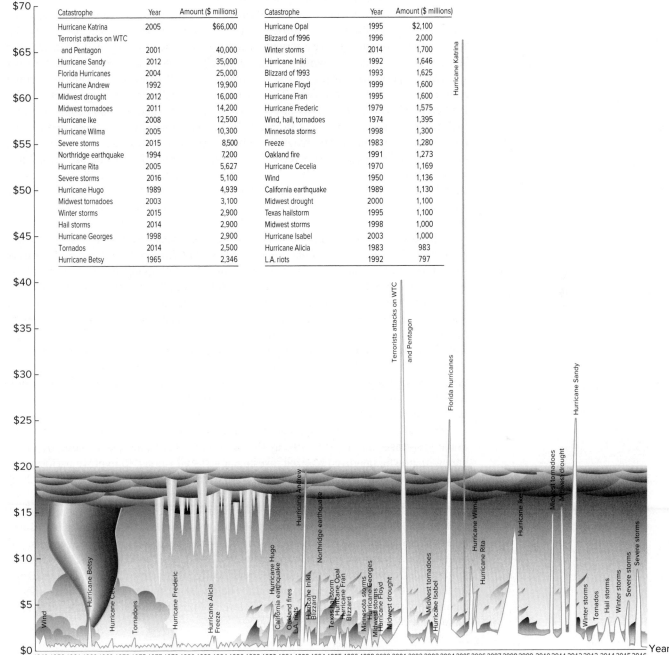

| Catastrophe | Year | Amount ($ millions) |
|---|---|---|
| Hurricane Katrina | 2005 | $66,000 |
| Terrorist attacks on WTC and Pentagon | 2001 | 40,000 |
| Hurricane Sandy | 2012 | 35,000 |
| Florida Hurricanes | 2004 | 25,000 |
| Hurricane Andrew | 1992 | 19,900 |
| Midwest drought | 2012 | 16,000 |
| Midwest tornadoes | 2011 | 14,200 |
| Hurricane Ike | 2008 | 12,500 |
| Hurricane Wilma | 2005 | 10,300 |
| Severe storms | 2015 | 8,500 |
| Northridge earthquake | 1994 | 7,200 |
| Hurricane Rita | 2005 | 5,627 |
| Severe storms | 2016 | 5,100 |
| Hurricane Hugo | 1989 | 4,939 |
| Midwest tornadoes | 2003 | 3,100 |
| Winter storms | 2015 | 2,900 |
| Hail storms | 2014 | 2,900 |
| Hurricane Georges | 1998 | 2,900 |
| Tornados | 2014 | 2,500 |
| Hurricane Betsy | 1965 | 2,346 |

| Catastrophe | Year | Amount ($ millions) |
|---|---|---|
| Hurricane Opal | 1995 | $2,100 |
| Blizzard of 1996 | 1996 | 2,000 |
| Winter storms | 2014 | 1,700 |
| Hurricane Iniki | 1992 | 1,646 |
| Blizzard of 1993 | 1993 | 1,625 |
| Hurricane Floyd | 1999 | 1,600 |
| Hurricane Fran | 1995 | 1,600 |
| Hurricane Frederic | 1979 | 1,575 |
| Wind, hail, tornadoes | 1974 | 1,395 |
| Minnesota storms | 1998 | 1,300 |
| Freeze | 1983 | 1,280 |
| Oakland fire | 1991 | 1,273 |
| Hurricane Cecelia | 1970 | 1,169 |
| Wind | 1950 | 1,136 |
| California earthquake | 1989 | 1,130 |
| Midwest drought | 2000 | 1,100 |
| Texas hailstorm | 1995 | 1,100 |
| Midwest storms | 1998 | 1,000 |
| Hurricane Isabel | 2003 | 1,000 |
| Hurricane Alicia | 1983 | 983 |
| L.A. riots | 1992 | 797 |

**Sources:** Richard L. Sandor, Centre Financial Products, 1949–1994; and authors' research, 1995–2016.

overall profitable year since the 1960s. The combined ratio in 2004 was 98.7. In 2005 the P&C industry reported a combined ratio of 100.9. The losses resulted from $81.9 billion in catastrophe losses primarily resulting from the record-breaking hurricane season, which included losses from Hurricanes Katrina, Wilma, and Rita. These losses added an esti-mated 8 points to the industry's combined ratios. If catastrophe losses are excluded, the combined ratios for 2005 and 2004 would have been 92.9 and 94.5, respectively. Losses from the record 2005 hurricane season prompted both Allstate and State Farm to stop writing new homeowner policies and drop some existing customers altogether. In 2006 and 2007 small levels of catastrophic losses, combined with strong performance in virtually all other major lines of P&C insurance, resulted in a combined ratio of 92.4, and 95.6, respectively, the best underwriting performance since 1936.

Losses rose significantly in 2008 through 2012 due to jumps in catastrophe losses (including $12.5 billion from Hurricane Ike, $25.0 billion from Hurricane Sandy, and $14.2 billion from the Midwest tornados) and losses in the mortgage and financial guarantee segments associated with the financial crisis. Note from Table 15–4, these two segments experienced losses of 151.8 percent and 20.9 percent of premiums written, respectively, in 2012, down from 214.6 percent and 416.9 percent, respectively, during the height of the financial crisis in 2008. These losses pushed the 2008 combined ratio to 105.1 percent (up 9.5 points from 2007). Excluding losses from these two sectors, the industry's combined ratio would have been 101.0 percent for the year. Significantly, lower catastrophe losses and a recovering economy resulted in an industry combined ratio of 101.0 percent in 2009 and 102.4 percent in 2010. While 2009 saw the third straight year of negative premium growth (the first since the Great Depression), premiums written in 2010 began to recover. Further, few major catastrophes occurred during these two years.

The United States experienced one of the worst years ever in terms of catastrophes in 2011. Insured catastrophe losses totaled $33.6 billion, the fifth most expensive year on record for insured catastrophe losses on an inflation-adjusted basis. Overall net income after taxes fell 46 percent, from $35.2 billion in 2010 to $19.2 billion. Such high catastrophe losses, along with high underwriting losses in key noncatastrophe exposed lines such as workers' compensation, pushed the industry's combined ratio to 108.2 (its highest level since 2001). As a result of large decreases in catastrophe losses and a marked acceleration in premium growth, profitability in the P&C insurance industry rebounded during 2012. Despite the impact of Hurricane Sandy (which made landfall in the Northeast United States in late October and caused insured losses of $25.0 billion) and smaller investment gains, net income grew to $33.5 billion in 2012. The combined ratio decreased to 103.2.

Profitability in the property–casualty insurance industry surged to its highest level in the post-crisis era in 2013–2016 as sharply lower catastrophe losses, modestly higher premium growth, improved realized investment gains all worked to improve performance. The P&C sector net written premiums were $477 billion in 2013 and $497 billion in 2014, and $514 billion in 2015, crossing the half trillion mark for a record high level. The P&C sector net written premiums for the first six months of 2016 continued to be strong at $268 billion. Solid gains were reported for both commercial and personal lines of business as premium rate increases and growth in the U.S. economy drove growth in aggregate premiums. The industry's combined ratio fell to 96.3, 97.0, 98.3, and 100.0, respectively, over this period. Despite these improvements, persistently low interest rates remain a challenge for the industry. Maintaining combined ratios below 100 is absolutely essential in order for the industry to continue posting reasonable levels of profitability in this challenging interest rate environment.

LG 15-7

## Regulation

Similar to life insurance companies, P&C insurers are chartered at the state level and regulated by state commissions. In addition, state guarantee funds provide (some) protection to policyholders, in a manner similar to that described earlier for life insurance companies, should a P&C insurance company fail. The National Association of Insurance Commissioners (NAIC) provides various services to state regulatory commissions. These include a standardized examination system, the Insurance Regulatory Information System (IRIS), to identify insurers with loss, combined, and other ratios operating outside normal ranges.

www.naic.org

An additional burden that P&C insurers face in some activity lines—especially auto insurance and workers' compensation insurance—is rate regulation. Given the social welfare importance of these lines, state commissioners often set ceilings on the premiums and premium increases in these lines (usually based on specific cost of capital and line risk exposure formulas for the insurance supplier). This has led some insurers to leave states such as New Jersey, Florida, and California, which have the most restrictive regulations.

In recent years, the P&C industry has come under attack for the way it handled claims from homeowners associated with Hurricane Katrina. Homeowners' policies excluded damage caused by flooding. Insurers insisted the storm surge from Hurricane Katrina was classified as flood damage and therefore was excluded from coverage under policy forms that had been reviewed by regulators in each state and had been in force for years. Lawyers for policyholders of State Farm Insurance Company claimed that insurers were trying to avoid paying out on their homeowners policies by claiming it was a flood when it was a combination of hurricane winds and a storm surge. They claimed that the storm surge was not a flood but a direct result of the hurricane's winds, which is a covered risk. Policyholders claimed that State Farm and other insurance companies used "deceptive" sales practices to sell those hurricane policies and collected extra premiums from them. A verdict in January 2007 not only held State Farm responsible for policy limits that totaled more than $220,000 on a loss deemed to be due to storm surge flooding, but also held the company liable for punitive damages.

## DO YOU UNDERSTAND:

6. *Why P&C insurers hold more capital and reserves than life insurers do?*

7. *Why life insurers' assets are, on average, longer in maturity than P&C insurers' assets?*

8. *What the main lines of insurance offered by P&C insurers are?*

9. *What the components of the combined ratio are?*

10. *How the operating ratio differs from the combined ratio?*

11. *Why the combined ratio tends to behave cyclically?*

## GLOBAL ISSUES

Like the other sectors of the financial institutions industry, the insurance sector is becoming increasingly global. Table 15–7 lists the top 10 countries in terms of total premiums written in 2015 (in U.S. dollars) and the percentage share of the world market. Table 15–8 lists the top 10 insurance companies worldwide by total revenues. While the United States, Japan, and western Europe dominate the global market, all regions are engaged in the insurance business and many insurers are engaged internationally.

Worldwide, 2012 was the third costliest year for the worldwide insurance industry (after 2011 and 2005). Natural disasters cost insurers $65 billion. However, losses in the United States accounted for 90 percent of the total; Europe and Asia experienced just $3.2 billion and $1.7 billion in losses, respectively. Insured losses worldwide were down

**TABLE 15–7** The World's Top 10 Countries in Terms of Insurance Premiums Written

| Rank | Country | Life Premiums Written (in billions of U.S. $) | Property–Casualty Premiums Written (in billions of U.S. $) | Total Premiums Written (in billions of U.S. $) | Share of World Market |
|------|---------|-----------------------------------------------|-----------------------------------------------------------|-----------------------------------------------|-----------------------|
| 1. | United States | $552.5 | $736.8 | $1,316.7 | 28.9% |
| 2. | Japan | 343.8 | 105.9 | 449.7 | 9.9 |
| 3. | China | 210.8 | 175.7 | 386.5 | 8.5 |
| 4. | United Kingdom | 214.5 | 105.7 | 320.2 | 7.0 |
| 5. | France | 150.1 | 80.4 | 230.5 | 5.1 |
| 6. | Germany | 96.7 | 116.6 | 213.3 | 4.7 |
| 7. | Italy | 124.8 | 40.2 | 165.0 | 3.6 |
| 8. | South Korea | 98.2 | 55.4 | 153.6 | 3.4 |
| 9. | Canada | 49.3 | 65.7 | 115.0 | 2.5 |
| 10. | Taiwan | 79.6 | 16.4 | 96.0 | 2.1 |

**Source:** Swiss Re, sigma, no. 4/2016.

**TABLE 15–8**     **World's 10 Largest Insurance Companies by Total Revenues**

| Rank | Company | Revenues (billions of U.S. $) | Home Country | Industry |
|---|---|---|---|---|
| 1. | Berkshire Hathaway | $210.8 | United States | Property–Casualty |
| 2. | AXA Group | 129.3 | France | Life |
| 3. | Allianz | 122.9 | Germany | Property–Casualty |
| 4. | Japan Post Holdings | 118.8 | Japan | Life |
| 5. | Ping An Insurance | 110.3 | China | Life |
| 6. | Assicurazioni Generali | 102.6 | Italy | Life |
| 7. | China Life Insurance | 101.3 | China | Life |
| 8. | State Farm Insurance | 75.7 | United States | Property–Casualty |
| 9. | MetLife | 70.0 | United States | Life |
| 10. | Munich Re Group | 69.4 | Germany | Property–Casualty |

**Source:** Insurance Information Institute website, 2016. www.iii.org

from a record $119 billion in 2011, when horrific earthquakes in Japan and New Zealand produced huge payouts on insured losses. In 2012, total economic costs from natural disasters worldwide amounted to $160 billion, compared with $400 billion in 2011. In that year, outside the United States, earthquakes in Italy produced total insured losses of $1.6 billion and flooding in China in July caused insured damage totaling $180 million. Finally, no catastrophic events in terms of loss of life occurred in 2012.

Global insured losses from natural catastrophes and human-caused disasters fell to $45 billion in 2013. Of the 2013 insured losses, $37 billion were generated by natural catastrophes, with hail in Europe and floods in many regions being the main drivers. Even though the economic environment improved only marginally, the worldwide insurance industry grew in 2014. Total direct premiums written were up 3.7 percent and the life insurance sector returned to positive growth, with premiums up 4.3 percent after a 1.8 percent decline in 2013. P&C premium growth grew to 2.9 percent from 2.7 percent. In 2014 overall losses totaled $110 billion, of which about $31 billion were insured. This was 38 percent lower than the 10-year-average loss of $63 billion. The year 2015 saw the lowest catastrophe losses of any year since 2009. Overall insured losses totaled $27 billion. The year's most devastating natural catastrophe was the magnitude 7.8 earthquake in Nepal northwest of the capital Kathmandu. World insurance premiums rose 3.8 percent in 2015, compared with 3.5 percent in 2014. Nonlife premiums rose 3.6 percent in 2015, following 2.4 percent growth in 2014. Life insurance premiums grew by 4.0 percent after inflation in 2015, slower than the 4.3 percent growth achieved in 2014. The first half of 2016 saw an increase in worldwide natural catastrophes. Total worldwide losses during this period were $70 billion (of which $27 billion were insured). This was significantly higher than the prior year's first half losses of $59 billion, of which $19 billion were insured. Then on August 24, a 6.2-magnitude earthquake shook central Italy, killing at least 120.

## SUMMARY

This chapter examined the activities and regulation of insurance companies. The first part of the chapter described the various classes of life insurance and recent trends in this sector. The second part discussed property–casualty companies. The various lines that comprise property–casualty insurance are becoming increasingly blurred as multiple activity line coverages are offered. Both life and property–casualty insurance companies are regulated at the state rather than the federal level.

## QUESTIONS

1. How does the primary function of an insurance company compare with that of a depository institution? (*LG 15-1*)

2. What is the adverse selection problem? How does adverse selection affect the profitable management of an insurance company? (*LG 15-1*)

3. Contrast the balance sheets of depository institutions with those of life insurance firms. (*LG 15-3*)

4. How has the composition of the assets of U.S. life insurance companies changed over time? (*LG 15-3*)

5. What are the similarities and differences among the four basic lines of life insurance products? (*LG 15-2*)

6. Explain how annuities represent the reverse of life insurance activities. (*LG 15-2*)

7. How can life insurance and annuity products be used to create a steady stream of cash disbursements and payments to avoid either the payment or receipt of a single lump sum cash amount? (*LG 15-2*)

8. If an insurance company decides to offer a corporate customer a private pension fund, how would this change the balance sheet of the insurance company? (*LG 15-3*)

9. How does the regulation of insurance companies compare with that of depository institutions? (*LG 15-4*)

10. How do state guarantee funds for life insurance companies compare with deposit insurance for depository institutions? (*LG 15-4*)

11. How do life insurance companies earn profits? (*LG 15-3*)

12. What are the two major lines of property–casualty (P&C) insurance firms? (*LG 15-5*)

13. How have P&C industry product lines based on net premiums written by insurance companies changed over time? (*LG 15-5*)

14. What are the three sources of underwriting risk in the P&C industry? (*LG 15-5*)

15. Identify four characteristics or features of the perils insured against by property–casualty insurance. Rank the features in terms of actuarial predictability and total loss potential. (*LG 15-5*)

16. How do increases in unexpected inflation affect P&C insurers? (*LG 15-5*)

17. Which of the insurance lines listed below will be charged a higher premium by insurance companies and why? (*LG 15-6*)
    a. Low-severity, high-frequency lines versus high-severity, low-frequency lines.
    b. Long-tail versus short-tail lines.

18. Contrast the balance sheet of a property–casualty insurance company with the balance sheet of a commercial bank. Explain the balance sheet differences in terms of the differences in the primary functions of the two organizations. (*LG 15-1*)

19. What does the loss ratio measure? What has been the long-term trend of the loss ratio? Why? (*LG 15-6*)

20. What does the expense ratio measure? Identify and explain the two major sources of expense risk to a property–casualty insurer. Why has the long-term trend in this ratio been decreasing? (*LG 15-6*)

21. How is the combined ratio defined? What does it measure? (*LG 15-6*)

22. What is the investment yield on premiums earned? Why has this ratio become so important to property–casualty insurers? (*LG 15-6*)

## PROBLEMS

1. Calculate the following: (*LG 15-2*)
   a. What is the amount of the annuity purchase required if you wish to receive a fixed payment of $200,000 for 20 years? Assume that the annuity will earn 10 percent per year.
   b. Calculate the annual cash flows (annuity payments) from a fixed-payment annuity if the present value of the 20-year annuity is $1 million and the annuity earns a guaranteed annual return of 10 percent. The payments are to begin at the end of the current year.
   c. Calculate the annual cash flows (annuity payments) from a fixed-payment annuity if the present value of the 20-year annuity is $1 million and the annuity earns a guaranteed annual return of 10 percent. The payments are to begin at the end of five years.

2. Calculate the following: (*LG 15-2*)
   a. What is the amount of the annuity purchase required if you wish to receive a fixed payment of $240,000 for 20 years? Assume that the annuity will earn 7 percent per year.

   b. Calculate the annual cash flows from a $2.5 million, 20-year fixed-payment annuity earning a guaranteed return of 7 percent per year if payments are to begin at the end of the current year.
   c. Calculate the annual cash flows from a $2.5 million, 20-year fixed-payment annuity earning a guaranteed return of 7 percent per year if payments are to begin at the end of year 6.

3. You deposit $10,000 annually into a life insurance fund for the next 10 years, at which time you plan to retire. Instead of a lump sum, you wish to receive annuities for the next 20 years. What is the annual payment you expect to receive beginning in year 11 if you assume an interest rate of 8 percent for the whole time period? (*LG 15-2*)

4. You deposit $10,000 annually into a life insurance fund for the next 10 years, after which time you plan to retire. (*LG 15-2*)
   a. If the deposits are made at the beginning of the year and earn an interest rate of 8 percent, what will be the amount in the retirement fund at the end of year 10?

**b.** Instead of a lump sum, you wish to receive annuities for the next 20 years (years 11 through 30). What is the constant annual payment you expect to receive at the beginning of each year if you assume an interest rate of 8 percent during the distribution period?

**c.** Repeat parts (a) and (b) assuming earning rates of 7 percent and 9 percent during the deposit period and earning rates of 7 percent and 9 percent during the distribution period.

5. You deposit $12,000 annually into a life insurance fund for the next 30 years, after which time you plan to retire. (*LG 15-2*)

**a.** If the deposits are made at the beginning of the year and earn an interest rate of 7 percent, what will be the amount of retirement funds at the end of year 30?

**b.** Instead of a lump sum, you wish to receive annuities for the next 20 years (years 31 through 50). What is the constant annual payment you expect to receive at the beginning of each year if you assume an interest rate of 7 percent during the distribution period?

**c.** Repeat parts (a) and (b) assuming earning rates of 6 percent and 8 percent during the deposit period and earning rates of 6 percent and 8 percent during the distribution period. During which period does the change in the earning rate have the greatest impact?

6. Calculate the following: (*LG 15-2*)

**a.** Suppose a 65-year-old person wants to purchase an annuity from an insurance company that would pay $20,000 per year until the end of that person's life. The insurance company expects this person to live for 15 more years and would be willing to pay 6 percent on the annuity. How much should the insurance company ask this person to pay for the annuity?

**b.** A second 65-year-old person wants the same $20,000 annuity, but this person is healthier and is expected to live for 20 more years. If the same 6 percent interest rate applies, how much should this healthier person be charged for the annuity?

**c.** In each case, what is the new purchase price of the annuity if the distribution payments are made at the beginning of the year?

7. Calculate the following: (*LG 15-2*)

**a.** Suppose a 60-year-old person wants to purchase an annuity from an insurance company that would pay $15,000 per year until the end of that person's life. The insurance company expects this person to live for 20 more years and would be willing to pay 5 percent on the annuity. How much should the insurance company ask this person to pay for the annuity?

**b.** A second 60-year-old person wants the same $15,000 annuity, but this person is much healthier and is expected to live for 30 more years. If the same 5 percent interest rate applies, how much should this healthier person be charged for the annuity?

**c.** In each case, what is the difference in the purchase price of the annuity if the distribution payments are made at the beginning of the year?

8. Calculate the following: (*LG 15-6*)

**a.** If the loss ratio on a line of property insurance is 73 percent, the loss adjustment expense is 12.5 percent, and the ratio of commissions and other acquisitions expenses is 18 percent, is this line profitable?

**b.** How does your answer to part (a) change if investment yields of 8 percent are added?

9. An insurance company's projected loss ratio is 77.5 percent, and its expense ratio is 23.9 percent. It estimates that dividends to policyholders will add another 5 percent. What is the minimum yield on investments required in order to maintain a positive operating ratio? (*LG 15-6*)

10. An insurance company's projected loss ratio is 64.8 percent and its expense ratio is 25.6 percent. The company estimates that dividends to policyholders will be 6 percent. What must be the minimum yield on investments to achieve a positive operating ratio? (*LG 15-6*)

11. An insurance company collected $3.6 million in premiums. and disbursed $1.96 million in losses. Loss adjustment expenses amounted to 6.6 percent and dividends paid to policyholders totaled 1.2 percent. The total income generated from their investments was $170,000 after all expenses were paid. What is the net profitability in dollars? (*LG 15-6*)

12. An insurance company collected $12.75 million in premiums and disbursed $9.18 million in losses. Loss adjustment expenses amounted to 20.1 percent and dividends paid to policyholders totaled 5 percent. The total income generated from the company's investments was $1,420,000 after all expenses were paid. What is the net profitability in dollars? (*LG 15-6*)

13. A property–casualty insurer brings in $6.25 million in premiums on its homeowners MP line of insurance. The line's losses amount to $4,343,750, expenses are $1,593,750, and dividends are $156,250. The insurer earns $218,750 in the investment of its premiums. Calculate the line's loss ratio, expense ratio, dividend ratio, combined ratio, investment ratio, operating ratio, and overall profitability. (*LG 15-6*)

14. A property–casualty insurer brings in $5.55 million in premiums on its homeowners multiple line of insurance. The line's losses amount to $3,962,700, expenses are $1,526,250, and dividends are $333,000. The insurer earns $349,650 in the investment of its premiums. Calculate the line's loss ratio, expense ratio, dividend ratio, combined ratio, investment ratio, operating ratio, and overall profitability. (*LG 15-6*)

## SEARCH THE SITE

Go to the Federal Reserve Board's website at **www.federalreserve.gov** and find the most recent distribution of life insurance industry assets for Table 15–2. Click on "Economic Research and Data." Click on "Financial Accounts of the United States." Click on "PDF." This will bring the file (Table L.116) onto your computer that contains the relevant data.

### Questions

1. How have the values of government securities, corporate securities, mortgages, and policy loans changed since 2016?
2. What are the likely reasons for these changes?

## SEARCH THE SITE

Go to the Insurance Information Institute's website at **www.iii.org** and use the following steps to find the most recent data on the world's largest life insurance companies by total revenue. Click on "Publications." Click on "International Insurance Fact Book 20XX." Click on "World Rankings." This will bring the file onto your computer that contains the relevant data.

### Questions

1. What are total revenues and assets of the top 10 insurance companies?
2. How have these values changed since 2015 as reported in Table 15–8?

# chapter
# 16

# Securities Firms and Investment Banks

## Learning Goals

**LG 16-1** *Know the different types of securities firms and investment banks.*

**LG 16-2** *Understand the major activity areas in which securities firms and investment banks engage.*

**LG 16-3** *Differentiate among the major assets and liabilities held by securities firms.*

**LG 16-4** *Know the main regulators of securities firms and investment banks.*

## SERVICES OFFERED BY SECURITIES FIRMS VERSUS INVESTMENT BANKS: CHAPTER OVERVIEW

Securities firms and investment banks primarily help net suppliers of funds (e.g., households) transfer funds to net users of funds (e.g., businesses) at a low cost and with a maximum degree of efficiency. Unlike other types of FIs, securities firms and investment banks do not transform the securities issued by the net users of funds into claims that may be "more" attractive to the net suppliers of funds (e.g., banks and their creation of bank deposits). Rather, they serve as brokers intermediating between fund suppliers and users.

Investment banking involves transactions such as the raising of debt and equity securities for corporations or governments. This includes the origination, underwriting, and placement of securities in money and capital markets for corporate or government issuers. Securities services involve assistance in the trading of securities in the secondary markets (brokerage services or market making). Together these services are performed by securities firms and investment banks. The largest companies in this industry perform multiple services (e.g., underwriting and brokerage services). These full-line firms are generally called investment banks. Many other firms concentrate their services in one area only (either securities trading or securities underwriting). That is, some firms in the industry specialize in the purchase, sale, and brokerage of existing securities (the retail side of the business) and are called securities firms, while other firms specialize in originating, underwriting, and distributing issues of new securities (the commercial side of the business) and are called investment banks. Both segments have undergone substantial structural changes in recent years. Some of the most recent consolidations include the acquisition of Bear Stearns by J.P. Morgan Chase, the bankruptcy of Lehman Brothers, and the acquisition of Merrill Lynch by Bank of America. Indeed, as discussed later in the chapter, the

**Figure 16–1** Total Values of Mergers and Acquisitions Managed by Investment Banks, 1990–2016

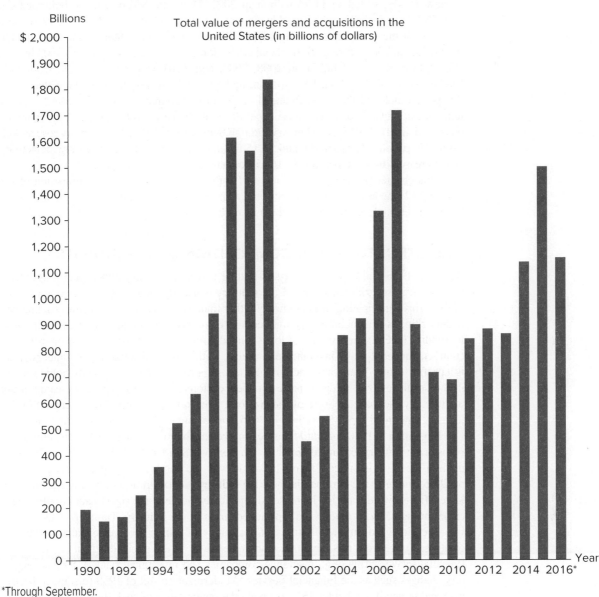

*Through September.

**Sources:** Thomson Financial website, various years. www.thomsonreuters.com

investment banking industry has seen the failure or acquisition of all but two of its largest firms (Goldman Sachs and Morgan Stanley) and these two firms converted to commercial bank holding companies in 2008.

Investment banking also includes corporate finance activities such as advising on mergers and acquisitions (M&As), as well as advising on the restructuring of existing corporations. Figure 16–1 reports M&As managed by investment banks for the period 1990–2016. Total dollar volume (measured by completed merger transaction value) of domestic M&As increased from less than $200 billion in 1990 to $1.83 trillion in 2000.[1] This merger wave was not restricted to the United States. For example, in 2000 there were over 36,700 merger and acquisition deals globally, valued at over $3.49 trillion. Nevertheless, reflecting the downturn in the U.S. economy, M&A transactions fell 53 percent in 2001 to $819 billion on

---

1. This reflected more than 10,800 deals in 2000.

only 7,525 deals (the first time since 1995 there were fewer than 10,000 deals). Similarly, worldwide M&As fell to $1.74 trillion in 2001. Domestic M&A activity bottomed out at $458 billion in 2002 (while worldwide activity fell to $1.20 trillion) before recovering (along with the economy), topping $1.71 trillion in the United States (and $4.5 trillion worldwide) in 2007. During the financial crisis, domestic M&A activity fell to $903 billion, $713 billion, and $687 billion in 2008, 2009, and 2010, respectively, while worldwide M&As fell to $2.9 trillion, $1.7 trillion, and $1.8 trillion, respectively. Note that while this period included the worst financial crisis since the Great Depression, M&A activity remained at higher levels than those experienced in the early 2000s. As the U.S. economy recovered in 2014, 2015, and (January through September) 2016, M&A activity rose as well (to $1.13 trillion, $1.50 trillion, and $1.15 trillion, respectively), while worldwide activity also increased (to $2.46 trillion, $3.16 trillion, and $2.30 trillion, respectively).

This chapter presents an overview of (1) the size, structure, and composition of the industry; (2) the key activities of securities firms and investment banks; (3) the industry's balance sheet and recent trends; and (4) its regulation.

## SIZE, STRUCTURE, AND COMPOSITION OF THE INDUSTRY

Because of the emphasis on securities trading and underwriting rather than longer-term investment in securities, the size of the industry is usually measured by the equity capital of the firms participating in the industry rather than by "asset size." Securities trading and underwriting is a financial service that requires relatively little investment in assets or liability funding (such as the issuance of loans funded through deposits or payments on insurance contracts funded through insurance premiums). Rather, securities trading and underwriting is a profit- (equity-) generating activity that does not require that FIs actually hold or invest in the securities they trade or issue for their customers. Accordingly, asset value is not traditionally the main measure of the size of a firm in this industry. Equity capital in this industry amounted to $235.0 billion in 2015, supporting total assets of $4.32 trillion.

Beginning in 1980 and until the stock market crash of October 19, 1987, the number of firms in the industry expanded dramatically, from 5,248 in 1980 to 9,515 in 1987. The aftermath of the crash included a major shakeout, with the number of firms declining to 6,016 by 2006 similar to the commercial banking industry, concentration of business among the largest firms over this period increased dramatically. Some of the significant growth in size came through M&As among the top-ranked firms in the industry. Table 16–1 lists major U.S. securities industry M&A transactions, many of which involve repeated ownership changes. Notice from this table that many recent M&As are interindustry mergers among financial service firms (e.g., insurance companies and investment banks). Recent regulatory changes such as the Financial Services Modernization Act of 1999 (discussed briefly here and in detail in Chapter 13) have been the major cause of such mergers. In fact, note in Table 16–1 that a majority of the securities industry mergers and acquisitions occurring in the 2000s include securities firms that are part of a financial services holding company.

The financial crisis resulted in a second major change in the structure of the industry. The five largest investment banks in existence at the beginning of 2008 (Lehman Brothers, Bear Stearns, Merrill Lynch, Goldman Sachs, and Morgan Stanley) were all gone as investment banks by the end of the year. Lehman Brothers failed at the start of the financial crisis, Bear Stearns and Merrill Lynch were acquired by financial services holding companies (J.P. Morgan Chase and Bank of America, respectively), and Goldman Sachs and Morgan Stanley requested and were granted commercial bank charters. As at least a partial result of the four investment banks being purchased by or converting to a commercial bank, in 2015 commercial bank holding companies' fee income from securities brokerage topped $10.50 billion, over 28 percent of the industry total. This is up from 2012 when fee income was $9.15 billion, but down from pre–financial crisis levels of $14.10 billion. Table 16–2 lists some of the top bank holding companies in terms of securities brokerage fee income. Further, the number of securities firms continued to fall to 4,115 by 2016. The investment banking industry was irrevocably changed.

**TABLE 16–1**  Major U.S. Securities Industry Merger and Acquisition Transactions

| Rank | Deal | Price (in billions of dollars) | Year |
|---|---|---|---|
| 1. | Citicorp merges with Travelers Group (which owned Smith Barney and Salomon) | $83.0 | 1998 |
| 2. | J. P. Morgan acquires Bank One* | 60.0 | 2004 |
| 3. | Bank of America acquires Fleet Boston* | 49.3 | 2003 |
| 4. | Bank of America acquires Merrill Lynch | 47.1 | 2008 |
| 5. | Chase acquires J. P. Morgan* | 35.0 | 2000 |
| 6. | Bank of America acquires MBNA* | 35.0 | 2005 |
| 7. | Wachovia acquires Golden West Financial* | 25.5 | 2006 |
| 8. | Wachovia acquires Southtrust* | 14.3 | 2004 |
| 9. | BlackRock Inc. acquires Barclays Global Investors | 13.5 | 2009 |
| 10. | UBS acquires Paine Webber Group | 12.0 | 2000 |
| 11. | Credit Suisse First Boston acquires Donaldson Lufkin Jenrette | 11.5 | 2000 |
| 12. | Dean Witter merges with Morgan Stanley | 10.2 | 1997 |
| 13. | Deutsche Bank acquires Bankers Trust* | 10.1 | 1998 |
| 14. | Region's Financial acquires AmSouth | 10.0 | 2006 |
| 15. | CME Group acquires NYMEX Holdings | 9.5 | 2008 |
| 16. | Travelers Group acquires Salomon Inc. | 9.0 | 1997 |
| 17. | Intercontinental Exchange acquires NYSE | 8.2 | 2012 |
| 18. | J. P. Morgan acquires Bear Stearns | 0.2 | 2008 |

*These organizations owned Section 20 securities subsidiaries and/or established financial services holding companies (FSHCs) under the Financial Services Modernization Act.
**Source:** Authors' research.

**LG 16-1**

**broker-dealers**

*Firms that assist in the trading of existing securities.*

**underwriting**

*Assisting in the issue of new securities.*

In its changed state, the firms in the industry can be divided along a number of dimensions. First are the largest firms, the diversified financial service or national full-service investment banks that service both retail customers (especially by acting as **broker-dealers**—assisting in the trading of existing securities, or secondary market transactions) and corporate customers (by securities **underwriting**—assisting in the issue of new securities, or primary market transactions).

With the changes in the past few years, national full-service firms now fall into three subgroups. First are the commercial bank or financial services holding companies that are the largest of the full-service investment banks. They have extensive domestic and international operations and offer advice, underwriting, brokerage, trading, and asset management services. The largest of these firms include Bank of America (through its acquisition of Merrill Lynch), Morgan Stanley, and J.P. Morgan (through its many acquisitions, including that of Bear Stearns, for $236 million in 2008). Second are the national full-service firms that specialize more in corporate finance or primary market activities and are highly active in trading securities, or secondary market activities. A good example of this is Goldman Sachs. Third are the large investment banks. These firms maintain more limited branch

**TABLE 16–2**  Top Bank Holding Companies in Securities Brokerage Fee Income
*(in billions of dollars)*

| Bank Holding Company | Securities Brokerage Fee Income |
|---|---|
| Bank of America | $11.39 |
| Morgan Stanley | 6.51 |
| Wells Fargo | 5.01 |
| Goldman Sachs | 3.51 |
| J.P. Morgan Chase | 2.30 |
| Citigroup | 1.76 |

**DO YOU UNDERSTAND:**

1. *How securities firms and investment banks fit into the intermediation process?*

2. *The trend in the number of securities firms and investment banks since 1980?*

3. *What categories of firms exist in the securities firm and investment banking industry?*

4. *What the difference is between brokerage services and underwriting services?*

**discount broker**

*A stockbroker that conducts trades for customers but does not offer investment advice.*

networks concentrated in major cities operating with predominantly institutional client bases. These firms include Lazard Ltd. and Greenhill & Co.

The rest of the industry is comprised of firms that perform a mix of primary and secondary market services for a particular segment of the financial markets:

1. Regional securities firms, which are often classified as large, medium, and small and concentrate on servicing customers in a particular region, such as New York or California (e.g., Raymond James Financial).
2. Specialized **discount brokers** (such as Charles Schwab), which effect trades for customers without offering investment advice or tips.
3. Specialized electronic trading securities firms (such as E*Trade), which provide a platform for customers to trade without the use of a broker. Rather, trades are enacted on a computer via the Internet.[2] The number of people living in U.S. households that used an online investing/stock trading service increased from 11.63 million in 2008 to 14.01 million in 2015. New features, such as the ability to trade from mobile phones and tablets, and the increased speed with which trades can be made are some of the main reasons for the increase.
4. Venture capital and private equity firms, which pool money from individual investors and other FIs (e.g., insurance companies) to fund relatively small and new businesses (e.g., biotechnology).[3]
5. Other firms in this industry include research boutiques, floor specialists, companies with large clearing operations, and other firms that do not fit into one of the categories above. This would include firms such as KCG (a leading firm in off-exchange trading of U.S. equities) and floor specialist Hilliard Lyons.

## SECURITIES FIRM AND INVESTMENT BANK ACTIVITY AREAS

**LG 16-2**

Securities firms and investment banks engage in as many as eight key activity areas: investment banking, venture capital, market making, trading, investing, cash management, mergers and acquisitions, and other service functions. As we describe each of these below, note that while each activity is available to a firm's customers independently, many of the activities can be and are conducted simultaneously (such as mergers and acquisitions, issuing debt and equity, and advisory services) for a firm's customers.

### Investment Banking

Investment banking refers to activities related to underwriting and distributing new issues of debt and equity securities. New issues can be either first-time issues of a company's debt or equity securities or the new issues of a firm whose debt or equity is already trading—secondary security offerings or seasoned issues (see Chapter 8 for a detailed discussion). As discussed in Chapter 8, an investment bank will often bring in a number of other investment banks (a so-called syndicate) to help sell and distribute a new issue. In 2012, a total of $6.19 trillion of debt and equity was underwritten by investment banks. This was up from $4.95 trillion underwritten in 2008, but well below the pre-crisis amounts of $7.51 trillion and $7.84 trillion in 2007 and 2006, respectively. Further, in just the first nine months of 2016, $5.96 trillion of debt and equity was underwritten by investment banks. Table 16–3 lists the top five underwriters of debt and equity for the first nine months of 2016 based on the dollar value of issues underwritten. The top five underwriters represented 26.7 percent of the industry total, suggesting that the industry is dominated by a small number of "top tier" underwriting firms. Top tier rating and the implied reputation this brings has a huge effect in this business. At times, investment banks have refused to participate in an issue

---

2. Discount brokers and electronic trading securities firms usually charge lower commissions than do full-service brokers such as Merrill Lynch.

3. Venture capital firms generally play an active management role in the firms in which they invest, often including a seat on the board of directors, and hold significant equity stakes. This differentiates them from traditional investment banking and securities firms.

**TABLE 16–3**  Top Underwriters of Global Debt and Equity, Ranked by All Issues, 2016* *(in billions of dollars)*

| Rank | Underwriter | Value | Number of Issues | Market Share[†] |
|---|---|---|---|---|
| 1. | J.P. Morgan | $ 388.8 | 1,537 | 6.5% |
| 2. | Citigroup | 331.8 | 1,296 | 5.6 |
| 3. | Bank of America | 322.5 | 1,325 | 5.4 |
| 4. | Barclays Capital | 292.9 | 1,022 | 4.9 |
| 5. | Goldman Sachs | 255.8 | 897 | 4.3 |
| Top 5 | | $1,591.8 | 6,077 | 26.7% |
| Industry total | | $5,961.5 | 18,599 | |

*Through September.
[†]Based on value of issues underwritten.

**Source:** Thomson Reuters Deals Intelligence, 2016. www.thomsonreuters.com

because their name would not be placed where they desired it on the "tombstone" advertisement announcing an issue (see Chapter 8).

Securities underwriting can be undertaken through either public or private offerings. A public offering represents the sale of a security to the public at large. In a private offering, an investment bank acts as a **private placement** agent for a fee, placing the securities with one or a few large institutional investors such as life insurance companies. Issuers of privately placed securities are not required to register with the SEC since the placements (sales of securities) are made only to large, sophisticated investors. In a public offering, the securities may be underwritten on a best efforts or a firm commitment basis, and the securities may be offered to the public at large. With best efforts underwriting, investment bankers act as *agents* on a fee basis related to their success in placing the issue with investors. In firm commitment underwriting, the investment bank acts as a *principal,* purchasing the securities from the issuer at one price and seeking to place them with public investors at a slightly higher price. Factors causing preference for a best efforts versus a firm commitment offering to the issuing firm include general volatility in the market, stability and maturity of the financial health of the issuing firm, and the perceived appetite for new issues in the market place. The investment bank will also consider these factors when negotiating the fees and/or pricing spread in making its decision regarding the offering process. Finally, in addition to investment banking operations in the corporate securities markets, the investment bank may participate as an underwriter (primary dealer) in government, municipal, and mortgage-backed securities. See Chapters 6, 7, and 8 for a detailed discussion of these services. Table 16–4 shows the top ranked underwriters for 2015 and (January through September) 2016 in the different areas of securities underwriting.

**private placement**

*A securities issue placed with one or a few large institutional investors.*

**TABLE 16–4**  Who's Number 1 in Each Market

| Type | Jan.–Sept. 2016 | | Full Year 2015 | |
|---|---|---|---|---|
| | Amount in Billions | Top-Ranked Manager | Amount in Billions | Top-Ranked Manager |
| Global debt | $ 5,518.0 | J.P. Morgan | $ 5,229.9 | J.P. Morgan |
| Convertible debt | 58.2 | Morgan Stanley | 90.1 | J.P. Morgan |
| Investment-grade debt | 2,652.7 | J.P. Morgan | 2,641.4 | J.P. Morgan |
| Mortgage debt | 352.9 | Wells Fargo | 447.8 | Credit Suisse |
| Asset-backed securities | 222.8 | J.P. Morgan | 344.1 | Citigroup |
| IPOs | 81.2 | Morgan Stanley | 188.4 | Morgan Stanley |
| Municipal new issues | 323.4 | Bank of America Merrill Lynch | 377.6 | Bank of America Merrill Lynch |
| Syndicated loans | 2,905.4 | J.P. Morgan | 4,662.5 | J.P. Morgan |
| Equity | 420.9 | J.P. Morgan | 779.9 | Goldman Sachs |

**Source:** Thomson Reuters Deals Intelligence, 2016. www.thomsonreuters.com

## EXAMPLE 16–1   Best Efforts versus Firm Commitment Securities Offering

An investment bank agrees to underwrite an issue of 20,000,000 shares of stock for Murray Construction Corp. on a firm commitment basis. The investment bank pays $15.50 per share to Murray Construction Corp. for the 20,000,000 shares of stock. It then sells those shares to the public for $16.35 per share. How much money does Murray Construction Corp. receive? What is the profit to the investment bank? If the investment bank can only sell the shares for 14.75, how much money does Murray Construction Corp. receive? What is the profit to the investment bank?

If the investment bank sells the stock for $16.35 per share, Murray Construction Corp. receives $15.50 × 20,000,000 shares = $310,000,000. The profit to the investment bank is ($16.35 – $15.50) × 20,000,000 shares = $17,000,000. The stock price of Murray Construction Corp. is $16.35, since that is what the public agrees to pay. From the perspective of Murray Construction Corp., the $17,000,000 represents the commission that it must pay to issue the stock.

If the investment bank sells the stock for $14.75 per share, Murray Construction Corp. still receives $15.50 × 20,000,000 shares = $310,000,000. The profit to the investment bank is ($14.75 – $15.50) × 20,000,000 shares = –$15,000,000. The stock price of Murray Construction Corp. is $14.75, since that is what the public agrees to pay. From the perspective of the investment bank, the –$15,000,000 represents a loss for the firm commitment it made to Murray Construction Corp. to issue the stock.

Suppose instead the investment bank agrees to underwrite these 20,000,000 shares on a best efforts basis. The investment bank is able to sell 18,400,000 shares for $15.50 per share, and it charges Murray Construction Corp. $0.375 per share sold. How much money does Murray Construction Corp. receive? What is the profit to the investment bank? If the investment bank can only sell the shares for 14.75, how much money does Murray Construction Corp. receive? What is the profit to the investment bank?

If the investment bank sells the stock for $15.50 per share, Murray Construction Corp. receives ($15.50 − $0.375) × 18,400,000 shares = $278,300,000, the investment bank's profit is $0.375 × 18,400,000 shares = $6,900,000, and the stock price is $15.50 per share, since that is what the public pays.

If the investment bank sells the stock for $14.75 per share, Murray Construction Corp. receives ($14.75 − $0.375) × 18,400,000 shares = $264,500,000, the investment bank's profit is still $0.375 × 18,400,000 shares = $6,900,000, and the stock price is $14.75 per share, since that is what the public pays.

### Venture Capital

**venture capital**

*A professionally managed pool of money used to finance new and often high-risk firms.*

A difficulty for new and small firms in obtaining debt financing from commercial banks is that CBs are generally not willing or able to make loans to new companies with no assets and business history. In this case, new and small firms often turn to investment banks (and other firms) that make venture capital investments to get capital financing as well as advice. **Venture capital** is a professionally managed pool of money used to finance new and often high-risk firms. Venture capital is generally provided to back an untried company and its managers in return for an equity investment in the firm. Venture capital firms do not make outright loans. Rather, they purchase an equity interest in the firm that gives them the same rights and privileges associated with an equity investment made by the firm's other owners. As equity holders, venture capital firms are not generally passive investors. They provide valuable expertise to the firm's managers and sometimes even help in recruiting senior managers for the firm. They also generally expect to be fully informed about the firm's operations, any problems, and whether the joint goals of all the firm's owners are being met.

The terms *venture capital* and *private equity* are often used interchangeably. However, there are distinct differences in the two types of investment institutions. For example, venture capital firms, generally using the pooled investment resources of institutions and wealthy individuals, concern themselves more with startup business concerns, while private equity firms acquire the investment funds they use from sources such as equity securities and nonpublicly traded stocks as well as the institutional and individual investment pooling used by venture capital firms. Further, venture capital firms tend to utilize teams of either scientific or business professionals to help identify new and emerging technologies in which to place their money. Private equity firms deal more with existing companies that have already proven themselves in the business field. As a result of the financial crisis, the differences between venture capital firms and private equity firms have become less distinct. With fewer new ventures being brought forth, there has been greater competition between the two types of investment institutions, with both searching for and funding the same types of new and small firms.

**institutional venture capital firms**

*Business entities whose sole purpose is to find and fund the most promising new firms.*

There are many types of venture capital firms. **Institutional venture capital firms** are business entities whose sole purpose is to find and fund the most promising new firms. Private-sector institutional venture capital firms include limited partner venture capital firms (that are established by professional venture capital firms, acting as general partners in the firm: organizing and managing the firm and eventually liquidating their equity investment), financial venture capital firms (subsidiaries of investment or commercial banks), and corporate venture capital firms (subsidiaries of nonfinancial corporations which generally specialize in making start-up investments in high-tech firms). Limited partner venture capital firms dominate the industry. In addition to these private-sector institutional venture capital firms, the federal government, through the SBA, operates Small Business Investment Companies (SBICs). SBICs are privately organized venture capital firms licensed by the SBA that make equity investments (as well as loans) to entrepreneurs for start-up activities and expansions. As federally sponsored entities, SBICs have relied on their unique opportunity to obtain investment funds from the U.S. Treasury at very low rates relative to private-sector institutional venture capital firms. In contrast to institutional venture capital firms, **angel venture capitalists (angels)** are wealthy individuals who make equity investments. Angel venture capitalists have invested much more in new and small firms than institutional venture capital firms.

**angel venture capitalists (angels)**

*Wealthy individuals who make equity investments.*

Venture capital firms receive many unsolicited proposals of funding from new and small firms. A majority of these requests are rejected. Venture capital firms look for two things in making their decisions to invest in a firm. The first is a high return. Venture capital firms are willing to invest in high-risk new and small firms. However, they require high levels of returns (sometimes as high as 700 percent within five to seven years) to take on these risks. The second is an easy exit. Venture capital firms realize a profit on their investments by eventually selling their interests in the firm. They want a quick and easy exit opportunity when it comes time to sell. Basically, venture capital firms provide equity funds to new, unproven, and young firms. This separates venture capital firms from commercial banks, which prefer to invest in existing, financially secure businesses.

Although venture capital business boomed in the 1990s and 2000s, this area took a hit after the financial crisis. The Volcker Rule, part of the Wall Street Reform and Consumer Protection Act of 2010, restricts banks from making big bets with their own money and thus has sharply reduced banks' investments in their own funds. As a result of the rule, Goldman Sachs had to shrink the size of its own investment in its funds to just 3 percent from as much as 37 percent. Bank of America decided to exit the private equity business altogether and Citigroup explored several options for its private equity funds after reducing its investments in hedge funds. For years, investment banks have attracted clients to invest in their venture capital funds by risking their own funds as well as the funds of their partners. However, this changed when the Volcker Rule was implemented in July 2014. As a result, investors have become more cautious about putting their money into venture capital funds.

### Market Making

Market making involves the creation of a secondary market in an asset by a securities firm or investment bank. Thus, in addition to being primary dealers in government securities and underwriters of corporate bonds and equities, investment banks make a secondary market in these instruments. Market making can involve either agency or principal transactions. *Agency transactions* are two-way transactions made on behalf of *customers*— for example, acting as a *stockbroker* or dealer for a fee or commission (as discussed in Chapter 8). On the NYSE, a market maker in a stock such as IBM may, upon the placement of orders by its customers, buy the stock at $185 from one customer and immediately resell it at $186 to another customer. The $1 difference between the buy and sell price is usually called the bid-ask spread and represents a large proportion of the market maker's profit. In *principal transactions,* the market maker seeks to profit on the price movements of securities and takes either long or short inventory positions for its own account. (Or the market maker may take an inventory position to stabilize the market in the securities.) In the previous example, the market maker would buy the IBM stock at $185 and hold it in its own portfolio in expectation of a price increase. Normally, market making can be a fairly profitable business. However, in periods of market stress or high volatility, these profits can rapidly disappear. For example, on the NYSE, in return for having monopoly power in market making for individual stocks (e.g., IBM), market makers have an "affirmative obligation" to buy stocks from sellers even when the market is crashing. This caused a number of actual and near bankruptcies for NYSE market makers at the time of the financial crisis. Finally, competition from Internet-based exchanges such as Instinet and Direct Edge has cut into trader's profits. For example, in 2016 only 9 percent of the total share volume on the NYSE is handled by floor specialists with no electronic aid; this is down from 100 percent in the early 1990s. Additionally, the number of floor traders on the NYSE has fallen to less than 1,000, from about 5,000 at the exchange's peak in the early 2000s.

Investment banks are major market makers in the derivatives securities markets. For example, in 2016 J.P. Morgan Chase managed over $53 trillion in derivative securities (28 percent of all derivative securities held by financial institutions). In just the first six months of 2016, Goldman Sachs earned over $2.8 billion making the market in these securities. Derivative securities, however, are also potentially the riskiest of the financial securities in which investment banks make the market. Indeed, at the center of the financial crisis were losses associated with off-balance-sheet mortgage-backed (derivative) securities created and held by these and other FIs. Losses from the falling value of subprime mortgages and derivative securities backed by these mortgages reached $1 trillion worldwide through 2009 and resulted in the failure, acquisition, or bailout of some of the largest investment banks (e.g., Lehman Brothers and Bear Stearns) and a near meltdown of the world's financial and economic systems.

### Trading

Trading is closely related to the market-making activities performed by securities firms and investment banks just described; a trader takes an active net position in an underlying instrument or asset. There are at least six types of trading activities:

1. *Position Trading*—involves purchases of large blocks of securities on the expectation of a favorable price move. Position traders maintain long or short positions for intervals of up to several weeks or even months. Rather than attempting to profit from very short-term movements in prices, as day traders do, position traders take relatively longer views of market trends. Such positions also facilitate the smooth functioning of the secondary markets in such securities.

2. *Pure Arbitrage*—entails buying an asset in one market at one price and selling it immediately in another market at a higher price. Pure arbitrageurs often attempt to profit from price discrepancies that may exist between the spot, or cash, price of a security and its corresponding futures price. Some important theoretical pricing relationships in futures markets should exist with spot markets and prices (see Chapter 10). When these relationships get out of line, pure arbitrageurs enter the market to exploit them.

3. *Risk Arbitrage*—involves buying securities in anticipation of some information release—such as a merger or takeover announcement or a Federal Reserve interest rate announcement. It is termed *risk arbitrage* because if the event does not actually occur—for example, if a merger does not take place or the Federal Reserve does not change interest rates—the trader stands to lose money.

4. *Program Trading*—is defined by the NYSE as the simultaneous buying and selling of a portfolio of at least 15 different stocks valued at more than $1 million, using computer programs to initiate such trades. Program trading is a type of pure arbitrage trading in that it is often associated with seeking to profit from differences between the cash market price (e.g., the Standard & Poor's 500 Stock Market Index) and the *futures* market price of a particular instrument.[4] Because computers are used to continuously monitor stock and futures prices—and can even initiate buy or sell orders—these trades are classified separately as *program trading*.

5. *Stock Brokerage*—involves the trading of securities on behalf of individuals who want to transact in the money or capital markets. To conduct such transactions, individuals contact their broker (such as Merrill Lynch), who then sends the orders to its representative at the exchange to conduct the trades (see Chapter 8). Large brokerage firms often have several licenses on the floor of a stock exchange (e.g., NYSE), through which their commission brokers (see Chapter 8) trade orders from the firm's clients or for the firm's own account.

6. *Electronic Brokerage*—offered by major brokers, involves direct access, via the Internet, to the trading floor, therefore bypassing traditional brokers. Many securities firms and investment banks offer online trading services to their customers as well as direct access to a client representative (stockbroker). Thus, customers may now conduct trading activities from their homes and offices through their accounts at securities firms. Because services provided by a typical brokerage firm are bypassed, the cost per share is generally lower and the price may be advantageous compared with trading directly on the exchanges. Users of the system can often use the network to discover existing sizes and quotes of offers to buy or sell. Interested parties can then negotiate with each other using the system's computers.

Securities trading can be conducted on behalf of a customer as an agent or on behalf of the firm as a principal. When trading at the retail level occurs on behalf of customers, it is often called *brokerage* (or stock brokering).

### Investing

Investing involves managing pools of assets such as closed- and open-end mutual funds (in competition with commercial banks, life insurance companies, and pension funds). Securities firms can manage such funds either as agents for other investors or as principals for themselves and their stockholders. As we discuss in more detail in Chapter 17, the objective in funds management is to select asset portfolios to beat some return-risk performance benchmark such as the S&P 500 Index. Since this business generates fees that are based on the size of the pool of assets managed, it tends to produce a more stable flow of income than does either investment banking or trading (discussed earlier).

---

4. An example is investing cash in the S&P Index and selling futures contracts on the S&P Index. Since stocks and futures contracts trade in different markets, their prices are not always equal.

## Cash Management

**cash management accounts (CMAs)**

*Money market mutual funds sold by investment banks that offer checkwriting privileges.*

Securities firms and investment banks offer bank deposit–like **cash management accounts (CMAs)** to individual investors and, since the 1999 Financial Services Modernization Act (see Chapter 13), deposit accounts themselves (Merrill Lynch being the first to offer a direct deposit account in June 2000 via the two banks it owns). Most of these accounts allow customers to write checks against some type of mutual fund account (e.g., money market mutual fund). These accounts can even be covered directly or indirectly by federal deposit insurance from the FDIC. CMAs were adopted by other security firms under various names (e.g., house account) and spread rapidly. Many of these accounts offer ATM services and debit cards. As a result of CMAs, the distinction between commercial banks and investment banks became blurred. However, the advantage of brokerage firm CMAs over commercial bank deposit accounts is that they make it easier to buy and sell securities. The broker can take funds out of the CMA account when an investor buys a security and deposit funds back into the CMA when the investor sells securities. In 2013 regulators proposed new rules that would significantly diminish these accounts as close substitutes to commercial bank deposit accounts. Under the new rules, the net asset values (NAVs) of money market mutual fund (MMMF) shares would float as the value of the underlying investments change. (As discussed in Chapter 17, NAVs of MMMFs are currently set at $1 per share.) Floating NAVs for MMMF shares would transform cash management accounts into floating value accounts. These new regulations would significantly reduce the advantages of CMAs. CMAs were instrumental in this industry's efforts to provide commercial banking services prior to the passage of the 1999 Financial Services Modernization Act. Since the passage of this regulation, securities firms are allowed to make loans, offer credit and debit cards, provide ATM services, and, most important, sell securities.

## Mergers and Acquisitions

As noted earlier, investment banks frequently provide advice on, and assistance in, mergers and acquisitions. For example, they assist in finding merger partners, underwrite any new securities to be issued by the merged firms, assess the value of target firms, recommend terms of the merger agreement, and even assist target firms in preventing a merger (e.g., writing restrictive provisions into a potential target firm's securities contracts). As mentioned in the chapter overview, mergers and acquisitions activity stood at $1.15 trillion for the first nine months of 2016. Panel A of Table 16–5 lists the top 10 investment bank merger advisors ranked by dollar volume of the U.S. mergers in which they were involved. Panel B of Table 16–5 lists the top 10 investment banks ranked by dollar volume of worldwide M&A activity. Notice that many of the top U.S. ranked investment banks reported in Panel A of Table 16–5 are also top ranked for worldwide activity in Panel B.

## Other Service Functions

Other service functions include custody and escrow services, clearance and settlement services, and research and advisory services—for example, giving advice on divestitures, spin-offs, and asset sales. In addition, investment banks are making increasing inroads into traditional bank service areas such as small-business lending and the trading of loans (see Chapters 7 and 24). In performing these functions, investment banks normally act as agents for a fee. Fees charged are often based on the total bundle of services performed for the client by the firm. The portion of the fee or commission allocated to research and advisory services is called *soft dollars.* When one area in the firm, such as an investment advisor, uses client commissions to buy research from another area in the firm, it receives a benefit because it is relieved from the need to produce and pay for the research itself. Thus, advisors using soft dollars face a conflict of interest between their need to obtain research and their clients' interest in paying the

**DO YOU UNDERSTAND:**

5. What the key areas of activities for securities firms are?

6. What the difference is between a best efforts and a firm commitment offering?

7. What the six trading activities performed by securities firms are?

**TABLE 16–5** The 10 Largest Mergers and Acquisition Firms Ranked by Value of Mergers, 2016*

| Panel A: Mergers Completed in United States | | | |
|---|---|---|---|
| Rank | Investment Bank | Value (in billions of dollars) | Number of Deals |
| 1. | Goldman Sachs | $ 532.1 | 98 |
| 2. | Bank of America Merrill Lynch | 405.2 | 66 |
| 3. | Citigroup | 395.4 | 49 |
| 4. | Morgan Stanley | 390.1 | 87 |
| 5. | Barclays | 355.8 | 76 |
| 6. | J.P. Morgan Chase | 353.6 | 101 |
| 7. | Credit Suisse | 323.4 | 52 |
| 8. | Centerview Partners | 258.5 | 52 |
| 9. | Deutsche Bank AG | 224.8 | 35 |
| 10. | Lazard | 211.6 | 44 |
| Industry total | | $1,154.5 | 6,078 |

| Panel B: Worldwide Mergers | | | |
|---|---|---|---|
| Rank | Investment Bank | Value (in billions of dollars) | Number of Deals |
| 1. | Goldman Sachs | $ 885.0 | 200 |
| 2. | Morgan Stanley | 690.5 | 204 |
| 3. | Bank of America Merrill Lynch | 637.0 | 136 |
| 4. | J.P. Morgan Chase | 625.5 | 195 |
| 5. | Citigroup | 501.6 | 129 |
| 6. | Barclays | 415.4 | 126 |
| 7. | Credit Suisse | 411.9 | 126 |
| 8. | Lazard | 411.4 | 163 |
| 9. | Deutsche Bank AG | 337.6 | 98 |
| 10. | Centerview Partners | 268.9 | 34 |
| Industry total | | $2,299.1 | 23,747 |

*Through September.

**Source:** Thomson Reuters Deals Intelligence, 2016. www.thomsonreuters.com

lowest commission rate available. Because of the conflict of interest that exists, the SEC (the primary regulator of investment banks and securities firms, see below) requires these firms to disclose soft dollar arrangements to their clients.

# RECENT TRENDS AND BALANCE SHEETS

## Recent Trends

In this section, we look at the balance sheet and trends in the securities firm and investment banking industry since the 1987 stock market crash. Trends in this industry depend heavily on the state of the stock market. For example, a major effect of the 1987 stock market crash was a sharp decline in stock market trading volume and, thus, in the brokerage commissions earned by securities firms over the 1987–1991 period (see Figure 16–2). Commission income began to recover only in and after 1992 with record stock market trading volumes being achieved in 1992 through 2000 (when the Dow Jones and S&P indexes hit new highs—see Chapter 8). Improvements in the U.S. economy in the mid-2000s resulted in an even greater increase in stock market values and trading and thus commission income. However, rising oil prices and the subprime mortgage market collapse and the eventual full market crash in 2008 through 2009 pushed stock market values down. As a result, commission income in the securities industry declined as well. As the economy and the stock

**Figure 16–2**    Commission Income as a Percentage of Total Revenues

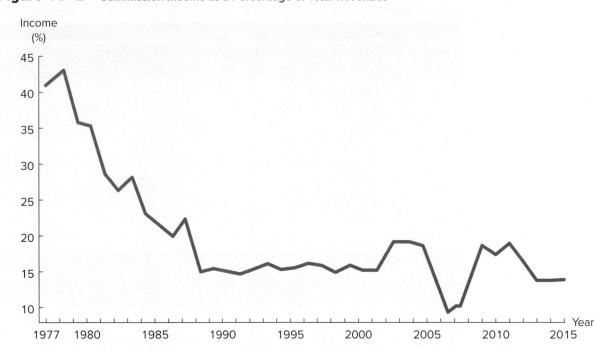

**Sources:** Securities and Exchange Commission; Standard & Poor's *Industry Surveys* (various issues); and the Securities Industry and Financial Markets Association.

market recovered in the early and mid-2010s, commission income again rose to between 15 and 20 percent of total revenues.

Also affecting the profitability of the investment banking industry was the decline in bond and equity underwriting during the 1987–1990 period. This was partly a result of the stock market crash, partly a result of a decline in M&As, and partly a reflection of investor concerns about junk bonds (which crashed during this period). Between 1991 and 2001, however, the securities industry showed a resurgence in underwriting activity and profitability. For example, domestic underwriting activity over the 1990–2001 period grew from $192.7 billion in 1990 to $1,623.9 billion in 2001 (see Table 16–6). The principal reasons for this were enhanced trading profits and increased growth in new issue underwritings. In particular, corporate debt issues became highly attractive to corporate treasurers because of relatively low long-term interest rates. Further, debt is less risky than equity, so there is less risk of an adverse price movement with debt compared to equity. Finally, debt is more likely to be bought in larger blocks by fewer investors, a transaction characteristic that makes the selling process less costly. In addition to debt securities, growth in the asset-backed securities market as a result of increased securitization of mortgages (and growth of mortgage debt) added to the value of underwriting.

As a result of enhanced trading profits and growth in new issues underwriting, pretax profits for the industry topped $9 billion in every year over the period 1996–2000 (see Figure 16–3). This is despite the collapse of Russian ruble and bond markets in 1998, economic turmoil in Asia in 1997, and economic uncertainty in the United States in the early 2000s. Indeed, despite a downturn in the U.S. economy toward the end of 2000, pretax profits in the securities industry soared to an all-time high of $31.6 billion in 2000. Only the continued slowdown of the U.S. economy in 2001, an accompanying drop in stock market values, and terrorist attacks on the World Trade Center (which housed the offices of many securities firms and investment banks) in September 2001 brought an end to record profits. While still strong by historical standards, industry pretax profits for 2001 fell 24 percent, to $16.0 billion. The Bank of New York alone estimated its costs associated with the terrorist attacks at $125 million. Citigroup estimated it lost $100 million to $200 million in business

**TABLE 16–6** **U.S. Corporate Underwriting Activity** *(in billions of dollars)*

| | Straight Corporate Debt | Con-vertible Debt | Asset-Backed Debt | Non-Agency MBS | Total Debt | Common Stock | Preferred Stock | Total Equity | All IPOs | Total Under-writing |
|---|---|---|---|---|---|---|---|---|---|---|
| 1986 | $ 134.9 | $ 9.8 | $ 10.0 | $ 62.2 | $ 216.9 | $ 43.2 | $ 13.9 | $ 57.1 | $ 22.3 | $ 274.0 |
| 1987 | 108.5 | 10.3 | 8.9 | 83.3 | 211.0 | 41.5 | 11.4 | 52.9 | 24.0 | 263.9 |
| 1988 | 99.2 | 4.1 | 14.3 | 83.5 | 201.1 | 29.7 | 7.6 | 37.3 | 23.6 | 239.4 |
| 1989 | 101.1 | 5.8 | 22.2 | 35.1 | 164.2 | 22.9 | 7.7 | 30.6 | 13.7 | 194.8 |
| 1990 | 76.5 | 5.5 | 43.6 | 43.2 | 168.8 | 19.2 | 4.7 | 23.9 | 10.1 | 192.7 |
| 1995 | 279.8 | 12.0 | 113.1 | 36.5 | 441.4 | 82.0 | 15.1 | 97.1 | 30.2 | 538.5 |
| 2000 | 587.5 | 49.6 | 337.0 | 102.1 | 1,076.2 | 189.1 | 15.4 | 204.5 | 76.1 | 1,280.7 |
| 2001 | 776.1 | 78.3 | 383.3 | 216.5 | 1,454.2 | 128.4 | 41.3 | 169.7 | 40.8 | 1,623.9 |
| 2003 | 775.8 | 72.7 | 600.2 | 345.3 | 1,794.0 | 118.5 | 37.8 | 156.3 | 43.7 | 1,950.3 |
| 2006 | 1,059.0 | 62.8 | 1,253.1 | 773.2 | 3,148.1 | 156.8 | 33.4 | 190.2 | 57.5 | 3,338.3 |
| 2007 | 1,128.3 | 76.4 | 509.7 | 773.9 | 2,488.2 | 187.5 | 60.0 | 247.5 | 91.1 | 2,735.7 |
| 2008 | 707.2 | 42.0 | 139.5 | 45.1 | 933.8 | 164.7 | 77.9 | 242.6 | 11.0 | 1,176.4 |
| 2010 | 1,012.1 | 20.7 | 124.8 | 22.9 | 1,180.5 | 185.1 | 13.3 | 198.4 | 47.8 | 1,378.9 |
| 2012 | 1,360.1 | 19.7 | 199.4 | 39.3 | 1,618.5 | 244.5 | 34.4 | 278.9 | 55.4 | 1,897.4 |
| 2015 | 1,489.5 | 19.7 | 193.6 | 177.4 | 1,880.0 | 224.4 | 32.3 | 256.7 | 38.7 | 2,175.4 |
| YTD '15* | 1,198.4 | 17.2 | 188.1 | 141.9 | 1,545.6 | 188.7 | 28.7 | 217.4 | 30.4 | 1,793.4 |
| YTD '16* | 1,255.3 | 13.6 | 143.1 | 140.4 | 1,552.4 | 127.4 | 17.3 | 144.7 | 15.5 | 1,712.6 |
| % change | 4.7% | −20.9% | −23.9% | −1.3% | 0.4% | −32.5% | −39.7% | −33.4% | −49.0% | −4.5% |

*Through August.
**Note:** IPOs are a subset of common stock.
**Sources:** Securities Industry and Financial Markets Association, *Industry Statistics,* various dates. www.sifma.org

from branches that were closed and because of the four days the stock market did not trade. Morgan Stanley, the largest commercial tenant in the World Trade Center, said the cost of property damage and relocation of its employees was $150 million. Also impacting profit, the securities industry was rocked by several allegations of securities law violations as well as a loss of investor confidence in Wall Street and corporate America as a result of a number of corporate governance failures and accounting scandals including Enron, Merck, WorldCom, and other major U.S. corporations.

**Figure 16–3** Securities Industry Pretax Profits, 1990–2015

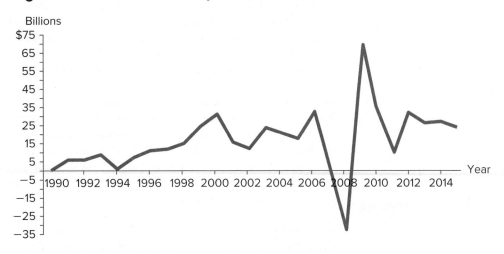

**Sources:** Securities Industry and Financial Markets Association, various dates. www.sifma.org

With the recovery of the U.S. economy in the mid-2000s, the U.S. securities industry again earned record profits as revenue growth strengthened and became more broadly based. Domestic underwriting surged to $3,338.3 billion in 2006, from $1,623.9 billion in 2001 (see Table 16–6). Further, the industry maintained its profitability mainly through deep cuts in expenses. Total expenses fell 10.4 percent from 2002 levels, largely due to lower interest expenses. Interest expense fell from $48.4 billion in 2002 to $37.5 billion in 2003, rising to $44.2 billion in 2004. The result was an increase in pretax profits to $24.1 billion in 2003 and $20.7 billion in 2004 (see Figure 16–3). Interest rate increases in 2005 caused interest expense incurred by the securities industry to increase. The result was that, while gross revenues remained high, the increased interest expense caused pretax profits to fall to $17.6 billion in 2005. A surge in revenues from trading gains and corporate advisory services caused pretax profits to bounce back to a record level of $33.1 billion in 2006.

Signs of the impending financial crisis arose in 2007. The industry began 2007 on a strong note but, hit by the subprime mortgage market meltdown that began in the summer of 2007, it ended the year with pretax profits of just $0.78 billion. Many revenue lines showed solid growth in 2007 and total revenues reached a record high of $474.2 billion in 2007. However, trading and investment account losses were large, totaling $6 billion in 2007, compared to a gain of $43 billion in 2006. Further, expenses grew faster than revenues, to a record $473.4 billion in 2007. The worst of the financial crisis hit in 2008 as the industry reported a record loss for the year of $34.1 billion. Revenues were $290.5 billion, down 38.7 percent from 2007. Nearly all revenue lines decreased from 2007 levels, with trading and investment account losses being the largest (−$65.0 billion in 2008).

As quickly as industry profits plunged during the financial crisis, they recovered in 2009. Pretax profits were a record $71.4 billion. Revenues totaled $288.1 billion for the year. Commission and fee income was $49.0 billion of the total, reflecting improved trading volume. Trading revenues, which had been negative for six consecutive quarters, grew to $45.3 billion. Industry expenses for 2009 were $212.4 billion, 33.7 percent below 2008 levels. Of this, interest expenses fell to just $21.9 billion, 82.2 percent below 2008 levels. While still in a fragile state, the industry seemed to be recovering along with the economy.

The U.S. and world economies grew very slowly after the financial crisis. While interest rates remained at historic lows, concerns about the health of Euro-zone economies and the U.S. fiscal cliff kept economic growth at a standstill. Memories of the financial crisis were still fresh in the minds of investors. Events such as the May 2010 "flash crash," the October 2011 collapse of MF Global Holdings, and the August 2012 trading glitch at Knight Capital caused individual and institutional investors to limit capital market activity. Industry pretax profits fell to $34.4 billion, $14.2 billion, and $32.0 billion in 2010, 2011, and 2012, respectively.

By the mid-2010s, while the industry had put most problems from the financial crisis behind it, the industry was affected by post-crisis consequences, with increased regulation on risk taking and capital requirements. Since 2013, many companies undertook strategic initiatives to respond to new regulations and to de-risk their firms. This led to balance sheet reductions as well as to downsizing or disposition of select businesses, trading products, and investments. In addition, corporate strategies increasingly focused on client services and away from making large bets through principal investments like hedge funds or risky trading activity for using the firm's capital. As regulations became stricter following the 2008 crisis, many large banks across the globe sold assets or were selling, and/or discontinuing, lines of operations, and are focusing more on their core competencies. A result of the new regulations is that profitability is down: pretax profits in 2013, 2014, and 2015 fell to $26.3 billion, $27.0 billion, and $23.8 billion, respectively.

**LG 16-3**

### Balance Sheets

The short-term nature of many of the assets in the portfolios of securities firms demonstrates that an important activity is trading/brokerage. As a broker, the securities firm receives a commission for handling the trade but does not take either an asset or liability position. Thus, many of the assets appearing on the balance sheets of securities firms are cash like money market instruments, not capital market positions. In the case of depository institutions, assets tend to be medium term from the lending position of the depository institutions. The consolidated balance sheet for the industry is shown in Table 16–7. Looking at the asset portfolio, receivables from other broker-dealers accounted for 32.38 percent of total assets, reverse repurchase agreements—securities purchased under agreements to resell (i.e., the broker gives a short-term loan to the repurchase agreement seller, see Chapter 5)—accounted for 26.48 percent of assets, and long positions in securities and commodities accounted for 22.54 percent of assets. Because of the extent to which this industry's balance sheet consists of financial market securities, the industry is subjected to particularly large levels of market risk and interest rate risk. Further, to the extent that many of these securities are foreign-issued securities, FI managers must be concerned with foreign exchange risk and sovereign risk as well (see Chapter 19).

A major similarity between securities firms and all other types of FIs is a high degree of financial leverage. That is, all of these firms hold high levels of debt that is used to finance an asset portfolio consisting primarily of financial securities. A difference in the funding is that securities firms tend to use liabilities that are extremely short-term and market based. With respect to liabilities, repurchase agreements—securities sold under agreement to repurchase—were the major source of funds (these are securities temporarily lent in exchange for cash received). Repurchase agreements amounted to 35.59 percent of total liabilities and equity. The other major sources of funds were payables to customers (19.33 percent), payables to other broker-dealers (15.67 percent), and securities and commodities sold short for future delivery (8.66 percent). Nearly 38 percent of the total liability financing was payables incurred in the transaction process. In contrast, depository institutions have fixed-term time and savings deposit liabilities.

**TABLE 16–7** Assets and Liabilities of Broker-Dealers as of 2015 *(in billions of dollars)*

|  |  | Percentage of Total Assets |
|---|---|---|
| **Assets** | | |
| Cash | $ 115.1 | 2.66% |
| Receivables from other broker-dealers | 1,400.1 | 32.38 |
| Receivables from customers | 257.2 | 5.95 |
| Receivables from noncustomers | 105.8 | 2.45 |
| Long positions in securities and commodities | 974.8 | 22.54 |
| Securities and investments not readily marketable | 32.6 | 0.75 |
| Securities purchased under agreements to resell | 1,145.3 | 26.48 |
| Exchange membership | 0.2 | 0.00 |
| Other assets | 293.5 | 6.79 |
| Total assets | $4,324.6 | 100.00% |
| **Liabilities** | | |
| Bank loans payable | $ 78.8 | 1.82% |
| Payables to other broker-dealers | 677.6 | 15.67 |
| Payables to noncustomers | 47.6 | 1.10 |
| Payables to customers | 835.8 | 19.33 |
| Short positions in securities and commodities | 374.5 | 8.66 |
| Securities sold under repurchase agreements | 1,539.1 | 35.59 |
| Other nonsubordinated liabilities | 418.0 | 9.66 |
| Subordinated liabilities | 118.1 | 2.73 |
| Total liabilities | $4,089.5 | 94.56% |
| **Capital** | | |
| Equity | $ 235.1 | 5.44% |
| Total capital (equity capital and subordinate debt) | 353.2 | 8.17% |
| Number of firms | 4,115 | |

**Source:** *Focus Report,* Office of Economic Analysis, U.S. Securities and Exchange Commission, 2016, Washington, DC. www.sec.gov

Equity capital amounted to only 5.44 percent of total assets, while total capital (equity capital plus subordinated liabilities) accounted for 8.17 percent of total assets. These levels are generally below the levels held by commercial banks (11.3 percent in 2016). One reason for their lower equity capital levels is that securities firm and investment bank balance sheets contain mostly tradable (liquid) securities compared to the relatively illiquid loans that represent a significant portion of banks' asset portfolios. However, this low level of capital can leave stand-alone investment banks vulnerable to runs. For example, in the summer of 2007, two Bear Stearns hedge funds suffered heavy losses on investments in the subprime mortgage market. The two funds filed for bankruptcy in the fall of 2007. Bear Stearns's market value was hurt badly from these losses. Because Bear Stearns operated with low levels of capital, the losses became so great that by March 2008 Bear Stearns was struggling to finance its day-to-day operations. Rumors of Bear Stearns's equity crisis became a reality as investors began quickly selling off their stock and draining what little equity the firm had left. Bear Stearns had no choice but to basically sell itself to the highest bidder to avoid declaring bankruptcy or completely closing down and leaving investors totally empty-handed. J.P. Morgan Chase purchased the company for $236 million; Bear Stearns's skyscraper in New York was worth over $2 billion alone.

---

### DO YOU UNDERSTAND:

8. What the trend in profitability in the securities industry has been over the last 25 years?

9. What the major assets held by broker-dealers are?

10. Why broker-dealers tend to hold less equity capital than commercial banks and thrifts?

---

# REGULATION

**LG 16-4**

www.sec.gov

The primary regulator of the securities industry has been the Securities and Exchange Commission (SEC), established in 1934 largely in response to abuses by securities firms that many at the time felt were partly responsible for the economic problems in the United States. The primary role of the SEC includes administration of securities laws, review and evaluation of registrations of new securities offerings (ensuring that all relevant information is revealed to potential investors), review and evaluation of annual and semiannual reports summarizing the financial status of all publicly held corporations, and the prohibition of any form of security market manipulation. The National Securities Markets Improvement Act (NSMIA) of 1996 reaffirmed the significance of the SEC as the primary regulator of securities firms. According to the NSMIA, states are not allowed to require federally registered securities firms to be registered in a state as well. States are also prohibited from requiring registrations of securities firms' transactions and from imposing substantive requirements on private placements. Prior to NSMIA, most securities firms were subject to regulation from both the SEC and the state in which they operated. NSMIA provides that states may still require securities firms to pay fees and file documents submitted to the SEC, but most of the regulatory burden imposed by states has been removed. Thus, NSMIA effectively gives the SEC primary regulatory jurisdiction over securities firms.

The early 2000s saw a reversal of this trend toward the dominance of the SEC with states—especially their attorneys general—increasingly intervening through securities-related investigations. Several highly publicized securities violations resulted in criminal cases brought against securities law violators by state prosecutors. For example, the New York State attorney general forced Merrill Lynch to pay a $100 million penalty because of allegations that Merrill Lynch brokers gave investors overly optimistic reports about the stock of its investment banking clients. In the spring of 2003 the issue culminated in an agreement between regulators and 10 of the nation's largest securities firms, with the latter agreeing to pay a record $1.4 billion in penalties to settle charges involving investor abuses. The long awaited settlement centered on charges that securities firms routinely issued overly optimistic stock research to investors in order to gain favor with corporate clients and win their investment banking business. The investigations of the SEC and other regulators, including the Financial Industry Regulatory Authority (FINRA) and state regulators, unveiled multiple examples of how Wall Street stock analysts tailored their research reports and ratings to win investment banking business. The agreement also forced broker-age companies to make structural changes in the way they handle research—for example, preventing analysts from attending certain investment banking meetings. It also required that securities firms have separate reporting and supervisory structures for their research and banking operations and that analysts' pay be tied to the quality and accuracy of their research rather than the amount of investment banking business they generate.

Despite all of these changes, the industry continued to find itself in the midst of scandal and prosecution. In January 2011, a former analyst at Primary Global Research LLC, Bob Nguyen, admitted he recruited employees of public companies specifically to help hedge funds and other investors obtain confidential information. In July 2012, the Commodity Futures Trading Commission filed a lawsuit in federal court accusing Pere-grine Financial and its founder, Russell Wasendorf Sr., of committing fraud and customer-funds violations, and making false statements. The scandal left Wasendorf hospitalized after a suicide attempt while regulators tried to find out what happened to $215 million of customer funds allegedly missing from the firm. In December 2012, Morgan Stanley agreed to pay $5 million to settle allegations that one of its senior investment bankers tried to improperly influence research analysts in the days before Facebook went pub-lic in May 2012. Allegations charged that the senior investment banker arranged phone calls from Facebook to analysts in a way that favored large investors over small investors and violated restrictions on investment bankers' role in the IPO process. In October 2013, J.P. Morgan and the Justice Department agreed to a $13 billion settlement ($9 billion in penalties and $4 billion in consumer relief) to resolve claims that the bank misled investors about the quality of mortgages it sold to them during the housing boom. (However, less than two weeks after the settlement announcement, the agreement was at risk of collapsing because of disagreements related to a criminal probe of the bank and its effort to get pen-alties reimbursed by a government-controlled fund.) A week earlier, J.P. Morgan agreed to pay $920 million and admitted wrongdoing to settle claims with four regulators tied to the London "whale" trading blunder that cost the bank more than $6 billion in 2012. The bank also agreed to pay $80 million to settle claims related to its credit card practices and $410 million for manipulating electricity markets. More recently, in December 2014 Citi-group, Goldman Sachs, and eight other securities firms were fined a total of $43.5 million for offering favorable stock research in hopes of winning underwriting business in an ini-tial public offering by Toys "R" Us. In March 2015, J.P. Morgan Chase admitted to misfil-ing more than 50,000 payment change notices in bankruptcy courts that were "improperly signed, under penalty of perjury, by persons who had not reviewed the accuracy of the notices." The bank agreed to pay more than $50 million to homeowners as part of a settle-ment with the U.S. Department of Justice over its mortgage practices.

www.finra.org

While the SEC sets the overall regulatory standards for the industry, the Financial Industry Regulatory Authority (FINRA) is involved in the day-to-day regulation of trading practices. In contrast to the SEC which is a government-run regulator, FINRA is an inde-pendent, not-for-profit organization authorized by Congress to protect America's investors by making sure the securities industry operates fairly and honestly. Specifically, FINRA writes and enforces rules governing the activities of securities firms, examines firms for compliance with those rules, works to foster market transparency, and supports investor education. FINRA monitors trading abuses (such as insider trading), trading rule viola-tions, and securities firms' capital (solvency positions)—such as the 2 percent net worth to assets minimum capital ratio. FINRA also performs market regulation under contract for the major U.S. stock exchanges. For example, in January 2013 FINRA announced that it is expanding its oversight of dark pool trading (see Chapter 8). As of 2016, about 15 percent of all stock trades in the United States occurred through dark pools, up from 3 percent in 2007. As more financial trading has occurred in dark pools, regulators and investors have become concerned that firms are placing orders on exchanges and in dark pools at the same time to move stock prices to their advantage. FINRA's expanded oversight is intended to monitor and determine whether orders placed in dark pools are indeed attempts at moving stock prices. FINRA also announced that it is increasing its surveillance of high-speed and rapid-fire trading across exchanges. As a result of the increased oversight, in 2014 Goldman Sachs announced that it would close its dark pool, one of the world's largest. The company stated that the revenue the dark pool was generating for the bank was not worth the risks that had been highlighted by a series of trading glitches and growing criticism of dark pools. Also, as a result of the new oversight, UBS agreed to pay $14.5 million to settle accusations by the SEC that a subsidiary violated federal securities laws in its operation of a dark pool. The UBS subsidiary allegedly allowed traders to buy and sell stocks priced at increments smaller than a penny and it failed to adequately disclose this system to all investors in its market.

Also overseeing this industry at the federal level is the U.S. Congress. The U.S. Senate Permanent Subcommittee on Investigations was created with the broad mandate to determine whether any changes are required in U.S. law to better protect the public. In the spring of 2010, a subcommittee hearing focused on the contributing role of investment banks in the financial crisis. Investment banks such as Goldman Sachs bundled toxic mortgages into complex financial instruments, many of which were rated AAA by credit-rating agencies, and sold them to investors. Goldman Sachs, in an attempt to manage its own risk on these securities, shorted the mortgage market, setting itself up for gains that would offset losses on the mortgage securities. The subcommittee brought up evidence and internal Goldman documents that showed Goldman knew the housing market was on the brink of collapse but continued to sell mortgage-backed securities to investors. All the while, Goldman allegedly bet against the securities it built and sold with the knowledge that the housing market's collapse would bring the firm a sizable payday.

The financial crisis reshaped much of the securities firms and investment banking industry. In response, regulators were charged with reshaping regulations to prevent events similar to those that led to the market collapse and the near collapse of this industry. The 2010 Wall Street Reform and Consumer Protection Act set forth many changes in the way securities firms and investment banks are regulated. The bill's Financial Services Oversight Council of financial regulators was given oversight of the industry in its charge to identify emerging systemic risks. Also under the act, effective July 21, 2011, the dollar threshold for determining whether an investment advisor must register under federal or state law increased: generally, all advisors with assets under management of under $100 million must register with state regulators and those with over $100 million under management must register with the SEC. Prior to that date, only advisors with assets under management of under $25 million registered with a state regulator. The bill also gave new authority for the Federal Reserve to supervise all firms that could pose a threat to financial stability and called for stronger capital and other prudential standards for all financial firms—and even higher standards for large, interconnected firms.

The bill gave authority to the government to resolve nonbank financial institutions whose failure could have serious systemic effects and revised the Federal Reserve's emergency lending authority to improve accountability. Investment banks also saw stricter oversight as the bill called for the regulation of securitization markets, stronger regulation of credit-rating agencies, a requirement that issuers and originators retain a financial interest in securitized loans, comprehensive regulation of all over-the-counter derivatives, and new authority for the Federal Reserve to oversee payment, clearing, and settlement systems. The act further mandated that over-the-counter (OTC) derivatives trading be moved to listed futures markets and cleared through a registered derivatives clearing organization (DCO) or exchange. The process was implemented in three stages during 2013. The first stage, for Category 1 entities (which included mostly swap dealers and major swap participants), was implemented on March 11, 2013. The second stage, for Category 2 entities (which included a much larger group of more than 100 firms), was implemented on June 11 and the third stage, for Category 3 entities (which included all others involved in swap transactions), was implemented on September 11. Under the new regulations, investment banks and brokerage firms may face an increase in their information technology capital and operating costs, as well as an increase in compliance and legal costs. Further, under the new rules, these FIs could face potential risks to principal investing and capital levels for market making.

Finally, the Securities Investor Protection Corporation (SIPC) protects investors against losses of up to $500,000 on securities firm failures. SIPC is not an agency or establishment of the U.S. government and it has no authority to investigate or regulate its member broker-dealers. Rather, the SIPC was created under the Securities Investor Protection Act of 1970 as a nonprofit membership corporation. SIPC oversees the liquidation of member broker-dealers that close when the broker-dealer is bankrupt or in financial trouble and customer assets are missing. While agencies such as the SEC and FINRA deal with cases of investment fund fraud, the SIPC's focus is both different and narrow: restoring customer cash and securities left in the hands of bankrupt or otherwise financially troubled brokerage firms. The fund does not protect against losses on customers' accounts due to poor investment choices that reduce the value of their portfolio. The SIPC is funded with premium contributions from member firms.

**www.sipc.org**

### DO YOU UNDERSTAND:

11. *What the major result of NSMIA is?*

12. *What regulatory changes resulted from the financial crisis?*

## GLOBAL ISSUES

More so than other sectors of the financial institutions industry, securities firms and investment banks operate globally. Both U.S. and European investment banks compete for business worldwide. This can be seen in Table 16–3 as four of the top five underwriters of global debt and equity are U.S. investment banks (J.P. Morgan Chase, Citigroup, Bank of America, and Goldman Sachs) and one is a European bank (Barclays Capital). Through September 2016, in M&A deals involving U.S. targets, 7 of the top 10 advisors were U.S. investment banks (including Goldman Sachs and J.P. Morgan Chase) and 3 were European banks (including Barclays Capital and Deutsche Bank). Further, U.S. investment banks held 6 of the top 10 spots on M&A deals in Europe and held 4 of the top 5 spots on deals in Asia.

As domestic securities trading and underwriting grew in the 1990s and 2000s, so did foreign securities trading and underwriting. Figures 16–4 and 16–5 show the foreign transactions in U.S. securities and U.S. transactions in foreign securities from 1991 to 2016. For example, foreign investors' transactions involving U.S. stocks increased from $211.2 billion in 1991 to $12,037.9 billion in 2008, before falling to $6,654.0 billion in 2009, during the financial crisis. As of 2016, stock transactions had increased back to $11,064.1 billion only slightly below the pre-crisis level. Similarly, U.S. investors' transactions involving stocks listed on foreign exchanges grew from $152.6 billion in 1991 to $5,423.0 billion in 2008, before falling to $3,228.9 in 2009 and recovering to $5,193.7 billion in 2016.

Table 16–8 reports the total dollar value of international security offerings from 1995 to 2016. Over this period, total offerings increased from $443.3 billion in 1995 to $3,781.7 billion in 2007, and then decreased in 2008 during the financial crisis to $3,349.7 billion. As the economy recovered in 2009, so did international securities offerings, increasing to $3,877.2 billion in 2009. But the recovery was short-lived, as new issues decreased to $2,840.0 billion in 2011 and stood at just $3,137.4 billion in 2015. Of the amounts in 2015, U.S. security issuers offered $651.2 billion in international markets, up from $72.9 billion in 1995.

One result of the financial crisis in the late 2000s was that large investment banks around the world became more concerned than ever with capital, liquidity, and leverage. However, they did not want to lose ground in the global competition for clients. The result was that global investment banks looked for strategic alliances that would allow them to compete in foreign markets or they exited foreign markets altogether. For example, in 2008 Morgan Stanley, in need of capital to bolster its balance sheet, sold a 21 percent stake in the firm to the Japanese financial institution, Mitsubishi UFJ. In March 2009, the two announced plans to form a joint venture that combined each firm's Japan-based securities business. Morgan Stanley took 40 percent ownership and managerial control of the institutional business and Mitsubishi took the remaining ownership and control of the retail operations. This kind of arrangement provides U.S.-based investment banks with a foothold alongside a domestic firm in the foreign market. In contrast to the strategic alliance

**Figure 16–4**   Foreign Transactions in U.S. Securities Markets

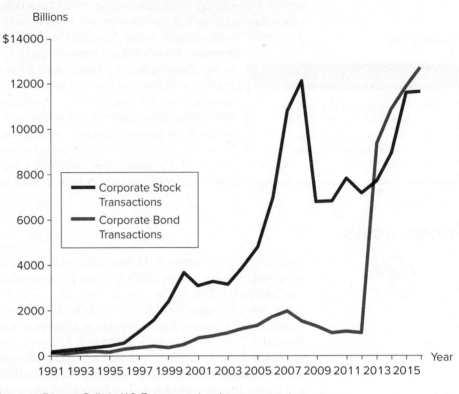

Billions

**Sources:** *Treasury Bulletin,* U.S. Treasury, various issues. www.ustreas.gov

**Figure 16–5**   U.S. Transactions in Foreign Securities Markets

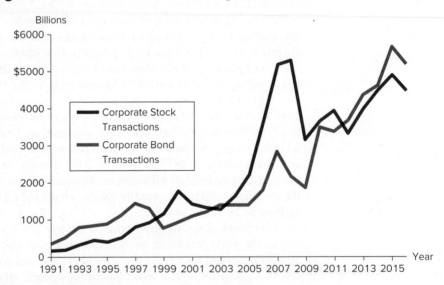

Billions

**Sources:** *Treasury Bulletin,* U.S. Treasury, various issues. www.ustreas.gov

between Morgan Stanley and Mitsubishi UFJ, Citigroup decided to abandon several foreign markets. During the financial crisis, Citigroup had to deal with growing U.S. government ownership, a deteriorating credit environment, and an unwieldy structure. Rather than trying to compete globally in this environment, Citigroup sold its Japanese domestic securities unit and its Japanese asset management unit, Nikko Asset Management, to subsidiaries

**TABLE 16-8** Value of International Security Offerings *(in billions of dollars)*

| Type of Offering | 1995 | 1999 | 2004 | 2007 | 2008 | 2009 | 2011 | 2014 | 2015 |
|---|---|---|---|---|---|---|---|---|---|
| **Total international offerings** | | | | | | | | | |
| Straight debt | $410.3 | $1,104.1 | $2,000.7 | $3,282.3 | $3,013.0 | $3,411.6 | $2,551.7 | $3,270.1 | $2,685.6 |
| Convertible debt | 9.8 | 31.5 | 50.1 | 90.0 | 53.8 | 55.5 | 36.3 | 55.1 | 38.4 |
| Common equity | 22.2 | 95.5 | 145.3 | 387.7 | 272.1 | 395.9 | 235.8 | 353.4 | 395.7 |
| Preferred equity | 1.0 | 7.5 | 2.7 | 21.7 | 10.9 | 14.2 | 16.2 | 16.0 | 17.7 |
| Total offerings | $443.3 | $1,238.5 | $2,198.8 | $3,781.7 | $3,349.7 | $3,877.2 | $2,840.0 | $3,694.7 | $3,137.4 |
| **International offerings by U.S. issuers** | | | | | | | | | |
| Straight debt | $64.3 | $270.5 | $200.9 | $363.7 | $236.8 | $255.5 | $272.2 | $597.3 | $651.2 |
| Convertible debt | 1.9 | 1.0 | 0.0 | 1.2 | 0.0 | 0.2 | 0.9 | 3.9 | 1.9 |
| Common equity | 6.7 | 9.3 | 0.2 | 4.7 | 20.0 | 1.6 | 0.9 | 1.6 | 1.0 |
| Preferred equity | 0.1 | 0.9 | 6.0 | 2.4 | 2.3 | 1.1 | 6.8 | 0.1 | 3.4 |
| Total offerings | $72.9 | $281.6 | $201.1 | $371.9 | $259.1 | $258.5 | $280.8 | $602.8 | $657.5 |

**Source:** *2016 Fact Book,* Securities Industry and Financial Markets Association. www.sifma.org

of Sumitomo Mitsui Financial Group. It also sold NikkoCiti Trust and Banking Corp. to Nomura Trust & Banking Co. Moves such as the sale of international properties, originally acquired to allow the investment bank to expand globally, will likely continue to play a part in the reshaping of the global investment banking industry.

As discussed in Chapter 5, one of the more grievous actions by some global investment banks during the financial crisis was the manipulation of the LIBOR. LIBOR is the average of the interest rates submitted by major banks in the United States, Europe, and the United Kingdom in a variety of major currencies such as the dollar, euro, and yen. The After the Crisis box summarizes the allegations that several large banks tried to manipulate the LIBOR rate during the financial crisis.

The scandal became widely public in June 2012 when British investment bank Barclays agreed to pay $450 million to settle allegations by U.S. and British authorities that some of its traders attempted to manipulate LIBOR rates to increase the bank's profits and reduce concerns about its stability during the financial crisis. Then in December 2012, UBS agreed to pay about $1.5 billion to settle charges that it manipulated LIBOR. Also in December, the U.S. Justice Department charged Tom Hayes, a former UBS and Citigroup trader, with conspiracy to commit fraud by manipulating the LIBOR (in June 2013, he was charged with eight counts of fraud as part of the UK investigation). In February 2013, the Royal Bank of Scotland decided to settle charges that it manipulated LIBOR at a cost of $610 million. Also in early 2013, Deutsche Bank stated that it had set aside money to cover potential fines associated with its role in the manipulation of the LIBOR. While several big banks pleaded guilty to and accepted penalties for manipulating LIBOR, the first criminal conviction of an individual occurred in August 2015. Former bank trader Tom Hayes was sentenced to 14 years in prison after a London jury convicted him of trying to fraudulently rig the LIBOR. The unanimous jury verdict delivered one of the harshest penalties against a banker since the financial crisis. Finally, in 2016 U.S. and British regulators fined six major global banks (Barclays, J.P. Morgan Chase, Citigroup, the Royal Bank of Scotland, UBS, and Bank of America) a total of nearly $6 billion for rigging the foreign exchange market and LIBOR interest rates. Forex traders from the banks had met in online chat room groups, one brazenly named "the Cartel" and another "Mafia," to set rates that cheated customers while adding to their own profits.

Also in 2013, U.S. investigators uncovered evidence that several investment banks had instructed a small group of brokers at ICAP to manipulate a benchmark for interest rate swaps, ISDAfix, in order to reap millions of dollars in trading

**DO YOU UNDERSTAND:**

13. *What the trends in foreign transactions in U.S. securities and U.S. transactions in foreign securities have been during the period of 1990–2016?*

14. *What the trends in international securities offerings have been during the late 1990s–2010s?*

## AFTER THE CRISIS

### Traders Influenced LIBOR Rates

A group of traders and brokers successfully managed to manipulate key interbank lending rates that affected loans around the world, one of the banks being investigated told Canadian regulators (reported in the *Wall Street Journal*). Canada's Competition Bureau said in a court filing in Ottawa that a bank it did not identify told the agency's investigators that people involved "were able to move" interest rates. According to *The Wall Street Journal,* the "cooperating party" was Swiss bank UBS, which said earlier that it had been granted some immunity by Switzerland's antitrust authority in return for cooperating with its probe into the potential manipulation of the London Interbank Offered Rate, or LIBOR.

No banks or individuals were charged with wrongdoing. Lawyers acting for the cooperating bank told the regulator that traders at six banks on the yen LIBOR panel—Citigroup, Deutsche Bank, HSBC Holdings, J.P. Morgan Chase, Royal Bank of Scotland, and UBS—influenced the rates. The traders used e-mails and instant messages to tell each other whether they wanted "to see a higher or lower yen LIBOR (rate) to aid their trading position(s)," *The Wall Street Journal* reported. They then "entered into agreements to submit artificially high or artificially low" quotes. However, the *Journal* reported that not all attempts to affect LIBOR submissions were successful.

The Competition Bureau said it had been investigating certain financial firms as part of a widening global probe into how banks set key interbank lending rates. The Canadian regulator said it had investigated whether the traders also "conspired" with individuals at interdealer broker firms. Two London-based interdealer brokers ICAP PLC and RP Martin Holdings Ltd. were under investigation. Regulators since late 2010 had been investigating banks that helped set interbank lending rates known as LIBOR and TIBOR in London and Tokyo, which are used to set interest rates on hundreds of trillions of dollars of securities. More than a dozen traders and brokers in London and Asia were fired, suspended, or put on leave as part of the probe, the *Financial Times* reported.

**Source:** Sakthi Prasad, Reuters Business News, February 17, 2012.

---

profits at the expense of companies and pension funds. Among the investment banks implicated were Barclays, UBS, Bank of America, J.P. Morgan Chase, and the Royal Bank of Scotland—the same banks implicated for rigging the LIBOR. The rigging of ISDAfix adds to growing evidence that a small group of influential investment banks have gained financially by distorting key financial gauges in world markets on everything from interest rates to currencies to commodities.

## SUMMARY

This chapter presented an overview of security firms, which primarily offer retail services to investors, and investment banking firms, which primarily offer activities and services related to corporate customers. Firms in this industry help bring new issues of debt and equity to the financial markets. In addition, this industry facilitates the trading and market making of securities after they are issued. The chapter discussed the structure of the industry and changes in the degree of concentration in firm size in the industry over the last three decades. Balance sheet information that highlighted the major assets and liabilities of the firms was also analyzed.

## QUESTIONS

1. In what ways are securities firms and investment banks financial intermediaries? (*LG 16-1*)

2. How has the size of the securities firm and investment banking industry changed since the late 1980s? (*LG 16-1*)

3. What are the different firms in the securities industry and how do they differ from each other? (*LG 16-1*)

4. Contrast the activities of securities firms with other FIs. (*LG 16-2*)

5. What are the key activity areas for securities firms? How does each activity area assist in the generation of profits and what are the major risks for each area? (*LG 16-2*)

6. Explain the difference between the investing and investment banking activities performed by securities firms and investment banks. (*LG 16-2*)

7. How does a public offering differ from a private placement? (*LG 16-2*)

8. How does a best efforts underwriting differ from a firm commitment underwriting? If you operated a company issuing stock for the first time, which type of underwriting would you prefer? Why might you still choose the alternative? (*LG 16-2*)

9. What is venture capital? (*LG 16-2*)

10. What are the different types of venture capital firms? How do institutional venture capital firms differ from angel venture capital firms? (*LG 16-2*)

11. What are the advantages and disadvantages to a new or small firm of getting capital funding from a venture capital firm? (*LG 16-2*)

12. What is the difference between pure arbitrage and risk arbitrage? If an investor observes the price of a stock trading in one exchange to be different from its price in another exchange, what form of arbitrage is applicable and how could the investor participate in that arbitrage? (*LG 16-2*)

13. How do agency transactions differ from principal transactions for market makers? (*LG 16-2*)

14. Why have brokerage commissions earned by securities firms fallen since 1977? (*LG 16-2*)

15. What three factors accounted for the resurgence in profits for securities firms from 1991 to 2000? (*LG 16-3*)

16. What factors contributed to the significant decrease in profits for securities firms in the early 2000s and the resurgence in profits in the middle of the first decade of the 2000s? (*LG 16-3*)

17. How did the financial crisis affect the performance of securities firms and investment banks? (*LG 16-3*)

18. What was the largest single asset and largest single liability of securities firms in 2015? (*LG 16-3*)

19. An investor notices that an ounce of gold is priced at $1,018 in London and $1,025 in New York. What action could the investor take to try to profit from the price discrepancy? Which of the six trading activities would this be? What might be some impediments to the success of the transaction? (*LG 16-2*)

20. An investment bank agrees to underwrite a $5,000,000 bond issue for the JCN corporation on a firm commitment basis. The investment bank pays JCN on Thursday and plans to begin a public sale on Friday. What type of interest rate movement does the investment bank fear while holding these securities? (*LG 16-2*)

21. Using Table 16–6, which type of security accounts for most underwriting in the United States? Which is likely to be more costly to underwrite: corporate debt or equity? Why? (*LG 16-3*)

22. What was the significance of the National Securities Markets Improvement Act of 1996? (*LG 16-4*)

23. Identify the major regulatory organizations that are involved with the daily operations of the investment securities industry, and explain their role in providing smoothly operating markets. (*LG 16-4*)

24. What have been the trends in global securities trading and underwriting in the 1990s–2010s? (*LG 16-3*)

## PROBLEMS

1. An investment bank agrees to underwrite an issue of 15 million shares of stock for Looney Landscaping Corp. (*LG 16-2*)
   a. The investment bank underwrites the stock on a firm commitment basis, and agrees to pay $12.50 per share to Looney Landscaping Corp. for the 15 million shares of stock. The investment bank then sells those shares to the public for $13.25 per share. How much money does Looney Landscaping Corp. receive? What is the profit to the investment bank? If the investment bank can sell the shares for only $11.95, how much money does Looney Landscaping Corp. receive? What is the profit to the investment bank?
   b. Suppose, instead, that the investment bank agrees to underwrite the 15 million shares on a best efforts basis. The investment bank is able to sell 13.6 million shares for $12.50 per share, and it charges Looney Landscaping Corp. $0.275 per share sold. How much money does Looney Landscaping Corp. receive? What is the profit to the investment bank? If the investment bank can sell the shares for only $11.95, how much money does Looney Landscaping Corp. receive? What is the profit to the investment bank?

2. An investment bank agrees to underwrite a $500 million, 10-year, 8 percent semiannual bond issue for KDO Corporation on a firm commitment basis. The investment bank pays KDO on Thursday and plans to begin a public sale on Friday. What type of interest rate movement does the investment bank fear while holding these securities? If interest rates rise 0.05 percent, or five basis points, overnight, what will be the impact on the profits of the investment bank? What if the market interest rate falls five basis points? (*LG 16-2*)

3. An investment bank pays $23.50 per share for 3,000,000 shares of the KDO company. It then sells these shares to the public for $25. How much money does KDO receive? What is the investment banker's profit? What is the stock price of KDO? (*LG 16-2*)

4. An investment bank pays $33.50 per share for 4 million shares of GM in a firm commitment stock offering. It then can sell those shares to the public for $32 per share. How much money does GM receive? What is the profit to the investment bank? What is the stock price of GM? (*LG 16-2*)

5. The MEP company has issued 5,000,000 new shares. Its investment bank agrees to underwrite these shares on a best

efforts basis. The investment bank is able to sell 4,200,000 shares for $54 per share. It charges MEP $1.25 per share sold. How much money does MEP receive? What is the investment bank's profit? What is the stock price of MEP? (*LG 16-2*)

6. XYZ, Inc. has issued 10 million new shares of stock. An investment bank agrees to underwrite these shares on a best efforts basis. The investment bank is able to sell 8.4 million shares for $27 per share, and it charges XYZ $0.675 per share sold. How much money does XYZ receive? What is the profit to the investment bank? What is the stock price of XYZ? (*LG 16-2*)

---

# SEARCH THE SITE

Go to the Securities Industry and Financial Markets Association website at **www.sifma.org** and find the most recent data on U.S. corporate underwriting activity using the following steps. Click on "Research." Click on "Statistics." On the Statistics page, click on "SIFMA Fact Book." This will download a file to your computer that contains the relevant data.

### Questions

1. What is the most recent level of total U.S. underwriting activity?
2. What is the distribution of underwriting by type of security underwritten (e.g., straight corporate debt, convertible debt, etc.)?
3. How has the distribution of underwriting activity changed since 2016, as reported in Table 16–6?

# Investment Companies

## Learning Goals

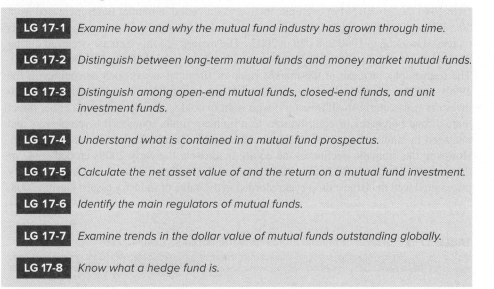

**LG 17-1**  *Examine how and why the mutual fund industry has grown through time.*

**LG 17-2**  *Distinguish between long-term mutual funds and money market mutual funds.*

**LG 17-3**  *Distinguish among open-end mutual funds, closed-end funds, and unit investment funds.*

**LG 17-4**  *Understand what is contained in a mutual fund prospectus.*

**LG 17-5**  *Calculate the net asset value of and the return on a mutual fund investment.*

**LG 17-6**  *Identify the main regulators of mutual funds.*

**LG 17-7**  *Examine trends in the dollar value of mutual funds outstanding globally.*

**LG 17-8**  *Know what a hedge fund is.*

## INVESTMENT COMPANIES: CHAPTER OVERVIEW

Investment companies are financial institutions that pool the financial resources of individuals and companies and invest those resources in (diversified) portfolios of assets. Open-end mutual funds (the largest portion of investment company business) sell new shares to investors and redeem outstanding shares on demand at their fair market values. They provide opportunities for small investors to invest in a liquid and diversified portfolio of financial securities at a lower price per unit of risk than could be achieved by investing in individual securities. A single share of a mutual fund could represent ownership in over a thousand different companies. Whereas the investment in the mutual fund might cost $100, buying over a thousand individual shares of stock could cost over $100,000 dollars. Further, since mutual funds can buy and sell securities in large blocks, their trading costs are much lower than those of the individual investor buying a few shares at a time.

Hedge funds are a type of investment pool that solicits funds from (wealthy) individuals and other investors (e.g., commercial banks) and invests these funds on their behalf. Hedge funds are similar to mutual funds in that they are pooled investment vehicles that accept investors' money and generally invest it on a collective basis. Investments in hedge funds, however, are restricted to more wealthy clients. This chapter presents an overview of the services offered by investment companies and highlights their rapid growth in the last several decades.

# SIZE, STRUCTURE, AND COMPOSITION OF THE MUTUAL FUND INDUSTRY

LG 17-1   *Historical Trends*

The first mutual fund was established in Boston in 1924. The industry grew very slowly at first, so that by 1970, 361 funds held about $50 billion in assets. Since then, the number of funds and the asset size of the industry have increased dramatically. This growth is attributed to the advent of money market mutual funds in 1972 (as investors looked for ways to earn market rates on short-term funds when regulatory ceilings constrained the interest rates they earned on bank deposits), to tax-exempt money market mutual funds first established in 1979, and to an explosion of special-purpose equity, bond, emerging market, and derivative funds (as capital market values soared in the 1990s). Money market mutual funds invest in securities with an original maturity under one year, while long-term funds invest in securities with an original maturity generally over one year.

Table 17–1 documents the tremendous increase in mutual funds for various years from 1940 though 2016. For example, total assets invested in mutual funds increased from $0.5 billion in 1940 to $12,000.6 billion in 2007. In addition, the number of mutual funds increased from 68 in 1940 to 8,026 in 2007.[1] The majority of this increase occurred during the bull market run in the 1990s (total mutual fund assets in 1990 were $1,065.2 billion). The tremendous increase in the market value of financial assets such as equities in the 1990s and the relatively low transaction cost opportunity that mutual funds provide to investors (particularly small investors) who want to hold such assets (through either direct mutual fund purchases or contributions to retirement funds sponsored by employers and managed by mutual funds—see Chapter 18) caused the mutual fund industry to boom. However, the dramatic decline in the equity markets in the early 2000s eroded some of this growth. The 2008–2009 financial crisis and the collapse in stock and other security prices produced the largest drop ever recorded in the value of industry assets. During 2008,

**TABLE 17–1**   Growth of Mutual Funds for Various Years, 1940–2016*

| Year | Total Net Assets (in billions) | Number of Funds |
|------|-------------------------------|-----------------|
| 1940 | $      0.5 | 68 |
| 1950 | 2.5 | 98 |
| 1960 | 17.0 | 161 |
| 1970 | 47.6 | 361 |
| 1980 | 134.8 | 564 |
| 1990 | 1,065.2 | 3,079 |
| 1995 | 2,811.3 | 5,725 |
| 2000 | 6,964.6 | 8,155 |
| 2001 | 6,974.9 | 8,305 |
| 2002 | 6,383.5 | 8,243 |
| 2005 | 8,891.1 | 7,974 |
| 2006 | 10,396.5 | 8,117 |
| 2007 | 12,000.6 | 8,026 |
| 2008 | 9,602.6 | 8,022 |
| 2009 | 11,113.0 | 7,663 |
| 2010 | 11,831.9 | 7,555 |
| 2012 | 13,045.2 | 7,582 |
| 2013 | 15,017.7 | 7,707 |
| 2014 | 15,875.3 | 7,928 |
| 2016 | 16,350.1 | 8,105 |

*Data pertain to conventional fund members of the Investment Company Institute.

**Sources:** Investment Company Institute, *Investment Company Fact Book,* various issues. www.ici.org

---

1. Most mutual fund companies offer more than one type of fund.

mutual fund losses on investments in financial securities and liquidation of mutual fund shares by investors resulted in a drop in industry assets of $2.4 trillion (or 20 percent). At the end of 2008, total assets fell to $9,602.6 billion. Investor demand for certain types of mutual funds plummeted, driven in large part by deteriorating financial market conditions. Equity funds suffered substantial outflows, while the inflow to U.S. government money market funds reached record highs. As the economy recovered in 2009, so did assets invested in mutual funds, growing to $11,113.0 billion by the end of the year and to $16,350.1 billion in 2016.

Additionally, growth has been driven by the rise in retirement funds under management by mutual funds. The retirement fund market has increased from $4.0 trillion in 1990 to over $24.5 trillion in 2016. Mutual funds manage approximately a quarter of this market and have experienced growth along with it. Many of these retirement funds are institutional funds. Institutional funds are mutual funds that manage retirement plans for an institution's employees (see Chapter 18). Also popular among retirement funds are *target date funds* (also known as lifecycle funds) and *lifestyle funds* (also known as target risk funds). Target date funds follow a predetermined reallocation of risk over time, and lifestyle funds maintain a predetermined risk level. The funds are aimed at a specific retirement year and are an aggregation of many—sometimes as many as 25—mutual funds. Lifecycle funds diversify and rebalance investors' portfolios as they approach retirement. They start with an aggressive mix of equities and bonds in the decades before retirement and rebalance to maintain diversification. The funds become more conservative as retirement nears, selling stocks and buying bonds.

As Figure 17–1 illustrates, in terms of asset size, the mutual fund (money market and long-term mutual funds) industry is larger than the insurance industry but smaller than the depository institutions industry. This makes mutual funds the second most important FI group in the United States as measured by asset size. Other types of FIs have noticed the tremendous growth in this area of FI services and have sought to directly compete by either buying existing mutual fund groups or managing mutual fund assets for a fee. For example, banks' share of all mutual fund assets managed grew to 5 percent in 2016. Much of this growth has occurred through banks' buying mutual fund companies, for example, Mellon buying Dreyfus, as well as converting internally managed trust funds into open-end mutual funds. Insurance companies are also participants in this market. In March 2001, for example, State Farm began offering a family of 10 mutual funds nationwide. The funds are available from more than 9,000 registered State Farm agents, on the Internet, or by application sent in response to phone requests made to a toll-free number. As of 2016, insurance companies managed 5 percent of the mutual fund industry's assets.

Low barriers to entry in the U.S. mutual fund industry have allowed new entrants to offer funds to compete for investor attention. Despite this, the share of industry assets held by the largest mutual fund sponsors has changed little since 1990. For example, the largest 25 companies that sponsor mutual funds managed 75 percent of the industry's assets in 2016, just slightly larger than 1995. The composition of the list of the 25 largest fund sponsors, however, has changed, with 15 of the largest fund companies in 2016 not among the largest in 1990.

**LG 17-2**

## Different Types of Mutual Funds

**equity funds**

*Funds consisting of common and preferred stock securities.*

**bond funds**

*Funds consisting of fixed-income capital market debt securities.*

The mutual fund industry is usually considered to have two sectors: short-term funds and long-term funds. Long-term funds comprise **equity funds** (composed of common and preferred stock securities), **bond funds** (composed of fixed-income securities with a maturity of over one year), and **hybrid funds** (composed of both stock and bond securities). Short-term funds comprise taxable **money market mutual funds (MMMFs)** and tax-exempt money market mutual funds (containing various mixes of those money market securities with an original maturity of less than one year, discussed in Chapter 5). Long-term equity funds typically are well diversified, and the risk is more systematic or market based. Bond funds have extensive interest rate risk because of their long-term, fixed-rate nature. Sector,

**Figure 17–1** Financial Assets of Major Financial Intermediaries: 1990, 2007, and 2016

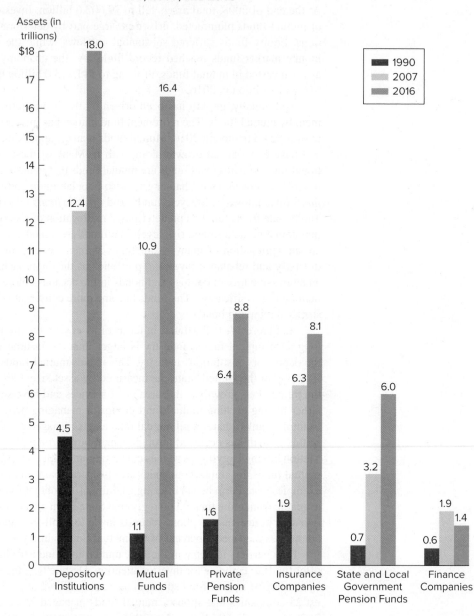

Assets (in trillions)

Legend:
- 1990
- 2007
- 2016

Depository Institutions: 4.5, 12.4, 18.0
Mutual Funds: 1.1, 10.9, 16.4
Private Pension Funds: 1.6, 6.4, 8.8
Insurance Companies: 1.9, 6.3, 8.1
State and Local Government Pension Funds: 0.7, 3.2, 6.0
Finance Companies: 0.6, 1.9, 1.4

**Sources:** Federal Reserve Board, Statistical Releases, "Financial Accounts of the United States," March 1991, December 2007, and November 2016. www.federalreserve.gov

**hybrid funds**

*Funds consisting of both stock and bond securities.*

**money market mutual funds (MMMFs)**

*Funds consisting of various mixtures of money market securities.*

or industry-specific, funds have systematic (market) and unsystematic risk, regardless of whether they are equity or bond funds. The principal type of risk for short-term funds is interest rate risk because of the predominance of fixed-income securities. Because of the shortness of maturity of the assets, which often is less than 60 days, this risk is mitigated to a large extent. Short-term funds generally have virtually no liquidity or default risk because of the types of assets held.

Tables 17–2 and 17–3 report the growth of bond and equity as well as hybrid mutual funds relative to money market mutual funds from 1980 through 2016. As can be seen, the 1990s saw a strong trend toward investing in equity mutual funds, reflecting the rise in share values during the 1990s. As a result, in 1999 some 74.2 percent of all mutual fund assets were in long-term funds while the remaining funds, 25.8 percent, were in money market mutual funds. However, in the early 2000s, as interest rates rose, the U.S. economy

**TABLE 17–2**  Growth in Long-Term versus Short-Term Mutual Funds, 1980–2016 *(in billions of dollars)*

| | 1980 | 1990 | 1999 | 2002 | 2007 | 2008 | 2009 | 2011 | 2013 | 2016 |
|---|---|---|---|---|---|---|---|---|---|---|
| **Panel A: Equity, Hybrid, and Bond Mutual Funds** | | | | | | | | | | |
| Holdings at market value | $61.8 | $608.4 | $4,538.5 | $3,638.4 | $7,829.0 | $5,435.3 | $6,961.6 | $7,870.9 | $12,333.0 | $13,208.8 |
| Household sector | 52.1 | 511.6 | 2,894.9 | 2,218.3 | 4,596.4 | 3,325.9 | 4,175.1 | 4,452.3 | 6,250.3 | 6,672.9 |
| Nonfinancial corporate business | 1.5 | 9.7 | 127.0 | 95.8 | 191.1 | 125.8 | 189.7 | 165.9 | 211.0 | 244.1 |
| State and local governments | 0.0 | 4.8 | 33.4 | 24.3 | 34.3 | 33.3 | 35.2 | 58.0 | 78.5 | 88.5 |
| Depository institutions | 0.0 | 3.3 | 14.9 | 23.1 | 31.7 | 21.6 | 47.4 | 43.5 | 60.1 | 59.7 |
| Insurance companies | 1.1 | 30.7 | 98.7 | 79.6 | 195.2 | 125.4 | 146.1 | 155.5 | 1,667.7 | 1,661.7 |
| Private pension funds | 7.1 | 40.5 | 1,056.5 | 931.9 | 2,110.6 | 1,366.0 | 1,817.3 | 2,053.2 | 3,007.6 | 3,317.6 |
| State and local government retirement funds | 0.0 | 7.8 | 140.9 | 167.4 | 296.4 | 181.1 | 229.2 | 206.9 | 505.9 | 566.3 |
| Rest of world | 0.0 | 0.0 | 169.5 | 98.0 | 373.5 | 256.2 | 321.7 | 735.6 | 552.0 | 597.9 |
| **Panel B: Money Market Mutual Funds** | | | | | | | | | | |
| Total assets | $76.4 | $493.3 | $1,579.6 | $2,223.9 | $3,033.1 | $3,757.3 | $3,258.6 | $2,642.5 | $2,717.8 | $2,702.5 |
| Household sector | 64.3 | 391.6 | 816.0 | 1,071.7 | 1,347.2 | 1,572.6 | 1,300.7 | 1,026.4 | 1,139.2 | 989.1 |
| Nonfinancial corporate business | 7.0 | 19.7 | 154.9 | 335.7 | 544.4 | 702.6 | 630.8 | 462.4 | 559.1 | 577.0 |
| Nonfarm noncorporate business | 0.0 | 6.7 | 40.7 | 61.3 | 74.3 | 79.2 | 72.1 | 77.7 | 82.7 | 94.6 |
| State and local governments | 0.0 | 0.0 | 51.2 | 58.7 | 82.9 | 80.5 | 85.1 | 149.2 | 158.9 | 180.2 |
| Insurance companies | 1.9 | 18.1 | 19.5 | 27.6 | 42.3 | 72.0 | 62.8 | 48.8 | 69.5 | 75.4 |
| Private pension funds | 2.6 | 17.8 | 76.9 | 84.5 | 93.5 | 95.7 | 96.4 | 153.7 | 154.7 | 154.8 |
| State and local government retirement funds | 0.0 | 2.8 | 11.8 | 15.5 | 12.4 | 14.3 | 14.2 | 46.0 | 48.6 | 48.8 |
| Funding corporations | 0.6 | 36.6 | 400.5 | 552.6 | 790.1 | 1,070.6 | 926.7 | 598.8 | 396.8 | 470.3 |
| Rest of world | 0.0 | 1.2 | 8.1 | 16.3 | 46.0 | 69.7 | 70.0 | 79.5 | 108.2 | 112.3 |

**Sources:** *Federal Reserve Bulletin,* "Flow of Fund Accounts," various issues. www.federalreserve.gov

**TABLE 17–3**  Number of Mutual Funds, 1980–2016

| Year | Equity | Hybrid | Bond | Taxable Money Market | Tax-Exempt Money Market | Total |
|---|---|---|---|---|---|---|
| 1980* | 288 | n.a. | 170 | 96 | 10 | 564 |
| 1990 | 1,099 | 193 | 1,046 | 506 | 235 | 3,079 |
| 2000 | 4,372 | 519 | 2,225 | 704 | 335 | 8,155 |
| 2007 | 4,742 | 478 | 2,001 | 545 | 260 | 8,026 |
| 2009 | 4,598 | 473 | 1,888 | 476 | 228 | 7,663 |
| 2012 | 4,501 | 560 | 1,941 | 400 | 180 | 7,582 |
| 2014 | 4,648 | 666 | 2,196 | 364 | 163 | 7,928 |
| 2015 | 4,764 | 717 | 2,154 | 336 | 145 | 8,116 |
| 2016 | 4,787 | 720 | 2,182 | 310 | 106 | 8,105 |

*Data from 1980 are not comparable to current classification. All funds were reclassified in 1984.

**Source:** Investment Company Institute, *Trends in Mutual Fund Investing,* November 2016. www.ici.org

weakened, and stock returns fell, the growth of money market funds increased relative to the growth of long-term funds. In 2002, some 62.1 percent of all mutual fund assets were in long-term funds; the remaining funds, 37.9 percent, were in money market mutual funds. In the mid-2000s, the U.S. economy grew and stock values increased. As a result, the share of long-term funds grew (to 72.1 percent of all funds in 2007), while money market funds decreased (to 27.9 percent in 2007).

The 2008–2009 financial crisis and the collapse in stock prices produced a sharp drop in long-term mutual fund activity. Equity funds suffered substantial outflows, while the inflow to U.S. government money market funds reached record highs. At the end of 2008, the share of long-term equity and bond funds plunged to 59.1 percent of all funds, while money market funds increased to 40.9 percent. As discussed below, part of the move to money market funds was the fact that during the worst of the financial crisis, the U.S. Treasury extended government insurance to all money market mutual fund accounts on a temporary basis. In 2009, as the economy and the stock market recovered, the share of long-term equity and bond funds increased back to 68.1 percent of all funds, while money market funds fell to 31.9 percent. By 2016, the share of long-term equity and bond funds was 83.0 percent of all funds, while money market funds decreased to 17.0 percent.

Money market mutual funds provide an alternative investment opportunity to interest-bearing deposits at commercial banks, which may explain the increase in MMMFs in the 1980s and early 2000s when the spread earned on MMMFs investments relative to deposits was mostly positive. Figure 17–2 illustrates the net cash flows invested in taxable money market mutual funds and the interest rate spread between MMMFs and the average rate on MMDAs. Both investments are relatively safe and earn short-term returns. The major difference between the two is that interest-bearing deposits (below $250,000) are fully insured by the FDIC but, because of bank regulatory costs (such as reserve requirements, capital adequacy requirements, and deposit insurance premiums), generally offer lower returns than noninsured MMMFs.[2] Thus, the net gain in switching to MMMFs is a higher return in exchange for the loss of FDIC deposit insurance coverage. Many investors appeared willing to give up FDIC insurance coverage to obtain additional returns in the late 1980s and late 1990s through 2001.

An exception occurred during the financial crisis of 2008–2009. In September 2008, the Primary Reserve Fund, a large and reputedly conservative money market fund, had holdings of $785 million in commercial paper issued by Lehman Brothers. As a result of Lehman's failure, shares in the Primary Reserve Fund "broke the buck" (i.e., fell below $1), meaning that its investors lost part of their principal investment. This was the first-ever incidence of a share price dip below a dollar for any money market mutual fund open to the general public. This type of fund had built a reputation for safe investment. Exposure to Lehman's failure scared investors, leading to a broad run on money market mutual funds. Within a few days, more than $200 billion had flowed out of these funds. The U.S. Treasury stopped the run by extending government insurance to all money market mutual fund accounts held in participating money market funds as of the close of business on September 19, 2008. The insurance coverage lasted for one year (through September 18, 2009). As seen in Figure 17–2, this action is associated with a change in the trend from net outflows to net inflows of funds into money market mutual funds.

Table 17–3 reports the growth in the mutual fund industry based on the number of funds in existence from 1980 through 2016. All categories of funds have generally increased in number in this time period, from a total of 564 in 1980 to 8,026 in 2007. *Tax-exempt* money market funds first became available in 1979. This was the major reason for their relatively small number (10 funds) in 1980. Also, the number of equity funds boomed in the 1990s: equity funds numbered 4,742 in 2007, up from 1,099 in 1990, while bond funds numbered 2,001 in 2007, up from 1,046 in 1990. But again, the 2008–2009 financial crisis and the collapse in financial markets produced a significant drop in the number of mutual funds.

---

2. Some mutual funds are covered by private insurance and/or by implicit or explicit guarantees from mutual fund management companies.

**Figure 17–2** Interest Rate Spread and Net New Cash Flow to Taxable Retail Money Market Funds, 1985–2016

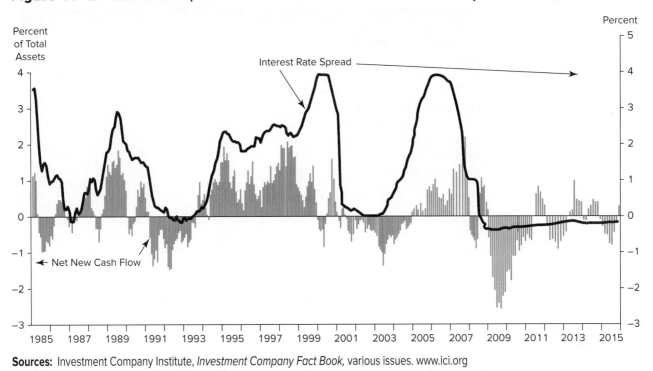

**Sources:** Investment Company Institute, *Investment Company Fact Book,* various issues. www.ici.org

The number of equity and bond funds was 4,598 and 1,888, respectively, by the end of 2009. The total number of funds dropped below 8,000 for the first time since 1999. In terms of the number of funds, the industry still had not recovered from the crisis. As of 2012, the number of equity funds had fallen to 4,501 and the total number of mutual funds stood at 7,582. As the U.S. economy recovered in the mid-2010s, the trends reversed. In 2016, the number of equity funds increased to 4,787 and the total number of funds was 8,105.

Notice that in Table 17–2, households (i.e., small investors) own the majority of both long- and short-term funds, 50.5 percent for long-term mutual funds and 36.6 percent for short-term mutual funds in 2016. This is to be expected, given that by pooling investments from a large number of small investors, fund managers are able to hold well-diversified portfolios of assets. In addition, managers can obtain lower transaction costs because of the volume of transactions, both in dollars and numbers, and they benefit from research, information, and monitoring activities at reduced costs. Many small investors are able to gain benefits of the money and capital markets by using mutual funds. Once an account is opened in a fund, a small amount of money can be invested on a periodic basis. In many cases, the amount of the investment would be insufficient for direct access to the money and capital markets. On the other hand, corporations are more likely to be able to diversify by holding a large bundle of individual securities and assets, and money and capital markets are easily accessible by direct investment. Further, an argument can be made that the goal of corporations should be to maximize shareholder wealth, not to be diversified.

As of 2016, some 55.9 million U.S. households (44.4 percent) owned mutual funds. This was down from 56.3 million (52.0 percent) in 2001. Table 17–4 lists some characteristics of household mutual fund owners as of 2016. Most are long-term owners, with 56 percent making their first purchases before 1990. While mutual fund investors come from all age groups, ownership is concentrated among individuals in their prime saving and investing years. Sixty-three percent of households owning mutual funds in 2016 were headed by individuals between the ages of 35 and 64. Interestingly, the number of families headed by a person with less than a college degree investing in mutual funds is 50 percent. In 72 percent of married households owning mutual funds, the spouse also worked full- or

**TABLE 17–4**   Selected Characteristics of Household Owners of Mutual Funds*

|  | 1995 | 2016 |
|---|---|---|
| **Demographic characteristics:** | | |
| Median age | 44 years | 51 years |
| Median household income | $60,000 | $94,300 |
| Median household financial assets | $50,000 | $200,000 |
| **Percentage of households:** | | |
| Married or living with a partner | 71 | 71 |
| Four-year college degree or more | 58 | 50 |
| Employed | 80 | 76 |
| **Fund types owned:** | | |
| Equity | 73 | 86 |
| Bond[†] | 49 | 46 |
| Hybrid | n.a. | 35 |
| Money market | 52 | 55 |

*Characteristics of primary financial decision maker in the household.
†This number is for bond and income funds.
**Sources:** Investment Company Institute, *Investment Company Fact Book,* various issues. www.ici.org

part-time. The typical fund-owning household has $94,300 invested in a median number of four mutual funds. Compared to 1995, 2016 has seen a slight increase in the median age of mutual fund holders (from 44 years to 51 years) and a large increase in median household financial assets owned (from $50,000 to $200,000). Further, holdings of equity funds have increased from 73 percent to 86 percent of all households. Finally, saving for retirement was one of the financial goals for 92 percent of mutual fund–owning households and 74 percent indicated that retirement saving was the household's primary financial goal.

LG 17-3

### Other Types of Investment Company Funds

While mutual funds dominate the investment company industry, two other types of funds are managed by these firms: closed-end funds and unit investment trusts.

**open-end mutual fund**

*A fund for which the supply of shares is not fixed but can increase or decrease daily with purchases and redemptions of shares.*

**Closed-End Funds.**   Mutual funds are **open ended** in that the number of shares outstanding fluctuates daily with the amount of share redemptions and new purchases. Shares are redeemable (meaning that investors buy and sell shares from and to the mutual fund company at their approximate net asset value [NAV, see below] that is set once a day, after markets close). Thus, the demand for shares determines the number of shares outstanding. Open-end mutual funds can be compared with regular corporations whose stock shares are traded on stock exchanges and to **closed-end investment companies,** both of which have a fixed number of shares outstanding at any given time. Closed-end funds generally do not continuously offer their shares for sale. Rather, they sell a fixed number of shares at one time (in an initial public offering), after which the shares typically trade on a secondary market. For example, **real estate investment trusts (REITs)** are closed-end investment companies that specialize in investing in real estate company shares and/or in buying mortgages.

**closed-end investment companies**

*Specialized investment companies that have a fixed supply of outstanding shares.*

For most closed-end company funds, investors generally buy and sell the company's shares that trade continuously during the day on a stock exchange as they do for corporate stocks. Since the number of shares available for purchase, at any moment in time, is fixed, the NAV of the fund's shares is determined by the value of the underlying shares as well as by the demand for the investment company's shares themselves. When demand for the investment company's shares is high (as was the case in the mid- and late 1990s when stock markets boomed) because the supply of shares in the fund is fixed, the shares can trade for more than the NAV of the securities held in the fund's asset portfolio. In this case, the fund is said to be *trading at a premium* (i.e., more than the fair market value of the securities held). When demand for the shares is low (as was the case in 2001 and 2008–2009 when

**real estate investment trust (REIT)**

*A closed-end investment company that specializes in investing in mortgages, property, or real estate company shares.*

stock market values fell), the value of the closed-end fund's shares can fall to less than the NAV of its assets. In this case, its shares are said to be *trading at a discount* (i.e., less than the fair market value of the securities held). In 2016, $266 billion was invested in 545 closed-end funds, compared to $16,350 billion invested in 8,105 open-end mutual funds.

**unit investment trust (UIT)**

*A fund that sells a fixed number of redeemable shares that are redeemed on a set termination date.*

**Unit Investment Trusts.**   **Unit investment trusts (UITs)** have characteristics of both mutual funds and closed-end funds. Like mutual funds, UITs issue redeemable shares (so-called units). Like closed-end funds, UITs typically issue only a fixed number of shares. Unlike mutual funds and closed-end funds, however, UITs have a termination date that is set when the UIT is established and differs according to the investments held in the portfolio. UITs are generally fixed portfolios of securities (up to 20 specific stocks or bonds) that see little or no change over the life of the UIT. Thus, investors know what they are investing in for the period of their investment. Upon termination of the UIT, proceeds from the sale of the securities are either paid to UIT holders or reinvested in another UIT. In 2016, $4.25 billion was invested in 5,188 UITs.

## MUTUAL FUND RETURNS AND COSTS

The return to mutual fund investors can vary widely, depending on the objective of the fund, fees charged on the fund, and general market conditions. This section provides an overview of these issues.

LG 17-4

### Mutual Fund Prospectuses and Objectives

Regulations require that mutual fund managers specify the investment objectives of their funds in a prospectus available to potential investors. This prospectus also includes a list of the securities that the fund holds. The aggregate figures for long-term funds (in Table 17–2) tend to obscure the fact that many different funds fall into this group of funds. Table 17–5 classifies 13 major categories of investment objectives for mutual funds, with the assets allocated to each of these major categories. The fund objective described in its prospectus provides general information about the types of securities the mutual fund holds as assets. For example, "capital appreciation" funds hold securities (mainly equities)

**TABLE 17–5**   Total Net Asset Value of Mutual Funds by Investment Classification

| Classification | Combined Assets (billions of dollars) | Percentage of Total |
|---|---|---|
| **Total net assets** | **$15,651.9** | **100.0%** |
| Capital appreciation | 1,842.8 | **11.8%** |
| World equity | 2,102.4 | 13.4 |
| Total return | 4,203.1 | 26.9 |
| **Total equity funds** | **$ 8,148.3** | **52.1%** |
| **Total hybrid funds** | **$ 1,336.6** | **8.5%** |
| Investment grade | 1,512.7 | 9.7 |
| High-yield bond | 325.6 | 2.1 |
| World bond | 431.5 | 2.7 |
| Government bond | 265.8 | 1.7 |
| Multisector | 283.5 | 1.8 |
| State municipal | 159.8 | 1.0 |
| National municipal | 433.6 | 2.8 |
| **Total bond funds** | **$ 3,412.3** | **21.8%** |
| Taxable funds | 2,499.8 | 16.0 |
| Tax-exempt funds | 254.9 | 1.6 |
| **Total money market funds** | **$ 2,754.7** | **17.6%** |

**Source:** Investment Company Institute, *2016 Investment Company Fact Book.* www.ici.org

of the highest growth and highest-risk firms. Again, within each of these 13 categories of mutual funds are a multitude of different funds offered by mutual fund companies. Historically, mutual funds have had to send out lengthy prospectuses describing their objectives and investments. In 1998, the SEC adopted a new procedure in which key sections of all fund prospectuses must be written in "plain English" instead of overly legal language. The idea is to increase the ability of investors to understand the risks related to the investment objectives or profile of a fund. An individual's preferences for a mutual fund's objective often change over time. It is quite likely that people in the early years of investing, 20 and 30 years old, would prefer a fairly aggressive high-growth type of fund. As these people mature into their forties and fifties and retirement becomes a bit more imminent, they may switch to a fund with more of a balance between income and growth. In their later years, investors may try to protect their savings by switching to higher-yield stock and bond funds.

Table 17–6 lists the largest 20 mutual funds in total assets held in November 2016, including the fund objective; total assets; 12-month, 5-year, and 10-year returns; net asset value (NAV—see later); and any initial fees (discussed below). Vanguard's 500 Index Fund Admiral Shares (which invests in 500 of the largest U.S. companies, which span many different industries and account for about three-fourths of the U.S. stock market's value) was the largest fund at the time. Vanguard, American Funds, and Fidelity offered 18 of the top 20 funds measured by asset size. Many of the top funds list either growth or growth and income as the fund's objective, and all of the top 20 funds performed well in 2016 as the stock market saw high returns and the economy recovered from the financial crisis. Further, despite a severe financial crisis in 2008 and 2009, all of the top 20 funds earned positive annual returns over the period 2006–2016. Over the three time periods (12 months, 5 years, and 10 years), the S&P 500 Index saw annual returns of 4.18 percent, 12.06 percent, and 4.55 percent, respectively. Of the top mutual funds, all outperformed the S&P 500 Index over the 12-month period, 12 outperformed it over the 5-year period, and 16 funds outperformed the S&P 500 Index over the 10-year period.

www.fidelity.com

www.vanguard.com

www.americanfunds.com

**TABLE 17–6**    **The Largest Mutual Funds in Assets Managed**

| Name of Fund | Objective | Total Assets (in millions of dollars) | 12-Month | Total Return 5-Year | 10 year | NAV | Initial Fees |
|---|---|---|---|---|---|---|---|
| Vanguard 500 Index;Adm | S&P 500 Index | $169,749 | 15.39% | 16.33% | 7.23% | $200.62 | 0.00% |
| Vanguard Tot Stk Idx;Adm | Growth/Income | 140,730 | 14.98 | 16.33 | 7.53 | 54.19 | 0.00 |
| Vanguard Instl Indx;Inst | S&P 500 Index | 114,076 | 15.41 | 16.35 | 7.24 | 198.50 | 0.00 |
| Vanguard Tot Stk Inx;Inv | Growth/Income | 100,943 | 14.85 | 16.20 | 7.41 | 54.16 | 0.00 |
| Vanguard Instl Index;InsP | S&P 500 Index | 89,057 | 15.43 | 16.37 | 7.26 | 198.51 | 0.00 |
| Vanguard Tot I Stk;Inv | International | 87,010 | 9.53 | 6.71 | 2.15 | 14.69 | 0.00 |
| Fidelity Contrafund | Growth | 75,749 | 10.51 | 15.41 | 8.62 | 100.29 | 0.00 |
| Vanguard T StMk Idx;Inst | Growth/Income | 73,870 | 15.00 | 16.34 | 7.54 | 54.20 | 0.00 |
| American Funds Growth;A | Growth | 73,178 | 8.43 | 15.20 | 6.80 | 43.77 | 5.75 |
| American Funds Inc;A | Income | 72,848 | 7.34 | 9.46 | 5.31 | 21.26 | 5.75 |
| Vanguard Wellington;Adm | Balanced | 72,324 | 12.03 | 11.60 | 7.23 | 67.28 | 0.00 |
| American Funds CIB;A | International/Income | 69,166 | 4.67 | 7.64 | 4.34 | 56.90 | 5.75 |
| Vanguard T IntlStIdx;Inst | International | 64,511 | 9.70 | 6.84 | — | 98.27 | 0.00 |
| Fidelity 500 Index;Pr | S&P 500 Index | 56,852 | 15.40 | 16.33 | 7.21 | 76.41 | 0.00 |
| American Funds InvCoA | Growth/Income | 56,519 | 10.95 | 14.38 | 5.98 | 36.64 | 5.75 |
| Dodge & Cox Stock | Growth/Income | 55,832 | 14.53 | 17.10 | 5.52 | 182.21 | 0.00 |
| Dodge & Cox Intl Stock | International | 55,245 | 5.62 | 8.17 | 2.88 | 38.79 | 0.00 |
| American Funds Bal;A | Balanced | 54,031 | 5.64 | 10.80 | 6.18 | 24.94 | 5.75 |
| American Funds CWGI;A | Global | 51,069 | 4.62 | 10.22 | 4.71 | 44.63 | 5.75 |
| American Funds Wash;A | Growth/Income | 50,334 | 8.57 | 13.23 | 5.94 | 41.33 | 5.75 |

**Index Funds.** A growing number of the long-term mutual funds are index funds in which fund managers buy securities in proportions similar to those included in a specified major stock index (such as the Vanguard Institutional Index Fund: Institutional Shares, which seeks to match the investment performance of the Standard & Poor's 500 Composite Stock Price Index). These funds are in contrast to actively managed funds, which are managed by an individual manager or a team of managers attempting to beat a benchmark index for their fund. In 2016, 406 index funds managed total net assets of $2.2 trillion. Because little research or aggressive management is necessary for index funds, management fees (discussed below) are lower. However, returns are often higher than more actively managed funds. For example, from data analyzed by Morningstar and Forbes over the period 2004–2014, it was found that actively managed funds generally underperformed index funds across nearly all asset classes examined. Active funds that invest in value stocks of midsized companies were the only fund category of the 12 categories Morningstar studied that had a 10-year success rate above their index fund counterparts. Active funds with below-average costs were more likely to outperform higher-cost active funds over the decade studied. However, low-cost active funds still had lower average annualized returns compared with the average index fund in nine of the 12 categories studied in the report.[3]

**Exchange Traded Funds.** Exchange traded funds (ETFs) are long-term mutual funds that are also designed to replicate a particular stock market index. (In February 2008 the SEC gave approval for the first actively managed ETF and a growing number of them are now actively managed.) While legally classified as open-end mutual funds, ETFs are similar to closed-end funds in that a fixed number of shares are outstanding at any point in time. Further, unlike open-end funds, where the price per share (or net asset value, NAV, see below) is determined only once a day after markets have closed, ETFs trade intraday on a stock exchange at prices that are determined by the market. Like a mutual fund, an ETF offers investors a proportionate share in a pool of stocks, bonds, and other assets. Table 17–7 summarizes some of the main differences and similarities of open-end mutual funds, closed-end mutual funds, and ETFs.

ETFs may be bought or sold through a broker or in a brokerage account, like trading shares of any publicly traded company. While ETFs are registered with the SEC as investment companies, they differ from traditional mutual funds both in how their shares are issued and redeemed and in how their shares or units are traded. Specifically, ETF shares are created when an institutional investor deposits a specified block of securities with the ETF. In return for this deposit, the institutional investor receives a fixed amount of ETF shares, some or all of which may then be sold on a stock exchange. The institutional investor may obtain its deposited securities by redeeming the same number of ETF shares it received from the ETF. Individual investors can buy and sell the ETF shares only when they are listed on an exchange. Unlike an

**TABLE 17–7** Differences among Open-End Mutual Funds, Closed-End Mutual Funds, and ETFs

| | Open-End Mutual Fund | Closed-End Mutual Fund | ETF |
|---|---|---|---|
| Number of shares | No limit on shares | Fixed number of shares | Fixed number of shares |
| Trading | Shares not traded on an exchange, but bought from and sold to fund | Shares traded on an exchange | Shares traded on an exchange |
| Price | Price based on NAV | Price based on supply and demand, not NAV | Price based on NAV |
| Intraday trading | Trades at market close only | Trading occurs all day | Trading occurs all day |

---

3. Morningstar's Active/Passive Barometer: A New Yardstick for an Old Debate, Morningstar Manager Research, June 2015.

institutional investor, a retail investor cannot purchase or redeem shares directly from the ETF, as with a traditional mutual fund.

ETFs include funds such as SPDRs and Vanguard's Large-Cap VIPERS funds.[4] Like index funds, the share price of an ETF changes over time in response to a change in the stock prices underlying a stock index. Further, since both ETFs and index funds are intended to track a specific index, management of the funds is relatively simple and management fees are lower than those for actively managed mutual funds. Unlike index funds, however, ETFs can be traded during the day, they can be purchased on margin, and they can be sold short by an investor who expects a drop in the underlying index value. Because ETFs behave like stocks, investors are subject to capital gains taxes only when they sell their shares. Thus, ETF investors can defer capital gains for as long as they hold the ETF. These features of ETFs (intraday tradability, transparency, tax efficiency, and access to specific markets or asset classes) have contributed to their growing popularity. ETFs also have gained favor due to the rising popularity of passive investments (discussed below), increasing use of asset allocation models, and a move toward external fee-based models of compensation. As a result, assets invested in the 1,687 ETFs in existence in 2016 totaled $2.39 trillion, up from $66 billion invested in a total of 80 funds in 2000. Most ETFs are registered as investment companies under the Investment Company Act of 1940 and are regulated by the SEC. Thus, they are subject to the same regulatory requirements as other mutual funds.

Generally, the price at which an ETF trades closely tracks the market value of the securities held in the portfolio. One reason for this fairly close relationship is the ability for authorized participants (APs) to create or redeem ETF shares at net asset value at the end of each trading day. An AP is typically a large financial institution that enters into a legal contract with an ETF distributor to create and redeem shares of the fund. APs are the only investors allowed to interact directly with the fund. Thus, they play a key role in the primary market for ETF shares. APs receive no compensation from the ETF distributor and have no legal obligation to create or redeem the ETF's shares. Rather, APs derive their compensation by acting as dealers in ETF shares. That is, APs stand ready to create and redeem shares in the primary market when doing so is a more effective way of managing their firms' aggregate exposure than trading in the secondary market. Creations and redemptions are processed through the National Securities Clearing Corporation (NSCC) and have the same guarantee as a domestic stock trade. Most ETFs do not create or redeem shares on many trading days. Rather than the creation and redemption of shares through an AP, investors trade shares in secondary markets. On average, daily aggregate ETF creations and redemptions are a fraction (10 percent) of their total primary market activity and secondary market trading, and account for less than 0.5 percent of the funds' total net assets.

### Investor Returns from Mutual Fund Ownership

The return for the investor from investing in mutual fund shares reflects three aspects of the underlying portfolio of mutual fund assets. First, the portfolio earns income and dividends on those assets. Second, capital gains occur when the mutual fund sells an asset at prices higher than the original purchase price of the asset. Third, the sale of additional mutual fund shares and the profitable investment made with the funds from these shares can produce a capital appreciation that adds to the value of all shares in the mutual fund. With respect to capital appreciation, mutual fund assets are normally **marked to market** daily. This means that the managers of the fund calculate the current value of each mutual fund share by computing the daily market value of the fund's total asset portfolio less any

**marked to market**

*Describes the prices on outstanding futures contracts that are adjusted each day to reflect current futures market conditions.*

---

4. SPDRs, Standard & Poor's Depository Receipts, hold a portfolio of the equity securities that comprise the Standard & Poor's 500 Composite Stock Price Index. SPDRs seek investment results that, before expenses, generally correspond to the price and yield performance of the Standard & Poor's 500 Composite Stock Price Index. Vanguard Large-Cap Index Participation Equity Receipts (VIPERs) seek to track the performance of a benchmark index that measures the investment return of large-capitalization stocks.

**net asset value (NAV)**

*The net asset value of a share in a mutual fund—equal to the market value of the assets in the mutual fund portfolio divided by the number of shares outstanding.*

liabilities and then dividing this amount by the number of mutual fund shares outstanding. The resulting value is called the **net asset value (NAV)** of the fund's shares. This is the price that investors obtain when they sell shares back to the fund that day or the price they pay to buy new shares in the fund on that day. NAVs are published just once a day, after markets are closed.

**LG 17-5**

---

### EXAMPLE 17–1  Calculation of NAV of an Open-End Mutual Fund

Suppose today a mutual fund contains 4,000 shares of Sears, Roebuck currently trading at $22.00, 1,200 shares of ExxonMobil currently trading at $77.00, and 1,500 shares of AT&T currently trading at $33.75. The mutual fund has no liabilities and 15,000 shares outstanding held by investors. Thus, today, the NAV of the fund's shares[5] is calculated as:

$$NAV = \frac{\text{Total market value of assets under management}}{\text{Number of mutual fund shares outstanding}}$$

$$= (4{,}000 \times \$22.00 + 1{,}200 \times \$77.00 + 1{,}500 \times \$33.75) \div 15{,}000 = \$15.402$$

If tomorrow Sears's shares increase to $26.50, ExxonMobil's shares increase to $78, and AT&T's shares increase to $35, the NAV (assuming the number of shares outstanding remains the same) would increase to:

$$NAV = (4{,}000 \times \$26.50 + 1{,}200 \times \$78 + 1{,}500 \times \$35) \div 15{,}000 = \$16.807$$

---

### EXAMPLE 17–2  Calculation of NAV of an Open-End Mutual Fund when the Number of Shares Increases

Consider the mutual fund in Example 17–1, but suppose that today 1,000 additional investors buy one share each of the mutual fund at the NAV of $15.402. This means that the fund manager has $15,402 additional funds to invest. Suppose that the fund manager decides to use these additional funds to buy additional shares in Sears. At today's market price, the manager could buy 700 additional shares ($15,402/$22.00) of Sears. Thus, its new portfolio of shares has 4,700 in Sears, 1,200 in ExxonMobil, and 1,500 in AT&T. Given the same rise in share values as assumed in Example 17–1, tomorrow's NAV will now be:

$$NAV = (4{,}700 \times 26.50 + 1{,}200 \times 78 + 1{,}500 \times 35) \div 16{,}000 = \$16.916$$

Note that the fund's value changed over the day due to both capital appreciation and investment size. A comparison of the NAV in Example 17–1 with the one in this example indicates that the additional shares and the profitable investments made with the new funds from these shares resulted in a slightly higher NAV than had the number of shares remained static ($16.916 versus $16.807).

---

Mutual fund investors can get information on the performance of mutual funds from several places. For example, for a comprehensive analysis of mutual funds, Morningstar, Inc. offers information on over 10,000 open-end and closed-end funds. Morningstar does not own, operate, or hold an interest in any mutual fund. Thus, it is recognized as a leading provider of unbiased data and performance analysis (e.g., returns) for the industry. Similarly, Lipper Analytical services, a subsidiary of Reuters, tracks the performance of more than 115,000 funds worldwide.

**www.morningstar.com**

**www.lipperweb.com**

---

5. We omit any fees that the mutual fund company charges for managing the mutual fund. These fees and their impact on returns are discussed later in the chapter.

## *Mutual Fund Costs*

Mutual funds charge shareholders a price or fee for the services they provide (i.e., management of a diversified portfolio of financial securities). Two types of fees are incurred by investors: sales loads and fund operating expenses. The total cost to the shareholder of investing in a mutual fund is the sum of the annualized sales load and other fees charged. We discuss these next.

**Load versus No-Load Funds.**   An investor who buys a mutual fund share may be subject to a one-time sales or commission charge, sometimes as high as 5.75 percent. In this case, the fund is called a **load fund.**[6] Funds that have no up-front sales or commission charges are called **no-load funds.**

 The argument in favor of load funds is that they provide the investor with more personal attention and advice on fund selection than no-load funds. However, the cost of increased personal attention may not be worthwhile. High fees do not guarantee good performance. For example, Table 17–6 lists initial fees for the largest U.S. stock funds in 2016. Notice that only American Funds assesses a load fee on mutual fund share purchases. After adjusting for this fee, the 12-month returns on the 7 American Funds mutual funds fall from a range of 10.95 percent to 4.62 percent to a range of 8.39 percent to 0.67 percent. As Figure 17–3 indicates, investors increasingly recognized this cost disadvantage for load funds in the 1990s as stock market values increased broadly and dramatically. In 1985, load funds represented almost 70 percent of mutual fund sales and no-load funds represented just over 30 percent. By 1998 new sales of no-load mutual fund shares actually exceeded those of load fund shares and by the mid-2000s total assets invested in no-load funds far exceeded those invested in load funds. Of course, because the load fee is a one-time charge, it must be converted to an annualized charge incurred by the shareholder over the life of the investment. If the shareholder's investment horizon is long term, the annualized load fee can end

**load fund**

*A mutual fund with an up-front sales or commission charge that the investor must pay.*

**no-load fund**

*A mutual fund that does not charge up-front sales or commission charges on the sale of mutual fund shares to investors.*

**Figure 17–3**   **Load versus No-Load Fund Assets as a Share of Fund Assets**

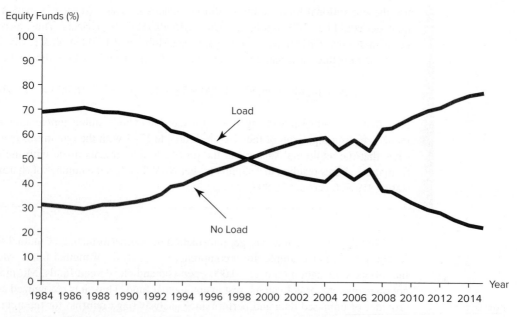

**Source:** Investment Company Institute, *Investment Company Fund Fact Book,* various issues. www.ici.org

---

6. Another kind of load, called a *back-end load,* is sometimes charged when mutual fund shares are sold by investors. Back-end loads, also referred to as deferred sales charges, are an alternative way to compensate the fund managers or sales force for their services. Some mutual funds waive back-end fees if the investor holds the funds for a stated period of time.

up being quite small. If the investment horizon is short, however, the load fee can leave the shareholder with little profit.

The demand for no-load funds by mutual fund investors has not gone unnoticed. Many companies, particularly discount brokers, now offer mutual fund "supermarkets" through which investors can buy and sell the mutual fund shares offered by several different mutual fund sponsors. The most important feature of a fund "supermarket" is its nontransaction fee program, whereby an investor may purchase mutual funds with no transaction fees from a large number of fund companies. The broker is generally paid for services from the fund's 12b-1 fees (discussed below). The nontransaction fee fund offerings at a discount broker often number in the thousands, providing an investor the convenience of purchasing no-load funds from different families at a single location.

**Fund Operating Expenses.**   In contrast to one-time up-front load charges on the initial investment in a mutual fund, annual fees are charged to cover fund-level expenses, calculated as a percentage of the fund assets. One type of fee (called a management fee) is charged to meet operating costs (such as administration and shareholder services). Management fees are generally the largest fee charged to mutual fund owners. In addition, mutual funds generally require a small percentage of investable funds—as a fee—to meet distribution expenses and shareholder servicing costs. These fees are known as **12b-1 fees** after the SEC rule covering such charges. Distribution fees include fees paid for marketing and selling fund shares. The SEC does not limit the size of 12b-1 fees that funds may charge. However, under Financial Industry Regulatory Authority (FINRA) rules, 12b-1 fees that are used to pay marketing and distribution expenses (as opposed to shareholder service expenses) cannot exceed 0.75 percent of a fund's average net assets per year. FINRA imposes an annual cap of 0.25 percent on shareholder service fees. Because these fees, charged to cover fund operating expenses, are paid out of the fund's assets, investors indirectly bear these expenses. These fees are generally expressed as a percentage of the average net assets invested in the fund.

Because the sales load is a one-time charge, it must be converted to an annualized payment incurred by the shareholder over the life of his or her investment. With this conversion, the total shareholder cost of investing in a fund is the sum of the annualized sales load plus any annual fees. For example, suppose an investor purchased funds shares with a 4 percent front-end load and expects to hold the shares for 10 years. The annualized sales load incurred by the investor is:

$$4\%/10 \text{ years} = 0.4\% \text{ per year}$$

Further, suppose the fund has a total fund expense ratio (including 12b-1 fees) of 1 percent per year. The annual total shareholder cost for this fund is calculated as:

$$0.4\% + 1\% = 1.4\% \text{ per year}$$

Funds sold through financial professionals such as brokers have recently adopted alternative payment methods. These typically include an annual 12b-1 fee based on asset values that may also be combined with a front-end or back-end sales charge. In many cases, funds offer several different share classes (all of which invest in the same underlying portfolio of assets), but each share class may offer investors different methods of paying for broker services. Indeed, in 2016 approximately two-thirds of all mutual funds had two or more share classes, compared to 1980 when all funds had only one share class. Most funds sold in multiple classes offer investors three payment plans through three share classes (A, B, and C), each having different mixes of sales loads and 12b-1 fees.

*Class A shares* represent the traditional means for paying for investment advice. That is, Class A shares carry a front-end load that is charged at the time of purchase as a percentage of the sales price. The front-end load on Class A shares is charged on new sales and is not generally incurred when Class A shares are exchanged for another mutual fund within the same fund family. In addition to the front-end load, Class A shares usually have an annual 12b-1 fee that is used to compensate brokers and sales professionals for ongoing

---

**12b-1 fees**

*Fees relating to the distribution costs of mutual fund shares.*

## EXAMPLE 17–3    Calculation of Mutual Fund Costs

The cost of mutual fund investing to the shareholder includes both the one-time sales load and any annual fees charged. Suppose an individual invests $10,000 in a load mutual fund. The load fee entails an up-front commission charge of 4 percent of the amount invested and is deducted from the original funds invested. Thus, the individual's actual investment, after the load fee is deducted, is:

$$\$10,000(1 - 0.04) = \$9,600$$

In addition, annual fund operating expenses are 0.85 percent (representing a management fee of 0.75 percent and a 12b-1 fee of 0.10 percent). The annual fees are charged on the average net asset value invested in the fund and are recorded at the end of each year. Investments in the fund return 5 percent each year paid on the last day of the year. If the investor reinvests the annual returns paid on the investment, after one year the operating fees deducted and the value of the investment are:

$$\text{Annual operating expenses} = \text{Average net asset value} \times \text{Annual operating expenses}$$
$$= [\$9,600 + \$9,600(1.05)]/2 \times 0.0085 = \$83.640$$
$$\text{Value of investment at end of year 1} = \$9,600(1.05) - \$83.640 = \$9,996.360$$

The investor's return on the mutual fund investment after one year is:

$$(\$9,996.360 - \$10,000)/\$10,000 = -0.04\%$$

In year 2, the investor's fees deducted and investment value at the end of the year are:

$$\text{Annual operating expenses} = [\$9,996.360 + \$9,996.360(1.05)]/2 \times 0.0085 = \$87.093$$
$$\text{Value of investment at end of year 2} = \$9,996.360(1.05) - \$87.093 = \$10,409.085$$

After two years the investor has paid a total of $400 in load fees and $170.733 in operating expenses, and he has made $409.085 above the original $10,000 investment. The investor's annual return on the mutual fund is 2.02 percent.[7]

---

assistance and service provided to fund shareholders. The 12b-1 fee for Class A shares is typically between 25 and 35 basis points of the portfolio's assets.

Unlike Class A shares, *Class B shares* are offered for sale at the NAV without a front-end load. Class B share investors pay for advice and assistance from brokers through a combination of annual 12b-1 fees (usually 1 percent) and a back-end load. The back-end load is charged when shares are redeemed (sold) and is typically based on the lesser of the original cost of the shares or the market value at the time of sale. After six to eight years, Class B shares typically convert to Class A shares, lowering the level of the annual 12b-1 fees from 1 percent to that of A shares.

*Class C shares* are offered at the NAV with no front-end load, and typically recover distribution costs through a combination of annual 12b-1 fees of 1 percent and a back-end load, set at 1 percent in the first year of purchase. After the first year no back-end load is charged on redemption. The Class C shares usually do not convert to Class A shares, and thus the annual 1 percent payment to the broker continues throughout the period of time that the shares are held.

As discussed below, the lack of complete disclosure and the inability of most mutual fund investors to understand the different fees charged for various classes of mutual fund shares came under scrutiny in the early 2000s.

### DO YOU UNDERSTAND:

1. Where mutual funds rank in terms of asset size of all FI industries?

2. What the difference is between short-term and long-term mutual funds?

3. What the trends have been (since 1980) regarding the number of mutual funds?

4. What the three largest mutual fund companies are? How have their funds performed in recent years?

5. What the difference is between an open-end mutual fund and a closed-end fund?

---

7.  That is, $\$10,000 = \$10,409.085/(1 + i)^2 => i = 2.02\%$.

Indeed, the potential for overcharging fees to various classes of mutual fund shareholders led the SEC to create new rules pertaining to these charges (see below). Possibly as a result of these scandals and new rules, more than 850 mutual funds decreased their management fees in 2005 and over 700 lowered their fees in 2006. Increased competition from ETFs and closed-end funds, which are less costly than open-end mutual funds and do not include sales charges, is another reason for the continued drop in mutual fund fees. The average fees and expenses paid by mutual fund investors continue to fall. Investors paid 0.68 percent on the average stock fund in 2015, down from 1.98 percent in 1990 and 1.18 percent in 2004. Bond fund investors paid an average of 0.54 percent, down from 1.89 percent in 1990 and 0.92 percent in 2004.

# MUTUAL FUND BALANCE SHEETS AND RECENT TRENDS

## Long-Term Funds

Note the asset distribution of long-term mutual funds in Table 17–8. As might be expected, the distribution of assets reflects the relative popularity of bonds and equities at various times. Underscoring the attractiveness of equities in 2007 was the fact that corporate equities represented 70.0 percent of total long-term mutual fund asset portfolios, while credit market instruments were the next most popular asset (28.1 percent of the asset portfolio). In contrast, consider the distribution of assets in 2008 when the equity markets were plummeting and the economy was in recession. Corporate equities made up only 55.5 percent of long-term mutual fund portfolios, and credit market instruments were 41.9 percent of total assets. Note too that total financial assets fell from $7,829.0 billion in 2007 (before the start of the financial crisis) to just $5,435.3 billion in 2008 (at the height of the crisis), a drop of 30.6 percent. As the economy and financial markets recovered, financial assets held by long-term mutual funds increased to $7,873.0 billion, of which only 60.5 percent were corporate equities. By 2016, while total assets had far surpassed pre-crisis levels, only 65.3 percent was invested in corporate equities. Thus, even eight years after the start of the financial crisis, long-term funds had not switched their holdings of corporate equities back to their pre-crisis levels.

**TABLE 17–8**   **Distribution of Assets in Long-Term Mutual Funds from 1990–2016** *(in billions of dollars)*

| | 1990 | 1995 | 2000 | 2007 | 2008 | 2010 | 2013 | 2016 | Percentage of Total, 2016 |
|---|---|---|---|---|---|---|---|---|---|
| Total financial assets | $608.4 | $1,852.8 | $4,434.6 | $7,829.0 | $5,435.3 | $7,873.0 | $10,221.8 | $13,208.8 | 100.0% |
| Security RPs | 6.1 | 50.2 | 106.4 | 132.2 | 124.7 | 137.5 | 319.1 | 85.1 | 0.6 |
| Credit market instruments | 360.1 | 761.1 | 1,073.5 | 2,120.8 | 2,181.7 | 2,895.3 | 4,133.7 | 4,061.1 | 30.7 |
| Open-market paper | 28.5 | 50.2 | 106.4 | 114.1 | 51.6 | 66.3 | 106.4 | 85.1 | 0.6 |
| Treasury securities | 87.1 | 205.3 | 123.7 | 179.2 | 187.9 | 290.7 | 469.9 | 857.1 | 6.5 |
| Agency securities | 72.6 | 109.9 | 275.3 | 565.4 | 592.7 | 769.8 | 1,033.7 | 613.4 | 4.6 |
| Municipal securities | 112.6 | 210.2 | 230.5 | 372.2 | 389.6 | 525.5 | 641.2 | 669.0 | 5.1 |
| Corporate and foreign bonds | 59.3 | 185.5 | 337.6 | 889.9 | 959.9 | 1,243.0 | 1,882.5 | 1,836.5 | 13.9 |
| Other loans and advances | 0.0 | 10.2 | 24.3 | 82.3 | 94.8 | 74.6 | 117.1 | 139.5 | 1.1 |
| Corporate equities | 233.2 | 1,024.9 | 3,226.9 | 5,476.9 | 3,014.1 | 4,762.7 | 5,668.1 | 8,620.7 | 65.3 |
| Miscellaneous assets | 8.9 | 6.3 | 3.5 | 16.8 | 20.0 | 2.9 | −16.2 | 302.4 | 2.3 |

**Sources:** Federal Reserve Board website, "Flow of Fund Accounts," various issues. www.federalreserve.gov

### Money Market Funds

Look at the distribution of assets of money market mutual funds from 1990 through 2016 in Table 17–9. In 2016, $2,459.6 billion (91.0 percent of total assets) were invested in short-term (under one year to maturity) financial securities—such as foreign deposits, domestic checkable deposits and currency, time and savings deposits, repurchase agreements (RPs or repos), open-market paper (mostly commercial paper), and U.S. government securities. This is up from 2007 (at the start of the financial crisis) when $2,094.3 billion (or 69.0 percent) of financial assets were invested in short-term securities. As financial markets tumbled in 2008, money market mutual funds moved investments out of corporate and foreign bonds (12.4 percent of the total in 2007 and 6.1 percent in 2008) into safer securities such as U.S. government securities (13.6 percent of the total investments in 2007 and 35.5 percent in 2008). Short-term maturity asset holdings reflect the objective of these funds to retain the depositlike nature of the share liabilities they issue. In fact, most customer-oriented money market mutual fund shares have their values fixed at $1. The principal type of risk for short-term funds is interest rate risk, because of the predominance of fixed-income securities. Because of the shortness of maturity of the assets, this risk is mitigated to a large extent. Further, asset value fluctuations due to interest rate changes and any small default risk and capital gains or losses are adjusted by increasing or reducing the number of $1 shares owned by the investor.

In addition to these typical risks faced by fund mangers, money market mutual funds experienced unusual liquidity risk at the start of the financial crisis. On September 16, 2008 (one day after Lehman Brothers filed for bankruptcy), Primary Reserve Fund, the oldest money market fund in the United States, saw its shares fall to an equivalent of 97 cents (below the $1.00 book value) after writing off debt issued by Lehman Brothers. Resulting investor anxiety about Primary Reserve Fund spread to other funds and investors

**TABLE 17–9**   Distribution of Assets in Money Market Mutual Funds, 1990–2016 *(in billions of dollars)*

| | 1990 | 1995 | 2000 | 2007 | 2008 | 2010 | 2013 | 2016 | Percentage of Total, 2016 |
|---|---|---|---|---|---|---|---|---|---|
| Total financial assets | $493.3 | $741.3 | $1,812.1 | $3,033.1 | $3,757.3 | $2,755.4 | $2,541.9 | $2,702.5 | 100.0% |
| Foreign deposits | 26.7 | 19.7 | 91.1 | 127.3 | 129.3 | 105.9 | 37.1 | 12.9 | 0.5 |
| Checkable deposits and currency | 11.2 | −3.5 | 2.2 | 1.9 | 7.5 | 14.2 | 27.5 | 13.3 | 0.5 |
| Time and savings deposits | 21.9 | 52.3 | 142.4 | 270.6 | 355.2 | 458.9 | 444.3 | 429.9 | 15.9 |
| Security RPs | 58.2 | 87.8 | 183.0 | 605.9 | 542.4 | 479.4 | 450.4 | 643.4 | 23.8 |
| Credit market instruments | 371.3 | 545.5 | 1,290.9 | 1,936.4 | 2,675.0 | 1,673.4 | 1,550.9 | 1,594.6 | 59.0 |
| Open-market paper | 204.0 | 235.5 | 608.6 | 674.6 | 618.5 | 394.2 | 356.6 | 276.6 | 10.0 |
| Treasury securities | 44.9 | 70.0 | 90.4 | 178.1 | 577.7 | 335.4 | 449.0 | 517.5 | 19.2 |
| Agency securities | 36.4 | 90.8 | 185.2 | 235.9 | 756.2 | 402.8 | 345.0 | 566.0 | 20.9 |
| Municipal securities | 84.0 | 127.7 | 244.7 | 471.0 | 494.6 | 386.8 | 309.6 | 216.2 | 8.0 |
| Corporate and foreign bonds | 2.0 | 21.5 | 161.9 | 376.8 | 228.0 | 154.2 | 90.7 | 18.3 | 0.7 |
| Miscellaneous assets | 4.0 | 43.4 | 102.5 | 90.9 | 47.9 | 23.6 | 31.7 | 8.4 | 0.3 |

**Sources:** Federal Reserve Board website, "Flow of Fund Accounts," various issues. www.federalreserve.gov

industrywide liquidated their MMMF shares. In just one week investors liquidated over $200 billion of the industry's total of $4 trillion invested in MMMFs. In response, on September 19, 2008, the federal government took steps to restore confidence in the MMMF industry. Specifically, the Department of Treasury opened the Temporary Guarantee Program for MMMFs, which provided up to $50 billion in coverage to MMMF shareholders

DO YOU UNDERSTAND:

6. *What major assets have been held by mutual funds in the 1990s–2010s?*

7. *How the asset distribution for money market mutual funds and long-term mutual funds differs?*

for amounts they held in the funds as of the close of business that day. The guarantee was triggered if a participating fund's net asset value fell below $0.995. The program was designed to address the severe liquidity strains in the industry and immediately stabilized the industry and stopped the outflows. As a consequence of this unprecedented turn of events, in 2016 regulators adopted new rules under which the net asset values of MMMF shares issued by institutional prime money market funds would float as the value of the underlying investments changed. A floating NAV would mean money market funds would behave more like short-term bond funds, with share prices rising and falling with changing market conditions.

---

**EXAMPLE 17–4** Calculation of Number of Shares Outstanding in a Money Market Mutual Fund

Because of a drop in interest rates, the market value of the assets held by a particular MMMF increases from $100 to $110. The market value balance sheet for the mutual fund before and after the drop in interest rates is:

(a) Before interest rate drop:

| Assets | | Liabilities and Equity | |
|---|---|---|---|
| Market value of MMMF assets | $100 | Market value of MMMF fund shares (100 shares × $1) | $100 |

(b) After interest rate drop:

| Assets | | Liabilities and Equity | |
|---|---|---|---|
| Market value of MMMF assets | $110 | Market value of MMMF fund shares (110 shares × $1) | $110 |

The interest rate drop results in 10 (110 − 100) new equity-type shares that are held by investors in the MMMF, reflecting the increase in the market value of the MMMF's assets of $10 (i.e., 10 new shares of $1 each).

---

## MUTUAL FUND REGULATION

LG 17-6

www.sec.gov

Because mutual funds manage and invest small investor savings, this industry is heavily regulated. Indeed, many regulations have been enacted to protect investors against possible abuses by mutual fund managers. The SEC is the primary regulator of mutual funds. Specifically, the Securities Act of 1933 requires a mutual fund to file a registration statement with the SEC and sets rules and procedures regarding a fund's prospectus that it sends to investors. In addition, the Securities Exchange Act of 1934 makes the purchase and sale of mutual fund shares subject to various antifraud provisions. This act requires mutual funds to furnish full and accurate information on all financial and corporate matters to prospective fund purchasers. The 1934 act also appointed the National Association of Securities Dealers (NASD) to supervise mutual fund share distributions. In 1940, Congress passed the Investment Advisers Act and Investment Company Act. The Investment Company Act established rules to prevent conflicts of interest, fraud, and excessive fees or charges for fund shares.

More recently, the Insider Trading and Securities Fraud Enforcement Act of 1988 required mutual funds to develop mechanisms and procedures to avoid insider trading abuses. In addition, the Market Reform Act of 1990, passed in the wake of the 1987 stock market crash, allows the SEC to introduce circuit breakers to halt trading on exchanges and to restrict program trading when it is deemed necessary. Finally, the National Securities Markets Improvement Act (NSMIA) of 1996 (discussed in Chapter 16) also applies to mutual fund companies. Specifically, the NSMIA exempts mutual fund companies from oversight by state securities regulators, thus reducing their regulatory burden.

Despite the many regulations imposed on mutual fund companies, several allegations of trading abuse and the improper assignment of fees were revealed and prosecuted in the early 2000s. The abusive activities fell into four general categories: market timing, late trading, directed brokerage, and improper assessment of fees.

*Market timing* is short-term trading of mutual funds that seeks to take advantage of short-term discrepancies between the price of a mutual fund's shares and out-of-date values on the securities in the fund's portfolio. It is especially common in international funds, where traders can exploit differences in time zones. *Late trading* allegations have involved cases in which some investors were able to buy or sell mutual fund shares long after the price had been set at 4:00 p.m. Eastern time each day (i.e., after the close of the NYSE and NASDAQ). *Directed brokerage* arrangements between mutual fund companies and brokerage houses afforded brokers the opportunity to improperly influence investors on their funds recommendations. For example, some mutual fund companies agreed to direct orders for stock and bond purchases and sales to brokerage houses that agreed to promote sales of the mutual fund company's products. Finally, the disclosure of 12b-1 fees allowed brokers to *improperly assess fees* by tricking investors into believing they were buying no-load funds. Before 12b-1 fees, all funds sold through brokers carried front-end load fees. As discussed earlier, with 12b-1 fees, fund companies introduced share classes, some of which carried back-end loads that declined over time and others which charged annual fees of up to 1 percent of asset values. Fund classes that charged annual 12b-1 fees would see performance decrease by that amount and thus not perform as well as an identical fund that carried a lower 12b-1 fee. The shareholder, however, saw only the fund's raw return (before annual fees) and not the dollar amount of the fee paid.

As a result of these illegal and abusive activities, new rules and regulations were imposed (in 2004 and 2005) on mutual fund companies. The rules were intended to give investors more information about conflicts of interest, improve fund governance, and close legal loopholes that some fund managers had abused. The SEC also took steps to close a loophole that allowed improper trading to go unnoticed at some mutual funds. Prior to the new rules, the SEC required that funds report trading by senior employees in individual stocks but not in shares of mutual funds they manage. The SEC now requires portfolio managers to report trading in funds they manage. To address the problem of market timing, the SEC now requires funds to provide expanded disclosure of the risks of frequent trading in fund shares and of their policies and procedures regarding such activities. Mutual funds also now have to be more open about their use of fair value pricing (a practice of estimating the value of rarely traded securities or updating the values of non-U.S. securities that last traded many hours before U.S. funds calculate their share prices each day) to guard against stale share prices that could produce profits for market timers. The SEC has also proposed that mutual funds or their agents receive all trading orders by 4:00 p.m. Eastern time, when the fund's daily price is calculated. This "hard closing," which would require fund orders to be in the hands of the mutual fund companies by 4:00 p.m., is intended to halt late trading abuses.

To ensure that the required rule changes took place, starting October 5, 2004, the SEC required that mutual funds hire chief compliance officers to monitor whether a mutual fund company is following the rules. The chief compliance officer reports directly to mutual fund directors, and not to executives of the fund management company. To further insulate the chief compliance officer from being bullied into keeping quiet about improper behavior, only the fund board can fire the compliance officer. Duties of the compliance officer include policing personal trading by fund managers, ensuring the accuracy of information provided to regulators and investors, reviewing fund business practices such as allocating trading commissions, and reporting any wrongdoing directly to fund directors.

New SEC rules also called for shareholder reports to include the fees shareholders paid, as well as management's discussion of the fund's performance over that period. As of September 1, 2004, mutual fund companies must provide clear information to investors on brokerage commissions and discounts, including improved disclosure on up-front sales charges for broker-sold mutual funds. Investors now get a document showing the amount they paid for a fund, the amount their broker was paid, and how the fund compares with industry averages based on fees, sales loads, and brokerage commissions. Finally, in March 2009, the SEC adopted amendments to the form used by mutual funds to register under the Investment Company Act of 1940 and to offer their securities under the Securities Act of 1933 in order to enhance the disclosures that are provided to mutual fund investors. The amendments (first proposed in November 2007) require key information to appear in plain English in a standardized order at the front of the mutual fund statutory prospectus. The new amendment also includes a new option for satisfying prospectus delivery obligations with respect to mutual fund securities under the Securities Act. Under the option, key information is sent or given to investors in the form of a summary prospectus and the statutory prospectus is provided on an Internet website. The improved disclosure framework is intended to provide investors with information that is easier to use and more readily accessible, while retaining the comprehensive quality of the information that was previously available.

After the financial crisis, in a February 2013 letter sent to the Financial Stability Oversight Council (FSOC) (set up as a result of the Wall Street Reform and Consumer Protection Act to oversee the financial system), the leaders of all 12 regional Federal Reserve banks called for a significant overhaul of the money market industry. The letter stated that, even four years after the financial crisis, without reform, money market mutual fund activities could spread the risk of significant credit problems from the funds to banks and the broader financial system. New York Fed President William Dudley stated that the risk of a run on money market funds was potentially higher in 2013 than before the crisis because banks increasingly used these funds as a source of financing and because Congress blocked the Fed and Treasury from using certain emergency tools that could stabilize the funds during a market panic. As a result of the calls for reform, in 2014 the SEC adopted amendments to the rules that govern money market mutual funds. The amendments make structural and operational reforms to address risks of investor runs in money market funds, while preserving the benefits of the funds. The new rules require a floating net asset value (NAV) for institutional prime money market funds. Floating NAV allows the daily share prices of these funds to fluctuate along with changes in the market value of fund assets. Further, liquidity fees and redemption gates were instituted, giving money market fund boards the ability to impose fees and gates during periods of stress. The final rules also include enhanced diversification and disclosure and stress testing requirements, as well as updated reporting by money market funds and private funds that operate like money market funds.

Also, in 2015 the SEC proposed rules and amendments to modernize and enhance the reporting and disclosure of information by investment companies and investment advisors. The new rules would enhance the quality of information available to investors and would allow the commission to more effectively collect and use data provided by investment companies and investment advisors. The SEC also proposed a comprehensive package of rule reforms designed to enhance effective liquidity risk management by open-end funds, including mutual funds and exchange-traded funds (ETFs). Under the proposed reforms, mutual funds and ETFs would be required to implement liquidity risk management programs and enhance disclosure regarding fund liquidity and redemption practices. The proposal is designed to better ensure that investors can redeem their shares and receive their assets in a timely manner. A fund's liquidity risk management program would be required to contain multiple elements, including classification of the liquidity of fund portfolio assets based on the amount of time an asset would be able to be converted to cash without a market impact; assessment, periodic review, and management of a fund's liquidity risk; establishment of a fund's three-day liquid asset minimum; and board approval and review.

**DO YOU UNDERSTAND:**

8. *Who the primary regulator of mutual fund companies is?*

9. *How the NSMIA affected mutual funds?*

## MUTUAL FUND GLOBAL ISSUES

As discussed throughout the chapter, mutual funds have been the fastest-growing sector in the U.S. financial institutions industry throughout the 1990s and into the 2000s. Only the worldwide financial crisis and the worst worldwide recession since the Great Depression curtailed the growth in this industry. Worldwide investment in mutual funds is shown in Table 17–10. Combined assets invested in non-U.S. mutual funds are approximately equal to that invested in U.S. mutual funds alone. However, recent growth in non-U.S. funds has exceeded that in U.S. funds. Worldwide (other than in the United States) investments in mutual funds increased over 187 percent, from $4.916 trillion in 1999 to $14.130 trillion in 2007. This compares to growth of 75 percent in U.S. funds. Likewise, non-U.S. mutual funds experienced bigger losses in total assets during the financial crisis. Worldwide funds fell to $9.316 trillion (34.1 percent) in 2008, while U.S. funds fell to $9.603 trillion (20.0 percent). By 2016, as worldwide economies improved, worldwide investments in mutual funds increased to $21.16 trillion (an increase of 127 percent from 2008), while U.S. investments increased to $18.13 trillion (an increase of 88.8 percent). In addition, as this industry developed in countries throughout the world, the number of mutual funds worldwide (other than in the United States) increased by 126 percent, from 43,537 in 2000 to 98,255 in 2016. Much more established in the United States, the number of mutual funds decreased by 0.6 percent over this period.

As may be expected, the worldwide mutual fund market is most active in those countries with the most sophisticated securities markets (e.g., Japan, France, Australia, Germany, and the United Kingdom).[8] Note that the large value of mutual funds in Luxembourg is a result of the country's introduction of legislation in 1988 that gave fund managers maximum freedom in their fund's management. The legislation let managers make virtually any investments they want to (including investments in options, futures, and venture capital) as long as they were clear enough about their intentions with investors. In addition, Luxembourg had an infrastructure of lawyers, accountants, banks, and computer technicians that made it an easy place to operate mutual funds.

Although U.S. mutual fund companies sponsor funds abroad, barriers to entry overseas are typically higher than in the United States. The U.S. mutual fund industry has worked to lower the barriers that prevent U.S. mutual fund firms from marketing their services abroad more widely and to improve competition in the often diverse fund markets around the world. The U.S. mutual fund industry has, for example, worked to achieve a true cross-border market for mutual fund companies in Europe and to ensure that publicly offered mutual fund companies can be used as funding vehicles in the retirement fund market in Europe and Japan. The industry has also sought to reduce barriers for U.S. mutual fund sponsors seeking to offer mutual fund company products in China and other Asian countries.

**DO YOU UNDERSTAND:**

**10.** What the trends have been (in the 1990s through 2010s) regarding assets invested in worldwide mutual funds?

## HEDGE FUNDS

**LG 17-8**

Hedge funds are investment pools that invest funds for (wealthy) individuals and other investors (e.g., commercial banks). They are similar to mutual funds in that they are pooled investment vehicles that accept investors' money and generally invest it on a collective basis. Hedge funds, however, are not subject to the numerous regulations that apply to mutual funds for the protection of individuals, such as regulations requiring a certain degree of liquidity, regulations requiring that mutual fund shares be redeemable at any time, regulations protecting against conflicts of interest, regulations to ensure fairness in the pricing of funds shares, disclosure regulations, and regulations limiting the use of

---

8. It might be noted that, as many European countries move away from state-sponsored pension plans to privately funded pension plans and retirement vehicles, the rate of growth in mutual funds in these countries is likely to rapidly accelerate.

**TABLE 17-10** Worldwide Assets of Open-End Investment Companies* *(in millions of U.S. dollars)*

| Non-U.S. Countries | 1999 | 2000 | 2007 | 2008 | 2010 | 2013 | 2016 |
|---|---|---|---|---|---|---|---|
| Argentina | $ 6,990 | $ 7,425 | $ 6,789 | $ 3,867 | $ 5,179 | $ 11,163 | $ 16,512 |
| Australia | 371,207 | 341,955 | 1,192,992 | 841,133 | 1,455,850 | 1,737,739 | 1,597,258 |
| Austria | 56,254 | 56,549 | 138,709 | 93,269 | 94,670 | 87,476 | 155,330 |
| Belgium | 65,461 | 70,313 | 149,842 | 105,057 | 96,288 | 79,993 | 88,424 |
| Brazil | 117,758 | 148,538 | 615,365 | 479,321 | 980,448 | 1,135,933 | 984,352 |
| Bulgaria | n.a. | n.a. | n.a. | 226 | 302 | 364 | 482 |
| Canada | 269,825 | 279,511 | 698,397 | 410,031 | 636,947 | 888,003 | 980,303 |
| Chile | 4,091 | 4,597 | 24,444 | 17,587 | 38,243 | 36,672 | 42,480 |
| China | n.a. | n.a. | 434,063 | 276,303 | 364,985 | 422,398 | 1,154,330 |
| Costa Rica | n.a. | 919 | 1,203 | 1,098 | 1,470 | 1,965 | 2,513 |
| Croatio | n.a. | n.a. | n.a. | n.a. | n.a. | n.a. | 2,262 |
| Czech Republic | 1,473 | 1,990 | 7,595 | 5,260 | 5,508 | 4,848 | 8,482 |
| Denmark‡ | 27,558 | 32,485 | 104,082 | 65,182 | 89,800 | 103,746 | 112,487 |
| Finland | 10,318 | 12,698 | 81,136 | 48,750 | 71,210 | 74,315 | 89,806 |
| France | 656,132 | 721,973 | 1,989,690 | 1,591,082 | 1,617,176 | 1,453,347 | 1,866,100 |
| Germany | 237,312 | 238,029 | 372,072 | 237,986 | 333,713 | 332,005 | 1,916,532 |
| Greece | 36,397 | 29,154 | 29,809 | 12,189 | 8,627 | 5,849 | 4,117 |
| Hong Kong | 182,265 | 195,924 | 818,421 | n.a. | n.a. | n.a. | n.a. |
| Hungary | 1,725 | 1,953 | 12,577 | 9,188 | 11,532 | 7,985 | 14,570 |
| India | 13,065 | 13,507 | 108,582 | 62,805 | 111,421 | 102,826 | 177,378 |
| Ireland | 95,174 | 137,024 | 951,371 | 720,486 | 1,014,104 | 1,316,755 | 2,128,143 |
| Italy | 475,661 | 424,014 | 419,687 | 263,588 | 234,313 | 181,307 | 203,272 |
| Japan | 502,752 | 431,996 | 713,998 | 575,327 | 785,504 | 777,307 | 1,475,209 |
| Korea | 167,177 | 110,613 | 329,979 | 221,992 | 266,495 | 269,689 | 382,169 |
| Liechtenstein | n.a. | n.a. | 25,103 | 20,489 | 35,387 | 34,839 | 44,616 |
| Luxembourg | 661,084 | 747,117 | 2,685,065 | 1,860,763 | 2,512,874 | 2,722,342 | 3,843,406 |
| Malta | n.a. | n.a. | n.a. | n.a. | n.a. | 2,024 | 3,475 |
| Mexico | 19,468 | 18,488 | 75,428 | 60,435 | 98,094 | 121,544 | 107,104 |
| Netherlands | 94,539 | 93,580 | 113,759 | 77,379 | 85,924 | 76,662 | 781,512 |
| New Zealand | 8,502 | 7,802 | 14,924 | 10,612 | 19,562 | 33,043 | 46,360 |
| Norway | 15,107 | 16,228 | 74,709 | 41,157 | 84,505 | 101,949 | 109,576 |
| Pakistan | n.a. | n.a. | 4,956 | 1,985 | 2,290 | 3,251 | 4,155 |
| Philippines | 117 | 108 | 2,090 | 1,263 | 2,184 | 4,591 | 5,357 |
| Poland | 762 | 1,546 | 45,542 | 17,782 | 25,595 | 22,817 | 31,064 |
| Portugal | 19,704 | 16,588 | 29,732 | 13,572 | 11,004 | 7,897 | 21,247 |
| Romania | n.a. | 8 | 390 | 326 | 1,713 | 2,823 | 5,172 |
| Russia | 177 | 177 | 7,175 | 2,026 | 3,917 | n.a. | n.a. |
| Slovakia | n.a. | n.a. | 4,762 | 3,841 | 4,349 | 2,882 | 6,205 |
| Slovenia | n.a. | n.a. | 4,219 | 2,067 | 2,663 | 2,354 | 2,445 |
| South Africa | 18,235 | 16,921 | 95,221 | 69,417 | 141,615 | 142,070 | 132,844 |
| Spain | 207,603 | 172,438 | 396,534 | 270,893 | 216,915 | 194,332 | 276,642 |
| Sweden | 83,250 | 78,085 | 194,955 | 113,331 | 205,449 | 218,232 | 271,782 |
| Switzerland | 82,512 | 83,059 | 176,282 | 135,052 | 261,893 | 364,352 | 485,510 |
| Taiwan | 31,153 | 32,074 | 58,323 | 46,116 | 59,032 | 60,132 | 64,667 |
| Trinidad and Tobago | n.a. | n.a. | n.a. | n.a. | 98,094 | 121,544 | 6,814 |
| Turkey | n.a. | n.a. | 22,609 | 15,404 | 19,545 | 17,414 | 13,729 |
| United Kingdom | 375,199 | 361,008 | 897,460 | 504,681 | 854,413 | 1,006,707 | 1,491,980 |
| **Total non-U.S.** | **$ 4,916,006** | **$ 4,916,006** | **$14,130,041** | **$ 9,316,409** | **$12,878,520** | **$14,180,565** | **$21,158,173** |
| **Total U.S.** | **$ 6,846,339** | **$ 6,964,667** | **$12,000,645** | **$ 9,602,605** | **$11,831,878** | **$13,675,893** | **$18,130,222** |
| **Total world** | **$11,762,345** | **$11,871,061** | **$26,130,686** | **$18,919,014** | **$24,710,398** | **$27,856,458** | **$39,288,395** |

*Funds of funds are not included except for France, Italy, and Luxembourg. Data include home-domiciled funds, except for Hong Kong, Korea, and New Zealand, which include home and foreign-domiciled funds.

‡Before 2003, data include special funds reserved for institutional investors.

**Note:** Components may not add to total because of rounding.

**Sources:** Investment Company Institute, *Investment Company Fact Book,* various issues. www.ici.org

leverage. Further, hedge funds do not have to disclose their activities to third parties. Thus, they offer a high degree of privacy for their investors. Until 2010, hedge funds were not required to register with the SEC. Thus, they were subject to virtually no regulatory oversight (e.g., by the SEC under the Securities Act and Investment Advisers Act) and generally took significant risk. Even after 2010, hedge funds offered in the United States avoid regulations by limiting the asset size of the fund (see below).

Historically, hedge funds have avoided regulations by limiting the number of investors to less than 100 individuals (below that required for SEC registration), who must be deemed "accredited investors." To be accredited, an investor must have a net worth of over $1 million or have an annual income of at least $200,000 ($300,000 if married). Institutional investors can be qualified as accredited investors if total assets exceed $5 million. These stiff financial requirements allowed hedge funds to avoid regulation under the theory that individuals with such wealth should be able to evaluate the risk and return on their investments. According to the SEC, these types of investors should be expected to make more informed decisions and take on higher levels of risk. However, as a result of some heavily publicized hedge fund failures and near failures—the result of fraud by fund managers (e.g., Bernard L. Madoff Investment Securities,) and the financial crisis (e.g., Bear Stearns High Grade Structured Credit Strategies Fund)—in 2010 federal regulators increased the oversight of hedge funds.

Because hedge funds have been exempt from many of the rules and regulations governing mutual funds, they can use aggressive strategies that are unavailable to mutual funds, including short selling, leveraging, program trading, arbitrage, and derivatives trading. Further, since hedge funds that do not exceed $100 million in assets under management do not register with the SEC, their actual data cannot be independently tracked. Therefore, hedge fund data are self-reported. It is estimated that in 2016 there were over 10,000 hedge funds in the United States, with managed assets estimated at $2.98 trillion. Table 17–11 lists the estimated 10 largest hedge fund firms by total assets managed in 2016.

Hedge funds grew in popularity in the 1990s as investors saw returns of over 40 percent after management fees (often more than 25 percent of the fund's profits). They came to the forefront of the news in the late 1990s when one large hedge fund, Long-Term Capital Management (LTCM), nearly collapsed. The near collapse of LTCM not only hurt its investors, but arguably came close to damaging the world's financial system. So great was the potential impact of the failure of LTCM that the Federal Reserve felt it was necessary to intervene by brokering a $3.6 billion bailout of LTCM by a consortium of some of the world's largest financial institutions.

Some hedge funds take positions (using sophisticated computer models) speculating that some prices will rise faster than others. For example, a hedge fund may buy (take a long position in) a bond expecting that its price will rise. At the same time the fund will borrow (taking a short position) in another bond and sell it, promising to return the

**TABLE 17–11**   Largest Hedge Fund Firms by Assets Managed

| Name of Fund | Country | Total Assets (in billions) |
| --- | --- | --- |
| Bridgewater Associates | United States | $104.2 |
| Man Group | United Kingdom | 76.4 |
| AQR Capital Management | United States | 47.2 |
| Och-Ziff Capital Management | United States | 44.6 |
| Two Sigma Investments | United States | 35.0 |
| Millennium Management | United States | 34.0 |
| Winton Capital Management | United Kingdom | 34.0 |
| D.E. Shaw & Co. | United States | 33.1 |
| Viking Global Investors | United States | 33.1 |
| BlackRock Advisors | United States | 31.1 |

**Source:** Institutional Investor. www.institutionalinvestor.com

borrowed bond in the future. Generally, bond prices tend to move up and down together. Thus, if prices go up as expected, the hedge fund will gain on the bond it purchased while losing money on the bond it borrowed. The hedge fund will make a profit if the gain on the bond it purchased is larger than the loss on the bond it borrowed. If, contrary to expectations, bond prices fall, the hedge fund will make a profit if the gains on the bond it borrowed are greater than the losses on the bond it bought. Thus, regardless of the change in prices, the simultaneous long and short positions in bonds will minimize the risk of overall losses for the hedge fund.

### Types of Hedge Funds

Most hedge funds are highly specialized, relying on the specific expertise of the fund managers to produce a profit. Hedge fund managers follow a variety of investment strategies. Some of these strategies use leverage and derivatives, while others are more conservative and involve little or no leverage. Generally, hedge funds are set up with specific parameters so that investors can forecast a risk-return profile. Figure 17–4 shows the general categories of hedge funds by risk classification.

*More risky* funds are the most aggressive and may produce profits in many types of market environments. Funds in this group are classified by objectives such as aggressive growth, emerging markets, macro, market timing, and short selling. Aggressive growth funds invest in equities expected to experience acceleration in growth of earnings per share. Generally, high price-to-earnings ratio, low or no dividend companies are included. These funds hedge by shorting equities where earnings disappointment is expected or by shorting stock indexes. Emerging market funds invest in equity or debt securities of emerging markets, which tend to have higher inflation and volatile growth. Macro funds aim to profit from changes in global economies, typically brought about by shifts in government policy that impact interest rates. These funds include investments in equities, bonds, currencies, and commodities. They use leverage and derivatives to accentuate the impact of market moves. Market timing funds allocate assets among different asset classes depending on the manager's view of the economic or market outlook. Thus, portfolio emphasis may swing widely between asset classes. The unpredictability of market movements and the difficulty of timing entry and exit from markets add significant risk to this strategy. Short-selling funds sell securities in anticipation of being able to buy them back in the future at a lower price based on the manager's assessment of the overvaluation of the securities or in anticipation of earnings disappointments.

*Moderate risk* funds are more traditional funds, similar to mutual funds, with only a portion of the portfolio being hedged. Funds in this group are classified by objectives such as distressed securities, fund of funds, opportunistic, multistrategy, and special situations. Distressed securities funds buy equity, debt, or trade claims, at deep discounts, of companies in or facing bankruptcy or reorganization. Profit opportunities come from the market's

**Figure 17–4** **Classification of Hedge Funds**

lack of understanding of the true value of these deep-discount securities and from the fact that the majority of institutional investors cannot own below-investment-grade securities. Funds of funds mix hedge funds and other pooled investment vehicles. This blending of different strategies and asset classes aims to provide a more stable long-term investment return than any of the individual funds. Returns and risk can be controlled by the mix of underlying strategies and funds. Capital preservation is generally an important consideration for these funds. Opportunistic funds change their investment strategy as opportunities arise to profit from events such as IPOs, sudden price changes resulting from a disappointing earnings announcement, and hostile takeover bids. These funds may utilize several investing styles at any point in time and are not restricted to any particular investment approach or asset class. Multistrategy funds take a diversified investment approach by implementing various strategies simultaneously to realize short- and long-term gains. This style of investment allows the manager to overweight or underweight different strategies to best capitalize on current investment opportunities. Special-situation funds invest in event-driven situations such as mergers, hostile takeovers, reorganizations, or leveraged buyouts. These funds may undertake the simultaneous purchase of stock in a company being acquired and sale of stock in its bidder, hoping to profit from the spread between the current market price and the final purchase price of the company.

*Risk-avoidance* funds are also more traditional funds, emphasizing consistent but moderate returns while avoiding risk. Funds in this group are classified by objectives such as income, market neutral–arbitrage, market neutral–securities hedging, and value. Income funds invest with the primary focus on yield or current income rather than solely on capital gains. These funds use leverage to buy bonds and some fixed-income derivatives, profiting from principal appreciation and interest income. Market neutral–arbitrage funds attempt to hedge market risk by taking offsetting positions, often in different securities of the same issuer, for example, long convertible bonds and short the firm's equity. Their focus is on obtaining returns with low or no correlation to both equity and bond markets. Market neutral–securities hedge funds invest equally in long and short equity portfolios in particular market sectors. Market risk is reduced, but effective stock analysis is critical to obtaining a profit. These funds use leverage to magnify their returns. They also sometimes use market index futures to hedge systematic risk. Value funds invest in securities perceived to be selling at deep discounts relative to their intrinsic values. Securities include those that may be out of favor or underfollowed by analysts.

Using traditional risk-adjusted measures of performance (such as Sharpe ratios), the performance of hedge funds has been very strong compared to that of traditional financial investments like stocks and bonds.[9] Many hedge funds posted strong returns during the early 2000s even as stock returns were plummeting. A few hedge funds even performed well during the financial crisis. Table 17–12 lists the top hedge fund managers and their hedge fund company by 2009 earnings. The average hedge fund lost 15.7 percent in 2008, the worst performance on record. Nearly three-quarters of all hedge funds experienced losses. Nevertheless, many funds outperformed many of the underlying markets such as the S&P 500 Index. Note that two of the hedge funds listed in Table 17–12 earned positive returns for 2008 as well as 2009 and one, BlueGold Global, earned 209.4 percent in 2008, a year where the S&P 500 Index earned a return of −37.0 percent. Indeed, only two of the listed hedge funds performed worse during the beginning of the financial crisis than the S&P 500 Index. Performance improved significantly in 2009, with the average fund earning over 20 percent for the year, the highest level since 2003 and the second best return in 10 years. However, the 2009 return on the S&P 500 Index was 26.46 percent. Note that while mutual fund performance is generally measured by returns relative to some benchmark (and therefore can perform "well" even by losing 10 percent if the benchmark

---

9. However, data deficiencies in the reporting and collection of hedge fund returns somewhat reduce confidence in all measures of hedge fund performance. Further, the inability to explain returns of individual hedge funds with standard multifactor risk models leaves open the possibility that it is not possible to properly measure the risk associated with at least some hedge fund strategies. If so, risk-adjusted returns earned by hedge funds may be overstated.

**TABLE 17–12**  Top Hedge Funds by Fund Earnings, 2008–2009

| Fund, Manager Name(s) | Fund Company | 2009 Return | 2008 Return |
|---|---|---|---|
| Appaloosa Investment I, David Tepper | Appaloosa Management. | 117.3% | −26.7% |
| Redwood Capital Master, Jonathan Kolatch | Redwood Capital Management | 69.1 | −33.0 |
| Glenview Institutional Partners, Larry Robbins | Glenview Capital Management | 67.1 | −49.0 |
| PARS IV, Changhong Zhu | Pacific Investment Management | 61.0 | −17.0 |
| Tennenbaum Opportunities V, TCP Investment Committee | Tennenbaum Capital Partners | 58.5 | −51.2 |
| Kensington Global Strategies, Kenneth Griffin | Citadel Investment Group | 57.0 | −55.0 |
| BlueGold Global, Pierre Andurand, Dennis Crema | BlueGold Capital Management | 54.6 | 209.4 |
| Waterstone Market Neutral Master, Shawn Bergerson | Waterstone Capital Management | 50.3 | 12.0 |
| Canyon Value Realization, Mitchell Julis, Joshua Friedman | Canyon Partners | 49.6 | −29.0 |
| Discovery Global Opportunity, Robert Citrone | Discovery Capital Management | 47.9 | −31.0 |

**Source:** Bloomberg, 2009. www.bloomberg.com

loses 10.5 percent), performance of hedge funds is measured by the growth in total assets managed. Assets under management in the hedge fund industry fell by nearly 30 percent (to $1.5 trillion) in 2008. The decline was the largest on record and was attributed to a combination of negative performance, a surge in redemptions, and the liquidation of funds.

Hedge fund performance continued to lag into the 2010s. In 2010, the average hedge fund earned 10.3 percent. In 2011 the average was 5.0 percent and in 2012 the average was 6.2 percent. The returns on the S&P 500 Index for these three years were 15.1 percent, 2.0 percent, and 14.5 percent, respectively. As discussed below, hedge funds generally charge fees of 2 percent of the money they manage (compared to 1 percent for mutual funds) whether the fund makes money or not. Further, managers may take up to 20 percent of any profit the hedge fund earns. With performance as seen in these years, the question for the industry is whether investors will begin to lose faith in hedge funds and start liquidating their sizeable investments in these funds. In 2012, the industry saw net outflows of funds invested of $31 billion. In August 2012, Reuters reported that one hedge fund administrator's redemption indicator hit its second-highest level of the year. Also, major investors in John Paulson's prominent but struggling hedge funds (e.g., Citigroup's private bank) had requested to redeem hundreds of millions of dollars. Hedge funds trailed the S&P 500 Index again in 2013 as U.S. markets rallied to record levels. Hedge funds returned an average of 7.4 percent, while the S&P returned 29.5 percent. In 2014, the average hedge fund returned just 2.5 percent, while the S&P 500 rose 11.4 percent. In 2015, the average hedge fund earned just 0.04 percent (the lowest returns since 2011), while the S&P fell 0.73 percent. Table 17–13 lists the top hedge fund managers and their hedge fund company for 2015 and 2014. Finally, in the first 10 months of 2016, the average hedge fund earned

**TABLE 17–13**  Top Hedge Funds by Fund Earnings, 2014–2015

| Fund, Fund Manager | Fund Company | 2015 Return | 2014 Return |
|---|---|---|---|
| Perceptive Life, Joseph Edelman | Perceptive Advisors | 51.8% | 18.9% |
| Melvin Capital, Gabriel Plotkin | Melvin Capital Management | 47.0 | n.a. |
| Segantii Asia-Pacific Equity Multi-Strategy, Simon Sadler, Kurt Ersoy | Segantii Capital Management | 29.6 | 34.8 |
| Sylebra Capital Partners Master, Jeff Fieler, Daniel Gibson | Sylebra Capital Management | 27.0 | n.a. |
| Teton Capital Paltners, Quincy Lee | Teton Capital Partners | 23.5 | 8.1 |
| Element Capital, Jeffrey Talpins | Element Capital Management | 22.7 | 8.1 |
| Golden China, George Jiang | Greenwoods Asset Management | 21.9 | 30.0 |
| Blackstone Senfina, Parag Pande | Blackstone Group | 21.0 | n.a. |
| Tybourne Equity, Eashwar Krishnan | Tybourne Capital Management | 21.0 | n.a. |
| Quantitative Global Trading, Jaffray Woodriff, Michael Geismar | Quantitative Investment Management | 20.8 | −12.3 |

**Source:** Bloomberg, 2016, www.bloomberg.com

4.09 percent, while the S&P returned 5.87 percent. Frustrated by such poor returns and high fees, hedge fund investors pulled out 1 percent of industry capital in the third quarter of 2016, with outflows totaling $28 billion. Third-quarter redemptions nearly tripled from the $8.2 billion investors redeemed during the second quarter, raising the amount of money pulled out in the first 10 months of 2016 to $51.5 billion. This puts the hedge fund sector on track to see its first annual outflow since the financial crisis.

Despite their name, hedge funds do not always "hedge" their investments to protect the fund and its investors against market price declines and other risks. For example, the failures of two of Bear Stearns's hedge funds (Bear Stearns High-Grade Structured Credit Fund and Bear Stearns High-Grade Structured Credit Enhanced Leveraged Fund) were the result of managers' failure to accurately predict how the subprime bond market would behave under extreme circumstances. The market moved against them and their investors lost $1.6 billion when the funds, heavily invested in mortgage securities, collapsed in the summer of 2007. The failures were the first sign of the upcoming financial crisis that would eventually cripple financial markets and the overall economy.

The strategy employed by the Bear Stearns funds was quite simple. Specifically, the funds purchased collateralized debt obligations (CDOs) that paid an interest rate over and above the cost of borrowing. Thus, every incremental unit of leverage added to the hedge funds' total expected return. To capitalize on this, fund managers used as much leverage as they could raise. Because the use of leverage increased the portfolio's exposure, fund managers purchased insurance on movements in credit markets. These insurance instruments, called credit default swaps, are designed to cover losses during times when credit concerns could cause bonds to fall in value, effectively hedging away some of the risk. In instances when credit markets (or the underlying bonds' prices) remain relatively stable, or even when they behave in line with historically based expectations, this strategy generates consistent, positive returns with very little deviation.

Unfortunately, as the problems with subprime debt began to unravel, the subprime mortgage-backed securities market behaved well outside of what the portfolio managers expected. This started a chain of events that imploded the fund. The subprime mortgage market began to see substantial increases in delinquencies from homeowners, which caused sharp decreases in the market values of these types of bonds. Since the Bear Stearns hedge fund managers failed to expect these sorts of extreme price movements, they also failed to purchase sufficient credit insurance to protect against these losses. Because they had leveraged their positions substantially, the funds began to experience large losses. The large losses made the creditors who provided the debt financing uneasy. The lenders required Bear Stearns to provide additional cash on their loans because the collateral (subprime bonds) was rapidly falling in value. However, the funds had no cash holdings. Thus, fund managers needed to sell bonds in order to generate cash. Quickly, it became public knowledge that Bear Stearns was in trouble, and competing funds moved to drive the prices of subprime bonds even lower to force Bear Stearns into an asset fire-sale. As prices on bonds fell, the funds experienced losses, which caused them to sell more bonds, which lowered the prices of the bonds even more, which caused the funds to sell more bonds, and so on. It did not take long before the funds had experienced a complete loss of capital.

### Fees on Hedge Funds

Hedge fund managers generally charge two types of fees: management fees and performance fees. As with mutual funds, the management fee is computed as a percentage of the total assets under management and typically runs between 1.5 and 2.0 percent. Performance fees are unique to hedge funds. Performance fees give the fund manager a share of any positive returns on a hedge fund. The average performance fee on hedge funds is approximately 20 percent but varies widely. For example, Steven Cohen's SAC Capital Advisors charges a performance fee of 50 percent. Table 17–14 lists the top 10 earnings figures for hedge fund managers in 2016. Performance fees are paid to the hedge fund manager before returns are paid to the fund investors. Hedge funds often specify a *hurdle rate,*

**TABLE 17–14**   Highest-Paid Hedge Fund Managers *(in millions of dollars)*

| Name | Firm | Earnings |
|---|---|---|
| Kenneth Griffin | Citadel | $1,700 |
| James Simons | Renaissance Technologies | 1,650 |
| Steven Cohen | Point 72 Asset Management | 1,550 |
| David Tepper | Appaloosa Management | 1,200 |
| David Shaw | D.E. Shaw Group | 700 |
| John Overdeck | Two Sigma Investments | 600 |
| David Siegel | Two Sigma Investments | 600 |
| Israel Englander | Millennium Management | 550 |
| Raymond Dalio | Bridgewater Associates | 500 |
| George Soros | Soros Fund Management | 300 |

which is a minimum annualized performance benchmark that must be realized before a performance fee can be assessed. Further, a *high-water mark* is usually used for hedge funds in which the manager does not receive a performance fee unless the value of the fund exceeds the highest net asset value it has previously achieved. High-water marks are used to link the fund manager's incentives more closely to those of the fund investors and to reduce the manager's incentive to increase the risk of trades.

Given hedge funds' recent record of low returns, fees are one of the key issues affecting the industry today. Investors are increasingly dissatisfied with fees and consequently pushing for more favorable arrangements. This discontent has resulted in the rejection of managers and withdrawal of funds altogether. For example, in 2014 CalPERS liquidated its entire hedge fund portfolio ($4 billion) in an effort to cut back on fees. As a result, the standard 2/20 fee model is slowly giving way to new structures. Rather than simply lowering fees, many hedge funds have adopted new structures altogether. For example, Adage Capital Management changed to a flat 0.5 percent management fee and 20 percent performance fee on trading gains or losses in excess of the S&P 500. If the fund's performance falls below the S&P 500 benchmark, it refunds up to half of those fees to investors. Investors reacted positively to this change as the fund doubled in size in the four years after the change. Other fee structure changes have included a hurdle rate requiring a minimum net return to be generated before the manager is allowed to collect performance fees. The hurdle rate is often tied to a benchmark rate, such as the S&P 500.

### Offshore Hedge Funds

Hedge funds that are organized in the United States are designated as domestic hedge funds. These funds require investors to pay income taxes on all earnings from the hedge fund. Funds located outside the United States and structured under foreign laws are designated as offshore hedge funds. Many offshore financial centers encourage hedge funds to locate in their countries. The major centers include the Cayman Islands, Bermuda, Dublin, and Luxembourg. The Cayman Islands is estimated to be the location of approximately 75 percent of all hedge funds. Offshore hedge funds are regulated in that they must obey the rules of the host country. However, the rules in most of these countries are not generally burdensome and provide anonymity to fund investors. Further, offshore hedge funds are not subject to U.S. income taxes on distributions of profit or to U.S. estate taxes on fund shares.

When compared to domestic hedge funds, offshore hedge funds have been found to trade more intensely, due to the low or zero capital gains tax for offshore funds. Further, offshore hedge funds tend to engage less often in positive feedback trading (rushing to buy when the market is booming and rushing to sell when the market is declining) than domestic hedge funds. Finally, offshore hedge funds have been found to herd (mimic each other's behavior when trading while ignoring information about the fundamentals of valuation) less than domestic hedge funds. Many hedge fund managers maintain both domestic and offshore hedge funds. Given the needs of their client investors, hedge fund managers want to have both types of funds to attract all types of investors.

### Regulation of Hedge Funds

While mutual funds are very highly regulated, hedge funds have generally been unregulated. Mutual funds in the United States are required to be registered with the SEC. Although hedge funds fall within the same statutory category as mutual funds, they operate under two exemptions from registration requirements as set forth in the Investment Company Act of 1940. First, funds are exempt if they have less than 100 investors. Second, funds are exempt if the investors are "accredited." To comply with SEC exemptions, hedge funds are also sold only via private placements. Thus, hedge funds may not be offered or advertised to the general investing public.

In 2010, the Wall Street Reform and Consumer Protection Act required hedge fund advisors with private pools of capital exceeding $100 million in assets to register with the SEC as investment advisors and become subject to all rules which apply to registered advisors by July 2011. Thus, previous exemptions from registration provided under the Investment Company Act of 1940 no longer apply to most hedge fund advisors. (Under the act, hedge fund managers who have less than $100 million in assets under management are overseen by the state where the manager is domiciled and become subject to state regulation.) This registration subjects hedge funds to periodic inspections by SEC examiners. Further, hedge funds are required to report information to the SEC about their trades and portfolios that is "necessary for the purpose of assessing systemic risk posed by a private fund." The data are kept confidential and can be shared only with the Financial Stability Oversight Council, set up to monitor potential shocks to the economic system. Finally, should the government determine a hedge fund has grown too large or risky, the hedge fund is placed under the supervision of the Federal Reserve. Despite these new regulations and the requirement that large hedge funds be registered with the SEC, the regulations imposed on hedge funds continue to be much less onerous than those imposed on mutual funds.

Nevertheless, hedge funds are prohibited from abusive trading practices and a number of funds got mixed up in the scandals plaguing the mutual fund industry in the 2000s. For example, in March 2007, the SEC charged 14 defendants in a scheme involving insiders at UBS Securities, Morgan Stanley, and several hedge funds and hedge fund managers. The SEC claimed that the defendants made $15 million in illicit profits through thousands of illegal trades, using inside information misappropriated from UBS. Just two months prior to this announcement, regulators announced an investigation of UBS and other banks that leased office space to hedge fund traders. Regulators stated a concern about the relationship between the banks and their hedge fund "hotel guests," looking at whether the banks had been using the real estate relationships as a way to entice hedge funds to do business with them, possibly at the expense of the funds' investors. Specifically, there was an investigation into whether hedge funds located in bank buildings were paying higher than normal trading fees to banks to compensate them for the office space and failing to disclose this expense to investors.

More recently, the late 2000s saw two highly publicized scandals associated with hedge funds. The first was that of Bernard L. Madoff Investment Securities. The Madoff investment scandal occurred after the discovery that the asset management business of former NASDAQ chair Bernard Madoff was actually a giant "Ponzi" scheme. According to a federal criminal complaint, client statements showing $65 billion in stock holdings were fictitious, and there was no indication that any stocks were purchased since the mid-1990s. Alerted by his sons, federal authorities arrested Madoff on December 11, 2008. The firm was placed in liquidation and a trustee was appointed on December 15, 2008, after Bernard Madoff confessed to having stolen customer property over a period of many years. On March 12, 2009, Madoff pled guilty to 11 felonies and admitted to operating what has been called the largest investor fraud ever committed by an individual. On June 29, 2009, he was sentenced to 150 years in prison with restitution of $170 billion. Although Madoff did not operate as a hedge fund, he operated through various funds of hedge funds.

Another highly publicized scandal occurring in the late 2000s involved Galleon Group LLC, one of the largest hedge fund management firms in the world before announcing its closure in October 2009. The firm was at the center of a 2009 insider trading scandal that resulted in investors pulling capital from the firm rapidly. Twenty people, including Galleon Group LLC co-founder Raj Rajaratnam, were criminally charged in what federal authorities call the biggest prosecution of alleged hedge fund insider trading in the United States. Prosecutors said they had evidence from wiretaps, trading records, and cooperating witnesses to prove widespread trafficking in illegal insider information—including an insider trading operation that paid sources for nonpublic information—that netted the hedge fund more than $20 million.

Finally, in July 2013, the Manhattan U.S. Attorney's office filed criminal charges against SAC Capital for insider trading that was "substantial, pervasive and on a scale without precedent in the hedge fund industry." Prosecutors accused SAC of allowing multiple portfolio managers and analysts to obtain or trade on inside information on various stocks while employed there. Six of the eight former employees cited in the complaint had already pleaded guilty to the charges. SAC's founder and chair, Steven Cohen, was also charged personally by the SEC for failure to supervise two employees now facing trial for insider trading and sought to ban him for life from managing outside investors' money. In September, federal prosecutors proposed settling the criminal case against SAC. To settle, the government sought a guilty plea from SAC and a financial penalty of as much as $2 billion.

## DO YOU UNDERSTAND:

11. *What the difference is between a mutual fund and a hedge fund?*

12. *What performance fees charged by hedge funds are?*

13. *How the regulatory status of hedge funds is changing?*

## SUMMARY

This chapter presented an overview of the mutual fund and hedge fund industries. Mutual funds and hedge funds pool funds from individuals and corporations and invest in diversified asset portfolios. Due to the tremendous increase in the value of financial assets such as equities from 1992 through 2007 and the cost-effective opportunity that these funds offer for investors to participate in these markets, mutual funds and hedge funds have increased tremendously in size, number of funds, and number of shareholders.

## QUESTIONS

1. What is a mutual fund? In what sense is it a financial institution? (*LG 17-1*)

2. What benefits do mutual funds have for individual investors? (*LG 17-1*)

3. What are long-term mutual funds? In what assets do these funds usually invest? What factors caused the strong growth in this type of fund during the 1990s and the decline in growth in the early and late 2000s? (*LG 17-2*)

4. What are money market mutual funds? In what assets do these funds typically invest? What factors caused the strong growth in this type of fund over various periods from 1992 through 2009? (*LG 17-2*)

5. Using the data in Table 17–2, discuss the growth and ownership holdings over the last 36 years of long-term funds versus money market funds. (*LG 17-2*)

6. How does the risk of short-term funds differ from that of long-term funds? (*LG 17-2*)

7. What are the economic reasons for the existence of mutual funds? (*LG 17-1*)

8. What are the principal demographics of household owners of mutual funds? (*LG 17-2*)

9. What is the difference between an open-end mutual fund and a closed-end fund? What is the difference between an open-end mutual fund and a unit investment trust? (*LG 17-3*)

10. What is the difference between an open-end mutual fund and an ETF closed-end fund? What is the difference between an open-end mutual fund and a unit investment trust? (*LG 17-3*)

11. What change in regulatory guidelines occurred in 2009 that had the primary purpose of giving investors a better understanding of the risks and objectives of a mutual fund? (*LG 17-4*)

12. What are the three components of the return that an investor receives from a mutual fund? (*LG 17-5*)

13. How is the net asset value (NAV) of a mutual fund determined? What is meant by the term *marked-to-market daily?* (*LG 17-5*)

14. How might an individual's preference for a mutual fund's objective change over time? (*LG 17-4*)

15. What is the difference between a load fund and a no-load fund? Is the argument that load funds are more closely managed and therefore have higher returns supported by the evidence presented in Table 17–6? (*LG 17-5*)

16. What is a 12b-1 fee? Suppose that you have a choice between two mutual funds, one a load fund with no annual 12b-1 fees, and the other a no-load fund with a maximum 12b-1 fee. How would the length of your expected holding period influence your choice between these two funds? (*LG 17-5*)

17. Why did the proportion of equities in long-term mutual funds increase from 38.3 percent in 1990 to 70.0 percent in 2007 and decrease back to 55.5 percent in 2008? How might an investor's preference for a mutual fund's objective change over time? (*LG 17-4*)

18. Who are the primary regulators of the mutual fund industry? How do their regulatory goals differ from those of other types of financial institutions? (*LG 17-6*)

19. Discuss the improper trading abuses and improper assignment of fees for which mutual funds were prosecuted in the early 2000s. (*LG 17-6*)

20. How have global mutual funds grown relative to U.S.-based mutual funds? (*LG 17-7*)

21. What is a hedge fund and how is it different from a mutual fund? (*LG 17-8*)

22. What are the different categories of hedge funds? (*LG 17-8*)

23. What types of fees do hedge funds charge? (*LG 17-8*)

24. What is the difference between domestic hedge funds and offshore hedge funds? Describe the advantages of offshore hedge funds over domestic hedge funds. (*LG 17-8*)

## PROBLEMS

1. An investor purchases a mutual fund for $50. The fund pays dividends of $1.50, distributes a capital gain of $2, and charges a fee of $2 when the fund is sold one year later for $52.50. What is the net rate of return from this investment? (*LG 17-5*)

2. Open-end Fund A has 165 shares of ATT valued at $35 each and 30 shares of Toro valued at $75 each. Closed-end Fund B has 75 shares of ATT and 72 shares of Toro. Both funds have 1,000 shares outstanding. (*LG 17-5*)
   a. What is the NAV of each fund using these prices?
   b. If the price of ATT stock increases to $36.25 and the price of Toro stock declines to $72.292, how does that impact the NAV of both funds?
   c. Assume that another 155 shares of ATT valued at $35 are added to Fund A. The funds needed to buy the new shares are obtained by selling 676 more shares in Fund A. What is the effect on Fund A's NAV if the prices remain unchanged from the original prices?

3. A mutual fund has 300 shares of General Electric, currently trading at $30, and 400 shares of Microsoft, Inc., currently trading at $54. The fund has 1,000 shares outstanding. (*LG 17-5*)
   a. What is the NAV of the fund?
   b. If investors expect the price of General Electric to increase to $34 and the price of Microsoft to decline to $48 by the end of the year, what is the expected NAV at the end of the year?
   c. Assume that the price of General Electric shares is realized at $34. What is the maximum price to which Microsoft can decline and still maintain the NAV as estimated in (a)?

4. Suppose today a mutual fund contains 2,000 shares of J.P. Morgan Chase, currently trading at $64.75, 1,000 shares of Walmart, currently trading at $63.10, and 2,500 shares of Pfizer, currently trading at $31.50. The mutual fund has no liabilities and 10,000 shares outstanding held by investors. (*LG 17-5*)
   a. What is the NAV of the fund?

   b. Calculate the change in the NAV of the fund if tomorrow J.P. Morgan shares increase to $66, Walmart's shares increase to $68, and Pfizer's shares decrease to $30.
   c. Suppose that today 1,000 additional investors buy one share each of the mutual fund at the NAV of $27.135. This means that the fund manager has $27,135 in additional funds to invest. The fund manager decides to use these additional funds to buy additional shares in J.P. Morgan Chase. Calculate tomorrow's NAV given the same rise in share values as assumed in (b).

5. An investor purchases a mutual fund share for $100. The fund pays dividends of $3, distributes a capital gain of $4, and charges a fee of $2 when the fund is sold one year later for $105. What is the net rate of return from this investment? (*LG 17-5*)

6. Suppose an individual invests $20,000 in a load mutual fund for two years. The load fee entails an up-front commission charge of 2.5 percent of the amount invested and is deducted from the original funds invested. In addition, annual fund operating expenses (or 12b-1 fees) are 0.55 percent. The annual fees are charged on the average net asset value invested in the fund and are recorded at the end of each year. Investments in the fund return 7 percent each year paid on the last day of the year. If the investor reinvests the annual returns paid on the investment, calculate the annual return on the mutual funds over the two-year investment period. (*LG 17-5*)

7. Suppose an individual invests $10,000 in a load mutual fund for two years. The load fee entails an up-front commission charge of 4 percent of the amount invested and is deducted from the original funds invested. In addition, annual fund operating expenses (or 12b-1 fees) are 0.85 percent. The annual fees are charged on the average net asset value invested in the fund and are recorded at the end of each year. Investments in the fund return 5 percent each year paid on the last day of the year. If the investor reinvests the annual returns paid on the investment, calculate the annual return on the mutual fund over the two-year investment period. (*LG 17-5*)

# SEARCH THE SITE

Go to the Investment Company Institute website and find the latest information available for Total Net Assets, Number of Funds, and Number of Shareholder Accounts in U.S. mutual funds. Go to the Investment Company Institute website at **www.ici.org.** Click on "Research & Statistics." Click on "Fact Books." Click on the most recent year "20XX Investment Company Fact Book." This will download a file onto your computer that will contain the most recent information on U.S. mutual funds. In the Data Tables of the Fact Book, go to the table listing Industry Total Net Assets, Number of Funds, Number of Share Classes, and Number of Shareholder Accounts.

## Questions

1. What is the most recent value for Total Net Assets and Number of Funds?
2. How has each of these changed since 2016 as reported in Table 17–1?

**chapter**

# Pension Funds

## Learning Goals

**LG 18-1**   *Describe the difference between a private pension fund and a public pension fund.*

**LG 18-2**   *Distinguish between and calculate the benefits from a defined benefit and a defined contribution pension fund.*

**LG 18-3**   *Identify the characteristics and calculate the benefits from the different types of private pension funds.*

**LG 18-4**   *Identify the different types of public pension funds.*

**LG 18-5**   *Examine the main regulations governing pension funds.*

**LG 18-6**   *Review the major issues for pension funds in the global markets.*

## PENSION FUNDS DEFINED: CHAPTER OVERVIEW

Pension funds are similar to life insurance companies (discussed in Chapter 15) and mutual funds (discussed in Chapter 17) in that all three attract small savers' funds and invest them in the financial markets to be liquidated at a later date. Indeed, as discussed in this chapter, insurance companies and mutual funds are main providers of pension funds. Pension funds are unique, however, in that they offer savings plans through which fund participants accumulate tax-deferred savings during their working years before withdrawing them during their retirement years. Funds originally invested in and accumulated in a pension plan are exempt from current taxation. Rather, tax payments are not made until funds are actually distributed to the fund participant, often later in his or her life.

Pension funds were first established in the United States in 1759 to benefit the widows and children of church ministers. It was not until 1875 that the American Express Company established the first corporate pension fund. By 1940, only 400 pension funds were in existence, mainly for employees in the railroad, banking, and public utilities industries. Since then the industry has boomed, so that currently over 680,000 pension funds exist. In 2016, U.S. households had 34 percent of their financial assets invested in pension funds, compared to just over 5 percent in 1950.

The pension fund industry comprises two distinct sectors. **Private pension funds** are those funds administered by a private corporation (e.g., insurance company, mutual fund). Because pension funds are such a large percentage of the insurance industry's business

**TABLE 18–1** Pension Fund Reserves, 1990–2016 *(in billions of dollars)*

|  | 1990 | 1995 | 2000 | 2005 | 2007 | 2008 | 2010 | 2013 | 2016 |
|---|---|---|---|---|---|---|---|---|---|
| Federal government | $1,232.3 | $1,598.6 | $2,002.6 | $2,494.6 | $2,713.8 | $2,758.1 | $3,147.6 | $3,435.5 | $3,821.4 |
| Private pension funds | | | | | | | | | |
|   Life insurance companies | 569.8 | 890.6 | 1,526.3 | 2,197.4 | 2,531.6 | 2,223.2 | 2,563.0 | 2,820.1 | 2,928.3 |
|   Other private pension funds | 1,833.0 | 2,845.2 | 4,314.6 | 5,398.1 | 6,122.8 | 5,281.4 | 6,625.7 | 7,603.7 | 8,875.3 |
| State and local govt. retirement funds | 800.0 | 1,382.9 | 2,006.4 | 3,140.9 | 3,588.5 | 3,799.0 | 4,408.7 | 4,877.3 | 6,108.0 |
| Total | $4,435.1 | $6,717.3 | $9,849.9 | $13,231.0 | $14,956.7 | $14,061.7 | $16,745.0 | $18,736.6 | $21,733.0 |

**Sources:** Federal Reserve Board, "Flow of Fund Accounts," various issues. www.federalreserve.gov

**private pension funds**

*Funds administered by a private corporation.*

**public pension funds**

*Funds administered by a federal, state, or local government.*

(see below), they are often listed separately from other private pension funds. **Public pension funds** are those funds administered by a federal, state, or local government (e.g., Social Security). In 2016, total financial assets invested in pension funds were $21,733.0 billion: $11,803.6 billion in private funds (including life insurance companies), $6,108.0 billion in state and local government funds, and $3,821.4 billion in federal government funds (see Table 18–1). Growth of private funds was particularly significant since the 1990s as the long-term viability of the major public pension fund, Social Security, came into question.

The financial crisis of 2008–2009 produced significant losses to pension funds, forcing many soon-to-be retirees to adjust their retirement plans or scrap them altogether. The plunge in stock prices decreased the value of worldwide pension assets from $25 trillion to $20 trillion. U.S. pension plans, which account for 61 percent of global pension assets, were especially hard hit—U.S. retirement account values fell by over $2 trillion. For individuals, lost retirement funds were especially painful—especially for consumers, who watched the value of their homes plummet, and for others who saw one or more persons in the household lose their jobs. These losses forced American workers to postpone retirement plans, work longer than they planned, take second jobs, downsize the lifestyles they had enjoyed for decades, or even all of the above.

This chapter provides an overview of the pension fund industry. In particular, we examine the size, structure, and composition of the industry. We also describe recent trends in private and public pension fund growth as well as the differences between these two major types of funds. Finally, we describe the major regulations under which the industry operates.

## SIZE, STRUCTURE, AND COMPOSITION OF THE INDUSTRY

**pension plan**

*Document that governs the operations of a pension fund.*

In this section, we describe the various characteristics of pension funds, including insured versus noninsured pension funds and defined benefit versus defined contribution pension funds. We then present an overview of the private pension funds and public pension funds that comprise this industry.

### Defined Benefit versus Defined Contribution Pension Funds

**defined benefit pension fund**

*Pension fund in which the employer agrees to provide the employee with a specific cash benefit upon retirement.*

A **pension plan** governs the operations of a pension fund. Pension funds can be distinguished by the way contributions are made and benefits are paid. A pension fund is either a defined benefit fund or a defined contribution fund. In a **defined benefit pension fund,** the corporate employer (or fund sponsor) agrees to provide the employee a specific cash benefit upon retirement, based on a formula that considers such factors as years of employment and salary during employment. The formula is generally one of three types: flat benefit, career average, or final pay formula. These three types of defined benefit funds are discussed in more detail next.

**flat benefit formula**

*Pension fund that pays a flat amount for every year of employment.*

**Flat Benefit Formula.**    A **flat benefit formula** pays a flat amount for every year of employment.

---

**EXAMPLE 18–1**   Calculation of Retirement Benefit for a Defined Benefit Fund Using a Flat Benefit Formula

An employee with 20 years of service at a company is considering retirement at some point in the next 10 years. The employer uses a flat benefit formula by which the employee receives an annual benefit payment of $2,000 times the number of years of service. For retirement now, in 5 years, and in 10 years, the employee's annual retirement benefit payment is:

|  | **Retirement Benefit** |
|---|---|
| Retire now | $2,000 \times 20 = $40,000 |
| Retire in 5 years | $2,000 \times 25 = $50,000 |
| Retire in 10 years | $2,000 \times 30 = $60,000 |

---

**career average formula**

*Pension fund that pays retirement benefits based on the employee's average salary over the entire period of employment.*

**Career Average Formula.**   Two variations of **career average formulas** exist; both base retirement benefits on the average salary over the entire period of employment. Under one formula, retirees earn benefits based on a percentage of their average salary during the entire period they belonged to the pension fund. Under the alternative formula, the retirement benefit is equal to a percentage of the average salary times the number of years employed.

---

**EXAMPLE 18–2**   Calculation of Retirement Benefit for a Defined Benefit Fund Using a Career Average Formula

An employee with 20 years of service at a company is considering retirement some time in the next 10 years. The employer uses a career average benefit formula by which the employee receives an annual benefit payment of 4 percent of his career average salary times the number of years of service. For retirement now, in 5 years, and in 10 years, the employee's annual retirement benefit payment is:

|  | **Average Salary** | **Retirement Benefit** |
|---|---|---|
| Retire now | $48,000 | $48,000 \times 0.04 \times 20 = $38,400 |
| Retire in 5 years | $50,000* | $50,000 \times 0.04 \times 25 = $50,000 |
| Retire in 10 years | $52,000* | $52,000 \times 0.04 \times 30 = $62,400 |

*These are based on estimates of the employee's future salary.

---

**final pay formula**

*Pension fund that pays retirement benefits based on a percentage of the average salary during a specified number of years at the end of the employee's career times the number of years of service.*

**Final Pay Formula.**   A **final pay formula** pays a retirement benefit based on a percentage of the average salary during a specified number of years at the end of the employee's career times the number of years of service.

---

**EXAMPLE 18–3**   Calculation of Retirement Benefit for a Defined Benefit Fund Using a Final Pay Formula

An employee with 20 years of service at a company is considering retirement at some time in the next 10 years. The employer uses a final pay benefit formula by which the employee receives an annual benefit payment of 2.5 percent of her average salary during her last five years of service times her total years employed. For retirement now, in 5 years, and in 10 years, the employee's (estimated) annual retirement benefit payment is:

| | Average Salary during Last Five Years of Service | Retirement Benefit |
|---|---|---|
| Retire now | $75,000 | $75,000 × 0.025 × 20 = $37,500 |
| Retire in 5 years | $80,000* | $80,000 × 0.025 × 25 = $50,000 |
| Retire in 10 years | $85,000* | $85,000 × 0.025 × 30 = $63,750 |

*These are based on estimates of the employee's future salary.

Notice that of the three benefit formulas, the final pay formula usually produces the biggest retirement benefit increases as years of service increase. This formula generally provides better protection against erosion of pension income by inflation. Benefit payments are based on the employee's career-end salary, which is generally the highest and often reflects current levels of price and wage inflation. This type of plan is also generally more costly to the employer.

Under defined benefit pension funds, the employer should set aside sufficient funds to ensure that it can meet the promised payments. When sufficient funds are available, the pension fund is said to be **fully funded.** Frequently, pension funds do not have sufficient funds available to meet all future promised payments, in which case the fund is said to be **underfunded.** While underfunding is not illegal, the pension fund is required by law to meet all of its payment obligations (see discussion below). Occasionally, pension funds have more than enough funds available to meet the required future payouts. In this case, the fund is said to be **overfunded.**

With a **defined contribution pension fund,** the employer (or plan sponsor) does not precommit to providing a specified retirement income. Rather, the employer contributes a specified amount to the pension fund during the employee's working years. The final retirement benefit is then based on total employer contributions, any additional employee contributions, and any gains or losses on the investments purchased by the fund with these contributions. For *fixed-income funds,* a minimum rate of return is often guaranteed, with the possibility of higher returns if fund assets earn above minimum rates of return. For *variable-income funds,* all investment profits and losses are passed through to fund participants. Thus, defined contribution funds provide benefits to employees in the form of higher potential returns than offered by defined benefit funds, but employees also must accept the increased risk of uncertain pension fund payouts.

### Insured versus Noninsured Pension Funds

Pension funds administered by life insurance companies (24.8 percent of the industry's assets) are termed **insured pension funds**. The designation as an insured pension fund is not necessarily derived from the type of administrator but from the classification of assets in which pension fund contributions are invested. Specifically, no separate pool of assets backs the pension plan. Rather, pension plan funds are pooled and invested in the general assets of the insurance company. The amount of the insurance company's assets devoted to pension funds is reported on the liability side of the balance sheet under "pension fund reserves." For example, in 2016 (see Table 18–2), life insurance companies managed a total of $2,928.3 billion in pension fund assets (reported in the liability account as "pension fund reserves"). These reserves represented 45.0 percent of the industry's total liabilities and equity. Pension fund assets were distributed among various assets on life insurance companies' balance sheets (e.g., U.S. government securities, corporate and foreign bonds, corporate equities), rather than being reported as a separate pool of pension fund assets segregated from other life insurance assets.

**Noninsured pension funds** are managed by a trust department of a financial institution appointed by the sponsoring business, participant, or union. Trustees invest the contributions and pay the retirement benefits in accordance with the terms of the pension fund. In contrast to insured pension funds, assets managed in noninsured pension funds are

**fully funded**

*A pension fund that has sufficient funds available to meet all future payment obligations.*

**underfunded**

*A pension fund that does not have sufficient funds available to meet all future promised payments.*

**overfunded**

*A pension fund that has more than enough funds available to meet the required future payouts.*

**defined contribution pension fund**

*Pension fund in which the employer agrees to make a specified contribution to the pension fund during the employee's working years.*

**insured pension fund**

*A pension fund administered by a life insurance company.*

**noninsured pension fund**

*A pension fund administered by a financial institution other than a life insurance company.*

**TABLE 18–2**  Life Insurance Company Balance Sheet *(in billions of dollars)*

| | | |
|---|---:|---:|
| **Total Assets** | **$6,511.9** | **100.0%** |
| Checkable deposits and currency | 76.2 | 1.2 |
| Money market securities | 54.7 | 0.8 |
| Credit market instruments | 3,185.8 | 48.9 |
|    Open market paper | 37.5 | 0.6 |
|    Treasury securities | 205.0 | 3.1 |
|    Agency- and GSE-backed securities | 336.6 | 5.2 |
|    Municipal securities | 164.4 | 2.5 |
|    Corporate and foreign bonds | 2,442.3 | 37.5 |
| Other loans and advances | 163.9 | 2.5 |
| Mortgages | 439.7 | 6.8 |
| Corporate equities | 317.7 | 4.9 |
| Mutual fund shares | 1,644.0 | 25.2 |
| Miscellaneous assets | 629.9 | 9.7 |
| **Total Liabilities** | **$6,115.0** | **93.9%** |
| Other loans and advances | 65.3 | 1.0 |
| Life insurance reserves | 1,496.5 | 23.0 |
| **Pension Fund Reserves** | **$2,928.3** | **45.0%** |
| Taxes payable | –32.8 | –0.5 |
| Miscellaneous liabilities | 1,657.7 | 25.4 |

**Source:** Federal Reserve Board, "Flow of Fund Accounts," 2016. www.federalreserve.gov

owned by the sponsor and are thus segregated and listed as separate pools of assets on the trustees' balance sheet. While the day-to-day investment decisions for a noninsured pension fund are controlled by the trustee, the sponsor of the pension fund normally specifies general guidelines the trustee should follow.

Premiums paid into insured pension funds, and the assets purchased with these premiums, become the legal property of the insurance company managing the pension funds. In contrast, premiums paid into noninsured pension funds, and the assets purchased with these premiums, are the legal property of the sponsoring corporation. Because insurance companies, as the asset owners (of insured pension funds), incur the risk associated with value fluctuations in their pension fund assets, they generally concentrate their asset investments in less risky securities (bonds and low-risk mortgages). Noninsured pension fund managers, by contrast, do not incur the risk associated with asset value fluctuations. Thus, the trustees overseeing these pension funds generally invest pension premiums received in riskier securities (e.g., equities). As a result, noninsured pension funds generally offer the potential for higher rates of return but are also riskier than insured pension funds. However, the higher rates of return allow the employee to reduce contributions necessary to achieve a given amount of funds at retirement.

**LG 18-1**

### Private Pension Funds

Private pension funds are created by private entities (e.g., manufacturing, mining, or transportation firms) and are administered by private corporations (financial institutions). Of the $11,803.6 billion of financial assets in private pension funds in 2016, life insurance companies administered $2,928.3 billion, mutual funds administered $3,317.6 billion, and other financial institutions such as banks administered $5,557.7 billion. Private fund contributions come from fund participants and/or their employers.

Defined contribution funds are increasingly dominating the private pension fund market. Indeed, many defined benefit funds are converting to defined contribution funds. Figure 18–1 shows private pension fund assets from 1984 to 2016. From Figure 18–1 note that as equity market values fell in 2001 and in 2008 (during the financial crisis), pension

**Figure 18-1** Private Pension Fund Assets, 1984–2016

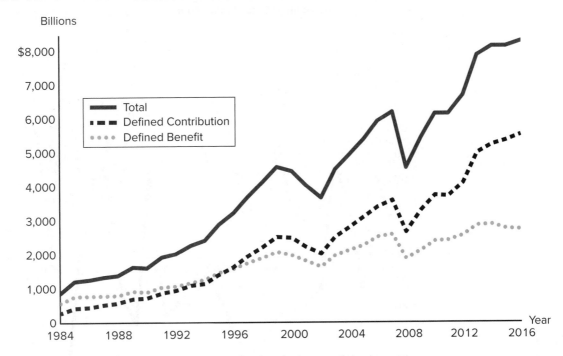

**Sources:** Federal Reserve Board, "Flow of Fund Accounts," various issues. www.federalreserve.gov

fund asset values, particularly for defined contribution funds, fell as well. As the economy recovered and equity market values increased in the mid- and then late 2000s, so did the value of pension fund assets. As we discuss below, this is because the main asset held by private pension funds is corporate equities. Note also that defined contribution funds are increasing in importance relative to defined benefit funds. Figure 18–2 shows the acquisition of new financial assets in defined benefit and defined contribution funds from 1990 through 2016. In 21 of the 27 years, defined benefit funds actually experienced a reduction in new assets held, while defined contribution funds saw a continuous increase in new asset investments. One reason for this shift is that defined contribution funds do not require the employer to guarantee retirement benefits, and thus corporate stockholders and managers do not need to monitor the pension fund's performance once the required contributions are made.

This shift in assets—from defined benefit funds to defined contribution funds—resulted in a massive shift in the risk of retirement benefits, from employers to employees, during the financial crisis. In a defined benefit pension fund, benefits are paid out at a fixed and known amount. Thus, the employees do not bear the risk of low investment returns on contributions or of outliving their retirement income. In a defined contribution plan, investment risk and investment rewards are assumed by each employee and not by the employer. As stock markets plunged in value, so did the value of assets and pension payouts in defined contribution funds. As mentioned earlier, the massive decreases in pension fund values forced many American workers to postpone retirement plans, work longer than they had planned, take second jobs, and downsize the lifestyles they had enjoyed for decades.

**LG 18-3**

**401(k) and 403(b) plans**

*Employer-sponsored plans that supplement a firm's basic retirement plan.*

**Types of Private Pension Funds.** Private defined benefit and defined contribution pension funds come in various types. Employees may participate in 401(k) and 403(b) plans, individual retirement accounts (IRAs), and Keogh accounts.

*401(k) and 403(b) Plans.* **401(k) and 403(b) plans** are employer-sponsored plans that supplement a firm's basic retirement plan, allowing for both employee and employer contributions (e.g., Supplementary Retirement Accounts offered by TIAA-CREF). While

**Figure 18–2**  Net Acquisition of Financial Assets, Defined Benefit and Defined Contribution Funds

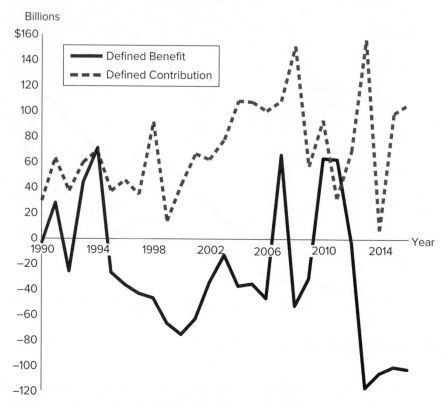

**Sources:** Federal Reserve Board, "Flow of Fund Accounts," various issues. www.federalreserve.gov

401(k) plans are offered to employees of taxable firms (contributions made by employers or plan sponsors are tax deductible), 403(b) plans are for employees of certain tax-exempt employers (e.g., hospitals and educational institutions). Contributions to these plans are taken on a pretax basis and thus reduce the employee's taxable salary. Further, employers often contribute an additional percentage of the employee's salaries or contributions to the funds (e.g., match amount). Both the contributions and earnings then grow tax deferred until they are withdrawn. Most of these plans are transferable to another 401(k) or 403(b) plan, or an IRA, if the employee changes jobs. Figure 18–3 shows the growth in 401(k) plans: from $385 billion in 1990, to $2,982 billion in 2007, and $4,860 billion in 2013. In 2016, there were over 81,000 401(k) plans and over 55 million participants.

Participants in 401(k) and 403(b) plans generally make their own choice of the allocation of assets from both employee and employer contributions (e.g., the choice among investing in equity, bonds, and money market securities). However, in December 2001 the U.S. Labor Department released a statement that for the first time allowed financial service companies to provide specific advice to retirement plan participants provided that the advice comes from a qualified financial expert that is independent of the plan provider. Previously, to avoid conflicts of interest (such as a plan provider steering plan participants to investments that generate higher fees for the company and reduce net returns for the investor), retirement plan providers generally could do no more than come up with general recommendations of what investors should buy or sell, avoiding naming specific mutual funds. Table 18–3 shows the allocation of assets by age of participants in 401(k) plans in 2016. Younger participants invest the majority of their contributions in equities, while older participants invest more heavily in fixed-income bond and guaranteed investment

**Figure 18–3** Assets in 401(k) Plans

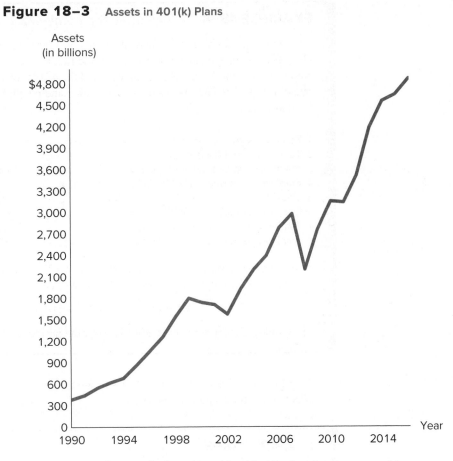

**Sources:** Investment Company Institute, *Mutual Fund Fact Book,* various years. www.ici.org

contract (GIC) funds.[1] Included in this group are also target date funds, which rebalance portfolios to become less focused on growth and more focused on income as the fund approaches the target date of the fund. Target date funds follow a predetermined reallocation of risk over time. The funds are aimed at a specific retirement year and are an aggregation of many mutual funds, sometimes as many as 25. The choice of asset allocation affects the fund's payout during retirement, similar to defined contribution funds.

**TABLE 18–3** 401(k) Asset Allocation by Age

| Age Cohort | Equity and Balanced Funds | Bond Funds | Company Stock | Money Funds | GICs | Other or Unknown |
|---|---|---|---|---|---|---|
| 20s | 79.1% | 5.1% | 6.1% | 1.3% | 2.6% | 5.8% |
| 30s | 75.5 | 6.4 | 6.8 | 2.0 | 3.2 | 6.1 |
| 40s | 71.7 | 7.3 | 7.9 | 2.5 | 4.3 | 6.3 |
| 50s | 64.7 | 9.0 | 8.7 | 3.4 | 7.7 | 6.5 |
| 60s | 60.2 | 10.9 | 7.3 | 4.6 | 11.0 | 6.0 |
| All | 66.6 | 8.7 | 8.0 | 3.3 | 7.1 | 6.3 |

**Source:** Investment Company Institute, *401(k) Plan Asset Allocation, Account Balances, and Loan Activity.* www.ici.org

1. A GIC is a long-term liability issued by insurance companies. A GIC guarantees not only a rate of interest over some given period but also the annuity rate on a beneficiary's contract (see Chapter 15).

## EXAMPLE 18–4    Calculating the Return on a 401(k) Plan

An employee contributes 10 percent of his $75,000 salary into the company's 401(k) plan. The company matches 40 percent of the first 6 percent of the employee's salary. The employee is in the 31 percent tax bracket and the 401(k) plan expects to yield an 8 percent rate of return. The employee's own contribution and his plan return for one year are calculated as follows.

1. Employee's gross contribution = $75,000 × 0.10 =                   $ 7,500
2. Tax savings[2] = $7,500 × 0.31 =                                          $ 2,325
3. Employee's net of tax contribution                                       $ 5,175
4. Employer's contribution = $75,000 × 0.40 × 0.06 =           $ 1,800
5. Total 401(k) plan investment at year's start                        $ 9,300
6. One-year earnings = $9,300 × 0.08 =                                  $   744
7. Total 401(k) investment at year-end                                  $10,044 [= (1) + (4) + (6)]
   Employee's one-year return = ($10,044 – $5,175)/$5,175 = 94.09%

Assuming the employee's salary, tax rate, and 401(k) yield remain constant over a 20-year career, when the employee retires, the 401(k) will be worth:

$$\$9,300\left(\left[\left(1+0.08\right)^{20}-1\right]/0.08\right)=\$425,586$$

The employee's net of tax contributions over the period total $5,175 × 20 = $103,500.

---

The allocation of a fund's assets across different types of securities can have a significant effect on the fund's returns and risks.

## EXAMPLE 18–5    Impact of Asset Allocation on a 401(k) Plan Return

An employee contributes $10,000 to a 401(k) plan each year, and the company matches 20 percent of this annually, or $2,000. The employee can allocate the contributions among equities (earning 10 percent annually), bonds (earning 6 percent annually), and money market securities (earning 4 percent annually). The employee expects to work at the company 30 years. The employee can contribute annually along one of the three following patterns:[3]

|                            | Option 1 | Option 2 | Option 3 |
|----------------------------|----------|----------|----------|
| Equities                   | 60%      | 50%      | 40%      |
| Bonds                      | 40       | 30       | 50       |
| Money market securities    | 0        | 20       | 10       |
|                            | 100%     | 100%     | 100%     |

The terminal value of the 401(k) plan, assuming all returns and contributions remain constant (at $12,000) over the 30 years,[4] will be:

**Option 1:**
$$12{,}000(0.6)([(1+0.10)^{30}-1]/0.10)+12{,}000(0.4)([(1+0.06)^{30}-1]/0.06)$$
$$=\$1{,}563{,}836$$

**Option 2:**
$$12{,}000(0.5)([(1+0.10)^{30}-1]/0.10)+12{,}000(0.3)([(1+0.06)^{30}-1]/0.06)$$
$$+12{,}000(0.2)([(1+0.04)^{30}-1]/0.04)=\$1{,}406{,}177$$

**CALCULATOR HINTS**

$N = 30$
$I = 10$
$PV = 0$
$PMT = 7{,}200$

CPT $FV = 1{,}184{,}357$

$+$

$N = 30$
$I = 6$
$PV = 0$
$PMT = 4{,}800$

CPT $FV = \underline{379{,}479}$

$= 1{,}563{,}836$

2. The employee will have to pay taxes on the funds as he withdraws funds during retirement. However, the tax rate is likely to be lower and tax payments are delayed by several years.
3. In reality, the employee has a larger number of possible choices in terms of fund asset allocation.
4. For simplicity, we assume that the employee's contribution remains constant over the 30 years. Realistically, as an employee's salary increases over his or her working years, contributions to the retirement funds increase as well.

**CALCULATOR HINTS**

$N = 30$
$I = 3$
$PV = 0$
$PMT = 7,200$
CPT $FV = 342,543$

$+$

$N = 30$
$I = 6$
$PV = 0$
$PMT = 4,800$
CPT $FV = \underline{379,479}$
$\phantom{CPT FV} = 722,022$

**Option 3:**

$$12,000(0.4)([(1 + 0.10)^{30} - 1]/0.10) + 12,000(0.5)([(1 + 0.06)^{30} - 1]/0.06)$$
$$+ 12,000(0.1)([(1 + 0.04)^{30} - 1]/0.04) = \$1,331,222$$

Notice that Option 1, which includes the largest investment in equities, produces the largest terminal value for the 401(k) plan, while Option 3, with the smallest investment in equities, produces the smallest terminal value. However, as discussed in Chapter 3, equity investments are riskier than bond and money market investments. Thus, the larger the portion of funds invested in equities, the higher the return risk of the pension plan—that is, the more uncertain the final (terminal) value of the plan. For example, suppose the economy slumped and equity investments earned only a 3 percent annual return over the 30 years the employee worked. In this case, the terminal value of the 401(k) plan would be:

**Option 1:**

$$12,000(0.6)([(1 + 0.03)^{30} - 1]/0.03) + 12,000(0.4)([(1 + 0.06)^{30} - 1]/0.06)$$
$$= \$722,022$$

**Option 2:**

$$12,000(0.5)([(1 + 0.03)^{30} - 1]/0.03) + 12,000(0.3)([(1 + 0.06)^{30} - 1]/0.06)$$
$$+ 12,000(0.2)([(1 + 0.04)^{30} - 1]/0.04) = \$704,666$$

**Option 3:**

$$12,000(0.4)([(1 + 0.03)^{30} - 1]/0.03) + 12,000(0.5)([(1 + 0.06)^{30} - 1]/0.06)$$
$$+ 12,000(0.1)([(1 + 0.04)^{30} - 1]/0.04) = \$770,013$$

In this case, Option 3, which involves the smallest investment in risky equities, produces the largest terminal value for the 401(k) plan.

**individual retirement accounts (IRAs)**

*Self-directed retirement accounts set up by employees who may also be covered by employer-sponsored pension plans.*

*Individual Retirement Accounts.*  **Individual retirement accounts (IRAs)** are self-directed retirement accounts set up by employees who may also be covered by employer-sponsored pension plans as well as self-employed individuals. Contributions to IRAs are made strictly by the employee. IRAs were first allowed in 1981 as a method of creating a tax-deferred retirement account to supplement an employer-sponsored plan. As of 2017, a maximum of $5,500 may be contributed to an IRA per year, and nonworking spouses may contribute an additional $5,500. If either spouse is covered by an employer-sponsored pension plan, the couple's adjusted gross income must be less than $196,000 for the contribution to be tax deductible.[5] IRAs may also be used by employees changing jobs. Any funds held by an employee in the old employer's pension fund may be invested in a tax-qualified IRA to maintain the tax-deferred status. In 2016, IRA account assets were greater than $7.3 trillion.

In 1998, a newer type of IRA, a Roth IRA, was established. Like a regular IRA, in 2016 Roth IRAs allow a maximum $5,500 after-tax contribution per individual ($11,000 per household) and the cap will increase as that on regular IRAs increases. Unlike a regular IRA, contributions to a Roth IRA are taxed in the year of contribution, and withdrawals from the account are tax-free (provided funds have been invested for at least five years and the account holder is at least 59½ years old). Roth IRAs are available only to individuals or households with an adjusted gross income of less than $133,000 or less than $196,000, respectively. Table 18–4 summarizes the main differences between a Roth IRA and a traditional IRA. As of 2006, Roth 401(k) and 403(b) retirement options also became available. As in a Roth IRA, contributions are taxed in the year of contribution and withdrawals are tax-free.

5. Individuals over 50 years of age can contribute $6,500 per year. If an employee's earnings exceed the limit, he or she can still invest in an IRA. However, the contribution is not tax deductible.

**TABLE 18–4**   Differences between a Roth IRA and a Traditional IRA

| Terms | Roth IRA | Traditional IRA |
|---|---|---|
| Tax benefits | Tax-free growth<br>Tax-free qualified withdrawals | Tax-deferred growth<br>Contributions may be tax deductible |
| Eligibility—age | Any age with employment compensation | Under age 70½ with employment compensation |
| Eligibility—income | 2017 single filers<br>Full contribution: up to $118,000<br>Partial contribution: $118,000 to $133,000<br>2017 joint filers<br>Full contribution: up to $186,000<br>Partial contribution: $186,000 to $196,000 | Full deductibility of a contribution for 2017 is available to active participants whose 2017 modified adjusted gross income (MAGI) is $99,000 or less (joint) and $61,000 or less (single); partial deductibility for MAGI up to $119,000 (joint) and $71,000 (single). In addition, full deductibility of a contribution is available for working or nonworking spouses who are not covered by an employer-sponsored plan whose MAGI is less than $99,000 for 2017; partial deductibility for MAGI up to $119,000. |
| Maximum contribution | 2016: $5,500 ($6,500 if you are 50 or older) or 100% of employment compensation, whichever is less | |
| Catch-up contribution | Individuals aged 50 or older (in the calendar year of their contribution) can contribute an additional $1,000 each year | |
| Contribution deadline | April 15 of the following tax year | April 15 of the following tax year |
| Taxation at withdrawal | Contributions are always withdrawn tax-free<br>Earnings are federally tax-free after the five-year aging requirement has been satisfied and one of the following conditions has been met: age 59½, death, disability, or qualified first-time home purchase | Withdrawals of pretax contributions and any earnings are taxable when distributed |
| Penalties at withdrawal | A nonqualified distribution is subject to taxation of earnings and a 10 percent additional tax unless an exception applies | Withdrawals before age 59½ may be subject to a 10 percent early withdrawal penalty unless an exception applies |
| Minimum required distributions (MRDs) | Not subject to minimum required distributions during the lifetime of the original owner | MRDs starting at 70½ |

Most IRA contributions are invested in mutual funds purchased through a broker or a mutual fund company. Choices of funds include stocks, bonds, futures, and U.S. Treasuries. Depository institutions usually handle CDs for their IRA customers. Whether a Roth IRA is a better option than a traditional IRA depends on the individual's expectation of his or her future tax bracket. Traditionally, retirees moved into a lower tax bracket. However, recently more retirees maintain high levels of income even in retirement. These individuals may be better off paying taxes on their IRA contributions during their working years (as under a Roth IRA). There are many websites available that calculate the advantage of a Roth IRA versus a traditional IRA for individuals (e.g., www.quicken.com). Appendix 18A (available through Connect or your course instructor) shows how an IRA can grow during an individual's working years to produce a significant sum of money for retirement.

*Keogh Accounts.*   A Keogh account is a retirement account available to self-employed individuals. Contributions by the individual may be deposited in a tax-deferred account administered by a life insurance company, a bank, or other financial institution. As with 401(k) plans, the participant in a Keogh account is given some discretion as to how the funds are to be invested.

The two types of Keogh plans are profit-sharing and money-purchase plans. Money-purchase plans require a mandatory contribution (at a constant percentage of the employee's income) each year whether the individual has profits or not. Profit-sharing plan contributions can vary by year. The most attractive feature of a Keogh retirement plan is the high maximum contribution allowed. Money-purchase plan contributions can be as high as the lesser of $53,000 or 25 percent of the individual's self-employment income. Profit-sharing plan contributions can vary from 0 to 25 percent of the individual's income, up to $53,000.[6]

**LG 18-1**

## Public Pension Funds

Pension funds sponsored by the federal or state and local governments are referred to as public pension funds. In 2016, these funds managed assets of more than $9.93 trillion.

**LG 18-4**

**State or Local Government Pension Funds.**   Employees of state or local governments may contribute to pension funds sponsored by these employers. Most are funded on a "pay as you go" basis, meaning that contributions collected from current employees are the source of payments to the current retirees. As a result of the increasing number of retirees relative to workers, some of these pension funds (e.g., the state of Illinois) have experienced a situation in which contributions have not been high enough to cover the increases in required benefit payments (the pension funds are underfunded). Some state and local governments have proposed tax increases to address this underfunding. Others have considered modifying the pay as you go method of funding contributions to operate their funds more like private pension funds. Without some modifications, many of the state and local government funds will increasingly be unable to maintain their promised payments to retirees, especially as the longevity of the population increases.

**Federal Government Pension Funds.**   The federal government sponsors two types of pension funds. The *first type* are funds for federal government employees: civil service employees, military personnel, and railroad employees. Civil service funds cover all federal employees who are not members of the armed forces. This group is not covered by Social Security. Similar to private pension funds, the federal government is the main contributor to the fund, but participants may contribute as well. In addition to Social Security, career military personnel receive retirement benefits from a federal government–sponsored military pension fund. Contributions to the fund are made by the federal government, and participants are eligible for benefits after 20 years of military service. Employees of the nation's railroad system are eligible to participate in the federal railroad pension system. Originated in the 1930s, contributions are made by railroad employers, employees, and the federal government.

The *second type* of fund, and the largest federal government pension fund, is Social Security. Also known as the Old Age and Survivors Insurance Fund, Social Security provides retirement benefits to almost all employees and self-employed individuals in the United States. Social Security was established in 1935 with the objective of providing

---

6. Keogh contribution caps are linked to the cost of living. In 2016, the cap was $53,000.

minimum retirement income to all retirees. Social Security is funded on a pay as you go basis; current employer and employee Social Security taxes are used to pay benefits to current retirees. Historically, Social Security tax contributions have generally exceeded disbursements to retirees. Any surpluses are held in a trust fund that can be used to cover required disbursements in years when contributions are insufficient to cover promised disbursements. Contributions, also known as the FICA tax, are a specified percentage of an individual's gross income (in 2016, 7.65 percent, for employees, and 15.30 percent, for self-employed individuals, of the first $115,500 earned). Employee contributions are matched with equivalent employer contributions.[7]

As the percentage of the population that is retired has increased and the percentage of the population that is working has decreased, Social Security tax revenue has dropped relative to benefits being paid out (i.e., Social Security is an underfunded pension fund). Indeed, in 2010 Social Security payouts exceeded revenues (excluding interest) for the first time, six years earlier than had been projected in 2009. Further, 2016 projections were that the Social Security system will be bankrupt (annual contributions and trust fund assets will be insufficient to cover required disbursements to retirees) by 2034. At that point, the extra reserves in the funds would be depleted and Social Security would be able to pay out in benefits only as much as it collects in payroll tax revenue. That would cause a 21 percent automatic cut in benefits. In other words, beneficiaries would receive only 79 cents for every $1 in benefits they would normally get. As a result, the federal government is currently considering new methods and ideas (discussed later) for fully funding the Social Security system.

## FINANCIAL ASSET INVESTMENTS AND RECENT TRENDS

Employer and employee contributions made to pension funds are invested in financial assets. These investments are tracked by the Federal Reserve because of the increasing importance of pension funds as participants in national and international security markets.

### Private Pension Funds

Financial assets (pension fund reserves) held by private pension funds in 1975 and 2016 are reported in Table 18–5. Financial assets held by pension funds totaled $244.3 billion in 1975 and $8,838.6 billion in 2016. In 2016, some 62.11 percent of pension fund assets were in corporate equities or equity mutual fund shares. This compares to 44.61 percent in 1975. In fact, pension funds are the largest institutional investor in the U.S. stock market. Certainly the booming stock market was a major reason for the increased investment in equities by pension funds in the 1990s. For example, in 1999 corporate equities and equity mutual fund shares composed 64.71 percent of private pension fund assets. The fall in stock market values in 2001–2002 resulted in a drop in this percentage to 55.87 percent at the end of 2002. The even larger financial crisis that followed years later resulted in a change in this percentage from 72.56 percent at the end of the second quarter of 2008 to 62.43 percent at the end of the first quarter of 2009.

Figure 18–4 shows differences between defined benefit and defined contribution fund investment portfolio allocations. In 2016, defined benefit funds had 30.73 percent of their funds invested in U.S. government securities and corporate and foreign bonds compared to 6.37 percent for defined contribution funds. Also, defined benefit funds had 35.52 percent of their assets invested in corporate equities compared to 21.57 percent by defined contribution funds. In contrast, defined contribution funds had 52.59 percent of their funds invested in mutual fund shares compared to 14.83 percent for defined benefit funds.

---

7. Self-employed individuals contribute at twice the rate of employees because employers pay a matched amount. The combined rate of the employee and employer is equal to the self-employment contribution rate.

**TABLE 18–5** Financial Assets Held by Private Pension Funds, 1975 and 2016 *(in billions)*

| | 1975 | | 2016 | |
|---|---|---|---|---|
| **Total financial assets** | $244.3 | 100.00% | $8,838.6 | 100.00% |
| Checkable deposits and currency | 4.4 | 1.77 | 21.1 | 0.24 |
| Time and savings deposits | 14.5 | 5.84 | 37.6 | 0.43 |
| Money market mutual shares | 0.0 | 0.00 | 154.8 | 1.75 |
| Security RPs | 4.3 | 1.73 | 2.6 | 0.03 |
| Credit market instruments | 71.3 | 28.70 | 1,267.6 | 14.34 |
| Open market paper | 9.1 | 3.66 | 47.3 | 0.54 |
| Treasury securities | 12.4 | 4.99 | 322.9 | 3.65 |
| Agency- and GSE-backed securities | 5.5 | 2.22 | 152.8 | 1.73 |
| Corporate and foreign bonds | 41.9 | 16.87 | 723.9 | 8.19 |
| Mortgages | 2.4 | 0.96 | 20.7 | 0.23 |
| Corporate equities | 108.0 | 43.48 | 2,172.1 | 24.57 |
| Mutual fund shares | 2.8 | 1.13 | 3,317.6 | 37.54 |
| Miscellaneous assets | 43.1 | 17.35 | 1,865.2 | 21.10 |

**Sources:** Federal Reserve Board, "Flow of Fund Accounts," various issues. www.federalreserve.gov

Defined benefit pension funds offer employees a guaranteed payout, while defined contribution funds do not. The promise made of a guaranteed retirement payment is likely a major reason for the larger percentage of investments in fixed-income securities made by defined benefit funds. Defined contribution funds do not offer a guaranteed retirement payout—thus, defined contribution fund administrators are more likely to invest in risky equities and equity mutual fund shares. The introduction of equities into these funds helps reduce the funding contributions required of the plan sponsor.

### Public Pension Funds

Financial assets held by state and local government pension funds in 1975 and 2016 are reported in Table 18–6. Like private pension funds, state and local pension funds held most of their assets in corporate equities or equity mutual fund shares (67.81 percent in 2016).

**Figure 18–4** Financial Assets in Defined Benefit and Defined Contribution Pension Funds

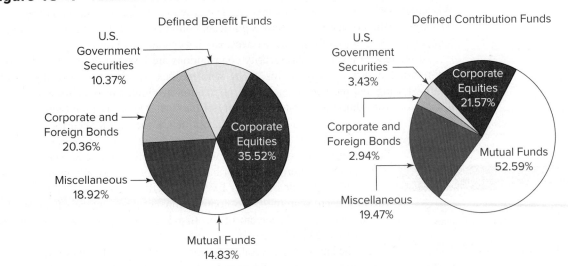

**Source:** Federal Reserve Board, "Flow of Fund Accounts," November 2016. www.federalreserve.gov

**TABLE 18-6**  Financial Assets Held by State and Local Government
Pension Funds, 1975 and 2016 *(in billions)*

|  | 1975 | | 2016 | |
|---|---|---|---|---|
| **Total financial assets** | $104.0 | 100.00% | $4,012.8 | 100.00% |
| Checkable deposits and currency | 0.3 | 0.29 | 4.3 | 0.11 |
| Time and savings deposits | 1.2 | 1.15 | 36.5 | 0.91 |
| Money market mutual shares | 0.0 | 0.00 | 48.8 | 1.22 |
| Security RPs | 0.0 | 0.00 | 3.4 | 0.08 |
| Credit market instruments | 78.2 | 75.05 | 883.9 | 22.02 |
| Open market paper | 0.0 | 0.00 | 39.7 | 0.99 |
| Treasury securities | 2.5 | 2.40 | 173.9 | 4.33 |
| Agency securities | 5.3 | 5.09 | 94.5 | 2.35 |
| Municipal securities | 1.9 | 1.82 | 2.4 | 0.06 |
| Corporate and foreign bonds | 61.0 | 58.54 | 565.2 | 14.09 |
| Mortgages | 7.5 | 7.20 | 8.2 | 0.20 |
| Corporate equities | 24.3 | 23.32 | 2,154.7 | 53.70 |
| Mutual fund shares | 0.0 | 0.00 | 566.3 | 14.11 |
| Miscellaneous assets | 0.2 | 0.19 | 314.9 | 7.85 |

**Sources:** Federal Reserve Board, "Flow of Fund Accounts," various issues. www.federalreserve.gov

Second in importance were U.S. government securities and bonds (20.77 percent in 2016). In 1975, only 23.32 percent of pension fund assets were in equities and 66.03 percent were in U.S. government securities and bonds.

In the early 2010s, state and local government pension funds faced a total shortfall of at least $4 trillion in their funding of employees' pensions and retirement benefits, and the financial problems were only growing. Illinois was in the worst shape, with over $83 billion of its pension obligations unfunded in fiscal year 2016. During the 2000s, many states contributed only the minimum required funds to their pensions. In 2000, states were required to pay only $27 billion total into their funds. By fiscal year 2008, that amount had more than doubled to a $64 billion deposit. As stock market returns fell and the U.S. economy entered a steep recession, state revenues fell dramatically. Yet states were calculating required pension contributions using assumptions based on interest rates and stock market growth rates experienced during boom markets. These unrealistic assumptions regarding reinvestment rates meant that states significantly undercontributed to their pension funds. Under these circumstances, the minimum contributions made in "good times" were insufficient to keep up with promised payouts. In fiscal 2000, half of the 50 states had fully funded their pension systems. By fiscal year 2016, only two states—South Dakota, and Wisconsin—were able to cover their costs. The growing bill from promised pension payouts coming due to states could have significant consequences for taxpayers, resulting in higher taxes, less money for public services, and lower state bond ratings.

www.ssa.gov

At the federal level, Social Security contributions are invested in relatively low-risk, low-return Treasury securities. This, along with the fact that the growth of the population is slowing and the percentage of the population in retirement is increasing, has led to questions regarding the long-term viability of the Social Security fund (and the Social Security system in general). To bolster public confidence, the Social Security system was restructured in the mid-1990s by raising contributions and reducing retirees' benefits. For example, full retirement age was 65 for many years. However, beginning with individuals born in 1938 or later, that age will gradually increase until it reaches 67 for people born after 1959. Further, the wage contribution increases virtually each year (e.g., the contribution as a percentage of an employee's income was 6.2 percent of the first $72,600 in 1998 and 7.65 percent of the first $127,200 in 2017).

In the late 1990s, several proposals were also introduced as possible ways of bolstering the Social Security fund's resources. For example, in December 2001 the Bush administration's Presidential Commission on Social Security

**DO YOU UNDERSTAND:**

**5.** *What the major financial assets held by private pension funds are?*

**6.** *What the major financial assets held by public pension funds are?*

Reform proposed changes to the Social Security system that included personal retirement accounts. After 12 years and several more suggestions for reform yet no major changes, in 2013 President Obama proposed changing the way the government adjusts Social Security benefits by switching to a measure called the chained consumer price index (CPI). Using a chained CPI, Social Security benefits would increase by a bit less each year than under the current formula; this rate of a gradual change would allow savings to grow over time. According to Congressional Budget Office calculations, if the chained CPI were implemented, Social Security benefits would be about $30 a month lower by 2023. By 2033, Social Security payments would be 3 percent lower than they would be using the current measure of inflation. Despite these calls for reform, no major reform of Social Security has been realized and, as mentioned, in 2010 Social Security payouts exceeded revenues for the first time, six years earlier than the year 2016, which had been projected in 2009. Social Security's total costs are projected to exceed its total revenue (including interest) by 2023.

# REGULATION

LG 18-5

www.dol.gov

The major piece of regulation governing private pension funds is the Employee Retirement Income Security Act (ERISA) of 1974 (also called the Pension Reform Act). While ERISA does not mandate that employers establish pension funds for their employees, it does require them to meet certain standards if a fund is to be eligible for tax-deferred status. ERISA was passed when many workers, who had contributed to pension funds for years, were failing to receive their pension benefits in a timely fashion. ERISA charged the Department of Labor with the task of overseeing pension funds. The principal features of ERISA involve pension plan funding, vesting of benefits, fiduciary responsibility, pension fund transferability, and pension fund insurance.

**Funding.**   Prior to ERISA, there were no statutory requirements forcing defined benefit fund administrators to adequately fund their pension funds. Specifically, funds sometimes operated such that employees' annual contributions to pension funds were insufficient to meet promised annual pension obligations. ERISA established guidelines for funding and set penalties for fund deficiencies. Contributions to pension funds must be sufficient to meet all annual costs and expenses and to fund any unfunded historical liabilities over a 30-year period. Further, any new underfunding arising from low investment returns or other losses has to be funded over a 15-year period. For some companies the required obligations resulting from ERISA were significant. For example, after ERISA was enacted, General Motors had to put $7.3 billion into its underfunded pension funds, while Ford Motor Company had to add $3.3 billion. Indeed, this provision of ERISA is one reason many companies switched from defined benefit to defined contribution retirement plans, as discussed earlier.

Despite these changes in required funding, unrealistic assumptions regarding reinvestment rates have led to significant underfunding of many pension funds. Other than the two bear markets of the 2000s, stock markets surged for a period of about 20 years. As a result, pension fund managers could realistically assume that funds would earn a rate of return of at least 8 or even 9 percent. However, since the mid-2000s, these rates are too optimistic. Yet many pension funds continue to use them as the higher rates make underfunding appear to be smaller. However, after a prolonged period of near zero interest rates and falling stock market values, the result is huge increases in underfunded pension funds.

Underfunded pension liabilities for single-employer plans surged to $823 billion in 2012 and $759 billion in 2013, the largest values ever (see Figure 18–5). Not all of this underfunding posed a major risk to participants and the pension insurance fund, however. Most companies that sponsored defined benefit plans were financially healthy and would be able to meet their pension obligations to their workers. However, the federally sponsored pension fund insurance agency, Pension Benefit Guaranty Corporation (PBGC) see below, estimated its loss exposure to reasonably possible terminations (e.g., underfunded plans sponsored by companies with credit ratings below investment grade) at approximately $223 billion in 2016, down from $295 billion in 2012. This exposure was concentrated in

**Figure 18–5** Total Underfunding of Insured Single-Employer Plans

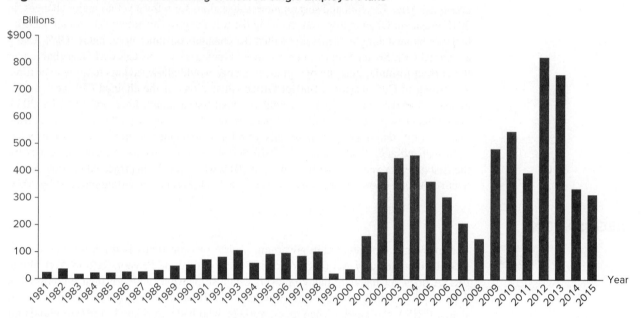

**Sources:** Pension Benefit Guaranty Corporation website, various dates. www.pbgc.gov

the manufacturing (primarily automobile/auto parts and primary and fabricated metals), transportation (primarily airlines), communications, utilities, and services sectors.

**vested employee**

*An employee who is eligible to receive pension benefits because he or she has worked for a stated period of time.*

**Vesting of Benefits.** Frequently, while employers start contributing to an employee's pension fund as soon as the employee is eligible to participate, benefits may not be paid to the employee until he or she has worked for the employer for a stated period of time (or until the employee is **vested**). For example, prior to ERISA, some plans required their employees to work 15 and even 25 years before they were eligible to receive pension benefits. ERISA requires that a plan must have a minimum vesting requirement and sets a maximum vesting period of 10 years.

**Fiduciary Responsibilities.** A pension plan fiduciary is a trustee or investment advisor charged with management of the pension fund. ERISA set standards governing pension fund management. Specifically, ERISA required that pension fund contributions be invested with the same diligence, skill, and care as a "prudent person" in like circumstances (the *prudent-person rule*). Fund assets are required to be managed with the sole objective of providing the promised benefits to participants. To ensure that a fund operates in this manner, ERISA requires pension funds to report on the current status (e.g., market value of assets held, income and expenses of the fund) of the pension fund.

Despite ERISA's fiduciary standards governing pension fund management, in 2002 Congress moved to implement changes in pension and corporate governance rules after the Enron failure caused thousands of workers to lose their retirement savings, which were heavily weighted in company stock. Enron matched its employees' 401(k) contributions with company stock but barred workers from selling this stock until age 50. Further, when Enron's stock price was rising, employees included more shares of the company's stock in their pension funds. However, as the stock price plunged when Enron's accounting problems were revealed, management barred employees from selling their shares of Enron. It was estimated that Enron employees lost $3 billion in retirement funds after the energy trader filed for bankruptcy and its stock price fell to less than $1 (from a high of over $80). Historically, labor laws limited the assets of traditional pension funds that may be held in employer stock or property to 10 percent. But the laws exempted 401(k) funds from that provision, hoping to encourage employers to offer retirement plans. The 2002 changes rescinded this exemption.

**Transferability.**    ERISA allowed employees to transfer pension credits from one employer's fund to another's when switching jobs.

**www.pbgc.gov**

**Insurance.**    ERISA established the Pension Benefit Guarantee Corporation (PBGC), an insurance fund for pension fund participants similar to the FDIC. The PBGC insures participants of defined benefit funds if the proceeds from the fund are unable to meet its promised pension obligations. As of 2016, the PBGC was responsible for the pensions of some 840,000 people from more than 4,700 failed single-employer plans, down from 1,500,000 in 2012. During 2016, the PBGC assumed responsibility for more than 46,000 people in 76 underfunded single-employer plans. Some of the largest failures were plans sponsored by Sears, Alcoa, Alpha Natural Resources, and Computer Sciences Corp. There is a maximum benefit guarantee that changes over time. Thus, workers covered by a failed pension plan may not be paid in full. For example, in 2017 the maximum annual coverage for workers who will begin receiving payments from PBGC at age 65 is $64,432.

When PBGC was created in 1974, the single-employer premium was a flat-rate $1 per plan participant. Congress raised the premium to $2.60 in 1979 and to $8.50 in 1986. In 1987, the basic premium was raised to $16 and an additional variable-rate premium was imposed on underfunded plans up to a maximum of $50. In 1991, Congress set the maximum at $72 per participant for underfunded plans and $19 per participant for fully funded plans.

Despite these premium increases, however, PBGC has generally operated at a deficit since its inception. This reflects the fact that unlike the FDIC, the PBGC has little regulatory power over the pension funds it insures. Thus, it cannot use portfolio restrictions or on-site supervision to restrict the risk taking of fund managers.[8] Partly in response to the growing PBGC deficit, the 1994 Retirement Protection Act was passed. Under the act (in 1997), the $72 premium cap was phased out (80 percent of underfunded plans were at the cap in 1997). Thus, underfunded programs were subjected to even higher premiums (some as high as several hundred dollars per participant).[9] Thus, like the FDIC in 1993, the PBGC has changed to a more overtly risk-based premium plan. As a result of these changes, in 2000 the PBGC's insurance fund operated at a record surplus of $9.7 billion. However, bankruptcies of several large companies (e.g., United Airlines, LTV Steel, Bethlehem Steel) in the early 2000s resulted in the agency posting a deficit of $23.3 billion and a call for additional reform at the beginning of 2005.

This call resulted in the passage of the Pension Protection Act of 2006, which called for increasing the annual premiums paid by companies to $30 per worker from $19 and the imposition of automatic increases in premiums each year (which would be tied to average wage increases of U.S. workers). As of 2018, rates are $74 per participant for single-employer plans and $28 per participant for multi-employer plans. Underfunded pension plans pay an additional variable rate charge of $38 per $1,000 of unfunded vested benefits. In addition, the act gives companies 5 years (rather than the previous 20 years) to make up shortfalls in their defined benefit pension plans. Finally, the Pension Protection Act requires companies to tell investors and employees well before any pension fund becomes significantly underfunded. This gives interested parties a chance to pressure companies to increase pension funding.

## GLOBAL ISSUES

**LG 18-6**

Pension systems around the world take many forms. For example, even within Europe there is wide variation in pension systems. The United Kingdom, the Netherlands, Ireland, Denmark, and Switzerland all have a tradition of state- (or public-) funded pension schemes, while Spain, Portugal, and Italy have less developed pension systems, and France uses a pay-as-you-go pension system. The systems of other countries vary greatly in their details. However, the extent to which a person's contributions (made to the system during

---

8. To the extent that regulation restricts the asset and liability activities of a firm or FI, these restrictions are similar to imposing an "implicit" premium or tax on the activities of the firm.
9. Underfunded plans pay a surcharge of $9 per participant per $1,000 of underfunding.

his or her working years) are linked to the benefits that he or she receives in retirement is one characteristic that distinguishes systems. For example, France and Germany are among the countries where the relationship between the benefits people receive in retirement and the taxes they pay during their working years is relatively weak. Such countries have typically offered generous benefits to those who take early retirement. As a result of drains on the pension funds from early retirement options and soaring national deficits incurred as a result of the financial crisis, many of these countries have begun to experience problems in the financing of public pensions and they have had to undertake reforms that strengthen the link between contributions and benefits. At the other extreme are countries such as Sweden, Italy, the United Kingdom, and Chile, which impose a tight relationship between a person's payments into the system and the benefits received during retirement. Some of these countries have strengthened this link by shifting some of the financing of state pensions into private sources. Although these countries are relatively well prepared to handle the problem of an aging population, several are considering reforming their systems.

Reforms of pension systems in other countries have included benefit reductions, measures to encourage later retirement, and expansions of private funding for government pensions. For example, in many countries reforms include raising the age at which a person is eligible for pension benefits. This type of reform recognizes increased life expectancy. Finland has taken the step of indexing its full pension retirement age to life expectancy, and several countries have taken steps to encourage people to remain in the labor force as they get older. Some have done so by strengthening the link between contributions and benefits. For example, Sweden introduced notional accounts by which participants can see their potential pension benefits rise as they work longer and contribute more to the system. Other countries have taken steps to reduce payments to persons who retire before the established retirement age. Many countries have traditionally offered generous benefits to people who choose to retire early, although early retirees typically receive a smaller annual pension than persons who wait until they are older to retire. However, the difference in retirement payments in many countries has not been sufficient to discourage large numbers of people from retiring early.

The European debt crisis forced many countries to reform their pension systems. For example, France's parliament approved a bill that increased the retirement age from 60 to 62. As part of the bailout plan organized by the International Monetary Fund, Greece made changes that increased the retirement age and cut automatic bonuses that retirees received at Christmas, Easter, and during the summer. Spain proposed to stop inflation-linked increases in pensions and raised its retirement age from 65 to 67. The retirement age for British workers was raised to 68, at which time they can start getting their full pension. Politicians from Athens to Madrid targeted pension reform as a way to offset government debt. The reforms sparked weeks of strikes and protests. Unions across Europe took to the streets to protest the new rules. On June 23, 2010, French workers held more than 200 demonstrations nationwide. A strike in Madrid on June 29, 2010, led to clashes with police. Strikes in Greece shut down airports, ferry service, banks, and hospitals. Protests since the start of September 2010 repeatedly brought more than one million people onto the streets. Yet, with nearly everyone in Europe eligible for a public pension, governments approved the plans that were necessary to continue to finance national pension funds.

> ## DO YOU UNDERSTAND:
>
> **9.** *How retirement systems in other countries vary?*
>
> **10.** *The pension reforms undertaken in other countries?*

## SUMMARY

This chapter provided an overview of the pension fund industry. Pension funds provide a way of accumulating retirement funds similar to life insurance contracts and mutual funds. Pension funds, however, have a tax advantage in that an employee's contributions to pension funds are exempt from current taxation. The chapter reviewed the types of funds offered by private companies (financial institutions) and by federal and state or local governments. Given the problems with the funding of public pension funds and the phenomenal increase in stock market values, growth in private pension funds has been larger than any other type of financial institution. We looked at the distribution of asset investments for both private and public pension funds and highlighted their differences. The chapter also reviewed the major piece of regulation governing the industry, ERISA, and the role played by the Pension Benefit Guaranty Corporation (PBGC).

## QUESTIONS

1. Describe the difference between a private pension fund and a public pension fund. (*LG 18-1*)

2. Describe the difference between an insured pension fund and a noninsured pension fund. What type of financial institutions would administer each of these? (*LG 18-1*)

3. Describe the difference between a defined benefit pension fund and a defined contribution pension fund. (*LG 18-2*)

4. What are the three types of formulas used to determine pension benefits for defined benefit pension funds? Describe each. (*LG 18-2*)

5. What have the trends been for assets invested in defined benefit versus defined contribution pension funds in the last three decades? (*LG 18-2*)

6. Describe the trend in assets invested in 401(k) plans in the 1990s through 2010s. (*LG 18-3*)

7. What is the difference between an IRA and a Keogh account? (*LG 18-3*)

8. Describe the "pay as you go" funding method that is used by many federal and state or local government pension funds.

What is the problem with this method that may damage the long-term viability of such funds? (*LG 18-4*)

9. Describe the different pension funds sponsored by the federal government. (*LG 18-4*)

10. What are the major assets held by private pension funds in 1975 versus 2016? Explain the differences. (*LG 18-1*)

11. How do the financial asset holdings of defined benefit pension funds differ from those of defined contribution pension funds? Explain the differences. (*LG 18-2*)

12. Describe the issues associated with the long-term viability of the Social Security fund. (*LG 18-4*)

13. What was the motivation for the passage of ERISA? (*LG 18-5*)

14. Describe the major features of ERISA. (*LG 18-5*)

15. What types of pension reforms have countries tried as their populations age and contributions to pension funds decrease? (*LG 18-6*)

## PROBLEMS

1. Your employer uses a flat benefit formula to determine retirement payments to its employees. The fund pays an annual benefit of $2,500 per year of service. Calculate your annual benefit payments for 25, 28, and 30 years of service. (*LG 18-2*)

2. An employer uses a career average formula to determine retirement payments to its employees. The annual retirement payout is 5 percent of an employee's career average salary times the number of years of service. Calculate the annual benefit payment under the following scenarios. (*LG 18-2*)

| Years Worked | Career Average Salary |
|---|---|
| 30 | $60,000 |
| 33 | 62,500 |
| 35 | 64,000 |

3. An employee with 25 years of service at a company is considering retirement at some time in the next 10 years. The employer uses a final pay benefit formula by which the employee receives an annual benefit payment of 3.5 percent of her average salary during her last five years of service times her total years employed. The employee's average salary over the last 5 years of service is as follows:

| | Average Salary during Last Five Years of Service |
|---|---|
| Retire now | $125,000 |
| Retire in 5 years | 135,000 |
| Retire in 10 years | 140,000 |

Calculate the annual benefit payment for retirement now, in 5 years, and in 10 years. (*LG 18-2*)

4. **eXcel** **Using a Spreadsheet to Calculate Pension Benefit Payments:** Your employer uses a career average formula to determine retirement payments to its employees. You have 20 years of service at the company and are considering retirement some time in the next 10 years. Your average salary over the 20 years has been $50,000 and you expect this to increase at a rate of 1 percent per year. Your employer uses a career average formula by which you receive an annual benefit payment of 5 percent of your career average salary times the number of years of service. Calculate the annual benefit if you retire now, in 2 years, 5 years, 8 years, and 10 years. (*LG 18-2*)

| Retire | Average Salary | => | The Payment Will Be |
|---|---|---|---|
| Now | $50,000 | | $50,000 \times 0.05 \times 20 = \$50,000$ |
| In 2 years | 51,005 | | $51,005 \times 0.05 \times 22 = \$56,105$ |
| In 5 years | 52,551 | | $52,551 \times 0.05 \times 25 = \$65,688$ |
| In 8 years | 54,143 | | $54,143 \times 0.05 \times 28 = \$78,800$ |
| In 10 years | 55,231 | | $55,231 \times 0.05 \times 30 = \$82,847$ |

5. **eXcel** **Using a Spreadsheet to Calculate Pension Benefit Payments:** Your employer uses a final pay formula to determine retirement payments to its employees. You have 20 years of service at the company and are considering retirement some time in the next 10 years. Your employer uses a final pay formula by which you receive an annual benefit payment of 4 percent of your average salary over the last three

years of service times the number of years employed. Calculate the annual benefit if you retire now, in 2 years, 5 years, 8 years, and 10 years using the estimated annual salary during the last three years of service listed below. (*LG 18-2*)

| Retire | Average Salary | => | The Payment Will Be |
|--------|---------|---|---------------------|
| Now | $50,000 | | $50,000 \times 0.04 \times 20 = \$40,000$ |
| In 2 years | 51,005 | | $51,005 \times 0.04 \times 22 = \$44,884$ |
| In 5 years | 52,551 | | $52,551 \times 0.04 \times 25 = \$52,551$ |
| In 8 years | 54,143 | | $54,143 \times 0.04 \times 28 = \$60,640$ |
| In 10 years | 55,231 | | $55,231 \times 0.04 \times 30 = \$66,277$ |

6. An employer uses a final pay formula to determine retirement payouts to its employees. The annual payout is 3 percent of the average salary over the employees' last three years of service times the total years employed. Calculate the annual benefit under the following scenarios. (*LG 18-2*)

| Years Worked | Average Salary during the Last Three Years of Service |
|--------------|--------------------------------------------------------|
| 17 | $40,000 |
| 20 | 47,000 |
| 22 | 50,000 |

7. Your company sponsors a 401(k) plan into which you deposit 12 percent of your $60,000 annual income. Your company matches 50 percent of the first 5 percent of your earnings. You expect the fund to yield 10 percent next year. If you are currently in the 31 percent tax bracket, what is your annual investment in the 401(k) plan and your one-year return? (*LG 18-3*)

8. Using the information in Problem 7, and assuming all variables remain constant over the next 25 years, what will your 401(k) fund value be in 25 years (when you expect to retire)? (*LG 18-3*)

9. Your company sponsors a 401(k) plan into which you deposit 10 percent of your $120,000 annual income. Your company matches 75 percent of the first 10 percent of your earnings. You expect the fund to yield 12 percent next year. If you are currently in the 31 percent tax bracket, what is your annual investment in the 401(k) plan and your one-year return? (*LG 18-3*)

10. Using the information in Problem 9, and assuming all variables remain constant over the next 15 years, what will your 401(k) fund value be in 15 years (when you expect to retire)? (*LG 18-3*)

11. An employee contributes $15,000 to a 401(k) plan each year, and the company matches 10 percent of this annually, or $1,500. The employee can allocate the contributions among equities (earning 12 percent annually), bonds (earning 5 percent annually), and money market securities (earning 3 percent annually). The employee expects to work at the company 20 years. The employee can contribute annually along one of the three following patterns:

| | Option 1 | Option 2 | Option 3 |
|---|---------|----------|----------|
| Equities | 60% | 50% | 40% |
| Bonds | 40 | 45 | 50 |
| Money market securities | 0 | 5 | 10 |
| | 100% | 100% | 100% |

Calculate the terminal value of the 401(k) plan for each of the 3 options, assuming all returns and contributions remain constant over the 20 years. (*LG18-3*)

## SEARCH THE SITE

Go to the Federal Reserve Board's website at **www.federalreserve.gov.** Find the most recent information on the net flow of funds to defined benefit and defined contribution pension funds using the following steps. Click on "Economic Research and Data." Click on "Financial Accounts of the United States." Click on the most recent date, PDF file. This will bring up the file onto your computer with the relevant data in Table F.118.b and F.118.c.

### Questions

1. How has the flow of funds to defined benefit and defined contribution pension funds changed since 2016 as reported in Figure 18–2?
2. Is the flow of funds into these two types of pension funds currently positive or negative? Why would these trends occur?

## APPENDIX 18A: Calculation of Growth in IRA Value during an Individual's Working Years

# This appendix is available through Connect or your course instructor.

# Types of Risks Incurred by Financial Institutions

## Learning Goals

**LG 19-1**  *Describe the major risks faced by financial institutions.*

**LG 19-2**  *Recognize that insolvency risk is a consequence of the other types of risk.*

**LG 19-3**  *Understand how the various risks faced by financial institutions are related.*

## WHY FINANCIAL INSTITUTIONS NEED TO MANAGE RISK: CHAPTER OVERVIEW

**LG 19-1** As has been mentioned in previous chapters, a major objective of FI management is to increase the FI's returns for its owners. This often comes, however, at the cost of increased risk. As discussed in Chapter 12, regulators' evaluation of the overall safety and soundness of a depository institution (DI) is summarized in the CAMELS rating assigned to the DI.[1] This chapter provides an overview of the various risks facing FIs: credit risk, liquidity risk, interest rate risk, market risk, off-balance-sheet risk, foreign exchange risk, country or sovereign risk, technology risk, operational risk, and insolvency risk. Table 19–1 presents a brief definition of each of these risks. As will become clear, the effective management of these risks is central to an FI's performance. Indeed, it can be argued that the main business of FIs is to manage these risks. As a result, FI managers must devote significant time to understanding and managing the various risks to which their FIs are exposed. By the end of this chapter, you will have a basic understanding of the variety and complexity of the risks facing managers of modern FIs. In the remaining chapters of the text, we look at the management of the most important of these risks in more detail.

---

1. Where $C$ = capital adequacy, $A$ = asset quality, $M$ = management, $E$ = earnings, $L$ = liquidity, and $S$ = sensitivity to market risk, and ratings range from 1 (best) to 5 (worst).

**TABLE 19–1**  Risks Faced by Financial Institutions

1. **Credit risk**—the risk that promised cash flows from loans and securities held by FIs may not be paid in full.
2. **Liquidity risk**—the risk that a sudden and unexpected increase in liability withdrawals may require an FI to liquidate assets in a very short period of time and at low prices.
3. **Interest rate risk**—the risk incurred by an FI when the maturities of its assets and liabilities are mismatched and interest rates are volatile.
4. **Market risk**—the risk incurred in trading assets and liabilities due to changes in interest rates, exchange rates, and other asset prices.
5. **Off-balance-sheet risk**—the risk incurred by an FI as the result of its activities related to contingent assets and liabilities.
6. **Foreign exchange risk**—the risk that exchange rate changes can affect the value of an FI's assets and liabilities denominated in foreign currencies.
7. **Country or sovereign risk**—the risk that repayments by foreign borrowers may be interrupted because of interference from foreign governments or other political entities.
8. **Technology risk**—the risk incurred by an FI when its technological investments do not produce anticipated cost savings.
9. **Operational risk**—the risk that existing technology or support systems may malfunction, that fraud that impacts the FI's activities may occur, and/or that external shocks such as hurricanes and floods may occur.
10. **Insolvency risk**—the risk that an FI may not have enough capital to offset a sudden decline in the value of its assets relative to its liabilities.

# CREDIT RISK

**credit risk**

*The risk that the promised cash flows from loans and securities held by FIs may not be paid in full.*

**Credit risk** arises because of the possibility that promised cash flows on financial claims held by FIs, such as loans and bonds, will not be paid in full. Virtually all types of FIs face this risk. However, in general, FIs that make loans or buy bonds with long maturities are more exposed than are FIs that make loans or buy bonds with short maturities. This means, for example, that depository institutions and life insurers are more exposed to credit risk than are money market mutual funds and property–casualty insurers, since depository institutions and life insurers tend to hold longer maturity assets in their portfolios than mutual funds and property–casualty insurers. For example, commercial and investment banks incurred billions of dollars of losses in the mid- and late 2000s as a result of credit risk on subprime mortgages and mortgage-backed securities. If the principal on all financial claims held by FIs were paid in full on maturity and interest payments were made on their promised payment dates, FIs would always receive back the original principal lent plus an interest return—that is, they would face no credit risk. Should a borrower default, however, both the principal loaned and the interest payments expected to be received are at risk.

Many financial claims issued by individuals or corporations and held by FIs promise a limited or fixed upside return (principal and interest payments to the lender) with a high probability, but they also may result in a large downside risk (loss of loan principal and promised interest) with a much smaller probability. Some examples of financial claims issued with these return-risk trade-offs are fixed-coupon bonds issued by corporations and bank loans. In both cases, an FI holding these claims as assets earns the coupon on the bond or the interest promised on the loan if no borrower default occurs. In the event of default, however, the FI earns zero interest on the asset and may well lose all or part of the principal lent, depending on its ability to lay claim to some of the borrower's assets through legal bankruptcy and insolvency proceedings. Accordingly, a key role of FIs involves screening and monitoring loan applicants to ensure that FI managers fund the most creditworthy loans (see Chapter 20).

**EXAMPLE 19–1**   Impact of Credit Risk on an FI's Equity Value

Consider an FI with the following balance sheet:

| Cash | $ 20m | Deposits | $ 90m |
|---|---|---|---|
| Gross loans | 80m | Equity (net worth) | 10m |
| | $100m | | $100m |

Suppose that the managers of the FI recognize that $5 million of its $80 million in loans is unlikely to be repaid due to an increase in credit repayment difficulties of its borrowers. Eventually, the FI's managers must respond by charging off or writing down the value of these loans on the FI's balance sheet. This means that the value of loans falls from $80 million to $75 million, an economic loss that must be charged off against the stockholder's equity capital or net worth (i.e., equity capital falls from $10 million to $5 million). Thus, both sides of the balance sheet shrink by the amount of the loss:

| Cash | | $20m | Deposits | $90m |
|---|---|---|---|---|
| Gross loans | 80m | | Equity after charge-off | 5m |
| Less: Loan loss | – 5m | | | |
| Loans after charge-off | | 75m | | |
| | | $95m | | $95m |

The effects of credit risk are evident in Figures 19–1 and 19–2, which show commercial bank charge-off (or write-off) rates (loans charged off as a percentage of total

**Figure 19–1**   **Charge-Off Rates for Commercial Bank Lending Activities**

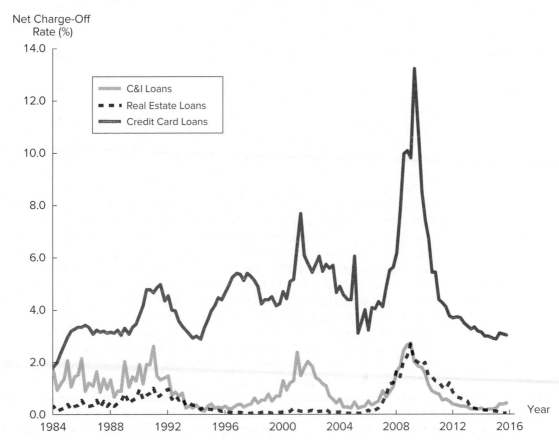

**Sources:** FDIC, *Quarterly Banking Profile,* various issues. www.fdic.gov

**Figure 19–2**    Credit Card Loss Rates and Personal Bankruptcy Filings

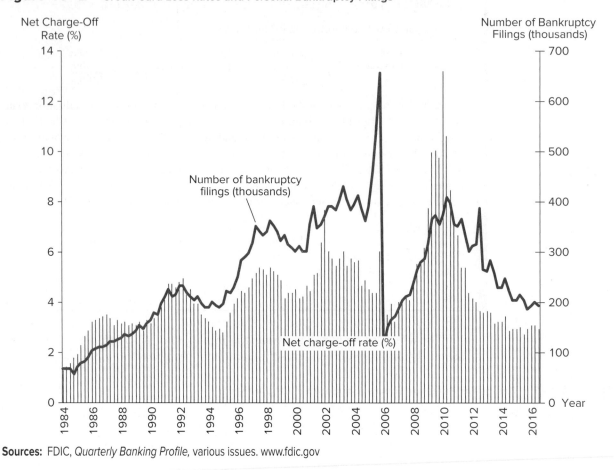

**Sources:** FDIC, *Quarterly Banking Profile,* various issues. www.fdic.gov

loans) for various types of loans between 1984 and 2016. Notice, in particular, the high rate of charge-offs experienced on credit card loans throughout this period. Indeed, credit card charge-offs by commercial banks increased persistently from the mid-1980s until late 1993 and again from 1995 through early 1998. While high relative to real estate and commercial and industrial (C&I) loan charge-off rates, by 1999, credit card charge-offs leveled off, and they even declined after 1999. With the downturn in the U.S. economy and an impending change in bankruptcy laws making it more difficult to declare bankruptcy, credit card charge-offs rose rapidly in 2001 and remained high through 2004. Note particularly that in October 2005, the Bankruptcy Reform Act was signed into law. This act makes it more difficult for consumers to declare bankruptcy. As a result, there was a surge in bankruptcy filings in the summer and early fall of 2005 just before the new rules went into effect and a huge drop-off in bankruptcy filings just after the enactment of the new rules. The financial crisis of 2008–2009 and the resulting economic recession produced a huge surge in credit card charge-off rates, which rose to an all-time high of 13.21 percent in March 2010. Despite these losses, credit card loans (including unused balances) extended by commercial banks continued to grow, from $1.856 trillion in March 1997 to $4.367 trillion in September 2008. As of June 2016, credit card loans had fallen to $3.659 trillion.

Even as losses due to credit risk increase, financial institutions continue to willingly give loans. This is because the FI charges a rate of interest on a loan that compensates for the risk of the loan. Thus, an important element in the credit risk management process is its pricing. Further, the potential loss an FI can experience from lending suggests that FIs need to collect information about borrowers whose assets are in their portfolios

**firm-specific
credit risk**

*The risk of default for the
borrowing firm associated
with the specific types of
project risk taken by that firm.*

**systemic credit risk**

*The risk of default associated with general economywide or macro-conditions affecting all borrowers.*

and to monitor those borrowers over time. Thus, managerial (monitoring) efficiency and credit risk management strategies directly affect the returns and risks of the loan portfolio. Moreover, one of the advantages that FIs have over individual investors is their ability to diversify credit risk exposures from a single asset by exploiting the law of large numbers in their asset investment portfolios. Diversification across assets, such as loans exposed to credit risk, reduces the overall credit risk in the asset portfolio and thus increases the probability of partial or full repayment of principal and/or interest. In particular, diversification reduces individual **firm-specific credit risk,** such as the risk specific to holding the bonds or loans of General Motors, while still leaving the FI exposed to **systemic credit risk,** such as factors that simultaneously increase the default risk of all firms in the economy (e.g., an economic recession).

Chapter 20 describes methods to measure the default risk of individual bonds and loans and investigates methods to measure the risk of portfolios of such claims. Chapter 24 discusses various methods—for example, loan sales and loan reschedulings—used to manage and control credit risk exposures.

**DO YOU UNDERSTAND:**

1. *Why credit risk exists for FIs?*
2. *How diversification affects an FI's credit risk exposure?*

## LIQUIDITY RISK

**liquidity risk**

*The risk that a sudden and unexpected increase in liability withdrawals may require an FI to liquidate assets in a very short period of time and at low prices.*

**Liquidity risk** arises when an FI's liability holders, such as depositors or insurance policyholders, demand immediate cash for the financial claims they hold with an FI or when holders of off-balance-sheet loan commitments (or credit lines) suddenly exercise their right to borrow (draw down their loan commitments). For example, when liability holders demand cash immediately—that is, "put" their financial claim back to the FI—the FI must either liquidate assets or borrow additional funds to meet the demand for the withdrawal of funds. The most liquid asset of all is cash, which FIs can use directly to meet liability holders' demands to withdraw funds. Although FIs limit their cash asset holdings because cash earns no interest, low cash holdings are generally not a problem. Day-to-day withdrawals by liability holders are generally predictable, and large FIs can normally expect to borrow additional funds to meet any sudden shortfalls of cash in the money and financial markets (see Chapter 22).

At times, however, FIs face a liquidity crisis. For example, because of a lack of confidence in an FI or some unexpected need for cash, liability holders may be led to demand larger withdrawals than usual. When all, or many, FIs face abnormally large cash demands, the cost of purchased or borrowed funds rises and the supply of such funds becomes restricted. As a consequence, FIs may have to sell some of their less liquid assets to meet the withdrawal demands of liability holders. This results in a more serious liquidity risk, especially as some assets with "thin" markets generate lower prices when the sale is immediate than when an FI has more time to negotiate the sale of an asset. As a result, the liquidation of some assets at low or "fire-sale" prices (the price the FI receives if the assets must be liquidated immediately at less than their fair market value) could threaten an FI's profitability and solvency. For example, in the summer of 2008, IndyMac bank failed in part due to a bank run that continued for several days, even after being taken over by the FDIC. The bank had announced on July 7 that, due to its deteriorating capital position, its mortgage operations would stop and it would operate only as a retail bank. News reports over the weekend highlighted the possibility that IndyMac would become the largest bank failure in over 20 years. Worried that they would not have access to their money, bank depositors rushed to withdraw money from IndyMac even though their deposits were insured up to $100,000 by the FDIC.[2] The run was so large that within a week of the original announcement, the FDIC had to step in and take over the bank.

---

2. One reason for the bank run is that, although deposits were insured up to $100,000 (since increased to $250,000), it may take some days to transfer deposits to the bank of an acquirer. IndyMac was eventually acquired by OneWest Bank Group.

**TABLE 19–2**   **Adjusting to a Deposit Withdrawal Using Asset Sales** *(in millions)*

| Before the Withdrawal | | | | After the Withdrawal | | | |
|---|---|---|---|---|---|---|---|
| **Assets** | | **Liabilities/Equity** | | **Assets** | | **Liabilities/Equity** | |
| Cash assets | $ 10 | Deposits | $ 90 | Cash assets | $ 0 | Deposits | $75 |
| Nonliquid | | | | Nonliquid | | | |
| assets | 90 | Equity | 10 | assets | 80 | Equity | 5 |
| | $100 | | $100 | | $80 | | $80 |

---

**EXAMPLE 19–2**   **Impact of Liquidity Risk on an FI's Equity Value**

Consider the simple FI balance sheet in Table 19–2. Before deposit withdrawals, the FI has $10 million in cash assets and $90 million in nonliquid assets (such as small business loans). These assets were funded with $90 million in deposits and $10 million in owner's equity. Suppose that depositors unexpectedly withdraw $15 million in deposits (perhaps due to the release of negative news about the profits of the FI) and the FI receives no new deposits to replace them. To meet these deposit withdrawals, the FI first uses the $10 million it has in cash assets and then seeks to sell some of its nonliquid assets to raise an additional $5 million in cash. Assume that the FI cannot borrow any more funds in the short-term money markets (see Chapter 5), and because it cannot wait to get better prices for its assets in the future (as it needs the cash now to meet immediate depositor withdrawals), the FI has to sell any nonliquid assets at 50 cents on the dollar. Thus, to cover the remaining $5 million in deposit withdrawals, the FI must sell $10 million in non-liquid assets, incurring a loss of $5 million from the face value of those assets. The FI must then write off any such losses against its capital or equity funds. Since its capital was only $10 million before the deposit withdrawal, the loss on the fire sale of assets of $5 million leaves the FI with $5 million.

---

**DO YOU UNDERSTAND:**

3.  *Why an FI might face a sudden liquidity crisis?*

4.  *What circumstances might lead an FI to liquidate assets at fire-sale prices?*

Chapter 21 examines the nature of normal, abnormal, and run-type liquidity risks and their impact on banks, thrifts, insurance companies, and other FIs in more detail. In addition, it looks at ways in which an FI can measure liquidity risk and better manage liquidity and liability risk exposures. Recall that Chapter 13 discussed the roles of deposit insurance and other liability guarantees in deterring deposit or other liability runs in depository institutions.

## INTEREST RATE RISK

**interest rate risk**

*The risk incurred by an FI when the maturities of its assets and liabilities are mismatched and interest rates are volatile.*

Chapter 1 discussed asset transformation as a special or key function of FIs. *Asset transformation* involves an FI buying primary securities or assets and issuing secondary securities or liabilities to fund the assets. The primary securities that FIs purchase often have maturity characteristics different from the secondary securities that FIs sell. In mismatching the maturities of its assets and liabilities as part of its asset transformation function, an FI potentially exposes itself to **interest rate risk.**

---

**EXAMPLE 19–3**   **Impact of an Interest Rate Increase on an FI's Profit When the Maturity of Assets Exceeds the Maturity of Liabilities**

Consider an FI that issues $100 million of liabilities with one year to maturity to finance the purchase of $100 million of assets with a two-year maturity. We show this in the following time lines:

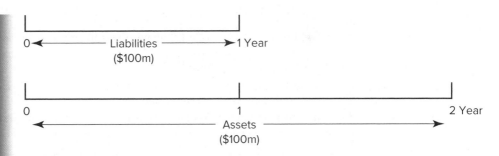

Suppose that the cost of funds (liabilities) for the FI is 9 percent in year 1 and the interest return on the assets is 10 percent per year. Over the first year, the FI can lock in a profit spread of 1 percent (10 percent – 9 percent) times $100 million by borrowing short term (for one year) and lending long term (for two years). Thus, its profit is $1 million (0.01 × 100m).

Its profit for the second year, however, is uncertain. If the level of interest rates does not change, the FI can *refinance* its liabilities at 9 percent and lock in a 1 percent or $1 million profit for the second year as well. The risk always exists, however, that interest rates will change between years 1 and 2. If interest rates rise and the FI can borrow new one-year liabilities at only 11 percent in the second year, its profit spread in the second year is actually negative; that is, 10 percent – 11 percent = –1 percent, or the FI loses $1 million (–0.01 × 100m). The positive spread earned in the first year by the FI from holding assets with a longer maturity than its liabilities is offset by a negative spread in the second year. Note that if interest rates were to rise by more than 2 percent in the second year, the FI would stand to make losses over the two-year period as a whole. As a result, when an FI holds longer-term assets relative to liabilities, it potentially exposes itself to **refinancing risk.** Refinancing risk is a type of interest rate risk in that the cost of refinancing can be more than the return earned on asset investments. As interest rates rose in the mid-2010s, good examples of this exposure were provided by banks that borrowed short-term deposits (deposits whose interest rates changed or adjusted frequently), while investing in fixed-rate loans (loans whose interest rates changed or adjusted infrequently).

**refinancing risk**

*The risk that the cost of rolling over or reborrowing funds will rise above the returns being earned on asset investments.*

---

**EXAMPLE 19–4**    Impact of an Interest Rate Decrease on an FI's Profit When the Maturity of Liabilities Exceeds the Maturity of Assets

An alternative balance sheet structure would have the FI borrowing $100 million for a longer term than the $100 million of assets in which it invests. This is shown as follows:

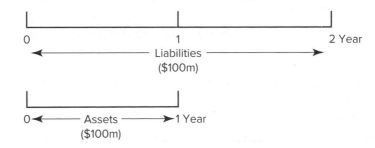

In this case, the FI is also exposed to interest rate risk; by holding shorter-term assets relative to liabilities, it faces uncertainty about the interest rate at which it can *reinvest* funds in the second year. As before, suppose that the cost of funds for the FI is 9 percent per year over the two years and the interest rate on assets is 10 percent in the first year. Over the first year, the FI can lock in a profit spread of 1 percent, or $1 million. If in the second year interest rates on $100 million invested in new one-year assets decreases to

**reinvestment risk**

*The risk that the returns on funds to be reinvested will fall below the cost of funds.*

8 percent, the FI's profit spread is negative 1 percent (8 percent − 9 percent), or the FI loses $1 million (−0.01 × $100m). The positive spread earned in the first year by the FI from holding assets with a shorter maturity than its liabilities is offset by a negative spread in the second year. Thus, the FI is exposed to **reinvestment risk;** by holding shorter-term assets relative to liabilities, it faces uncertainty about the interest rate at which it can reinvest funds borrowed over a longer period. In recent years, good examples of this exposure are banks operating in the Euromarkets that have borrowed fixed-rate deposits while investing in floating-rate loans—loans whose interest rates are changed or adjusted frequently.

**price risk**

*The risk that the price of the security will change when interest rates change.*

In addition to a potential refinancing or reinvestment effect, an FI faces **price risk** or *market value* uncertainty as well when interest rates change. Remember that the economic or fair market value of an asset or liability is conceptually equal to the present value of the current and future cash flows on that asset or liability. Therefore, rising interest rates increase the discount rate on future asset (liability) cash flows and reduce the market price or present value of that asset or liability. Conversely, falling interest rates increase the present value of the cash flows from assets and liabilities. Moreover, mismatching maturities by holding longer-term assets than liabilities means that when interest rates rise, the economic or present value of the FI's assets falls by a larger amount than its liabilities. This exposes the FI to the risk of economic loss and potentially to the risk of insolvency.

If holding assets and liabilities with mismatched maturities exposes FIs to interest rate risk, FIs can seek to hedge or protect themselves against interest rate risk by matching the maturity of their assets and liabilities.[3] This has resulted in the general philosophy that matching maturities is somehow the best policy for FIs averse to risk. Note, however, that matching maturities is not necessarily consistent with an active asset transformation function for FIs. That is, FIs cannot be asset transformers (i.e., transforming short-term deposits into long-term loans) and direct balance sheet matchers or hedgers at the same time. Although it does reduce exposure to interest rate risk, matching maturities may reduce the FI's profitability because returns from acting as specialized risk-bearing asset transformers are reduced. As a result, some FIs emphasize asset–liability maturity mismatching more than others. For example, depository institutions traditionally hold longer-term assets than liabilities, whereas life insurers tend to match the long-term nature of their liabilities with long-term assets. Finally, matching maturities hedges interest rate risk only in a very approximate rather than complete fashion. The reasons for this are technical, relating to the difference between the average life (or duration) and maturity of an asset or liability and whether the FI partly funds its assets with equity capital as well as liabilities. In the preceding simple examples, the FI financed its assets completely with borrowed funds. In the real world, FIs use a mix of liabilities and stockholders' equity to finance asset purchases. When assets and liabilities are not equal, hedging risk (i.e., insulating FIs' stockholder's equity values) may be achieved by not exactly matching the maturities (or average lives) of assets and liabilities (see Chapter 22). We discuss the *causes* of interest rate risk and methods used to *measure* interest rate risk in detail in Chapter 22. We discuss the instruments and methods to *hedge* interest rate risk in Chapters 10 and 23.

**DO YOU UNDERSTAND:**

5. *What refinancing risk is?*

6. *Why a rise in the level of interest rates adversely affects the market value of both assets and liabilities?*

7. *What the concept of maturity matching means?*

## MARKET RISK

**market risk**

*The risk incurred in trading assets and liabilities due to changes in interest rates, exchange rates, and other asset prices.*

**Market risk** arises when FIs actively trade assets and liabilities (and derivatives) rather than holding them for longer-term investment, funding, or hedging purposes. Market risk is closely related to interest rate and foreign exchange risk in that as these risks increase or decrease, the overall risk of the FI is affected. However, market risk adds another dimension of risk: trading activity. Market risk is the incremental risk incurred by an FI when

---

3. This assumes that FIs can directly "control" the maturity of their assets and liabilities. As interest rates fall, many mortgage borrowers seek to "prepay" their existing loans and refinance at a lower rate. This prepayment risk—which is directly related to interest rate movements—can be viewed as a further interest rate–related risk (see Chapters 7 and 24).

interest rate and foreign exchange risks are combined with an active trading strategy, especially one that involves short trading horizons such as a day.[4]

Conceptually, an FI's trading portfolio can be differentiated from its investment portfolio on the basis of time horizon and liquidity. The trading portfolio contains assets, liabilities, and derivative contracts that can be quickly bought or sold on organized financial markets. The investment portfolio (or in the case of banks, the "banking book") contains assets and liabilities that are relatively illiquid and held for longer periods. Table 19–3 shows a hypothetical breakdown between banking book and trading book assets and liabilities. Note that capital produces a cushion against losses on either the banking or trading books (see Chapter 22). As can be seen, the banking book contains the majority of loans and deposits plus other illiquid assets. The trading book contains long and short positions in instruments such as bonds, commodities, foreign exchange, equities, and derivatives.

As discussed in Chapters 11 through 18, the traditional roles of many financial institutions have changed in recent years. For example, for large commercial banks such as money center banks, the decline in income from traditional deposit taking and lending activities has been matched by an increased reliance on income from trading. Similarly, the decline in underwriting and brokerage income for large investment banks has also been met by more active and aggressive trading in securities, derivatives, and other assets. Mutual fund managers, who actively manage their asset portfolios, are also exposed to market risk. Of course, with time, every asset and liability can be sold. While bank regulators have normally viewed tradable assets as those being held for horizons of less than one year, private FIs take an even shorter-term view. In particular, FIs are concerned about the fluctuation in value—or value at risk (VAR)—of their trading account assets and liabilities for periods as short as one day—so-called daily earnings at risk (DEAR)—especially if such fluctuations pose a threat to their solvency.

An extreme case of the type of risk involved in active trading is, of course, the financial crisis of 2008–2009. As mortgage borrowers defaulted on their mortgages, financial institutions that held these mortgages and mortgage-backed securities started announcing huge losses on them. These securitized loans—and particularly, securitized subprime mortgage loans—led to the huge financial losses resulting from market risk. Investment banks and securities firms were major purchasers of mortgages and mortgage-backed securities in the early 2000s, which allowed them to increase their business of packaging the loans as securities. As mortgage borrowers defaulted on their mortgages, the securitized mortgage market froze and FIs were left holding these "toxic" assets at deeply reduced market values. By mid-September 2008, financial markets had frozen. Banks stopped lending to each other at anything but exorbitantly high rates, and some mark-to-market securities had to be priced in some cases using asset pricing models rather than trades because trades did not take place. Banks that were active traders faced extreme market risk.

## DO YOU UNDERSTAND:

8. *What market risk is?*
9. *What conditions have led to an increase in market risk for FIs?*

**TABLE 19–3** The Investment (Banking) Book and Trading Book of a Commercial Bank

|  | Assets | Liabilities |
|---|---|---|
| Banking book | Loans | Capital |
|  | Other illiquid assets | Deposits |
| Trading book | Bonds (long) | Bonds (short) |
|  | Commodities (long) | Commodities (short) |
|  | FX (long) | FX (short) |
|  | Equities (long) | Equities (short) |
|  | Derivatives* (long) | Derivatives* (short) |

*Derivatives are off-balance-sheet (as discussed in Chapter 10).

4. This market or trading risk is not the same as the concept of "market risk" used in asset portfolio management (often called beta [$\beta$] risk).

The financial market crisis illustrates trading or market risk—the risk that when an FI takes an open or unhedged long (buy) or short (sell) position in bonds, equities, commodities, and derivatives, prices may change in a direction opposite to that expected. As a result, as the volatility of asset prices increases, the market risks faced by FIs that adopt open trading positions increase. This requires FI management (and regulators) to establish controls or limits on positions taken by traders as well as to develop models to measure the market risk exposure of an FI on a day-to-day basis.

## OFF-BALANCE-SHEET RISK

**off-balance-sheet risk**

*The risk incurred by an FI as the result of activities related to contingent assets and liabilities.*

One of the most striking trends involving FIs has been the growth in their off-balance-sheet (OBS) activities and thus, their **off-balance-sheet risks.** The value of on-balance-sheet items for commercial banks in 2016 was $15.029 trillion, while the face or notional value of their off-balance-sheet derivative items was $189.832 trillion. Although all FIs to some extent engage in off-balance-sheet activities, most attention has been drawn to the activities of banks, especially large banks that invest heavily in off-balance-sheet assets and liabilities, particularly derivative securities. Off-balance-sheet activities have been less of a concern to smaller depository institutions and many insurers. An off-balance-sheet activity, by definition, does not appear on an FI's current balance sheet since it does not involve holding a current primary claim (asset) or the issuance of a current secondary claim (liability). Instead, off-balance-sheet activities affect the *future,* rather than the current, shape of an FI's balance sheet. They involve the creation of **contingent assets and liabilities** that give rise to their potential placement in the future on the balance sheet. As such, they have a direct impact on the FI's future profitability and performance. Thus, accountants place them "below the bottom line" on an FI's balance sheet.

**contingent assets and liabilities**

*Assets and liabilities off the balance sheet that potentially can produce positive or negative future cash flows for an FI.*

An example of an off-balance-sheet activity is the issuance of standby **letter of credit** guarantees by insurance companies and banks to back the issuance of municipal bonds. Many state and local governments could not issue such securities without bank or insurance company letter of credit guarantees that promise principal and interest payments to investors should the municipality default on its obligations in the future. Thus, the letter of credit guarantees payment should a municipal government (e.g., New York State) face financial problems in paying either the promised interest and/or principal payments on the bonds it issues. If a municipal government's cash flow is sufficiently strong to pay off the principal and interest on the debt it issues, the letter of credit guarantee issued by the FI expires unused. Nothing appears on the FI's balance sheet today or in the future. However, the fee earned for issuing the letter of credit guarantee appears on the FI's income statement (see Chapter 12).

**letter of credit**

*A credit guarantee issued by an FI for a fee on which payment is contingent on some future event occurring, most notably default of the agent that purchases the letter of credit.*

The ability to earn fee income while not loading up or expanding the balance sheet has become an important motivation for FIs to pursue off-balance-sheet business. Unfortunately, this activity is not risk free. Off-balance-sheet securities played a prominent role in the U.S. subprime mortgage crisis. According to critics, these securities hid the underlying risk in mortgage investments because the ratings on various securities, such as mortgage-backed securities (MBSs) and collateralized mortgage obligations (CMOs), were based on misleading or incorrect information about the creditworthiness of the borrowers. For a variety of reasons, market participants did not accurately measure the risk inherent in these financial innovations or understand their potential impact on the overall stability of the financial system. For example, the pricing model for CMOs clearly did not reflect the level of risk they introduced into the system. During the financial crisis, the average recovery rate for "high-quality" CMOs was approximately 32 cents on the dollar, while the recovery rate for "low-quality" CMOs was approximately five cents for every dollar. These huge losses dramatically impacted the balance sheets of FIs worldwide, leaving them with very little capital to continue operations. As off-balance-sheet financial assets became more and more complex, and harder and harder to value, investors were reassured by the fact that both the international bond rating agencies and bank regulators, who came to rely on them, accepted as valid some complex mathematical models which theoretically showed the risks were much smaller than they actually proved to be in practice. In fact, the new products became so complicated that the authorities could no longer calculate the risks and started relying on the risk management methods of the banks themselves. Similarly, the rating agencies relied on the information provided by the originators of synthetic products—a massive abdication of responsibility.

Letters of credit and CMOs are just two examples of off-balance-sheet activities. Others include loan commitments by banks, mortgage servicing contracts by depository institutions, and positions in forwards, futures, swaps, and other derivative securities by almost all large FIs. While some of these activities are structured to reduce an FI's exposure to credit, interest rate, or foreign exchange risks, mismanagement or speculative use of these instruments can result in major losses to FIs. Indeed, as seen during the financial crisis of 2008–2009, significant losses in off-balance-sheet activities (e.g., credit default swaps) can cause an FI to fail, just as major losses due to balance sheet default and interest rate risks can cause an FI to fail.

**DO YOU UNDERSTAND:**

10. *Why FIs are motivated to pursue off-balance-sheet business? What are the risks?*

11. *Why letter of credit guarantees are an off-balance-sheet item?*

---

### EXAMPLE 19–5    Impact of Off-Balance-Sheet Risk on an FI's Equity Value

Consider Table 19–4. In Panel A, the value of the FI's net worth ($E$) is calculated in the traditional way as the difference between the market values of its on-balance-sheet assets ($A$) and liabilities ($L$):

$$E = A - L$$
$$10 = 100 - 90$$

Under this calculation, the market value of the stockholders' equity stake in the FI is 10 and the ratio of the FI's capital to assets (or capital-to-assets ratio) is 10 percent. Regulators and FIs often use this ratio as a simple measure of solvency (see Chapter 13 for more details).

A more accurate picture of the FI's economic solvency should consider the market values of both its on-balance-sheet and OBS activities (Panel B of Table 19–4). Specifically, the FI manager should value contingent or future asset and liability claims as well as current assets and liabilities. In our example, the current market value of the FI's contingent assets ($CA$) is 50; the current market value of its contingent liabilities ($CL$) is 55. Since $CL$ exceeds $CA$ by 5, this difference is an additional obligation, or claim, on the

**TABLE 19–4**    Valuation of an FI's Net Worth with and without Consideration of Off-Balance-Sheet Activities

| Assets | | Liabilities | |
|---|---|---|---|
| **Panel A: Traditional valuation of an FI's net worth** | | | |
| Market value of assets ($A$) | 100 | Market value of liabilities ($L$) | 90 |
| | | Net worth ($E$) | 10 |
| | 100 | | 100 |
| **Panel B: Valuation of an FI's net worth with on- and off-balance-sheet activities valued** | | | |
| Market value of assets ($A$) | 100 | Market value of liabilities ($L$) | 90 |
| | | Net worth ($E$) | 5 |
| Market value of contingent assets ($CA$) | 50 | Market value of contingent liabilities ($CL$) | 55 |
| | 150 | | 150 |

FI's net worth. That is, stockholders' true net worth ($E$) is really 5 rather than 10 when we ignored off-balance-sheet activities:

$$
\begin{aligned}
E &= (A - L) + (CA - CL) \\
&= (100 - 90) + (50 - 55) \\
&= 5
\end{aligned}
$$

Thus, economically speaking, contingent assets and liabilities are contractual claims that directly impact the economic value of the equity holders' stake in an FI. Indeed, from both the stockholders' and regulators' perspectives, large increases in the value of OBS liabilities can render the FI economically insolvent just as effectively as losses due to mismatched interest rate gaps and default or credit losses from on-balance-sheet activities.

We detailed the specific nature of the risks of off-balance-sheet activities and instruments more fully in Chapter 12. We also look at how some of these instruments (forwards, futures, swaps, and options) can be used to manage risk in Chapter 23.

## FOREIGN EXCHANGE RISK

FIs have increasingly recognized that both direct foreign investment and foreign portfolio investment can extend the operational and financial benefits available from purely domestic investments. Thus, U.S. pension funds that held approximately 5 percent of their assets in foreign securities in the early 1990s now hold close to 13 percent of their assets in foreign securities. At the same time, many large U.S. banks, investment banks, and mutual funds have become more global in their orientation. To the extent that the returns on domestic and foreign investments are imperfectly correlated, FIs can reduce risk through domestic–foreign activity/investment diversification.

The returns on domestic and foreign direct investments and portfolio investments are not perfectly correlated for two reasons. The first is that the underlying technologies of various economies differ, as do the firms in those economies. For example, one economy may be agriculturally based and another industry based. Given different economic infrastructures, one economy could be expanding while another is contracting—in the mid-2010s, for example, the U.S. economy was expanding while the European economy was recessionary. The second reason is that exchange rate changes are not perfectly correlated across countries: the dollar–euro exchange rate may be appreciating while the dollar–yen exchange rate may be depreciating.

One potential benefit to an FI from becoming increasingly global in its outlook is an ability to expand abroad directly through branching or acquisitions or by indirectly developing a financial asset portfolio that includes foreign as well as domestic securities. Even so, foreign investment activities expose an FI to **foreign exchange risk.** Foreign exchange risk is the risk that exchange rate changes can adversely affect the value of an FI's assets and liabilities denominated in foreign currencies.

Chapter 9 introduced the basics of FX markets and risks by discussing how events in other countries affect an FI's return-risk opportunities. Foreign exchange risks can occur either directly as the result of trading in foreign currencies, making foreign currency loans (a loan in British pounds to a corporation), buying foreign-issued securities (British pound–denominated bonds or euro-denominated government bonds), or issuing foreign currency–denominated debt (British pound–denominated certificates of deposit) as a source of funds.

To understand how foreign exchange risk arises, suppose that a U.S. FI makes a loan to a British company in pounds (£). Should the British pound depreciate in value relative to the U.S. dollar, the principal and interest payments received by the U.S. FI would be devalued in dollar terms. Indeed, were the British pound to fall far enough over the investment period, when cash flows are converted back into dollars, the overall return could be negative. That is, on the conversion of principal and interest payments from pounds into dollars,

**foreign exchange risks**

*The risk that exchange rate changes can affect the value of an FI's assets and liabilities denominated in foreign currencies.*

**Figure 19–3** The Foreign Asset and Liability Position: A Net Long Asset Position in Pounds

foreign exchange losses can offset the promised value of local currency interest payments at the original exchange rate at which the investment occurred.

In general, an FI can hold assets denominated in a foreign currency and/or issue foreign liabilities. Consider a U.S. FI that holds £100 million British pound loans as assets and funds £80 million of them with British pound certificates of deposit. The difference between the £100 million in pound loans and the £80 million in pound CDs is funded by dollar CDs (i.e., £20 million pounds worth of dollar CDs). See Figure 19–3. In this case, the U.S. FI is net long £20 million in British assets. That is, it holds more foreign assets than liabilities. The U.S. FI suffers losses if the exchange rate for pounds falls or depreciates against the dollar over this period. In dollar terms, the value of the British pound loan assets falls or decreases in value by more than the British pound CD liabilities do. That is, the FI is exposed to the risk that its net foreign assets may have to be liquidated at an exchange rate lower than the one that existed when the FI entered into the foreign asset–liability position.

Instead, the FI could have £20 million more foreign liabilities than assets. In this case, it would be holding a net short position in foreign assets, as shown in Figure 19–4. Under this circumstance, the FI is exposed to foreign exchange risk if the pound appreciates against the dollar over the investment period. This occurs because the value of its British pound liabilities in dollar terms rose faster than the return on its pound assets. Consequently, to be approximately hedged, the FI must match its assets and liabilities in each foreign currency.

Note that the FI is fully hedged only if we assume that it holds foreign assets and liabilities of exactly the same maturity. Consider what happens if the FI matches the size of its foreign currency book (British pound assets = British pound liabilities = £100 million in that currency) but mismatches the maturities so that the pound assets are of six-month maturity and the liabilities are of three-month maturity. The FI would then be exposed to foreign interest rate risk—the risk that British interest rates would rise when it has to roll over its £100 million British CD liabilities at the end of the third month. Consequently, an FI that matches both the size and maturities of its exposures in assets and liabilities of a given currency is hedged or immunized against foreign currency and foreign interest rate risk. To the extent that FIs mismatch their portfolio and maturity exposures in different currency assets and liabilities, they face both foreign currency and foreign interest rate risks. As already noted, if foreign exchange rate and interest rate changes are not perfectly correlated across countries, an FI can diversify away part, if not all, of its foreign currency risk.

**DO YOU UNDERSTAND:**

**12.** *Why the returns on domestic and foreign portfolio investments are not, in general, perfectly correlated?*

**Figure 19–4** The Foreign Asset and Liability Position: A Net Short Asset Position in Pounds

## COUNTRY OR SOVEREIGN RISK

**country or
sovereign risk**

*The risk that repayments
from foreign borrow-
ers may be interrupted
because of interference
from foreign governments.*

A globally oriented FI that mismatches the size and maturities of its foreign assets and liabilities is exposed to foreign currency risk. Even beyond this risk, and even when investing in dollars, holding assets in a foreign country can expose an FI to an additional type of foreign investment risk called **country or sovereign risk.** Country or sovereign risk is different from the type of credit risk that is faced by an FI that purchases domestic assets such as the bonds and loans of domestic corporations. For example, when a domestic corporation is unable or unwilling to repay a loan, an FI usually has recourse to the domestic bankruptcy court and eventually may recoup at least a portion of its original investment when the assets of the defaulted firm are liquidated or restructured. By comparison, a foreign corporation may be unable to repay the principal or interest on a loan even if it would like to do so. Most commonly, the government of the country in which the corporation is headquartered may prohibit or limit debt repayments due to foreign currency shortages and adverse political events. Thus, sovereign risk is a broader measure of the risk faced by FIs that operate abroad. Measuring such exposure or risk includes an analysis of macroeconomic issues such as trade policy, the fiscal stance (deficit or surplus) of the government, government intervention in the economy, its monetary policy, capital flows and foreign investment, inflation, and the structure of its financial system.

For example, in 2001 the government of Argentina, which had pegged its peso to the dollar on a one-to-one basis since the early 1990s, had to default on its government debt largely because of an overvalued peso and the adverse effect this had on its exports and foreign currency earnings. In December 2001 Argentina ended up defaulting on $130 billion in government-issued debt, and in 2002 it passed legislation that led to defaults on $30 billion of corporate debt owed to foreign creditors. Argentina's economic problems continued into the 2000s and even the 2010s. In September 2003, it defaulted on a $3 billion loan to the IMF, and in early 2015 Argentina was still asking holdouts to accept a haircut of 65 percent on the bond principal. Another case of extreme sovereign risk is the European crisis of the 2010s. Despite massive injections of bailout funds by Euro-zone countries and the International Monetary Fund, in March 2012 Greek government debtholders lost 53.5 percent of their $265 billion investment as Greece restructured much of its sovereign debt. The restructuring produced the largest-ever sovereign debt default.

In the event of restrictions or outright prohibitions on the payment of debt obligations by sovereign governments, the FI claimholder has little if any recourse to local bankruptcy courts or to an international civil claims court. The major leverage available to an FI, to ensure or increase repayment probabilities, is its control over the future supply of loans or funds to the country concerned. Such leverage may be very weak, however, in the face of a country's collapsing currency and government.

**DO YOU UNDERSTAND:**

13. *How an FI can be subject to
    sovereign risk even if it lends
    to the highest-quality foreign
    corporations?*

14. *How an FI can discipline a
    country that threatens not to
    repay its loans?*

## TECHNOLOGY AND OPERATIONAL RISK

**www.bis.org**

Technology and operational risks are closely related and in recent years have caused great concern to FI managers and regulators alike. The Bank for International Settlements (BIS), the principal organization of central banks in the major economies of the world, defines operational risk (inclusive of technological risk) as "the risk of loss resulting from inadequate or failed internal processes, people, and systems or from external events."[5] A number of FIs add reputational risk and strategic risk (e.g., due to a failed merger) as part of a broader definition of operational risk.

Technological innovation has been a major concern of FIs in recent years (see Chapter 11). Banks, insurance companies, and investment companies have sought to improve their operational efficiency with major investments in internal and external communications,

---

5. See Basel Committee on Bank Supervision, *Sound Practices for the Management and Supervision of Operational Risk,* Bank for International Settlements, December 2010, p. 23. www.bis.org

computers, and an expanded technological infrastructure. For example, most banks provide depositors with the capabilities to check account balances, transfer funds between accounts, manage finances, pay bills, and more from their various personal electronic devices. At the wholesale level, electronic transfers of funds through the automated clearinghouses (ACHs) and wire transfer payment networks such as the Clearing House Interbank Payments System (CHIPS) have been developed. Indeed, a global financial service firm such as Citigroup has operations in more than 100 countries connected in real time by a proprietary satellite system.

The major objectives of technological expansion are to lower operating costs, increase profits, and capture new markets for an FI. In current terminology, the object is to allow the FI to exploit, to the fullest extent possible, potential economies of scale and economies of scope in selling its products (see Chapter 11). For example, an FI could use the same information on the quality of customers stored in its computers to expand the sale of both loan products and insurance products—the same information (e.g., age, job, size of family, or income) can identify both potential loan and life insurance customers.

**technology risk**

*The risk incurred by an FI when its technological investments do not produce anticipated cost savings.*

**Technology risk** occurs when technological investments do not produce the anticipated cost savings in the form of either economies of scale or economies of scope. Diseconomies of scale, for example, arise because of excess capacity, redundant technology, and/or organizational and bureaucratic inefficiencies that become worse as an FI grows in size. Diseconomies of scope arise when an FI fails to generate perceived synergies or cost savings through major new technological investments. Technological risk can result in major losses in an FI's competitive efficiency and ultimately result in its long-term failure. Similarly, gains from technological investments can produce performance superior to an FI's rivals as well as allow it to develop new and innovative products enhancing its long-term survival chances.

**operational risk**

*The risk that existing technology or support systems may malfunction or break down.*

**Operational risk** is partly related to technology risk and can arise when existing technology malfunctions or "back-office" support systems break down. For example, the biggest known theft of credit card numbers was discovered in 2009, when as many as 130 million credit and debit card numbers were stolen from Heartland Payment Systems. Malware planted on Heartland's network recorded card data as they arrived from retailers. Another notable instance is that of Target Stores in 2013. Hackers infected the company's payment card readers, making off with 110 million records at the height of the Christmas shopping season. Even though such computer and data problems are rare, their occurrence can cause major dislocations for the FIs involved and potentially disrupt the financial system in general.

Operational risk is not exclusively the result of technological failure. Other sources of operational risk can result in direct costs (e.g., loss of income), indirect costs (e.g., client withdrawals and legal costs), and opportunity costs (e.g., forgone business opportunities) that reduce an FI's profitability and market value. A good example of operational risk involved $6.2 billion in losses incurred by J.P. Morgan Chase's trader, Bruno Iksil, also known as "the London Whale." Iksil took large credit default swap (CDS) positions in expectation that the financial crisis in Europe would cause anxiety in the financial markets. Instead, bailouts, austerity measures, and interventions prevented any major disruption from occurring in Europe. To maintain the proper balance and deal with expiring contracts, Iksil needed to continually make new trades. But the CDS market was too small and the amounts Iksil was trading were too large to let J.P. Morgan operate in secrecy. Once the story got out, hedge fund traders took positions designed to gain from the trades that Iksil had to make to keep the position going. That activity negatively altered prices on the CDSs that Iksil needed. Eventually the only choice was to close the CDS position and take the loss. Activities such as these by employees of FIs result in an overall loss of reputation and, in turn, a loss of business for FI employers. Indeed, the Federal Reserve defines reputational risk as the potential that negative publicity regarding an institution's business practices, whether true or not, will cause a decline in the customer base, costly litigation, or revenue reductions. The Fed includes this type of operational risk as part of its principles of sound management in banking institutions.

**DO YOU UNDERSTAND:**

15. *How operational risk is related to technology risk?*

16. *How technological expansion can help an FI better exploit economies of scale and economies of scope?*

## INSOLVENCY RISK

LG 19-2

**insolvency risk**

*The risk that an FI may not have enough capital to off-set a sudden decline in the value of its assets relative to its liabilities.*

**Insolvency risk** is a consequence or an outcome of one or more of the risks described above: interest rate, market, credit, off-balance-sheet, technological, foreign exchange, sovereign, and liquidity. Technically, insolvency occurs when the capital or equity resources of an FI's owners are driven to, or near to, zero due to losses incurred as the result of one or more of the risks described previously. Consider the case of Washington Mutual (WaMu), which incurred heavy losses from its on- and off-balance-sheet holdings during the financial crisis. By early September 2008, WaMu's market capital was worth only $3.5 billion, down from $43 billion at the end of 2006. In September 2008, the bank was taken over by the FDIC and sold to J.P. Morgan Chase. In contrast, in March 2009 Citigroup's stock price fell to below $1 per share and the once largest bank in the United States was near failure. Proving that some banks are too big to fail, Citigroup received a substantial government guarantee against losses (up to $306 billion) and a $20 billion injection of cash to prevent failure. Indeed, between October 2008 and December 2009 over 700 banks had received a total of $205 billion in federal government funds (through the Capital Purchase Program) in an effort to prop up capital and support lending.[6]

In general, the more equity capital to borrowed funds an FI has—that is, the lower its leverage—the better able it is to withstand losses due to risk exposures such as adverse liquidity changes, unexpected credit losses, and so on. Thus, both the management and regulators of FIs focus on an FI's capital (and its "adequacy") as a key measure of its ability to remain solvent and grow in the face of a multitude of risk exposures. Chapter 13 discusses the issue of what is considered to be an adequate level of capital to manage an FI's overall risk exposure.

**DO YOU UNDERSTAND:**

17. When insolvency risk occurs?

18. How insolvency risk is related to credit risk and liquidity risk?

## OTHER RISKS AND INTERACTION AMONG RISKS

LG 19-3

This overview chapter concentrated on 10 major risks continuously impacting an FI manager's decision-making process and risk management strategy. These risks were credit risk, liquidity risk, interest rate risk, market risk, off-balance-sheet risk, foreign exchange risk, country or sovereign risk, technology risk, operational risk, and insolvency risk. Even though the discussion generally described each independently, in reality these risks are interdependent. For example, when interest rates rise, corporations and consumers find maintaining promised payments on their debt more difficult. Thus, over some range of interest rate movements, credit and interest rate risks are positively correlated. Furthermore, the FI may have been counting on the funds from promised payments on its loans for liquidity management purposes. Thus, liquidity risk is also correlated with interest rate and credit risks. The inability of a customer to make promised payments also affects the FI's income and profits and, consequently, its equity or capital position. Thus, each risk and its interaction with other risks ultimately affects solvency risk. The interaction of the various risks also means that FI managers face making complicated trade-offs. In particular, as they take actions to manage one type of risk, FI managers must consider the possible impact of such actions on other risks.

Various other risks also impact an FI's profitability and risk exposure. Discrete risks include a sudden change in taxation, such as the Tax Reform Act of 1986, which subjected banks to a minimum corporate tax rate of 20 percent (the alternative minimum tax) and limited their ability to expense the cost of funds used to purchase tax-free municipal bonds. Such changes can affect the attractiveness of some types of assets over others, as well as the liquidity of an FI's balance sheet. For example, banks' demand for municipal bonds fell quite dramatically following the 1986 tax law change. As a result, the municipal bond market became quite illiquid for a time.

Changes in regulatory policy constitute another type of discrete or event-type risk. These include lifting the regulatory barriers to lending or to entry or on products offered (see Chapter 13). The 1999 Financial Services Modernization Act is one example, as is the 2010 Wall Street Reform and Consumer Protection Act. Other discrete or event risks involve sudden

---

6. Of this total investment, $226.7 billion had been repaid through October 2016.

and unexpected changes in financial market conditions due to war, revolution, or sudden market collapse, such as the 1929, 1987, and 2008 stock market crashes or the September 2001 terrorist attacks in the United States. These can have a major impact on an FI's risk exposure. Other event risks include theft, malfeasance, and breach of fiduciary trust. All of these can ultimately cause an FI to fail or be severely harmed. Yet, each is difficult to model and predict.

More general macroeconomic risks such as increased inflation, inflation volatility, and unemployment can directly and indirectly impact an FI's level of interest rate, credit, and liquidity risk exposure. For example, the U.S. unemployment rate was over 10 percent in the summer of 2009, the highest level since September 1992. Since December 2007 (as the recession began), the U.S. economy lost over 6 million jobs, half of which were lost in the period November 2008 through June 2009. With so many people out of work, the credit risk exposure of FIs increased dramatically as borrowers had trouble keeping up with their loan payments after losing their jobs.

> **DO YOU UNDERSTAND:**
>
> 19. *What the term* event risk *means?*
> 20. *The event and general macroeconomic risks facing FIs?*

## SUMMARY

This chapter provided an overview of the major risks that modern FIs face. FIs face *credit risk* or default risk if their clients default on their loans and other obligations. They encounter *liquidity risk* as a result of excessive withdrawals of liabilities by customers. They face *interest rate risk* when the maturities of their assets and liabilities are mismatched. They incur *market risk* for their trading portfolios of assets and liabilities if adverse movements in the prices of these assets or liabilities occur. FIs also engage in significant amounts of off-balance-sheet activities, thereby exposing them to *off-balance-sheet risks*—changing values of their contingent assets and liabilities. If FIs conduct foreign business, they are subject to *foreign exchange risk.* Business dealings in foreign countries or with foreign companies also subject FIs to *country* or *sovereign risk.* The advent of sophisticated technology and automation increasingly exposes FIs to both *technological* and *operational risks.* FIs face *insolvency risk* when their overall equity capital is insufficient to withstand the losses that they incur as a result of such risk exposures. The effective management of these risks—including the interaction among them—determines the ability of a modern FI to survive and prosper over the long run. The chapters that follow analyze these risks in greater detail, beginning with those risks incurred on the balance sheet.

## QUESTIONS

1. What is *credit risk?* Which types of FIs are more susceptible to this type of risk? Why? (*LG 19-1*)

2. What is the difference between firm-specific credit risk and systemic credit risk? How can an FI alleviate firm-specific credit risk? (*LG 19-1*)

3. In the 1980s, many thrifts that failed had made loans to oil companies located in Louisiana, Texas, and Oklahoma. When oil prices fell, these companies, the regional economy, and the thrifts all experienced financial problems. What types of risk were inherent in the loans that these thrifts had made? (*LG 19-1*)

4. What is *liquidity risk?* What routine operating factors allow FIs to deal with this risk in times of normal economic activity? What market reality can create severe financial difficulty for an FI in times of extreme liquidity crises? (*LG 19-1*)

5. Which type of cash withdrawal presents very little liquidity risk? Which type of cash withdrawal is a source of significant liquidity risk for DIs? (*LG 19-1*)

6. What is the process of *asset transformation* performed by a financial institution? Why does this process often lead to the creation of *interest rate risk?* What is interest rate risk? (*LG 19-1*)

7. What is *refinancing risk?* How is refinancing risk part of interest rate risk? If an FI funds long-term fixed-rate assets with short-term liabilities, what will be the impact on earnings of an increase in the rate of interest? A decrease in the rate of interest? (*LG 19-1*)

8. What is *reinvestment risk?* How is reinvestment risk part of interest rate risk? If an FI funds short-term assets with long-term liabilities, what will be the impact on earnings of a decrease in the rate of interest? An increase in the rate of interest? (*LG 19-1*)

9. The sales literature of a mutual fund claims that the fund has no risk exposure since it invests exclusively in default risk-free federal government securities. Is this claim true? Why or why not? (*LG 19-1*)

**10.** How can interest rate risk adversely affect the economic or market value of an FI? (*LG 19-1*)

**11.** How does a policy of matching the maturities of assets and liabilities work (*a*) to minimize interest rate risk and (*b*) against the asset-transformation function for FIs? (*LG 19-1*)

**12.** Corporate bonds usually pay interest semiannually. If an FI decided to change from semiannual to annual interest payments, how would this affect the bond's interest rate risk? (*LG 19-1*)

**13.** Consider two bonds, a 10-year premium bond with a coupon rate higher than its required rate of return and a zero coupon bond that pays only a lump sum payment after 10 years with no interest over its life. Which do you think would have more interest rate risk—that is, which bond's price would change by a larger amount for given changes in interest rates? Explain your answer. (*LG 19-1*)

**14.** Consider again the two bonds in Question 13. If the investment goal is to leave the assets untouched until maturity, such as for a child's education or for one's retirement, which of the two bonds has more interest rate risk? What is the source of this risk? (*LG 19-1*)

**15.** A money market mutual fund bought $1,000,000 of two-year Treasury notes six months ago. During this time, the value of the securities has increased, but for tax reasons the mutual fund wants to postpone any sale for two more months. What type of risk does the mutual fund face for the next two months? (*LG 19-1*)

**16.** What is the nature of an off-balance-sheet activity? How does an FI benefit from such activities? Identify the various risks that these activities generate for an FI and explain how these risks can create varying degrees of financial stress for the FI at a later time. (*LG 19-1*)

**17.** What is *foreign exchange risk?* What does it mean for an FI to be *net long* in foreign assets? What does it mean for an FI to be *net short* in foreign assets? In each case, what must happen to the foreign exchange rate to cause the FI to suffer losses? (*LG 19-1*)

**18.** What two factors provide potential benefits to FIs that expand their asset holdings and liability funding sources beyond their domestic borders? (*LG 19-1*)

**19.** If the Swiss franc is expected to depreciate in the near future, would a U.S.-based FI in Bern City, Switzerland, prefer to be net long or net short in its asset positions? Discuss. (*LG 19-1*)

**20.** If an FI has the same amount of foreign assets and foreign liabilities in the same currency, has that FI necessarily reduced the risk involved in these international transactions to zero? Explain. (*LG 19-1*)

**21.** A U.S. insurance company invests $1,000,000 in a private placement of British bonds. Each bond pays £300 in interest per year for 20 years. If the current exchange rate is £1.5612 for US$1, what is the nature of the insurance company's exchange rate risk? Specifically, what type of exchange rate movement concerns this insurance company? (*LG 19-1*)

**22.** If you expect the Swiss franc to depreciate in the near future, would a U.S.-based FI in Basel, Switzerland, prefer to be net long or net short in its asset positions? Discuss. (*LG 19-1* )

**23.** What is *country* or *sovereign risk?* What remedy does an FI realistically have in the event of a collapsing country or currency? (*LG 19-1*)

**24.** What is the difference between technology risk and operational risk? How does internationalizing the payments system among banks increase operational risk? (*LG 19-1*)

**25.** Bank 1, with $130 million in assets and $20 million in costs, acquires Bank 2, which has $50 million in assets and $10 million in costs. After the acquisition, the bank has $180 million in assets and $35 million in costs. Did this acquisition produce economies of scale or economies of scope? (*LG 19-1* )

**26.** Characterize the risk exposure(s) of the following FI transactions by choosing one or more of the following: (*LG 19-1*)
 **a.** Credit risk
 **b.** Interest rate risk
 **c.** Off-balance-sheet risk
 **d.** Foreign exchange rate risk
 **e.** Country/sovereign risk
 **f.** Technology risk
 (1) A bank finances a $10 million, six-year, fixed-rate commercial loan by selling one-year certificates of deposit.
 (2) An insurance company invests its policy premiums in a long-term municipal bond portfolio.
 (3) A French bank sells two-year fixed-rate notes to finance a two-year fixed-rate loan to a British entrepreneur.
 (4) A Japanese bank acquires an Austrian bank to facilitate clearing operations.
 (5) A mutual fund completely hedges its interest rate risk exposure using forward contingent contracts.
 (6) A bond dealer uses his own equity to buy Mexican debt on the less developed countries (LDC) bond market.
 (7) A securities firm sells a package of mortgage loans as mortgage-backed securities.

**27.** Why can *insolvency risk* be classified as a consequence or outcome of any or all of the other types of risks? (*LG 19-2*)

**28.** Discuss the interrelationships among the different sources of FI risk exposure. Why would the construction of an FI risk management model to measure and manage only one type of risk be incomplete? (*LG 19-3*)

## PROBLEMS

**1.** A financial institution has the following market value balance sheet structure: (*LG 19-1*)

| Assets | | Liabilities and Equity | |
|---|---|---|---|
| Cash | $ 1,000 | Certificate of deposit | $10,000 |
| Bond | 10,000 | Equity | 1,000 |
| Total assets | $11,000 | Total liabilities and equity | $11,000 |

**a.** The bond has a 10-year maturity, a fixed-rate coupon of 10 percent paid at the end of each year, and a par value of $10,000. The certificate of deposit has a 1-year maturity and a 6 percent fixed rate of interest. The FI expects no additional asset growth. What will be the net interest income (NII) at the end of the first year? (*Note:* Net interest income equals interest income minus interest expense.)

**b.** If at the end of year 1 market interest rates have increased 100 basis points (1 percent), what will be the net interest income for the second year? Is the change in NII caused by reinvestment risk or refinancing risk?

**c.** Assuming that market interest rates increase 1 percent, the bond will have a value of $9,446 at the end of year 1. What will be the market value of the equity for the FI? Assume that all of the NII in part (*a*) is used to cover operating expenses or is distributed as dividends.

**d.** If market interest rates had *decreased* 100 basis points by the end of year 1, would the market value of equity be higher or lower than $1,000? Why?

**e.** What factors have caused the changes in operating performance and market value for this FI?

**2.** Consider the following income statement for WatchoverU Savings Inc. (in millions): (*LG 19-1*)

| Assets | | Liabilities | |
|---|---|---|---|
| Floating-rate mortgages (currently 10% annually) | $ 50 | NOW accounts (currently 6% annually) | $ 70 |
| 30-year fixed-rate loans (currently 7% annually) | 50 | Time deposits (currently 6% annually) | 20 |
| | | Equity | 10 |
| Total | $100 | | $100 |

**a.** What is WatchoverU's expected net interest income at year-end?

**b.** What will be the net interest income at year-end if interest rates rise by 2 percent?

**3.** If a bank invested $50 million in a two-year asset paying 10 percent interest per year and simultaneously issued a $50 million one-year liability paying 8 percent interest per year, what would be the impact on the bank's net interest income if, at the end of the first year, all interest rates increased by 1 percentage point? (*LG 19-1*)

**4.** Assume that a bank has assets located in Germany worth €150 million earning an average of 8 percent. It also holds €100 in liabilities and pays an average of 6 percent per year. The current spot rate is €1.50 for $1. If the exchange rate at the end of the year is €2.00 for $1: (*LG 19-1*)

**a.** What happened to the dollar? Did it appreciate or depreciate against the euro (€)?

**b.** What is the effect of the exchange rate change on the net interest margin (interest received minus interest paid) in dollars from its foreign assets and liabilities?

**c.** What is the effect of the exchange rate change on the value of the assets and liabilities in dollars?

**5.** Six months ago, Qualitybank issued a $100 million, one-year-maturity CD, denominated in British pounds (Euro CD). On the same date, $60 million was invested in a £-denominated loan and $40 million in a U.S. Treasury bill. The exchange rate on this date was £1.5382 for $1. If you assume no repayment of principal and if today's exchange rate is £1.1905 for $1: (*LG 19-1*)

**a.** What is the current value of the Euro CD principal in dollars and pounds?

**b.** What is the current value of the British loan principal in dollars and pounds?

**c.** What is the current value of the U.S. Treasury bill in dollars and pounds?

**d.** What is Qualitybank's profit/loss from this transaction in dollars and pounds?

**6.** Suppose you purchase a 10-year AAA-rated Swiss bond for par that is paying an annual coupon of 8 percent and has a face value of 1,000 Swiss francs (SF). The spot rate is US$0.66667 for SF1. At the end of the year, the bond is downgraded to AA and the yield increases to 10 percent. In addition, the SF depreciates to US$0.74074 for SF1. (*LG 19-1*)

**a.** What is the loss or gain to a Swiss investor who holds this bond for a year?

**b.** What is the loss or gain to a U.S. investor who holds this bond for a year?

# SEARCH THE SITE

Go to the FDIC website at **www.fdic.gov.** Find the most recent breakdown for charge-off rates for C&I loans of commercial banks using the following steps. Click on "Analysts." From there click on "FDIC Quarterly Banking Profile." Click on "Quarterly Banking Profile," and then click on "Commercial Bank Section." Finally, click on "TABLE V-A. Loan Performance, FDIC-Insured Commercial Banks." This will bring up the files that contain the relevant data.

## Questions

1. How has the charge-off rate changed since 2016 as reported in Figure 19–1?
2. Compare the charge-off rate of C&I loans with real estate and credit card loans. Which has changed the most since 2016?

# Managing Credit Risk on the Balance Sheet

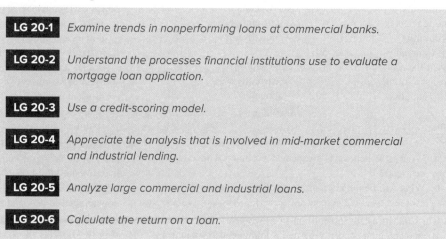

**Learning Goals**

**LG 20-1**  *Examine trends in nonperforming loans at commercial banks.*

**LG 20-2**  *Understand the processes financial institutions use to evaluate a mortgage loan application.*

**LG 20-3**  *Use a credit-scoring model.*

**LG 20-4**  *Appreciate the analysis that is involved in mid-market commercial and industrial lending.*

**LG 20-5**  *Analyze large commercial and industrial loans.*

**LG 20-6**  *Calculate the return on a loan.*

## CREDIT RISK MANAGEMENT: CHAPTER OVERVIEW

In Chapter 19, we provided a basic description of the risks that emanate from financial markets as well as from the traditional activities of financial institutions. In the next three chapters, we provide a more detailed analysis of four of these risks. We also discuss how these risks can be managed. Specifically, we look at the measurement and management of credit risk, liquidity risk, interest rate risk, and insolvency risk. We start our analysis with credit risk.

As discussed in Chapter 1, financial institutions (FIs) are special because of their ability to efficiently transform financial claims of household savers into claims issued to corporations, individuals, and governments. FIs' ability to process and evaluate information and control and monitor borrowers allows them to transform these claims at the lowest possible cost to all parties. One specific type of financial claim transformation discussed in Chapter 1 is credit allocation. FIs transform claims of household savers (in the form of deposits) into loans issued to corporations, individuals, and governments. The FI accepts the credit risk on these loans in exchange for a fair return sufficient to cover the cost of funding paid (e.g., covering the cost of borrowing or issuing deposits) to household savers, the credit risk involved in lending, and a profit margin reflecting competitive conditions.

Credit risk management is important for FI managers because it involves the determination of several features of a loan or debt instrument: interest rate, maturity, collateral, and other covenants. Riskier projects require more analysis before loans are approved or debt instruments are purchased. If credit risk analysis is inadequate, default rates could be higher and push a bank into insolvency, especially if the markets are competitive and the margins are low. Indeed, the default of one major borrower can have a significant impact on the value and reputation of many FIs. For example, the total exposure of U.S. banks to WorldCom at the time of its bankruptcy in 2002 was over $700 million. Losses from this single failure resulted in a drop in earnings per share at J.P. Morgan Chase of 5 cents (or nearly 2 percent). Likewise, at then Bank One (Bank One is now a part of J.P. Morgan Chase) earnings per share dropped 3 cents (or 1 percent), and at Bank of America earnings per share decreased by 5 cents (or 1 percent). Similarly, a single major economic event can cause losses to many FIs' loan portfolios. For example, in 2005 Hurricanes Katrina and Rita resulted in over $1.3 billion in bad loans for major banks operating in areas hit by the storm. And, of course, the financial crisis of 2008–2009 resulted in the largest ever credit risk–related losses for U.S. financial institutions. Losses from the falling value of on- and off-balance-sheet credit instruments (e.g., mortgages, mortgage-backed securities, credit cards) topped $2.3 trillion worldwide. In just the first quarter of 2009, the annualized net charge-off rate on total loans and leases at U.S. banks was 1.94 percent, slightly below the 1.95 percent rate in the fourth quarter of 2008 (which was the highest quarterly net charge-off rate in the 25 years that insured institutions have reported these data).

Many financial institutions were unable to survive the mortgage crisis. For example, Countrywide Financial, the country's largest mortgage issuer, nearly failed in the summer of 2007 due to defaults by its subprime mortgage borrowers. Only a $2 billion equity investment by Bank of America in 2007 and then an acquisition by Bank of America in 2008 kept this savings institution alive. (This acquisition proved costly for Bank of America. Even into 2014 Bank of America paid a record $17 billion settlement to the U.S. Justice Department over questionable mortgages issued by Countrywide before the acquisition. The settlement was the largest ever reached between the United States and a single company, and was approximately equal to Bank of America's total profit for the previous three years.) IndyMac bank, the ninth-largest mortgage lender in the United States in 2007, was seized by the FDIC in July 2008. At a cost to the FDIC of between $4 billion and $8 billion, IndyMac represented the largest bank failure in over 20 years. Overall, in 2008–2010, 322 U.S. banks failed—compared to 3 from 2005 to 2007. Further, the Federal Deposit Insurance Corporation reported that it had 884 banks on its list of troubled institutions at year-end 2010, up from 90 in the first quarter of 2008.

Most recently, bank loan portfolios were exposed to losses from the European debt crisis. In early 2012, U.S. banks' exposure to Greek debt was relatively insignificant, at approximately $5.8 billion. However, the risks posed to U.S. banks and the banking system from a Greek debt default and a contagion crisis in other Euro-zone countries were huge. U.S. banks had more than $50 billion worth of debt exposure to both Spain and Ireland, $6.6 billion to Portugal, and over $66 billion to Italy—all countries in risk of debt default in the event of a continued economic slowdown. Further, U.S. banks had even larger exposures to the larger countries in Europe and to European banks. These seemingly unending credit-related events stress FIs' need to manage their loan portfolios to protect the overall FI from failure due to credit risk.

In this chapter we look at the types of loans (real estate, individual [consumer], commercial and industrial [C&I], and others) as well as the characteristics of those loans made by U.S. FIs. We also examine various methods and models used to measure credit risk or default risk on individual loans (and bonds), including qualitative and quantitative models (e.g., credit-scoring models and newer models of credit risk measurement). Indeed, technological advances have been at least one driving force behind the advances and new models of credit risk measurement and management in recent years. In Appendix 20A (available through Connect or your course instructor), we consider methods for evaluating the risk of the *overall loan portfolio,* or loan concentration risk. Methods for hedging and managing an FI's credit risk, such as the use of credit derivative swaps, are left to Chapters 23 and 24. Finally in this chapter, we look at how both interest and fees are incorporated to calculate the return on a loan. Measurement of the credit risk on individual loans or bonds is crucial if an FI manager is to (1) price a loan or value a bond correctly and (2) set appropriate limits on the amount of credit extended to any one borrower or the loss exposure accepted from any particular counterparty.

## CREDIT QUALITY PROBLEMS

**junk bond**

*A bond rated as speculative or less than investment grade by bond-rating agencies such as Moody's.*

LG 20-1

Over the past three decades, the credit quality of many FIs' lending and investment decisions has attracted a great deal of attention. For most of the 1980s, tremendous problems occurred with bank and thrift residential and farm mortgage loans. In the late 1980s and early 1990s, attention shifted to the problems relating to commercial real estate loans (to which banks, thrifts, and insurance companies were all exposed) and **junk bonds** (bonds rated as speculative or less than investment-grade securities by rating agencies such as Moody's or S&P—see Chapter 6 for the assignment and meaning of bond ratings). In the late 1990s, concern shifted to the rapid increase in auto loans and credit cards as well as the declining quality in commercial lending standards as high-yield business loan delinquencies started to increase. In the late 1990s and early 2000s, attention has focused on problems with telecommunication companies, new technology companies, and a variety of sovereign countries, including at various times Argentina, Brazil, and Russia. Despite these credit concerns, the credit quality of most FIs improved throughout the 1990s. For example, for FDIC-insured commercial banks, the ratio of nonperforming loans to assets declined significantly from 1992 through 2000 (see Figure 20–1).

The recession in the U.S. economy in the early 2000s led to a reversal in this trend as nonperforming loan rates increased, particularly on C&I loans. However, the nonperformance of loans in all categories was still below that of the early 1990s. As the U.S. economy improved in the mid-2000s, nonperforming loan rates fell. But mortgage delinquencies, particularly on subprime mortgages, surged in the last quarter of 2006 and all of 2007 as homeowners who had stretched themselves financially to buy a home or refinance a mortgage in the early 2000s fell behind on their loan payments. Trouble in the mortgage markets continued to escalate as the number of foreclosures hit a record 1.5 million in the first six months of 2009 and over 8 percent of all real estate loans held by commercial

**Figure 20–1**   **Nonperforming Asset Ratio for U.S. Commercial Banks**

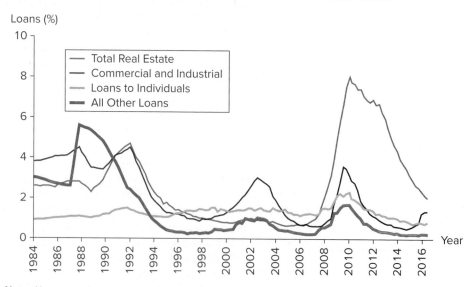

**Note:** Noncurrent loan rates represent the percentage of loans that are past due 90 days or more or in nonaccrual status.

**Sources:** Federal Deposit Insurance Corporation, *Quarterly Banking Profile*, various issues. www.fdic.gov

banks were nonperforming (i.e., were past due 90 days or more). Problems in the mortgage markets spread to other sectors as well. In 2008 consumer bankruptcy filings rose to 1.06 million, up from 801,840 in 2007 and 602,000 in 2006. By late 2009, over 2.30 percent of all individual (consumer) loans held by commercial banks were nonperforming. Business loan losses grew as well, peaking at 3.57 percent in the third quarter of 2009. For example, when Chrysler went into bankruptcy in May 2009 it owed banks, including Citigroup and J.P. Morgan Chase, $6.9 billion. President Obama's plan for Chrysler's bankruptcy cut that to $1 billion, for a loss to banks of $5.9 billion. The banks ended up realizing 33 cents on the dollar for these loans—a loss of $4.6 billion. As the U.S. economy slowly recovered in 2010–2016, nonperforming loan rates edged downward but still remained at levels higher than those seen throughout much of the 30-year period.

The potential loss an FI can experience from lending suggests that FIs need to collect information about borrowers whose assets are in their portfolios and monitor those borrowers over time. Thus, managerial efficiency and credit risk management strategies directly affect the return and risks of the loan portfolio. One of the advantages that FIs have over individual investors is the ability to diversify some credit risk by exploiting the law of large numbers in their asset investment portfolios (see Chapter 1). That is, diversification across assets exposed to credit risk reduces the overall credit risk in the asset portfolio and thus increases the probability of partial or full repayment of principal and/or interest.[1]

A credit quality problem, in the worst case, can cause an FI to become insolvent, or it can result in such a significant drain on earnings and net worth that it can adversely affect the FI's profitability and its ability to compete with other domestic and international FIs. For example, on average, commercial banks hold over 50 percent of their assets in the form of loans (mortgage loans, C&I loans, consumer loans, and other loans), while they finance their total assets with an average of 11 percent equity (see Chapter 11). Large losses on these loans could quickly wipe out a bank's equity capital. Consider an FI with the following balance sheet:

| | | | |
|---|---|---|---|
| Cash and other assets | $ 48m | Deposits | $ 89m |
| Gross loans | 52m | Equity (net worth) | 11m |
| | $100m | | $100m |

Suppose that the managers of the FI recognize that $11 million of its $52 million in loans is unlikely to be repaid due to an increase in credit repayment difficulties of its borrowers. Eventually, the FI's managers must respond by charging off or writing down the value of these loans on the FI's balance sheet. This means that the value of loans falls from $52 million to $41 million, an economic loss that must be charged off against the stockholders' equity capital or net worth (i.e., equity capital falls from $11 million to zero). Thus, both sides of the balance sheet shrink by the amount of the loss:

| | | | | |
|---|---|---|---|---|
| Cash and other assets | | $48m | Deposits | $89m |
| Gross loans | 52m | | Equity after charge-off | 0m |
| Less: Loan loss | −11m | | | |
| Loans after charge-off | | 41m | | |
| | | $89m | | $89m |

We discuss credit analysis next.

## CREDIT ANALYSIS

This section discusses credit analysis for real estate lending, consumer and small-business lending, mid-market commercial and industrial lending, and large commercial and industrial lending. It also provides insights into the credit risk evaluation process from the perspective of a credit officer (or an FI manager) evaluating a loan application.

---

1. That is, the risk of a portfolio of loans is less than the sum of individual risks of each loan because individual loans' risks are not perfectly correlated with each other. The lower the degree of correlation among loans' risks, the lower the risk of a loan portfolio.

LG 20-2

## Real Estate Lending

Because of the importance of residential mortgages to banks, savings institutions, credit unions, and insurance companies, residential mortgage loan applications are among the most standardized of all credit applications. In Chapter 7, we outlined the different types of characteristics of real estate loans (e.g, adjustable-rate versus fixed-rate mortgages, interest rate payments versus fee payments,[2] and down payments). In this chapter, we look at the evaluation process that FIs (such as commercial banks, savings institutions, and finance companies) use to determine whether a real estate loan application should be approved. Two considerations dominate an FI's decision to approve a mortgage loan application: (1) the applicant's ability and willingness to make timely interest and principal repayments and (2) the value of the borrower's collateral.

Ability and willingness of the borrower to repay debt outstanding is usually established by application of qualitative and quantitative models. The character of the applicant is also extremely important. Stability of residence, occupation, family status (e.g., married, single), previous history of savings, and credit (or bill payment) history are frequently used in assessing character. The loan officer must also establish whether the applicant has sufficient income. In particular, the loan amortization (i.e., principal and interest payments) should be reasonable when compared with the applicant's income and age. The loan officer should also consider the applicant's monthly expenditures. Family responsibilities and marital stability are also important. Monthly financial obligations relating to auto, personal, and credit card loans should be ascertained, and an applicant's personal balance sheet and income statement should be constructed.

**GDS (gross debt service) ratio**

*Total accommodation expenses (mortgage, lease, condominium, management fees, real estate taxes, etc.) divided by gross income.*

Two ratios are very useful in determining a customer's ability to maintain mortgage payments: the **GDS (gross debt service) ratio** and the **TDS (total debt service) ratio.** The gross debt service ratio is the customer's total annual accommodation expenses (mortgage, lease, condominium management fees, real estate taxes, etc.) divided by annual gross income. The total debt service ratio is the customer's total annual accommodation expenses plus all other debt service payments divided by annual gross income. These can be represented as follows:

$$GDS = \frac{\text{Annual mortgage payments} + \text{Property taxes}}{\text{Annual gross income}}$$

**TDS (total debt service) ratio**

*Total accommodation expenses plus all other debt service payments divided by gross income.*

$$TDS = \frac{\text{Annual total debt payments}}{\text{Annual gross income}}$$

As a general rule, for an FI to consider an applicant, the GDS and TDS ratios must be less than an acceptable threshold. The threshold is commonly 25 to 30 percent for the GDS ratio and 35 to 40 percent for the TDS ratio.[3]

---

### EXAMPLE 20–1   Calculation of the GDS and TDS Ratios

Consider two customers who have applied for a mortgage from an FI with a GDS threshold of 25 percent and a TDS threshold of 40 percent.

| Customer | Gross Annual Income | Monthly Mortgage Payments | Annual Property Taxes | Monthly Other Debt Payments |
|---|---|---|---|---|
| 1 | $150,000 | $3,000 | $3,500 | $2,000 |
| 2 | 60,000 | 500 | 1,500 | 200 |

The GDS and TDS ratios for the mortgage applicants are as follows:

---

2. Often called "points" (see Chapter 7).
3. The numerator of the GDS is often increased to include home heating and homeowners' association and other fees. When the GDS ratio is used for consumer credit, rent is substituted for mortgage payments, when applicable.

| Customer | GDS | TDS |
|----------|-----|-----|
| 1 | $\dfrac{3{,}000(12) + 3{,}500}{150{,}000} = 26.33\%$ | $\dfrac{3{,}000(12) + 3{,}500 + 2{,}000(12)}{150{,}000} = 42.33\%$ |
| 2 | $\dfrac{500(12) + 1{,}500}{60{,}000} = 12.50\%$ | $\dfrac{500(12) + 1{,}500 + 200(12)}{60{,}000} = 16.50\%$ |

Despite a higher level of gross income, Customer 1 does not meet the GDS or TDS thresholds because of relatively high mortgage, tax, and other debt payments. Customer 2, while earning less, has fewer required payments and meets both the FI's GDS and TDS thresholds.

**LG 20-3**

**credit-scoring system**

*A mathematical model that uses observed characteristics of the loan applicant to calculate a score that represents the applicant's probability of default.*

FIs often combine the various factors affecting the ability and willingness to make loan repayments into a single credit score. A **credit-scoring system** (illustrated below) is a quantitative model that uses observed characteristics of the applicant to calculate a "score" representing the applicant's probability of default (versus repayment). Credit-scoring models are used to calculate the probability of default or to sort borrowers into different default risk classes. The primary benefit of credit-scoring models is to improve the accuracy of predicting borrowers' performance without using additional resources. This benefit results in fewer defaults and charge-offs to the FI. The models use data on observed economic and financial borrower characteristics to assist an FI manager in (1) identifying factors of importance in explaining default risk, (2) evaluating the relative degree of importance of these factors, (3) improving the pricing of default risk, (4) screening bad loan applicants, and (5) more efficiently calculating the necessary reserves to protect against future loan losses.

Credit-scoring systems are developed by using borrower characteristics (e.g., income, age, loan payment history) for some past period. The credit-scoring model weights each characteristic to identify a boundary number (score) or range such that if past loan customers had an overall credit score (derived from the weighted characteristics) greater than the boundary number (score) they did not default on the loan, whereas if they had a credit score less than the boundary number they defaulted on the loan. The boundary number or range is derived by statistical analysis, such as logit or discriminant analysis.[4] Assuming new loan customers act like past customers, the credit-scoring system can then be used to calculate a credit score for new loan applicants and assign them to a high or low default risk group. The applicant's total score must be above the boundary score or range to be considered acceptable for a loan.

The theory behind credit scoring is that by selecting and combining different economic and financial characteristics, an FI manager may be able to separate good from bad loan customers based on the characteristics of borrowers who have defaulted in the past. One advantage of a credit-scoring system is that a loan applicant's credit quality is expressed as a single numerical value, rather than as a judgmental assessment of several separate factors. This is beneficial for FIs that must evaluate small loan applicants quickly, at low cost, and consistently and who would otherwise have to employ many more credit analysts (each of whom might well apply inconsistent standards across different loan applicants as well as adding to the FI's labor costs).

If the FI uses a scoring system, the loan officer can give an immediate answer—yes, maybe, or no—and the reasons for that answer. A maybe occurs in borderline cases or when the loan officer is uncertain of the classification of certain input information. A credit-scoring system allows an FI to reduce the ambiguity and turnaround time and increase the transparency of the credit approval process.

---

4. For example, those credit-scoring systems based on a statistical technique called discriminant analysis are also referred to as discriminant analysis models. Discriminant analysis places borrowers into two groups (defaulting and nondefaulting) and, by seeking to maximize the difference in the variance of the characteristics (e.g., income) between these groups while minimizing the variance within each group, seeks to derive appropriate weights for the characteristics that discriminate between the defaulting and nondefaulting groups. This is the discriminant function that results from discriminant analysis.

## EXAMPLE 20–2    Credit Scoring of a Real Estate Loan

An FI uses the following credit-scoring model to evaluate real estate loan applications:

| Characteristic | Characteristic Values and Weights | | | | |
|---|---|---|---|---|---|
| Annual gross income | <$10,000 | $10,000–$25,000 | $25,000–$50,000 | $50,000–$100,000 | >$100,000 |
| Score | 0 | 15 | 35 | 50 | 75 |
| TDS | >50% | 35%–50% | 15%–35% | 5%–15% | <5% |
| Score | 0 | 10 | 20 | 35 | 50 |
| Relations with FI | None | Checking account | Savings account | Both | |
| Score | 0 | 30 | 30 | 60 | |
| Major credit cards | None | 1 or more | | | |
| Score | 0 | 20 | | | |
| Age | <25 | 25–60 | >60 | | |
| Score | 5 | 30 | 35 | | |
| Residence | Rent | Own with mortgage | Own outright | | |
| Score | 5 | 20 | 50 | | |
| Length of residence | <1 year | 1–5 years | >5 years | | |
| Score | 0 | 20 | 45 | | |
| Job stability | <1 year | 1–5 years | >5 years | | |
| Score | 0 | 25 | 50 | | |
| Credit history | No record | Missed a payment in last 5 years | Met all payments | | |
| Score | 0 | −15 | 50 | | |

The loan is automatically rejected if the applicant's total score is less than 120 (i.e., applicants with a score of 120 or less have, in the past, mainly defaulted on their loan). The loan is automatically approved if the total score is greater than 190 (i.e., applicants with a score of 190 or more have, in the past, mainly paid their loan in complete accordance with the loan agreement). A score between 120 and 190 is reviewed by a loan committee for a final decision.

A loan customer listing the following information on the loan application receives the following points:

| Characteristic | Value | Score |
|---|---|---|
| Annual gross income | $67,000 | 50 |
| TDS | 12% | 35 |
| Relations with FI | None | 0 |
| Major credit cards | 4 | 20 |
| Age | 37 | 30 |
| Residence | Own/mortgage | 20 |
| Length of residence | 2½ years | 20 |
| Job stability | 2½ years | 25 |
| Credit history | Met all payments | 50 |
| Total score | | 250 |

The real estate loan for this customer would be automatically approved.

Rather than develop and use a proprietary credit-scoring model, many (particularly smaller) FIs use FICO scores to evaluate mortgage (and consumer) loans. Developed by Bill Fair and Earl Isaac (Fair Isaac Corp.), the FICO score uses five factors to determine a loan applicant's score. In order of importance, they are:

1. Payment history (35% of the FICO score).
2. Debt/amounts owed (30% of the FICO score).
3. Age of credit history (15% of the FICO score).
4. New credit/inquiries (10% of the FICO score).
5. Mix of accounts/types of credit (10% of the FICO score).

The FICO scale runs from 300 to 850. A score of 800 or above indicates an exceptional FICO score (approximately 1% of consumers with a credit score of 800+ are likely to become seriously delinquent in the future). A score of 579 or below indicates a poor FICO score and is considered to be poor credit (approximately 61% of consumers with a credit score under 579 are likely to become seriously delinquent in the future). The vast majority of people have scores between 600 and 800. A score of 720 or higher is generally sufficient to receive favorable interest rates on a mortgage.

Verification of the borrower's financial statements is essential. For example, if the answer is yes to a loan application, the loan officer states that the FI is prepared to grant the loan subject to a verification of his or her creditworthiness and obtains the applicant's permission to make all necessary inquiries. The collateral backing the mortgage is normally considered only after the loan officer has established that the applicant can service the loan. If collateral secures a loan, the FI must make sure that its claim, should the borrower default, is free and clear from other claims. This process is referred to as **perfecting** a security interest in the **collateral.** Even if collateral secures the loan, no FI should become involved in a loan that is likely to go into default. In such a case, the FI would at best seize the property in a **foreclosure** (where the FI takes possession of the mortgaged property in satisfaction of the defaulting borrower's indebtedness, forgoing claim to any deficiency) or **power of sale** (where the FI takes the proceeds of the forced sale of a mortgaged property in satisfaction of the indebtedness and returns to the mortgagor the excess over the indebtedness or claims any shortfall as an unsecured creditor).

Finally, before an FI accepts a mortgage, it must satisfy itself regarding the property involved in the loan by doing the following:

- Confirming the title and legal description of the property.
- Obtaining a surveyor's certificate confirming that the house is within the property boundaries.
- Checking with the tax office to confirm that no property taxes are unpaid.
- Requesting a land title search to determine that there are no other claims against the property.
- Obtaining an independent appraisal to confirm that the purchase price is in line with the market value.

## Consumer (Individual) and Small-Business Lending

The techniques used for mortgage loan credit analysis are very similar to those applied to individual and small-business loans. Individual consumer loans are scored like mortgages, often without the borrower ever meeting the loan officer. Unlike mortgage loans for which the focus is on a property, however, nonmortgage consumer loans focus on the individual's ability to repay. Thus, credit-scoring models for such loans would put more weight on personal characteristics such as annual gross income, the TDS score, and so on.

Small-business loans are more complicated because the FI is frequently asked to assume the credit risk of an individual whose business cash flows require considerable analysis, often with incomplete accounting information available to the credit officer. Typically, loans are made to small businesses to help start up the company. This creates several problems. There is less history to base the loan on. Numerical scoring rules may

**perfecting collateral**

*The process of ensuring that collateral used to secure a loan is free and clear to the lender should the borrower default on the loan.*

**foreclosure**

*The process of taking possession of the mortgaged property in satisfaction of a defaulting borrower's indebtedness and forgoing claim to any deficiency.*

**power of sale**

*The process of taking the proceeds of the forced sale of a mortgaged property in satisfaction of the indebtedness and returning to the mortgagor the excess over the indebtedness or claiming any shortfall as an unsecured creditor.*

be less useful in this case. A start-up business that fails may also have less collateral value compared to a larger company. Because of this, the personal assets of the small-business owner may be used as collateral on the loan. A loan to a small business will necessarily be small, so the size of the profits to be earned by the FI from the loan is not likely to be very substantial. A $50,000 loan with a 3 percent interest spread over the cost of funds provides only $1,500 of gross revenues before loan loss provisions, monitoring costs, and allocation of overheads. This low profitability has caused many FIs to build small-business scoring models similar to, but more sophisticated than, those used for mortgages and consumer credit. These models often combine computer-based financial analysis of borrower financial statements with behavioral analysis of the owner of the small business.

### Mid-Market Commercial and Industrial Lending

In recent years, mid-market commercial and industrial lending has offered some of the most profitable opportunities for credit-granting FIs. Although definitions of mid-market corporates vary, they typically have sales revenues from $5 million to $100 million a year, have a recognizable corporate structure (unlike many small businesses), but do not have ready access to deep and liquid capital markets (as do large corporations). Commercial loans can be made for periods as short as a few weeks to as long as eight years or more. Traditionally, short-term commercial loans (those with an original maturity of one year or less) are used to finance firms' working capital needs and other short-term funding needs, while long-term commercial loans are used to finance credit needs that extend beyond one year, such as the purchase of real assets (machinery), new venture start-up costs, and permanent increases in working capital. They can be made in quite small amounts, such as $100,000 to small businesses, or in packages as large as $1 billion or more to major corporations.

**LG 20-4**

Credit analysis of a mid-market corporate customer differs from that of a small business because, while still assessing the character of the firm's management, its main focus is on the business itself. The credit process begins with an account officer gathering information by meeting existing customers, checking referrals, and meeting with new business prospects. Having gathered information about the credit applicant, an account officer decides whether it is worthwhile to pursue the new business, given the applicant's needs, the FI's credit policies, the current economy, and the competitive lending environment. If it is, the account officer structures and prices the credit agreement with reference to the FI's credit granting policy. This includes several areas of analysis, including the five C's of credit, cash flow analysis, ratio analysis, and financial statement comparisons (described below). At any time in this process, conditions could change or new information could be revealed, significantly changing the borrower's situation and forcing the account officer to begin the process again.

Once the applicant and an account officer tentatively agree on a loan, the account officer must obtain internal approval from the FI's credit risk management team. Generally, even for the smallest mid-market credit, at least two officers must approve a new loan customer. Larger credit requests must be presented formally (either in hard copy or through a computer network) to a credit approval officer and/or committee before they can be signed. This means that, during the negotiations, the account officer must be very well acquainted with the FI's overall credit philosophy and current strategy.

**Five C's of Credit.**    To analyze the loan applicant's credit risk, the account officer must understand the customer's character, capacity, collateral, conditions, and capital (sometimes referred to as the *five C's of credit*). Character refers to the probability that the loan applicant will try to honor the loan obligations. Capacity is a subjective judgment regarding the applicant's ability to pay the FI according to the terms of the loan. Collateral is represented by assets that the loan applicant offers as security backing the loan. Conditions refer to any general economic trends or special developments in certain geographic regions or sectors of the economy that might affect the applicant's ability to meet the loan obligations. Capital is measured by the general financial condition of the applicant as indicated by an analysis of the applicant's financial statements and leverage. Some important questions that provide information on the five C's follow.

*Production  (measures of capacity and conditions)*

- On what production inputs does the applicant depend?
- To what extent does this cause supply risk?
- How do input price risks affect the applicant?
- How do costs of production compare with those of the competition?
- How does the quality of goods and services produced compare with those of the competition?

*Management  (measures of character and conditions)*

- Is management trustworthy?
- Is management skilled at production? Marketing? Finance? Building an effective organization?
- To what extent does the company depend on one or a few key players?
- Is there a succession plan for senior management?
- Are credible and sensible accounting, budgeting, and control systems in place?

*Marketing  (measures of conditions)*

- How are the changing needs of the applicant's customers likely to affect the applicant?
- How creditworthy are the applicant's customers?
- At what stage of their life cycles are the applicant's products and services?
- What are the market share and share growth of the applicant's products and services?
- What is the applicant's marketing policy?
- Who are the applicant's competitors? What policies are they pursuing? Why are they able to remain in business?
- How is the applicant meeting changing market needs?

*Capital (measures of capital and collateral)*

- How much equity is currently funding the firm's assets?
- How much access does the firm have to equity and debt markets?
- Will the company back the loan with the firm's assets?

**Cash Flow Analysis.**    As an initial step of the loan analysis, FIs require corporate loan applicants to provide cash flow information, which provides the FI with relevant information about the applicant's cash receipts and disbursements compared to the principal and interest payments on the loan. In general, some activities increase cash (cash receipts) and some decrease cash (cash disbursements). Table 20–1 classifies the firm's basic cash receipts (sources of cash) and disbursements (uses of cash). Cash receipts include increasing liabilities (or equity) or decreasing noncash assets. For example, if a firm sells new common stock, the firm has used primary markets to raise cash. Likewise, a drop in accounts receivable means that the firm has collected cash from its credit sales—also a cash receipt.

**TABLE 20–1    Sources and Uses of Cash**

| Sources of Cash | Uses of Cash |
| --- | --- |
| Decrease a noncash current asset | Increase a noncash current asset |
| Decrease a fixed asset | Increase a fixed asset |
| Increase a current liability | Decrease a current liability |
| Increase long-term debt | Decrease long-term debt |
| Net income | Net losses |
| Depreciation | Pay dividends |
| Sell common or preferred stock | Repurchase common or preferred stock |

**TABLE 20–2** The Statement of Cash Flows

**A. Cash flows from operating activities**

Net income
Additions (sources of cash):
   Depreciation
   Decrease noncash current assets
   Increase accrued wages and taxes
   Increase accounts payable
Subtractions (uses of cash):
   Increase noncash current assets
   Decrease accrued wages and taxes
   Decrease accounts payable

**B. Cash flows from investing activities**

Additions:
   Decrease fixed assets
   Decrease other long-term assets
Subtractions:
   Increase fixed assets
   Increase other long-term assets

**C. Cash flows from financing activities**

Additions:
   Increase notes payable
   Increase long-term debt
   Increase common and preferred stock
Subtraction:
   Decrease notes payable
   Decrease long-term debt
   Decrease common and preferred stock
   Pay dividends

**D. Net change in cash and marketable securities**

The firm uses cash to decrease a liability (paying off a bank loan) or to increase noncash assets (buying inventory). The statement of cash flows separates these cash flows into four categories or sections: cash flows from operating activities, cash flows from investing activities, cash flows from financing activities, and net change in cash and marketable securities. The basic setup of a statement of cash flows is presented in Table 20–2.

Cash flows from operations are those cash inflows and outflows that result directly from producing and selling the firm's products. These cash flows include: net income and changes in working capital accounts other than cash and operations-related short-term debt. Most loan officers consider this top section of the statement of cash flows to be the most important. It shows quickly and compactly the firm's cash flows generated by and used for the production process. That is, it shows whether the production and sale of the firm's product results in a net cash inflow for the firm. Loan officers look for positive cash flows from operations as a sign of a successful firm—positive cash flows from the firm's operations are precisely what gives the firm value. Unless the firm has a stable, healthy pattern in its cash flows from operations, it is not financially healthy no matter what its level of cash flows from investing activities or cash flows from financing activities.

Cash flows from investing activities are cash flows associated with buying or selling fixed or other long-term assets. This section of the statement of cash flows shows cash inflows and outflows from long-term investing activities—most significantly the firm's investment in fixed assets.

Cash flows from financing activities are cash flows that result from debt and equity financing transactions. These include raising cash by issuing short-term debt, long-term debt, and stock and using cash to pay dividends, pay off debt, and buy back stock. Loan officers normally look for the "cash flows from financing activities" figure to show small

**TABLE 20–3**   Financial Statements Used to Construct a Cash Flow Statement (*in thousands of dollars*)

**Panel A: Balance Sheets**

| Assets | 2018 | 2019 | Change from 2018 to 2019 | Liabilities/Equity | 2018 | 2019 | Change from 2018 to 2019 |
|---|---|---|---|---|---|---|---|
| Cash | $ 133 | $ 72 | $ (61) | Notes payable | $ 657 | $ 967 | $ 310 |
| Accounts receivable | 1,399 | 1,846 | 447 | Accounts payable | 908 | 1,282 | 374 |
| Inventory | 1,255 | 1,779 | 524 | Accruals | 320 | 427 | 107 |
| Current assets | 2,787 | 3,697 | 910 | Current liabilities | 1,885 | 2,676 | 791 |
| Gross fixed assets | 876 | 1,033 | 157 | Long-term debt | 375 | 300 | (75) |
| Less: depreciation | (277) | (350) | (73) | Common stock | 700 | 700 | 0 |
| Net fixed assets | 599 | 683 | 84 | Retained earnings | 465 | 754 | 289 |
| Temporary investments | 39 | 50 | 11 | Total | $3,425 | $4,430 | $1,005 |
| Total assets | $3,425 | $4,430 | $1,005 | | | | |

**Panel B: Income Statement**

| | 2019 |
|---|---|
| Net sales (all on credit) | $12,430 |
| Cost of goods sold | (8,255) |
| Gross profit | 4,175 |
| Cash operating expenses | (3,418) |
| Depreciation | (73) |
| Operating profit | 684 |
| Interest expense | (157) |
| Taxes | (188) |
| Net income | 339 |
| Dividends | (50) |
| Change in retained earnings | $ 289 |

amounts of net borrowing along with dividend payments. If, however, a firm is going through a major period of expansion, net borrowing could reasonably be much higher.

The bottom line of the statement of cash flows shows the sum of cash flows from operations, investing activities, and financing activities. The bottom line will reconcile to the net change in cash and marketable securities account on the balance sheet over the period of analysis.

Even though a company may report a large amount of net income on its income statement during a year, the firm may actually receive a positive, negative, or zero amount of cash. Accounting rules under generally accepted accounting principles (GAAP) create this sense of discord: net income is the result of accounting rules, or GAAP, that do not necessarily reflect the firm's cash flows. While the income statement shows a firm's accounting-based income, the statement of cash flows more often reflects reality today and is thus more important to managers and investors as they seek to answer such important questions as: Does the firm generate sufficient cash to pay its operating expenses? Does the firm generate sufficient cash to purchase assets needed for sustained growth? Does the firm generate sufficient cash to pay down its outstanding debt obligations, thus avoiding financial distress?

When evaluating the cash flow statement, FIs want to see that the loan applicant can pay back the loan with cash flows produced from the applicant's operations. FIs do not (except as a last resort) want the loan applicant to pay back the loan by selling fixed assets or issuing additional debt. Thus, the cash flows from the operating activities section of the cash flow statement are most critical to the FI in evaluating the loan applicant.

**Ratio Analysis.**   In addition to cash flow information, an applicant requesting specific levels of credit substantiates these business needs by presenting historical audited financial statements and projections of future needs. Historical financial statement analysis can be

---

### EXAMPLE 20–3    Computation of Cash Flow Statement

Consider the financial statement for the loan applicant presented in Table 20–3. The cash flow statement reconciles the change in the firm's cash assets account from 2018 to 2019 as equal to –$61 (see the first row of Panel A). Construction of the cash flow statement begins with all cash flow items associated with the operating activities of the applicant. Panel A of Table 20–4 shows that the cash flows from operations total –$78. Next, cash flows from investment activities (i.e., fixed-asset investments and other nonoperating investments of the firm) are calculated in Table 20–4, Panel B, as –$168. Finally, cash flows from financing activities are shown in Panel C as $185. The sum of these cash flow activities, reportesd in Panel D, –$61, equals the change in the cash account from 2018 to 2019 (Table 20–3, Panel A, first row). Given that the loan should be repaid from cash flows from operations, which are negative (i.e., –$78), this loan applicant will likely be rejected.

---

useful in determining whether cash flow and profit projections are plausible on the basis of the history of the applicant and in highlighting the applicant's risks.

Calculation of financial ratios is useful when performing financial statement analysis on a mid-market corporate applicant. Although stand-alone accounting ratios are used for determining the size of the credit facility, the analyst may find relative ratios more informative when determining how the applicant's business is changing over time (i.e., time series analysis) or how the applicant's ratios compare to those of its competitors (i.e., cross-sectional analysis). Ratio analysis almost always includes a comparison of one firm's ratios relative to the ratios of other firms in the industry, or cross-sectional

**TABLE 20–4**    Cash Flow Statement *(in thousands of dollars)*

|  |  | Cash Flow Impact |
|---|---|---|
| **Panel A: Cash flows from operating activities** |  |  |
| Net sales | $12,430 | ↑ |
| Change in accounts receivable | (447) | ↓ |
| Cash receipts from sales | 11,983 |  |
| Cost of goods sold | (8,255) | ↓ |
| Change in inventory | (524) | ↓ |
| Change in accounts payable | 374 | ↑ |
| Cash margin | 3,578 |  |
| Cash operating expenses | (3,418) | ↓ |
| Change in accruals | 107 | ↑ |
| Cash before interest and taxes | 267 |  |
| Interest expense | (157) | ↓ |
| Taxes | (188) | ↓ |
| Cash flows from operations | (78) |  |
| **Panel B: Cash flows from investing activities** |  |  |
| Change in gross fixed assets | (157) | ↓ |
| Change in temporary investments | (11) | ↓ |
| Cash flows from investing activities | (168) |  |
| **Panel C: Cash flows from financing activities** |  |  |
| Retirement of long-term debt | (75) | ↓ |
| Change in notes payable | 310 | ↑ |
| Change in common stock | 0 | — |
| Dividends paid | (50) | ↓ |
| Cash flows from financing activities | 185 |  |
| **Panel D: Net increase (decrease) in cash** | (61)* |  |

*This is equal to the change in cash for 2018–2019 reported in Panel A of Table 20–3.

analysis. Key to cross-sectional analysis is identifying similar firms that compete in the same markets, have similar size assets, and operate in a similar manner to the firm being analyzed. Since no two firms are identical, obtaining such a comparison group is no easy task. Thus, the choice of companies to use in cross-sectional analysis is at best subjective. Comparative ratios that can be used in cross-sectional analysis are available from many sources. Value Line Investment Surveys, Robert Morris Associates, and Hoover's Online are examples of three major sources of financial ratios for numerous industries that operate within the United States and worldwide.

Hundreds of ratios could be calculated from any set of accounting statements. The following are a few that most credit analysts find useful. Values of the ratios using the 2019 financial statements in Table 20–3 are also presented.

*Liquidity Ratios*

$$\text{Current ratio} = \frac{\text{Current assets}}{\text{Current liabilities}} = \frac{3{,}697}{2{,}676} = 1.38 \text{ times}$$

$$\text{Quick ratio (acid-test ratio)} = \frac{\text{Current assets} - \text{Inventory}}{\text{Current liabilities}} = \frac{3{,}679 - 1{,}779}{2{,}676} = 0.72 \text{ times}$$

Liquidity provides the defensive cash and near-cash resources for firms to meet claims for payment. Liquidity ratios express the variability of liquid resources relative to potential claims. When considering the liquidity of a loan applicant, high levels of liquidity effectively guard against liquidity crises but at the cost of lower returns on investment. Note that a company with a very predictable cash flow can maintain low levels of liquidity without much liquidity risk. Account officers frequently request detailed cash flow projections from an applicant that specify exactly when cash inflows and outflows are anticipated.

*Asset Management Ratios*

$$\text{Number of days sales in receivables} = \frac{\text{Accounts receivable} \times 365}{\text{Credit sales}} = \frac{1{,}846 \times 365}{12{,}430} = 54.21 \text{ days}$$

$$\text{Number of days in inventory} = \frac{\text{Inventory} \times 365}{\text{Cost of goods sold}} = \frac{1{,}779 \times 365}{8{,}255} = 78.66 \text{ days}$$

$$\text{Sales to working capital} = \frac{\text{Sales}}{\text{Working capital}} = \frac{12{,}430}{3{,}697 - 2{,}676} = 12.17 \text{ times}$$

$$\text{Sales to fixed assets} = \frac{\text{Sales}}{\text{Fixed assets}} = \frac{12{,}430}{683} = 18.20 \text{ times}$$

$$\text{Sales to total assets (assets turnover)} = \frac{\text{Sales}}{\text{Total assets}} = \frac{12{,}430}{4{,}430} = 2.81 \text{ times}$$

The asset management ratios give the account officer clues as to how well the applicant uses its assets relative to its past performance and the performance of the industry. For example, ratio analysis may reveal that the number of days that finished goods are in inventory is increasing. This suggests that finished goods inventories, relative to the sales they support, are not being used as well as in the past. If this increase is the result of a deliberate policy to increase inventories to offer customers a wider choice and if it results in higher future sales volumes or increased margins that more than compensate for increased capital tied up in inventory, the increased relative size of finished goods inventories is good for the applicant and, thus, the FI. An FI should be concerned, on the other hand, if increased finished goods inventories are the result of declining sales but steady purchases of supplies and production. Inventory aging schedules give more information than single ratios and should be requested by the account officer concerned about deteriorating ratios.

What a loan applicant often describes in words differs substantially from what the ratio analysis reveals. For example, a company that claims to be a high-volume producer but has low sales-to-assets ratios relative to the industry bears further investigation. In discussing the analysis with the applicant, the account officer not only gains a better appreciation of the applicant's strategy and needs but also may help the applicant better understand the company relative to financial and industry norms.

*Debt and Solvency Ratios*

$$\text{Debt-to-asset ratio} = \frac{\text{Short-term liabilities} + \text{Long-term liabilities}}{\text{Total assets}} = \frac{2{,}676 + 300}{4{,}430} = 67.18\%$$

$$\text{Times interest earned ratio} = \frac{\text{Earnings available to meet interest charges}}{\text{Interest charges}} = \frac{684}{157} = 4.36 \text{ times}$$

$$\text{Cash-flow-to-debt ratio} = \frac{\text{EBIT} + \text{Depreciation}}{\text{Debt}} = \frac{684 + 73}{2{,}676 + 300} = 25.44\%$$

**EBIT**

*Earnings before interest and taxes.*

where **EBIT** represents earnings before interest and taxes (i.e., operating profit).

Debt and solvency ratios give the account manager an idea of the extent to which the applicant finances its assets with debt versus equity. Specifically, the lower the debt-to-asset ratio, the less debt and more equity the applicant uses to finance its assets (i.e., the bigger the applicant's equity cushion). Similarly, the higher the times interest earned ratio and the cash-flow-to-debt ratio, the more equity and less debt the applicant uses to finance its assets.

Adequate levels of equity capital are as critical to the health of a credit applicant as they are to the health of FIs. The account officer analyzing a credit application or renewal wishes to know whether a sufficient equity cushion exists to absorb fluctuations in the loan applicant's earnings and asset values and whether sufficient cash flow exists to make debt service payments. Clearly, the larger the fluctuations or variability of cash flows, the larger is the need for an equity cushion. Note that from a secured debtor's point of view (e.g., a bank lender), the unsecured creditors and subordinate lenders (such as subordinate bond holders) form part of the quasi-equity cushion in liquidation. The secured creditor must make sure, however, that it enjoys true seniority in cash payments so that the firm's assets are not liquidated in paying down the claims of the subordinate (junior) creditors and equity holders.

Whether a debt burden is too large can be analyzed with the help of a times interest earned ratio. This ratio measures the dollars available to meet interest payment obligations (earnings available to meet interest expense). A value of 1 for this ratio means that $1 of earnings is available to meet each dollar of interest payment obligations. A value of less (greater) than 1 means that the applicants have less (more) than $1 of earnings available to pay each dollar of interest payment obligations. This ratio can be tailored to the applicant's situation, depending on what really constitutes fixed charges that must be paid. One version of it follows: (EBIT + Lease payments)/[Interest + Lease payments + Sinking fund/$(1 - T)$], where $T$ is the marginal tax rate.[5] Here, it is assumed that sinking fund payments must be made.[6] They are adjusted by the division of $(1 - T)$ into a before-tax cash outflow so they can be added to other before-tax cash outflows. The variability of cash flows (the cash flow ratio) provides a clue as to how much higher than 1 a times interest earned ratio should be.

The cash-flow-to-debt ratio is a variant of the times interest earned ratio. It measures the cash flows available for debt service in proportion to the debt principal being serviced and can be compared to the interest rate on the debt. If this ratio is equal to the interest rate on the debt, the applicant's cash flows are just sufficient to pay the required interest on the debt principal. The more the ratio exceeds the interest rate on the debt, the larger is the debt-service cushion.

---

5. Another version adds to the denominator investments for replacing equipment that is needed for the applicant to remain in business.

6. *Sinking funds* are required periodic payments into a fund that is used to retire the principal amounts on bonds outstanding (see Chapter 6).

*Profitability Ratios.*

$$\text{Gross margin} = \frac{\text{Gross profit}}{\text{Sales}} = \frac{4{,}175}{12{,}430} = 33.59\%$$

$$\text{Operating profit margin} = \frac{\text{Operating profit}}{\text{Sales}} = \frac{684}{12{,}430} = 5.50\%$$

$$\text{Return on assets} = \frac{\text{EAT}}{\text{Total assets}} = \frac{339}{4{,}430} = 7.65\%$$

$$\text{Return on equity} = \frac{\text{EAT}}{\text{Total equity}} = \frac{339}{1{,}454} = 23.31\%$$

$$\text{Dividend payout} = \frac{\text{Dividends}}{\text{EAT}} = \frac{50}{339} = 14.75\%$$

**EAT**

*Earnings after taxes.*

where **EAT** represents earnings after taxes, or net income.

For all but the dividend payout ratio, the higher the value of the ratio, the higher the profitability of the firm. The dividend payout ratio measures how much of the profit is retained in the firm versus paid out to the stockholders as dividends. The lower the dividend payout ratio, the more profits (percentage wise) are retained in the firm. A profitable firm that retains its earnings increases its level of equity capital as well as its creditworthiness. The analyst should be concerned about large swings in profitability as well as profit trends.[7]

*Cautions with Ratio Analysis.* While ratio analysis provides useful information about a loan applicant's financial condition, it also has limitations that require care and judgment in its use. For example, many firms operate in more than one industry. For these companies, it is difficult to construct a meaningful set of industry averages. Further, different accounting practices can distort industry comparisons. For example, the loan applicant may be using straight line depreciation for its fixed assets, while industry competitors are using an accelerated cost recovery method (ACRS), which causes depreciation to accrue quickly. ACRS methods will cause fixed asset values to be written down quickly and leave their book value lower than straight line depreciation. This can distort the analysis of fixed asset–based ratios. In addition, it is sometimes difficult to generalize whether a particular value for a ratio is good or bad. For example, a high current ratio can be a sign of a highly liquid firm or one that holds excessive cash. FI loan officers need to be aware of the problems with ratio analysis in analyzing the loan applicant's financial statements and making a loan decision.

**Common-Size Analysis and Growth Rates.** In addition to the ratios listed previously, an analyst can compute sets of ratios by dividing all income statement amounts by total sales revenue and all balance sheet amounts by total assets. These calculations yield common-size financial statements that can be used to identify changes in corporate performance. Year-to-year growth rates also give useful ratios for identifying trends. Common-size financial statements may provide quantitative clues as to the direction in which the firm is moving as well as the direction that the analysis should take.

Having reviewed the financial and other conditions of the applicant, the FI can include loan covenants (similar to bond covenants discussed in Chapter 6) as a part of the loan agreement. Loan covenants reduce the risk of the loan to the lender. They can include a variety of conditions such as maintenance of various ratios at or within stated ranges, key-person insurance policies on employees critical to the success of the project funded by the loan, and so on.

**Following Approval.** The credit process does not end when the applicant signs the loan agreement. As is the case for mortgage loans, before allowing a drawdown (the actual release of the funds to the borrower) of a mid-market credit, the account officer must make sure that

---

7. *Market value ratios* such as the growth rate in the share price, price-earnings ratio, and dividend yield are also valuable indicators if they are available. For a mid-market corporation, however, they are probably unavailable since the debt and equity claims of most mid-market corporations are not publicly traded. The account officer may find it informative to substitute a similar listed firm (a comparability test).

**conditions precedent**

*Those conditions specified in the credit agreement that must be fulfilled before drawdowns are permitted.*

**conditions precedent** have been cleared. Conditions precedent are those conditions specified in the credit agreement that must be fulfilled before drawdowns are permitted. These include various title searches, perfecting of collateral, and the like. Following drawdown, the credit must be monitored throughout the loan's life to ensure that the borrower is living up to its commitments and to detect any deterioration in the borrower's creditworthiness so as to protect the FI's interest in the loan being repaid in full with the promised interest return.

Typically, the borrower's credit needs will change from time to time. A growing company has an expanding need for credit. A company moving into the international arena needs foreign exchange. A contractor may have periodic guarantee requests. Even if the credit agreements being offered do not change, a corporation's credit needs are usually reviewed on an annual basis to ensure that they comply with the terms of the original credit agreement. FIs typically wish to maintain close contact with customers to meet their ongoing financial service requirements—both credit and noncredit—so that the relationship will develop into a permanent, mutually beneficial one (the customer relationship effect).

**LG 20-5**

### Large Commercial and Industrial Lending

An FI's bargaining strength is severely diminished when it deals with large creditworthy corporate customers. Large corporations are able to issue debt and equity directly in the capital markets as well as to make private placements of securities. Also, they typically maintain credit relationships with several FIs and have significant in-house financial expertise. They manage their cash positions through the money markets by issuing their own commercial paper (see Chapter 5) to meet fund shortfalls and use excess funds to buy Treasury bills, banker's acceptances, and other companies' commercial paper. Moreover, large corporate clients are not seriously restricted by international borders but have operations and access to international capital markets and FIs in many parts of the world. Large corporate clients are very attractive to FIs because, although spreads and fees are small in percentage terms, the transactions are often large enough to make them very profitable as long as a default does not occur and they offer the potential for cross-selling other FI products to the client.

Specifically, the FI's relationship with large corporate clients goes beyond lending. The FI's role as broker, dealer, and advisor to a corporate client may rival or exceed the importance of its role as a lender. A large corporate client is likely to investigate several avenues for obtaining credit and to compare, for example, the flexibility and cost of a bond, a private placement, and borrowing from different FIs. The client may periodically poll FIs to determine opportune times to tap financial markets, even if this means inventorying funds. The FI's loan account officer must often liaise with the FI's investment banker to obtain information and indicative pricing on new security issues. Clearly, the amount of time this involves means that an FI's senior corporate account officer manages far fewer accounts than colleagues providing mid-market credits.

In providing a credit service to large corporations, credit management remains an important issue. Large corporations frequently use loan commitments (a contractual commitment to loan to a firm a certain maximum amount at a given interest rate), performance guarantees (such as letters of credit—see Chapter 5), and term loans, as do mid-market corporates. If the FI is contracting in spot and forward foreign exchange or swaps, or is engaging in other derivative activities with the corporate client as a counterparty, it must do so within the credit limits established by a regular credit review process.

An additional complicating factor is that large corporate accounts often consist of several related corporate entities under a common management. For example, a holding company may wholly own, control, or have substantial stakes in various operating subsidiaries. A subsidiary's credit risk may be better than, the same as, or worse than that of a holding company as a whole. An FI lending to a holding company with no assets other than its equity stake in its subsidiaries puts itself in a subordinate lending position relative to the lenders to the operating subsidiaries, which have direct claims over those subsidiaries' operating assets.

An account officer preparing a credit review for a large corporate customer often faces a complex task. The standard methods of analysis that we introduced when discussing mid-market corporates apply to large corporate clients but with additional complications. The corporate business often crosses more than one business activity and location. Hence, industry comparisons are difficult at best. Additional analytical aids are available to account officers. Specifically, large corporations are tracked by rating agencies and market analysts, who can provide account officers with a great deal of information to aid in their credit analysis. Also, because of these customers' additional complexities and large credit risk exposures, FIs can use sophisticated credit-scoring models in the credit review process based on accounting and/or financial market data. We discuss two such credit-scoring models below.

**Credit-Scoring Models.** Credit-scoring models use data on observed borrower characteristics either to calculate the probability of default or to sort borrowers into different default risk classes. By selecting and combining different economic and financial borrower characteristics, an FI manager may be able to:

1. Numerically establish which factors are important in explaining default risk.
2. Evaluate the relative degree or importance of these factors.
3. Improve the pricing of default risk.
4. Screen high-risk loan applicants.
5. Calculate any reserves needed to meet expected future loan losses.

To employ credit-scoring models in this manner, the FI manager must identify objective economic and financial measures of risk for any particular class of borrower. For consumer loans, the objective characteristics in a credit-scoring model might include income, assets, age, occupation, and location. For commercial loans, cash flow information and financial ratios such as the debt-to-equity ratio are usually key factors. After data are identified, a statistical technique quantifies or scores the default risk probability or default risk classification.

*Altman's Z Score.* E. I. Altman developed a Z-score model for analyzing publicly traded manufacturing firms in the United States. The indicator variable $Z$ is an overall measure of the borrower's default risk classification. This classification, in turn, depends on the values of various financial ratios of the borrower ($X_j$) and the weighted importance of these ratios based on the observed experience of defaulting versus nondefaulting borrowers derived from a discriminant analysis model.[8]

Altman's credit-scoring model takes the following form:

$$Z = 1.2X_1 + 1.4X_2 + 3.3X_3 + 0.6X_4 + 1.0X_5$$

where

$X_1 = $ Working capital/Total assets

$X_2 = $ Retained earnings/Total assets[9]

$X_3 = $ Earnings before interest and taxes/Total assets

$X_4 = $ Market value of equity/Book value of total liabilities

$X_5 = $ Sales/Total assets

---

**EXAMPLE 20–4**   Calculation of Altman's Z Score

Suppose that the financial ratios of a potential borrowing firm take the following values:

$$X_1 = 0.2$$
$$X_2 = 0$$
$$X_3 = -0.20$$
$$X_4 = 0.10$$
$$X_5 = 2.0$$

The ratio $X_2$ is zero and $X_3$ is negative, indicating that the firm has had negative earnings or losses in recent periods. Also, $X_4$ indicates that the borrower is highly leveraged. However,

---

8. E. I. Altman, "Managing the Commercial Lending Process," in *Handbook of Banking Strategy,* ed. R. C. Aspinwall and R. A. Eisenbeis (New York: John Wiley & Sons, 1985), pp. 473–510. See also footnote 4 in this chapter for a discussion of this technique. Other models include linear probability models and logit models. See A. Saunders and M. M. Cornett, *Financial Institutions Management: A Risk Management Approach,* 9th ed. (New York: McGraw-Hill, 2018).
9. Working capital is Current assets – Current liabilities.

the working capital ratio ($X_1$) and the sales/assets ratio ($X_5$) indicate that the firm is reasonably liquid and is maintaining its sales volume. The $Z$ score provides an overall score or indicator of the borrower's credit risk since it combines and weights these five factors according to their past importance in explaining (discriminating between) borrower default and borrower repayment. For the borrower in question:

$$Z = 1.2(0.2) + 1.4(0) + 3.3(-0.20) + 0.6(0.10) + 1.0(2.0)$$
$$Z = 0.24 + 0 - 0.66 + 0.06 + 2.0$$
$$Z = 1.64$$

With a $Z$ score less than 1.81 (i.e., in the high default risk region), the FI should not make a loan to this borrower until it improves its earnings.

According to Altman's credit-scoring model, any firm with a $Z$ score of less than 1.81 should be considered a high default risk firm; between 1.81 and 2.99, an indeterminate default risk firm; and greater than 2.99, a low default risk firm.

Use of the $Z$-score model to make credit risk evaluations has a number of problems. The first problem is that this model usually discriminates only among three cases of borrower behavior: high, indeterminate, and low default risk. As discussed in Chapter 19, in the real world various gradations of default exist, from nonpayment or delay of interest payments (nonperforming assets) to outright default on all promised interest and principal payments. This problem suggests that a more accurate or finely calibrated sorting among borrowers may require defining more classes in the scoring model.

The second problem is that there is no obvious economic reason to expect that the weights in the Z-score model—or, more generally, the weights in any credit-scoring model—will be constant over any but very short periods. Further, discriminant analysis models are very sensitive to the weights for the different variables. Since different industries have different operating characteristics, there is no reason that the functions would be similar for different industries. In the retail market, the demographics of the market play a big role in the value of the weights. For example, credit card companies often evaluate different models for different areas of the country. Because of the sensitivity of the models, extreme care should be taken in the process of selecting the correct sample to validate the model for use. The same concern also applies to the scoring model's explanatory variables ($X_j$). Specifically, due to changing financial market conditions, other borrower-specific financial ratios may come to be increasingly relevant in explaining default risk probabilities.

The third problem is that this model ignores important, hard-to-quantify factors that may play a crucial role in the default or no-default decision. For example, the reputation of the borrower and the nature of long-term borrower–lender relationships could be important borrower-specific characteristics, as could macro factors such as the phase of the business cycle. Credit-scoring models like the Z-score model often ignore these variables. Moreover, traditional credit-scoring models rarely use publicly available information, such as the prices of the outstanding public debt and equity of the borrower.

A fourth problem relates to the infrequency (e.g., quarterly or annually) with which accounting variables are updated. This allows scores to be changed at generally infrequent intervals.

**www.moodysanalytics.com**   *Moody's Analytics Credit Monitor Model.*   In recent years, following the pioneering work on options by Merton, Black, and Scholes, we now recognize that when a firm raises funds either by issuing bonds or by increasing its bank loans, it holds a very valuable default or repayment option.[10] That is, if a borrower's investments fail to pay off, so that it cannot repay its bond holders or the loan to the FI, it has the option to default on its debt

---

10.  R. C. Merton, "On the Pricing of Corporate Debt: The Risk Structure of Interest Rates," *Journal of Finance* 29 (1974), pp. 449–70; F. Black and M. Scholes, "The Pricing of Options and Corporate Liabilities," *Journal of Political Economy* 81 (1973), pp. 737–59.

repayments and turn any remaining assets over to the debtholder. Because of limited liability, the borrower's loss is limited, on the downside, by the amount of equity that is invested in the firm. On the other hand, if things go well, the borrower can keep most of the upside returns on asset investments after the promised principal and interest on the debt have been paid. The KMV Corporation (purchased by Moody's in 2002 and now part of Moody's Analytics Enterprise Risk Solutions) has turned this relatively simple idea into a credit-monitoring model. Many of the largest U.S. banks are now using this model to determine the expected default frequency (EDF), that is, the probability of default, of large corporations.[11]

The expected default frequency that is calculated reflects the probability that the market value of the firm's assets will fall below the promised repayments on debt liabilities in one year. If the value of a firm's assets falls below its debt liabilities, it can be viewed as being economically insolvent. Simulations by Moody's Analytics have shown that this model outperforms both accounting-based models and S&P rating changes as predictors of corporate failure and distress.[12] An example for AMR Corp., which filed for Chapter 11 bankruptcy protection on November 29, 2011, is shown in Figure 20–2. Note that the Moody's Analytics score (EDF) is rising earlier than rating agencies are downgrading the firm's debt. Indeed, the rating agencies were very slow to react to, if not totally insensitive to, the increase in AMR Corp's risk. Thus, the Moody's Analytics EDF score gives a better "early warning" of impending default. In an effort to get control over credit-rating firms that give high-quality

**Figure 20–2** Moody's Analytics EDF, Moody's, and S&P Ratings for AMR Corporation

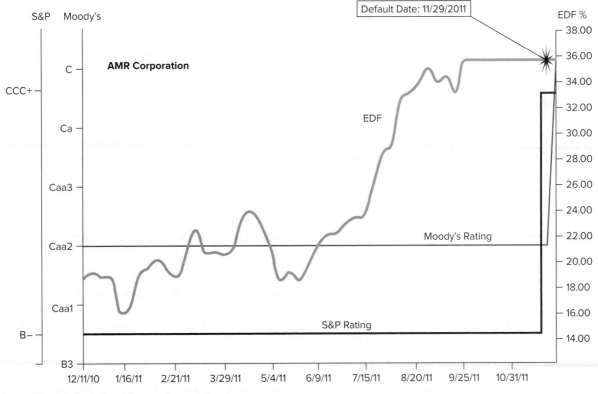

**Source:** Moody's Analytics. www.moodysanalytics.com

11. See KMV Corporation, *Credit Monitor* (San Francisco: KMV Corporation, 1994).
12. The Moody's Analytics database contains 30 years of information on over 6,000 public and 220,000 private company default events for a total of 60,000 public and 2.8 million private companies, healthy and distressed, around the world.

ratings to high-risk firms, in April 2009 the Credit Rating Agency Reform Act was passed. This act gave the SEC regulatory authority over credit-rating firms and was intended to increase competition and oversight of credit-rating firms.

# CALCULATING THE RETURN ON A LOAN

LG 20-6

An important element in the credit management process, once the decision to make a loan has been made, is its pricing. This includes adjustments for the perceived credit risk or default risk of the borrower. This section demonstrates two ways to calculate the return on a loan: the traditional *return on assets approach* and a newer approach used by many FIs including banks, thrifts, and insurance companies called *risk-adjusted return on capital* (RAROC), which considers loan returns in the context of the risk of the loan to the FI. While we demonstrate the return calculations using examples of commercial and industrial loans, the techniques can be used to calculate the return on other loans (such as credit card or mortgage loans) as well.

## Return on Assets (ROA)

A number of factors impact the promised return that an FI achieves on any given dollar loan (asset) amount. These factors include the following:

1. The interest rate on the loan.
2. Any fees relating to the loan.
3. The credit risk premium ($m$) on the loan.
4. The collateral backing the loan.
5. Other nonprice terms (such as compensating balances and reserve requirements).

   In this section, we consider an example of how to calculate the promised return on a C&I loan. Suppose that an FI makes a spot one-year, $1 million loan. The loan rate is set as follows:

$$\begin{array}{r} \text{Base lending rate } (BR) = \phantom{0}8\% \\ +\text{ Risk premium } (m) = \phantom{0}2\% \\ \hline BR + m = 10\% \end{array}$$

### LIBOR

*The London Interbank Offered Rate, the rate for interbank dollar loans in the foreign or Eurodollar market of a given maturity.*

### prime lending rate

*The base lending rate periodically set by banks.*

### compensating balance

*A proportion of a loan that a borrower is required to hold on deposit at the lending institution.*

The base lending rate ($BR$) could reflect the FI's weighted average cost of capital or its marginal cost of funds, such as the commercial paper rate, the federal funds rate, or **LIBOR**—the London Interbank Offered Rate, which is the rate for interbank dollar loans in the foreign or Eurodollar market of a given maturity. Alternatively, the base lending rate could reflect the **prime lending rate.** Traditionally, the prime rate has been the rate charged to the bank's lowest risk customers. Now it is more a rate to which positive or negative risk premiums ($m$) can be added. In other words, FIs now charge their best and largest borrowers below prime rate to compete with the commercial paper market.

   Direct and indirect fees and charges relating to a loan fall into three general categories:

1. A loan origination fee ($f$) charged to the borrower for processing the application.
2. A compensating balance requirement ($b$) to be held as generally non-interest-bearing demand deposits. **Compensating balances** represent a percentage of a loan that a borrower cannot actively use for expenditures. Instead, these balances must be kept on deposit at the FI. For example, a borrower facing a 10 percent compensating balance requirement on a $100 loan would have to place $10 on deposit (traditionally in a demand deposit) with the FI and could use only $90 of the $100 borrowed. This requirement raises the effective cost of loans for the borrower since less than the full loan amount ($90 in this case) can actually be used by the borrower and the deposit rate earned on compensating balances is less than the borrowing rate. Thus, compensating balance requirements act as an additional source of return on lending for an FI.[13]

---

13. They also create a more stable supply of deposits and, thus, mitigate liquidity problems.

**3.** A reserve requirement charge (*RR*) imposed by the Federal Reserve on the bank's demand deposits, including any compensating balances (see Chapter 13).

Although credit risk may be the most important factor ultimately affecting the return on a loan, FI managers should not ignore these other factors in evaluating loan profitability and risk. Indeed, FIs can compensate for high credit risk in a number of ways other than charging a higher explicit interest rate or risk premium on a loan or restricting the amount of credit available. In particular, higher fees, high compensating balances, and increased collateral backing offer implicit and indirect methods to compensate an FI for lending risk. Indeed, fee income has become increasingly important in the cost-benefit analysis of consumer and business lending. Consequently, the contractually promised gross return on the loan, *k*, per dollar lent (or $1 + k$)—or ROA per dollar lent—will equal:[14]

$$1 + k = 1 + \frac{f + (BR + m)}{1 - b(1 - RR)}$$

The numerator of this formula is the promised gross cash inflow to the FI per dollar lent, reflecting direct fees (*f*) plus the loan interest rate ($BR + m$) discussed earlier. In the denominator, for every \$1 that the FI lends, it retains *b* as non-interest-bearing compensating balances. Thus, $1 - b$ represents the net proceeds of each \$1 of loan received by the borrower from the FI, ignoring reserve requirements. However, since *b* (the compensating balance) is held by the borrower at the FI in a demand deposit account, the Federal Reserve requires the FI to hold non-(or low-)interest-bearing reserves at the rate *RR* against these compensating balances. Thus, the FI's net benefit from requiring compensating balances must consider the cost of holding additional reserves. The net outflow by the FI per \$1 of loans is, thus, $1 - b(1 - RR)$, or 1 minus the reserve-adjusted compensating balance requirement.

---

**EXAMPLE 20–5** Calculation of ROA on a Loan

Suppose a bank does the following:

**1.** Sets the loan rate on a prospective loan at 10 percent (where $BR = 6\%$ and $m = 4\%$).
**2.** Charges a ⅛ percent (or 0.125 percent) loan origination fee (*f*) to the borrower.
**3.** Imposes a 8 percent compensating balance requirement (*b*) to be held as non-interest-bearing demand deposits.
**4.** Sets aside reserves (*RR*) at a rate of 10 percent of deposits, held at the Federal Reserve (i.e., the Fed's cash-to-deposit reserve ratio is 10 percent).

Placing the numbers from our example into this formula, we have:

$$1 + k = 1 + \frac{0.00125 + (0.06 + 0.04)}{1 - (0.08)(0.9)}$$

$$1 + k = 1 + \frac{0.10125}{0.928}$$

$$1 + k = 1.1091, \text{ or } k = 10.91\%$$

This is, of course, larger than the simple promised interest return on the loan, $BR + m = 10$ percent.

---

In the special case in which fees (*f*) are zero and the compensating balance (*b*) is zero:

$$f = 0$$
$$b = 0$$

---

14. This formula ignores present value aspects that could easily be incorporated. For example, fees are earned in up-front undiscounted dollars, while interest payments and risk premiums are normally paid on loan maturity and, thus, should be discounted by the FI's cost of funds.

the contractually promised return formula reduces to:

$$1 + k = 1 + (BR + m)$$

That is, the credit risk premium is the fundamental factor driving the promised return on a loan, once the base rate on the loan has been set.

Note that as commercial lending markets have become more competitive, both origination fees ($f$) and compensating balances ($b$) have become less important. For example, when compensating balances are still required, FIs may now allow them to be held as time deposits and earn interest. As a result, borrowers' opportunity losses from compensating balances have been reduced to the difference between the loan rate and the compensating balance time-deposit rate. In addition, compensating balance requirements are very rare on international loans such as Eurodollar loans. Finally, note that for a given promised gross return on a loan, $k$, FI managers can use the pricing formula to find various combinations of fees, compensating balances, and risk premiums they may offer their customers that will generate the same returns.

### RAROC Models

An increasingly popular model used to evaluate the return on a loan to a large customer is the risk-adjusted return on capital (RAROC) model. Bankers Trust (acquired by Deutsche Bank in 1998) pioneered RAROC, which has now been adopted by virtually all the large banks in the United States and Europe, although with some proprietary differences among them.

The essential idea behind RAROC is that rather than evaluating the actual or promised annual cash flow on a loan as a percentage of the amount lent (or ROA), as described in the last subsection, the lending officer balances the loan's expected income against the loan's expected risk. Thus, the numerator of the RAROC equation is net income (or ROA – Cost of funding the loan) on the loan. Further, rather than dividing expected annual loan income by assets lent, it is divided by some measure of asset (loan) value at risk or what is often called value (or capital) at risk, since loan losses have to be written against an FI's capital (see Chapter 12):

$$\text{RAROC} = \frac{\text{One-year income on a loan}}{\text{Loan (asset) risk or value at risk}}$$

A loan is approved by the FI only if RAROC is sufficiently high relative to a benchmark return on equity capital, where ROE measures the return stockholders require on their equity investment in the FI. The idea here is that a loan should be made only if the risk-adjusted return on the loan adds to the FI's equity value as measured by the ROE required by the FI's stockholders. Thus, for example, if an FI's ROE is 10 percent, a loan should be made only if the estimated RAROC is higher than the 10 percent required by the FI's stockholders as a reward for their investment. Alternatively, if the RAROC on an existing loan falls below an FI's RAROC benchmark, the lending officer should seek to adjust the loan's terms (e.g., via the required loan rate or fees) to make it "profitable" again. Therefore, RAROC serves as both a credit-risk measure and a loan pricing tool for the FI manager.

One problem in estimating RAROC is the measurement of loan risk (the denominator in the RAROC equation). In calculating RAROC, most FIs divide one-year loan income by a loan risk measure calculated as the product of the dollar value of the loan, an "unexpected" default rate, and the proportion of the loan that cannot be recaptured on a borrower's default—the so-called loss given default. Thus,

$$\text{RAROC} = \frac{\text{One-year income on a loan}}{\text{Dollar value of a loan} \times \text{Unexpected default rate} \times \text{Loss given default}}$$

**DO YOU UNDERSTAND:**

8. *What factors impact the rate of return on loans issued by FIs?*

9. *What the difference between the ROA and the RAROC on a loan is?*

The denominator in the RAROC equation is, therefore, an estimate of the unexpected overall loss on the loan in extreme conditions such as the worst year in the next 100 years, which is the product of the unexpected default rate and the loss given default.

---

**EXAMPLE 20–6** Calculation of RAROC

Suppose a borrower of $100,000 has risk characteristics that put the firm in a risk class that has experienced an average historical default rate of 0.2 percent. However, one year in every 100 (or 1 percent of the time), such as in a major recession, the bank expects 4 percent of these types of loans to default. This 4 percent can be viewed as the unexpected or 1 in 100 years default rate.[15] Moreover, upon default, the FI has historically recovered only 20 percent of the defaulted loans. As a result, the loss given default is 80 percent. Accordingly, for this borrower, the loan loss risk per dollar lent is $0.032 (0.04 \times 0.80)$, or the value (or capital) at risk to the FI (the denominator of the RAROC equation) is $100,000(0.04 \times 0.80) = \$3,200$.

Suppose the cost of funds for the FI is 9.80 percent and the loan rate is 10 percent on the $100,000 loan. After adjusting for fees of 0.1 percent, the expected one-year income on the loan, or the numerator of the RAROC equation, is $100,000 times 0.3 cents per dollar lent $(10\% - 9.80\% + 0.10\%)$, or 0.003. The extreme case loss rate for borrowers of this type is 4 percent (i.e., the default that has or is projected to occur once in every 100 years), and the dollar proportion of loans of this type that cannot be recaptured on default (loss given default) has historically been 80 percent. Then:

$$\text{RAROC} = \frac{100,000(0.003)}{(100,000)(0.04)(0.8)} = \frac{300}{3,200} = 9.375\%$$

If the FI's ROE is less than 9.375 percent (e.g., it is 9 percent), the loan can be viewed as being profitable. If the ROE is higher than 9.375 percent (e.g., 9.5 percent), it should be rejected and/or the loan officer should seek higher spreads and fees on the loan.[16]

---

15. The extreme loss rate is usually calculated by taking the average annual loss rate over some historical period and estimating the annual standard deviation of loan loss rates around that mean. If the standard deviation is multiplied by 2.33, as long as loan loss rates are normally distributed, this reflects the 99th percentile worst-loss case scenario. In practice, loss rates are not normally distributed, so many FIs use higher multiples of $\sigma$. For example, Bank of America uses a multiple of $6 \times \sigma$.

16. For more on RAROC, see A. Saunders and L. Allen, *Credit Risk Measurement: New Approaches to Value at Risk and Other Paradigms,* 2nd ed. (New York: John Wiley & Sons, 2002).

## SUMMARY

This chapter provided an in-depth look at the measurement and on-balance-sheet management of credit risks. The chapter then discussed the role of credit analysis and how it differs across different types of loans, especially mortgage loans, individual loans, mid-market corporate loans, and large corporate loans. Both qualitative and quantitative approaches to credit analysis were discussed, as well as methods to evaluate the risk of loan portfolios.

## QUESTIONS

1. Why is credit risk analysis an important component of FI risk management? (*LG 20-1*)

2. What are the primary considerations used by FIs to evaluate mortgage loans? (*LG 20-2*)

3. What are the purposes of credit-scoring models? How do these models assist an FI manager to better administer credit? (*LG 20-3*)

4. How does an FI evaluate its credit risks with respect to consumer and small-business loans? (*LG 20-3*)

5. In what ways does the credit analysis of a mid-market borrower differ from that of a small-business borrower? (*LG 20-4*)

6. What are some of the special risks and considerations when lending to small businesses rather than large businesses? (*LG 20-4, LG 20-5*)

**7.** Why must an account officer be well versed in the FI's credit policy before talking to potential mid-market business borrowers? *(LG 20-4)*

**8.** How does ratio analysis help answer questions about the production, management, and marketing capabilities of a prospective borrower? *(LG 20-4)*

**9.** Why should a credit officer be concerned if a mid-market business borrower's liquidity ratios differ from the industry norm? *(LG 20-4)*

**10.** What are conditions precedent? *(LG20-4)*

**11.** Why is an FI's bargaining strength weaker when dealing with large corporate borrowers than mid-market business borrowers? *(LG20-5)*

**12.** Consider the coefficients of Altman's Z score. Can you tell by the size of the coefficients which ratio appears most important in assessing the creditworthiness of a loan applicant? Explain. *(LG 20-5)*

**13.** Why could a lender's expected return be lower when the risk premium is increased on a loan? *(LG 20-6)*

**14.** What are compensating balances? What is the relationship between the amount of compensating balance requirement and the return on the loan to the FI? *(LG20-6)*

***The following questions are related to the Appendix material.***

**15.** How does loan portfolio risk differ from individual loan risk? *(LG 20-6)*

**16.** Explain how modern portfolio theory can be applied to lower the credit risk of an FI's portfolio. *(LG 20-6)*

## PROBLEMS

**1.** Jane Doe earns $30,000 per year and has applied for an $80,000, 30-year mortgage at 8 percent interest, paid monthly. Property taxes on the house are expected to be $1,200 per year. If her bank requires a gross debt service ratio of no more than 30 percent, will Jane be able to obtain the mortgage? *(LG 20-2)*

**2.** Suppose you are a loan officer at Carbondale Local Bank. Joan Doe listed the following information on her mortgage application: *(LG 20-2, LG 20-3)*

| Characteristic | Value |
| --- | --- |
| Annual gross income | $45,000 |
| TDS | 10% |
| Relations with FI | Checking account |
| Major credit cards | 5 |
| Age | 27 |
| Residence | Own/Mortgage |
| Length of residence | 2½ years |
| Job stability | 5½ years |
| Credit history | Missed 2 payments 1 year ago |

Use the information below to determine whether or not Joan Doe should be approved for a mortgage from your bank.

| Characteristic | Characteristic Values and Weights | | | | |
| --- | --- | --- | --- | --- | --- |
| Annual gross income | <$10,000 | $10,000–$25,000 | $25,000–$50,000 | $50,000–$100,000 | >$100,000 |
| Score | 0 | 10 | 20 | 35 | 60 |
| TDS | >50% | 35%–50% | 15%–35% | 5%–15% | <5% |
| Score | −10 | 0 | 20 | 40 | 60 |
| Relations with FI | None | Checking account | Savings account | Both | |
| Score | 0 | 10 | 10 | 20 | |
| Major credit cards | None | Between 1 and 4 | 5 or more | | |
| Score | 0 | 20 | 10 | | |
| Age | <25 | 25–60 | >60 | | |
| Score | 5 | 25 | 35 | | |
| Residence | Rent | Own with mortgage | Own outright | | |
| Score | 5 | 20 | 50 | | |

| Characteristic | Characteristic Values and Weights | | |
| --- | --- | --- | --- |
| Length of residence | <1 year | 1–5 years | >5 years |
| Score | 0 | 25 | 40 |
| Job stability | <1 year | 1–5 years | >5 years |
| Score | 0 | 25 | 50 |
| Credit history | No record | Missed a payment in last 5 years | Met all payments |
| Score | 0 | −15 | 40 |

The loan is automatically rejected if the applicant's *total* score is less than or equal to 120. The loan is automatically approved if the total score is greater than or equal to 190. A score between 120 and 190 (noninclusive) is reviewed by a loan committee for a final decision.

**3.** In 2018, Webb Sports Shop had cash flows from investing activities of $2,567,000 and cash flows from financing activities of $3,459,000. The balance in the firm's cash account was $950,000 at the beginning of 2018 and $1,025,000 at the end of the year. Calculate Webb Sports Shop's cash flow from operations for 2018. *(LG 20-4)*

**4.** Use the balance sheet and income statement below to construct a statement of cash flows for 2019 for Clancy's Dog Biscuit Corp. *(LG 20-4)*

**Clancy's Dog Biscuit Corporation**
**Balance Sheet as of December 31, 2018 and 2019**
**(in millions of dollars)**

| Assets | 2018 | 2019 | Liabilities & Equity | 2018 | 2019 |
| --- | --- | --- | --- | --- | --- |
| Current assets: | | | Current liabilities: | | |
| Cash and marketable securities | $ 5 | $ 5 | Accrued wages and taxes | $ 6 | $ 10 |
| Accounts receivable | 19 | 20 | Accounts payable | 15 | 16 |
| Inventory | 29 | 36 | Notes payable | 13 | 14 |
| Total | $ 53 | $ 61 | Total | $ 34 | $ 40 |

| Fixed assets: | | | Long-term debt: | $ 53 | $ 57 |
|---|---|---|---|---|---|
| Gross plant and | | | Stockholders' equity: | | |
| equipment | $ 88 | $106 | Preferred stock | | |
| Less: Depreciation | 11 | 15 | (2 million | | |
| Net plant | | | shares) | $ 2 | $ 2 |
| and equipment | $ 77 | $ 91 | Common | | |
| | | | stock and | | |
| | | | paid-in surplus | | |
| | | | (5 million shares) | 11 | 11 |
| Other long-term | | | Retained | | |
| assets | 15 | 15 | earnings | 45 | 57 |
| Total | $ 92 | $106 | Total | $ 58 | $ 70 |
| Total | | | Total liabilities | | |
| assets | $145 | $167 | and equity | $145 | $167 |

### Clancy's Dog Biscuit Corporation
### Income Statement
### for Years Ending December 31, 2018 and 2019
### (in millions of dollars)

| | 2018 | 2019 |
|---|---|---|
| Net sales | $80 | $76 |
| Less: Cost of goods sold | 39 | 44 |
| Gross profits | 41 | 32 |
| Less: Depreciation and other operating expenses | 4 | 4 |
| Earnings before interest and taxes (EBIT) | 37 | 28 |
| Less: Interest | 5 | 5 |
| Earnings before taxes (EBT) | 32 | 23 |
| Less: Taxes | 10 | 7 |
| Net income | $22 | $16 |
| Less: Preferred stock dividends | $ 1 | $ 1 |
| Net income available to common stockholders | 21 | 15 |
| Less: Common stock dividends | 3 | 3 |
| Addition to retained earnings | $18 | $12 |

5. Harper Outdoor Furniture Inc. has net cash flows from operating activities for the last year of $340 million. The income statement shows that net income is $315 million and depreciation expense is $46 million. During the year, the change in inventory on the balance sheet was $38 million, the change in accrued wages and taxes was $15 million, and the change in accounts payable was $20 million. At the beginning of the year the balance of accounts receivable was $50 million. Calculate the end-of-year balance for accounts receivable. (*LG 20-4*)

6. Consider the following company's balance sheet and income statement. (*LG 20-4*)

### Balance Sheet

| Assets | | Liabilities and Equity | |
|---|---|---|---|
| Cash | $ 4,000 | Accounts payable | $ 30,000 |
| Accounts | | Notes | |
| receivable | 52,000 | payable | 12,000 |
| Inventory | 40,000 | Total current | |
| | | liabilities | 42,000 |
| Total current | | Long-term debt | 36,000 |
| assets | 96,000 | | |
| Fixed assets | 44,000 | Equity | 62,000 |
| | | Total liabilities | |
| Total assets | $140,000 | and equity | $140,000 |

### Income Statement

| | |
|---|---|
| Sales (all on credit) | $200,000 |
| Cost of goods sold | 130,000 |
| Gross margin | 70,000 |
| Selling and administrative expenses | 20,000 |
| Depreciation | 8,000 |
| EBIT | 42,000 |
| Interest expense | 4,800 |
| Earnings before tax | 37,200 |
| Taxes | 11,160 |
| Net income | $ 26,040 |

For this company, calculate the following:
a. Current ratio.
b. Number of days' sales in receivables.
c. Sales to total assets.
d. Number of days in inventory.
e. Debt-to-asset ratio.
f. Cash-flow-to-debt ratio.
g. Return on assets.
h. Return on equity.

7. In Problem 6, how might we determine whether these ratios reflect a well-managed, creditworthy company? (*LG 20-4*)

**Use the following financial statements for Lake of Egypt Marina to answer Problem 8.** (*LG 20-4*)

### Lake of Egypt Marina Inc.
### Balance Sheet as of December 31, 2018 and 2019
### (in millions of dollars)

| Assets | 2018 | 2019 | Liabilities & Equity | 2018 | 2019 |
|---|---|---|---|---|---|
| Current assets: | | | Current liabilities: | | |
| Cash and | | | Accrued | | |
| marketable | | | wages and | | |
| securities | $ 65 | $ 75 | taxes | $ 43 | $ 40 |
| Accounts | | | Accounts | | |
| receivable | 110 | 115 | payable | 80 | 90 |
| Inventory | 190 | 200 | Notes payable | 70 | 80 |
| Total | $365 | $390 | Total | $193 | $210 |
| Fixed assets: | | | Long-term debt: | $280 | $300 |
| Gross plant | | | | | |
| and equipment | $471 | $580 | Stockholders' equity: | | |
| Less: Depreciation | 100 | 110 | Preferred stock | | |
| | | | (2 million shares) | $ 5 | $ 5 |
| Net plant | | | Common stock | | |
| and equipment | $371 | $470 | and paid-in | | |
| | | | surplus | | |
| | | | (65 million shares) | 65 | 65 |
| Other long-term | | | | | |
| assets | 49 | 50 | | | |
| Total | $420 | $520 | Retained earnings | 242 | 330 |
| | | | Total | $312 | $400 |
| Total | | | Total liabilities | | |
| assets | $785 | $910 | and equity | $785 | $910 |

### Lake of Egypt Marina Inc.
### Income Statement
### for Years Ending December 31, 2018 and 2019
### (in millions of dollars)

| | 2018 | 2019 |
|---|---|---|
| Net sales (all credit) | $432 | $515 |
| Less: Cost of goods sold | 200 | 260 |

| | | |
|---|---|---|
| Gross profits | 232 | 255 |
| Less: Depreciation and other operating expenses | 20 | 22 |
| Earnings before interest and taxes (EBIT) | 212 | 233 |
| Less: Interest | 30 | 33 |
| Earnings before taxes (EBT) | 182 | 200 |
| Less: Taxes | 55 | 57 |
| Net income | $127 | $143 |
| Less: Preferred stock dividends | $ 5 | $ 5 |
| Net income available to common stockholders | 122 | 138 |
| Less: Common stock dividends | 65 | 65 |
| Addition to retained earnings | $ 57 | $ 73 |

8. Calculate the following ratios for Lake of Egypt Marina Inc. as of year-end 2019. (*LG 20-4*)

| | Lake of Egypt Marina Inc. Industry |
|---|---|
| a. Current ratio | 2.0 times |
| b. Quick ratio | 1.2 times |
| c. Days sales in receivables | 32.50 days |
| d. Days sales in inventory | 101.39 |
| e. Sales to working capital | 4.25 times |
| f. Sales to fixed assets | 1.15 times |
| g. Total assets turnover | 1.18 times |
| h. Debt to assets | 62.50% |
| i. Times interest earned | 9.50 times |
| j. Cash flow to debt | 62.55% |
| k. Gross margin | 55.55% |
| l. Profit margin | 28.75% |
| m. ROA | 19.75% |
| n. ROE | 36.88% |
| o. Dividend payout ratio | 35% |

Using these ratios for Lake of Egypt Marina Inc. and the industry, what can you conclude about Lake of Egypt Marina's financial performance for 2019? (Ratios l, m, n, and o use net income available to common stockholders.)

9. Industrial Corporation has a net income-to-sales (profit margin) ratio of 0.03, a sales-to-assets (asset utilization) ratio of 1.5, and a debt-to-asset ratio of 0.66. What is Industrial's return on equity? (*LG 20-4*)

10. The following is ABC Inc.'s balance sheet (in thousands): (*LG 20-5*)

| Assets | | Liabilities and Equity | |
|---|---|---|---|
| Cash | $ 20 | Accounts payable | $ 30 |
| Accounts receivable | 90 | Notes payable | 90 |
| Inventory | 90 | Accruals | 30 |
| | | Long-term debt | 150 |
| Plant and equipment | 500 | Equity | 400 |
| Total | $700 | Total | $700 |

Also, sales equal $500, cost of goods sold equals $360, interest payments equal $62, taxes equal $56, and net income equals $22. The beginning retained earnings is $0, the market value of equity is equal to its book value, and the company pays no dividends.

a. Calculate Altman's $Z$ score for ABC, Inc. if ABC has a 50 percent dividend payout ratio and the market value of equity is equal to its book value. Recall the following:

Net working capital = Current assets − Current liabilities

Current assets = Cash + Accounts receivable + Inventories

Current liabilities = Accounts payable + Accruals + Notes payable

EBIT = Revenues − Cost of goods sold − Depreciation

Taxes = (EBIT − Interest)(Tax rate)

Net income = EBIT − Interest − Taxes

Retained earnings = Net income(1 − Dividend payout ratio)

b. Should you approve ABC Inc.'s application to your bank for $500,000 for a capital expansion loan?

c. If ABC's sales were $450,000, taxes were $16,000, and the market value of equity fell to one-quarter of its book value (assume cost of goods sold and interest are unchanged), how would that change ABC's income statement? With the new data, does your credit decision change?

d. What are some of the shortcomings of using a discriminant function model to evaluate credit risk?

11. Suppose that the financial ratios of a potential borrowing firm took the following values: $X_1$ = Net working capital/Total assets = 0.10, $X_2$ = Retained earnings/Total assets = 0.20, $X_3$ = Earnings before interest and taxes/Total assets = 0.22, $X_4$ = Market value of equity/Book value of long-term debt = 0.60, $X_5$ = Sales/Total assets ratio = 0.9. Calculate and interpret the Altman's $Z$ score for this firm. (*LG 20-5*)

12. Countrybank offers one-year loans with a stated rate of 10 percent but requires a compensating balance of 10 percent. What is the true cost of this loan to the borrower? (*LG 20-6*)

13. Metrobank offers one-year loans with a 9 percent stated rate, charges a ¼ percent loan origination fee, imposes a 10 percent compensating balance requirement, and must pay a 6 percent reserve requirement to the Federal Reserve. What is the return to the bank on these loans? (*LG 20-6*)

14. An FI is planning to give a loan of $5,000,000 to a firm in the steel industry. It expects to charge an up-front fee of 0.10 percent and a service fee of 5 basis points. The loan has a maturity of 8 years. The cost of funds (and the RAROC benchmark) for the FI is 10 percent. The FI has estimated the risk premium on the steel manufacturing sector to be approximately 0.18 percent, based on two years of historical data. The current market interest rate for loans in this sector is 10.1 percent. The 99th (extreme case) loss rate for borrowers of this type has historically run at 3 percent, and the dollar proportion of loans of this type that cannot be recaptured on default has historically been 90 percent. Using the RAROC model, should the FI make the loan? (*LG 20-6*)

*The following problem is related to the Appendix material.*

15. A bank has two loans of equal size outstanding, A and B, and the bank has identified the returns they would earn in two different states of nature, 1 and 2, representing default and no default, respectively.

| | State | |
|---|---|---|
| | 1 | 2 |
| Security A | 0.02 | 0.14 |
| Security B | 0.00 | 0.18 |

If the probability of state 1 is 0.2 and the probability of state 2 is 0.8, calculate: (*LG 20-6*)

a. The expected return of each security.

b. The expected return on the portfolio in each state.

c. The expected return on the portfolio.

# SEARCH THE SITE

Go to the FDIC website at **www.fdic.gov.** Find the most recent breakdown for nonperformance rates for C&I loans of commercial banks using the following steps. Click on "Analysts." From there click on "FDIC Quarterly Banking Profile." Click on "Quarterly Banking Profile," and then click on "Commercial Bank Section." Finally, click on "TABLE V-A. Loan Performance, FDIC-Insured Commercial Banks." This will bring up the files that contain the relevant data.

### Questions

1. How has the nonperformance rate changed since 2016?
2. Compare the nonperformance rate of C&I loans with real estate and credit card loans. Which has changed the most since 2016?

## APPENDIX 20A: Loan Portfolio Risk and Management

This appendix is available through Connect or your course instructor.

**chapter**

# Managing Liquidity Risk on the Balance Sheet

## Learning Goals

| | |
|---|---|
| **LG 21-1** | *Identify the causes of liquidity risk.* |
| **LG 21-2** | *Define the two methods financial institutions use to manage liquidity risk.* |
| **LG 21-3** | *Describe how depository institutions measure liquidity risk.* |
| **LG 21-4** | *Examine the components of a liquidity plan.* |
| **LG 21-5** | *Explain why abnormal deposit drains occur.* |
| **LG 21-6** | *Consider the extent to which insurance companies are exposed to liquidity risk.* |
| **LG 21-7** | *Clarify the extent to which investment funds are exposed to liquidity risk.* |

## LIQUIDITY RISK MANAGEMENT: CHAPTER OVERVIEW

This chapter looks at the problems created by liquidity risk. Unlike other risks that threaten the very solvency of an FI, liquidity risk is a normal aspect of the everyday management of an FI. For example, banks must manage liquidity so they can pay out cash as deposit holders request withdrawals of their funds. In extreme cases, liquidity risk problems develop into solvency risk problems. Moreover, some FIs are more exposed to liquidity risk than others. At one extreme, depository institutions are highly exposed. At the other extreme, mutual funds, hedge funds, pension funds, and property–casualty insurance companies have relatively low liquidity risk exposure. However, these FIs are certainly exposed to some liquidity risk. While the focus of the discussion is around liquidity risk at depository institutions, we discuss the unique aspects of liquidity risk in other types of institutions as well. The financial crisis of 2008–2009 was, in part, due to liquidity risk. As mortgage and mortgage-backed securities markets started to experience large losses, credit markets froze and banks stopped lending to each other at anything but high overnight rates. The overnight London Interbank Offered Rate (LIBOR, a benchmark that reflects the rate at which banks lend to one another) more than doubled, rising from 2.57 percent on September 29, 2008, to an all-time high of 6.88 percent on September 30, 2009. Banks generally rely on each other for cash needed to meet their daily liquidity needs. Interest rates on interbank borrowings are generally low because of confidence that financial institutions will repay each other. However, this confidence broke down during the financial crisis. Without interbank funding, banks became reluctant to lend to other credit markets, resulting in a more general and widespread liquidity crisis. To stem the post-2007 liquidity crisis, central banks around the world had to pump short-term cash into strained markets as they reeled amid the growing crisis that reshaped the contours of the global financial system.

# CAUSES OF LIQUIDITY RISK

**LG 21-1**

**fire-sale price**

*The price received for an asset that has to be liquidated (sold) immediately.*

Liquidity risk arises for two reasons—a liability-side reason and an asset-side reason. The liability-side reason occurs when an FI's liability holders, such as depositors or insurance policyholders, seek to cash in their financial claims immediately. When liability holders demand cash by withdrawing deposits, the FI needs to borrow additional funds or liquidate assets to meet the withdrawal. The most liquid asset is cash. FIs use this asset to pay claim holders who seek to withdraw funds. However, FIs tend to minimize their holdings of cash reserves as assets because those reserves pay no or little interest. To generate interest revenues, most FIs invest in less liquid and/or longer-maturity assets. While most assets can be turned into cash eventually, for some assets this can be done only at a high cost when the asset must be liquidated immediately. The price the asset holder must accept for immediate sale may be far less than it would receive with a longer horizon over which to negotiate a sale. Some assets may be liquidated only at low **fire-sale prices,** thus threatening the solvency of the FI. Alternatively, rather than liquidating assets, an FI may seek to purchase or borrow additional funds. However, replacing deposits with purchased funds may also be costly in that purchased funds would be obtained at relatively higher interest rates than what is paid on lost deposits.

The second cause of liquidity risk is asset-side liquidity risk, such as the ability to fund the exercise of off-balance-sheet loan commitments. As we describe in Chapter 12, a loan commitment allows a customer to borrow (take down) funds from an FI (over a commitment period) on demand. When a borrower draws on its loan commitment, the FI must fund the loan on the balance sheet immediately. This creates a demand for liquidity. As with liability withdrawals, an FI can meet such a liquidity need by running down its cash assets, selling off other liquid assets, or borrowing additional funds.

To understand the connection between liquidity risk and insolvency risk, consider the simple FI balance sheet in Table 21–1. Before deposit withdrawals, the FI has $10 million in cash assets and $90 million in nonliquid assets. These assets are funded with $ 90 million in deposits and $10 million in owners' equity. Suppose that depositors unexpectedly withdraw $20 million in deposits (perhaps due to the release of negative news about the profits of the FI) and the FI receives no new deposits to replace them. To meet these deposit withdrawals, the FI first uses the $10 million it has in cash assets and then seeks to sell some of its nonliquid assets to raise an additional $10 million in cash. Suppose also that the FI cannot borrow any more funds in the short-term money markets (see Chapter 5), and because it cannot wait to get better prices for its assets in the future (as it needs the cash now to meet immediate depositor withdrawals), the FI has to sell any nonliquid assets at 50 cents on the dollar. Thus, to cover the remaining $10 million in deposit withdrawals, the FI must

**TABLE 21–1** Adjusting to a Deposit Withdrawal Using Asset Sales *(in millions)*

| Before the Withdrawal | | | | After the Withdrawal | | | |
|---|---|---|---|---|---|---|---|
| **Assets** | | **Liabilities/Equity** | | **Assets** | | **Liabilities/Equity** | |
| Cash assets | $ 10 | Deposits | $ 90 | Cash assets | $ 0 | Deposits | $70 |
| Nonliquid assets | 90 | Equity | 10 | Nonliquid assets | 70 | Equity | 0 |
| | $100 | | $100 | | $70 | | $70 |

sell $20 million in nonliquid assets, incurring a loss of $10 million from the face value of those assets. The FI must then write off any such losses against its capital or equity funds. Since its capital was only $10 million before the deposit withdrawal, the loss on the fire-sale of assets of $10 million leaves the FI economically insolvent (i.e., with zero equity capital or net worth).

## LIQUIDITY RISK AND DEPOSITORY INSTITUTIONS

### Liability-Side Liquidity Risk

As discussed in Chapter 11, a depository institution's (DI) balance sheet typically has a large amount of short-term liabilities, such as demand deposits and other transaction accounts, that fund relatively long-term, illiquid assets such as commercial loans and mortgages. Demand deposit accounts and other transaction accounts are contracts that give the holders the right to put their financial claims back to the DI on any given day and demand immediate repayment of the face value in cash.[1] Thus, an individual demand deposit account holder with a balance of $10,000 can demand to be repaid immediately in cash, as can a corporation with $100 million in its demand deposit account. In theory, at least, a DI that has 50 percent of its liabilities in demand deposits and other transaction accounts must stand ready to pay out the entire amount by liquidating an equivalent amount of assets (or borrowing additional funds) on any given banking day.

**core deposits**

*Deposits that provide a relatively stable, long-term funding source to a depository institution.*

In reality, a DI knows that *normally* only a small proportion of its demand deposits will be withdrawn on any given day. Most demand deposits remain with the DI, thus behaving as **core deposits** on a day-by-day basis, providing a relatively stable or long-term source of funding for the DI. Moreover, deposit withdrawals may in part be offset by the inflow of new deposits. The DI manager must monitor the resulting net deposit withdrawals or **net deposit drains.** Specifically, over time a DI manager can normally predict—with a good degree of accuracy—the probability of different-sized net deposit drains (the difference between deposit withdrawals and deposit additions) on any given banking day.

**net deposit drain**

*The amount by which cash withdrawals exceed additions; a net cash outflow.*

For example, suppose the probability distribution of net deposit drains is strongly peaked at the 5 percent net (deposit) withdrawal level—this DI expects approximately 5 percent of its net deposit funds to be withdrawn on any given day with the highest probability. Assume also that the distribution has a standard deviation of 1 percent. If the distribution is normal, we can state with 95 percent confidence that the rate of deposits withdrawals will be between 3 percent and 7 percent (i.e., plus or minus two standard deviations). A net deposit drain means that a DI is receiving insufficient additional deposits (and other cash inflows) to offset deposit withdrawals, which means that the liability side of its balance sheet is contracting. Table 21–2 illustrates a 5 percent, equal to $3.5 million, net deposit drain.

**TABLE 21–2**   **The Effect of Net Deposit Drains on the Balance Sheet** *(in millions)*

| Before the Drain | | | | After the Drain | | | |
|---|---|---|---|---|---|---|---|
| **Assets** | | **Liabilities/Equity** | | **Assets** | | **Liabilities/Equity** | |
| Cash assets | $ 10 | Deposits | $ 70 | Cash assets | $ 6.5 | Deposits | $66.5 |
| Nonliquid assets | 90 | Borrowed funds | 10 | Nonliquid assets | 90 | Borrowed funds | 10 |
| | | Equity | 20 | | | Equity | 20 |
| | $100 | | $100 | | $96.5 | | $96.5 |

1.  Accounts with this type of put option include demand deposits, NOW accounts (interest-bearing checking accounts with minimum balance requirements), and money market accounts (interest-bearing checking accounts with minimum balance requirements and restrictions as to the number of checks written). We describe these accounts in more detail in Chapter 12. Banks typically liquidate deposit account contracts immediately upon request of the customer. Many deposit account contracts, however, give a bank some powers to delay withdrawals by requiring notification of withdrawal a certain number of days before withdrawal or by imposing penalty fees such as loss of interest.

LG 21-2

An FI can manage a drain on deposits in two major ways: (1) purchased liquidity management and/or (2) stored liquidity management. Traditionally, DI managers relied on *stored liquidity* as the primary mechanism of liquidity management. Today, many DIs—especially the largest banks with access to the money market and other nondeposit markets for funds—rely on *purchased liquidity*. Smaller DIs—such as community banks—more often look to *stored liquidity*.

**Purchased Liquidity Management.**   A DI manager who purchases liquidity to offset a deposit drain turns to the markets for purchased funds, such as the federal funds market and/or the repurchase (repo) agreement markets (discussed in Chapter 5), which are interbank markets for short-term loans. Alternatively, a DI manager could issue additional fixed-maturity certificates of deposit (see Chapter 12) or additional notes and bonds. For example, the DI in Table 21–2 could fully fund its net deposit drain as long as the total amount of the funds raised equals $3.5 million. This can be expensive for the DI, however, since it must pay *market rates* for funds to offset net drains on low interest rate deposits.[2] Thus, the higher the cost of purchased funds relative to rates earned on assets, the less attractive this approach to liquidity management becomes. Further, since most of these purchased funds are not covered by deposit insurance, their availability may be limited should the DI incur insolvency difficulties. Table 21–3 shows the DI's balance sheet if it responds to deposit drains by using purchased liquidity techniques.

**purchased liquidity management**

*An adjustment to a deposit drain that occurs on the liability side of the balance sheet.*

Note that **purchased liquidity management** has allowed the DI to maintain its overall balance sheet size of $100 million without disturbing the size and composition of the asset side of its balance sheet—that is, the complete adjustment to the deposit drain occurs on the liability side of the balance sheet. In other words, purchased liquidity management can insulate the asset side of the balance sheet from normal drains on the liability side of the balance sheet. This is one of the reasons for the enormous growth in recent years of DI-purchased liquidity management techniques and associated purchased fund markets such as fed funds, repurchase agreements, and CDs among DIs. (We describe and discuss these instruments and markets in Chapter 5.) In the early 2000s regulators expressed concerns about the increased use of these (wholesale) funding sources by DIs. Indeed, with the liquidity crunch experienced during the financial crisis, additional (wholesale) funds were hard, and sometimes impossible, to obtain.

**stored liquidity management**

*An adjustment to a deposit drain that occurs on the asset side of the balance sheet.*

**Stored Liquidity Management.**   Instead of meeting the net deposit drain by purchasing liquidity in the money markets, the DI can use **stored liquidity management.** That is, the FI can liquidate some of its assets, thus utilizing its stored liquidity. U.S. banks traditionally have held or "stored" cash reserves in their vaults and at the Federal Reserve for this very purpose. The Federal Reserve sets a minimum requirement for the cash reserves that banks must hold (see Chapter 13).[3] Even so, banks still tend to hold cash reserves in excess of the minimum required amount to meet liquidity drains.

**TABLE 21–3**   Adjusting to a Deposit Drain by Purchasing Funds *(in millions)*

| Assets | | Liabilities/Equity | |
|---|---|---|---|
| Cash assets | $ 10 | Deposits | $ 66.5 |
| Nonliquid assets | 90 | Borrowed funds | 13.5 |
| | | Equity | 20 |
| | $100 | | $100 |

---

2. However, the rates paid are normally slow to adjust to changes in market interest rates and lie below purchased fund rates.
3. Currently, the Fed requires a minimum 3 percent cash reserve on the first $110.2 million and 10 percent on the rest of a DI's demand deposit and transaction account holdings. The $110.2 million figure is adjusted annually along with the increase or decrease in DI deposits. The first $15.2 million of the $110.2 million is not subject to reserve requirements. See Chapter 13.

**TABLE 21–4**   **Composition of a DI's Balance Sheet** *(in millions)*

| Assets | | Liabilities/Equity | |
|---|---|---|---|
| Cash assets | $ 9 | Deposits | $ 70 |
| Nonliquid assets | 91 | Borrowed funds | 10 |
| | | Equity | 20 |
| | $100 | | $100 |

**TABLE 21–5**   **Reserve Asset Adjustment to Deposit Drain** *(in millions)*

| Assets | | Liabilities/Equity | |
|---|---|---|---|
| Cash assets | $ 5.5 | Deposits | $66.5 |
| Nonliquid assets | 91 | Borrowed funds | 10 |
| | | Equity | 20 |
| | $96.5 | | $96.5 |

Suppose in our example that on the asset side of the balance sheet the DI normally holds $9 million of its assets in cash (of which $3 million is to meet Federal Reserve minimum reserve requirements and $6 million is an "excess" cash reserve). We depict the situation before the net drain in liabilities in Table 21–4. As depositors withdraw $3.5 million in deposits, the DI meets this by using the excess cash stored in its vaults or held on deposit at other DIs or at the Federal Reserve. If the reduction of $3.5 million in deposit liabilities is met by a $3.5 million reduction in cash assets held by the DI, its balance sheet is as shown in Table 21–5.

When the DI uses its cash as the liquidity adjustment mechanism, both sides of its balance sheet contract. In this example, both the DI's total assets and liabilities/equity shrink from $100 million to $96.5 million. The cost to the DI of using stored liquidity, apart from decreased asset size, is that it must hold excess low interest rate assets in the form of cash on its balance sheet.[4] Thus, the cost of using cash to meet liquidity needs is the forgone return (or opportunity cost) of being unable to invest these funds in loans and other higher income-earning assets.

Finally, note that although stored liquidity management and purchased liquidity management are alternative strategies for meeting deposit drains, a DI can combine the two methods by using some purchased liquidity management and some stored liquidity management to meet liquidity needs.

**EXAMPLE 21–1**    **Impact of Stored Liquidity versus Purchased Liquidity Management on a DI's Net Income**

Suppose a DI has the following balance sheet:

| Assets | | Liabilities and Equity | |
|---|---|---|---|
| Cash | $ 1m (equal to required reserves) | Core deposits | $ 6m |
| Loans | 9m | Subordinated debt | 2m |
| | | Equity | 2m |
| | $10m | | $10m |

The average cost of core deposits is 6 percent and the average yield on loans is 8 percent. Increases in interest rates are expected to cause a net drain of $2 million in core deposits over the next six months. New short-term debt (such as subordinated debt) can be obtained at a cost of 7.5 percent. If the DI uses stored liquidity management to manage liquidity

---

4. DIs could hold highly liquid interest-bearing assets such as T-bills, but they are still less liquid than cash, and immediate liquidation may result in some small capital value losses and transaction costs.

risk, it reduces its loan portfolio (selling loans for cash) to offset this expected decline in deposits. Assuming there is no capital loss on the sale of the loans, the DI's net income will change as follows:

| | |
|---|---|
| Decrease in interest income–loans | $-0.08 \times \$2m = -\$160,000$ |
| Decrease in interest expense–core deposits | $-(-0.06) \times \$2m = \underline{\ \$120,000}$ |
| Change in net income | $-\$\ \ 40,000$ |

If the DI uses purchased liquidity management to manage liquidity risk, it issues short-term, subordinated debt to pay off the expected decline in deposits. In this case, the DI's net income will change by:

| | |
|---|---|
| Decrease in interest expense–core deposits | $-0.06 \times \$2m = \ \ \$120,000$ |
| Increase in interest expense–short-term debt | $-(-0.075) \times \$2m = \underline{-\$150,000}$ |
| Change in net income | $-\$\ \ 30,000$ |

The DI is more profitable if it manages the drain in core deposits using purchased liquidity management. The decrease in net income is $30,000 versus $40,000 if it uses stored liquidity management.

### Asset-Side Liquidity Risk

Just as deposit drains can cause a DI liquidity problems, so can loan requests, resulting from the exercise, by borrowers, of loan commitments and other credit lines. In recent years, depository institutions—especially commercial banks—increased their loan commitments tremendously, with the belief they would not be exercised. Unused loan commitments to cash grew from 529.4 percent in 1994 to 1014.6 percent in October 2008 (before falling back to 608.6 percent during the financial crisis). Table 21–6 shows the effect of a $5 million exercise of a loan commitment by a borrower. As a result, the DI must fund $5 million in additional loans on the balance sheet. Consider the Before columns in Table 21–6 (the balance sheet before the commitment exercise) and the After columns (as the loan is added to the balance sheet after the exercise). In particular, the exercise of the loan commitment means that the DI needs to provide $5 million immediately to the borrower (nonliquid assets increase from $91 to $96 million). This can be done either by purchased liquidity management (borrowing an additional $5 million in the money market and lending these funds to the borrower) or by stored liquidity management (decreasing the DI's excess cash assets from $9 million to $4 million). We present balance sheets that result from each of these two policies in Table 21–7.

**TABLE 21–6**  The Effects of a Loan Commitment Exercise *(in millions)*

| Before | | | | After | | | |
|---|---|---|---|---|---|---|---|
| Cash assets | $ 9 | Deposits | $ 70 | Cash assets | $ 9 | Deposits | $ 70 |
| Nonliquid assets | 91 | Borrowed funds | 10 | Nonliquid assets | 96 | Borrowed funds | 10 |
| | | Equity | 20 | | | Equity | 20 |
| | $100 | | $100 | | $105 | | $100 |
| Off-balance-sheet | | | | Off-balance-sheet | | | |
| loan commitment | $ 5 | | | loan commitment | $ 0 | | |

**TABLE 21–7**  Adjusting the Balance Sheet to a Loan Commitment Exercise *(in millions)*

| Purchased Liquidity Management | | | | Stored Liquidity Management | | | |
|---|---|---|---|---|---|---|---|
| Cash assets | $ 9 | Deposits | $ 70 | Cash assets | $ 4 | Deposits | $ 70 |
| Nonliquid assets | 96 | Borrowed funds | 15 | Nonliquid assets | 96 | Borrowed funds | 10 |
| | | Equity | 20 | | | Equity | 20 |
| | $105 | | $105 | | $100 | | $100 |

*Measuring a DI's Liquidity Exposure*

Having discussed the sources of liquidity risk for a DI, we next look at several methods currently used to measure the extent of a DI's liquidity risk exposure. These methods take into account the DI's excess cash reserves and its ability to raise additional purchased funds.

**Financing Gap and the Financing Requirement.**   A first way to measure liquidity risk exposure is to determine the DI's financing gap. As we discussed earlier, even though demand depositors can withdraw their funds immediately, they do not do so in normal circumstances. On average, most demand deposits stay at DIs for quite long periods, often two years or more. Thus, a DI manager often thinks of the average deposit base, including demand deposits, as a core source of funds that over time can fund a DI's average amount of loans. We define a **financing gap** as the difference between a DI's average loans and average (core) deposits, or:

$$\text{Financing gap} = \text{Average loans} - \text{Average deposits}$$

If this financing gap is positive, the DI must find liquidity to fund the gap. This funding can come via either purchased liquidity management (i.e., borrowing funds) or stored liquidity management (i.e., liquidating assets), as discussed previously. Thus:

$$\text{Financing gap} = -\text{Liquid assets} + \text{Borrowed funds}$$

We can write this relationship as:

$$\text{Financing gap} + \text{Liquid assets} = \text{Financing requirement (borrowed funds)}$$

As expressed in this fashion, the liquidity and managerial implications of the **financing requirement** (the financing gap plus a DI's liquid assets) are that the level of core deposits and loans as well as the amount of liquid assets determines the DI's borrowing or purchased fund needs. In particular, the larger a DI's financing gap and liquid asset holdings, the higher the amount of funds it needs to borrow in the money markets and the greater is its exposure to liquidity problems from such a reliance.

The balance sheet in Table 21–8 indicates the relationship between the financing gap, liquid assets, and the borrowed funds financing requirement. This is seen in the following equation:

$$\begin{array}{ccc} \text{Financing gap} & + & \text{Liquid assets} & = & \text{Financing requirement} \\ (\$5 \text{ million}) & & (\$5 \text{ million}) & & (\$10 \text{ million}) \end{array}$$

A widening financing gap can warn of future liquidity problems for a DI since it may indicate increased deposit withdrawals (core deposits falling below $20 million in Table 21–8) and increasing loans due to more exercise of loan commitments (loans rising above $25 million). If the DI does not reduce its liquid assets—that is, if they stay at $5 million—the manager must resort to more money market borrowings. As these borrowings rise, sophisticated lenders in the money market may be concerned about the DI's creditworthiness. They may react by imposing higher-risk premiums on borrowed funds or establishing stricter credit limits by not rolling over funds lent to the DI. If the DI's financing requirements dramatically exceed such limits, it may become insolvent.

**financing gap**

*The difference between a DI's average loans and average (core) deposits.*

**financing requirement**

*The financing gap plus a DI's liquid assets.*

**TABLE 21–8**   The Financing Requirement of a DI *(in millions)*

| Assets | | | Liabilities | |
|---|---|---|---|---|
| Loans | $25 | | Core deposits | $20 |
| | | Financing gap    (5) | | |
| Liquid assets | 5 | | | |
| | | | **Financing requirement (borrowed funds)** | 10 |
| Total | $30 | | Total | $30 |

**TABLE 21–9**   Net Liquidity Position *(in millions)*

| | |
|---|---:|
| **Sources of Liquidity** | |
| **1.** Total cash-type assets | $ 2,000 |
| **2.** Maximum borrowed funds limit | 12,000 |
| **3.** Excess cash reserves | 500 |
| Total | $14,500 |
| **Uses of Liquidity** | |
| **1.** Funds borrowed | $ 6,000 |
| **2.** Federal Reserve borrowing | 1,000 |
| Total | $ 7,000 |
| Total net liquidity | $ 7,500 |

**Sources and Uses of Liquidity.**   As discussed earlier, a DI's liquidity risk arises from the ongoing conducting of business, such as a withdrawal of deposits or new loan demand, and the subsequent need to meet these demands by liquidating assets or borrowing funds. Therefore, a second measure of liquidity risk exposure a DI manager might use to measure the DI's liquidity position on a daily basis is a *net liquidity statement*. A net liquidity statement lists sources and uses of liquidity and, thus, provides a measure of a DI's net liquidity position. Such a statement for a hypothetical U.S. bank is presented in Table 21–9.

The DI can obtain liquid funds in three ways. First, it can sell its liquid assets such as T-bills immediately with little price risk and low transaction costs. Second, it can borrow funds in the money/purchased funds market up to a maximum amount (this is an internal guideline based on the manager's assessment of the credit limits that the purchased or borrowed funds market is likely to impose on the bank). Third, it can use any excess cash reserves over and above the amount held to meet regulatory imposed reserve requirements. In Table 21–9, the DI's *sources* of liquidity total $14,500 million. Compare this to the DI's *uses* of liquidity—in particular, the amount of borrowed or purchased funds it has already utilized (e.g., fed funds, RPs borrowed) and the amount of cash it has already borrowed from the Federal Reserve through discount window loans. These total $7,000 million. As a result, the DI has a positive net liquidity position of $7,500 million. These liquidity sources and uses can be tracked easily on a day-by-day basis.

The net liquidity position in Table 21–9 lists management's expected sources and uses of liquidity for a hypothetical bank. All DIs report their historical sources and uses of liquidity in their annual and quarterly reports. Appendix 21A to this chapter (available through Connect or your course instructor) presents the September 2016 *Sources and Uses of Funds* Statement for J.P. Morgan Chase. As a DI manager deals with liquidity risk, historical sources and uses of liquidity statements can be useful tools for determining where future liquidity issues may arise.

**Peer Group Ratio Comparisons.**   A third way to measure a DI's liquidity exposure is to compare certain of its key ratios and balance sheet features—such as loans to deposits, core deposits to total assets, borrowed funds to total assets, and commitments to lend to assets ratios—with those for DIs of a similar size and geographic location (see Chapter 12). A high ratio of loans to deposits and borrowed funds to total assets and/or a low ratio of core deposits to total assets means that the DI relies heavily on the short-term money market rather than on core deposits to fund loans. This could mean future liquidity problems if the DI is at or near its borrowing limits in the purchased funds market. Similarly, a high ratio of loan commitments to assets indicates the need for a high degree of liquidity to fund any unexpected takedowns of these loans by customers—thus, high-commitment DIs often face more liquidity risk exposure than do low-commitment DIs.

Table 21–10 lists the 2016 values of these ratios for the banks we reviewed in Chapter 12: Heartland Bank and Trust Company (HBT) and Bank of America Corporation (BOA). Neither of these banks relied heavily on borrowed funds (short-term money market

**TABLE 21–10**  Liquidity Exposure Ratios for Two DIs

|  | Heartland Bank and Trust Company | Bank of America |
|---|---|---|
| Borrowed funds to total assets | 6.15% | 9.54% |
| Core deposits to total assets | 81.71 | 76.44 |
| Loans to deposits | 78.50 | 68.26 |
| Commitments to lend to total assets | 16.19 | 48.44 |

instruments) to fund loans. Their ratio of borrowed funds to total assets was 6.15 percent and 9.54 percent, respectively. Their ratio of core deposits (the stable deposits of the DI, such as demand deposits, NOW accounts, MMDAs, other savings accounts, and retail CDs) to total assets, on the other hand, was 81.71 percent and 76.44 percent, respectively. As a major money center bank, Bank of America gets slightly more of its liquid funds from the borrowed funds markets than core deposit markets. HBT, a smaller, consumer-oriented bank, uses core deposits much more than borrowed funds to get its liquid funds. Further, the ratios of loans to deposits for HBT and BOA were 78.50 percent and 68.26 percent, respectively. The result is that Bank of America is subject to less liquidity risk than HBT. Furthermore, HBT had a ratio of loan commitments to total assets of only 16.19 percent, while BOA had a much greater ratio of 48.44 percent. If these commitments are taken down (see Chapters 11 and 19), BOA must come up with the cash to fulfill these commitments, more so than HBT. Thus, BOA was exposed to substantially greater liquidity risk from unexpected takedowns of these commitments.

**liquidity index**

*A measure of the potential losses a DI could suffer as the result of a sudden (or fire-sale) disposal of assets.*

**Liquidity Index.**  A final way to measure liquidity risk is to use a **liquidity index.** This index measures the potential losses a DI could suffer from a sudden or fire-sale disposal of assets compared to the amount it would receive at a fair market value established under normal market conditions, which might take a lengthy period of time as a result of a careful search and bidding process. The larger the differences between immediate fire-sale asset prices ($P_i$) and fair market prices $\left(P_i^*\right)$, the less liquid is the DI's portfolio of assets. Define an index I such that:

$$I = \sum_{i=1}^{N}[(w_i)(P_i/P_i^*)]$$

where

$w_i$ = Percentage of each asset in the DI's portfolio

$\sum w_i$ = 1

$P_i$ = Price if a DI liquidates asset $i$ today

$P_i^*$ = Price if a DI liquidates asset $i$ at some future point in time (e.g., in one month)

The liquidity index will always lie between 0 and 1. The liquidity index for a particular DI could also be compared with indexes calculated for a peer group of similar DIs.

---

**EXAMPLE 21–2**  Calculation of the Liquidity Index

Suppose that a bank has two assets: 50 percent in one-month Treasury bills and 50 percent in real estate loans. If the bank must liquidate its T-bills today ($P_1$), it receives $99 per $100 of face value. If it can wait to liquidate them on maturity (in one month's time), it will receive the fair market price of $100 per $100 of face value ($P_1^*$). If the bank has to liquidate its real estate loans today, it receives $85 per $100 of face value ($P_2$). Liquidation at the end of one month (closer to maturity) will result in a fair market price of $92 per

$100 of face value ($P_2^*$). Thus, the one-month liquidity index value for this bank's asset portfolio is:

$$I = (1/2)(0.99/1.00) + (1/2)(0.85/0.92)$$
$$= 0.495 + 0.462$$
$$= 0.957$$

Suppose alternatively that a slow or thin real estate market causes the bank to be able to liquidate the real estate loans at only $65 per $100 of face value ($P_2$) on an immediate sale. The one-month liquidity index for the bank's asset portfolio is:

$$I = (1/2)(0.99/1.00) + (1/2)(0.65/0.92)$$
$$= 0.495 + 0.353$$
$$= 0.848$$

The value of the one-month liquidity index decreases due to the larger discount on the immediate or fire-sale price—from the fair (full value) market price of real estate—over the one-month period. The larger the discount from fair value, the smaller the liquidity index or higher the liquidity risk the bank faces.

**New Liquidity Risk Measures Implemented by the Bank for International Settlements.** During the financial crisis, many DIs struggled to maintain adequate liquidity. Indeed, extraordinary levels of liquidity assistance were required from central banks in order to maintain the financial system. Even with this extensive support, a number of DIs failed or were forced into mergers. Recognizing the need for DIs to improve their liquidity risk management and control their liquidity risk exposure, the Bank for International Settlement's (BIS) Basel Committee on Banking Supervision developed two new regulatory standards for liquidity risk supervision. The standards are intended to "enhance tools, metrics, and benchmarks that supervisors can use to assess the resilience of banks' liquidity cushions and constrain any weakening in liquidity maturity profiles, diversity of funding sources, and stress testing practices."[5] The two new liquidity ratios to be maintained by DIs are the *liquidity coverage ratio* (to be implemented in 2019) and the *net stable funds ratio* (implemented in 2018). The rule applies to large, internationally active banking organizations with $250 billion or more in total consolidated assets or $10 billion or more in total on-balance-sheet foreign exposure, and to consolidated subsidiary depository institutions of these banking organizations with $10 billion or more in total assets.

The liquidity coverage ratio (LCR) aims to ensure that a DI maintains an adequate level of high-quality liquid assets (HQLA) that can be converted into cash to meet liquidity needs for a 30-day time horizon under an "acute liquidity stress scenario" specified by supervisors. The specified scenario incorporates both institution-specific and systemic shocks that are based on actual circumstances experienced in the global financial crisis. Thus, maintenance of the LCR is intended to ensure that DIs can survive a severe liquidity stress scenario for at least 30 days. The LCR, which is reported to DI supervisors monthly, is as follows:

$$\text{Liquidity coverage ratio} = \frac{\text{Stock of high-quality liquid assets}}{\text{Total net cash outflows over the next 30 calendar days}} \geq 100\%$$

The net stable funding ratio (NSFR) takes a longer-term look at liquidity on a DI's balance sheet. The NSFR evaluates liquidity over the entire balance sheet and provides incentives for DIs to use stable sources of financing. This longer-term liquidity ratio requires that a minimum amount of stable funding be held over a one-year time horizon based on liquidity risk factors assigned to liquidity exposures of on-and off-balance-sheet assets.

---

5. "International Framework for Liquidity Risk Measurement, Standards and Monitoring," Bank for International Settlements, December 2009. www.bis.org

The NSFR is intended to ensure that long-term assets are funded with stable liabilities. It limits reliance on short-term wholesale funding, which was a major problem in the financial crisis. Basically, stable funding is sought for all illiquid assets and securities held, where *stable funding* is defined as equity and liability financing that is expected to be a reliable source of funds over a one-year time horizon. The NSFR ratio, which will be reported to DI supervisors quarterly starting in 2018, is:

$$\text{Net stable funding ratio} = \frac{\text{Available amount of stable funding}}{\text{Required amount of stable funding}} > 100\%$$

Appendix 21B (available through Connect or your course instructor) provides more detail on how to calculate these two additional measures of liquidity risk.

In 2013, the BIS also introduced additional guidelines for monitoring intraday liquidity risk at internationally active banks. The guidelines specify six operational elements that should be included in a bank's strategy for managing intraday liquidity risk.[6] According to these guidelines, banks should:

1. Have the capacity to measure expected daily gross liquidity inflows and outflows, anticipate the intraday timing of these flows where possible, and forecast the range of potential net funding shortfalls that might arise at different points during the day.
2. Have the capacity to monitor intraday liquidity positions against expected activities and available resources (balances, remaining intraday credit capacity, available collateral).
3. Arrange to acquire sufficient intraday funding to meet intraday objectives.
4. Have the ability to manage and mobilize collateral as necessary to obtain intraday funds.
5. Have a robust capability to manage the timing of liquidity outflows in line with intraday objectives.
6. Be prepared to deal with unexpected disruptions to intraday liquidity flows.

**LG 21-4**

**Liquidity Planning.** Liquidity planning is a key component in measuring (and being able to deal with) liquidity risk and its associated costs. Specifically, liquidity planning allows managers to make important borrowing priority decisions before liquidity problems arise. Such forward planning can lower the cost of funds (by determining an optimal funding mix) and can minimize the amount of excess reserves that a DI needs to hold.

A liquidity plan has a number of components. The first component is the delineation of managerial details and responsibilities. Responsibilities are assigned to key management personnel should a liquidity crisis occur. The plan identifies those managers responsible for interacting with various regulatory agencies such as the Federal Reserve, the FDIC, and the Office of the Comptroller of the Currency (OCC). It also specifies areas of managerial responsibility in disclosing information to the public, including depositors. The second component of a liquidity plan is a detailed list of fund providers most likely to withdraw as well as the pattern of fund withdrawals. For example, in a crisis, financial institutions such as mutual funds and pension funds are more likely than correspondent banks and small business corporations to withdraw funds quickly from banks and thrifts. In turn, correspondent banks and small corporations are more likely than individual depositors to withdraw funds quickly. This makes liquidity exposure sensitive to the effects of future funding composition changes. In addition, FIs such as depository institutions face particularly heavy seasonal withdrawals of deposits in the quarter before Christmas. The third component of liquidity planning is the identification of the size of potential deposit and fund withdrawals over various time horizons in the future (one week, one month, one quarter, etc.) as well as alternative private market funding sources to meet such withdrawals (e.g., emergency loans from other FIs and the Federal Reserve). The fourth component of the plan sets internal limits on separate subsidiaries' and branches' borrowings as well as bounds for acceptable risk premiums to pay in each market (fed funds, RPs, CDs, etc.).

www.federalreserve.gov
www.fdic.gov

---

6. "Monitoring Tools for Intraday Liquidity Management," Bank for International Settlements, April 2013. www.bis.org

**TABLE 21–11** Deposit Distribution and Possible Withdrawals Involved in a DI's Liquidity Plan *(in millions)*

| Deposits | | | $250 |
|---|---|---|---|
| From: | | | |
| Mutual funds | | | 60 |
| Pension funds | | | 50 |
| Correspondent banks | | | 15 |
| Small businesses | | | 70 |
| Individuals | | | 55 |

| Expected Withdrawals | Average | | Maximum |
|---|---|---|---|
| One week | $40 | | $105 |
| One month | 55 | | 140 |
| Three months | 75 | | 200 |

| The Sequence of Deposit Withdrawal Funding | One Week | One Month | Three Months |
|---|---|---|---|
| 1. New deposits | $10 | $35 | $75 |
| 2. Investment portfolio asset liquidation | 50 | 60 | 75 |
| 3. Borrowings from other FIs | 30 | 35 | 45 |
| 4. Borrowings from Fed | 15 | 10 | 5 |

In addition, the plan details a sequencing of assets for disposal in anticipation of various degrees or intensities of deposit/fund withdrawals. Such a plan may evolve from a DI's asset–liability management committee and may be relayed to various key departments of the DI (e.g., the money desk and the treasury department) that play vital day-to-day roles in liability funding.

Consider, for example, Table 21–11. The data are for a DI that holds $250 million in deposits from mutual funds, pension funds, correspondent banks, small businesses, and individuals. The table includes the average and maximum expected withdrawals over the next one-week, one-month, and one-quarter periods. The liquidity plan for the DI outlines how to cover expected deposit withdrawals should they materialize. In this case, the DI will seek to cover expected deposit withdrawals over the next three months first with new deposits, then with the liquidation of marketable securities in its investment portfolio, then with borrowings from other FIs, and finally, if necessary, with borrowings from the Federal Reserve.

## Liquidity Risk, Unexpected Deposit Drains, and Bank Runs

**LG 21-5**

Under normal banking conditions, and with appropriate management planning, neither net deposit withdrawals nor the exercise of loan commitments poses significant liquidity problems for DIs. This is because, typically, borrowed funds availability or excess cash reserves are adequate to meet anticipated needs. For example, even in December and the summer vacation season, when net deposit withdrawals are high, DIs anticipate these *seasonal* effects by holding larger than normal excess cash reserves or borrowing more than normal on the wholesale money markets.

Major liquidity problems can arise, however, if deposit drains are abnormally large and unexpected. Abnormal deposit drains may occur for a number of reasons, including:

1. Concerns about a DI's solvency relative to that of other DIs.
2. Failure of a related DI, leading to heightened depositor concerns about the solvency of surviving DIs (*a contagion effect*).
3. Sudden changes in investor preferences regarding holding nonbank financial assets (such as T-bills or mutual fund shares) relative to DI deposits.

**bank run**

*A sudden and unexpected increase in deposit withdrawals from a DI.*

In such cases, sudden and unexpected surges in net deposit withdrawals risk triggering a **bank run,** which could force a DI into insolvency.

**Deposit Drains and Bank Run Liquidity Risk.**   At the core of bank run liquidity risk is the fundamental and unique nature of the demand deposit contract. Specifically, demand deposit contracts are first-come, first-served contracts in the sense that a depositor's place in line determines the amount he or she will be able to withdraw from a DI. For example, suppose that a DI has 100 depositors, each of whom deposited $1. Suppose that each has a reason to believe—correctly or incorrectly—that the DI has assets worth only $90 on its balance sheet. A frequent reason for depositors to believe this is the announcement of trouble in the DI's loan portfolio. As a result, each depositor has an incentive to be the first to go to the DI and withdraw his or her $1 deposit because the DI pays depositors sequentially as it liquidates its assets. If it has $90 in assets, it can pay in full only the first 90 depositors in the line. The 10 depositors at the end of the line get *nothing at all.*[7] Thus, demand deposits are in essence either full-pay or no-pay contracts.

Because demand deposit contracts pay in full only a certain proportion of depositors when a DI's assets are valued at less than its deposits—and because depositors realize this—any line outside a DI encourages other depositors to join the line immediately even if they do not need cash today for normal consumption purposes. Thus, even the DI's core depositors, who really do not need to withdraw deposits for current consumption needs, rationally seek to withdraw their funds immediately when they observe a sudden increase in the lines at their DI.

As a bank run develops, the demand for net deposit withdrawals grows. The DI may initially meet this by decreasing its cash reserves, selling off liquid or readily marketable assets such as T-bills and T-bonds, and seeking to borrow in the money markets. As a bank run increases in intensity, more depositors join the withdrawal line, and a liquidity crisis develops. Specifically, the DI finds it difficult, if not impossible, to borrow in the money markets at virtually any price. Also, it has sold all its liquid assets, cash, and bonds as well as any salable loans (see Chapter 24). The DI is likely to have left only relatively illiquid loans on the asset side of the balance sheet to meet depositor claims for cash. However, these loans can be sold or liquidated only at very large discounts from face value. A DI needing to liquidate long-term assets at fire-sale prices to meet continuing deposit drains faces the strong possibility that the proceeds from such asset sales will be insufficient to meet depositors' cash demands. The DI's liquidity problem then turns into a solvency problem; that is, the DI must close its doors.

The incentives for depositors to run first and ask questions later create a fundamental instability in the banking system, in that an otherwise sound DI can be pushed into insolvency and failure by unexpectedly large depositor drains and liquidity demands. This is especially so in periods of contagious runs or **bank panics** (such as the panic involving the Greek debt and banking crisis of 2010), when depositors lose faith in the banking system as a whole and engage in a run on all DIs in a banking system.

**bank panic**

*A systemic or contagious run on the deposits of the banking industry as a whole.*

### Bank Runs, the Discount Window, and Deposit Insurance

Regulators have recognized the inherent instability of the banking system due to the all-or-nothing payoff features of deposit contracts. As a result, regulatory mechanisms are in place to ease DIs' liquidity problems and to deter bank runs and panics. The two major liquidity risk insulation mechanisms are *deposit insurance* and the *discount window*.

**Deposit Insurance.**   Because of the serious effects that a contagious run on DIs could have on the economy (e.g., inability to transfer wealth from period to period, inability to implement monetary policy, inability to allocate credit to various sectors of the economy in special need of financing—see Chapter 1), government regulators of depository institutions have established guarantee programs offering deposit holders varying degrees of insurance protection

---

7. We assume no deposit insurance exists that guarantees payment of deposits or no discount window borrowing is available to fund a temporary need for funds. The presence of deposit insurance and the discount window alter the incentive to engage in a bank run, as we describe later in this chapter.

to deter runs. Specifically, the FDIC was created in 1933 in the wake of the banking panics of 1930–1933, when some 10,000 commercial banks failed. The original level of individual depositor insurance coverage at depository institutions was $2,500, which was increased (six times since 1934) to $100,000 in 1980, and to $250,000 in October 2008. With deposit insurance guarantees in place, if a deposit holder believes his or her claim is totally secure, even if the DI is in trouble, the holder has no incentive to run. The deposit holder's place in line no longer affects his or her ability to retrieve funds deposited in the DI. Thus, deposit insurance deters runs as well as contagious runs and panics.

**www.fdic.gov**

During the financial crisis of 2008–2009, in an attempt to deter bank runs and panics and thus provide stability to the U.S. banking system, the Troubled Asset Relief Program (or TARP) gave the U.S. Treasury funds to buy "toxic" mortgages and other securities from financial institutions and also called for the FDIC to increase deposit insurance to $250,000 from $100,000 per person per institution. The $250,000 cap concerns a depositor's beneficial interest and ownership of deposited funds. In actuality, by structuring deposit funds in a DI in a particular fashion, a depositor can achieve many times the $250,000 coverage cap on deposits. To see this, consider the different categories of deposit fund ownership available to an individual shown in Table 21–12. Each of these categories represents a distinct accumulation of funds toward the $250,000 insurance cap. Note the coverage ceiling is *per DI*.

**TABLE 21–12** Deposit Ownership Categories

- Individual ownership, such as a simple checking account.
- Joint ownership, such as the savings account of a husband and wife.
- Revocable trusts, in which the beneficiary is a qualified relative of the settlor, and the settlor has the ability to alter or eliminate the trust.
- Irrevocable trusts whose beneficial interest is not subject to being altered or eliminated.
- Employee benefit plans whose interests are vested and thus not subject to being altered or eliminated.
- Public units–accounts of federal, state, and municipal governments.
- Corporations and partnerships.
- Unincorporated businesses and associates.
- Individual retirement accounts (IRAs).
- Keogh accounts.
- Executor or administrator accounts.
- Accounts held by DIs in an agency or fiduciary capacity.

**Source:** U.S. Department of the Treasury, "Modernizing the Financial System: Recommendations for Safer More Competitive Banks" (Washington, DC: Treasury Department). www.ustreas.gov

---

### EXAMPLE 21–3   Calculation of Insured Deposits

A married couple with one child and with individual retirement account (IRA) and Keogh private pension plans for both the husband and the wife at the DI could accrue a total coverage cap of $2.0 million as a family:

| | |
|---|---:|
| Husband's deposit account | $ 250,000 |
| Wife's deposit account | 250,000 |
| Joint deposit account | 250,000 |
| Child's deposit account held in trust | 250,000 |
| Husband's IRA | 250,000 |
| Wife's IRA | 250,000 |
| Husband's Keogh account | 250,000 |
| Wife's Keogh account | 250,000 |
| Total deposit insurance coverage | $2,000,000 |

By expanding the range of ownership in this fashion, the coverage cap for a family per DI can rapidly approach $2 million or more.

---

The primary intention of deposit insurance is to deter DI runs and panics. A secondary and related objective has been to protect the smaller, less informed saver against the reduction in wealth that would occur if that person were last in line were the DI to fail. Under the current deposit insurance contract, the small, less informed depositor is defined by the $250,000 ceiling. Theoretically at least, larger, more informed depositors with more than $250,000 on deposit are at risk if a DI fails. As a result, these large uninsured depositors should be sensitive to DI risk and seek to discipline riskier DIs by demanding higher interest rates on their deposits or withdrawing their deposits completely. Until recently, the manner in which DI failures have been resolved meant that both large and small depositors were often fully protected against losses. This was especially so where large banks got into trouble and were viewed as too-big-to-fail. That is, they were too big to be liquidated by regulators either because of the draining effects on the resources of the insurance fund or for fear of contagious or systemic runs spreading to other major banks. Thus, although uninsured depositors tended to lose in thrift and small-bank failures, in large-bank failures the failure resolution methods employed by regulators usually resulted in implicit 100 percent deposit insurance. As a result, for large banks in particular, neither small nor large depositors had sufficient incentives to impose market discipline on riskier banks.

**The Discount Window.**    Deposit insurance is not the only mechanism by which regulators mitigate DI liquidity risk. A second mechanism has been the central banks' provision of a lender of last resort facility through the discount window. Suppose that a DI has an unexpected deposit drain near the end of a reserve requirement period but cannot meet its reserve target (see Chapter 13). It can seek to borrow from the central bank's discount window facility to offset this liquidity drain. Alternatively, discount window loans can also meet short-term seasonal liquidity needs due to crop-planting cycles. Normally, DIs make such loans by discounting short-term high-quality securities such as Treasury bills and banker's acceptances with the central bank. The interest rate at which such securities are discounted is called the *discount rate* and is set by the central bank.

www.federalreserve.gov

In the wake of the terrorist attacks of September 11, 2001, the Federal Reserve's discount window supplied funds to the banking system in unprecedented amounts. The magnitude of destruction resulting from the attacks caused severe disruptions to the U.S. banking system, particularly in DIs' abilities to send electronic payments. The physical disruptions caused by the attacks included outages of telephone switching equipment in lower Manhattan's financial district, impaired records processing and communications systems at individual banks, the evacuation of buildings that were the sites for the payment operations of several large DIs, and the suspended delivery of checks by air couriers. These disruptions left some DIs unable to execute payments to other DIs through the Fed's Fedwire system (see Chapter 4), which in turn resulted in an unexpected shortfall of funds for other DIs. The Federal Reserve took several steps to address the problems in the payments system on and after September 11, 2001. Around noon on the eleventh, the Board of Governors of the Fed released a statement saying that the Fed was open and operating and that the discount window was available to meet liquidity needs of all FIs. The Fed staff also contacted FIs frequently during the next few days, encouraging them to make payments and to consider the use of the discount window to cover unexpected shortfalls that they might encounter. Thus, the Fed's discount window was a primary tool used to restore payments coordination during this period.

The Fed took additional unprecedented steps, expanding the usual function of the discount window, to address the financial crisis. While the discount window had traditionally been available to DIs, in the spring of 2008 (as Bear Stearns nearly failed) investment banks gained access to the discount window through the Primary Dealer Credit Facility (PDCF). In the first three days, securities firms borrowed an average of $31.3 billion per day from the Fed. The largest expansion of the discount window's availability to all FIs occurred in the wake of the Lehman Brothers failure, as a series of actions were taken in

**Figure 21–1** The Spread between the Discount Rate and the Fed Funds Rate

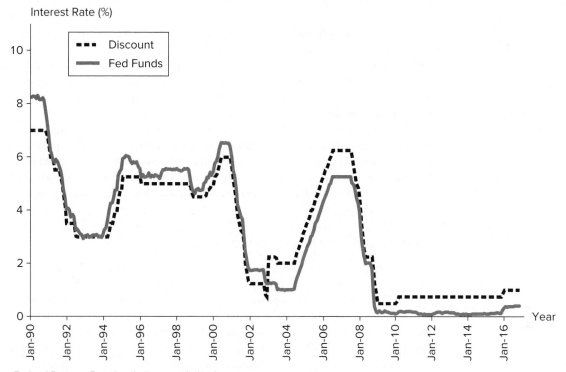

**Source:** Federal Reserve Board website. www.federalreserve.gov

response to the increasingly fragile state of financial markets. After March 2008, several new broad-based lending programs were implemented, providing funding to a wide array of new parties, including U.S. money market mutual funds, commercial paper issuers, insurance companies, and others. These programs rapidly expanded the current lending programs offered via the Fed.

Further, over the next 18 months, in response to a weakening economy and a growing financial crisis, the Fed significantly reduced the level of short-term interest rates by lowering its target federal funds rate to near zero. The overall reduction in the target federal funds rate since late 2007 has been dramatic, going from 5.26 percent in September 2007 to a range of 0 percent to 0.25 percent as of December 16, 2008 (see Figure 21–1). It also significantly reduced the spread (premium) between the discount rate and the federal funds target to just a quarter of a point, bringing the discount rate down to a half percent. With lower rates at the Fed's discount window and interbank liquidity scarce as many lenders cut back their lending, more financial institutions chose to borrow at the window. The magnitude and diversity of nontraditional lending programs and initiatives developed during the crisis were unprecedented in Federal Reserve history. The lending programs were all designed to "unfreeze" and stabilize various parts of the credit markets, with the overall goal that parties receiving credit via these new Fed programs would, in turn, provide funding to creditworthy individuals and firms.

> ## DO YOU UNDERSTAND:
>
> 3. *The benefits and costs of using (a) purchased liquidity management and (b) stored liquidity management to meet a deposit drain?*
>
> 4. *What the major sources of DI liquidity are? What the major uses are?*
>
> 5. *What factors determine a DI's financing requirement?*
>
> 6. *How to measure liquidity risk?*

## LIQUIDITY RISK AND INSURANCE COMPANIES

 *Life Insurance Companies*

Like depository institutions, life insurance companies hold cash reserves and other liquid assets in order to meet policy payments and cancellations (surrenders) and other working capital needs that arise in the course of writing insurance. Least predictable among these is the early cancellation of an insurance policy which results in the insurer having to pay the

**surrender value**

*The amount that an insurance policyholder receives when cashing in a policy early.*

insured the **surrender value** of that policy.[8] In the normal course of business, premium income and returns on an insurer's asset portfolio are sufficient to meet the cash outflows required when policyholders surrender their policies early (see Chapter 15). When premium income is insufficient to meet surrenders, however, a life insurer can sell some of its relatively liquid assets, such as government bonds. In this case, bonds act as a buffer or reserve asset source of liquidity for the insurer. Nevertheless, a drop in market values of insurers' financial assets, such as the drop in the market values of many securities in 2001 and 2008, can result in investment losses for insurance companies and raise the possibility of increased insurance company failures.

Concerns about the solvency of an insurer can result in a run in which new premium income dries up and existing policyholders as a group seek to cancel their policies by cashing them in early. To meet exceptional demands for cash, a life insurer could be forced to liquidate other assets in its portfolio, such as commercial mortgage loans and other securities, potentially at fire-sale prices.[9] Forced asset liquidations can push an insurer, like a DI, into insolvency.

### Property–Casualty Insurance Companies

As discussed in Chapter 15, property–casualty (P&C) insurers sell policies that insure against certain contingencies impacting either real property or individuals. These contingencies are relatively short term and unpredictable, unlike those covered by life insurers. With the help of mortality tables, claims on life insurance policies are generally predictable. P&C claims (such as the estimated $35 billion in insurance losses associated with Hurricane Sandy in 2012) are virtually impossible to predict. Thus, P&C insurers have a greater need for liquidity than life insurers. As a result, P&C insurers tend to hold shorter-term, more liquid assets than do life insurers. P&C insurers' contracts and premium-setting intervals are usually relatively short term as well, so that problems caused by policy surrenders are less severe. P&C insurers' greatest liquidity exposure occurs when policyholders cancel or fail to renew policies with an insurer because of pricing, competition, or safety and solvency concerns. This may cause an insurer's premium cash inflow, when added to its investment returns, to be insufficient to meet its policyholders' claims.

Alternatively, large unexpected claims may materialize and exceed the flow of premium income and income returns from assets. Disasters such as Hurricane Andrew in 1991 and Hurricane Katrina in 2005 have caused severe liquidity crises and failures among smaller P&C insurers.[10] A more recent example is the near failure of insurance giant AIG, which in late summer 2008 was hit by $18 billion in losses from guarantees (credit default swaps, or CDSs) it wrote on mortgage derivatives. As the mortgage debt securities' values declined, AIG was forced to post more collateral to signal to CDS contract counterparties that it could pay off the mortgage guarantees it wrote. Despite these actions by AIG, Standard & Poor's announced that it would downgrade AIG's credit rating. The rating downgrade required AIG to post up to an additional $14.5 billion in collateral, funds which it did not have. AIG made an unprecedented approach to the Federal Reserve seeking $40 billion in short-term financing. The company announced that a financing entity—funded by the Federal Reserve Bank of New York and AIG—had purchased $46.1 billion of the complex debt securities insured by AIG. The deal also included a broader restructuring of the federal government's bailout of AIG, which originally included an $85 billion bridge loan and $37.8 billion in Fed financing.

---

8. A surrender value is usually some proportion or percentage less than 100 percent of the face value of the insurance contract. The surrender value continues to grow as funds invested in the policy earn interest (returns). Earnings to the policyholder are taxed if and when the policy is actually surrendered or cashed in before the policy matures.

9. Life insurers also provide a considerable amount of loan commitments, especially in the commercial property area. As a result, they face asset-side loan commitment liquidity risk in a similar fashion to DIs.

10. Claims also may arise in long-tail lines when a contingency takes place during the policy period but a claim is not lodged until many years later. As mentioned in Chapter 15, the claims regarding damage caused by asbestos contacts are in this category.

### Guarantee Programs for Life and Property–Casualty Insurance Companies

Both life insurance and property–casualty insurance companies are regulated at the state level (see Chapter 15). Unlike banks and thrifts, neither life nor P&C insurers have a federal guarantee fund. Beginning in the 1960s, most states began to sponsor state guarantee funds for firms selling insurance in that state. As discussed in Chapter 15, these state guarantee funds differ in a number of important ways from deposit insurance. First, although these programs are sponsored by state insurance regulators, they are actually run and administered by the private insurance companies themselves. Second, unlike the Depository Institution Insurance Fund, in which the FDIC established a permanent fund by requiring DIs to pay annual premiums to the fund in excess of insurance fund payouts to resolve failures, no permanent guarantee fund exists for the insurance industry, with the sole exception of the P&C and life guarantee funds for the state of New York. This means that contributions are paid into the guarantee fund by surviving firms only *after* an insurance company has failed.

Third, the size of the required contributions that surviving insurers make to protect policyholders in failed insurance companies differs widely from state to state. In those states that have no permanent guarantee fund, each surviving insurer is normally levied a pro rata amount, according to the size of its statewide premium income. This amount either helps pay off small policyholders after the assets of the failed insurer have been liquidated or acts as a cash injection to make the acquisition of a failed insurer attractive. The definition of small policyholders generally varies across states from $100,000 to $500,000.

Finally, because no permanent fund exists and the annual pro rata contributions are often legally capped, a delay usually occurs before small policyholders receive the cash surrender values of their policies or other payment obligations from the guarantee fund. This contrasts with deposit insurance, where insured depositors normally receive immediate coverage (payout) of their claims.

Thus, the private nature of insurance industry guarantee funds, their lack of permanent reserves, and low caps on annual contributions mean that they provide less credible protection to claimants than do bank and thrift insurance funds. As a result, the incentives for insurance policyholders to engage in a run, should they perceive that an insurer has asset quality problems or insurance underwriting problems, is quite strong even in the presence of such guarantee funds.

---

## LIQUIDITY RISK AND INVESTMENT FUNDS

**LG 21-7**

Investment funds such as mutual funds and hedge funds sell shares as liabilities to investors and invest the proceeds in assets such as bonds and equities. Open-end investment funds must stand ready to buy back issued shares from investors at their current market price or net asset value (see Chapter 17). Thus, at a given market price, the supply of open-end fund shares is perfectly elastic. The price at which an open-end investment fund stands ready to sell new shares or redeem existing shares is the net asset value (NAV). As discussed in Chapter 17, the NAV is the current or market value of the fund's assets less any accrued liabilities divided by the number of shares in the fund.

An investment fund's willingness to provide instant liquidity to shareholders while it invests funds in equities, bonds, and other long-term instruments could expose it to liquidity problems similar to those faced by depository institutions when the number of withdrawals (or in this case, mutual fund shares redeemed) rises to abnormally high or unexpected levels. Indeed, investment funds can be subject to dramatic liquidity needs if investors become nervous about the true value of a fund's assets. If the market value of the underlying assets falls and is expected to continue to fall, fund holders will want to liquidate their positions as fast as possible. However, the fundamental difference in the way that investment fund contracts are valued compared to the valuation of DI deposit contracts reduces the incentives for investment fund shareholders to engage in depositlike runs. Specifically, if an investment fund were to be closed and liquidated, its assets would be distributed to fund shareholders on an equal or pro rata basis rather than on the first-come, first-served basis employed under deposit and insurance policy contracts.

To illustrate this difference, we can compare the incentives for investment fund investors to engage in a run with those of DI depositors. Table 21–13 shows a simple balance sheet of an open-end investment fund and a DI. When they perceive that a DI's assets are valued below its liabilities, depositors have an incentive to engage in a run on the DI to be first in line to withdraw. In the example in Table 21–13, only the first 90 DI depositors receive $1 back for each $1 deposited. The last 10 receive nothing at all.

Now consider the investment fund with 100 shareholders who invested $1 each for a total of $100 with assets worth $90. If these shareholders tried to cash in their shares, none would receive $1. Instead, an investment fund values its balance sheet liabilities on a market value basis. The price of any share liquidated by an investor, $P$, is:

$$P = \frac{\text{Value of assets}}{\text{Shares outstanding}} = \text{NAV}$$

Thus, unlike deposit contracts that have fixed face values of $1, the value of an investment fund's shares reflects the changing value of its assets divided by the number of shares outstanding.

In Table 21–13, the value of each shareholder's claim is:

$$P = \frac{\$90}{100} = \$0.90$$

That is, each investment fund shareholder participates in the fund's loss of asset value on a pro rata, or proportional, basis. Technically, whether first or last in line, each investment fund shareholder who cashes in shares on any given day receives the same net asset value per share of the fund. In this case, it is 90 cents, representing a loss of 10 cents per share for all shareholders. All investment fund shareholders realize this and know that investors share asset losses on a pro rata basis. As a result, being first in line to withdraw investment fund shares, on any given day, has no overall advantage. Of course, rapidly falling asset values will result in a greater incentive for investors to cash in their shares as quickly as possible before values fall any further. However, this rush, or run, by investors is due to a drop in the underlying value of their investments and not the threat of receiving nothing because they are not first in line to cash in.

This is not to say that mutual funds bear no liquidity risk. Money market mutual funds (MMMFs) experienced tremendous liquidity risk at the start of the financial crisis. On September 16, 2008 (one day after Lehman Brothers filed for bankruptcy), Reserve Primary Fund, the oldest money market fund in the United States, saw its shares fall to 97 cents (below the $1.00 book value) after writing off debt issued by Lehman Brothers. Resulting investor anxiety about Reserve Primary Fund spread to other funds, and investors industrywide liquidated their MMMF shares. In just one week investors liquidated $170 billion of the industry's total $14 trillion invested in MMMFs. In response, on September 19, the federal government took steps to restore confidence in the MMMF industry. Specifically, the Department of Treasury opened the Temporary Guarantee Program for MMMFs, which provided up to $50 billion in coverage to MMMF shareholders for amounts they held in the funds as of close of business that day. Further, in July 2014, the SEC adopted new rules to address risks of investor runs in money market mutual funds. The new rules require a floating NAV for institutional prime money market funds. This change allows the daily share

**TABLE 21–13**   Run Incentives of DI Depositors versus Investment Fund Investors

| Depository Institution | | Open-End Investment Fund | |
|---|---|---|---|
| **Assets** | **Liabilities** | **Assets** | **Liabilities** |
| Assets        $90 | $100 deposits (100 depositors with $1 deposits) | Assets        $90 | $100 shares (100 shareholders with $1 shares) |

DO YOU UNDERSTAND:

11. *What the impact would be on a DI's liquidity needs if it offered deposit contracts of an open-end investment fund type rather than the traditional all-or-nothing demand deposit contract?*

12. *How the incentives of an investment fund's investors to engage in runs compare with the incentives of DI depositors?*

prices of these funds to fluctuate along with changes in the market value of fund assets. Using NAV will reduce the risk of runs in money market funds and provide important new tools that will help further protect investors and the financial system.

Some of the biggest liquidity crises experienced by individual FIs recently have occurred with hedge funds, which are highly specialized investment funds with a limited number of wealthy investors, usually 100 or less. For example, in the summer of 2007, two Bear Stearns hedge funds suffered heavy losses on investments in the subprime mortgage market. The two funds filed for bankruptcy in the fall of 2007. Bear Stearns's market value was hurt badly from these losses. The losses became so great that by March 2008 Bear Stearns was struggling to finance its day-to-day operations. Bear Stearns had no choice but to basically sell itself to the highest bidder to avoid declaring bankruptcy or completely closing down and leaving investors totally empty-handed. J.P. Morgan Chase purchased the company for $236 million. Bear Stearns's skyscraper in New York was worth over $2 billion alone.

## SUMMARY

This chapter provided an in-depth look at the measurement and on-balance-sheet management of liquidity risks. Liquidity risk is a common problem that DI managers face. Well-developed policies for holding liquid assets or having access to markets for purchased funds are normally adequate to meet liability withdrawals. Very large unexpected withdrawals, however, can cause asset liquidity problems to be compounded by incentives for liability claimholders to engage in runs at the first sign of a liquidity problem. The incentives for depositors and life insurance policyholders to engage in runs can push normally sound FIs into insolvency.

## QUESTIONS

1. How does the degree of liquidity risk differ for different types of financial institutions? (*LG 21-1*)

2. Why would a DI be forced to sell assets at fire-sale prices? (*LG 21-1*)

3. What are the two reasons liquidity risk arises? How does liquidity risk arising from the liability side of the balance sheet differ from liquidity risk arising from the asset side of the balance sheet? What is meant by fire-sale prices? (*LG 21-2*)

4. The probability distribution of the net deposit drain of a DI has been estimated to have a mean of 2 percent. (*LG 21-2*)
   a. Is this DI increasing or decreasing in size? Explain.
   b. If a DI has a net deposit drain, what are the two ways it can offset this drain of funds? How do the two methods differ?

5. What are core deposits? What role do core deposits play in predicting the probability distribution of net deposit drains? (*LG 21-2*)

6. How is asset-side liquidity risk likely to be related to liability-side liquidity risk? (*LG 21-2*)

7. How is a DI's distribution pattern of net deposit drains affected by the following? (*LG 21-1*)
   a. The holiday season.
   b. Summer vacations.
   c. A severe economic recession.
   d. Double-digit inflation.

8. What are two ways a DI can offset the liquidity effects of a net deposit drain of funds? How do the two methods differ?

What are the operational benefits and costs of each method? (*LG 21-2*)

9. What are two ways a DI can offset the effects of asset-side liquidity risk, such as the drawing down of a loan commitment? (*LG 21-2*)

10. Define each of the following four measures of liquidity risk. Explain how each measure would be implemented and utilized by a DI. (*LG 21-3*)
    a. Financing gap and financing requirement.
    b. Sources and uses of liquidity.
    c. Peer group ratio comparisons.
    d. Liquidity index.

11. What are the several components of a DI's liquidity plan? How can such a plan help a DI reduce liquidity shortages? (*LG 21-4*)

12. What is a bank run? What are some possible withdrawal shocks that could initiate a bank run? What feature of the demand deposit contract provides deposit withdrawal momentum that can result in a bank run? (*LG 21-5*)

13. Describe the unprecedented steps the Federal Reserve took with respect to the discount window operations during the financial crisis. (*LG 21-5*)

14. Why does deposit insurance deter bank runs? (*LG 21-5*)

15. What is the greatest cause of liquidity exposure that property–casualty insurers face? (*LG 21-6*)

16. How is the liquidity problem faced by investment funds different from the liquidity problem faced by DIs and insurance companies? (*LG 21-7*)

## PROBLEMS

1. The AllStar Bank has the following balance sheet:

| Assets (in millions) | | Liabilities | |
|---|---|---|---|
| Cash | $ 30 | Deposits | $ 90 |
| Other assets | 140 | Borrowed funds | 40 |
| | $170 | Other liabilities | 40 |
| | | | $170 |

   Its largest customer decides to exercise a $15 million loan commitment. Show how the new balance sheet changes if AllStar uses (a) stored liquidity management or (b) purchased liquidity management. (*LG 21-2*)

2. Consider the balance sheet for the DI listed below:

| Assets (in millions) | | Liabilities | |
|---|---|---|---|
| Cash | $10 | Deposits | $68 |
| Securities | 15 | Equity | 7 |
| Loans | 50 | | |

   The DI is expecting a $15 million net deposit drain. Show the DI's balance sheet under these two conditions: (*LG 21-2*)
   a. The DI purchases liabilities to offset this expected drain.
   b. The stored liquidity management is used to meet the liquidity shortfall.

3. A DI has assets of $10 million consisting of $1 million in cash and $9 million in loans. It has core deposits of $6 million. It also has $2 million in subordinated debt and $2 million in equity. Increases in interest rates are expected to result in a net drain of $1 million in core deposits over the year. (*LG 21-2*)
   a. The average cost of deposits is 2 percent and the average yield on loans is 5 percent. The DI decides to reduce its loan portfolio to offset this expected decline in deposits. What is the cost and what will be the total asset size of the firm from this strategy after the drain?
   b. If the cost of issuing new short-term debt is 3.5 percent, what is the cost of offsetting the expected drain if the DI increases its liabilities? What will be the total asset size of the DI from this strategy after the drain?

4. The Plainbank has $10 million in cash and equivalents, $30 million in loans, and $15 million in core deposits. Calculate (*a*) the financing gap and (*b*) the financing requirement. (*LG 21-3*)

5. A DI has $10 million in T-bills, a $5 million line of credit to borrow in the repo market, and $5 million in excess cash reserves (above reserve requirements) with the Fed. The DI currently has borrowed $6 million in fed funds and $2 million from the Fed discount window to meet seasonal demands. (*LG 21-3*)
   a. What is the DI's total available (sources of) liquidity?
   b. What is the DI's current total uses of liquidity?
   c. What is the net liquidity of the DI?
   d. What conclusions can you derive from the result?

6. The Acme Corporation has been acquired by the Conglomerate Corporation. To help finance the takeover, Conglomerate is going to liquidate the overfunded portion of Acme's pension fund. The assets listed below are going to be liquidated. Listed are their face values, liquidation values today, and their anticipated liquidation values one year from now (their fair market values). (*LG 21-3*)

| Asset | Face Value | Current Liquidation Value | One-Year Liquidation Value |
|---|---|---|---|
| IBM stock | $10,000 | $ 9,900 | $10,500 |
| GE bonds | 5,000 | 4,000 | 4,500 |
| Treasury securities | 15,000 | 13,000 | 14,000 |

   Calculate the one-year liquidity index for these securities.

7. A DI has the following assets in its portfolio: $20 million in cash reserves with the Fed, $20 million in T-bills, and $50 million in mortgage loans. If it needs to dispose of its assets at short notice, it will receive only 99 percent of the fair market value of the T-bills and 90 percent of the fair market value of its mortgage loans. If the DI waits one month to liquidate these assets, it would receive the full fair market value for each security. Calculate the one-month liquidity index using the previous information. (*LG 21-3*)

8. An investment fund has the following assets in its portfolio: $40 million in fixed-income securities and $40 million in stocks at current market values. In the event of a liquidity crisis, it can sell its assets at a 96 percent discount if they are disposed of in two days. It will receive 98 percent if disposed of in four days. Two shareholders, A and B, own 5 percent and 7 percent of equity (shares), respectively. (*LG 21-7*)
   a. Market uncertainty has caused shareholders to sell their shares back to the investment fund. What will the two shareholders receive if the investment fund must sell all its assets in two days? In four days?
   b. How does this differ from a bank run? How have bank regulators mitigated the problem of bank runs?

9. An investment fund has $1 million in cash and $9 million invested in securities. It currently has 1 million shares outstanding. (*LG 21-7*)
   a. What is the NAV of this fund?
   b. Assume that some of the shareholders decide to cash in their shares of the fund. How many shares, at its current NAV, can the fund take back without resorting to a sale of assets?
   c. As a result of anticipated heavy withdrawals, it sells 10,000 shares of IBM stock currently valued at $40. Unfortunately, it receives only $35 per share. What is the net asset value after the sale? What are the fund's cash assets after the sale?
   d. Assume after the sale of IBM shares, 100,000 shares are sold back to the fund. What is the current NAV? Is there a need to sell more stocks to meet this redemption?

*The following problems are related to the Appendix material.*

10. Central Bank has the following balance sheet (in millions of dollars): *(LG 21-3)*

| Assets | | Liabilities and Equity | |
|---|---|---|---|
| Cash | $ 15 | Stable retail deposits | $ 140 |
| | | Less stable retail | |
| Deposits at the Fed | 30 | deposits | 70 |
| | | CDs maturing in | |
| Treasury bonds | 145 | 6 months | 100 |
| Qualifying marketable | | Unsecured wholesale | |
| securities | 50 | funding from: | |
| | | Stable small business | |
| GNMA bonds | 60 | deposits | 125 |
| Loans to AA– rated | | Less stable small | |
| corporations | 540 | business deposits | 100 |
| | | Nonfinancial | |
| Mortgages | 285 | corporates | 500 |
| Premises | 40 | Equity | 130 |
| Total | $1,165 | Total | $1,165 |

Cash inflows over the next 30 days from the FI's performing assets are $7.5 million. Calculate the LCR for Central Bank.

11. WallsFarther Bank has the following balance sheet (in millions of dollars): *(LG 21-3)*

| Assets | | Liabilities and Equity | |
|---|---|---|---|
| Cash | $ 12 | Stable retail deposits | $ 55 |
| Deposits at the Fed | 19 | Less stable retail deposits | 20 |
| | | Unsecured wholesale | |
| Treasury securities | 125 | funding from: | |
| | | Stable small business | |
| GNMA securities | 94 | deposits | 80 |
| Loans to AA rated | | Less stable small | |
| corporations | 138 | business deposits | 49 |
| Loans to BB rated | | | |
| corporations | 106 | Nonfinancial corporates | 250 |
| Premises | 20 | Equity | 60 |
| Total | $514 | Total | $514 |

Cash inflows over the next 30 days from the FI's performing assets are $5.5 million. Calculate the LCR for WallsFarther Bank.

12. FirstBank has the following balance sheet (in millions of dollars): *(LG21-3)*

| Assets | | Liabilities and Equity | |
|---|---|---|---|
| Cash | $ 12 | Stable retail deposits | $ 55 |
| Deposits at the Fed | 19 | Less stable retail deposits | 20 |
| | | Unsecured wholesale | |
| Treasury securities | 125 | funding from: | |
| | | Stable small business | |
| GNMA securities | 94 | deposits | 80 |
| Loans to A rated | | | |
| corporations | | Less stable small | |
| (maturity > 1 year) | 138 | business deposits | 49 |
| Loans to B rated | | | |
| corporations | | Nonfinancial | |
| (maturity < 1 year) | 106 | corporates | 250 |
| Premises | 20 | Equity | 60 |
| Total | $514 | Total | $514 |

Calculate the NSFR for FirstBank.

13. BancTwo has the following balance sheet (in millions of dollars): *(LG21-3)*

| Assets | | Liabilities and Equity | |
|---|---|---|---|
| Cash | $ 20 | Stable retail deposits | $ 190 |
| | | Less stable retail | |
| Deposits at the Fed | 30 | deposits | 70 |
| | | CDs maturing in 6 | |
| Treasury bonds | 145 | months | 100 |
| Qualifying marketable | | | |
| securities | | Unsecured wholesale | |
| (maturity < 1 year) | 50 | funding from: | |
| | | Stable small business | |
| FNMA bonds | 60 | deposits | 125 |
| Loans to AA– rated | | | |
| corporations | | Less stable small | |
| (maturity > 1 year) | 540 | business deposits | 100 |
| Mortgages | | Nonfinancial | |
| (unencumbered) | 285 | corporates | 450 |
| Premises | 35 | Equity | 130 |
| Total | $1,165 | Total | $1,165 |

Calculate the NSFR for BancTwo.

# SEARCH THE SITE

Go to the Federal Reserve Board's website at **www.federalreserve.gov,** and find the most recent data for the fed funds rate and the discount window rate using the following steps. Click on "Economic Research and Data." Click on "Statistical Releases and Historical Data." Under "Interest Rates," click on "weekly." This will bring up a table listing the most recent data.

## Questions

1. Using information in this file, update Figure 21–1.
2. Calculate the percentage change in each rate since 2016, as reported in Figure 21–1. Which rate has increased or decreased more? Why?

**APPENDIX 21A: Sources and Uses of Funds Statement: J.P. Morgan Chase, September 2016**

**APPENDIX 21B: New Liquidity Risk Measures Implemented by the Bank for International Settlements**

Appendixes 21A and 21B are available through Connect or your course instructor.

# Managing Interest Rate Risk and Insolvency Risk on the Balance Sheet

## Learning Goals

**LG 22-1** *Define the repricing gap measure of interest rate risk.*

**LG 22-2** *Understand the weaknesses of the various interest rate risk models.*

**LG 22-3** *Define the duration gap measure of interest rate risk.*

**LG 22-4** *Discuss how capital protects against credit risk and interest rate risk.*

**LG 22-5** *Highlight the differences between the book value and market value of equity.*

# chapter 222

## INTEREST RATE AND INSOLVENCY RISK MANAGEMENT: CHAPTER OVERVIEW

In this third chapter on managing risk on an FI's balance sheet, we provide a detailed analysis of interest rate risk and insolvency risk. Chapter 19 established the fact that while performing their asset-transformation functions, financial institutions (FIs) often mismatch the maturities of their assets and liabilities. In so doing, they expose themselves to interest rate risk. This chapter analyzes two methods used to measure an FI's interest rate risk exposure: the repricing model and the duration model. The repricing gap model examines the impact of interest rate changes on an FI's net interest income (NII). However, as we explain later in the chapter, the FI's duration gap is a more comprehensive measure of interest rate risk exposure than the repricing gap. We also discuss in this chapter the on-balance-sheet management of interest rate risk.[1]

Insolvency risk is the result, a consequence, or an outcome of excessive amounts of one or more of the risks taken by an FI (e.g., liquidity risk, credit risk, and interest rate risk). Technically, insolvency occurs when the internal capital or equity resources of an FI's owners are at or near zero as a result of bad balance sheet outcomes due to one or more of these risks. Indeed, insolvency risk experienced by depository institutions (DIs) during the financial market crisis hit the banking industry very badly. Over the period 2008–2016, 520 DIs failed (at a cost to the FDIC of $73 billion).

---

1. In Chapter 23, we examine how derivative securities can be used to hedge interest rate risk.

# INTEREST RATE RISK MEASUREMENT AND MANAGEMENT

While many factors influence the level and movement of interest rates, it is the central bank's monetary policy strategy that most directly underlies the level and movement of interest rates, which in turn affect an FI's cost of funds and return on assets. As discussed in Chapter 4, when the Fed finds it necessary to slow down the economy, it tightens monetary policy by taking actions that raise interest rates. The normal result is a decrease in business and household spending (especially that financed by credit or borrowing). Conversely, if business and household spending declines to the extent that the Fed finds it necessary to stimulate the economy, it allows interest rates to fall (an expansionary monetary policy). The drop promotes borrowing and spending. While these actions by the Fed to increase or decrease interest rates hamper or promote borrowing and spending, they also create interest rate risk for financial institutions. For example, in 2008, as the U.S. economy fell into its deepest recession since the Great Depression, the Fed, in a historic move, unexpectedly announced that it would drop its target fed funds rate to a range between zero and a quarter of 1 percent and lower its discount window rate to a half a percent, the lowest level since the 1940s. Even into 2015, because of the economy's continued weakness, the Fed announced that it expected to keep the fed funds rate below 1 percent. In essence, as long as rates stay low and the Fed makes statements that it does not intend to raise rates, interest rate risk is low. Rather, the critical concern for interest rate risk management is: when will the Fed increase interest rates? It was December 2015 before the Fed eventually raised interest rates (for the first time in 10 years). Even beyond the low rates set by the U.S. Federal Reserve, the Bank of Japan, the European Central Bank, and several smaller European central banks ventured into the once uncharted territory of negative interest rates. When central banks set negative interest rates, the lender pays the borrower, i.e., instead of getting paid for depositing funds with the central bank, the commercial bank now pays the central bank to deposit funds.

In this section, we analyze two methods used to measure an FI's interest rate risk: the repricing gap and the duration gap model. The repricing gap model, sometimes called the funding gap model, concentrates on the impact of interest rate changes on an FI's net interest income (NII), which is the difference between an FI's interest income and interest expense (see Chapter 12) and thus the FI's net interest income. This contrasts with the market value–based duration gap model, which incorporates the impact of interest rate changes on the overall market value of an FI's balance sheet and ultimately on its owners' equity or net worth. Until recently, U.S. bank regulators had been content to base their evaluations of bank interest rate risk exposures on the repricing gap model alone. As discussed later in this chapter, regulators and other analysts now recognize the serious weaknesses of the repricing gap model. As a result, while the repricing gap model is still used to measure interest rate risk in most FIs, it is increasingly being used in conjunction with the duration gap model. In fact, the largest banks are now using the duration gap model as their main measure of interest rate risk.

**LG 22-1**

**repricing or funding gap**

*The difference between those assets whose interest rates will be repriced or changed over some future period (RSAs) and liabilities whose interest rates will be repriced or changed over some future period (RSLs).*

## Repricing Gap Model

The **repricing or funding gap** model is a simple model used by small (and thus most) FIs in the United States. This model is essentially a book value accounting cash flow analysis of the interest income earned on an FI's assets and the interest expense paid on its liabilities (or its net interest income) over some particular period. Under the repricing gap approach, DIs report quarterly on their Call Reports, interest-rate sensitivity reports that show the repricing gaps for assets and liabilities with various maturities; for example:

1. One day
2. More than 1 day to 3 months
3. More than 3 months to 6 months
4. More than 6 months to 12 months
5. More than 1 year to 5 years
6. More than 5 years

**TABLE 22–1** Repricing Gaps for an FI *(in millions of dollars)*

|  | Assets | Liabilities | Gaps |
|---|---|---|---|
| **1.** 1 day | $ 20 | $ 30 | $–10 |
| **2.** More than 1 day–3 months | 30 | 40 | –10 |
| **3.** More than 3 months–6 months | 70 | 85 | –15 |
| **4.** More than 6 months–12 months | 90 | 70 | +20 |
| **5.** More than 1 year–5 years | 40 | 30 | +10 |
| **6.** More than 5 years | 10 | 5 | +5 |
|  | $260 | $260 |  |

**rate sensitivity**

*The time to repricing of an asset or liability.*

The gap in each maturity bucket (or bin) is calculated by estimating the difference between the rate-sensitive assets (RSAs) and rate-sensitive liabilities (RSLs) on the balance sheet. **Rate sensitivity** means that the asset or liability is repriced (either because it matures and the funds will be rolled over into a new asset or liability, or because it is a financial instrument with a variable interest rate) at or near current market interest rates within the maturity horizon of the bucket under consideration. Repricing can be the result of a rollover of an asset or liability (e.g., a loan is paid off at or prior to maturity and the funds are used to issue a new loan at current market rates), or it can occur because the asset or liability is a variable-rate instrument (e.g., a variable-rate mortgage whose interest rate is reset every quarter based on movements in a prime rate). Table 22–1 shows the assets and liabilities of an FI categorized into each of the six previously defined maturity buckets.

The advantage of the repricing model lies in its information value and its simplicity in pointing to an FI's net interest income exposure (or profit exposure) to interest rate changes in each different maturity bucket. For example, suppose that an FI has a negative $10 million difference between assets and liabilities being repriced in one day (or the one-day bucket). Assets and liabilities that are repriced each day are likely to be interbank borrowings on the federal funds or repurchase agreement markets (see Chapter 5). Thus, a negative gap (RSA < RSL) exposes the FI to **refinancing risk,** in that a rise in these short-term rates would lower the FI's net interest income since the FI has more rate-sensitive liabilities than assets in that bucket. Refinancing risk is a type of interest rate risk in that the cost of refinancing can be more than the return earned on asset investments. In other words, assuming equal changes in interest rates on RSAs and RSLs, interest expense will increase by more than interest revenue. Conversely, if the FI has a positive $20 million difference between its assets and liabilities being repriced in 6 months to 12 months, it has a positive gap (RSA > RSL) for this period and is exposed to **reinvestment risk.** By holding shorter-term assets relative to liabilities, it faces uncertainty about the interest rate at which it can reinvest funds borrowed over a longer period. Thus, a drop in rates over this period would lower the FI's net interest income, since interest income would decrease by more than interest expense. Specifically, let:

**refinancing risk**

*The risk that the cost of rolling over or reborrowing funds will rise above the returns being earned on asset investments.*

**reinvestment risk**

*The risk that the returns on funds to be reinvested will fall below the cost of the funds.*

$\Delta NII_i$ = Change in net interest income in the *i*th maturity bucket

$GAP_i$ = Dollar size of the gap between the book value of rate-sensitive assets and rate-sensitive liabilities in maturity bucket *i*

$\Delta R_i$ = Change in the level of interest rates impacting assets and liabilities in the *i*th maturity bucket

Then:

$$\Delta NII_i = (GAP_i)\Delta R_i = (RSA_i - RSL_i)\Delta R_i$$

In this first bucket, if the gap is negative $10 million and short-term interest rates (such as the fed funds and/or repo rates) rise by 1 percent, the annualized change in the FI's future net interest income is:

$$\Delta NII_i = (-\$10 \text{ million}) \times 0.01 = -\$100,000$$

That is, the negative gap and associated refinancing risk result in a loss of $100,000 in net interest income for the FI.

This approach is very simple and intuitive. We will see later in this section, however, that market or present-value losses (and gains) also occur on assets and liabilities when interest rates change. These effects are not accounted for in the funding gap model because asset and liability values are reported at their *historic* book values rather than on a market value basis. Thus, in the repricing gap model, interest rate changes affect only the current interest income earned and interest expense paid on an asset or liability, rather than the market value of assets and liabilities on the balance sheet.[2]

The FI manager can also estimate cumulative gaps (CGAP) over various repricing categories or buckets. A common cumulative gap of interest is the one-year repricing gap estimated from Table 22–1 as:

$$CGAP = (-\$10m) + (-\$10m) + (-15m) + \$20m = -15 \text{ million}$$

If $\Delta R_i$ is the average interest rate change affecting assets and liabilities that can be repriced within a year, the cumulative effect on the bank's net interest income is:

$$\Delta NII = \left( \sum_{i=1\,\text{day}}^{1\,\text{year}} RSA_i - \sum_{i=1\,\text{day}}^{1\,\text{year}} RSL_i \right) \Delta R_i$$
$$= (CGAP)\Delta R_i$$
$$= (-\$15 \text{ million})(0.01) = -\$150,000$$

We next look at an example of calculating the cumulative one-year gap using an FI in the form of a commercial bank. Remember that the manager considers whether each asset or liability will, or can, have its interest rate changed within the next year. If it will or can, it is a rate-sensitive asset or liability. If not, it is a rate-insensitive asset or liability.

**Measuring and Managing Interest Rate Risk Using the Repricing Gap.**   Consider the simplified bank balance sheet in Table 22–2. Rather than the original maturities, the reported maturities are those remaining on different assets and liabilities at the time the repricing gap is estimated.

*Rate-Sensitive Assets.*   Looking down the asset side of the balance sheet in Table 22–2, we see the following one-year rate-sensitive assets (RSAs):

**TABLE 22–2**   **Simple Bank Balance Sheet and Repricing Gap** *(in millions of dollars)*

| Assets | | Liabilities | |
|---|---|---|---|
| **1.** Cash and due from | $  5 | **1.** Two-year time deposits | $ 40 |
| **2.** Short-term consumer loans (one-year maturity) | 50 | **2.** Demand deposits | 40 |
| **3.** Long-term consumer loans (two-year maturity) | 25 | **3.** Passbook savings | 30 |
| **4.** Three-month T-bills | 30 | **4.** Three-month CDs | 40 |
| **5.** Six-month T-notes | 35 | **5.** Three-month banker's acceptances | 20 |
| **6.** Three-year T-bonds | 60 | **6.** Six-month commercial paper | 60 |
| **7.** 10-year fixed-rate mortgages | 20 | **7.** One-year time deposits | 20 |
| **8.** 30-year floating-rate mortgages | 40 | **8.** Equity capital (fixed) | 20 |
| **9.** Premises | 5 | | |
| | $270 | | $270 |

2. For example, a 30-year bond purchased 10 years ago when rates were 13 percent would be reported as having the same book (accounting) value as when rates were 7 percent. Using market values, capital gains and losses would be reflected on the balance sheet as rates change.

1. *Short-term consumer loans: $50 million,* which are repriced at the end of the year and just make the one-year cutoff.
2. *Three-month T-bills: $30 million,* which are repriced on maturity (rollover) every three months.
3. *Six-month T-notes: $35 million,* which are repriced on maturity (rollover) every six months.
4. *30-year floating-rate mortgages: $40 million,* which are repriced (i.e., the mortgage rate is reset) every nine months. Thus, these long-term assets are RSAs in the context of the repricing model with a one-year repricing horizon.

Summing these four items produces total one-year RSAs of $155 million. The remaining $115 million of assets are not rate sensitive over the one-year repricing horizon—that is, a change in the level of interest rates will not affect the size of the interest income generated by these assets over the next year.[3] The $5 million in the cash and due from category and the $5 million in premises are nonearning assets. Although the $105 million in long-term consumer loans, three-year Treasury bonds, and 10-year, fixed-rate mortgages generate interest income, the size of revenue generated will not change over the next year, since the interest rates or coupons earned on these assets are not expected to change (i.e., they are fixed over the next year).

*Rate-Sensitive Liabilities.*  Looking down the liability side of the balance sheet in Table 22–2, we see that the following liability items clearly fit the one-year rate or repricing sensitivity test:

1. *Three-month CDs: $40 million,* which mature in three months and are repriced on rollover.
2. *Three-month banker's acceptances: $20 million,* which mature in three months and are repriced on rollover.
3. *Six-month commercial paper: $60 million,* which matures and is repriced every six months.
4. *One-year time deposits: $20 million,* which are repriced at the end of the one-year gap horizon.

Summing these four items produces one-year rate-sensitive liabilities (RSLs) of $140 million. The remaining $130 million is not rate sensitive over the one-year period. The $20 million in equity capital and $40 million in demand deposits (see the following discussion) do not pay interest and are therefore classified as noninterest paying. The $30 million in passbook savings (see the following discussion) and $40 million in two-year time deposits generate interest expense over the next year, but the level of the interest expense generated will not change if the general level of interest rates change. Thus, we classify these items as rate-insensitive liabilities. We can make strong arguments for and against their inclusion as rate-sensitive liabilities.

*Against Inclusion.*  Historically, demand deposits were prohibited from paying explicit interest. However, as of July 2011 the federal prohibition against the payment of interest on demand deposits was repealed. Despite this change, few depository institutions are paying any interest on demand deposits. Further, although explicit interest is paid on transaction accounts such as NOW accounts, the rates paid by FIs do not fluctuate directly with changes in the general level of interest rates (particularly when the general level of rates is rising). Moreover, many demand deposits act as **core deposits** for FIs, meaning they are a long-term source of funds.

**core deposits**

*Those deposits that act as a long-term source of funds for an FI.*

*For Inclusion.*  Even though they pay no explicit interest, demand deposits pay implicit interest because FIs do not charge fees to fully cover their costs for checking services. Further, if interest rates rise, individuals draw down (or run off) their demand deposits, forcing the bank to replace them with higher-yielding, interest-bearing, rate-sensitive funds. This is most likely to occur when the interest rates on alternative instruments are high. In such

3. We are assuming that the assets are noncallable over the year and that there will be no prepayments (runoffs, see below) on the mortgages within a year.

an environment, the opportunity cost of holding funds in demand deposit accounts is likely to be larger than it is in a low–interest rate environment.

Similar arguments for and against the inclusion of retail passbook savings accounts also can be made. Although Federal Reserve Regulation Q ceilings on the maximum rates to be charged for these accounts were abolished in March 1986, banks still adjust these rates only infrequently. However, savers tend to withdraw funds from these accounts when rates rise, forcing banks to replace them with more expensive fund substitutions.[4]

The four repriced liabilities ($40 + $20 + $60 + $20) sum to $140 million, and the four repriced assets ($50 + $30 + $35 + $40) sum to $155 million. Given this, the cumulative one-year repricing gap (CGAP) for the bank is:

$$CGAP = (\text{One-year RSA}) - (\text{One-year RSA})$$
$$= RSA - RSL$$
$$= \$155 \text{ million} - \$140 \text{ million} = \$15 \text{ million}$$

Interest rate sensitivity can also be expressed as a percentage of assets ($A$), commonly referred to as the gap ratio:

$$\text{GAP ratio} = \frac{CGAP}{A} = \frac{\$15 \text{ million}}{\$270 \text{ million}} = 0.056 = 5.6\%$$

Expressing the repricing gap in this way is useful since it tells us (1) the direction of the interest rate exposure (positive or negative CGAP) and (2) the scale of that exposure as indicated by dividing the gap by the asset size of the institution. In our example, the bank has a CGAP equal to 5.6 percent of the value of its total assets. This version of the gap ratio is used by regulators to measure interest rate risk.[5]

Table 22–3 shows an interest rate sensitivity report for Security Federal Corp. (headquartered in Aiken, South Carolina). In this report, Security Federal shows the repricing gap for periods ranging from three months or less to over ten years.

*Equal Changes in Rates on RSAs and RSLs.*   The CGAP provides a measure of an FI's interest rate sensitivity. Table 22–4 highlights the relation between CGAP and changes in NII when interest rate changes for RSAs are equal to interest rate changes for RSLs. For example, when CGAP is positive (or the FI has more RSAs than RSLs), NII will rise when interest rates rise (row 1, Table 22–4), since interest income increases more than interest expense does.

**TABLE 22–3**   **Security Federal Corp., Interest Rate Sensitivity Report** *(Dollars in Thousands)*

| SECURITY FEDERAL CORPORATION AND SUBSIDIARIES | | | | | | | |
|---|---|---|---|---|---|---|---|
| Management's Discussion and Analysis of Financial Condition and Results of Operations | | | | | | | |
| | Three Months or Less | Over 3–12 Months | Over 1–3 Years | Over 3–5 Years | Over 5–10 Years | Over 10 Years | Total |
| **Interest-earning assets:** | | | | | | | |
| Loans | $ 96,342 | $ 91,818 | $ 71,470 | $ 52,632 | $ 14,952 | $ 11,696 | $338,910 |
| Mortgage-backed securities: | | | | | | | |
|   Held to maturity, at cost | 818 | 2,118 | 3,678 | 1,983 | 2,839 | 18,437 | 29,873 |
|   Available for sale, at fair value | 78,452 | 15,974 | 13,996 | 9,694 | 21,970 | 42,711 | 182,797 |

*continued*

4. The Federal Reserve's repricing report has traditionally viewed transaction accounts and passbook savings accounts as rate-insensitive liabilities, as we have done in this example. However, with the growth of the Internet and competition from money market mutual funds, the mobility of these funds is highly sensitive to (relative) rates paid by banks versus other nonbank FIs (such as money market mutual funds).

5. An alternative version of the gap ratio is defined as rate-sensitive assets divided by rate-sensitive liabilities. A gap ratio greater than 1 indicates that there are more rate sensitive assets than liabilities (similar to a gap > 0). Thus, the FI is set to see increases in net interest income when interest rates increase. A gap ratio less than 1 indicates that there are more rate sensitive liabilities than assets (similar to a gap < 0). Thus, the FI is set to see increases in net interest income when interest rates decrease. In our example, the gap ratio is 1.107 meaning that in the one-year-and-less time bucket, the FI has $1.107 of RSAs for every $1 of RSLs.

**TABLE 22–3**  **Security Federal Corp., Interest Rate Sensitivity Report** *(Dollars in Thousands) (Continued)*

| | Three Months or Less | Over 3–12 Months | Over 1–3 Years | Over 3–5 Years | Over 5–10 Years | Over 10 Years | Total |
|---|---|---|---|---|---|---|---|
| Investment securities | | | | | | | |
| Available for sale, at fair value | 86,350 | 3,804 | 6,960 | 5,588 | 80,240 | 9,775 | 192,717 |
| FHLB stock, at cost | — | 2,215 | — | — | — | — | 2,215 |
| Other interest-earning Assets | 490 | 2,095 | 1,350 | — | — | — | 3,935 |
| Total interertemst-earning assets | $ 262,452 | $ 118,024 | $ 97,454 | $ 69,897 | $120,001 | $ 82,619 | $750,447 |
| **Interest-bearing liabilities:** | | | | | | | |
| Deposits: | | | | | | | |
| Certificate accounts | $ 49,293 | $ 92,093 | $ 79,162 | $ 15,574 | $ — | $ — | $236,122 |
| NOW accounts | 4,771 | 14,314 | 76,342 | — | — | — | 95,427 |
| Money market accounts | 36,643 | 112,218 | 80,156 | — | — | — | 229,017 |
| Statement savings accounts | 1,560 | 4,679 | 24,953 | — | — | — | 31,192 |
| Borrowings | 23,307 | 5,000 | 17,900 | — | $ — | 6,084 | 52,291 |
| Total interest-bearing liabilities | $ 115,574 | $ 228,304 | $ 278,513 | $ 15,574 | — | $ 6,084 | $644,049 |
| Current period GAP | $146,878 | $(110,280) | $(181,059) | $ 54,323 | $120,001 | $ 76,535 | $106,398 |
| Cumulative GAP | $ 146,878 | $ 36,598 | $(144,461) | $(90,138) | $ 29,863 | $106,398 | $106,398 |
| Cumulative GAP as a percentage of total interest-earning assets | 19.6% | 4.9% | (19.2)% | (12.0)% | 4.0% | 14.2% | 14.2% |

---

**EXAMPLE 22–1**  **Impact of Rate Changes on Net Interest Income When CGAP Is Positive**

Suppose that, for the bank depicted in Table 22–2, interest rates rise by 1 percent on both RSAs and RSLs. The CGAP would project the expected annual change in net interest income ($\Delta NII$) of the bank as:

$$\Delta NII = (RSA \times \Delta R) - (RSL \times \Delta R) = CGAP \times \Delta R$$
$$= (\$155 \text{ million} \times 0.01) - (\$140 \text{ million} \times 0.01) = (\$15 \text{ million}) \times 0.01$$
$$= (\$1.55 \text{ million} - \$1.40 \text{ million}) = \$150{,}000$$

Similarly, if interest rates fall equally for RSAs and RSLs (row 2, Table 22–4), NII will fall when CGAP is positive. As rates fall, interest income falls by more than interest expense. Thus, NII falls. Suppose that for our bank, rates fall by 1 percent. The CGAP predicts that NII will fall by:

$$\Delta NII = [\$155 \text{ million} \times (-0.01)] - [\$140 \text{ million} \times (-0.01)] = \$15 \text{ million} \times -0.01$$
$$= -\$1.55 \text{ million} - (-\$1.40 \text{ million}) = -\$150{,}000$$

---

**CGAP effect**

*The relation between changes in interest rates and changes in net interest income.*

It is evident from this equation that the larger the absolute value of CGAP, the larger the expected change in NII (i.e., the larger the increase or decrease in the FI's interest income relative to interest expense). In general, when CGAP is positive, the change in NII is positively related to the change in interest rates. Thus, an FI would want its CGAP to be positive when interest rates are expected to rise. Conversely, when CGAP is negative, if interest rates rise by equal amounts for RSAs and RSLs (row 3, Table 22–4), NII will fall (since the bank has more RSLs than RSAs). If interest rates fall equally for RSAs and RSLs (row 4, Table 22–4), NII will increase when CGAP is negative. As rates fall, interest expense decreases by more than interest income. In general then, when CGAP is negative, the change in NII is negatively related to the change in interest rates. Thus, an FI would want its CGAP to be negative when interest rates are expected to fall. We refer to these relationships as **CGAP effects.**

**TABLE 22–4**  Impact of CGAP on the Relation between Changes in Interest Rates and Changes in Net Interest Income, Assuming Rate Changes for RSAs Equal Rate Changes for RSLs

| Row | CGAP | Change in Interest Rate | Change in Interest Income | | Change in Interest Expense | Change in NII |
|-----|------|-------------------------|---------------------------|-----|----------------------------|---------------|
| 1 | >0 | ↑ | ↑ | > | ↑ | ↑ |
| 2 | >0 | ↓ | ↓ | > | ↓ | ↓ |
| 3 | <0 | ↑ | ↑ | < | ↑ | ↓ |
| 4 | <0 | ↓ | ↓ | < | ↓ | ↑ |

*Unequal Changes in Rates on RSAs and RSLs.*    The previous section considered changes in net interest income as interest rates changed, assuming that the change in rates on RSAs was exactly equal to the change in rates on RSLs (in other words, assuming the interest rate spread between rates on RSAs and RSLs remained unchanged). This is not often the case. Rather, rate changes on RSAs generally differ from those on RSLs (i.e., the spread between interest rates on assets and liabilities changes along with the levels of these rates). See Panel a of Figure 22–1, which plots monthly CD rates (liabilities) and prime lending rates (assets) for the period 1990–2016. Panel b shows the monthly spread between the two rates. Notice that although the rates generally move in the same direction, they are not perfectly correlated. In this case, as we consider the impact of rate changes on NII, we have a spread effect in addition to the CGAP effect.

If the spread between the rate on RSAs and RSLs increases, when interest rates rise (fall), interest income increases (decreases) by more (less) than interest expense. The result is an increase in NII. Conversely, if the spread between the rates on RSAs and RSLs decreases, when interest rates rise (fall), interest income increases (decreases) less (more) than interest expense, and NII decreases. In general, the **spread effect** is such that, regardless of the direction of the change in interest rates, a positive relation exists between changes in the spread (between rates on RSAs and RSLs) and changes in NII. Whenever the spread increases (decreases), NII increases (decreases).

**spread effect**

*The effect that a change in the spread between rates on RSAs and RSLs has on net interest income (NII) as interest rates change.*

---

**EXAMPLE 22–2**    Impact of Spread Effect on Net Interest Income

To understand spread effect, assume for a moment that both RSAs and RSLs equal $155 million. Suppose that rates rise by 1.2 percent on RSAs and by 1 percent on RSLs (i.e., the spread between the rate on RSAs and RSLs increases by 1.2 percent − 1 percent = 0.2 percent). The resulting change in NII is calculated as:

$$\Delta NII = (RSA \times \Delta R_{RSA}) - (RSL \times \Delta R_{RSL})$$
$$= \Delta \text{Interest income} - \Delta \text{Interest expense}$$
$$= (\$155 \text{ million} \times 1.2\%) - (\$155 \text{ million} \times 1.0\%)$$
$$= \$155 \text{ million} (1.2\% - 1.0\%)$$
$$= \$310,000$$

---

See Table 22–5 for various combinations of CGAP and spread changes and their effects on NII. The first four rows in Table 22–5 consider a bank with a positive CGAP; the last four rows consider a bank with a negative CGAP. Notice in Table 22–5 that the CGAP and spread effects can both have the same effect on NII. For example, in row 6 of Table 22–5, if CGAP is negative and interest rates increase, the CGAP effect says NII will decrease. If, at the same time, the spread between RSAs and RSLs decreases as interest rates increase, the spread effect also says NII will decrease. In these cases,

**Figure 22–1** Three-Month CD Rates versus Prime Rates for 1990–2016

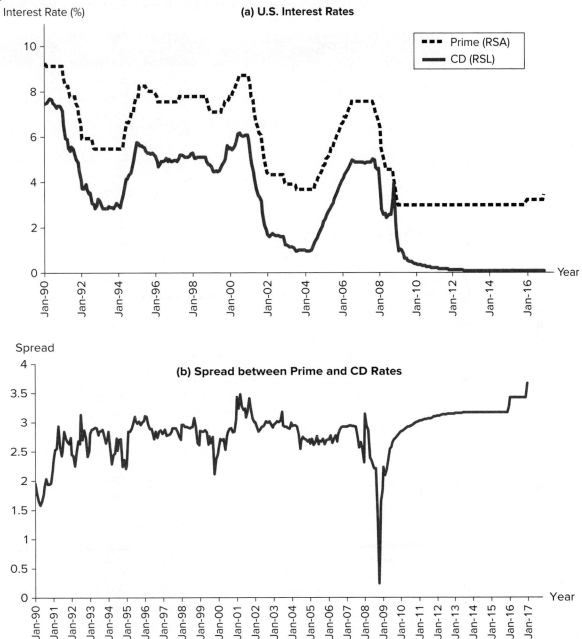

RSA = Rate-sensitive assets.
RSL = Rate-sensitive liabilities.
**Sources:** Federal Reserve Bulletin, various issues. www.federalreserve.gov

FI managers can accurately predict the direction of the change in NII as interest rates change (rows indicated with one arrow under the Change in NII column). When the two work in opposite directions, however, the change in NII cannot be predicted without knowing the size of the CGAP and the expected change in the spread (see the rows indicated by two arrows, ↑ ↓, under the Change in NII column). For example, in row 5 of Table 22–5, if CGAP is negative and interest rates increase, the CGAP effect says NII will decrease. If, at the same time, the spread between RSAs and RSLs increases as interest rates increase, the spread effect says NII will increase.

**TABLE 22–5**   Impact of CGAP on the Relation between Changes in Interest Rates and Changes in Net Interest Income, Allowing for Different Rate Changes on RSAs and RSLs

| Row | CGAP | Change in Interest Rates | Change in Spread | Change in NII |
|-----|------|--------------------------|------------------|---------------|
| 1 | >0 | ↑ | ↑ | ↑ |
| 2 | >0 | ↑ | ↓ | ↑↓ |
| 3 | >0 | ↓ | ↑ | ↑↓ |
| 4 | >0 | ↓ | ↓ | ↓ |
| 5 | <0 | ↑ | ↑ | ↑↓ |
| 6 | <0 | ↑ | ↓ | ↓ |
| 7 | <0 | ↓ | ↑ | ↑ |
| 8 | <0 | ↓ | ↓ | ↑↓ |

---

**EXAMPLE 22–3**   Combined Impact of CGAP and the Spread Effect on Net Interest Income

Suppose that for the FI in Table 22–2, interest rates fall by 1.0 percent on RSAs and by 1.2 percent on RSLs. Now the change in NII is calculated as:

$$\Delta NII = [\$155 \text{ million} \times (-0.010)] - [\$140 \text{ million} \times (-0.012)]$$
$$= \$1.55 \text{ million} - (-\$1.68 \text{ million})$$
$$= \$0.13 \text{ million, or } \$130,000$$

Even though the CGAP effect (i.e., RSA > RSA) is putting negative pressure on NII (in Example 22–1, the CGAP effect of a 1 percent decrease in the rate on both RSAs and RSLs produced a *decrease* in NII of $150,000), the increase in the spread, and the resulting spread effect, is so big that NII *increases* by $130,000.

---

Some FIs accept quite large interest rate exposures relative to their asset sizes. For example, the one-year repricing gap to total interest-earning assets ratio of Security Federal Corporation was 19.6 percent at the end of 2015 and the one-year gap to total interest-earning assets ratio was 4.9 percent (i.e., it had more RSAs than RSLs). If interest rates rose in 2016, Security Federal Corporation was set up to see net interest income increases due to the repricing of its large amount of RSAs (relative to RSLs) at higher rates. Thus, Security Federal's management set up its balance sheet in expectation of interest rate increases over the five years. Conversely, Security Federal reported a three-year repricing gap to total assets ratio of –19.2 percent and a five-year ratio of –12.0 percent. Thus, Security Federal was set up to see net interest income increases at lower interest rates. That is, Security Federal's management set up its balance sheet in expectation of interest rate decreases over the next five years.

The repricing gap is the measure of interest rate risk historically used by FIs, and it is still the main measure of interest rate risk used by small community banks and thrifts. The repricing gap model is conceptually easy to understand and can easily be used to forecast changes in profitability for a given change in interest rates. The repricing gap can be used to allow an FI to structure its assets and liabilities or to go off the balance sheet to take advantage of a projected interest rate change. However, the repricing gap model has some major weaknesses that have resulted in regulators calling for the use of more comprehensive models (e.g., the duration gap model) to measure the interest rate risk of an FI. We next discuss some of the major weaknesses of the repricing model.

**LG 22-2**

**Weaknesses of the Repricing Model.**   Despite the fact that this model of interest rate risk is used by the vast majority of depository institutions in the United States, the repricing model has four major weaknesses: (1) it ignores market value effects of interest rate changes, (2) it ignores cash flow patterns within a maturity bucket, (3) it fails to deal with the problem of rate-insensitive asset and liability cash flow runoffs and prepayments, and (4) it ignores cash flows from off-balance-sheet activities. This section discusses each of these weaknesses.

*Market Value Effects.* As discussed in the next section, interest rate changes have a market (or present) value effect in addition to an income effect on asset and liability values. That is, the present values of the cash flows on assets and liabilities change, in addition to the immediate interest received or paid on them, as interest rates change. In fact, the present values (and, where relevant, the market prices) of virtually all assets and liabilities on an FI's balance sheet change as interest rates change. As such, the repricing gap is only a *partial* and short-term measure of an FI's true overall interest rate risk exposure.

*Cash Flow Patterns within a Maturity Bucket.* The problem of defining buckets over a range of maturities ignores information regarding the distribution of assets and liabilities within that bucket. For example, the dollar values of RSAs and RSLs within any maturity bucket range may be equal. However, on average, liabilities may be repriced toward the end of the bucket's range and assets may be repriced toward the beginning, in which case a change in interest rates will have an effect on asset and liability cash flows that will not be accurately measured by the repricing gap approach.

*The Problem of Runoffs and Prepayments.* Even if an asset or liability is rate insensitive, virtually all assets and liabilities pay some interest and/or principal back in any given year. As a result, the FI receives a cash flow or **runoff** from its rate-insensitive portfolio that can be reinvested at current market rates. That is, most assets and liabilities (e.g., long-term mortgages) pay some principal and/or interest back to the FI in any given year. This runoff cash flow component of a rate-insensitive asset and liability is itself rate *sensitive*. The FI manager can easily deal with this in the repricing gap model by identifying for each asset and liability item the estimated dollar cash flow that will be run off within the next year (or other time frame) and adding these amounts to the value of rate-sensitive assets and liabilities.

Similarly, the repricing model assumes that there is no prepayment of RSAs and RSLs. In reality, however, cash flows from RSAs and RSLs do not act in such a predictable fashion. For example, a mortgage may be paid off early, either to buy a new house or to refinance the mortgage should interest rates fall. For a variety of reasons, mortgage borrowers relocate or refinance their mortgages (especially when current mortgage rates are below mortgage coupon rates). This propensity to prepay means that realized cash flows on RSAs and RSLs can often deviate substantially from the stated or expected cash flows in a no-prepayment world. As with runoffs, the FI manager can deal with prepayments in the repricing gap model by estimating the amount of prepayment on each asset and liability within the next year (or other time frame) and adding these amounts to the values of RSAs and RSLs.

*Cash Flows from Off-Balance-Sheet Activities.* The RSAs and RSLs used in the repricing model generally include only assets and liabilities listed on the balance sheet. Changes in interest rates will affect the cash flows on many off-balance-sheet instruments as well. For example, an FI might have hedged its interest rate risk with an interest rate futures contract (see Chapter 23). As interest rates change, these futures contracts—as part of the marking-to-market process—produce a daily cash flow (either positive or negative) for the FI that may offset any on-balance-sheet gap exposure. These offsetting cash flows from futures contracts are ignored by the simple repricing model and should (and could) be included in the model.

---

**LG 22-3**

### Duration Gap Model

In Chapter 3, we demonstrated how to calculate duration and showed that the duration measure has economic meaning as the sensitivity of an asset or liability's value to small changes in interest rates. That is:

$$D = -\frac{\%\Delta \text{ in the market value of a security}}{\Delta R/(1 + R)}$$

---

**runoff**

*Periodic cash flow of interest and principal amortization payments on long-term assets such as conventional mortgages that can be reinvested at market rates.*

**duration gap**

*A measure of overall interest rate risk exposure for an FI.*

For FIs, the major relevance of duration is its use as a measure of interest rate risk exposure. The duration gap model can be used instead of the repricing model discussed earlier to evaluate an FI's overall interest rate exposure—to measure the FI's **duration gap.**

**The Duration Gap for a Financial Institution.**   To estimate the overall duration gap of an FI, we first determine the duration of an FI's asset portfolio ($A$) and the duration of its liability portfolio ($L$). Specifically, the duration of a portfolio of assets or liabilities is the market value weighted average of the durations of the components of the portfolio. These can be calculated as:

$$D_A = X_{1A}D_1^A + X_{2A}D_2^A + ... + X_{nA}D_n^A$$

and:

$$D_L = X_{1L}D_1^L + X_{2L}D_2^L + ... + X_{nL}D_n^L$$

where

$$X_{1j} + X_{2j} + ... + X_{nj} = 1$$
$$j = A, L$$

The $X_{ij}$'s in the equation represent the market value proportions of each asset or liability held in the respective asset and liability portfolios. Thus, if new 30-year Treasury bonds were 1 percent of a life insurer's portfolio and $D_1^A$, the duration of those bonds, was equal to 9.25 years, $X_{1A}D_1^A = 0.01(9.25) = 0.0925$. More simply, the duration of a portfolio of assets or liabilities is a market value weighted average of the individual durations of the assets or liabilities on the FI's balance sheet.

Consider an FI's simplified market value balance sheet:

| Assets ($) | Liabilities/Equity ($) |
|---|---|
| Assets ($A$) = $100 | Liabilities ($L$) = $ 90 |
|  | Equity ($E$) = ___10 |
| $\overline{\$100}$ | $\$100$ |

From the balance sheet:

$$A = L + E$$

and:

$$\Delta A = \Delta L + \Delta E$$

or:

$$\Delta E = \Delta A - \Delta L$$

That is, when interest rates change, the change in the FI's equity or net worth ($E$) equals the difference between the change in the market values of assets and liabilities on each side of the balance sheet.

Since $\Delta E = \Delta A - \Delta L$, we need to determine how $\Delta A$ and $\Delta L$—the changes in the market values of assets and liabilities on the balance sheet—are related to their duration.[6] From the duration model (assuming annual compounding of interest):

$$\frac{\Delta A}{A} = -D_A \frac{\Delta R}{(1 + R)}$$

and:

$$\frac{\Delta L}{L} = -D_L \frac{\Delta R}{(1 + R)}$$

---

6. In what follows, we use the $\Delta$ (change) notation instead of d (derivative notation) to recognize that interest rate changes tend to be discrete rather then infinitesimally small. For example, in real-world financial markets the smallest observed rate change is usually one basis point, or 1/100 of 1 percent.

Here we have simply substituted $\Delta A/A$ or $\Delta L/L$, the percentage change in the market values of assets or liabilities, for $\Delta P/P$, the percentage change in any single bond's price, and $D_A$ or $D_L$, the duration of the FI's asset or liability portfolio, for $D_i$, the duration on any given bond, deposit, or loan. The term $\Delta R/(1 + R)$ reflects the shock to interest rates as before.[7] To show dollar changes, these equations can be rewritten as:

$$\Delta A = A \times -D_A \times \frac{\Delta R}{(1 + R)}$$

and:

$$\Delta L = L \times -D_L \times \frac{\Delta R}{(1 + R)}$$

Since $\Delta E = \Delta A - \Delta L$, we can substitute these two expressions into this equation. Rearranging and combining these equations[8] results in a measure of the change in the market value of equity:

$$\Delta E = -(D_A - kD_L) \times A \times \frac{\Delta R}{(1 + R)}$$

where

> $k = L/A$ = Measure of the FI's leverage—the amount of borrowed funds or liabilities rather than owners' equity used to fund its asset portfolio

The effect of interest rate changes on the market value of an FI's equity or net worth ($\Delta E$) breaks down into three effects:

1. *The leverage-adjusted duration gap* $= D_A - kD_L$. This gap is measured in years and reflects the degree of duration mismatch in an FI's balance sheet. Specifically, the larger this gap *in absolute terms,* the more exposed the FI is to interest rate risk.
2. *The size of the FI.* The term $A$ measures the size of the FI's assets. The larger the asset size of the FI, the larger the dollar size of the potential net worth exposure from any given interest rate shock.
3. *The size of the interest rate shock* $= \Delta R/(1 + R)$. The larger the shock, the greater the FI's exposure.[9]

---

7. For simplicity, we assume that the interest rate changes are the same for both assets and liabilities. This assumption is standard in Macauley duration analysis (see Chapter 3).

8. $\Delta E = \left[ A \times (-D_A) \times \dfrac{\Delta R}{(1 + R)} \right] - \left[ L \times (-D_L) \times \dfrac{\Delta R}{(1 + R)} \right]$

Assuming that the level of interest rates and expected shock to interest rates are the same for both assets and liabilities:

$$\Delta E = [(-D_A) A + (D_L) L] \frac{\Delta R}{(1 + R)}$$

or:

$$\Delta E = -(D_A A - D_L L) \frac{\Delta R}{(1 + R)}$$

To rearrange the equation in a slightly more intuitive fashion, we multiply and divide both the terms $D_A A$ and $D_L L$ by $A$ (assets):

$$\Delta E = -[(A/A)D_A - (L/A)D_L] \times A \times [\Delta R/(1 + R)]$$

Therefore:

$$\Delta E = -[D_A - (L/A)D_L] \times A \times [\Delta R/(1 + R)]]$$

and thus:

$$\Delta E = -(D_A - kD_L) \times A \times [\Delta R/(1 + R)]$$

where

$$k = L/A$$

9. We assume that the level of rates and the expected shock to interest rates are the same for both assets and liabilities. This assumption is standard in Macauley duration analysis. Although restrictive, this assumption can be relaxed. Specifically, if $\Delta R_A$ is the shock to assets and $\Delta R_L$ is the shock to liabilities, we can express the duration gap model as:

$$\Delta E = -\left[ \left( D_A \times A \times \frac{\Delta R_A}{1 + R_A} \right) - \left( D_L \times L \times \frac{\Delta R_L}{1 + R_L} \right) \right]$$

**TABLE 22–6**   Fannie Mae Duration Gap

| | For the Three Months Ended September 30, 2016 | | |
|---|---|---|---|
| | **Duration Gap** | **Rate Slope Shock 25 Bps** | **Rate Level Shock 50 Bps** |
| | **(in months)** | **Exposure (dollars in billions)** | |
| Average ................................................................ | 0.3 | $0.0 | $ 0.0 |
| Minimum................................................................ | (0.3) | 0.0 | 0.0 |
| Maximum................................................................ | 0.9 | 0.1 | 0.1 |
| Standard deviation................................................ | 0.3 | 0.0 | 0.0 |
| | **For the Three Months Ended September 30, 2015** | | |
| | **Duration Gap** | **Rate Slope Shock 25 Bps** | **Rate Level Shock 50 Bps** |
| | **(in months)** | **Exposure (dollars in billions)** | |
| Average ................................................................ | (0.2) | $ 0.0 | $ 0.0 |
| Minimum................................................................ | (0.8) | 0.0 | 0.0 |
| Maximum................................................................ | 0.7 | 0.1 | 0.1 |
| Standard deviation................................................ | 0.3 | 0.0 | 0.0 |

Given this, we express the exposure of the net worth of the FI as:

$$\Delta E = -\text{Leverage adjusted duration gap} \times \text{Asset size} \times \text{Interest rate shock}$$

Interest rate shocks are largely external to the FI and often result from changes in the Federal Reserve's monetary policy or from international capital movements (as discussed in Chapter 4). The size of the duration gap and the size of the FI, however, are largely under the control of its management. Table 22–6 shows the duration gap and the market value impact on Fannie Mae's net portfolio for interest rate shocks for the three months ended September 30, 2016, and the three months ended September 30, 2015. For both periods, the effective duration gap was approximately zero months.

We next use an example to explain how a manager can utilize information on an FI's duration gap to restructure the balance sheet to immunize stockholders' net worth against interest rate risk (i.e., set the balance sheet up *before* a change in interest rates, so that $\Delta E$ is nonnegative for a forecasted change in interest rates). The general rules we illustrate are as follows. If the duration gap (DGAP) is negative, there is a positive relation between changes in interest rates and changes in the market value of the FI. Thus, if interest rates increase (decrease), the market value of the FI increases (decreases). If the DGAP is positive, there is a negative relation between changes in interest rates and changes in the market value of the FI. Thus, if interest rates decrease (increase), the market value of the FI increases (decreases). Table 22–7 highlights this relation between DGAP and changes in an FI's equity value.

**TABLE 22–7**   Impact of DGAP on the Relation between Changes in Interest Rates and Changes in Equity Value

| DGAP | Change in Interest Rates | Change in Asset Value | | Change in Liability Value | Change in Equity Value |
|---|---|---|---|---|---|
| >0 | ↑ | ↓ | > | ↓ | ↓ |
| >0 | ↓ | ↑ | > | ↑ | ↑ |
| <0 | ↑ | ↓ | < | ↓ | ↑ |
| <0 | ↓ | ↑ | < | ↑ | ↓ |

**EXAMPLE 22–4**   Duration Gap Measurement and Exposure

Suppose that the FI manager calculates that:

$$D_A = 5 \text{ years}$$
$$D_L = 3 \text{ years}$$

Then the manager learns from an economic forecasting unit that rates are expected to rise from 10 percent to 11 percent in the immediate future. That is:

$$\Delta R = 1\% = 0.01$$
$$1 + R = 1.10$$

The FI's initial balance sheet is:

| Assets ($ millions) | Liabilities ($ millions) |
|---|---|
| $A = \$100$ | $L = \$\ 90$ |
| | $E = \underline{\ \ \ 10}$ |
| $\overline{\$100}$ | $\$100$ |

The FI manager calculates the potential loss to equity holders' net worth ($E$) if the forecast of rising rates proves true:

$$\Delta E = -(D_A - kD_L) \times A \times \frac{\Delta R}{(1 + R)}$$

$$= -[5 - (0.9)(3)] \times \$100 \text{ million} \times \frac{0.01}{1.1} = -\$2.09 \text{ million}$$

The FI could lose $2.09 million in net worth if rates rise by 1 percent. The FI started with $10 million in equity, so the loss of $2.09 million is almost 21 percent of its initial net worth. The market value balance sheet after the rise in rates by 1 percent then appears as follows:[10]

| Assets ($ millions) | Liabilities ($ million) |
|---|---|
| $A = \$95.45$ | $L = \$87.54$ |
| | $E = \underline{\ \ \ 7.91}$ |
| $\overline{\$95.45}$ | $\$95.45$ |

Even though the rise in interest rates would not push the FI into economic insolvency, it reduces the FI's net-worth-to-assets ratio from 10 percent (10/100) to 8.29 percent (7.91/95.45). To counter this effect, the manager might reduce the FI's duration gap. In an extreme case, this gap might be reduced to zero:

$$\Delta E = (0) \times A \times \Delta R/(1 + R) = 0$$

To do this, the FI should not directly set $D_A = D_L$, which ignores the fact that the FI's assets ($A$) do not equal its borrowed liabilities ($L$) and that $k$ (which reflects the ratio $L/A$) is not equal to 1. To see the importance of factoring in leverage (or $L/A$), suppose that the manager increases the duration of the FI's liabilities to five years, the same as $D_A$. Then:

$$\Delta E = -[5 - (0.9)(5)] \times \$100 \text{ million} \times (0.01/1.1) = -0.45 \text{ million}$$

The FI is still exposed to a loss of $0.45 million if rates rise by 1 percent.

An appropriate strategy involves changing $D_L$ until:

$$D_A = kD_L = 5 \text{ years}$$

For example:

$$\Delta E = -[5 - (0.9)5.55] \times \$100 \text{ million} \times (0.01/1.1) = 0$$

In this case, the FI manager sets $D_L = 5.55$ years, or slightly longer than $D_A = 5$ years, to compensate for the fact that only 90 percent of assets are funded by borrowed liabilities, with the other 10 percent funded by equity. Note that the FI manager has at least three other ways to reduce the duration gap to zero:

1. *Reduce $D_A$*. Reduce $D_A$ from 5 years to 2.7 years (equal to $kD_L$, or [0.9][3]) so that

$$(D_A - kD_L) = [2.7 - (0.9)(3)] = 0$$

10. These values are calculated as follows:

$$\frac{\Delta A}{A} = -5\left(\frac{0.01}{1.1}\right) = -0.04545 = -4.545\%$$

$$100 + (-0.04545)\,100 = 95.45$$

and:

$$\frac{\Delta L}{L} = -3\left(\frac{0.01}{1.1}\right) = -0.02727 = -2.727\%$$

$$90 + (-0.02727)\,90 = 87.54$$

2. *Reduce $D_A$ and increase $D_L$.* Shorten the duration of assets and lengthen the duration of liabilities at the same time. One possibility is to *reduce $D_A$* to 4 years and to *increase $D_L$* to 4.44 years so that

$$(D_A - kD_L) = [4 - (0.9)(4.44)] = 0$$

3. *Change $k$ and $D_L$.* Increase $k$ (leverage) from 0.9 to 0.95 and increase $D_L$ from 3 years to 5.26 years so that:

$$(D_A - kD_L) = [5 - (0.95)(5.26)] = 0$$

The preceding example demonstrates how the duration model can be used to immunize an FI's entire balance sheet against interest rate risk (i.e., so that the value of the FI's equity is unaffected by changes in interest rates).

**LG 22-2**

**Difficulties in Applying the Duration Model to Real-World FI Balance Sheets.** Critics of the duration model have often claimed that it is difficult to apply in real-world situations. However, duration measures and immunization strategies are useful in most real-world situations. In fact, the model recently proposed by the Federal Reserve and the Bank for International Settlements (BIS) to monitor bank interest rate risk is heavily based on the duration model. We next consider the various criticisms of the duration model and discuss ways that an FI manager would deal with these criticisms in practice.

*Duration Matching Can Be Costly.*   Critics charge that although in principle an FI manager can change $D_A$ and $D_L$ to immunize the FI against interest rate risk, restructuring the balance sheet of a large and complex FI can be both time-consuming and costly. This argument may have been true historically, but the growth of purchased funds, asset securitization, and loan sales markets has considerably eased the speed and lowered the transaction costs of major balance sheet restructurings. (See Chapter 24 for a discussion of these strategies.) Moreover, an FI manager could still manage interest rate risk exposure using the duration model by employing techniques other than direct portfolio rebalancing to immunize against interest rate risk. Managers can obtain many of the same results of direct duration matching by taking offsetting (hedging) positions in the markets for derivative securities, such as futures, forwards, options, and swaps (see Chapter 23).

*Immunization Is a Dynamic Problem.*   Even though assets and liabilities are duration matched today, the same assets and liabilities may not be matched tomorrow. This is because the duration of assets and liabilities changes as they approach maturity, and, most importantly, the rate at which their durations change through time may not be the same on the asset and liability sides of the balance sheet. As a result, the manager has to continuously restructure the balance sheet to remain immunized. In theory, the strategy requires the portfolio manager to rebalance the portfolio continuously to ensure that the durations of its assets and liabilities are matched. Because continuous rebalancing may not be easy to do and involves costly transaction fees, most FI managers seek to be only approximately dynamically immunized against interest rate changes by rebalancing at discrete intervals, such as quarterly. That is, FI managers accept the trade-off between being perfectly immunized and the transaction costs of maintaining an immunized balance sheet dynamically.

*Large Interest Rate Changes and Convexity.*   Duration measures the price sensitivity of fixed-income securities for small changes in interest rates of the order of one basis point (or one hundredth of 1 percent). But suppose that interest rate shocks are much larger, of the order of 2 percent or 200 basis points. In this case, duration becomes a less accurate predictor of how much the prices of securities will change and, therefore, a less accurate measure of the interest rate sensitivity and the interest rate gap of an FI. Figure 22–2 is

**Figure 22–2**   Duration Estimated versus True Bond Price

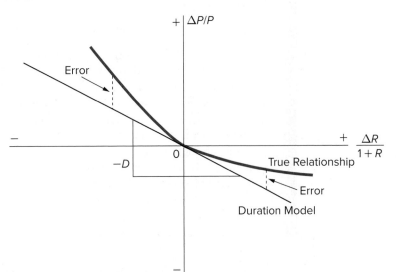

**convexity**

*The degree of curvature of the price–yield curve around some interest rate level.*

a graphic representation of the reason for this. Note the change in an asset's or liability's price, such as that of a bond, due to yield (interest rate) changes according to the duration model and the "true relationship," as calculated directly, using the exact present value calculation for a bond.

Specifically, the duration model predicts that the relationship between an interest rate change (or shock) and a bond's price change will be proportional to the bond's duration (*D*). By precisely calculating the true change in the bond's price, however, we would find that for large interest rate increases, duration overpredicts the *fall* in the bond's price, and for large interest rate decreases, it underpredicts the *increase* in the bond's price. That is, the duration model predicts symmetric effects for rate increases and decreases on the bond's price. As Figure 22–2 shows, in actuality, the capital *loss* effect of rate increases tends to be smaller than the capital *gain* effect of rate decreases. This is the result of the bond's price–yield relationship exhibiting a property called **convexity** rather than linearity, as assumed by the basic duration model (see the more detailed discussion in Chapter 3). Nevertheless, an FI manager sufficiently concerned about the impact of large rate changes on the FI's balance sheet can capture the convexity effect by directly measuring it and incorporating it into the duration gap model.[11]

---

**EXAMPLE 22–5**   The Impact of Convexity for Large Interest Rate Changes

Consider a four-year bond that pays 8 percent coupons annually and has a yield to maturity of 10 percent. Table 22–8 shows that the market value of this bond is $936.603 (see point A in Figure 22–3) and the duration of this bond is 3.562 years. Suppose interest rates change such that the yield to maturity on the bond increases to 12 percent. The true market value of the bond (point B in Figure 22–3) decreases to:

$$V_b = \left(\frac{80}{1+0.12}\right)^1 + \left(\frac{80}{1+0.12}\right)^2 + \left(\frac{80}{1+0.12}\right)^3 + \left(\frac{80}{1+0.12}\right)^4 = \$878.506$$

---

11. Technically speaking, convexity can be viewed as the *rate of change* of the bond's value with respect to any interest rate change, whereas duration measures the *change* in a bond's value with respect to a change in interest rates.

This is a drop of $58.097. According to the duration model, however, the change in the bond's value is:

$$P = 936.603 \times (-3.562) \times (0.02/1.10) = -\$60.658$$

or the new bond value is $875.945 (point C in Figure 22–3).

The difference in these two values, $2.561 ($878.506 – $875.945), (or, 0.29 percent [$2.561/$878.506]), is due to the convexity in the "true" market value calculation versus the linearity in the duration model. This linearity assumption leads to inaccuracies in the duration value calculations that increase with the size of the interest rate change.[12]

Reversing the experiment reveals that if the yield on the bond decreases from 10 percent to 8 percent, the true or actual price of the bond increases to $1,000.000 (point D in Figure 22–3). This is an increase in value of $63.397. The duration model, however, predicts a $60.658 increase in the bond, or that the new bond value is $997.261 (point E in Figure 22–3). The duration model has underpredicted the bond price increase by $2.739, or by over 0.27 percent of the true price increase.

**TABLE 22–8**   **Duration of a Four-Year Bond with an 8 Percent Coupon Paid Annually and a 10 Percent Yield**

| $t$ | $CF_t$ | $PV$ of $CF$ | $PV$ of $C \times t$ |
|---|---|---|---|
| 1 | 80 | 72.727 | 72.727 |
| 2 | 80 | 66.116 | 132.231 |
| 3 | 80 | 60.105 | 180.316 |
| 4 | 1,080 | 737.655 | 2,950.618 |
| | | $936.603 | $3,335.892 |

$$D = \frac{3,335.892}{936.603} = 3.562 \text{ years}$$

**Figure 22–3**   **The Price–Yield Curve for the Four-Year Bond**

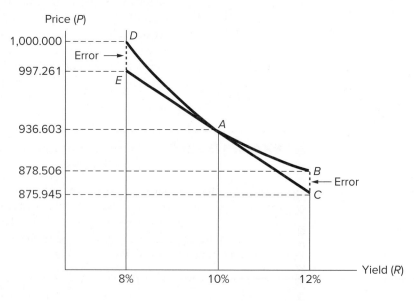

12. Even allowing for convexity, there still may be a very small difference between the true change in the value of a bond and the value change predicted by the duration model adjusted for convexity. This is because convexity itself varies as the level of interest rates changes. In practice, few investors or fund managers concern themselves with this issue.

In the previous example, an important question for the FI manager is whether a 0.27 percent error is big enough to be concerned about. This depends on the size of the interest rate change and the size of the portfolio under management. Clearly, 0.27 percent of a large number will still be a large number!

# INSOLVENCY RISK MANAGEMENT

In the previous two chapters and in this chapter, we have examined three major areas of risk exposure facing a modern FI manager. To ensure survival, an FI manager needs to protect the institution against the risk of insolvency—to shield it from those risks that are sufficiently large to cause the institution to fail. The primary means of protection against the risk of insolvency and failure is an FI's equity capital. However, capital also serves as a source of funds and as a necessary requirement for growth under the existing minimum capital-to-assets ratios set by regulators.

Indeed, part of the Troubled Asset Relief Program (TARP) of 2008–2009 was the Capital Purchase Program, which was designed to encourage U.S. financial institutions to build capital to increase the flow of financing to U.S. businesses and consumers and to support the U.S. economy. Under the program, the Treasury purchased over $205 billion in senior preferred stock issued by FIs. The senior preferred shares qualify as Tier I capital and rank senior to common stock. However, financial institutions had to meet certain standards. For example, they had to (1) ensure that incentive compensation for senior executives did not encourage unnecessary and excessive risks that threatened the value of the financial institution; (2) agree to pay back any bonus or incentive compensation paid to a senior executive based on statements of earnings, gains, or other criteria that were later proven to be materially inaccurate; (3) refrain from making any golden parachute payment to a senior executive based on the Internal Revenue Code provision; and (4) agree not to deduct for tax purposes executive compensation in excess of $500,000 for each senior executive. In addition to capital injections received as part of the Capital Purchase Program, TARP provided additional emergency funding to Citigroup ($25 billion) and Bank of America ($20 billion). Through December 2016, $245 billion of TARP capital injections had been allocated to DIs, of which $239.6 billion had been paid back, along with a return of $35.7 billion in dividends and assessments.

FI managers may often prefer low levels of capital because they allow the institution to generate a higher return on equity for the firm's stockholders. The moral hazard problem of deposit insurance (see Chapter 13) exacerbates this tendency. However, this strategy results in a greater chance of insolvency. Since regulators are more concerned with the safety of the financial system than stockholder returns, there is a need for minimum capital requirements (Chapter 13 discussed the regulatory requirements on an FI's capital). In the remainder of this chapter, we focus on how various risks affect the level of an FI's capital.

## Capital and Insolvency Risk

**net worth**

*A measure of an FI's capital that is equal to the difference between the market value of its assets and the market value of its liabilities.*

**book value**

*The value of assets and liabilities based on their historical costs.*

**Capital.**    To understand how an FI's equity capital protects against insolvency risk, we must define *capital* more precisely. The problem is that equity capital has many definitions: an economist's definition of capital may differ from an accountant's definition, which in turn may differ from a regulator's definition. Specifically, the economist's definition of an FI's capital, or owners' equity stake, is the difference between the market values of its assets and its liabilities. This is also called an FI's **net worth** (see Chapter 12). This is the *economic* meaning of capital. But regulators and accountants have found it necessary to adopt definitions that depart by a greater or lesser degree from economic net worth. The concept of an FI's economic net worth is really a *market value accounting* concept. With the exception of the investment banking industry, regulatory- and accounting-defined capital and required leverage ratios are based in whole or in part on historical or **book value** accounting concepts.

We begin by looking at the role of economic capital or net worth as a device to protect against two of the major types of risk described in the previous chapters and in this chapter:

**TABLE 22–9**   An FI's Market Value Balance Sheet *(in millions of dollars)*

| Assets | | Liabilities | |
|---|---|---|---|
| Long-term securities | $ 80 | Liabilities (short-term floating-rate deposits) | $ 90 |
| Long-term loans | 20 | Net worth | 10 |
| | $100 | | $100 |

credit risk and interest rate risk. We then compare this market value concept with the book value concept of capital. Because it can actually distort an FI's true solvency position, the book value of capital concept can be misleading to managers, owners, liability holders, and regulators alike. We also examine some possible reasons FI regulators continue to rely on book value concepts when such economic value transparency problems exist.

**The Market Value of Capital.**   To understand how economic net worth insulates an FI against the risk of insolvency, consider the following example. Table 22–9 presents a simple balance sheet, where an FI's assets and liabilities are valued in market value terms. On a **market value or mark-to-market value basis,** asset and liability values are adjusted each day to reflect current market conditions. Thus, the economic value of the FI's equity is $10 million, which is the difference between the market value of its assets and liabilities, and it is economically solvent. Let's consider the impact of two classic types of FI risk—credit and interest rate—on this FI's net worth.

*Market Value of Capital and Credit Risk.*   The balance sheet in Table 22–9 indicates that the FI has $20 million in long-term loans. Suppose that as the result of a recession, a number of its borrowers have cash flow problems and are unable to keep up their promised loan repayment schedules. A decline in the current and expected future cash flows on loans lowers the market value of the FI's loan portfolio below $20 million. Suppose that loans are really worth only $12 million (the price the FI would receive if it could sell these loans in a secondary market). This means the market value of the loan portfolio has fallen from $20 million to $12 million. The revised market value balance sheet is presented in Table 22–10.

The loss of $8 million in the market value of loans appears on the liability side of the balance sheet as a loss of $8 million of the FI's net worth—the loss of asset value is directly charged against the equity owners' capital or net worth. As you can see, the liability holders are fully protected because the total market value of their $90 million in liability claims is still $90 million. This is due to the fact that liability holders legally are senior claimants and equity holders are junior claimants to the FI's assets. Consequently, equity holders bear losses on the asset portfolio first. In fact, in this example, liability holders are hurt only when losses on the loan portfolio exceed $10 million (which was the FI's original net worth).

Let's consider a larger credit risk shock in which the market value of the loan portfolio plummets from $20 million to $8 million, a loss of $12 million (see Table 22–11). This larger loss renders the FI insolvent. The market value of its assets ($88 million) is now less than the value of its liabilities ($90 million). The owners' net worth stake has been completely wiped out—reduced from $10 million to $0 million, resulting in zero net

**market value or mark-to-market value basis**

*Balance sheet values that reflect current rather than historical prices.*

**TABLE 22–10**   An FI's Market Value Balance Sheet after a Decline in the Value of Loans *(in millions of dollars)*

| Assets | | Liabilities | |
|---|---|---|---|
| Long-term securities | $80 | Liabilities | $90 |
| Long-term loans | 12 | Net worth | 2 |
| | $92 | | $92 |

**TABLE 22–11**　An FI's Market Value Balance Sheet after a Major Decline in the Value of the Loan Portfolio *(in millions of dollars)*

| Assets | | Liabilities | |
|---|---|---|---|
| Long-term securities | $80 | Liabilities | $88 |
| Long-term loans | 8 | Net worth | 0 |
| | $88 | | $88 |

worth. Therefore, this hurts liability holders, but only a bit. Specifically, the equity holders bear the first $10 million of the $12 million loss in value of the loan portfolio. Only after the equity holders are completely wiped out do the liability holders begin to lose. In this example, the economic value of their claims on the FI has fallen from $90 million to $88 million, or a loss of $2 million (a percentage loss of 2.22 percent). After insolvency, the remaining $88 million in assets is liquidated and distributed to deposit holders. Note here that we are ignoring insurance guarantees afforded to some FI (e.g., bank) liability holders.[13]

This example clearly demonstrates the concept of net worth or capital as an "insurance" fund protecting liability holders against insolvency risk. The larger the FI's net worth relative to the size of its assets, the more insolvency protection its liability holders and, in some cases, liability guarantors such as the FDIC have. This is the reason that regulators focus on capital requirements such as the ratio of net worth to assets in assessing an FI's insolvency risk exposure and in setting deposit insurance premiums (see Chapter 13).

*Market Value of Capital and Interest Rate Risk.*　Consider the market value balance sheet in Table 22–9 before interest rates rise. As we discussed earlier in the chapter, rising interest rates reduce the market value of the FI's long-term securities and loans, while floating-rate instruments find their market values largely unaffected if interest rates on such securities are instantaneously reset. Suppose that a rise in interest rates reduces the market value of the FI's long-term securities to $75 million from $80 million and the market value of its long-term loans to $17 million from $20 million. Because all deposit liabilities are assumed to be short-term floating-rate deposits, their market values are unchanged at $90 million. After the shock to interest rates, the market value balance sheet is represented in Table 22–12. The loss of $8 million in the market value of the FI's assets is once again reflected on the liability side of the balance sheet by an $8 million decrease in net worth to $2 million. Thus, as with increased credit risk, the equity holders first bear losses in asset values due to adverse interest rate changes. Only if the fall in the market value of assets exceeds $10 million are the liability holders, as senior claimants to the FI's assets, adversely affected.

These examples show that market valuation of the balance sheet produces an economically accurate picture of net worth and, thus, an FI's solvency position. The equity holders directly bear the credit and interest rate risks that result in losses in the market value

**TABLE 22–12**　An FI's Market Value Balance Sheet after a Rise in Interest Rates *(in millions of dollars)*

| Assets | | Liabilities | |
|---|---|---|---|
| Long-term securities | $75 | Liabilities | $90 |
| Long-term loans | 17 | Net worth | 2 |
| | $92 | | $92 |

13. In the presence of deposit insurance, the insurer, such as the FDIC, bears some of the depositors' losses. For details, see Chapter 13.

**TABLE 22–13**  **An FI's Book Value Balance Sheet** *(in millions of dollars)*

| Assets | | Liabilities | |
|---|---|---|---|
| Long-term securities | $ 80 | Short-term liabilities | $ 90 |
| Long-term loans | 20 | Equity | 10 |
| | $100 | | $100 |

of assets and liabilities in the sense that such losses are charges against the value of their ownership claims in the FI. The market value of equity is more relevant than book value because, in the event of bankruptcy, the liquidation (market) value determines the FI's ability to pay various claimants. As long as the owners' capital or equity stake is adequate, or sufficiently large, liability holders (and implicitly regulators that back the claims of liability holders) are protected against insolvency risk. If regulators were to close an FI before its economic net worth became zero, neither liability holders, nor those regulators guaranteeing the claims of liability holders, would stand to lose. Thus, many academics and analysts advocate the use of market value accounting and market value of capital closure rules for all FIs, especially because the book value of capital rules are closely associated with the savings institutions disaster in the 1980s (discussed in Chapter 13).

To see why book value of capital rules may incorrectly measure insolvency risk, consider the same credit and interest rate risk scenarios discussed above, but this time in a world where book value accounting and capital regulations hold sway.

**The Book Value of Capital.**  Table 22–13 uses the same initial balance sheet as in Table 22–9, but assumes that assets and liabilities are now valued at their historical book values. In Table 22–13, the $80 million in long-term securities and $20 million in long-term loans reflect the historical or original book values of those assets—that is, they reflect the (historical) values at the time the loans were made and the securities were purchased, which may have been many years ago when the economy was in a different stage of the business cycle and interest rates were at different levels. Similarly, on the liability side, the $90 million in liabilities also reflects their historical cost, so that the equity of the FI is now the book value of the stockholders' claims rather than the market value of those claims. For example, the book value of capital—the difference between the book value of an FI's assets and the book value of its liabilities—usually comprises the following three components in banking:

1. **Par value of shares**—the face value of the common shares issued by the FI (the par value is usually $1 per share) times the number of shares outstanding.
2. **Surplus value of shares**—the difference between the price the public paid for common shares when originally offered (e.g., $5 per share) and their par values (e.g., $1), times the number of shares outstanding.
3. **Retained earnings**—the accumulated value of past profits not yet paid in dividends to shareholders. Since these earnings could be paid in dividends, they are part of the equity owners' stake in the FI. Consequently for an FI,

$$\text{Book value of capital} = \text{Par value} + \text{Surplus} + \text{Retained earnings}$$

As the balance sheet in Table 22–13 is constructed, the book value of capital equals $10 million. However, invariably, the book value of equity *does not equal* the market value of equity (the difference between the market value of assets and liabilities). This inequality between the book and market values of equity can be best understood by examining the effects of the same credit and interest rate shocks on the FI, but assuming book value rather than market value accounting methods.

*The Book Value of Capital and Credit Risk.*  Suppose that some of the $20 million in loans are in difficulty due to the inability of businesses to maintain their repayment schedules. We assumed in Table 22–10 that the revaluation of the promised cash flows of loans leads to an immediate downward adjustment of the loan portfolio's market value from $20 million to $12 million, and a market value loss of $8 million. By contrast, under historical book value accounting methods, such as generally accepted accounting principles (GAAP), FIs have more discretion in reflecting and timing the recognition of loan loss on their balance sheets, and thus more control over the impact of such losses on capital.

Indeed, managers of FIs may well resist writing down the values of bad assets as long as possible to try to present a more favorable picture to depositors, shareholders, and regulators. Such resistance might be expected if managers believe that the recognition of such losses could threaten their careers. Similarly, FI managers can selectively sell assets to inflate their reported capital. For example, managers can sell assets that have market values above their book values, resulting in an increase in the book value of capital. Only pressure from auditors and regulators such as bank, thrift, and insurance examiners may force loss recognition and write-downs of the values of problem assets. For example, the Wall Street Reform and Consumer Protection Act of 2010 includes a push for DIs to accrue more loan loss reserves during good times. Prior to the financial crisis, DIs had been restricted by accounting standards and the SEC from building capital for loan loss reserves that were likely to occur but difficult to predict. Therefore, banks felt pressured to keep reserves low. The restrictions worsened the effects of the financial crisis for DIs as the reserves they had set aside prior to the crisis did not cover their losses during the financial crisis and left them scrambling for capital.

*Book Value of Capital and Interest Rate Risk.* Although book value accounting systems recognize credit risk problems, albeit only partially and usually with a long and discretionary time lag, their failure to recognize the impact of interest rate risk is even more extreme. In the market value accounting example in Table 22–12, a rise in interest rates lowered the market values of long-term securities and loans by $8 million and led to a fall in the market value of net worth from $10 million to $2 million. In a book value accounting world, when all assets and liabilities reflect their original cost of purchase, the rise in interest rates has no effect on the value of assets, liabilities, or the book value of equity—the balance sheet remains unchanged. Table 22–13 reflects the position both before and after the interest rate rise. This was the case for those thrifts that continued to report long-term fixed-rate mortgages at historical book values even though interest rates rose dramatically in the early 1980s. As a result, these FIs continued to record a positive book value of capital position. On a market value net worth basis, however, their mortgages were worth far less than the book values shown on their balance sheets. Indeed, more than half of the firms in the industry were economically insolvent, many massively so.

**The Discrepancy between the Market and Book Values of Equity.** The degree to which the book value of an FI's capital deviates from its true economic market value depends on a number of factors, especially:

1. **Interest rate volatility**—the higher the interest rate volatility, the greater the discrepancy.
2. **Examination and enforcement**—the more frequent are on-site and off-site examinations and the stiffer the examiner/regulator standards regarding charging off problem loans, the smaller the discrepancy.
3. **Asset trading**—the more assets that are traded, the easier it is to assess the true market value of the asset portfolio.

In actual practice, we can get an idea of the discrepancy between book values (BV) and market values (MV) of equity for large publicly traded FIs even when the FI does not mark its balance sheet to market. Specifically, in an efficient capital market, the FI's stock price reflects the market value of the FI's outstanding equity shares. This valuation is based on the FI's current and expected future net earnings or dividend flows. The market value of equity per share (MV) is therefore:

$$MV = \frac{\text{Market value of equity ownership in shares outstanding}}{\text{Number of shares}}$$

**www.fasb.org**

**LG 22-5**

**TABLE 22–14**   Market-to-Book Value Ratios for U.S. Depository Institutions

| Bank Name | Market-to-Book Ratio |
| --- | --- |
| Bank of America | 0.955× |
| Bank of New York Mellon | 1.412 |
| BB&T | 1.544 |
| Citigroup | 0.826 |
| Comerica | 1.552 |
| Deutsche Bank | 0.341 |
| J.P. Morgan Chase | 1.394 |
| KeyCorp | 1.888 |
| Northern Trust | 2.424 |
| PNC Financial | 1.379 |
| Regions Financial | 1.103 |
| State Street Corp. | 1.629 |
| SunTrust Banks | 1.231 |
| U.S. Bancorp | 2.149 |
| Wells Fargo | 1.608 |

**Source:** Authors' research.

By contrast, the historical or book value of the FI's equity per share (BV) is equal to:

$$BV = \frac{\text{Par value of equity} + \text{Surplus value} + \text{Retained earnings}}{\text{Number of shares}}$$

**market-to-book ratio**

*A ratio that shows the discrepancy between the stock market value of an FI's equity and the book value of its equity.*

The ratio MV/BV is often called the **market-to-book ratio** and shows the degree of discrepancy between the market value of an FI's equity capital as perceived by investors in the stock market and the book value of capital on its balance sheet. The higher the market-to-book ratio, the more the book value of capital understates an FI's true equity or economic net worth position as perceived by investors in the capital market. If the market-to-book value is less than 1, the FI's equity is perceived by investors in the stock market to be worth less than the book value of its capital. Table 22–14 lists the market-to-book ratios for selected U.S. depository institutions. The values range from a low of 0.341 times for Deutsche Bank to 2.424 times for Northern Trust.

**Arguments against Market Value Accounting.**   The first argument against market value (MV) accounting it that it is difficult to implement. This may be especially true for small commercial banks and thrifts with large amounts of nontraded assets such as small loans in their balance sheets. When market prices or values for assets cannot be determined accurately, marking to market may be done only with error. A counterargument to this is that the error resulting from the use of market valuation of nontraded assets is still likely to be less than that resulting from the use of original book or historical valuation since the market value approach does not require all assets and liabilities to be traded. As long as current and expected cash flows on an asset or liability and an appropriate discount rate can be specified, approximate market values can always be imputed. Indeed, with the increase of loan sales and asset securitization (see Chapter 24), indicative market prices are available on an increasing variety of loans.

Further, during the financial crisis, the Financial Accounting Standards Board clarified its position on the application of market value accounting where there are limited or no observable inputs for marking certain assets to market, as was the case with many of the mortgage-backed securities at the center of the crisis. The guidance does not eliminate market value accounting, but it does provide management with much more discretion with respect to applying the convention when pricing illiquid assets. This discretion includes the ability to use internal assumptions with respect to future cash flows, which means employing generally more benign estimates than what the "market" is currently imposing. The guidance specifically allows management to use internal cash flow models and assumptions to estimate fair value when there are limited market data available.

A second argument against market value accounting is that it introduces an unnecessary degree of variability into an FI's earnings—and thus net worth—because paper capital gains and losses on assets are passed through the income statement. Critics argue that reporting unrealized capital gains and losses is distortionary if the FI actually plans to hold these assets to maturity. FI managers argue that in many cases, they do hold loans and other assets to maturity and, therefore, never actually realize capital gains or losses. Further, regulators have argued that they may be forced to close banks too early under the prompt corrective action requirements imposed by the FDIC Improvement Act (FDICIA) of 1991 (see Chapter 13), especially if an interest rate spike is only temporary (as much empirical evidence shows) and capital losses on securities can be quickly turned into capital gains as rates fall again. The counterargument is that FIs are increasingly trading, selling, and securitizing assets rather than holding them to maturity. Further, the failure to reflect capital gains and losses from interest rate changes means that the FI's equity position fails to reflect its true interest rate risk exposure.

In April 2009, the Financial Accounting Standards Board (which sets accounting rules for U.S. firms) eased its stance on marking-to-market such that DIs (as well as other firms) that meet certain conditions are no longer required to take earnings hits when asset markets are flawed. Specifically, the FASB ruling allows DIs to avoid market losses by stating that they intend to hold on to the asset and that it is more likely than not that they will. The rule says that once an asset is other than temporarily impaired, only losses related to the underlying creditworthiness shall affect earnings and regulatory capital. Losses attributed to market conditions are disclosed and accounted for elsewhere. The rule draws a distinction that is especially relevant to mortgage-backed securities, a market that had largely dried up during the financial crisis.

A third argument against market value accounting is that FIs are less willing to accept longer-term asset exposures, such as mortgage loans and C&I loans, if these assets must be continually marked to market to reflect changing credit quality and interest rates. For example, as discussed earlier in the chapter, long-term assets are more interest rate sensitive than are short-term assets. The concern is that market value accounting may interfere with FIs' special functions (see Chapter 1) as lenders and monitors and may even result in (or accentuate) a major credit crunch. Of the three arguments against market value accounting, this one is probably the most persuasive to regulators concerned about small business finance and economic growth.

---

**DO YOU UNDERSTAND:**

6. *Why an FI can be economically insolvent when its book value of net worth is positive?*

7. *What the major components of an FI's book value of equity are?*

8. *Whether book value accounting for loan losses is backward or forward looking?*

9. *What a market-to-book ratio that is less than 1 implies about an FI's performance?*

10. *What the arguments against the use of market value accounting are?*

---

## SUMMARY

This chapter provided a look at the measurement and on-balance-sheet management of interest rate and insolvency risks. The chapter first introduced two methods used to measure an FI's interest rate risk exposure: the repricing gap model and the duration gap model. The repricing gap model concentrates only on the net interest income effects of rate changes and ignores balance sheet or market value effects. As such it gives a partial, but potentially misleading, picture of an FI's interest rate risk exposure. The duration gap model is superior to the simple repricing gap model because it incorporates the effects of interest rate changes on the market values of assets and liabilities. The chapter concluded with an analysis of the role of an FI's capital in insulating it against credit, interest rate, and other risks. According to economic theory, shareholder equity capital or economic net worth should be measured on a market value basis as the difference between the market value of an FI's assets and liabilities. In actuality, regulators use a mixture of book value and market value accounting rules. For example, FIs are required to mark-to-market investment securities held as trading assets, while being able to carry most loans at their book values. This mix of book value and market value accounting for various assets and liabilities creates a potential distortion in the measured net worth of the FI.

## QUESTIONS

1. How do monetary policy actions by the Federal Reserve impact interest rates? (*LG 22-1*)

2. What is the repricing gap? In using this model to evaluate interest rate risk, what is meant by rate sensitivity? On what financial performance variable does the repricing gap model focus? Explain. (*LG 22-1*)

3. What is a maturity bucket in the repricing gap model? Why is the length of time selected for repricing assets and liabilities important when using the repricing gap model? (*LG 22-1*)

4. What is the CGAP effect? According to the CGAP effect, what is the relation between changes in interest rates and changes in net interest income when CGAP is positive? When CGAP is negative? (*LG 22-1*)

5. Which of the following is an appropriate change to make on a bank's balance sheet when GAP is negative, spread is expected to remain unchanged, and interest rates are expected to rise? (*LG 22-1*)
   a. Replace fixed-rate loans with rate-sensitive loans.
   b. Replace marketable securities with fixed-rate loans.
   c. Replace fixed-rate CDs with rate-sensitive CDs.
   d. Replace equity with demand deposits.
   e. Replace marketable securities with vault cash.

6. If a bank manager was quite certain that interest rates were going to rise within the next six months, how should the bank manager adjust the bank's repricing gap to take advantage of this anticipated rise? What if the manager believed rates would fall? (*LG 22-1*)

7. Which of the following assets or liabilities fit the one-year rate or repricing sensitivity test? (*LG 22-1*)
   a. 91-day U.S. Treasury bills.
   b. 1-year U.S. Treasury notes.
   c. 20-year U.S. Treasury bonds.
   d. 20-year floating-rate corporate bonds with annual repricing.
   e. 30-year floating-rate mortgages with repricing every two years.
   f. 30-year floating-rate mortgages with repricing every six months.
   g. Overnight fed funds.
   h. 9-month fixed-rate CDs.
   i. 1-year fixed-rate CDs.
   j. 5-year floating-rate CDs with annual repricing.
   k. Common stock.

8. What is the gap-to-total-assets ratio? What is the value of this ratio to interest rate risk managers and regulators? (*LG 22-1*)

9. What is the spread effect? (*LG 22-1*)

10. Consider the repricing gap model. (*LG 22-2*)
    a. What are some of its weaknesses?
    b. How have large banks solved the problem of choosing the optimal time period for repricing?

11. How is duration related to the interest elasticity of a fixed-income security? What is the relationship between duration and the price of the fixed-income security? (*LG 22-3*)

12. If you use duration only to immunize your portfolio, what three factors affect changes in an FI's net worth when interest rates change? (*LG 22-3*)

13. If interest rates rise and an investor holds a bond for a time longer than the duration, will the return earned exceed or fall short of the original required rate of return? (*LG 22-3*)

14. If a bank manager was quite certain that interest rates were going to rise within the next six months, how should the bank manager adjust the bank's duration gap to take advantage of this anticipated rise? What if the manager believed rates would fall? (*LG 22-3*)

15. What are the criticisms of using the duration model to immunize an FI's portfolio? (*LG 22-2*)

16. What is convexity? (*LG 22-3*)

17. What is the difference between book value accounting and market value accounting? How do interest rate changes affect the value of bank assets and liabilities under the two methods? (*LG 22-5*)

18. What are the differences between the economist's definition of capital and the accountant's definition of capital? (*LG 22-4*)
    a. How does economic value accounting recognize the adverse effects of credit risk?
    b. How does book value accounting recognize the adverse effects of credit risk?

19. What are some of the arguments for and against the use of market value versus book value of capital? (*LG 22-5*)

20. Why is the market value of equity a better measure of a bank's ability to absorb losses than book value of equity? (*LG 22-5*)

## PROBLEMS

1. Calculate the repricing gap and impact on net interest income of a 1 percent increase in interest rates for the following positions: (*LG 22-1*)
   a. Rate-sensitive assets = $100 million; Rate-sensitive liabilities = $50 million.
   b. Rate-sensitive assets = $50 million; Rate-sensitive liabilities = $150 million.
   c. Rate-sensitive assets = $75 million; Rate-sensitive liabilities = $70 million.
   d. What conclusions can you draw about the repricing gap model from the above results?

2. Consider the following balance sheet positions for a financial institution: (*LG 22-1*)
   - Rate-sensitive assets = $200 million; Rate-sensitive liabilities = $100 million.
   - Rate-sensitive assets = $100 million; Rate-sensitive liabilities = $150 million.
   - Rate-sensitive assets = $150 million; Rate-sensitive liabilities = $140 million.
   a. Calculate the repricing gap and the impact on net interest income of a 1 percent increase in interest rates for each position.

**b.** Calculate the impact on net interest income on each of the above situations assuming a 1 percent decrease in interest rates.

**c.** What conclusion can you draw about the repricing gap model from these results?

**3.** Consider the following balance sheet for Watchover Savings Inc. (in millions): (*LG 22-1*)

| Assets | | Liabilities and Equity | |
|---|---|---|---|
| Floating-rate mortgages | | NOW deposits (currently | |
| (currently 10% p.a.) | $ 60 | 6% p.a.) | $105 |
| 30-year fixed-rate loans | | 5-year time deposits | |
| (currently 7% p.a.) | 90 | (currently 6% p.a.) | 25 |
| | | Equity | 20 |
| Total | $150 | Total | $150 |

**a.** What is Watchover's expected net interest income at year-end?

**b.** What will be the net interest income at year-end if interest rates rise by 2 percent?

**c.** Using the one-year cumulative repricing gap model, what is the expected net interest income for a 2 percent increase in interest rates?

**4.** Consider the following balance sheet for Watchovia Bank (in millions): (*LG 22-1*)

| Assets | | Liabilities and Equity | |
|---|---|---|---|
| Floating-rate mortgages (currently | | 1-year time deposits (currently | |
| 10% annually) | $ 50 | 6% annually) | $ 70 |
| 30-year fixed-rate loans (currently | | 3-year time deposits (currently | |
| 7% annually) | 50 | 7% annually) | 20 |
| | | Equity | 10 |
| Total assets | $100 | Total liabilities and equity | $100 |

**a.** What is Watchovia's expected net interest income at year-end?

**b.** What will net interest income be at year-end if interest rates rise by 2 percent?

**c.** Using the one-year cumulative repricing gap model, what is the expected net interest income for a 2 percent increase in interest rates?

**d.** What will net interest income be at year-end if interest rates on RSAs increase by 2 percent but interest rates on RSLs increase by 1 percent? Is it reasonable for changes in interest rates on RSAs and RSLs to differ? Why?

**5.** A bank has the following balance sheet:

| | Assets | Average Rate | Liabilities and Equity | | Average Rate |
|---|---|---|---|---|---|
| Rate sensitive | $ 550,000 | 7.75% | Rate sensitive | $ 375,000 | 6.25% |
| Fixed rate | 755,000 | 8.75 | Fixed rate | 805,000 | 7.50 |
| Nonearning | 265,000 | | Nonpaying | 390,000 | |
| Total | $1,570,000 | | Total | $1,570,000 | |

Suppose interest rates rise such that the average yield on rate-sensitive assets increases by 45 basis points and

the average yield on rate-sensitive liabilities increases by 35 basis points. (*LG 22-1*)

**a.** Calculate the bank's repricing GAP and percentage gap.

**b.** Assuming the bank does not change the composition of its balance sheet, calculate the resulting change in the bank's interest income, interest expense, and net interest income.

**c.** Explain how the CGAP and spread effects influenced the change in net interest income.

**6.** Use the following information about a hypothetical government security dealer named J.P. Groman. (Market yields are in parentheses; amounts are in millions.) (*LG 22-1*)

| Assets | | Liabilities and Equity | |
|---|---|---|---|
| Cash | $ 10 | Overnight repos | $170 |
| 1-month T-bills (7.05%) | 75 | Subordinated debt | |
| 3-month T-bills (7.25%) | 75 | 7-year fixed (8.55%) | 150 |
| 2-year T-notes (7.50%) | 50 | | |
| 8-year T-notes (8.96%) | 100 | | |
| 5-year munis (floating rate) (8.20% reset every six months) | 25 | Equity | 15 |
| Total | $335 | Total | $335 |

**a.** What is the repricing or funding gap if the planning period is 30 days? 91 days? 2 years? (Recall that cash is a non-interest-earning asset.)

**b.** What is the impact over the next 30 days on net interest income if all interest rates rise by 50 basis points?

**c.** The following one-year runoffs are expected: $10 million for two-year T-notes, $20 million for the eight-year T-notes. What is the one-year repricing gap?

**d.** If runoffs are considered, what is the effect on net interest income at year-end if interest rates rise by 50 basis points?

**7.** Consider the following. (*LG 22-3*)

**a.** What is the duration of a two-year bond that pays an annual coupon of 10 percent and whose current yield to maturity is 14 percent? Use $1,000 as the face value.

**b.** What is the expected change in the price of the bond if interest rates are expected to decline by 0.5 percent?

**8.** Consider the following. (*LG 22-3*)

**a.** Calculate the leverage-adjusted duration gap of an FI that has assets of $1 million invested in 30-year, 10 percent semiannual coupon Treasury bonds selling at par and whose duration has been estimated at 9.94 years. It has liabilities of $900,000 financed through a two-year, 7.25 percent semiannual coupon note selling at par.

**b.** What is the impact on equity values if all interest rates fall 20 basis points—that is, $\Delta R/(1 + R/2) = -0.0020$?

**9.** Use the data provided for Gotbucks Bank Inc. to answer this question.

**Gotbucks Bank Inc.** *(dollars in millions)*

| Assets | | Liabilities and Equity | |
|---|---|---|---|
| Cash | $ 30 | Core deposits | $ 20 |
| Federal funds | 20 | Federal funds | 50 |
| Loans (floating) | 105 | Euro CDs | 130 |
| Loans (fixed) | 65 | Equity | 20 |
| Total assets | $220 | Total liabilities and equity | $220 |

Notes to the balance sheet: Currently, the fed funds rate is 8.5 percent. Variable-rate loans are priced at 4 percent over LIBOR (currently at 11 percent). Fixed-rate loans are selling at par and have five-year maturities with 12 percent interest paid annually. Core deposits are all fixed rate for two years at 8 percent paid annually. Euro CDs currently yield 9 percent. (*LG 22-3*)

  **a.** What is the duration of Gotbucks Bank's (GBI) fixed-rate loan portfolio if the loans are priced at par?

  **b.** If the average duration of GBI's floating-rate loans (including fed fund assets) is 0.36 year, what is the duration of the bank's assets? (Note that the duration of cash is zero.)

  **c.** What is the duration of GBI's core deposits if they are priced at par?

  **d.** If the duration of GBI's Euro CDs and fed fund liabilities is 0.401 year, what is the duration of the bank's liabilities?

  **e.** What is GBI's duration gap? What is its interest rate risk exposure? If *all* yields increase by 1 percent, what is the impact on the market value of GBI's equity? (That is, $\Delta R/(1 + R) = 0.01$ for all assets and liabilities.)

10. An insurance company issued a $90 million one-year, zero-coupon note at 8 percent add-on annual interest (paying one coupon at the end of the year) and used the proceeds plus $10 million in equity to fund a $100 million face value, two-year commercial loan at 10 percent annual interest. Immediately after these transactions were (simultaneously) undertaken, all interest rates went up 1.5 percent. (*LG 22-3*)

  **a.** What is the market value of the insurance company's loan investment after the changes in interest rates?

  **b.** What is the duration of the loan investment when it was first issued?

  **c.** Using duration, what is the expected change in the value of the loan if interest rates are predicted to increase to 11.5 percent from the initial 10 percent?

  **d.** What is the market value of the insurance company's $90 million liability when interest rates rise by 1.5 percent?

  **e.** What is the duration of the insurance company's liability when it is first issued?

11. Use the following balance sheet information to answer this question. (*LG 22-3*)

**Balance Sheet** (*dollars in thousands*)
**and Duration** (*in years*)

|  | Duration | Amount |
|---|---|---|
| T-bills | 0.5 | $   90 |
| T-notes | 0.9 | 55 |
| T-bonds | 4.393 | 176 |
| Loans | 7 | 2,724 |
| Deposits | 1 | 2,092 |
| Federal funds | 0.01 | 238 |
| Equity |  | 715 |

  **a.** What is the average duration of all the assets?

  **b.** What is the average duration of all the liabilities?

  **c.** What is the FI's leverage-adjusted duration gap? What is the FI's interest rate risk exposure?

  **d.** If the entire yield curve shifted upward 0.5 percent (i.e., $\Delta R/(1 + R) = 0.0050$), what is the impact on the FI's market value of equity?

  **e.** If the entire yield curve shifted downward 0.25 percent (i.e., $\Delta R/(1 + R) = -0.0025$), what is the impact on the FI's market value of equity?

12. Two banks are being examined by regulators to determine the interest rate sensitivity of their balance sheets. Bank A has assets composed solely of a 10-year $1 million loan with a coupon rate and yield of 12 percent. The loan is financed with a 10-year, $1 million CD with a coupon rate and yield of 10 percent. Bank B has assets composed solely of a 7-year, 12 percent zero-coupon bond with a current (market) value of $894,006.20 and a maturity (principal) value of $1,976,362.88. The bond is financed with a 10-year, 8.275 percent coupon $1,000,000 face value CD with a yield to maturity of 10 percent. The loan and the CDs pay interest annually, with principal due at maturity. (*LG 22-3*)

  **a.** If market interest rates increase 1 percent (100 basis points), how do the market values of the assets and liabilities of each bank change? That is, what will be the net effect on the market value of the equity for each bank?

  **b.** What accounts for the differences in the changes in the market value of equity between the two banks?

  **c.** Verify your results above by calculating the duration for the assets and liabilities of each bank, and estimate the changes in value for the expected change in interest rates. Summarize your results.

# Managing Risk off the Balance Sheet with Derivative Securities

## Learning Goals

**LG 23-1**  *Know how risk can be hedged with forward contracts.*

**LG 23-2**  *Know how risk can be hedged with futures contracts.*

**LG 23-3**  *Distinguish a microhedge from a macrohedge.*

**LG 23-4**  *Know how risk can be hedged with option contracts.*

**LG 23-5**  *Know how risk can be hedged with swap contracts.*

**LG 23-6**  *Understand how the different hedging methods compare.*

## DERIVATIVE SECURITIES USED TO MANAGE RISK: CHAPTER OVERVIEW

Chapters 20 through 22 described ways financial institutions (FIs) measure and manage various risks on the balance sheet. Rather than managing risk by making on-balance-sheet changes, FIs are increasingly turning to off-balance-sheet instruments such as forwards, futures, options, and swaps to hedge these risks. As the use of these derivatives has increased, so have the fees and revenues FIs have generated. For example, revenue from derivatives transactions at commercial banks totaled $12.7 billion in the first half of 2016. We discussed the basic characteristics of derivative securities and derivative securities markets in Chapter 10. In Chapter 10 we also noted that traders of derivatives can be either speculators or hedgers. Speculators in derivative contracts buy to profit from a price increase or sell to profit from a price decrease. Speculators buy derivative contracts with the hope of later being able to sell them at a higher price. Conversely, speculators sell derivative contracts with the hope of being able to buy back identical and offsetting derivative contracts at a lower price. Thus, speculators put their money at risk in the hope of profiting from an anticipated price change. This chapter considers the role that derivative securities contracts play in managing an FI's interest rate, foreign exchange, and credit risk exposures. Here we focus on derivative trading by hedgers who take a position in a derivative contract as protection against an increase or decrease in the price of a security such as a bond or stock in the future. Hedgers buy a derivative contract to lock in a price now to protect against future rising securities prices. Hedgers sell a derivative contract to lock in a price now to protect against future falls in securities prices. Although large banks and other FIs are responsible for a significant amount of derivatives trading activity, FIs of all sizes have used these instruments to hedge their asset–liability risk exposures.

The rapid growth of derivatives use by both FIs and nonfinancial firms has been controversial. In the 1990s and 2000s, critics charged that derivative contracts contain potential losses that can materialize to haunt their holders, particularly banks and insurance companies that deal heavily in these instruments. As will be discussed in this chapter, when employed appropriately, derivatives can be used to hedge (or reduce) an FI's risk. However, when misused, derivatives can increase the risk of an FI's insolvency. In the 1990s, a number of scandals involving FIs, firms, and municipalities (such as Bankers Trust and the Allied Irish Bank) led to a tightening of the accounting (reporting) requirements for derivative contracts. Then in the late 2000s, billions of dollars of losses on derivative securities and the near collapse of the world's financial markets led to a call for major regulations to be imposed on the trading of derivative securities. The regulations intended to bring many over-the-counter derivative contracts made between financial institutions under federal regulation and to empower securities and commodities regulators to police them.

## FORWARD AND FUTURES CONTRACTS

To present the essential nature and characteristics of forward and futures contracts, we first review the comparison of these derivative contracts with spot contracts (see also Chapter 10).

**spot contract**

*An agreement to transact involving the immediate exchange of assets and funds.*

**Spot Contract.**    A **spot contract** is an agreement between a buyer and a seller at time 0, when the seller of the asset agrees to deliver it immediately for cash and the buyer agrees to pay in cash for that asset. Thus, the unique feature of a spot contract is the immediate and simultaneous exchange of cash for securities, or what is often called *delivery versus payment.* A spot bond quote of $97 for a 20-year maturity bond means that the buyer must pay the seller $97 per $100 of face value for immediate delivery of the 20-year bond.[1]

**forward contract**

*An agreement to transact involving the future exchange of a set amount of assets at a set price.*

**Forward Contract.**    A **forward contract** is a contractual agreement between a buyer and a seller to exchange a prespecified asset for cash at some later date at a price set at time 0. Market participants take a position in forward contracts because the future (spot) price or interest rate on an asset is uncertain. Rather than risk that the future spot price will move against them—that the asset will become more expensive to buy in the future—forward traders pay a financial institution a fee to arrange a forward contract. Such a contract lets the market participant hedge the risk that future spot prices on an asset will move against him or her by guaranteeing a future price for the asset *today.* For example, in a three-month forward contract to deliver 20-year bonds, the buyer and seller agree on a price and amount today (time 0), but the delivery (or exchange) of the 20-year bond for cash does not occur until three months hence. If the forward price agreed to at time 0 was $97 per $100 of face value, in three months' time the seller delivers $100 of 20-year bonds and receives $97 from the buyer. This is the price the buyer must pay and the seller must accept no matter what happens to the spot price of 20-year bonds during the three months between the time the contract was entered into and the time the bonds are delivered for payment (i.e., whether the spot price falls to $96 or below or rises to $98 or above). As of 2016, commercial banks held over $32.1 trillion in forward contracts off their balance sheets.

Forward contracts often involve underlying assets that are nonstandardized (e.g., six-month pure discount bonds). As a result, the buyer and seller involved in a forward contract must locate and deal directly with each other to set the terms of the contract rather than transacting the sale in a centralized market. Accordingly, once a party has agreed to a

---

1. Throughout this chapter, as we refer to the prices of various securities, we do not include the transaction fees charged by brokers and dealers for conducting trades for investors and hedgers.

forward position, canceling the deal prior to expiration is generally difficult (although an offsetting forward contract can normally be arranged).

**futures contract**

*An agreement to transact involving the future exchange of a set amount of assets for a price that is settled daily.*

**marked to market**

*Describes the prices on outstanding futures contracts that are adjusted each day to reflect current futures market conditions.*

**Futures Contract.** A **futures contract** is usually arranged by an organized exchange. It is an agreement between a buyer and a seller at time 0 to exchange a standardized, pre-specified asset for cash at some later date. As such, a futures contract is very similar to a forward contract. The difference relates to the price. In a forward contract, the price is fixed over the life of the contract ($97 per $100 of face value with payment in three months), but in a futures contract, it is **marked to market** daily. This means that the contract's price and the future contract holder's account are adjusted each day as the futures price for the contract changes. Therefore, actual daily cash settlements occur between the buyer and seller in response to this marking-to-market process (i.e., gains and losses must be realized daily). This can be compared to a forward contract for which cash payment from buyer to seller occurs only at the end of the contract period.[2] In 2016, commercial banks held over $6.7 trillion in futures contracts off their balance sheets.

### Hedging with Forward Contracts

**naive hedge**

*A hedge of a cash asset on a direct dollar-for-dollar basis with a forward or futures contract.*

To understand the usefulness of forward contracts in hedging an FI's interest rate risk,[3] consider a simple example of a **naive hedge** (a hedge of a cash asset on a direct dollar-for-dollar basis with a forward or futures contract). Suppose that an FI portfolio manager holds a $1 million face value portfolio of 20-year government bonds on the balance sheet. At time 0, the market values these bonds at $97 per $100 of face value, or $970,000 in total. Assume that the manager receives a forecast that interest rates are expected to rise by 2 percent from their current level of 8 percent to 10 percent over the next three months. If the predicted change in interest rates is correct, rising interest rates mean that bond prices will fall and the manager stands to make a capital loss on the bond portfolio. Having read Chapters 3 and 22, the manager is an expert on duration and has calculated the 20-year maturity bond portfolio's duration to be exactly nine years. Thus, the manager can predict a capital loss, or change in bond portfolio values ($\Delta P$), from the duration equation of Chapter 3:[4]

$$\frac{\Delta P}{P} = -D \times \frac{\Delta R}{1 + R}$$

where

$\Delta P$ = Capital loss on portfolio = ?
$P$ = Initial value of portfolio = $970,000
$D$ = Duration of portfolio = 9 years
$\Delta R$ = Change in forecast yield = 0.02
$1 + R$ = 1 plus the current yield on 20-year bond portfolio = 1.08

$$\frac{\Delta P}{\$970,000} = -9 \times \left(\frac{0.02}{1.08}\right)$$

$$\Delta P = -9 \times \$970,000 \times \left(\frac{0.02}{1.08}\right) = -\$161,667$$

As a result, the FI portfolio manager expects to incur a capital loss on the bond portfolio of $161,667—as a percentage loss ($\Delta P/P$) = 16.67%—or a drop in price from $97 per $100 face value to $80.833 per $100 face value. To offset this loss—in fact, to reduce the risk of capital loss to zero—the manager may hedge this position by taking an

2. Another difference between forwards and futures is that forward contracts are bilateral contracts subject to counterparty default risk, but the default risk on futures is significantly reduced by the futures exchange guaranteeing to indemnify counterparties against credit or default risk.

3. Throughout the chapter we illustrate how derivative securities can be used to hedge interest rate risk. Derivatives are also used to hedge many other types of risks affecting FIs (e.g., foreign exchange risk, credit risk, and so on).

4. For simplicity, we ignore issues relating to convexity here (see Chapter 22).

off-balance-sheet hedge, such as selling $1 million face value of 20-year bonds for forward delivery in three months' time. Suppose that at time 0, the portfolio manager can find a buyer willing to pay $97 for every $100 of 20-year bonds delivered in three months' time.

Now consider what happens to the FI portfolio manager if the gloomy forecast of a 2 percent rise in interest rates is accurate. The portfolio manager's bond portfolio position has fallen in value by 16.67 percent, equal to a capital loss of $161,667. After the rise in interest rates, however, the manager can buy $1 million face value of 20-year bonds in the spot market at $80.833 per $100 of face value, or a total cost of $808,333, and deliver these bonds to the forward contract buyer. Remember that the forward contract buyer agreed to pay $97 per $100 of face value for the $1 million of face value bonds delivered, or $970,000. As a result, the portfolio manager makes a profit on the forward transaction of:

$$\begin{array}{ccc} \$970,000 & - & \$808,333 & = & \$161,667 \\ \text{(price paid by} & & \text{(cost of purchasing bonds} & & \\ \text{forward buyer to} & & \text{in the spot market at} & & \\ \text{forward seller} & & t = \text{month 3 for delivery} & & \\ & & \text{to the forward buyer)} & & \end{array}$$

As you can see, the on-balance-sheet loss of $161,667 is exactly offset by the off-balance-sheet gain of $161,667 from selling the forward contract. In fact, for any change in interest rates, a loss (gain) on the balance sheet is offset by a partial or complete gain (loss) on the forward contract. Indeed, the success of a hedge does not hinge on the manager's ability to accurately forecast interest rates. Rather, the reason for the hedge is the lack of ability to perfectly predict interest rate changes. The hedge allows the FI manager to protect against interest rate changes even if they are not perfectly predicted. Thus, the FI's net interest rate exposure is zero, or, in the parlance of finance, it has **immunized** its assets against interest rate risk.

**immunize**

*To fully hedge or protect an FI against adverse movements in interest rates (or asset prices).*

### Hedging with Futures Contracts

Even though some hedging of interest rate risk does take place using forward contracts—such as forward rate agreements commonly used by insurance companies and banks prior to mortgage loan originations—many FIs hedge interest rate risk either at the micro level (called *microhedging*) or at the macro level (called *macrohedging*) using futures contracts. Before looking at futures contracts, we explain the difference between microhedging and macrohedging.

**LG 23-3**

**microhedging**

*Using a derivative securities contract to hedge a specific asset or liability.*

**basis risk**

*A residual risk that occurs because the movement in a spot (cash) asset's price is not perfectly correlated with the movement in the price of the asset delivered under a futures or forward contract.*

**macrohedging**

*Hedging the entire duration gap of an FI.*

**Microhedging.**   An FI is **microhedging** when it employs a derivative securities contract to hedge a particular asset or liability risk. For example, we earlier considered a simple example of microhedging asset-side portfolio risk in which an FI manager wanted to insulate the value of the institution's bond portfolio fully against a rise in interest rates. An example of microhedging on the liability side of the balance sheet occurs when an FI, attempting to lock in a cost of funds to protect itself against a possible rise in short-term interest rates, takes a short (sell) position in futures contracts on CDs or T-bills. When microhedging, the FI manager often tries to pick a futures or forward contract whose underlying deliverable asset closely matches the asset (or liability) position being hedged. The earlier example of exactly matching the asset in the portfolio with the deliverable security underlying the forward contract (20-year bonds) was unrealistic. Because such exact matching often cannot be achieved, the usual situation produces a residual "unhedgeable" risk termed **basis risk.** This risk occurs mainly because the prices of the assets or liabilities that an FI wishes to hedge are imperfectly correlated over time with the prices of the futures or forward contracts used to hedge risk.

**Macrohedging.**   **Macrohedging** occurs when an FI manager wishes to use futures or other derivative securities to hedge the entire balance sheet duration gap. This contrasts with microhedging in which an FI manager identifies specific assets and liabilities and seeks individual futures and other derivative contracts to hedge those individual risks. Note that macrohedging and microhedging can lead to quite different hedging strategies and results. In particular, a macrohedge takes a whole portfolio view and allows for individual asset and liability interest sensitivities or durations to net out one another. FIs that attempt to manage their risk exposure by hedging each balance sheet position will find that hedging is excessively costly, because the use of a series of microhedges ignores the FI's internal hedges that are already on the balance sheet. That is, if a long-term fixed-rate asset position is exposed to interest rate increases, there may be a matching long-term fixed-rate liability position that also is exposed to interest rate decreases. Putting on two microhedges to reduce the risk exposures of each of these positions fails to recognize that the FI has already hedged much of its risk by taking matched balance sheet positions. The efficiency of the macrohedge is that it focuses only on those mismatched positions that are candidates for off-balance-sheet hedging activities. This can result in a very different aggregate futures position than when an FI manager disregards this netting or portfolio effect and hedges only individual asset and liability positions on a one-to-one basis.

**Microhedging with Futures.**   The number of futures contracts that an FI should buy or sell in a microhedge depends on the interest rate risk exposure created by a particular asset or liability on the balance sheet. The key is to take a position in the futures market to offset a loss on the balance sheet due to a move in interest rates with a gain in the futures market. Table 23–1 shows part of an interest rate futures quote from *The Wall Street Journal Online* for August 3, 2016 (see also Table 10–4). In this list, a June 2017 Eurodollar futures contract can be bought (long) or sold (short) on August 3, 2016, for 99.075 percent of the face value of the Eurodollar CD contract, or the yield on the Eurodollar CD contract deliverable in June 2017 will be 0.925 percent (100% − 99.075%). The minimum contract size on one of these futures is $1,000,000, so a position in one contract can be taken at a price of $990,750.

The subsequent profit or loss from a position in June 2017 Eurodollar futures taken on August 3, 2016, is graphically described in Figure 23–1. A short position in the futures will

**TABLE 23–1**   **Futures Contracts on Interest Rates, August 3, 2016**

Interest Rate Futures |

Wednesday, August 03, 2016

**Treasury Bonds (CBOT)-$100,000; pts 32nds of 100%**

| | Open | High | Low | Settle | Chg | LIFETIME High | LIFETIME Low | Open Int |
|---|---|---|---|---|---|---|---|---|
| Sep 16 | 171-310 | 172-210 | 171-140 | 172-050 | −6.0 | 177-110 | 158-200 | 562,270 |
| Dec 16 | 170-140 | 171-040 | 170-020 | 170-230 | −6.0 | 175-190 | 159-290 | 958 |

Est vol 395,934; vol 570,038; open int, 563,228

**Eurodollar (CME)-$1,000,000; pts of 100%**

| | Open | High | Low | Settle | Chg | LIFETIME High | LIFETIME Low | Open Int |
|---|---|---|---|---|---|---|---|---|
| Sep 16 | 99.1800 | 99.1850 | 99.1550 | 99.1650 | −.0150 | 99.4100 | 98.9200 | 1,174,950 |
| Dec 16 | 99.1350 | 99.1400 | 99.1050 | 99.1250 | −.0100 | 99.3800 | 98.7500 | 1,393,526 |
| Mar 17 | 99.1100 | 99.1100 | 99.0800 | 99.1000 | −.0100 | 99.3700 | 98.6000 | 1,016,815 |
| **Jun 17** | **99.0750** | **99.0850** | **99.0450** | **99.0750** | **−.0050** | **99.3500** | **98.4550** | **927,677** |
| Sep 17 | 99.0450 | 99.0550 | 99.0200 | 99.0500 | −.0050 | 99.3200 | 98.3250 | 816,393 |
| Dec 17 | 99.0050 | 99.0150 | 98.9750 | 99.0100 | −.0050 | 99.2700 | 98.2050 | 1,213,547 |
| Mar 18 | 98.9800 | 98.9950 | 98.9550 | 98.9900 | ... | 99.2400 | 98.1100 | 615,874 |
| Jun 18 | 98.9500 | 98.9600 | 98.9200 | 98.9550 | ... | 99.2000 | 98.0250 | 464,573 |
| Sep 18 | 98.9050 | 98.9250 | 98.8850 | 98.9200 | ... | 99.1550 | 97.9500 | 428,536 |
| Dec 18 | 98.8500 | 98.8800 | 98.8350 | 98.8750 | +.0050 | 99.1050 | 97.8700 | 534,731 |
| Mar 19 | 98.8150 | 98.8500 | 98.8050 | 98.8400 | +.0050 | 99.0650 | 97.8100 | 390,000 |
| Jun 19 | 98.7750 | 98.8100 | 98.7650 | 98.8000 | +.0050 | 99.0200 | 97.7450 | 287,696 |
| Sep 19 | 98.7300 | 98.7650 | 98.7250 | 98.7600 | +.0100 | 98.9750 | 97.6850 | 231,594 |
| Dec 19 | 98.6750 | 98.7150 | 98.6700 | 98.7100 | +.0100 | 98.9050 | 97.6250 | 224,505 |
| Mar 20 | 98.6350 | 98.6750 | 98.6300 | 98.6650 | +.0050 | 98.8600 | 97.5750 | 142,250 |
| Jun 20 | 98.5800 | 98.6250 | 98.5800 | 98.6150 | +.0050 | 98.8150 | 97.5250 | 92,368 |
| Sep 20 | 98.5300 | 98.5750 | 98.5300 | 98.5650 | +.0050 | 98.7700 | 97.4700 | 82,732 |
| Dec 20 | 98.4700 | 98.5200 | 98.4700 | 98.5100 | +.0050 | 98.7150 | 97.4200 | 90,244 |
| Mar 21 | 98.4250 | 98.4700 | 98.4250 | 98.4600 | ... | 98.6700 | 97.3750 | 53,826 |
| Jun 21 | 98.3850 | 98.4200 | 98.3700 | 98.4100 | ... | 98.6200 | 97.3300 | 47,830 |
| Sep 21 | 98.3300 | 98.3700 | 98.3200 | 98.3600 | ... | 98.5750 | 97.2900 | 21,024 |
| Dec 21 | 98.2750 | 98.3200 | 98.2650 | 98.3050 | −.0050 | 98.5200 | 97.2500 | 17,020 |
| Mar 22 | 98.2350 | 98.2750 | 98.2250 | 98.2650 | −.0050 | 98.4800 | 97.2200 | 10,521 |
| Jun 22 | 98.2000 | 98.2350 | 98.1850 | 98.2250 | −.0050 | 98.4350 | 97.1900 | 5,456 |
| Sep 22 | 98.1900 | 98.1950 | 98.1550 | 98.1850 | −.0050 | 98.3950 | 97.1600 | 5,294 |
| Dec 22 | 98.1150 | 98.1450 | 98.1100 | 98.1450 | −.0050 | 98.3500 | 97.1350 | 5,584 |
| Mar 23 | 98.1100 | 98.1150 | 98.0850 | 98.1200 | −.0050 | 98.3200 | 97.1200 | 4,537 |
| Jun 23 | 98.0800 | 98.0950 | 98.0500 | 98.0850 | −.0050 | 98.2850 | 97.1000 | 860 |
| Sep 23 | 98.0500 | 98.0500 | 98.0500 | 98.0600 | −.0050 | 98.2000 | 97.0800 | 1,253 |
| Dec 23 | 98.0150 | 98.0200 | 98.0000 | 98.0200 | −.0100 | 98.1200 | 97.1850 | 747 |

Est vol 1,343,406; vol 1,043,249; open int, 9,073,939, n.a..

**Source:** *The Wall Street Journal Online,* August 4, 2016. www.wsj.com

**Figure 23–1**    Profit or Loss on a Futures Position in Eurodollar Futures,
                   Taken on August 3, 2016

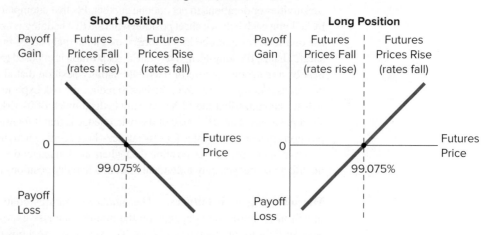

produce a profit (for the seller of the contract) when interest rates rise (meaning that the value of the underlying Eurodollar contract decreases). Therefore, a short position in the futures market is the appropriate hedge when the FI stands to lose on the balance sheet if interest rates are expected to rise (e.g., the FI holds Eurodollar CDs in its asset portfolio).[5] In fact, if the FI is perfectly hedged, any loss in value from a change in the price on an asset on the balance sheet over the period of the hedge (e.g., in Figure 23–2, a change from a beginning asset price of 99.075 percent at the beginning of the hedge) is exactly offset by a gain on the short position in the Eurodollar futures contract. A long position in the futures market produces a profit when interest rates fall (meaning that the value of the underlying Eurodollar CD contract increases).[6] Therefore, a long position is the appropriate hedge when the FI stands to lose on the balance sheet if interest rates are expected to fall.[7] Table 23–2 summarizes the long and short positions.

**Figure 23–2**    FI Value Change On and Off the Balance Sheet from a
                   Perfect Short Hedge

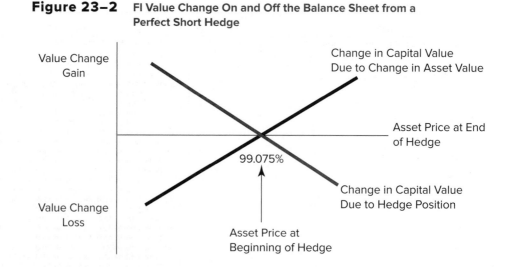

5. We assume that the balance sheet has no liability of equal size and maturity (or duration) as the CD. If the FI has such a liability, any loss in value from the CD could be offset with an equivalent decrease in value from the liability. In this case, there is no interest rate risk exposure and thus there is no need to hedge.

6. Notice that if rates move in an opposite direction from that expected, losses are incurred on the futures position—that is, if rates rise and futures prices drop, the long hedger loses. Similarly, if rates fall and futures prices rise, the short hedger loses.

7. This might be the case when the FI is financing itself with long-term, fixed-rate certificates of deposit.

**TABLE 23–2**   Summary of Gains and Losses on Microhedges Using Futures Contracts

| Type of Hedge | Change in Interest Rates | Cash Market | Futures Market |
|---|---|---|---|
| Long hedge (buy) | Decrease | Loss | Gain |
| Short hedge (sell) | Increase | Loss | Gain |

Appendix 23A to this chapter (available through Connect or your course instructor) presents mathematical details and numerical examples of hedging with futures contracts.

## OPTIONS

This section discusses the role of options in hedging interest rate risk. FIs have a wide variety of option products to use in hedging, including exchange-traded options, over-the-counter (OTC) options, options embedded in securities, and caps, collars, and floors. Not only have the types of option products increased in recent years, but the use of options has increased as well. In 2016, commercial banks held over $5.8 trillion in exchange-traded options and $26.4 trillion in OTC options as part of their off-balance-sheet exposures. We begin by reviewing the four basic option strategies: buying a call, writing (selling) a call, buying a put, and writing (selling) a put. We pay particular attention to how interest rates affect the value of the options.

### Basic Features of Options

In describing the features of the four basic option strategies that FIs might employ to hedge interest rate risk, we summarize their return payoffs in terms of interest rate movements (see Chapter 10 for the details). Specifically, we consider bond options in which the underlying assets are futures contracts on bonds. Thus, underlying the futures contracts are bonds whose payoff values are inversely linked to interest rate movements in a manner similar to bond prices and interest rates in general (see Chapter 3).

**Buying a Call Option on a Bond.**   The first strategy of buying (or taking a long position in) a call option on a bond is shown in Figure 23–3. Notice two important things about bond call options:

1.  As interest rates fall, bond prices rise, and the call option buyer has a large profit potential. The more rates fall (the higher bond prices rise), the larger the profit on the exercise of the option.

**Figure 23–3**   Payoff Function for the Buyer of a Call Option on a Bond

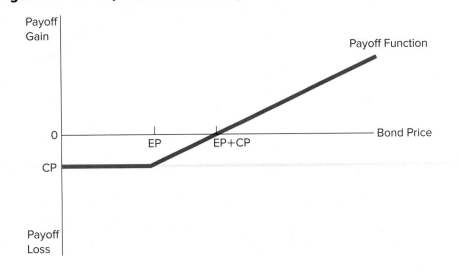

**2.** As interest rates rise, bond prices fall and the potential for a negative payoff (loss) for the buyer of the call option increases. If rates rise so that bond prices fall below the exercise price, EP, the call buyer is not obligated to exercise the option. Thus, the buyer's losses are truncated by the amount of the up-front premium payment (call premium, CP) made to purchase the call option.

Thus, buying a call option is a strategy to take when interest rates are expected to fall. Notice that unlike interest rate futures, whose prices and payoffs move symmetrically with changes in the level of interest rates, the payoffs on bond call options move asymmetrically with changes in interest rates.[8] As we discuss below, this often results in options being the preferred hedging instruments over futures contracts.

**Writing a Call Option on a Bond.**   The second strategy is writing (or taking a short position in) a call option on a bond, as shown in Figure 23–4. Notice two important things about this payoff function:

**1.** When interest rates rise and bond prices fall, the potential for the writer of the call to receive a positive payoff or profit increases. The call buyer is less likely to exercise the option, which would force the option writer to sell the underlying bond at the exercise price, EP. However, this profit has a maximum equal to the call premium (CP) charged up front to the buyer of the option.
**2.** When interest rates fall and bond prices rise, the probability that the writer will take a loss increases. The call buyer will exercise the option, forcing the option writer to sell the underlying bonds. Since bond prices are theoretically unbounded in the upward direction, although they must return to par at maturity, these losses could be very large.

Thus, writing a call option is a strategy to take when interest rates are expected to rise. Caution is warranted, however, because profits are limited but losses are unlimited. As discussed below, this makes writing a call option an unacceptable strategy to use when hedging interest rate risk.

**Figure 23–4**   **Payoff Function for the Writer of a Call Option on a Bond**

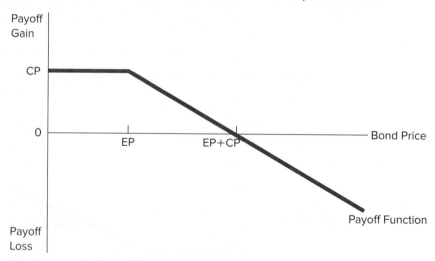

8. This does not necessarily mean that options are less risky than spot or futures positions. Options can, in fact, be riskier than other investments since they exist for only a limited period of time and are leveraged investments (i.e., their value is only a fraction of the underlying security). To compare an option position to a spot position one must consider an equal dollar investment in the two positions over a common period of time.

**Figure 23–5**  Payoff Function for the Buyer of a Put Option on a Bond

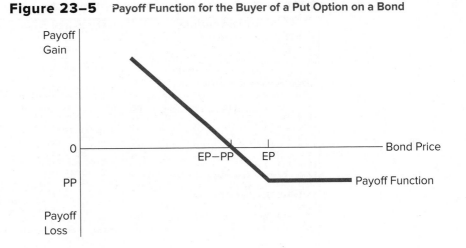

**Buying a Put Option on a Bond.**    The third strategy is buying (or taking a long position in) a put option on a bond, as shown in Figure 23–5. Note the following:

1. When interest rates rise and bond prices fall, the probability that the buyer of the put will make a profit from exercising the option increases. Thus, if bond prices fall, the buyer of the put option can purchase bonds in the bond market at that price and put them (sell them) back to the writer of the put at the higher exercise price. As a result, the put option buyer has unlimited profit potential. The higher the rates rise, the more the bond prices fall, and the larger the profit on the exercise of the option.
2. When interest rates fall and bond prices rise, the probability that the buyer of a put will lose increases. If rates fall so that bond prices rise above the exercise price, EP, the put buyer does not have to exercise the option. Thus, the maximum loss is limited to the size of the up-front put premium (PP).

Thus, buying a put option is a strategy to take when interest rates are expected to rise.

**Writing a Put Option on a Bond.**    The fourth strategy is writing (or taking a short position in) a put option on a bond, as shown in Figure 23–6. Note the following:

1. When interest rates fall and bond prices rise, the writer has an enhanced probability of making a profit. The put buyer is less likely to exercise the option, which would force the option writer to buy the underlying bond. However, the writer's maximum profit is constrained to equal the put premium (PP).

**Figure 23–6**  Payoff Function for the Writer of a Put Option on a Bond

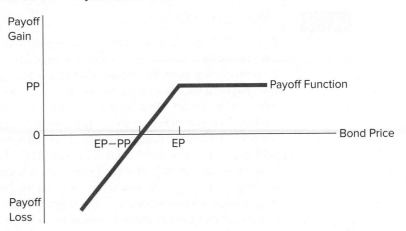

**TABLE 23–3**   Futures Options on Interest Rates, August 3, 2016  Futures Options

### FUTURES OPTIONS

INTEREST RATE Futures Options

For Wednesday, August 3, 2016

All prices are settlement prices. Open interest is from the previous trading day.

#### 30-YEAR US TREASURY BOND OPTIONS

| Strike | Call | | | Put | | |
|---|---|---|---|---|---|---|
| | SEP | OCT | DEC | SEP | OCT | DEC |
| 17000 | 3'06 | 3'04 | 4'28 | 0'60 | 2'22 | 3'46 |
| 17100 | 2'28 | 2'34 | 3'60 | 1'18 | 2'52 | 4'14 |
| 17200 | 1'56 | 2'04 | 3'30 | 1'46 | 3'22 | 4'48 |
| **17300** | **1'25** | **1'43** | **3'03** | **2'15** | **3'61** | **5'21** |
| 17400 | 1'00 | 1'22 | 2'43 | 2'54 | 4'40 | 5'61 |
| 17500 | 0'45 | 1'04 | 2'21 | 3'35 | 5'22 | 6'38 |
| Est.vol | Volume | Open Int | | Est.vol | Volume | Open Int |
| 37334 | 36470 | 228545 | | 30451 | 26297 | 220041 |

#### 10-YEAR US TREASURY NOTE

| Strike | Call | | | Put | | |
|---|---|---|---|---|---|---|
| | SEP | OCT | DEC | SEP | OCT | DEC |
| 13100 | 1'48 | 1'22 | 1'50 | 0'11 | 0'45 | 1'09 |
| 13150 | 1'22 | 1'03 | 1'33 | 0'17 | 0'58 | 1'24 |
| 13200 | 0'63 | 0'51 | 1'18 | 0'26 | 1'10 | 1'41 |
| 13250 | 0'44 | 0'38 | 1'04 | 0'39 | 1'29 | 1'59 |
| 13300 | 0'29 | 0'28 | 0'56 | 0'56 | 1'51 | 2'15 |
| 13350 | 0'18 | 0'20 | 0'46 | 1'13 | 2'11 | 2'37 |
| 13400 | 0'11 | 0'14 | 0'37 | 1'38 | 2'37 | 2'60 |
| 13450 | 0'07 | 0'10 | 0'30 | 2'02 | 3'01 | 3'21 |
| Est.vol | Volume | Open Int | | Est.vol | Volume | Open Int |
| 89481 | 106300 | 1063053 | | 50758 | 98329 | 936900 |

#### 5-YEAR US TREASURY NOTE

| Strike | Call | | | Put | | |
|---|---|---|---|---|---|---|
| | Sep | Oct | Dec | Sep | Oct | Dec |
| 12100 | 0'625 | 1'095 | 1'240 | 0'065 | 0'165 | 0'310 |
| 12125 | 0'495 | 0'615 | 1'130 | 0'095 | 0'205 | 0'360 |
| 12150 | 0'375 | 0'505 | 1'030 | 0'135 | 0'255 | 0'420 |
| 12175 | 0'270 | 0'410 | 0'580 | 0'190 | 0'320 | 0'490 |
| 12200 | 0'185 | 0'330 | 0'500 | 0'265 | 0'400 | 0'570 |
| Est.vol | Volume | Open Int | | Est.vol | Volume | Open Int |
| 5174 | 16839 | 191859 | | 22298 | 13207 | 668820 |

#### EURODOLLAR

| Strike | Call | | | Put | | |
|---|---|---|---|---|---|---|
| | Sep | Dec | Mar | Sep | Dec | Mar |
| 9850 | 0.6650 | 0.6275 | 0.6505 | 0.5875 | 0.5750 | 0.5900 |
| 9862 | 0.5400 | 0.5050 | 0.4850 | 0.4825 | 0.4800 | 0.4975 |
| 9875 | 0.4150 | 0.3825 | 0.3700 | 0.3875 | 0.3925 | 0.4150 |
| 9887 | 0.2925 | 0.2675 | 0.2675 | 0.3025 | 0.3150 | 0.3375 |
| 9900 | 0.1700 | 0.1620 | 0.1800 | 0.2275 | 0.2450 | 0.2700 |
| 9912 | 0.0675 | 0.0850 | 0.1100 | 0.1650 | 0.1850 | 0.2125 |
| 9925 | 0.0100 | 0.0325 | 0.0600 | 0.1150 | 0.1350 | 0.1625 |
| Est.vol | Volume | Open Int | | Est.vol | Volume | Open Int |
| 209732 | 147078 | 10016110 | | 313719 | 317189 | 11733652 |

**Source:** *The Wall Street Journal,* August 4, 2016. www.wsj.com

**2.** When interest rates rise and bond prices fall, the writer of the put is exposed to potentially large losses. The put buyer will exercise the option, forcing the option writer to buy the underlying bond at the exercise price, EP. Since bond prices are theoretically unbounded in the downward direction, these losses can be unlimited.

Thus, writing a put option is a strategy to take when interest rates are expected to fall. However, profits are limited and losses are potentially unlimited (i.e., the investor could potentially lose his or her entire investment in the option). As with the writing of a call option (discussed in more detail below), this makes writing a put option an unacceptable strategy to use when hedging interest rate risk.

### Actual Interest Rate Options

**www.cbot.com**

**www.cme.com**

FIs have a wide variety of OTC and exchange-traded options available. Table 23–3, from Table 10–6 and *The Wall Street Journal Online,* reports data on some of the exchange-traded interest rate futures options traded on the Chicago Board of Trade (CBOT) and the Chicago Mercantile Exchange (CME) on August 3, 2016. We discussed these contracts and the operations of the markets in detail in Chapter 10.

### Hedging with Options

Figures 23–7 and 23–8 describe graphically the way that buying a put option on a bond can potentially hedge the interest rate risk exposure of an FI that holds bonds as part of its asset investment portfolio. Figure 23–7 shows the gross payoff of a bond and the payoff from buying a put option on it. In this case, any losses on the bond (as rates rise and bond values decrease) are offset with profits from the put option that was bought (points to the left of point *X* in Figure 23–7). If rates fall, the bond value increases, yet the accompanying losses on the purchased put option positions are limited to the option premiums paid (points to the right of point *X*). Figure 23–8 shows the net overall payoff from the bond investment combined with the put option hedge. Note in Figure 23–8 that buying a put option truncates the downside losses on the bond following a rise in interest rates to some maximum amount and scales down the upside profits by the cost of bond price risk insurance—the put premium—leaving some positive upside profit potential. Notice too that the combination of being long in the bond and buying a put option on a bond

**Figure 23–7** Buying a Put Option to Hedge the Interest Rate Risk on a Bond

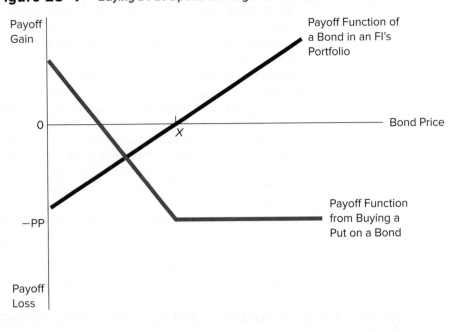

**Figure 23–8** Net Payoff of Buying a Bond Put and Investing in a Bond

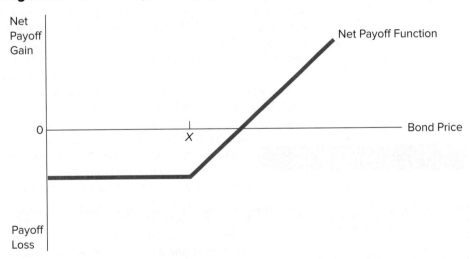

mimics the payoff function of buying a call option (compare Figures 23–3 and 23–8). Conversely, an FI can buy a call option on a bond to hedge interest rate risk exposure from a bond that is part of the FI's liability portfolio. Option contracts can also be used to hedge the aggregate duration gap exposure (macrohedge), foreign exchange risk, and credit risk of an FI as well. Appendix 23B to this chapter (available through Connect or your course instructor) presents mathematical details and numerical examples of hedging with options.

## Caps, Floors, and Collars

As discussed in Chapter 10, caps, floors, and collars are derivative securities that have many uses, especially in helping an FI hedge interest rate risk exposure as well as risks unique to its individual customers. Buying a cap means buying a call option or a succession of call options on interest rates. Specifically, if interest rates rise above the cap rate, the seller of the cap—usually a bank—compensates the buyer—for example, another FI—in return for an up-front premium. As a result, buying an interest rate cap is like buying insurance against an (excessive) increase in interest rates.

Buying a floor is similar to buying a put option on interest rates. If interest rates fall below the floor rate, the seller of the floor compensates the buyer in return for an up-front premium. As with caps, floor agreements can have one or many exercise dates.

A collar occurs when an FI takes a simultaneous position in a cap and a floor, such as buying a cap and selling a floor. The idea here is that the FI wants to hedge itself against rising rates, but wants to finance the cost of the cap. One way to do this is to sell a floor and use the premiums on the floor to pay the premium on the purchased cap. Thus, these three over-the-counter instruments are special cases of options. FI managers use them like options to hedge the interest rate risk of an FI's portfolio.

In general, FIs purchase interest rate caps if they are exposed to losses when interest rates rise. Usually, this happens if they are funding assets with floating-rate liabilities such as notes indexed to the LIBOR (or some other cost of funds) and they have fixed-rate assets or they are net long in bonds, or—in a macrohedging context—their duration gap is greater than zero, or $D_A - kD_L > 0$. By contrast, FIs purchase floors when they have fixed costs of debt and have variable rates (returns) on assets or they are net short in bonds, or $D_A - kD_L < 0$. Finally, FIs purchase collars when they are concerned about excessive volatility of interest rates or more commonly to finance cap or floor positions. Appendix 23C to this chapter (available through Connect or your course instructor) presents details and examples of hedging with caps, floors, and collars.

## RISKS ASSOCIATED WITH FUTURES, FORWARDS, AND OPTIONS

Financial institutions can be either users of derivative contracts for hedging and other purposes or dealers that act as counterparties in trades with customers for a fee. In 2016, approximately 1,442 banks were users of derivatives, with four big dealer banks (J.P. Morgan Chase, Citigroup, Goldman Sachs, and Bank of America) accounting for some 90.4 percent of the $189.8 trillion derivatives held by the user banks. However, these securities entail risk for the user banks. This section discusses the various types of risks involved with futures, forwards, and options trading.

Contingent credit risk is likely to be present when FIs expand their positions in forward, futures, and option contracts. This risk relates to the fact that the counterparty to one of these contracts may default on payment obligations, leaving the FI unhedged and having to replace the contract at today's interest rates, prices, or exchange rates. Further, such defaults are most likely to occur when the counterparty is losing heavily on the contract and the FI is in the money on the contract. This type of default risk is much more serious for forward contracts than for futures contracts. This is so because forward contracts are nonstandard contracts entered into bilaterally by negotiating parties such as two FIs and all cash flows are required to be paid at one time (on contract maturity). Thus, they are essentially over-the-counter arrangements with no external guarantees should one or the other party default on the contract. For example, the contract seller might default on a forward foreign exchange contract that promises to deliver £10 million in three months' time at the exchange rate $1.70 to £1 if the cost to purchase £1 for delivery is $1.90 when the forward contract matures. By contrast, futures contracts are standardized contracts guaranteed by organized exchanges such as the New York Futures Exchange (NYFE). Futures contracts, like forward contracts, make commitments to deliver foreign exchange (or some other asset) at some future date. If a counterparty defaults on a futures contract, however, the exchange assumes the defaulting party's position and payment obligations. Thus, unless a systemic financial market collapse threatens the exchange itself, futures are essentially default risk free. In addition, default risk is reduced by the daily marking to market of futures contracts. This prevents the accumulation of losses and gains that occur with forward contracts.[9]

### DO YOU UNDERSTAND:

5. How interest rate increases affect the payoff from buying a call option on a bond? How they affect the payoff from writing a call option on a bond?

6. How interest rate increases affect the payoff from buying a put option on a bond? How they affect the payoff from writing a put option on a bond?

7. What the outcome is if an FI hedges by buying put options on futures and interest rates rise (i.e., bond prices fall)?

8. The difference among a cap, a floor, and a collar used to hedge interest rate risk?

9. The risks involved with hedging with forwards, futures, and options?

---

9. More specifically, the default risk of a futures contract is less than that of a forward contract for at least four reasons: (1) daily marking to market of futures, (2) margin requirements on futures that act as a security bond, (3) price limits that spread extreme price fluctuations over time, and (4) default guarantees by the futures exchange itself.

Option contracts can also be traded by an FI over the counter (OTC) or bought/sold on organized exchanges. If the options are standardized options traded on exchanges, such as bond options, they are virtually default risk free. If they are specialized options purchased OTC such as interest rate caps, some element of default risk exists.

# SWAPS

The market for swaps has grown enormously in recent years—the value of swap contracts outstanding by U.S. commercial banks was more than $111.9 trillion in 2016. The five generic types of swaps, in order of their notional principal outstanding, are *interest rate swaps, currency swaps, credit risk swaps, commodity swaps,* and *equity swaps* (see Chapter 10). In this section, we consider the role of the two major generic types of swaps—interest rate and currency—in hedging FI risk. We then examine the credit risk characteristics of these instruments.

**LG 23-5**

## Hedging with Interest Rate Swaps

To explain the role of a swap transaction in hedging FI interest rate risk, we use a simple example. Consider two FIs: the first is a money center bank that has raised $100 million of its funds by issuing four-year, medium-term notes with 10 percent annual fixed coupons rather than relying on short-term deposits to raise funds (see Table 23–4). On the asset side of its portfolio, the bank makes commercial and industrial (C&I) loans whose rates are indexed to annual changes in the London Interbank Offered Rate (LIBOR). FIs often index most large commercial and industrial loans to either LIBOR or the federal funds rate in the money market.

As a result of having floating-rate loans and fixed-rate liabilities in its asset–liability structure, the money center bank has a negative duration gap; the duration of its assets is shorter than that of its liabilities. That is (using the equation in Chapter 22),

$$D_A - kD_L < 0$$

The bank could make changes either on or off the balance sheet. On the balance sheet, one way for the bank to hedge this exposure would be to shorten the duration or interest rate sensitivity of its liabilities by transforming them into short-term floating-rate liabilities that better match the rate sensitivity of its asset portfolio. For example, the bank could attract an additional $100 million in short-term deposits that are indexed to the LIBOR rate (at, say, LIBOR plus 2.5 percent) in a manner similar to its loans. The proceeds of these deposits could then be used to pay off the medium-term notes. This would reduce the duration gap between the bank's assets and liabilities. Alternatively, the bank could go off the balance sheet and sell an interest rate swap—that is, enter into a swap agreement to make the floating-rate payment side of a swap agreement.

The second party of the swap is a savings bank that has invested $100 million in fixed-rate residential mortgages of long duration. To finance this residential mortgage portfolio, the savings bank relies on short-term certificates of deposit with an average duration of one year (see Table 23–5). On maturity, these CDs must be rolled over at the current market rate. Consequently, the savings bank's asset–liability balance sheet structure is the reverse of the money center bank's:

$$D_A - kD_L > 0$$

**TABLE 23–4**  **Money Center Bank Balance Sheet**

| Assets | | Liabilities | |
|---|---|---|---|
| C&I loans (rate indexed to LIBOR) | $100 million | Medium-term notes (coupons fixed at 10% annually) | $100 million |

**TABLE 23–5**  Savings Bank Balance Sheet

| Assets | | Liabilities | |
|---|---|---|---|
| Fixed-rate mortgages | $100 million | Short-term CDs (one year) | $100 million |

On the balance sheet, the savings bank could hedge its interest rate risk exposure by transforming the short-term floating-rate nature of its liabilities into fixed-rate liabilities that better match the long-term maturity (duration) structure of its assets. For example, the savings bank could issue long-term notes with a maturity equal or close to that on the mortgages (at, say, 9 percent). The proceeds of the sale of the notes could then be used to pay off the CDs and reduce the repricing gap. Alternatively, the savings bank could go off the balance sheet and buy a swap—that is, take the fixed-payment side of a swap agreement.

The opposing balance sheet and interest rate risk exposures of the money center bank and the savings bank provide the necessary conditions for an interest rate swap agreement between the two parties. This swap agreement can be arranged directly between the parties. However, it is likely that an FI—another bank or an investment bank—would act as either a broker or an agent, receiving a fee for bringing the two parties together or intermediating fully by accepting the credit risk exposure and guaranteeing the cash flows underlying the swap contract. By acting as a principal as well as an agent, the FI can add a credit risk premium to the fee. However, the credit risk exposure of a swap to an FI is somewhat less than that on a loan (this is discussed later in this chapter). Conceptually, when a third-party FI fully intermediates the swap, that FI is really entering into two separate swap agreements, in this case, one with the money center bank and one with the savings bank.

**plain vanilla**

*A standard agreement without any special features.*

For simplicity, we consider an example below of a **plain vanilla** fixed–floating rate swap (a standard swap agreement without any special features) in which a third-party intermediary acts as a simple broker or agent by bringing together two DIs with opposing interest rate risk exposures to enter into a swap agreement or contract. We depict a possible fixed–floating rate swap transaction in Figure 23–9. The expected net financing costs for the DIs are listed in Table 23–6.

**Figure 23–9**  Fixed–Floating Rate Swap

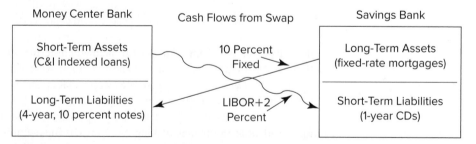

**TABLE 23–6**  Financing Cost Resulting from Interest Rate Swap *(in millions of dollars)*

| | Money Center Bank | | Savings Bank | |
|---|---|---|---|---|
| Cash outflows from balance sheet financing | 1. | $-10\% \times \$100$ | 5. | $-(\text{CD rate}) \times \$100$ |
| Cash inflows from swap | 2. | $10\% \times \$100$ | 6. | $(\text{LIBOR} + 2\%) \times \$100$ |
| Cash outflows from swap | 3. | $-(\text{LIBOR} + 2\%) \times \$100$ | 7. | $-10\% \times \$100$ |
| Net cash flows | 4. | $-(\text{LIBOR} + 2\%) \times \$100$ | 8. | $-(8\% + \text{CD rate} - \text{LIBOR}) \times \$100$ |
| Rate available on | | | | |
| Variable-rate debt | | LIBOR + 2½% | | |
| Fixed-rate debt | | | | 9% |

---

## EXAMPLE 23–1    Expected Cash Flows on an Interest Rate Swap

In this example, the notional (or face) value of the swap is $100 million—equal to the assumed size of the money center bank's medium-term note issue—and the four-year maturity is equal to the maturity of its note liabilities. The annual coupon cost of these note liabilities is 10 percent (item 1 in Table 23–6). The money center bank's problem is that the variable return on its assets may be insufficient to cover the cost of meeting these fixed coupon payments if market interest rates *fall.* By comparison, the fixed returns on the savings bank's mortgage asset portfolio may be insufficient to cover the interest cost of its CDs should market rates *rise* (item 5 in Table 23–6). The swap agreement might dictate that the savings bank send (item 7 in Table 23–6) fixed payments of 10 percent per year of the notional $100 million value of the swap to the money center bank (item 2 in Table 23–6) to allow the money center bank to cover fully the coupon interest payments on its note issue. In return, the money center bank sends annual payments indexed to the one-year LIBOR to help the savings bank cover the cost of refinancing its one-year renewable CDs. Suppose that the money center bank agrees to send (item 3 in Table 23–6) the savings bank annual payments at the end of each year equal to one-year LIBOR plus 2 percent (item 6 in Table 23–6).[10]

As a result of the swap, the money center bank has transformed its four-year, fixed-rate liability notes into a variable-rate liability matching the variability of returns on its C&I loans (item 4 in Table 23–6). Further, through the interest rate swap, the money center bank effectively pays LIBOR plus 2 percent for its financing. Had it gone to the debt market, the money center bank would pay LIBOR plus 2.5 percent (a savings of 0.5 percent with the swap). The savings bank also has transformed its variable-rate CDs into fixed-rate payments similar to those received on its fixed-rate mortgages (item 8 in Table 23–6). As a result, it has successfully microhedged.

---

Note in Example 23–1 that in the absence of default/credit risk, only the money center bank is really fully hedged. This happens because the annual 10 percent payments it receives from the savings bank at the end of each year allow it to meet the promised 10 percent coupon rate payments to its note holders regardless of the return it receives on its variable-rate assets. By contrast, the savings bank receives variable-rate payments based on LIBOR plus 2 percent. It is quite possible that the CD rate that the savings bank must pay on its deposit liabilities does not exactly track the LIBOR-indexed payments sent by the money center bank—that is, the savings bank is subject to basis risk exposure on the swap contract. This basis risk can come from two sources. First, CD rates do not exactly match the movements of LIBOR rates over time since the former are determined in the domestic money market and the latter in the Eurodollar market. Second, the credit/default risk premium on the savings bank's CDs may increase over time. Thus, the plus 2 percent add-on to LIBOR may be insufficient to hedge the savings bank's cost of funds. The savings bank might be better hedged by requiring the money center bank to send it floating payments based on U.S. domestic CD rates rather than LIBOR. To do this, the money center bank would probably require additional compensation since it would then bear basis risk. Its asset returns would be sensitive to LIBOR movements while its swap payments were indexed to U.S. CD rates.

Further, in order for the swap to be the most efficient choice for the FIs, there must be some barrier that prevents the two firms from directly transacting in the other's cash market (which equivalently raises the costs of these cross-market transactions). This barrier may consist of regulatory restrictions or tax considerations. If, however, the barrier results

---

10. These rates implicitly assume that this is the cheapest way each party can hedge its interest rate exposure. For example, LIBOR plus 2 percent is the lowest-cost way that the money center bank can transform its fixed-rate liabilities into floating-rate liabilities.

from information asymmetries, these potential gains to trade can be expected to disappear as the swap market develops.

### Hedging with Currency Swaps

Swaps are long-term contracts that can also be used to hedge an FI's exposure to currency risk. The following section considers a plain vanilla example of how **currency swaps** can immunize FIs against foreign exchange rate risk when they mismatch the currencies of their assets and liabilities.

**Fixed–Fixed Currency Swaps.** Consider a U.S. FI with all of its $80 million fixed-rate assets denominated in dollars. It is financing part of its asset portfolio with a £50 million issue of four-year, medium-term British pound notes that have a fixed annual coupon of 10 percent. By comparison, an FI in the United Kingdom has all its £50 million assets denominated in pounds. It is funding those assets with a $80 million issue of four-year, medium-term dollar notes with a fixed annual coupon of 10 percent.

These two FIs are exposed to opposing currency risks. The U.S. FI is exposed to the risk that the dollar will depreciate against the pound over the next four years, which would make it more costly to cover the annual coupon interest payments and the principal repayment on its pound-denominated notes. On the other hand, the UK FI is exposed to the risk that the dollar will appreciate against the pound, making it more difficult to cover the dollar coupon and principal payments on its four-year, $80 million note issue from the pound cash flows on its assets.

The FIs can hedge the exposures either on or off the balance sheet. Assume that the dollar/pound exchange rate is fixed at $1.6/£1. On the balance sheet, the U.S. FI can issue $80 million in four-year, medium-term dollar notes (at, say, 10.5 percent). The proceeds of the sale can be used to pay off the £50 million of four-year, medium-term pound notes. Similarly, the UK FI can issue £50 million in four-year, medium-term pound notes (at, say, 10.5 percent), using the proceeds to pay off the $80 million of four-year, medium-term dollar notes. Both FIs have taken actions on the balance sheet so that they are no longer exposed to movements in the exchange rate between the two currencies.

---

**EXAMPLE 23–2** Expected Cash Flows on a Fixed–Fixed Currency Swap

Off the balance sheet, the UK and U.S. FIs can enter into a currency swap by which the UK FI sends annual payments in pounds to cover the coupon and principal repayments of the U.S. FI's pound note issue, and the U.S. FI sends annual dollar payments to the UK FI to cover the interest and principal payments on its dollar note issue. We summarize this currency swap in Figure 23–10 and Table 23–7. As a result of the swap, the UK FI transforms fixed-rate dollar liabilities into fixed-rate pound liabilities that better match the pound

**Figure 23–10** Fixed–Fixed Pound/Dollar Currency Swap

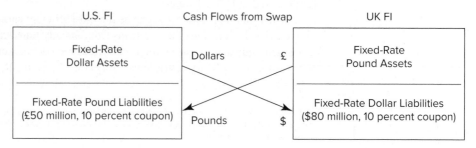

fixed-rate cash flows from its asset portfolio. Similarly, the U.S. FI transforms fixed-rate pound liabilities into fixed-rate dollar liabilities that better match the fixed-rate dollar cash flows from its asset portfolio. Further, both FIs transform the pattern of their payments at a lower rate than had they made changes on the balance sheet. Both FIs effectively obtain financing at 10 percent while hedging against exchange rate risk. Had they gone to the market, they would have paid 10.5 percent to do this. In undertaking this exchange of cash flows, the two parties normally agree on a fixed exchange rate for the cash flows at the beginning of the period.[11] In this example, the fixed exchange rate is $1.6/£1.

By combining an interest rate swap of the fixed-floating type described earlier with a currency swap, we can also produce a fixed–floating currency swap that is a hybrid of the two plain vanilla swaps we have considered so far.

### Credit Swaps

In recent years the fastest-growing types of swaps have been those developed to better allow FIs to hedge their credit risk, so-called credit swaps or credit default swaps (CDSs). In 2000, commercial banks' total notional principal for outstanding credit derivative contracts was $426 billion. By March 2008, this amount had risen to $16.44 trillion before falling to $13.44 trillion in 2009 during the financial crisis. By September 2011, the notional principal of credit derivative contracts increased only slightly, to $15.66 trillion. Of this amount, $15.31 trillion was CDSs. Due to post–financial crisis regulations imposed on commercial banks involving the trading of swaps, the notional value of credit derivatives held by banks dropped to $6.85 trillion in June 2016, with $6.41 of this amount being CDS contracts.

Credit swaps are important for two reasons. First, credit risk is still more likely to cause an FI to fail than either interest rate risk or FX risk. Second, CDSs allow FIs to maintain long-term customer lending relationships without bearing the full credit risk exposure from those relationships. Indeed, then Federal Reserve Board chair Alan Greenspan credited this market with helping the banking system maintain its strength through an economic recession in the early 2000s. He argued that credit swaps were effectively used to shift a significant part of banks' risk from their corporate loan portfolios. However, the Fed chair also commented that these derivative securities are prone to induce speculative excesses that need to be contained through regulation, supervision, and private-sector action. While commercial banks have been the main buyers of credit risk protection through credit swaps, insurance companies (such as AIG) have been the net sellers of credit risk protection. Thus, they have been more willing than banks to bear credit risk. The result is that the FI bearing the credit risk of a loan is often different from the FI that issued the loan. Indeed, in some recessionary periods, insurance companies have suffered large losses as buyers

**TABLE 23–7** Financing Costs Resulting from the Fixed–Fixed Currency Swap Agreement *(in millions of dollars)*

|  | U.S. FI | UK FI |
|---|---|---|
| Cash outflows from balance sheet financing | $-10\% \times £50$ | $-10\% \times \$80$ |
| Cash inflows from swap | $10\% \times £50$ | $10\% \times \$80$ |
| Cash outflows from swap | $-10\% \times \$80$ | $-10\% \times £50$ |
| Net cash flows | $-10\% \times \$80$ | $-10\% \times £50$ |
| Rate available on |  |  |
|    Dollar-denominated notes | 10.5% |  |
|    Pound-denominated notes |  | 10.5% |

11. As with interest rate swaps, this exchange rate reflects the contracting parties' expectations as to future exchange rate movements.

of credit risk, while banks have been well protected. And as discussed in Chapter 10 and below, during the financial crisis of 2008–2009, insurance or re-insurance company losses from CDSs were so large that some could not pay the promised obligations and, as a result, banks (and other buyers of credit swaps) were exposed to significantly higher credit risk.

The buyer of a CDS makes periodic payments to the seller until the end of the life of the swap or until the credit event specified in the contract occurs. These payments are typically made every quarter, six months, or year. The settlement of the swap in the event of a default involves either physical delivery of the bonds (or loans) or a cash payment. Generally, a CDS specifies that a number of different bonds (loans) can be delivered in the event of a default. The bonds (loans) typically have the same seniority, but they may not sell for the same percentage of face value immediately after a default. This gives the holder of a CDS a cheapest-to-deliver option. When a default happens, the buyer of protection will review alternative deliverable bonds (or loans) and choose the one that can be purchased most cheaply for delivery.

Below we look at two types of CDSs: (1) the total return swap and (2) the pure credit swap. We then look at credit risk concerns with the swaps themselves.

**Total Return Swaps.**   Although FIs spend significant resources attempting to evaluate and price expected changes in a borrower's credit risk over the life of a loan, a borrower's credit situation (credit quality) sometimes deteriorates unexpectedly after the loan terms are determined and the loan is issued. A lender can use a total return swap to hedge this possible change in credit risk exposure. **A total return swap** involves swapping an obligation to pay interest at a specified fixed or floating rate for payments representing the total return on a loan or a bond (interest and principal value changes) of a specified amount. The swap can be designed to cover any change in value of the principal as well as just the interest. This type of swap often is used when there is exposure to a change in the credit risk of the counterparty.

**total return swap**

*A swap involving an obligation to pay interest at a specified fixed or floating rate for payments representing the total return on a specified amount.*

---

**EXAMPLE 23–3**   Calculation of Cash Flows on a Total Return Swap

Suppose that an FI lends $100 million to a Brazilian manufacturing firm at a fixed rate of 10 percent. If the firm's credit risk increases unexpectedly over the life of the loan, the market value of the loan and, consequently, the FI's net worth will fall. The FI can hedge an unexpected increase in the borrower's credit risk by entering into a total return swap in which it agrees to pay a total return based on an annual fixed rate ($f$) plus changes in the market value of Brazilian (U.S. dollar–denominated) government debt (changes in the value of these bonds reflect the political and economic events in the firm's home country and thus will be correlated with the credit risk of the Brazilian borrowing firm). Also, the bonds are in the same currency (U.S. dollars) as the loans. In return, the FI receives a variable market rate payment of interest annually (e.g., one-year LIBOR rate). Figure 23–11 and Table 23–8 illustrate the cash flows associated with the typical total return swap for the FI.

Using the total return swap, the FI agrees to pay a fixed rate of interest annually and the capital gain or loss on the market value of the Brazilian (U.S. dollar) bond over the

**Figure 23–11**   Cash Flows on a Total Return Swap

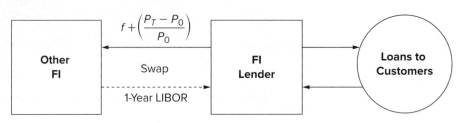

1-Year LIBOR

period of the hedge. In Figure 23–11, $P_0$ denotes the market value of the bond at the beginning of the swap period and $P_T$ represents the market value of the bond at the end of the swap period. If the Brazilian bond decreases in value over the period of the hedge ($P_0 > P_T$), the FI pays a relatively small (possibly negative) amount to the counterparty equal to the fixed payment on the swap minus the capital loss on the bond.[12] For example, suppose the Brazilian (U.S. dollar) bond is priced at par ($P_0 = 100$) at the beginning of the swap period. At the end of the swap period or the payment date, the Brazilian bond has a secondary market value of 90 ($P_T = 90$) due to an increase in Brazilian country risk. Suppose that the fixed-rate payment ($f$) as part of the total return swap is 12 percent. Then the FI would send to the swap counterparty the fixed rate of 12 percent minus 10 percent (the capital loss on the Brazilian bond), or a total of 2 percent, and would receive in return a floating payment (e.g., LIBOR = 11 percent) from the counterparty to the swap. Thus, the net profit on the swap to the FI lender is 9 percent (11 percent minus 2 percent) times the notional amount of the swap contract. This gain can be used to offset the loss of market value on the loan to the Brazilian firm. This example is illustrated in Table 23–8.

Thus, the FI benefits from the total return swap if the Brazilian bond value deteriorates as a result of a political or economic shock. Assuming that the Brazilian firm's credit risk deteriorates along with the local economy, the FI will offset some of this loss of the Brazilian loan on its balance sheet with a gain from the total return swap.

Note that hedging credit risk in this fashion allows the FI to maintain its customer relationship with the Brazilian firm (and perhaps earn fees from selling other financial services to that firm) without bearing a large amount of credit risk exposure. Moreover, since the Brazilian loan remains on the FI's balance sheet, the Brazilian firm may not even know its loan is being hedged. This would not be the case if the FI sought to reduce its risk by selling all or part of the loan (see Chapter 24). Finally, the swap does not completely hedge credit risk in this case. Specifically, basis risk is present to the extent that the credit risk of the Brazilian firm's U.S. dollar loan is imperfectly correlated with Brazilian country risk, reflected in the price of the Brazilian (U.S. dollar) bonds.

**Pure Credit Swaps.**   While total return swaps can be used to hedge credit risk exposure, they contain an element of interest rate risk as well as credit risk. For example, in Table 23–8, if the LIBOR rate changes, the *net* cash flows on the total return swap

**TABLE 23–8**   Cash Flows on a Total Return Swap

| | Annual Cash Flow for Year 1 through Final Year | Additional Payment by FI | Total Return |
|---|---|---|---|
| Cash inflow on swap to FI lender | 1-year LIBOR (11%) | — | 1-year LIBOR (11%) |
| Cash outflow on swap to other FI | Fixed rate ($f$) (12%) | $P_T - P_0$ (90 − 100) | $\left[ f + \dfrac{P_T - P_0}{P_0} \right]$ $\left( 12\% + \dfrac{90 - 100}{100} = 12\% - 10\% = 2\% \right)$ |
| | | Net profit | 9% |

12. Total return swaps are typically structured so that the capital gain or loss is paid at the end of the swap. However, an alternative structure does exist in which the capital gain or loss is paid at the end of each interest period during the swap.

**Figure 23–12**   A Pure Credit Swap

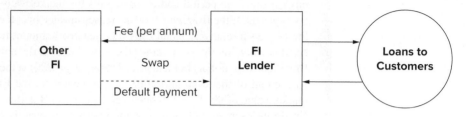

also change—even though the credit risks of the underlying loans (and bonds) have not changed.

To strip out the "interest rate" sensitive element of total return swaps, an alternative swap has been developed called a **pure credit swap**. In this case, as shown in Figure 23–12, the FI lender will send (each swap period) a fixed fee or payment (like an insurance premium) to the FI counterparty. If the FI lender's loan does not default, it will receive nothing back from the FI counterparty. However, if the loan defaults, the FI counterparty will cover the default loss by making a default payment that is often equal to the par value of the original loan (e.g., $P_0 = \$100$) minus the secondary market value of the defaulted loan (e.g., $P_T = \$40$). That is, the FI counterparty will pay $P_0 - P_T$ (or $60, in this example). Thus, a pure credit swap is like buying credit insurance and/or a multi-period credit option.

**pure credit swap**

*A swap in which an FI receives the par value of the loan on default in return for paying a periodic swap fee.*

### Credit Risk Concerns with Swaps

The financial crisis showed just how much risk the swap market can present to FIs and the global financial system. At the heart of the 2008–2009 financial crisis were derivative securities, mainly credit swaps, held by financial institutions. Specifically, in the late 2000s, FIs such as Lehman Brothers and AIG had written and, in the case of AIG, also insured billions of dollars of credit swap contracts. When mortgages underlying these contracts fell drastically in value, credit swap writers found themselves unable to make good on their promised payments to the swap holders. The result was a significant increase in risk and a decrease in profits for the FIs that had purchased these swap contracts. Given the events surrounding the financial crisis and the role that swaps played in the crisis, it is critical that both regulators and market participants have a heightened awareness of the credit risks on swap agreements.

This raises the following questions. What, exactly, is the default risk on swaps? Is it high or low? Is it the same as or different from the credit risk on loans? In fact, the credit risk on swaps and the credit risk on loans differ in three major ways, so that the credit risk on a swap is much less than that on a loan of equivalent dollar size.[13] We discuss these differences next.

**Netting and Swaps.**   One factor that mitigates the credit risk on swaps is the netting of swap payments. On each swap payment date, one party makes a fixed payment and the other makes a floating payment. In general, however, each party calculates the net difference between the two payments, and one party makes a single payment for the net difference to the other. This netting of payments implies that the default exposure of the in-the-money party is limited to the net payment rather than either the total fixed or floating payment itself.

---

13. As with loans, swap participants deal with the credit risk of counterparties by setting bilateral limits on the notional amount of swaps entered into (similar to credit rationing on loans) and adjusting the fixed and/or floating rates by including credit risk premiums. For example, a low credit-quality, fixed-rate payer may have to pay an additional spread to a high credit–quality, floating-rate payer.

For instance, in Example 23–1, if the LIBOR rate on the first swap payment date is 3.5 percent, from Table 23–6 the money center bank's cash inflows and cash outflows from the swap are $10m (= 10% × $100m) and $5.5m (= [3.5% + 2%] × $100m), respectively. Conversely, the savings bank's cash inflows and outflows from the swap are $5.5m and $10m, respectively. Rather than have both FIs receive cash *and* pay cash, the cash flows from the swap are netted. Thus, the savings bank pays a net cash flow of $4.5m to be received by the money center bank.

**Payment Flows Are Interest, Not Principal.**   Currency swaps involve swaps of interest and principal, but interest rate swaps involve swaps of interest payments only measured against some notional (or face) principal value. This suggests that the default risk on such interest rate swaps is less than on a regular loan, in which both its interest and principal payments are exposed to credit risk.

**Standby Letters of Credit.**   When swaps are made between parties of different credit standings so that one party perceives a significant risk of default by the other party, the poor-quality credit risk party may be required to buy a standby letter of credit (or another form of performance guarantee) from a third-party high-quality (AAA-rated) FI. In this case, should default occur, the standby letter of credit party would provide the swap payments in lieu of the defaulting party.

> **DO YOU UNDERSTAND:**
>
> 10. What the difference is between an interest rate swap and a currency swap?
> 11. What the major differences are between the credit risk on swaps and the credit risk on loans?

## COMPARISON OF HEDGING METHODS

**LG 23-6**

As described previously, an FI has many alternative derivative instruments with which it can hedge a particular risk. In this section, we look at some general features of the different types of contracts that may lead to an FI preferring one derivative instrument over another. We summarize these in Table 23–9.

### Writing versus Buying Options

Many FIs prefer to buy rather than write options. Of the two reasons for this, one is economic and the other is regulatory.

**TABLE 23–9**   Comparison of Hedging Methods

**Writing versus buying options**
- Writing options truncates upside profit potential while downside loss potential is unlimited.
- Buying options truncates downside loss potential while upside profit potential is unlimited.
- Commercial banks are prohibited by regulators from writing options in certain areas of risk management.

**Futures versus options hedging**
- Futures hedging produces symmetric gains and losses when interest rates move against the on-balance-sheet securities, *as well as* when interest rates move in favor of on-balance-sheet securities.
- Options hedging protects the FI against value losses when interest rates move against the on-balance-sheet securities, but, unlike with futures hedging, does not fully reduce value gains when interest rates move in favor of on-balance-sheet securities.

**Swaps versus forwards, futures, and options**
- Futures, and most options, are standardized contracts with fixed principal amounts. Swaps (and forwards) are OTC contracts negotiated directly by the counterparties to the contract.
- Futures contracts are marked to market daily. Swaps and forwards require payments only at times specified in the swap or forward agreement.
- Swaps can be written for relatively long time horizons. Futures and option contracts do not trade for more than two or three years into the future and active trading in these contracts generally extends to contracts with a maturity of less than one year.
- Swap and forward contracts are subject to default risk. Most futures and option contracts are not subject to default risk.

**Figure 23–13**    Writing a Call Option to Hedge the Interest Rate Risk on a Bond

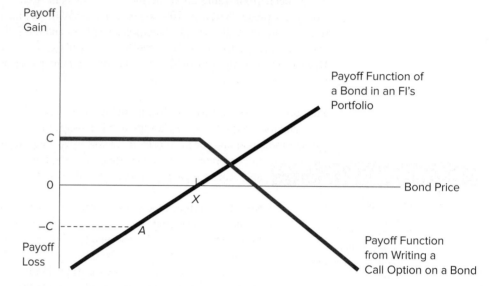

**Economic Reasons for Not Writing Options.**    In writing an option, the upside profit potential is truncated but the downside losses are not. On an *expected* basis, the writing of an appropriate call or put option would lead to a fair rate of return. However, the *actual* price or interest rate movement on the underlying asset may move against the option writer. It is this actual price or rate change that leads to the possibility of unlimited losses. Although such risks may be offset by writing a large number of options at different exercise prices and/or hedging an underlying portfolio of bonds, the writer's downside risk exposure may still be significant. Figures 23–13 and 23–14 indicate this. An FI is long in a bond in its portfolio and seeks to hedge the interest rate risk on that bond by writing a bond call option (Figure 23–13). Note that writing the call may hedge the FI when rates fall and bond prices rise—that is, the increase in the value of the bond is offset by losses on the written call. When the reverse occurs and interest rates rise, the FI's profits from writing the call may be insufficient to offset the loss on its bonds. This occurs because the upside profit (per call written) is truncated and equals the premium income (*C*). If the decrease in the bond value is larger than the premium income (to the left of point *A* in Figure 23–13), the FI is unable to offset the associated capital value loss on the bond with profits from writing options. As shown in Figure 23–14, the result is a net loss for the FI—and the larger the increase in interest rates, the larger the loss to the FI.

**Figure 23–14**    Net Payoff of Writing a Call Option on a Bond and Buying a Bond

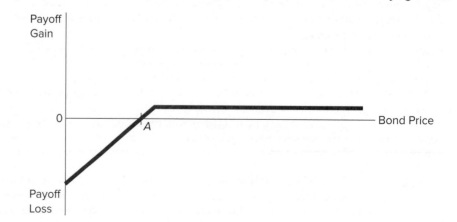

By contrast, hedging the FI's risk by buying a put option on a bond generally offers the manager a more attractive alternative. Refer again to Figures 23–7 and 23–8. The net overall payoff from the bond investment combined with the put option hedge truncates the downside losses on the bond following a rise in interest rates to some maximum amount and scales down the upside profits by the put premium.

**Regulatory Reasons for Not Writing Options.**   Many FIs also buy options rather than write options for regulatory reasons. Regulators consider writing options, especially **naked options**, which do not identifiably hedge an underlying asset or liability position, to be risky because of their unlimited loss potential. Indeed, bank regulators prohibit commercial banks from writing puts or calls in certain areas of risk management.

**naked options**

*Option positions that do not identifiably hedge an underlying asset or liability.*

### Futures versus Options Hedging

To understand the factors that impact the choice between using futures rather than options contracts to hedge, compare the payoff gains illustrated in Figures 23–15 and 23–16 (for futures contracts) with those in Figures 23–7 and 23–8 (for option contracts). A hedge with futures contracts produces symmetric gains and losses with interest rate increases and decreases. That is, if the FI in Figure 23–15 loses value on the bond due to an interest rate increase (to the left of point $X$), it enjoys a gain on the futures contract to offset this loss. If the FI gains value on the bond due to an interest rate decrease (to the right of point $X$), a loss on the futures contract offsets this gain. The result (shown in Figure 23–16) is no profit or loss for the FI regardless of what happens to interest rates.

By comparison, a hedge with an option contract offsets losses but only partly offsets gains—gains and losses from hedging with options are no longer symmetric for interest rate increases and decreases. For example, in Figure 23–7, if the FI loses value on the bond due to an interest rate increase (to the left of point $X$), a gain on the option contract offsets the loss. However, if the FI gains value on the bond due to an interest rate decrease (to the right of point $X$), the gain is offset only to the extent that the FI loses the fixed option premium (because it never exercises the option). Thus, (as shown in Figure 23–8) the option hedge protects the FI against value losses when interest rates move against the on-balance-sheet securities but, unlike futures hedging, does not fully reduce value gains when interest rates move in favor of on-balance-sheet securities. Thus, many FIs prefer option-type contracts to futures/forward type contracts.

**Figure 23–15**   **Selling a Futures Contract to Hedge the Interest Rate Risk on a Bond**

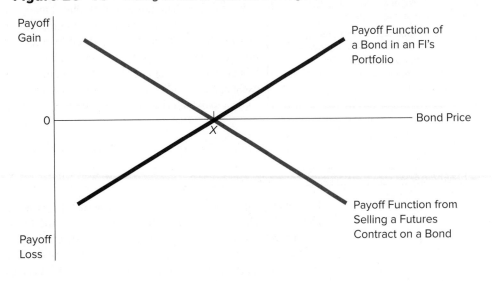

**Figure 23–16**    Net Payoff of Selling a Futures Contract and Buying a Bond

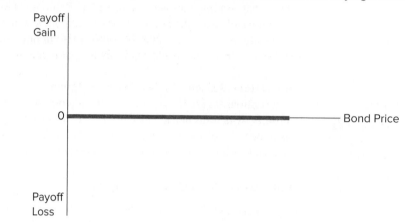

### Swaps versus Forwards, Futures, and Options

We have shown in this chapter that swaps can be used to alter the cash flows of an FI from a particular asset and liability structure. In this respect, swaps are comparable to forwards, futures, and options. Indeed, conceptually a swap is just a succession of forward rate contracts. Further, all of the derivative instruments can be viewed as relatively low-cost hedging alternatives when compared to changing the overall composition of the FI's balance sheet of assets and liabilities.

There are, however, some significant contractual differences between swaps and forward, futures, and option contracts that assist the FI manager in his or her choice of hedging method. First, futures and many options are standardized contracts with fixed principal amounts. Swaps (and most forwards), on the other hand, are OTC contracts negotiated directly by the counterparties to the contract. This feature allows for flexibility in the principal amount of the swap contract. Second, futures contracts are marked to market daily, while swaps and forwards require payments only at times specified in the swap or forward agreement. Thus, hedging risk exposure with futures can result in large cash inflows and outflows for the FI if price movements result in margin calls at the end of the day as a result of this marking-to-market process. Third, swaps can be written for relatively long time horizons, sometimes as long as 20 years. Futures and option contracts do not trade for more than two or three years into the future and active trading in these contracts generally extends to contracts with a maturity of less than 1 year. Thus, swaps provide the FI with better long-term contractual protection against risk exposures than futures and options. Finally, swap and forward contracts are subject to default risk, while most futures and option contracts are not. Swap and forward contracts are negotiated between two counterparties, and should one party fail to abide by the terms of the contract, the counterparty incurs this default risk. Futures and option contracts, however, are guaranteed by the exchange on which they trade. Thus, futures and (exchange-traded) options are subject to default risk only when the entire exchange has a default risk problem.

## SUMMARY

This chapter analyzed the risk-management role of forwards, futures, options, and swaps. These (off-balance-sheet) derivative securities provide FIs with a low-cost alternative to managing risk exposure directly on the balance sheet. We first looked at the use of forward and futures contracts as hedging instruments. We saw that while they are close substitutes, they are not perfect substitutes. A number of characteristics such as maturity, liquidity, flexibility, marking to market, and capital requirements differentiate these products and make one or the other more attractive to any particular FI manager. We next discussed the use of option-type contracts available to FI managers to hedge interest rate risk. In particular, we noted that the unique nature of the asymmetric payoff structure of option-type contracts often makes them more attractive to FIs than other hedging instruments such as forwards and futures. Finally, we evaluated the role of swaps as risk-management vehicles for FIs. We analyzed the major types of swaps, such as interest rate and currency swaps. Swaps have special features of long maturity, flexibility, and liquidity that make them attractive alternatives relative to shorter-term hedging vehicles such as futures and options.

## QUESTIONS

1. What are some of the major differences between futures and forward contracts? (*LG 23-1, LG 23-2*)

2. In each of the following cases, indicate whether it would be appropriate for an FI to buy or sell a forward contract to hedge the appropriate risk. (*LG 23-1*)
   a. A commercial bank plans to issue CDs in three months.
   b. An insurance company plans to buy bonds in two months.
   c. A thrift is going to sell Treasury securities next month.
   d. A U.S. bank lends to a French company; the loan is payable in euros.
   e. A mutual fund plans to sell its holding of stock in a German company.
   f. A finance company has assets with a duration of 6 years and liabilities with a duration of 13 years.

3. What is a naive hedge? How does a naive hedge protect an FI from risk? (*LG 23-1*)

4. Suppose that you purchase a Treasury bond futures contract at $95 per $100 of face value. (*LG 23-2*)
   a. What is your obligation when you purchase this futures contract?
   b. If an FI purchases this contract, in what kind of hedge is it engaged?
   c. Assume that the Treasury bond futures price falls to 94. What is your loss or gain?
   d. Assume that the Treasury bond futures price rises to 97. Mark your position to market.

5. What are the differences between a microhedge and a macrohedge for an FI? Why is it generally more efficient for FIs to employ a macrohedge than a series of microhedges? (*LG 23-3*)

6. What is basis risk? What are the sources of basis risk? *LG 23-2*

7. Answer the following: (*LG 23-4*)
   a. What are the two ways to use call and put options on T-bonds to generate positive cash flows when interest rates decline?
   b. When and how can an FI use options on T-bonds to hedge its assets and liabilities against interest rate declines?
   c. Is it more appropriate for FIs to hedge against a decline in interest rates with long calls or short puts?

8. Consider Table 23–3. What are the prices paid for the following futures options: (*LG 23-4*)
   a. December U.S. Treasury-bond calls at 17400.
   b. December 5-year Treasury puts at 12125.
   c. December Eurodollar calls at 9887.

9. Consider Table 23–3 again. (*LG 23-4*)
   a. What happens to the price of a call when:
      (1) The exercise price increases?
      (2) The time until expiration increases?
   b. What happens to the price of the put when these two variables increase?

10. How does hedging with options differ from hedging with forward or futures contracts? (*LG 23-6*)

11. In each of the following cases, identify what risk the manager of an FI faces and whether the risk should be hedged by buying a put or a call option. (*LG 23-4*)
    a. A commercial bank plans to issue CDs in three months.
    b. An insurance company plans to buy bonds in two months.
    c. A thrift plans to sell Treasury securities next month.
    d. A U.S. bank lends to a French company with the loan payable in euros.
    e. A mutual fund plans to sell its holding of stock in a British company.
    f. A finance company has assets with a duration of six years and liabilities with a duration of 13 years.

12. Suppose that an FI manager writes a call option on a T-bond futures contract with an exercise price of 114 at a quoted price of 0-55. What type of opportunities or obligations does the manager have? (*LG 23-4*)

13. Suppose that a pension fund manager anticipates the purchase of a 20-year, 8 percent coupon T-bond at the end of two years. Interest rates are assumed to change only once every year at year end. At that time, it is equally probable that interest rates will increase or decrease 1 percent. When purchased in two years, the T-bond will pay interest semiannually. Currently, it is selling at par. (*LG 23-4*)
    a. What is the pension fund manager's interest rate risk exposure?
    b. How can the pension fund manager use options to hedge that interest rate risk exposure?

14. How can caps, floors, and collars be used to hedge interest rate risk? (*LG 23-4*)

15. Explain the similarity between a swap and a forward contract. (*LG 23-6*)

16. Distinguish between a swap *seller* and a swap *buyer*. (*LG 23-5*)

17. Give two reasons why credit swaps have been the fastest-growing form of swaps in recent years. (*LG 23-5*)

**18.** What is a total return swap? (*LG 23-5*)

**19.** How does a pure credit swap differ from a total return swap? (*LG 23-5*)

**20.** Why is the credit risk on a swap lower than the credit risk on a loan? (*LG 23-5*)

## PROBLEMS

**1.** A bank purchases a six-month $1 million Eurodollar deposit at an interest rate of 6.5 percent per year. It invests the funds in a six-month Swedish krona bond paying 7.5 percent per year. The current spot rate of U.S. dollars for Swedish krona is $0.18/SKr. (*LG 23-1*)

    **a.** The six-month forward rate on the Swedish krona is being quoted at $0.1810/SKr. What is the net spread earned on this investment if the bank covers its foreign exchange exposure using the forward market?

    **b.** At what forward rate will the spread be only 1 percent per year?

**2.** An insurance company owns $50 million of floating-rate bonds yielding LIBOR plus 1 percent. These loans are financed with $50 million of fixed-rate guaranteed investment contracts (GICs) costing 10 percent. A finance company has $50 million of auto loans with a fixed rate of 14 percent. They are financed with $50 million of debt with a variable rate of LIBOR plus 4 percent. If the finance company is going to be the swap buyer and the insurance company the swap seller, what is an example of a feasible swap? (*LG 23-5*)

**3.** A commercial bank has $200 million of floating-rate loans yielding the T-bill rate plus 2 percent. These loans are financed with $200 million of fixed-rate deposits costing 9 percent. A savings association has $200 million of mortgages with a fixed rate of 13 percent. They are financed with $200 million of CDs with a variable rate of T-bill plus 3 percent. (*LG 23-5*)

    **a.** Discuss the type of interest rate risk each FI faces.

    **b.** Propose a swap that would result in each FI having the same type of assets and liabilities (i.e., one has fixed assets and fixed liabilities, and the other has assets and liabilities all tied to some floating rate).

    **c.** Show that this swap would be acceptable to both parties.

    **d.** What are some practical difficulties in arranging this swap?

**4.** A British bank issues a $100 million, three-year Eurodollar CD at a fixed annual rate of 7 percent. The proceeds of the CD are lent to a British company for three years at a fixed rate of 9 percent. The spot exchange rate of pounds for U.S. dollars is £1.50/US$. (*LG 23-5*)

    **a.** Is this expected to be a profitable transaction ex ante? What are the cash flows if exchange rates are unchanged over the next three years? What is the risk exposure of the bank's underlying cash position? How can the British bank reduce that risk exposure?

    **b.** If the U.S. dollar is expected to appreciate against the pound to £1.65/$1, £1.815/$1, and £2.00/$1 over the next three years, respectively, what will be the cash flows on this transaction?

    **c.** If the British bank swaps U.S. dollar payments for British pound payments at the current spot exchange rate, what are the cash flows on the swap? What are the cash flows on the entire hedged position? Assume that the U.S. dollar appreciates at the same rates as in part (b).

**5.** Bank 1 can issue five-year CDs at an annual rate of 11 percent fixed or at a variable rate of LIBOR + 2 percent. Bank 2 can issue five-year CDs at an annual fixed rate of 13 percent or at a variable rate of LIBOR + 3 percent. (*LG 23-5*)

    **a.** Is a mutually beneficial swap possible between the two banks?

    **b.** What is the comparative advantage of the two banks?

    **c.** What is an example of a feasible swap?

*The following problems are related to Appendix 23A, 23B, and 23C materials.*

**6.** Answer the following. (*LG 23-2, LG 23-3*)

    **a.** What is the duration of a 20-year 8 percent coupon (paid semiannually) Treasury bond (deliverable against the Treasury bond futures contract) selling at par?

    **b.** What is the predicted impact on the Treasury bond price based on its duration if interest rates increase 50 basis points annually (25 basis points semiannually)?

    **c.** What is the meaning of the following Treasury bond futures price quote: 101-130?

**7.** An FI holds a 15-year, $10,000,000 par value bond that is priced at 104 and yields 7 percent. The FI plans to sell the bond but for tax purposes must wait two months. The bond has a duration of 9.4 years. The FI's market analyst is predicting that the Federal Reserve will raise interest rates within the next two months and doing so will raise the yield on the bond to 8 percent. Most other analysts are predicting no change in interest rates, so presently plenty of two-month forward contracts for 15-year bonds are available at 104. The FI would like to hedge against this interest rate forecast with an appropriate position in a forward contract. What will this position be? Show that if rates rise by 1 percent as forecast, the hedge will protect the FI from loss. (*LG 23-2*)

**8.** Hedge Row Bank has the following balance sheet (in millions):

| Assets | | Liabilities | |
|---|---|---|---|
| Assets | $150 | Liabilities | $135 |
| | | Equity | 15 |
| Total | $150 | Total | $150 |

The duration of the assets is six years and the duration of the liabilities is four years. The bank is expecting interest rates to fall from 10 percent to 9 percent over the next year. (*LG 23-2*)

    **a.** What is the duration gap for Hedge Row Bank?

    **b.** What is the expected change in net worth for Hedge Row Bank if the forecast is accurate?

**c.** What will be the effect on net worth if interest rates increase 100 basis points?

**d.** If the existing interest rate on the liabilities is 6 percent, what will be the effect on net worth of a 1 percent increase in interest rates?

**9.** Tree Row Bank has assets of $150 million, liabilities of $135 million, and equity of $15 million. The asset duration is six years and the duration of the liabilities is four years. Market interest rates are 10 percent. Tree Row Bank wishes to hedge the balance sheet with Treasury bond futures contracts, which currently have a price quote of $95 per $100 face value for the benchmark 20-year, 8 percent coupon bond underlying the contract, a market yield of 8.5295 percent, and a duration of 10.3725 years. (*LG 23-2, LG 23-3*)

**a.** Should the bank go short or long on the futures contracts to establish the correct macrohedge?

**b.** How many contracts are necessary to fully hedge the bank?

**c.** Verify that the change in the futures position will offset the change in the cash balance sheet position for a change in market interest rates of plus 100 basis points and minus 50 basis points.

**d.** If the bank had hedged with Treasury bill futures contracts that had a market value of $98 per $100 of face value and a duration of 0.25 year, how many futures contracts would have been necessary to fully hedge the balance sheet?

**e.** What additional issues should be considered by the bank in choosing between T-bond or T-bill futures contracts?

**10.** How would your answer for part (b) in Problem 9 change if the relationship of the price sensitivity of futures contracts to the price sensitivity of underlying bonds were $[\Delta R_f/(1 + R_f)/\Delta R/(1 + R)] = br = 0.92$? (*LG 23-2*)

**11.** A mutual fund plans to purchase $500,000 of 30-year Treasury bonds in four months. These bonds have a duration of 12 years and are priced at 96-08 (32nds). The mutual fund is concerned about interest rates changing over the next four months and is considering a hedge with T-bond futures contracts that mature in six months. The T-bond futures contracts are selling for 98-24 (32nds) and have a duration of 8.5 years. (*LG 23-2*)

**a.** If interest rate changes in the spot market exactly match those in the futures market, what type of futures position should the mutual fund create?

**b.** How many contracts should be used?

**c.** If the implied rate on the deliverable bond in the futures market moves 12 percent more than the change in the discounted spot rate, how many futures contracts should be used to hedge the portfolio?

**d.** What causes futures contracts to have a different price sensitivity than the assets in the spot markets?

**12.** Consider the following balance sheet (in millions) for an FI: (*LG 23-1, LG 23-2*)

| Assets | | Liabilities | |
|---|---|---|---|
| Duration = 10 years | $950 | Duration = 2 years | $860 |
| | | Equity = | 90 |

**a.** What is the FI's duration gap?

**b.** What is the FI's interest rate risk exposure?

**c.** How can the FI use futures and forward contracts to create a macrohedge?

**d.** What is the impact on the FI's equity value if the relative change in interest rates is an increase of 1 percent? That is, $\Delta R/(1 + R) = 0.01$.

**e.** Suppose that the FI in part (c) macrohedges using Treasury bond futures that are currently priced at 96. What is the impact on the FI's futures position if the relative change in all interest rates is an increase of 1 percent? That is, $\Delta R/(1 + R) = 0.01$. Assume that the deliverable Treasury bond has a duration of nine years.

**f.** If the FI wants to macrohedge, how many Treasury bond futures contracts does it need?

**13.** Refer to Problem 12. How does consideration of basis risk change your answers? (*LG 23-2*)

**a.** Compute the number of T-bond futures contracts required to construct a macrohedge if T-bond futures are priced at 96 and the duration of the T-bond underlying the futures contract is 9 years. Also, assume that $[\Delta R_f/(1 + R_f)/\Delta R/(1 + R)] = br = 0.90$.

**b.** Explain what is meant by $br = 0.90$.

**c.** If $br = 0.90$, what information does this provide on the number of futures contracts needed to construct a macrohedge?

**14.** Village Bank has $240 million worth of assets with a duration of 14 years and liabilities worth $210 million with a duration of four years. In the interest of hedging interest rate risk, Village Bank is contemplating a macrohedge with interest rate T-bond futures contracts now selling for 102-21 (32nds). The T-bond underlying the futures contract has a duration of nine years. If the spot and futures interest rates move together, how many futures contracts must Village Bank sell to fully hedge the balance sheet? (*LG 23-2*)

**15.** An FI has a $100 million portfolio of six-year Eurodollar bonds that have an 8 percent coupon. The bonds are trading at par and have a duration of five years. The FI wishes to hedge the portfolio with T-bond options that have a delta of –0.625. The underlying long-term Treasury bonds for the option have a duration of 10.1 years and trade at a market value of $96,157 per $100,000 of par value. Each put option has a premium of 3.25 (percent of $100,000). (*LG 23-4*)

**a.** How many bond put options are necessary to hedge the bond portfolio?

**b.** If interest rates increase 100 basis points, what is the expected gain or loss on the put option hedge?

**c.** What is the expected change in market value on the bond portfolio?

**d.** How far must interest rates move before the payoff on the hedge will exactly offset the cost of placing the hedge?

**e.** How far must interest rates move before the gain on the bond portfolio will exactly offset the cost of placing the hedge?

**16.** Corporate Bank has $840 million of assets with a duration of 12 years and liabilities worth $720 million with a duration of seven years. Assets and liabilities are yielding 7.56 percent. The bank is concerned about preserving the value of its equity in the event of an increase in interest rates and is contemplating a macrohedge with interest rate options. The call and put options have a face value of $100,000, are priced at $1\frac{44}{64}$ and $\frac{56}{64}$, respectively, and have a delta ($\delta$) of 0.4 and –0.4, respectively. The price of an underlying T-bond is $104.53125\left(104\frac{68}{128}\right)$, its duration is 8.17 years, and its yield to maturity is 7.56 percent. (*LG 23-4*)

a. What type of option should Corporate Bank use for the macrohedge?

b. How many options should be purchased?

c. What is the effect on the economic value of the equity if interest rates rise 50 basis points?

d. What is the dollar change in value of the option position if interest rates rise by 50 basis points?

e. What will be the cost of the hedge if each option has a premium of $0.875 per $100 of face value?

f. How much must interest rates move against the hedge for the increased value of the bank to offset the cost of the hedge?

g. How much must interest rates move in favor of the hedge, or against the balance sheet, before the payoff from the hedge will exactly cover the cost of the hedge?

17. An FI has a $200 million asset portfolio that has an average duration of 6.5 years. The average duration of its $160 million in liabilities is 4.5 years. Assets and liabilities are yielding 10 percent. The FI uses put options on T-bonds to hedge against unexpected interest rate increases. The average delta ($\delta$) of the put options has been estimated at –0.3 and the average duration of the T-bonds is seven years. The current market value of the T-bonds is $96,000. Put options on T-bonds are selling at a premium of $1.25 per face value of $100. (*LG 23-4*)

a. What is the modified duration of the T-bonds if the current level of interest rates is 10 percent?

b. How many put option contracts should the FI purchase to hedge its exposure against rising interest rates? The face value of the T-bonds is $100,000.

c. If interest rates increase 50 basis points, what will be the change in value of the equity of the FI?

d. If interest rates increase 50 basis points, what will be the change in value of the T-bond option hedge position?

e. What must be the change in interest rates before the change in value of the balance sheet (equity) will offset the cost of placing the hedge?

f. How much must interest rates change before the payoff of the hedge will exactly cover the cost of placing the hedge?

18. A mutual fund plans to purchase $10 million of 20-year T-bonds in two months. The bonds are yielding 7.68 percent. These bonds have a duration of 11 years. The mutual fund is concerned about interest rates changing over the next two months and is considering a hedge with a two-month option on a T-bond futures contract. Two-month calls with a strike price of 105 are priced at 1-25, and puts of the same maturity and exercise price are quoted at 2-09. The delta of the call is 0.5 and the delta of the put is –0.7. The current price of a deliverable T-bond is 103-08 per $100 of face value, its duration is nine years, and its yield to maturity is 7.68 percent. (*LG 23-4*)

a. What type of option should the mutual fund purchase?

b. How many options should it purchase?

c. What is the cost of these options?

d. If rates change +/–50 basis points, what will be the impact on the price of the desired T-bonds?

e. By how much does the value of the call position change if interest rates change +/–50 basis points?

19. An FI has purchased a $200 million cap of 9 percent at a premium of 0.65 percent of face value. A $200 million floor of 4 percent is also available at a premium of 0.69 percent of face value. (*LG 23-4*)

a. If interest rates rise to 10 percent, what is the amount received by the FI? What are the net savings after deducting the premium?

b. If the FI also purchases a floor, what are the net savings if interest rates rise to 11 percent? What are the net savings if interest rates fall to 3 percent?

c. If, instead, the FI sells (writes) the floor, what are the net savings if interest rates rise to 11 percent? What if they fall to 3 percent?

d. What amount of floors should the FI sell in order to compensate for its purchase of caps, given the above premiums?

**APPENDIX 23A: Hedging with Futures Contracts**

**APPENDIX 23B: Hedging with Options**

**APPENDIX 23C: Hedging with Caps, Floors, and Collars**

Appendixes 23A, 23B, and 23C are available through Connect or your course instructor.

**chapter**

# 24

# Managing Risk off the Balance Sheet with Loan Sales and Securitization

## Learning Goals

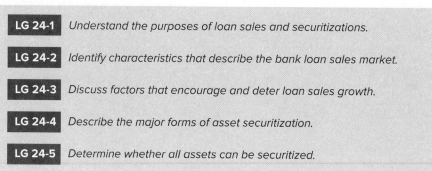

**LG 24-1**   *Understand the purposes of loan sales and securitizations.*

**LG 24-2**   *Identify characteristics that describe the bank loan sales market.*

**LG 24-3**   *Discuss factors that encourage and deter loan sales growth.*

**LG 24-4**   *Describe the major forms of asset securitization.*

**LG 24-5**   *Determine whether all assets can be securitized.*

## WHY FINANCIAL INSTITUTIONS SELL AND SECURITIZE LOANS: CHAPTER OVERVIEW

**LG 24-1**   **Loan sales and securitization**—the packaging and selling of loans and other assets backed by loans issued by the FI—are mechanisms that FIs have used to hedge their credit risk, interest rate risk, and liquidity risk exposures. In addition, loan sales and securitization have allowed FI asset portfolios to become more liquid, provided an important source of fee income (with FIs acting as servicing agents for the assets sold), and helped reduce the adverse effects of regulatory "taxes" such as capital requirements, reserve requirements, and deposit insurance premiums on FI profitability. Loan sales involve splitting up larger loans and loan portfolios, whereas loan securitization involves the grouping of smaller loans into larger pools. While loan sales have been in existence for many years, the use of loan sales (by removing existing loans from the balance sheet) is increasingly being recognized as a valuable tool in an FI manager's portfolio of credit risk management techniques. In Chapter 1, we discussed the role of FIs as both asset transformers and asset brokers. By increasingly relying on loan sales and securitization, FIs such as depository institutions have begun moving away from being strictly asset transformers that originate and hold assets to maturity toward becoming more reliant on servicing and other fees. This makes depository institutions look increasingly similar to securities firms and investment banks in terms of the enhanced importance of asset brokerage over asset transformation functions.

**TABLE 24–1**    Basic Description of Loan Sales and Other Forms
of Mortgage Securitization

**Loan sale**—an FI originates a loan and subsequently sells it.

**Pass-through securities**—mortgages or other assets originated by an FI are pooled and investors are offered an interest in the pool in the form of pass-through certificates or securities. Examples of pass-through securities are Government National Mortgage Association (GNMA) or Federal National Mortgage Association (FNMA) securities.

**Collateralized mortgage obligations (CMOs)**—similar to pass-throughs, CMOs are securities backed by pools of mortgages or other assets originated by an FI. Pass-throughs give investors common rights in terms of risks and returns, but CMOs assign varying combinations of risk and return to different groups of investors in the CMO by repackaging the pool.

**Mortgage-backed bonds (MBBs)**—a bond issue backed by a group of mortgages on an FI's balance sheet. With MBBs, the mortgages remain on the FI's balance sheet and funds used to pay the MBB holders' coupons and principal repayments may or may not come from the collateralized mortgages.

**loan sales and securitization**

*The packaging and selling of loans and other assets backed by securities issued by an FI.*

In Chapter 7, we discussed the basics of asset sales and securitization and the markets in which these securities trade. This chapter investigates the role of loan sales and other forms of asset securitization in improving the return–risk trade-off for FIs. However, as seen in the mid- and late 2000s with assets backed with subprime mortgages, asset securitization can result in huge losses if the underlying assets do not pay as promised. This chapter describes the process associated with loan sales and the major forms, or vehicles, of asset securitization and analyzes their unique characteristics. Table 24–1 presents a definition of the loan sale and securitization mechanisms that this chapter discusses.

## LOAN SALES

**loan sale**

*Sale of a loan originated by a bank with or without recourse to an outside buyer.*

**recourse**

*The ability of a loan buyer to sell the loan back to the originator should it go bad.*

**correspondent banking**

*A relationship between a small bank and a large bank in which the large bank provides a number of deposit, lending, and other services.*

A **loan sale** occurs when an FI originates a loan and sells it with or without recourse to an outside buyer. If the loan is sold without recourse, the FI not only removes it from its balance sheet (purchasing new investments with the freed-up funds), but it also has no explicit liability if the loan eventually goes bad. The loan buyer (not the FI that originated the loan) bears all the credit risk. If, however, the loan is sold with **recourse**, under certain conditions the buyer can put the loan back to the selling FI. Therefore, the FI retains a contingent (credit risk) liability. In practice, most loan sales are without recourse because a loan sale is technically removed from the balance sheet only when the buyer has no future credit risk claim on the FI. Loan sales usually involve no creation of new types of securities, such as those described later in the chapter when we consider the securitization activities of FIs.

FIs have sold loans among themselves for more than 100 years. In fact, a large part of **correspondent banking** involves small FIs making loans that are too big for them to hold on their balance sheets—either for lending concentration risk or capital adequacy reasons—and selling (or syndicating) parts of these loans to large FIs with whom they have had a long-term deposit-lending correspondent relationship. In turn, the large banks often sell (or syndicate) parts of their loans (called *participations*) to smaller FIs. The syndicated loan market—that is, the market for buying and selling loans once they have been originated—can be segmented into three categories: market makers, active traders, and occasional sellers/investors. Market makers are generally the large commercial banks (e.g., J.P. Morgan Chase and Goldman Sachs), which commit capital to create liquidity and take outright positions in the markets. Institutions that actively engage in primary loan origination have an advantage in trading on the secondary market, mainly because of their acquired skill in accessing and understanding loan documentation. Active traders are mainly investment banks, commercial banks, and vulture funds (see below). Other financial institutions such as insurance companies also trade but to a lesser extent. Occasional participants are either sellers of loans (who seek to remove loans from their balance sheets

**highly leveraged transaction (HLT) loan**

*A loan that finances a merger and acquisition; a leveraged buyout results in a high leverage ratio for the borrower.*

to meet regulatory constraints or to manage their exposures) or buyers of loans (who seek exposure to sectors or countries, especially when they do not have the critical size to do so in the primary loan markets).

Even though this market has existed for many years, it grew slowly until the early 1980s when it entered a period of spectacular growth, largely due to expansion in **highly leveraged transaction (HLT) loans** to finance leveraged buyouts (LBOs) and mergers and acquisitions (M&As). Specifically, the volume of loans sold by U.S. banks increased from less than $20 billion in 1980 to $285 billion in 1989. Many of these loans were sold at far less than their original book value (i.e., they were classified as *distressed loans,* or loans trading below 90 cents on the dollar). These losses reduced bank capital to the extent that many banks (and savings institutions) failed (see Chapter 14). In the early 1990s, the volume of loan sales declined dramatically, along with the decline in LBO and M&A activity. In 1991, the volume of loan sales had fallen to approximately $10 billion. In the late 1990s, the volume of loan sales expanded again, partly due to an expanding economy and a resurgency in M&As. For example, the loan market research firm Loan Pricing Corporation reported that secondary trading volume in 1999 was more than $79 billion. Loan sales continued to grow to almost $120 billion in the early 2000s as FIs sold distressed loans. Triggered by an economic slowdown, distressed loan sales jumped from 11 percent of total loan sales in 1999 to 36 percent in 2001, and 42 percent in 2002. As the U.S. economy improved in the early and mid-2000s, the percentage of distressed loan sales fell (e.g., to 17 percent in 2006). Even as the economy slowed in 2007 and 2008, while loans sales surged to over $500 billion, distressed loan sales remained low. In 2007, distressed loans were just 9 percent of total loan sales, and in 2008 they were under 8 percent of all loan sales. Loan sales fell only slightly (to $474 billion) in 2009, during the worst of the financial crisis. However, as might be expected during a recession, the percent of distressed loans increased significantly, to almost 30 percent. Loan sales decreased slightly in 2010, as the U.S. economy began to improve. However, distressed loans remained high, over 20 percent. In 2011 and 2012, the U.S. economy continued to struggle and loan sales growth remained flat. However, the percent of distressed loans decreased significantly, to 8.7 and 5.5 percent in 2011 and 2012, respectively, as many financial institutions had already sold off their marketable distressed loans in 2009 and 2010. Figure 24–1 shows the growth in loan sales over the period 1991–2016.

**Figure 24–1**  **Recent Trends in the Loan Sales Market**

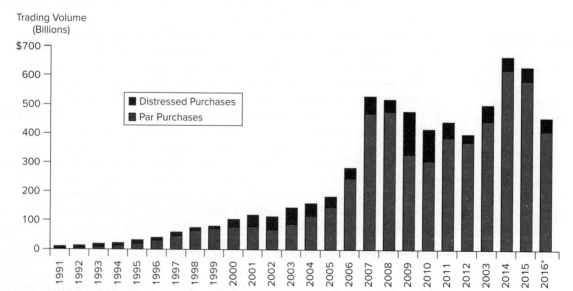

*Through three quarters

**Sources:** Thomson Reuters LPC website, 2016. thomsonreuters.com

### Types of Loan Sales Contracts

The two basic types of loan sales contracts are *participations* and *assignments*. Currently, assignments represent the bulk of loan sales.

**participation in a loan**

*The act of buying a share in a loan syndication with limited contractual control and rights over the borrower.*

**Participations.** The unique characteristics of **participations in loans** are:

- The holder (buyer) is not a party to the underlying (primary) credit agreement, so that the initial contract between the loan seller (which may be a syndicate of FIs) and the borrower remains in place after the sale.
- The loan buyer can exercise only partial control over changes in the loan contract's terms. The holder can vote on only material changes to the loan contract, such as the interest rate or collateral backing.

The economic implication of these characteristics is that the buyer of the loan participation has a double risk exposure—to the borrower as well as to the original lender (or lenders). Specifically, if the selling FI fails, the loan participation bought by an outside party may be characterized as an unsecured obligation of the FI rather than a true sale. Alternatively, the borrowers' claims against a failed selling FI may be netted against its loans, reducing the amount of loans outstanding and adversely impacting the buyer of a participation in those loans. As a result of these exposures, the buyer bears a double monitoring cost as well.

**assignment**

*The purchase of a share in a loan syndication with some contractual control and rights over the borrower.*

**Assignments.** Because of the monitoring costs and the risks involved in participations, loans are sold on an assignment basis in more than 90 percent of the cases on the U.S. domestic market. The key features of an **assignment** are:

- All ownership rights are transferred on sale, meaning that the loan buyer holds a direct claim on the borrower.
- U.S. domestic loans are normally transferred with a Uniform Commercial Code filing, meaning there is documentation of a change of ownership in which the buyer has first claim on the borrower's assets in the event of bankruptcy.

Although ownership rights are generally much clearer in a loan sale by assignment, contractual terms frequently limit the seller's (e.g., an FI's) scope regarding to whom the loan can be sold. A loan sale by assignment means the borrower (e.g., IBM) must negotiate any changes on the loan with an FI it may have had no prior relationship with or knowledge of. To protect the borrower (IBM), the original loan contract may require either the FI agent or the borrower (IBM) to agree to the sale. (An FI agent is an FI that distributes interest and principal payments to lenders in loan syndications with multiple lenders.) The loan contract may also restrict the sale to a certain class of institutions, such as those that meet certain net worth/net asset size conditions (say, Allstate Insurance Company). Currently, the trend appears to be toward originating loan contracts with very limited assignment restrictions. This is true in both the U.S. domestic and foreign loan sales markets. The most tradable loans are those that can be assigned without buyer restrictions. In evaluating ownership rights, the buyer of the loan (Allstate) also needs to verify the original loan contract and to establish the full implications of the purchase regarding the buyer's (Allstate's) rights to collateral if the borrower (IBM) defaults. Because of these contractual problems, trading frictions, and costs, some loan sales take as long as three months to complete, although for most loan sales the developing market standard is that loan sales should be completed within 10 days.

LG 24-2

### The Loan Sales Market

**LDC loans**

*Loans made to a less developed country (LDC).*

The U.S. loan sales market has three segments: two involve sales and trading of domestic loans and the third involves sales of **LDC loans** (less developed country loans that have been made to certain Asian, African, and Latin American countries).

**Traditional Short-Term Segment.**   In the traditional short-term segment of the market, FIs sell loans with short maturities, often one to three months. This market has characteristics similar to those of the market for commercial paper (see Chapter 5) in that loan sales have similar maturities and issue sizes. Loan sales, however, usually have yields that are 1 to 10 basis points above those of commercial paper of a similar rating and, unlike commercial paper, are secured by the assets of the borrowing firm. However, commercial paper issuers generally are blue chip corporations that have the best credit ratings. Banks may sell the loans of less creditworthy borrowers, thereby raising required yields. Indeed, since commercial paper issuers tend to be well-known companies, information, monitoring, and credit assessment costs are lower for commercial paper issues than for loan sales. Moreover, since there is an active secondary market in commercial paper, but not for loan sales, the commercial paper buyer takes on less liquidity risk than does the buyer of a loan sale. The key characteristics of the loans bought and sold in the short-term loan sales market are:

- The loans are secured by assets of the borrowing firm or other external guarantors.
- They have been made to investment-grade borrowers or better.
- They are issued for a short term (90 days or less).
- They are sold in units of $1 million and up.
- Loan rates are closely tied to the commercial paper rate.

Traditional short-term loan sales dominated the market until 1984 and the emergence of the HLT and LDC loan markets. The growth of the commercial paper market (see Chapter 5) has also reduced the importance of this market segment.

**HLT Loan Sales.**   With the increase in M&As and LBOs financed via highly leveraged transactions (HLTs), especially from 1985 to 1989, a new segment in the loan sales market, HLT loan sales or highly leveraged loan market, appeared.[1] HLT loans mainly differ according to whether they are nondistressed (bid price exceeds 90 cents per $1 of loans) or distressed (bid price is less than 90 cents per $1 of loans or the borrower is in default).

Virtually all HLT loans have the following characteristics:

- They are secured by assets of the borrowing firm (usually given senior security status).
- They have long maturity (often three- to six-year maturities).
- They have floating rates tied to the London Interbank Offered Rate (LIBOR), the prime rate, or a CD rate (HLT rates are normally 200–275 basis points above these rates).
- They have strong covenant protection.

**financial distress**

*The state when a borrower is unable to meet a payment obligation to lenders and other creditors.*

Nevertheless, HLTs tend to be quite heterogeneous with respect to the size of the issue, the interest payment date, interest indexing, and prepayment features. After origination, some HLT borrowers such as Macy's and El Paso Electric have suffered periods of **financial distress** in that they were unable to make timely payments on many of the bonds they had issued and loans they had outstanding. As a result, a distinction between the market for distressed and nondistressed HLTs is usually made.

**vulture fund**

*A specialized fund that invests in distressed loans.*

**The Buyers.**   Of the wide array of potential buyers, some are interested in only a certain segment of the market for regulatory and strategic reasons. In particular, an increasingly specialized group of buyers of distressed loans includes investment banks and **vulture funds.** For the nondistressed market and the traditional U.S. domestic loan sales market, the seven major buyers are investment banks, vulture funds, other domestic banks, foreign banks, insurance companies and pension funds, closed-end bank loan mutual funds, and nonfinancial corporations.

---

1. What constitutes an HLT loan has often caused dispute. In October 1989, however, the three U.S. federal bank regulators adopted a definition of an HLT as a loan that (1) involves a buyout, acquisition, or recapitalization and (2) either doubles the company's liabilities and results in a leverage ratio higher than 50 percent, results in a leverage ratio higher than 75 percent, or is designated as an HLT by a syndication agent.

*Investment Banks.*    Investment banks are predominantly buyers of loans because (1) analysis of these loans utilizes investment skills similar to those required for junk bond trading and (2) investment banks are often closely associated with the borrower in underwriting the original junk bond/HLT deals. As such, large investment banks—for example, Bank of America Merrill Lynch and Goldman Sachs—are relatively more informed agents in this market, either by acting as market makers or in taking short-term positions on movements in the market prices of these loans.

*Vulture Funds.*    Vulture funds are specialized investment funds established to invest in distressed loans, often with an agenda that does not include helping the distressed firm survive. These investments can be active, especially for those seeking to use the loans purchased for bargaining in a restructuring deal, which generates restructuring returns that strongly favor the loan purchaser. Alternatively, such loans may be held as passive investments or high-yield securities in a well-diversified portfolio of distressed securities. Investment banks, in fact, manage many vulture funds. Most secondary market trading in U.S. loan sales occurs in this segment of the market.

*Other Domestic Banks.*    Interbank loan sales are at the core of the traditional market and historically have revolved around correspondent banking and regional banking/branching restrictions. Restrictions on nationwide banking in the past led banks to originate regionally undiversified and borrower undiversified loan portfolios. Small banks often sold loan participations to their large correspondents to improve regional/borrower diversification and to avoid regulatory imposed single-borrower loan concentration ceilings. (A loan to a single borrower should not exceed 10 percent of a bank's capital.) This arrangement also worked in the other direction, with the larger banks selling participations to smaller banks.

   The traditional interbank market, however, has been shrinking as a result of three factors. First, the traditional correspondent banking relationship is breaking down as markets become more competitive. Second, concerns about counterparty risk and moral hazard have increased. In particular, moral hazard is the risk that the selling bank will seek to offload its "bad" loans (via loan sales), keeping the "good" loans in its portfolio. Third, the barriers to nationwide banking have been removed, particularly following the full implementation of interstate banking in 1997 (after the passage of the Riegle-Neal Interstate Banking and Branching Efficiency Act in 1994) and the (continuing) contraction in the number of small banks (see Chapter 13). Nevertheless, some small banks find the loan sales market enormously useful as a way to regionally diversify their loan portfolios.

*Foreign Banks.*    Foreign banks remain the dominant buyer of domestic U.S. loans. Because of the cost of branching, the loan sales market allows foreign banks to achieve a well-diversified domestic U.S. loan portfolio without developing a nationwide banking network.

*Insurance Companies and Pension Funds.*    Subject to meeting liquidity and credit quality restrictions (such as buying only BBB rated loans or above), insurance companies (such as Aetna) and pension funds are important buyers of long-term loans.

*Closed-End Bank Loan Mutual Funds.*    First established in 1988, these leveraged mutual funds, such as Highland Capital Management of Dallas, Texas, invest in domestic U.S. bank loans. Although they could purchase loans in the loan sales market, the largest funds have moved into primary loan syndications as well because of the attractive fee income available. These mutual funds increasingly participate in funding loans originated by commercial banks. Indeed, some money center banks, such as J.P. Morgan Chase, have actively encouraged closed-end fund participation in primary loan syndications.

*Nonfinancial Corporations.*    Some corporations—primarily the financial services arms of the very largest U.S. and European companies (e.g., GE Capital and ITT Financial)—buy loans. This activity amounts to no more than 5 percent of total U.S. domestic loan sales.

**The Sellers.**   The sellers of domestic loans and HLT loans are major money center banks, small regional or community banks, foreign banks, investment banks, and the U.S. government.

*Major Money Center Banks.*   The largest money center banks have dominated loan selling. In recent years, market concentration in loan selling has been accentuated by the increase in HLTs (and the important role that major money center banks have played in originating loans in HLT deals) as well as growth in real estate loan sales.

*Small Regional or Community Banks.*   As mentioned earlier, small banks sell loans and loan participations to larger FIs for diversification and regulatory purposes. Although they are not a major player in the loan sales market, small banks have found loan sales to be essential for diversifying their credit risk.

*Foreign Banks.*   To the extent that foreign banks are sellers rather than buyers of loans, these loans come from branch networks such as the Japanese-owned banks in California or through selling loans originated in their home country in U.S. loan sales markets.

*Investment Banks.*   Investment banks such as Merrill Lynch (a subsidiary of Bank of America) act as loan sellers either as part of their loan origination activities or as active traders in the market.

*The U.S. Government and Its Agencies.*   In recent years, the U.S. government and its agencies have shown an increased willingness to engage in loan sales. This has been aided by the passage of the Debt Collection Improvement Act of 1996, which authorizes federal agencies to sell delinquent and defaulted loan assets. The Department of Housing and Urban Development also has been an increasingly large seller of mortgage loans on multifamily apartment properties. However, the largest loan sales by a government agency to date have been made by the Resolution Trust Corporation (RTC). Established in 1989 and disbanded at the end of 1995, the RTC had to resolve more than 700 problem savings institutions through merger, closure, or conservatorship. With respect to the U.S. commercial and industrial loan sales market, RTC dispositions had a relatively moderate supply-side effect largely because the bulk of RTC's asset sales were real estate assets (such as multifamily mortgages). The tendency of the RTC was to combine good and bad loans into loan packages and sell them at auction to bidders.

### Secondary Market for Less Developed Country Debt

Since the mid-1980s, a secondary market for trading less developed country (LDC) debt has developed among large commercial and investment banks in New York and London. The volume of trading has grown dramatically, from around $2 billion per year in 1984 to over $6 billion today. Like domestic loan sales, the removal of LDC loans from the balance sheet allows an FI to free up assets for other investments. Further, being able to sell these loans—even if at a price below the face value of the original loan—may signify that the FI's balance sheet is sufficiently strong to bear the loss. In fact, a number of studies have found that announcements of FIs writing down the value of LDC loans—prior to their charge-off and sale—have a positive effect on FI stock prices. For example, on May 19, 1987, Citicorp announced that the bank was adding a staggering $3 billion to its reserves against losses on loans to developing countries. In the week following the announcement, Citicorp's stock rose from $50.625 to $55.375.

In recent years, there have been a large number of changes in the structure of the market. Now there are three market segments: sovereign bonds, performing loans, and nonperforming loans.[2] The first segment of the LDC debt market is that for sovereign bonds (i.e., government-issued debt). Sovereign bonds have historically been issued in foreign currencies, either U.S. dollars or euros. LDC sovereign debt tends to have lower credit ratings than other sovereign debt because of the increased economic and political risks. The second segment of the LDC debt market is that for performing LDC loans. Performing loans are original or restructured outstanding sovereign loans on which the sovereign country is currently maintaining promised payments to lenders or debt holders. Any discounts from 100 percent reflect expectations that these countries may face repayment problems in the future. The third segment of the LDC market is that for nonperforming loans. Nonperforming loans reflect the secondary market prices for the sovereign loans of countries where there are no interest or principal payments currently being made. These are normally traded at very deep discounts from 100 percent.

## LG 24-3 *Factors Encouraging Future Loan Sales Growth*

The introduction to this chapter stated that one reason that FIs sell loans is to manage their credit risk better. Loan sales remove assets (and credit risk) from the balance sheet[3] and allow an FI to achieve better asset diversification. Other than credit risk management, however, FIs are encouraged to sell loans for a number of other economic and regulatory reasons.

**Fee Income.**   An FI can often report any fee income earned from originating loans as current income, but interest earned on direct lending can be accrued (as income) only over time (see Chapter 12). As a result, originating and quickly selling loans can boost an FI's reported income under current accounting rules.

**Liquidity Risk.**   In addition to credit risk, holding loans on the balance sheet can increase the overall illiquidity of an FI's assets. This illiquidity is a problem because FI liabilities tend to be highly liquid. Asset illiquidity can expose the FI to harmful liquidity problems when depositors unexpectedly withdraw their deposits. To mitigate a liquidity problem, an FI's management can sell some of its loans to outside investors (see Chapter 21). Thus, the FI loan market has created a secondary market that has significantly reduced the illiquidity of loans held as assets on the balance sheet.

**Capital Costs.**   The capital adequacy requirements imposed on FIs are a burden as long as required capital exceeds the amount the FI believes to be privately beneficial. Thus, FIs struggling to meet a required capital-to-assets ($K/A$) ratio can boost this ratio by reducing assets ($A$) rather than boosting capital ($K$)—see Chapter 13. One way to downsize or reduce $A$ and boost the $K/A$ ratio is through loan sales.

**Reserve Requirements.**   Regulatory requirements, such as reserves that a bank must hold at the central bank, represent a form of tax that adds to the cost of funding the loan portfolio. Regulatory taxes such as reserve requirements[4] create an incentive for banks to

---

2. A fourth, but very small, market is that for Brady bonds. Brady bonds reflect programs under which the U.S. and other FIs have exchanged their dollar loans for dollar bonds issued by the relevant less developed countries (LDCs). These bonds have a much longer maturity than that promised on the original loans and a lower promised original coupon (yield) than the interest rate on the original loan. However, the principal usually has been collateralized through the issuing country's purchasing U.S. Treasury bonds and holding them in a special-purpose escrow account. Should that country default on its Brady bonds, the buyers of the bonds could access the dollar bonds held as collateral. These loan-for-bond restructuring programs, also called *debt-for-debt swaps,* were developed under the auspices of the U.S. Treasury's 1989 Brady Plan and international organizations such as the IMF. Once loans were swapped for bonds by banks and other FIs, they could be sold on the secondary market. The Brady bond process ended in the 1990s. Yet a small amount of these bonds still exist and trade.
3. However, if FIs primarily sell high-quality loans, the average quality of the remaining loans may actually decrease.
4. Under current reserve requirement regulations (Regulation D, amended May 1986), bank loan sales with recourse are regarded as a liability and hence are subject to reserve requirements. The reservability of loan sales extends to a bank issuing a credit guarantee and a recourse provision. Loans sold without recourse (or credit guarantees by the selling bank) are free of reserve requirements. With the elimination of reserve requirements on nontransaction accounts and the lowering of reserve requirements on transaction accounts in 1991, the reserve tax effect is likely to become a less important feature driving bank loan sales (as well as the recourse/nonrecourse mix) in the future.

remove loans from the balance sheet by selling them without recourse to outside parties. Such removal allows banks to shrink both their assets and deposits and, thus, the amount of reserves they have to hold against their deposits.

 **LG 24-3**   *Factors Deterring Future Loan Sales Growth*

The loan sales market has experienced a number of up-and-down phases in recent years. Notwithstanding the value of loan sales as a credit risk management tool and other reasons described above, a number of factors may deter the market's growth and development in the future. We discuss these next.

**Access to the Commercial Paper Market.**   Since 1987, large banks have enjoyed much greater powers to underwrite commercial paper directly, without experiencing legal challenges by the securities industry claiming that underwriting by banks is contrary to the Glass-Steagall Act. These underwriting powers were expanded in 1999 with the passage of the Financial Services Modernization Act, which eliminated Glass-Steagall restrictions on underwriting activities such as commercial paper underwriting (see Chapter 13). This means that the need to underwrite or sell short-term bank loans as an imperfect substitute for commercial paper underwriting has now become much less important. In addition, more and more smaller middle market firms are gaining direct access to the commercial paper market. As a result, such firms have less need to rely on bank loans to finance their short-term expenditures, with fewer loan originations generally resulting in fewer loans being sold.

**Customer Relationship Effects.**   As the financial institutions industry consolidates and expands the range of financial services sold, customer relationships have become even more important. To the extent that a loan customer (borrower) views the sale of its loan by its FI as an adverse statement about the customer's value to the FI, loan sales can harm revenues generated by the FI as current and potential future customers take their business elsewhere.

**Legal Concerns.**   A number of legal concerns are currently hampering the loan sales market's growth, especially for distressed loans. In particular, although FIs are normally secured creditors, other creditors may attack this status through **fraudulent conveyance** proceedings if the borrowing firm enters bankruptcy. Fraudulent conveyance is any transfer of assets (such as a loan sale) at less than fair value made by a firm while it is insolvent. Fraudulent conveyance prevents an insolvent firm from giving away its assets or selling them at unreasonably low prices and thereby depriving its remaining creditors of fair treatment on liquidation or bankruptcy. For example, fraudulent conveyance proceedings have been brought against the secured lenders to firms such as Revco, Circle K, Allied Stores, and RJR Nabisco. In these cases, the sale of loans to a particular party were found to be illegal. More recently, in late 2011 the FHFA (the conservator of Fannie Mae and Freddie Mac) sued 17 different financial institutions (including Bank of America, J.P. Morgan Chase, Goldman Sachs, and Citigroup) for misrepresenting the quality of mortgage-backed securities sold to Fannie Mae and Freddie Mac. As of late 2013, the FHFA had secured $28 billion from banks, including $6.97 billion from Bank of America, $4 billion from J.P. Morgan Chase, $3.68 billion from Royal Bank of Scotland, and $1.35 billion from Goldman Sachs. Further, in October 2012 the U.S. Justice Department filed a complaint against Bank of America claiming that the bank and its Countrywide Financial unit generated thousands of defective loans and sold them to Fannie Mae and Freddie Mac. The lawsuit was the sixth brought against a major U.S. bank by the Justice Department in less than 18 months. As discussed earlier, contractual terms in loan contracts can limit the loan originator's scope regarding to whom the loan

**fraudulent conveyance**

*A transaction such as a sale of securities or transference of assets to a particular party that is determined to be illegal.*

---

**DO YOU UNDERSTAND:**

1. What the reasons are for the rapid growth and subsequent decline in loan sales over the last three decades?

2. Which loans should have the highest yields—loans sold with recourse or loans sold without recourse?

3. What the two basic types of loan sales contracts by which loans can be transferred between seller and buyer are? Describe each.

4. What institutions are the major buyers in the traditional U.S. domestic loan sales market? What institutions are the major sellers in this market?

5. What some of the economic and regulatory reasons are that FIs choose to sell loans?

6. What some of the factors are that will likely encourage loan sales growth in the future?

7. What some of the factors are that will likely deter the growth of the loan sales market in the future?

can be sold. Fraudulent conveyance proceedings are challenges of loan sales as defined in the original loan contract. Such lawsuits represent one of the factors that have slowed the growth of the distressed loan market.

# LOAN SECURITIZATION

**LG 24-4**

Loan securitization involves a change of strategy from a traditional FI's policy of holding the loans it originates on its balance sheet until maturity. Instead, loan securitization consists of packaging loans or other assets into newly created securities and selling these asset-backed securities (ABS) to investors. By packaging and selling loans to outside parties, the FI removes considerable liquidity, interest rate, and credit risk from its asset portfolio. Rather than holding loans on the balance sheet until maturity, shortly after origination, the originate-to-distribute model entails the FI's sale of the loan and other asset-backed securities for cash, which can then be used to originate new loans/assets, thereby starting the securitization cycle over again. Thus, the process of securitization allows FIs' asset portfolios to become more liquid, provides an important source of fee income (with FIs acting as servicing agents for the assets sold), and helps reduce the effects of regulatory taxes such as capital requirements, reserve requirements, and deposit insurance premiums.

Credit derivatives, such as asset securitization and credit default swaps, allow investors to separate the credit risk exposure from the lending process itself. That is, FIs can assess the creditworthiness of loan applicants, originate loans, fund loans, and even monitor and service loans without retaining exposure to loss from credit events, such as default or missed payments. This decoupling of the risk from the lending activity allows the market to efficiently transfer risk across counterparties. However, it also loosens the incentives to carefully perform each of the steps of the lending process. This loosening of incentives was an important factor leading to the global financial crisis of 2008–2009, which witnessed the aftereffects of poor loan underwriting, inferior documentation and due diligence, failure to monitor borrower activity, and fraudulent activity on the part of both lenders and borrowers. Although bank regulators attempt to examine the off-balance-sheet activities of banks to ascertain their safety and soundness, there is far less scrutiny off the balance sheet than there is for on-balance-sheet activities (i.e., traditional lending and deposit taking). To the extent that counterparty credit risk was not fully disclosed to, or monitored by, regulators, the increased use of these innovations transferred risk in ways that were not necessarily scrutinized or understood. It was in this context of increased risk and inadequate regulation that the credit crisis developed.

This section discusses the three major forms of securitization—pass-through securities, collateralized mortgage obligations (CMOs), and mortgage-backed bonds—and analyzes their unique characteristics. Although depository institutions mainly undertake loan securitization, the insurance industry has also entered into this area. In addition, although all three forms of securitization originated in the real estate lending market, these techniques are currently being applied to loans other than mortgages—for example, credit card loans, auto loans, student loans, and commercial and industrial (C&I) loans. The Securities Industry and Financial Market Association, a bond industry trade group representing member and associate securities firms, banks, and government agencies, reported that $1,212.0 billion of mortgage-backed securities were issued in 2016.

www.sifma.org

## Pass-Through Security

FIs frequently pool the mortgages and other loans they originate and offer investors an interest in the pool in the form of *pass-through certificates* or *securities*. Pass-through mortgage securities "pass through" promised payments by households of principal and interest on pools of mortgages created by financial institutions to secondary market investors (mortgage-backed security bond holders) holding an interest in these pools. We illustrate this process in Figure 24–2. After a financial institution accepts mortgages (step 1 in Figure 24–2), it pools them and sells interests in

**Figure 24–2**   Pass-Through Mortgage Security

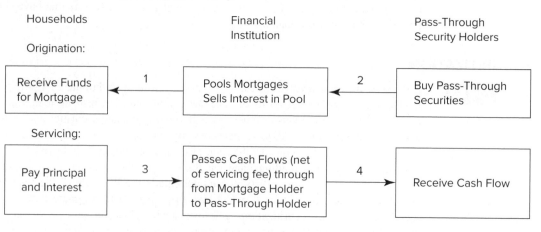

these pools to pass-through security holders (step 2 in Figure 24–2). Each pass-through mortgage security represents a fractional ownership share in a mortgage pool. Thus, a 1 percent owner of a pass-through mortgage security issue is entitled to a 1 percent share of the principal and interest payments made over the life of the mortgages underlying the pool of securities. The originating financial institutions (e.g., bank or mortgage company) or a third-party servicer receives principal and interest payments from the mortgage holder (step 3 in Figure 24–2) and passes these payments (minus a servicing fee) through to the pass-through security holders (step 4).

Although many different types of loans (and other assets) on FIs' balance sheets are currently being securitized as pass-throughs, the original use of this type of securitization is a result of government-sponsored programs to enhance the liquidity of the residential mortgage market. These programs indirectly subsidize the growth of home ownership in the United States. We begin by analyzing the government-sponsored securitization of residential mortgage loans. Three government agencies or government-sponsored enterprises (introduced in Chapter 7) are directly involved in the creation of mortgage-backed pass-through securities. Informally, they are known as Ginnie Mae (GNMA), Fannie Mae (FNMA), and Freddie Mac (FHLMC).

Fannie Mae and Freddie Mac were particularly hard hit by the subprime mortgage market collapse in the mid- and late 2000s, as these government-sponsored agencies are deeply involved in the market that securitizes subprime mortgages. The two agencies recorded approximately $9 billion in losses in the last half of 2007 related to the market for subprime mortgage–backed securities. In March 2008, government regulators reduced capital requirements on Fannie Mae and Freddie Mac to 20 percent from 30 percent in a bid to add liquidity to the troubled mortgage market. Regulators estimated that this reduction, in combination with the release of portfolio caps announced in February 2008, was expected to provide up to $200 billion of immediate liquidity to the mortgage-backed securities market and allow Fannie Mae and Freddie Mac to purchase or guarantee about $2 trillion in mortgages in 2008. Continued losses, however, would constrain the agencies' ability to buy or guarantee mortgages and, in turn, mortgage-backed securities.

These fears and concerns became a reality during the financial crisis. In July 2008, Fannie's and Freddie's share prices fell sharply, resulting in a situation in which market participants refused to extend credit to Fannie and Freddie under any terms. Even though Fannie and Freddie maintained access to the debt markets (albeit at higher-than-usual interest rates), their inability to raise new capital cast doubts on their long-term viability. As a result, the federal government concluded that "the companies cannot continue to operate safely and soundly and fulfill their critical public mission, without significant action" to address their financial weaknesses. The Housing and Economic Recovery Act of 2008 (P.L. 110-289), enacted on July 30, 2008, authorized the government to take over the

www.ginniemae.gov

www.fanniemae.com

www.freddiemac.com

government-sponsored enterprises (GSEs). On September 7, 2008, the Federal Housing Finance Agency (FHFA) established a conservatorship for both Fannie and Freddie.

In February 2011, the Obama administration recommended phasing out the GSEs and gradually reducing the government's involvement in the mortgage market. In the proposal, any dismantling of Fannie and Freddie would happen gradually to avoid a shake-up in the mortgage markets. Steps to reduce the government's role in the mortgage market likely would raise borrowing costs for home buyers, adding pressure on the still-fragile U.S. housing markets. Consequently, the implementation of the proposal is likely to take years and be driven by the pace of the housing market's recovery.

Complicating these efforts, as the U.S. economy and housing market slowly recovered, so did the GSEs. In 2012, FNMA and FHLMC reported net income of $17.2 billion and $11.0 billion, respectively, the best year ever for both companies. By 2015, net income for the two GSEs was $7.2 billion and $2.3 billion, respectively, and for the first three quarters of 2016 net income was $11.0 billion and $6.4 billion, respectively. Further, by mid-2013 the companies' stocks were trading at $4.08 and $3.75, respectively, up from $0.20–$0.30 at the beginning of the year. In early 2017, the companies' shares traded at $4.12 and $3.97, respectively. The two GSEs had repaid $66 billion of the loans received in 2008 to the U.S. Treasury and the government projected a total of $238 billion in revenues due to the government from the two, a $50 billion profit. The GSEs were making money and were expected to remain profitable. The prospect of steady profits confounded legislative efforts to shrink the federal role in securitizing home loans.

**The Incentives and Mechanics of Pass-Through Security Creation.** In order to analyze the securitization process, we trace the mechanics of a mortgage pool securitization to provide insights into the return–risk benefits of this process to the mortgage originating FI, as well as the attractiveness of these securities to investors. Given that more than $7.88 trillion of mortgage-backed securities are outstanding—a large proportion sponsored by GNMA—we analyze the creation of a GNMA pass-through security next.[5]

Suppose that an FI has just originated 1,000 new residential mortgages in its local area. The average size of each mortgage is $100,000. Thus, the total size of the new mortgage pool is:

$$1,000 \times \$100,000 = \$100 \text{ million}$$

Each mortgage, because of its small size, receives credit risk insurance protection from the FHA. This insurance costs a small fee to the originating FI. In addition, each of these new mortgages has an initial stated maturity of 30 years and a mortgage rate—often called the *mortgage coupon*—of 9 percent per year. Suppose that the FI originating these loans relies mostly on liabilities such as demand deposits as well as its own capital or equity to finance its assets. Under current capital adequacy requirements, each $1 of new residential mortgage loans must be backed by some capital. As discussed in Chapter 13, regular 1- to 4-family residential mortgages are separated into two risk categories ("category 1 residential mortgage exposures" and "category 2 residential mortgage exposures"). Category 1 residential mortgages include traditional, first-lien, prudently underwritten mortgage loans. Category 2 residential mortgages include junior liens and non-traditional mortgage products. The risk weight assigned to the residential mortgage exposure then depends on the mortgage's loan-to-value ratio. For example, if the loans in the $100 million mortgage pool are classified as category 1 mortgages and have a loan-to-value ratio between 60 and 80 percent, they are assigned a risk weight of 50 percent and the risk-based capital requirement is 8 percent (see Chapter 13). Therefore, the FI capital needed to back the $100 million mortgage portfolio is:

$$\text{Capital requirement} = \$100 \text{ million} \times 0.5 \times 0.08 = \$4 \text{ million}$$

---

5. At the end of 2016, outstanding mortgage pools were $7.88 trillion, with GNMA pools amounting to $1,732.0 billion; FNMA, $3,043.7 billion; FHLMC, $1,899.2 billion; and private pools and other, $1,210.1 billion.

**www.federalreserve.gov**

We assume that the remaining $96 million needed to fund the mortgages comes from the issuance of demand deposits. Current regulations require that for every dollar of demand deposits held by the FI, a 10 percent cash reserve has to be held at the Federal Reserve Bank or in the vault (see Chapter 13). Assuming that the FI funds the cash reserves on the asset side of the balance sheet with demand deposits, the bank must issue $106.67 million [$96 million/(1 – 0.1)] in demand deposits (i.e., $96 million to fund mortgages and $10.67 million to fund the required cash reserves on these demand deposits). The reserve requirement on demand deposits is essentially an additional tax, over and above the capital requirement, on funding the FI's residential mortgage portfolio. Note that since a 0 percent reserve requirement currently exists on CDs and time deposits, the FI needs to raise fewer funds if it uses CDs to fund its mortgage portfolio.

**www.fdic.gov**

Given these considerations, the FI's initial postmortgage balance sheet may look like the one in Table 24–2. In addition to the capital and reserve requirement taxes, the FI also must pay an annual insurance premium to the FDIC based on the size of its deposits (see Chapter 13). Assuming a deposit insurance premium of 45 basis points (for a low-quality bank),[6] the fee would be:

$$\$106.67 \text{ million} \times 0.0045 = \$480,015$$

Although the FI is earning a 9 percent mortgage coupon on its mortgage portfolio, it is facing three levels of regulatory taxes:

1. Capital requirements
2. Reserve requirements
3. FDIC insurance premiums

Thus, one incentive to securitize is to reduce the regulatory "tax" burden on the FI to increase its after-tax return.

In addition to facing regulatory taxes on its residential mortgage portfolio earnings, the FI in Table 24–2 has two risk exposure problems:

1. *Interest rate risk exposure.* The FI funds the 30-year mortgage portfolio from (short-term) demand deposits. Thus, it has a maturity mismatch (see Chapters 19 and 22). This is true even if the mortgage assets have been funded with short-term CDs, time deposits, or other purchased funds.
2. *Liquidity risk exposure.* The FI is holding an illiquid asset portfolio of long-term mortgages and no excess reserves. As a result, it is exposed to the type of potential liquidity problems discussed in Chapter 21, including the risk of having to conduct mortgage asset "fire sales" to meet large unexpected demand deposit withdrawals.

One possible solution to these interest rate and liquidity risk problems is to lengthen the FI's on-balance-sheet liabilities by issuing longer-term deposits or other liability claims such as medium-term notes. Another solution is to engage in interest rate swaps to transform the FI's liabilities into those of a long-term, fixed-rate nature (see Chapter 23). These techniques, however, do not resolve the problem of regulatory taxes and the burden they impose on the FI's returns.

In contrast, creating GNMA pass-through securities can largely resolve the interest rate and liquidity risk problems on the one hand and reduce the burden of regulatory

**TABLE 24–2**  **FI Balance Sheet** *(in millions of dollars)*

| Assets | | Liabilities | |
|---|---|---|---|
| Cash reserves | $ 10.67 | Demand deposits | $106.67 |
| Long-term mortgages | 100.00 | Capital | 4.00 |
| | $110.67 | | $110.67 |

6. As of 2016, the deposit insurance premium was 9 basis points for the highest quality banks (see Chapter 13).

taxes on the other. This requires the FI to securitize the $100 million in residential mortgages by issuing GNMA pass-through securities. In our example, the FI can do this since each of the 1,000 underlying mortgages has FHA/VA mortgage insurance, the same stated mortgage maturity of 30 years, and coupons of 9 percent. Therefore, they are eligible for securitization under the GNMA program if the FI is an approved lender (which we assume it is—see Chapter 7).

The steps followed in this securitization process are summarized in Figure 24–3. The FI begins the securitization process by packaging the $100 million in mortgage loans. The packaged mortgage loans are removed from the balance sheet by placing them with a third-party trustee off the balance sheet. This third-party trustee may be another FI of high creditworthiness or a legal trustee. Next, the FI determines that (1) GNMA will guarantee, for a fee, the timing of interest and principal payments on the bonds issued to back the mortgage pool and (2) the FI itself will continue to service the pool of mortgages for a fee, even after they are placed in trust. Then, GNMA issues pass-through securities backed by the underlying $100 million pool of mortgages. These GNMA securities or pass-through bonds are sold to outside investors in the capital market, and the proceeds (net of any underwriting fees) go to the originating FI.

**Prepayment Risk on GNMA Pass-Throughs.**   Mortgage loan securitization reduces (or removes) the regulatory tax burden, interest rate risk exposure, and liquidity risk exposure that FIs face when they issue mortgages. It does, however, introduce a new risk—so-called prepayment risk—to the pass-through security holder. Following the sale, each mortgagee makes a payment every month to the FI. The FI aggregates these payments and passes the funds through to GNMA bond investors via the trustee net of servicing fee and insurance fee deductions. Most fixed-rate mortgages are **fully amortized** over the mortgage's life. This means that so long as the mortgagee does not seek to prepay the mortgage early

**full amortization**

*The equal, periodic repayment on a loan that reflects part interest and part principal over the life of the loan.*

**Figure 24–3**   **Summary of a GNMA Pass-Through**

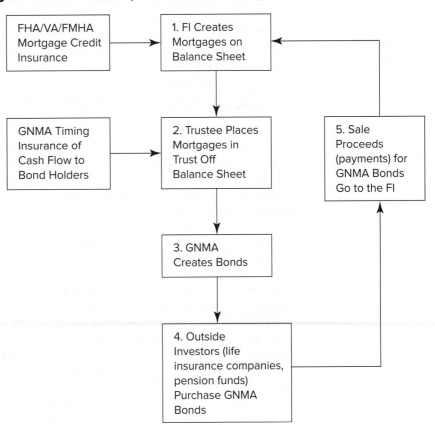

**TABLE 24–3**  The FI's Balance Sheet Postsecuritization *(in millions of dollars)*

| Assets | | Liabilities | |
|---|---|---|---|
| Cash reserves | $ 10.67 | Demand deposits | $106.67 |
| Cash proceeds from | | | |
| mortgage securitization | 100.00 | Capital | 4.00 |
| | $110.67 | | $110.67 |

**prepay**

*To pay back a loan before its maturity to the FI that originated the loan.*

within the 30-year period, either to buy a new house or to refinance the mortgage should interest rates fall, bond holders can expect to receive a constant stream of payments each month analogous to the stream of income on fixed-coupon, fixed-income bonds. In reality, however, mortgagees do not act in such a predictable fashion. For a variety of reasons, they relocate or refinance their mortgages (especially when current mortgage rates are below mortgage coupon rates). This propensity to **prepay** means that *realized* coupons/cash flows on pass-through securities can often deviate substantially from the stated or expected coupon flows in a no-prepayment world (see below). This unique prepayment risk provides the attraction of pass-throughs to some (less risk-averse) GNMA pass-through investors but leads other more risk-averse investors to avoid these instruments. Collateralized mortgage obligations, discussed in the next section, provide a way to reduce this prepayment risk.

Assuming that an FI incurs no fees or underwriting costs in the securitization process, its balance sheet might be similar to the one in Table 24–3 immediately after the securitization has taken place. A dramatic change in the FI's balance sheet exposure has occurred. First, $100 million cash has replaced $100 million illiquid mortgage loans. Second, the maturity mismatch is reduced as long-term mortgages are replaced by cash (a short-term asset). Third, the FI has an enhanced ability to deal with and reduce its regulatory taxes. Specifically, it can reduce its capital, since capital standards require none be held against cash on the balance sheet compared to the residential mortgages in the pool, which require 8 percent capital be held against 50 percent of the face value of the mortgage (i.e., on a $100,000 mortgage, an FI must hold $4,000 ($100,000 × 0.5 × 0.08) in capital—see Chapter 13). The FI also reduces its reserve requirement and deposit insurance premiums if it uses part of the cash proceeds from the GNMA sale to pay off or retire demand deposits and downsize its balance sheet.

Of course, keeping an all or highly liquid asset portfolio and/or downsizing is a way to reduce regulatory taxes, but these strategies are hardly likely to enhance an FI's profits. The real logic of securitization is that the FI can use cash proceeds from the mortgage/GNMA sale to create or originate new mortgages, which in turn can be securitized. In so doing, the FI is acting more as an asset (mortgage) broker than a traditional asset transformer, as we discussed in Chapter 1. The advantage of being an asset broker is that the FI profits from mortgage pool servicing fees plus up-front points and fees from mortgage origination. At the same time, the FI no longer must bear the illiquidity and maturity mismatch risks and regulatory taxes that arise when it acts as an asset transformer and holds mortgages to maturity on its balance sheet. Put more simply, the FI's profitability becomes more fee dependent than interest rate–spread dependent.

**Prepayment Risk on Pass-Through Securities.**    As we discussed earlier, the cash flows on the pass-through directly reflect the interest and principal cash flows on the underlying mortgages minus service and insurance fees. However, over time, mortgage rates change. As coupon rates on new mortgages fall, there is an increased incentive for individuals in the pool to pay off old, high-cost mortgages and refinance at lower rates. However, refinancing involves transaction costs and recontracting costs. As a result, mortgage rates may have to fall by some amount below the current coupon rate before there is a significant increase in prepayment in the pool. This was particularly evident from the early 2000s to the middle of the first decade as new residential mortgage rates fell to their lowest levels

**Figure 24–4** The Prepayment Relationship

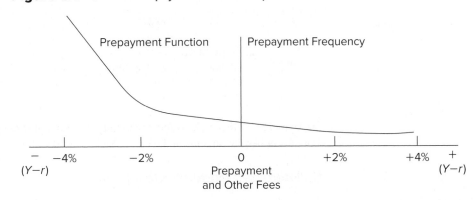

in 30 years. Figure 24–4 plots the prepayment frequency of a pool of mortgages in relation to the spread between the current mortgage coupon rate ($Y$) and the mortgage coupon rate ($r$) in the existing pool. Notice when the current mortgage rate ($Y$) is above the rate in the pool ($Y > r$), mortgage prepayments are small, reflecting monthly forced turnover as people have to relocate because of jobs, divorces, marriages, and other considerations. Even when the current mortgage rate falls below $r$, those remaining in the mortgage pool do not rush to prepay because up-front refinancing, contracting, and penalty costs are likely to outweigh any present value savings from lower mortgage rates. However, as current mortgage rates continue to fall, the propensity for mortgage holders to prepay increases significantly. Conceptually, mortgage holders have a very valuable call option on the mortgage when this option is in the money. That is, when current mortgage rates fall sufficiently lower so that the present value savings of refinancing outweigh the exercise price (the cost of prepayment penalties and other fees and costs), the mortgage will be called by the mortgage holder.

Since the FI has sold the mortgage cash flows to GNMA investors and must by law pass through all payments received (minus servicing and guaranty fees), investors' cash flows directly reflect the rate of prepayment. As a result, instead of receiving an equal monthly cash flow, *PMT*, as is done under a no-prepayment scenario, the actual cash flows (*CF*) received on these securities by investors fluctuate monthly with the rate of prepayments (see Figure 24–5).

In a no-prepayment world, each month's cash flows are the same: $PMT_1 = PMT_2 = \ldots = PMT_{360}$. However, in a world with prepayments, each month's realized cash flows from the mortgage pool can differ. In Figure 24–5 we show a rising level of cash flows from month 2 onward peaking in month 60, reflecting the effects of early prepayments by some of the 1,000 mortgagees in the pool. This leaves less outstanding principal and interest to be paid in later years. For example, if 300 mortgagees fully prepay by month 60, only 700 mortgagees will remain in the pool at that date. The effect of prepayments is to lower dramatically the principal and interest cash flows received in the later months of the pool's life. For instance, in Figure 24–5, the cash flow received by GNMA bond holders in month 360 is very small relative to month 60 and even months 1 and 2. This reflects the decline in the pool's outstanding principal. Thus, the pass-through security places on the investor in the mortgage pool a

**Figure 24–5** The Effects of Prepayments on Pass-Through Bond Holders' Cash Flows

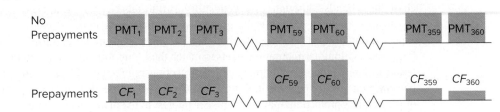

**Figure 24–6**   The Creation of a CMO

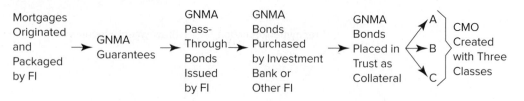

prepayment risk that reflects the uncertainty, in terms of timing, of the cash flows received from his or her investments in the bonds backed by the mortgage pool.

### Collateralized Mortgage Obligation

**collateralized mortgage obligation (CMO)**

*A mortgage-backed bond issued in multiple classes or tranches.*

Although pass-throughs are still the primary mechanism for securitization, the **collateralized mortgage obligation (CMO)** is a second vehicle for securitizing FI assets that is used increasingly. Innovated in 1983 by FHLMC and Credit Suisse First Boston, the CMO is a device for making mortgage-backed securities more attractive to investors. The CMO does this by repackaging the cash flows from mortgages and pass-through securities in a different fashion to attract different types of investors with different degrees of aversion to prepayment risk. A pass-through security gives each investor a pro rata share of any promised and prepaid cash flows on a mortgage pool. The CMO is a multiclass pass-through with a number of different bond holder classes or tranches differentiated by the order in which each class is paid off. Thus, a CMO is a type of derivative security with mortgages as the primary asset. Unlike a pass-through, each bond holder class has a different guaranteed coupon just as a regular T-bond has, but more importantly, the allocation of early cash flows due to mortgage prepayments is such that at any one time, all prepayments go to retire the principal outstanding of only one class of bond holders at a time, leaving the other classes' prepayment protected for a period of time. Thus, a CMO serves as a way to distribute or reduce prepayment risk.

#### Creation of CMOs

CMOs can be created either by packaging and securitizing whole mortgage loans or, more frequently, by placing existing pass-throughs in a trust off the balance sheet. The trust or third-party FI holds the GNMA pass-throughs as collateral against issues of new CMO securities. The trust issues these CMOs in three or more different classes. For example, the first CMO that Freddie Mac issued in 1983, secured by 20,000 conventional home mortgages worth $1 billion, had three classes: A, $215 million; B, $350 million; and C, $435 million. We show a three-class or tranche CMO in Figure 24–6.

Class A CMO holders will be the least prepayment protected since after paying any guaranteed coupons to the three classes of bond holders, A, B, and C, all remaining cash flows from the mortgage pool have to be used to repurchase the principal outstanding of class A bond holders. Thus, these bonds have the shortest average life with a minimum of prepayment protection. They are, therefore, of great interest to investors seeking short-duration mortgage-backed assets to reduce the duration of their mortgage-related asset portfolios. In recent years depository institutions have been large buyers of CMO Class A securities.

After Class A bonds have been retired, remaining cash flows (after coupon payments) are used to retire the bonds of Class B. As a result, Class B holders will have higher prepayment protection than Class A and expected durations of five to seven years, depending on the level of interest rates. Pension funds and life insurance companies primarily purchase these bonds, although some depository institutions buy this bond class as well.

Class C holders will have the greatest prepayment protection. Because of their long expected duration, Class C bonds are highly attractive to insurance companies and pension funds seeking long-term duration assets to match their long-term duration liabilities. Indeed, because of their failure to offer prepayment protection, regular GNMA pass-throughs may not be very attractive to these institutions. Class C CMOs, with their high but imperfect degree of prepayment protection, may be of greater interest to the managers of these institutions.

**EXAMPLE 24–1**  Calculation of Payments to Three Classes
of CMO Bond Holders

Suppose that an investment bank buys a $150 million issue of GNMAs and places them in trust as collateral. It then issues a CMO with the following three classes:

*Class A:* Annual fixed coupon 7 percent, class size $50 million.
*Class B:* Annual fixed coupon 8 percent, class size $50 million.
*Class C:* Annual fixed coupon 9 percent, class size $50 million.

Suppose that in month 1 the promised amortized cash flows (*PMT*) on the mortgages underlying the GNMA pass-through collateral are $1 million, but an additional $1.5 million cash flow results from early mortgage prepayments. Thus, in the first month, the cash flows available to pay promised coupons to the three classes of bond holders are:

$$PMT + \text{Prepayments} = \$1 \text{ million} + \$1.5 \text{ million} = \$2.5 \text{ million}$$

This cash flow is available to the trustee, who uses it in the following fashion:

1. **Coupon payments.** Each month the trustee pays the guaranteed coupons to the three classes of bond holders at annualized coupon rates of 7 percent, 8 percent, and 9 percent, respectively. Given the stated principal of $50 million for each class, the Class A (7 percent annual coupon) bond holders receive approximately $291,667 in coupon payments in month 1; the Class B (8 percent annual coupon) bond holders receive approximately $333,333 in month 1; and the Class C (9 percent annual coupon) bond holders receive approximately $375,000 in month 1. Thus, the total promised coupon payments to the three classes amounts to $1,000,000 (equal to *PMT,* the no-prepayment principal and interest cash flows in the GNMA pool).
2. **Principal payments.** The trustee has $2.5 million available to pay as a result of promised mortgage payments plus early prepayments, but the total payment of coupon interest amounts to only $1 million. For legal and tax reasons, the remaining $1.5 million must be paid to the CMO bond holders. The unique feature of the CMO is that the trustee pays this remaining $1.5 million to Class A bond holders only. This retires early some of these bond holders' principal outstanding. At the end of month 1, only $48.5 million ($50 million – $1.5 million) of Class A bonds remains outstanding, compared to $50 million of Class B and $50 million of Class C bonds. These payment flows are shown graphically in Figure 24–7.

Suppose that in month 2 the promised amortized cash flows (PMT) on the mortgages underlying the GNMA pass-through collateral are $991,250, but again an additional $1.5 million cash flow results from early mortgage prepayments. Thus, in month 2, the cash flows available to pay promised coupons to the three classes of bond holders are:

$$PMT + \text{Prepayments} = \$991,250 + \$1.5 \text{ million} = \$2,491,250$$

**Figure 24–7**  Allocation of Cash Flows to Owners of CMO Classes

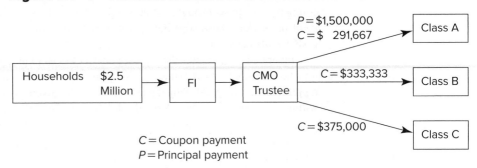

*C* = Coupon payment
*P* = Principal payment

This cash flow is available to the trustee, who uses it in the following fashion:

1. **Coupon payments.** The trustee pays the guaranteed coupons to the three classes of bond holders at annualized coupon rates of 7 percent, 8 percent, and 9 percent, respectively. Given the remaining principal of $48.5 million for Class A (7 percent annual coupon) bonds, these bond holders receive approximately $282,917 in coupon payments in month 2. Given Class B and C bonds' stated principal of $50 million, the Class B (8 percent annual coupon) bond holders again receive approximately $333,333 in month 2; and the Class C (9 percent annual coupon) bond holders again receive approximately $375,000 in month 2. Thus, the total promised coupon payments to the three classes amounts to $991,250 (equal to *PMT,* the no-prepayment principal and interest cash flows in the GNMA pool).

2. **Principal payments.** The trustee has $2,491,250 available to pay as a result of promised mortgage payments plus early prepayments. Again, the remaining $1.5 million must be paid to the CMO bond holders. The trustee again pays this remaining $1.5 million to Class A bond holders only. This retires early some of these bond holders' principal outstanding. At the end of month 2, only $47 million ($48.5 million – $1.5 million) of Class A bonds remains outstanding, compared to $50 million of Class B and $50 million of Class C.

This continues until the full amount of the principal of Class A bonds is paid off. Once this happens, any subsequent prepayments go to retire the principal outstanding to Class B bond holders and, after they are paid off, to Class C bond holders.

Clearly, issuing CMOs is often equivalent to engaging in double securitization. An FI packages mortgages and issues a GNMA pass-through. An investment bank such as Goldman Sachs or another CMO issuer such as FHLMC, a commercial bank, or a savings bank may buy this entire issue or a large part of it. Goldman Sachs, for example, then places these GNMA securities as collateral with a trust and issues three new classes of bonds backed by the GNMA securities as collateral. (These trusts are sometimes called real estate mortgage investment conduits, or REMICS, see below). As a result, the investors in each CMO class have a claim to the GNMA collateral should the issuer fail. The investment bank or other issuer creates the CMO to make a profit by repackaging the cash flows from the single-class GNMA pass-through into cash flows more attractive to different groups of investors. The sum of the prices at which the three CMO bond classes can be sold normally exceeds that of the original pass-through:

$$\sum_{i=1}^{3} P_{iCMO} > P_{GNMA}$$

Gains from repackaging come from the way CMOs restructure prepayment risk to make it more attractive to different classes of investors. Specifically, under a CMO, each class has a guaranteed or fixed coupon.[7] By restructuring the GNMA as a CMO, an FI can offer investors who buy bond Class C a high degree of mortgage prepayment protection compared to a pass-through; those who buy Class B receive an average degree of prepayment protection; those who buy Class A have virtually no prepayment protection. Thus, CMOs redistribute prepayment risk among investors.

Figure 24–8 illustrates the typical pattern of outstanding principal balances for a three-tranche (class) CMO over time. With no prepayment, the outstanding principal balance is represented in Figure 24–8 by the curved line *MN.* Given any positive flow of prepayments, within a few years, the class A bonds clearly would be fully retired, point *X* in Figure 24–8.

---

7. Coupons may be paid monthly, quarterly, or semiannually.

**Figure 24–8** **Pattern of Principal Balances Outstanding for Three-Class CMO**

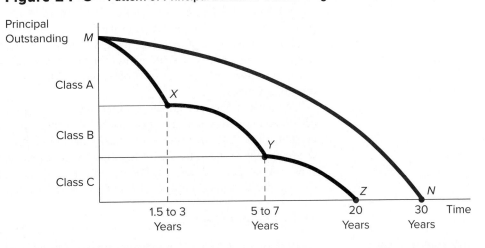

In practice, this often occurs one and a half to three years after issue. After the trustee retires Class A, only Classes B and C remain. As the months pass, the trustee uses any excess cash flows over and above the promised coupon payments to Class B bond holders to retire bond class B's principal. Eventually, all of the principal on Class B bonds is retired (point *Y* in Figure 24–8)—in practice, five to seven years after CMO issue. After Class B bonds are retired, all remaining cash flows are dedicated to paying the promised coupon of Class C bond holders and retiring the full amount of principal on Class C bonds (point *Z* in Figure 24–8). In practice, Class C bonds can have an average life of as long as 20 years.

CMOs can always have more than the three classes described earlier. Indeed, issues of up to 17 different classes have been made. Clearly, the 17th-class bond holders would have an enormous degree of prepayment protection, since the first 16 classes would have had their bonds retired before the principal outstanding on this bond class would be affected by early prepayments. In addition, trustees have created other special types of classes as products to attract investor interest. Frequently, CMO issues contain a Z class as the last regular class. The Z implicitly stands for zero, but these are not really zero-coupon bonds. This class has a stated coupon such as 10 percent and accrues interest for the bond holder on a monthly basis at this rate. The trustee does not pay this interest, however, until all other classes of bonds are fully retired. When the other classes have been retired, the Z class bond holder receives the promised coupon and principal payments plus accrued interest payments. Thus, the Z class has characteristics of both a zero-coupon bond (no coupon payments for a long period) and a regular bond.

Another type of CMO class that is partially protected from prepayment risk is a planned amortization class, or PAC. A PAC is designed to produce constant cash flows within a range (or band) of prepayment rates. The greater predictability of the cash flows on these classes of bonds occurs because they must satisfy a principal repayment schedule, compared to other CMO classes in which principal repayment might or might not occur. PAC bond holders have priority over all other classes in the CMO issue in receiving principal payments from the underlying mortgages. Thus, the greater certainty of the cash flows for the PAC bonds comes at the expense of the non-PAC bonds, called support bonds, which absorb the prepayment risk. Just as sequential bonds were created to allow investors to specify maturity ranges for their investments, PACs can be divided sequentially to provide more narrow paydown structures. Although PAC bonds are somewhat protected from prepayment risk, they are not completely risk-free. If prepayments are fast enough or slow enough, the cash flows of the PAC bonds will change.[8]

8. The PAC band is the range of constant prepayment speeds defined by a minimum and maximum under which the scheduled payments will remain unchanged. The minimum and maximum prepayment speeds are stated in the contract governing the CMO. As long as the prepayment speed remains within this stated range, the PAC payments are known and guaranteed. If prepayment falls outside of the stated range, cash flows on the PAC can vary.

One drawback of CMOs is that originators may not be able to pass through all interest payments on a tax-free basis when they issue multiple debt securities. This creates a tax problem for various originators. A provision of the 1986 Tax Reform Act authorized the creation of a new type of mortgage-backed security called a REMIC (real estate mortgage investment conduit). A REMIC allows for the pass-through of all interest and principal payments before taxes are levied. Today, most CMOs are created as REMICs because of this tax advantage.

As noted, CMOs are attractive to secondary mortgage market investors because they can choose a particular CMO class that fits their maturity needs. While there is no guarantee that the CMO securities will actually mature in exact accordance with the horizon desired by the investor, the CMO significantly increases the probability of receiving cash flows over a specified horizon. For example, a third-class CMO holder knows that he or she will not be paid off until all first- and second-class holders are paid in full.

### Mortgage-Backed Bond

**mortgage- (asset-) backed bonds (MBBs)**

*Bonds collateralized by a pool of assets.*

As discussed in Chapter 7, **mortgage- (asset-) backed bonds (MBBs)** differ from pass-throughs and CMOs in two key dimensions. First, while pass-throughs and CMOs help FIs remove mortgages from their balance sheets, mortgages backing MBBs normally remain on the balance sheet. Second, pass-throughs and CMOs have a direct link between the cash flows on the underlying mortgages and the cash flows on the bond instrument issued. In contrast, the relationship for MBBs is one of collateralization—the cash flows on the mortgages backing the bond are not necessarily directly connected to interest and principal payments on the MBB. Thus, a MBB is also a type of derivative with mortgages as the primary security.

An FI issues an MBB to reduce risk to the MBB holders, who have a first claim to a segment of the FI's mortgage assets. The FI segregates a group of mortgage assets on its balance sheet and pledges this group of assets as collateral against the MBB issue. A trustee normally monitors the segregation of assets and ensures that the market value of the collateral exceeds the principal owed to MBB holders. That is, FIs back most MBB issues by excess collateral. This excess collateral backing of the bond, in addition to the priority rights of the bond holders, generally ensures the sale of these bonds with a high investment grade credit rating. In contrast, the FI, when evaluated as a whole, could be rated as BB or even lower. A high credit rating results in lower coupon payments than would be required if significant default risk had lowered the credit rating. To explain the potential benefits and the sources of any gains to an FI from issuing MBBs, we examine the following simple example.

---

### EXAMPLE 24–2   Gains to an FI from Issuing MBBs

Consider an FI with $20 million in long-term mortgages as assets. It is financing these mortgages with $10 million in short-term uninsured deposits (e.g., wholesale deposits over $250,000) and $10 million in insured deposits (e.g., retail deposits of $250,000 or less). In this example, we ignore the issues of capital and reserve requirements. Look at the balance sheet structure shown in Table 24–4.

This balance sheet poses problems for the FI manager. First, the FI has significant interest rate risk exposure due to the mismatch of the maturities of its assets and liabilities. Second, because of this interest rate risk and the potential default and prepayment risk on the FI's mortgage assets, uninsured depositors are likely to require a positive and potentially significant risk premium to be paid on their deposits. By contrast, the insured depositors may require approximately the risk-free rate on their deposits because they are fully insured by the FDIC (see Chapter 21).

To reduce its interest rate risk exposure and to lower its funding costs, the FI can segregate $12 million of the mortgages on the asset side of its balance sheet and pledge them as collateral backing a $10 million long-term MBB issue. Because the $10 million in MBBs is backed by mortgages worth $12 million, the mortgage-backed bond issued by the FI may cost less to issue, in terms of required yield, than uninsured deposit rates currently being paid—it may well be rated AA, while uninsured deposits might be rated BB. The FI can then use the proceeds of the $10 million bond issue to replace the $10 million of uninsured deposits.

Consider the FI's balance sheet after the issue of the MBBs (Table 24–5). It might seem that the FI has miraculously engineered a restructuring of its balance sheet that has resulted in a better match of the maturities of its assets and liabilities and a decrease in funding costs. The bond issue has lengthened the average maturity of liabilities by replacing short-term wholesale deposits with long-term MBBs and has lowered funding costs because AA rated bond coupon rates are below BB rated uninsured deposit rates. This outcome, however, occurs only because the insured depositors do not worry about risk exposure since they are 100 percent insured by the FDIC. The result of the MBB issue and the segregation of $12 million of assets as collateral backing the $10 million bond issue is that the insured deposits of $10 million are now backed by only $8 million in free or unpledged assets. If smaller depositors were not insured by the FDIC, they would surely demand very high risk premiums for holding these risky deposits. The implication of this is that the FI gains only because the FDIC is willing to bear enhanced credit risk through its insurance guarantees to depositors.[9] As a result, the FI is actually gaining at the expense of the FDIC. Consequently, it is not surprising that the FDIC is concerned about the growing use of this form of securitization by risky banks and thrifts.

**TABLE 24–4**   **Balance Sheet of Potential MBB Issuer** *(in millions of dollars)*

| Assets | | Liabilities | |
|---|---|---|---|
| Long-term mortgages | $20 | Insured deposits | $10 |
| | | Uninsured deposits | 10 |
| | $20 | | $20 |

**TABLE 24–5**   **FI's Balance Sheet after MBB Issue** *(in millions of dollars)*

| Assets | | Liabilities | |
|---|---|---|---|
| Collateral (market value of segregated mortgages) | $12 | MBB issue | $10 |
| Other mortgages | 8 | Insured deposits | 10 |
| | $20 | | $20 |

MBB issuance also has a number of costs. First, MBBs tie up mortgages on the FI's balance sheet for a long time, thus decreasing the asset portfolio's liquidity. Further, the balance sheet becomes more illiquid due to the need to overcollateralize MBBs to ensure a high-quality credit risk rating for the issue; in our example, the overcollateralization was $2 million. Second, the MBB issuer (the FI) is subject to any prepayment risk on the mortgages underlying the MBB. Third, the FI continues to be liable for capital adequacy and reserve requirement taxes by keeping the mortgages on the balance sheet. Because of these costs, MBBs are the least used of the three basic vehicles of securitization.

---

9. The FDIC does not make the risk-based deposit insurance premium to banks and thrifts sufficiently large to reflect this risk.

## SECURITIZATION OF OTHER ASSETS

The major use of the three securitization vehicles—pass-throughs, CMOs, and mortgage-backed bonds—has been to package fixed-rate residential mortgage assets. The standard features on mortgages have make the packaging and securitization of these securities relatively easy. But these techniques can and have been used for other assets, including the following:

- Automobile loans
- Credit card receivables (CARDs)
- Small-business loans guaranteed by the Small Business Administration
- Commercial and industrial loans
- Student loans
- Equipment loans
- Junk bonds
- Adjustable rate mortgages

At the end of 2016, securitized automobile loans totaled $193.5 billion, credit card receivables totaled $133.9 billion, student loans totaled $190.8 billion, and equipment loans totaled $50.3 billion.

## CAN ALL ASSETS BE SECURITIZED?

**LG 24-5**

The extension of securitization technology to assets other than fixed-rate residential mortgages raises questions about the limits of securitization and whether all assets and loans can eventually be securitized. Conceptually, the answer is that they can, so long as doing so is profitable or the benefits to the FI from securitization outweigh its costs. With heterogeneous loans, it is important to standardize the salient features of loans. Default risks, if significant, have to be reduced by diversification. Expected maturities have to be reasonably similar. As mechanisms are developed to overcome these difficulties, it is perfectly reasonable to expect securitization to grow. Table 24–6 summarizes the overall benefits versus the costs of securitization.

From Table 24–6, given any set of benefits, the more costly and difficult it is to find asset packages of sufficient size and homogeneity, the more difficult and expensive it is to securitize. For example, C&I loans have maturities running from a few months to eight years or more. Further, they have varying interest rate terms (fixed, LIBOR floating, federal funds rate floating) and fees. In addition, C&I loans contain different contractual covenants (covering items such as dividend payments by firms) and are made to firms in a wide variety of industries. Despite this, FIs have still been able to issue securitization packages called CLOs (collateralized loan obligations containing high-quality, low–default risk loans) and CDOs (collateralized debt obligations containing a diversified collection of

**TABLE 24–6**　Benefits versus Costs of Securitization

| Benefits | Costs |
|---|---|
| 1. New funding source (bonds versus deposits). | 1. Public/private credit risk insurance and guarantees. |
| 2. Increased liquidity of bank loans. | 2. Overcollateralization. |
| 3. Enhanced ability to manage the duration gap and thus interest rate risk. | 3. Valuation and packaging (the cost of asset heterogeneity). |
| 4. A savings to the issuer (if off balance sheet) on reserve requirements, deposit insurance premiums, and capital adequacy requirements. | |

junk bonds or risky bank loans). The interest and principal payments on a CDO are linked to the timing of default losses and repayments on a pool of underlying loans or bonds. A synthetic CDO is a type of CDO in which the underlying credit exposures are credit default swaps (CDSs) rather than a pool of loans or bonds. Thus, the periodic payments are linked to the cash flows from the credit default swaps. If the credit event occurs in the underlying portfolio, the synthetic CDO (and any investors) become responsible for the losses. Synthetic CDOs are securitized securities that can offer extremely high returns to investors. However, investors can lose more than their initial investments if several credit events occur in the underlying portfolio. The riskiest of the CDOs, sometimes called "toxic waste," pay out only if everything goes right.

The best CDOs will pay out unless the entire portfolio defaults. Generally, it has been much harder to securitize low-quality loans into CDOs. Specifically, the harder it is to value a loan or asset pool, the greater the costs of securitization due to the need for over-collateralization or credit risk insurance. The major sellers of CDOs are commercial and investment banks, through their SIVs or SPVs (see Chapter 13). The major buyers are hedge funds, commercial banks, investment banks, and pension funds. While the banks that create and sell the CDOs distribute the cash flows from the underlying assets to the CDO buyers, the valuation of these credit derivatives is not based solely on the estimated cash flows from underlying assets. Rather, the valuation of CDOs involves the use of metrics and algorithms developed by traders and mathematicians.

Of all of the instruments that caused damage to FIs and the world's financial markets in general during the financial crisis, the most damaging one was arguably the CDO backed by subprime debt. Many FIs had invested heavily in these CDOs. The volume of CDO issues grew from $10 billion in 1995 to over $500 billion in 2006 (before the financial crisis). This market decreased in size significantly after the crisis, to $11.0 billion in 2011, $45.5 billion in 2012, and $78.0 billion in 2013. However, by 2015 this market had recovered significantly as over $141 billion was outstanding only to fall back to $75 billion in 2016. Cash flow CDOs have as their underlying collateral real securities, such as bonds, CDO tranches, and asset-backed securities tranches. The most naive investors simply looked at the ratings on these CDO tranches and then bought the tranche if they liked the rating. They did not attempt or did not have the models to confirm if the price they were asked to pay was a fair value.[10] Other investors accepted what CDO arrangers and the ratings agencies recommended for valuation technology. However, these models consistently underestimated the worst-case scenario and overvalued CDO tranches.[11] The best practice in valuing cash flow CDOs is to simulate the performance of the mortgage loans underlying the CDO tranches, loan by loan, and then simulate the losses and cash flows of the CDO tranches in the CDO structure. Most investors until recently have done no analysis—because they did not have such software capabilities at their disposal. As a result, they consistently overpaid for cash flow CDO tranches and they took on risk that they did not understand.

The potential boundary to securitization may well be defined by the relative degree of heterogeneity and the credit quality of an asset type or group. It is not surprising that 30-year, fixed-rate residential mortgages were the first assets to be securitized since they are the most homogeneous of all assets in FI balance sheets. For example, the existence of secondary markets for houses provides price information that allows reasonably accurate market valuations of the underlying asset and extensive data are available on mortgage default rates by locality.

**DO YOU UNDERSTAND:**

**12.** *Whether or not all assets and loans can be securitized? Explain your answer.*

10. These investors ignored the fact that the ratings agencies are paid by the CDO arranger and that they have a bias in favor of a rating that is better than the real risk level. Unless CDO tranches were rated favorably, arrangers could not make money by packaging securities freely available in the market and then reselling them at a higher price in the form of tranches.

11. Note that this technique also maximizes CDO arrangers' profits by getting investors to buy CDO tranches that they would not purchase if they had an accurately measured value.

# SUMMARY

This chapter discussed the increasing role of loan sales in addition to the legal and regulatory factors that are likely to affect the future growth of this market. The chapter also discussed three major forms of securitization—pass-through securities, collateralized mortgage obligations (CMOs), and mortgage-backed bonds (MBBs)—and described recent innovations in the securitization of other FI assets. Loan sales provide a simple alternative to the full securitization of loans through bond packages. In particular, they provide a valuable tool to an FI that wishes to manage its credit risk exposure better. Recently, by increasingly relying on securitization, banks and thrifts have begun to move away from being asset transformers and toward becoming asset brokers. Thus, over time we have seen the traditional differences between commercial banking and investment banking diminish as more and more loans and assets are securitized.

# QUESTIONS

1. Why have FIs been very active in loan securitization issuance of pass-through securities while they have reduced their volume of loan sales? Under what circumstances would you expect loan sales to dominate loan securitization? (*LG 24-1*)

2. What is the difference between loans sold with recourse and without recourse from the perspective of both sellers and buyers? (*LG 24-1*)

3. What are some of the key features of short-term loan sales? (*LG 24-2*)

4. Why are yields higher on loan sales than they are for similar maturity and issue size commercial paper issues? (*LG 24-2*)

5. What is the difference between loan participations and loan assignments? (*LG 24-2*)

6. What are highly leveraged transactions? What constitutes the federal regulatory definition of an HLT? (*LG 24-2*)

7. Who are the buyers and sellers of U.S. loans? Why do they participate in this activity? (*LG 24-2*)

8. In addition to managing credit risk, what are some other reasons for the sale of loans by FIs? (*LG 24-3*)

9. What are the three levels of regulatory taxes faced by FIs when making loans? How does securitization reduce the levels of taxation? (*LG 24-3*)

10. How do loan sales and securitization help an FI manage its interest rate and liquidity risk exposures? (*LG 24-4*)

11. What specific changes occur on the balance sheet at the completion of the securitization process? What adjustments occur to the risk profile of the FI? (*LG 24-4*)

12. What is prepayment risk? How does prepayment risk affect the cash flow stream on a fully amortized mortgage loan? What are the two primary factors that cause early payment? (*LG 24-4*)

13. What is a collateralized mortgage obligation (CMO)? How is it similar to a pass-through security? How does it differ? In what way does the creation of a CMO use market segmentation to redistribute prepayment risk? (*LG 24-4*)

14. What are the differences between CMOs and MBBs? (*LG 24-4*)

15. How do FIs use securitization to manage their interest rate, credit, and liquidity risks? (*LG 24-4*)

16. Why do buyers of Class C tranches of collateralized mortgage obligations (CMOs) receive a lower return than purchasers of Class A tranches? (*LG 24-4*)

17. Can all assets and loans be securitized? Explain your answer. (*LG 24-5*)

# PROBLEMS

1. A bank has made a three-year, $10 million loan that pays annual interest of 8 percent. The principal is due at the end of the third year. (*LG 24-2*)
   a. The bank is willing to sell this loan with recourse at an 8.5 percent discount rate. What should it receive for this loan?
   b. The bank also has the option to sell this loan without recourse at a discount rate of 8.75 percent. What should it expect for selling this loan?
   c. If the bank expects a 0.50 percent probability of default on this loan over its three-year life, is it better off selling this loan with or without recourse? It expects to receive no interest payments or principal if the loan is defaulted.

2. City Bank has made a 10-year, $2 million loan that pays annual interest of 10 percent per year. The principal is expected at maturity. (*LG 24-2*)
   a. What should it expect to receive from the sale of this loan if the current market rate on loans is 12 percent?
   b. The prices of loans of this risk are currently being quoted in the secondary market at bid-offer prices of 88–89 cents (on each dollar). Translate these quotes into actual prices for the above loan.
   c. Do these prices reflect a distressed or nondistressed loan? Explain.

3. An FI is planning the purchase of a $5 million loan to raise the existing average duration of its assets from 3.5 years to

5 years. It currently has total assets worth $20 million, $5 million in cash (0 duration), and $15 million in loans. All the loans are fairly priced. (*LG 24-2*)

a. Assuming it uses the cash to purchase the loan, should it purchase the loan if its duration is seven years?

b. What asset duration loans should it purchase in order to raise its average duration to five years?

4. An FI is planning to issue $100 million in commercial loans. It will finance all of it by issuing demand deposits. (*LG 24-2*)

a. What is the minimum capital required if there are no reserve requirements?

b. What is the minimum demand deposits it needs to attract in order to fund this loan if you assume there is a 10 percent average reserve requirement on demand deposits, all reserves are held in the form of cash, and $8 million of funding is through equity?

c. Show a simple balance sheet with total assets and total liabilities and equity, assuming this is the only project funded by the bank.

5. Consider $200 million of 30-year mortgages with a coupon of 10 percent paid quarterly. (*LG 24-4*)

a. What is the quarterly mortgage payment?

b. What are the interest repayments over the first year of life of the mortgages? What are the principal repayments?

c. Construct a 30-year CMO using this mortgage pool as collateral. There are three tranches (where A offers the least protection against prepayment and C offers the most). A $50 million tranche A makes quarterly payments of 9 percent; a $100 million tranche B makes quarterly payments of 10 percent; and a $50 million tranche C makes quarterly payments of 11 percent.

d. Assuming no amortization of principal and no prepayments, what are the total promised coupon payments to the three classes? What are the principal payments to each of the three classes for the first year?

e. If, over the first year, the trustee receives quarterly prepayments of $10 million on the mortgage pool, how are the funds distributed?

f. How can the CMO issuer earn a positive spread on the CMO?

6. Consider $100 million of 30-year mortgages with a coupon of 5 percent per year paid quarterly. (*LG 24-4*)

a. What is the quarterly mortgage payment?

b. What are the interest and principal repayments over the first year of life of the mortgages?

c. Construct a 30-year CMO using this mortgage pool as collateral. The pool has three tranches, where tranche A offers the least protection against prepayment and tranche C offers the most protection against prepayment. Tranche A of $25 million receives quarterly payments

at 4 percent per year, tranche B of $50 million receives quarterly payments at 5 percent per year, and tranche C of $25 million receives quarterly payments at 6 percent per year.

d. Assume nonamortization of principal and no prepayments. What are the total promised coupon payments to the three classes? What are the principal payments to each of the three classes for the first year?

e. If, over the first year, the trustee receives quarterly prepayments of $5 million on the mortgage pool, how are these funds distributed?

f. How are the cash flows distributed if prepayments in the first half of the second year are $10 million quarterly?

7. Assume an FI originates a pool of short-term real estate loans worth $20 million with maturities of five years and paying interest rates of 9 percent (paid annually). (*LG 24-4*)

a. What is the average payment received by the FI (both principal and interest) if no prepayment is expected over the life of the loans?

b. If the loans are converted into real estate certificates and the FI charges a 50 basis points servicing fee (including insurance), what are the payments expected by the holders of the securities, if no prepayment is expected?

8. What is the impact on GNMA pricing if a pass-through is not fully amortized? What is the present value of a $10 million pool of 15-year mortgages with an 8.5 percent per year monthly mortgage coupon if market rates are 5 percent? The GNMA guarantee fee is 6 basis points and the FI servicing fee is 44 basis points. (*LG 24-4*)

a. Assume that the GNMA pass-through is fully amortized.

b. Assume that the GNMA pass-through is only half amortized. There is a lump sum payment at the maturity of the GNMA pass-through that equals 50 percent of the mortgage pool's face value.

9. Consider a GNMA mortgage pool with principal of $20 million. The maturity is 30 years with a monthly mortgage payment of 10 percent per year. Assume no prepayments. (*LG 24-4*)

a. What is the monthly mortgage payment (100 percent amortizing) on the pool of mortgages?

b. If the GNMA insurance fee is 6 basis points and the servicing fee is 44 basis points, what is the yield on the GNMA pass-through?

c. What is the monthly payment on the GNMA in part (b)?

d. Calculate the first monthly servicing fee paid to the originating FIs.

e. Calculate the first monthly insurance fee paid to GNMA.

10. Calculate the value of (a) the mortgage pool and (b) the GNMA pass-through security in Problem 9 if market interest rates increase 50 basis points. Assume no prepayments. (*LG 24-4*)

# SEARCH THE SITE

Go to the Loan Pricing Corporation (Thomson Reuters) website at **www.loanpricing.com,** and find the most recent information on secondary loan market trading volume and lead secondary loan market arrangers.

To get secondary market volume, click on "Analysis" and then click on "U.S. Secondary Loan Market Volume." To get the lead arrangers, click on "Analysis" and then click on "View LPC League Tables."  Then select the desired "Time Frame," "Year," and under, "Select Region," choose "U.S. Bookrunner."

## Questions

1. How has the dollar volume of secondary market loan market trading changed since 2016, as reported in Figure 24–1?
2. What is the percentage of distressed versus par secondary loan market volume?
3. Who are the lead arrangers of secondary loan market trading and what percentage of the total market does each one possess?

Altman, E. I. "Managing the Commercial Lending Process." *Handbook of Banking Strategy,* R. C. Aspinwall and R. A. Eisenbeis, eds. (New York: John Wiley & Sons, 1985), pp. 473–510.

Bank for International Settlements. "A New Capital Adequacy Framework," June 1999.

———. "The New Basel Capital Accord," January 2001.

———. "Liquidity Coverage Ratio Disclosure Standards," March 2014.

———. "Basel III" The Net Stable Funding Ratio," April 2014.

———. "International Framework for Liquidity Risk Measurement, Standards and Monitoring," December 2009.

———. "Sound Practices for the Management and Supervision of Operational Risk," December 2010.

———. "Standardized Measurement Approach for Operational Risk," March 2016.

Bao, J., M. O'Hara, and X. Zhou. "The Volker Rule and Market-Making in Times of Stress," SSRN working paper, http://ssrn.com/abstract=2836714.

———. "Monitoring Tools for Intraday Liquidity Management," April 2013.

*Best's Review,* July 2016.

Black, F., and M. Scholes. "The Pricing of Options and Corporate Liabilities," *Journal of Political Economy* 81 (May–June 1973), pp. 637–654 and 737–759.

Brealey, R. A., S. C. Myers, and A. J. Marcus. *Fundamentals of Corporate Finance* (New York: McGraw-Hill, 1999), pp. 225–229.

Cox, J., and M. Rubenstein. *Options Markets* (Englewood Cliffs, NJ: Prentice-Hall, 1985).

Federal Deposit Insurance Corporation. "The CAMELS Evaluation Components," *DOS Manual of Examination Policies,* October 2016.

Gilkerson, J.H., and S.D. Smith. "The Convexity Trap: Pitfalls in Financing Mortgage Portfolios and Related Securities," Federal Reserve Bank of Atlanta, Economic Review, November-December 1992, pp. 17–27.

KMV Corporation. *Credit Monitor* (San Francisco: KMV Corporation, 1994).

Merton, R. C. "On Option Pricing of Corporate Debt: The Risk Structure of Interest Rates," *Journal of Finance* 29 (1974), pp. 447–470.

Office of the Comptroller of the Currency. "Regulatory Capital Rules: Standardized Approach for Risk-Weighted Assets; Market Discipline and Disclosure Requirements," June 2012.

———. Bank Derivatives Report, First Quarter, 2016.

Organization for Economic Cooperation and Development. "Country Risk Classifications," October 2013.

Saunders, A., and L. Allen. *Credit Risk Measurement: New Approaches to Value at Risk and Other Paradigms,* 2nd ed. (New York: John Wiley & Sons, 2002).

Saunders, A., and M. M. Cornett. *Financial Institutions Management: A Risk Management Approach,* 9th ed. (New York: McGraw-Hill, 2018).

Steelman, A., and J. A. Weinberg. "The Financial Crisis: Toward an Explanation and Policy Response," *Federal Reserve Bank of Richmond Annual Report 2008,* April 2009.

U.S. Treasury, Bureau of Public Debt. "Treasury Offering Announcement," May 24, 2016.

———. "Treasury Auction Results," May 24, 2016.

**Notes:** Page numbers with an *f* indicate a figure; an *n,* a note, and a *t,* a table.